South Carolina Rules of Court

Volume I – State

2012

WEST®
A Thomson Reuters business

Mat #41130574

ISBN: 978–0–314–94382–8

PREFACE

South Carolina Rules of Court, Volume I, State, 2012 replaces the 2011 edition. This pamphlet provides, in convenient form, court rules governing state practice in South Carolina, with amendments received through December 1, 2011.

THE PUBLISHER

January 2012

*

ADDITIONAL INFORMATION OR RESEARCH ASSISTANCE

For additional information or research assistance call the West reference attorneys at 1-800-REF-ATTY (1-800-733-2889). Contact West's editorial department directly with your questions and suggestions by e-mail at west.editor@thomson.com.

Visit West's home page at west.thomson.com.

*

TABLE OF CONTENTS

*

[illegible]

SOUTH CAROLINA APPELLATE COURT RULES

Westlaw Electronic Research

These rules may be searched electronically on Westlaw in the SC-RULES *database; updates to these rules may be found on Westlaw in* SC-RULESUPDATES. *For search tips and a summary of database content, consult the Westlaw Scope Screen for each database.*

APPENDICES TO PART IV

V. RULES GOVERNING THE JUDICIARY, EMPLOYEES OF THE JUDICIAL DEPARTMENT, AND OTHERS ASSISTING THE JUDICIARY

I. APPLICABILITY AND GENERAL PROVISIONS

RULE 101. SCOPE AND TITLE

(a) Scope. These Rules are divided into six parts. Part I governs the applicability of these Rules and contains general provisions. Part II governs practice and procedure in appeals, petitions, and motions in the Supreme Court and the Court of Appeals. Part III is reserved for future use. Part IV governs the admission to practice, conduct, discipline, continuing legal education, and other obligations and duties of attorneys in this State. Part V governs the conduct, discipline, continuing legal education, and other obligations of judges in the courts of this State; and rules governing employees of the Judicial Department. Part VI contains rules governing judicial administration.

(b) Title. These Rules shall be entitled South Carolina Appellate Court Rules, and may be cited by rule number and the letters SCACR, i.e., Rule ___, SCACR.

[Adopted and amended effective September 1, 1990.]

RULE 102. EFFECTIVE DATE AND REPEALER

(a) Effective Date. These Rules take effect on September 1, 1990. They govern all matters occurring after they take effect and also all further proceeding in matters then pending, except to the extent that in the opinion of the Court their application in a particular matter pending when these rules take effect would not be feasible or would work an injustice, in which event the former procedure applies. Part II, however, shall not apply in any appeal where a notice of intent to appeal was served prior to the effective date of these rules; if a notice was served before the effective date, the appeal shall proceed to conclusion under the Supreme Court Rules. Where the time to serve a notice of intent to appeal under Supreme Court Rules 1, § 1A, or 50 has expired before these Rules take effect, these Rules shall not revive the right to appeal or to petition for a writ of certiorari in a post-conviction relief case.

(b) Repealer. The Supreme Court Rules and the Miscellaneous Rules shall be repealed when these Rules become effective.

[Adopted effective September 1, 1990.]

II. RULES OF APPELLATE PRACTICE

A. Appeals

RULE 201. RIGHT TO APPEAL

(a) Judgments, Orders and Decisions Subject to Appeal. Appeal may be taken, as provided by law, from any final judgment, appealable order or decision. The procedure for petitioning for a writ of certiorari to review final judgments in post-conviction relief cases is provided by Rule 243. Further, the review of decisions of the State Board of Canvassers in election cases shall be by petition for a writ of certiorari under S.C. Code Ann. §§ 7–17–250 and 7–17–270.

(b) Who May Appeal. Only a party aggrieved by an order, judgment, sentence or decision may appeal.

[Adopted effective September 1, 1990. Amended effective May 3, 2007; April 29, 2009.]

RULE 202. DESIGNATION OF PARTIES AND DEFINITIONS

(a) Designation of Parties. The party appealing shall be known as the appellant and the adverse party as the respondent.

(b) Definitions. For the purpose of Part II of the South Carolina Appellate Court Rules, the following definitions shall apply:

(1) *Lower Court:* the circuit court (including masters–in–equity), family court or probate court from which the appeal is taken.

(2) *Administrative Tribunal:* the administrative law court or agency from which the appeal is taken.

[Adopted effective September 1, 1990. Amended effective May 3, 2007.]

RULE 203. NOTICE OF APPEAL

(a) Notice. A party intending to appeal must serve and file a notice of appeal and otherwise comply with these Rules. Service and filing are defined by Rule 262.

(b) Time for Service.

(1) *Appeals From the Court of Common Pleas.* A notice of appeal shall be served on all respondents within thirty (30) days after receipt of written notice of entry of the order or judgment. When a timely motion for judgment n.o.v. (Rule 50, SCRCP), motion to alter or amend the judgment (Rules 52 and 59, SCRCP), or a motion for a new trial (Rule 59, SCRCP) has been made, the time for appeal for all parties shall be stayed and shall run from receipt of written notice of entry of the order granting or denying such motion. When a form or other short order or judgment indicates that a more full and complete order or judgment is to follow, a party need not appeal until receipt of written notice of entry of the more complete order or judgment.

(2) *Appeals From the Court of General Sessions.* After a plea or trial resulting in conviction or a proceeding resulting in revocation of probation, a notice of appeal shall be served on all respondents within ten (10) days after the sentence is imposed. In all other cases, a notice of appeal shall be served on all respondents within ten (10) days after receipt of written notice of entry of the order or judgment. When a timely post-trial motion is made under Rule 29(a), SCRCrimP, the time to appeal shall be stayed and shall begin to run from receipt of written notice of entry of an order granting or denying such motion. In those cases in which the State is allowed to appeal a pre-trial order or ruling, the notice of appeal must be served within ten (10) days of receiving actual notice of the ruling or order; provided, however, that the notice of appeal must be served before the jury is sworn or, if tried without a jury, before the State begins the presentation of its case in chief.

(3) *Appeals From the Family Court.* A notice of appeal in a domestic relations action shall be served in the same manner provided by Rule 203(b)(1). A notice of appeal in a juvenile action shall be served in the same manner as provided by Rule 203(b)(2).

(4) *Appeals From Masters and Special Referees.* The notice of appeal from an order or judgment issued by a master or special referee shall be served in the same manner as provided by Rule 203(b)(1).

(5) *Appeals From Probate Court.* When a direct appeal is authorized by S.C. Code Ann. § 62–1–308(g), the notice of appeal shall be served in the same manner as provided by Rule 203(b)(1).

(6) *Appeals From Administrative Tribunals.* When a statute allows a decision of the administrative law court or agency (administrative tribunal) to be appealed directly to the Supreme Court or the Court of Appeals, the notice of appeal shall be served on the agency, the administrative law court (if it has been involved in the case) and all parties of record within thirty (30) days after receipt of the decision. If a timely petition for rehearing is filed with the administrative tribunal, the time to appeal for all parties shall be stayed and shall run from receipt of the decision granting or denying that motion. If a decision indi-

cates that a more full and complete decision is to follow, a party need not appeal until receipt of the more complete decision.

(c) Cross–Appeals. A respondent may institute a cross-appeal by serving a notice of appeal on all adverse parties, or in the case of an appeal from the administrative tribunal, by serving a notice of appeal on the agency, the administrative law court (if it has been involved in the case) and all parties of record, within five (5) days after receipt of appellant's notice of appeal, or within the time prescribed by Rule 203(b), whichever period last expires.

(d) Filing.

(1) *Appeals from the Circuit Court, Family Court and Probate Court.*

(A) Where to File. The notice of appeal shall be filed with the clerk of the lower court and with the Clerk of the Supreme Court in the following cases:

(i) Any final judgment from the circuit court which includes a sentence of death.

(ii) Any final judgment involving a challenge on state or federal grounds to the constitutionality of a state law or county or municipal ordinance where the principal issue is one of the constitutionality of the law or ordinance; provided, however, in any case where the Supreme Court finds that the constitutional issue raised is not a significant one, the Supreme Court may transfer the case to the Court of Appeals.

(iii) Any final judgment from the circuit court involving the authorization, issuance, or proposed issuance of general obligation debt, revenue, institutional, industrial, or hospital bonds of the State, its agencies, political subdivisions, public service districts, counties, and municipalities, or any other indebtedness now or hereafter authorized by Article X of the Constitution of this State.

(iv) Any final judgment from the circuit court pertaining to elections and election procedure.

(v) Any order limiting an investigation by a State Grand Jury under S.C. Code Ann. § 14–7–1630.

(vi) Any order of the family court relating to an abortion by a minor under S.C. Code Ann. § 44–41–33.

In all other cases, the notice of appeal shall be filed with the clerk of the lower court and the Clerk of the Court of Appeals.

(B) When and What to File. The notice of appeal shall be filed with the clerk of the lower court and the clerk of the appellate court within ten (10) days after the notice of appeal is served. The notice filed with the appellate court shall be accompanied by the following:

(i) Proof of service showing that the notice has been served on all respondents;

(ii) A copy of the order(s) and judgment(s) to be challenged on appeal if they have been reduced to writing;

(iii) A filing fee as set by order of the Supreme Court;[1] this fee is not required for criminal appeals or appeals by the State of South Carolina or its departments or agencies;

(iv) If the appeal is from a guilty plea, an Alford [2] plea or a plea of nolo contendere, a written explanation showing that there is an issue which can be reviewed on appeal. This explanation should identify the issue(s) to be raised on appeal and the factual basis for the issue(s) including how the issue(s) was raised below and the ruling of the lower court on that issue(s). If an issue was not raised to and ruled on by the lower court, the explanation shall include argument and citation to legal authority showing how this issue can be reviewed on appeal. If the appellant fails to make a sufficient showing, the notice of appeal may be dismissed;

(v) If the notice of appeal is from a post-conviction relief case and the lower court determined that the post-conviction relief action is barred as successive or being untimely under the statute of limitations, the written explanation required by Rule 243(c), SCACR; and,

(vi) If the notice of appeal is from a habeas corpus proceeding and the lower court determined that habeas corpus relief was improper because the issues could have been raised in a timely application under the Post–Conviction Relief Act (see Simpson v. State, 329 S.C. 43, 495 S.E.2d 429 (1998)), a written explanation as to why this determination was improper. This explanation must contain sufficient facts, argument and citation to legal authority to show that there is an arguable basis for asserting that the determination by the lower court was improper. If the appellant fails to make a sufficient showing, the notice of appeal may be dismissed.

(2) *Appeals from Administrative Tribunals.*

(A) Where to File. Appeals from a decision of the Public Service Commission setting public utility rates pursuant to Title 58 of the South Carolina Code of Laws shall be filed with the Clerk of the Supreme Court. Unless otherwise required by statute, all other appeals from administrative tribunals shall be filed with the Clerk of the Court of Appeals.

(B) When and What to File. The notice of appeal shall be filed with the clerk of the appellate court within the time required to serve the notice of appeal under Rule 203(b)(6). The notice filed with the appellate court shall be accompanied by the following:

(i) Proof of service showing that the notice has been served on the agency, the administrative law court (if it has been involved in the case), and all parties of record;

(ii) A copy of the decision(s) to be challenged on appeal; and

(iii) A filing fee as set by order of the Supreme Court;[1] this fee is not required for criminal appeals or appeals by the State of South Carolina or its departments or agencies.

(3) *Effect of Failure to Timely File.* If the notice of appeal is not timely filed or the filing fee is not paid in full, the appeal shall be dismissed, and shall not be reinstated except as provided by Rule 260.

(e) Form and Content. The notice of appeal shall be substantially in the form designated in the Appendix to these Rules.

(1) *Appeals from the Circuit Court, Family Court and Probate Court.* In appeals from lower courts, the notice of appeal shall contain the following information:

(A) The name of the court, judge, and county from which the appeal is taken.

(B) The docket number of the case in the lower court.

(C) The date of the order, judgment, or sentence from which the appeal is taken; and if appropriate for the determination of the timeliness of the appeal, a statement of when the appealing party received notice of the order or judgment from which the appeal is taken, or, if a cross-appeal, when the respondent received appellant's notice of appeal.

(D) The name of the party taking the appeal.

(E) The names, mailing addresses, and telephone numbers of all attorneys of record and the names of the party or parties represented by each.

(2) *Appeals from Administrative Tribunals.* In appeals from administrative tribunals, the notice of appeal shall contain the following information:

(A) The name of the agency and the name of the administrative law judge (if applicable).

(B) The docket number of the case before the administrative law court, or if the appeal is from an agency, the docket number before the agency.

(C) The date of the decision from which the appeal is taken; and if appropriate for the determination of the timeliness of the appeal, a statement of when the appealing party received the decision from which the appeal is taken, or, if a cross-appeal, when the respondent received appellant's notice of appeal.

(D) The name of the party taking the appeal.

(E) The names, mailing addresses, and telephone numbers of all attorneys of record and the names of the party or parties represented by each.

[Adopted effective September 1, 1990. Amended effective July 1, 1993; June 1, 1999; May 3, 2007; May 1, 2008; April 29, 2009.]

1 By order dated April 17, 1990, this filing fee was set at one hundred ($100.00) dollars.

2 North Carolina v. Alford, 400 U.S. 25, 91 S.Ct. 160, 27 L.Ed.2d 162 (1970)

RULE 204. TRANSFER OF CASES

(a) Improperly Filed Cases. In the event that the notice of appeal is filed in the wrong appellate court, the appellate court in which the matter is filed shall issue an order transferring the case to the appropriate appellate court.

(b) Certification by Supreme Court. In any case which is pending before the Court of Appeals, the Supreme Court may, in its discretion, on motion of any party to the case, on request by the Court of Appeals, or on its own motion, certify the case for review by the Supreme Court before it has been determined by the Court of Appeals. Certification is normally appropriate where the case involves an issue of significant public interest or a legal principle of major importance. The effect of such certification shall be to transfer jurisdiction over the case to the Supreme Court for all purposes.

[Adopted effective June 1, 1999.]

RULE 205. EFFECT OF APPEAL

Upon the service of the notice of appeal, the appellate court shall have exclusive jurisdiction over the appeal; the lower court or administrative tribunal shall have jurisdiction to entertain petitions for writs of supersedeas as provided by Rule 241. Nothing in these Rules shall prohibit the lower court, commission or tribunal from proceeding with matters not affected by the appeal.

[Adopted effective September 1, 1990. Renumbered effective June 1, 1999. Amended effective May 3, 2007; April 29, 2009.]

RULE 206. CASES INVOLVING MULTIPLE NOTICES OF APPEAL

Where more than one party serves a notice of appeal, the party whose notice of appeal is first received by the appellate court shall be designated as the primary appellant and shall be responsible for performing all duties required of the appellant under Rules 207 and 210. Upon receipt of notification that the primary appellant has received the transcript of proceeding, the clerk of the appellate court shall establish a briefing schedule.

[Adopted effective September 1, 1990. Renumbered and amended effective June 1, 1999.]

RULE 207. TRANSCRIPT OF PROCEEDING

(a) Appeals From a Lower Court.

(1) *Ordering the Transcript.* Where a transcript of the proceeding must be prepared by the court report-

er, appellant shall, within the time provided for ordering the transcript, make satisfactory arrangements (including agreement regarding payment for the transcript), in writing with the court reporter for furnishing the transcript. In appeals from the court of common pleas, masters in equity, special referees or the family court in domestic actions, the transcript must be ordered within ten (10) days after the date of service of the notice of appeal. In appeals from the court of general sessions or the family court in juvenile actions, the transcript must be ordered within thirty (30) days of the date of service of the notice of appeal. Appellant shall contemporaneously furnish all counsel of record, the Office of Court Administration, and the clerk of the appellate court with copies of all correspondence with the court reporter. Unless the parties otherwise agree in writing, appellant must order a transcript of the entire proceedings below. If a party to the appeal unjustifiably refuses to agree to ordering less than the entire transcript, appellant may move to be awarded costs for having unnecessary portions transcribed; this motion must be made no later than the time the final briefs are due under Rule 211.

(2) *Delivery of Transcript.* The court reporter shall transcribe and deliver the transcript to appellant no later than sixty (60) days after the date of the request. Records shall be transcribed by the court reporter in the order in which the requests for transcripts are made.

(3) *Extension for Court Reporter.* If a court reporter anticipates continuous engagement in the performance of other official duties which make it impossible to prepare a transcript in compliance with this Rule, the reporter shall promptly notify the Office of Court Administration in writing of the fact, setting forth the caption of the case involved, the length of time required to complete the transcript, and the nature and probable duration of the conflicting official duties. The Office of Court Administration may grant an extension of up to ninety (90) days. An extension in excess of ninety (90) days shall not be allowed except by order of the Chief Justice.

(4) *Notice of Extension.* Upon the granting of any extension of time for delivery of the transcript, the Office of Court Administration shall notify all parties and the clerk of the appellate court.

(5) *Failure to Receive Transcript.* If appellant has not received the transcript within the allotted time nor received notification of an extension within ten (10) days after the allotted time, appellant shall notify the Office of Court Administration, the clerk of the appellate court, and the court reporter in writing.

(6) *Failure to Comply.* The willful failure of a court reporter to comply with the provisions of this Rule shall constitute contempt of court enforceable by order of the Supreme Court.

(b) Appeals From an Administrative Tribunal.

(1) *Ordering the Transcript.* Within ten (10) days after the date of service of the notice of appeal, appellant shall, in writing, make satisfactory arrangements with the administrative law court or the agency (administrative tribunal) to obtain a transcript of the proceeding before that body. Appellant shall contemporaneously furnish all counsel of record, and the clerk of the appellate court with copies of all correspondence with the administrative tribunal. Unless the parties otherwise agree in writing, appellant must order a transcript of the entire proceedings before the administrative tribunal. If a party to the appeal unjustifiably refuses to agree to order less than the entire transcript, appellant may move to be awarded costs for having unnecessary portions transcribed; this motion must be made no later than the time the final briefs are due under Rule 211. The administrative tribunal may establish reasonable rates for providing the transcript or a copy thereof.

(2) *Delivery of Transcript.* The administrative tribunal shall insure that the transcript is delivered to the appellant within (60) days after the date of the request.

(3) *Extension.* If the administrative tribunal cannot deliver the transcript in the time specified, it shall promptly seek an extension from the appellate court. The request for an extension shall be in writing and shall comply with Rule 240, SCACR.

(4) *Failure to Receive Transcript.* If appellant has not received the transcript within the allotted time nor received notification of an extension within ten (10) days after the allotted time, appellant shall notify the clerk of the appellate court, and the administrative tribunal in writing.

(c) Duty of Appellant. The transcript received from the court reporter or the administrative tribunal must be retained by appellant during the entire appeal and for a period of at least one (1) year after the remittitur (See Rule 221) is sent to the lower court or administrative tribunal.

[Adopted effective September 1, 1990. Amended effective February 4, 1997. Renumbered and amended effective June 1, 1999. Amended effective May 3, 2007; April 29, 2009.]

RULE 208. INITIAL BRIEFS

(a) Time for Serving and Filing Initial Briefs.

(1) *Brief of Appellant.* Within thirty (30) days after receiving the transcript or, if no transcript is ordered, within thirty (30) days after serving the notice of appeal, appellant shall serve one copy of his brief on all parties to the appeal, and file with the clerk of the appellate court one copy of the brief with proof of service.

(2) *Brief of Respondent.* Within thirty (30) days after service of appellant's brief, respondent shall serve one copy of his brief on all parties to the appeal and file with the clerk of the appellate court one copy of the brief with proof of service.

(3) *Reply Brief.* An appellant may file and serve a brief in reply to the brief of respondent. If a reply brief is prepared, appellant shall, within ten (10) days after service of respondent's brief, serve one copy of the reply brief on all parties to the appeal and file with the clerk of the appellate court one copy of the reply brief with proof of service.

(4) *Failure to File.* Upon the failure of the appellant to file and serve his brief within the time prescribed, the clerk of the appellate court shall sign an order dismissing the appeal, and the appeal shall not be reinstated except as provided by Rule 260. Upon the failure of respondent to timely file a brief, the appellate court may take such action as it deems proper.

(b) Content. The initial briefs under this Rule and the final briefs under Rule 211 shall contain:

(1) *Brief of Appellant.* The brief of appellant shall contain under appropriate headings and in the order here indicated:

(A) Table of Contents and Cases. A table of contents, with page references, and a table of cases (alphabetically arranged), statutes, and other authorities cited, with references to the pages of the brief where they are cited.

(B) Statement of Issues on Appeal. A statement of each of the issues presented for review. The statement shall be concise and direct as to each issue, and may be stated in question form. Broad general statements may be disregarded by the appellate court. Ordinarily, no point will be considered which is not set forth in the statement of the issues on appeal.

(C) Statement of the Case. The statement shall contain a concise history of the proceedings, insofar as necessary to an understanding of the appeal. The statement shall not contain contested matters and shall contain, as a minimum, the following information: the date of the commencement of the action or matter; the nature of the action or matter; the nature of the defense or of the response; the action of the court, jury, master, or administrative tribunal; the date(s) of trial or hearing; the mode of trial; the amount involved on appeal; the date and nature of the order, judgment or decision appealed from; the date of the service of the notice of appeal; the date of and description of such orders, judgments, decisions and proceedings of the lower court or administrative tribunal that may have affected the appeal, or may throw light upon the questions involved in the appeal; and any changes made in the parties by death, substitution, or otherwise. Any matters stated or alleged in appellant's statement shall be binding on appellant.

(D) Argument. The brief shall be divided into as many parts as there are issues to be argued. At the head of each part, the particular issue to be addressed shall be set forth in distinctive type, followed by discussion and citations of authority. A party may also include a separate statement of facts relevant to the issues presented for review, with reference to the record on appeal, which may include contested matters and summarize the party's contentions.

(E) Conclusion. A short conclusion stating the precise relief requested.

(2) *Brief of Respondent.* The brief of respondent shall conform to the requirements of Rule 208(b)(1)(A)–(E), except that a statement of the issues or of the case need not be made unless the respondent is dissatisfied with the statement of the issues or of the case by appellant. If a respondent does not include his own statement of the case, he shall be bound by the matters stated or alleged in appellant's statement of the case. If a respondent does include his own statement of the case, he shall be bound by the matters stated or alleged in his statement of the case. Respondent's brief may also contain argument asking the court to affirm for any ground appearing on the record as provided by Rule 220(c).

(3) *Reply Brief.* All reply briefs shall contain a table of contents, with page references, and a table of cases (alphabetically arranged), statutes, and other authorities cited, with references to the pages of the reply brief where they are cited.

(4) *References to Record.* The brief shall contain references to the transcript, pleadings, orders, exhibits, or other materials which may be properly included in the Record on Appeal [see Rule 210(c)] to support the salient facts alleged. References shall also be made to where relevant objections and rulings occurred in the transcript. In the initial briefs, these references should be to the page and line number of the transcript prepared by the court reporter or by the page of the material to be referenced; e.g., Answer p. 7, Motion for Judgment p. 2, Transcript p. 231. Intelligible abbreviations may be used. After the Record on Appeal is prepared, these references shall be revised as provided by Rule 211(b)(1).

(5) *Length of Briefs.* Except in cases in which a sentence of death has been imposed, principal briefs shall not exceed fifty (50) pages, and reply briefs shall not exceed twenty-five (25) pages. On motion, the appellate court may grant a party permission to exceed those limitations.

(6) *Joining in Briefs.* In cases involving more than one appellant or respondent, including cases consolidated for appeal, any number of parties may join in a single brief, and any party may adopt by reference all or any part of the brief of another.

(7) *Supplemental Citations.* When pertinent and significant authorities come to the attention of a party after his initial brief(s) has been served and filed, the party shall promptly advise the clerk of the appellate court, by letter, with a copy to all counsel, setting forth the citations. There shall be a reference either to the

page of the brief or to an issue to which the citations pertain, but the letter shall, without argument, state the reasons for the supplemental citations. Any response shall be made promptly and shall be similarly limited.

(8) *Form.* All briefs shall comply with the requirements of Rule 267, except that the cover of initial briefs may be made of white paper of not less than twenty pound weight and the initial briefs shall not be bound but shall be securely stapled or fastened on the top left hand corner.

[Adopted effective September 1, 1990. Amended effective July 1, 1993. Renumbered and amended effective June 1, 1999. Amended effective May 3, 2007; April 29, 2009.]

RULE 209. DESIGNATION OF MATTER TO BE INCLUDED IN THE RECORD ON APPEAL

(a) Time to Serve and File. At the same time a party serves his initial brief(s) under Rule 208, to include a reply brief, he shall also serve on all parties to the appeal a Designation of Matter to be Included in the Record on Appeal which shall set forth with specificity those parts of the transcript, pleadings, orders, exhibits, or other materials which he proposes to include in the record on appeal. One copy of this Designation with proof of service shall immediately be filed with the clerk of the appellate court.

(b) Content. The Designation must clearly identify what the party desires to have included in the Record on Appeal, and the Designation may only propose to include portions of the transcript, pleadings, orders, exhibits, or other materials which may be properly included in the Record on Appeal [See Rule 210(c)]. A party shall not include any matter in his Designation which is not relevant to the appeal.

(c) Certification. The Designation shall be accompanied by a certificate signed by the party's counsel of record that the Designation contains no matter which is irrelevant to the appeal.

[Adopted effective September 1, 1990. Renumbered and amended effective June 1, 1999. Amended effective July 1, 2000.]

RULE 210. RECORD ON APPEAL

(a) Time for Service. Within thirty (30) days after service of the last brief, the appellant shall serve a copy of the Record on Appeal on each party who has served a brief. Proof of service of the Record shall be immediately filed with the clerk of the appellate court.

(b) Time for Filing. The appellant must file with the clerk of the appellate court fifteen (15) copies of the Record on Appeal no later than the date his brief(s) are due under Rule 211. As provided by Rule 267(d), one copy filed with the appellate court shall be filed unbound. The appellate court may require an appellant to file additional copies of the Record on Appeal.

(c) Content. The Record on Appeal shall include all matter designated to be included by any party under Rule 209 and shall comply with the requirements of Rule 267. The Record shall not, however, include matter which was not presented to the lower court or tribunal. Matter contained in the Record on Appeal shall be arranged in the following order: the title page, index, orders, judgments, decrees, decisions, pleadings, transcript, charges, exhibits and other materials or documents, and a certificate by appellant. Each page of the Record on Appeal shall be numbered consecutively beginning with the index. Where a portion of a page of the trial transcript, or a page of an exhibit or document, is to be included in the Record on Appeal, the entire page shall be included. When a portion of an order, judgment, decision or pleading is to be included in the Record on Appeal, the entire order, judgment, decision or pleading shall be included in the Record, to include the caption and signature(s); provided, however, that the portion of a pleading showing verification or service shall not be included unless relevant to the appeal. If the original court reporter's numbering has been deleted, the Record on Appeal shall contain ellipses or other notation indicating when pages of the court reporter's transcript have been omitted.

Where witness testimony is included in the Record on Appeal, the first page of each witness's direct, cross, redirect and recross examination must show the name of the witness, the phase of examination and the name of the counsel conducting the examination. If this information is not already reflected on the page, the top of the page shall be annotated with the required information in the following form: John H. Doe—Direct (Cross) (Redirect) (Recross) Examination by Mr. Smith.

(d) Title. The title page shall contain the caption as set forth in Rule 267. Nothing shall be printed on the title page except the caption.

(e) Index. Every Record on Appeal shall contain an index to the principal matters therein to include orders, judgments, decisions, pleadings, pretrial matters, opening statements, testimony, motions, closing arguments, jury charges, post-trial motions and exhibits. For witness testimony, the index shall show the pages on which direct, cross, redirect and recross examination begins.

(f) Exhibits. Photographs, plats and diagrams, and other paper exhibits shall be inserted in the Record on Appeal where they can reasonably be reduced or drawn to a size which permits them to be printed and inserted in the Record on Appeal, without folding more than one time. Where they are larger, or do not reasonably lend themselves to accurate reproduction, they need not be included in the Record on Appeal, but shall be filed separately. All exhibits other than paper exhibits must be retained in the trial court and delivered to the appellate court only upon receipt of an order from the clerk of the appellate court.

(g) Certificate of Counsel. Appellant or his counsel shall certify that the Record on Appeal contains all material proposed to be included by any of the parties and not any other material.

(h) Review Limited to Record on Appeal. Except as provided by Rule 212 and Rule 208(b)(1)(C) and (2), the appellate court will not consider any fact which does not appear in the Record on Appeal.

[Adopted effective September 1, 1990. Amended effective July 1, 1993. Renumbered and amended effective June 1, 1999. Amended effective May 3, 2007; May 1, 2008; April 29, 2009.]

RULE 211. FINAL BRIEFS

(a) Time to Serve and File. Within twenty (20) days after the service of the Record on Appeal, each party shall serve a copy of his final brief(s) on every other party to the appeal, and file fifteen (15) copies of the final brief(s) with the clerk of the appellate court. As provided by Rule 267(d), one copy filed with the appellate court shall be filed unbound. The party must also file with the clerk proof that the final brief(s) has been served, and a certificate that his final brief(s) complies with Rule 211(b). The appellate court may require a party to file additional copies of its brief(s).

(b) Content. The final brief(s) shall be identical to the brief(s) previously served under Rule 208, except for the following:

(1) *References to the Record.* The references in the initial brief shall be revised to indicate where the material appears in the Record on Appeal. These revised references may be in place of or in addition to the initial references, and shall be in the form indicated by the following examples: (R. p. 15, line 4) (R. p. 75, lines 8–20) (R. p. 90, line 1–p. 101, line 14) (R. pp. 29–31).

(2) *Correction of Typographical Errors and Misspellings.* The party may correct obvious typographical errors and misspellings which were contained in the initial brief. No other changes may be made.

[Adopted effective September 1, 1990. Amended effective July 1, 1993. Renumbered and amended effective June 1, 1999. Amended effective May 3, 2007; May 1, 2008; April 29, 2009.]

RULE 212. SUPPLEMENTAL RECORD

(a) By the Court. The appellate court may require copies of all or any part of the transcript of proceedings or other matter which was before the lower court or administrative tribunal to be sent up for its inspection and consideration. It may likewise require a report of the trial or hearing, or of any matter relative thereto, to be made by the trial judge or administrative tribunal. These matters shall become part of the Record on Appeal.

(b) By a Party. With the written consent of all attorneys of record, a party may supplement the Record on Appeal at any time before argument commences. Without such consent or after argument commences, a party desiring to supplement the Record on Appeal must move the appellate court for leave to do so. In response to that motion, the other party(s) shall designate any supplemental materials which that party desires to add if the Court grants the motion.

(c) Appendix. Supplemental materials filed under Rule 212(b) shall be included in an Appendix to the Record on Appeal. Unless otherwise agreed by the parties or ordered by the Court, the Appendix shall be compiled, served and filed by the party initially proposing it.

[Adopted effective September 1, 1990. Renumbered effective June 1, 1999. Amended effective May 3, 2007.]

RULE 213. AMICUS CURIAE BRIEF

A brief of an amicus curiae may be filed only by leave of the appellate court granted on motion, or at the request of the appellate court. The brief may be conditionally filed with the motion for leave to file. A motion for leave shall identify the interest of the applicant and shall state the reasons why a brief of an amicus curiae is desirable. The brief shall be limited to argument of the issues on appeal as presented by the parties and shall comply with the requirements of Rules 208(b) and 211. If leave to file an amicus curiae brief is granted, the appellate court will specify the period in which a response to the brief may be filed.

[Adopted effective September 1, 1990. Renumbered effective June 1, 1999.]

RULE 214. CONSOLIDATION

Where there is more than one appeal from the same order, judgment, decision or decree, or where the same question is involved in two or more appeals in different cases, the appellate court may, in its discretion, order the appeal to be consolidated.

[Adopted effective September 1, 1990. Renumbered effective June 1, 1999. Amended effective May 3, 2007.]

RULE 215. SUBMISSION WITHOUT ORAL ARGUMENT

Unless otherwise ordered by the appellate court, all appeals in civil cases which do not involve a constitutional question and in which the amount involved is $1000 or less, and all appeals in civil cases where there has been no final judgment, shall be submitted to the appellate court without oral argument. Further, the appellate court may decide any other case without oral argument if it determines that oral argument would not aid the court in resolving the issues.

[Adopted effective September 1, 1990.]

RULE 216. NOTICE OF ORAL ARGUMENT

(a) Preliminary List.

(1) *When Mailed.* Not later than forty (40) days prior to the commencement of any term of court, the clerk of the appellate court shall mail to the parties or their counsel a list of all cases which may be reached for hearing at the term.

(2) *Scheduling Conflicts.* Upon receipt of the preliminary list, counsel shall immediately notify the clerk of the appellate court in writing of any anticipated conflict which may prevent his appearance, with copies to all parties on appeal.

(b) Roster.

(1) *When Mailed.* Not later than fifteen days prior to the commencement of any term of Court, the clerk of the appellate court shall mail to the parties or their counsel a roster showing the dates fixed for the hearing of the cases in which oral argument will be heard.

(2) *Continuances.* Once a case is placed on the roster, it shall not be continued except by order of the appellate court or the Chief Judge or Chief Justice thereof.

[Adopted effective September 1, 1990.]

RULE 217. MOTION TO ARGUE AGAINST PRECEDENT

Permission of the appellate court shall not be required to argue against precedent in the brief. Oral argument against precedent shall not be permitted except upon leave of the appellate court in which the case is then pending, pursuant to motion in accordance with Rule 240 filed at least fifteen (15) days prior to oral argument.

[Adopted effective September 1, 1990. Amended effective April 29, 2009.]

RULE 218. ORAL ARGUMENT

(a) Conduct of Argument. The appellant shall open and close the argument. The opening argument shall include a statement of the relevant facts. Unless otherwise permitted by the court, counsel will not be permitted to read from books, briefs, records or authorities cited.

(b) Failure to Appear. If any party fails to appear, the court will hear argument on behalf of the parties present. If no party appears, the case will be decided on the briefs unless the court shall otherwise order.

(c) Length of Argument. The length of time allotted for oral argument shall be determined by the court. The clerk shall notify all parties of the time allotted.

[Adopted effective September 1, 1990.]

RULE 219. HEARING OR REHEARING OF CASES BY THE COURT OF APPEALS EN BANC

(a) When Hearing or Rehearing *En Banc* Will Be Ordered. It shall require the affirmative vote of six (6) members of the Court of Appeals to hear or rehear an appeal or other proceeding *en banc.* A hearing or rehearing *en banc* is not favored and ordinarily will not be ordered except (1) when consideration by the full court is necessary to secure or maintain uniformity of its decisions, or (2) when the proceeding involves a question of exceptional importance.

(b) Suggestion of a Party for Hearing or Rehearing *En Banc*. If a party desires to suggest that a matter be heard initially *en banc*, the suggestion shall made in writing, and must be served and filed not later than twenty (20) days prior to the hearing date. If a suggestion for rehearing *en banc* is to be made, it shall be included in the petition for rehearing. No response shall be filed by other parties unless the Court shall so order. The Clerk of the Court of Appeals shall transmit the suggestion to all judges of the Court. A vote will not be taken to determine if the matter shall be heard or reheard *en banc* unless a member of the Court calls for a vote on the suggestion. If no vote is taken on the suggestion, the parties shall be advised that the suggestion has been rejected.

[Adopted effective September 1, 1990. Amended effective August 31, 1997; April 28, 2011.]

RULE 220. OPINIONS

(a) Opinions. The appellate court shall make its decisions in writing by published opinions or memorandum opinions, with any concurring or dissenting opinions attached. Published opinions shall appear in the Official Reports of the Supreme Court and the Court of Appeals; memorandum opinions shall not be published in the official reports and shall be of no precedential value. Published opinions shall be sent to the official reporter and other reporters or publishers when the time for rehearing has expired or, if a petition for rehearing has been filed, when the petition has been finally decided by the appellate court. The court may affirm, reverse, or modify the decision below or remand all or any issues for further proceedings.

(b) Decision by the Court. In every decision rendered by an appellate court, every point distinctly stated in the case which is necessary to the decision of the appeal and fairly arising upon the record of the court must be stated in writing and must, with the reason for the court's decision, be preserved in the record of the case. This rule does not apply to the following:

(1) The Supreme Court may file a memorandum opinion dismissing an appeal, affirming or reversing the judgment appealed from, or granting other appropriate relief when, in unanimous decision, the Supreme

Court determines that a published opinion would have no precedential value and any one or more of the following circumstances exists and is dispositive of issues submitted to the Court for decision: (A) that a judgment of the trial court is based on findings of fact which are or are not clearly erroneous; (B) that the evidence to support a jury verdict is or is not insufficient; (C) that the order of an administrative agency is or is not supported by such quantum of evidence as prescribed by the statute or law under which judicial review is permitted; or (D) that no error of law appears.

(2) The Court of Appeals need not address a point which is manifestly without merit.

(c) Affirmance on Any Ground Appearing in Record. The appellate court may affirm any ruling, order, decision or judgment upon any ground(s) appearing in the Record on Appeal.

[Adopted effective September 1, 1990. Amended effective May 3, 2007.]

RULE 221. REHEARING AND REMITTITUR

(a) Rehearing. Petitions for rehearing must be actually received by the appellate court no later than fifteen (15) days after the filing of the opinion, order, judgment, or decree of the court. A petition for rehearing shall be in accordance with Rule 240, and shall state with particularity the points supposed to have been overlooked or misapprehended by the court. No petition for rehearing shall be allowed from an order denying a petition for a writ of certiorari under Rule 242, SCACR.

(b) Remittitur. The remittitur shall contain a copy of the judgment of the appellate court, shall be sealed with the seal and signed by the clerk of the court, and unless otherwise ordered by the court shall not be sent to the lower court or administrative tribunal until fifteen (15) days have elapsed (the day of filing being excluded) since the filing of the opinion, order, judgment, or decree of the court finally disposing of the appeal. If a petition for rehearing is received before the remittitur is sent, the remittitur shall not be sent pending disposition of the petition by the court. Where a petition for rehearing has been denied, the Court of Appeals shall not send the remittitur to the lower court or administrative tribunal until the time to petition for a writ of certiorari under Rule 242(c) has expired. If a petition for writ of certiorari is filed, the Court of Appeals shall not send the remittitur until notified that the petition has been denied. If the writ is granted by the Supreme Court, the Court of Appeals shall not send the remittitur.

(c) Rehearing of Motions. The appellate court will not entertain petitions for rehearing on a motion or petition unless the action of the court on the motion or petition has the effect of dismissing or finally deciding a party's appeal.

[Adopted effective September 1, 1990. Amended effective July 1, 2000; May 3, 2007; April 29, 2009.]

RULE 222. COSTS ON APPEAL

(a) To Whom Allowed. Unless otherwise ordered by the appellate court or agreed by the parties, costs shall be taxed against the appellant when the appeal is dismissed or judgment on appeal is affirmed. When a judgment is reversed, costs shall be taxed against the respondent unless the court orders otherwise. When an appeal is affirmed or reversed in part or is vacated, costs shall be allowed only as ordered by the appellate court.

(b) Costs Allowed. The party entitled to recover costs under this rule may, to the extent the party actually incurred these costs, recover the following: (1) the filing fee paid under Rule 203(d); (2) the cost of the court reporter's transcript; (3) premiums paid for costs of supersedeas bonds or other bonds obtained to preserve rights pending appeal; (4) the cost of printing the Record on Appeal under Rule 209; and (5) the cost of printing the party's final brief(s) under Rule 210. In addition, the party shall be entitled to recover an attorney's fee in an amount which shall be set by order of the Supreme Court.[1] The allowance of additional costs will generally not be allowed except in the most extraordinary of circumstances.

(c) Costs for Printing Irrelevant Matter. A party who has unjustifiably designated irrelevant matter to be included in the Record on Appeal shall not be entitled to tax the cost of printing this matter in the Record on Appeal. Further, a party not otherwise entitled to costs under this Rule shall be entitled to collect the cost the party incurred for printing irrelevant matter which another party unjustifiably designated to be included in the Record on Appeal.

(d) Motion for Costs. A party desiring costs to be taxed shall, within fifteen (15) days of the issuance of the remittitur, serve and file a motion requesting that costs be assessed under this Rule. The motion shall comply with Rule 240. If costs are being sought under (b) above, the motion shall be accompanied by a sworn, itemized statement of costs incurred in the form prescribed in the Appendix to these rules. Any return or reply to the motion shall be served and filed in the manner provided by Rule 240. The return may oppose the request for costs or seek a reduction of the amount of costs to be awarded. The remittitur shall not be stayed by the filing of a motion for costs.

(e) Taxation. Costs on appeal shall be taxed only in the appellate court. If costs are taxed, they shall become part of the judgment of the appellate court and shall be added to the remittitur. If a petition for a writ of certiorari is sought under Rule 242, the Court of Appeals shall tax costs only in those cases in which the petition for a writ of certiorari is denied. In all cases in which a writ of certiorari is granted, costs shall be awarded in the manner provided by Rule 242(j).

(f) Applicability. This Rule does not apply to criminal cases or post-conviction relief cases.

[Adopted effective September 1, 1990. Amended effective August 31, 1997; September 1, 2001; April 29, 2009.]

1 By order dated July 24, 1997, the amount of attorney's fee was set at $1,000.

RULE 223. ARBITRATION OF APPEALS

(a) Arbitration by Consent. Except criminal cases and civil cases in which the State or one of its political subdivisions is a party, the parties may agree to arbitration of the appeal in lieu of having the case decided by an appellate court. Before any case may be disposed of by arbitration, counsel for all litigants must agree in writing to disposition of the case in that manner. The arbitration panel shall consist of three (3) retired justices, retired judges, active or retired attorneys, or a combination thereof who shall consent in writing to serve. The parties shall select their own arbitrators. The parties agreeing to submit their appeal to arbitration shall file a completed consent to arbitration form supplied by the Clerk of the Supreme Court. Each arbitrator shall receive actual expenses and compensation in the amount of $150 for each case acted upon, to be charged against the losing party.

(b) Submission; Oral Argument. Counsel may agree to submit the case to the arbitrators on the basis of the transcript and the briefs filed or may require oral arguments. If a hearing is held it shall be at such place and time as counsel agree upon and need not be in Columbia.

(c) Decision. The arbitrators shall, within fifteen (15) days after argument, file their decision with the Supreme Court which shall be that the order or judgment on appeal be either (1) affirmed, (2) reversed, (3) modified, or (4) remanded. When the order or judgment is affirmed or reversed outright, no statement of reasons shall be required. If the order or judgment is modified or the case is remanded, a brief recitation of the modification or the purpose for which the remand is made shall be stated. No formal opinion shall be filed or published by the Supreme Court and the action of the arbitrator shall not serve as a precedent for any court of the State. In event of disagreement among the arbitrators a vote of two shall prevail.

(d) Judgment. The Supreme Court shall give to the decision of the arbitrators the same weight and force as a determination by the Supreme Court and judgment shall be entered and enforced accordingly. In no case shall the arbitrators' decision be subject to review. By consenting to arbitration, counsel and the parties waive all jurisdictional objections.

[Adopted effective September 1, 1990.]

RULES 224 TO 239. [RESERVED]

B. Petitions and Motions

RULE 240. MOTIONS AND PETITIONS GENERALLY

(a) Applicability. This Rule governs all motions or petitions filed in the appellate court, including but not limited to: motions for extension of time, motions to reinstate, petitions for rehearing, motions to be relieved as counsel or for substitution of counsel, petitions for supersedeas, motions to remand or dismiss and petitions for hearing en banc. Where Rules 241 through 246 provide different or additional requirements or procedures, those requirements or procedures shall apply.

(b) Stay of Time Limits. Unless otherwise provided by these Rules, or ordered by the appellate court, the time limits imposed by these Rules shall not be stayed by the filing of a motion or petition. A motion to dismiss an appeal or a motion to relieve counsel shall, however, automatically stay the time limits for perfecting the appeal until the motion is decided.

(c) Form and Content of Motions and Petitions. All motions or petitions filed in an appellate court shall be in writing, shall state the grounds thereof, and shall comply with the requirements of Rule 267. The pages of the motion or petition and all supporting documents shall be consecutively numbered. Each motion or petition shall include the following:

(1) A certificate or affidavit of service reflecting the date of service upon all parties. The original certificate or affidavit of service must be filed with the original motion or petition.

(2) A memorandum with citation of authorities in support of the motion.

(3) Where the Record on Appeal or Appendix has not been filed, or where the facts relied upon in support of the motion are not contained in the Record on Appeal or Appendix, the parties shall file affidavits and other documents in support of their positions.

(d) Filing of Motions and Petitions. An original and six (6) copies of the motion shall be filed with the clerk of the appellate court, and a copy shall be served upon each party. The copies filed with the appellate court shall be accompanied by the filing fee set by order of the Supreme Court. [1] This filing fee shall not be required for motions or petitions in criminal appeals, petitions for writs of certiorari under Rules 242 and 243, certified questions under Rule 244, petitions to

1 By order dated October 2, 1985, the filing fee for motions and petitions was set at twenty-five ($25.00) dollars.

invoke the original jurisdiction of the Supreme Court under Rule 245, or motions or petitions filed by the State of South Carolina or its departments or agencies. In extraordinary cases, the appellate court may relieve a party from paying the filing fee.

(e) Return to Motion. Any party opposing a motion or petition shall have ten (10) days from the date of service thereof to file an original and six (6) copies of his return with the clerk and serve on all parties a copy of the return; provided, however, a return to a petition or motion for rehearing under Rule 221 need not be filed unless requested by the court. The court may in its discretion enlarge or limit the time for filing the return. The provisions of Rule 240(c) shall apply to a return. Failure of a party to timely file a return may be deemed a consent by that party to the relief sought in the motion or petition.

(f) Reply. The moving party shall have five (5) days from the date of service of a return to file an original and six (6) copies of a reply with the clerk and serve on all parties a copy of the reply. The provisions of Rule 240(c) apply to a reply.

(g) Failure to Comply. Failure of the moving party to perform any act required by this Rule may be deemed an abandonment of the motion or petition.

(h) Hearing. Unless otherwise ordered by the court, motions or petitions shall be decided without oral argument.

(i) Rehearing. The court will not entertain petitions for rehearing on a motion or petition unless the action of the court on the motion or petition has the effect of dismissing or finally deciding a party's appeal.

(j) Authority of an Individual Judge or Justice. Except where these rules require the concurrence of two or more members of an appellate court, an individual judge or justice may grant or deny any motion or petition on behalf of the court. Any review of an order issued by an individual judge or justice shall be by petition for rehearing.

[Adopted effective September 1, 1990. Amended effective July 1, 1993; May 3, 2007. Renumbered from Rule 224 effective April 29, 2009.]

RULE 241. STAY AND SUPERSEDEAS IN CIVIL ACTIONS

(a) General Rule. As a general rule, the service of a notice of appeal in a civil matter acts to automatically stay matters decided in the order, judgment, decree or decision on appeal, and to automatically stay the relief ordered in the appealed order, judgment, or decree or decision. This automatic stay continues in effect for the duration of the appeal unless lifted by order of the lower court, the administrative tribunal, appellate court, or judge or justice of the appellate court. The lower court or administrative tribunal retains jurisdiction over matters not affected by the appeal including the authority to enforce any matters not stayed by the appeal.

(b) Exceptions. The exceptions to the general rule are found in statutes, court rules, and case law. Where specific conditions must be met before the exception applies, those conditions must be strictly complied with. A list of some, but not all, of the exceptions to the general rule is:

(1) Money judgments as provided in S.C. Code Ann. § 18–9–130.

(2) Judgments directing the assignment or delivery of documents or personal property as provided in S.C. Code Ann. § 18–9–150.

(3) Judgments directing the execution of conveyances or other instruments as provided in S.C. Code Ann. § 18–9–160.

(4) Judgments directing the sale or delivery of possession of real property as provided in S.C. Code Ann. § 18–9–170.

(5) Judgments directing the sale of perishable property as provided in S.C. Code Ann. § 18–9–220.

(6) Family court orders regarding a child or requiring payment of support for a spouse or child as provided in S.C. Code Ann. § 63–3–630.

(7) Worker's compensation awards as provided in S.C. Code Ann. § 42–17–60.

(8) An appeal from an order granting an injunction or temporary restraining order.

(9) Family court orders awarding temporary suit costs or attorney's fees as provided in S.C. Code Ann. § 63–3–530(A)(2).

(10) Ejectment orders as provided in S.C. Code Ann. § 27–37–130 and S.C. Code Ann. § 27–40–800.

(11) Appeals from administrative tribunals as provided in S.C. Code Ann. § 1–23–380(A)(2) and § 1–23–600(G)(5).

(c) Supersedeas or Lifting of Automatic Stay.

(1) After service of notice of appeal, any party may move for an order lifting the automatic stay in cases which involve the general rule. In a case subject to an exception, any party may move for an order imposing a supersedeas of matters decided in the order, judgment, decree or decision on appeal after service of the notice of appeal. The effect of the granting of a supersedeas is to suspend or stay the matters decided in the order, judgment, decree or decision on appeal and, where a prior order or decision was in effect at the time the appealed order, judgment, decree or decision was filed, to revive the terms of the prior order or decision.

(2) In determining whether an order should issue pursuant to this Rule, the lower court, administrative tribunal, appellate court, or judge or justice of the appellate court should consider whether such an order is necessary to preserve jurisdiction of the appeal or to prevent a contested issue from becoming moot.

(3) The granting of supersedeas or the lifting of the automatic stay under this Rule may be conditioned upon such terms, including but not limited to the filing of a bond or undertaking, as the lower court, administrative tribunal, appellate court, or judge or justice of the appellate court may deem appropriate. Further, where it appears that the granting or lifting of a stay, or the issuance of a writ of supersedeas is insufficient to afford complete relief, the lower court, administrative tribunal, appellate court, or judge or justice of the appellate court may order other affirmative relief upon such terms as are deemed appropriate.

(4) If an order is issued pursuant to Rule 241(c)(1), the terms of that order continue in effect during the pendency of the appeal unless modified or revoked by the lower court, the administrative tribunal or the appellate court or judge or justice of the appellate court which issued it, or by a superior court. The granting of any relief pursuant to this Rule shall not be construed to affect the validity of the judgment, order, decree, decision and any liens until the judgment, order, decree or decision is reversed or modified by the appellate court.

(d) Procedure for Obtaining Lift of Stay or Supersedeas.

(1) Except where extraordinary circumstances make it impracticable, an application for an order lifting the automatic stay or for supersedeas must first be made to the lower court or administrative tribunal which entered the order or decision on appeal. The issuance of an ex parte order or decision, or an unnecessary delay by the lower court or administrative tribunal in ruling on this application shall constitute an extraordinary circumstance.

(2) After the lower court or administrative tribunal has ruled, any party may petition the appellate court where the appeal is pending or an individual judge or justice for review of this order. The individual judge or justice may grant or deny the relief on a temporary basis, and refer the matter to the full appellate court to hear and determine the matter, or he or she may issue a final order. Upon the issuance of a final order by an individual judge or justice, an aggrieved party may petition the full appellate court for review of that decision.

(3) A person seeking an order lifting an automatic stay or granting a writ of supersedeas must file a written petition verified by the client. The petition shall be captioned the same as the appeal. In addition to the petition and verification, the moving party must contemporaneously file a certified copy of the order, judgment, decree or decision of the lower court or administrative tribunal and a copy of the notice of appeal with its proof of service.

(4) The petition shall contain:

(A) the factual background necessary for an understanding of the petition. If the facts are subject to dispute, the petition shall be supported by affidavits or other sworn statements;

(B) the grounds for the petition, and legal arguments with supporting points and authority;

(C) a showing that an application for this relief was made to the lower court or administrative tribunal, and was unjustifiably denied or that the relief granted failed to afford the relief which the petitioner requested. A certified copy of the lower court's or administrative tribunal's ruling must be included. If no application was made to the lower court or administrative tribunal, then the petition shall state the extraordinary circumstances which made it impracticable to make such an application.

(5) The petition and accompanying documents shall be served on the opposing party(ies). Upon application to the full appellate court, one original and six copies, and a certificate of service shall be filed with the clerk of the appellate court. If the relief is sought from an individual judge or justice, the original and two copies must be filed with the judge or justice. The individual judge or justice shall forward the original documents, including a copy of any order issued by the judge or justice in the matter, to the clerk of the appellate court as soon as possible.

(6) A supersedeas or order lifting the automatic stay may be issued ex parte only where exigent circumstances require that action be taken before there is time for a hearing. An ex parte order shall issue only if:

(A) it clearly appears from specific facts shown by affidavits or included in the verified petition that immediate and irreparable injury, loss or damage will result before the opposing party can respond; and

(B) the moving party's attorney certifies in writing, as an officer of the court, the efforts which have been made to give notice, or the reasons supporting the claim that notice should not be required.

(7) Any party aggrieved by the decision of the lower court, the administrative tribunal, or an individual judge or justice may petition under this Rule for a review of that decision.

[Adopted effective September 1, 1990. Amended effective May 3, 2007; February 5, 2009. Renumbered from Rule 225 effective April 29, 2009.]

RULE 242. CERTIORARI TO THE COURT OF APPEALS

(a) Authority of the Supreme Court. The Supreme Court, or any two (2) justices thereof, may in its discretion, on motion of any party to the case or on its own motion, issue a writ of certiorari to review a final decision of the Court of Appeals.

(b) Considerations Governing Review. A writ of certiorari is not a matter of right, but of sound judicial discretion, and will be granted only where there are special and important reasons. The following, while neither controlling nor fully measuring the Supreme Court's discretion or power to grant review in general, indicate the character of reasons which will be considered:

(1) Where there are novel questions of law.

(2) Where there is a dissent in the decision of the Court of Appeals.

(3) Where the decision of the Court of Appeals is in conflict with a prior decision of the Supreme Court.

(4) Where substantial constitutional issues are directly involved.

(5) Where a federal question is included and the decision of the Court of Appeals conflicts with a decision of the United States Supreme Court.

(c) Time for Petitioning and Filing Fee. A decision of the Court of Appeals is not final for the purpose of review by the Supreme Court until the petition for rehearing or reinstatement has been acted on by the Court of Appeals. A petition for writ of certiorari shall be served on opposing counsel and filed with proof of service with the Clerk of the Court of Appeals and the Clerk of the Supreme Court within thirty (30) days after the petition for rehearing or reinstatement is finally decided by the Court of Appeals. An original and six (6) copies of the petition shall be filed with the Supreme Court. The copies filed with the Supreme Court shall be accompanied by the filing fee set by order of the Supreme Court.[1] No filing fee shall be required in criminal cases or petitions filed by the State of South Carolina or its agencies or departments.

(d) Content of Petition. The petition for writ of certiorari shall contain the following:

(1) Certification by counsel for petitioner that a petition for rehearing or reinstatement was made and finally ruled on by the Court of Appeals.

(2) The questions presented for review, expressed in the terms and circumstances of the case but without unnecessary detail. Only those questions raised in the Court of Appeals and in the petition for rehearing shall be included in the petition for writ of certiorari as a question presented to the Supreme Court. A question presented will be deemed to include every subsidiary question fairly comprised therein.

(3) A concise statement of the case, containing the facts material to the consideration of the questions presented.

(4) A direct and concise argument in support of the petition. The argument on each question shall include citation of authority and specific reference to pertinent portions of the Record on Appeal. Failure of a petitioner to present with accuracy, brevity, and clarity the information and arguments that are essential to a ready and adequate understanding of the points requiring consideration will be a sufficient reason for denying the petition. The total length of a petition shall not exceed twenty-five (25) pages.

(e) Appendix. At the same time the petition is filed, the petitioner shall also file two (2) copies of the Appendix with the Clerk of the Supreme Court. As provided by Rule 267(d), one copy filed with the Supreme Court shall be filed unbound. The Appendix shall include the following:

(1) A copy of the Record on Appeal and brief(s), or in post-conviction relief matters, a copy of the Appendix, petition for writ of certiorari, return, reply and any briefs filed under Rule 243, SCACR.

(2) If the matter was dismissed by the Court of Appeals for procedural or other reasons, the Appendix shall include any documents relevant to the dismissal including any motion to dismiss and any return or reply that may have been filed.

(3) A copy of the decision of the Court of Appeals on which certiorari is sought.

(4) A copy of the petition for rehearing or reinstatement filed in the Court of Appeals and the Court's ruling on that petition.

If the Appendix contains any of the documents specified in (2) above, a copy of the Appendix must be served on the opposing counsel and proof of service of the Appendix must be filed when the petition for writ of certiorari is filed.

(f) Return to Petition. Within thirty (30) days after service of the petition, respondent shall serve a copy of his return on opposing counsel, and shall file with the Clerk of the Supreme Court one original and six (6) copies of his return and proof of service showing that the return has been served. The return shall include an argument on each question and may include a counter-statement of the case and of the questions presented for review. The total length of a return shall not exceed twenty-five (25) pages. If review is being sought regarding a post-conviction relief case, the respondent need not file a return unless requested by the Supreme Court.

(g) Reply. The petitioner shall have ten (10) days from the date of service of the return to file with the Clerk of the Supreme Court an original and six (6) copies of a reply and proof of service showing that the reply has been served. The total length of the reply shall not exceed fifteen (15) pages.

(h) Consolidation. Where several cases that involve identical or closely related questions are sought to be reviewed on certiorari, the filing of a single petition for writ of certiorari shall suffice to cover all the cases.

(i) Consideration by the Supreme Court. The petition will be considered by the Supreme Court without oral argument. The petition may be granted or denied on any question presented. If the petition is granted, the Clerk shall notify each party or his attorney, specifying the question or questions to be considered, and the parties shall prepare briefs addressing the question(s). Petitioner shall have thirty (30) days from the date the petition is granted to serve a copy of his brief on all parties to the appeal, and file with the Clerk of the Supreme Court fifteen (15) copies of his brief, along with proof of service. At the time he files his brief, petitioner shall also file thirteen (13) additional copies of the Appendix. Within thirty (30) days after service of petitioner's brief, respondent shall serve a copy of his brief on all parties to the appeal, and file with the Clerk of the Supreme Court fifteen (15) copies of his brief, along with proof of service. Petitioner may file a reply brief. If a reply brief is prepared, petitioner shall, within ten (10) days after service of respondent's brief, serve a copy of his reply brief on all parties to the appeal and file with the Clerk of the Supreme Court fifteen (15) copies of his reply brief, along with proof of service. The briefs shall, to the extent possible, comply with the requirements of Rule 208(b). Oral argument shall not be permitted unless ordered by the Supreme Court.

(j) Costs When a Writ of Certiorari Has Been Granted.

(1) *To Whom Awarded.* Unless otherwise ordered by the Supreme Court or agreed to by the parties, costs shall be assessed against the appellant if the decision of the Supreme Court has the effect of affirming the judgment of the lower court or tribunal which was reviewed by the Court of Appeals. When the decision of the Supreme Court has the effect of reversing the judgment of the lower court or tribunal which was on appeal, costs shall be assessed against the respondent before the Court of Appeals. When the decision of the Supreme Court has the effect of affirming or reversing in part or vacating the judgment of the lower court or tribunal which was on appeal, costs shall be allowed only as ordered by the Supreme Court.

(2) *Costs Allowed.* The party entitled to recover costs may recover all those costs specified in Rule 222(b), to include the attorney's fee provided by that rule. Additionally, the party may, to the extent the party actually incurred these costs, recover: (1) the filing fee paid under Rule 242(c); (2) the cost of printing the Appendix under Rule 242(e) and (i); and (3) the cost of printing the party's brief(s) under Rule 242(i). The party may also recover an additional attorney's fee in an amount which shall be set by order of the Supreme Court.[2] The allowance of additional costs will generally not be allowed except in the most extraordinary circumstances.

(3) *Costs for Printing Irrelevant Matter.* A party who has unjustifiably designated irrelevant matter to be included in the Record on Appeal shall not be entitled to tax the cost of printing this matter in the Record on Appeal or in the Appendix. Further, a party not otherwise entitled to costs under this Rule shall be entitled to collect the cost the party incurred for printing irrelevant matter in the Record on Appeal and/or the Appendix which another party unjustifiably designated to be included in the Record on Appeal.

(4) *Motion for Costs.* A party desiring costs to be taxed shall, within fifteen (15) days of the issuance of the remittitur, serve and file a motion requesting that costs be assessed under this Rule. The motion shall comply with Rule 240. If costs are being sought under (2) above, the motion shall be accompanied by a sworn, itemized statement of costs incurred in the form prescribed in the Appendix to these rules. Any return or reply to the motion shall be served and filed in the manner provided by Rule 240. The return may oppose the request for costs or seek a reduction of the amount of costs to be awarded. The remittitur shall not be stayed by the filing of a motion for costs.

(5) *Taxation.* Costs under this Rule shall be taxed by the Supreme Court. If costs are taxed, they shall become part of the judgment of the appellate court and shall be added to the remittitur.

(6) *Applicability.* Costs shall not be awarded in criminal cases or post-conviction relief cases.

[Adopted effective September 1, 1990. Amended effective August 31, 1997; July 1, 2000; September 1, 2001; May 3, 2007; May 1, 2008. Renumbered from Rule 226 effective April 29, 2009.]

1 By order dated April 17, 1990, this filing fee was set at one hundred ($100.00) dollars.

2 By order dated July 24, 1997, the amount of attorney's fee was set at $1,000.

RULE 243. CERTIORARI TO REVIEW POST-CONVICTION RELIEF ACTIONS

(a) Review by Writ of Certiorari. A final decision entered under the Post–Conviction Relief Act shall be reviewed by the Supreme Court upon petition of either party for a writ of certiorari, according to the procedure set forth in this Rule.

(b) Notice of Appeal and Ordering Transcript. In the same manner and under the same time limitations as provided for appeals from the Court of Common Pleas in Rules 203 and 207, the petitioner shall serve and file a notice of appeal and shall obtain from the court reporter a transcript of the proceedings in the lower court.

(c) Explanation Required. If the lower court has determined that the post-conviction relief action is barred as successive or being untimely under the statute of limitations, the petitioner must, at the time the notice of appeal is filed, provide an explanation as to why this determination was improper. This explanation must contain sufficient facts, argument and citation to legal authority to show that there is an arguable basis for asserting that the determination by the lower court was improper. If the petitioner fails to make a sufficient showing, the notice of appeal may be dismissed.

(d) Service and Filing of Petition and Appendix. Within thirty (30) days of receipt of the transcript, petitioner shall serve a copy of the Appendix and petition for writ of certiorari on opposing counsel and shall file with the Clerk of the Supreme Court an original plus six (6) copies of the petition, two (2) copies of the Appendix, and proof of service showing the Appendix and petition have been served. As provided by Rule 267(d), one copy of the Appendix filed with the Supreme Court shall be filed unbound.

(e) Content of Petition. The petition shall contain:

(1) The questions presented for review, expressed in the terms and circumstances of the case but without unnecessary detail.

(2) A concise statement of the case, containing the facts material to the consideration of the questions presented.

(3) A direct and concise argument in support of the petition. The argument on each question shall include citation of authority and specific reference to pertinent portions of the lower court record. The total length of a petition shall not exceed twenty-five pages.

(f) Content of Appendix. The Appendix shall contain:

(1) The entire lower court record.

(2) A copy of the final order entered after the post-conviction proceeding.

(3) An index setting forth the principal matters contained in the Appendix. This index shall be in the same form required for a Record on Appeal under Rule 210(e).

(g) Return of Respondent. Within thirty (30) days after service of the petition and Appendix, respondent shall serve a copy of his return on opposing counsel, and shall file with the Clerk of the Supreme Court an original and six (6) copies of his return and proof of service showing that the return has been served. The return may rephrase the questions, offer additional sustaining grounds, and present a concise counter-statement. The total length of a return shall not exceed twenty-five (25) pages.

(h) Reply. The petitioner shall have ten (10) days from the date of service of the return to file with the Clerk of the Supreme Court an original and six (6) copies of a reply and proof of service showing that the reply has been served. The total length of the reply shall not exceed fifteen (15) pages.

(i) Special Procedures Where a White v. State Review Is Sought. Where the petition seeks review under White v. State, 263 S.C. 110, 208 S.E.2d 35 (1974), the following procedure shall be followed:

(1) When the post-conviction relief judge has affirmatively found that the right to a direct appeal was not knowingly and intelligently waived, the petition shall contain a question raising this issue along with all other post-conviction relief issues petitioner seeks to have reviewed. At the same time the petition is served, petitioner shall serve and file a brief addressing the direct appeal issues. This brief shall, to the extent possible, comply with the requirements of Rule 208(b). Respondent's return to the petition shall address the post-conviction relief issues, including whether the direct appeal was knowingly and intelligently waived. At the same time the return is due, respondent shall also serve and file a brief addressing the direct appeal issues. Within ten (10) days after service of respondent's brief, petitioner may file a reply brief on the direct appeal issues.

(2) When the post-conviction relief judge has found that the applicant is *not* entitled to a White v. State review, the petition shall raise the question of waiver of the right to a direct appeal along with all other post-conviction relief issues petitioner seeks to have reviewed. The petition shall also contain a "Statement of Issues on Appeal" listing the issues to be raised if a White v. State review is granted; this statement of issues shall comply with the requirements of Rule 208(b)(1)(B). Briefing of the direct appeal issues will not be allowed unless certiorari is granted on the issue.

(j) Procedure Upon Grant of Certiorari. Upon the concurrence of any two justices, the petition may be granted on any question presented. The petition will be considered by the Supreme Court without oral argument. If the petition is granted, the Clerk shall notify each party or his attorney, specifying the question or questions to be considered, and the parties shall prepare briefs addressing the question(s). Petitioner shall have thirty (30) days from the date the petition is granted to serve a copy of his brief on all parties to the appeal, and file with the Clerk of the Supreme Court fifteen (15) copies of his brief, along with proof of service. At the time he files his brief, petitioner shall also file thirteen (13) additional copies of the Appendix. Within thirty (30) days after service of petitioner's brief, respondent shall serve a copy of his brief on all parties to the appeal, and file with the Clerk of the Supreme Court fifteen (15) copies of his brief, along with proof of service. Petitioner may file a reply brief. If a reply brief is prepared, petitioner shall, within ten (10) days after service of respondent's brief, serve a copy of his reply brief on all parties to the appeal and file with the Clerk of the Supreme Court fifteen (15) copies of his reply brief, along with proof of service. The briefs shall, to the extent possible, comply with the requirements of Rule 208(b). Oral argument shall not be permitted unless ordered by the Supreme Court.

(k) Bail Pending Appellate Review. A post-conviction relief applicant may be admitted to bail after the service of the notice of appeal by either the applicant or the State. Where the sentence originally imposed did not exceed imprisonment for ten (10) years, the petition for bail shall be made to the lower court. In all other cases, the petition for bail shall be made to the Supreme Court. The petition and any return or reply shall comply with the requirements of Rule 240. The authority to grant bail will be exercised with caution and only in exceptional cases. In deciding whether to exercise the discretionary authority to admit an applicant to bail, the following factors will be considered: the probability the applicant will prevail on appellate review and the nature of the relief he or she will receive; the seriousness of the criminal offense committed; the danger the applicant may pose to the community if he or she is released; the likelihood that the applicant may flee if released; and the character and circumstances of the applicant. If bail is granted, the court may require the posting of a bond and impose other conditions. A party aggrieved by the decision of the lower court regarding bail may petition the Supreme Court for review of that decision.

(*l*) Transfer of Cases to the Court of Appeals. The Supreme Court may transfer a case filed under this rule to the Court of Appeals. If transferred, the Court of Appeals shall proceed with the case in the same manner as the Supreme Court would have done under this rule with the exception that a petition for a writ of certiorari may be granted by one judge of a three-judge panel. Review of any final decision of the Court of Appeals shall be by a petition for a writ of certiorari under Rule 242, SCACR.

[Adopted effective September 1, 1990. Amended effective July 1, 1993; July 1, 2000; May 1, 2005; May 3, 2007; January 10, 2008; May 1, 2008. Renumbered from Rule 227 effective April 29, 2009.]

RULE 244. CERTIFICATION OF QUESTIONS OF LAW

(a) Scope of Certification. The Supreme Court in its discretion may answer questions of law certified to it by any federal court of the United States or the highest appellate court or an intermediate appellate court of any other state, when requested by the certifying court if there are involved in any proceeding before that court questions of law of this state which may be determinative of the cause then pending in the certifying court when it appears to the certifying court there is no controlling precedent in the decisions of the Supreme Court.

(b) Procedure. The certification order shall be signed by the presiding judge or the chief judge, and forwarded to the Supreme Court by the clerk of the certifying court under its official seal. A certification order shall set forth the questions of law to be answered, all findings of fact relevant to the questions certified, and a statement showing fully the nature of the controversy in which the questions arose. The Supreme Court may request the original or copies of all or of any portion of the record before the certifying court to be filed with the Court, if, in the opinion of the Supreme Court, the record or a portion thereof may be necessary in deciding to accept or in answering the questions.

(c) Action by the Supreme Court. Within forty-five (45) days of receiving a certification order, the Supreme Court shall notify the certifying court and the parties of its decision to answer or refuse to answer the questions certified. At the same time the Supreme Court gives notice of its decision to answer the questions, it shall also inform the certifying court and the parties of the approximate date the questions will come before the Supreme Court for consideration.

(d) Briefs. The plaintiff in the trial court or the appealing party in the appellate court shall serve and file his brief within thirty (30) days from the date of receipt of the notice from the Supreme Court specified in Rule 244(c) and the opposing party shall serve and file a respondent's brief within thirty (30) days after service of copies of the plaintiff's or appellant's brief. Within ten (10) days after service of the respondent's brief, the plaintiff or appellant may serve and file a reply brief. The briefs shall, to the extent possible, have the same content as briefs under Rule 208(b), and shall be served and filed in the same number and manner as provided by Rule 211, to include proof of service.

(e) Rescission of Certification. The Supreme Court, in its discretion, may rescind its agreement to answer a certified question. Upon deciding to rescind, the Supreme Court shall notify the parties and the certifying court of its action.

(f) Decision. The written opinion of the Supreme Court stating the law governing the questions certified shall be sent to the certifying court and to the parties by the Clerk under the seal of the Supreme Court. The decision shall be accorded the same force and effect as any other decision of the Supreme Court and shall be published with the opinions of the Supreme Court.

(g) Certification to Other Courts. An appellate court, on its own motion or the motion of any party, may order certification of questions of law to the highest court of any state when it appears to the court that there are involved in any proceeding before the court questions of law of the receiving state which may be determinative of the cause then pending in the court and it appears to the court that there are no controlling precedents in the decisions of the highest court or intermediate appellate courts of the receiving state. The procedures for certification from this State to the receiving state shall be those provided in the laws of the receiving state.

[Adopted effective September 1, 1990. Amended effective July 1, 2000. Renumbered from Rule 228 effective April 29, 2009.]

RULE 245. ORIGINAL JURISDICTION OF THE SUPREME COURT

(a) When Appropriate. The Supreme Court will not entertain matters in its original jurisdiction when the matter can be determined in a lower court in the first instance, without material prejudice to the rights of the parties. If the public interest is involved, or if special grounds of emergency or other good reasons exist why the original jurisdiction of the Supreme Court should be exercised, the facts showing the reasons must be stated in the petition with supporting affidavits.

(b) Extraordinary Writs. A party seeking the issuance of an extraordinary writ in the original jurisdiction of the Supreme Court shall serve and file a petition. The petition and any return shall comply with the requirements of Rule 240.

(c) Actions. A party seeking to have the Supreme Court entertain an action in its original jurisdiction (petitioner) shall serve on all other parties (respondents) a petition for original jurisdiction, a complaint setting forth the claim for relief in the manner specified by Rule 8, SCRCP, and a notice advising each respondent he has twenty (20) days from the date of service to serve and file a return to the petition. Service shall be in the same manner as required for summons and complaints in Rule 4, SCRCP. The petitioner shall file an original and six (6) copies of the petition, notice and complaint with the Clerk of the Supreme Court, along with proof of service on each respondent. Any party opposing the petition shall have twenty (20) days from the date of service to file an original and six (6) copies of his return with the Clerk of the Supreme Court and serve on all parties a copy of the return. Failure of a party to timely file a return may be deemed a consent by that party to the matter being heard in the original jurisdiction. Unless otherwise ordered by the Supreme Court, the petition shall be decided without oral argument. If the petition is granted, the respondent shall have thirty (30) days to serve and file an answer to the complaint. The Supreme Court may provide for discovery, fact finding and/or a briefing schedule as necessary.

[Adopted effective September 1, 1990. Renumbered from Rule 229 effective April 29, 2009.]

RULE 246. STAY IN CRIMINAL CASES

(a) Stays Pending Appeal. The service of a notice of appeal by a criminal defendant shall operate as a stay of the execution of the sentence until the appeal is finally disposed of; provided, however, a sentence of confinement shall not be stayed until the defendant has posted bail under S.C. Code Ann. §§ 18–1–80 and –90 (1985). Where the sentence exceeds imprisonment for ten (10) years, the defendant may only be admitted to bail by an appellate court. Where the State has taken an appeal, the appeal shall automatically operate as a stay of further proceedings in the lower court.

(b) Stays of Sentences After Affirmance. No stay of any sentence in a criminal case which has been affirmed by the judgment of an appellate court shall be granted, except by order of an appellate court, or a judge or justice thereof, upon motion pursuant to Rule 240.

[Adopted effective September 1, 1990. Renumbered from Rule 230 effective April 29, 2009.]

RULE 247. CERTIORARI TO REVIEW DNA TESTING DECISIONS

(a) Review by Writ of Certiorari. A final order of the circuit or family court denying or granting DNA testing under the Access to Justice Post–Conviction DNA Testing Act (S.C. Code Ann. §§ 17–28–10 to –120) shall be reviewed upon petition of either party for a writ of certiorari according to the procedure set forth in this rule.

(b) Notice of Appeal and Ordering Transcript. The notice of appeal shall be served on all respondents within ten (10) days after receipt of written notice of entry of the final order. If review will involve testing relating to a case in which a sentence of death was imposed or will involve a challenge on state or federal grounds to the constitutionality of a state law or county or municipal ordinance, the notice of appeal shall be filed with the Supreme Court. In all other cases, the notice of appeal shall be filed with the Court of Appeals. Under Rule 204, SCACR, the Supreme Court may certify a case for review by the Supreme Court. Further, in the same manner and under the same time limitations as provided for appeals from the Court of General Sessions or the Family Court in juvenile delinquency cases in Rule 207, the petitioner shall obtain from the court reporter a transcript of the proceedings in the lower court.

(c) Service and Filing of Petition and Appendix. Within thirty (30) days of receipt of the transcript, petitioner shall serve a copy of the Appendix and petition for a writ of certiorari on opposing counsel and shall file with the Clerk of the appellate court in which the matter is pending an original plus six (6) copies of the petition, two (2) copies of the Appendix, and proof of service showing the Appendix and petition have been served. As provided by Rule 267(d), one copy of the Appendix filed with the appellate court shall be filed unbound.

(d) Content of Petition. The petition shall contain:

(1) The questions presented for review, expressed in the terms and circumstances of the case but without unnecessary detail.

(2) A concise statement of the case containing the facts material to the consideration of the questions presented.

(3) A direct and concise argument in support of the petition. The argument on each question shall include citation of authority and specific reference to pertinent portions of the lower court record. The total length of a petition shall not exceed twenty-five (25) pages.

(e) Content of Appendix. The Appendix shall contain:

(1) The entire lower court record.

(2) A copy of the final order entered in the proceeding.

(3) An index setting forth the principal matters contained in the appendix. This index shall be in the same form required for a Record on Appeal under Rule 210(e).

(f) Return of Respondent. Within thirty (30) days after service of the petition and Appendix, respondent shall serve a copy of a return on opposing counsel, and shall file with the Clerk of the appellate court in which the matter is pending an original and six (6) copies of the return and proof of service showing that the return has been served. The return may rephrase the questions, offer additional sustaining grounds, and present a concise counter-statement. The total length of a return shall not exceed twenty-five (25) pages.

(g) Reply. The petitioner shall have ten (10) days from the date of service of the return to file with the Clerk of the appellate court in which the matter is pending an original and six (6) copies of a reply and proof of service showing that the reply has been served. The total length of the reply shall not exceed fifteen (15) pages.

(h) Procedure Upon Grant of Certiorari. Upon the concurrence of any two justices of the Supreme Court or one judge of a three-judge panel of the Court of Appeals, the petition may be granted on any question presented. The petition will be considered by the appellate court without oral argument. If the petition is granted, the Clerk shall notify each party or his attorney, specifying the question or questions to be considered, and the parties shall prepare briefs addressing the question(s). Petitioner shall have thirty (30) days from the date the petition is granted to serve a copy of a brief on all parties to the appeal, and file with the Clerk of the appellate court fifteen (15) copies of the brief, along with proof of service. At the time the brief is filed, petitioner shall also file thirteen (13) additional copies of the Appendix. Within thirty (30) days after service of petitioner's brief, respondent shall serve a copy of a brief on all parties to the appeal, and file with the Clerk of the appellate court fifteen (15) copies of the brief, along with proof of service. Petitioner may file a reply brief. If a reply brief is prepared, petitioner shall, within ten (10) days after service of respondent's brief, serve a copy of the reply brief on all parties to the appeal and file with the Clerk of the appellate court fifteen (15) copies of the reply brief, along with proof of service. The briefs shall, to the extent possible, comply with the requirements of Rule 208(b). Oral argument shall not be permitted unless ordered by the appellate court.

(i) Review of Decisions of the Court of Appeals. A final decision of the Court of Appeals under this rule may be reviewed as provided by Rule 242, SCACR.

[Adopted effective April 29, 2009.]

C. General Provisions

RULE 260. DISMISSAL AND REINSTATEMENT

(a) Involuntary Dismissal and Reinstatement. Whenever it appears that an appellant or a petitioner has failed to comply with the requirements of these Rules, the clerk shall issue an order of dismissal, which shall have the same force and effect as an order of the appellate court. A case shall not be reinstated except by leave of the court, upon good cause shown, after notice to all parties. The clerk shall remit the case to the lower court or administrative tribunal in accordance with Rule 221 unless a motion to reinstate the appeal has been actually received by the court within fifteen (15) days of filing of the order of dismissal (the day of filing being excluded).

(b) Agreed Dismissal. If the parties to an appeal or other proceeding shall sign and file with the clerk of the appellate court an agreement that the proceeding be dismissed, the appellate court may enter an order of dismissal. The agreement may contain a provision altering the costs to be assessed under Rule 222 and/or other settlement terms subject to the provisions of Rule 261.

(c) Withdrawal. An appeal or other proceeding may be dismissed on motion of the appellant or petitioner upon such terms as may be fixed by the court.

[Adopted effective September 1, 1990. Amended effective July 1, 2000; May 3, 2007. Renumbered from Rule 231 effective April 29, 2009.]

RULE 261. AGREEMENTS AND SETTLEMENTS

(a) Agreements Generally. Any agreement submitted to the appellate court for its consideration shall be in writing and signed by the parties or their attorneys. Further, any agreement submitted to the appellate court shall be public unless a motion to seal is filed and the appellate court determines that the matters should be sealed under the standard provided by Rule 41.1, SCRCP.

(b) Settlement Agreements. If a settlement agreement relates to a matter that is pending before an appellate court, the settlement agreement need not be submitted to the appellate court unless approval by the appellate court, a lower court or tribunal is required before the agreement can be effective, or the parties desire to have the agreement approved by the appellate court.

(c) Agreements Regarding Rules. Any agreement to modify a requirement of these Appellate Court Rules must be approved by the appellate court.

(d) Vacation of Prior Opinions, Orders or Judgments. In the agreement, the parties may request vacation of opinions, orders, decisions and judgments previously issued in the matter. The agreement must set forth the facts that warrant this extraordinary relief. If the matter is pending before the Supreme Court and the agreement requests the vacation of an order or opinion of the Court of Appeals, the Supreme Court, in its discretion, may seek a recommendation from the Court of Appeals regarding the request for vacation. If an agreement containing a request for vacation is rejected, the parties may resubmit the agreement without the request for vacation.

[Adopted effective September 1, 1990. Amended effective July 1, 2000; May 5, 2003; May 3, 2007. Renumbered from Rule 232 and amended effective April 29, 2009.]

RULE 262. FILING AND SERVICE

(a) Filing. Except for petitions for rehearing (Rule 221) and motions for reinstatement (Rule 260), filing may be accomplished by:

(1) Delivering the document to the clerk of the appellate court. Whenever a document is filed with the appellate court, at least one copy of the document must contain an original signature as set forth in Rule 267(b); or

(2) By depositing the document in the U.S. mail, properly addressed to the clerk, with sufficient first class postage attached. The date of filing shall be the date of delivery or the date of mailing. Any document filed with the appellate court shall be accompanied by proof of service of such document on all parties. An electronically transmitted facsimile copy of a document may be accepted for filing; however, an original of the document must be immediately sent by U.S. mail to the clerk.

(b) Service. Whenever under these Rules service is required or permitted to be made upon a party represented by an attorney the service shall be made upon the attorney unless service upon the party himself is ordered by the appellate court. Service upon the attorney or upon a party shall be made by delivering a copy to him or by mailing it to him at his last known address or, if no address is known, by leaving it with the clerk of court. Delivery of a copy within this Rule means: handing it to the attorney or to the party; or leaving it at his office with his clerk or other person in charge thereof; or, if there be no one in charge, leaving it in a conspicuous place therein; or, if the office is closed or the person to be served has no office, leaving a copy at his dwelling place or usual place of abode with some person of suitable age and discretion then residing therein. Service by mail is complete upon mailing.

[Adopted effective September 1, 1990. Amended effective July 1, 2000. Renumbered from Rule 233 effective April 29, 2009.]

RULE 263. TIME

(a) Computation. In computing any period of time prescribed or allowed by these Rules, by order of court, or by any applicable statute, the day of the act, event, or default after which the designated period of time begins to run is not to be included. The last day of the period so computed is to be included, unless it is a Saturday, Sunday or a state or federal holiday, in which event the period runs until the end of the next day which is neither a Saturday, Sunday nor such holiday. When the period of time prescribed or allowed is less than seven (7) days, intermediate Saturdays, Sundays and holidays shall be excluded in the computation. A half holiday shall be considered as other days and not as a holiday. No additional time shall be allowed after service by mail or upon a statutory agent. Rule 6(e), SCRCP, is not applicable to these rules, and no additional time shall be allowed by reason of service by mail or upon a statutory agent.

(b) Extending and Diminishing Time Prescribed by These Rules. The time prescribed by these Rules for performing any act except the time for serving the notice of appeal under Rules 203 and 243 may be extended or shortened by the appellate court, or by any judge or justice thereof. The time prescribed by these Rules for performing any act or taking any action may not be extended by agreement of the parties.

[Adopted effective September 1, 1990. Amended effective July 1, 2000. Renumbered from Rule 234 effective April 29, 2009.]

RULE 264. SUBSTITUTION OF ATTORNEYS OR GUARDIANS

(a) Continued Representation. The attorneys and/or guardians ad litem of the respective parties in the court below shall be deemed the attorneys and guardians of the same parties in the appellate court until withdrawal is approved and notice is given as provided in this Rule.

(b) Withdrawal. An attorney of record in a matter pending before an appellate court may not withdraw from representation of his client without justifiable cause, or the consent of his client; and then only after proper written notice to his client, on petition to and by written order of the appellate court, and with notice to the adverse party.

[Adopted effective September 1, 1990. Renumbered from Rule 235 effective April 29, 2009.]

RULE 265. SUBSTITUTION OF PARTIES

(a) Service of Notice in the Event of the Death or Incompetency of a Party. If a party against whom an appeal may be taken dies or becomes incompetent before a notice of appeal is served, an appellant may serve the party's personal representative, guardian ad litem, committee or his attorney of record. If a party entitled to appeal shall die or become incompetent before serving a notice of appeal, the notice may be served by his personal representative, guardian ad litem, committee or his attorney of record. In either event, if there is no attorney of record, the time for serving the notice shall be tolled until a personal representative, guardian ad litem or committee is properly appointed.

(b) Substitution Upon Death or Incompetency of a Party. If a party to an appeal dies or becomes incompetent, the appellate court may, upon motion or on its own initiative, order substitution of the proper parties or remand the case to the trial court for the substitution of the proper parties as provided by Rule 25, SCRCP.

(c) Other Substitution. If substitution of a party is desired for any reason other than death or incompetency, substitution shall be by motion to the appellate court.

(d) Substitution of Official Party. If a public officer in his official capacity is a party to an action pending in an appellate court and during its pendency he ceases to hold office, his successor in office shall be automatically substituted as a party. Proceedings following substitution shall be in the name of the substituted party. An order of substitution may be entered at any time upon the suggestion of the substituted party or any other party, but the omission to enter such an order shall not affect the substitution.

[Adopted effective September 1, 1990. Amended effective June 30, 1991. Renumbered from Rule 236 effective April 29, 2009.]

RULE 266. SUBSEQUENT APPLICATIONS FOR RELIEF

When any justice or judge of any of the courts of this State has declined to grant any order or writ in any case, and thereafter application for the same order or writ, or an order or writ of a similar character, is made to an appellate court or any member thereof, it shall be incumbent upon the party, or his attorney, to show in the application the former refusal and the judge or justice who refused the same, and if the refusal has been reduced to writing, a copy of the order shall be attached to the application.

[Adopted effective September 1, 1990. Renumbered from Rule 237 effective April 29, 2009.]

RULE 267. FORM OF PAPERS

(a) Captions. All documents filed in the appellate court shall be headed by a caption. Except as provided below for appeals from administrative tribunals, the caption shall contain the name of the appellate court where the document is to be filed (i.e., Supreme Court or Court of Appeals); if the matter involves review of a lower court decision, the name of the county and judge from which the appeal is taken including the title of the judge (e.g., Circuit Court Judge, Family Court Judge, Master-in-Equity, Probate Judge, Special Referee, Special Circuit Court Judge); the title of the case (the party commencing the action in the lower court shall always appear first in the title regardless of whom is appellant or petitioner); the title of the document (e.g., RECORD ON APPEAL; APPENDIX; BRIEF OF APPELLANT; PETITION FOR WRIT OF CERTIORARI; MOTION TO DISMISS); and the name, address and phone number of the counsel submitting the document, or in the case of a Record on Appeal or Appendix, the names, addresses and phone numbers of all counsel in the case. The caption should be substantially in the form shown by this example:

THE STATE OF SOUTH CAROLINA
In the Supreme Court

APPEAL FROM RICHLAND COUNTY
Howard S. Barnes, Circuit Court Judge

Paul L. Doe, ... Appellant (or Respondent),

v.

Mary M. Roe, ... Respondent (or Appellant).

RECORD ON APPEAL

John T. Smith, Esquire
P.O. Box 123
Columbia, SC 29000
(803) 000–0000
Attorney for Appellant

Wanda D. Jones, Esquire
P.O. Box 456
Columbia, SC 29000
(803) 000–0000
Attorney for Respondent

In appeals from administrative tribunals, the caption shall contain the name of the appellate court where the document is to be filed (i.e. Supreme Court or Court of Appeals); the name of the tribunal from which the appeal is taken (e.g., Administrative Law Court, Public Service Commission, etc.); the name of the administrative law judge (if applicable); the title of the case (the title shall remain the same as the title before the tribunal regardless of whom is the appellant); the title of the document (e.g., RECORD ON APPEAL; BRIEF OF APPELLANT; MOTION TO DISMISS); and the name, address and phone number of the counsel submitting the document, or in the case of a Record on Appeal, the names, addresses and phone numbers of all counsel in the case. The caption should be substantially in the form shown by this example:

THE STATE OF SOUTH CAROLINA
In the Court of Appeals
[In the Supreme Court]

APPEAL FROM THE ADMINISTRATIVE LAW COURT [OR NAME OF AGENCY]

George E. Brown, Administrative Law Judge

Case No. 05–ALJ–00–0000–CC

South Carolina
Department of Revenue, Respondent,

v.

Jane C. Roe, Appellant.

BRIEF OF APPELLANT

John E. Smith, Esquire
P.O. Box 123
Greenville, SC 29000
(864) 000–0000
Attorney for Appellant

Wanda D. Jones, Esquire
P.O. Box 456
Columbia, SC 29000
(803) 000–0000
Attorney for Respondent

On motions or petitions, the name, address and phone number of counsel submitting the document shall be placed at the end of the document with his signature.

(b) Signatures. The original of a document or paper filed by a party or his attorney shall be signed by the party or the attorney. The signature of a party or attorney constitutes a certificate by him that he has read the document or paper; that to the best of his knowledge, information and belief there is good ground to support it; and that it is not interposed for delay.

(c) Paper and Type Size. All papers or documents filed with the appellate court shall be typewritten or machine duplicated. Type size shall be standard 12–point or larger and double spaced on white bond paper of not less than twenty pound weight, 8 ½ inches by 11 inches. With the exception of exhibits as provided in Rule 210(f), no photographic reduction of the Record on Appeal, brief or other paper is acceptable which reduces the size of the alphabet below that of pica type. Paper shall be of good quality, opaque and unglazed. Duplication through use of chemically treated paper, commonly referred to as "wet image or process copy", does not comply with this rule. Copy may be typed or reproduced on both sides if type or reproduction does not show through; provided, however, if the Record on Appeal or Appendix exceeds 100 pages, copy must be typed or reproduced on both sides of the paper. All copies must be clean, neat and clearly legible.

(d) Margins and Bindings. Typewritten papers or reproductions must have a blank margin of an inch and a half on the left. If more than two sheets are used, they shall be securely fastened on the left margin. While petitions or motions need not be bound, Records on Appeal, Appendices in post-conviction relief matters and briefs must be bound in volumes not exceeding 250 sheets each. If staples or clasps are used to bind the volumes, the spines of the volumes shall be bound with heavy tape. One copy of every Final Brief, Record on Appeal, Supplemental Record, or Appendix filed with the appellate court shall be filed unbound.

(e) Covers. Covers of the Record on Appeal and briefs shall be of a material not less than 50 pound weight and not glassine. The cover of the Record on Appeal shall be white; that of the brief of appellant blue; that of respondent red; that of an intervenor or amicus curiae green; and that of any reply brief gray. The front cover of a brief or Record on Appeal shall contain only the caption.

(f) Compliance. The clerk of the appellate court shall insure compliance with this Rule before accepting any papers for filing.

[Adopted effective September 1, 1990. Amended effective July 1, 1993; July 1, 2000; September 1, 2001; May 3, 2007; May 1, 2008. Renumbered from Rule 238 effective April 29, 2009.]

RULE 268. CITATION OF SOUTH CAROLINA AUTHORITY

To provide guidance on citing South Carolina authority, the following forms of citation are given. Once cited in the form given, the authority may thereafter be cited in an abbreviated form. Additional guidance on citation of authority may be found in *A Uniform System of Citation* published by the Harvard Law Review Association, *A Guide to South Carolina Legal Research and Citation* published by the S.C. Bar C.L.E. Division, or other publications.

(a) South Carolina Constitution. The South Carolina Constitution should be cited in the following manner: S.C. Const. art. IV, § 4.

(b) Statutes and Regulations.

(1) Statutes which appear in a hardbound volume of the Code of Laws of South Carolina should be cited in the following form: S.C.Code Ann. § 1–2–345 (1976). Where the statute appears in a replacement hardbound volume, the citation should include the date appearing on the spine of the volume or the copyright date of the volume in the following form: S.C.Code Ann. § 11–35–1210 (1986). Statutes which appear in the supplement to the Code of Laws of South Carolina should be cited in the following form: S.C.Code Ann. § 6–7–890 (Supp.1988).

(2) Statutes which have not yet been codified should be cited by the number of the Act, and the year and page number where it appears in the South Carolina Acts and Joint Resolutions in the following form: Act No. 100, 1985 S.C. Acts 277.

(3) Regulations which appear in the Code of Laws of South Carolina should be cited in the following manner: 23 S.C.Code Ann.Regs. 19–501 (1976). Regulations which appear in the supplement to the Code of Laws of South Carolina should be cited in the following manner: 24A S.C.Code Ann.Regs. 61–40 (Supp.1988). The date used in the citation shall be the latest copyright date of the volume or supplement.

(c) Court Rules. Court rules should be cited by the rule number and the abbreviations shown:

(1) South Carolina Appellate Court Rules: Rule ___, SCACR.

(a) Rules of Professional Conduct: Rule ___, RPC, Rule 407, SCACR.

(b) Rules for Lawyer Disciplinary Enforcement: Rule ___, RLDE, Rule 413, SCACR.

(c) Code of Judicial Conduct: Rule ___, CJC, Rule 501, SCACR.

(d) Rules for Judicial Disciplinary Enforcement: Rule ___, RJDE, Rule 502, SCACR.

(2) South Carolina Rules of Civil Procedure: Rule ___, SCRCP.

(3) South Carolina Rules of Criminal Procedure: Rule ___, SCRCrimP.

(4) South Carolina Rules of Family Court: Rule ___, SCRFC.

(5) South Carolina Rules of Probate Court: Rule ___, SCRPC.

(6) South Carolina Rules of Magistrates Court: Rule ___, SCRMC.

(7) South Carolina Rules of Evidence: Rule ___, SCRE.

(d) Appellate Court Decisions.

(1) Published opinions or orders of the Supreme Court or Court of Appeals should be cited in the following manner: State v. Williams, 297 S.C. 404, 377 S.E.2d 309 (1989); Andrews v. Piedmont Air Lines, 297 S.C. 367, 377 S.E.2d 127 (Ct.App.1989). If a published opinion does not appear in a reporter, it should be cited in the following manner: Donahue v. Donahue, Op. No. 23083 (S.C.Sup.Ct. filed Sept. 25, 1989); Satcher v. Berry, Op. No. 1383 (S.C.Ct.App. filed July 31, 1989). Further, if the opinion has been published in the Advance Sheets published by the Supreme Court, the opinion should be cited in the following manner: State v. Victor, Op. No. 23118 (S.C.Sup.Ct. filed Dec. 11, 1989) (Davis Adv.Sh. No. 29 at 5). If a published order does not appear in a reporter, it should be cited by its order number: State v. Smith, 89–OR–25 (S.C.Ct.App. dated March 1, 1989), or by reference to the date of the order if no order number has been assigned: State v. Smith, S.C.Sup.Ct. Order dated March 1, 1989. Further, if the order has been published on the front of the Advance Sheets the order should be cited in the following manner: State v. Foster, S.C.Sup.Ct. Order dated June 9, 1989 (Davis Adv.Sh. No. 14).

(2) Memorandum opinions and unpublished orders have no precedential value and should not be cited except in proceedings in which they are directly involved. Memorandum opinions may be cited in the following form: Burns v. Burns, Op. No. 89–MO–110 (S.C.Ct.App. filed July 31, 1989). Unpublished orders may be cited in a similar manner as provided for published orders under Rule 268(d)(1).

(3) The South Carolina Equity Reports, beginning with 1 Desaussure Equity and ending with 14 Richardson Equity should be cited in the following manner: Taylor v. Taylor, 4 S.C.Eq. (4 Des.Eq.) 165 (1811). The following table of cross references is provided:

Reporter	Citation to be Used
1 Desaussure	1 S.C. Eq. (1 Des. Eq.)
2 Desaussure	2 S.C. Eq. (2 Des. Eq.)
3 Desaussure	3 S.C. Eq. (3 Des. Eq.)
4 Desaussure	4 S.C. Eq. (4 Des. Eq.)
Harper	5 S.C. Eq. (Harp. Eq.)
1 McCord	6 S.C. Eq. (1 McCord Eq.)
2 McCord	7 S.C. Eq. (2 McCord Eq.)
Bailey	8 S.C. Eq. (Bail. Eq.)
Richardson's Cases	9 S.C. Eq. (Rich. Cas.)
1 Hill	10 S.C. Eq. (1 Hill Eq.)
2 Hill	11 S.C. Eq. (2 Hill Eq.)
Riley	12 S.C. Eq. (Ril. Eq.)
Dudley	13 S.C. Eq. (Dud. Eq.)
Rice	14 S.C. Eq. (Rice Eq.)
Cheves	15 S.C. Eq. (Chev. Eq.)
McMullen	16 S.C. Eq. (McMul. Eq.)
Speers	17 S.C. Eq. (Speers Eq.)
1 Richardson	18 S.C. Eq. (1 Rich. Eq.)
2 Richardson	19 S.C. Eq. (2 Rich. Eq.)
1 Strobhart	20 S.C. Eq. (1 Strob. Eq.)
2 Strobhart	21 S.C. Eq. (2 Strob. Eq.)
3 Strobhart	22 S.C. Eq. (3 Strob. Eq.)
4 Strobhart	23 S.C. Eq. (4 Strob. Eq.)
3 Richardson	24 S.C. Eq. (3 Rich. Eq.)
4 Richardson	25 S.C. Eq. (4 Rich. Eq.)
5 Richardson	26 S.C. Eq. (5 Rich. Eq.)
6 Richardson	27 S.C. Eq. (6 Rich. Eq.)
7 Richardson	28 S.C. Eq. (7 Rich. Eq.)
8 Richardson	29 S.C. Eq. (8 Rich. Eq.)
9 Richardson	30 S.C. Eq. (9 Rich. Eq.)
10 Richardson	31 S.C. Eq. (10 Rich. Eq.)
11 Richardson	32 S.C. Eq. (11 Rich. Eq.)
12 Richardson	33 S.C. Eq. (12 Rich. Eq.)
13 Richardson	34 S.C. Eq. (13 Rich. Eq.)
14 Richardson	35 S.C. Eq. (14 Rich. Eq.)

(4) The South Carolina Law Reports beginning with 1 Bay and ending with 15 Richardson should be cited in the following manner: Roche v. Chaplin, 17 S.C.L. (1 Bail.) 419 (1830). The following table of cross references is provided:

Reporter	Citation to be Used
1 Bay	1 S.C.L. (1 Bay)
2 Bay	2 S.C.L. (2 Bay)
1 Brevard	3 S.C.L. (1 Brev.)
2 Brevard	4 S.C.L. (2 Brev.)
3 Brevard	5 S.C.L. (3 Brev.)
1 Treadway	6 S.C.L. (1 Tread.)
2 Treadway	7 S.C.L. (2 Tread.)
1 Mill (Constitutional)	8 S.C.L. (1 Mill)
2 Mill (Constitutional)	9 S.C.L. (2 Mill)
1 Nott and McCord	10 S.C.L. (1 Nott & McC.)
2 Nott and McCord	11 S.C.L. (2 Nott & McC.)
1 McCord	12 S.C.L. (1 McCord)
2 McCord	13 S.C.L. (2 McCord)
3 McCord	14 S.C.L. (3 McCord)
4 McCord	15 S.C.L. (4 McCord)

Reporter	Citation to be Used
Harper	16 S.C.L. (Harp.)
1 Bailey	17 S.C.L. (1 Bail.)
2 Bailey	18 S.C.L. (2 Bail.)
1 Hill	19 S.C.L. (1 Hill)
2 Hill	20 S.C.L. (2 Hill)
3 Hill	21 S.C.L. (3 Hill)
Riley	22 S.C.L. (Ril.)
Dudley	23 S.C.L. (Dud.)
Rice	24 S.C.L. (Rice)
Cheves	25 S.C.L. (Chev.)
1 McMullen	26 S.C.L. (1 McMul.)
2 McMullen	27 S.C.L. (2 McMul.)
1 Speers	28 S.C.L. (1 Speers)
2 Speers	29 S.C.L. (2 Speers)
1 Richardson	30 S.C.L. (1 Rich.)
2 Richardson	31 S.C.L. (2 Rich.)
1 Strobhart	32 S.C.L. (1 Strob.)
2 Strobhart	33 S.C.L. (2 Strob.)
3 Strobhart	34 S.C.L. (3 Strob.)
4 Strobhart	35 S.C.L. (4 Strob.)
5 Strobhart	36 S.C.L. (5 Strob.)
3 Richardson	37 S.C.L. (3 Rich.)
4 Richardson	38 S.C.L. (4 Rich.)
5 Richardson	39 S.C.L. (5 Rich.)
6 Richardson	40 S.C.L. (6 Rich.)
7 Richardson	41 S.C.L. (7 Rich.)
8 Richardson	42 S.C.L. (8 Rich.)
9 Richardson	43 S.C.L. (9 Rich.)
10 Richardson	44 S.C.L. (10 Rich.)
11 Richardson	45 S.C.L. (11 Rich.)
12 Richardson	46 S.C.L. (12 Rich.)
13 Richardson	47 S.C.L. (13 Rich.)
14 Richardson	48 S.C.L. (14 Rich.)
15 Richardson	49 S.C.L. (15 Rich.)

[Adopted effective September 1, 1990. Amended effective September 3, 1995; September 1, 2001. Renumbered from Rule 239 effective April 29, 2009.]

RULE 269. FRIVOLOUS APPEALS, PETITIONS, MOTIONS, OR RETURNS

Where an appeal, petition, motion or return is frivolous or taken solely for the purposes of delay, or is not in compliance with these Rules, the appellate court may upon its own motion or that of a party, after ten (10) days notice, impose upon offending attorneys or parties such sanctions as the circumstances of the case and discouragement of like conduct in the future may require. This Rule does not apply to any matters where counsel is required by law to pursue an appeal or petition for writ of certiorari even though the matter may be frivolous.

[Adopted effective September 1, 1990. Renumbered from Rule 240 effective April 29, 2009.]

RULE 270. FORMS

The Supreme Court should prescribe the content and format of the forms required by these Rules. The use of *these* forms *is recommended, but is not required.*

[Adopted effective September 1, 1990. Renumbered from Rule 241 effective April 29, 2009.]

APPENDICES TO PART II

APPENDIX A. TABLE OF COMPARATIVE RULES

This Table indicates the source or the most similar provision(s) under the former Supreme Court Rules for each of the Rules in the 100 and 200 series.

SCACR	TITLE	SOURCE OR FORMER RULE
101	SCOPE AND TITLE	None
102	EFFECTIVE DATE AND REPEALER	None
201	RIGHT TO APPEAL	
	(a) Judgments and Orders Subject to Appeal	Rule 72, SCRCP
	(b) Who May Appeal	S.C. Code § 18–1–30
202	DESIGNATION OF PARTIES	S.C. Code § 18–1–120
203	NOTICE OF APPEAL	
	(a) Notice	Sup. Ct. Rule 1, § 1B
	(b) Time for Service	Sup. Ct. Rule 1, § 1A
	(c) Cross–Appeals	None
	(d) Filing	Sup. Ct. Rule 1, § 1C S.C. Code § 14–8–200
	(e) Form and Content	Sup. Ct. Rule 1, § 1E
204	TRANSFER OF CASES	S.C. Code §§ 14–8–210(b), and 14–8–260
205	EFFECT OF APPEAL	Sup. Ct. Rule 18, § 3
206	CASES INVOLVING MULTIPLE NOTICES OF APPEAL	None, but prior practice
207	TRANSCRIPT OF PROCEEDINGS	
	(a) Ordering the Transcript	Sup. Ct. Rule 1, § 2A–B
	(b) Delivery of Transcript	Sup. Ct. Rule 1, § 2A
	(c) Extension for Court Reporter	Sup. Ct. Rule 1, § 2D
	(d) Notice of Extension	Sup. Ct. Rule 1, § 2E
	(e) Failure to Receive Transcript	Sup. Ct. Rule 1, § 2F
	(f) Failure to Comply	Sup. Ct. Rule 1, § 2G
	(g) Duty of Appellant	None
208	INITIAL BRIEFS	
	(a) Time for Serving and Filing Initial Briefs	Sup.Ct. Rule 8, § 9
	(b) Content	Sup.Ct. Rules 1, § 3A; 4, § 3A and 8, §§ 2–4
209	DESIGNATION OF MATTER TO BE INCLUDED IN THE RECORD ON APPEAL	None, but see Sup.Ct. Rule 1, § 3
210	RECORD ON APPEAL	
	(a) Time for Service	Sup.Ct. Rule 1, § 4
	(b) Time for Filing	Sup.Ct. Rule 1, § 4
	(c) Content	Sup.Ct. Rule 4
	(d) Title	Sup.Ct. Rule 4, § 2
	(e) Index	Sup.Ct. Rule 4, § 2
	(f) Exhibits	Sup.Ct. Rule 4, § 5
	(g) Certificate of Counsel	Sup.Ct. Rule 4, § 2
	(h) Review Limited to Record on Appeal	Sup.Ct. Rule 8, § 7
211	FINAL BRIEFS	None
212	SUPPLEMENTAL RECORD	Sup.Ct. Rule 2
213	AMICUS CURIAE BRIEF	None, but prior practice
214	CONSOLIDATION	Sup.Ct. Rule 26

SCACR	TITLE	SOURCE OR FORMER RULE
215	SUBMISSION WITHOUT ORAL ARGUMENT	Sup.Ct. Rule 29
216	NOTICE OF ORAL ARGUMENT	Sup.Ct. Rule 22
217	MOTION TO ARGUE AGAINST PRECEDENT	Sup.Ct. Rule 8, § 10
218	ORAL ARGUMENT	Sup.Ct. Rules 10, 12, and 13
219	HEARING OF CASES BY THE COURT OF APPEALS EN BANC	S.C. Code § 14–8–90
220	OPINIONS	
	(a) Opinions	None, but prior practice
	(b)(1) Decisions by Court (Sup. Ct.)	Sup.Ct. Rule 23 and S.C. Code § 18–9–280
	(b)(2) Decisions by Court (Ct. App.)	S.C. Code § 14–8–250
	(c) Affirmance on Any Ground Appearing in Record	Sup.Ct. Rule 4, § 8
221	REHEARING AND REMITTITUR	
	(a) Rehearing	Sup.Ct. Rule 17, § 2
	(b) Remittitur	Sup.Ct. Rule 17, § 1
	(c) Rehearing of Motions	None, but prior practice
222	COSTS ON APPEAL	Sup.Ct. Rule 38
223	ARBITRATION OF APPEALS	None, but allowed by prior order of the Supreme Court
224	MOTIONS AND PETITIONS GENERALLY	
	(a–e) Applicability, etc.	Sup.Ct. Rule 16
	(f) Reply	None
	(g–h) Failure to Comply, etc.	Sup.Ct. Rule 16
	(i) Authority of an Individual Judge or Justice	S.C. Const. Art. V, § 20
225	STAY AND SUPERSEDEAS IN CIVIL ACTIONS	Sup.Ct. Rules 18, § 3B; and 41
226	CERTIORARI TO THE COURT OF APPEALS	Sup.Ct. Rule 55
227	CERTIORARI TO REVIEW POST–CONVICTION RELIEF ACTIONS	Sup.Ct. Rule 50(9)
228	CERTIFICATION OF QUESTIONS OF LAW	Sup.Ct. Rule 46
229	ORIGINAL JURISDICTION OF THE SUPREME COURT	Sup.Ct. Rule 20
230	STAY IN CRIMINAL CASES	
	(a) Stays Pending Appeal	None, but prior practice
	(b) Stays of Sentences After Affirmance	Sup.Ct. Rule 28
231	DISMISSAL AND REINSTATEMENT	Sup.Ct. Rules 1, §§ 5 and 6; 8, § 9; and 18, § 2
232	AGREEMENTS AND SETTLEMENTS	Sup.Ct. Rule 15
233	FILING AND SERVICE	
	(a) Filing	None, but prior practice
	(b) Service	Sup.Ct. Rule 1, § 8; Rule 5 (b)(1), SCRCP
234	TIME	
	(a) Computation	Rule 6(a), SCRCP
	(b) Extending and Diminishing Time Prescribed by these Rules	Sup.Ct. Rule 18, § 1
235	SUBSTITUTION OF ATTORNEYS OR GUARDIANS	Sup.Ct. Rule 3, § 1

SCACR	TITLE	SOURCE OR FORMER RULE
236	SUBSTITUTION OF PARTIES	Sup.Ct. Rule 3, § 2
237	SUBSEQUENT APPLICATIONS FOR RELIEF	Sup.Ct. Rule 30
238	FORM OF PAPERS	
	(a) Captions	Sup.Ct. Rule 4, § 2
	(b) Signatures	Rule 11(a), SCRCP
	(c)-(f) Paper and Type Size, etc.	Sup.Ct. Rule 5
239	CITATION OF SOUTH CAROLINA AUTHORITY	Sup.Ct. Rule 8, §§ 11–12
240	FRIVOLOUS APPEAL, PETITIONS, MOTIONS OR RETURNS	None
241	FORMS	Sup.Ct. Rule 39

APPENDIX B. APPEALS CHART

This chart shows the major steps in processing an appeal under the South Carolina Appellate Court Rules and is intended to provide an overview of the direct appeal process. It does not give all of the detailed requirements for perfecting an appeal, nor does it show the steps necessary in special situations (cross appeals, multiple appellants, cases requiring no transcript from the court reporter, petitions for writs of certiorari to the Court of Appeals, etc.). Counsel should always consult the text of the Rules.

PART II
APPENDIX B

APPEALS CHART

This chart shows the major steps in processing an appeal under the South Carolina Appellate Court Rules and is intended to provide an overview of the direct appeal process. It does not give all of the detailed requirements for perfecting an appeal, nor does it show the steps necessary in special situations (cross appeals, multiple appellants cases requiring no transcript from the court reporter, petitions for writs of certiorari to the Court of Appeals, etc.). Counsel should always consult the text of the Rules.

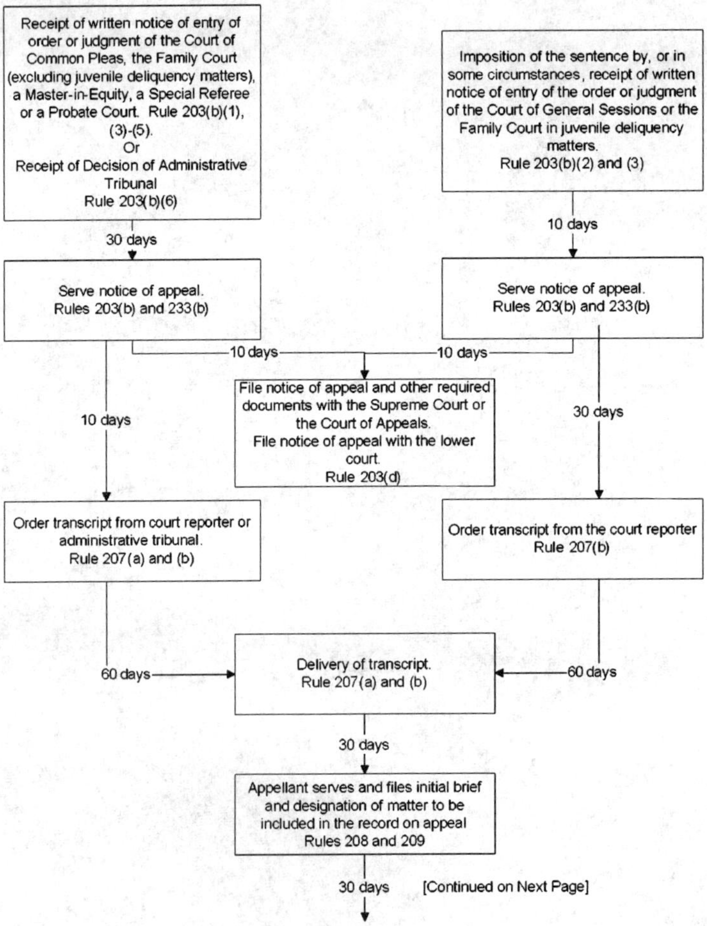

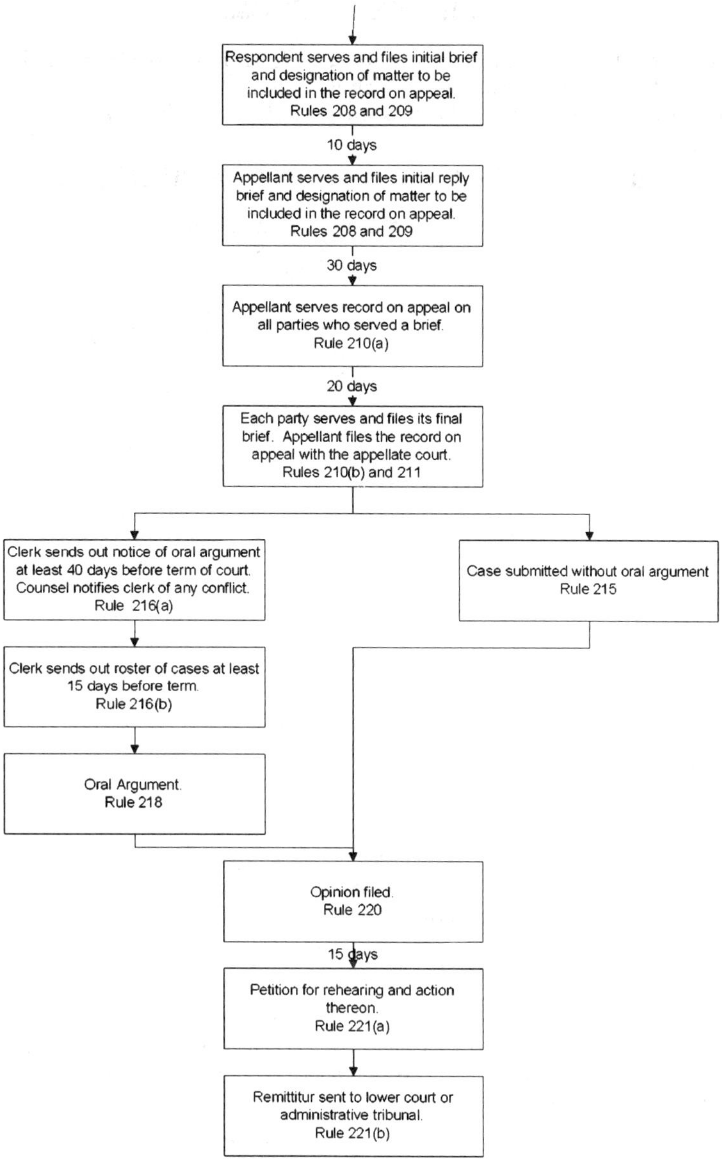
Respondent serves and files initial brief and designation of matter to be included in the record on appeal. Rules 208 and 209
10 days
Appellant serves and files initial reply brief and designation of matter to be included in the record on appeal. Rules 208 and 209
30 days
Appellant serves record on appeal on all parties who served a brief. Rule 210(a)
20 days
Each party serves and files its final brief. Appellant files the record on appeal with the appellate court. Rules 210(b) and 211
Clerk sends out notice of oral argument at least 40 days before term of court. Counsel notifies clerk of any conflict. Rule 216(a)
Case submitted without oral argument Rule 215
Clerk sends out roster of cases at least 15 days before term. Rule 216(b)
Oral Argument. Rule 218
Opinion filed. Rule 220
15 days
Petition for rehearing and action thereon. Rule 221(a)
Remittitur sent to lower court or administrative tribunal. Rule 221(b)

APPENDIX C. FORMS

This Appendix contains forms which may be used for Rules 201–241, SCACR. These forms are in the nature of examples which can be modified to meet the needs of a particular case. In the forms, optional language is shown in brackets.

FORM 1. NOTICE OF APPEAL IN A CIVIL CASE

THE STATE OF SOUTH CAROLINA
In The Court of Appeals
[In The Supreme Court]

APPEAL FROM GREENVILLE COUNTY
Court of Common Pleas

George E. Brown, Circuit Court Judge

Case No. 2000–CP–00–0000

Stephen L. Doe, as Personal Representative of the Estate of
John B. Doe, ... Respondent,

v.

Jane C. Roe, ... Appellant.

NOTICE OF APPEAL

Jane C. Roe appeals the order [judgment] of the Honorable George E. Brown dated September 1, 2000. Appellant received written notice of entry of this order [judgment] on September 3, 2000.

September 15, 2000

s/ John E. Smith

John E. Smith
Post Office Box 123
Greenville, South Carolina 29000
(864) 000–0000
Attorney for Appellant

Other Counsel of Record:

Mary P. Jones
Post Office Box 456
Greenville, South Carolina 29000
Attorney for Respondent
(864) 000–0000

FORM 2. NOTICE OF APPEAL FOR A CROSS APPEAL IN A CIVIL CASE

THE STATE OF SOUTH CAROLINA
In The Court of Appeals
[In The Supreme Court]

APPEAL FROM ORANGEBURG COUNTY
Family Court

Rebecca T. Green, Family Court Judge

Case No. 2000–DR–00–0000

John E. Jones, ... Respondent-Appellant,

v.

Frances T. Jones, ... Appellant-Respondent.

NOTICE OF APPEAL

John E. Jones appeals the order [judgment] of the Honorable Rebecca T. Green dated September 10, 2000. Respondent-Appellant received a notice of appeal from Appellant-Respondent on September 20, 2000.

September 25, 2000

s/ Thomas A. Doe

Thomas A. Doe
Post Office Box 456
Orangeburg, South Carolina 29000
(803) 000–0000
Attorney for Respondent-Appellant

Other Counsel of Record:

Samuel N. Smith
Post Office Box 123
Orangeburg, South Carolina 29000
(803) 000–0000
Attorney for Appellant-Respondent

FORM 3. NOTICE OF APPEAL FROM COMMON PLEAS REGARDING A CONVICTION IN MAGISTRATES OR MUNICIPAL COURT

THE STATE OF SOUTH CAROLINA
In The Court of Appeals
[In The Supreme Court]

APPEAL FROM CHARLESTON COUNTY
Court of Common Pleas

Howard S. Barnes, Circuit Court Judge

Case No. 2000–CP–00–0000

The State, ... Respondent,

v.

Thomas L. Smith, ... Appellant.

NOTICE OF APPEAL

Thomas L. Smith appeals the order of the Honorable Howard S. Barnes dated September 1, 2000, which affirmed his conviction in magistrates [municipal] court. Appellant received written notice of the order on September 10, 2000.

September 15, 2000

s/ Robert F. Jones

Robert F. Jones
Post Office Box 456
Charleston, South Carolina 29000
(803) 000–0000
Attorney for Appellant

Other Counsel of Record:

Frank P. White
Assistant Solicitor
Post Office Box 789
Charleston, South Carolina 29000
(803) 000–0000
Attorney for Respondent

FORM 4. NOTICE OF APPEAL FROM A SENTENCE IMPOSED BY THE COURT OF GENERAL SESSIONS

THE STATE OF SOUTH CAROLINA
In The Court of Appeals
[In The Supreme Court]

APPEAL FROM RICHLAND COUNTY
Court of General Sessions

Howard S. Barnes, Circuit Court Judge

Case No. 2000–GS–00–0000

The State, ... Respondent,

v.

Thomas L. Smith, ... Appellant.

NOTICE OF APPEAL

Thomas L. Smith appeals his conviction and sentence in this case. The sentence was imposed by the Honorable Howard S. Barnes on September 3, 2000. [This appeal is taken from the order of the Honorable Howard S. Barnes, dated September 10, 2000, which denied appellant's motion for a new trial. Appellant received written notice of entry of this order on September 11, 2000.]*

September 12, 2000

s/ Wanda D. Jones

Wanda D. Jones
Post Office Box 456
Columbia, South Carolina 29000
(803) 000–0000
Attorney for Appellant

Other Counsel of Record:

John T. Doe
Assistant Solicitor
Post Office Box 789
Columbia, South Carolina 29000
(803) 000–0000
Attorney for Respondent

* The bracketed language should be added to the body of the Notice of Appeal when the appeal is taken from a written order deciding a post-trial motion under Rule 29(a), SCRCrimP.

FORM 5. NOTICE OF APPEAL FROM THE FAMILY COURT IN A JUVENILE DELINQUENCY MATTER

THE STATE OF SOUTH CAROLINA
In The Court of Appeals
[In The Supreme Court]

APPEAL FROM RICHLAND COUNTY
Family Court

Rebecca T. Green, Family Court Judge

Case No. 2000–JU–00–0000

In the Interest of Mary A. S.,
a Juvenile under the Age of Seventeen, ... Appellant.

NOTICE OF APPEAL

Mary A. S. appeals the judgment of the Honorable Rebecca T. Green committing her to the Department of Juvenile Justice for an indeterminate period not to exceed her twenty-first birthday. Judgment was imposed on September 10, 2000. [This appeal is taken from the order of the Honorable Rebecca T. Green, dated September 17, 2000, which denied appellant's motion for a new trial. Appellant received written notice of entry of this order on September 18, 2000.]*

September 19, 2000

s/ Wanda D. Jones

Wanda D. Jones
Post Office Box 456
Columbia, South Carolina 29000
(803) 000–0000
Attorney for Appellant

Other Counsel of Record:

John T. Doe
Assistant Solicitor
Post Office Box 789
Columbia, South Carolina 29000
(803) 000–0000
Attorney for Respondent

* The bracketed language should be added to the body of the Notice of Appeal when the appeal is taken from a written order deciding a post-trial motion under Rule 29(a), SCRCrimP.

FORM 6. NOTICE OF APPEAL FROM ADMINISTRATIVE TRIBUNAL

THE STATE OF SOUTH CAROLINA

In The Court of Appeals

[In The Supreme Court]

APPEAL FROM THE ADMINISTRATIVE LAW COURT [OR NAME OF AGENCY]

George E. Brown, Administrative Law Judge

Case No. 05–ALJ–00–0000–CC

South Carolina Department of Revenue, Respondent,

v.

Jane C. Roe, Appellant.

NOTICE OF APPEAL

Jane C. Roe appeals the decision of the Honorable George E. Brown dated September 1, 2006. Appellant received a copy of this decision on September 3, 2006.

September 15, 2006

s/ John E. Smith
John E. Smith
Post Office Box 123
Greenville, South Carolina 29000
(864) 000–0000
Attorney for Appellant

Other Counsel of Record:
Mary P. Jones
Post Office Box 456
Greenville, South Carolina 29000
(864) 000–0000
Attorney for Respondent

[Amended effective June 17, 2010.]

FORM 7. PROOF OF SERVICE OF A NOTICE OF APPEAL

THE STATE OF SOUTH CAROLINA
In The Court of Appeals
[In The Supreme Court]

APPEAL FROM GREENVILLE COUNTY
Court of Common Pleas

George E. Brown, Circuit Court Judge

Case No. 2000–CP–00–0000

Stephen L. Doe, as Personal Representative of the Estate of
John B. Doe, ... Respondent,

v.

Jane C. Roe, ... Appellant.

PROOF OF SERVICE

I certify that I have served the Notice of Appeal on Stephen L. Doe by depositing a copy of it in the United States Mail, postage prepaid, on September 15, 2000, addressed to his attorney of record, Mary P. Jones, Post Office Box 456, Greenville, South Carolina 29000 [by personally delivering a copy of it to his attorney of record, Mary P. Jones, at her office at 123 Oak Street, Greenville, South Carolina 29000, on September 15, 2000].

September 15, 2000

s/ John E. Smith

John E. Smith
Post Office Box 123
Greenville, South Carolina 29000
(864) 000–000–0000
Attorney for Appellant

FORM 8. LETTER TO THE APPELLATE COURT CLERK FILING THE NOTICE OF APPEAL

September 16, 2000

The Honorable Tanya A. Gee

Clerk, South Carolina Court of Appeals

Post Office Box 11629

Columbia, South Carolina 29211

[The Honorable Daniel E. Shearouse

Clerk, Supreme Court of South Carolina

Post Office Box 11330

Columbia, South Carolina 29211]

RE: Stephen L. Doe, as Personal Representative of the Estate of John B. Doe, Respondent, v. Jane C. Roe, Appellant, Case No. 2000–CP–00–0000

Dear Ms. Gee [Mr. Shearouse]:

Enclosed for filing is a notice of appeal in the above case. Also enclosed are the following:

(1) Proof of service of the notice of appeal on the respondent[s].

(2) A copy of the order[s] [judgment] which is [are] to be challenged on appeal.

(3) A filing fee of $100.*

[(4) This appeal is being filed with the Supreme Court because . . . (see Rule 203(d) for when an appeal can be filed with the Supreme Court).]

Sincerely,

s/ John E. Smith
John E. Smith
Post Office Box 123
Greenville, South Carolina 29000
(864) 000–0000
Attorney for Appellant

cc: Mary P. Jones
Post Office Box 456
Greenville, South Carolina 29000
(864) 000–0000
Attorney for Respondent

[Amended effective June 17, 2010.]

* Under Rule 203(d)(1)(B)(iii) and (d)(2)(B)(iii), SCACR, a filing fee is not required if the appeal is from a criminal case including juvenile delinquency matters, or if the appeal is taken by the State of South Carolina, its departments or agencies. Further, no filing fees are required in post-conviction relief cases. Rule 240(d), SCACR.

FORM 9. LETTER TO CLERK OF LOWER COURT FILING NOTICE OF APPEAL

September 16, 2000

The Honorable ____________________
Clerk of Court for __________ County
Post Office Box __________
__________, South Carolina 29000

RE: Stephen L. Doe, as Personal Representative
of the Estate of John B. Doe, Respondent, v.
Jane C. Roe, Appellant, Case No. 2000–CP–00–0000

Dear ____________________:

Enclosed for filing is a notice of appeal in the above case.

Sincerely,

s/ John E. Smith
John E. Smith
Post Office Box 123
Greenville, South Carolina 29000
(864) 000–0000
Attorney for Appellant

cc: Mary P. Jones
Post Office Box 456
Greenville, South Carolina 29000
(864) 000–0000
Attorney for Respondent

FORM 10. AGREEMENT TO ORDER LESS THAN THE ENTIRE TRANSCRIPT

THE STATE OF SOUTH CAROLINA
In The Court of Appeals
[In The Supreme Court]

APPEAL FROM GREENVILLE COUNTY
Court of Common Pleas

George E. Brown, Circuit Court Judge

Case No. 2000–CP–00–0000

Stephen L. Doe, as Personal Representative of the Estate of
John B. Doe, ... Respondent,

v.

Jane C. Roe, ... Appellant.

AGREEMENT TO ORDER LESS
THAN THE ENTIRE TRANSCRIPT

The undersigned agree that the following portions of the proceedings will not be ordered from the court reporter:

(1) Selection and swearing of the jury;

(2) Opening statements of counsel for appellant and respondent;

(3) Closing arguments of counsel for appellant and respondent.

s/ John E. Smith

John E. Smith
Post Office Box 123
Greenville, South Carolina 29000
(864) 000–0000
Attorney for Appellant

s/ Mary P. Jones

Mary P. Jones
Post Office Box 456
Greenville, South Carolina 29000
(864) 000–0000
Attorney for Respondent

FORM 11. LETTER ORDERING TRANSCRIPT FROM COURT REPORTER

September 18, 2000

(Court Reporter)

Post Office Box ________

Greenville, South Carolina 29000

RE: Stephen L. Doe, as Personal Representative of the Estate of John B. Doe, Respondent, v. Jane C. Roe, Appellant, Case No. 2000–CP–00–0000

Dear ________:

On August 15, 2000, the above case was tried before the Honorable George E. Brown, Circuit Court Judge, in Greenville County. My records indicate that you were the court reporter for this case.

I request that you provide me with a transcript of the proceedings. Please transcribe the entire record [except for the following parts:

(1) Selection and swearing of the jury;

(2) Opening statements of counsel for appellant and respondent;

(3) Closing arguments of counsel for appellant and respondent].*

* Unless all the parties to the appeal agree, a transcript of the entire proceedings must be ordered. Form 10 contains a sample agreement to order less than the entire transcript.

I agree to pay the per page charge for this transcript as provided by Rule 607, SCACR.

Sincerely,

s/ John E. Smith

John E. Smith

Post Office Box 123

Greenville, South Carolina 29000

(864) 000–0000

Attorney for Appellant

cc: Mary P. Jones, Esquire

S.C. Court Administration

Clerk, Court of Appeals [Supreme Court]

[Amended effective June 17, 2010.]

FORM 12. NOTICE THAT TRANSCRIPT HAS NOT BEEN TIMELY RECEIVED

December 27, 2000

The Honorable Rosalyn W. Frierson
Director, South Carolina Court Administration
1015 Sumter Street, Suite 200
Columbia, South Carolina 29201

RE: Stephen L. Doe, as Personal Representative
of the Estate of John B. Doe, Respondent, v.
Jane C. Roe, Appellant, Case No. 2000–CP–00–0000

Dear Ms. Frierson:

On September 18, 2000, the transcript of the proceedings in this case was ordered. On November 17, 2001, the Office of Court Administration granted a thirty (30) day extension.

As of this day, appellant has not received the transcript from the court reporter.

Sincerely,

s/ John E. Smith

John E. Smith
Post Office Box 123
Greenville, South Carolina 29000
(864) 000–0000
Attorney for Appellant

cc: ____ (Court Reporter)
Mary P. Jones, Esquire
Clerk, Court of Appeals [Supreme Court]

FORM 13. BRIEF OF APPELLANT*

THE STATE OF SOUTH CAROLINA

In The Court of Appeals

[In The Supreme Court]

APPEAL FROM GREENVILLE COUNTY

Court of Common Pleas

George E. Brown, Circuit Court Judge

Case No. 2000–CP–00–0000

Stephen L. Doe, as Personal Representative of the Estate of John B. Doe,	Respondent,
v.	
Jane C. Roe,	Appellant.

[INITIAL] BRIEF OF APPELLANT

[Amended effective June 17, 2010.]

* Under Rule 267(e), SCACR, the cover of the final briefs should be the following colors: brief of appellant—blue; brief of respondent—red; reply brief—gray; and amicus curiae or intervenor—green.

John E. Smith
Post Office Box 123
Greenville, South Carolina 29000
(864) 000–0000
Attorney for Appellant

TABLE OF CONTENTS

TABLE OF AUTHORITIES*

CASES

STATUTES

OTHER AUTHORITIES

* The authorities cited are fictitious and intended to show the form of citation only.

STATEMENT OF ISSUES ON APPEAL

1. DID THE TRIAL COURT ERR IN FAILING TO FIND THIS ACTION IS BARRED BY RES JUDICATA?

2. DID THE TRIAL COURT ERR IN CHARGING THE JURY THAT FRAUD MUST BE PROVED BY A PREPONDERANCE OF THE EVIDENCE?

STATEMENT OF THE CASE

On February 1, 2000, John B. Doe brought this action alleging fraud against Jane C. Roe. Roe answered alleging Doe's claim was precluded by judgment in a prior contract action between the parties. The contract action was tried on November 15, 1990, and judgment was entered on December 1, 1990.

Doe died before the trial of this case. By order of the court dated February 15, 2000, Stephen L. Doe, as personal representative, was substituted as plaintiff.

On August 15, 2000, the case was tried by a jury which found for Doe and awarded him $10,000.00 in damages. On September 15, 2000, Roe served the Notice of Appeal on Doe.

FACTS

[Counsel may wish to set out the facts relevant to the arguments at this point in the brief. This, however, is optional, and the relevant facts may be included in the discussion of each argument. In either case, the brief must contain references to where the salient facts can be found in the Record on Appeal. In Initial Briefs, these references shall be made in the manner specified by Rule 208(b)(4), SCACR. In the Final Briefs, these references shall be to the page and line number of the Record on Appeal (i.e. , R.p. 37, lines 7–8). Rules 211(b)(1), SCACR.]

Arguments

I. BECAUSE RESPONDENT COULD HAVE RAISED FRAUD IN HIS PRIOR BREACH OF CONTRACT SUIT AGAINST APPELLANT, HE IS BARRED BY RES JUDICATA FROM BRINGING THIS SUIT.

[Set out discussion and citations of authority.]

II. BECAUSE FRAUD MUST BE PROVED BY CLEAR AND CONVINCING EVIDENCE, THE TRIAL COURT ERRED WHEN IT CHARGED THE JURY THAT THE RESPONDENT MUST PROVE FRAUD BY A PREPONDERANCE OF THE EVIDENCE.

[Set out discussion and citations of authority.]

CONCLUSION

For the reasons stated, this Court should reverse the judgment of the circuit court.

Respectfully submitted,

January 20, 2001

/s/ John E. Smith
John E. Smith
Post Office Box 123
Greenville, South Carolina 29000
(864) 000–0000
Attorney for Appellant

FORM 14. DESIGNATION OF MATTER TO BE INCLUDED IN THE RECORD ON APPEAL

THE STATE OF SOUTH CAROLINA
In The Court of Appeals
[In The Supreme Court]

APPEAL FROM GREENVILLE COUNTY
Court of Common Pleas

George E. Brown, Circuit Court Judge

Case No. 2000–CP–00–0000

Stephen L. Doe, as Personal Representative of the Estate of
John B. Doe, ... Respondent,
v.
Jane C. Roe, ... Appellant.

DESIGNATION OF MATTER
TO BE INCLUDED IN THE RECORD ON APPEAL

Appellant proposes the following be included in the Record on Appeal:

1. Order of September 1, 2000;
2. Order of December 1, 1990;
3. Complaint;
4. Answer;
5. Transcript of Proceedings pp. 2–6; 15–17; 29–36; 42–44; 61–80; and 90–99;
6. Defendant's Request to Charge No. 4;
7. Defendant's Exhibits 1, 6, and 7.

I certify that this designation contains no matter which is irrelevant to this appeal.

January 20, 2001

/s/ John E. Smith

John E. Smith
Post Office Box 123
Greenville, South Carolina 29000
(864) 000–0000

FORM 15. RECORD ON APPEAL

THE STATE OF SOUTH CAROLINA
In The Court of Appeals
[In The Supreme Court]

APPEAL FROM GREENVILLE COUNTY
Court of Common Pleas

George E. Brown, Circuit Court Judge

Case No. 2000–CP–00–0000

Stephen L. Doe, as Personal Representative of the Estate of
John B. Doe, ... Respondent,

v.

Jane C. Roe, ... Appellant.

RECORD ON APPEAL

John E. Smith
Post Office Box 123
Greenville, South Carolina 29000
(864) 000–0000
Attorney for Appellant

Mary P. Jones
Post Office Box 456
Greenville, South Carolina 29000
(864) 000–0000
Attorney for Respondent

INDEX

<u>Order of September 1, 2000</u>

[Set out entire order including caption and signature.]

<u>Order of December 1, 1990</u>

[Set out entire order including caption and signature.]

<u>Complaint</u>

[Set out entire complaint including caption and signature.]

Answer

[Set out entire answer including caption and signature.]

Testimony of Stephen L. Doe

[Set out testimony including entire page of trial transcript where a portion of the page is to be included.]

Deposition of John B. Doe

[Set out testimony including entire page of trial transcript where a portion of the page is to be included.]

Testimony of Louise M. Miller

[Set out testimony including entire page of trial transcript where a portion of the page is to be included.]

Testimony of Jane C. Roe

[Set out testimony including entire page of trial transcript where a portion of the page is to be included.]

Testimony of Mark N. Brown

[Set out testimony including entire page of trial transcript where a portion of the page is to be included.]

Charge

[Set out the portions of the jury charge designated to be included. Where a portion of a page of the charge is to be included, include the entire page.]

Request to Charge

[Set out request to charge.]

Defendant's Exhibit 1

[Set out exhibit.]

Defendant's Exhibit 6

[Set out exhibit.]

Defendant's Exhibit 7

[Set out exhibit.]

Certificate of Counsel

The undersigned hereby certifies that the Record on Appeal contains all material proposed to be included by any of the parties and not any other material.

March 20, 2001

/s/ John E. Smith

John E. Smith
Post Office Box 123
Greenville, South Carolina 29000
(803) 000–0000
Attorney for Appellant

FORM 16. CERTIFICATE OF COUNSEL IN FINAL BRIEF

THE STATE OF SOUTH CAROLINA
In The Court of Appeals
[In The Supreme Court]

APPEAL FROM GREENVILLE COUNTY
Court of Common Pleas

George E. Brown, Circuit Court Judge

Case No. 2000–CP–00–0000

Stephen L. Doe, as Personal Representative of the Estate of
John B. Doe, ... Respondent,

v.

Jane C. Roe, ... Appellant.

CERTIFICATE OF COUNSEL

The undersigned certified that this Final Brief complies with Rule 211(b), SCACR.

April 5, 2001

s/ John E. Smith

John E. Smith
Post Office Box 123
Greenville, South Carolina 29000
(864) 000–0000
Attorney for Appellant

FORM 17. ITEMIZED STATEMENT OF COSTS

THE STATE OF SOUTH CAROLINA

In The Court of Appeals

[In The Supreme Court]

)
)
)
v.)
)
)
)

The Appellate Court is requested to tax the following costs against

____

(Name of Party)

COSTS TAXABLE UNDER RULE 222, SCACR	NO. OF PAGES	RATE	REQUESTED	ALLOWED (For Court Use Only)
Cost of Printing or Copying Final Brief				
Cost of Printing or Copying Final Reply Brief				
Cost of Printing or Copying Record on Appeal				
Filing Fee Paid Under Rule 203(d), SCACR				
Cost of Court Reporter's Transcript				
Attorney's Fee Provided By Rule 222(b), SCACR				
Other (specify and explain):				
COSTS TAXABLE UNDER RULE 242(j), SCACR				
Cost of Printing or Copying Brief				
Cost of Printing or Copying Reply Brief				
Cost of Printing or Copying Appendix				
Filing fee paid under Rule 242(c), SCACR				
Attorney's fee provided by Rule 242(j)(2), SCACR				
Other (specify and explain):				
		TOTAL		

I, ________, do swear or affirm that the foregoing costs are correct and were necessarily incurred in this action. A copy of this statement was (mailed to/served upon) opposing counsel.

____

(Signature)

Attorney for ______________________________

Subscribed and sworn to before me this ___ day of ________, 20 ___.

____

Notary Public for ______________________

My Commission Expires: ______________________

(Seal)

[Amended effective June 17, 2010.]

FORM 18. PETITION FOR A WRIT OF CERTIORARI TO THE COURT OF APPEALS

THE STATE OF SOUTH CAROLINA
In The Supreme Court

APPEAL FROM GREENVILLE COUNTY
Court of Common Pleas

George E. Brown, Circuit Court Judge

Opinion No. 0000 (S.C. Ct. App. filed Feb. 10, 2002)

Stephen L. Doe, as Personal Representative of the Estate of
John B. Doe, ... Respondent,

v.

Jane C. Roe, ... Petitioner.

PETITION FOR A WRIT OF CERTIORARI

John E. Smith
Post Office Box 123
Greenville, South Carolina 29000
(864) 000–0000
Attorney for Petitioner

Other Counsel of Record:

Mary P. Jones
Post Office Box 456
Greenville, South Carolina 29000
(864) 000–0000
Attorney for Respondent

INDEX

CERTIFICATE OF COUNSEL

Counsel for petitioner certifies that the Petition for Rehearing was made and finally ruled on by the Court of Appeals on March 2, 2002.

QUESTIONS PRESENTED

1. Did the Court of Appeals err in holding that this action is not barred by res judicata?
2. Did the Court of Appeals err in holding that petitioner had failed to timely object to the trial judge's charge on the burden of proof?

STATEMENT OF THE CASE

On February 1, 2000, John B. Doe brought this action ....

[Set forth facts relevant to the questions presented. Counsel may wish to simply give a brief history of the case at this point and set forth the facts in the argument on each question. Reference should be made to where the salient facts can be found in the Record on Appeal (i.e., R.p. 37, lines 7–8).]

The Court of Appeals affirmed the judgment of the circuit court. Stephen L. Doe, as Personal Representative of the Estate of John B. Doe v. Jane C. Roe, Op. No. 0000 (S.C. Ct. App. filed Feb. 10, 2002). Petitioner seeks a writ of certiorari to review that decision.

ARGUMENT

1. THE COURT OF APPEALS SHOULD HAVE HELD THAT THIS ACTION IS BARRED BY RES JUDICATA.

   [Set out discussion and citations of authority.]

2. PETITIONER DID TIMELY OBJECT TO THE TRIAL JUDGE'S ERRONEOUS CHARGE ON THE BURDEN OF PROOF.

   [Set out discussion and citations of authority.]

CONCLUSION

For the reasons stated, petitioner asks the Court to grant the petition for a writ of certiorari.

Respectfully submitted,

March 27, 2002

/s/ John E. Smith

John E. Smith
Post Office Box 123
Greenville, South Carolina 29000
(864) 000–0000
Attorney for Petitioner

FORM 19. PETITION FOR A WRIT OF CERTIORARI IN POST-CONVICTION RELIEF ACTIONS

THE STATE OF SOUTH CAROLINA
In The Supreme Court

APPEAL FROM RICHLAND COUNTY
Court of Common Pleas

George E. Brown, Circuit Court Judge

Case No. 2000–CP–00–0000

Thomas L. Smith, #123456 .... Petitioner,

v.

State of South Carolina, ... Respondent.

PETITION FOR A WRIT OF CERTIORARI

Frederick C. Roe
Post Office Box 567
Columbia, South Carolina 29000
(803) 000–0000
Attorney for Petitioner

Other Counsel of Record:

John T. Doe
Assistant Attorney General
Post Office Box 789
Columbia, South Carolina 29000
(803) 000–0000
Attorney for Respondent

INDEX

QUESTIONS PRESENTED

1. Did the circuit court err in holding that petitioner's trial counsel was not ineffective in failing to object to the malice charge?
2. Did the circuit court err in holding that petitioner's trial counsel was not ineffective in failing to move for a continuance?

STATEMENT OF THE CASE

On April 1, 1994, petitioner was convicted of murder and was sentenced to life imprisonment. On direct appeal, his conviction was affirmed by the South Carolina Supreme Court. State v. Smith, 1998–MO–000 (S.C. S.Ct. filed August 1, 1998).

Petitioner then brought this action seeking post-conviction relief in July 1999. He alleged . . . .

> [Set forth facts relevant to the questions presented. Counsel may wish to simply give a brief history of the case at this point and set forth the facts in the argument on each question. Reference should be made to where salient facts can be found in the Appendix (i.e., App. p. 10, lines 1–6).]

The circuit court denied the application on September 1, 2000, and a notice of appeal was served on September 9, 2000. Petitioner now seeks a writ of certiorari to review this denial.

ARGUMENT

1. COUNSEL WAS INEFFECTIVE IN FAILING TO OBJECT TO THE MALICE INSTRUCTION.
   [Set forth discussion and citations of authority.]
2. COUNSEL WAS INEFFECTIVE IN FAILING TO MOVE FOR A CONTINUANCE.
   [Set forth discussion and citations of authority.]

CONCLUSION

For the reasons stated, petitioner asks this Court to grant the petition for a writ of certiorari.

Respectfully submitted,

November 1, 2001

/s/ Frederick C. Roe

Frederick C. Roe
Post Office Box 567
Columbia, South Carolina 29000
(803) 000–0000
Attorney for Petitioner

FORM 20. APPENDIX IN POST–CONVICTION RELIEF ACTIONS

THE STATE OF SOUTH CAROLINA
In The Supreme Court

APPEAL FROM RICHLAND COUNTY
Court of Common Pleas

George E. Brown, Circuit Court Judge

Case No. 2000–CP–00–0000

Thomas L. Smith, #1213456 . . . . Petitioner,
v.
State of South Carolina, ... Respondent.

APPENDIX

Frederick C. Roe
Post Office Box 567
Columbia, South Carolina 29000
(803) 000–0000
Attorney for Petitioner

John T. Doe
Assistant Attorney General
Post Office Box 789
Columbia, South Carolina 29000
(803) 000–0000
Attorney for Respondent

INDEX

[The remaining portion of the Appendix is composed of a copy of the documents listed in the Index.]

III. [RESERVED]

IV. RULES GOVERNING THE PRACTICE OF LAW

RULE 401. STUDENT PRACTICE RULE

(a) This Rule is adopted solely in aid of the clinical legal education programs at the University of South Carolina School of Law and the Charleston School of Law.

(b) An eligible law student may appear in any inferior court or before any administrative tribunal on behalf of any indigent person, with that person's written consent, or on behalf of the State or any of its departments, agencies, institutions, or political subdivisions, with the written approval of the Attorney General. If referred to the clinical legal education program by a state or federal court, department, agency, institution, or other department of the University of South Carolina School of Law or the Charleston School of Law, an eligible law student may also appear in an inferior court or before an administrative tribunal on behalf of a non-indigent person or non-profit organization with the written consent of the person or the written approval of the organization's governing body or executive officer. The consent or approval shall be filed in the record of the case and shall be brought to the attention of the judge or the presiding officer. In all cases, a supervising lawyer is required to be personally present throughout the proceeding.

(c) An eligible law student may engage in other activities, under a lawyer's general supervision, but outside the lawyer's presence, including:

(1) preparation of the pleadings, briefs and other legal documents to be approved and signed by the supervising lawyer;

(2) assisting indigent inmates of correctional institutions in preparing applications and supporting documents for post-conviction relief. If there is an attorney of record in the matter, all such assistance must be supervised by that attorney and all documents submitted to the court on behalf of the inmate must be signed by the attorney. Solicitation of representation of indigent inmates shall be a violation of this Rule;

(3) mediate a dispute in a court annexed mediation program; provided the eligible law student has successfully completed a 40 hour mediation training program approved by the Board of Arbitrator and Mediator Certification of the Supreme Court's Commission on Alternative Dispute Resolution, and provided the eligible law student is supervised on-site by an attorney who is licensed to practice law in South Carolina and holds a current certification in mediation from the Board of Arbitrator and Mediator Certification.

(d) In order to make an appearance pursuant to this Rule, a law student must:

(1) be enrolled in the University of South Carolina School of Law or the Charleston School of Law;

(2) have completed the equivalent of four (4) semesters of legal studies;

(3) be certified by the Dean of the respective School of Law as being of good character and competent legal ability, and as being currently enrolled in a clinical course. The certification shall be filed with the Clerk of the Supreme Court and shall remain in effect for eighteen (18) months or until the announcement of the results of the first Bar examination following the student's graduation, whichever is earlier. The certification of students who pass the Bar examination shall remain in effect until they are admitted to the Bar. The certification may be withdrawn by the respective Dean at any time upon written notice to the Clerk or may be terminated by the Supreme Court without notice or hearing and without any showing of cause;

(4) neither ask for nor receive any compensation or remuneration of any kind for services performed pursuant to this Rule. Nothing in this provision shall be interpreted to prevent the law student from receiving course credit from the respective School of Law for his participation in the clinical programs, or to preclude the clinical programs from seeking attorney's fees where appropriate; and

(5) certify in writing that the student is familiar with, and will be governed by the Rules of Professional Conduct adopted by the Supreme Court. Any student who violates the Rules of Professional Conduct or fails to abide by the conditions of this Rule shall be subject to disciplinary action by the Supreme Court.

(e) The supervising lawyer shall be approved by the Dean of the respective School of Law and shall assume personal professional responsibility for the student's guidance and for supervising the quality of the student's work.

[Adopted effective September 1, 1990. Amended effective December 13, 1991; February 12, 2001; March 7, 2007; October 10, 2008.]

RULE 402. ADMISSION TO PRACTICE LAW

(a) Board of Law Examiners.

(1) *Members.* The Board of Law Examiners shall consist of seven (7) members of the South Carolina Bar who are actively engaged in the practice of law in South Carolina and who have been active members of the South Carolina Bar for at least seven (7) years. The Board members shall be appointed by the Supreme Court for three (3) year terms and shall be eligible for reappointment. At least one member shall be appointed from each Congressional District. In case of a

vacancy on the Board, the Supreme Court shall appoint a member of the South Carolina Bar to serve the remainder of the unexpired term.

(2) *Associate Members.* The Supreme Court may appoint associate members to assist the members of the Board. These associate members must be members of the South Carolina Bar who are actively engaged in the practice of law in South Carolina and who have been active members of the South Carolina Bar for at least five (5) years. These associate members shall assist the members of the Board in preparing the essay Examinations and model answers, administering the Bar Examination, and grading the Examination, and shall have such additional duties as may be determined by the members of the Board. While the Supreme Court shall not be limited in whom it appoints, the members of the Board shall nominate persons to serve as associate members.

(3) *Chair; Secretary.* The Supreme Court shall appoint a chair from among the members of the Board. The Clerk of the Supreme Court shall serve as secretary of the Board ex officio.

(4) *Duties.* The Board of Law Examiners shall determine whether applicants for admission to the practice of law in South Carolina possess the necessary legal knowledge for admission. The members of the Board are authorized to make rules and regulations for conducting the Examination, including a list of the subjects upon which applicants may be tested and regulations providing for the accommodation of disabled applicants. These rules and regulations shall not become effective until at least ninety (90) days after they are approved by the Supreme Court.

(b) Committee on Character and Fitness.

(1) *Members.* The Committee on Character and Fitness shall consist of twelve (12) active members of the South Carolina Bar who shall be appointed by the Supreme Court for five (5) year terms. In case of a vacancy on the Committee, the Supreme Court shall appoint an active member of the Bar to serve the remainder of the unexpired term.

(2) *Chair; Secretary.* The Supreme Court shall appoint a chair and a secretary of the Committee from among the Committee's membership.

(3) *Panels and Meetings.* The members shall be divided by the chair into panels composed of three (3) members. The chair may rotate membership on the panels, and may substitute members between panels. Panels shall meet when scheduled by the chair or the Committee, and the full Committee may meet to consider administrative matters. Meetings of the Committee other than periodic meetings may be called by the chair upon the chair's own motion and shall be called by the chair upon the written request of three members of the Committee.

(4) *Quorum.* A quorum for a meeting of the full Committee shall be seven (7) members, and a quorum for a panel shall be three (3) members.

(5) *Duties.* The Committee on Character and Fitness shall investigate and determine whether an applicant for admission to the Bar possesses the qualifications prescribed by this Rule as to age, legal education, and character. The applicant must establish to the reasonable satisfaction of a majority of a panel that the applicant is qualified. In conducting investigations, a panel may take and hear testimony, compel by subpoena the attendance of witnesses, and require the applicant to appear for a hearing before a panel or for a personal interview before a single member of the Committee. An applicant will not be denied admission by the Committee without being afforded the opportunity for a hearing before a panel. Any member of the Committee may administer oaths and issue subpoenas. The Committee may adopt rules that shall become effective upon approval by the Supreme Court. In addition, the Committee shall perform the duties specified by Rule 33 of the Rules for Lawyer Disciplinary Enforcement contained in Rule 413, SCACR, and any other duties as directed by the Supreme Court.

(c) Qualifications for Admission. No person shall be admitted to the practice of law in South Carolina unless the person:

(1) is at least twenty-one (21) years of age;

(2) is of good moral character;

(3) has received a JD or LLB degree from a law school which was approved by the Council of Legal Education of the American Bar Association at the time the degree was conferred. An approved law school includes a school that is provisionally approved by the Council. An applicant who has not provided proof of graduation by July 10th for the July Bar Examination or February 10th for the February Bar Examination shall not be allowed to sit for the examination. An applicant, however, who has not graduated may sit for the examination if the law school certifies in writing that the applicant has completed all requirements for graduation by July 10th for the July Bar Examination or February 10th for the February Bar Examination; the applicant must provide proof of graduation by April 1 following the February Bar Examination or October 1 following the July Bar Examination;

(4) has been found qualified by a panel of the Committee on Character and Fitness;

(5) has passed the Bar Examination given by the Board of Law Examiners;

(6) has received a scaled score of at least seventy-seven (77) on the Multistate Professional Responsibility Examination (MPRE) administered by the National Conference of Bar Examiners. If the score was obtained prior to the filing of the application, the MPRE must have been taken within four (4) years of the date on which the application is filed. While an

application can be filed without proof of completion of this requirement, applicants are warned that failure to timely submit proof of completion of this requirement can significantly delay admission as provided by subsection (k) of this rule;

(7) is not disbarred, suspended from the practice of law, or the subject of any pending disciplinary proceeding in another jurisdiction;

(8) has successfully completed the Bridge the Gap Program sponsored by the South Carolina Bar. While an application can be filed without proof of completion of this requirement, applicants are warned that failure to timely submit proof of completion of this requirement can significantly delay admission as provided by subsection (k) of this rule; and

(9) has paid the fees and taken the oath or affirmation specified by this rule.

(d) Application to Take the Bar Examination.

(1) *Filing Application; Fees.* Any person desiring to take the Bar Examination shall file an application, in duplicate, with the Clerk of the Supreme Court. The application form shall be approved by the Committee on Character and Fitness. Applications shall be accepted from December 1 to January 31 for the July Examination and from August 1 to September 30 for the February Examination. The non-refundable application fee shall be:

(i) $400 for applications filed from December 1 to January 10 or from August 1 to August 31.

(ii) $750 for applications filed during the remainder of the application periods.

If the applicant has been admitted to practice law for more than one (1) year in another state, the District of Columbia, or another country at the time the application is filed, the applicant shall file one (1) additional copy of the application along with an additional fee of $500. A portion of this fee will be used to obtain a character report from the National Conference of Bar Examiners.

An application will not be considered filed until both the fully completed application and fee(s) are received by the Clerk of the Supreme Court. The application fee(s) shall be made payable to the Clerk of the Supreme Court of South Carolina, and the application and fee(s) shall be sent to the Clerk, Supreme Court of South Carolina, Post Office Box 11330, Columbia, South Carolina 29211. An applicant who withdraws or fails to sit for an Examination shall not be entitled to a refund of the application fee(s) or to have the application fee(s) credited to a later Examination. An applicant who has failed the Examination must comply with the requirements of section (i) below.

For the purpose of this rule, filing means: (1) delivering the document to the Clerk of the Supreme Court; or (2) depositing the document in the U.S. mail, properly addressed to the Clerk of the Supreme Court, with sufficient first class postage attached. The date of filing shall be the date of delivery or the date of mailing.

Petitions seeking permission to file a late application are strongly discouraged, and only petitions documenting extraordinary circumstances justifying the late filing will be granted. If a petition for late filing is submitted, the petition must comply with the provisions of Rule 240, SCACR, must contain facts showing that extraordinary circumstances exist, and must be accompanied by a fully completed bar application, along with all required original attachments. Under no circumstances will petitions be accepted for filing after March 15 for the July Bar Examination or November 15 for the February Bar Examination. Unless otherwise directed by the Court, the filing fee for a late application will be $1,500, plus an additional $500 fee if the applicant has been admitted to practice law for more than one (1) year in another state, the District of Columbia, or another country at the time the application is filed. The filing fee is non-refundable and may not be credited to a later examination.

(2) *Duty to Keep Application Current.* Until they have been admitted, applicants are under a continuing obligation to keep their applications current and must update responses whenever there is an addition to or a change to information previously filed with the Clerk. These updates must be made in writing and must include all relevant documentation.

(3) *Special Accommodations for Disabled Applicants.* An applicant needing special accommodations for the Bar Examination due to a disability shall submit a written request for such accommodations to the Board of Law Examiners. The procedure and forms to be used in making a written request shall be specified in the Rules of the Board of Law Examiners. Unless the chair of the Board determines there is good cause to allow a late request, written requests for special accommodations must be submitted by November 1 for the February Examination and April 1 for the July Examination.

(e) Determination by Committee On Character and Fitness. The Committee on Character and Fitness shall consider the application and any further information it deems relevant to determine if the applicant has the requisite qualifications and character to be admitted to practice law in this state. The Committee shall notify the Clerk of the Supreme Court whether it finds the applicant qualified or unqualified and, if found to be unqualified, the Clerk shall send the applicant a letter notifying the applicant of this finding. An applicant found to be unqualified shall not be allowed to sit for the Examination. If the Committee has not made a determination of the applicant's qualification by July 1 for the July Examination or February 1 for the February Examination, the applicant shall be allowed to sit for the Examination, and the Committee shall make its determination after the Examination is administered.

(f) Determination of Fitness of Certain Law Students. A student enrolled in a law school approved or provisionally approved by the Council of Legal Education of the American Bar Association who has a character problem that might disqualify the student from being admitted to practice law may have the matter resolved by filing a provisional application. The application shall be made on a form approved by the Committee on Character and Fitness and shall be filed in duplicate with the Clerk of the Supreme Court. Each request must be accompanied by a non-refundable fee of $100. The Committee may begin an immediate investigation of the individual's character and shall promptly notify the individual of its determination. No adverse inference concerning an applicant's character and fitness shall be drawn because the applicant filed a provisional application, nor does the filing of a provisional application relieve an applicant from fully complying with the normal application process.

(g) Review by Supreme Court of Fitness Determination; Re-application. Any applicant dissatisfied with the determination of the Committee on Character and Fitness may petition the Supreme Court for review within fifteen (15) days of the date of the letter notifying the applicant of the Committee's determination. The petition shall comply with the requirements of Rule 240, SCACR, to include the filing fee required by that rule. An applicant who is found not to be qualified by the Committee or whose petition for review of the Committee's determination has been denied may not reapply for admission until two (2) years after the date of the letter notifying the applicant of the Committee's determination.

(h) False and Misleading Information by Applicants. An applicant who knowingly provides false or misleading information in an application (to include any attachments to the application), document, or statement submitted or made to the Committee on Character and Fitness, the Board of Law Examiners, or the staff of the Court shall be guilty of contempt of the Supreme Court of South Carolina and may be punished accordingly. In addition, if it is determined that an applicant has knowingly submitted false or misleading information, the Court may bar the applicant from reapplying for up to five years. Further, if the applicant has already been admitted, the Court may vacate the admission or discipline the lawyer under Rule 413, SCACR. For the purpose of this rule, false or misleading information shall also include the knowing omission of material information by an applicant in the application (to include any attachments to the application) or in response to an inquiry by the Committee, Board or staff of the Court.

(i) Bar Examination.

(1) *When Given.* The Bar Examination shall be conducted twice each year on the last consecutive Monday, Tuesday, and Wednesday in February and July.

(2) *Content; Grading; Passing.* The Bar Examination shall consist of seven (7) sections. Six (6) of these sections shall be composed of essay questions prepared by the Board of Law Examiners. The Chair of the Board shall assign a member of the Board to prepare and grade or supervise the preparation and grading of each essay section. The Multistate Bar Examination shall be the seventh (7th) section. To pass the Multistate portion of the Examination, an applicant must attain a scaled score of at least 125. To pass an essay section, the applicant must obtain a score of seventy (70). Once an applicant reaches seventy (70) points on an essay section, that section will receive a passing grade and will not be graded further. An applicant must pass six (6) of the seven (7) sections to pass the Bar Examination; provided, however, that an applicant who receives a scaled score of 110 or less on the Multistate Bar Examination shall fail the Bar Examination without any grading of the essay questions. The Board shall notify the Clerk of the Supreme Court of the results of the essay sections.

(3) *Anonymous Grading; Prohibited Comments in Answer Sheets and Booklets.* Applicants taking the Bar Examination shall be assigned an identification number that shall be used for the purposes of taking and grading the Examination. Except for the identification number and any other information the applicant may be directed to provide by those administering the Examination, answer sheets or booklets for the Examination shall contain no other information revealing the identity of the applicant. Any reference to the applicant's economic status, social standing, employment, personal hardship or other extraneous information in the answer sheets or booklets is prohibited.

(4) *Notification of Results.* The Clerk of the Supreme Court shall send a letter to each applicant advising the applicant whether the applicant passed or failed the Bar Examination. Additionally, the names of those passing the Examination and the identification numbers of those failing the Examination shall be posted on the South Carolina Judicial Department Website.

(5) *Access to Examination Answers; Re-grading or Other Review.* No applicant shall be given access to the answers the applicant submitted during the examination. The results reported by the Board of Law Examiners are final, and no applicant shall be allowed to seek re-grading or any other review of the results of the examination.

(6) *Request for Verification of Multistate Bar Examination.* While no review or inspection of the Multistate Bar Examination (MBE) will be permitted, an applicant may request a hand grading of the MBE. Any such request must be filed with the Clerk of the Supreme Court along with the applicable fee[1] within fifteen days of the date of the letter of notification in (4) above.

(7) *Prohibited Contacts.* An applicant shall not, either directly or through an agent, contact any member or associate member of the Board of Law Examiners or any member of the Supreme Court regarding the questions on any section of the Bar Examination, grading procedures, or an applicant's answers. This provision does not prohibit an applicant from seeking verification of the MBE score as permitted by (6) above.

(8) *Cheating on the Bar Examination.* An applicant who cheats, aids or assists another applicant in cheating on the Bar Examination, or attempts to cheat or aid or assist another in cheating, shall be guilty of contempt of the Supreme Court of South Carolina and may be punished accordingly. In addition, if it is determined that an applicant has cheated or aided or assisted another in cheating, the applicant shall fail the examination and the Court may prohibit the applicant from reapplying for up to five years. Further, if the applicant has already been admitted, the Court may vacate the admission or discipline the lawyer under Rule 413, SCACR.

(j) Re-Examination.

(1) *Application and Filing Fees.* Any applicant who has failed to pass the Bar Examination may apply to be re-examined. The application shall be made on a form approved by the Committee on Character and Fitness. The filing periods and filing fee(s) applicable to initial applications shall be applicable to applications for re-examination. Any request for special accommodations on the Examination must be submitted in the manner provided by section (d)(3) above.

(2) *Special Requirements for Applicants Who Have Failed the Bar Examination Three or More Times.* An applicant who has failed the Examination three or four times shall not be eligible to sit for a Bar Examination until at least one year following the administration of the last failed Examination. An applicant who has failed the Examination five or more times shall not be eligible to sit for the Bar Examination until at least two years following the administration of the last failed Bar Examination. Further, any applicant who has failed the Bar Examination three or more times must complete a course of study before being eligible to retake the Bar Examination. A new course of study must be completed after each subsequent failure. The course of study shall consist of one of the following:

(i) at least twelve (12) semester hours, or its equivalent, of classes at a law school approved or provisionally approved by the Council of Legal Education of the American Bar Association. The courses must be related to the subjects that are tested on the Bar Examination, and the applicant must complete all course requirements that would be required of a law student including a passing grade for the course. The supplemental application shall include certification from the law school that the applicant has completed the required number of hours, or if the course of study has not been completed at the time the supplemental application is filed, certification from the law school that the applicant is currently enrolled in courses which will give the applicant sufficient hours to complete the course of study before the Examination. The law school must provide certification that the required number of hours has been completed before the applicant will be re-examined.

(ii) study under the direct supervision of an attorney for at least twenty (20) hours per week for at least six months immediately preceding the Examination. The supervising attorney must be an active member of the South Carolina Bar who has been admitted to practice for at least five (5) years and is engaged in the active practice of law in South Carolina. The proposed course of study must specify the topics to be covered, the books and materials to be used, and the dates and locations of study, and must be submitted by the supervising attorney to the Board of Law Examiners for its approval. For the July Examination, the proposed course of study must be submitted not later than December 15. For the February Examination, the proposed course of study must be submitted not later than July 15. The Board of Law Examiners may approve, disapprove or modify the proposed course of study to include increasing the number of hours required. The supplemental application shall include certification from the supervising attorney that the applicant is current on the approved course of study. The supervising lawyer must provide certification that the applicant has completed the course of study before the applicant will be re-examined.

(k) Admission.

(1) *Admission Ceremonies.* Admission ceremonies shall be conducted by the Supreme Court in February, May, September and November. Applicants must have submitted proof of completion of all requirements for admission (see subsection (c) of this rule) at least ten (10) days prior to the scheduled date of the ceremony to participate in that ceremony. Applicants who take the February Bar Examination are expected to have all requirements for admission completed for the May ceremony following the examination, and applicants who take the July Bar Examination are expected to have all requirements for admission completed for the November ceremony following the examination. Applicants will be notified of the date and time of the admission ceremony.

(2) *Special Admission Ceremonies.* On petition, the Court may schedule applicants for admission on other dates based on compelling circumstances such as illness or irreconcilable conflicts that prevent the applicant from appearing at one of the ceremonies established in (1) above. Applicants who are ineligible to participate in one of the admission ceremonies

established in (1) above due to their failure to timely submit proof of completion of Bridge the Gap or the MPRE are not eligible to be admitted at a special admission ceremony.

(3) *Fee and Oath.* To be admitted, the applicant must pay a fee of $50 and take and subscribe the following oath or affirmation:

Lawyer's Oath

I do solemnly swear (or affirm) that:

I am duly qualified, according to the Constitution of this State, to exercise the duties of the office to which I have been appointed, and that I will, to the best of my ability, discharge those duties and will preserve, protect and defend the Constitution of this State and of the United States;

I will maintain the respect and courtesy due to courts of justice, judicial officers, and those who assist them;

To my clients, I pledge faithfulness, competence, diligence, good judgment and prompt communication;

To opposing parties and their counsel, I pledge fairness, integrity, and civility, not only in court, but also in all written and oral communications;

I will not pursue or maintain any suit or proceeding which appears to me to be unjust nor maintain any defenses except those I believe to be honestly debatable under the law of the land, but this obligation shall not prevent me from defending a person charged with a crime;

I will employ for the purpose of maintaining the causes confided to me only such means as are consistent with trust and honor and the principles of professionalism, and will never seek to mislead an opposing party, the judge or jury by a false statement of fact or law;

I will respect and preserve inviolate the confidences of my clients, and will accept no compensation in connection with a client's business except from the client or with the client's knowledge and approval;

I will maintain the dignity of the legal system and advance no fact prejudicial to the honor or reputation of a party or witness, unless required by the justice of the cause with which I am charged;

I will assist the defenseless or oppressed by ensuring that justice is available to all citizens and will not delay any person's cause for profit or malice;

[So help me God.]

The oath or affirmation shall be administered in open Court and all persons admitted to the Bar shall sign their names in a book, kept for that purpose, in the office of the Clerk of the Supreme Court.

(*l*) Failure to be Admitted.

(1) *More than One (1) Year.* An applicant who is not admitted within one (1) year of the date of the letter advising the applicant that the applicant has passed the Bar Examination must file a supplemental application with the Clerk of the Supreme Court. The supplemental application shall be on a form prescribed by the Committee on Character and Fitness, and the applicant may not be admitted to the South Carolina Bar unless the Committee makes a re-determination that the applicant is qualified. The filing shall be accompanied by a fee of $100.

(2) *More than Two (2) Years.* An applicant who is not admitted within two (2) years of the date of the letter advising the applicant that the applicant has passed the Bar Examination may not be admitted without retaking the Bar Examination. The applicant must file a new application and pay the application fee(s) specified in section (d) above. On motion based on extraordinary circumstances, the Court may allow the applicant to be admitted without retaking the Bar Examination. The motion shall comply with the requirements of Rule 240, SCACR, to include the filing fee specified by that rule. If the applicant is granted permission to be admitted without retaking the Examination, the applicant shall pay a fee of $100.

(m) Admission of Certain Law Professors. A person serving as the Dean or as a tenured professor of the University of South Carolina School of Law or the Charleston School of Law may be admitted to practice law in this State without taking the Bar Examination (section (c)(5) above), the Multistate Professional Responsibility Examination (section (c)(6) above), or the Bridge the Gap Program (section (c)(8) above) if the Dean or professor:

(1) has been admitted to practice law in the highest court of another state or the District of Columbia for at least five (5) years;

(2) has been a full-time and continuous member of the faculty of the Law School with the rank of assistant professor of law or higher for the previous three (3) or more complete academic years; and

(3) has been recommended for admission by the Dean of the Law School, or in the case of the Dean, by the President of the University of South Carolina or the Chairman of the Board of Directors of the Charleston School of Law.

The application for admission shall be made on a form prescribed by the Committee on Character and Fitness, and shall be filed in triplicate with the Clerk of the Supreme Court. The application shall be accompanied by a non-refundable application fee of $400. A portion of this fee will be used to obtain a character report from the National Conference of Bar Examiners. The Dean or professor must comply with all other requirements of section (c) above. If found qualified by the Committee on Character and Fitness, the Dean or professor shall be admitted upon taking the oath and paying the fee specified by section (k) above.

(n) Confidentiality.

(1) The files and records maintained by the Board of Law Examiners, the Committee on Character and Fitness, and the Clerk of the Supreme Court relating to Bar applications, Examinations, and admissions shall be confidential, and shall not be disclosed except

as necessary for the Board, the Committee or the Clerk to carry out their responsibilities. The Board of Law Examiners, the Committee on Character and Fitness, and the Clerk may disclose information to the National Conference of Bar Examiners and to the Bar admission authorities in other jurisdictions, and may disclose the names of those persons who have passed the Bar Examination or those who are or will be admitted and the date of their admission. The Supreme Court may authorize the release of confidential information to other persons or agencies.

(2) Notwithstanding the above, beginning with the results of the February 2011 Bar Examination, the Clerk may release the following information to law schools regarding applicants taking the South Carolina Bar Examination who are graduates of that law school: the names of the applicants who took the Examination and whether they passed or failed the Examination, the number of times each applicant has taken the South Carolina Bar Examination, the Law School Admission Council number for each applicant, and the overall pass rate of the applicants on each section of the Bar Examination. Any information released to law schools pursuant to this rule shall be kept confidential by the law school, shall only be used for statistical analysis, and shall only be released for purposes of reporting aggregated information to accrediting bodies. Each law school requesting the release of the above information shall, on a form approved by the Supreme Court, agree to comply with the confidentiality and use restrictions placed on this information.

(*o*) Immunity.

(1) The Board of Law Examiners, the Committee on Character and Fitness, and the members, associate members, employees, and agents of the Board or Committee, are absolutely immune from all civil liability for conduct and communications occurring in the performance of their official duties relating to the Examination, character and fitness qualification, and licensing of persons seeking to be admitted, readmitted or reinstated to the practice of law.

(2) Records, statements of opinion, testimony and other information regarding an applicant for admission, readmission or reinstatement to the Bar communicated by any entity, including any person, firm, or institution, to the Board of Law Examiners, the Committee on Character and Fitness, or to the members, associate members, employees or agents of the Board or Committee, are absolutely privileged, and civil suits predicated thereon may not be instituted.

[Adopted effective September 1, 1990. Amended effective September 25, 1990; November 1, 1991. Paragraph (c)(4) rescinded effective November 5, 1992. Amended effective August 26, 1993; October 5, 1995; January 7, 1998; November 18, 1998; November 15, 2001; January 24, 2002; April 4, 2002; January 27, 2003; September 1, 2003; October 22, 2003; October 18, 2005; June 1, 2007; September 17, 2008; March 6, 2009; April 10, 2009; April 29, 2009; October 1, 2009; January 1, 2010; March 24, 2010; December 3, 2010; January 6, 2011; September 8, 2011.]

[1] This fee is currently ten dollars ($10.00) and should be payable by check to the National Conference of Bar Examiners.

Note

The forms for the application for admission to practice law in South Carolina and for the character affidavit are available at http://www.sccourts.org.

RULE 403. TRIAL EXPERIENCES

(a) General Rule. Although admitted to practice law in this State, an attorney shall not appear as counsel in any hearing, trial, or deposition in a case pending before a court of this State until the attorney's trial experiences required by this rule have been approved by the Supreme Court. An attorney whose trial experiences have not been approved may appear as counsel if the attorney is accompanied by an attorney whose trial experiences have been approved under this rule or who is exempt from this rule, and the other attorney is present throughout the hearing, trial, or deposition. Attorneys admitted to practice law in this State on or before March 1, 1979, are exempt from the requirements of this rule. Attorneys holding a limited certificate to practice law in this State need not comply with the requirements of this rule.

(b) Trial Experiences Defined. A trial experience is defined as the:

(1) actual participation in an entire contested testimonial-type trial or hearing if the attorney is accompanied by an attorney whose trial experiences have been approved under this rule or who is exempt from this rule, and the other attorney is present throughout the hearing or trial;

(2) observation of an entire contested testimonial-type trial or hearing; or

(3) participation in a judicial observation and experience program approved by the Chief Justice's Commission on the Profession, provided the student participates in the program for a minimum of two weeks.

(c) Trial Experiences Required. An attorney must complete four (4) trial experiences. The required trial experiences are:

(1) one (1) civil jury trial in a Court of Common Pleas or in the United States District Court for the District of South Carolina;

(2) one (1) criminal jury trial in General Sessions Court or in the United States District Court for the District of South Carolina;

(3) one (1) trial in the Family Court; and

(4) one (1) trial experience which must be either a trial in equity before a circuit judge, master-in-equity, or special referee, or an administrative proceeding before an Administrative Law Judge or administrative officer of this State or of the United States. The administrative proceeding must be governed by either

the South Carolina Administrative Procedures Act or the Federal Administrative Procedure Act, and the hearing must take place within South Carolina.

Each of the trial experiences set forth in (1) and (2) above must include an opening statement, a closing argument and direct and cross examination of at least three witnesses. Trial experiences in the Family Court set forth in (3) must include direct and cross examination of at least two witnesses.

(d) When Trial Experiences May be Completed.

(1) Rule 403(b)(1) and (2) trial experiences may be completed any time after the completion of one-half (½) of the credit hours needed for law school graduation.

(2) Rule 403(b)(3) trial experiences, involving participation in a judicial observation and experience program approved by the Chief Justice's Commission on the Profession, may be completed after a law student has completed one year of law school. The supervising judge may sign the certificate giving credit for the trial experience upon completion of the program.

(e) Certificate to be Filed. The attorney shall file with the Supreme Court a Certificate showing that the trial experiences have been completed. This Certificate, which shall be on a form approved by the Supreme Court, shall state the names of the cases, the dates and the tribunals involved and shall be attested to by the respective judge, master, referee or administrative officer. A filing fee of $25 shall accompany the Certificate.

(f) Attorneys Admitted in Another State. An attorney who has been admitted to practice law in another state, territory or the District of Columbia for three (3) years may satisfy the requirements of this rule by providing proof of equivalent experience in the other jurisdiction for each category of cases specified in (c) above. This proof of equivalent experience shall be made in the form of an affidavit and shall include at least the name of the case, the case number, a brief description of the facts of the case and the type of trial experience used to satisfy the requirements of (c) above. To provide the definitive evidence required of attorneys under this section, a letter from a judge of a court of record in the other jurisdiction with personal knowledge of the attorney, attesting to that attorney's trial competence, may be substituted for detailed evidence of such experience. The affidavit shall be filed with the Supreme Court. A filing fee of $25 shall accompany the affidavit.

(g) Judge Advocate General Lawyers. The Judge Advocate General's Corps of any service of the Armed Forces of the United States (including the United States Coast Guard) shall be considered a jurisdiction for the purposes of (f) above. Further, for the purposes of (f) above, an attorney who has been a judge advocate for three years or more, either active or reserve, may use a court-martial with members as equivalent experience for the trial experience required in (c)(2), and may use a separation action or other adverse personnel action before a formal board of officers as equivalent experience for the trial experience required by (c)(4). Additionally, an attorney who has served on active duty as a judge advocate for three (3) years or more may submit a letter from a military judge or staff judge advocate with personal knowledge of the attorney attesting to the attorney's trial competence, and this letter shall have the same effect as the letter from a judge under (f) above. The military judge or staff judge advocate submitting the letter must have the rank of Colonel or above in the Army, Air Force, or Marines or Captain or above in the Navy or Coast Guard. All other requirements of (f) must be complied with.

(h) Circuit Court Law Clerks and Federal District Court Law Clerks. A person employed full time for nine (9) months as a law clerk for a South Carolina circuit court judge or as a law clerk for a United States District Court Judge in the District of South Carolina may be certified as having completed the requirements of this rule by participating in or observing one (1) experience described in (c)(3) or (4) above. A part-time law clerk may be certified in a similar manner if the law clerk has been employed as a law clerk for at least 1350 hours. The law clerk must submit a statement from a judge or other court official certifying that the law clerk has been employed as a law clerk for the period required by this rule. A Certificate (see (e) above) must be submitted for the trial.

(i) Appellate Court Law Clerks and Staff Attorneys. A person employed full time for eighteen (18) months as a law clerk or staff attorney for the Supreme Court of South Carolina or the South Carolina Court of Appeals, or the United States Court of Appeals for the Fourth Circuit may be certified as having completed the requirements of this rule by participating in or observing one (1) experience described in (c)(3) or (4) above. A part-time law clerk or staff attorney may be certified in a similar manner if the law clerk or staff attorney has been employed as a law clerk or staff attorney for at least 2700 hours. The law clerk or staff attorney must submit a statement from a judge, justice or other court official certifying that the law clerk has been employed as a law clerk or staff attorney for the period required by this rule. A Certificate (see (e) above) must be submitted for the trial.

(j) Bankruptcy Law Clerks. A person employed full time for nine (9) months as a law clerk for a United States Bankruptcy Judge in South Carolina may be certified as having completed the requirements of this rule by participating in or observing the three (3) trial experiences described in (c)(1), (2) and (3) above. A part-time law clerk may be certified in a similar manner if the law clerk has been employed as a law clerk for at least 1350 hours. The law clerk must submit a statement from a judge or other court official certifying that the law clerk has been employed as a law clerk for the period required by this rule. A

Certificate (see (e) above) must be submitted for the trials.

(k) Approval or Disapproval. The Court will notify the attorney if the trial experiences submitted in the Certificate or affidavit have been approved or disapproved.

(*l*) Confidentiality. The confidentiality provisions of Rule 402(i), SCACR, shall apply to all files and records of the Clerk of the Supreme Court relating to the administration of this rule. The Clerk may, however, disclose whether an attorney's trial experiences have been approved and the date of that approval.

[Adopted effective September 1, 1990. Amended effective January 6, 2000; February 17, 2000; August 16, 2000; August 22, 2001; September 1, 2003; December 17, 2003; April 7, 2004; February 17, 2005; March 26, 2007; September 6, 2007; February 21, 2008; November 21, 2008; June 28, 2010.]

Note

The form for the certificate to show completion of trial experience is available at http://www.sccourts.org.

RULE 404. ADMISSION PRO HAC VICE AND APPEARANCES BY NON-SOUTH CAROLINA LAWYERS IN ARBITRATION, MEDIATION OR OTHER ALTERNATIVE DISPUTE RESOLUTION PROCEEDINGS IN SOUTH CAROLINA

(a) Admission; Tribunal Defined. Upon written application, an attorney who is not admitted to practice law in South Carolina and who is admitted and authorized to practice law in the highest court of another state or the District of Columbia may appear pro hac vice in any action or proceeding before a tribunal of this state if an attorney admitted to practice law in South Carolina is associated as attorney of record. For the purpose of this rule, a "tribunal" includes any court of this state, and the South Carolina Administrative Law Court and any South Carolina agency authorized to hear and determine contested cases as defined under S.C. Code Ann. § 1-23-310.

(b) Prohibitions on Admission Pro Hac Vice. An attorney may not appear pro hac vice if the attorney is a resident of South Carolina, is regularly employed in South Carolina, or is regularly engaged in the practice of law or in substantial business or professional activities in South Carolina, unless the attorney has filed an application for admission under Rule 402, SCACR. Notwithstanding any other provision herein, an attorney who files more than six applications for admission pro hac vice in a calendar year, including applications for purposes of Rule 404(h), is considered regularly engaged in the practice of law in South Carolina.

(c) Application for Admission Pro Hac Vice. An attorney desiring to appear pro hac vice shall file with the tribunal in which the matter is pending, prior to making an appearance, an Application for Admission Pro Hac Vice which contains the following information:

(1) the applicant's residence and office addresses;

(2) the state and federal courts to which the applicant has been admitted to practice and the dates of admission;

(3) whether the applicant is a member in good standing in those courts, and a certificate of good standing of the Bar of the highest court of the state or the District of Columbia where the applicant regularly practices law;

(4) whether the applicant is currently suspended or disbarred in any court, and if so, a description of the circumstances under which the suspension or disbarment occurred;

(5) whether the applicant has been formally notified of any complaints pending before a disciplinary agency in any jurisdiction and, if so, provide a detailed description of the nature and status of any pending disciplinary complaints;

(6) an identification of all law firms with which the applicant is associated and a description of all the applicant's pending pro hac vice appearances in South Carolina to include the name and address of the tribunal;

(7) the names of each case or proceeding in South Carolina in which the applicant has filed an application to appear as counsel pro hac vice, the name and address of the tribunal, the date of each application, and whether it was granted;

(8) the name, address, and telephone number of the active member(s) of the South Carolina Bar who is (are) the attorney(s) of record; and

(9) an affirmation that the applicant will comply with the applicable statutes, law and procedural rules of the State of South Carolina; be familiar with and comply with the South Carolina Rules of Professional Conduct; and submit to the jurisdiction of the South Carolina courts and the South Carolina disciplinary process.

The tribunal in its discretion may order a hearing on the application and shall enter an order granting or refusing the application. If the application is refused, the tribunal shall state its reasons.

(d) Fee; Record of Appearances Pro Hac Vice. Each time an Application for Admission Pro Hac Vice under this rule is made, the attorney seeking to appear pro hac vice shall provide a copy of the application to the South Carolina Supreme Court Office of Bar Admissions accompanied by a $250 fee. Upon receipt of the application, the Clerk of the South Carolina Supreme Court shall certify to the tribunal in which a pro hac vice appearance has been requested that the fee has been received. The Office of Bar Admissions shall maintain a record of all pro hac vice applications as a public record.

(e) Conduct of Attorney Appearing Pro Hac Vice. An attorney appearing pro hac vice is subject to the jurisdiction of the South Carolina courts with respect to South Carolina law governing the conduct of attorneys to the same extent as an attorney admitted to practice law in this state. The attorney shall comply with the South Carolina Rules of Professional Conduct and is subject to the disciplinary jurisdiction of the Supreme Court of South Carolina. The tribunal in which an attorney is appearing pro hac vice or the Supreme Court of South Carolina may withdraw permission for the attorney to appear pro hac vice based on a violation of South Carolina law; a violation of the South Carolina Rules of Professional Conduct; a violation of a court order or the rules of the tribunal; the submission of an Application for Admission Pro Hac Vice which contains false, misleading or incomplete information; the pendency of a lawyer disciplinary proceeding or the imposition of a suspension, disbarment or other lawyer disciplinary sanction in this or another jurisdiction; the withdrawal or suspension of permission to appear pro hac vice in this or another jurisdiction; or other good cause.

(f) Responsibilities of Attorney of Record for Attorney Appearing Pro Hac Vice. The South Carolina attorney of record shall at all times be prepared to go forward with the case; sign all papers subsequently filed; and attend all subsequent proceedings in the matter, unless the tribunal specifically excuses the South Carolina attorney of record from attendance.

(g) Non-South Carolina Lawyers Appearing in an Arbitration, Mediation or Other Alternative Dispute Resolution Proceeding in South Carolina. Pursuant to Rule 5.5(c)(3) of the Rules of Professional Conduct, Rule 407, SCACR, a lawyer admitted to practice law in another jurisdiction may perform legal services on a temporary basis in this jurisdiction if those services are in or reasonably related to a pending or potential arbitration, mediation, or other alternative dispute resolution proceeding in this or another jurisdiction, if the services arise out of or are reasonably related to the lawyer's pre-existing representation of a client in a jurisdiction in which the lawyer is admitted to practice.

(h) Limitations on Provision of Legal Services Pursuant to Rule 5.5(c)(3). A lawyer who is not admitted to practice in South Carolina who seeks to provide legal services pursuant to Rule 5.5(c)(3) in more than three matters in a calendar year shall be presumed to be providing legal services on a regular, not temporary, basis.

(i) Fee; Record of Provision of Legal Services Pursuant to Rule 5.5(c)(3). For each matter in which a lawyer seeks to provide legal services pursuant to Rule 5.5(c)(3), the lawyer shall file a verified statement with the South Carolina Supreme Court Office of Bar Admissions stating that the lawyer has not filed more than three statements pursuant to this rule in a 365–day period. The statement shall be accompanied by a $250 fee and shall be served on opposing counsel, if known. If opposing counsel is not known at the time the verified statement is filed, the statement shall be filed on opposing counsel within ten days of learning the identity of opposing counsel.

[Adopted effective September 1, 1990. Amended effective July 1, 2002; March 1, 2005; April 14, 2005; October 1, 2005; July 20, 2006; July 27, 2009.]

Note

The form for verified application for admission Pro Hac Vice in the State of South Carolina pursuant to this rule is available at http://www.sccourts.org.

RULE 405. LIMITED CERTIFICATE OF ADMISSION TO PRACTICE LAW IN SOUTH CAROLINA

(a) The Supreme Court may issue a limited certificate of admission to practice law in South Carolina to any person who:

(1) is at least twenty-one (21) years of age;

(2) is a person of good moral character;

(3) has received a JD or LLB degree from a law school which was approved by the Council of Legal Education of the American Bar Association at the time the degree was conferred;

(4) has been admitted to practice law in the highest court of another state or the District of Columbia;

(5) is a member in good standing in each jurisdiction where he is admitted to practice law;

(6) has not been disbarred or suspended from the practice of law and is not the subject of any pending disciplinary proceeding in any other jurisdiction;

(7) is employed in the legal department or under the supervision of the legal department of a corporation, company, partnership, or association (business employer) which does not provide legal services in South Carolina to the public or its employees. If not a South Carolina corporation, company, partnership or association, the business employer must be qualified or otherwise lawfully engaged in business in South Carolina;

(8) performs most of his duties for the business employer in South Carolina and has his principal office in South Carolina; and

(9) provides legal services in South Carolina solely for the business employer or the parent or subsidiary of such employer.

(b) An attorney issued a limited certificate of admission to practice law may represent his employer:

(1) before any State agency in an administrative proceeding if authorized by the agency's regulations;

(2) before the magistrate's court in civil proceedings upon presentation of a copy of the certificate to the court;

(3) before any other South Carolina court or tribunal only if:

(i) he associates as co-counsel a member of the South Carolina Bar licensed under Rule 402. The associated attorney shall be present at all trials, hearings, depositions, and other proceedings, and shall be required to sign all pleadings, motions, and other documents required to be signed by an attorney; and

(ii) a copy of the certificate is presented to the court or other tribunal.

(c) An attorney granted a limited certificate of admission to practice law is not prevented from appearing in any matter pro se or from fulfilling the duties of a member of the reserve components of the armed forces or the National Guard.

(d) An attorney desiring a limited certificate of admission to practice law shall file with the Clerk of the Supreme Court an application in duplicate on a form prescribed by the Supreme Court.

(e) The application shall be accompanied by a certificate of good standing from each jurisdiction in which the attorney has been admitted to practice law, a non-refundable application fee of $400 and a statement signed by a representative of the attorney's employer stating that the attorney and the business employer meet the requirements of subsections (a)(7) to (9) of this Rule.

(f) Any questions concerning the fitness or qualifications of an attorney applying for a limited certificate of admission to practice law may be referred by the Court to the Committee on Character and Fitness for a hearing and recommendation.

(g) The performance of legal services in this State by an attorney issued a limited certificate of admission to practice law shall be deemed the active engagement in the practice of law and shall subject the attorney to all duties and obligations of active members of the South Carolina Bar and to all rules on the practice of law, including the Rules of Professional Conduct, Rule 407, SCACR, and the Rules for Lawyer Disciplinary Enforcement, Rule 413, SCACR. If an attorney granted a limited certificate engages in the practice of law in excess of that permitted by this rule, the attorney may be subject to discipline under Rule 413, SCACR, suspension or revocation of the limited certificate by the Supreme Court, or being held in contempt of the Supreme Court for engaging in the unauthorized practice of law.

(h) The limited certificate of admission to practice law shall expire if the attorney ceases to be an employee of the business employer, is otherwise admitted to the Bar of this State, fails to fulfill the obligations required of active members of the South Carolina Bar, is suspended or disbarred from the practice of law in this or any other jurisdiction, or fails at any time to be a member of the bar in good standing before the highest court of at least one other state or the District of Columbia.

(i) Upon the expiration of the limited certificate of admission to practice law, the attorney shall immediately surrender the certificate to the Clerk of the Supreme Court. The failure to immediately surrender the certificate upon expiration may subject the attorney to discipline under Rule 413, SCACR, or to being held in contempt of the Supreme Court.

(j) Notwithstanding any other provision of this Rule, the performance of legal services in this State solely for the corporation, company, partnership, or association prior to December 31, 1989, shall be deemed to have been the authorized practice of law in this State for all purposes if, at the time of the performance of the legal services, the attorney met the requirements of section (a) above.

(k) The confidentiality provisions of Rule 402(n), SCACR, shall apply to all files and records of the Board of Law Examiners, the Committee on Character and Fitness, and the Clerk of the Supreme Court relating to a limited certificate to practice law under this rule.

(*l*) An attorney granted a limited certificate to practice law under this Rule may, subject to the limitations contained in section (m) below, provide *pro bono* legal services if the attorney:

(1) is associated with an approved legal services organization which receives, or is eligible to receive, funds from the Legal Services Corporation or is working on a case or project through the South Carolina Bar Pro Bono Program;

(2) performs all activities authorized by this Rule under the supervision of an attorney (Supervising Attorney) who is an active member of the South Carolina Bar employed by, or participating as a volunteer for, the legal services organization or the South Carolina Bar Pro Bono Program and who assumes professional responsibility for the conduct of the matter, litigation, or administrative proceeding in which the attorney participates; and

(3) neither asks for nor receives compensation of any kind for the legal services provided to the client.

(m) In representing a client through an approved legal services organization or the South Carolina Bar Pro Bono Program, the attorney may:

(1) appear in any court or before any tribunal in this State if the client consents, in writing, to that appearance and the Supervising Attorney has given written approval for the appearance. The written consent and approval must be filed with the court or tribunal and must be brought to the attention of the judge or presiding officer prior to the appearance;

(2) prepare pleadings and other documents to be filed in any court or before any tribunal in this State on behalf of the client. Such pleadings shall also be signed by the Supervising Attorney; and

(3) otherwise engage in the practice of law as is necessary for the representation of the client.

[Adopted effective September 1, 1990. Amended effective November 1, 1991; September 21, 1992; August 26, 1993; September 18, 1996; January 1, 1997; October 22, 1997; April 18, 2002; July 1, 2002; April 7, 2004; September 16, 2009; December 3, 2010.]

Note

The form for an Application for a Limited Certificate of Admission to Practice Law in South Carolina is available at http://www.sccourts.org.

RULE 406. DISPOSITION OF FEES

One fourth of all fees collected by the bar admissions office, to include bar application or reinstatement fees, shall be remitted by the Judicial Department to the General Fund of the State of South Carolina; provided, however, the amount remitted to the General Fund in any fiscal year shall not exceed the amount remitted in Fiscal Year 2002–2003. The remaining portion shall be deposited by the Judicial Department in an escrow account to be held by the State Treasurer, and shall be used for expenses incurred by the bar admissions office, the Committee on Character and Fitness and the Board of Law Examiners, and for such other expenses of the Judicial Department as the Chief Justice may direct.

[Adopted effective September 1, 1990. Amended effective December 17, 2003.]

RULE 407. SOUTH CAROLINA RULES OF PROFESSIONAL CONDUCT

PREAMBLE: A LAWYER'S RESPONSIBILITIES

[1] A lawyer, being a member of the legal profession, is a representative of clients, an officer of the legal system and a public citizen having special responsibility for the quality of justice.

[2] As a representative of clients, a lawyer performs various functions. As advisor, a lawyer provides a client with an informed understanding of the client's legal rights and obligations and explains their practical implications. As advocate, a lawyer zealously asserts the client's position under the rules of the adversary system. As negotiator, a lawyer seeks a result advantageous to the client but consistent with requirements of honest dealings with others. As an evaluator, a lawyer acts by examining a client's legal affairs and reporting about them to the client or to others.

[3] In addition to these representational functions, a lawyer may serve as a third-party neutral, a nonrepresentational role helping the parties to resolve a dispute or other matter. Some of these Rules apply directly to lawyers who are or have served as third-party neutrals. See, e.g., Rules 1.12 and 2.4. In addition, there are Rules that apply to lawyers who are not active in the practice of law or to practicing lawyers even when they are acting in a nonprofessional capacity. For example, a lawyer who commits fraud in the conduct of a business is subject to discipline for engaging in conduct involving dishonesty, fraud, deceit or misrepresentation. See Rule 8.4.

[4] In all professional functions a lawyer should be competent, prompt and diligent. A lawyer should maintain communication with a client concerning the representation. A lawyer should keep in confidence information relating to representation of a client except so far as disclosure is required or permitted by the Rules of Professional Conduct or other law.

[5] A lawyer's conduct should conform to the requirements of the law, both in professional service to clients and in the lawyer's business and personal affairs. A lawyer should use the law's procedures only for legitimate purposes and not to harass or intimidate others. A lawyer should demonstrate respect for the legal system and for those who serve it, including judges, other lawyers and public officials. While it is a lawyer's duty, when necessary, to challenge the rectitude of official action, it is also a lawyer's duty to uphold legal process.

[6] As a public citizen, a lawyer should seek improvement of the law, access to the legal system, the administration of justice and the quality of service rendered by the legal profession. As a member of a learned profession, a lawyer should cultivate knowledge of the law beyond its use for clients, employ that knowledge in reform of the law and work to strengthen legal education. In addition, a lawyer should further the public's understanding of and confidence in the rule of law and the justice system because legal institutions in a constitutional democracy depend on popular participation and support to maintain their authority. A lawyer should be mindful of deficiencies in the administration of justice and of the fact that the poor, and sometimes persons who are not poor, cannot afford adequate legal assistance. Therefore, all lawyers should devote professional time and resources and use civic influence to ensure equal access to our system of justice for all those who because of economic or social barriers cannot afford or secure adequate legal counsel. A lawyer should aid the legal profession in pursuing these objectives and should help the bar regulate itself in the public interest.

[7] Many of a lawyer's professional responsibilities are prescribed in the Rules of Professional Conduct, as well as substantive and procedural law. However, a lawyer is also guided by personal conscience and the approbation of professional peers. A lawyer should strive to attain the highest level of skill, to improve the law and the legal profession and to exemplify the legal profession's ideals of public service.

[8] A lawyer's responsibilities as a representative of clients, an officer of the legal system and a public

citizen are usually harmonious. Thus, when an opposing party is well represented, a lawyer can be a zealous advocate on behalf of a client and at the same time assume that justice is being done. So also, a lawyer can be sure that preserving client confidences ordinarily serves the public interest because people are more likely to seek legal advice, and thereby heed their legal obligations, when they know their communications will be private.

[9] In the nature of law practice, however, conflicting responsibilities are encountered. Virtually all difficult ethical problems arise from conflict between a lawyer's responsibilities to clients, to the legal system and to the lawyer's own interest in remaining an ethical person while earning a satisfactory living. The Rules of Professional Conduct often prescribe terms for resolving such conflicts. Within the framework of these Rules, however, many difficult issues of professional discretion can arise. Such issues must be resolved through the exercise of sensitive professional and moral judgment guided by the basic principles underlying the Rules. These principles include the lawyer's obligation zealously to protect and pursue a client's legitimate interests, within the bounds of the law, while maintaining a professional, courteous and civil attitude toward all persons involved in the legal system.

[10] The legal profession is largely self-governing. Although other professions also have been granted powers of self-government, the legal profession is unique in this respect because of the close relationship between the profession and the processes of government and law enforcement. This connection is manifested in the fact that ultimate authority over the legal profession is vested largely in the courts.

[11] To the extent that lawyers meet the obligations of their professional calling, the occasion for government regulation is obviated. Self–regulation also helps maintain the legal profession's independence from government domination. An independent legal profession is an important force in preserving government under law, for abuse of legal authority is more readily challenged by a profession whose members are not dependent on government for the right to practice.

[12] The legal profession's relative autonomy carries with it special responsibilities of self-government. The profession has a responsibility to assure that its regulations are conceived in the public interest and not in furtherance of parochial or self-interested concerns of the bar. Every lawyer is responsible for observance of the Rules of Professional Conduct. A lawyer should also aid in securing their observance by other lawyers. Neglect of these responsibilities compromises the independence of the profession and the public interest which it serves.

[13] Lawyers play a vital role in the preservation of society. The fulfillment of this role requires an understanding by lawyers of their relationship to our legal system. The Rules of Professional Conduct, when properly applied, serve to define that relationship.

[Adopted effective September 1, 1990. Amended effective October 1, 2005.]

SCOPE

[1] The Rules of Professional Conduct are rules of reason. They should be interpreted with reference to the purposes of legal representation and of the law itself. Some of the Rules are imperatives, cast in the terms "shall" or "shall not." These define proper conduct for purposes of professional discipline. Others, generally cast in the term "may," are permissive and define areas under the Rules in which the lawyer has discretion to exercise professional judgment. No disciplinary action should be taken when the lawyer chooses not to act or acts within the bounds of such discretion. Other Rules define the nature of relationships between the lawyer and others. The Rules are thus partly obligatory and disciplinary and partly constitutive and descriptive in that they define a lawyer's professional role. Many of the Comments use the term "should." Comments do not add obligations to the Rules but provide guidance for practicing in compliance with the Rules.

[2] The Rules presuppose a larger legal context shaping the lawyer's role. That context includes court rules and statutes relating to matters of licensure, laws defining specific obligations of lawyers and substantive and procedural law in general. The Comments are sometimes used to alert lawyers to their responsibilities under such other law.

[3] Compliance with the Rules, as with all law in an open society, depends primarily upon understanding and voluntary compliance, secondarily upon reinforcement by peer and public opinion and finally, when necessary, upon enforcement through disciplinary proceedings. The Rules do not, however, exhaust the moral and ethical considerations that should inform a lawyer, for no worthwhile human activity can be completely defined by legal rules. The Rules simply provide a framework for the ethical practice of law.

[4] Furthermore, for purposes of determining the lawyer's authority and responsibility, principles of substantive law external to these Rules determine whether a client-lawyer relationship exists. Most of the duties flowing from the client-lawyer relationship attach only after the client has requested the lawyer to render legal services and the lawyer has agreed to do so. But there are some duties, such as that of confidentiality under Rule 1.6, that attach when the lawyer agrees to consider whether a client-lawyer relationship shall be established. See Rule 1.18. Whether a client-lawyer relationship exists for any specific purpose can depend on the circumstances and may be a question of fact.

[5] Under various legal provisions, including constitutional, statutory and common law, the responsibilities of government lawyers may include authority concerning legal matters that ordinarily reposes in the client in private client-lawyer relationships. For example, a lawyer for a government agency may have authority on behalf of the government to decide upon settlement or whether to appeal from an adverse judgment. Such authority in various respects is generally vested in the attorney general and the state's attorney in state government, and their federal counterparts, and the same may be true of other government law officers. Also, lawyers under the supervision of these officers may be authorized to represent several government agencies in intragovernmental legal controversies in circumstances where a private lawyer could not represent multiple private clients. These Rules do not abrogate any such authority.

[6] Failure to comply with an obligation or prohibition imposed by a Rule is a basis for invoking the disciplinary process. The Rules presuppose that disciplinary assessment of a lawyer's conduct will be made on the basis of the facts and circumstances as they existed at the time of the conduct in question and in recognition of the fact that a lawyer often has to act upon uncertain or incomplete evidence of the situation. Moreover, the Rules presuppose that whether or not discipline should be imposed for a violation, and the severity of a sanction, depend on all the circumstances, such as the willfulness and seriousness of the violation, extenuating factors and whether there have been previous violations.

[7] Violation of a Rule should not itself give rise to a cause of action against a lawyer nor should it create any presumption in such a case that a legal duty has been breached. In addition, violation of a Rule does not necessarily warrant any other nondisciplinary remedy, such as disqualification of a lawyer in pending litigation. The Rules are designed to provide guidance to lawyers and to provide a structure for regulating conduct through disciplinary agencies. They are not designed to be a basis for civil liability. Furthermore, the purpose of the Rules can be subverted when they are invoked by opposing parties as procedural weapons. The fact that a Rule is a just basis for a lawyer's self-assessment, or for sanctioning a lawyer under the administration of a disciplinary authority, does not imply that an antagonist in a collateral proceeding or transaction has standing to seek enforcement of the Rule. Nevertheless, since the Rules do establish standards of conduct by lawyers, a lawyer's violation of a Rule may be evidence of breach of the applicable standard of conduct.

[8] The Comment accompanying each Rule explains and illustrates the meaning and purpose of the Rule. The Preamble and this note on Scope provide general orientation. The Comments are intended as guides to interpretation, but the text of each Rule is authoritative.

[Adopted effective September 1, 1990. Amended effective October 1, 2005.]

CLIENT–LAWYER RELATIONSHIP

RULE 1.0. TERMINOLOGY

(a) "Belief" or "believes" denotes that the person involved actually supposed the fact in question to be true. A person's belief may be inferred from circumstances.

(b) "Confirmed in writing," when used in reference to the informed consent of a person, denotes informed consent that is given in writing by the person or a writing that a lawyer promptly transmits to the person confirming an oral informed consent. See paragraph (g) for the definition of "informed consent." If it is not feasible to obtain or transmit the writing at the time the person gives informed consent, then the lawyer must obtain or transmit it within a reasonable time thereafter.

(c) "Consult" or "consultation" denotes communication of information reasonably sufficient to permit the client to appreciate the significance of the matter in question.

(d) "Depository institution" means any bank, credit union or savings and loan association authorized by federal or state laws to do business in South Carolina and insured by the Federal Deposit Insurance Corporation, the National Credit Union Share Insurance Fund, or any successor insurance corporation(s) established by federal or state law.

(e) "Firm" or "law firm" denotes a lawyer or lawyers in a law partnership, professional corporation, sole proprietorship or other association, or in a legal services organization; lawyers employed in the legal department of a corporation, government, or other organization; and lawyers associated with an enterprise who represent clients within the scope of that association.

(f) "Fraud" or "fraudulent" denotes conduct that is fraudulent under the substantive or procedural law of the applicable jurisdiction or which has a purpose to deceive.

(g) "Informed consent" denotes the agreement by a person to a proposed course of conduct after the lawyer has communicated reasonably adequate information and explanation about the material risks of and reasonably available alternatives to the proposed course of conduct.

(h) "Knowingly," "known," or "knows" denotes actual knowledge of the fact in question. A person's knowledge may be inferred from circumstances.

(i) "Partner" denotes a member of a partnership, a shareholder in a law firm organized as a professional corporation, or a member of an association authorized to practice law.

(j) "Reasonable" or "reasonably" when used in relation to conduct by a lawyer denotes the conduct of a reasonably prudent and competent lawyer.

(k) "Reasonable belief" or "reasonably believes" when used in reference to a lawyer denotes that the lawyer believes the matter in question and that the circumstances are such that the belief is reasonable.

(l) "Reasonably should know" when used in reference to a lawyer denotes that a lawyer of reasonable prudence and competence would ascertain the matter in question.

(m) "Screened" denotes the isolation of a lawyer from any participation in a matter through the timely imposition of procedures within a firm that are reasonably adequate under the circumstances to protect information that the isolated lawyer is obligated to protect under these Rules or other law.

(n) "Serious crime" denotes any felony; any lesser crime that reflects adversely on the lawyer's honesty, trustworthiness or fitness as a lawyer in other respects; or, any crime a necessary element of which, as determined by the statutory or common law definition of the crime, involves interference with the administration of justice, false swearing, misrepresentation, fraud, deceit, bribery, extortion, misappropriation, theft, willful failure to file income tax returns, or an attempt, conspiracy or solicitation of another to commit a serious crime.

(o) "Substantial" when used in reference to degree or extent denotes a material matter of clear and weighty importance.

(p) "Tribunal" denotes a court, an arbitrator in a binding arbitration proceeding, or a legislative body, administrative agency or other body acting in an adjudicative capacity. A legislative body, administrative agency or other body acts in an adjudicative capacity when a neutral official, after the presentation of evidence or legal argument by a party or parties, will render a binding legal judgment directly affecting a party's interests in a particular matter.

(q) "Writing" or "written" denotes a tangible or electronic record of a communication or representation, including handwriting, typewriting, printing, photostating, photography, audio or videorecording and e-mail. A "signed" writing includes an electronic sound, symbol or process attached to or logically associated with a writing and executed or adopted by a person with the intent to sign the writing.

[Adopted effective September 1, 1990. Amended effective October 1, 2005; February 19, 2009; June 28, 2010.]

Comment

Confirmed in Writing

[1] If it is not feasible to obtain or transmit a written confirmation at the time the client gives informed consent, then the lawyer must obtain or transmit it within a reasonable time thereafter. If a lawyer has obtained a client's informed consent, the lawyer may act in reliance on that consent so long as it is confirmed in writing within a reasonable time thereafter.

Firm

[2] Whether two or more lawyers constitute a firm within paragraph (d) can depend on the specific facts. For example, two practitioners who share office space and occasionally consult or assist each other ordinarily would not be regarded as constituting a firm. However, if they present themselves to the public in a way that suggests that they are a firm or conduct themselves as a firm, they should be regarded as a firm for purposes of the Rules. The terms of any formal agreement between associated lawyers are relevant in determining whether they are a firm, as is the fact that they have mutual access to information concerning the clients they serve. Furthermore, it is relevant in doubtful cases to consider the underlying purpose of the Rule that is involved. A group of lawyers could be regarded as a firm for purposes of the Rule that the same lawyer should not represent opposing parties in litigation, while it might not be so regarded for purposes of the Rule that information acquired by one lawyer is attributed to another.

[3] With respect to the law department of an organization, including the government, there is ordinarily no question that the members of the department constitute a firm within the meaning of the Rules of Professional Conduct. There can be uncertainty, however, as to the identity of the client. For example, it may not be clear whether the law department of a corporation represents a subsidiary or an affiliated corporation, as well as the corporation by which the members of the department are directly employed. A similar question can arise concerning an unincorporated association and its local affiliates.

[4] Similar questions can also arise with respect to lawyers in legal aid and legal services organizations. Depending upon the structure of the organization, the entire organization or different components of it may constitute a firm or firms for purposes of these Rules.

Fraud

[5] When used in these Rules, the terms "fraud" or "fraudulent" refer to conduct that is characterized as such under the substantive or procedural law of the applicable jurisdiction or conduct which has a purpose to deceive. This does not include merely negligent misrepresentation or negligent failure to apprise another of relevant information. For purposes of these Rules, it is not necessary that anyone has suffered damages or relied on the misrepresentation or failure to inform.

Informed Consent

[6] Many of the Rules of Professional Conduct require the lawyer to obtain the informed consent of a client or other person (e.g., a former client or, under certain circumstances, a prospective client) before accepting or continuing representation or pursuing a course of conduct. See, e.g., Rules 1.2(c), 1.6(a), 1.7(b), and 1.18(d). The communication necessary to obtain such consent will vary according to the Rule involved and the circumstances giving rise to the need to obtain informed consent. The lawyer must make reasonable efforts to ensure that the client or other person possesses information reasonably adequate to make an informed decision. Ordinarily, this will require communication that includes a

disclosure of the facts and circumstances giving rise to the situation, any explanation reasonably necessary to inform the client or other person of the material advantages and disadvantages of the proposed course of conduct and a discussion of the client's or other person's options and alternatives. In some circumstances it may be appropriate for a lawyer to advise a client or other person to seek the advice of other counsel. A lawyer need not inform a client or other person of facts or implications already known to the client or other person; nevertheless, a lawyer who does not personally inform the client or other person assumes the risk that the client or other person is inadequately informed and the consent is invalid. In determining whether the information and explanation provided are reasonably adequate, relevant factors include whether the client or other person is experienced in legal matters generally and in making decisions of the type involved, and whether the client or other person is independently represented by other counsel in giving the consent. Normally, such persons need less information and explanation than others, and generally a client or other person who is independently represented by other counsel in giving the consent should be assumed to have given informed consent.

[7] Obtaining informed consent will usually require an affirmative response by the client or other person. In general, a lawyer may not assume consent from a client's or other person's silence. Consent may be inferred, however, from the conduct of a client or other person who has reasonably adequate information about the matter. A number of Rules require that a person's consent be confirmed in writing. See Rules 1.7(b), 1.9(a), and 1.18(d). For a definition of "writing" and "confirmed in writing," see paragraphs (*o*) and (b). Other Rules require that a client's consent be obtained in a writing signed by the client. See, e.g., Rules 1.8(a) and (g). For a definition of "signed," see paragraph (*o*).

Screened

[8] This definition applies to situations where screening of a personally disqualified lawyer is permitted to remove imputation of a conflict of interest under Rules 1.8(*l*), 1.10(e), 1.11, 1.12 or 1.18.

[9] The purpose of screening is to assure the affected parties that confidential information known by the personally disqualified lawyer remains protected. The personally disqualified lawyer should acknowledge the obligation not to communicate with any of the other lawyers in the firm with respect to the matter. Similarly, other lawyers in the firm who are working on the matter should be informed that the screening is in place and that they may not communicate with the personally disqualified lawyer with respect to the matter. Additional screening measures that are appropriate for the particular matter will depend on the circumstances. To implement, reinforce and remind all affected lawyers of the presence of the screening, it may be appropriate for the firm to undertake such procedures as a written undertaking by the screened lawyer to avoid any communication with other firm personnel and any contact with any firm files or other materials relating to the matter, written notice and instructions to all other firm personnel forbidding any communication with the screened lawyer relating to the matter, denial of access by the screened lawyer to firm files or other materials relating to the matter and periodic reminders of the screen to the screened lawyer and all other firm personnel.

[10] In order to be effective, screening measures must be implemented as soon as practical after a lawyer or law firm knows or reasonably should know that there is a need for screening.

RULE 1.1. COMPETENCE

A lawyer shall provide competent representation to a client. Competent representation requires the legal knowledge, skill, thoroughness and preparation reasonably necessary for the representation.

[Adopted effective September 1, 1990. Amended effective October 1, 2005.]

Comment

Legal Knowledge and Skill

[1] In determining whether a lawyer employs the requisite knowledge and skill in a particular matter, relevant factors include the relative complexity and specialized nature of the matter, the lawyer's general experience, the lawyer's training and experience in the field in question, the preparation and study the lawyer is able to give the matter and whether it is feasible to refer the matter to, or associate or consult with, a lawyer of established competence in the field in question. In many instances, the required proficiency is that of a general practitioner. Expertise in a particular field of law may be required in some circumstances.

[2] A lawyer need not necessarily have special training or prior experience to handle legal problems of a type with which the lawyer is unfamiliar. A newly admitted lawyer can be as competent as a practitioner with long experience. Some important legal skills, such as the analysis of precedent, the evaluation of evidence and legal drafting, are required in all legal problems. Perhaps the most fundamental legal skill consists of determining what kind of legal problems a situation may involve, a skill that necessarily transcends any particular specialized knowledge. A lawyer can provide adequate representation in a wholly novel field through necessary study. Competent representation can also be provided through the association of a lawyer of established competence in the field in question.

[3] In an emergency a lawyer may give advice or assistance in a matter in which the lawyer does not have the skill ordinarily required where referral to or consultation or association with another lawyer would be impractical. Even in an emergency, however, assistance should be limited to that reasonably necessary in the circumstances, for ill-considered action under emergency conditions can jeopardize the client's interest.

[4] A lawyer may accept representation where the requisite level of competence can be achieved by reasonable preparation. This applies as well to a lawyer who is appointed as counsel for an unrepresented person. See also Rule 6.2.

Thoroughness and Preparation

[5] Competent handling of a particular matter includes inquiry into and analysis of the factual and legal elements of the problem, and use of methods and procedures meeting the standards of competent practitioners. It also includes adequate preparation. The required attention and preparation are determined in part by what is at stake; major litigation and complex transactions ordinarily require more extensive treatment than matters of lesser complexity and consequence. An agreement between the lawyer and the client regarding the scope of the representation may limit the matters for which the lawyer is responsible. See Rule 1.2(c).

Maintaining Competence

[6] To maintain the requisite knowledge and skill, a lawyer should keep abreast of changes in the law and its practice, engage in continuing study and education and comply with all continuing legal education requirements to which the lawyer is subject.

RULE 1.2. SCOPE OF REPRESENTATION AND ALLOCATION OF AUTHORITY BETWEEN CLIENT AND LAWYER

(a) Subject to paragraphs (c) and (d), a lawyer shall abide by a client's decisions concerning the objectives of representation and, as required by Rule 1.4, shall consult with the client as to the means by which they are to be pursued. A lawyer may take such action on behalf of the client as is impliedly authorized to carry out the representation. A lawyer shall abide by a client's decision whether to make or accept an offer of settlement of a matter. In a criminal case, the lawyer shall abide by the client's decision, after consultation with the lawyer, as to a plea to be entered, whether to waive jury trial and whether the client will testify.

(b) A lawyer's representation of a client, including representation by appointment, does not constitute an endorsement of the client's political, economic, social or moral views or activities.

(c) A lawyer may limit the scope of the representation if the limitation is reasonable under the circumstances and the client gives informed consent.

(d) A lawyer shall not counsel a client to engage, or assist a client, in conduct that the lawyer knows is criminal or fraudulent, but a lawyer may discuss the legal consequences of any proposed course of conduct with a client and may counsel or assist a client to make a good faith effort to determine the validity, scope, meaning or application of the law.

[Adopted effective September 1, 1990. Amended effective October 1, 2005.]

Comment

Allocation of Authority between Client and Lawyer

[1] Paragraph (a) recognizes that the client has the ultimate authority to determine the purposes to be served by legal representation, within the limits imposed by law and the lawyer's professional obligations. A lawyer is not required to pursue objectives or employ means simply because a client may wish that the lawyer do so. The decisions specified in paragraph (a), such as whether to make or accept an offer of settlement of a civil matter, must also be made by the client. See Rule 1.4(a)(1) for the lawyer's duty to communicate with the client about such decisions. With respect to the means by which the client's objectives are to be pursued, the lawyer shall consult with the client as required by Rule 1.4(a)(2) and may take such action as is impliedly authorized to carry out the representation.

[2] On occasion, however, a lawyer and a client may disagree about the means to be used to accomplish the client's objectives. Clients normally defer to the special knowledge and skill of their lawyer with respect to the means to be used to accomplish their objectives, particularly with respect to technical, legal and tactical matters. Conversely, lawyers usually defer to the client regarding such questions as the expense to be incurred and concern for third persons who might be adversely affected. Because of the varied nature of the matters about which a lawyer and client might disagree and because the actions in question may implicate the interests of a tribunal or other persons, this Rule does not prescribe how such disagreements are to be resolved. Other law, however, may be applicable and should be consulted by the lawyer. The lawyer should also consult with the client and seek a mutually acceptable resolution of the disagreement. If such efforts are unavailing and the lawyer has a fundamental disagreement with the client, the lawyer may withdraw from the representation. See Rule 1.16(b)(4). Conversely, the client may resolve the disagreement by discharging the lawyer. See Rule 1.16(a)(3).

[3] At the outset of a representation, the client may authorize the lawyer to take specific action on the client's behalf without further consultation. Absent a material change in circumstances and subject to Rule 1.4, a lawyer may rely on such an advance authorization. The client may, however, revoke such authority at any time.

[4] In a case in which the client appears to be suffering diminished capacity, the lawyer's duty to abide by the client's decisions is to be guided by reference to Rule 1.14.

Independence from Client's Views or Activities

[5] Legal representation should not be denied to people who are unable to afford legal services, or whose cause is controversial or the subject of popular disapproval. By the same token, representing a client does not constitute approval of the client's views or activities.

Agreements Limiting Scope of Representation

[6] The scope of services to be provided by a lawyer may be limited by agreement with the client or by the terms under which the lawyer's services are made available to the client. When a lawyer has been retained by an insurer to represent an insured, for example, the representation may be limited to matters related to the insurance coverage. A limited representation may be appropriate because the client has limited objectives for the representation. In addition, the terms upon which representation is undertaken may exclude specific means that might otherwise be used to accomplish the client's objectives. Such limitations may exclude actions that the client thinks are too costly or that the lawyer regards as repugnant or imprudent.

[7] Although this Rule affords the lawyer and client substantial latitude to limit the representation, the limitation must be reasonable under the circumstances. If, for example, a client's objective is limited to securing general information about the law the client needs in order to handle a common and typically uncomplicated legal problem, the lawyer and client may agree that the lawyer's services will be limited to a brief telephone consultation. Such a limitation, however, would not be reasonable if the time allotted was not sufficient to yield advice upon which the client could rely. Although an agreement for a limited representation does not exempt a lawyer from the duty to provide competent representation, the limitation is a factor to be considered when determining the legal knowledge, skill, thoroughness and preparation reasonably necessary for the representation. See Rule 1.1.

[8] All agreements concerning a lawyer's representation of a client must accord with the Rules of Professional Conduct and other law. See, e.g., Rules 1.1, 1.8 and 5.6.

Criminal, Fraudulent and Prohibited Transactions

[9] Paragraph (d) prohibits a lawyer from knowingly counseling or assisting a client to commit a crime or fraud. This prohibition, however, does not preclude the lawyer from giving an honest opinion about the actual consequences that appear likely to result from a client's conduct. Nor does the fact that a client uses advice in a course of action that is criminal or fraudulent of itself make a lawyer a party to the course of action. There is a critical distinction between presenting an analysis of legal aspects of questionable conduct and recommending the means by which a crime or fraud might be committed with impunity.

[10] When the client's course of action has already begun and is continuing, the lawyer's responsibility is especially delicate. The lawyer is required to avoid assisting the client, for example, by drafting or delivering documents that the lawyer knows are fraudulent or by suggesting how the wrongdoing might be concealed. A lawyer may not continue assisting a client in conduct that the lawyer originally supposed was legally proper but then discovers is criminal or fraudulent. The lawyer must, therefore, withdraw from the representation of the client in the matter. See Rule 1.16(a). In some cases, withdrawal alone might be insufficient. It may be necessary for the lawyer to give notice of the fact of withdrawal and to disaffirm any opinion, document, affirmation or the like. See Rule 4.1.

[11] Where the client is a fiduciary, the lawyer may have special obligations in dealings with a beneficiary. However, under S.C. Code Ann. § 62–1–109, the representation of a fiduciary does not necessarily create any duties or obligations to other interested persons.

[12] Paragraph (d) applies whether or not the defrauded party is a party to the transaction. Hence, a lawyer must not participate in a sham transaction such as, for example, a transaction to effectuate criminal or fraudulent avoidance of tax liability. Paragraph (d) does not preclude undertaking a criminal defense incident to a general retainer for legal services to a lawful enterprise. The last clause of paragraph (d) recognizes that determining the validity or interpretation of a statute or regulation may require a course of action involving disobedience of the statute or regulation or of the interpretation placed upon it by governmental authorities.

[13] If a lawyer comes to know or reasonably should know that a client expects assistance not permitted by the Rules of Professional Conduct or other law or if the lawyer intends to act contrary to the client's instructions, the lawyer must consult with the client regarding the limitations on the lawyer's conduct. See Rule 1.4(a)(5).

RULE 1.3. DILIGENCE

A lawyer shall act with reasonable diligence and promptness in representing a client.

[Adopted effective September 1, 1990. Amended effective October 1, 2005.]

Comment

[1] A lawyer should pursue a matter on behalf of a client despite opposition, obstruction or personal inconvenience to the lawyer, and take whatever lawful and ethical measures are required to vindicate a client's cause or endeavor. A lawyer must also act with commitment and dedication to the interests of the client and with zeal in advocacy upon the client's behalf. A lawyer is not bound, however, to press for every advantage that might be realized for a client. For example, a lawyer may have authority to exercise professional discretion in determining the means by which a matter should be pursued. See Rule 1.2. The lawyer's duty to act with reasonable diligence does not require the use of offensive tactics or preclude the treating of all persons involved in the legal process with courtesy and respect.

[2] A lawyer's work load must be controlled so that each matter can be handled competently.

[3] Perhaps no professional shortcoming is more widely resented than procrastination. A client's interests often can be adversely affected by the passage of time or the change of conditions; in extreme instances, as when a lawyer overlooks a statute of limitations, the client's legal position may be destroyed. Even when the client's interests are not affected in substance, however, unreasonable delay can cause a client needless anxiety and undermine confidence in the lawyer's trustworthiness. A lawyer's duty to act with reasonable promptness, however, does not preclude the lawyer from agreeing to a reasonable request for a postponement that will not prejudice the lawyer's client.

[4] Unless the relationship is terminated as provided in Rule 1.16, a lawyer should carry through to conclusion all matters undertaken for a client. If a lawyer's employment is limited to a specific matter, the relationship terminates when the matter has been resolved. If a lawyer has served a client over a substantial period in a variety of matters, the client sometimes may assume that the lawyer will continue to serve on a continuing basis unless the lawyer gives notice of withdrawal. Doubt about whether a client-lawyer relationship still exists should be clarified by the lawyer, preferably in writing, so that the client will not mistakenly suppose the lawyer is looking after the client's affairs when the lawyer has ceased to do so. For example, if a lawyer has handled a judicial or administrative proceeding that produced a result adverse to the client and the lawyer and the client have not agreed that the lawyer will handle the matter on appeal, the lawyer should consult with the client about the possibility of appeal before relinquishing responsibility for the matter. See Rule 1.4(a)(2). Whether the lawyer is obligated to prosecute the appeal for the client depends on the scope of the representation the lawyer has agreed to provide to the client. See Rule 1.2.

[5] To prevent neglect of client matters in the event of a practitioner's death or disability, it is the better practice, and the duty of diligence may require, that each lawyer or law firm prepare a plan, in conformity with applicable rules, that designates another competent lawyer to review client files, notify each client of the lawyer's death or disability, and determine whether there is a need for immediate protective action. Cf. Rule 31 of the South Carolina Rules for Lawyer Disciplinary Enforcement (providing for court appointment of a lawyer to inventory files and take other protective action in absence of a plan providing for another lawyer to inventory files and take other protective action in absence of a plan providing for another lawyer to protect the interests of the clients of a deceased or disabled lawyer).

RULE 1.4. COMMUNICATION

(a) A lawyer shall

(1) promptly inform the client of any decision or circumstance with respect to which the client's in-

formed consent, as defined in Rule 1.0(g), is required by these Rules;

(2) reasonably consult with the client about the means by which the client's objectives are to be accomplished;

(3) keep the client reasonably informed about the status of the matter;

(4) promptly comply with reasonable requests for information; and

(5) consult with the client about any relevant limitation on the lawyer's conduct when the lawyer knows that the client expects assistance not permitted by the Rules of Professional Conduct or other law.

(b) A lawyer shall explain a matter to the extent reasonably necessary to permit the client to make informed decisions regarding the representation.

[Adopted effective September 1, 1990. Amended effective October 1, 2005.]

Comment

[1] Reasonable communication between the lawyer and the client is necessary for the client effectively to participate in the representation.

Communicating with Client

[2] If these Rules require that a particular decision about the representation be made by the client, paragraph (a)(1) requires that the lawyer promptly consult with and secure the client's consent prior to taking action unless prior discussions with the client have resolved what action the client wants the lawyer to take. For example, a lawyer who receives from opposing counsel an offer of settlement in a civil controversy or a proffered plea bargain in a criminal case must promptly inform the client of its substance unless the client has previously indicated that the proposal will be acceptable or unacceptable or has authorized the lawyer to accept or to reject the offer. See Rule 1.2(a).

[3] Paragraph (a)(2) requires the lawyer to reasonably consult with the client about the means to be used to accomplish the client's objectives. In some situations-depending on both the importance of the action under consideration and the feasibility of consulting with the client-this duty will require consultation prior to taking action. In other circumstances, such as during a trial when an immediate decision must be made, the exigency of the situation may require the lawyer to act without prior consultation. In such cases the lawyer must nonetheless act reasonably to inform the client of actions the lawyer has taken on the client's behalf. Additionally, paragraph (a)(3) requires that the lawyer keep the client reasonably informed about the status of the matter, such as significant developments affecting the timing or the substance of the representation.

[4] A lawyer's regular communication with clients will minimize the occasions on which a client will need to request information concerning the representation. When a client makes a reasonable request for information, however, paragraph (a)(4) requires prompt compliance with the request, or if a prompt response is not feasible, that the lawyer, or a member of the lawyer's staff, acknowledge receipt of the request and advise the client when a response may be expected. Client telephone calls should be promptly returned or acknowledged.

Explaining Matters

[5] The client should have sufficient information to participate intelligently in decisions concerning the objectives of the representation and the means by which they are to be pursued, to the extent the client is willing and able to do so. Adequacy of communication depends in part on the kind of advice or assistance that is involved. For example, when there is time to explain a proposal made in a negotiation, the lawyer should review all important provisions with the client before proceeding to an agreement. In litigation a lawyer should explain the general strategy and prospects of success and ordinarily should consult the client on tactics that are likely to result in significant expense or to injure or coerce others. On the other hand, a lawyer ordinarily will not be expected to describe trial or negotiation strategy in detail. The guiding principle is that the lawyer should fulfill reasonable client expectations for information consistent with the duty to act in the client's best interests, and the client's overall requirements as to the character of representation. In certain circumstances, such as when a lawyer asks a client to consent to a representation affected by a conflict of interest, the client must give informed consent, as defined in Rule 1.0(g).

[6] Ordinarily, the information to be provided is that appropriate for a client who is a comprehending and responsible adult. However, fully informing the client according to this standard may be impracticable, for example, where the client is a child or suffers from diminished capacity. See Rule 1.14. When the client is an organization or group, it is often impossible or inappropriate to inform every one of its members about its legal affairs; ordinarily, the lawyer should address communications to the appropriate officials of the organization. See Rule 1.13. Where many routine matters are involved, a system of limited or occasional reporting may be arranged with the client.

Withholding Information

[7] In some circumstances, a lawyer may be justified in delaying transmission of information when the client would be likely to react imprudently to an immediate communication. Thus, a lawyer might withhold a psychiatric diagnosis of a client when the examining psychiatrist indicates that disclosure would harm the client. A lawyer may not withhold information to serve the lawyer's own interest or convenience or the interests or convenience of another person. Rules or court orders governing litigation may provide that information supplied to a lawyer may not be disclosed to the client. Rule 3.4(c) directs compliance with such rules or orders.

RULE 1.5. FEES

(a) A lawyer shall not make an agreement for, charge, or collect an unreasonable fee or an unreasonable amount for expenses. The factors to be considered in determining the reasonableness of a fee include the following:

(1) the time and labor required, the novelty and difficulty of the questions involved, and the skill requisite to perform the legal service properly;

(2) the likelihood that the acceptance of the particular employment will preclude other employment by the lawyer;

(3) the fee customarily charged in the locality for similar legal services;

(4) the amount involved and the results obtained;

(5) the time limitations imposed by the client or by the circumstances;

(6) the nature and length of the professional relationship with the client;

(7) the experience, reputation, and ability of the lawyer or lawyers performing the services; and

(8) whether the fee is fixed or contingent.

(b) The scope of the representation and the basis or rate of the fee and expenses for which the client will be responsible shall be communicated to the client, preferably in writing, before or within a reasonable time after commencing the representation, except when the lawyer will charge a regularly represented client on the same basis or rate. Any changes in the basis or rate of the fee or expenses shall be communicated to the client, preferably in writing.

(c) A fee may be contingent on the outcome of the matter for which the service is rendered, except in a matter in which a contingent fee is prohibited by paragraph (d) or other law. A contingent fee agreement shall be in a writing signed by the client and shall state the method by which the fee is to be determined, including the percentage or percentages that shall accrue to the lawyer in the event of settlement, trial or appeal; litigation and other expenses to be deducted from the recovery; and whether such expenses are to be deducted before or after the contingent fee is calculated. The agreement must clearly notify the client of any expenses the client will be expected to pay. Upon conclusion of a contingent fee matter, the lawyer shall provide the client with a written statement stating the outcome of the matter and, if there is a recovery, showing the remittance to the client and the method of its determination.

(d) A lawyer shall not enter into an arrangement for, charge, or collect:

(1) any fee in a domestic relations matter, the payment or amount of which is contingent upon the securing of a divorce or upon the amount of alimony or support, or property settlement in lieu thereof, provided that a lawyer may charge a contingency fee in collection of past due alimony or child support; or

(2) a contingent fee for representing a defendant in a criminal case.

(e) A division of a fee between lawyers who are not in the same firm may be made only if:

(1) the division is in proportion to the services performed by each lawyer or each lawyer assumes joint responsibility for the representation;

(2) the client agrees to the arrangement, including the share each lawyer will receive, and the agreement is confirmed in writing; and

(3) the total fee is reasonable.

[Adopted effective September 1, 1990. Amended effective October 1, 2005.]

Comment

Reasonableness of Fee and Expenses

[1] Paragraph (a) requires that lawyers charge fees that are reasonable under the circumstances. The factors specified in (1) through (8) are not exclusive. Nor will each factor be relevant in each instance. The South Carolina version of the rule differs from the Model Rule by making the test in paragraph (a)(2) objective rather than subjective. Paragraph (a) also requires that expenses for which the client will be charged must be reasonable. A lawyer may seek reimbursement for the cost of services performed in-house, such as copying, or for other expenses incurred in-house, such as telephone charges, either by charging a reasonable amount to which the client has agreed in advance or by charging an amount that reasonably reflects the cost incurred by the lawyer.

Basis or Rate of Fee

[2] When the lawyer has regularly represented a client, they ordinarily will have evolved an understanding concerning the basis or rate of the fee and the expenses for which the client will be responsible. In a new client-lawyer relationship, however, an understanding as to fees and expenses must be promptly established, preferably in writing. Generally, it is desirable to furnish the client with at least a simple memorandum or copy of the lawyer's customary fee arrangements that states the general nature of the legal services to be provided, the basis, rate or total amount of the fee and whether and to what extent the client will be responsible for any costs, expenses or disbursements in the course of the representation. A written statement concerning the terms of the engagement reduces the possibility of misunderstanding.

[3] Contingent fees, like any other fees, are subject to the reasonableness standard of paragraph (a) of this Rule. In determining whether a particular contingent fee is reasonable, or whether it is reasonable to charge any form of contingent fee, a lawyer must consider the factors that are relevant under the circumstances. Applicable law may impose limitations on contingent fees, such as a ceiling on the percentage allowable, or may require a lawyer to offer clients an alternative basis for the fee. Applicable law also may apply to situations other than a contingent fee, for example, government regulations regarding fees in certain tax matters.

Terms of Payment

[4] A lawyer may require advance payment of a fee, but is obliged to return any unearned portion. Note further, however, that in certain circumstances in which a legitimate interest is served, the client and lawyer may enter into an arrangement under which there is a nonrefundable retainer fee. This nonrefundable retainer fee may be retained if it is reasonable under the factors listed in Rule 1.5. The lawyer may deposit the nonrefundable fee immediately into the law firm's operating account. However, if, at the end of the representation, it would be unreasonable for the lawyer to retain the entire fee, the lawyer must then refund that portion of the fee that is unreasonable. See Rule 1.16(d). A lawyer may accept property in payment for services, such as an ownership interest in an enterprise, providing this does not involve acquisition of a proprietary interest in the cause of action or subject matter of the litigation contrary to Rule 1.8(i). However, a fee paid in property instead of money may

be subject to the requirements of Rule 1.8(a) because such fees often have the essential qualities of a business transaction with the client.

[5] An agreement may not be made whose terms might induce the lawyer improperly to curtail services for the client or perform them in a way contrary to the client's interest. For example, a lawyer should not enter into an agreement whereby services are to be provided only up to a stated amount when it is foreseeable that more extensive services probably will be required, unless the situation is adequately explained to the client. Otherwise, the client might have to bargain for further assistance in the midst of a proceeding or transaction. However, it is proper to define the extent of services in light of the client's ability to pay. A lawyer should not exploit a fee arrangement based primarily on hourly charges by using wasteful procedures.

Prohibited Contingent Fees

[6] Paragraph (d) prohibits a lawyer from charging a contingent fee in a domestic relations matter when payment is contingent upon the securing of a divorce or upon the amount of alimony or support or property settlement to be obtained. This provision does not preclude a contract for a contingent fee for legal representation in connection with the recovery of post-judgment balances due under support, alimony or other financial orders because such contracts do not implicate the same policy concerns.

Division of Fee

[7] A division of fee is a single billing to a client covering the fee of two or more lawyers who are not in the same firm. A division of fee facilitates association of more than one lawyer in a matter in which neither alone could serve the client as well, and most often is used when the fee is contingent and the division is between a referring lawyer and a trial specialist. Paragraph (e) permits the lawyers to divide a fee either on the basis of the proportion of services they render or each lawyer assumes responsibility for the representation as a whole. In addition, the client must agree to the arrangement, including the share that each lawyer is to receive, and the agreement must be confirmed in writing. Contingent fee agreements must be in a writing signed by the client and must otherwise comply with paragraph (c) of this Rule. Joint responsibility for the representation entails financial and ethical responsibility for the representation as if the lawyers were associated in a partnership. A lawyer who assumes joint responsibility should be available to both the client and the other fee-sharing lawyer as needed throughout the representation and should remain knowledgeable about the progress of the legal matter. A lawyer should only refer a matter to a lawyer whom the referring lawyer reasonably believes is competent to handle the matter. See Rule 1.1.

[8] Paragraph (e) does not prohibit or regulate division of fees to be received in the future for work done when lawyers were previously associated in a law firm. Also, when a client has hired two or more lawyers in succession on a matter and later refuses to consent to a discharged lawyer receiving an earned share of the legal fee, paragraph (e) should not be applied to prevent a lawyer who has received a fee from sharing that fee with the discharged lawyer to the extent that the discharged lawyer has earned the fee for work performed on the matter and is entitled to payment.

Disputes over Fees

[9] If a procedure has been established for resolution of fee disputes, such as an arbitration or mediation procedure established by the bar, the lawyer must comply with the procedure when it is mandatory, and, even when it is voluntary, the lawyer should conscientiously consider submitting to it. See Rule 416, SCACR. Law may prescribe a procedure for determining a lawyer's fee, for example, in representation of an executor or administrator, a class or a person entitled to a reasonable fee as part of the measure of damages. The lawyer entitled to such a fee and a lawyer representing another party concerned with the fee should comply with the prescribed procedure.

RULE 1.6. CONFIDENTIALITY OF INFORMATION

(a) A lawyer shall not reveal information relating to the representation of a client unless the client gives informed consent, the disclosure is impliedly authorized in order to carry out the representation or the disclosure is permitted by paragraph (b).

(b) A lawyer may reveal information relating to the representation of a client to the extent the lawyer reasonably believes necessary:

(1) to prevent the client from committing a criminal act;

(2) to prevent reasonably certain death or substantial bodily harm;

(3) to prevent the client from committing a crime or fraud that is reasonably certain to result in substantial injury to the financial interests or property of another and in furtherance of which the client has used or is using the lawyer's services;

(4) to prevent, mitigate or rectify substantial injury to the financial interests or property of another that is reasonably certain to result or has resulted from the client's commission of a crime or fraud in furtherance of which the client has used the lawyer's services;

(5) to secure legal advice about the lawyer's compliance with these Rules;

(6) to establish a claim or defense on behalf of the lawyer in a controversy between the lawyer and the client, to establish a defense to a criminal charge or civil claim against the lawyer based upon conduct in which the client was involved, or to respond to allegations in any proceeding concerning the lawyer's representation of the client; or

(7) to comply with other law or a court order.

[Adopted effective September 1, 1990. Amended effective October 1, 2005.]

Comment

[1] This Rule governs the disclosure by a lawyer of information relating to the representation of a client during the lawyer's representation of the client. See Rule 1.18 for the lawyer's duties with respect to information provided to the lawyer by a prospective client, Rule 1.9(c)(2) for the lawyer's duty not to reveal information relating to the lawyer's prior representation of a former client and Rules 1.8(b) and 1.9(c)(1) for the lawyer's duties with respect to the use of such information to the disadvantage of clients and former clients.

[2] A fundamental principle in the client-lawyer relationship is that, in the absence of the client's informed consent, the lawyer must not reveal information relating to the representation. See Rule 1.0(g) for the definition of informed consent. Confidentiality contributes to the trust that is the hallmark of the client-lawyer relationship. The client is thereby encouraged to seek legal assistance and to communicate fully and frankly with the lawyer even as to embarrassing or legally damaging subject matter. The lawyer needs this information to represent the client effectively and, if necessary, to advise the client to refrain from wrongful conduct. Almost without exception, clients come to lawyers in order to determine their rights and what is, in the complex of laws and regulations, deemed to be legal and correct.

[3] The principle of client-lawyer confidentiality is given effect by related bodies of law: the attorney-client privilege, the work product doctrine and the rule of confidentiality established in professional ethics. The attorney-client privilege and work-product doctrine apply in judicial and other proceedings in which a lawyer may be called as a witness or otherwise required to produce evidence concerning a client. The rule of client-lawyer confidentiality applies in situations other than those where evidence is sought from the lawyer through compulsion of law. The confidentiality rule, for example, applies not only to matters communicated in confidence by the client but also to all information relating to the representation, whatever its source. A lawyer may not disclose such information except as authorized or required by the Rules of Professional Conduct or other law. See also Scope.

[4] The requirement of maintaining confidentiality of information relating to representation applies to government lawyers who may disagree with the policy goals that their representation is designed to advance.

[5] Paragraph (a) prohibits a lawyer from revealing information relating to the representation of a client. This prohibition also applies to disclosures by a lawyer that do not in themselves reveal protected information but could reasonably lead to the discovery of such information by a third person. A lawyer's use of a hypothetical to discuss issues relating to the representation is permissible so long as there is no reasonable likelihood that the listener will be able to ascertain the identity of the client or the situation involved.

Authorized Disclosure

[6] Except to the extent that the client's instructions or special circumstances limit that authority, a lawyer is impliedly authorized to make disclosures about a client when appropriate in carrying out the representation. In some situations, for example, a lawyer may be impliedly authorized to admit a fact that cannot properly be disputed or to make a disclosure that facilitates a satisfactory conclusion to a matter. Lawyers in a firm may, in the course of the firm's practice, disclose to each other information relating to a client of the firm, unless the client has instructed that particular information be confined to specified lawyers.

Disclosure Adverse to Client

[7] Although the public interest is usually best served by a strict rule requiring lawyers to preserve the confidentiality of information relating to the representation of their clients, the confidentiality rule is subject to limited exceptions. The lawyer may learn that a client intends prospective conduct that is criminal. As stated in paragraph (b)(1), the lawyer has professional discretion to reveal information in order to prevent such consequences. Paragraph (b)(2) recognizes the overriding value of life and physical integrity and permits disclosure reasonably necessary to prevent reasonably certain death or substantial bodily harm. Such harm is reasonably certain to occur if it will be suffered imminently or if there is a present and substantial threat that a person will suffer such harm at a later date if the lawyer fails to take action necessary to eliminate the threat. Thus, a lawyer who knows that a client has accidentally discharged toxic waste into a town's water supply may reveal this information to the authorities if there is a present and substantial risk that a person who drinks the water will contract a life-threatening or debilitating disease and the lawyer's disclosure is necessary to eliminate the threat or reduce the number of victims.

[8] Paragraph (b)(3) does not limit the breadth of Paragraph (b)(1), but describes one specific example of a situation in which disclosure is permitted to prevent a criminal act by the client. Paragraph (b)(3) is a limited exception to the rule of confidentiality that permits the lawyer to reveal information to the extent necessary to enable affected persons or appropriate authorities to prevent the client from committing a crime or fraud, as defined in Rule 1.0(e), that is reasonably certain to result in substantial injury to the financial or property interests of another and in furtherance of which the client has used or is using the lawyer's services. Such a serious abuse of the client-lawyer relationship by the client forfeits the protection of this Rule. The client can, of course, prevent such disclosure by refraining from the wrongful conduct. Although paragraph (b)(3) does not require the lawyer to reveal the client's misconduct, the lawyer may not counsel or assist the client in conduct the lawyer knows is criminal or fraudulent. See Rule 1.2(d). See also Rule 1.16 with respect to the lawyer's obligation or right to withdraw from the representation of the client in such circumstances, and Rule 1.13(c), which permits the lawyer, where the client is an organization, to reveal information relating to the representation in limited circumstances.

[9] Paragraph (b)(4) addresses the situation in which the lawyer does not learn of the client's crime or fraud until after it has been consummated. Although the client no longer has the option of preventing disclosure by refraining from the wrongful conduct, there will be situations in which the loss suffered by the affected person can be prevented, rectified or mitigated. In such situations, the lawyer may disclose information relating to the representation to the extent necessary to enable the affected persons to prevent or mitigate reasonably certain losses or to attempt to recoup their losses. Paragraph (b)(4) does not apply when a person who has committed a crime or fraud thereafter employs a lawyer for representation concerning that offense.

[10] A lawyer's confidentiality obligations do not preclude a lawyer from securing confidential legal advice about the lawyer's personal responsibility to comply with these Rules. In most situations, disclosing information to secure such advice will be impliedly authorized for the lawyer to carry out the representation. Even when the disclosure is not impliedly authorized, paragraph (b)(5) permits such disclosure because of the importance of a lawyer's compliance with the Rules of Professional Conduct.

[11] Where a legal claim or disciplinary charge alleges complicity of the lawyer in a client's conduct or other misconduct of the lawyer involving representation of the client, the lawyer may respond to the extent the lawyer reasonably believes necessary to establish a defense. The same is true with respect to a claim involving the conduct or representation of a former client. Such a charge can arise in

a civil, criminal, disciplinary or other proceeding and can be based on a wrong allegedly committed by the lawyer against the client or on a wrong alleged by a third person, for example, a person claiming to have been defrauded by the lawyer and client acting together. The lawyer's right to respond arises when an assertion of such complicity has been made. Paragraph (b)(6) does not require the lawyer to await the commencement of an action or proceeding that charges such complicity, so that the defense may be established by responding directly to a third party who has made such an assertion. The right to defend also applies, of course, where a proceeding has been commenced.

[12] A lawyer entitled to a fee is permitted by paragraph (b)(6) to prove the services rendered in an action to collect it. This aspect of the rule expresses the principle that the beneficiary of a fiduciary relationship may not exploit it to the detriment of the fiduciary.

[13] Other law may require that a lawyer disclose information about a client. Whether such a law supersedes Rule 1.6 is a question of law beyond the scope of these Rules. When disclosure of information relating to the representation appears to be required by other law, the lawyer must discuss the matter with the client to the extent required by Rule 1.4. If, however, the other law supersedes this Rule and requires disclosure, paragraph (b)(7) permits the lawyer to make such disclosures as are necessary to comply with the law.

[14] A lawyer may be ordered to reveal information relating to the representation of a client by a court or by another tribunal or governmental entity claiming authority pursuant to other law to compel the disclosure. Absent informed consent of the client to do otherwise, the lawyer should assert on behalf of the client all nonfrivolous claims that the order is not authorized by other law or that the information sought is protected against disclosure by the attorney-client privilege or other applicable law. In the event of an adverse ruling, the lawyer must consult with the client about the possibility of appeal to the extent required by Rule 1.4. Unless review is sought, however, paragraph (b)(7) permits the lawyer to comply with the court's order.

[15] Paragraph (b) permits disclosure only to the extent the lawyer reasonably believes the disclosure is necessary to accomplish one of the purposes specified. Where practicable, the lawyer should first seek to persuade the client to take suitable action to obviate the need for disclosure. In any case, a disclosure adverse to the client's interest should be no greater than the lawyer reasonably believes necessary to accomplish the purpose. If the disclosure will be made in connection with a judicial proceeding, the disclosure should be made in a manner that limits access to the information to the tribunal or other persons having a need to know it and appropriate protective orders or other arrangements should be sought by the lawyer to the fullest extent practicable.

[16] Paragraph (b) permits but does not require the disclosure of information relating to a client's representation to accomplish the purposes specified in paragraphs (b)(1) through (b)(7). In exercising the discretion conferred by this Rule, the lawyer may consider such factors as the nature of the lawyer's relationship with the client and with those who might be injured by the client, the lawyer's own involvement in the transaction and factors that may extenuate the conduct in question. A lawyer's decision not to disclose as permitted by paragraph (b) does not violate this Rule. Disclosure may be required, however, by other Rules. Some Rules require disclosure only if such disclosure would be permitted by paragraph (b). See Rules 1.2(d), 4.1(b), 8.1 and 8.3. Rule 3.3, on the other hand, requires disclosure in some circumstances regardless of whether such disclosure is permitted by this Rule. See Rule 3.3(c).

Acting Competently to Preserve Confidentiality

[17] A lawyer must act competently to safeguard information relating to the representation of a client against inadvertent or unauthorized disclosure by the lawyer or other persons who are participating in the representation of the client or who are subject to the lawyer's supervision. See Rules 1.1, 5.1 and 5.3.

[18] When transmitting a communication that includes information relating to the representation of a client, the lawyer must take reasonable precautions to prevent the information from coming into the hands of unintended recipients. This duty, however, does not require that the lawyer use special security measures if the method of communication affords a reasonable expectation of privacy. Special circumstances, however, may warrant special precautions. Factors to be considered in determining the reasonableness of the lawyer's expectation of confidentiality include the sensitivity of the information and the extent to which the privacy of the communication is protected by law or by a confidentiality agreement. A client may require the lawyer to implement special security measures not required by this Rule or may give informed consent to the use of a means of communication that would otherwise be prohibited by this Rule.

Former Client

[19] The duty of confidentiality continues after the client-lawyer relationship has terminated. See Rule 1.9(c)(2). See Rule 1.9(c)(1) for the prohibition against using such information to the disadvantage of the former client.

RULE 1.7. CONFLICT OF INTEREST: CURRENT CLIENTS

(a) Except as provided in paragraph (b), a lawyer shall not represent a client if the representation involves a concurrent conflict of interest. A concurrent conflict of interest exists if:

(1) the representation of one client will be directly adverse to another client; or

(2) there is a significant risk that the representation of one or more clients will be materially limited by the lawyer's responsibilities to another client, a former client or a third person or by a personal interest of the lawyer.

(b) Notwithstanding the existence of a concurrent conflict of interest under paragraph (a), a lawyer may represent a client if:

(1) the lawyer reasonably believes that the lawyer will be able to provide competent and diligent representation to each affected client;

(2) the representation is not prohibited by law;

(3) the representation does not involve the assertion of a claim by one client against another client represented by the lawyer in the same litigation or other proceeding before a tribunal; and

(4) each affected client gives informed consent, confirmed in writing.

[Adopted effective September 1, 1990. Amended effective October 1, 2005.]

Comment

General Principles

[1] Loyalty and independent judgment are essential elements in the lawyer's relationship to a client. Concurrent conflicts of interest can arise from the lawyer's responsibilities to another client, a former client or a third person or from the lawyer's own interests. For specific Rules regarding certain concurrent conflicts of interest, see Rule 1.8. For former client conflicts of interest, see Rule 1.9. For conflicts of interest involving prospective clients, see Rule 1.18. For definitions of "informed consent" and "confirmed in writing," see Rule 1.0(g) and (b).

[2] Resolution of a conflict of interest problem under this Rule requires the lawyer to: 1) clearly identify the client or clients; 2) determine whether a conflict of interest exists; 3) decide whether the representation may be undertaken despite the existence of a conflict, i.e., whether the conflict is consentable; and 4) if so, consult with the clients affected under paragraph (a) and obtain their informed consent, confirmed in writing. The clients affected under paragraph (a) include both of the clients referred to in paragraph (a)(1) and the one or more clients whose representation might be materially limited under paragraph (a)(2).

[3] A conflict of interest may exist before representation is undertaken, in which event the representation must be declined, unless the lawyer obtains the informed consent of each client under the conditions of paragraph (b). To determine whether a conflict of interest exists, a lawyer should adopt reasonable procedures, appropriate for the size and type of firm and practice, to determine in both litigation and non-litigation matters the persons and issues involved. See also Comment to Rule 5.1. Ignorance caused by a failure to institute such procedures will not excuse a lawyer's violation of this Rule. As to whether a client-lawyer relationship exists or, having once been established, is continuing, see Comment to Rule 1.3 and Scope.

[4] If a conflict arises after representation has been undertaken, the lawyer ordinarily must withdraw from the representation, unless the lawyer has obtained the informed consent of the client under the conditions of paragraph (b). See Rule 1.16. Where more than one client is involved, whether the lawyer may continue to represent any of the clients is determined both by the lawyer's ability to comply with duties owed to the former client and by the lawyer's ability to represent adequately the remaining client or clients, given the lawyer's duties to the former client. See Rule 1.9. See also Comments [5] and [27].

[5] Unforeseeable developments, such as changes in corporate and other organizational affiliations or the addition or realignment of parties in litigation, might create conflicts in the midst of a representation, as when a company sued by the lawyer on behalf of one client is bought by another client represented by the lawyer in an unrelated matter. Depending on the circumstances, the lawyer may have the option to withdraw from one of the representations in order to avoid the conflict. The lawyer must seek court approval where necessary and take steps to minimize harm to the clients. See Rule 1.16. The lawyer must continue to protect the confidences of the client from whose representation the lawyer has withdrawn. See Rule 1.9(c).

Identifying Conflicts of Interest: Directly Adverse

[6] Loyalty to a current client prohibits undertaking representation directly adverse to that client without that client's informed consent. Thus, absent consent, a lawyer may not act as an advocate in one matter against a person the lawyer represents in some other matter, even when the matters are wholly unrelated. The client as to whom the representation is directly adverse is likely to feel betrayed, and the resulting damage to the client-lawyer relationship is likely to impair the lawyer's ability to represent the client effectively. In addition, the client on whose behalf the adverse representation is undertaken reasonably may fear that the lawyer will pursue that client's case less effectively out of deference to the other client, i.e., that the representation may be materially limited by the lawyer's interest in retaining the current client. Similarly, a directly adverse conflict may arise when a lawyer is required to cross-examine a client who appears as a witness in a lawsuit involving another client, as when the testimony will be damaging to the client who is represented in the lawsuit. On the other hand, simultaneous representation in unrelated matters of clients whose interests are only economically adverse, such as representation of competing economic enterprises in unrelated litigation, does not ordinarily constitute a conflict of interest and thus may not require consent of the respective clients.

[7] Directly adverse conflicts can also arise in transactional matters. For example, if a lawyer is asked to represent the seller of a business in negotiations with a buyer represented by the lawyer, not in the same transaction but in another, unrelated matter, the lawyer could not undertake the representation without the informed consent of each client.

Identifying Conflicts of Interest: Material Limitation

[8] Even where there is no direct adverseness, a conflict of interest exists if there is a significant risk that a lawyer's ability to consider, recommend or carry out an appropriate course of action for the client will be materially limited as a result of the lawyer's other responsibilities or interests. For example, a lawyer asked to represent several individuals seeking to form a joint venture is likely to be materially limited in the lawyer's ability to recommend or advocate all possible positions that each might take because of the lawyer's duty of loyalty to the others. The conflict in effect forecloses alternatives that would otherwise be available to the client. The mere possibility of subsequent harm does not itself require disclosure and consent. The critical questions are the likelihood that a difference in interests will eventuate and, if it does, whether it will materially interfere with the lawyer's independent professional judgment in considering alternatives or foreclose courses of action that reasonably should be pursued on behalf of the client.

Lawyer's Responsibilities to Former Clients and Other Third Persons

[9] In addition to conflicts with other current clients, a lawyer's duties of loyalty and independence may be materially limited by responsibilities to former clients under Rule 1.9 or by the lawyer's responsibilities to other persons, such as fiduciary duties arising from a lawyer's service as a trustee, executor or corporate director.

Personal Interest Conflicts

[10] The lawyer's own interests should not be permitted to have an adverse effect on representation of a client. For

example, if the probity of a lawyer's own conduct in a transaction is in serious question, it may be difficult or impossible for the lawyer to give a client detached advice. Similarly, when a lawyer has discussions concerning possible employment with an opponent of the lawyer's client, or with a law firm representing the opponent, such discussions could materially limit the lawyer's representation of the client. In addition, a lawyer may not allow related business interests to affect representation, for example, by referring clients to an enterprise in which the lawyer has an undisclosed financial interest. See Rule 1.8 for specific Rules pertaining to a number of personal interest conflicts, including business transactions with clients. See also Rule 1.10 (personal interest conflicts under Rule 1.7 ordinarily are not imputed to other lawyers in a law firm).

Interest of Person Paying for a Lawyer's Service

[11] A lawyer may be paid from a source other than the client, including a co-client, if the client is informed of that fact and consents and the arrangement does not compromise the lawyer's duty of loyalty or independent judgment to the client. See Rule 1.8(f). If acceptance of the payment from any other source presents a significant risk that the lawyer's representation of the client will be materially limited by the lawyer's own interest in accommodating the person paying the lawyer's fee or by the lawyer's responsibilities to a payer who is also a co-client, then the lawyer must comply with the requirements of paragraph (b) before accepting the representation, including determining whether the conflict is consentable and, if so, that the client has adequate information about the material risks of the representation.

Prohibited Representations

[12] Ordinarily, clients may consent to representation notwithstanding a conflict. However, as indicated in paragraph (b) some conflicts are nonconsentable, meaning that the lawyer involved cannot properly ask for such agreement or provide representation on the basis of the client's consent. When the lawyer is representing more than one client, the question of consentability must be resolved as to each client.

[13] Consentability is typically determined by considering whether the interests of the clients will be adequately protected if the clients are permitted to give their informed consent to representation burdened by a conflict of interest. Thus, under paragraph (b)(1), representation is prohibited if in the circumstances the lawyer cannot reasonably conclude that the lawyer will be able to provide competent and diligent representation. See Rule 1.1 (competence) and Rule 1.3 (diligence).

[14] Paragraph (b)(2) describes conflicts that are nonconsentable because the representation is prohibited by applicable law. For example, in some states substantive law provides that the same lawyer may not represent more than one defendant in a capital case, even with the consent of the clients, and under federal criminal statutes certain representations by a former government lawyer are prohibited, despite the informed consent of the former client. In addition, decisional law in some states limits the ability of a governmental client, such as a municipality, to consent to a conflict of interest.

[15] Paragraph (b)(3) describes conflicts that are nonconsentable because of the institutional interest in vigorous development of each client's position when the clients are aligned directly against each other in the same litigation or other proceeding before a tribunal. Whether clients are aligned directly against each other within the meaning of this paragraph requires examination of the context of the proceeding. Although this paragraph does not preclude a lawyer's multiple representation of adverse parties to a mediation (because mediation is not a proceeding before a "tribunal" under Rule 1.0(n)), such representation may be precluded by paragraph (b)(1).

Informed Consent

[16] Informed consent is defined in Rule 1.0(g). The information required depends on the nature of the conflict and the nature of the risks involved. When representation of multiple clients in a single matter is undertaken, the information should include the implications of the common representation, including possible effects on loyalty, confidentiality and the attorney-client privilege and the advantages and risks involved. See Comments [28] and [29] (effect of common representation on confidentiality).

[17] Under some circumstances it may be impossible to make the disclosure necessary to obtain consent. For example, when the lawyer represents different clients in related matters and one of the clients refuses to consent to the disclosure necessary to permit the other client to make an informed decision, the lawyer cannot properly ask the latter to consent. In some cases the alternative to common representation can be that each party may have to obtain separate representation with the possibility of incurring additional costs. These costs, along with the benefits of securing separate representation, are factors that may be considered by the affected client in determining whether common representation is in the client's interests.

Consent Confirmed in Writing

[18] Paragraph (b) requires the lawyer to obtain the informed consent of the client, confirmed in writing. Such a writing may consist of a document executed by the client or one that the lawyer promptly records and transmits to the client following an oral consent. See Rule 1.0(b). See also Rule 1.0(*o*) (writing includes electronic transmission). If it is not feasible to obtain or transmit the writing at the time the client gives informed consent, then the lawyer must obtain or transmit it within a reasonable time thereafter. See Rule 1.0(b). The requirement of a writing does not supplant the need in most cases for the lawyer to talk with the client, to explain the risks and advantages, if any, of representation burdened with a conflict of interest, as well as reasonably available alternatives, and to afford the client a reasonable opportunity to consider the risks and alternatives and to raise questions and concerns. The better practice is to include within any writing the risks, advantages and alternatives discussed as a matter of full disclosure. Rather, the writing is required in order to impress upon clients the seriousness of the decision the client is being asked to make and to avoid disputes or ambiguities that might later occur in the absence of a writing.

Revoking Consent

[19] A client who has given consent to a conflict may revoke the consent and, like any other client, may terminate the lawyer's representation at any time. Whether revoking consent to the client's own representation precludes the lawyer from continuing to represent other clients depends on the circumstances, including the nature of the conflict, whether the client revoked consent because of a material change in circumstances, the reasonable expectations of the other clients and whether material detriment to the other clients or the lawyer would result.

Consent to Future Conflict

[20] Whether a lawyer may properly request a client to waive conflicts that might arise in the future is subject to the test of paragraph (b). The effectiveness of such waivers is generally determined by the extent to which the client reasonably understands the material risks that the waiver entails. The more comprehensive the explanation of the types of future representations that might arise and the actual and reasonably foreseeable adverse consequences of those representations, the greater the likelihood that the client will have the requisite understanding. Thus, if the client agrees to consent to a particular type of conflict with which the client is already familiar, then the consent ordinarily will be effective with regard to that type of conflict. If the consent is general and open-ended, then the consent ordinarily will be ineffective, because it is not reasonably likely that the client will have understood the material risks involved. On the other hand, if the client is an experienced user of the legal services involved and is reasonably informed regarding the risk that a conflict may arise, such consent is more likely to be effective, particularly if, e.g., the client is independently represented by other counsel in giving consent and the consent is limited to future conflicts unrelated to the subject of the representation. In any case, advance consent cannot be effective if the circumstances that materialize in the future are such as would make the conflict nonconsentable under paragraph (b).

Conflicts in Litigation

[21] Paragraph (b)(3) prohibits representation of opposing parties in the same litigation, regardless of the clients' consent. On the other hand, simultaneous representation of parties whose interests in litigation may conflict, such as coplaintiffs or codefendants, is governed by paragraph (a)(2). A conflict may exist by reason of substantial discrepancy in the parties' testimony, incompatibility in positions in relation to an opposing party or the fact that there are substantially different possibilities of settlement of the claims or liabilities in question. Such conflicts can arise in criminal cases as well as civil. The potential for conflict of interest in representing multiple defendants in a criminal case is so grave that ordinarily a lawyer should decline to represent more than one codefendant. On the other hand, common representation of persons having similar interests in civil litigation is proper if the requirements of paragraph (b) are met.

[22] Ordinarily a lawyer may take inconsistent legal positions in different tribunals at different times on behalf of different clients. The mere fact that advocating a legal position on behalf of one client might create precedent adverse to the interests of a client represented by the lawyer in an unrelated matter does not create a conflict of interest. A conflict of interest exists, however, if there is a significant risk that a lawyer's action on behalf of one client will materially limit the lawyer's effectiveness in representing another client in a different case; for example, when a decision favoring one client will create a precedent likely to seriously weaken the position taken on behalf of the other client. Factors relevant in determining whether the clients need to be advised of the risk include: where the cases are pending, whether the issue is substantive or procedural, the temporal relationship between the matters, the significance of the issue to the immediate and long-term interests of the clients involved and the clients' reasonable expectations in retaining the lawyer. If there is significant risk of material limitation, then absent informed consent of the affected clients, the lawyer must refuse one of the representations or withdraw from one or both matters.

[23] When a lawyer represents or seeks to represent a class of plaintiffs or defendants in a class-action lawsuit, unnamed members of the class are ordinarily not considered to be clients of the lawyer for purposes of applying paragraph (a)(1) of this Rule. Thus, the lawyer does not typically need to get the consent of such a person before representing a client suing the person in an unrelated matter. Similarly, a lawyer seeking to represent an opponent in a class action does not typically need the consent of an unnamed member of the class whom the lawyer represents in an unrelated matter.

[23a] A lawyer serving as a part-time prosecutor is not necessarily disqualified from simultaneously representing other civil or criminal defense clients in private practice. If the prosecutions handled by the lawyer are limited in nature and scope, the lawyer may be able to represent other clients in criminal or civil matters that are not related to any of the cases that the lawyer has prosecuted.

Nonlitigation Conflicts

[24] Conflicts of interest under paragraphs (a)(1) and (a)(2) arise in contexts other than litigation. For a discussion of directly adverse conflicts in transactional matters, see Comment [7]. Relevant factors in determining whether there is significant potential for material limitation include the duration and intimacy of the lawyer's relationship with the client or clients involved, the functions being performed by the lawyer, the likelihood that disagreements will arise and the likely prejudice to the client from the conflict. The question is often one of proximity and degree. See Comment [8].

[25] For example, conflict questions may arise in estate planning and estate administration. A lawyer may be called upon to prepare wills for several family members, such as husband and wife, and, depending upon the circumstances, a conflict of interest may be present. In estate administration the identity of the client also may be unclear. The issue is addressed in S.C. Code Ann. § 62–1–109. In order to comply with conflict of interest rules, the lawyer should make clear the lawyer's relationship to the parties involved.

[26] Whether a conflict is consentable depends on the circumstances. For example, a lawyer may not represent multiple parties to a negotiation whose interests are fundamentally antagonistic to each other, but common representation is permissible where the clients are generally aligned in interest even though there is some difference in interest among them. Thus, a lawyer may seek to establish or adjust a relationship between clients on an amicable and mutually advantageous basis; for example, in helping to organize a business in which two or more clients are entrepreneurs, working out the financial reorganization of an enterprise in which two or more clients have an interest or arranging a property distribution in settlement of an estate. The lawyer seeks to resolve potentially adverse interests by developing the parties' mutual interests. Otherwise, each party might have to obtain separate representation, with the possibility of incurring additional cost, complication or even litigation. Given these and other relevant factors, the clients may prefer that the lawyer act for all of them.

Special Considerations in Common Representation

[27] In considering whether to represent multiple clients in the same matter, a lawyer should be mindful that if the common representation fails because the potentially adverse interests cannot be reconciled, the result can be additional cost, embarrassment and recrimination. Ordinarily, the lawyer will be forced to withdraw from representing all of the clients if the common representation fails. In some situa-

tions, the risk of failure is so great that multiple representation is plainly impossible. For example, a lawyer cannot undertake common representation of clients where contentious litigation or negotiations between them are imminent or contemplated. Moreover, because the lawyer is required to be impartial between commonly represented clients, representation of multiple clients is improper when it is unlikely that impartiality can be maintained. Generally, if the relationship between the parties has already assumed antagonism, the possibility that the clients' interests can be adequately served by common representation is not very good. Other relevant factors are whether the lawyer subsequently will represent both parties on a continuing basis and whether the situation involves creating or terminating a relationship between the parties.

[28] A particularly important factor in determining the appropriateness of common representation is the effect on client-lawyer confidentiality and the attorney-client privilege. With regard to the attorney-client privilege, the prevailing rule is that, as between commonly represented clients, the privilege does not attach. Hence, it must be assumed that if litigation eventuates between the clients, the privilege will not protect any such communications, and the clients should be so advised.

[29] As to the duty of confidentiality, continued common representation will almost certainly be inadequate if one client asks the lawyer not to disclose to the other client information relevant to the common representation. This is so because the lawyer has an equal duty of loyalty to each client, and each client has the right to be informed of anything bearing on the representation that might affect that client's interests and the right to expect that the lawyer will use that information to that client's benefit. See Rule 1.4. The lawyer should, at the outset of the common representation and as part of the process of obtaining each client's informed consent, advise each client that information will be shared and that the lawyer will have to withdraw if one client decides that some matter material to the representation should be kept from the other. In limited circumstances, it may be appropriate for the lawyer to proceed with the representation when the clients have agreed, after being properly informed, that the lawyer will keep certain information confidential. For example, the lawyer may reasonably conclude that failure to disclose one client's trade secrets to another client will not adversely affect representation involving a joint venture between the clients and agree to keep that information confidential with the informed consent of both clients.

[30] When seeking to establish or adjust a relationship between clients, the lawyer should make clear that the lawyer's role is not that of partisanship normally expected in other circumstances and, thus, that the clients may be required to assume greater responsibility for decisions than when each client is separately represented. Any limitations on the scope of the representation made necessary as a result of the common representation should be fully explained to the clients at the outset of the representation. See Rule 1.2(c).

[31] Subject to the above limitations, each client in the common representation has the right to loyal and diligent representation and the protection of Rule 1.9 concerning the obligations to a former client. The client also has the right to discharge the lawyer as stated in Rule 1.16.

Organizational Clients

[32] A lawyer who represents a corporation or other organization does not, by virtue of that representation, necessarily represent any constituent or affiliated organization, such as a parent or subsidiary. See Rule 1.13(a). Thus, the lawyer for an organization is not barred from accepting representation adverse to an affiliate in an unrelated matter, unless the circumstances are such that the affiliate should also be considered a client of the lawyer, there is an understanding between the lawyer and the organizational client that the lawyer will avoid representation adverse to the client's affiliates, or the lawyer's obligations to either the organizational client or the new client are likely to limit materially the lawyer's representation of the other client.

[33] A lawyer for a corporation or other organization who is also a member of its board of directors should determine whether the responsibilities of the two roles may conflict. The lawyer may be called on to advise the corporation in matters involving actions of the directors. Consideration should be given to the frequency with which such situations may arise, the potential intensity of the conflict, the effect of the lawyer's resignation from the board and the possibility of the corporation's obtaining legal advice from another lawyer in such situations. If there is material risk that the dual role will compromise the lawyer's independence of professional judgment, the lawyer should not serve as a director or should cease to act as the corporation's lawyer when conflicts of interest arise. The lawyer should advise the other members of the board that in some circumstances matters discussed at board meetings while the lawyer is present in the capacity of director might not be protected by the attorney-client privilege and that conflict of interest considerations might require the lawyer's recusal as a director or might require the lawyer and the lawyer's firm to decline representation of the corporation in a matter.

RULE 1.8. CONFLICT OF INTEREST: CURRENT CLIENTS: SPECIFIC RULES

(a) A lawyer shall not enter into a business transaction with a client or knowingly acquire an ownership, possessory, security or other pecuniary interest adverse to a client unless:

(1) the transaction and terms on which the lawyer acquires the interest are fair and reasonable to the client and are fully disclosed and transmitted in writing in a manner that can be reasonably understood by the client;

(2) the client is advised in writing of the desirability of seeking and is given a reasonable opportunity to seek the advice of independent legal counsel on the transaction; and

(3) the client gives informed consent, in a writing signed by the client, to the essential terms of the transaction and the lawyer's role in the transaction, including whether the lawyer is representing the client in the transaction.

(b) A lawyer shall not use information relating to representation of a client to the disadvantage of the client unless the client gives informed consent, except as permitted or required by these Rules.

(c) A lawyer shall not solicit any substantial gift from a client, including a testamentary gift, or prepare on behalf of a client an instrument giving the lawyer or a person related to the lawyer any substantial gift unless the lawyer or other recipient of the gift is related to the client. For purposes of this paragraph, related persons include a spouse, child, grandchild, parent, grandparent or other relative or individual with whom the lawyer or the client maintains a close, familial relationship.

(d) Prior to the conclusion of representation of a client, a lawyer shall not make or negotiate an agreement giving the lawyer literary or media rights to a portrayal or account based in substantial part on information relating to the representation.

(e) A lawyer shall not provide financial assistance to a client in connection with pending or contemplated litigation, except that:

(1) a lawyer may advance court costs and expenses of litigation, the repayment of which may be contingent on the outcome of the matter; and

(2) a lawyer representing an indigent client may pay court costs and expenses of litigation on behalf of the client.

(f) A lawyer shall not accept compensation for representing a client from one other than the client unless:

(1) the client gives informed consent;

(2) there is no interference with the lawyer's independence of professional judgment or with the client-lawyer relationship; and

(3) information relating to representation of a client is protected as required by Rule 1.6.

(g) A lawyer who represents two or more clients shall not participate in making an aggregate settlement of the claims of or against the clients, or in a criminal case an aggregated agreement as to guilty or nolo contendere pleas, unless each client gives informed consent, in a writing signed by the client. The lawyer's disclosure shall include the existence and nature of all the claims or pleas involved and of the participation of each person in the settlement.

(h) A lawyer shall not:

(1) make an agreement prospectively limiting the lawyer's liability to a client for malpractice unless the client is independently represented in making the agreement; or

(2) settle a claim or potential claim for such liability with an unrepresented client or former client unless that person is advised in writing of the desirability of seeking and is given a reasonable opportunity to seek the advice of independent legal counsel in connection therewith.

(i) A lawyer shall not acquire a proprietary interest in the cause of action or subject matter of litigation the lawyer is conducting for a client, except that the lawyer may:

(1) acquire a lien authorized by law to secure the lawyer's fee or expenses; and

(2) contract with a client for a reasonable contingent fee in a civil case.

(j) While lawyers are associated in a firm, a prohibition in the foregoing paragraphs (a) through (i) that applies to any one of them shall apply to all of them.

(k) A lawyer related to another lawyer as parent, child, sibling or spouse shall not personally represent a client in a representation directly adverse to a person whom the lawyer knows is represented by the other lawyer unless the client gives informed consent.

(*l*) In any adversarial proceeding, a lawyer shall not serve as both an advocate and an advisor to the hearing officer, trial judge or trier of fact. A lawyer serving as an advocate in a particular matter shall not directly or indirectly engage in an ex parte communication with the hearing officer, trial judge or trier of fact concerning the proceeding.

(m) A lawyer shall not have sexual relations with a client when the client is in a vulnerable condition or is otherwise subject to the control or undue influence of the lawyer, when such relations could have a harmful or prejudicial effect upon the interests of the client, or when sexual relations might adversely effect the lawyer's representation of the client.

[Adopted effective September 1, 1990. Amended effective November 7, 1996; October 1, 2005.]

Comment

Business Transactions Between Client and Lawyer

[1] A lawyer's legal skill and training, together with the relationship of trust and confidence between lawyer and client, create the possibility of overreaching when the lawyer participates in a business, property or financial transaction with a client, for example, a loan or sales transaction or a lawyer investment on behalf of a client. The requirements of paragraph (a) must be met even when the transaction is not closely related to the subject matter of the representation, as when a lawyer drafting a will for a client learns that the client needs money for unrelated expenses and offers to make a loan to the client. The Rule applies to lawyers engaged in the sale of goods or services related to the practice of law, for example, the sale of insurance or the provision of investment or fiduciary services to existing clients of the lawyer's legal practice. See Rule 5.7. It also applies to lawyers purchasing property from estates they represent. It does not apply to ordinary fee arrangements between client and lawyer, which are governed by Rule 1.5, although its requirements must be met when the lawyer accepts an interest in the client's business or other nonmonetary property as payment of all or part of a fee. In addition, the Rule does not apply to standard commercial transactions between the lawyer and the client for products or services that the client generally markets to others, for example, banking or brokerage services, medical services, products manufactured or distributed by the client, and utilities' services. In such transactions, the lawyer has no advantage in dealing with the client, and the restrictions in paragraph (a) are unnecessary and impracticable.

[2] Paragraph (a)(1) requires that the transaction itself be fair to the client and that its essential terms be communicated

to the client, in writing, in a manner that can be reasonably understood. Paragraph (a)(2) requires that the client also be advised, in writing, of the desirability of seeking the advice of independent legal counsel. It also requires that the client be given a reasonable opportunity to obtain such advice. Paragraph (a)(3) requires that the lawyer obtain the client's informed consent, in a writing signed by the client, both to the essential terms of the transaction and to the lawyer's role. When necessary, the lawyer should discuss both the material risks of the proposed transaction, including any risk presented by the lawyer's involvement, and the existence of reasonably available alternatives and should explain why the advice of independent legal counsel is desirable. See Rule 1.0(g) (definition of informed consent).

[3] The risk to a client is greatest when the client expects the lawyer to represent the client in the transaction itself or when the lawyer's financial interest otherwise poses a significant risk that the lawyer's representation of the client will be materially limited by the lawyer's financial interest in the transaction. Here the lawyer's role requires that the lawyer must comply, not only with the requirements of paragraph (a), but also with the requirements of Rule 1.7. Under that Rule, the lawyer must disclose the risks associated with the lawyer's dual role as both legal adviser and participant in the transaction, such as the risk that the lawyer will structure the transaction or give legal advice in a way that favors the lawyer's interests at the expense of the client. Moreover, the lawyer must obtain the client's informed consent. In some cases, the lawyer's interest may be such that Rule 1.7 will preclude the lawyer from seeking the client's consent to the transaction.

[4] If the client is independently represented in the transaction, paragraph (a)(2) of this Rule is inapplicable, and the paragraph (a)(1) requirement for full disclosure is satisfied either by a written disclosure by the lawyer involved in the transaction or by the client's independent counsel. The fact that the client was independently represented in the transaction is relevant in determining whether the agreement was fair and reasonable to the client as paragraph (a)(1) further requires.

Use of Information Related to Representation

[5] Use of information relating to the representation to the disadvantage of the client violates the lawyer's duty of loyalty. Paragraph (b) applies when the information is used to benefit either the lawyer or a third person, such as another client or business associate of the lawyer. For example, if a lawyer learns that a client intends to purchase and develop several parcels of land, the lawyer may not use that information to purchase one of the parcels in competition with the client or to recommend that another client make such a purchase. The Rule does not prohibit uses that do not disadvantage the client. For example, a lawyer who learns a government agency's interpretation of trade legislation during the representation of one client may properly use that information to benefit other clients. Paragraph (b) prohibits disadvantageous use of client information unless the client gives informed consent, except as permitted or required by these Rules. See Rules 1.2(d), 1.6, 1.9(c), 3.3, 4.1(b), 8.1 and 8.3.

Gifts to Lawyers

[6] A lawyer may accept a gift from a client if the transaction meets general standards of fairness. For example, a simple gift such as a present given at a holiday or as a token of appreciation is permitted. If a client offers the lawyer a more substantial gift, paragraph (c) does not prohibit the lawyer from accepting it, although such a gift may be voidable by the client under the doctrine of undue influence, which treats client gifts as presumptively fraudulent. In any event, due to concerns about overreaching and imposition on clients, a lawyer may not suggest that a substantial gift be made to the lawyer or for the lawyer's benefit, except where the lawyer is related to the client as set forth in paragraph (c).

[7] If effectuation of a substantial gift requires preparing a legal instrument such as a will or conveyance, the client should have the detached advice that another lawyer can provide. The sole exception to this Rule is where the client is a relative of the donee.

[8] This Rule does not prohibit a lawyer from seeking to have the lawyer or a partner or associate of the lawyer named as executor of the client's estate or to another potentially lucrative fiduciary position if the lawyer complies with Rule 1.8. Nevertheless, such appointments will be subject to the general conflict of interest provision in Rule 1.7 when there is a significant risk that the lawyer's interest in obtaining the appointment will materially limit the lawyer's independent professional judgment in advising the client concerning the choice of an executor or other fiduciary. In obtaining the client's informed consent to the conflict, the lawyer should advise the client concerning the nature and extent of the lawyer's financial interest in the appointment, as well as the availability of alternative candidates for the position.

Literary Rights

[9] An agreement by which a lawyer acquires literary or media rights concerning the conduct of the representation creates a conflict between the interests of the client and the personal interests of the lawyer. Measures suitable in the representation of the client may detract from the publication value of an account of the representation. Paragraph (d) does not prohibit a lawyer representing a client in a transaction concerning literary property from agreeing that the lawyer's fee shall consist of a share in ownership in the property, if the arrangement conforms to Rule 1.5 and paragraphs (a) and (i).

Financial Assistance

[10] Lawyers may not subsidize lawsuits or administrative proceedings brought on behalf of their clients, including making or guaranteeing loans to their clients for living expenses, because to do so would encourage clients to pursue lawsuits that might not otherwise be brought and because such assistance gives lawyers too great a financial stake in the litigation. These dangers do not warrant a prohibition on a lawyer lending a client court costs and litigation expenses, including the expenses of medical examination and the costs of obtaining and presenting evidence, because these advances are virtually indistinguishable from contingent fees and help ensure access to the courts. Similarly, an exception allowing lawyers representing indigent clients to pay court costs and litigation expenses regardless of whether these funds will be repaid is warranted.

Person Paying for a Lawyer's Services

[11] Lawyers are frequently asked to represent a client under circumstances in which a third person will compensate the lawyer, in whole or in part. The third person might be a relative or friend, an indemnitor (such as a liability insurance company) or a co-client (such as a corporation sued along with one or more of its employees). Because third-party payers frequently have interests that differ from those of the client, including interests in minimizing the amount spent on the representation and in learning how the representation is progressing, lawyers are prohibited from accepting or con-

tinuing such representations unless the lawyer determines that there will be no interference with the lawyer's independent professional judgment and there is informed consent from the client. See also Rule 5.4(c) (prohibiting interference with a lawyer's professional judgment by one who recommends, employs or pays the lawyer to render legal services for another).

[12] Sometimes, it will be sufficient for the lawyer to obtain the client's informed consent regarding the fact of the payment and the identity of the third-party payer. If, however, the fee arrangement creates a conflict of interest for the lawyer, then the lawyer must comply with Rule. 1.7. The lawyer must also conform to the requirements of Rule 1.6 concerning confidentiality. Under Rule 1.7(a), a conflict of interest exists if there is significant risk that the lawyer's representation of the client will be materially limited by the lawyer's own interest in the fee arrangement or by the lawyer's responsibilities to the third-party payer (for example, when the third-party payer is a co–client). Under Rule 1.7(b), the lawyer may accept or continue the representation with the informed consent of each affected client, unless the conflict is nonconsentable under that paragraph. Under Rule 1.7(b), the informed consent must be confirmed in writing.

Aggregate Settlements

[13] Differences in willingness to make or accept an offer of settlement are among the risks of common representation of multiple clients by a single lawyer. Under Rule 1.7, this is one of the risks that should be discussed before undertaking the representation, as part of the process of obtaining the clients' informed consent. In addition, Rule 1.2(a) protects each client's right to have the final say in deciding whether to accept or reject an offer of settlement and in deciding whether to enter a guilty or nolo contendere plea in a criminal case. The rule stated in this paragraph is a corollary of both these Rules and provides that, before any settlement offer or plea bargain is made or accepted on behalf of multiple clients, the lawyer must inform each of them about all the material terms of the settlement, including what the other clients will receive or pay if the settlement or plea offer is accepted. See also Rule 1.0(g) (definition of informed consent). Lawyers representing a class of plaintiffs or defendants, or those proceeding derivatively, may not have a full client-lawyer relationship with each member of the class; nevertheless, such lawyers must comply with applicable rules regulating notification of class members and other procedural requirements designed to ensure adequate protection of the entire class.

Limiting Liability and Settling Malpractice Claims

[14] Paragraph (h) is not intended to apply to customary qualifications and limitations in legal opinions and memoranda. Nevertheless, agreements prospectively limiting a lawyer's liability for malpractice are prohibited unless the client is independently represented in making the agreement because they are likely to undermine competent and diligent representation. Also, many clients are unable to evaluate the desirability of making such an agreement before a dispute has arisen, particularly if they are then represented by the lawyer seeking the agreement. This paragraph does not, however, prohibit a lawyer from entering into an agreement with the client to arbitrate legal malpractice claims, provided such agreements are enforceable and the client is fully informed of the scope and effect of the agreement. Nor does this paragraph limit the ability of lawyers to practice in the form of a limited-liability entity, where permitted by law, provided that each lawyer remains personally liable to the client for his or her own conduct and the firm complies with any conditions required by law, such as provisions requiring client notification or maintenance of adequate liability insurance. Nor does it prohibit an agreement in accordance with Rule 1.2 that defines the scope of the representation, although a definition of scope that makes the obligations of representation illusory will amount to an attempt to limit liability.

[15] Agreements settling a claim or a potential claim for malpractice are not prohibited by this Rule. Nevertheless, in view of the danger that a lawyer will take unfair advantage of an unrepresented client or former client, the lawyer must first advise such a person in writing of the appropriateness of independent representation in connection with such a settlement. In addition, the lawyer must give the client or former client a reasonable opportunity to find and consult independent counsel.

Family Relationships Between Lawyers

[16] When lawyers representing different clients in the same matter or in substantially related matters are closely related by blood or marriage, there may be a significant risk that client confidences will be revealed and that the lawyer's family relationship will interfere with both loyalty and independent professional judgment. As a result, each client is entitled to know of the existence and implications of the relationship between the lawyers before the lawyer agrees to undertake the representation. Thus, a lawyer related to another lawyer, e.g., as parent, child, sibling or spouse, ordinarily may not represent a client in a matter where the related lawyer personally is representing another party, unless each client gives informed consent. The disqualification arising from a close family relationship is personal and ordinarily is not imputed to members of firms with whom the lawyers are associated. See Rule 1.10.

Acquiring Proprietary Interest in Litigation

[17] Paragraph (i) states the traditional general rule that lawyers are prohibited from acquiring a proprietary interest in litigation. Like paragraph (e), the general rule has its basis in common law champerty and maintenance and is designed to avoid giving the lawyer too great an interest in the representation. In addition, when the lawyer acquires an ownership interest in the subject of the representation, it will be more difficult for a client to discharge the lawyer if the client so desires. The Rule is subject to specific exceptions developed in decisional law and continued in these Rules. The exception for certain advances of the costs of litigation is set forth in paragraph (e). In addition, paragraph (i) sets forth exceptions for liens authorized by law to secure the lawyer's fees or expenses and contracts for reasonable contingent fees. The law of each jurisdiction determines which liens are authorized by law. These may include liens granted by statute, liens originating in common law and liens acquired by contract with the client. When a lawyer acquires by contract a security interest in property other than that recovered through the lawyer's efforts in the litigation, such an acquisition is a business or financial transaction with a client and is governed by the requirements of paragraph (a). Contracts for contingent fees in civil cases are governed by Rule 1.5.

Imputation of Prohibitions

[18] Under paragraph (j), a prohibition on conduct by an individual lawyer in paragraphs (a) through (i) also applies to all lawyers associated in a firm with the personally prohibited lawyer. For example, one lawyer in a firm may not enter into a business transaction with a client of another member of the firm without complying with paragraph (a), even if the first

lawyer is not personally involved in the representation of the client. The prohibitions set forth in paragraphs (k) and (*l*) are personal and are not applied to associated lawyers.

Serving as an Advocate and Advisor in Adversarial Proceedings

[19] Rule 1.8(*l*) addresses primarily administrative proceedings in which a lawyer who serves as an advisor to a public administrative body is permitted to prosecute matters which are adjudicated by that body. This rule prohibits a lawyer who has served or is serving as an advisor on a particular matter from also prosecuting or defending that particular matter. It does not prevent one lawyer from prosecuting an administrative matter in which another lawyer in the same office serves as an advisor to the hearing body, as long as the lawyers do not communicate with one another or share information about the particular case. Communications between the prosecuting lawyer and the advising lawyer with respect to a particular matter would operate as an indirect ex parte communication with the hearing officer, trial judge, or trier of fact, because the information gained by the advising lawyer would be available to the hearing officer, trial judge, or trier of fact.

For example, a lawyer advising the Board of Dentistry may not prosecute a disciplinary action against Dentist Doe while at the same time advising the Board on matters relative to the Doe matter. The lawyer may advise the Board on the Doe matter while another lawyer employed by the same employer prosecutes the Doe matter, but the two lawyers may not share information with one another, except in the regular course of discovery, with notice to Doe. The lawyers must operate as if they are in separate firms, even though they are employed by a common employer. Similarly, general counsel employed by a state supported university may not defend the university in a dispute brought by an employee under the university's internal employee grievance system while at the same time serving as an advisor to the internal panel which is adjudicating the employee grievance matter. One lawyer in general counsel's office may advise the employee grievance body on the particular matter while another lawyer in the same office defends the university in the matter, as long as the two lawyers do not share information concerning the matter. The lawyers must operate as if they are in separate firms, even though they are employed by a common employer.

[20] Lawyers in private practice would be prohibited, under Rule 1.7, from representing an adjudicatory body in a particular matter while another lawyer in the same law firm prosecutes or defends the same matter before the adjudicatory body. Because of the nature of public employment of lawyers, however, some accommodation must be made to permit the sharing of responsibilities among lawyers of a common employer. The erection of a screen preventing the sharing of information among lawyers employed by a common public employer permits the efficient carrying out of administrative functions, while at the same time protecting the rights of individuals whose rights are being adjudicated in the proceedings.

Sexual Relations with Clients

[21] The relationship between lawyer and client is a fiduciary one in which the lawyer occupies the highest position of trust and confidence. Except in a few, limited circumstances, such as when the lawyer and client are married to each other, a sexual relationship between lawyer and client presents a significant danger of harm to client interests and should be avoided. Sexual relationships between a lawyer and a client pose three types of potential problems. First, a question may arise as to the voluntariness of a client's consent to a sexual relationship. Lawyers are in a position of extraordinary trust and may not use that power and influence to entice a vulnerable client into an otherwise undesired sexual relationship. Second, sexual relationships are inappropriate when the existence of the relationship could prejudice a client's legal interests, especially when the client is involved in a domestic relations case. Third, a lawyer engaged in an intimate sexual relationship with a client may not be able to exercise the proper degree of professional judgment and independence required to fully represent the client. In any of these circumstances, a sexual relationship between lawyer and client is not appropriate, and the client's own emotional involvement renders it unlikely that a client can give adequate informed consent to the relationship.

RULE 1.9. DUTIES TO FORMER CLIENTS

(a) A lawyer who has formerly represented a client in a matter shall not thereafter represent another person in the same or a substantially related matter in which that person's interests are materially adverse to the interests of the former client unless the former client gives informed consent, confirmed in writing.

(b) A lawyer shall not knowingly represent a person in the same or a substantially related matter in which a firm with which the lawyer formerly was associated had previously represented a client

(1) whose interests are materially adverse to that person; and

(2) about whom the lawyer had acquired information protected by Rules 1.6 and 1.9(c) that is material to the matter;

unless the former client gives informed consent, confirmed in writing.

(c) A lawyer who has formerly represented a client in a matter or whose present or former firm has formerly represented a client in a matter shall not thereafter:

(1) use information relating to the representation to the disadvantage of the former client except as these Rules would permit or require with respect to a client, or when the information has become generally known; or

(2) reveal information relating to the representation except as these Rules would permit or require with respect to a client.

[Adopted effective September 1, 1990. Amended effective October 1, 2005.]

Comment

[1] After termination of a client-lawyer relationship, a lawyer has certain continuing duties with respect to confidentiality and conflicts of interest and thus may not represent another client except in conformity with this Rule. Under this Rule, for example, a lawyer could not properly seek to rescind on behalf of a new client a contract drafted on behalf of the former client. So also a lawyer who has prosecuted an

accused person could not properly represent the accused in a subsequent civil action against the government concerning the same transaction. Nor could a lawyer who has represented multiple clients in a matter represent one of the clients against the others in the same or a substantially related matter after a dispute arose among the clients in that matter, unless all affected clients give informed consent. See Comment [9]. Current and former government lawyers must comply with this Rule to the extent required by Rule 1.11.

[2] The scope of a "matter" for purposes of this Rule may depend on the facts of a particular situation or transaction. The lawyer's involvement in a matter can also be a question of degree. When a lawyer has been directly involved in a specific transaction, subsequent representation of other clients with materially adverse interests in that transaction clearly is prohibited. On the other hand, a lawyer who recurrently handled a type of problem for a former client is not precluded from later representing another client in a factually distinct problem of that type even though the subsequent representation involves a position adverse to the prior client. Similar considerations can apply to the reassignment of military lawyers between defense and prosecution functions within the same military jurisdictions. The underlying question is whether the lawyer was so involved in the matter that the subsequent representation can be justly regarded as a changing of sides in the matter in question.

[3] Matters are "substantially related" for purposes of this Rule if they involve the same transaction or legal dispute or if there otherwise is a substantial risk that confidential factual information as would normally have been obtained in the prior representation would materially advance the client's position in the subsequent matter. For example, a lawyer who has represented a businessperson and learned extensive private financial information about that person may not then represent that person's spouse in seeking a divorce. Similarly, a lawyer who has previously represented a client in securing environmental permits to build a shopping center would be precluded from representing neighbors seeking to oppose rezoning of the property on the basis of environmental considerations, but would not be precluded, on the grounds of substantial relationship, from defending a tenant of the completed shopping center in resisting eviction for nonpayment of rent. Information that has been disclosed to the public or to other parties adverse to the former client ordinarily will not be disqualifying. Information acquired in a prior representation may have been rendered obsolete by the passage of time, a circumstance that may be relevant in determining whether two representations are substantially related. In the case of an organizational client, general knowledge of the client's policies and practices ordinarily will not preclude a subsequent representation; on the other hand, knowledge of specific facts gained in a prior representation that are relevant to the matter in question ordinarily will preclude such representation. A former client is not required to reveal the confidential information learned by the lawyer in order to establish a substantial risk that the lawyer has confidential information to use in the subsequent matter. A conclusion about the possession of such information may be based on the nature of the services the lawyer provided the former client and information that would in ordinary practice be learned by a lawyer providing such services.

Lawyers Moving Between Firms

[4] When lawyers have been associated within a firm but then end their association, the question of whether a lawyer should undertake representation is more complicated. There are several competing considerations. First, the client previously represented by the former firm must be reasonably assured that the principle of loyalty to the client is not compromised. Second, the rule should not be so broadly cast as to preclude other persons from having reasonable choice of legal counsel. Third, the rule should not unreasonably hamper lawyers from forming new associations and taking on new clients after having left a previous association. In this connection, it should be recognized that today many lawyers practice in firms, that many lawyers to some degree limit their practice to one field or another, and that many move from one association to another several times in their careers. If the concept of imputation were applied with unqualified rigor, the result would be radical curtailment of the opportunity of lawyers to move from one practice setting to another and of the opportunity of clients to change counsel.

[5] Paragraph (b) operates to disqualify the lawyer only when the lawyer involved has actual knowledge of information protected by Rules 1.6 and 1.9(c). Thus, if a lawyer while with one firm acquired no knowledge or information relating to a particular client of the firm, and that lawyer later joined another firm, neither the lawyer individually nor the second firm is disqualified from representing another client in the same or a related matter even though the interests of the two clients conflict. See Rule 1.10(b) for the restrictions on a firm once a lawyer has terminated association with the firm.

[6] Application of paragraph (b) depends on a situation's particular facts, aided by inferences, deductions or working presumptions that reasonably may be made about the way in which lawyers work together. A lawyer may have general access to files of all clients of a law firm and may regularly participate in discussions of their affairs; it should be inferred that such a lawyer in fact is privy to all information about all the firm's clients. In contrast, another lawyer may have access to the files of only a limited number of clients and participate in discussions of the affairs of no other clients; in the absence of information to the contrary, it should be inferred that such a lawyer in fact is privy to information about the clients actually served but not those of other clients. In such an inquiry, the burden of proof should rest upon the firm whose disqualification is sought.

[7] Independent of the question of disqualification of a firm, a lawyer changing professional association has a continuing duty to preserve confidentiality of information about a client formerly represented. See Rules 1.6 and 1.9(c).

[8] Paragraph (c) provides that information acquired by the lawyer in the course of representing a client may not subsequently be used or revealed by the lawyer to the disadvantage of the client. However, the fact that a lawyer has once served a client does not preclude the lawyer from using generally known information about that client when later representing another client.

[9] The provisions of this Rule are for the protection of former clients and can be waived if the client gives informed consent, which consent must be confirmed in writing under paragraphs (a) and (b). See Rule 1.0(g). With regard to the effectiveness of an advance waiver, see Comment [20] to Rule 1.7. With regard to disqualification of a firm with which a lawyer is or was formerly associated, see Rule 1.10.

RULE 1.10. IMPUTATION OF CONFLICTS OF INTEREST: GENERAL RULE

(a) While lawyers are associated in a firm, none of them shall knowingly represent a client when any one of them practicing alone would be prohibited from doing so by Rules 1.7, 1.8(c), or 1.9, unless the prohibition is based on a personal interest of the prohibited lawyer and does not present a significant risk of materially limiting the representation of the client by the remaining lawyers in the firm.

(b) When a lawyer has terminated an association with a firm, the firm is not prohibited from thereafter representing a person with interests materially adverse to those of a client represented by the formerly associated lawyer and not currently represented by the firm, unless:

(1) the matter is the same or substantially related to that in which the formerly associated lawyer represented the client; and

(2) any lawyer remaining in the firm has information protected by Rules 1.6 and 1.9(c) that is material to the matter.

(c) A disqualification prescribed by this rule may be waived by the affected client under the conditions stated in Rule 1.7.

(d) The disqualification of lawyers associated in a firm with former or current government lawyers is governed by Rule 1.11.

(e) A lawyer representing a client of a public defender office, legal services association, or similar program serving indigent clients shall not be disqualified under this Rule because of the program's representation of another client in the same or a substantially related matter if:

(1) the lawyer is screened in a timely manner from access to confidential information relating to and from any participation in the representation of the other client; and

(2) the lawyer retains authority over the objectives of the representation pursuant to Rule 5.4(c).

[Adopted effective September 1, 1990. Amended effective October 1, 2005.]

Comment

Definition of "Firm"

[1] For purposes of the Rules of Professional Conduct, the term "firm" denotes lawyers in a law partnership, professional corporation, sole proprietorship or other association authorized to practice law; or lawyers employed in a legal services organization or the legal department of a corporation or other organization. See Rule 1.0(d). Whether two or more lawyers constitute a firm within this definition can depend on the specific facts. See Rule 1.0, Comments [2]—[4]. For purposes of imputing disqualification under this Rule, however, paragraph (e) treats legal services organizations differently from other law firms by permitting screening.

Principles of Imputed Disqualification

[2] The rule of imputed disqualification stated in paragraph (a) gives effect to the principle of loyalty to the client as it applies to lawyers who practice in a law firm. Such situations can be considered from the premise that a firm of lawyers is essentially one lawyer for purposes of the rules governing loyalty to the client, or from the premise that each lawyer is vicariously bound by the obligation of loyalty owed by each lawyer with whom the lawyer is associated. Paragraph (a) operates only among the lawyers currently associated in a firm. When a lawyer moves from one firm to another, the situation is governed by Rules 1.9(b) and 1.10(b).

[3] The rule in paragraph (a) does not prohibit representation where neither questions of client loyalty nor protection of confidential information are presented. Where one lawyer in a firm could not effectively represent a given client because of strong political beliefs, for example, but that lawyer will do no work on the case and the personal beliefs of the lawyer will not materially limit the representation by others in the firm, the firm should not be disqualified. On the other hand, if an opposing party in a case were owned by a lawyer in the law firm, and others in the firm would be materially limited in pursuing the matter because of loyalty to that lawyer, the personal disqualification of the lawyer would be imputed to all others in the firm.

[4] The rule in paragraph (a) also does not prohibit representation by others in the law firm where the person prohibited from involvement in a matter is a nonlawyer, such as a paralegal or legal secretary. Nor does paragraph (a) prohibit representation if the lawyer is prohibited from acting because of events before the person became a lawyer, for example, work that the person did while a law student. Such persons, however, ordinarily must be screened from any personal participation in the matter to avoid communication to others in the firm of confidential information that both the nonlawyers and the firm have a legal duty to protect. See Rules 1.0(*l*) and 5.3.

[5] Rule 1.10(b) operates to permit a law firm, under certain circumstances, to represent a person with interests directly adverse to those of a client represented by a lawyer who formerly was associated with the firm. The Rule applies regardless of when the formerly associated lawyer represented the client. However, the law firm may not represent a person with interests adverse to those of a present client of the firm, which would violate Rule 1.7. Moreover, the firm may not represent the person where the matter is the same or substantially related to that in which the formerly associated lawyer represented the client and any other lawyer currently in the firm has material information protected by Rules 1.6 and 1.9(c).

[6] Rule 1.10(c) removes imputation with the informed consent of the affected client or former client under the conditions stated in Rule 1.7. The conditions stated in Rule 1.7 require the lawyer to determine that the representation is not prohibited by Rule 1.7(b) and that each affected client or former client has given informed consent to the representation, confirmed in writing. In some cases, the risk may be so severe that the conflict may not be cured by client consent. For a discussion of the effectiveness of client waivers of conflicts that might arise in the future, see Rule 1.7, Comment [20]. For a definition of informed consent, see Rule 1.0(g).

[7] Where a lawyer has joined a private firm after having represented the government, imputation is governed by Rule 1.11(b) and (c), not this Rule. Under Rule 1.11(d), where a lawyer represents the government after having served clients in private practice, nongovernmental employment or in another government agency, former-client conflicts are not imputed to government lawyers associated with the individually disqualified lawyer. Judicial law clerks are governed by Rule 1.12.

[8] A conflict arising under Rule 1.8(c) is specifically imputed to other lawyers within the firm under this Rule. Otherwise, where a lawyer is prohibited from engaging in certain transactions under Rule 1.8, paragraph (j) of that Rule, and not this Rule, determines whether that prohibition also applies to other lawyers associated in a firm with the personally prohibited lawyer.

[9] Rule 1.10(e) allows programs providing legal services to indigents to avoid imputed disqualification by screening lawyers from conflicting matters within the office. See Rule 1.0(*l*) for screening procedures. The authorization of screening is intended to increase the number of persons to whom each program can provide legal services, while at the same time protecting the clients from prejudice. Paragraph (e) applies only to programs of the type delineated and does not authorize screening by private law firms to avoid imputed disqualification.

RULE 1.11. SPECIAL CONFLICTS OF INTEREST FOR FORMER AND CURRENT GOVERNMENT OFFICERS AND EMPLOYEES

(a) Except as law may otherwise expressly permit, a lawyer who has formerly served as a public officer or employee of the government:

(1) is subject to Rule 1.9(c); and

(2) shall not otherwise represent a client in connection with a matter in which the lawyer participated personally and substantially as a public officer or employee, unless the appropriate government agency gives its informed consent, confirmed in writing, to the representation.

(b) When a lawyer is disqualified from representation under paragraph (a), no lawyer in a firm with which that lawyer is associated may knowingly undertake or continue representation in such a matter unless:

(1) the disqualified lawyer is timely screened from any participation in the matter and is apportioned no part of the fee therefrom; and

(2) written notice is promptly given to the appropriate government agency to enable it to ascertain compliance with the provisions of this rule.

(c) Except as law may otherwise expressly permit, a lawyer having information that the lawyer knows is confidential government information about a person acquired when the lawyer was a public officer or employee, may not represent a private client whose interests are adverse to that person in a matter in which the information could be used to the material disadvantage of that person. As used in this Rule, the term "confidential government information" means information that has been obtained under governmental authority and which, at the time this Rule is applied, the government is prohibited by law from disclosing to the public or has a legal privilege not to disclose and which is not otherwise available to the public. A firm with which that lawyer is associated may undertake or continue representation in the matter only if the disqualified lawyer is timely screened from any participation in the matter and is apportioned no part of the fee therefrom.

(d) Except as law may otherwise expressly permit, a lawyer currently serving as a public officer or employee:

(1) is subject to Rules 1.7 and 1.9; and

(2) shall not:

(i) participate in a matter in which the lawyer participated personally and substantially while in private practice or nongovernmental employment, unless the appropriate government agency gives its informed consent, confirmed in writing; or

(ii) negotiate for private employment with any person who is involved as a party or as lawyer for a party in a matter in which the lawyer is participating personally and substantially, except that a lawyer serving as a law clerk to a judge, other adjudicative officer or arbitrator may negotiate for private employment as permitted by Rule 1.12(b) and subject to the conditions stated in Rule 1.12(b).

(e) As used in this Rule, the term "matter" includes:

(1) any judicial or other proceeding, application, request for a ruling or other determination, contract, claim, controversy, investigation, charge, accusation, arrest or other particular matter involving a specific party or parties, and

(2) any other matter covered by the conflict of interest rules of the appropriate government agency.

[Adopted effective September 1, 1990. Amended effective October 1, 2005.]

Comment

[1] A lawyer who has served or is currently serving as a public officer or employee is personally subject to the Rules of Professional Conduct, including the prohibition against concurrent conflicts of interest stated in Rule 1.7. In addition, such a lawyer may be subject to statutes and government regulations regarding conflict of interest. Such statutes and regulations may circumscribe the extent to which the government agency may give consent under this Rule. See Rule 1.0(g) for the definition of informed consent.

[2] Paragraphs (a)(1), (a)(2) and (d)(1) restate the obligations of an individual lawyer who has served or is currently serving as an officer or employee of the government toward a former government or private client. Rule 1.10 is not applicable to the conflicts of interest addressed by this Rule. Rather, paragraph (b) sets forth a special imputation rule for former government lawyers that provides for screening and notice. Because of the special problems raised by imputation within a government agency, paragraph (d) does not impute the conflicts of a lawyer currently serving as an officer or employee of the government to other associated government officers or employees, although ordinarily it will be prudent to screen such lawyers.

[3] Paragraphs (a)(2) and (d)(2) apply regardless of whether a lawyer is adverse to a former client and are thus designed not only to protect the former client, but also to prevent a

lawyer from exploiting public office for the advantage of another client. For example, a lawyer who has pursued a claim on behalf of the government may not pursue the same claim on behalf of a later private client after the lawyer has left government service, except when authorized to do so by the government agency under paragraph (a). Similarly, a lawyer who has pursued a claim on behalf of a private client may not pursue the claim on behalf of the government, except when authorized to do so by paragraph (d). As with paragraphs (a)(1) and (d)(1), Rule 1.10 is not applicable to the conflicts of interest addressed by these paragraphs.

[4] This Rule represents a balancing of interests. On the one hand, where the successive clients are a government agency and another client, public or private, the risk exists that power or discretion vested in that agency might be used for the special benefit of the other client. A lawyer should not be in a position where benefit to the other client might affect performance of the lawyer's professional functions on behalf of the government. Also, unfair advantage could accrue to the other client by reason of access to confidential government information about the client's adversary obtainable only through the lawyer's government service. On the other hand, the rules governing lawyers presently or formerly employed by a government agency should not be so restrictive as to inhibit transfer of employment to and from the government. The government has a legitimate need to attract qualified lawyers as well as to maintain high ethical standards. Thus a former government lawyer is disqualified only from particular matters in which the lawyer participated personally and substantially. The provisions for screening and waiver in paragraph (b) are necessary to prevent the disqualification rule from imposing too severe a deterrent against entering public service. The limitation of disqualification in paragraphs (a)(2) and (d)(2) to matters involving a specific party or parties, rather than extending disqualification to all substantive issues on which the lawyer worked, serves a similar function.

[5] When a lawyer has been employed by one government agency and then moves to a second government agency, it may be appropriate to treat that second agency as another client for purposes of this Rule, as when a lawyer is employed by a city and subsequently is employed by a federal agency. However, because the conflict of interest is governed by paragraph (d), the latter agency is not required to screen the lawyer as paragraph (b) requires a law firm to do. The question of whether two government agencies should be regarded as the same or different clients for conflict of interest purposes is beyond the scope of these Rules. See Rule 1.13 Comment [6].

[6] Paragraphs (b) and (c) contemplate a screening arrangement. See Rule 1.0(*l*) (requirements for screening procedures). These paragraphs do not prohibit a lawyer from receiving a salary or partnership share established by prior independent agreement, but that lawyer may not receive compensation directly relating the lawyer's compensation to the fee in the matter in which the lawyer is disqualified.

[7] Notice, including a description of the screened lawyer's prior representation and of the screening procedures employed, generally should be given as soon as practicable after the need for screening becomes apparent.

[8] Paragraph (c) operates only when the lawyer in question has knowledge of the information, which means actual knowledge; it does not operate with respect to information that merely could be imputed to the lawyer.

[9] Paragraphs (a) and (d) do not prohibit a lawyer from jointly representing a private party and a government agency when doing so is permitted by Rule 1.7 and is not otherwise prohibited by law.

[10] For purposes of paragraph (e) of this Rule, a "matter" may continue in another form. In determining whether two particular matters are the same, the lawyer should consider the extent to which the matters involve the same basic facts, the same or related parties, and the time elapsed.

RULE 1.12. FORMER JUDGE, ARBITRATOR, MEDIATOR OR OTHER THIRD-PARTY NEUTRAL

(a) Except as stated in paragraph (d), a lawyer shall not represent anyone in connection with a matter in which the lawyer participated personally and substantially as a judge or other adjudicative officer or law clerk to such a person or as an arbitrator, mediator or other third-party neutral, unless all parties to the proceeding give informed consent, confirmed in writing.

(b) A lawyer shall not negotiate for employment with any person who is involved as a party or as lawyer for a party in a matter in which the lawyer is participating personally and substantially as a judge or other adjudicative officer or as an arbitrator, mediator or other third-party neutral. A lawyer serving as a law clerk to a judge or other adjudicative officer may negotiate for employment with a party or lawyer involved in a matter in which the clerk is participating personally and substantially, but only after the lawyer has notified the judge or other adjudicative officer.

(c) If a lawyer is disqualified by paragraph (a), no lawyer in a firm with which that lawyer is associated may knowingly undertake or continue representation in the matter unless:

(1) the disqualified lawyer is timely screened from any participation in the matter and is apportioned no part of the fee therefrom; and

(2) written notice is promptly given to the parties and any appropriate tribunal to enable them to ascertain compliance with the provisions of this rule.

(d) An arbitrator selected as a partisan of a party in a multimember arbitration panel is not prohibited from subsequently representing that party.

[Adopted effective September 1, 1990. Amended effective October 1, 2005.]

Comment

[1] This Rule generally parallels Rule 1.11. The term "personally and substantially" signifies that a judge who was a member of a multimember court, and thereafter left judicial office to practice law, is not prohibited from representing a client in a matter pending in the court, but in which the former judge did not participate. So also the fact that a former judge exercised administrative responsibility in a court does not prevent the former judge from acting as a lawyer in a matter where the judge had previously exercised remote or incidental administrative responsibility that did not

affect the merits. Compare the Comment to Rule 1.11. The term "adjudicative officer" includes such officials as judges pro tempore, referees, special masters, hearing officers and other parajudicial officers, and also lawyers who serve as part-time judges. Compliance Canons A(2), B(2) and C of the Model Code of Judicial Conduct provide that a part-time judge, judge pro tempore or retired judge recalled to active service, may not "act as a lawyer in any proceeding in which he served as a judge or in any other proceeding related thereto." Although phrased differently from this Rule, those Rules correspond in meaning.

[2] Like former judges, lawyers who have served as arbitrators, mediators or other third-party neutrals may be asked to represent a client in a matter in which the lawyer participated personally and substantially. This Rule forbids such representation unless all of the parties to the proceedings give their informed consent, confirmed in writing. See Rule 1.0(g) and (b). Other law or codes of ethics governing third-party neutrals may impose more stringent standards of personal or imputed disqualification. See Rule 2.4.

[3] Although lawyers who serve as third-party neutrals do not have information concerning the parties that is protected under Rule 1.6, they typically owe the parties an obligation of confidentiality under law or codes of ethics governing third-party neutrals. Thus, paragraph (c) provides that conflicts of the personally disqualified lawyer will be imputed to other lawyers in a law firm unless the conditions of this paragraph are met.

[4] Requirements for screening procedures are stated in Rule 1.0(*l*). Paragraph (c)(1) does not prohibit the screened lawyer from receiving a salary or partnership share established by prior independent agreement, but that lawyer may not receive compensation directly related to the matter in which the lawyer is disqualified.

[5] Notice, including a description of the screened lawyer's prior representation and of the screening procedures employed, generally should be given as soon as practicable after the need for screening becomes apparent.

RULE 1.13. ORGANIZATION AS CLIENT

(a) A lawyer employed or retained by an organization represents the organization acting through its duly authorized constituents.

(b) If a lawyer for an organization knows that an officer, employee or other person associated with the organization is engaged in action, intends to act or refuses to act in a matter related to the representation that is a violation of a legal obligation to the organization, or a violation of law which reasonably might be imputed to the organization, and that is likely to result in substantial injury to the organization, then the lawyer shall proceed as is reasonably necessary in the best interest of the organization.

Unless the lawyer reasonably believes that it is not necessary in the best interest of the organization to do so, the lawyer shall refer the matter to higher authority in the organization, including, if warranted by the circumstances, to the highest authority that can act on behalf of the organization as determined by applicable law.

(c) Except as provided in paragraph (d), if,

(1) despite the lawyer's efforts in accordance with paragraph (b), the highest authority that can act on behalf of the organization insists upon or fails to address in a timely and appropriate manner an action, or a refusal to act, that is clearly a violation of law, and

(2) the lawyer reasonably believes that the violation is reasonably certain to result in substantial injury to the organization, then the lawyer may reveal information relating to the representation whether or not Rule 1.6 permits such disclosure, but only if and to the extent the lawyer reasonably believes necessary to prevent substantial injury to the organization.

(d) Paragraph (c) shall not apply with respect to information relating to a lawyer's representation of an organization to investigate an alleged violation of law, or to defend the organization or an officer, employee or other constituent associated with the organization against a claim arising out of an alleged violation of law.

(e) A lawyer who reasonably believes that he or she has been discharged because of the lawyer's actions taken pursuant to paragraphs (b) or (c), or who withdraws under circumstances that require or permit the lawyer to take action under either of those paragraphs, shall proceed as the lawyer reasonably believes necessary to assure that the organization's highest authority is informed of the lawyer's discharge or withdrawal.

(f) In dealing with an organization's directors, officers, employees, members, shareholders or other constituents, a lawyer shall explain the identity of the client when the lawyer knows or reasonably should know that the organization's interests are adverse to those of the constituents with whom the lawyer is dealing.

(g) A lawyer representing an organization may also represent any of its directors, officers, employees, members, shareholders or other constituents, subject to the provisions of Rule 1.7. If the organization's consent to the dual representation is required by Rule 1.7, the consent shall be given by an appropriate official of the organization other than the individual who is to be represented, or by the shareholders.

[Adopted effective September 1, 1990. Amended effective October 1, 2005.]

Comment

The Entity as the Client

[1] An organizational client is a legal entity, but it cannot act except through its officers, directors, employees, shareholders and other constituents. Officers, directors, employees and shareholders are the constituents of the corporate organizational client. The duties defined in this Comment apply equally to unincorporated associations. "Other constituents" as used in this Comment means the positions equivalent to officers, directors, employees and shareholders held by persons acting for organizational clients that are not corporations.

[2] When one of the constituents of an organizational client communicates with the organization's lawyer in that person's organizational capacity, the communication is protected by Rule 1.6. Thus, by way of example, if an organizational client requests its lawyer to investigate allegations of wrongdoing, interviews made in the course of that investigation between the lawyer and the client's employees or other constituents are covered by Rule 1.6. This does not mean, however, that constituents of an organizational client are the clients of the lawyer. The lawyer may not disclose to such constituents information relating to the representation except for disclosures explicitly or impliedly authorized by the organizational client in order to carry out the representation or as otherwise permitted by Rule 1.6.

[3] When constituents of the organization make decisions for it, the decisions ordinarily must be accepted by the lawyer even if their utility or prudence is doubtful. Decisions concerning policy and operations, including ones entailing serious risk, are not as such in the lawyer's province. Paragraph (b) makes clear, however, that when the lawyer knows that the organization is likely to be substantially injured by action of an officer or other constituent that violates a legal obligation to the organization or is in violation of law that might be imputed to the organization, the lawyer must proceed as is reasonably necessary in the best interest of the organization. As defined in Rule 1.0(g), knowledge can be inferred from circumstances, and a lawyer cannot ignore the obvious.

[4] In determining how to proceed under paragraph (b), the lawyer should give due consideration to the seriousness of the violation and its consequences, the responsibility in the organization and the apparent motivation of the person involved, the policies of the organization concerning such matters, and any other relevant considerations. Ordinarily, referral to a higher authority would be necessary. In some circumstances, however, it may be appropriate for the lawyer to ask the constituent to reconsider the matter; for example, if the circumstances involve a constituent's innocent misunderstanding of law and subsequent acceptance of the lawyer's advice, the lawyer may reasonably conclude that the best interest of the organization does not require that the matter be referred to higher authority. If a constituent persists in conduct contrary to the lawyer's advice, it will be necessary for the lawyer to take steps to have the matter reviewed by a higher authority in the organization. If the matter is of sufficient seriousness and importance or urgency to the organization, referral to higher authority in the organization may be necessary even if the lawyer has not communicated with the constituent. Any measures taken should, to the extent practicable, minimize the risk of revealing information relating to the representation to persons outside the organization. Even in circumstances where a lawyer is not obligated by Rule 1.13 to proceed, a lawyer may bring to the attention of an organizational client, including its highest authority, matters that the lawyer reasonably believes to be of sufficient importance to warrant doing so in the best interest of the organization.

[5] Paragraph (b) also makes clear that, when it is reasonably necessary to enable the organization to address the matter in a timely and appropriate manner, the lawyer must refer the matter to higher authority, including, if warranted by the circumstances, the highest authority that can act on behalf of the organization under applicable law. The organization's highest authority to whom a matter may be referred ordinarily will be the board of directors or similar governing body. However, applicable law may prescribe that under certain conditions the highest authority reposes elsewhere, for example, in the independent directors of a corporation.

Relation to Other Rules

[6] The authority and responsibility provided in this Rule are concurrent with the authority and responsibility provided in other Rules. In particular, this Rule does not limit or expand the lawyer's responsibility under Rules 1.6, 1.8, 1.16, 3.3 or 4.1. Paragraph (c) of this Rule supplements Rule 1.6(b) by providing an additional basis upon which the lawyer may reveal information relating to the representation, but does not modify, restrict, or limit the provisions of Rule 1.6(b)(1)–(7). Under paragraph (c) the lawyer may reveal such information only when the organization's highest authority insists upon or fails to address threatened or ongoing action that is clearly a violation of law, and then only to the extent the lawyer reasonably believes necessary to prevent reasonably certain substantial injury to the organization. It is not necessary that the lawyer's services be used in furtherance of the violation, but it is required that the matter be related to the lawyer's representation of the organization. If the lawyer's services are being used by an organization to further a crime or fraud by the organization, Rules 1.6(b)(3) and 1.6(b)(4) may permit the lawyer to disclose confidential information. In such circumstances Rule 1.2(d) may also be applicable, in which event, withdrawal from the representation under Rule 1.16(a)(1) may be required.

[7] Paragraph (d) makes clear that the authority of a lawyer to disclose information relating to a representation in circumstances described in paragraph (c) does not apply with respect to information relating to a lawyer's engagement by an organization to investigate an alleged violation of law or to defend the organization or an officer, employee or other person associated with the organization against a claim arising out of an alleged violation of law. This is necessary in order to enable organizational clients to enjoy the full benefits of legal counsel in conducting an investigation or defending against a claim.

[8] A lawyer who reasonably believes that he or she has been discharged because of the lawyer's actions taken pursuant to paragraph (b) or (c), or who withdraws in circumstances that require or permit the lawyer to take action under either of these paragraphs, must proceed as the lawyer reasonably believes necessary to assure that the organization's highest authority is informed of the lawyer's discharge or withdrawal.

Government Agency

[9] The duty defined in this Rule applies to governmental organizations. Defining precisely the identity of the client and prescribing the resulting obligations of such lawyers may be more difficult in the government context and is a matter beyond the scope of these Rules. See Scope [18]. Although in some circumstances the client may be a specific agency, it may also be a branch of government, such as the executive branch, or the government as a whole. For example, if the action or failure to act involves the head of a bureau, either the department of which the bureau is a part or the relevant branch of government may be the client for purposes of this Rule. Moreover, in a matter involving the conduct of government officials, a government lawyer may have authority under applicable law to question such conduct more extensively than that of a lawyer for a private organization in similar circumstances. Thus, when the client is a governmental organization, a different balance may be appropriate between maintaining confidentiality and assuring that the

wrongful act is prevented or rectified, for public business is involved. In addition, duties of lawyers employed by the government or lawyers in military service may be defined by statutes and regulation. This Rule does not limit that authority. See Scope.

Clarifying the Lawyer's Role

[10] There are times when the organization's interest may be or become adverse to those of one or more of its constituents. In such circumstances the lawyer should advise any constituent, whose interest the lawyer finds adverse to that of the organization of the conflict or potential conflict of interest, that the lawyer cannot represent such constituent, and that such person may wish to obtain independent representation. Care must be taken to assure that the individual understands that, when there is such adversity of interest, the lawyer for the organization cannot provide legal representation for that constituent individual, and that discussions between the lawyer for the organization and the individual may not be privileged.

[11] Whether such a warning should be given by the lawyer for the organization to any constituent individual may turn on the facts of each case.

Dual Representation

[12] Paragraph (g) recognizes that a lawyer for an organization may also represent a principal officer or major shareholder.

Derivative Actions

[13] Under generally prevailing law, the shareholders or members of a corporation may bring suit to compel the directors to perform their legal obligations in the supervision of the organization. Members of unincorporated associations have essentially the same right. Such an action may be brought nominally by the organization, but usually is, in fact, a legal controversy over management of the organization.

[14] The question can arise whether counsel for the organization may defend such an action. The proposition that the organization is the lawyer's client does not alone resolve the issue. Most derivative actions are a normal incident of an organization's affairs, to be defended by the organization's lawyer like any other suit. However, if the claim involves serious charges of wrongdoing by those in control of the organization, a conflict may arise between the lawyer's duty to the organization and the lawyer's relationship with the board. In those circumstances, Rule 1.7 governs who should represent the directors and the organization.

RULE 1.14. CLIENT WITH DIMINISHED CAPACITY

(a) When a client's capacity to make adequately considered decisions in connection with a representation is diminished, whether because of minority, mental impairment or for some other reason, the lawyer shall, as far as reasonably possible, maintain a normal client-lawyer relationship with the client.

(b) When the lawyer reasonably believes that the client has diminished capacity, is at risk of substantial physical, financial or other harm unless action is taken and cannot adequately act in the client's own interest, the lawyer may take reasonably necessary protective action, including consulting with individuals or entities that have the ability to take action to protect the client and, in appropriate cases, seeking the appointment of a guardian ad litem, conservator or guardian.

(c) Information relating to the representation of a client with diminished capacity is protected by Rule 1.6. When taking protective action pursuant to paragraph (b), the lawyer is impliedly authorized under Rule 1.6(a) to reveal information about the client, but only to the extent reasonably necessary to protect the client's interests.

[Adopted effective September 1, 1990. Amended effective October 1, 2005.]

Comment

[1] The normal client-lawyer relationship is based on the assumption that the client, when properly advised and assisted, is capable of making decisions about important matters. When the client is a minor or suffers from a diminished mental capacity, however, maintaining the ordinary client-lawyer relationship may not be possible in all respects. In particular, a severely incapacitated person may have no power to make legally binding decisions. Nevertheless, a client with diminished capacity often has the ability to understand, deliberate upon, and reach conclusions about matters affecting the client's own well-being. For example, children as young as five or six years of age, and certainly those of ten or twelve, are regarded as having opinions that are entitled to weight in legal proceedings concerning their custody. So also, it is recognized that some persons of advanced age can be quite capable of handling routine financial matters while needing special legal protection concerning major transactions.

[2] The fact that a client suffers a disability does not diminish the lawyer's obligation to treat the client with attention and respect. Even if the person has a legal representative, the lawyer should as far as possible accord the represented person the status of client, particularly in maintaining communication.

[3] The client may wish to have family members or other persons participate in discussions with the lawyer. When necessary to assist in the representation, the presence of such persons generally does not affect the applicability of the attorney-client evidentiary privilege. Nevertheless, the lawyer must keep the client's interests foremost and, except for protective action authorized under paragraph (b), must look to the client, and not family members, to make decisions on the client's behalf.

[4] If a legal representative has already been appointed for or by the client, the lawyer should ordinarily look to the representative for decisions on behalf of the client. In matters involving a minor, whether the lawyer should look to the parents as natural guardians may depend on the type of proceeding or matter in which the lawyer is representing the minor. If the lawyer represents the guardian as distinct from the ward, and is aware that the guardian is acting adversely to the ward's interest, the lawyer may have an obligation to prevent or rectify the guardian's misconduct. See Rule 1.2(d).

Taking Protective Action

[5] If a lawyer reasonably believes that a client is at risk of substantial physical, financial or other harm unless action is taken, and that a normal client-lawyer relationship cannot be maintained as provided in paragraph (a) because the client lacks sufficient capacity to communicate or to make adequate-

ly considered decisions in connection with the representation, then paragraph (b) permits the lawyer to take protective measures deemed necessary. Such measures could include: consulting with family members, using a reconsideration period to permit clarification or improvement of circumstances, using voluntary surrogate decisionmaking tools such as durable powers of attorney or consulting with support groups, professional services, adult-protective agencies or other individuals or entities that have the ability to protect the client. In taking any protective action, the lawyer should be guided by such factors as the wishes and values of the client to the extent known, the client's best interests and the goals of intruding into the client's decisionmaking autonomy to the least extent feasible, maximizing client capacities and respecting the client's family and social connections.

[6] In determining the extent of the client's diminished capacity, the lawyer should consider and balance such factors as: the client's ability to articulate reasoning leading to a decision, variability of state of mind and ability to appreciate consequences of a decision; the substantive fairness of a decision; and the consistency of a decision with the known long-term commitments and values of the client. In appropriate circumstances, the lawyer may seek guidance from an appropriate diagnostician.

[7] If a legal representative has not been appointed, the lawyer should consider whether appointment of a guardian ad litem, conservator or guardian is necessary to protect the client's interests. Thus, if a client with diminished capacity has substantial property that should be sold for the client's benefit, effective completion of the transaction may require appointment of a legal representative. In addition, rules of procedure in litigation sometimes provide that minors or persons with diminished capacity must be represented by a guardian or next friend if they do not have a general guardian. In many circumstances, however, appointment of a legal representative may be more expensive or traumatic for the client than circumstances in fact require. Evaluation of such circumstances is a matter entrusted to the professional judgment of the lawyer. In considering alternatives, however, the lawyer should be aware of any law that requires the lawyer to advocate the least restrictive action on behalf of the client.

Disclosure of the Client's Condition

[8] Disclosure of the client's diminished capacity could adversely affect the client's interests. For example, raising the question of diminished capacity could, in some circumstances, lead to proceedings for involuntary commitment. Information relating to the representation is protected by Rule 1.6. Therefore, unless authorized to do so, the lawyer may not disclose such information. When taking protective action pursuant to paragraph (b), the lawyer is impliedly authorized to make the necessary disclosures, even when the client directs the lawyer to the contrary. Nevertheless, given the risks of disclosure, paragraph (c) limits what the lawyer may disclose in consulting with other individuals or entities or seeking the appointment of a legal representative. At the very least, the lawyer should determine whether it is likely that the person or entity consulted with will act adversely to the client's interests before discussing matters related to the client. The lawyer's position in such cases is an unavoidably difficult one.

Emergency Legal Assistance

[9] In an emergency where the health, safety or a financial interest of a person with seriously diminished capacity is threatened with imminent and irreparable harm, a lawyer may take legal action on behalf of such a person even though the person is unable to establish a client-lawyer relationship or to make or express considered judgments about the matter, when the person or another acting in good faith on that person's behalf has consulted with the lawyer. Even in such an emergency, however, the lawyer should not act unless the lawyer reasonably believes that the person has no other lawyer, agent or other representative available. The lawyer should take legal action on behalf of the person only to the extent reasonably necessary to maintain the status quo or otherwise avoid imminent and irreparable harm. A lawyer who undertakes to represent a person in such an exigent situation has the same duties under these Rules as the lawyer would with respect to a client.

[10] A lawyer who acts on behalf of a person with seriously diminished capacity in an emergency should keep the confidences of the person as if dealing with a client, disclosing them only to the extent necessary to accomplish the intended protective action. The lawyer should disclose to any tribunal involved and to any other counsel involved the nature of his or her relationship with the person. The lawyer should take steps to regularize the relationship or implement other protective solutions as soon as possible. Normally, a lawyer would not seek compensation for such emergency actions taken.

RULE 1.15. SAFEKEEPING PROPERTY

(a) A lawyer shall hold property of clients or third persons that is in a lawyer's possession in connection with a representation separate from the lawyer's own property. Funds shall be kept in a separate account maintained in the state where the lawyer's office is situated, or elsewhere with the consent of the client or third person. Other property shall be identified as such and appropriately safeguarded. Complete records of such account funds and other property shall be kept by the lawyer and shall be preserved for a period of six years after termination of the representation. A lawyer shall comply with Rule 417, SCACR (Financial Recordkeeping).

(b) A lawyer may deposit the lawyer's own funds in a client trust account for the sole purpose of paying service charges on that account, but only in an amount necessary for that purpose.

(c) A lawyer shall deposit into a client trust account unearned legal fees and expenses that have been paid in advance, to be withdrawn by the lawyer only as fees are earned or expenses incurred.

(d) Upon receiving funds or other property in which a client or third person has an interest, a lawyer shall promptly notify the client or third person. Except as stated in this rule or otherwise permitted by law or by agreement with the client, a lawyer shall promptly deliver to the client or third person any funds or other property that the client or third person is entitled to receive and, upon request by the client or third person, shall promptly render a full accounting regarding such property.

(e) When in the course of representation a lawyer is in possession of property in which two or more persons (one of whom may be the lawyer) claim interests, the property shall be kept separate by the lawyer until the dispute is resolved. The lawyer shall promptly distribute all portions of the property as to which the interests are not in dispute.

(f)(1) A lawyer shall not disburse funds from an account containing the funds of more than one client or third person ("trust account") unless the funds to be disbursed have been deposited in the account and are collected funds.

(2) Notwithstanding Subsection (f)(1) above, a lawyer may disburse funds from a trust account at the lawyer's risk in reliance on the following deposits when the deposit is made:

(i) in cash or other items treated by the depository institution as equivalent to cash;

(ii) by verified and documented electronic funds transfer;

(iii) by a properly endorsed government check;

(iv) by a certified check, cashier's check, or other check drawn by a depository institution or an insurance company, provided the insurance company check does not exceed $50,000;

(v) by any other instrument payable at or through a depository institution, but only if the amount of such other instrument does not exceed $5,000 and the lawyer has a reasonable and prudent belief that the deposit of such other instrument will be collected promptly; or

(vi) by any other instrument payable at or through a depository institution and at least ten (10) days have passed since the date of deposit without notice to the lawyer that the credit for, or collection of, such other instrument has been delayed or is impaired.

If the actual collection of deposits described in Subsections (i) through (vi) above does not occur, the lawyer shall, as soon as practical but in no event more than five (5) business days after notice of noncollection, deposit replacement funds in the account.

(g) A lawyer shall not use or pledge any entrusted property to obtain credit or other personal benefit for the lawyer or any person other than the legal or beneficial owner of that property.

(h) Every lawyer maintaining a law office trust account shall file with the financial institution a written directive requiring the institution to report to the Commission on Lawyer Conduct when any properly payable instrument drawn on the account is presented for payment against insufficient funds. No law office trust account shall be maintained in a financial institution that does not agree to make such reports. The inadvertent failure of the institution to provide the report required by this rule shall not be construed to establish a breach of duty of care, or contract with, the Court or any third party who may sustain a loss as a result of an overdraft of a lawyer trust account.

[Adopted effective September 1, 1990. Amended effective October 1, 2005; August 13, 2007; February 19, 2009; June 28, 2010; October 6, 2010.]

Comment

[1] A lawyer should hold property of others with the care required of a professional fiduciary. Securities should be kept in a safe deposit box, except when some other form of safekeeping is warranted by special circumstances. All property that is the property of clients or third persons, including prospective clients, must be kept separate from the lawyer's business and personal property and, if monies, in one or more trust accounts. Separate trust accounts may be warranted when administering estate monies or acting in similar fiduciary capacities. A lawyer should maintain on a current basis books and records in accordance with prudent accounting practice and must comply with any recordkeeping rules established by law or court order. See, e.g., Rule 417, SCACR (Financial Recordkeeping).

[2] While normally it is impermissible to commingle the lawyer's own funds with client funds, paragraph (b) provides that it is permissible when necessary to pay service charges on that account. Accurate records must be kept regarding which part of the funds are the lawyer's.

[3] Lawyers often receive funds from which the lawyer's fee will be paid. The lawyer is not required to remit to the client funds that the lawyer reasonably believes represent fees owed. However, a lawyer may not hold funds to coerce a client into accepting the lawyer's contention. The disputed portion of the funds must be kept in a trust account and the lawyer should suggest means for prompt resolution of the dispute, such as arbitration. The undisputed portion of the funds shall be promptly distributed.

[4] Paragraph (e) also recognizes that third parties may have lawful claims against specific funds or other property in a lawyer's custody, such as a client's creditor who has a lien on funds recovered in a personal injury action. A lawyer may have a duty under applicable law to protect such third-party claims against wrongful interference by the client. In such cases, when the third-party claim is not frivolous under applicable law, the lawyer must refuse to surrender the property to the client until the claims are resolved. A lawyer should not unilaterally assume to arbitrate a dispute between the client and the third party, but, when there are substantial grounds for dispute as to the person entitled to the funds, the lawyer may file an action to have a court resolve the dispute.

[5] The requirement in Rule 1.15(f)(1) that funds be deposited and collected in the lawyer's trust account prior to disbursement is fundamental to proper trust accounting.

[6] Based on the lawyer's relationship with the depository institution or other considerations, deposited funds of various types may be made "available" for immediate withdrawal by the depository institution; however, lawyers should be aware that "available funds" are not necessarily collected funds since the credit given for the available funds may be revoked if the deposited item does not clear.

[7] Subsections (i) through (vi) of Rule 1.15(f)(2) represent categories of trust account deposits which carry a limited risk of failure so that disbursements may be made in reliance on such deposits without violating the fundamental rule of disbursing only on collected funds. In any of those circum-

stances, however, a lawyer's disbursement of funds from a trust account in reliance on deposits that are not yet collected funds is at the risk of the lawyer making the disbursement. The lawyer's risk includes deposited instruments that are forged, stolen, or counterfeit. If any of the deposits fail for any reason, the lawyer, upon receipt of notice or actual knowledge, must promptly act to protect the property of the lawyer's clients and third persons. If the lawyer accepting any such items personally pays the amount of any failed deposit within five (5) business days of receipt of notice that the deposit has failed, the lawyer will not be considered to have committed professional misconduct based upon the disbursement of uncollected funds.

[8] A lawyer's disbursement of funds from a trust account in reliance on deposits that are not yet collected funds in any circumstances other than Subsections (i) through (vi) of Rule 1.15(f)(2) may be grounds for a finding of professional misconduct.

[9] The obligations of a lawyer under this Rule are independent of those arising from activity other than rendering legal services. For example, a lawyer who serves only as an escrow agent is governed by the applicable law relating to fiduciaries even though the lawyer does not render legal services in the transaction and is not governed by this Rule.

[10] The Lawyers' Fund for Client Protection provides a means through the collective efforts of the Bar to reimburse persons who have lost money or property as a result of dishonest conduct of a lawyer. Under Rule 411, SCACR, each active or senior member of the Bar is required to make an annual contribution to this fund.

[11] A lawyer's obligations with regard to identified but unclaimed funds are set forth in the Uniform Unclaimed Property Act, S.C. Code Ann. § 27–18–10, et seq.

RULE 1.16. DECLINING OR TERMINATING REPRESENTATION

(a) Except as stated in paragraph (c), a lawyer shall not represent a client or, where representation has commenced, shall withdraw from the representation of a client if:

(1) the representation will result in violation of the Rules of Professional Conduct or other law;

(2) the lawyer's physical or mental condition materially impairs the lawyer's ability to represent the client; or

(3) the lawyer is discharged.

(b) Except as stated in paragraph (c), a lawyer may withdraw from representing a client if:

(1) withdrawal can be accomplished without material adverse effect on the interests of the client;

(2) the client persists in a course of action involving the lawyer's services that the lawyer reasonably believes is criminal or fraudulent;

(3) the client has used the lawyer's services to perpetrate a crime or fraud;

(4) the client insists upon taking action that the lawyer considers repugnant or with which the lawyer has a fundamental disagreement;

(5) the client fails substantially to fulfill an obligation to the lawyer regarding the lawyer's services or payment therefor and has been given reasonable warning that the lawyer will withdraw unless the obligation is fulfilled;

(6) the representation will result in an unreasonable financial burden on the lawyer or has been rendered unreasonably difficult by the client; or

(7) other good cause for withdrawal exists.

(c) A lawyer must comply with applicable law requiring notice to or permission of a tribunal when terminating a representation. When ordered to do so by a tribunal, a lawyer shall continue representation notwithstanding good cause for terminating the representation.

(d) Upon termination of representation, a lawyer shall take steps to the extent reasonably practicable to protect a client's interests, such as giving reasonable notice to the client, allowing time for employment of other counsel, surrendering papers and property to which the client is entitled and refunding any advance payment of fee or expense that has not been earned or incurred. The lawyer may retain papers relating to the client to the extent permitted by other law. The lawyer may retain a reasonable nonrefundable retainer.

[Adopted effective September 1, 1990. Amended effective October 1, 2005.]

Comment

[1] A lawyer should not accept representation in a matter unless it can be performed competently, promptly, without improper conflict of interest and to completion. Ordinarily, a representation in a matter is completed when the agreed-upon assistance has been concluded. See Rules 1.2(c) and 6.5. See also Rule 1.3, Comment [4].

Mandatory Withdrawal

[2] A lawyer ordinarily must decline or withdraw from representation if the client demands that the lawyer engage in conduct that is illegal or violates the Rules of Professional Conduct or other law. The lawyer is not obliged to decline or withdraw simply because the client suggests such a course of conduct; a client may make such a suggestion in the hope that a lawyer will not be constrained by a professional obligation.

[3] When a lawyer has been appointed to represent a client, withdrawal ordinarily requires approval of the appointing authority. See also Rule 6.2. Similarly, court approval or notice to the court is often required by applicable law before a lawyer withdraws from pending litigation. Difficulty may be encountered if withdrawal is based on the client's demand that the lawyer engage in unprofessional conduct. The court may request an explanation for the withdrawal, while the lawyer may be bound to keep confidential the facts that would constitute such an explanation. The lawyer's statement that professional considerations require termination of the representation ordinarily should be accepted as sufficient. Lawyers should be mindful of their obligations to both clients and the court under Rules 1.6 and 3.3.

Discharge

[4] A client has a right to discharge a lawyer at any time, with or without cause, subject to liability for payment for the lawyer's services. Where future dispute about the withdrawal may be anticipated, it may be advisable to prepare a written statement reciting the circumstances.

[5] Whether a client can discharge appointed counsel may depend on applicable law. A client seeking to do so should be given a full explanation of the consequences. These consequences may include a decision by the appointing authority that appointment of successor counsel is unjustified, thus requiring self-representation by the client.

[6] If the client has severely diminished capacity, the client may lack the legal capacity to discharge the lawyer, and in any event the discharge may be seriously adverse to the client's interests. The lawyer should make special effort to help the client consider the consequences and may take reasonably necessary protective action as provided in Rule 1.14.

Optional Withdrawal

[7] A lawyer may withdraw from representation in some circumstances. The lawyer has the option to withdraw if it can be accomplished without material adverse effect on the client's interests. Withdrawal is also justified if the client persists in a course of action that the lawyer reasonably believes is criminal or fraudulent, for a lawyer is not required to be associated with such conduct even if the lawyer does not further it. Withdrawal is also permitted if the lawyer's services were misused in the past even if that would materially prejudice the client. The lawyer may also withdraw where the client insists on taking action that the lawyer considers repugnant or with which the lawyer has a fundamental disagreement.

[8] A lawyer may withdraw if the client refuses to abide by the terms of an agreement relating to the representation, such as an agreement concerning fees or court costs or an agreement limiting the objectives of the representation. The South Carolina version of paragraph (b)(5) specifically recognizes that nonpayment for services may be a basis for withdrawal.

Assisting the Client upon Withdrawal

[9] Even if the lawyer has been unfairly discharged by the client, a lawyer must take all reasonable steps to mitigate the consequences to the client. The lawyer may retain papers as security for a fee only to the extent permitted by law. See Rule 1.15. Whether a client and lawyer may enter into an arrangement under which there is a nonrefundable retainer fee is governed by case law. Even when permitted, a nonrefundable retainer still must comply with Rule 1.5 and not be unreasonable. See Rule 1.5, Comment [4].

RULE 1.17. SALE OF LAW PRACTICE

A lawyer or a law firm may sell or purchase a law practice, including good will, if the following conditions are satisfied:

(a) The seller ceases to engage in the private practice of law in the geographic area in which the practice has been conducted;

(b) The entire practice is sold to one or more lawyers or law firms;

(c) The seller gives written notice to each of the seller's active clients regarding:

(1) the proposed sale;

(2) the client's right to retain other counsel or to take possession of the file; and

(3) the fact that the client's consent to the transfer of the client's files will be presumed if the client does not take any action or does not otherwise object within ninety (90) days of receipt of the notice;

(d) A notice is published in a newspaper of general circulation in the geographic area in which the practice has been conducted regarding:

(1) the proposed sale;

(2) the client's right to retain other counsel or to take possession of the client's file;

(3) the fact that active clients will be or have been given written notice regarding the proposed sale and that their consent to the sale will be presumed if they do not take any action or object within ninety (90) days of the date of the mailing of the written notice;

(4) the fact that the selling lawyer will retain the files of inactive clients unless those clients give permission for the transfer of their files or, if the parties to the sale elect to give written notice to an inactive client in the same manner provided by paragraph (c) above, the inactive client's consent to the sale will be presumed if the client does not take any action or does not otherwise object within ninety (90) days of the date of the mailing of the notice; and

(e) The fees charged clients shall not be increased by reason of the sale.

The agreement for the sale of a law practice may include reasonable restrictions on the seller's right to practice without violating Rule 5.6.

[Adopted effective January 8, 1998. Amended effective October 1, 2005.]

Comment

[1] The practice of law is a profession, not merely a business. Clients are not commodities that can be purchased and sold at will. Pursuant to this Rule, when a lawyer or an entire firm ceases to practice and other lawyers or firms take over the representation, the selling lawyer or firm may obtain compensation for the reasonable value of the practice as may withdrawing partners of law firms. See Rules 5.4 and 5.6.

Termination of Practice by the Seller

[2] The requirement that all of the private practice be sold is satisfied if the seller in good faith makes the entire practice available for sale to the purchasers. The fact that a number of the seller's clients decide not to be represented by the purchasers but take their matters elsewhere, therefore, does not result in a violation. Return to private practice as a result of an unanticipated change in circumstances does not necessarily result in a violation. For example, a lawyer who has sold the practice to accept an appointment to judicial office does not violate the requirement that the sale be attendant to cessation of practice if the lawyer later resumes private practice upon being defeated in a contested or a retention election for the office or resigns from a judiciary position.

[3] The requirement that the seller cease to engage in the private practice of law in the geographic area does not

prohibit employment as a lawyer on the staff of a public agency or a legal services entity that provides legal services to the poor, or as in-house counsel to a business.

[4] The Rule permits a sale of an entire practice attendant upon retirement from the private practice of law within the jurisdiction. Its provisions, therefore, accommodate the lawyer who sells the practice upon the occasion of moving to another state or geographic area within this state.

Sale of Entire Practice

[5] The Rule requires that the seller's entire practice be sold. The prohibition against sale of less than an entire practice protects those clients whose matters are less lucrative and who might find it difficult to secure other counsel if a sale could be limited to substantial fee-generating matters. The purchasers are required to undertake all client matters in the practice, subject to client consent. This requirement is satisfied, however, even if a purchaser is unable to undertake a particular client matter because of a conflict of interest.

Client Confidences, Consent and Notice

[6] Negotiations between seller and prospective purchaser prior to disclosure of information relating to a specific representation of an identifiable client no more violate the confidentiality provisions of Rule 1.6 than do preliminary discussions concerning the possible association of another lawyer or mergers between firms, with respect to which client consent is not required. Providing the purchaser access to client-specific information relating to the representation and to the file, however, requires client consent. The Rule provides that before such information can be disclosed by the seller to the purchaser regarding an active client, the client must be given actual written notice of the contemplated sale, including the identity of the purchaser, and must be told that the decision to consent or make other arrangements must be made within 90 days. If nothing is heard from the active client within that time, consent to the sale is presumed.

[7] It is not envisioned that files of inactive clients will be transferred to the purchaser as part of the sale of the practice, because of the continuing duties to inactive clients. Should the parties choose to transfer files of inactive clients of the seller as part of the sale of the law practice, notice must be given to each inactive client in the same manner as set forth in paragraph (c) or (d). For purposes of this Rule, an inactive client refers to a client whose file has been closed due to the completion or termination of the representation.

[8] All the elements of client autonomy, including the client's absolute right to discharge a lawyer and transfer the representation to another, survive the sale of the practice.

Fee Arrangements Between Client and Purchaser

[9] The sale may not be financed by increases in fees charged the clients of the practice. Existing agreements between the seller and the client as to fees and the scope of the work must be honored by the purchaser.

Other Applicable Ethical Standards

[10] Lawyers participating in the sale of a law practice are subject to the ethical standards applicable to involving another lawyer in the representation of a client. These include, for example, the seller's obligation to exercise competence in identifying a purchaser qualified to assume the practice and the purchaser's obligation to undertake the representation competently (see Rule 1.1); the obligation to avoid disqualifying conflicts, and to secure the client's informed consent for those conflicts that can be agreed to (see Rule 1.7 regarding conflicts and Rule 1.0(g) for the definition of informed consent); and the obligation to protect information relating to the representation (see Rules 1.6 and 1.9).

[11] If approval of the substitution of the purchasing lawyer for the selling lawyer is required by the rules of any tribunal in which a matter is pending, such approval must be obtained before the matter can be included in the sale (see Rule 1.16).

Applicability of the Rule

[12] This Rule applies to the sale of a law practice by representatives of a deceased, disabled or disappeared lawyer. Thus, the seller may be represented by a non-lawyer representative not subject to these Rules. Since, however, no lawyer may participate in a sale of a law practice which does not conform to the requirements of this Rule, the representatives of the seller as well as the purchasing lawyer can be expected to see to it that they are met.

[13] Admission to or retirement from a law partnership or professional association, retirement plans and similar arrangements, and a sale of tangible assets of a law practice, do not constitute a sale or purchase governed by this Rule. Nor does this Rule govern the transfer of ownership interests or clients between members of a law firm.

[14] This Rule does not apply to the transfers of legal representation between lawyers when such transfers are unrelated to the sale of a practice.

RULE 1.18. DUTIES TO PROSPECTIVE CLIENT

(a) A person with whom a lawyer discusses the possibility of forming a client-lawyer relationship with respect to a matter is a prospective client only when there is a reasonable expectation that the lawyer is likely to form the relationship.

(b) Even when no client-lawyer relationship ensues, a lawyer who has had discussions with a prospective client shall not use or reveal information learned in the consultation, except as Rule 1.9 would permit with respect to information of a former client.

(c) A lawyer subject to paragraph (b) shall not represent a client with interests materially adverse to those of a prospective client in the same or a substantially related matter if the lawyer received information from the prospective client that could be significantly harmful to that person in the matter, except as provided in paragraph (d). If a lawyer is disqualified from representation under this paragraph, no lawyer in a firm with which that lawyer is associated may knowingly undertake or continue representation in such a matter, except as provided in paragraph (d).

(d) When the lawyer has received disqualifying information as defined in paragraph (c), representation is permissible if:

(1) both the affected client and the prospective client have given informed consent, confirmed in writing, or

(2) the lawyer who received the information took reasonable measures to avoid exposure to more disqualifying information than was reasonably necessary to determine whether to represent the prospective client; and

(i) the disqualified lawyer is timely screened from any participation in the matter and is apportioned no part of the fee therefrom; and

(ii) written notice is promptly given to the prospective client.

[Adopted effective October 1, 2005.]

Comment

[1] Prospective clients, like clients, may disclose information to a lawyer, place documents or other property in the lawyer's custody, or rely on the lawyer's advice. A lawyer's discussions with a prospective client usually are limited in time and depth and leave both the prospective client and the lawyer free (and sometimes required) to proceed no further. Hence, prospective clients should receive some but not all of the protection afforded clients.

[2] Not all persons who communicate information to a lawyer are entitled to protection under this Rule. A person who communicates information unilaterally to a lawyer without any reasonable expectation that the lawyer is willing to discuss the possibility of forming a client-lawyer relationship, therefore is not a "prospective client" within the meaning of paragraph (a).

[3] It is often necessary for a prospective client to reveal information to the lawyer during an initial consultation prior to the decision about formation of a client-lawyer relationship. The lawyer often must learn such information to determine whether there is a conflict of interest with an existing client and whether the matter is one that the lawyer is willing to undertake. Paragraph (b) prohibits the lawyer from using or revealing that information, except as permitted by Rule 1.9, even if the client or lawyer decides not to proceed with the representation. The duty exists regardless of how brief the initial conference may be.

[4] In order to avoid acquiring disqualifying information from a prospective client, a lawyer considering whether or not to undertake a new matter should limit the initial interview to only such information as reasonably appears necessary for that purpose. Where the information indicates that a conflict of interest or other reason for non-representation exists, the lawyer should so inform the prospective client or decline the representation. If the prospective client wishes to retain the lawyer, and if consent is possible under Rule 1.7, then consent from all affected present or former clients must be obtained before accepting the representation.

[5] A lawyer may condition conversations with a prospective client on the person's informed consent that no information disclosed during the consultation will prohibit the lawyer from representing a different client in the matter. See Rule 1.0(g) for the definition of informed consent. If the agreement expressly so provides, the prospective client may also consent to the lawyer's subsequent use of information received from the prospective client.

[6] Even in the absence of an agreement, under paragraph (c), the lawyer is not prohibited from representing a client with interests adverse to those of the prospective client in the same or a substantially related matter unless the lawyer has received from the prospective client information that could be significantly harmful if used in the matter.

[7] Under paragraph (c), the prohibition in this Rule is imputed to other lawyers as provided in Rule 1.10, but, under paragraph (d)(1), imputation may be avoided if the lawyer obtains the informed consent, confirmed in writing, of both the prospective and affected clients. In the alternative, imputation may be avoided if the conditions of paragraph (d)(2) are met and all disqualified lawyers are timely screened and written notice is promptly given to the prospective client. See Rule 1.0(*l*) (requirements for screening procedures). Paragraph (d)(2)(i) does not prohibit the screened lawyer from receiving a salary or partnership share established by prior independent agreement, but that lawyer may not receive compensation directly related to the matter in which the lawyer is disqualified.

[8] Notice, including a description of the screened lawyer's prior representation and of the screening procedures employed, generally should be given as soon as practicable after the need for screening becomes apparent. When disclosure is likely to significantly injure the client, a reasonable delay may be justified.

[9] For the duty of competence of a lawyer who gives assistance on the merits of a matter to a prospective client, see Rule 1.1. For a lawyer's duties when a prospective client entrusts valuables or papers to a lawyer's care, see Rule 1.15.

COUNSELOR

RULE 2.1. ADVISOR

In representing a client, a lawyer shall exercise independent professional judgment and render candid advice. In rendering advice, a lawyer may refer not only to law but to other considerations such as moral, economic, social and political factors, that may be relevant to the client's situation.

[Adopted effective September 1, 1990. Amended effective October 1, 2005.]

Comment

Scope of Advice

[1] A client is entitled to straightforward advice expressing the lawyer's honest assessment. Legal advice often involves unpleasant facts and alternatives that a client may be disinclined to confront. In presenting advice, a lawyer endeavors to sustain the client's morale and may put advice in as acceptable a form as honesty permits. However, a lawyer should not be deterred from giving candid advice by the prospect that the advice will be unpalatable to the client.

[2] Advice couched in narrow legal terms may be of little value to a client, especially where practical considerations, such as cost or effects on other people, are predominant. Purely technical legal advice, therefore, can sometimes be inadequate. It is proper for a lawyer to refer to relevant moral and ethical considerations in giving advice. Although a lawyer is not a moral advisor as such, moral and ethical considerations impinge upon most legal questions and may decisively influence how the law will be applied.

[3] A client may expressly or impliedly ask the lawyer for purely technical advice. When such a request is made by a client experienced in legal matters, the lawyer may accept it at face value. When such a request is made by a client inexperienced in legal matters, however, the lawyer's responsibility as advisor may include indicating that more may be involved than strictly legal considerations.

[4] Matters that go beyond strictly legal questions may also be in the domain of another profession. Family matters can

involve problems within the professional competence of psychiatry, clinical psychology or social work; business matters can involve problems within the competence of the accounting profession or of financial specialists. Where consultation with a professional in another field is itself something a competent lawyer would recommend, the lawyer should make such a recommendation. At the same time, a lawyer's advice at its best often consists of recommending a course of action in the face of conflicting recommendations of experts.

Offering Advice

[5] In general a lawyer is not expected to give advice until asked by the client. However, when a lawyer knows that a client proposes a course of action that is likely to result in substantial adverse legal consequences to the client, the lawyer's duty to the client under Rule 1.4 may require that the lawyer offer advice if the client's course of action is related to the representation. Similarly, when a matter is likely to involve litigation, it may be necessary under Rule 1.4 to inform the client of forms of dispute resolution that might constitute reasonable alternatives to litigation. A lawyer ordinarily has no duty to initiate investigation of a client's affairs or to give advice that the client has indicated is unwanted, but a lawyer may initiate advice to a client when doing so appears to be in the client's interest.

RULE 2.2. [RESERVED]

RULE 2.3. EVALUATION FOR USE BY THIRD PERSONS

(a) A lawyer may provide an evaluation of a matter affecting a client for the use of someone other than the client if the lawyer reasonably believes that making the evaluation is compatible with other aspects of the lawyer's relationship with the client.

(b) When the lawyer knows or reasonably should know that the evaluation is likely to affect the client's interests materially and adversely, the lawyer shall not provide the evaluation unless the client gives informed consent.

(c) Except as disclosure is authorized in connection with a report of an evaluation, information relating to the evaluation is otherwise protected by Rule 1.6

[Adopted effective September 1, 1990. Amended effective October 1, 2005.]

Comment

Definition

[1] An evaluation may be performed at the client's direction or when impliedly authorized in order to carry out the representation. See Rule 1 2. Such an evaluation may be for the primary purpose of establishing information for the benefit of third parties; for example, an opinion concerning the title of property rendered at the behest of a vendor for the information of a prospective purchaser, or at the behest of a borrower for the information of a prospective lender. In some situations, the evaluation may be required by a government agency; for example, an opinion concerning the legality of the securities registered for sale under the securities laws. In other instances, the evaluation may be required by a third person, such as a purchaser of a business.

[2] A legal evaluation should be distinguished from an investigation of a person with whom the lawyer does not have a client-lawyer relationship. For example, a lawyer retained by a purchaser to analyze a vendor's title to property does not have a client-lawyer relationship with the vendor. So also, an investigation into a person's affairs by a government lawyer, or by special counsel by a government lawyer, or by special counsel employed by the government, is not an evaluation as that term is used in this Rule. The question is whether the lawyer is retained by the person whose affairs are being examined. When the lawyer is retained by that person, the general rules concerning loyalty to client and preservation of confidences apply, which is not the case if the lawyer is retained by someone else. For this reason, it is essential to identify the person by whom the lawyer is retained. This should be made clear not only to the person under examination, but also to others to whom the results are to be made available.

Duties Owed to Third Person and Client

[3] When the evaluation is intended for the information or use of a third person, a legal duty to that person may or may not arise. That legal question is beyond the scope of this Rule. However, since such an evaluation involves a departure from the normal client-lawyer relationship, careful analysis of the situation is required. The lawyer must be satisfied as a matter of professional judgment that making the evaluation is compatible with other functions undertaken in behalf of the client. For example, if the lawyer is acting as advocate in defending the client against charges of fraud, it would normally be incompatible with that responsibility for the lawyer to perform an evaluation for others concerning the same or a related transaction. Assuming no such impediment is apparent, however, the lawyer should advise the client of the implications of the evaluation, particularly the lawyer's responsibilities to third persons and the duty to disseminate the findings.

Access to and Disclosure of Information

[4] The quality of an evaluation depends on the freedom and extent of the investigation upon which it is based. Ordinarily a lawyer should have whatever latitude of investigation seems necessary as a matter of professional judgment. Under some circumstances, however, the terms of the evaluation may be limited. For example, certain issues or sources may be categorically excluded, or the scope of search may be limited by time constraints or the non-cooperation of persons having relevant information. Any such limitations that are material to the evaluation should be described in the report. If after a lawyer has commenced an evaluation, the client refuses to comply with the terms upon which it was understood the evaluation was to have been made, the lawyer's obligations are determined by law, having reference to the terms of the client's agreement and the surrounding circumstances. In no circumstances is the lawyer permitted to knowingly make a false statement of material fact or law in providing an evaluation under this Rule. See Rule 4.1

Obtaining Client's Informed Consent

[5] Information relating to an evaluation is protected by Rule 1.6. In many situations, providing an evaluation to a third party poses no significant risk to the client; thus, the lawyer may be impliedly authorized to disclose information to carry out the representation. See Rule 1.6(a). Where, however, it is reasonably likely that providing the evaluation will affect the client's interests materially and adversely, the lawyer must first obtain the client's informed consent.

Financial Auditors' Requests for Information

[6] When a question concerning the legal situation of a client arises at the instance of the client's financial auditor and the question is referred to the lawyer, the lawyer's response may be made in accordance with procedures recognized in the legal profession. Such a procedure is set forth in the American Bar Association Statement of Policy Regarding Lawyers' Responses to Auditors' Requests for Information, adopted in 1975.

RULE 2.4. LAWYER SERVING AS THIRD PARTY NEUTRAL

(a) A lawyer serves as a third party neutral when the lawyer assists two or more persons who are not clients of the lawyer to reach a resolution of a dispute or other matter that has arisen between them. Service as a third party neutral may include service as an arbitrator, a mediator or in such other capacity as will enable the lawyer to assist the parties to resolve the matter.

(b) A lawyer serving as a third party neutral shall inform unrepresented parties that the lawyer is not representing them. When the lawyer knows or reasonably should know that a party does not understand the lawyer's role in the matter, the lawyer shall explain the difference between the lawyer's role as a third party neutral and a lawyer's role as one who represents a client.

(c) When one or more of the parties in a mediation is a current or former client of the neutral lawyer or the neutral's law firm, a lawyer may serve as a neutral only if the matter in which the lawyer serves as a neutral is not the same matter in which the lawyer or law firm represents or represented the party and all parties give informed consent confirmed in writing.

[Adopted effective October 1, 2005.]

Comment

[1] Alternative dispute resolution has become a substantial part of the civil justice system. Aside from representing clients in dispute resolution processes, lawyers often serve as third party neutrals. A third party neutral is a person, such as a mediator, arbitrator, conciliator or evaluator, who assists the parties, represented or unrepresented, in the resolution of a dispute or in the arrangement of a transaction. Whether a third party neutral serves primarily as a facilitator, evaluator or decision maker depends on the particular process that is either selected by the parties or mandated by a court.

[2] The role of a third party neutral is not unique to lawyers, although, in some court-connected contexts, only lawyers are allowed to serve in this role or to handle certain types of cases. In performing this role, the lawyer may be subject to court rules or other law that apply either to third party neutrals generally or to lawyers serving as third party neutrals. Lawyer–neutrals may also be subject to various codes of ethics, such as the Code of Ethics for Arbitration in Commercial Disputes prepared by a joint committee of the American Bar Association and the American Arbitration Association or the Model Standards of Conduct for Mediators jointly prepared by the American Bar Association, the American Arbitration Association and the Society of Professionals in Dispute Resolution.

[3] Unlike non-lawyers who serve as third party neutrals, lawyers serving in this role may experience unique problems as a result of differences between the role of a third party neutral and a lawyer's service as a client representative. The potential for confusion is significant when the parties are unrepresented in the process. Thus paragraph (b) requires a lawyer neutral to inform unrepresented parties that the lawyer is not representing them. For some parties, particularly parties who frequently use dispute resolution processes, this information will be sufficient. For others, particularly those who are using the process for the first time, more information will be required. Where appropriate, the lawyer should inform unrepresented parties of the important differences between the lawyer's role as third party neutral and a lawyer's role as a client representative, including the inapplicability of the attorney client evidentiary privilege. The extent of disclosure required under this paragraph will depend on the particular parties involved and the subject matter of the proceeding, as well as the particular features of the dispute-resolution process selected.

[4] A lawyer who serves a third party neutral subsequently may be asked to serve as a lawyer representing a client in the same matter. The conflicts of interest that arise for both the individual lawyer and the lawyer's law firm are addressed in Rule 1.12.

[5] Lawyers who represent clients in alternative dispute resolution processes are governed by the Rules of Professional Conduct. When the dispute resolution process takes place before a tribunal, as in binding arbitration (see Rule 1.0(n)), the lawyer's duty of candor is governed by Rule 3.3. Otherwise, the lawyer's duty of candor toward both the third party neutral and other parties is governed by Rule 4.1.

ADVOCATE

RULE 3.1. MERITORIOUS CLAIMS AND CONTENTIONS

A lawyer shall not bring or defend a proceeding, or assert or controvert an issue therein, unless there is a basis in law and fact for doing so that is not frivolous, which includes a good faith argument for an extension, modification or reversal of existing law. A lawyer for the defendant in a criminal proceeding, or the respondent in a proceeding that could result in incarceration, may nevertheless so defend the proceeding as to require that every element of the case be established.

[Adopted effective September 1, 1990. Amended effective October 1, 2005.]

Comment

[1] The advocate has a duty to use legal procedure for the fullest benefit of the client's cause, but also a duty not to abuse legal procedure. The law, both procedural and substantive, establishes the limits within which an advocate may proceed. However, the law is not always clear and never is static. Accordingly, in determining the proper scope of advocacy, account must be taken of the law's ambiguities and potential for change.

[2] The filing of an action or defense or similar action taken for a client is not frivolous merely because the facts have not

first been fully substantiated or because the lawyer expects to develop vital evidence only by discovery. What is required of lawyers, however, is that they inform themselves about the facts of their clients' cases and the applicable law and determine that they can make good faith arguments in support of their clients' positions. Such action is not frivolous even though the lawyer believes that the client's position ultimately will not prevail. The action is frivolous, however, if the lawyer is unable either to make a good faith argument on the merits of the action taken or to support the action taken by good faith argument for an extension, modification or reversal of existing laws.

[3] The lawyer's obligations under this Rule are subordinate to federal or state constitutional law that entitles a defendant in a criminal matter to the assistance of counsel in presenting a claim or contention that otherwise would be prohibited by this Rule.

RULE 3.2. EXPEDITING LITIGATION

A lawyer shall make reasonable efforts to expedite litigation consistent with the interests of the client.

[Adopted effective September 1, 1990. Amended effective October 1, 2005.]

Comment

[1] Dilatory practices bring the administration of justice into disrepute. Although there will be occasions when a lawyer may properly seek a postponement for personal reasons, it is not proper for a lawyer to routinely fail to expedite litigation solely for the convenience of the lawyer. Nor will a failure to expedite be reasonable if done for the purpose of frustrating an opposing party's attempt to obtain rightful redress or repose. It is not a justification that similar conduct is often tolerated by the bench and bar. The question is whether a competent lawyer acting in good faith would regard the course of action as having some substantial purpose other than delay. Realizing financial or other benefit from otherwise improper delay in litigation is not a legitimate interest of the client.

RULE 3.3. CANDOR TOWARD THE TRIBUNAL

(a) A lawyer shall not knowingly:

(1) make a false statement of fact or law to a tribunal or fail to correct a false statement of material fact or law previously made to the tribunal by the lawyer;

(2) fail to disclose to the tribunal legal authority in the controlling jurisdiction known to the lawyer to be directly adverse to the position of the client and not disclosed by opposing counsel; or

(3) offer evidence that the lawyer knows to be false. If a lawyer, the lawyer's client, or a witness called by the lawyer, has offered material evidence and the lawyer comes to know of its falsity, the lawyer shall take reasonable remedial measures, including, if necessary, disclosure to the tribunal. A lawyer may refuse to offer evidence, other than the testimony of a defendant in a criminal matter, that the lawyer reasonably believes is false.

(b) A lawyer who represents a client in an adjudicative proceeding and who knows that a person intends to engage, is engaging or has engaged in criminal or fraudulent conduct related to the proceeding shall take reasonable remedial measures, including, if necessary, disclosure to the tribunal.

(c) The duties stated in paragraphs (a) and (b) apply when the lawyer is representing a client before a tribunal as well as in an ancillary proceeding conducted pursuant to the tribunal's adjudicative authority, such as a deposition. These duties continue to the conclusion of the proceeding, and apply even if compliance requires disclosure of information otherwise protected by Rule 1.6.

(d) In an ex parte proceeding, a lawyer shall inform the tribunal of all material facts known to the lawyer that will enable the tribunal to make an informed decision, whether or not the facts are adverse.

[Adopted effective September 1, 1990. Amended effective October 1, 2005.]

Comment

[1] This Rule governs the conduct of a lawyer who is representing a client in the proceedings of a tribunal. See Rule 1.0(n) for the definition of "tribunal." It also applies when the lawyer is representing a client in an ancillary proceeding conducted pursuant to the tribunal's adjudicative authority, such as a deposition. Thus, for example, paragraph (a)(3) requires a lawyer to take reasonable remedial measures if the lawyer comes to know that a client who is testifying in a deposition has offered evidence that is false.

[2] This Rule sets forth the special duties of lawyers as officers of the court to avoid conduct that undermines the integrity of the adjudicative process A lawyer acting as an advocate in an adjudicative proceeding has an obligation to present the client's case with persuasive force. Performance of that duty while maintaining confidences of the client, however, is qualified by the advocate's duty of candor to the tribunal. Consequently, although a lawyer in an adversary proceeding is not required to present an impartial exposition of the law or to vouch for the evidence submitted in a cause, the lawyer must not allow the tribunal to be misled by false statements of law or fact or evidence that the lawyer knows to be false.

Representations by a Lawyer

[3] An advocate is responsible for pleadings and other documents prepared for litigation, but is usually not required to have personal knowledge of matters asserted therein, for litigation documents ordinarily present assertions by the client, or by someone on the client's behalf, and not assertions by the lawyer. Compare Rule 3.1. However, an assertion purporting to be on the lawyer's own knowledge, as in an affidavit by the lawyer or in a statement in open court, may properly be made only when the lawyer knows the assertion is true or believes it to be true on the basis of a reasonably diligent inquiry. There are circumstances where failure to make a disclosure is the equivalent of an affirmative misrepresentation. The obligation prescribed in Rule 1.2(d) not to counsel a client to commit or assist the client in committing a fraud applies in litigation. Regarding compliance with Rule 1.2(d), see the Comment to that Rule. See also the Comment to Rule 8.4(b).

Legal Argument

[4] Legal argument based on a knowingly false representation of law constitutes dishonesty toward the tribunal. A lawyer is not required to make a disinterested exposition of the law, but must recognize the existence of pertinent legal authorities. Furthermore, as stated in paragraph (a)(2), an advocate has a duty to disclose directly adverse authority in the controlling jurisdiction that has not been disclosed by the opposing party. The underlying concept is that legal argument is a discussion seeking to determine the legal premises properly applicable to the case.

Offering Evidence

[5] Paragraph (a)(3) requires, that the lawyer refuse to offer evidence that the lawyer knows to be false, regardless of the client's wishes. This duty is premised on the lawyer's obligation as an officer of the court to prevent the trier of fact from being misled by false evidence. A lawyer does not violate this Rule if the lawyer offers the evidence for the purpose of establishing its falsity.

[6] If a lawyer knows that the client intends to testify falsely or wants the lawyer to introduce false evidence, the lawyer should seek to persuade the client that the evidence should not be offered. If the persuasion is ineffective and the lawyer continues to represent the client, the lawyer must refuse to offer the false evidence. If only a portion of a witness's testimony will be false the lawyer may call the witness to testify but may not elicit or otherwise permit the witness to present the testimony that the lawyer knows is false.

[7] The duties stated in paragraphs (a) and (b) apply to all lawyers, including defense counsel in criminal cases. Counsel, however, may allow the accused to give a narrative statement if the accused so desires, even if counsel knows that the testimony or statement will be false. See also Comment [9]. When a narrative statement is offered under these circumstances, the lawyer may not examine the witness or use the false testimony in the closing argument.

[8] The prohibition against offering false evidence only applies if the lawyer knows that the evidence is false. A lawyer's reasonable belief that evidence is false does not preclude its presentation to the trier of fact. A lawyer's knowledge that evidence is false, however, can be inferred from the circumstances. See Rule 1.0(g). Thus, although a lawyer should resolve doubts about the veracity of testimony or other evidence in favor of the client, the lawyer cannot ignore an obvious falsehood.

[9] Although (a)(3) only prohibits a lawyer from offering evidence the lawyer knows to be false, it permits the lawyer to refuse to offer testimony or other proof that the lawyer reasonably believes is false. Offering such proof may reflect adversely on the lawyer's ability to discriminate in the quality of evidence and thus impair the lawyer's effectiveness as an advocate. Because of the special protections historically provided criminal defendants, however, this Rule does not permit a lawyer to refuse to offer the testimony of such a client where the lawyer reasonably believes but does not know that the testimony will be false. Unless the lawyer knows the testimony will be false, the lawyer must honor the client's decision to testify. See also Comment [7].

Remedial Measures

[10] Having offered material evidence in the belief that it was true, a lawyer may subsequently come to know that the evidence is false. Or, a lawyer may be surprised when the lawyer's client, or another witness called by the lawyer, offers testimony the lawyer knows to be false, either during the lawyer's direct examination or in response to cross examination by the opposing lawyer. In such situations or if the lawyer knows of the falsity of testimony elicited from the client during a deposition, the lawyer must take reasonable remedial measures. In such situations, the advocate's proper course is to remonstrate with the client confidentially, advise the client of the lawyer's duty of candor to the tribunal and seek the client's cooperation with respect to the withdrawal or correction of the false statements or evidence. If that fails, the advocate must take further remedial action. If withdrawal from the representation is not permitted or will not undo the effect of the false evidence, the advocate must make disclosure to the tribunal. It is for the tribunal then to determine what should be done making a statement about the matter to the trier of fact, ordering a mistrial or perhaps nothing.

[11] The disclosure of a client's false testimony can result in grave consequences to the client, including not only a sense of betrayal but also loss of the case and perhaps a prosecution for perjury. But the alternative is that the lawyer cooperate in deceiving the court, thereby subverting the truth finding process which the adversary system is designed to implement. See Rule 1.2(d). Furthermore, unless it is clearly understood that the lawyer will act upon the duty to disclose the existence of false evidence, the client can simply reject the lawyer's advice to reveal the false evidence and insist that the lawyer keep silent. Thus the client could in effect coerce the lawyer into being a party to fraud on the court.

Preserving Integrity of The Adjudicative Process

[12] Lawyers have a special obligation to protect a tribunal against criminal or fraudulent conduct that undermines the integrity of the adjudicative process, such as bribing, intimidating or otherwise unlawfully communicating with a witness, juror, court official or other participant in the proceeding, unlawfully destroying or concealing documents or other evidence or failing to disclose information to the tribunal when required by law to do so. Thus, paragraph (b) requires a lawyer to take reasonable remedial measures, including disclosure if necessary, whenever the lawyer knows that a person, including the lawyer's client, intends to engage, is engaging or has engaged in criminal or fraudulent conduct related to the proceeding.

Duration of Obligation

[13] A practical time limit on the obligation to rectify false evidence or false statements of law and fact has to be established. The conclusion of the proceeding is a reasonably definite point for the termination of the obligation. A proceeding has concluded within the meaning of this Rule when a final judgment in the proceeding has been affirmed on appeal or the time for review has passed.

Ex Parte Proceedings

[14] Ordinarily an advocate has the limited responsibility of presenting one side of the matters that a tribunal should consider in reaching a decision; the conflicting position is expected to be presented by the opposing party. However, in any ex parte proceeding, such as an application for a temporary restraining order, there is no balance of presentation by opposing advocates. The object of an ex parte proceeding is nevertheless to yield a substantially just result. The judge has an affirmative responsibility to accord the absent party just consideration. The lawyer for the represented party has the correlative duty to make disclosures of

material facts known to the lawyer and that the lawyer reasonably believes are necessary to an informed decision.

Withdrawal

[15] Normally, a lawyer's compliance with the duty of candor imposed by this Rule does not require that the lawyer withdraw from the representation of a client whose interests will be or have been adversely affected by the lawyer's disclosure. The lawyer may, however, be required by Rule 1.16(a) to seek permission of the tribunal to withdraw if the lawyer's compliance with this Rule's duty of candor results in such an extreme deterioration of the client-lawyer relationship that the lawyer can no longer competently represent the client. Also see Rule 1.16(b) for the circumstances in which a lawyer will be permitted to seek a tribunal's permission to withdraw. In connection with a request for permission to withdraw that is premised on a client's misconduct, a lawyer may reveal information relating to the representation only to the extent reasonably necessary to comply with this Rule or as otherwise permitted by Rule 1.6.

RULE 3.4. FAIRNESS TO OPPOSING PARTY AND COUNSEL

A lawyer shall not:

(a) unlawfully obstruct another party's access to evidence or unlawfully alter, destroy or conceal a document or other material having potential evidentiary value. A lawyer shall not counsel or assist another person to do any such act;

(b) falsify evidence, counsel or assist a witness to testify falsely, or offer an inducement to a witness that is prohibited by law;

(c) knowingly disobey an obligation under the rules of a tribunal, except for an open refusal based on an assertion that no valid obligation exists;

(d) in pretrial procedure, make a frivolous discovery request or fail to make a reasonably diligent effort to comply with a legally proper discovery request by an opposing party;

(e) in trial, allude to any matter that the lawyer does not reasonably believe is relevant or that will not be supported by admissible evidence, assert personal knowledge of facts in issue except when testifying as a witness, or state a personal opinion as to the justness of a cause, the credibility of a witness, the culpability of a civil litigant or the guilt or innocence of an accused; or

(f) request a person other than a client to refrain from voluntarily giving relevant information to another party unless:

(1) the person is a relative or an employee or other agent of a client; and

(2) the lawyer reasonably believes that the person's interests will not be adversely affected by refraining from giving such information.

[Adopted effective September 1, 1990. Amended effective October 1, 2005.]

Comment

[1] The procedure of the adversary system contemplates that the evidence in a case is to be marshaled competitively by the contending parties. Fair competition in the adversary system is secured by prohibitions against destruction or concealment of evidence, improperly influencing witnesses, obstructive tactics in discovery procedure, and the like.

[2] Documents and other items of evidence are often essential to establish a claim or defense. Subject to evidentiary privileges, the right of an opposing party, including the government, to obtain evidence through discovery or subpoena is an important procedural right. The exercise of that right can be frustrated if relevant material is altered, concealed or destroyed. Applicable law in many jurisdictions makes it an offense to destroy material for purposes of impairing its availability in a pending proceeding or one whose commencement can be foreseen. Falsifying evidence is also generally a criminal offense. Paragraph (a) applies to evidentiary material generally, including computerized information. A lawyer may take temporary possession of physical evidence of client crimes for the purpose of conducting a limited examination that will not alter or destroy material characteristics of the evidence or in any other manner alter or destroy the value of the evidence for possible use by the prosecution. In such a case, applicable law may require the lawyer to turn the evidence over to the police or other prosecuting authority, depending on the circumstances.

[3] With regard to paragraph (b), it is not improper to pay a witness's expenses or to compensate an expert witness on terms permitted by law. The common law rule in most jurisdictions is that it is improper to pay an occurrence witness any fee for testifying and that it is improper to pay an expert witness a contingent fee.

[4] Paragraph (f) permits a lawyer to advise employees of a client to refrain from giving information to another party, for the employees may identify their interests with those of the client. See also Rule 4.2.

RULE 3.5. IMPARTIALITY AND DECORUM OF THE TRIBUNAL

A lawyer shall not:

(a) seek to influence a judge, juror, member of the jury venire or other official by means prohibited by law;

(b) communicate ex parte with such a person during the proceeding unless authorized to do so by law or court order;

(c) communicate with a juror or member of the jury venire after discharge of the jury if:

(1) the communication is prohibited by law or court order;

(2) the juror has made known to the lawyer a desire not to communicate; or

(3) the communication involves misrepresentation, coercion, duress or harassment;

(d) engage in conduct intended to disrupt a tribunal; or

(e) participate in any judicial portrait fund or memorial except upon the following conditions:

(1) the soliciting entity shall be a law school or an established state, county or local bar organization or association which was not formed for the primary purpose of soliciting judicial portrait funds or memorials;

(2) except for an officer of the soliciting entity, no lawyer or judge other than the intended honoree shall be identified in any communication preparatory to the creation of, or during the solicitation for, the fund or memorial; and

(3) anonymity of donors shall be guaranteed, and any solicitation shall so state.

[Adopted and amended effective September 1, 1990. Amended effective October 1, 2005.]

Comment

[1] Many forms of improper influence upon a tribunal are proscribed by criminal law. Others are specified in the ABA Model Code of Judicial Conduct, with which an advocate should be familiar. A lawyer is required to avoid contributing to a violation of such provisions. The South Carolina version of paragraph (a) differs from the Model Rule in its reference to a "member of the jury venire" rather than "prospective juror" since any person technically could be the latter.

[2] During a proceeding a lawyer may not communicate ex parte with persons serving in an official capacity in the proceedings such as judges, masters or jurors, unless authorized to do so by law or court order.

[3] A lawyer may on occasion want to communicate with a juror or member of the jury venire after the jury has been discharged. The lawyer may do so unless the communication is prohibited by law or a court order but must respect the desire of the juror not to talk with the lawyer. The lawyer may not engage in improper conduct during the communication.

[4] The advocate's function is to present evidence and argument so that the cause may be decided according to law. Refraining from abusive or obstreperous conduct is a corollary of the advocate's right to speak on behalf of litigants. A lawyer may stand firm against abuse by a judge but should avoid reciprocation; the judge's default is no justification for similar dereliction by an advocate. An advocate can present the cause, protect the record for subsequent review and preserve professional integrity by patient firmness no less effectively than by belligerence or theatrics.

[5] The duty to refrain from disruptive conduct applies to any proceeding of a tribunal, including a deposition. See Rule 1.0(n) and Rule 3.3, Comment [1].

RULE 3.6. TRIAL PUBLICITY

(a) A lawyer who is participating or has participated in the investigation or litigation of a matter shall not make an extrajudicial statement that the lawyer knows or reasonably should know will be disseminated by means of public communication and will have a substantial likelihood of materially prejudicing an adjudicative proceeding in the matter.

(b) Notwithstanding paragraph (a), a lawyer may state:

(1) the claim, offense or defense involved and, except when prohibited by law, the identity of the persons involved;

(2) information contained in a public record;

(3) that an investigation of a matter is in progress;

(4) the scheduling or result of any step in litigation;

(5) a request for assistance in obtaining evidence and information necessary thereto;

(6) a warning of danger concerning the behavior of a person involved, when there is reason to believe that there exists the likelihood of substantial harm to an individual or to the public interest; and

(7) in a criminal case, in addition to subparagraphs (1) through (6):

(i) the identity, residence, occupation and family status of the accused;

(ii) if the accused has not been apprehended, information necessary to aid in apprehension of that person;

(iii) the fact, time and place of arrest; and

(iv) the identity of investigating and arresting officers or agencies and the length of the investigation.

(c) Notwithstanding paragraph (a), a lawyer may make a statement that a reasonable lawyer would believe is required to protect a client from the substantial undue prejudicial effect of recent publicity not initiated by the lawyer or the lawyer's client. A statement made pursuant to this paragraph shall be limited to such information as is necessary to mitigate the recent adverse publicity.

(d) No lawyer associated in a firm or government agency with a lawyer subject to paragraph (a) shall make a statement prohibited by paragraph (a).

[Adopted effective September 1, 1990. Amended effective May 8, 1996; October 1, 2005.]

Comment

[1] It is difficult to strike a balance between protecting the right to a fair trial and safeguarding the right of free expression. Preserving the right to a fair trial necessarily entails some curtailment of the information that may be disseminated about a party prior to trial, particularly where trial by jury is involved. If there were no such limits, the result would be the practical nullification of the protective effect of the rules of forensic decorum and the exclusionary rules of evidence. On the other hand, there are vital social interests served by the free dissemination of information about events having legal consequences and about legal proceedings themselves. The public has a right to know about threats to its safety and measures aimed at assuring its security. It also has a legitimate interest in the conduct of judicial proceedings, particularly in matters of general public concern. Furthermore, the subject matter of legal proceedings is often of direct significance in debate and deliberation over questions of public policy

[2] Special rules of confidentiality may validly govern proceedings in juvenile, domestic relations and mental disability proceedings, and perhaps other types of litigation. Rule 3.4(c) requires compliance with such rules.

[3] The Rule sets forth a basic general prohibition against a lawyer's making statements that the lawyer knows or should know will have a substantial likelihood of materially prejudicing an adjudicative proceeding. Recognizing that the public value of informed commentary is great and the likelihood of prejudice to a proceeding by the commentary of a lawyer who is not involved in the proceeding is small, the Rule applies only to lawyers who are, or who have been involved in the investigation or litigation of a case, and their associates.

[4] Paragraph (b) identifies specific matters about which a lawyer's statements would not ordinarily be considered to present a substantial likelihood of material prejudice, and should not in any event be considered prohibited by the general prohibition of paragraph (a). Paragraph (b) is not intended to be an exhaustive listing of the subjects upon which a lawyer may make a statement, but statements on other matters may be subject to paragraph (a).

[5] There are, on the other hand, certain subjects that are more likely than not to have a material prejudicial effect on a proceeding, particularly when they refer to a civil matter triable to a jury, a criminal matter, or any other proceeding that could result in incarceration. These subjects relate to:

(a) the character, credibility, reputation or criminal record of a party, suspect in a criminal investigation or witness, or the identity of a witness, or the expected testimony of a party or witness;

(b) in a criminal case or proceeding that could result in incarceration, the possibility of a plea of guilty to the offense or the existence or contents of any confession, admission, or statement given by a defendant or suspect or that person's refusal or failure to make a statement;

(c) the performance or results of any examination or test or the refusal or failure of a person to submit to an examination or test, or the identity or nature of physical evidence expected to be presented;

(d) any opinion as to the guilt or innocence of a defendant or suspect in a criminal case or proceeding that could result in incarceration;

(e) information that the lawyer knows or reasonably should know is likely to be inadmissible as evidence in a trial and that would, if disclosed, create a substantial risk of prejudicing an impartial trial; or

(f) the fact that a defendant has been charged with a crime, unless there is included therein a statement explaining that the charge is merely an accusation and that the defendant is presumed innocent until and unless proven guilty.

[6] Another relevant factor in determining prejudice is the nature of the proceeding involved. Criminal jury trials will be most sensitive to extrajudicial speech. Civil trials may be less sensitive. Non–jury hearings and arbitration proceedings may be even less affected. The Rule will still place limitations on prejudicial comments in these cases, but the likelihood of prejudice may be different depending on the type of proceeding.

[7] Finally, extrajudicial statements that might otherwise raise a question under this Rule may be permissible when they are made in response to statements made publicly by another party, another party's lawyer, or third persons, where a reasonable lawyer would believe a public response is required in order to avoid prejudice to the lawyer's client. When prejudicial statements have been publicly made by others, responsive statements may have the salutary effect of lessening any resulting adverse impact on the adjudicative proceeding. Such responsive statements should be limited to contain only such information as is necessary to mitigate undue prejudice created by the statements made by others.

[8] See Rule 3.8(f) for additional duties of prosecutors in connection with extrajudicial statements about criminal proceedings.

RULE 3.7. LAWYER AS WITNESS

(a) A lawyer shall not act as advocate at a trial in which the lawyer is likely to be a necessary witness unless:

(1) the testimony relates to an uncontested issue;

(2) the testimony relates to the nature and value of legal services rendered in the case; or

(3) disqualification of the lawyer would work substantial hardship on the client.

(b) A lawyer may act as advocate in a trial in which another lawyer in the lawyer's firm is likely to be called as a witness unless precluded from doing so by Rule 1.7 or Rule 1.9.

[Adopted effective September 1, 1990. Amended effective October 1, 2005.]

Comment

[1] Combining the roles of advocate and witness can prejudice the tribunal and the opposing party and can also involve a conflict of interest between the lawyer and client.

Advocate Witness Rule

[2] The tribunal has proper objection when the trier of fact may be confused or misled by a lawyer serving as both advocate and witness. The opposing party has proper objection where the combination of roles may prejudice that party's rights in the litigation. A witness is required to testify on the basis of personal knowledge, while an advocate is expected to explain and comment on evidence given by others. It may not be clear whether a statement by an advocate witness should be taken as proof or as an analysis of the proof.

[3] To protect the tribunal, paragraph (a) prohibits a lawyer from simultaneously serving as advocate and necessary witness except in those circumstances specified in paragraphs (a)(1) through (a)(3). Paragraph (a)(1) recognizes that if the testimony will be uncontested, the ambiguities in the dual role are purely theoretical. Paragraph (a)(2) recognizes that where the testimony concerns the extent and value of legal services rendered in the action in which the testimony is offered, permitting the lawyers to testify avoids the need for a second trial with new counsel to resolve that issue. Moreover, in such a situation the judge has firsthand knowledge of the matter in issue; hence, there is less dependence on the adversary process to test the credibility of the testimony.

[4] Apart from these two exceptions, paragraph (a)(3) recognizes that a balancing is required between the interests of the client and those of the tribunal and the opposing party. Whether the tribunal is likely to be misled or the opposing party is likely to suffer prejudice depends on the nature of the

case, the importance and probable tenor of the lawyer's testimony, and the probability that the lawyer's testimony will conflict with that of other witnesses. Even if there is risk of such prejudice, in determining whether the lawyer should be disqualified, due regard must be given to the effect of disqualification on the lawyer's client. It is relevant that one or both parties could reasonably foresee that the lawyer would probably be a witness. The conflict of interest principles stated in Rules 1.7, 1.9 and 1.10 have no application to this aspect of the problem.

[5] Because the tribunal is not likely to be misled when a lawyer acts as advocate in a trial in which another lawyer in the lawyer's firm will testify as a necessary witness, paragraph (b) permits the lawyer to do so except in situations involving a conflict of interest.

Conflict of Interest

[6] In determining if it is permissible to act as advocate in a trial in which the lawyer will be a necessary witness, the lawyer must also consider that the dual role may give rise to a conflict of interest that will require compliance with Rules 1.7 or 1.9. For example, if there is likely to be substantial conflict between the testimony of the client and that of the lawyer, the representation involves a conflict of interest that requires compliance with Rule 1.7. This would be true even though the lawyer might not be prohibited by paragraph (a) from simultaneously serving as advocate and witness because the lawyer's disqualification would work a substantial hardship on the client. Similarly, a lawyer who might be permitted to simultaneously serve as an advocate and a witness by paragraph (a)(3) might be precluded from doing so by Rule 1.9. The problem can arise whether the lawyer is called as a witness on behalf of the client or is called by the opposing party. Determining whether or not such a conflict exists is primarily the responsibility of the lawyer involved. If there is a conflict of interest, the lawyer must secure the client's informed consent, confirmed in writing. In some cases the lawyer will be precluded from seeking the client's consent. See Rule 1.7. See Rule 1.0(b) for the definition of "confirmed in writing" and Rule 1.0(g) for the definition of "informed consent."

[7] Paragraph (b) provides that a lawyer is not disqualified from serving as an advocate because a lawyer with whom the lawyer is associated in a firm is precluded from doing so by paragraph (a). If, however, the testifying lawyer would also be disqualified by Rule 1.7 or Rule 1.9 from representing the client in the matter, other lawyers in the firm will be precluded from representing the client by Rule 1.10 unless the client gives informed consent under the conditions stated in Rule 1.7.

RULE 3.8. SPECIAL RESPONSIBILITIES OF A PROSECUTOR

The prosecutor in a criminal case shall:

(a) refrain from prosecuting a charge that the prosecutor knows is not supported by probable cause;

(b) make reasonable efforts to assure that the accused has been advised of the right to, and the procedure for obtaining, counsel and has been given reasonable opportunity to obtain counsel;

(c) not seek to obtain from an unrepresented accused a waiver of important pretrial rights, such as the right to a preliminary hearing;

(d) make timely disclosure to the defense of all evidence or information known to the prosecutor that tends to negate the guilt of the accused or mitigates the offense, and, in connection with sentencing, disclose to the defense and to the tribunal all unprivileged mitigating information known to the prosecutor, except when the prosecutor is relieved of this responsibility by a protective order of the tribunal;

(e) not subpoena a lawyer in a grand jury or other criminal proceeding to present evidence about a past or present client unless the prosecutor reasonably believes:

(1) the information sought is not protected from disclosure by any applicable privilege;

(2) the evidence sought is essential to the successful completion of an ongoing investigation or prosecution; and

(3) there is no other feasible alternative to obtain the information;

(f) except for statements that are necessary to inform the public of the nature and extent of the prosecutor's action and that serve a legitimate law enforcement purpose, refrain from making extrajudicial comments that have a substantial likelihood of heightening public condemnation of the accused and exercise reasonable care to prevent investigators, law enforcement personnel, employees or other persons assisting or associated with the prosecutor in a criminal case from making an extrajudicial statement that the prosecutor would be prohibited from making under Rule 3.6 or this Rule.

[Adopted effective September 1, 1990. Amended effective May 8, 1996; October 1, 2005; December 1, 2005.]

Comment

[1] A prosecutor has the responsibility of a minister of justice and not simply that of an advocate. This responsibility carries with it specific obligations to see that the defendant is accorded procedural justice and that guilt is decided upon the basis of sufficient evidence. Precisely how far the prosecutor is required to go in this direction is a matter of debate and varies in different jurisdictions. Many jurisdictions have adopted the ABA Standards of Criminal Justice Relating to the Prosecution Function, which in turn are the product of prolonged and careful deliberation by lawyers experienced in both criminal prosecution and defense. Applicable law may require other measures by the prosecutor and knowing disregard of those obligations or a systematic abuse of prosecutorial discretion could constitute a violation of Rule 8.4.

[2] In some jurisdictions, a defendant may waive a preliminary hearing and thereby lose a valuable opportunity to challenge probable cause. Accordingly, prosecutors should not seek to obtain waivers of preliminary hearings or other important pretrial rights from unrepresented accused persons. Paragraph (c) does not apply, however, to an accused appearing *pro se* with the approval of the tribunal. Nor does it forbid the lawful questioning of a suspect who has knowingly waived the rights to counsel and silence.

[3] The exception in paragraph (d) recognizes that a prosecutor may seek an appropriate protective order from the tribunal if disclosure of information to the defense could result in substantial harm to an individual or to the public interest.

[4] Paragraph (e) is intended to limit the issuance of lawyer subpoenas in grand jury and other criminal proceedings to those situations in which there is a genuine need to intrude into the client lawyer relationship.

[5] Paragraph (f) supplements Rule 3.6, which prohibits extrajudicial statements that have a substantial likelihood of prejudicing an adjudicatory proceeding. In the context of a criminal prosecution, a prosecutor's extrajudicial statement can create the additional problem of increasing public condemnation of the accused. Although the announcement of an indictment, for example, will necessarily have severe consequences for the accused, a prosecutor can, and should, avoid comments which have no legitimate law enforcement purpose and have a substantial likelihood of increasing public opprobrium of the accused. Nothing in this Comment is intended to restrict the statements which a prosecutor may make which comply with Rule 3.6(b) or 3.6(c).

[6] Like other lawyers, prosecutors are subject to Rules 5.1 and 5.3, which relate to responsibilities regarding lawyers and nonlawyers who work for or are associated with the lawyer's office. Paragraph (f) reminds the prosecutor of the importance of these obligations in connection with the unique dangers of improper extrajudicial statements in a criminal case. In addition, paragraph (f) requires a prosecutor to exercise reasonable care to prevent persons assisting or associated with the prosecutor from making improper extrajudicial statements, even when such persons are not under the direct supervision of the prosecutor. Ordinarily, the reasonable care standard will be satisfied if the prosecutor issues the appropriate cautions to law-enforcement personnel and other relevant individuals.

RULE 3.9. ADVOCATE IN NONADJUDICATIVE PROCEEDINGS

A lawyer representing a client before a legislative body or administrative agency in a nonadjudicative proceeding shall disclose that the appearance is in a representative capacity and shall conform to the provisions of Rules 3.3(a) through (c), 3.4(a) through (c), and 3.5.

[Adopted effective September 1, 1990. Amended effective October 1, 2005.]

Comment

[1] In representation before bodies such as legislatures, municipal councils, and executive and administrative agencies acting in a rule making or policy making capacity, lawyers present facts, formulate issues and advance argument to the matters under consideration. The decision making body, like a court, should be able to rely on the integrity of the submissions made to it. A lawyer appearing before such a body must deal with it honestly and in conformity with applicable rules of procedure. See Rules 3.3(a) through (c), 3.4(a) through (c) and 3.5.

[2] Lawyers have no exclusive right to appear before nonadjudicative bodies, as they do before a court. The requirements of this Rule therefore may subject lawyers to regulations inapplicable to advocates who are not lawyers. However, legislatures and administrative agencies have a right to expect lawyers to deal with them as they deal with courts.

[3] This Rule only applies when a lawyer represents a client in connection with an official hearing or meeting of a governmental agency or a legislative body to which the lawyer or the lawyer's client is presenting evidence or argument. It does not apply to representation of a client in a negotiation or other bilateral transaction with a governmental agency or in connection with an application for a license or other privilege or the client's compliance with generally applicable reporting requirements, such as the filing of income tax returns. Nor does it apply to the representation of a client in connection with an investigation or examination of the client's affairs conducted by government investigators or examiners. Representation in such matters is governed by Rules 4.1 through 4.4.

TRANSACTIONS WITH PERSONS OTHER THAN CLIENTS

RULE 4.1. TRUTHFULNESS IN STATEMENTS TO OTHERS

In the course of representing a client a lawyer shall not knowingly:

(a) make a false statement of material fact or law to a third person; or

(b) fail to disclose a material fact when disclosure is necessary to avoid assisting a criminal or fraudulent act by a client, unless disclosure is prohibited by Rule 1.6.

[Adopted effective September 1, 1990. Amended effective October 1, 2005.]

Comment

Misrepresentation

[1] A lawyer is required to be truthful when dealing with others on a client's behalf, but generally has no affirmative duty to inform an opposing party of relevant facts. A misrepresentation can occur if the lawyer incorporates or affirms a statement of another person that the lawyer knows is false. Misrepresentations can also occur by partially true but misleading statements or omissions that are the equivalent of affirmative false statements. For dishonest conduct that does not amount to a false statement or for misrepresentations by a lawyer other than in the course of representing a client, see Rule 8.4.

[2] A government lawyer involved with or supervising a law enforcement investigation or operation does not violate this rule as a result of the use, by law enforcement personnel or others, of false identifications, backgrounds and other information for purposes of the investigation or operation.

Statements of Fact

[3] This Rule refers to statements of fact. Whether a particular statement should be regarded as one of fact can depend on the circumstances. Under generally accepted conventions in negotiation, certain types of statements ordinarily are not taken as statements of material fact. Estimates of price or value placed on the subject of a transaction and a party's intentions as to an acceptable settlement of a

claim are ordinarily in this category, and so is the existence of an undisclosed principal except where nondisclosure of the principal would constitute fraud. Lawyers should be mindful of their obligations under applicable law to avoid criminal and tortious misrepresentation.

Crime or Fraud by Client

[4] Under Rule 1.2(d), a lawyer is prohibited from counseling or assisting a client in conduct that the lawyer knows is criminal or fraudulent. Paragraph (b) states a specific application of the principle set forth in Rule 1.2(d) and addresses the situation where a client's crime or fraud takes the form of a lie or misrepresentation. Ordinarily, a lawyer can avoid assisting a client's crime or fraud by withdrawing from the representation. Sometimes it may be necessary for the lawyer to give notice of the fact of withdrawal and to disaffirm an opinion, document, affirmation or the like. In extreme cases, substantive law may require a lawyer to disclose information relating to the representation to avoid being deemed to have assisted the client's crime or fraud. If the lawyer can avoid assisting a client's crime or fraud only by disclosing this information, then under paragraph (b) the lawyer is required to do so unless the disclosure is prohibited by Rule 1.6.

RULE 4.2. COMMUNICATION WITH PERSON REPRESENTED BY COUNSEL

In representing a client, a lawyer shall not communicate about the subject of the representation with a person the lawyer knows to be represented by another lawyer in the matter unless the lawyer has the consent of the other lawyer or is authorized to do so by law or a court order.

[Adopted effective September 1, 1990. Amended effective October 1, 2005.]

Comment

[1] This Rule contributes to the proper functioning of the legal system by protecting a person who has chosen to be represented by a lawyer in a matter against possible overreaching by other lawyers who are participating in the matter, interference by those lawyers with the client lawyer relationship and the uncounselled disclosure of information relating to the representation.

[2] This Rule applies to communications with any person who is represented by counsel concerning the matter to which the communication relates.

[3] The Rule applies even though to represented person initiates or consents to the communication. A lawyer must immediately terminate communication with a person if, after commencing communication, the lawyer learns that the person is one with whom communication is not permitted by this Rule.

[4] This Rule does not prohibit communication with a represented person, or an employee or agent of such a person, concerning matters outside the representation. For example, the existence of a controversy between a government agency and a private party, or between two organizations, does not prohibit a lawyer for either from communicating with nonlawyer representatives of the other regarding a separate matter. Nor does this Rule preclude communication with a represented person who is seeking advice from a lawyer who is not otherwise representing a client in the matter without consent from or notice to the original lawyer. A lawyer may not make a communication prohibited by this Rule through the acts of another. See Rule 8.4(a). Parties to a matter may communicate directly with each other, and a lawyer is not prohibited from advising a client concerning a communication that the client is legally entitled to make. Also, a lawyer having independent justification or legal authorization for communicating with a represented person is permitted to do so including giving a second professional opinion without consent from or notice to the original lawyer.

[5] Communications authorized by law may include communications by a lawyer on behalf of a client who is exercising a constitutional or other legal right to communicate with the government. Communications authorized by law may also include investigative activities of lawyers representing governmental entities, directly or through investigative agents, prior to the commencement of criminal or civil enforcement proceedings. When communicating with the accused in a criminal matter, a government lawyer must comply with this Rule in addition to honoring the constitutional rights of the accused. The fact that a communication does not violate a state or federal constitutional right is insufficient to establish that the communication is permissible under this Rule.

[6] A lawyer who is uncertain whether a communication with a represented person is permissible may seek a court order. A lawyer may also seek a court order in exceptional circumstances to authorize a communication that would otherwise be prohibited by this Rule, for example, where communication with a person represented by counsel is necessary to avoid reasonably certain injury.

[7] In the case of a represented organization, this Rule prohibits communications with a constituent of the organization who supervises, directs or regularly consults with the organization's lawyer concerning the matter or has authority to obligate the organization with respect to the matter or whose act or omission in connection with the matter may be imputed to the organization for purposes of civil or criminal liability. Consent of the organization's lawyer is not required for communication with a former constituent. If a constituent of the organization is represented in the matter by his or her own counsel, the consent by that counsel to a communication will be sufficient for purposes of this Rule. Compare Rule 3.4(f). In communicating with a current or former constituent of an organization, a lawyer must not use methods of obtaining evidence that violate the legal rights of the organization. See Rule 4.4, Comment [2].

[8] The prohibition on communications with a represented person only applies in circumstances where the lawyer knows that the person is in fact represented in the matter to be discussed. This means that the lawyer has actual knowledge of the fact of the representation; but such actual knowledge may be inferred from the circumstances. See Rule 1.0(g). Thus, the lawyer cannot evade the requirement of obtaining the consent of counsel by closing eyes to the obvious.

[9] In the event the person with whom the lawyer communicates is not known to be represented by counsel in the matter, the lawyer's communications are subject to Rule 4.3.

RULE 4.3. DEALING WITH UNREPRESENTED PERSON

In dealing on behalf of a client with a person who is not represented by counsel, a lawyer shall not state or imply that the lawyer is disinterested. When the lawyer knows or reasonably should know that the unrepresented person misunderstands the lawyer's role in the matter, the lawyer shall make reasonable efforts to correct the misunderstanding. The lawyer shall not give legal advice to an unrepresented person, other than the advice to secure counsel, if the lawyer knows or reasonably should know that the interests of such a person are or have a reasonable possibility of being in conflict with the interests of the client.

[Adopted effective September 1, 1990. Amended effective October 1, 2005.]

Comment

[1] An unrepresented person, particularly one not experienced in dealing with legal matters, might assume that a lawyer is disinterested in loyalties or is a disinterested authority on the law even when the lawyer represents a client. In order to avoid a misunderstanding, a lawyer will typically need to identify the lawyer's client and, where necessary, explain that the client has interests opposed to those of the unrepresented person. For misunderstandings that sometimes arise when a lawyer for an organization deals with an unrepresented constituent, see Rule 1.13(d).

[2] The Rule distinguishes between situations involving unrepresented persons whose interests may be adverse to those of the lawyer's client and those to which the person's interests are not in conflict with the client's. In the former situation, the possibility that the lawyer will compromise the unrepresented person's interests is so great that the Rule prohibits the giving of any advice, apart from the advice to obtain counsel. Whether a lawyer is giving impermissible advice may depend on the experience and sophistication of the unrepresented person, as well as the setting in which the behavior and comments occur. This Rule does not prohibit a lawyer from negotiating the terms of a transaction or settling a dispute with an unrepresented person. So long as the lawyer has explained that the lawyer represents an adverse party and is not representing the person, the lawyer may inform the person of the terms on which the lawyer's client will enter into an agreement or settle a matter, prepare documents that require the person's signature and explain the lawyer's own view of the meaning of the document or the lawyer's view of the underlying legal obligations.

RULE 4.4. RESPECT FOR RIGHTS OF THIRD PERSONS

(a) In representing a client, a lawyer shall not use means that have no substantial purpose other than to embarrass, delay, or burden a third person, or use methods of obtaining evidence that violate the legal rights of such a person.

(b) A lawyer who receives a document relating to the representation of the lawyer's client and knows or reasonably should know that the document was inadvertently sent shall promptly notify the sender.

[Adopted effective September 1, 1990. Amended effective October 1, 2005.]

Comment

[1] Responsibility to a client requires a lawyer to subordinate the interests of others to those of the client, but that responsibility does not imply that a lawyer may disregard the rights of third persons. It is impractical to catalogue all such rights, but they include legal restrictions on methods of obtaining evidence from third persons and unwarranted intrusions into privileged relationships, such as the client lawyer relationship.

[2] Paragraph (b) recognizes that lawyers sometimes receive documents that were mistakenly sent or produced by opposing parties or their lawyers. If a lawyer knows or reasonably should know that a such a document was sent inadvertently, then this Rule requires the lawyer to promptly notify the sender in order to permit that person to take protective measures. Whether the lawyer is required to take additional steps, such as returning the original document, is a matter of law beyond the scope of these Rules, as is the question of whether the privileged status of a document has been waived. Similarly, this Rule does not address the legal duties of a lawyer who receives a document that the lawyer knows or reasonably should know may have been wrongfully obtained by the sending person. For purposes of this Rule, "document" includes e mail or other electronic modes of transmission subject to being read or put into readable form.

[3] Some lawyers may choose to return a document unread, for example, when the lawyer learns before receiving the document that it was inadvertently sent to the wrong address. Where a lawyer is not required by applicable law to do so, the decision to voluntarily return such a document is a matter of professional judgment ordinarily reserved to the lawyer. See Rules 1.2 and 1.4.

RULE 4.5. THREATENING CRIMINAL PROSECUTION

A lawyer shall not present, participate in presenting, or threaten to present criminal or professional disciplinary charges solely to obtain an advantage in a civil matter.

[Adopted effective September 1, 1990. Amended effective October 1, 2005.]

Comment

This Rule is not included in the Model Rules of Professional Conduct. The language of this Rule is based upon DR 7 105 of the Code of Professional Responsibility.

LAW FIRMS AND ASSOCIATIONS

RULE 5.1. RESPONSIBILITIES OF PARTNERS, MANAGERS, AND SUPERVISORY LAWYERS

(a) A partner in a law firm, and a lawyer who individually or together with other lawyers possesses comparable managerial authority in a law firm, shall make reasonable efforts to ensure that the firm has in effect measures giving reasonable assurance that all lawyers in the firm conform to the Rules of Professional Conduct.

(b) A lawyer having direct supervisory authority over another lawyer shall make reasonable efforts to ensure that the other lawyer conforms to the Rules of Professional Conduct.

(c) A lawyer shall be responsible for another lawyer's violation of the Rules of Professional Conduct if:

(1) the lawyer orders or, with knowledge of the specific conduct, ratifies the conduct involved; or

(2) the lawyer is a partner or has comparable managerial authority in the law firm in which the other lawyer practices, or has direct supervisory authority over the other lawyer, and knows of the conduct at a time when its consequences can be avoided or mitigated but fails to take reasonable remedial action.

[Adopted effective September 1, 1990. Amended effective October 1, 2005.]

Comment

[1] Paragraph (a) applies to lawyers who have managerial authority over the professional work of a firm. See Rule 1.0(d). This includes members of a partnership, the shareholders in a law firm organized as a professional corporation, and members of other associations authorized to practice law; lawyers having comparable managerial authority in a legal services organization or a law department of an enterprise or government agency; and lawyers who have intermediate managerial responsibilities in a firm. Paragraph (b) applies to lawyers who have supervisory authority over the work of other lawyers in a firm.

[2] Paragraph (a) requires lawyers with managerial authority within a firm to make reasonable efforts to establish internal policies and procedures designed to provide reasonable assurance that all lawyers in the firm will conform to the Rules of Professional Conduct. Such policies and procedures include those designed to detect and resolve conflicts of interest, identify dates by which actions must be taken in pending matters, account for client funds and property and ensure that inexperienced lawyers are properly supervised.

[3] Other measures that may be required to fulfill the responsibility prescribed in paragraph (a) can depend on the firm's structure and the nature of its practice. In a small firm of experienced lawyers, informal supervision and periodic review of compliance with the required systems ordinarily will suffice. In a large firm, or in practice situations in which difficult ethical problems frequently arise, more elaborate measures may be necessary. Some firms, for example, have a procedure whereby junior lawyers can make confidential referral of ethical problems directly to a designated senior partner or special committee. See Rule 5.2. Firms, whether large or small, may also rely on continuing legal education in professional ethics. In any event, the ethical atmosphere of a firm can influence the conduct of all its members and the partners may not assume that all lawyers associated with the firm will inevitably conform to the Rules.

[4] Paragraph (c) expresses a general principle of personal responsibility for acts of another. See also Rule 8.4(a).

[5] Paragraph (c)(2) defines the duty of a partner or other lawyer having comparable managerial authority in a law firm, as well as a lawyer who has direct supervisory authority over performance of specific legal work by another lawyer. Whether a lawyer has supervisory authority in particular circumstances is a question of fact. Partners and lawyers with comparable authority have at least indirect responsibility for all work being done by the firm, while a partner or manager in charge of a particular matter ordinarily also has supervisory responsibility for the work of other firm lawyers engaged in the matter. Appropriate remedial action by a partner or managing lawyer would depend on the immediacy of that lawyer's involvement and the seriousness of the misconduct. A supervisor is required to intervene to prevent avoidable consequences of misconduct if the supervisor knows that the misconduct occurred. Thus, if a supervising lawyer knows that a subordinate misrepresented a matter to an opposing party in negotiation, the supervisor as well as the subordinate has a duty to correct the resulting misapprehension.

[6] Professional misconduct by a lawyer under supervision could reveal a violation of paragraph (b) on the part of the supervisory lawyer even though it does not entail a violation of paragraph (c) because there was no direction, ratification or knowledge of the violation.

[7] Apart from this Rule and Rule 8.4(a), a lawyer does not have disciplinary liability for the conduct of a partner, associate or subordinate. Whether a lawyer may be liable civilly or criminally for another lawyer's conduct is a question of law beyond the scope of these Rules.

[8] The duties imposed by this Rule on managing and supervising lawyers do not alter the personal duty of each lawyer in a firm to abide by the Rules of Professional Conduct. See Rule 5.2.(a).

RULE 5.2. RESPONSIBILITIES OF A SUBORDINATE LAWYER

(a) A lawyer is bound by the Rules of Professional Conduct notwithstanding that the lawyer acted at the direction of another person.

(b) A subordinate lawyer does not violate the Rules of Professional Conduct if that lawyer acts in accordance with a supervisory lawyer's reasonable resolution of an arguable question of professional duty.

[Adopted effective September 1, 1990. Amended effective October 1, 2005.]

Comment

[1] Although a lawyer is not relieved of responsibility for a violation by the fact that the lawyer acted at the direction of a supervisor, that fact may be relevant in determining whether a lawyer had the knowledge required to render conduct a violation of the Rules. For example, if a subordinate filed a frivolous pleading at the direction of a supervisor, the subordinate would not be guilty of a professional violation unless the subordinate knew of the document's frivolous character.

[2] When lawyers in a supervisor-subordinate relationship encounter a matter involving professional judgment as to ethical duty, the supervisor may assume responsibility for making the judgment. Otherwise, a consistent course of action or position could not be taken. If the question can reasonably be answered only one way, the duty of both lawyers is clear and they are equally responsible for fulfilling it. However, if the question is reasonably arguable, someone has to decide upon the course of action. That authority ordinarily reposes in the supervisor, and a subordinate may be guided accordingly. For example, if a question arises wheth-

er the interests of two clients conflict under Rule 1.7, the supervisor's reasonable resolution of the question should protect the subordinate professionally if the resolution is subsequently challenged.

RULE 5.3. RESPONSIBILITIES REGARDING NONLAWYER ASSISTANTS

With respect to a nonlawyer employed or retained by or associated with a lawyer:

(a) a partner, and a lawyer who individually or together with other lawyers possesses comparable managerial authority in a law firm shall make reasonable efforts to ensure that the firm has in effect measures giving reasonable assurance that the person's conduct is compatible with the professional obligations of the lawyer;

(b) a lawyer having direct supervisory authority over the nonlawyer shall make reasonable efforts to ensure that the person's conduct is compatible with the professional obligations of the lawyer; and

(c) a lawyer shall be responsible for conduct of such a person that would be a violation of the Rules of Professional Conduct if engaged in by a lawyer if:

(1) the lawyer orders or, with the knowledge of the specific conduct, ratifies the conduct involved; or

(2) the lawyer is a partner or has comparable managerial authority in the law firm in which the person is employed, or has direct supervisory authority over the person, and knows of the conduct at a time when its consequences can be avoided or mitigated but fails to take reasonable remedial action.

[Adopted effective September 1, 1990. Amended effective October 1, 2005.]

Comment

[1] Lawyers generally employ assistants in their practice, including secretaries, investigators, law student interns, and paraprofessionals. Such assistants, whether employees or independent contractors, act for the lawyer in rendition of the lawyer's professional services. A lawyer must give such assistants appropriate instruction and supervision concerning the ethical aspects of their employment, particularly regarding the obligation not to disclose information relating to representation of the client, and should be responsible for their work product. The measures employed in supervising nonlawyers should take account of the fact that they do not have legal training and are not subject to professional discipline.

[2] Paragraph (a) requires lawyers with managerial authority within a law firm to make reasonable efforts to establish internal policies and procedures designed to provide reasonable assurance that nonlawyers in the firm will act in a way compatible with the Rules of Professional Conduct. See Comment [1] to Rule 5.1. Paragraph (b) applies to lawyers who have supervisory authority over the work of a nonlawyer. Paragraph (c) specifies the circumstances in which a lawyer is responsible for conduct of a nonlawyer that would be a violation of the Rules of Professional conduct if engaged in by a lawyer.

RULE 5.4. PROFESSIONAL INDEPENDENCE OF A LAWYER

(a) A lawyer or law firm shall not share legal fees with a nonlawyer, except that:

(1) an agreement by a lawyer with the lawyer's firm, partner, or associate may provide for the payment of money, over a reasonable period of time after the lawyer's death, to the lawyer's estate or to one or more specified persons;

(2) a lawyer who undertakes to complete unfinished legal business of a deceased lawyer may pay to the estate of the deceased lawyer that proportion of the total compensation which fairly represents the services rendered by the deceased lawyer;

(3) a lawyer who purchases the practice of a deceased, disabled, or disappeared lawyer may, pursuant to the provision of Rule 1.17, pay to the estate or other representative of that lawyer the agreed-upon purchase price;

(4) a lawyer or a law firm may include nonlawyer employees in a compensation or retirement plan, even though the plan is based in whole or in part on a profit-sharing arrangement.

(b) A lawyer shall not form a partnership with a nonlawyer if any of the activities of the partnership consist of the practice of law.

(c) A lawyer shall not permit a person who recommends, employs, or pays the lawyer to render legal services for another to direct or regulate the lawyer's professional judgment in rendering such legal services.

(d) A lawyer shall not practice with or in the form of a professional corporation or association authorized to practice law for a profit, if:

(1) a nonlawyer owns any interest therein, except that a fiduciary representative of the estate or trust of a lawyer may hold the stock or interest of the lawyer for a reasonable time during settlement or administration;

(2) a nonlawyer is a corporate director or officer thereof or occupies a position of similar responsibility in any form of association other than a corporation; or

(3) a nonlawyer has the right to direct or control the professional judgment of a lawyer.

[Adopted effective September 1, 1990. Amended effective October 1, 2005.]

Comment

[1] The provisions of this Rule express traditional limitations on sharing fees. These limitations are to protect the lawyer's professional independence of judgment. Where someone other than the client pays the lawyer's fee or salary, or recommends employment of the lawyer, that arrangement does not modify the lawyer's obligation to the client. As

stated in paragraph (c), such arrangements should not interfere with the lawyer's professional judgment.

[2] This Rule also expresses traditional limitations on permitting a third party to direct or regulate the lawyer's professional judgment in rendering legal services to another. See also Rule 1.8(f)(lawyer may accept compensation from a third party as long as there is no interference with the lawyer's independent professional judgment and the client gives informed consent).

RULE 5.5. UNAUTHORIZED PRACTICE OF LAW; MULTIJURISDICTIONAL PRACTICE OF LAW

(a) A lawyer shall not practice law in a jurisdiction in violation of the regulation of the legal profession in that jurisdiction or assist another in doing so.

(b) A lawyer who is not admitted to practice in this jurisdiction shall not:

(1) except as authorized by these Rules or other law, establish an office or other systematic and continuous presence in this jurisdiction for the practice of law; or

(2) hold out to the public or otherwise represent that the lawyer is admitted to practice law in this jurisdiction.

(c) A lawyer admitted in another United States jurisdiction, and not disbarred or suspended from practice in any jurisdiction, may provide legal services on a temporary basis in this jurisdiction that:

(1) are undertaken in association with a lawyer who is admitted to practice in this jurisdiction and who actively participates in the matter;

(2) are in or reasonably related to a pending or potential proceeding before a tribunal in this or another jurisdiction, if the lawyer, or a person the lawyer is assisting, is authorized by law or order to appear in such proceeding or reasonably expects to be so authorized;

(3) are in or reasonably related to a pending or potential arbitration, mediation, or other alternative dispute resolution proceeding in this or another jurisdiction, if the services arise out of or are reasonably related to the lawyer's representation of an existing client in a jurisdiction in which the lawyer is admitted to practice and are not services for which the forum requires pro hac vice admission; or

(4) are not within paragraph (c)(2) or (c)(3) and arise out of or are reasonably related to the lawyer's representation of an existing client in a jurisdiction in which the lawyer is admitted to practice.

(d) A lawyer admitted in another United States jurisdiction, and not disbarred or suspended from practice in any jurisdiction, may provide legal services in this jurisdiction that:

(1) are provided to the lawyer's employer or its organizational affiliates and are not services for which the forum requires pro hac vice admission; or

(2) are services that the lawyer is authorized to provide by federal law or other law of this jurisdiction.

[Adopted effective September 1, 1990. Amended effective October 1, 2005.]

Comment

[1] A lawyer may practice law only in a jurisdiction in which the lawyer is authorized to practice. A lawyer may be admitted to practice law in a jurisdiction on a regular basis or may be authorized by court rule or order or by law to practice for a limited purpose or on a restricted basis. Paragraph (a) applies to unauthorized practice of law by a lawyer, whether through the lawyer's direct action or by the lawyer assisting another person.

[2] The definition of the practice of law is established by law and varies from one jurisdiction to another. Whatever the definition, limiting the practice of law to members of the bar protects the public against rendition of legal services by unqualified persons. This Rule does not prohibit a lawyer from employing the services of paraprofessionals and delegating functions to them, so long as the lawyer supervises the delegated work and retains responsibility for their work. See Rule 5.3.

[3] A lawyer may provide professional advice and instruction to nonlawyers whose employment requires knowledge of the law; for example, claims adjusters, employees of financial or commercial institutions, social workers, accountants and persons employed in government agencies. Lawyers also may assist independent nonlawyers, such as paraprofessionals, who are authorized by the law of a jurisdiction to provide particular law-related services. In addition, a lawyer may counsel nonlawyers who wish to proceed pro se.

[4] Other than as authorized by law or this Rule, a lawyer who is not admitted to practice generally in this jurisdiction violates paragraph (b) if the lawyer establishes an office or other systematic and continuous presence in this jurisdiction for the practice of law. Presence may be systematic and continuous even if the lawyer is not physically present here. Such a lawyer must not hold out to the public or otherwise represent that the lawyer is admitted to practice law in this jurisdiction. See also Rules 7.1(a) and 7.5(b).

[5] There are occasions in which a lawyer admitted to practice in another United States jurisdiction, and not disbarred or suspended from practice in any jurisdiction, may provide legal services on a temporary basis in this jurisdiction under circumstances that do not create an unreasonable risk to the interests of their clients, the public or the courts. Paragraph (c) identifies four such circumstances. The fact that conduct is not so identified does not imply that the conduct is or is not authorized. With the exception of paragraphs (d)(1) and (d)(2), the Rule does not authorize a lawyer to establish an office or other systematic and continuous presence in this jurisdiction without being admitted to practice generally here.

[6] There is no single test to determine whether a lawyer's services are provided on a "temporary basis" in this jurisdiction, and may therefore be permissible under paragraph (c). Services may be "temporary" even though the lawyer provides services in this jurisdiction on a recurring basis, or for an extended period of time, as when the lawyer is representing a client in a single lengthy negotiation or litigation.

[7] Paragraphs (c) and (d) apply to lawyers who are admitted to practice law in any United States jurisdiction,

which includes the District of Columbia and any state, territory or commonwealth of the United States. The word "admitted" in paragraph (c) contemplates that the lawyer is authorized to practice in the jurisdiction in which the lawyer is admitted and excludes a lawyer who while technically admitted is not authorized to practice, because, for example, the lawyer is on inactive status.

[8] Paragraph (c)(1) recognizes that the interests of clients and the public are protected if a lawyer admitted only in another jurisdiction associates with a lawyer licensed to practice in this jurisdiction. For this paragraph to apply, however, the lawyer admitted to practice in this jurisdiction must actively participate in and share responsibility for the representation of the client.

[9] Lawyers not admitted to practice generally in a jurisdiction may be authorized by law or order of a tribunal or an administrative agency to appear before the tribunal or agency. This authority may be granted pursuant to formal rules governing admission pro hac vice or pursuant to informal practice of the tribunal or agency. Under paragraph (c)(2), a lawyer does not violate this Rule when the lawyer appears before a tribunal or agency pursuant to such authority. To the extent that a court rule or other law of this jurisdiction requires a lawyer who is not admitted to practice in this jurisdiction to obtain admission pro hac vice before appearing before a tribunal or administrative agency, this Rule requires the lawyer to obtain that authority.

[10] Paragraph (c)(2) also provides that a lawyer rendering services in this jurisdiction on a temporary basis does not violate this Rule when the lawyer engages in conduct in anticipation of a proceeding or hearing in a jurisdiction in which the lawyer is authorized to practice law or in which the lawyer reasonably expects to be admitted pro hac vice. Examples of such conduct include meetings with the client, interviews of potential witnesses, and the review of documents. Similarly, a lawyer admitted only in another jurisdiction may engage in conduct temporarily in this jurisdiction in connection with pending litigation in another jurisdiction in which the lawyer is or reasonably expects to be authorized to appear, including taking depositions in this jurisdiction.

[11] When a lawyer has been or reasonably expects to be admitted to appear before a court or administrative agency, paragraph (c)(2) also permits conduct by lawyers who are associated with that lawyer in the matter, but who do not expect to appear before the court or administrative agency. For example, subordinate lawyers may conduct research, review documents, and attend meetings with witnesses in support of the lawyer responsible for the litigation.

[12] Paragraph (c)(3) permits a lawyer admitted to practice law in another jurisdiction to perform services on a temporary basis in this jurisdiction if those services are in or reasonably related to a pending or potential arbitration, mediation, or other alternative dispute resolution proceeding in this or another jurisdiction, if the services arise out of or are reasonably related to the lawyer's pre-existing representation of a client in a jurisdiction in which the lawyer is admitted to practice. The lawyer, however, must obtain admission pro hac vice in the case of a court-annexed arbitration or mediation or otherwise if court rules or law so require. For the purposes of this rule, a lawyer who is not admitted to practice in South Carolina who seeks to provide legal services pursuant to Rule 5.5(c)(3) in more than three matters in a 365–day period shall be presumed to be providing legal services on a regular, not temporary, basis. A lawyer providing legal services pursuant to paragraph (c)(3) must comply with the requirements of Rule 404, SCACR.

[13] Paragraph (c)(4) permits a lawyer admitted in another jurisdiction to provide certain legal services on a temporary basis in this jurisdiction that arise out of or are reasonably related to the lawyer's pre-existing representation of a client in a jurisdiction in which the lawyer is admitted but are not within paragraphs (c)(2) or (c)(3). These services include both legal services and services that nonlawyers may perform but that are considered the practice of law when performed by lawyers.

[14] Paragraph (c)(3) requires that the services arise out of or be reasonably related to the lawyer's pre-existing representation of a client in a jurisdiction in which the lawyer is admitted. A variety of factors evidence such a relationship. The lawyer's client may have been previously represented by the lawyer, or may be resident in or have substantial contacts with the jurisdiction in which the lawyer is admitted. The matter, although involving other jurisdictions, may have a significant connection with that jurisdiction. In other cases, significant aspects of the lawyer's work for the client might be conducted in that jurisdiction or a significant aspect of the matter may involve the law of that jurisdiction. The necessary relationship might arise when the client's activities or the legal issue involve multiple jurisdictions, such as when the officers of a multinational corporation survey potential business sites and seek the services of their lawyer in assessing the relative merits of each.

[15] Paragraph (d) identifies two circumstances in which a lawyer who is admitted to practice in another United States jurisdiction, and is not disbarred or suspended from practice in any jurisdiction, may establish an office or other systematic and continuous presence in this jurisdiction for the practice of law as well as provide legal services on a temporary basis. Except as provided in paragraphs (d)(1) and (d)(2), a lawyer who is admitted to practice law in another jurisdiction and who establishes an office or other systematic or continuous presence in this jurisdiction must become admitted to practice law generally in this jurisdiction.

[16] Paragraphs (d)(1) applies to a lawyer who is employed by a client to provide legal services to the client or its organizational affiliates, i.e., entities that control, are controlled by, or are under common control with the employer. This paragraph does not authorize the provision of personal legal services to the employer's officers or employees. The paragraph applies to in-house corporate lawyers, government lawyers and others who are employed to render legal services to the employer. The lawyer's ability to represent the employer outside the jurisdiction in which the lawyer is licensed generally serves the interests of the employer and does not create an unreasonable risk to the client and others because the employer is well situated to assess the lawyer's qualifications and the quality of the lawyer's work.

[17] If an employed lawyer establishes an office or other systematic presence in this jurisdiction for the purpose of rendering legal services to the employer, the lawyer may be subject to registration or other requirements, including assessments for client protection funds and mandatory continuing legal education.

[18] Paragraph (d)(2) recognizes that a lawyer may provide legal services in a jurisdiction in which the lawyer is not licensed when authorized to do so by federal or other law, which includes statute, court rule, executive regulation or judicial precedent.

[19] A lawyer who practices law in this jurisdiction pursuant to paragraphs (c) or (d) or otherwise is subject to the disciplinary authority of this jurisdiction. See Rule 8.5(a).

[20] In some circumstances, a lawyer who practices law in this jurisdiction pursuant to paragraphs (c) or (d) may have to inform the client that the lawyer is not licensed to practice law in this jurisdiction. For example, that may be required when the representation occurs primarily in this jurisdiction and requires knowledge of the law of this jurisdiction. See Rule 1.4(b).

[21] Paragraphs (c) and (d) do not authorize communications advertising legal services to prospective clients in this jurisdiction by lawyers who are admitted to practice in other jurisdictions. Whether and how lawyers may communicate the availability of their services to prospective clients in this jurisdiction is governed by Rules 7.1 to 7.5.

RULE 5.6. RESTRICTIONS ON RIGHT TO PRACTICE

A lawyer shall not participate in offering or making:

(a) a partnership, shareholders, operating, employment, or other similar type of agreement that restricts the right of a lawyer to practice after termination of the relationship, except an agreement concerning benefits upon retirement; or

(b) an agreement in which a restriction on the lawyer's right to practice is part of the settlement of a client controversy.

[Adopted effective September 1, 1990. Amended effective October 1, 2005.]

Comment

[1] An agreement restricting the right of lawyers to practice after leaving a firm not only limits their professional autonomy but also limits the freedom of clients to choose a lawyer. Paragraph (a) prohibits such agreements except for restrictions incident to provisions concerning retirement benefits for service with the firm.

[2] Paragraph (b) prohibits a lawyer from agreeing not to represent other persons in connection with settling a claim on behalf of a client.

[3] This Rule does not apply to prohibit restrictions that may be included in the terms of the sale of a law practice pursuant to Rule 1.17.

RULE 5.7. RESPONSIBILITIES REGARDING LAW RELATED SERVICES

(a) A lawyer shall be subject to the Rules of Professional Conduct with respect to the provision of law related services, as defined in paragraph (b), if the law related services are provided:

(1) by the lawyer in circumstances that are not distinct from the lawyer's provision of legal services to clients; or

(2) in other circumstances by an entity controlled by the lawyer individually or with others if the lawyer fails to take reasonable measures to assure that a person obtaining the law related services knows that the services are not legal services and that the protections of the client lawyer relationship do not exist.

(b) The term "law related services" denotes services that might reasonably be performed in conjunction with and in substance are related to the provision of legal services, and that are not prohibited as unauthorized practice of law when provided by a nonlawyer.

[Adopted effective October 1, 2005.]

Comment

[1] When a lawyer performs law-related services or controls an organization that does so, there exists the potential for ethical problems. Principal among these is the possibility that the person for whom the law-related services are performed fails to understand that the services may not carry with them the protections normally afforded as part of the client-lawyer relationship. The recipient of the law-related services may expect, for example, that the protection of client confidences, prohibitions against representation of persons with conflicting interests, and obligations of a lawyer to maintain professional independence apply to the provision of law related services when that may not be the case.

[2] Rule 5.7 applies to the provision of law related services by a lawyer even when the lawyer does not provide any legal services to the person for whom the law related services are performed and whether the law related services are performed through a law firm or a separate entity. The Rule identifies the circumstances in which all of the Rules of Professional Conduct apply to the provision of law related services. Even when those circumstances do not exist, however, the conduct of a lawyer involved in the provision of law related services is subject to those Rules that apply generally to lawyer conduct, regardless of whether the conduct involves the provision of legal services. See, e. g., Rule 8.4.

[3] When law related services are provided by a lawyer under circumstances that are not distinct from the lawyer's provision of legal services to clients, the lawyer in providing the law related services must adhere to the requirements of the Rules of Professional Conduct as provided in paragraph (a)(1). Even when the law related and legal services are provided in circumstances that are distinct from each other, for example through separate entities or different support staff within the law firm, the Rules of Professional Conduct apply to the lawyer as provided in paragraph (a)(2) unless the lawyer takes reasonable measures to assure that the recipient of the law related services knows that the services are not legal services and that the protections of the client lawyer relationship do not apply.

[4] Law-related services also may be provided through an entity that is distinct from that through which the lawyer provides legal services. If the lawyer individually or with others has control of such an entity's operations, the Rule requires the lawyer to take reasonable measures to assure that each person using the services of the entity knows that the services provided by the entity are not legal services and that the Rules of Professional Conduct that relate to the client lawyer relationship do not apply. A lawyer's control of an entity extends to the ability to direct its operation. Whether a lawyer has such control will depend upon the circumstances of the particular case.

[5] When a client-lawyer relationship exists with a person who is referred by a lawyer to a separate law-related service

entity controlled by the lawyer, individually or with others, the lawyer must comply with Rule 1.8(a).

[6] In taking the reasonable measures referred to in paragraph (a)(2) to assure that a person using law-related services understands the practical effect or significance of the inapplicability of the Rules of Professional Conduct, the lawyer should communicate to the person receiving the law-related services, in a manner sufficient to assure that the person understands the significance of the fact, that the relationship of the person to the business entity will not be a client lawyer relationship. The communication should be made before entering into an agreement for provision of or providing law related services, and preferably should be in writing.

[7] The burden is upon the lawyer to show that the lawyer has taken reasonable measures under the circumstances to communicate the desired understanding. For instance, a sophisticated user of law related services, such as a publicly held corporation, may require a lesser explanation than someone unaccustomed to making distinctions between legal services and law related services, such as an individual seeking tax advice from a lawyer accountant or investigative services in connection with a lawsuit.

[8] Regardless of the sophistication of potential recipients of law related services, a lawyer should take special care to keep separate the provision of law related and legal services in order to minimize the risk that the recipient will assume that the law related services are legal services. The risk of such confusion is especially acute when the lawyer renders both types of services with respect to the same matter. Under some circumstances the legal and law related services may be so closely entwined that they cannot be distinguished from each other, and the requirement of disclosure and consultation imposed by paragraph (a)(2) of the Rule cannot be met. In such a case a lawyer will be responsible for assuring that both the lawyer's conduct and, to the extent required by Rule 5.3, that of nonlawyer employees in the distinct entity that the lawyer controls complies in all respects with the Rules of Professional Conduct.

[9] A broad range of economic and other interests of clients may be served by lawyers engaging in the delivery of law-related services. Examples of law related services include providing title insurance, financial planning, accounting, trust services, real estate counseling, legislative lobbying, economic analysis, social work, psychological counseling, tax preparation, and patent, medical or environmental consulting.

[10] When a lawyer is obliged to accord the recipients of such services the protections of those Rules that apply to the client lawyer relationship, the lawyer must take special care to heed the proscriptions of the Rules addressing conflict of interest (Rules 1.7 through 1.11, especially Rules 1.7(a)(2) and 1.8 (a), (b) and (f)), and to scrupulously adhere to the requirements of Rule 1.6 relating to disclosure of confidential information. The promotion of the law related services must also to all respects comply with Rules 7.1 through 7.3, dealing with advertising and solicitation. In that regard, lawyers should take special care to identify the obligations that may be imposed as a result of a jurisdiction's decisional law.

[11] When the full protections of all of the Rules of Professional Conduct do not apply to the provision of law related services, principles of law external to the Rules, for example, the law of principal and agent, govern the legal duties owed to those receiving the services. Those other legal principles may establish a different degree of protection for the recipient with respect to confidentiality of information, conflicts of interest and permissible business relationships with clients. See also Rule 8.4 (Misconduct).

PUBLIC SERVICE

RULE 6.1. VOLUNTARY PRO BONO PUBLICO SERVICE

A lawyer should render public interest legal service. A lawyer may discharge this responsibility by providing professional services at no fee or reduced fee to persons of limited means or to public service or charitable groups or organizations, by service in activities for improving the law, the legal system or the legal profession, and by financial support for organizations that provide legal services to persons of limited means.

[Adopted effective September 1, 1990. Amended effective October 1, 2005.]

Comment

[1] The ABA House of Delegates has formally acknowledged "the basic responsibility of each lawyer engaged in the practice of law to provide public interest legal services" without fee, or at a substantially reduced fee, in one or more of the following areas: poverty law, civil rights law, public rights law, charitable organization representation and the administration of justice. This Rule expresses that policy but is not intended to be enforced through disciplinary process.

[2] The rights and responsibilities of individuals and organizations in the United States are increasingly defined in legal terms. As a consequence, legal assistance in coping with the web of statutes, rules and regulations is imperative for persons of modest and limited means, as well as for the relatively well to do.

[3] The basic responsibility for providing legal services for those unable to pay ultimately rests upon the individual lawyer, and personal involvement in the problems of the disadvantaged can be one of the most rewarding experiences in the life of a lawyer. Every lawyer, regardless of professional prominence or professional workload, should find time to participate in or otherwise support the provision of legal services to the disadvantaged. The provision of free legal services to those unable to pay reasonable fees continues to be an obligation of each lawyer as well as the profession generally, but the efforts of individual lawyers are often not enough to meet the need. Thus, it has been necessary for the profession and government to institute additional programs to provide legal services. Accordingly, legal aid offices, lawyer referral services, and other related programs have been developed, and others will be developed by the profession and government. Every lawyer should support all proper efforts to meet this need for legal services.

RULE 6.2. ACCEPTING APPOINTMENTS

A lawyer shall not seek to avoid appointment by a tribunal to represent a person except for good cause, such as:

(a) representing the client is likely to result in violation of the Rules of Professional Conduct or other law;

(b) representing the client is likely to result in an unreasonable financial burden on the lawyer; or

(c) the client or the cause is so repugnant to the lawyer as to be likely to impair the client-lawyer relationship or the lawyer's ability to represent the client.

[Adopted effective September 1, 1990. Amended effective October 1, 2005.]

Comment

[1] A lawyer ordinarily is not obliged to accept a client whose character or cause the lawyer regards as repugnant. The lawyer's freedom to select clients is, however, qualified. All lawyers have a responsibility to assist in providing pro bono publico service. See Rule 6.1. An individual lawyer fulfills this responsibility by accepting a fair share of unpopular matters or indigent or unpopular clients. A lawyer may also be subject to appointment by a court to serve unpopular clients or persons unable to afford legal services.

Appointed Counsel

[2] For good cause a lawyer may seek to decline an appointment to represent a person who cannot afford to retain counsel or whose cause is unpopular. Good cause exists if the lawyer could not handle the matter competently, see Rule 1.1, or if undertaking the representation would result in an improper conflict of interest, for example, when the client or the cause is so repugnant to the lawyer as to be likely to impair the client lawyer relationship or the lawyer's ability to represent the client. A lawyer may also seek to decline an appointment if acceptance would be unreasonably burdensome, for example, when it would impose a financial sacrifice so great as to be unjust.

[3] An appointed lawyer has the same obligations to the client as retained counsel, including the obligations of loyalty and confidentiality, and is subject to the same limitations on the client lawyer relationship, such as the obligation to refrain from assisting the client in violation of the Rules.

RULE 6.3. MEMBERSHIP IN LEGAL SERVICES ORGANIZATION

A lawyer may serve as a director, officer or member of a legal services organization, apart from the law firm in which the lawyer practices, notwithstanding that the organization serves persons having interests adverse to a client of the lawyer. The lawyer shall not knowingly participate in a decision or action of the organization:

(a) if participating in the decision or action would be incompatible with the lawyer's obligations to a client under Rule 1.7; or

(b) where the decision or action could have a material adverse effect on the representation of a client of the organization whose interests are adverse to a client of the lawyer.

[Adopted effective September 1, 1990. Amended effective October 1, 2005.]

Comment

[1] Lawyers should be encouraged to support and participate in legal service organizations. A lawyer who is an officer or a member of such an organization does not thereby have a client lawyer relationship with persons served by the organization. However, there is potential conflict between the interests of such persons and the interests of the lawyer's clients. If the possibility of such conflict disqualified a lawyer from serving on the board of a legal services organization, the profession's involvement in such organizations would be severely curtailed.

[2] It may be necessary in appropriate cases to reassure a client of the organization that the representation will not be affected by conflicting loyalties of a member of the board. Established, written policies in this respect can enhance the credibility of such assurances.

RULE 6.4. LAW REFORM ACTIVITIES AFFECTING CLIENT INTERESTS

A lawyer may serve as a director, officer or member of an organization involved in reform of the law or its administration notwithstanding that the reform may affect the interests of a client of the lawyer. When the lawyer knows that the interests of a client may be materially benefited by a decision in which the lawyer participates, the lawyer shall disclose that fact but need not identify the client.

[Adopted effective September 1, 1990. Amended effective October 1, 2005.]

Comment

[1] Lawyers involved in organizations seeking law reform generally do not have a client lawyer relationship with the organization. Otherwise, it might follow that a lawyer could not be involved in a bar association law reform program that might indirectly affect a client. See also Rule 1.2(b). For example, a lawyer specializing in antitrust litigation might be regarded as disqualified from participating in drafting revisions of rules governing that subject. In determining the nature and scope of participation in such activities, a lawyer should be mindful of obligations to clients under other Rules, particularly Rule 1.7. A lawyer is professionally obligated to protect the integrity of the program by making an appropriate disclosure within the organization when the lawyer knows a private client might be materially benefited.

RULE 6.5. NONPROFIT AND COURT ANNEXED LIMITED LEGAL SERVICES PROGRAMS

(a) A lawyer who, under the auspices of a program sponsored by a nonprofit organization or court, provides short term limited legal services to a client without expectation by either the lawyer or the client that the lawyer will provide continuing representation in the matter:

(1) is subject to Rules 1.7 and 1.9(a) only if the lawyer knows that the representation of the client involves a conflict of interest; and

(2) is subject to Rule 1.10 only if the lawyer knows that another lawyer associated with the lawyer in a law firm is disqualified by Rule 1.7 or 1.9(a) with respect to the matter.

(b) Except as provided in paragraph (a)(2), Rule 1.10 is inapplicable to a representation governed by this Rule.

[Adopted effective October 1, 2005.]

Comment

[1] Legal services organizations, courts and various non-profit organizations have established programs through which lawyers provide short term limited legal services such as advice or the completion of legal forms that will assist persons to address their legal problems without further representation by a lawyer. In these programs, such as legal advice hotlines, advice once clinics or pro se counseling programs, a client lawyer relationship is established, but there is no expectation that the lawyer's representation of the client will continue beyond the limited consultation. Such programs are normally operated under circumstances in which it is not feasible for a lawyer to systematically screen for conflicts of interest as is generally required before undertaking a representation. See, e.g., Rules 1.7, 1.9 and 1.10.

[2] A lawyer who provides short term limited legal services pursuant to this Rule must secure the client's informed consent to the limited scope of the representation. See Rule 1.2(c). If a short term limited representation would not be reasonable under the circumstances, the lawyer may offer advice to the client but must also advise the client of the need for further assistance of counsel. Except as provided in this Rule, the Rules of Professional Conduct, including Rules 1.6 and 1.9(c), are applicable to the limited representation.

[3] Because a lawyer who is representing a client in the circumstances addressed by this Rule ordinarily is not able to check systematically for conflicts of interest, paragraph (a) requires compliance with Rules 1.7 or 1.9(a) only if the lawyer knows that the representation presents a conflict of interest for the lawyer, and with Rule 1.10 only if the lawyer knows that another lawyer in the lawyer's firm is disqualified by Rules 1.7 or 1.9(a) in the matter.

[4] Because the limited nature of the services significantly reduces the risk of conflicts of interest with other matters being handled by the lawyer's firm, paragraph (b) provides that Rule 1.10 is inapplicable to a representation governed by this Rule except as provided by paragraph (a)(2). Paragraph (a)(2) requires the participating lawyer to comply with Rule 1.10 when the lawyer knows that the lawyer's firm is disqualified by Rules 1.7 or 1.9(a). By virtue of paragraph (b), however, a lawyer's participation in a short term limited legal services program will not preclude the lawyer's firm from undertaking or continuing the representation of a client with interests adverse to a client being represented under the program's auspices. Nor will the personal disqualification of a lawyer participating in the program be imputed to other lawyers participating in the program.

[5] If, after commencing a short term limited representation in accordance with this Rule, a lawyer undertakes to represent the client in the matter on an ongoing basis, Rules 1.7, 1.9(a) and 1.10 become applicable.

LAWYER ADVERTISING

RULE 7.1. COMMUNICATIONS CONCERNING A LAWYER'S SERVICES

A lawyer shall not make false, misleading, or deceptive communications about the lawyer or the lawyer's services. A communication violates this rule if it:

(a) contains a material misrepresentation of fact or law, or omits a fact necessary to make the statement considered as a whole not materially misleading;

(b) is likely to create an unjustified expectation about results the lawyer can achieve, or states or implies that the lawyer can achieve results by means that violate the Rules of Professional Conduct or other law;

(c) compares the lawyer's services with other lawyers' services, unless the comparison can be factually substantiated;

(d) contains a testimonial about, or endorsement of, the lawyer

(1) without identifying the fact that it is a testimonial or endorsement;

(2) for which payment has been made, without disclosing that fact;

(3) which is not made by an actual client, without identifying that fact; and

(4) which does not clearly and conspicuously state that any result the endorsed lawyer or law firm may achieve on behalf of one client in one matter does not necessarily indicate similar results can be obtained for other clients.

(e) contains a nickname, moniker, or trade name that implies an ability to obtain results in a matter.

[Adopted effective September 1, 1990. Amended effective January 1, 1998; October 1, 2005; August 22, 2011.]

Comment

[1] This Rule governs all communications about a lawyer's services, including advertising permitted by Rule 7.2. Whatever means are used to make known a lawyer's services, statements about them must be truthful.

[2] Truthful statements that are misleading are also prohibited by this Rule. A truthful statement is misleading if it omits a fact necessary to make the lawyer's communication considered as a whole not materially misleading. A truthful statement is also misleading if there is a substantial likelihood that it will lead a reasonable person to formulate a specific conclusion about the lawyer or the lawyer's services for which there is no reasonable factual foundation.

[3] An advertisement that truthfully reports a lawyer's achievements on behalf of clients or former clients may be misleading if presented so as to lead a reasonable person to form an unjustified expectation that the same results could be obtained for other clients in similar matters without reference to the specific factual and legal circumstances of each client's case. Similarly, an unsubstantiated comparison of the lawyer's services or fees with the services or fees of other lawyers may be misleading if presented with such specificity as would lead a reasonable person to conclude that the comparison can be substantiated. The inclusion of an appropriate disclaimer or qualifying language may preclude a finding that a statement is likely to create unjustified expectations or otherwise mislead a prospective client.

For instance, the prohibition in paragraph (b) on statements likely to create "unjustified expectations" may preclude, and the limitations in paragraph (d) on testimonials and endorsements does preclude, advertisements about results obtained on behalf of a client, such as the amount of a damage award or the lawyer's record in obtaining favorable verdicts, unless they state clearly and conspicuously that any result the lawyer or law firm may have achieved on behalf of clients in other matters does not necessarily indicate similar results can be obtained for other clients. Such information may create the unjustified expectation that similar results can be obtained for others without reference to the specific factual and legal circumstances.

[4] Paragraph (e) precludes the use of nicknames, such as the "Heavy Hitter" or "The Strong Arm," that suggest the lawyer or law firm has an ability to obtain favorable results for a client in any matter. A significant possibility exists that such nicknames will be used to mislead the public as to the results that can be obtained or create an unsubstantiated comparison with the services provided by other lawyers. See also Rule 8.4(f)(prohibition against stating or implying an ability to influence improperly a government agency or official or to achieve results by means that violate the Rules of Professional Conduct or other law).

RULE 7.2. ADVERTISING

(a) Subject to the requirements of this Rule and Rules 7.1 and 7.3, a lawyer may advertise services through written, recorded or electronic communication, including public media. All advertisements shall be predominately informational such that, in both quantity and quality, the communication of factual information rationally related to the need for and selection of a lawyer predominates and the communication includes only a minimal amount of content designed to attract attention to and create interest in the communication.

All advertisements shall predominantly informational such that, in both quantity and quality, the communication of factual information rationality related to the need for and selection of a lawyer predominates and the communication includes only a minimal amount of content designed to attract attention to and create interest in communication.

(b) A lawyer is responsible for the content of any advertisement or solicitation placed or disseminated by the lawyer and has a duty to review the advertisement or solicitation prior to its dissemination to reasonably ensure its compliance with the Rules of Professional Conduct. The lawyer shall keep a copy or recording of every advertisement or communication for two (2) years after its last dissemination along with a record of when and where it was disseminated.

(c) A lawyer shall not give anything of value to a person for recommending the lawyer's services except that a lawyer may

(1) pay the reasonable costs of advertisements or communications permitted by this Rule;

(2) pay the usual charges of a legal service plan or a not-for-profit lawyer referral service, which is itself not acting in violation of any Rule of Professional Conduct; and

(3) pay for a law practice in accordance with Rule 1.17.

(d) Any communication made pursuant to this Rule shall include the name and office address of at least one lawyer responsible for its content.

(e) No lawyer shall, directly or indirectly, pay all or a part of the cost of an advertisement by a lawyer not in the same firm unless the advertisement discloses the name and address of the nonadvertising lawyer, the relationship between the advertising lawyer and the nonadvertising lawyer, and whether the advertising lawyer may refer any case received through the advertisement to the nonadvertising lawyer.

(f) Every advertisement that contains information about the lawyer's fee shall disclose whether the client will be liable for any expenses in addition to the fee and, if the fee will be a percentage of the recovery, whether the percentage will be computed before deducting the expenses.

(g) A lawyer who advertises a specific fee or range of fees for a particular service shall honor the advertised fee or fee range for at least ninety (90) days following dissemination of the advertisement, unless the advertisement specifies a shorter period; provided that a fee advertised in a publication which is issued not more than annually, shall be honored for one (1) year following publication.

(h) All advertisements shall disclose the geographic location, by city or town, of the office in which the lawyer or lawyers who will actually perform the services advertised principally practice law. If the office location is outside a city or town, the county in which the office is located must be disclosed. A lawyer referral service shall disclose the geographic area in which the lawyer practices when a referral is made.

[Adopted effective September 1, 1990. Amended effective January 1, 1998; October 1, 2005; February 15, 2007; June 28, 2010; August 22, 2011.]

Comment

[1] To assist the public in obtaining legal services, lawyers should be allowed to make known their services not only through reputation but also through organized information campaigns in the form of advertising. Advertising involves an active quest for clients, contrary to the tradition that a lawyer should not seek clientele. However, the public's need to know about legal services can be fulfilled in part through advertising. This need is particularly acute in the case of persons of moderate means who have not made extensive use of legal services. The interest in expanding public information about legal services ought to prevail over considerations of tradition. Nevertheless, advertising by lawyers entails the risk of practices that are misleading or overreaching.

[2] This Rule permits public dissemination of information concerning a lawyer's name or firm name, address and telephone number; the kinds of services the lawyer will undertake; the basis on which the lawyer's fees are deter-

mined, including prices for specific services and payment and credit arrangements; a lawyer's foreign language ability; names of references and, with their consent, names of clients regularly represented; and other information that might invite the attention of those seeking legal assistance.

[3] Questions of effectiveness and taste in advertising are matters of speculation and subjective judgment. Some jurisdictions have had extensive prohibitions against television advertising, against advertising going beyond specified facts about a lawyer, or against "undignified" advertising. Television is now one of the most powerful media for getting information to the public, particularly persons of low and moderate income; prohibiting television advertising, therefore, would impede the flow of information about legal services to many sectors of the public. Limiting the information that may be advertised has a similar effect and assumes that the bar can accurately forecast the kind of information that the public would regard as relevant. Similarly, electronic media, such as the Internet, can be an important source of information about legal services, and lawful communication by electronic mail is permitted by this Rule, but see Rule 7.3(a) for the prohibition against the solicitation of a prospective client through a real time electronic exchange that is not initiated by the prospective client.

[4] Regardless of medium, a lawyer's advertisement should provide only useful, factual information presented in an objective and understandable fashion so as to facilitate a prospective client's ability to make an informed choice about legal representation. A lawyer should strive to communicate such information without the use of techniques intended solely to gain attention and which demonstrate a clear and intentional lack of relevance to the selection of counsel, as such techniques hinder rather than facilitate intelligent selection of counsel. A lawyer's advertisement should reflect the serious purpose of legal services and our judicial system. The state has a significant interest in protecting against a public loss of confidence in the legal system, including its participants, and in protecting specifically against harm to the jury system that might be caused by lawyer advertising. The effectiveness of the legal system depends upon the public's trust that the legal system will operate with fairness and justice. Public trust is likely to be diminished if the public believes that some participants are able to obtain results through inappropriate methods. Public confidence also is likely to be diminished if the public perceives that the personality of their advocate, rather than the legal merit of their claim, is a key factor in determining the outcome of their matter. It is necessary to ensure that lawyer advertisements do not have these detrimental impacts. This rule is intended to preserve the public's access to information relevant to the selection of counsel, while limiting those advertising methods that are most likely to have a harmful impact on public confidence in the legal system and which are of little or no benefit to the potential client.

[5] Neither this Rule nor Rule 7.3 prohibits communications authorized by law, such as notice to members of a class in class action litigation.

Record of Advertising

[6] Paragraph (b) imposes upon the lawyer who disseminates an advertisement or causes its dissemination the responsibility for reviewing each advertisement prior to dissemination to ensure its compliance with the Rules of Professional Conduct. It also requires that a record of the content and use of advertising be kept in order to facilitate enforcement of this Rule.

Paying Others to Recommend a Lawyer

[7] Lawyers are not permitted to pay others for channeling professional work. Paragraph (c)(1), however, allows a lawyer to pay for advertising and communications permitted by this Rule, including the cost of print directory listings, on-line directory listings, newspaper ads, television and radio airtime, domain-name registrations, sponsorship fees, banner ads, and group advertising. A lawyer may compensate employees, agents and vendors who are engaged to provide marketing or client-development services, such as publicists, public relations personnel, business development staff and website designers. See Rule 5.3 for the duties of lawyers and law firms with respect to the conduct of nonlawyers who prepare marketing materials for them.

[8] A lawyer may pay the usual charges of a legal service plan or a not for profit lawyer referral service, which is itself not acting in violation of the Rules of Professional Conduct. A legal service plan is a prepaid or group legal service plan or a similar delivery system that assists prospective clients to secure legal representation. A lawyer referral service, on the other hand, is any organization that holds itself out to the public as a lawyer referral service. Such referral services are understood by laypersons to be consumer-oriented organizations that provide unbiased referrals to lawyers with appropriate experience in the subject matter of the representation and afford other client protections, such as complaint procedures or malpractice insurance requirements. Consequently, this Rule only permits a lawyer to pay the usual charges of a not-for-profit lawyer referral service. The "usual charges" may include a portion of legal fees collected by a lawyer from clients referred by the service when that portion of fees is collected to support the expenses projected for the referral service.

[9] A lawyer who accepts assignments or referrals from a legal service plan or referrals from a lawyer referral service must act reasonably to assure that the activities of the plan or service are compatible with the lawyer's professional obligations. See Rule 5.3. Legal service plans and lawyer referral services may communicate with prospective clients, but such communication must be in conformity with these Rules. Thus, advertising must not be false or misleading, as would be the case if the communications of a group advertising program or a group legal services plan would mislead prospective clients to think that it was a lawyer referral service sponsored by a state agency or bar association. See also Rule 7.3(b).

RULE 7.3. DIRECT CONTACT WITH PROSPECTIVE CLIENTS

(a) A lawyer shall not by in person, live telephone or real time electronic contact solicit professional employment from a prospective client when a significant motive for the lawyer's doing so is the lawyer's pecuniary gain, unless the person contacted:

(1) is a lawyer; or

(2) has a family, close personal, or prior professional relationship with the lawyer.

(b) A lawyer shall not solicit professional employment from a prospective client by direct written, recorded or electronic communication or by in person, telephone, telegraph, facsimile or realtime electronic contact even when not otherwise prohibited by paragraph (a), if:

(1) the prospective client has made known to the lawyer a desire not to be solicited by the lawyer;

(2) the solicitation involves coercion, duress, harassment, fraud, overreaching, intimidation or undue influence;

(3) the solicitation concerns an action for personal injury or wrongful death or otherwise relates to an accident or disaster involving the person solicited or a relative of that person unless the accident or disaster occurred more than thirty (30) days prior to the solicitation;

(4) the solicitation concerns a specific matter and the lawyer knows, or reasonably should know, that the person solicited is represented by a lawyer in the matter; or

(5) the lawyer knows, or reasonably should know, that the physical, emotional, or mental state of the person makes it unlikely that the person would exercise reasonable judgment in employing a lawyer.

(c) Any lawyer who uses written, recorded, or electronic solicitation shall maintain a file for two years showing the following:

(1) the basis by which the lawyer knows the person solicited needs legal services; and

(2) the factual basis for any statements made in the written, recorded, or electronic communication.

(d) Every written, recorded or electronic communication from a lawyer soliciting professional employment from a prospective client known to be in need of legal services in a particular matter, and with whom the lawyer has no family, close personal or prior professional relationship, shall conform to Rules 7.1 and 7.2 and, in addition, must conform to the following provisions:

(1) The words "ADVERTISING MATERIAL," printed in capital letters and in prominent type, shall appear on the front of the outside envelope and on the front of each page of the material. Every such recorded or electronic communication shall clearly state both at the beginning and at the end that the communication is an advertisement. If the solicitation is made by computer, including, but not limited to, electronic mail, the words "ADVERTISING MATERIAL," printed in capital letters and in prominent type, shall appear in any subject line of the message and at the beginning and end of the communication.

(2) Each solicitation must include the following statements:

(A) "You may wish to consult your lawyer or another lawyer instead of me (us). You may obtain information about other lawyers by consulting directories, seeking the advice of others, or calling the South Carolina Bar Lawyer Referral Service at 799–7100 in Columbia or toll free at 1–800–868–2284. If you have already engaged a lawyer in connection with the legal matter referred to in this communication, you should direct any questions you have to that lawyer" and

(B) "The exact nature of your legal situation will depend on many facts not known to me (us) at this time. You should understand that the advice and information in this communication is general and that your own situation may vary."

Where the solicitation is written, the above statements must be in a type no smaller than that used in the body of the communication.

(3) Each solicitation must include the following statement: "ANY COMPLAINTS ABOUT THIS COMMUNICATION OR THE REPRESENTATIONS OF ANY LAWYER MAY BE DIRECTED TO THE COMMISSION ON LAWYER CONDUCT, 1015 SUMTER STREET, SUITE 305, COLUMBIA, SOUTH CAROLINA 29201—TELEPHONE NUMBER 803–734–2037." Where the solicitation is written, this statement must be printed in capital letters and in a size no smaller than that used in the body of the communication.

(e) Written communications mailed to prospective clients shall be sent only by regular U.S. mail, not by registered mail or other forms of restricted or certified delivery.

(f) Written communications mailed to prospective clients shall not be made to resemble legal pleadings or other legal documents.

(g) Any written communication prompted by a specific occurrence involving or affecting the intended recipient of the communication or a family member shall disclose how the lawyer obtained the information prompting the communication.

(h) A written communication seeking employment by a specific prospective client in a specific matter shall not reveal on the envelope, or on the outside of a self mailing brochure or pamphlet, the nature of the client's legal problem.

(i) If a lawyer reasonably believes that a lawyer other than the lawyer whose name or signature appears on the communication will likely be the lawyer who primarily handles the case or matter, or that the case or matter will be referred to another lawyer or law firm, any written communication concerning a specific matter shall include a statement so advising the potential client.

(j) Notwithstanding the prohibitions in paragraph (a), a lawyer may participate with a prepaid or group legal service plan operated by an organization not owned or directed by the lawyer that uses in person or telephone contact to solicit memberships or subscriptions for the plan from persons who are not known to need legal services in a particular matter covered by the plan. A lawyer may participate with a prepaid or group legal service plan only if the plan is established in compliance with all statutory and regulatory requirements imposed upon such plans under South Carolina law. Lawyers who participate in a legal service plan must make reasonable efforts to assure that the plan sponsors are in compliance with Rules 7.1, 7.2 and 7.3(b).

[Adopted effective September 1, 1990. Amended effective January 1, 1997; January 1, 1998; October 1, 2005; December 16 2010; August 22, 2011.]

Comment

[1] There is a potential for abuse inherent in direct in person or, live telephone or real time electronic contact by a lawyer with a prospective client known to need legal services. These forms of contact between a lawyer and a prospective client subject the layperson to the private importuning of the trained advocate in a direct interpersonal encounter. The prospective client, who may already feel overwhelmed by the circumstances giving rise to the need for legal services, may find it difficult to fully evaluate all available alternatives with reasoned judgment and appropriate self interest in the face of the lawyer's presence and insistence upon being retained immediately. The situation is fraught with the possibility of undue influence, intimidation, and overreaching.

[2] The use of general advertising and written recorded or electronic communications to transmit information from lawyer to prospective client, rather than direct in person live telephone or real time electronic contact, will help to assure that the information flows cleanly as well as freely. The contents of advertisements and communications permitted under Rule 7.2 can be permanently recorded so that they cannot be disputed and may be shared with others who know the lawyer. This potential for informal review is itself likely to help guard against statements and claims that might constitute false, misleading, deceptive, or unfair communications, in violation of Rule 7.1. The contents of direct in person live telephone or real time electronic conversations between a lawyer and a prospective client can be disputed and may not be subject to third party scrutiny. Consequently, they are much more likely to approach, and occasionally cross, the dividing line between accurate representations and those that are false and misleading.

[3] There is far less likelihood that a lawyer would engage in abusive practices against an individual who is a former client, or with whom the lawyer has a close personal or family relationship, or in situations in which the lawyer is motivated by considerations other than the lawyer's pecuniary gain. Nor is there a serious potential for abuse when the person contacted is a lawyer. Consequently, the general prohibition in Rule 7.3(a) and the requirements of Rule 7.3(d) are not applicable in those situations. Also, paragraph (a) is not intended to prohibit a lawyer from participating in constitutionally protected activities of public or charitable legal service organizations or bona fide political, social, civic, fraternal, employee or trade organizations whose purposes include providing or recommending legal services to its members or beneficiaries.

[4] But even permitted forms of solicitation can be abused. Thus, any solicitation which contains information which is false, misleading, deceptive or unfair within the meaning of Rule 7.1; which involves coercion, duress, harassment, fraud, overreaching, intimidating or undue influence within the meaning of Rule 7.3(b)(2); which involves contact with a prospective client who has made known to the lawyer a desire not to be solicited by the lawyer within the meaning of Rule 7.3(b)(1); which involves contact with a person the lawyer reasonably should know is represented by another lawyer in the matter; or which involves contact with a prospective client the lawyer reasonably should know is physically, emotionally or mentally incapable of exercising reasonable judgment in choosing a lawyer under Rule 7.3(b)(5) is prohibited. Moreover, if after sending a letter or other communication to a client as permitted by Rule 7.2, the lawyer receives no response, any further effort to communicate with the prospective client may violate the provisions of Rule 7.3(b).

[5] The public views direct solicitation in the immediate wake of an accident as an intrusion on the personal privacy and tranquility of citizens. The 30–day restriction in paragraph (b)(3) is meant to forestall the outrage and irritation with the legal profession engendered by crass commercial intrusion by attorneys upon a citizen's personal grief in a time of trauma. The rule is limited to a brief period, and lawyer advertising permitted under Rule 7.2 offers alternative means of conveying necessary information about the need for legal services and the qualifications of available lawyers and law firms to those who may be in need of legal services without subjecting the prospective client to direct persuasion that may overwhelm the client's judgment.

[6] This Rule is not intended to prohibit a lawyer from contacting representatives of organizations or groups that may be interested in establishing a group or prepaid legal plan for their members, insureds, beneficiaries or other third parties for the purpose of informing such entities of the availability of and details concerning the plan or arrangement which the lawyer or lawyer's firm is willing to offer. This form of communication is not directed to a prospective client. Rather, it is usually addressed to an individual acting in a fiduciary capacity seeking a supplier of legal services for others who may, if they choose, become prospective clients of the lawyer. Under these circumstances, the activity which the lawyer undertakes in communicating with such representatives and the type of information transmitted to the individual are functionally similar to and serve the same purpose as advertising permitted under Rule 7.2.

[7] The requirement in Rule 7.3(d) that certain communications be marked "Advertising Material" does not apply to communications sent in response to requests of potential clients or their spokespersons or sponsors. General announcements by lawyers, including changes in personnel or office location, do not constitute communications soliciting professional employment from a client known to be in need of legal services within the meaning of this Rule.

[8] Requiring communications to be marked as advertisements sent only by regular U.S. mail and prohibiting communications from resembling legal documents is designed to allow the recipient to choose whether or not to read the solicitation without fear or legal repercussions. In addition, the lawyer or law firm should reveal the source of information used to determine that the recipient has a potential legal problem. Disclosure of this information source will help the recipient understand the extent of knowledge the lawyer or law firm has regarding the recipient's particular situation and will avoid misleading the recipient into believing that the lawyer has particularized knowledge about the recipient's matter if the lawyer does not.

[9] Paragraph (j) of this Rule permits a lawyer to participate with an organization which uses personal contact to solicit members for its group or prepaid legal service plan,

provided that the personal contact is not undertaken by any lawyer who would be a provider of legal services through the plan. The organization referred to in paragraph (j) must not be owned by or directed, whether as manager or otherwise, by any lawyer or law firm that participates in the plan. For example, paragraph (j) would not permit a lawyer to create an organization controlled directly or indirectly by the lawyer and use the organization for the in person or telephone solicitation of legal employment of the lawyer through memberships in the plan or otherwise. The communication permitted by these organizations also must not be directed to a person known to need legal services in a particular matter, but is to be designed to inform potential plan members generally of another means of affordable legal services.

RULE 7.4. COMMUNICATION OF FIELDS OF PRACTICE AND SPECIALIZATION

(a) A lawyer who is certified under the Rule on Lawyer Competence, Rule 408, SCACR, is entitled to advertise or state publicly in any manner otherwise permitted by these rules that the lawyer is certified as a specialist in the pertinent specialty field by the Supreme Court of South Carolina.

(b) A lawyer who is not certified as a specialist but who concentrates in, limits his or her practice to, or wishes to announce a willingness to accept cases in a particular field may so advertise or publicly state in any manner otherwise permitted by these rules. To avoid confusing or misleading the public and to protect the objectives of the South Carolina certified specialization program, any such advertisement or statements shall be strictly factual and shall not contain any form of the words "certified," "specialist," "expert," or "authority" except as permitted by Rule 7.4(d).

(c) A lawyer admitted to engage in patent practice before the United States Patent and Trademark Office may use the designation "Patent Attorney" or a substantially similar designation. A lawyer engaged in the trademark practice may use the designation "trademarks," "trademark attorney," or "trademark lawyer" or any combination of those terms.

(d) A lawyer engaged in admiralty practice may use the designation "admiralty," "proctor in admiralty" or a substantially similar designation.

[Adopted effective September 1, 1990. Amended effective October 1, 2005.]

Comment

[1] Paragraph (b) of this Rule permits a lawyer to indicate areas of practice in communications about the lawyer's services, for example, in a telephone directory or other advertising. If a lawyer practices only in certain fields, or will not accept matters except in such fields, the lawyer is permitted to so indicate.

[2] Paragraph (c) recognizes the long-established policy of the Patent and Trademark Office for the designation of lawyers practicing before the Office. Paragraph (d) recognizes that designation of admiralty practice has a long historical tradition associated with maritime commerce and the federal courts.

RULE 7.5. FIRM NAMES AND LETTERHEADS

(a) A lawyer shall not use a firm name, letterhead or other professional designation that violates Rule 7.1. A trade name may be used by a lawyer in private practice if it does not imply a connection with a government agency or with a public or charitable legal services organization and is not otherwise in violation of Rule 7.1.

(b) A law firm with offices in more than one jurisdiction may use the same name or other professional designation in each jurisdiction, but identification of the lawyers in an office of the firm shall indicate the jurisdictional limitations on those not licensed to practice in the jurisdiction where the office is located.

(c) The name of a lawyer holding a public office shall not be used in the name of a law firm, or in communications on its behalf, during any substantial period in which the lawyer is not actively and regularly practicing with the firm.

(d) Lawyers may state or imply that they practice in a partnership or other organization only when that is the fact.

[Adopted effective September 1, 1990. Amended effective October 1, 2005.]

Comment

[1] A firm may be designated by the names of all or some of its members, by the names of deceased members where there has been a continuing succession in the firm's identity or by a trade name such as the "ABC Legal Clinic." A lawyer or law firm may also be designated by a distinctive website address or comparable professional designation. Although the United States Supreme Court has held that legislation may prohibit the use of trade names in professional practice, use of such names in law practice is acceptable so long as it is not misleading. If a private firm uses a trade name that includes a geographical name such as "Springfield Legal Clinic," an express disclaimer that it is a public legal aid agency may be required to avoid a misleading implication. It may be observed that any firm name including the name of a deceased partner is, strictly speaking, a trade name. The use of such names to designate law firms has proven a useful means of identification. However, it is misleading to use the name of a lawyer not associated with the firm or a predecessor of the firm or the name of a non lawyer.

[2] With regard to paragraph (d), lawyers sharing office facilities, but who are not in fact associated with each other in a law firm, may not denominate themselves as, for example, "Smith and Jones," for that title suggests that they are practicing law together in a firm.

MAINTAINING THE INTEGRITY OF THE PROFESSION

RULE 8.1. BAR ADMISSION AND DISCIPLINARY MATTERS

An applicant for admission to the bar, or a lawyer in connection with a bar admission application or in connection with a disciplinary matter, shall not:

(a) knowingly make a false statement of material fact; or

(b) fail to disclose a fact necessary to correct a misapprehension known by the person to have arisen in the matter, or knowingly fail to respond to a lawful demand for information from an admissions or disciplinary authority, except that this rule does not require disclosure of information otherwise protected by Rule 1.6.

[Adopted effective September 1, 1990. Amended effective October 1, 2005.]

Comment

[1] The duty imposed by this Rule extends to persons seeking admission to the bar as well as to lawyers. Hence, if a person makes a material false statement in connection with an application for admission, it may be the basis for subsequent disciplinary action if the person is admitted, and in any event may be relevant in a subsequent admission application. The duty imposed by this Rule applies to a lawyer's own admission or discipline as well as that of others. Thus, it is a separate professional offense for a lawyer to knowingly make a misrepresentation or omission in connection with a disciplinary investigation of the lawyer's own conduct. Paragraph (b) of this Rule also requires correction of any prior misstatement in the matter that the applicant or lawyer may have made and affirmative clarification of any misunderstanding on the part of the admissions or disciplinary authority of which the person involved becomes aware.

[2] This Rule is subject to the provisions of the fifth amendment of the United States Constitution and corresponding provisions of state constitutions. A person relying on such a provision in response to a question, however, should do so openly and not use the right of nondisclosure as a justification for failure to comply with this Rule.

[3] A lawyer representing an applicant for admission to the bar, or representing a lawyer who is the subject of a disciplinary inquiry or proceeding, is governed by the rules applicable to the client-lawyer relationship, including Rule 1.6 and, in some cases, Rule 3.3.

RULE 8.2. JUDICIAL AND LEGAL OFFICIALS

(a) A lawyer shall not make a statement that the lawyer knows to be false or with reckless disregard as to its truth or falsity concerning the qualifications or integrity of a judge, adjudicatory officer or public legal officer, or of a candidate for election or appointment to judicial or legal office.

(b) A lawyer who is a candidate for judicial office shall comply with the applicable provisions of the Code of Judicial Conduct.

[Adopted effective September 1, 1990. Amended effective October 1, 2005.]

Comment

[1] Assessments by lawyers are relied on in evaluating the professional or personal fitness of persons being considered for election or appointment to judicial office and to public legal offices, such as attorney general, prosecuting attorney and public defender. Expressing honest and candid opinions on such matters contributes to improving the administration of justice. Conversely, false statements by a lawyer can unfairly undermine public confidence in the administration of justice.

[2] When a lawyer seeks judicial office, the lawyer should be bound by applicable limitations on political activity.

[3] To maintain the fair and independent administration of justice, lawyers are encouraged to continue traditional efforts to defend judges and courts unjustly criticized.

RULE 8.3. REPORTING PROFESSIONAL MISCONDUCT

(a) A lawyer who is arrested for or has been charged by way of indictment, information or complaint with a serious crime shall inform the Commission on Lawyer Conduct in writing within fifteen days of being arrested or being charged by way of indictment, information or complaint.

(b) A lawyer who knows that another lawyer has committed a violation of the Rules of Professional Conduct that raises a substantial question as to that lawyer's honesty, trustworthiness or fitness as a lawyer in other respects, shall inform the appropriate professional authority.

(c) A lawyer who knows that a judge has committed a violation of applicable rules of judicial conduct that raises a substantial question as to the judge's honesty, trustworthiness, or fitness for office in other respects shall inform the appropriate authority.

(d) This Rule does not require disclosure of information otherwise protected by Rule 1.6.

(e) Inquiries or information received by the South Carolina Bar Lawyers Helping Lawyers Committee or an equivalent county bar association committee regarding the need for treatment for alcohol, drug abuse or depression, or by the South Carolina Bar law office management assistance program or an equivalent county bar association program regarding a lawyer seeking the program assistance, shall not be disclosed to the disciplinary authority without written permission of the lawyer receiving assistance. Any such inquiry or information shall enjoy the same confidence as information protected by the attorney-client privilege under applicable law.

[Adopted effective September 1, 1990. Amended effective February 8, 1996; March 21, 1997; April 4, 2002; October 1, 2005; June 28, 2010.]

Comment

[1] Self regulation of the legal profession requires that members of the profession initiate disciplinary investigation when they know of a violation of the Rules of Professional Conduct. Lawyers have a similar obligation with respect to judicial misconduct. An apparently isolated violation may indicate a pattern of misconduct that only a disciplinary investigation can uncover. Reporting a violation is especially important where the victim is unlikely to discover the offense. The South Carolina version of paragraph (c) modifies the model version by specifically including "honesty" and "trustworthiness" to parallel the requirement of paragraph (b).

[2] A report about misconduct is not required where it would involve violation of Rule 1.6. However, a lawyer should encourage a client to consent to disclosure where prosecution would not substantially prejudice the client's interests.

[3] If a lawyer were obliged to report every violation of the Rules, the failure to report any violation would itself be a professional offense. Such a requirement existed in many jurisdictions but proved to be unenforceable. This Rule limits the reporting obligation to those offenses that a self regulating profession must vigorously endeavor to prevent. A measure of judgment is, therefore, required in complying with the provisions of this Rule. The term "substantial" refers to the seriousness of the possible offense and not the quantum of evidence of which the lawyer is aware. A report should be made to the bar disciplinary agency unless some other agency, such as a peer review agency, is more appropriate in the circumstances. Similar considerations apply to the reporting of judicial misconduct.

[4] The duty to report professional misconduct does not apply to a lawyer retained to represent a lawyer whose professional conduct is in question. Such a situation is governed by the Rules applicable to the client lawyer relationship.

[5] Paragraph (e) encourages lawyers to seek assistance from the South Carolina Bar Lawyers Helping Lawyers Committee, from a South Carolina Bar law office management assistance program, or from an equivalent county bar association program without fear of being reported for violating the Rules of Professional Conduct. Information about a lawyer's or judge's misconduct or fitness may be received by a lawyer in the course of that lawyer's participation in an approved lawyers or judges assistance program. In that circumstance, providing for an exception to the reporting requirements of paragraphs (b) and (c) of this Rule encourages lawyers and judges to seek treatment through such a program. Conversely, without such an exception, lawyers and judges may hesitate to seek assistance from these programs, which may then result in additional harm to their professional careers and additional injury to the welfare of clients and the public. These Rules do not otherwise address the confidentiality of information received by a lawyer or judge participating in an approved lawyers assistance program; such an obligation, however, may be imposed by the rules of the program or other law.

RULE 8.4. MISCONDUCT

It is professional misconduct for a lawyer to:

(a) violate or attempt to violate the Rules of Professional Conduct, knowingly assist or induce another to do so, or do so through the acts of another;

(b) commit a criminal act that reflects adversely on the lawyer's honesty, trustworthiness or fitness as a lawyer in other respects;

(c) commit a criminal act involving moral turpitude;

(d) engage in conduct involving dishonesty, fraud, deceit or misrepresentation;

(e) engage in conduct that is prejudicial to the administration of justice;

(f) state or imply an ability to influence improperly a government agency or official or to achieve results by means that violate the Rules of Professional Conduct or other law; or

(g) knowingly assist a judge or judicial officer in conduct that is a violation of applicable rules of judicial conduct or other law.

[Adopted effective September 1, 1990. Amended effective October 1, 2005.]

Comment

[1] Lawyers are subject to discipline when they violate or attempt to violate the Rules of Professional Conduct, knowingly assist or induce another to do so or do so through the acts of another, as when they request or instruct an agent to do so on the lawyer's behalf. Paragraph (a), however, does not prohibit a lawyer from advising a client concerning action the client is legally entitled to take.

[2] Many kinds of illegal conduct reflect adversely on fitness to practice law, such as offenses involving fraud and the offense of willful failure to file an income tax return. Although a lawyer is personally answerable to the entire criminal law, a lawyer should be professionally answerable only for offenses that indicate lack of those characteristics relevant to law practice. Offenses involving violence, dishonesty, breach of trust, or serious interference with the administration of justice are in that category. The South Carolina version of this Rule also specifically includes criminal acts involving moral turpitude as professional misconduct. A pattern of repeated offenses, even ones of minor significance when considered separately, can indicate indifference to legal obligation.

[3] A lawyer who, in the course of representing a client, knowingly manifests by words or conduct, bias or prejudice based upon race, sex, religion, national origin, disability, age, sexual orientation or socioeconomic status, violates paragraph (d) when such actions are prejudicial to the administration of justice. Legitimate advocacy respecting the foregoing factors does not violate paragraph (d). A trial judge's finding that peremptory challenges were exercised on a discriminatory basis does not alone establish a violation of this rule.

[4] A lawyer may refuse to comply with an obligation imposed by law upon a good faith belief that no valid obligation exists. The provisions of Rule 1.2(d) concerning a good faith challenge to the validity, scope, meaning or application of the law apply to challenges of legal regulation of the practice of law.

[5] Lawyers holding public office assume legal responsibilities going beyond those of other citizens. A lawyer's abuse of public office can suggest an inability to fulfill the professional role of lawyers. The same is true of abuse of positions of private trust such as trustee, executor, administrator, guardian, agent and officer, director or manager of a corporation or other organization.

RULE 8.5. DISCIPLINARY AUTHORITY; CHOICE OF LAW

(a) Disciplinary Authority. A lawyer admitted to practice in this jurisdiction is subject to the disciplinary authority of this jurisdiction, regardless of where the lawyer's conduct occurs. A lawyer not admitted in this jurisdiction is also subject to the disciplinary authority of this jurisdiction if the lawyer provides or offers to provide any legal services in this jurisdiction. A lawyer may be subject to the disciplinary authority of both this jurisdiction and another jurisdiction for the same conduct.

(b) Choice of Law. In any exercise of the disciplinary authority of this jurisdiction, the rules of professional conduct to be applied shall be as follows:

(1) for conduct in connection with a matter pending before a tribunal, the rules of the jurisdiction in which the tribunal sits, unless the rules of the tribunal provide otherwise; and

(2) for any other conduct, the rules of the jurisdiction in which the lawyer's conduct occurred, or, if the predominant effect of the conduct is in a different jurisdiction, the rules of that jurisdiction shall be applied to the conduct. A lawyer shall not be subject to discipline if the lawyer's conduct conforms to the rules of a jurisdiction in which the lawyer reasonably believes the predominant effect of the lawyer's conduct will occur. Any communication made for the purpose of soliciting clients from within South Carolina or advertising a lawyer's services in South Carolina shall be deemed to have its predominant effect within South Carolina and shall be subject to provisions of Rules 7.1 through 7.5 of the Rules of Professional Conduct and Rule 418, SCACR, regardless of the jurisdiction in which the lawyer is licensed or in which matter may be pending.

(c) A lawyer giving advice or providing services that would be considered to be the practice of law if provided while the lawyer was affiliated with a law firm is subject to the Rules of Professional Conduct with respect to the giving of such advice or the providing of such services whether or not the lawyer is actively engaged in the practice of law or affiliated with a law firm. In giving such advice and in providing such services, a lawyer shall be considered to be representing a client for the purposes of the Rules of Professional Conduct.

[Adopted effective September 1, 1990. Amended effective October 1, 2005.]

Comment

Disciplinary Authority

[1] It is longstanding law that the conduct of a lawyer admitted to practice in this jurisdiction is subject to the disciplinary authority of this jurisdiction. Extension of the disciplinary authority of this jurisdiction to other lawyers who provide or offer to provide legal services in this jurisdiction is for the protection of the citizens of this jurisdiction. Reciprocal enforcement of a jurisdiction's disciplinary findings and sanctions will further advance the purposes of this Rule. See Rule 29 of the Rules for Lawyer Disciplinary Enforcement, Rule 413, SCACR. A lawyer who is subject to the disciplinary authority of this jurisdiction under Rule 8.5(a) appoints an official to be designated by this Court to receive service of process in this jurisdiction. The fact that the lawyer is subject to the disciplinary authority of this jurisdiction may be a factor in determining whether personal jurisdiction may be asserted over the lawyer for civil matters.

Choice of Law

[2] A lawyer may be potentially subject to more than one set of rules of professional conduct which impose different obligations. The lawyer may be licensed to practice in more than one jurisdiction with differing rules, or may be admitted to practice before a particular court with rules that differ from those of the jurisdiction or jurisdictions in which the lawyer is licensed to practice. Additionally, the lawyer's conduct may involve significant contacts with more than one jurisdiction.

[3] Paragraph (b) seeks to resolve such potential conflicts. Its premise is that minimizing conflicts between rules, as well as uncertainty about which rules are applicable, is in the best interest of both clients and the profession (as well as the bodies having authority to regulate the profession). Accordingly, it takes the approach of (i) providing that any particular conduct of a lawyer shall be subject to only one set of rules of professional conduct, (ii) making the determination of which set of rules applies to particular conduct as straightforward as possible, consistent with recognition of appropriate regulatory interests of relevant jurisdictions, and (iii) providing protection from discipline for lawyers who act reasonably in the face of uncertainty.

[4] Paragraph (b)(1) provides that as to a lawyer's conduct relating to a proceeding pending before a tribunal, the lawyer shall be subject only to the rules of the jurisdiction in which the tribunal sits unless the rules of the tribunal, including its choice of law rule, provide otherwise. As to all other conduct, including conduct in anticipation of a proceeding not yet pending before a tribunal, paragraph (b)(2) provides that a lawyer shall be subject to the rules of the jurisdiction in which the lawyer's conduct occurred, or if the predominant effect of the conduct is in another jurisdiction, the rules of that jurisdiction shall be applied to the conduct. In the case of conduct in anticipation of a proceeding that is likely to be before a tribunal, the predominant effect of such conduct could be where the conduct occurred, where the tribunal sits or in another jurisdiction.

[5] When a lawyer's conduct involves significant contacts with more than one jurisdiction, it may not be clear whether the predominant effect of the lawyer's conduct will occur in a jurisdiction other than the one in which the conduct occurred. So long as the lawyer's conduct conforms to the rules of a jurisdiction in which the lawyer reasonably believes the predominant effect will occur, the lawyer shall not be subject to discipline under this Rule.

[6] If two admitting jurisdictions were to proceed against a lawyer for the same conduct, they should, applying this rule, identify the same governing ethics rules. They should take all appropriate steps to see that they do apply the same rule to the same conduct, and in all events should avoid proceeding against a lawyer on the basis of two inconsistent rules.

[7] The choice of law provision applies to lawyers engaged in transnational practice, unless international law, treaties or other agreements between competent regulatory authorities in the affected jurisdictions provide otherwise.

[8] The Rules of Professional Conduct apply to a lawyer giving advice or providing services that are not prohibited as the unauthorized practice of law when provided by a non-lawyer but are considered the practice of law when provided by a lawyer. For instance, an accountant giving tax advice to a client is not normally engaged in the unauthorized practice of law. However, if a lawyer gives the same advice, he or she is giving legal advice and is subject to the Rules of Professional Conduct, whether working for a law firm, or an accounting

firm, a consulting firm, or another enterprise. Of course, this is also true if the lawyer is giving advice or providing services that would constitute the unauthorized practice of law by a non-lawyer. In giving both kinds of advice and in providing both kinds of services, a lawyer is considered to be representing a client for the purposes of determining which of these Rules govern the lawyer's conduct. This rule does not permit lawyers to engage in activities that would otherwise violate Rules 5.4 or 5.5 or any of the other Rules of Professional Conduct.

RULE 408. CONTINUING LEGAL EDUCATION AND SPECIALIZATION

PREAMBLE

In the modern legal environment, the law continues to grow more complex and it changes with increasing frequency. Continuing education is no longer a luxury, but is a necessity for all lawyers. Mindful of the improvements in the administration of justice that have resulted from our judicial continuing legal education and mandatory continuing legal education requirements, we believe that all judges and lawyers must meet certain minimum continuing legal education requirements if they are to maintain their competency. We have provided for the continuing legal education of elected and selected other judges in Rule 504. It is our intention that all active members of the Bar and those judges (other than federal judges) who are not required to satisfy the requirements of Rule 504 shall fulfill the mandatory continuing legal education requirements specified in this Rule.

(a) Continuing Legal Education Requirements. All persons admitted to the South Carolina Bar shall be required to attend at least fourteen (14) hours of approved continuing legal education (CLE) courses each year. The annual reporting period for purposes of this Rule shall run from March 1 through the last day in February. At least two (2) of the fourteen (14) hours required annually shall be devoted to legal ethics/professional responsibility. Failure to meet these requirements will result in suspension from the practice of law pursuant to Rule 419, SCACR. Only in cases involving extraordinary hardship or extenuating circumstances may this requirement be waived or modified. The following members of the South Carolina Bar shall be exempt from these requirements:

(1) specialists certified pursuant to this Rule who satisfy the continuing legal education (CLE) requirements of their specialty; provided, however, that at least two (2) hours of the CLE credits completed by certified specialists shall be devoted to legal ethics/professional responsibility;

(2) lawyers at least 60 years old who have been admitted to practice law for thirty (30) or more years, and who apply to the Commission on Continuing Legal Education and Specialization for this exemption. (Exemptions granted prior to June 23, 1994 remain in effect). Provided, however, that if a lawyer who receives an exemption or is entitled to an exemption under this provision is suspended for a definite period of more than six (6) months under Rule 413, SCACR, this exemption shall not apply or be granted during the suspension period;

(3) lawyers, including members of the judiciary, who are not enrolled as "active members" of the Bar. Provided, however, that except in the case of federal judges (including federal magistrates and federal administrative law judges), all judicial members of the Bar not required to fulfill the judicial continuing legal education requirements of Rule 504, SCACR, shall be considered "active members" for the purpose of satisfying the continuing legal education requirements of this Rule and shall not be entitled to an exemption therefrom based upon their status as "judicial members" of the Bar.

(b) Commission on Continuing Legal Education and Specialization.

(1) *Membership and Terms of Office.* The Commission on Continuing Legal Education and Specialization shall consist of twelve (12) members. The Supreme Court shall appoint to the Commission: one (1) member of the Supreme Court or Court of Appeals; one (1) circuit court judge; one (1) family court judge; two (2) attorneys from each of the four (4) judicial regions established by order of the Chief Justice dated January 9, 1992; and one (1) additional attorney from Region II. Of the members first appointed to the Commission, four (4) shall serve a term of one (1) year; four (4) shall serve a term of two (2) years; and four (4) shall serve a term of three (3) years. Members thereafter appointed shall be appointed for three (3) years, but shall continue to serve until their successors are appointed. A member appointed to fill an unexpired term shall serve only to the completion of that term and until his or her successor is appointed. Except for the initial appointments to the Commission, the House of Delegates of the South Carolina Bar shall nominate up to two (2) members of the South Carolina Bar to fill each attorney position on the Commission. No person shall be appointed for more than two (2) consecutive terms. The Supreme Court shall appoint a chairperson and a secretary of the Commission from among the Commission's membership.

(2) *Duties.* Subject to the continuing jurisdiction of the Supreme Court, the Commission shall have general jurisdiction over all matters pertaining to mandatory continuing legal education and specialization in the practice of law and shall:

(A) administer the programs established pursuant to this Rule and Rule 504, SCACR;

(B) select fields of specialization in which South Carolina lawyers may be certified;

(C) appoint and supervise Specialization Advisory Boards, each consisting of at least five (5) lawyers practicing in the specialty field. Each Specialization Advisory Board shall be charged with the responsibility for establishing standards and procedures for certification, recertification and decertification of lawyers in specialty fields approved by the Commission;

(D) subject to the approval of the Supreme Court, make and publish rules, regulations, bylaws, standards and procedures implementing its duties. No proposed rule, regulation, by-law, set of standards or procedures, or any substantive amendment to the preceding shall be adopted by the Commission or any Specialization Advisory Board unless it is first published in the *South Carolina Bar News* or its successor publication for the information and comments of members of the Bar at least ninety (90) days prior to the proposed effective date. A public hearing shall be ordered by the Commission or Specialization Authorization Board upon receipt, at least ten (10) days prior to the effective date, of a petition for a hearing signed by at least ten (10) members of the Bar. Notice of the hearing shall be given in the *South Carolina Bar News* or its successor publication. An adopted rule, regulation, by-law, set of standards or procedures, or any substantive amendment to the preceding shall not become effective until it is filed with and approved by the Supreme Court. The final versions shall be included in any publication of the South Carolina Appellate Court Rules. The procedures contained in this paragraph shall not apply to internal operating procedures of the Commission;

(E) direct a staff headed by an Executive Director appointed by the Supreme Court. The staff shall assist the Commission and the Specialization Advisory Boards in administering this Rule, including processing applications for certified specialist status and for recertification, processing decertification orders, advising Specialization Advisory Boards on CLE course accreditation, providing information about the requirements of this Rule, assisting the Commission and Specialization Advisory Boards in preparing reports, and performing other administrative assignments as directed by the Commission; and

(F) report, at least annually, to the Supreme Court and the South Carolina Bar;

(G) may promulgate regulations approving organizations which certify lawyers as specialists in specialty fields in which the Supreme Court of South Carolina does not certify specialists.

(c) Designation of Specialty Fields.

(1) Subject to approval by the Supreme Court, the Commission may designate a specialty field and define the scope of practice of the field. The designation may be made by the Commission on its own initiative or upon the petition of 100 members of the Bar. Prior to the Commission's designation of a specialty field, notice of the proposed designation must be published in the *South Carolina Bar News* or its successor publication and at least one (1) public hearing relating to the proposed designation must be held.

In designating and defining a specialty field, the Commission shall consider:

(A) whether the public interest would be served;

(B) whether there is sufficient interest to warrant the designation;

(C) whether appropriate standards of proficiency can be established for the specialty field;

(D) whether there is satisfactory evidence of the existence or prospect of an adequate program of continuing legal education in the specialty field; and

(E) whether the designation of the specialty field would fulfill the objectives and further the orderly growth of certified specialization in South Carolina.

(2) No standard governing lawyer certification shall be approved which shall in any way limit the right of any certified lawyer to practice in all fields of law. Any lawyer, alone or in association with any other lawyer, shall have the right to practice in all fields of law, even though certified as a specialist in a particular field. No lawyer shall be required to attain certified specialist status before practicing in any designated specialty field. Any lawyer, alone or in association with any other lawyer, shall have the right to practice in any field of law, even though not certified under the program as a specialist in that field.

All requirements for and all benefits to be derived from certification as a specialist are individual and may not be fulfilled nor attributed to a law firm of which the specialist may be a member.

Participation in the specialization program shall be on a completely voluntary basis.

(d) Specialization Advisory Boards. Each designated specialty field shall have a Specialization Advisory Board charged with the responsibility of establishing standards and procedures for the certification, recertification and decertification of lawyers in the specialty field. No rules or standards shall be adopted in contravention of the South Carolina Appellate Court Rules. Each Specialization Advisory Board shall:

(1) make and publish reasonable and nondiscriminatory standards concerning education, experience and other relevant matters for the certification of lawyers as specialists in its specialty field;

(2) provide procedures for investigating the qualifications of applicants and certificate holders;

(3) make and publish reasonable and nondiscriminatory standards for recertification and decertification;

(4) recommend to the Supreme Court, for the issuance of certificates, lawyers who have qualified for certification in the designated specialty fields;

(5) make and publish rules, regulations and by-laws to implement its authority and duties;

(6) cooperate with the Supreme Court, the Commission and other agencies of the Court and the Bar in establishing and enforcing standards of professional conduct for certified lawyers;

(7) cooperate with the Special Committee on Specialization of the American Bar Association and with agencies in other states engaged in regulating legal specialization;

(8) accredit CLE courses to be taken by certified specialists for recertification, subject to the right of a certified specialist to appeal accreditation decisions to the Commission and from the Commission to the Supreme Court; and

(9) report, at least annually, to the Commission.

(e) Minimum Standards for Specialist Certification.

(1) To qualify for certification in a designated specialty field, an applicant must, at a minimum:

(A) be an active member in good standing of the South Carolina Bar;

(B) submit the names of five (5) other attorneys who are familiar with the applicant's practice, not including attorneys who currently practice in the same law firm as the applicant, who can attest to the applicant's reputation for involvement and competency in the specialty field;

(C) have been engaged in the practice of law for at least five (5) years. If a Specialization Advisory Board finds that an applicant who has not been engaged in the practice of law for five (5) years has had specialized post-graduate education or concentrated experience in a particular area of practice and that the experience is equal to or greater than the experience the applicant would have gained in that area from five (5) years of practice, the Specialization Advisory Board may recommend to the Supreme Court that the requirement of five (5) years of practice be waived and that the applicant be certified as a specialist; and

(D) pay any fee required by the Commission.

(2) As determined by each Specialization Advisory Board, an applicant must:

(A) make a satisfactory showing of substantial involvement (i.e. actual performance) in the specialty field during a five (5) year period, or other reasonable period of not less than three (3) years, immediately preceding the application, which demonstrates according to objective and verifiable standards that the applicant has been substantially involved in the specialty field for which certification is sought; and

(B) successfully complete a program of instruction approved by the Specialization Advisory Board; and

(C) undergo and satisfactorily complete an examination approved and administered by the Specialization Advisory Board. The examination shall consist of oral and/or written parts and shall be designed to test the applicant's knowledge of and ability in the specialty field for which certification is sought.

(3) "Substantial involvement" shall be defined by each Specialization Advisory Board as to its particular field of law from a consideration of the complexity and the extent of necessary devotion to the particular field of practice. It is intended to be a measurement of the actual experience within that particular field. It may be measured by any of several standards such as the time spent on legal matters within the specialty field, the number or type of matters handled within a certain period of time, the time spent in teaching the law of the specialty field, or any combination of these or other appropriate factors. However, within each specialty field, experience requirements shall be measured by objective standards.

(4) The limit on the number of specialties in which a lawyer may be certified shall be determined by such practical limits as are imposed by the requirement of substantial involvement and such other standards as may be established by the Commission and approved by the Supreme Court as a prerequisite to certification.

(f) Standards for Renewal of Certification. Renewal of certification in a designated specialty field shall be required every five (5) years. Each applicant for recertification must:

(1) make a satisfactory showing of substantial involvement in the particular designated specialty field during the period of certification;

(2) make a satisfactory showing of attendance, during the preceding period of certification, at a minimum of sixty (60) hours of continuing legal education in the designated specialty field for which certification was granted. Only attendance at courses accredited by the pertinent Specialization Advisory Board shall count as credit toward the mandatory continuing legal education requirement for certified specialists. The Specialization Advisory Boards shall determine the number of credit hours to be given for each course and the specialty field entitled to credit. On the application of any interested person, the Specialization Advisory Boards, with the assistance of the staff described in section (b)(2)(E) of this Rule, shall make a determination of the qualification of, and credit to be allowed for, particular continuing legal education courses; and

(3) pay any fees prescribed by the Commission.

(g) Revocation of Certification. The Specialization Advisory Board may revoke certification of any lawyer if the certification program for that field is terminated or if it is determined after a hearing, on appropriate notice, that:

(1) certification was granted contrary to the rules of the Specialization Advisory Board, the Commission, or the Supreme Court; or

(2) certification was granted to a lawyer who was not eligible to have been certified in a specialty or who

made any false representation or misstatement of material fact; or

(3) the certified lawyer has failed to abide by all rules and regulations covering the program promulgated by the Specialization Advisory Board, as amended from time to time, including the continuing legal education requirement for maintenance of certified status; or

(4) the certified lawyer has failed to pay any fee prescribed by the Commission; or

(5) the certified lawyer no longer meets the qualifications established by a Specialization Advisory Board; or

(6) the lawyer fails to meet the standards of competence for his particular specialty. Competency in a specialty area shall be determined in the same manner violations of the Rules of Professional Conduct are determined by the Commission on Lawyer Conduct.

(h) Right of Hearing and Appeal.

(1) Except for denial of certification because of failure to receive a passing grade on a specialty field's written examination, a lawyer who is refused certified status, renewal of certification, or whose certified status is revoked shall have the right to a hearing before the appropriate Specialization Advisory Board and the right to appeal the Advisory Board's ruling to the Commission under rules and regulations prescribed by the Commission and approved by the Supreme Court. The exhaustion of this right to appeal shall be a condition precedent to judicial review.

Under rules and regulations prescribed by the Commission and approved by the Supreme Court, an examination and grade review process shall be established for lawyers who fail to receive a passing grade on a specialty field's written examination.

(2) Except as provided otherwise with respect to the issue of whether a lawyer passed a specialty field's written examination, decisions of the Commission may be appealed to the Supreme Court under rules and regulations prescribed by the Commission and approved by the Supreme Court. Decisions of the Commission concerning whether a lawyer passed or failed a specialty field's written examination shall be final.

(i) Responsibilities of Certified Specialists. When a client is referred by a lawyer to a lawyer who is certified under this program, on a matter within the lawyer's specialty field, the certified lawyer shall not take unfair advantage of the certification to enlarge the scope of the representation, and shall strictly comply with the requirements of the Rules of Professional Conduct.

Any certified specialist or any lawyer who holds himself or herself out as a specialist in a particular field shall be held to a standard of competence set by the Supreme Court for a certified specialist in that field.

(j) Financing. Fees approved by the Commission shall be charged for filing applications for certification or renewal of certification by a Specialization Advisory Board, issuance of the certificate evidencing certified status and mandatory continuing legal education registration. The fees shall be reasonable and in an amount as may be necessary to defray the expense of administering the specialization and mandatory continuing legal education programs, and may be changed from time to time.

(k) Confidentiality. The following records regarding lawyer specialization shall be confidential and shall not be disclosed except upon order of the Supreme Court of South Carolina:

(1) All statements or other matter submitted by persons asked to provide a reference for an applicant seeking certification or recertification as a specialist; and

(2) All files or records relating to any applicant who has been denied certification or recertification as a specialist.

[Adopted effective September 1, 1990. Amended effective July 1, 1992; January 7, 1993; August 26, 1993; January 5, 1994; May 5, 1994; June 23, 1994; October 6, 1994; January 1, 1997; March 4, 1997; July 16, 1997; January 22, 1999; September 6, 2000; January 11, 2001; October 12, 2001; May 3, 2006.]

Publisher's Notes

The CLE Regulations are published as "Appendix C" and the Regulations for Legal Specialization in South Carolina are published as "Appendix D" at the end of this part.

RULE 409. RESIGNATION

An attorney's resignation from membership in the Bar shall be referred by the Supreme Court to the Commission on Lawyer Conduct for investigation and a recommendation as to the propriety of accepting the resignation. The Court shall take such action on the resignation as it deems proper.

[Adopted effective September 1, 1990. Amended effective January 1, 1997.]

RULE 410. SOUTH CAROLINA BAR

(a) Name. There is hereby created and established an organization to be known as the South Carolina Bar.

(b) Purposes. The purposes of the organization shall be to uphold and defend the Constitution of the United States and the Constitution of the State of South Carolina; to protect, and maintain respect for, representative government; to continually improve the administration of justice throughout the State; to require the highest standards of ethical and professional conduct, and uphold the integrity and honor of the legal profession; to advance the science of jurisprudence; to promote consistent high quality of legal education and legal services to the public; to apply the knowledge, experience and ability of the legal profession to the promotion of the public good; to encourage goodwill and respect for integrity and excellence in public service among the members of the legal profession and the public; to perform any additional purposes and duties assigned to it by the Supreme Court of South Carolina; and to promote and correlate such policies and activities of the Bar as fall within these purposes in the interest of the legal profession and the public.

(c) Duties and Powers.

(1) The duties of the South Carolina Bar shall be to faithfully carry out its stated purposes as set forth in this rule as may be amended from time to time, with the powers as shall be reasonably necessary and proper for the carrying out of these purposes, including the power to adopt, and amend as necessary, the Bylaws by which it shall be governed, to establish classification of memberships, to recommend amendments or additions to this rule and to the Constitution approved by this Court to be effective upon formation of the South Carolina Bar, and to recommend changes in the license fees to be charged the members thereof.

(2) The annual license fee for active members who have been admitted to practice law in this State or any other jurisdiction for three years or more shall be $245.00 plus the amount specified in (3) below. The license fee for all other members shall be in lesser amounts as may be provided for in the Bylaws of the South Carolina Bar plus the amount specified in (3) below. The license fee shall be payable on or before January 1st of each year. All income and assets shall be handled separately by the South Carolina Bar, as prescribed in its Constitution and Bylaws.

(3) For each of the listed classes of membership, the following additional license fee shall be paid:

(A) Active Members (less than three years)—$20.00

(B) Active Members (three years or more)—$50.00

(C) Judicial Members—$50.00

(D) Inactive Members—$20.00

(E) Military Members—$20.00

(F) Limited Certificates—$20.00

The funds generated from this additional fee shall be placed in a separate account by the South Carolina Bar and shall be disbursed as directed by the Supreme Court to help defray the costs of operating the Commission on Judicial Conduct, the Commission on Lawyer Conduct and the Office of Disciplinary Counsel.

(d) Membership Required. No person shall engage in the practice of law in the State of South Carolina who is not licensed by this Court and a member in good standing of the South Carolina Bar except as otherwise provided in the rules of this Court.

(e) Attorney Information System (AIS). The AIS is a web-based system developed by the South Carolina Judicial Department to maintain and update information regarding members of the South Carolina Bar. Members use this system, which is accessed using a user name and password, to verify and update their individual contact information. The mailing and e-mail address shown in the AIS shall be used for all purposes of notifying and serving the member.

(f) Enrollment of Members and Duties Upon Enrollment. Every person admitted to the practice of law in South Carolina shall be added to the AIS immediately upon their admission. The Clerk of the Supreme Court is authorized to release information from the admissions/application records as necessary to populate the data fields in the AIS. Each new member shall verify and update his or her information in the AIS within five (5) days of being admitted or licensed. Additionally, the South Carolina Bar may require a new member to provide additional information on a form provided by the South Carolina Bar.

(g) Duty of Members to Verify and Update the AIS. Persons admitted to practice law in South Carolina shall have a continuing duty to verify and update their information contained in the AIS, and must ensure that the AIS information is current and accurate at all times. At a minimum, the contact information listed on the AIS must include a mailing address, an e-mail address and a telephone number. Members must update their contact information on the AIS within five (5) days of any change. Additionally, members must verify and update all of their information prior to paying their bar license fees every year. For those fields that the member cannot correct or update using the AIS, the member will make and submit a discrepancy report on the AIS so that the matter can be resolved. Members who have resigned, been disbarred or suspended, or whose admission or license has otherwise been terminated, and who do not intend to ever seek reinstatement or readmission, are not required to update their information.

(h) Foreign Legal Consultants.

(1) *Duty to Verify and Update the AIS.* While not members of the South Carolina Bar, persons who are licensed as foreign legal consultants under Rule 424, SCACR, shall be added to the AIS immediately upon their licensing, and the Clerk of the Supreme Court is authorized to release information from the admissions/application records as necessary to populate the data fields in the AIS. Foreign legal consultants shall have the same duty to update and verify their information on the AIS as specified for members under (f) and (g) above.

(2) *License Fees.* Foreign Legal Consultants shall pay a license fee of $295 to the South Carolina Bar by January 1st. Fifty dollars of this fee shall be placed in the separate account referenced in (c)(3) above to be disbursed as directed by the Supreme Court to help

defray the costs of operating the Commission on Judicial Conduct, the Commission on Lawyer Conduct, and the Office of Disciplinary Counsel.

[Adopted effective September 1, 1990. Amended effective April 18, 1997; September 6, 2000; April 3, 2002; September 1, 2003; October 22, 2003; February 21, 2006; July 19, 2007; October 17, 2011.]

Notes

Notes to 2003 Amendments

The first amendment to Rule 410, SCACR, increased the license fee in Rule 410(c)(2) as requested by the Bar and added subsection 410(c)(3) to impose an additional fee to help defray the costs of operating the attorney and judicial disciplinary systems in South Carolina.

The second amendment amended section (e) of the Rule.

Note to 2006 Amendment

This amendment specifies time limits for providing change of address information to the Bar and specifically requires all members, with the exception of retired members, to provide a current email address to the Bar.

RULE 411. LAWYERS' FUND FOR CLIENT PROTECTION

(a) Statement of Purpose. The Supreme Court is charged with the duty of defining and regulating the practice of law and of organizing and governing the association known as the South Carolina Bar which is composed of the attorneys at law of the State, which association acts as the administrative agency of the Court for the purpose of improving the administration of justice. Attorneys at law in this State, as officers of the Court, have the professional responsibility to preserve and protect the honor and integrity of the profession and have evidenced acceptance of this responsibility by recommending to the Court through the South Carolina Bar the establishment of the Lawyers' Fund for Client Protection of the South Carolina Bar.

The Supreme Court, in the exercise of its exclusive powers, and the attorneys at law in this State, in the exercise of their professional responsibility, have the duty to protect insofar as reasonably possible those persons who may be injured by the infrequent occurrence of attorney dishonesty. Therefore, the following Rule of the Supreme Court, recommended by the South Carolina Bar, is adopted for those purposes.

There is hereby established a special committee of the South Carolina Bar to be known as the Lawyers' Fund for Client Protection Committee whose functions shall be to receive, hold, manage, and disburse such funds as may from time to time be appropriated to it by the House of Delegates of the South Carolina Bar with the approval of the Supreme Court or voluntarily contributed or which may be otherwise received for the purpose of maintaining the integrity and protecting the good name of the legal profession by reimbursing, to the extent deemed by the Committee proper and feasible, losses caused by the dishonest conduct of members of the South Carolina Bar.

(b) Membership and Terms of Office of Lawyers' Fund for Client Protection Committee. The Lawyers' Fund for Client Protection Committee shall consist of ten (10) members of the South Carolina Bar and one (1) member selected from the general public appointed by the President and approved by the Supreme Court. The appointments shall be for a term of five (5) years, and no member who has served a full term shall be eligible for reappointment to the Committee until one (1) year after the termination of the member's last term. Vacancies shall be filled for the unexpired term in the same manner as the original appointments to the Committee.

(c) Duties of Lawyers' Fund for Client Protection Committee.

(1) The Committee shall be authorized, commencing on January 1, 1980, to consider applications for reimbursement of losses which arise after the effective date of this Rule and which are caused by the dishonest conduct of a member of the South Carolina Bar who was acting either as a lawyer or in a fiduciary capacity customary to the practice of law in the matter in which the loss arose, but only to the extent to which these losses are not bonded or to the extent these losses are not otherwise covered; and provided the Bar member has died, has been adjudicated a bankrupt, has been adjudicated mentally incompetent, has been disbarred or suspended from the practice of law, has voluntarily resigned from the practice of law, has left the jurisdiction of this state or cannot be found, or has become a judgment debtor of the applicant based upon his dishonest conduct as a lawyer; or provided that the application has been certified to the Committee by the Commission on Lawyer Conduct of the Supreme Court or the Board of Governors of the South Carolina Bar as an appropriate case for consideration because the loss was caused by the dishonest conduct of a member of the South Carolina Bar. For the purposes of this rule, dishonest conduct of a member of the South Carolina Bar shall include not only dishonest conduct committed by the member, but also dishonest conduct of any person who is not a member of the Bar employed by a member or the firm of a member to assist the member or firm in providing legal services. Reimbursement for losses caused by dishonest conduct of an employee of a member or firm shall only be allowed if the acts giving rise to the loss occurred during the course of that employment. Additionally, for purposes of this rule, dishonest conduct shall include the failure of a lawyer to return an unearned fee after the Resolution of Fee Disputes Board determines the lawyer is not entitled to retain the fee.

The Committee shall investigate applications, which are brought to its attention. The Committee shall be authorized and empowered to reject or allow applications in whole or in part to the extent that funds are available to it. The Committee shall have complete discretion in determining the order, extent, and manner of payments of applications. The payment to any applicant shall not exceed the sum of $40,000 per claim; provided, however, that the aggregate total of claims paid per attorney shall not exceed $200,000. In operating the Lawyers' Fund for Client Protection pursuant to this Rule, the South Carolina Bar does not create or acknowledge any legal responsibility for the acts of individual lawyers in the practice of law. All reimbursements of losses from the Lawyers' Fund for Client Protection shall be a matter of grace in the sole discretion of the Committee and not as a matter of right. No client or member of the public shall have any right in the Lawyers' Fund for Client Protection as a third party beneficiary or otherwise. No attorney shall be compensated for representing an applicant except as authorized by the Committee.

In order for an application to be considered by the Committee, the application must be received by the South Carolina Bar within three (3) years of the date the applicant discovered or reasonably ought to have discovered the dishonest conduct. No application may be considered after the expiration of six (6) years from the date of the dishonest conduct. An application for resolution of a fee dispute which is timely filed under Rule 416, SCACR, shall be considered timely filed for purposes of consideration under this rule in the event an unearned fee is not repaid.

The Committee is further authorized to disburse funds as ordered by the Supreme Court pursuant to Rule 31(f) contained in Rule 413, SCACR. Unless otherwise provided by the order of the Supreme Court, the Committee shall be entitled to reimbursement from the suspended, disbarred, disappeared, or deceased attorney or his estate.

(2) Subject to the approval of the Board of Governors of the South Carolina Bar, the Committee is authorized to prescribe rules of procedure for the management of its funds and affairs, for the presentation of applications, for the processing and payment of applications and for the subrogation or assignment to the South Carolina Bar of all rights of any reimbursed applicant, provided all rules prescribed shall be subject to approval by the Supreme Court.

(3) The Committee may use or employ the Lawyers' Fund for Client Protection for any of the following purposes within the scope of the Committee's objectives:

(A) to make reimbursements on approved applications to clients and members of the public;

(B) to purchase insurance to cover losses in whole or in part as is deemed appropriate, provided that the purchase of the insurance is approved by the Board of Governors of the South Carolina Bar;

(C) to invest any portions of the Fund as may not be needed currently to pay losses, in United States Government Bonds, notes, or bills with interest or other investment income to become a part of the Fund; or

(D) to deposit at interest in federally insured banks or savings and loan associations located in the State of South Carolina, with the interest or other income from the deposit to become a part of the Fund.

(4) The Committee shall establish a rule making confidential all applications, proceedings and reports involving applications for reimbursements until the Committee authorizes reimbursement to the applicant unless the lawyer whose alleged conduct predicates the application requests the matter be made public. This provision shall not be construed to deny access to relevant information to appropriate authorized agencies as authorized by the Committee's Rules of Procedure.

(5) The Commission on Lawyer Conduct of the Supreme Court shall allow a member of the Bar who is assigned to investigate the application for reimbursement to have access, during the investigation, to Board of Commissioners' files if any pertain to the alleged loss.

(6) The Committee shall provide a full report of its activities at least annually to the Board of Governors of the South Carolina Bar and to the Supreme Court. It shall make such other report of its activities and give such publicity to its activities as the Board of Governors or the Supreme Court may deem advisable.

(7) Members of the Committee and staff of the Committee shall be immune from liability and suit while acting within the scope of their duties under this Rule or any rules which may be promulgated by the Committee under (c)(2) above.

(d) Funding.

(1) The South Carolina Bar shall assess each "Active Member" and each "Senior Member" of the South Carolina Bar, as defined in the Bylaws of the South Carolina Bar, the sum of twenty ($20.00) dollars in each calendar year and shall make an appropriation to the Lawyers' Fund for Client Protection in that amount for each year of its operation; provided, however, that no assessment or appropriation may be made which will increase the assets of the fund to an amount in excess of $3,000,000. Payment and enforcement of collection shall be in the same manner and at the same time and with the same penalties for non-payment as provided for payment and collection of license fees in the Bylaws of the South Carolina Bar, but otherwise shall be treated as a separate assessment of "Active Members" and "Senior Members".

(2) All sums appropriated by the South Carolina Bar for the use of the Committee shall be held by the Treasurer of the South Carolina Bar in a separate account known as Lawyers' Fund for Client Protection, subject to the written direction of the Committee under Committee rules.

(3) The Committee is authorized to enforce claims which the Fund may have for restitution and to employ and compensate consultants, agents, legal counsel and other employees as it deems necessary and appropriate. Payment shall be made from the Fund only upon condition that the South Carolina Bar receive a pro-tanto assignment from the payee of the payee's assignable rights against the lawyer involved, the lawyer's personal representative, heirs, devisees and assigns, and against all other persons or legal entities against whom the payee may have a right of recovery by reason of the loss, and upon condition that the Fund shall be entitled to reimbursement on terms the Committee deems proper under the circumstances including reimbursement of costs incurred in prosecuting a claim against the lawyer, the lawyer's personal representative, etc. The net proceeds collected by reason of the assignment shall be for the sole benefit of the Fund and enforcement of this right shall be within the sole discretion of the Committee.

(4) The administrative expenses of the Committee shall be paid out of the general fund of the South Carolina Bar. Provided, however, that any direct administrative expenses, other than staff assistance costs, exceeding $2,000 in any fiscal year shall be paid out of the Lawyers' Fund for Client Protection.

(5) The Fund may be abolished by the same authority which created it. In the event of such abolition, all assets of the Fund shall be and remain the property of the South Carolina Bar to be used for its general purposes as determined by the Board of Governors.

(e) That, in addition to the foregoing, the Fund shall accept and hold on deposit funds received from disciplinary counsel, in addition to monies raised by the assessment established herein for purposes of restitution ordered by the Supreme Court of South Carolina, and shall thereafter disburse these additional monies as directed by order of the Court or upon directive from disciplinary counsel made in accordance with a Plan of Restitution between disciplinary counsel and a lawyer or former lawyer. Amounts disbursed under this paragraph shall not apply toward the maximum limits otherwise available to be paid to any applicant, except to reduce the total amount due for such an applicant, and the disbursement thereof shall not be limited by the time limits otherwise applicable to those making application to the Fund. Nothing in this paragraph shall give any victim of the misconduct of a lawyer or former lawyer a right to make a claim against monies received by the Fund under this paragraph, nor create any cause of action to contest disbursements made under this paragraph by an order of the Supreme Court of South Carolina or a Plan of Restitution arrived at between disciplinary counsel and a sanctioned lawyer or former lawyer. Nothing in this rule shall in any way affect the right of any victim of the misconduct of any lawyer or former lawyer to seek redress against a lawyer or former lawyer's representatives in any legal forum, except to reduce the amount owed by the amount of any payment made to the victim/applicant under the provisions of this rule. Any such Plan of Restitution shall consider and address amounts paid out by the Fund on account of a lawyer or a former lawyer and may, if the parties to that Plan of Restitution agree, include provision for repayment of all or portions of monies paid out by the Fund on account of such lawyer or former lawyer from monies raised by assessments rated under this rule.

[Adopted effective September 1, 1990. Amended effective January 24, 1994; November 16, 1994; May 3, 1995; January 1, 1997; August 21, 1998; September 24, 1998; October 20, 1998; November 4, 2004; April 4, 2007; June 28, 2010.]

RULE 412. INTEREST ON LAWYER TRUST ACCOUNTS (IOLTA)

(a) Definitions. As used herein, the term:

(1) "Nominal or short-term" describes funds of a client or third person that, pursuant to section (d) below, the lawyer has determined cannot provide a positive net return to the client or third person;

(2) "Foundation" means the South Carolina Bar Foundation, Inc.;

(3) "IOLTA account" means a trust account benefiting the South Carolina Bar Foundation established in an eligible institution for the deposit of pooled nominal or short-term funds of clients or third persons. The account product may be an interest-bearing checking account; a money market account with or tied to check-writing; a sweep account which is a government money market fund or daily overnight financial institution repurchase agreement invested solely in or fully collateralized by United States government securities; or an open-end money market fund solely invested in or fully collateralized by United States government securities.

(A) "Open-end money market fund" is a fund holding itself out as a money market fund as defined by applicable federal statutes and regulations under the Investment Act of 1940 and, at the time of the investment, having total assets of at least $250,000,000.

(B) "United States government securities" are United States treasury obligations and obligations issued or guaranteed as to principal and interest by the United States or any agency or instrumentality thereof, including obligations of Government Sponsored Enterprises.

(4) "Eligible Institution" means any bank or savings and loan association authorized by federal or state laws to do business in South Carolina and insured by the Federal Deposit Insurance Corporation or any successor insurance corporation(s) established by federal or state laws.

(5) "Reasonable fees" for IOLTA accounts are per check charges, per deposit charges, a fee in lieu of a

minimum balance, Federal deposit insurance fees, sweep fees and a reasonable IOLTA account administrative fee.

(b) Attorney Participation.

(1) All nominal or short-term funds belonging to clients or third persons that are placed in trust with any member of the South Carolina Bar practicing law from an office or other business location within the state of South Carolina shall be deposited into one or more IOLTA accounts, except as provided in Rule 1.15 of Rule 407, South Carolina Appellate Court Rules, with respect to funds maintained other than in a bank account and as provided in section (i) below.

(2) A law firm of which the lawyer is a member may maintain the account on behalf of any or all lawyers in the firm.

(c) Depository Procedures.

(1) The IOLTA account shall be established with an eligible institution that voluntarily chooses to participate. Funds deposited in each IOLTA account shall be subject to withdrawal upon request and without delay, subject only to any notice period which the institution is required or permitted to reserve by law or regulation and as provided in Rule 1.15 regarding safekeeping of client property.

(2) The rate of interest or dividends payable on any IOLTA trust account shall be no less than:

(A) the highest interest rate or dividend generally available from the institution to its non-IOLTA customers for each IOLTA account that meets the same minimum balance or other eligibility qualifications, if any. In determining the highest interest rate or dividend generally available from the institution to its non-IOLTA customers, the institution may consider factors, in addition to the IOLTA account balance, customarily considered by the institution when setting interest rates or dividends for its customers if such factors do not discriminate between IOLTA accounts and accounts of non-IOLTA customers and these factors do not include that the account is an IOLTA account. The institution also shall consider all product option types noted at (a)(3) for an IOLTA account offered by the financial institution to its non-IOLTA customers by either establishing the applicable product as an IOLTA account or paying the comparable interest rate or dividend on the IOLTA checking account in lieu of actually establishing the comparable highest interest rate or dividend product; or

(B) an eligible institution may choose to pay a rate equal to the greater of 0.65% or 65% (the "index") of the Federal Funds Target Rate (the "benchmark") as of the first business day of the IOLTA remitting period, which rate is deemed to be net of reasonable fees, on an IOLTA checking account. The index and benchmark are determined periodically, but not more frequently than every six months, by the Foundation to reflect an overall comparable rate for the South Carolina Bar Foundation. When applicable, the Foundation will express its benchmark in relation to the Federal Funds Target Rate.

(3) Eligible institutions may choose to pay rates higher than comparable rates described at (c)(2) above.

(d) Determination of Nominal or Short–Term Funds.

(1) The lawyer shall exercise good faith judgment in determining upon receipt whether the funds of a client or third person are nominal or short-term. Client or third person funds shall be deposited in a lawyer's or law firm's IOLTA account unless the funds can earn income for the client in excess of the costs incurred to secure such income.

In the exercise of this good faith judgment and determining whether a client's funds can earn income in excess of costs of securing that income for the benefit of the client or third person, and thus provide a positive net return to the client or third person, the lawyer or law firm shall consider the following factors:

(A) the amount of funds to be deposited;

(B) the expected duration of the deposit, including the likelihood of delay in the matter for which the funds are held;

(C) the rates of interest or yield at financial institutions where the funds are to be deposited;

(D) the cost of establishing and administering non–IOLTA accounts for the benefit of the client or third person, including service charges, the costs of the lawyer's services, and the costs of preparing any tax reports required for income accruing to the benefit of the client or third person;

(E) the capability of financial institutions, lawyers or law firms to calculate and pay income to individual clients or third persons; and

(F) any other circumstances that affect the ability of the client's or third persons' funds to earn a net return for the client or third person.

The lawyer or law firm shall review its IOLTA account at reasonable intervals to determine whether changed circumstances require further action with respect to the funds of any client or third person.

(2) The determination of whether a client's or third person's funds are nominal or short-term shall rest in the sound judgment of the lawyer or law firm. No lawyer shall be charged with ethical impropriety based on the exercise of such good faith judgment.

(3) Notification to the client is not required nor shall the client or third person have the power to elect whether nominal or short-term funds shall be placed in the IOLTA account.

(4) The provisions of section (c) shall not relieve a lawyer or law firm from an obligation imposed by Rule 1.15 of the Rules of Professional Conduct with respect to safekeeping of client property.

(e) IOLTA Refund Procedures.

The Foundation shall establish procedures for the processing of refund requests for such instances as bank or lawyer error.

(f) Notice to Foundation.

Lawyers or law firms shall advise the Foundation, at Post Office Box 608, Columbia, SC 29202-0608, by facsimile at (803) 779-6126, or in such other manner as the Foundation publishes in its materials is acceptable, of the establishment and closing of an IOLTA account for funds covered by this rule. Such notice shall include: the name of the institution where the IOLTA account is established; the IOLTA account number as assigned by the institution; the institution address; and the name and South Carolina Bar attorney number of the lawyer, or of each member of the South Carolina Bar in a law firm, practicing from an office or other business location within the state of South Carolina that has established the IOLTA account.

(g) Certification.

Each member shall certify annually on the member's license fee statement submitted pursuant to Rule 410, South Carolina Appellate Court Rules, that the member is in compliance with the provisions of this rule or, pursuant to section (i) below, has been approved by the Foundation as exempt from the provisions of this rule.

(h) Remittance and Reporting Instructions.

A lawyer or law firm depositing client funds in an IOLTA account shall direct the depository institution to:

(1) calculate and remit interest or dividends, net of reasonable service charges or fees, if any, on the average monthly balance in the account or as otherwise computed in accordance with the institution's standard accounting practice, monthly to the Foundation, which shall be the sole beneficial owner of the interest or dividends generated by the accounts;

(2) transmit monthly to the Foundation a report, listing by account the name of the lawyer or law firm for whom each remittance is made, the lawyer's or law firm's IOLTA account number as assigned by the institution, the rate and type of interest or dividend applied, the average account balance for the reporting period or the other amount from which interest or dividends are determined, the amount of each remittance, and the amount and type of any service charges or fees assessed during the remittance period, and the net amount of interest remitted for the period;

(3) transmit at least quarterly to the depositing lawyer or law firm, a report or statement in accordance with normal procedures for reporting to its depositors.

"Reasonable fees" as defined in (a)(5) may be deducted from interest or dividends on an IOLTA account provided that such charges or fees shall be calculated in accordance with an eligible institution's standard practice for non-IOLTA customers. No other fees or charges shall be assessed against the interest on an IOLTA account, but rather shall be the responsibility of, and may be charged to, the lawyer or law firm maintaining the IOLTA account. Fees or charges in excess of the interest or dividend earned on the account for any month shall not be taken from interest or dividends earned on other IOLTA accounts or from the principal of the account. Eligible institutions may elect to waive any or all fees on IOLTA accounts.

(i) Exempt Accounts.

The Foundation will establish procedures for a lawyer or law firm to maintain an interest-free trust account for client and third-person funds that are nominal or short-term when the lawyer's or law firm's account cannot reasonably be expected to produce or has not produced over time an interest income net of reasonable service charges or fees.

(j) Program Administration.

The Foundation shall, in accordance with its charter and by-laws, receive, administer, invest, disburse and separately account for all funds remitted to it through this program.

[Adopted effective September 1, 1990. Amended effective March 1, 2005; February 19, 2009; June 15, 2010.]

RULE 413. RULES FOR LAWYER DISCIPLINARY ENFORCEMENT

I. PURPOSE AND TERMINOLOGY

RULE 1. PURPOSE

The regulation of the conduct of lawyers is critical to preserving the integrity of the legal profession and enhancing public confidence in the judicial system. These rules provide the procedure for resolving allegations that a lawyer has committed ethical misconduct or that a lawyer suffers from a physical or mental condition which adversely affects the lawyer's ability to practice law.

[Adopted effective January 1, 1997.]

RULE 2. TERMINOLOGY

The following terminology is used throughout these rules:

(a) Admonition: a sanction imposed on a lawyer by an investigative panel of the Commission or by the Supreme Court. See Rule 7(b)(5) and Rule 19(d)(2). A confidential admonition cannot be imposed by an investigative panel after the filing and service of formal charges. If imposed by the Supreme Court after the disciplinary proceeding has become public under Rule 12(b), the order imposing the admonition shall not be published, but shall be a matter of public record. Only in cases of minor misconduct, when there is little or no injury to the public, the legal system, or the profession, should an admonition be imposed.

(b) Closed, But Not Dismissed: a manner of disposing of a matter where a panel of the Commission makes a finding that the matter should not be dismissed, but it is either impossible or impractical to proceed with the matter because it appears that the lawyer is deceased, disappeared, incarcerated, physically or mentally incapacitated, disbarred, or suspended from the practice of law, or for other good cause.

(c) Commission: the Commission on Lawyer Conduct.

(d) Commission Counsel: the lawyer drafting reports, providing legal advice to the Commission and performing other duties assigned by the Commission. See Rule 6.

(e) Complaint: information in any form from any source received by the Commission that alleges, or from which a reasonable inference can be drawn, that a lawyer committed misconduct or is incapacitated. If there is no written complaint from another person, disciplinary counsel's written statement of the allegations constitutes the complaint.

(f) Conviction: any conviction resulting from a trial or any type of plea, including a plea of nolo contendere or a plea pursuant to *North Carolina v. Alford,* 400 U.S. 25, 91 S.Ct. 160, 27 L.Ed.2d 162 (1970).

(g) Deferred Discipline Agreement: a confidential agreement between the lawyer and an investigative panel of the Commission for the lawyer to undergo treatment, participate in education programs or take other corrective action. It is only available as a response to misconduct that is minor and can be addressed through treatment or a rehabilitation program. A deferred discipline agreement can only be entered into prior to the filing and service of formal charges.

(h) Disciplinary Counsel: the lawyer in charge of screening and investigating complaints, prosecuting formal charges and performing other duties assigned by the Supreme Court. See Rule 5.

(i) Formal Charges: the document that charges the lawyer with specific acts of misconduct or with a specific incapacity.

(j) Hearing Panel: the panel of the Commission that conducts hearings on formal charges. See Rule 4.

(k) Hearing: the public proceeding at which the issues of law and fact raised by the formal charges and answer are tried. See Rule 26.

(*l*) Incapacity: a mental or physical condition that adversely affects a lawyer's ability to practice law. Incapacity is distinguished from a disability that does not adversely affect a lawyer's ability to practice law.

(m) Incapacity Inactive Status: non-disciplinary suspension of a lawyer from the practice of law based on incapacity.

(n) Interim Suspension: temporary suspension from the practice of law pending a final determination in any proceeding under these rules. See Rule 17.

(*o*) Investigation: an inquiry into allegations of misconduct, including a search for and examination of evidence concerning the allegations. See Rule 19.

(p) Investigative Panel: the panel of the Commission that considers the recommendations of disciplinary counsel with regard to the disposition of cases and acceptance of agreements for resolution of disciplinary matters. The investigative panel also determines whether formal charges will be filed. See Rule 4.

(q) Lawyer: anyone admitted to practice law in this state, including any formerly admitted lawyer with respect to acts committed prior to resignation or disbarment; any lawyer specially admitted by a court of this state for a particular proceeding; a lawyer not admitted in this jurisdiction if the lawyer provides or offers to provide any legal services in this jurisdiction; or anyone whose advertisements or solicitations are subject to regulation by Rule 418, SCACR.

(r) Letter of Caution: a written caution or warning about past or future conduct issued when it is determined that no misconduct has been committed or that only minor misconduct not warranting the imposition of a sanction has been committed. A letter of caution may be issued by disciplinary counsel, an investigative panel or the Supreme Court. The issuance of a letter of caution is not a sanction under these rules and does not constitute a finding of misconduct. The fact that a letter of caution has been issued shall not be considered in a subsequent disciplinary proceeding against the lawyer unless the caution or warning contained in the letter of caution is relevant to the misconduct alleged in the proceedings.

(s) Misconduct: any conduct by a lawyer constituting grounds for discipline. See Rule 7(a).

(t) Proceedings: all steps in the discipline and incapacity system set forth in these rules.

(u) Public Members: members of the Commission who have never been admitted to practice law in any jurisdiction and have never held a judicial office.

(v) Public Reprimand: a reprimand by the Supreme Court in the form of a written decision which shall be imposed in person or served upon the respondent by certified mail.

(w) Reasonable Cause: a reasonable ground for belief in the existence of facts warranting the filing of formal charges for discipline or a petition for transfer to incapacity inactive status.

(x) Record: all documents filed in the case beginning with the formal charges. The record includes a transcript of the hearing on the formal charges.

(y) Respondent: a lawyer against whom formal charges have been filed.

(z) Screening: examination of a complaint or other information coming to the attention of disciplinary counsel to determine whether the Commission has jurisdiction. See Rule 19(a).

(aa) Serious Crime: any felony; any lesser crime that reflects adversely on the lawyer's honesty, trustworthiness or fitness as a lawyer in other respects; or, any crime a necessary element of which, as determined by the statutory or common law definition of the crime, involves interference with the administration of justice, false swearing, misrepresentation, fraud, deceit, bribery, extortion, misappropriation, theft, willful failure to file income tax returns, or an attempt, conspiracy or solicitation of another to commit a serious crime.

(bb) Supreme Court: the Supreme Court of South Carolina.

[Adopted effective January 1, 1997. Amended effective May 22, 1997; August 7, 1997; July 1, 1999; June 8, 2000; September 1, 2003; October 4, 2006; April 4, 2007; January 1, 2010; June 28, 2010; January 19, 2011.]

II. ORGANIZATION AND STRUCTURE

RULE 3. THE COMMISSION ON LAWYER CONDUCT

(a) Commission Created. There is hereby created a Commission on Lawyer Conduct.

(b) Jurisdiction. The Commission shall have jurisdiction over all allegations that a lawyer has committed misconduct or is incapacitated.

(c) Appointment of Members. The Commission shall be composed of 50 members appointed by the Supreme Court. 34 members shall be active members of the South Carolina Bar. 16 members shall be public members.

(d) Terms. Attorney members shall serve for a term of 4 years and public members shall serve for a term of 2 years. Commission members shall be eligible for reappointment. A member assigned to a hearing panel may continue to participate in the hearing and decision of a matter despite the expiration of the member's term if the hearing began before the expiration of the term.

(e) Removal. The Supreme Court may remove any member of the Commission.

(f) Vacancies. A vacancy shall occur when a Commission member ceases to be eligible to represent the category from which the member was appointed, is removed, or becomes unable to serve for any reason. An appointment to fill the vacancy shall be made by the Supreme Court. A member selected to fill a vacancy shall hold office for the duration of the unexpired term.

(g) Powers Not Assumed. These rules shall not be construed to deny any court the powers necessary to maintain control over its proceedings. Nothing in these rules shall limit the authority of the Supreme Court to enjoin and to punish as contempt of court any person who engages in the unauthorized practice of law.

[Adopted effective January 1, 1997. Amended effective October 4, 2006; January 1, 2010.]

RULE 4. ORGANIZATION AND AUTHORITY OF THE COMMISSION

(a) Officers. The Supreme Court shall appoint one attorney member to serve as the chair and another to serve as the vice-chair of the Commission. The vice-chair shall perform the duties of the chair whenever the chair is absent or unable to act.

(b) Panels and Meetings. The attorney members of the Commission, other than the chair and vice-chair, shall be divided by the chair into 8 panels of 4 attorney members and 2 public members. The panels shall be assigned to serve as an investigative panel or a hearing panel as designated by the chair. If the panel is assigned to serve as an investigative panel, the chair shall add either the chair or the vice-chair to the panel to increase its membership to 7. The chair may rotate the assignments of the panels as investigative or hearing panels, and may rotate membership on the panels; provided, however, that no member shall sit on both the investigative and hearing panel for the same proceeding. Panels shall meet when scheduled by the Commission. The full Commission shall meet periodically as determined by the Commission to consider administrative matters. Meetings of the Commission other than periodic meetings may be called by the chair upon the chair's own motion and shall be called by the chair upon the written request of three members of the Commission.

(c) Quorum. 23 members of the full Commission, 5 members of an investigative panel and 3 members of a hearing panel shall constitute a quorum for the transaction of business. Where necessary to obtain a quorum for a panel, the chair of the Commission may appoint substitute members from another panel; provided, however, that no member who has served on an investigative panel in a matter may be appointed to serve on the hearing panel for that matter.

(d) Expenses. Subject to such policies as the Office of Finance and Personnel of the Judicial Department may establish, members shall be reimbursed for reasonable and necessary expenses incurred pursuant to their duties.

(e) Powers and Duties of the Commission.

(1) The Commission shall have the duty and authority to:

(A) adopt its own rules of procedure for discipline and incapacity proceedings subject to the approval of the Supreme Court; and

(B) propose amendments to the Rules of Professional Conduct and these Rules for Lawyer Disciplinary Enforcement to the Supreme Court.

(2) In addition to the duties assigned to Commission counsel in Rule 6, the Commission may delegate to Commission counsel the duty and authority to:

(A) maintain the Commission's records;

(B) maintain statistics concerning the operation of the Commission and make them available to the Commission and the Supreme Court;

(C) prepare an annual report of the Commission's activities for presentation to the Supreme Court and the public;

(D) inform the public of the existence and operation of the lawyer discipline system, including the Commission's address and telephone number and the disposition of each matter in which public discipline is imposed;

(E) monitor lawyers for compliance with conditions of reinstatement, readmission, discipline and deferred discipline, and refer lawyers who fail to comply to disciplinary counsel for contempt proceedings;

(F) provide advice and assistance to attorneys appointed to protect clients' interests; and,

(G) supervise attorneys, court reporters, and other staff as the Supreme Court may provide to the Commission.

(f) Powers and Duties of Investigative Panel. An investigative panel shall have the duty and authority to:

(1) review the recommendations of disciplinary counsel after investigation and either issue a letter of caution, issue notice of intent to impose a confidential admonition, enter into a deferred discipline agreement, consider an agreement for discipline by consent, authorize formal charges, refer the matter to another agency, or dismiss the complaint;

(2) designate a member of the panel to preside over the investigative panel in the absence of the chair or vice-chair of the Commission;

(3) declare a matter closed, but not dismissed prior to the filing of formal charges; and,

(4) after proper notice, re-open a matter that has been previously dismissed or closed but not dismissed.

(g) Powers and Duties of Hearing Panel. A hearing panel shall have the duty and authority to:

(1) rule on pre-hearing motions, conduct hearings on formal charges and make findings, conclusions, and recommendations to the Supreme Court for the disposition of the case, pursuant to Rule 26;

(2) designate a member of the panel to serve as the chair of the panel; and

(3) declare, after proper notice, a matter closed, but not dismissed, after the filing of formal charges.

(h) Recusal. A member of the Commission shall recuse himself or herself in any matter in which recusal would be required of a judicial officer under the Code of Judicial Conduct.

(i) Complaints Against Members of the Commission. If a complaint is filed against a lawyer member of the Commission, the Commission member against whom the complaint has been filed shall not participate in the investigation or adjudication of the matter. [Adopted effective January 1, 1997. Amended effective September 1, 2003; March 1, 2004; May 26, 2006; April 4, 2007; January 1, 2010; January 19, 2011.]

RULE 5. DISCIPLINARY COUNSEL

(a) Appointment. The Supreme Court shall appoint an active member of the South Carolina Bar as the disciplinary counsel. The disciplinary counsel may be removed by a majority vote of the Supreme Court. The disciplinary counsel shall not otherwise engage in the practice of law, except to the extent a staff attorney would be authorized to do so under Rule 506, SCACR, or serve in a judicial capacity.

(b) Powers and Duties. Disciplinary counsel shall have the authority and duty to:

(1) receive and screen complaints, dismiss complaints, issue letters of caution, refer complaints to other agencies when appropriate, conduct investigations, notify complainants about the status and disposition of their complaints, make recommendations to an investigative panel on the disposition of complaints after investigation, file formal charges when directed to do so by an investigative panel, prosecute formal charges, and file briefs and other appropriate petitions with the Supreme Court;

(2) maintain permanent records of the operations of disciplinary counsel's office, including receipt of complaints, screening, investigation, and filing of formal charges in lawyer discipline and incapacity matters, subject to the requirements of Rule 20;

(3) compile statistics to aid in the administration of the system, including but not limited to a log of all complaints received, investigative files, and statistical summaries of docket processing and case dispositions;

(4) supervise such other attorneys, investigators and staff as the Supreme Court or the Attorney General may provide;

(5) employ private investigators or experts as necessary to investigate and process matters before the Commission and the Supreme Court;

(6) investigate and, if appropriate, commence and prosecute contempt proceedings in the Supreme Court based on allegations that a lawyer who is disbarred, suspended or transferred to incapacity inactive status has engaged in the practice of law;

(7) initiate and prosecute proceedings before the Commission and the Supreme Court to enforce orders related to disciplinary proceedings or related to the

practice of law by lawyers and to seek restraining orders and sanctions in connection with violations thereof;

(8) dismiss a matter where a lawyer subject to a pending complaint dies prior to an agreement for discipline by consent or report of the hearing panel being submitted to the Supreme Court;

(9) serve as opposing counsel in proceedings before the Committee on Character and Fitness in which a lawyer seeks reinstatement or readmission;

(10) provide advice and assistance to attorneys appointed to protect clients' interests; and,

(11) perform other duties at the direction of the Commission or the Supreme Court.

(c) Appointment of Attorneys to Assist Disciplinary Counsel. The Supreme Court may appoint such additional active members of the South Carolina Bar as it deems appropriate to assist the disciplinary counsel in performing disciplinary counsel's duties under this rule. Subject to such policies as the Office of Finance and Personnel of the Judicial Department may establish, these attorneys shall be reimbursed for reasonable and necessary expenses incurred pursuant to their duties.

[Adopted effective January 1, 1997. Amended effective September 1, 2003; May 26, 2006; November 15, 2007; January 1, 2010; January 19, 2011.]

RULE 6. COMMISSION COUNSEL

(a) Appointment. The Supreme Court may appoint a Commission counsel to assist the Commission.

(b) Powers and Duties. The Commission may delegate functions to the Commission counsel, including but not limited to the duty and authority to:

(1) advise the hearing panel during its deliberations and draft decisions, orders, reports and other documents on behalf of the hearing panel;

(2) supervise other staff necessary to the performance of the Commission's duties; and

(3) perform other duties at the direction of the Commission.

[Adopted effective January 1, 1997.]

III. GENERAL PROVISIONS

RULE 7. GROUNDS FOR DISCIPLINE; SANCTIONS IMPOSED; DEFERRED DISCIPLINE AGREEMENT

(a) Grounds for Discipline. It shall be a ground for discipline for a lawyer to:

(1) violate or attempt to violate the Rules of Professional Conduct, Rule 407, SCACR, or any other rules of this jurisdiction regarding professional conduct of lawyers;

(2) engage in conduct violating applicable rules of professional conduct of another jurisdiction;

(3) willfully violate a valid order of the Supreme Court, Commission or panels of the Commission in a proceeding under these rules, willfully fail to appear personally as directed, willfully fail to comply with a subpoena issued under these rules, or knowingly fail to respond to a lawful demand from a disciplinary authority to include a request for a response or appearance under Rule 19(b)(1), (c)(3) or (c)(4);

(4) be convicted of a crime of moral turpitude or a serious crime;

(5) engage in conduct tending to pollute the administration of justice or to bring the courts or the legal profession into disrepute or conduct demonstrating an unfitness to practice law;

(6) violate the oath of office taken to practice law in this state and contained in Rule 402(k), SCACR;

(7) willfully violate a valid court order issued by a court of this state or of another jurisdiction;

(8) employ a person in violation of Rule 34;

(9) willfully fail to comply with the terms of a finally accepted deferred disciplinary agreement or any terms of a finally accepted agreement for discipline by consent; and,

(10) willfully fail to comply with a final decision of the Resolution of Fee Disputes Board.

(b) Sanctions. Misconduct shall be grounds for one or more of the following sanctions:

(1) disbarment;

(2) suspension for a definite period from the office of attorney at law. The period of the suspension shall not exceed 3 years and shall be set by the Supreme Court;

(3) public reprimand;

(4) admonition, provided that an admonition may be used in subsequent proceedings as evidence of prior misconduct solely upon the issue of sanction to be imposed;

(5) restitution to persons financially injured, repayment of unearned or inequitable attorney's fees or costs advanced by the client, and reimbursement to the Lawyers' Fund for Client Protection;

(6) assessment of the costs of the proceedings, including the cost of hearings, investigations, prosecution, service of process and court reporter services;

(7) assessment of a fine;

(8) limitations on the nature and extent of the lawyer's future practice;

(9) any other sanction or requirement as the Supreme Court may determine is appropriate.

[Adopted effective January 1, 1997. Amended effective August 7, 1997; June 8, 2000; September 1, 2003; September 22, 2004; April 4, 2007; January 1, 2010.]

RULE 8. PROOF

Charges of misconduct or incapacity shall be established by clear and convincing evidence, and the burden of proof of the charges shall be on the disciplinary counsel. The burden of proof in proceedings seeking reinstatement following disbarment, suspension or transfer to lawyer incapacity inactive status is on the lawyer by clear and convincing evidence.

[Adopted effective January 1, 1997.]

RULE 9. CIVIL RULES APPLICABLE

Except as otherwise provided in these rules, the South Carolina Rules of Evidence applicable to nonjury civil proceedings and the South Carolina Rules of Civil Procedure apply in lawyer discipline and incapacity cases when formal charges have been filed. The right to discovery, however, shall be limited to that provided by Rule 25.

[Adopted effective January 1, 1997. Amended effective September 1, 2003.]

RULE 10. RIGHT TO COUNSEL

The lawyer shall be entitled to retain counsel and to have the assistance of counsel at every stage of these proceedings. The Commission may appoint counsel to represent the lawyer in incapacity proceedings. See Rule 28(b)(3). After appearing as counsel for a lawyer in a matter under these rules, counsel for the lawyer may only withdraw upon leave of the chair, vice chair, or a panel of the Commission after 10 days notice to disciplinary counsel and the lawyer or, prior to formal charges having been filed, upon stipulation of the lawyer, the withdrawing counsel and disciplinary counsel. Provided, after a matter has been forwarded to the Supreme Court for action, counsel can only withdraw from representation upon leave of the Supreme Court after due notice to the client and disciplinary counsel.

[Adopted effective January 1, 1997. Amended effective September 1, 2003.]

RULE 11. EX PARTE CONTACTS

Members of the Commission and Commission counsel shall not engage in *ex parte* communications regarding a case, except that before making a determination to file formal charges in a case pursuant to Rule 19(d)(4), members of the investigative panel assigned to that case may communicate with disciplinary counsel as required to perform their duties in accordance with these rules, and the chair and vice-chair may entertain requests for permissive disclosure pursuant to Rule 12(c) made by disciplinary counsel without notice to the lawyer. Where disciplinary counsel makes a request to the chair or vice-chair pursuant to either Rule 12(c) or 19(b) without notice to the lawyer, the request shall so state and set forth the reason that notice is not being given. *Ex parte* communications shall include any communication which would be prohibited by Section 3B(7) of the Code of Judicial Conduct, Rule 501, SCACR, if engaged in by a judge.

[Adopted effective January 1, 1997. Amended effective September 1, 2003; January 1, 2010.]

RULE 12. ACCESS TO DISCIPLINARY INFORMATION

(a) General Rule. Except as otherwise provided in these rules or ordered by the Supreme Court, the members of the Commission, the staff of the Commission, disciplinary counsel, the staff of disciplinary counsel, the members of the Supreme Court and the staff of the Supreme Court shall not in any way reveal the existence of the complaint, while the matter remains confidential, except to persons directly involved in the matter and then only to the extent necessary for a proper disposition of the matter. A violation of this provision may be punished as a contempt of the Supreme Court.

(b) When Misconduct Proceedings Become Public. When formal charges are filed regarding allegations of misconduct, the formal charges and any answer shall become public 30 days after the filing of the answer or, if no answer is filed, 30 days after the expiration of the time to answer under Rule 23. Thereafter, except as otherwise provided by these rules or the Supreme Court, all subsequent records and proceedings relating to the misconduct allegations shall be open to the public inclusive of a letter of caution or admonition issued after the filing of formal charges. If allegations of incapacity are raised during the misconduct proceedings, all records, information and proceedings relating to these allegations shall be held confidential.

(c) Permissive Disclosure by Commission. The Commission may, however, disclose information at any stage of the proceedings:

(1) when the chair, vice-chair or a panel of the Commission has determined that there is a need to notify another person to protect that person or to notify a government agency in order to protect the public or the administration of justice;

(2) to appropriate law enforcement officials when the chair, vice-chair or a panel of the Commission determines that it is in possession of reliable information indicating that a person has violated the criminal laws of this State, any other state, the District of Columbia, or the United States;

(3) upon waiver in writing by the lawyer;

(4) to persons from whom and entities from which it appears that a lawyer has misappropriated monies or other property when the chair or vice-chair or a panel of the Commission has determined that the disclosure of the information will tend to prevent further misappropriation or likely facilitate restitution, recovery, or compensation from the Lawyers' Fund for Client

Protection, insurance coverage, title insurance, or other sources; or,

(5) to the appropriate disciplinary authority in any jurisdiction in which a lawyer is admitted to practice law or has applied for admission to practice law concerning a matter where there is evidence the lawyer committed misconduct under lawyer or judicial disciplinary rules of that jurisdiction or where a lawyer receives any sanction under Rule 7(b).

(d) Disclosure Necessary for Withdrawal as Counsel. When it is necessary to obtain the permission of a tribunal to withdraw from representation, a lawyer may reveal the fact that the client filed a complaint with the Commission to help establish good cause for withdrawal. If the motion to be relieved includes a reference to the existence of a complaint which is confidential under this rule, the lawyer may elect to give opposing counsel notice of the motion only, without revealing the existence of the complaint. If the lawyer's motion to be relieved is accompanied by a request that the records relating to the motion be sealed, the tribunal shall take steps to prevent disclosure of the existence of the complaint to any other person. After deciding the motion to be relieved, the tribunal shall insure that either the record is sealed or that all references to the complaint are deleted from the record available to the public. No members of the tribunal or its staff who learn of the existence of the complaint shall reveal that fact to any other person.

(e) Protective Orders. In order to protect the interests of a complainant, witness, third party or respondent, the hearing panel may, upon application of any person and for good cause shown, issue a protective order prohibiting the disclosure of specific information otherwise privileged or confidential and direct that the proceedings be conducted in a manner to preserve the confidentiality of the information that is the subject of the application.

(f) Work Product and Deliberations. Disciplinary counsel's work product, Commission deliberations, and records of the Commission's deliberations shall not be disclosed.

(g) Permissive disclosure by the parties. Either party may disclose in proceedings before a hearing panel statements and other evidence, gathered prior to the matter becoming public after the filing of formal charges, that were subject to discovery under Rule 25 to the extent admissible under South Carolina Rules of Civil Procedure or South Carolina Rules of Evidence.

[Adopted effective January 1, 1997. Amended effective March 6, 1997; September 1, 2003; January 1, 2010.]

RULE 13. IMMUNITY FROM CIVIL SUITS

Communications to the Commission, Commission counsel, disciplinary counsel, or their staffs relating to misconduct or incapacity and testimony given in the proceedings shall be absolutely privileged, and no civil lawsuit predicated thereon may be instituted against any complainant or witness. Members of the Commission, Commission counsel and staff, disciplinary counsel and staff, any attorney appointed to protect clients under Rule 31, and any supervising or monitoring attorney appointed under Rule 33 shall be absolutely immune from civil suit for all conduct in the course of their official duties.

[Adopted effective January 1, 1997. Amended effective May 22, 1997.]

RULE 14. TIME, SERVICE AND FILING

(a) Computation of Time. Computation of time under these rules shall be in the manner provided by Rule 263, SCACR.

(b) Extending and Diminishing Time Prescribed by These Rules.

(1) *By the Commission.* The chair of the Commission, the vice-chair of the Commission, or the chair of the hearing panel before which the matter is pending, may extend or shorten the period of time to perform any act required by Rules 19–26. Any request for an extension by an investigative panel or hearing panel shall be considered by the chair or vice-chair of the Commission. No extension over 30 days shall be granted except upon good cause shown. The grant or denial of an extension shall not be subject to an interlocutory appeal.

(2) *By Disciplinary Counsel.* Disciplinary counsel may extend the time for responses due from a lawyer under Rule 19 for one or more periods not to exceed 30 days in the aggregate for each.

(3) *By the Parties.* Disciplinary counsel and the lawyer may, by written agreement, extend the time to respond under Rule 19 or 23(a) after the execution and delivery by both parties of an agreement for discipline by consent or deferred disciplinary agreement for the duration of the period the agreement is awaiting a final disposition and for a period of 30 days thereafter if the Agreement is not accepted.

(4) *By the Supreme Court.* Except for those periods of time that may be extended by the Commission under (1) above, the Supreme Court or any justice thereof may grant an extension of time to perform any act required by these Rules. The Supreme Court or any justice thereof may shorten any time period prescribed by these rules.

(c) Service. Service upon the lawyer of formal charges in any disciplinary or incapacity proceedings shall be made by personal service upon the lawyer or the lawyer's counsel by any person authorized by the chair of the Commission, or by registered or certified mail, return receipt requested, to the lawyer's last known address. If service cannot be so made, service shall be deemed complete when deposited in the U.S. Mail, provided the formal charges were sent by registered or certified mail, return receipt requested, to the address the lawyer provided to the South Carolina Bar pursuant to Rule 410(e), SCACR, and to the lawyer's last known address, if those addresses differ. Service of all other documents shall be made in the manner provided by Rule 262(b), SCACR.

(d) Filing. When these rules require filing of a document with the Commission or the Supreme Court, the filing may be accomplished by:

(1) Delivering the document to the Commission or the clerk of the Supreme Court; or

(2) Depositing the document in the U.S. mail, properly addressed to the Commission or the clerk of the Supreme Court, with sufficient first class postage attached.

The date of filing shall be the date of delivery or the date of mailing. Any document filed with the Supreme Court or the Commission shall be accompanied by proof of service of such document on all other parties. An electronically transmitted facsimile copy of a document may be accepted for filing; however, an original of the document must be immediately sent by U.S. mail to the clerk of the Supreme Court or the Commission.

[Adopted effective January 1, 1997. Amended effective September 1, 2003; November 15, 2007; April 29, 2009; March 22, 2010.]

RULE 15. OATHS; SUBPOENA POWER

(a) Oaths. Oaths and affirmations may be administered by any member of the Commission, disciplinary counsel, or any other person authorized by law to administer oaths and affirmations.

(b) Subpoenas for Investigation.

(1) Disciplinary counsel may compel by subpoena the attendance of the lawyer or witnesses and the production of pertinent books, papers, documents (whether in typed, printed, written, digital, electronic, or other format), and other tangible evidence for the purposes of investigation.

(2) The Commission chair, vice-chair, or Commission counsel may issue subpoenas for specific witnesses or documents at the request of the lawyer under investigation or direct disciplinary counsel to subpoena witnesses or documents and provide the subpoenaed information to the Commission chair, vice-chair, or Commission counsel.

(c) Subpoenas for Deposition or Hearing. After formal charges are filed, disciplinary counsel and respondent may compel by subpoena the attendance of witnesses and the production of pertinent books, papers, and documents at a deposition or hearing held under these rules.

(d) Enforcement of Subpoenas. The willful failure to comply with a subpoena issued under this rule may be punished as a contempt of the Supreme Court. Upon proper application, the Supreme Court may enforce the attendance and testimony of any witnesses and the production of any documents subpoenaed.

(e) Quashing Subpoenas. Any attack on the validity of a subpoena shall be heard and determined by the investigative or hearing panel before which the matter is pending. Any resulting order shall not be subject to an interlocutory appeal; instead these decisions must be challenged by filing objections or a brief pursuant to Rule 27(a).

(f) Subpoena Pursuant to Law of Another Jurisdiction. Whenever a subpoena is sought in this State pursuant to the law or disciplinary rules of another jurisdiction for use in lawyer or judicial disciplinary or disability proceedings, and where the issuance of the subpoena has been duly approved under the applicable laws or rules of the other jurisdiction, the chair or vice-chair or a panel of the Commission upon a showing of good cause, may issue a subpoena to compel the attendance of witnesses and the production of documents in the county where the witness resides or is employed or elsewhere in this state as agreed by the witness. Service, enforcement, or challenges to such subpoenas shall be as provided in these rules.

[Adopted effective January 1, 1997. Amended effective April 18, 1997; September 1, 2003; November 15, 2007; January 1, 2010.]

RULE 16. LAWYERS CHARGED WITH OR CONVICTED OF A CRIME

(a) Transmittal of Charging Documents. The clerk of any court in this state shall transmit a certified copy of any indictment, information or complaint charging a lawyer with a crime to the disciplinary counsel within 10 days of the filing of such charging document.

(b) Transmittal of Certificate of Conviction. The clerk of any court in this state in which a lawyer is convicted of a crime shall, within 10 days after the conviction, transmit a certified copy of the judgment of conviction to disciplinary counsel.

(c) Action by Disciplinary Counsel. Upon receiving competent evidence that a lawyer has been charged or convicted of a crime, disciplinary counsel shall determine whether the crime involved is a serious crime as defined by Rule 2(aa). If the crime is a serious crime, disciplinary counsel may seek an interim suspension under Rule 17(a) if the lawyer has been charged with a serious crime, and shall seek an interim suspension under Rule 17(a) if the lawyer has been convicted of a serious crime. If the crime is not a serious crime, disciplinary counsel shall process the matter in the same manner as any other information coming to the attention of the Commission.

(d) Conviction as Conclusive Evidence. A certified copy of a judgment of conviction constitutes conclusive evidence that the lawyer committed the crime, and the sole issue in any disciplinary proceedings based on the conviction shall be the nature and extent of the discipline imposed.

(e) Stay of Hearing; Effect of Acquittal, Dismissal of Charges, or Reversal or Vacation of Conviction. The hearing under Rule 26 shall not be held until all direct appeals from the conviction are exhausted. An acquittal, dismissal of the criminal charges, or reversal or vacation of a conviction shall not automatically terminate any proceeding then pending against the lawyer, and the Commission may proceed on the basis of the available evidence other than the charge or the conviction.

[Adopted effective January 1, 1997.]

RULE 17. INTERIM SUSPENSION

(a) Criminal Prosecution or Conviction for a Serious Crime. Without the necessity of Commission action, the Supreme Court may place a lawyer on interim suspension upon notice of the filing of an indictment, information or complaint charging the lawyer with a serious crime, and shall immediately place a lawyer on interim suspension on receipt of a certified copy of a judgment of conviction or other competent evidence showing that the lawyer has been convicted of a serious crime. The fact that sentencing may be delayed or an appeal may be taken shall not prevent the Supreme Court from imposing an interim suspension.

(b) Other Misconduct or Incapacity. Upon receipt of sufficient evidence demonstrating that a lawyer poses a substantial threat of serious harm to the public or to the administration of justice, the Supreme Court may suspend the lawyer or transfer the lawyer to incapacity inactive status pending a final determination in any proceeding under these rules.

(c) Failure to Respond to Notice of Investigation, Subpoena, or Notice of Appearance. Upon receipt of sufficient evidence demonstrating that a lawyer has failed to fully respond to a notice of investigation, has failed to fully comply with a proper subpoena issued in connection with an investigation or formal charges, has failed to appear at and fully respond to inquiries at an appearance required pursuant to Rule 19(c)(3), or has failed to respond to inquiries or directives of the Commission or the Supreme Court, the Supreme Court may place that lawyer on interim suspension.

(d) Motion for Reconsideration. A lawyer placed on interim suspension or transferred to incapacity inactive status may apply to the Supreme Court for reconsideration of the order. A copy of the motion shall be filed with the Commission and served on the disciplinary counsel.

(e) Order to be Public. The order of interim suspension or transfer to incapacity inactive status shall be public. Unless the Supreme Court determines that it is appropriate to do so, an order transferring a lawyer to incapacity inactive status shall not disclose the nature of the incapacity.

[Adopted effective January 1, 1997. Amended effective September 1, 2003; January 1, 2010; June 1, 2010.]

RULE 18. NOTIFICATION TO COMPLAINANT; LIMITED RIGHT TO REVIEW

(a) Notification to Complainant. Disciplinary counsel shall provide written acknowledgment of every complaint, if the complainant is known, and notify the complainant in writing of the final disposition of a proceeding under these rules. Notification in writing shall be mailed within 20 days of the decision disposing of the proceeding.

(b) Limited Right to Review. Although entitled to notice, a complainant is not a party to the proceeding. However, upon notice of a dismissal by disciplinary counsel pursuant to Rule 19(d)(1), a complainant may seek review by the investigative panel. Disciplinary counsel shall inform the complainant of the following review process in the notice of dismissal. The complainant may seek review by submitting a request to the disciplinary counsel in writing within 30 days of the date of the notice of dismissal. Upon receipt of the request for review, disciplinary counsel shall provide the lawyer with a copy of the request. The lawyer may submit a written response within 15 days. Disciplinary counsel shall submit the complainant's request and the lawyer's response, if any, for consideration at the next meeting of the investigative panel. Notification in writing shall be mailed to the complainant and the lawyer within 20 days of the investigative panel's decision. The complainant is not entitled to appeal or otherwise seek review of a dismissal or referral by disciplinary counsel pursuant to Rule 19(a) or of any decision, action, or disposition by the investigative panel, the hearing panel, the Commission chair or vice-chair, or the Supreme Court.

[Adopted effective January 1, 1997. Amended effective August 7, 1997; August 13, 1998; January 1, 2010.]

IV. DISCIPLINARY PROCEEDINGS

RULE 19. SCREENING AND INVESTIGATION

(a) Screening. Disciplinary counsel shall evaluate all information coming to disciplinary counsel's attention by complaint or from other sources that alleges lawyer misconduct or incapacity. If the information would not constitute misconduct or incapacity if it were true, disciplinary counsel shall dismiss the complaint or, if appropriate, refer the matter to another agency. If the information raises allegations that would constitute lawyer misconduct or incapacity if true, disciplinary counsel shall conduct an investigation.

(b) Investigation. Disciplinary counsel shall conduct all investigations. Disciplinary counsel may issue subpoenas pursuant to Rule 15(b), conduct interviews and examine evidence to determine whether grounds exist to believe the allegations of complaints. Disciplinary counsel shall issue a notice of investigation to the lawyer with a copy of the complaint or information received requesting that the lawyer file a response to the allegations in the notice; provided, however, that disciplinary counsel may seek permission of the chair or vice-chair to dispense with the requirement to make this request or to dispense with the requirement to provide the lawyer with a copy of the complaint or information received. The lawyer shall file a written response within 15 days of notice to do so from disciplinary counsel. The written response must include the lawyer's verification that it is complete and accurate to the best of the lawyer's knowledge and belief.

(c) Requirements of Notice of Investigation.

(1) When issuing notice of investigation pursuant to Rule 19(b), disciplinary counsel shall give the following notice to the lawyer:

(A) a specific statement of the allegations being investigated and the rules or other ethical standards allegedly violated, with the provision that the investigation can be expanded if deemed appropriate by disciplinary counsel;

(B) the lawyer's duty to respond pursuant to Rule 19(b);

(C) the lawyer's opportunity to meet with disciplinary counsel pursuant to Rule 19(c)(3); and,

(D) the name of the complainant unless the investigative panel determines that there is good cause to withhold that information.

(2) The investigative panel may defer the giving of notice but, when notice is deferred, disciplinary counsel must give notice to the lawyer before making a recommendation as to a disposition.

(3) Before disciplinary counsel or the investigative panel determines its disposition of the complaint under Rule 19(d), either disciplinary counsel or the lawyer may request that the lawyer appear before disciplinary counsel to respond to questions. The appearance shall be on the record and the testimony shall be under oath or affirmation. If disciplinary counsel requests the lawyer's appearance, disciplinary counsel must give the lawyer 20 days' notice.

(4) Any person giving testimony pursuant to Rule 19 shall be entitled to obtain a transcript of his or her testimony from the transcribing court reporter upon paying the subscribed charges unless otherwise directed by an investigative panel for good cause shown.

(d) Disposition After Investigation.

(1) Upon completion of the investigation, if disciplinary counsel believes that no misconduct has been committed, and a written caution is not appropriate to conclude the matter, disciplinary counsel may dismiss the complaint.

(2) If disciplinary counsel believes that no misconduct has been committed, but a written caution or warning is appropriate to conclude the matter, disciplinary counsel may issue a letter of caution.

(3) If disciplinary counsel believes there is evidence supporting the allegations against a lawyer, disciplinary counsel may:

(A) propose an agreement for discipline by consent to the lawyer pursuant to Rule 21;

(B) recommend to an investigative panel that the matter be concluded with a letter of caution or a confidential admonition; or,

(C) recommend to an investigative panel that formal charges be filed.

(4) The investigative panel may adopt, reject or modify the recommendations of disciplinary counsel.

(A) If the investigative panel finds no violation or a violation pursuant to Rule 7 for which the imposition of a sanction is not warranted, it may dismiss or issue a letter of caution.

(B) If the investigative panel finds that there is reasonable cause to believe the lawyer committed misconduct for which the imposition of a sanction is warranted, it may accept an agreement for discipline by consent pursuant to Rule 21; it may execute a deferred discipline agreement; it may admonish the lawyer pursuant to the provisions of Rule 19(d)(5) or, it may direct disciplinary counsel to file formal charges.

(C) If the investigative panel finds that the matter should not be dismissed, but it is either impossible or impractical to proceed with the matter because it appears that the lawyer is deceased, disappeared, incarcerated, physically or mentally incapacitated, disbarred, or suspended from the practice of law, or for other good cause, the panel may designate the matter closed but not dismissed. If the lawyer files a written objection with the Commission and serves a copy of that objection on disciplinary counsel within 10 days of service of notice that the matter was closed, but not dismissed, the matter shall be deemed re-opened and in the investigation phase. Any objection need not contain any grounds for objecting. Before a matter can be re-opened after being closed, but not dismissed, an investigative panel of the Commission must make a finding that there has been a change in the circumstances that were the basis for the matter to be closed, but not dismissed, or that there is other good cause for it to be re-opened. Before a motion can be considered by an investigative panel of the Commission to re-open a matter that has been previously closed, but not dismissed, disciplinary counsel shall serve a copy of the motion to do so containing the grounds to re-open on the lawyer and then the lawyer shall have 10 days to respond thereto. Disciplinary counsel shall notify both the lawyer and the complainant when a matter is closed, but not dismissed, and when the matter is re-opened. If the panel declines to re-open the matter, disciplinary counsel shall so advise the lawyer.

(5) When the investigative panel finds reasonable cause to conclude that the lawyer has committed misconduct, but finds that public discipline is not warranted, it may issue notice to the lawyer that it intends to impose a confidential admonition as a final disposition of the matter(s). Notice to the lawyer shall include a copy of the confidential admonition and shall be served on the lawyer in accordance with Rule 14(c). The notice of intent shall state the lawyer's right to object and that any such objection need not include any grounds therefor. The confidential admonition shall thereafter be imposed unless the lawyer both files with the Commission and serves on disciplinary counsel a written objection within 30 days of mailing of the notice. If the lawyer objects to the imposition of the confidential admonition in conformity with the requirements of this rule, disciplinary counsel shall file formal charges.

[Adopted effective January 1, 1997. Amended effective April 18, 1997; August 7, 1997; June 8, 2000; September 1, 2003; May 26, 2006; April 4, 2007; January 1, 2010; January 19, 2011.]

RULE 20. MOTION BY DISCIPLINARY COUNSEL TO RE-OPEN DISMISSED COMPLAINTS

If a complaint has been dismissed, the allegations made in that complaint shall not be used for any purpose unless the complaint is re-opened by the Commission. A complaint dismissed prior to the filing of formal charges may be re-opened by an investigative panel upon motion of disciplinary counsel upon a finding by the investigative panel that there is new information concerning the matter dismissed, an additional complaint has been filed against the same lawyer involving related or similar allegations, or other good cause. Prior to a motion to re-open being decided, a copy of the motion to re-open containing the grounds therefor shall be served on the lawyer by disciplinary counsel, and the lawyer shall then have 10 days thereafter to file a written response with the Commission. The lawyer and the complainant shall be notified by disciplinary counsel as to the panel's decision on the motion to re-open.

[Adopted effective January 1, 1997. Amended effective September 1, 2003; January 1, 2010.]

RULE 21. DISCIPLINE BY CONSENT

(a) Agreement. At any stage in the proceedings, the lawyer and disciplinary counsel may agree to the imposition of a stated sanction(s) or the issuance of a letter of caution in exchange for the lawyer's admission of any or all of the allegations of misconduct involved in the proceedings. If the agreement is entered into after the filing of the formal charges, the agreement shall admit or deny the allegations contained in the formal charges. If the agreement is entered into before the filing of the formal charges, the agreement shall contain the specific factual allegations which the lawyer admits he or she has committed and the applicable provisions of the Rules of Professional Conduct or other ethical or disciplinary provisions that the lawyer has violated. The agreement shall be signed by disciplinary counsel, by the lawyer and, if the lawyer is represented by counsel, by the lawyer's counsel. The signature of the lawyer's counsel on the agreement shall indicate that counsel has advised the lawyer regarding the agreement and that counsel believes the lawyer is voluntarily entering into the agreement with a full understanding of the effect of the agreement.

(b) Affidavit. The lawyer shall also sign an affidavit stating that:

(1) the lawyer consents to the sanction(s) or letter of caution;

(2) the consent is voluntarily given;

(3) the matters admitted in the agreement and the facts stated in the affidavit are true.

(c) Submission to Panel. The agreement and affidavit shall be submitted to an investigative panel if formal charges have not been filed, or to a hearing panel if formal charges have been filed on any of the allegations. Provided, if formal charges have been filed but not heard, an investigative panel can consider the proposed agreement and affidavit if the parties both agree in writing. The panel shall either reject the agreement, or submit the agreement and affidavit to the Supreme Court if it determines the agreement should be accepted. An investigative panel shall, however, finally approve or disapprove an agreement for an admonition, a deferred discipline agreement or a letter of caution and, if approved, shall impose the sanction or issue the letter of caution without submitting the matter to the Supreme Court.

(d) Action by Supreme Court. If the panel submits the matter to the Supreme Court, the Supreme Court shall either reject the agreement or issue a decision disciplining the lawyer which shall be based on the agreement. The decision shall comply with the requirements of Rule 27(e).

(e) Effect of Rejection of Agreement. If an agreement is rejected by the panel or the Supreme Court, the proceedings shall continue. The rejected agreement and affidavit shall be withdrawn and shall not be used against the lawyer in any further proceedings.

(f) Confidentiality. The agreement, affidavit and any statement or other documents submitted in mitigation shall remain confidential until the Supreme Court enters a decision disciplining the lawyer at which time the agreement, affidavit and any statement or other documents submitted in mitigation shall be available to the public. An agreement and affidavit which are rejected or which result in the imposition of an admonition, a deferred discipline agreement or a letter of caution by an investigative panel, shall not be available to the public at any time, nor shall any statement or other documents in mitigation filed therewith.

(g) Briefs and Oral Arguments. The Supreme Court may require the parties to submit briefs or participate in oral arguments in connection with the agreement. Either the lawyer or disciplinary counsel may move before the Supreme Court for permission for the parties to file briefs, to have oral arguments, or both in connection with the agreement, but the Supreme Court, in its discretion, may proceed to take action on the agreement without briefs, without oral arguments, or without either, not withstanding a request from one or both of the parties.

[Adopted effective January 1, 1997. Amended effective May 22, 1997; August 7, 1997; June 24, 1999; July 21, 1999; June 8, 2000; September 1, 2003.]

RULE 22. FORMAL CHARGES

The formal charges shall give fair and adequate notice of the nature of the alleged misconduct or incapacity. Disciplinary counsel shall file the formal charges with the Commission. Disciplinary counsel shall cause a copy of the formal charges to be served upon the respondent or respondent's counsel and shall file proof of service with the Commission.

[Adopted effective January 1, 1997.]

RULE 23. ANSWER

(a) Time. The respondent shall file a written answer with the Commission and serve a copy on disciplinary counsel within 30 days after service of the formal charges, unless the time is extended by the hearing panel.

(b) Waiver of Privilege. The raising of a mental or physical condition as a defense constitutes a waiver of any medical privilege pursuant to Rule 28(d)(4).

[Adopted effective January 1, 1997.]

RULE 24. FAILURE TO ANSWER; FAILURE TO APPEAR

(a) Failure to Answer. Failure to answer the formal charges shall constitute an admission of the factual allegations.

(b) Failure to Appear. If the respondent should fail to appear when specifically so ordered by the hearing panel or the Supreme Court, the respondent shall be deemed to have admitted the factual allegations which were to be the subject of such appearance and to have conceded the merits of any motion or recommendations to be considered at such appearance. Absent good cause, the hearing panel or Supreme Court shall not continue or delay proceedings because of the respondent's failure to appear. A willful failure to appear before a hearing panel or the Supreme Court may be punished as a contempt of the Supreme Court.

[Adopted effective January 1, 1997.]

RULE 25. DISCOVERY

(a) Initial Disclosure. Within 20 days of the filing of an answer, disciplinary counsel and respondent shall exchange:

(1) the names and addresses of all persons known to have knowledge of the relevant facts;

(2) non-privileged evidence relevant to the formal charges;

(3) the names of expert witnesses expected to testify at the hearing and affidavits setting forth their opinions and the bases therefor; and,

(4) other material only upon good cause shown to the chair of the hearing panel.

Disciplinary counsel or the respondent may withhold such information only with permission of the chair of the hearing panel or the chair's designee, who shall authorize withholding of the information only for good cause shown, taking into consideration the materiality of the information possessed by the witness and the position the witness occupies in relation to the judge. The chair's review of the withholding request is to be in camera, but the party making the request must advise the opposing party of the request without disclosing the subject of the request.

(b) Pre–Hearing Disclosure. Within 20 days of the date of the filing of an answer, the chair of the hearing panel shall set a date for the exchange of witness lists and exhibits no later than 30 days prior to the scheduled hearing. Disciplinary counsel and respondent shall exchange exhibits to be presented at the hearing, names and addresses of witnesses to be called at the hearing, witness statements, and summaries of interviews with witnesses who will be called at the hearing (for purposes of this paragraph, a witness statement is a written statement signed or otherwise adopted or approved by the person making it, or a stenographic, mechanical, electrical, or other recording, or a transcription thereof, which is a substantially verbatim recital of an oral statement by the person making it and contemporaneously recorded). Copies of transcripts of testimony taken by a court reporter pursuant to Rule 15(b) or Rule 19(c) may be obtained by the parties from the court reporter at the expense of the requesting party and need not be made available to the requesting party by the opposing party unless not otherwise available or otherwise directed by the Commission under Rule 25(h).

(c) Depositions. Depositions shall only be allowed if agreed upon by the disciplinary counsel and the respondent, or if the chair of the hearing panel or the chair's designee grants permission to do so based on a showing of good cause. The chair or the chair's designee may place restrictions or conditions on the manner, time and place of any authorized deposition.

(d) Exculpatory Evidence. Notwithstanding any other provision of this rule, disciplinary counsel shall provide respondent with exculpatory evidence relevant to the formal charges.

(e) Duty of Supplementation. Both parties have a continuing duty to supplement information required to be exchanged under this rule.

(f) Completion of Discovery. All discovery shall be completed within 60 days of the filing of the answer.

(g) Failure to Disclose. If a party fails to timely disclose a witness's name and address, any statements by the witness, summaries of witness interviews, or other evidence required to be disclosed or exchanged under this rule, the hearing panel may grant a continuance of the hearing, preclude the party from calling the witness or introducing the document, or take such other action as may be appropriate. In the event disciplinary counsel has not timely disclosed exculpatory material, the hearing panel may require the matter to be disclosed and grant a continuance, or take such other action as may be appropriate.

(h) Resolution of Disputes. Disputes concerning discovery shall be determined by the hearing panel. Review of these decisions shall not be subject to an interlocutory appeal; instead these decisions must be challenged by filing objections or a brief pursuant to Rule 27(a).

(i) Pre–Hearing Conferences. The hearing panel may require the respondent and disciplinary counsel to participate in a pre-hearing conference in person or by telephone. Either party may request a pre-hearing conference. Scheduling of a pre-hearing conference is at the sole discretion of the chair of the hearing panel.

[Adopted effective January 1, 1997. Amended effective September 1, 2003; November 15, 2007; January 1, 2010.]

RULE 26. HEARING

(a) Scheduling. Upon receipt of the respondent's answer or upon expiration of the time to answer, the hearing panel of the Commission shall schedule a public hearing and notify disciplinary counsel and respondent of the date, time, and place of the hearing.

(b) Hearing Panel. The hearing shall be conducted by three or more members of the hearing panel of the Commission. See Rule 4(g).

(c) Conduct of Hearing.

(1) All testimony shall be given under oath or affirmation.

(2) Disciplinary counsel shall present evidence on the formal charges.

(3) Disciplinary counsel may call the respondent as a witness.

(4) Both parties shall be permitted to present evidence and produce and cross-examine witnesses.

(5) The hearing shall be recorded verbatim and a transcript shall be promptly prepared and filed with the Commission. A copy of the transcript shall be made available to the respondent at respondent's expense.

(6) Disciplinary counsel and the respondent may submit proposed findings, conclusions, and recommendations for dismissal, letter of caution, sanction(s), or transfer to lawyer incapacity inactive status to the members of the hearing panel who conducted the hearing.

(d) Submission of the Report. Within 60 days after the filing of the transcript, the hearing panel shall file with the Supreme Court the record of the proceeding and a report setting forth a written summary, proposed findings of fact, conclusions of law, any minority opinions, and recommendations for dismissal, letter of caution, sanction(s), or transfer to lawyer incapacity inactive status. The hearing panel shall at the same time serve the report upon the respondent and disciplinary counsel.

(e) Combining Cases for Hearing. Upon motion of either party after 10 days notice to the opposing party, a hearing panel may combine for hearing two or more formal charges pending against a lawyer which have not been heard or may reconvene to hear additional formal charges against a lawyer filed prior to the hearing panel issuing a panel report concerning formal charges against the lawyer already heard by that panel.

[Adopted effective January 1, 1997. Amended effective August 7, 1997; September 1, 2003; April 4, 2007; March 22, 2010.]

RULE 27. REVIEW BY SUPREME COURT

(a) Briefs of Disciplinary Counsel and Respondent. Within 30 days of the service of the hearing panel report, disciplinary counsel and/or respondent may serve and file a brief setting forth and arguing any exceptions taken to the findings, conclusions or recommendations made by the hearing panel. Within 30 days after service of the brief, the opposing party may serve and file a brief in response. Within 15 days of the service of the response, the party who filed the brief containing exceptions may serve and file a reply brief. The failure of a party to file a brief taking exceptions to the report constitutes acceptance of the findings of fact, conclusions of law, and recommendations.

(b) Form, Content and Number of Briefs. The form and content of the briefs shall, to the extent possible, comply with the requirements of Rules 208 and 267, SCACR. The number of briefs to be served and filed shall be the same as that required for final briefs under Rule 211(a), SCACR.

(c) Supplementary Filings and Oral Argument.

(1) If the Supreme Court desires an expansion of the record or additional findings, it shall remand the case to the hearing panel with appropriate directions and withhold action pending receipt of the additional filing.

(2) The Supreme Court may order additional briefs or oral arguments as to the entire case or specified issues.

(d) Stay for Further Proceedings. If, during review by the Supreme Court, the Commission receives another complaint against the respondent, disciplinary counsel shall advise the Supreme Court. The Supreme Court may stay its review pending the Commission's determination of the second complaint. The Supreme Court may impose a single sanction covering all recommendations for discipline from the Commission against a respondent.

(e) Decision.

(1) The Supreme Court shall file a written decision dismissing the case, containing a letter of caution, imposing a sanction(s), or transferring the lawyer to incapacity inactive status. Any order relating to incapacity shall comply with Rule 28(g). Unless otherwise ordered by the Supreme Court, the decision shall be effective upon filing.

(2) The Supreme Court may accept, reject, or modify in whole or in part the findings, conclusions and recommendations of the Commission.

(3) The Supreme Court may assess costs against the respondent if it finds the respondent has committed misconduct. Unless otherwise ordered by the Court, costs shall be paid within 30 days of the filing of the opinion or order assessing costs.

(f) Rehearing. A petition for rehearing must be served and filed within 15 days after the filing of the decision or order.

(g) Recusal. A justice of the Supreme Court shall not participate in any proceeding involving allegations of misconduct or incapacity against the justice, or in any proceeding where recusal is required under the Code of Judicial Conduct.

(h) Notice of Decision. The Commission shall transmit notice of all public discipline imposed against a lawyer, transfers to and from incapacity inactive status, and reinstatements to the National Discipline Data Bank maintained by the American Bar Association, the disciplinary enforcement agency of every other jurisdiction in which the lawyer is admitted, and the South Carolina Bar. The Commission shall transmit notice of a decision suspending, disbarring or transferring a lawyer to disability inactive status to the clerk of court in each county in which the lawyer maintained an office and the chief judge for administrative purposes having authority over any county in which the lawyer maintained an office. The Commission may also establish policies for giving notice of public discipline to other courts, agencies and organizations. The Commission shall not provide notice when an admonition is imposed.

[Adopted effective January 1, 1997. Amended effective August 7, 1997; September 9, 1999; June 8, 2000; April 29, 2009.]

RULE 28. CASES INVOLVING ALLEGATIONS OF MENTAL OR PHYSICAL INCAPACITY

(a) Initiation of Incapacity Proceeding. An incapacity proceeding may be initiated by complaint, by a claim of inability to defend in a disciplinary proceeding, or by an order of involuntary commitment or adjudication of incompetency.

(b) Proceedings to Determine Incapacity Generally. All incapacity proceedings shall be conducted in accordance with the procedures for disciplinary proceedings, except:

(1) the purpose of the incapacity proceedings shall be to determine whether the lawyer suffers from a physical or mental condition that adversely affects the lawyer's ability to practice law;

(2) all of the proceedings, information and documents shall be confidential except as provided in Rule 28(g);

(3) the Commission, if it deems it appropriate, may appoint counsel to represent the lawyer if the lawyer is without representation;

(4) the Commission may appoint a guardian ad litem for the lawyer;

(5) the hearing panel shall designate one or more qualified medical, psychiatric, or psychological experts to examine the lawyer prior to the hearing on the matter. The hearing panel may designate an expert agreed upon by disciplinary counsel and the lawyer. The expert or experts shall report to the hearing panel and the parties;

(6) if the Supreme Court concludes that the lawyer suffers from a physical or mental condition that adversely affects the lawyer's ability to practice law, it may enter any order appropriate to the circumstances, the nature of the incapacity and probable length of the period of incapacity, including:

(A) transferring the lawyer to incapacity inactive status;

(B) placing restrictions or conditions on the lawyer, to include limiting the lawyer's practice of law or requiring the lawyer to undergo appropriate treatment;

(C) deferring any disciplinary proceeding based on misconduct pending against the lawyer if the Supreme Court determines that the lawyer is unable to assist in his or her own defense pursuant to Rule 28(d)(2).

(c) Involuntary Commitment or Adjudication of Incompetency. If a lawyer has been judicially declared incompetent or is involuntarily committed on the grounds of incompetency or incapacity by a final judicial order after a judicial hearing, the Supreme Court, upon receipt of a certified copy of the order, shall enter an order immediately transferring the lawyer to incapacity inactive status. A copy of the order shall be served, in the manner the Supreme Court shall direct, upon the lawyer, the lawyer's guardian, or the director of the institution to which the lawyer has been committed.

(d) Inability to Properly Defend in a Disciplinary Proceeding.

(1) If in the course of a disciplinary proceeding based on misconduct, a lawyer alleges an inability to assist in the defense due to mental or physical incapacity, disciplinary counsel shall notify the Supreme Court. The Supreme Court shall immediately transfer the lawyer to incapacity inactive status pending a determination by the Supreme Court of the incapacity pursuant to Rule 28(b). A determination by the Commission that the lawyer is able to assist in his or her own defense is interlocutory and may not be appealed before entry of a final order in the proceeding.

(2) If, pursuant to Rule 28(b), the Supreme Court determines the claim of inability to defend is valid, the disciplinary proceeding based on misconduct shall be deferred. Any investigation of the disciplinary complaint may continue. The lawyer shall remain on incapacity inactive status until the Supreme Court grants a petition for reinstatement to active status as a lawyer. If the Supreme Court determines that a petition for reinstatement to active status should be granted, the Supreme Court shall also determine the disposition of the interrupted disciplinary proceedings.

(3) If, pursuant to Rule 28(b), the Supreme Court determines that the claim of inability to defend is invalid, the disciplinary proceeding based on misconduct shall resume. The lawyer shall, however, be retained on incapacity inactive status pending completion of the disciplinary proceedings.

(4) The raising of mental or physical condition as a defense to, or in mitigation of, formal charges constitutes a waiver of any medical privilege.

(e) Stipulated Disposition.

(1) After receipt of the examination report of the expert or experts designated by the hearing panel, disciplinary counsel and the lawyer may agree upon proposed findings of fact, conclusions, and recommended disposition. The stipulated disposition shall be submitted to the hearing panel for a recommendation to the Supreme Court of approval or rejection. The final decision on the recommendation shall be made by the Supreme Court.

(2) If the Supreme Court accepts the stipulated disposition, it shall enter an order in accordance with its terms. If the stipulated disposition is rejected by the Supreme Court, it shall be withdrawn and cannot be used against the lawyer in any proceedings. If the Supreme Court rejects the stipulated disposition, the Supreme Court shall order that the hearing proceed.

(f) Reinstatement From Incapacity Inactive Status.

(1) *Generally.* No lawyer transferred to incapacity inactive status may resume active status except by order of the Supreme Court.

(2) *Petition.* Any lawyer transferred to incapacity inactive status shall be entitled to petition for transfer to active status once a year or at whatever shorter intervals the Supreme Court may direct in the order transferring the lawyer to incapacity inactive status or any modifications thereof. The lawyer shall serve a copy of the petition on disciplinary counsel, and shall file 10 copies of the petition with the Clerk of the Supreme Court. The copies filed with the Clerk shall be accompanied by proof of service showing service on disciplinary counsel.

(3) *Examination.* Upon the filing of a petition for transfer to active status, the Supreme Court may take or direct whatever action it deems necessary or proper to determine whether the incapacity has been removed, including a direction for an examination of the lawyer by qualified medical or psychological experts designated by the Supreme Court. In its discretion, the Supreme Court may direct that the expense of the examination be paid by the lawyer.

(4) *Required Disclosure.* With the filing of a petition for reinstatement to active status, the lawyer shall be required to disclose the name of each psychiatrist, psychologist, physician and hospital or other institution by whom or in which the lawyer has been examined or treated since the transfer to incapacity inactive status. The lawyer shall furnish to the Supreme Court written consent to the release of information and records relating to the incapacity if requested by the Supreme Court or court-appointed medical or psychological experts.

(5) *Learning in the Law; Examinations and Training.* The Supreme Court may also direct that the lawyer establish proof of competency and learning in the law, which may include a requirement to successfully complete the examinations and training required by Rule 402(c)(5), (6), and (8), SCACR.

(6) *Granting of Petition for Transfer to Active Status.* The Supreme Court shall grant the petition for transfer to active status upon a showing by clear and convincing evidence that the incapacity has been removed.

(7) *Judicial Declaration of Competency.* If a lawyer transferred to incapacity inactive status on the basis of a judicial determination of incompetence has been declared to be competent, the Supreme Court may dispense with further evidence that the incapacity to practice law has been removed and may immediately direct reinstatement to active status.

(g) Orders to Be Public. An order transferring a lawyer to incapacity inactive status or reinstating a lawyer to active status following transfer to incapacity inactive status shall be public; the order shall not, however, disclose the nature of the incapacity. All other orders issued in an incapacity proceeding shall be confidential.

[Adopted effective January 1, 1997. Amended effective July 21, 1999; September 1, 2003.]

RULE 29. RECIPROCAL DISCIPLINE AND RECIPROCAL INCAPACITY INACTIVE STATUS

(a) Lawyers Disciplined or Transferred to Incapacity Inactive Status in Another Jurisdiction. Upon being disciplined or transferred to incapacity inactive status in another jurisdiction, a lawyer admitted to practice in this state shall promptly inform disciplinary counsel of the discipline or transfer. Upon notification from any source that a lawyer within the jurisdiction of the Commission has been disciplined or transferred to incapacity inactive status in another jurisdiction, disciplinary counsel shall obtain a certified copy of the disciplinary order and file it with the Commission and the Supreme Court.

(b) Notice to Lawyer and Disciplinary Counsel. Upon receipt of a certified copy of an order demonstrating that a lawyer admitted to practice in this state has been disciplined or transferred to incapacity inactive status in another jurisdiction, the Supreme Court shall issue a notice to the lawyer and disciplinary counsel:

(1) Containing a copy of the order from the other jurisdiction; and

(2) Directing that the lawyer or disciplinary counsel inform the Supreme Court, within 30 days from service of the notice, of any claim by the lawyer or disciplinary counsel predicated upon the grounds set forth in (d) below, that the imposition of the identical discipline or transfer to incapacity inactive status in this state would be unwarranted and the reasons for that claim.

(c) Effect of Stay in Other Jurisdiction. In the event the discipline or transfer imposed in the other jurisdiction has been stayed there, any reciprocal discipline or transfer imposed in this state shall be deferred until the stay expires.

(d) Discipline to Be Imposed. Upon the expiration of the time provided by (b)(2) above, the Supreme Court shall impose the identical discipline or incapacity inactive status unless the lawyer or disciplinary counsel demonstrates, or the Supreme Court finds, that it clearly appears upon the face of the record from which the discipline is predicated, that:

(1) The procedure was so lacking in notice or opportunity to be heard as to constitute a deprivation of due process;

(2) There was such infirmity of proof establishing the misconduct as to give rise to the clear conviction that the Supreme Court could not, consistent with its duty, accept as final the conclusion on that subject;

(3) The imposition of the same discipline by the Supreme Court would result in grave injustice;

(4) The misconduct established warrants substantially different discipline in this state; or

(5) The reason for the original transfer to incapacity inactive status no longer exists.

If the Supreme Court determines that any of those elements exist, it shall enter such other order as it deems appropriate. The burden is on the party seeking different discipline in this jurisdiction to demonstrate that the imposition of the same discipline is not appropriate.

(e) Conclusiveness of Adjudication in Other Jurisdictions. In all other aspects, a final adjudication in another jurisdiction that a lawyer has been guilty of misconduct or should be transferred to incapacity inactive status shall establish conclusively the misconduct or the incapacity for purposes of a disciplinary or incapacity proceeding in this state.

[Adopted effective January 1, 1997.]

V. ADDITIONAL REQUIREMENTS RELATING TO DISBARRED, SUSPENDED AND DECEASED LAWYERS

RULE 30. DUTIES FOLLOWING DISBARMENT OR SUSPENSION

(a) Notice to Clients. A disbarred or suspended lawyer shall promptly notify, or cause to be notified, by registered or certified mail, return receipt requested, all clients being represented in a pending matter. The notice shall advise the client of the disbarment or suspension and of the consequent inability to act as an attorney. The notice shall also advise the client to seek legal advice of the client's own choice elsewhere and, if the matter involves pending litigation or administrative proceedings, of the desirability of the prompt substitution of another lawyer to act as the client's attorney in the proceedings.

(b) Notice to Other Counsel. A disbarred or suspended lawyer shall promptly notify, or cause to be notified, any co-counsel in any pending matter and any opposing counsel in any pending matter, or in the absence of opposing counsel, the adverse parties, of the disbarment or suspension and of the consequent inability of the lawyer to act as an attorney. The notice shall state the place of residence of the client of the disbarred or suspended lawyer.

(c) Withdrawal From Representation. In the event the client does not obtain substitute counsel within 10 days of the date of the notice, it shall be the responsibility of the disbarred or suspended attorney to move in the court or agency in which the proceedings are pending for leave to withdraw.

(d) Refund of Fees and Return of Property. A disbarred or suspended attorney shall promptly refund any part of any fees paid in advance that has not been earned. The lawyer shall also deliver to all clients being represented in pending matters any papers or other property to which they are entitled and shall notify them and any counsel representing them of a suitable time and place where the papers and other property may be obtained, calling attention to any urgency for obtaining the papers or other property. If an attorney has been appointed under Rule 31, the return of client fees and property shall be accomplished by the appointed attorney.

(e) Duty to Maintain Records. The lawyer shall keep and maintain records showing compliance with the requirements of this rule, and shall make these records available to disciplinary counsel upon request.

(f) Surrender of Certificate. A lawyer who has been disbarred or indefinitely suspended from the practice of law shall, within fifteen (15) days after the disbarment or indefinite suspension, surrender his or her certificate of admission to practice law in this state to the Clerk of the Supreme Court. The certificate shall be destroyed by the Clerk.

(g) Affidavit to Be Filed. Within 15 days after the effective date of the disbarment or suspension, the respondent shall file and serve an affidavit with the Supreme Court and the disciplinary counsel showing:

(1) Compliance with the provisions of the order of disbarment or suspension and this rule;

(2) All other state, federal and administrative jurisdictions to which the lawyer is admitted to practice; and

(3) Residence or other addresses where communications may thereafter be directed.

(h) Failure to Comply. A disbarred or suspended lawyer who fails to comply with the requirements of this rule may be held in criminal or civil contempt by the Supreme Court. Further, if a disbarred or suspended lawyer fails to timely surrender the certificate to practice law or to timely file the affidavit as required by sections (f) and (g) of this rule, the time before the disbarred or suspended lawyer is eligible to seek reinstatement under Rules 32 or 33, RLDE, shall not begin to run until the certificate and affidavit are actually received by the Clerk of the Supreme Court.

[Adopted effective January 1, 1997. Amended effective March 25, 2008.]

RULE 31. APPOINTMENT OF ATTORNEY TO PROTECT CLIENTS' INTERESTS

(a) Appointment of Attorney. If a lawyer has been transferred to incapacity inactive status, has disappeared or died, or has been suspended or disbarred, and no partner, personal representative or other responsible party capable of conducting the lawyer's affairs is known to exist, disciplinary counsel shall petition the Supreme Court for an order appointing an attorney or attorneys to inventory the files of the inactive, disappeared, deceased, suspended or disbarred lawyer and to take action as appropriate to protect the interests of the lawyer and the lawyer's clients. If the Supreme Court determines that a lawyer suffers from a physical or mental condition that adversely affects the lawyer's ability to practice law but decides that a transfer to incapacity inactive status is not warranted, it may appoint an attorney to protect clients' interests. The order of appointment shall be public.

(b) Duties of Appointed Attorney. The appointed attorney shall:

(1) Take custody of the lawyer's files and trust or escrow accounts. The chair or vice chair may issue such orders as may be necessary to assist the appointed attorney in obtaining custody over such files and accounts, to include orders compelling the lawyer or a third party to take specific action regarding the files and accounts. The willful failure to comply with such an order may be punished as a contempt of the Supreme Court. A party who wishes to challenge such an order must immediately seek review of the order by petition to the Supreme Court.

(2) Notify each client in a pending matter, and in the discretion of the appointed attorney, in any other matter, at the client's address shown in the file, by first class mail, of the client's right to obtain any papers, money or other property to which the client is entitled and the time and place at which the papers, money or other property may be obtained, calling attention to any urgency in obtaining the papers, money or other property;

(3) Publish, in a newspaper of general circulation in the county or counties in which the lawyer resided or engaged in any substantial practice of law, once a week for three consecutive weeks, notice of the discontinuance or interruption of the lawyer's law practice. The notice shall include the name and address of the lawyer whose practice has been discontinued or interrupted; the time, date and location where clients may pick up their files; and the name, address and telephone number of the appointed attorney. The notice shall also be mailed, by first class mail, to any errors and omissions insurer or other entity having reason to be informed of the discontinuance or interruption of the law practice;

(4) Release to each client the papers, money or other property to which the client is entitled. Before releasing the property, appointed counsel shall obtain a receipt from the client for the property;

(5) With the consent of the client, file notices, motions or pleadings on behalf of the client where

jurisdictional time limits are involved and other legal counsel has not yet been obtained; and

(6) Perform any other acts directed in the order of appointment.

(c) Period of Appointment. An appointment shall be for a period of no longer than 9 months. Upon application by the appointed attorney, the Supreme Court may extend the period of appointment as necessary.

(d) Representation of Clients. Clients should be encouraged to engage other counsel as soon as possible but nothing in this paragraph shall be construed as preventing the appointed attorney from accepting employment by any client of the lawyer.

(e) Termination of Appointment. When the provisions of (b) above and the order of appointment have been complied with, the appointed attorney shall apply to the Supreme Court for termination of the appointment. The application shall contain the written releases of clients to whom files and other property were returned, information regarding the efforts made to contact the lawyer's remaining clients, an inventory of the files and other property remaining in the appointed attorney's possession and an itemized account of the expenses incurred in carrying out the order of the Supreme Court appointing the attorney. Upon approval of the application by the Supreme Court, all files and property remaining in the appointed attorney's possession shall be deposited with the Commission. Unless otherwise ordered by the Supreme Court, the files shall be retained by the Commission for a period of 3 years at which time they shall be destroyed in a manner which protects their confidentiality. Other client property remaining in the possession of the Commission after 3 years shall be disposed of in a manner as ordered by the Supreme Court.

(f) Compensation and Expenses. With the exception of reasonable and necessary expenses, such as postage, telephone bills, copies, supplies and the cost of publishing legal notice in the newspaper, an appointed attorney shall serve without compensation as a service to the legal profession. However, the Supreme Court may order that the appointed attorney be reimbursed a reasonable amount for other expenses, such as the appointed attorney's time or the time of support staff, when it determines that extraordinary time and services were necessary for the completion of the required duties or when the appointment has worked a substantial hardship on the appointed attorney's practice. The Supreme Court shall determine the reasonableness of necessary expenses and other expenses.[1] Expenses which are approved and awarded by the Supreme Court shall be paid from funds remaining in the lawyer's accounts. If no such funds exist, payment shall be made from the Lawyers' Fund for Client Protection under Rule 411, SCACR. If the appointed attorney's expenses are paid by the Lawyers' Fund for Client Protection, the Supreme Court may order the lawyer to reimburse that Fund.

(g) Protection of Client Information. An appointed attorney shall not be permitted to disclose any information contained in the files inventoried without the consent of the client to whom the file relates, except as necessary to carry out the order of appointment.

[Adopted effective January 1, 1997. Amended effective April 23, 1998; August 21, 2003; March 22, 2010; June 1, 2010.]

1 In an effort to balance the need to preserve the Lawyers' Fund for Client Protection with the need to, in certain situations, reimburse attorneys appointed pursuant to Rule 31, RLDE, Rule 413, SCACR, the following rates are currently established for reimbursement of the appointed attorney's fees, support staff costs and the cost of copies, but are subject to change at the discretion of the Court.

Appointed Attorney's Fees	$50.00 per hour
Support Staff	$10.00 per hour
Copies	$ 0.10 per page

RULE 32. REINSTATEMENT FOLLOWING A DEFINITE SUSPENSION OF LESS THAN NINE MONTHS

Unless otherwise provided for in the Supreme Court's suspension order, a lawyer who has been suspended for a definite period of less than 9 months shall be reinstated to the practice of law at the end of the period of suspension by filing with the Supreme Court, and serving upon disciplinary counsel and the Commission on Lawyer Conduct, an affidavit stating that the lawyer is currently in good standing with the Commission on Continuing Legal Education and Specialization and the South Carolina Bar, has fully complied with the requirements of the suspension order, and has paid any required fees and costs, including payment of necessary expenses and compensation approved by the Supreme Court to the attorney appointed pursuant to Rule 31, RLDE, to protect the interests of the lawyer's clients for necessary expenses, or to the Lawyers' Fund for Client Protection if the Fund has paid the appointed attorney under Rule 31(f), RLDE. If suspended for conduct resulting in a criminal conviction and sentence, the lawyer must also successfully complete all conditions of the sentence, including, but not limited to, any period of probation or parole. In such a case, the lawyer must attach to the affidavit documentation demonstrating compliance with this provision. The affidavit filed with the Supreme Court shall be accompanied by proof of service showing service on disciplinary counsel and the Commission on Lawyer Conduct, and a filing fee of $200. When all preconditions set out in this rule are met, the Court shall issue an order of reinstatement. The order shall be public.

[Adopted effective January 1, 1997. Amended effective July 21, 1999; December 7, 2000; January 17, 2001; August 9, 2001; April 7, 2004; January 1, 2010.]

RULE 33. REINSTATEMENT FOLLOWING A DEFINITE SUSPENSION FOR NINE MONTHS OR MORE OR DISBARMENT

(a) Generally. A lawyer who has been suspended for a definite period of 9 months or more, or has been disbarred shall be reinstated to the practice of law only upon order of the Supreme Court. A petition for reinstatement shall not be filed earlier than 5 years from the date of entry of the order of disbarment. A lawyer who has received a definite suspension for 9 months or more may file the petition for reinstatement no earlier than 270 days prior to the expiration of the period of suspension. All records and proceedings relating to reinstatement shall be open to the public.

(b) Petition. A petition for reinstatement must be under oath or affirmation under penalty of perjury and shall specify with particularity the manner in which the lawyer meets each of the criteria specified in (f) below.

(c) Service and Filing of Petition. The lawyer shall serve a copy of the petition on disciplinary counsel and on the Commission on Lawyer Conduct and shall file 10 copies of the petition with the Supreme Court. The copies filed with the Supreme Court shall be accompanied by a filing fee of $1,500 and proof of service showing service on disciplinary counsel and the Commission on Lawyer Conduct.

(d) Action by Supreme Court. Unless otherwise directed by the Supreme Court, the petition shall be referred to the Committee on Character and Fitness.

(e) Notice of Petition.

(1) *By the Lawyer.* Within ten (10) days of the matter being referred to the Committee on Character and Fitness by the Supreme Court, the lawyer shall publish a notice of the petition in a newspaper of general circulation in each county in which the lawyer maintained an office for the practice of law when the lawyer was suspended or disbarred. The notice shall inform members of the bar and the public about the application for reinstatement, and shall request that any individuals file notice of their opposition or concurrence with the Committee within 60 days of the date on which the matter was referred to the Committee. The notice shall specify the date by which any response must be filed with the Committee. In addition, the lawyer shall, within 10 days of the matter being referred to the Committee, serve a notice on the complainant(s) in the disciplinary proceeding that led to the lawyer's suspension or disbarment. This notice shall contain the same information contained in the notice required to be published in the newspaper. The lawyer shall promptly provide the Committee with a copy of the newspaper notice and shall provide the Committee with proof of service of the notice given to the complainants.

(2) *By the Clerk of Court.* The Clerk of the Supreme Court shall place a notice in the Advance Sheets of the Supreme Court indicating that the lawyer has applied for reinstatement. That notice shall contain the same information required to be published in the newspaper under (1) above.

(f) Criteria for Reinstatement and Readmission. A lawyer may be reinstated or readmitted only if the lawyer meets each of the following criteria:

(1) The lawyer has fully complied with the terms and conditions of all prior disciplinary orders.

(2) The lawyer has not engaged nor attempted to engage in the unauthorized practice of law during the period of suspension or disbarment.

(3) If the lawyer was suffering under a physical or mental infirmity at the time of suspension or disbarment, including alcohol or other drug abuse, the infirmity has been removed. Where alcohol or other drug abuse was a causative factor in the lawyer's misconduct, the lawyer shall not be reinstated unless:

(A) the lawyer has pursued appropriate rehabilitative treatment;

(B) the lawyer has abstained from the use of alcohol or other drugs for at least 1 year or the period of suspension, whichever is shorter; and

(C) the lawyer is likely to continue to abstain from alcohol or other drugs.

(4) The lawyer recognizes the wrongfulness and seriousness of the misconduct for which the lawyer was suspended or disbarred.

(5) The lawyer has not engaged in any other professional misconduct since suspension or disbarment.

(6) Notwithstanding the conduct for which the lawyer was disciplined, the lawyer has the requisite honesty and integrity to practice law.

(7) The lawyer has kept informed about recent developments in the law and is competent to practice.

(8) If disbarred, the lawyer has successfully completed the examinations and training required by Rule 402(c)(5), (6) and (8), SCACR. The lawyer may take the examinations and begin this training no earlier than 9 months prior to the earliest date on which the lawyer may apply for readmission. The lawyer shall attach proof of completion of these examinations and training to the petition for readmission.

(9) If suspended for a definite period of 9 months or more, the lawyer has, during the period of suspension, completed and reported continuing legal education and legal ethics/professional responsibility credits equal to those required of active members of the South Carolina Bar and is currently in good standing with the Commission on Continuing Legal Education and Specialization. The lawyer shall attach to the petition for reinstatement a statement from the Commission on Continuing Legal Education and Specialization confirming compliance with this requirement.

(10) If suspended or disbarred for conduct resulting in a criminal conviction and sentence, the lawyer has

successfully completed all conditions of the sentence, including, but not limited to, any period of probation or parole.

(11) The lawyer has paid necessary expenses and compensation approved by the Supreme Court to the attorney appointed pursuant to Rule 31, RLDE, to protect the interests of the lawyer's clients for necessary expenses, or to the Lawyers' Fund for Client Protection if the Fund has paid the appointed attorney under Rule 31(f), RLDE.

(g) Action by Committee on Character and Fitness. Within 180 days of the matter being referred to the Committee on Character and Fitness, a panel of the Committee shall conduct a hearing. If the petition for reinstatement is withdrawn after the start of the hearing, the lawyer must wait two years from the date the petition is withdrawn to reapply for reinstatement.

At the hearing before the panel, the lawyer shall have the burden of demonstrating by clear and convincing evidence that the lawyer has met each of the criteria in paragraph (f) above. Any member of the Committee may issue subpoenas to compel the attendance of witnesses and the production of pertinent books, papers and documents. The willful failure to comply with a subpoena issued under this rule may be punished as contempt of the Supreme Court. Upon proper application, the Supreme Court may enforce the attendance and testimony of any witness and the production of any documents subpoenaed. The hearing shall be open to the public. Disciplinary Counsel and the Commission shall be allowed to present evidence and make arguments to the panel. The panel shall file a report with the Supreme Court containing its findings and recommendations.

The Committee on Character and Fitness may promulgate rules and regulations governing practice and procedure before the Committee. These rules and regulations shall become effective when approved by the Supreme Court.

(h) Decision as to Reinstatement. The Supreme Court shall review the report filed by the panel of the Committee on Character and Fitness. The Supreme Court may require the parties to file briefs or may schedule oral argument on the matter. If the Supreme Court finds that the lawyer has complied with each of the criteria of paragraph (f), it may reinstate the lawyer. The decision to grant or deny reinstatement rests in the discretion of the Court. In making this determination, the seriousness of the prior misconduct will be considered and the petition for reinstatement may be denied based solely on the seriousness of the prior misconduct. Unless otherwise ordered by the Supreme Court in the order denying reinstatement, no lawyer shall be permitted to reapply for reinstatement within 2 years following an adverse ruling upon a petition for reinstatement or readmission. Orders granting or denying petitions for reinstatement shall be public.

(i) Conditions of Reinstatement. The Supreme Court may impose conditions on a lawyer's reinstatement. The conditions shall be imposed in cases where the lawyer has met the burden of proof justifying reinstatement, but the Supreme Court reasonably believes that further precautions should be taken to protect the public. The Supreme Court may impose any conditions that are reasonably related to the grounds for the lawyer's original suspension or disbarment, or to evidence presented at the hearing regarding the lawyer's failure to meet the criteria for reinstatement. The conditions may include, but are not limited to, any of the following: limitation upon practice (to one area of law or through association with an experienced supervising lawyer); participation in continuing legal education courses; monitoring of the lawyer's practice (for compliance with trust account rules, accounting procedures, or office management procedures); abstention from the use of drugs or alcohol; active participation in Alcoholics Anonymous or other alcohol or drug rehabilitation program; monitoring of the lawyer's compliance with any other orders (such as abstinence from alcohol or drugs, or participation in alcohol or drug rehabilitation programs). If the monitoring or supervising lawyer determines that the reinstated lawyer's compliance with any condition of reinstatement is unsatisfactory, the monitoring or supervising lawyer shall immediately notify the disciplinary counsel. The disciplinary counsel may then seek a revocation of the reinstatement, a modification of the terms of the reinstatement or other appropriate relief by filing a petition with the Supreme Court. The disciplinary counsel may also seek an interim suspension of the lawyer pending the Supreme Court's consideration of the petition if disciplinary counsel believes the lawyer poses a potential for harm to the public.

[Adopted effective January 1, 1997. Amended effective March 5, 1998; November 18, 1998; July 21, 1999; December 14, 1999; December 7, 2000; August 9, 2001; December 13, 2001; September 1, 2003; April 7, 2004; January 1, 2010.]

RULE 34. EMPLOYMENT OF DISBARRED OR SUSPENDED LAWYERS

A lawyer who is disbarred, suspended or transferred to incapacity inactive status shall not be employed directly or indirectly by a member of the South Carolina Bar as a paralegal, investigator or in any other capacity connected with the practice of law, nor be employed directly or indirectly in the State of South Carolina as a paralegal, investigator or in any capacity connected with the practice of law by a lawyer licensed in any other jurisdiction. Additionally, a lawyer who is disbarred, suspended or transferred to incapacity inactive status shall not serve as an arbitrator, mediator or third party neutral in any Alternative Dispute Resolution proceeding in this state nor shall any member of the South Carolina Bar directly or indirectly employ a lawyer who has been disbarred, suspended or transferred to incapacity inactive status as an arbitrator, mediator or third party neutral in any Alternative Dispute Resolution proceeding. Any member of the South Carolina Bar who, with knowledge that the person is disbarred, suspended or transferred to incapacity inactive status, employs such person in a manner prohibited by this rule shall be subject to discipline under these rules. A disbarred or suspended lawyer who violates this rule shall be deemed in contempt of the Supreme Court and may be punished accordingly.

[Adopted effective January 1, 1997. Amended effective March 3, 2005; May 3, 2006.]

RULE 414. LIMITED CERTIFICATE TO PRACTICE LAW FOR CLINICAL LAW PROGRAM TEACHERS

(a) This rule is adopted to foster and aid the clinical law programs of law schools. These programs provide legal services to those who are unable to afford private legal counsel and educate law students in providing these legal services.

(b) The Supreme Court may issue a limited certificate of admission to practice law in South Carolina to any person who:

(1) is employed full-time by a law school within this State which has been approved by the American Bar Association and is responsible for supervising or teaching in the clinical law program operated by the law school;

(2) provides legal services solely in connection with the supervision of or instruction in the law school's clinical law program;

(3) neither requests nor receives compensation or remuneration of any kind for legal services from the person for whom the services are rendered;

(4) is at least twenty-one years of age;

(5) is a person of good moral character;

(6) has received a JD or LLB degree from a law school that was approved by the Council of Legal Education of the American Bar Association at the time the degree was conferred;

(7) has been admitted to practice law in the highest court of another state or the District of Columbia for at least three (3) years;

(8) is a member in good standing in each jurisdiction where he is admitted to practice law;

(9) has not been disbarred or suspended from the practice of law and is not the subject of any pending disciplinary proceeding in any other jurisdiction; and,

(10) has not, within the last five (5) years, been denied admission to a bar for character or ethical reasons or disciplined for professional misconduct.

(c) An attorney desiring a limited certificate of admission shall file with the Clerk of the Supreme Court an application in duplicate on a form prescribed by the Supreme Court.

(d) The application shall be accompanied by a certificate of good standing from each jurisdiction in which the attorney has been admitted to practice law and a statement signed by the Dean of the law school at which the attorney is employed stating that the attorney meets the requirements of (b)(1)–(3) above.

(e) The performance of legal services in this State by an attorney issued a limited certificate of admission to practice law shall be deemed the active engagement in the practice of law and shall subject the attorney to all duties and obligations of active members of the South Carolina Bar and to all rules on the practice of law, including the Rules of Professional Conduct, Rule 407, SCACR, and the Rules for Lawyer Disciplinary Enforcement, Rule 413, SCACR. The attorney shall not, however, need to comply with the requirements of Rule 403, SCACR. If an attorney granted a limited certificate engages in the practice of law in excess of that permitted by this rule, the attorney may be subject to discipline under Rule 413, SCACR, a suspension or revocation of the limited certificate by the Supreme Court, or being held in contempt of the Supreme Court for engaging in the unauthorized practice of law.

(f) The limited certificate of admission to practice law shall expire if the attorney ceases to meet the requirements of (b)(1)–(3) above, is otherwise admitted to the Bar of this State, fails to fulfill the obligations required of active members of the South Carolina Bar, is suspended or disbarred from the practice of law in this or any other jurisdiction, or fails at any time to be a member of the bar in good standing before the highest court of at least one other state or the District of Columbia.

(g) Upon the expiration of the limited certificate of admission to practice law, the attorney shall immediately surrender the certificate to the Clerk of the Supreme Court. The failure to immediately surrender the certificate upon expiration may subject the attorney to discipline under Rule 413, SCACR, or to being held in contempt of the Supreme Court.

(h) The confidentiality provisions of Rule 402(n), SCACR, shall apply to all files and records of the Board of Law Examiners, the Committee on Character and Fitness, and the Clerk of the Supreme Court relating to a limited certificate to practice law under this rule.

[Adopted effective January 7, 1993. Amended effective August 26, 1993; January 1, 1997; April 18, 2002; September 16, 2009; December 3, 2010.]

RULE 415. LIMITED CERTIFICATE OF ADMISSION FOR THE RETIRED AND INACTIVE ATTORNEY PRO BONO PARTICIPATION PROGRAM

(a) The Supreme Court may issue a limited certificate to practice law in South Carolina to any person who:

(1) is or was admitted to practice law in South Carolina or any other state or territory of the United States or the District of Columbia and is retired from the active practice of law or is on inactive status;

(2) has not been retired or on inactive status for more than seven years;

(3) has been a member in good standing in each jurisdiction in which the retired or inactive attorney is or was admitted to practice law;

(4) has not been disciplined for professional misconduct in any jurisdiction within the past fifteen (15) years and is not the subject of any pending disciplinary proceeding;

(5) is associated with an approved legal services organization (Legal Services) which receives, or is eligible to receive, funds from the Legal Services Corporation; is working on a case or project through the South Carolina Bar Pro Bono Program (the Program); or is working with a program funded in whole or in part by a grant from the South Carolina Bar Foundation, Inc. (the Grantee), using interest and dividends remitted under the procedure established in Rule 412, SCACR;

(6) performs all activities authorized by this Rule under the supervision of an attorney who is an active member of the South Carolina Bar employed by, or participating as a volunteer for, Legal Services, the Program or the Grantee and who assumes professional responsibility for the conduct of the matter, litigation, or administrative proceeding in which the retired or inactive attorney participates and;

(7) agrees to abide by the South Carolina Rules of Professional Conduct and all other rules governing the practice of law in this State and to submit to the jurisdiction of the Supreme Court for disciplinary purposes.

(b) The limited certificate issued under this Rule authorizes the retired or inactive attorney to provide legal services solely to clients approved to receive services from Legal Services, the Program or the Grantee, or to provide other services through the Program such as Ask–A–Lawyer or educational clinics. The retired or inactive attorney issued a limited certificate may:

(1) appear in any court or before any tribunal in this State if the client consents, in writing, to that appearance and the supervising attorney has given written approval for the appearance. The written consent and approval must be filed with the court or tribunal and must be brought to the attention of the judge or presiding officer prior to the appearance;

(2) prepare pleadings and other documents to be filed in any court or before any tribunal in this State on behalf of the client. Such pleadings shall also be signed by the supervising attorney; and

(3) otherwise engage in the practice of law as is necessary for the representation of the client.

(c) An attorney desiring a limited certificate shall file with the Clerk of the Supreme Court an application in duplicate on a form prescribed by the Supreme Court accompanied by:

(1) a certification by Legal Services, the Program or the Grantee stating that;

(A) the retired or inactive attorney is currently associated with Legal Services, the Program or the Grantee;

(B) an active member of the South Carolina Bar employed by, or acting as a volunteer for, Legal Services, the Program or the Grantee will assume the duties of the supervising attorney required by this Rule; and

(C) the retired or inactive attorney meets the requirements of section (a) of this Rule;

(2) a certificate of good standing from each jurisdiction in which the retired or inactive attorney is or was admitted to practice law; and

(3) a sworn statement by the retired or inactive attorney that the retired or inactive attorney:

(A) has read and is familiar with the South Carolina Rules of Professional Conduct and all rules relating to the practice of law in this State and will abide by the provisions thereof; and

(B) will neither ask for nor receive compensation of any kind for the legal services rendered under this Rule.

(d) Any questions concerning the fitness or qualifications of the retired or inactive attorney may be referred by the Supreme Court to the Committee on Character and Fitness for a hearing and recommendation.

(e) If an attorney granted a limited certificate of practice engages in the practice of law in excess of that permitted by this rule, the attorney may be subject to discipline under Rule 413, SCACR, a suspension or revocation of the limited certificate by the Supreme Court, or being held in contempt of the Supreme Court for engaging in the unauthorized practice of law.

(f) The limited certificate shall be revoked immediately upon:

(1) notice by Legal Services, the Program or the Grantee stating that the retired or inactive attorney has ceased to be associated with Legal Services, the Program or the Grantee. Such notice must be sent to the retired or inactive attorney and must be filed with the Clerk of the Supreme Court within five (5) days after the association has ceased. The notice need not state a reason for the cessation of the association; or

(2) a determination by the Supreme Court, in its discretion, that the limited certificate should be revoked. Notice of the revocation shall be sent to the retired or inactive attorney and Legal Services, the

Program or the Grantee within five (5) days of the revocation.

(g) Upon the revocation of the limited certificate, the supervising attorney shall immediately file notice of the revocation in the official file of each matter pending before any court or tribunal in which the retired or inactive attorney was involved.

(h) The confidentiality provisions of Rule 402(n), SCACR, shall apply to all files and records of the Board of Law Examiners, the Committee on Character and Fitness, and the Clerk of the Supreme Court relating to a limited certificate to practice law under this rule.

[Adopted effective September 22, 1993. Amended effective January 6, 2000; December 13, 2001; September 16, 2008; September 16, 2009; December 3, 2010.]

RULE 416. RESOLUTION OF FEE DISPUTES BOARD

RULE 1. CREATION

There is hereby created the Resolution of Fee Disputes Board of the South Carolina Bar ("Board").

[Adopted effective January 1, 1994.]

RULE 2. JURISDICTION

The purpose of the Board is to establish procedures whereby a dispute concerning fees, costs or disbursements between a client and an attorney who is a member of the South Carolina Bar (the Bar) may be resolved expeditiously, fairly and professionally, thereby furthering the administration of justice, encouraging the highest standards of ethical and professional conduct, assisting in upholding the integrity and honor of the legal profession, and applying the knowledge, experience and ability of the legal profession to the promotion of the public good. As used in these Rules, "fee" is deemed to include a legal fee, costs of litigation and disbursements associated with a legal cause, claim or matter and "client" is defined as a person on whose behalf professional legal services have been rendered by an attorney who is a member of the South Carolina Bar. A dispute exists when the parties to an employment agreement between lawyer and client have a genuine difference as to the fair and proper amount of a fee. The amount in dispute, as used in these Rules, is the dollar amount of that difference. A dispute does not exist solely because of the failure of the client to pay a fee.

Under no circumstances will the Board participate in: (1) a fee dispute involving an amount in dispute of $50,000 or more; (2) disputes over fees which by law must be determined or approved, as between lawyer and client,by a court, commission, judge, or other tribunal. When an allegation of attorney misconduct arises out of a fee dispute other than as to the reasonableness of the fee, the Board, in its discretion, may refer the matter to the Commission on Lawyer Conduct. If the alleged misconduct does not arise out of a fee dispute, it shall be referred to the Commission on Lawyer Conduct.

If an attorney is suspended from the practice of law after a fee dispute has been filed with the Board, the Board shall retain jurisdiction over the dispute until the conclusion of the fee dispute process. This shall include all applicable appeals under Rule 20.

No fee dispute may be filed with the Board more than three (3) years after the dispute arose.

Jurisdictional issues shall be determined by the circuit chair.

[Adopted effective January 1, 1994. Amended effective January 1, 1997; September 11, 1998; November 5, 2003; September 7, 2007; June 28, 2010; December 6, 2011.]

RULE 3. APPOINTMENT AND TENURE

The Board shall be appointed by the President of the Bar ("President") and shall consist of not fewer than five (5) members of the Bar of this state from each judicial circuit of the state. Members of the Board shall be appointed for terms of three (3) years or until a successor has been appointed. Where additional members are subsequently appointed, those appointments shall be on a staggered basis so that the number of terms expiring shall be approximately the same each year. The expiration of a term will coincide with the date of expiration of the term of the incumbent President in the same year. A member of the Board may be reappointed.

[Adopted effective January 1, 1994.]

RULE 4. DUTIES

The Board is authorized to receive, inquire into, take proofs, and make findings and final determination of disputes between attorneys and clients. It shall be the duty of the Board to encourage the amicable resolution of fee disputes falling within its jurisdiction. Each member shall continue to serve until completion of ongoing work on the Board.

[Adopted effective January 1, 1994. Amended effective September 7, 2007.]

RULE 5. APPOINTMENT OF EXECUTIVE COUNCIL

From among the appointed Board members, the President shall appoint an Executive Council comprised of the following: One Executive Council member from each of the four Judicial Regions of the state and one additional member, appointed by the President, who will be chair of the Executive Council.

The chair shall have the authority to interpret these Rules until such time as the Executive Council considers the interpretation. The duties of the Executive Council will be to oversee and assist the functioning of the Board in the respective circuits of the state and to make recommendations to the Board of Governors as to procedures to be followed and rules to be amended.

Executive Council members should be experienced in the practice of law with not fewer than five (5) years active practice, and in the case of the chair, not fewer than ten (10) years active practice.

The terms of the Executive Council shall be for three (3) years. The expiration of a term will coincide with the date of expiration of the term of the incumbent President in the same year. Should the term of an Executive Council member on the Board expire and the member not be reappointed to the Board, the member's term on the Executive Council shall expire at the same time the member's term on the Board expires. In that event, the President shall appoint a replacement member to the Executive Council for the unexpired term. A member of the Executive Council may be reappointed.

The Executive Council shall meet at such times and places as may be called by the chair or by any four members thereof.

[Adopted effective January 1, 1994. Amended effective September 1, 2002.]

RULE 6. CIRCUIT PANEL

The members of the Board within a judicial circuit comprise the circuit panel. The President shall appoint one member of the circuit panel as circuit chair and such other members as co-chairs as needed, all of whose terms shall be at the pleasure of the President. Appointment of co-chairs shall be made upon recommendation of the circuit chair.

[Adopted effective January 1, 1994. Amended effective September 11, 1998.]

RULE 7. HEARING PANEL

The members of the Board appointed to hear or consider a specific case or proceeding will be the hearing panel. The hearing panel will be appointed by the circuit chair from the circuit panel except as provided in Rule 18 concerning conflicts of interest.

[Adopted effective January 1, 1994.]

RULE 8. ASSIGNED MEMBER

The member of the circuit panel who is assigned to conduct the initial investigation of an application shall be known as the "assigned member." The assigned member shall not be a member of the hearing panel which hears a dispute investigated by that assigned member or represent a party before that hearing panel. With the consent of the Executive Director of the Bar and as provided in Rule 11, a Bar staff person who is a Bar member or who is supervised by a Bar member may be appointed as the assigned member.

[Adopted effective January 1, 1994. Amended effective September 7, 2007.]

RULE 9. RULE EXCLUSIVE UPON CONSENT

(a) Any client-applicant for the services of the Board must consent in writing to be bound by a final decision of the Board. Thereafter, the attorney is also bound.

(b) No application will be accepted from an attorney unless accompanied by the client's written consent to jurisdiction and consent to be bound by the final decision of the Board. Thereafter, both parties are bound.

(c) Upon consent of the client-applicant to be bound by the final decision of the Board, exclusive jurisdiction over the fee dispute vests in the Board.

[Adopted effective January 1, 1994. Amended effective September 7, 2007.]

RULE 10. COMMENCEMENT OF PROCEEDINGS

All proceedings hereunder shall be commenced by filing an application in the Office of the Bar, on forms provided by the Bar. The application shall include a written statement of the facts and circumstances surrounding the dispute, furnishing complete names and addresses. If the client-applicant is not the person who paid for the lawyer's services, the third party payer, with the written consent of the client-applicant, may jointly file with the client applicant, with both signatures affixed to the application. If the materials submitted exceed twenty-five (25) pages, the client-applicant shall submit three additional sets of the materials.

If the responding party is an attorney, the Bar shall forward the completed application, as filed, to the attorney by electronic mail, with confirmation of delivery. If the responding party is not an attorney, the Bar shall forward the completed application, as filed, to the responding party by certified mail, return receipt requested. A copy shall be sent by regular mail or e-mail to the circuit chair in the circuit where the principal place of practice of the attorney is located. If the application involves attorneys in more than one circuit, a copy of the completed application shall be sent to the chair of the Executive Council, who shall designate which of these circuit chairs shall have jurisdiction and shall proceed with the matter.

If the amount in dispute exceeds $7,500, the circuit chair may appoint a hearing panel without assignment of the matter to an assigned member.

After the initial correspondence, all other correspondence will be sent by regular mail or, with the written consent of the client and lawyer, by e-mail. Such written consent may be withdrawn by written notice served on all other parties or attorneys. If served by regular mail, correspondence will be deemed served upon deposit in the U.S. Mail with proper postage affixed. If served by email, service is complete upon transmission, unless the party making service learns that the attempted service did not reach the person to be served. All parties have the duty to inform the circuit chair of any change of address.

[Adopted effective January 1, 1994. Amended effective September 11, 1998; September 7, 2007; December 6, 2011.]

RULE 11. INVESTIGATION BY ASSIGNED MEMBER

Upon receipt of the completed application, the circuit chair shall promptly appoint the assigned member. The assigned member shall conduct an investigation sufficient to enable the rendering of an informed recommendation. The assigned member's recommendation shall be written and contain the reasons for it. This report shall be submitted to the circuit chair, with a copy to the Bar office, as soon as possible and not later than ninety (90) days after appointment of the assigned member, unless the time is extended by the circuit chair pursuant to Rule 12. The circuit chair shall send a copy of the report to each of the parties and notification of the circuit chair's concurrence or nonconcurrence with the recommendations of the assigned member.

The attorney shall respond to the issues raised in the application within thirty (30) days of being contacted by the assigned member. The assigned member may extend the period for response once and by no more than 30 days.

The parties to the dispute and any witnesses on their behalves shall make themselves available for interview at a time and place designated by the assigned member within the time required for the assigned member to make a report. If a party or a witness cannot, for any reason, be present at the designated time and place, that witness or party shall submit a written response to the assigned member within fourteen (14) days of the date the assigned member designated as the interview date, unless the assigned member grants the party or witness an extension. The party or witness may also submit a statement in writing, provided such statement is delivered to the assigned member on or before the date designated for the interview of that party or witness. The response to questions along with the written statement, if any, together shall constitute the complete statement of the party or witness concerning the dispute. In the event a party fails to respond, then the assigned member must render a decision based upon the available materials.

The assigned member may encourage resolution of the dispute by compromise where the circumstances warrant such effort. Efforts at compromise may include mediation of the dispute by the assigned member. Compromise or consent agreements, whether written or oral, become the final decision of the Board fifteen (15) days after the date of a letter from the circuit chair to the parties confirming the agreement.

If the amount in dispute does not exceed $1,000, in lieu of appointment of an assigned member, the circuit chair may assign the dispute to the staff of the Bar for an expedited investigation and recommendation. The staff in its discretion may make findings based on written submissions by the parties or on such other information as may be necessary to render an informed recommendation. In the event of such assignment, the staff shall have the same powers and be governed by the same duties and procedures as would an assigned member.

[Adopted effective January 1, 1994. Amended effective September 11, 1998; September 7, 2007; December 6, 2011.]

RULE 12. SCHEDULE OF PROCEEDINGS

(a) All fee disputes should be resolved within six (6) months. The assigned member's report should be completed within thirty (30) to ninety (90) days after being forwarded by the circuit chair. A fee dispute may not exceed six (6) months without the written consent of the circuit chair for good cause shown. Any extension of time granted by the circuit chair must be for a specified period of time which shall be the least amount of time deemed necessary to resolve the dispute.

(b) If an assigned member does not respond to reminders from the Bar office, the Bar office will notify the circuit chair.

(c) If a fee dispute has been assigned and is pending, without an extension approved by the circuit chair,

(1) more than ninety (90) days, then the circuit chair may, at his or her discretion:

(A) reassign the fee dispute;

(B) if the amount exceeds $7,500, appoint a hearing panel, which shall schedule a hearing within thirty (30) days

(2) more than six (6) months, then the circuit chair shall, with the concurrence of the Executive Council Chair:

(A) reassign the fee dispute;

(B) if the amount exceeds $7,500, appoint a hearing panel, which shall schedule a hearing within thirty (30) days; or

(C) return all investigative notes and application to the designated Bar staff member for investigation as the assigned member.

In these events, the original assigned member shall immediately turn over notes and files to the circuit chair.

(d) If the circuit chair is delinquent, then the case may be reassigned to the Executive Council Chair or the Executive Council Chair's designee.

[Adopted effective January 1, 1994. Amended effective September 11, 1998; November 5, 2003; September 7, 2007; December 6, 2011.]

RULE 13. PROCEEDINGS OF THE BOARD

If the amount in dispute is $7,500 or less, the decision of the assigned member or Bar staff, with the concurrence of the circuit chair, shall be the final decision of the Board.

If the amount in dispute is more than $7,500, the decision of the assigned member with the concurrence of the circuit chair shall be served on the parties by first class mail, with proper postage affixed, or by e-mail, provided the parties have consented to services by e-mail in accordance with Rules 10. The decision is final unless a written request for a hearing panel is made by filing such request with the circuit chair within thirty (30) days after the date of mailing written notification of the decision. (For Hearing Panel Decision, see Rule 17.)

If the chair does not concur with the decision of the assigned member, a hearing panel will be appointed.

[Adopted effective January 1, 1994. Amended effective September 11, 1998; September 7, 2007; December 6, 2011.]

RULE 14. APPOINTMENT OF HEARING PANEL

When appropriate, a hearing panel of three (3) members shall be appointed by the circuit chair from the circuit panel in the judicial circuit where the principal place of practice of the attorney is located. A hearing panel should be appointed within ten (10) days of the date a written request for a hearing panel is filed with the circuit chair. The procedure for appointing hearing panel members shall be established by the Executive Council. One (1) member of the hearing panel shall be designated by the circuit chair as chair of the hearing panel. Upon appointment of the hearing panel, the parties to the proceeding shall be notified in writing by the circuit chair of the appointment of the hearing panel, giving the names and addresses of the members, including the identity of the chair, and further informing the parties involved that the hearing panel will resolve the dispute. Each party may proceed without counsel or be represented by counsel of the party's choosing and at the party's own expense. The Board is not required by law to appoint an attorney to represent a party; however, upon request of a party, a member of the Board may be appointed to represent the party before the hearing panel if, in the discretion of the circuit chair, good cause is shown. Good cause may include but is not limited to (1) the income level of the party, (2) the educational level of the party, or (3) interests of parity and justice.

[Adopted effective January 1, 1994. Amended effective September 1, 2002.]

RULE 15. PANEL HEARINGS

The chair of the hearing panel shall convene a hearing at a place within the circuit within forty-five (45) days of assignment by the circuit chair and at least thirty (30) days after giving notice to the parties by first class mail, with proper postage affixed, unless otherwise agreed by all parties and the panel members. The notice shall inform the parties that the hearing is *de novo* and that no reports or other information from the assigned member will be considered. The notice also shall inform the parties that they may have witnesses present and may present documentary evidence and should present all evidence they expect to present at the hearing.

If the circuit chair determines that a hearing panel or panel member is delinquent in scheduling or attending a hearing, the circuit chair has the authority to reassign the whole panel or reassign one or more panel members.

If a party or a witness cannot, for any reason, be present at the hearing, a written statement shall be submitted which shall be the complete statement of the party or witness. If a party fails to appear, then the hearing panel shall render its decision based on the available testimony and documentation.

Conduct of the hearings shall be pursuant to such rules and procedures as the Executive Council may prescribe. While it is not necessary to follow strictly the rules of evidence as generally applied in circuit court, hearings should be conducted in conformance generally with them. If the hearing cannot be completed within the allotted time, it may be adjourned by the panel chair and reconvened with no less than ten (10) days notice, unless the parties and panel members otherwise agree to a date and time certain.

A party to a fee dispute may, at the party's own expense, cause any hearing by the panel to be recorded and transcribed. The tape recording of the hearing shall be the property of the Board. If a party has a hearing transcribed, the party shall, at the party's own expense, provide a copy of the transcript to the Board.

[Adopted effective January 1, 1994. Amended effective September 11, 1998; September 1, 2002; September 7, 2007.]

RULE 16. VOLUNTARY TERMINATION

Prior to the final decision of the Board, the party who initiated the process may terminate the process. Termination of the process takes effect upon receipt in the Bar office of written acknowledgement from the initiating party.

This written acknowledgement of withdrawal will have the effect of ending the availability of the procedure with prejudice to the initiating party as to that dispute so that a party who initially filed an application with the Board may not make a second filing on the same dispute after withdrawing the first filing. Should that party fail to make a written acknowledgement of the withdrawal, the Board shall proceed to resolve the matter without delay.

Nothing herein is to be construed as limiting a party from filing an amended or supplemental form pertaining to the dispute, if requested or if needed, under such conditions as the hearing panel may provide or as may be established by the Executive Council.

[Adopted effective January 1, 1994. Amended effective September 1, 2002; September 7, 2007.]

RULE 17. HEARING PANEL

Upon conclusion of the panel hearing, the hearing panel members shall forthwith proceed to reach a decision and shall, within fifteen (15) days of the hearing, issue a written decision, including a factual statement of the controversy and the reasons for the decision reached. A decision of the majority of the hearing panel shall constitute a final decision of the Board. The written decision shall be filed with the Bar, and a copy sent to the circuit chair and each party to the dispute by first class mail, with proper postage affixed, or by email, provided the parties have consented to service by email in accordance with Rule 10. Service by mail is complete upon mailing.

[Adopted effective January 1, 1994. Amended effective September 11, 1998; September 1, 2002; September 7, 2007.]

RULE 18. CONFLICTS OF INTEREST

In case of a conflict of interest or disqualification of a circuit chair and vice-chair after disqualification of a circuit chair in a given case, the chair of the Executive Council shall then act as the circuit chair in that specific instance.

In case the chair of the Executive Council has a conflict of interest or is disqualified, the member of the Executive Council next senior in years of active practice in this state shall act as Executive Council chair in that specific instance.

In extraordinary cases where members of the circuit panel are disqualified for any reason, either voluntarily or involuntarily, in a specific dispute, and there do not remain enough members of the circuit panel to comprise the hearing panel, the chair of the Executive Council, or, in the event of the disqualification of the chair of the Executive Council, the President shall appoint the requisite number of members from the Board to the hearing panel.

Likewise, should any member of the circuit panel in a judicial circuit fail or refuse to discharge the duties of a member of the Board, the chair of the Executive Council shall appoint a substitute member from members of the Board.

[Adopted effective January 1, 1994. Amended effective September 7, 2007.]

RULE 19. COMPLIANCE

The decision of the Board shall be final and binding upon the parties and shall be enforceable in any court of competent jurisdiction. The parties shall comply with the terms of the final decision within thirty (30) days after mailing. In case of non-compliance, the circuit chair shall issue a Certificate of Non–Compliance which may be entered as a judgment pursuant to Rule 58(a), SCRCP. The circuit chair shall forward all non-compliance orders to the Bar. This order shall then be forwarded to the Commission on Lawyer Conduct under Rule 8.3 of the Rules of Professional Conduct, Rule 407, SCACR.

[Adopted effective January 1, 1994. Amended effective September 11, 1998; September 1, 2002.]

RULE 20. APPEALS

(a) A party aggrieved by the final decision of the Board may appeal the decision to the circuit court in the county where the principal place of practice of the attorney is located.

(b) To confer jurisdiction of an appeal on the circuit court, the appealing party must commence the appeal within thirty (30) days after the final decision is mailed to the appealing party, except that if based upon corruption, fraud, or other undue means, it must be commenced within thirty (30) days after such grounds are known or should have been known.

(c) In order to commence an appeal, the appealing party must:

(1) file with the clerk of the circuit court a notice of appeal along with a signed document certifying the names and addresses to which the appealing party mailed copies of the notice and the date the copies were mailed. The notice of appeal must contain (i) the names of all parties to the dispute, (ii) an indication that the appealing party is appealing from a final decision of the Resolution of Fee Disputes Board, (iii) a detailed statement of the grounds for the appeal and (iv) the name, current mailing address, and telephone number of the appealing party;

(2) pay the required filing fee to the clerk of court;

(3) mail each other party to the dispute a copy of the notice of appeal; and

(4) mail a copy of the notice to the South Carolina Bar Resolution of Fee Disputes Board.*

A notice of appeal is sufficient if it is in writing, is signed by the appealing party, and contains the information required in sub-paragraph (c)(*l*).

(d) Filing an appeal does not stay the issuance of a Certificate of Non–Compliance. However, if, upon the filing of a notice of appeal, a party pays the disputed sum to the Bar to be held in trust pending resolution of the appeal, no Certificate of Non–Compliance shall be issued. The Bar shall remit the disputed sum to the prevailing party within ten (10) days of the final disposition of the dispute.

(e) The Board shall supply to the circuit court a record on appeal, which shall include such of the following materials as were involved in the proceedings of the Board: the application, the decision of the assigned member, the concurrence or non-concurrence of the circuit chair, and the decision of the hearing panel.

(f) The court shall affirm or vacate the final decision of the Board. The court may vacate only where:

(1) the decision was procured by corruption, fraud, or other undue means;

(2) there was evident partiality or corruption in an assigned member or hearing panel member, or misconduct prejudicing the rights of any party;

(3) the assigned member or hearing panel members exceeded their powers;

(4) the hearing panel members refused to postpone the hearing, if any, upon sufficient cause being shown therefore, or the assigned member or hearing panel members refused to hear evidence material to the controversy, or otherwise conducted the proceeding so as to substantially prejudice the rights of a party; or

(5) the hearing panel chair did not provide notice of the hearing as required under Rule 15.

(g) In vacating the final decision, the court may order a reconsideration by a new assigned member appointed by the circuit chair or, if vacating the decision of a hearing panel, a rehearing before a new hearing panel appointed by the circuit chair. Any reconsideration or rehearing shall be de novo, and no reports or decisions of any prior assigned member or hearing panel shall be considered. When a final decision of the Board is vacated, any judgment which may have been entered pursuant to that decision also is vacated.

(h) The parties and the circuit court shall provide the Board notice of all proceedings on appeal and the final disposition of the appeal.

[Adopted effective January 1, 1994. Amended effective September 11, 1998; November 5, 2003; September 7, 2007; December 6, 2011.]

* The current address of the Board is Post Office Box 608, Columbia, SC 29202.

Notes

Note to 2003 Amendments

Amended by Order dated November 5, 2003. The amendment to 20(a) provides that an appeal from a decision of the Board does not stay the issuance of a Certificate of Non-Compliance and restricts the circuit court from vacating a decision of the Board only when one of the five grounds set forth in 20(a) have been met. The amendment to 20(c) provides that the parties and the circuit court shall provide the Board with notice of all proceedings and the final disposition.

RULE 21. PROCEEDINGS CONFIDENTIAL

All proceedings shall be confidential, except that where a party to a proceeding subsequently resorts to legal proceedings in a court of record to appeal or to enforce the final decision of the Board, compliance with these Rules concerning appeal or enforcement does not constitute a violation of the confidentiality of the proceeding.

[Adopted effective January 1, 1994.]

RULE 22. AMENDMENTS TO RULES

Upon approval by the Bar's House of Delegates, amendments to these Rules shall be submitted to the Supreme Court of South Carolina for approval. Any amendment to these rules is effective as to any fee dispute filed after the date of approval by the Supreme Court.

[Adopted effective January 1, 1994. Amended effective September 7, 2007; December 6, 2011.]

RULE 417. FINANCIAL RECORDKEEPING

RULE 1. RECORDKEEPING GENERALLY

A lawyer who practices in this jurisdiction shall maintain current financial records as provided in these Rules and required by Rule 1.15 of the South Carolina Rules of Professional Conduct, and shall retain the following records for a period of six years after termination of the representation:

(a) receipt and disbursement journals containing a record of deposits to and withdrawals from client trust accounts, specifically identifying the date, source, and description of each item deposited, as well as the date, payee, and purpose of each disbursement;

(b) ledger records for all client trust accounts showing, for each separate trust client or beneficiary, the source of all funds deposited, the names of all persons for whom the funds are or were held, the amount of such funds, the descriptions and amounts of charges or withdrawals, and the names of all persons or entities to whom such funds were disbursed;

(c) copies of retainer and compensation agreements with clients as required by Rule 1.5 of the South Carolina Rules of Professional Conduct;

(d) copies of accountings to clients or third persons showing the disbursement of funds to them or on their behalf;

(e) copies of bills for legal fees and expenses rendered to clients;

(f) copies of records showing disbursements on behalf of clients;

(g) the physical or electronic equivalents of all checkbook registers, bank statements, records of deposit, pre-numbered canceled checks, and substitute checks provided by a financial institution;

(h) records of all electronic transfers from client trust accounts, including the name of the person authorizing transfer, the date of transfer, the name of the recipient and confirmation from the financial institution of the trust account number from which money was withdrawn, and the date and the time the transfer was completed;

(i) copies of monthly trial balances and monthly reconciliations of the client trust accounts maintained by the lawyer; and

(j) copies of those portions of client files that are reasonably related to client trust account transactions.

[Adopted effective September 9, 2011.]

Comment

[1] Rule 1 enumerates the basic financial records that a lawyer must maintain with regard to all client trust accounts of a law firm. These include the standard books of account and the supporting records that are necessary to safeguard and account for the receipt and disbursement of client or third person funds as required by Rule 1.15 of the South Carolina Rules of Professional Conduct. Consistent with Rule 1.15, this Rule proposes that lawyers maintain client trust account records for a period of six years after termination of each particular legal engagement or representation.

[2] Rule 1(g) requires that the physical or electronic equivalents of all checkbook registers, bank statements, records of deposit, pre-numbered canceled checks, and substitute checks be maintained for a period of six years after termination of each legal engagement or representation. The "Check Clearing for the 21st Century Act" or "Check 21 Act", codified at 12 U.S.C. § 5001 et. seq., recognizes "substitute checks" as the legal equivalent of an original check. A "substitute check" is defined at 12 U.S.C. § 5002(16) as a paper reproduction of the original check that contains an image of the front and back of the original check; bears a magnetic ink character recognition ("MICR") line containing all the information appearing on the MICR line of the original check; conforms with generally applicable industry standards for substitute checks; and is suitable for automated processing in the same manner as the original check. Banks, as defined in 12 U.S.C. § 5002(2), are not required to return to customers the original canceled checks. Most banks now provide electronic images of checks to customers who have access to their accounts on internet-based websites. It is the lawyer's responsibility to download electronic images. Electronic images shall be maintained for the requisite number of years and shall be readily available for printing upon request or shall be printed and maintained for the requisite number of years.

[3] The ACH (Automated Clearing House) Network is an electronic funds transfer or payment system that primarily provides for the inter-bank clearing of electronic payments between originating and receiving participating financial institutions. ACH transactions are payment instructions to either debit or credit a deposit account. ACH payments are used in a variety of payment environments including bill payments, business-to-business payments, and government payments (e.g. tax refunds). In addition to the primary use of ACH transactions, retailers and third parties use the ACH system for other types of transactions including electronic check conversion (ECC). ECC is the process of transmitting MICR information from the bottom of a check, converting check payments to ACH transactions depending upon the authorization given by the account holder at the point-of-purchase. In this type of transaction, the lawyer should be careful to comply with the requirements of Rule 1(h).

[4] There are five types of check conversions where a lawyer should be careful to comply with the requirements of Rule 1(h). First, in a "point-of-purchase conversion," a paper check is converted into a debit at the point of purchase and the paper check is returned to the issuer. Second, in a "back-office conversion," a paper check is presented at the point of purchase and is later converted into a debit and the paper check is destroyed. Third, in an "account-receivable conversion," a paper check is converted into a debit and the paper check is destroyed. Fourth, in a "telephone-initiated debit" or "check-by-phone" conversion, bank account information is provided via the telephone and the information is converted to a debit. Fifth, in a "web-initiated debit," an electronic payment is initiated through a secure web environment. Rule 1(h) applies to each type of electronic funds transfer described. All electronic funds transfers shall be recorded and a lawyer should not re-use a check number which has been previously used in an electronic transfer transaction.

[5] The potential for these records to serve as safeguards is realized only if the procedures set forth in Rule 1(i) are regularly performed. The trial balance is the sum of balances of each client's ledger card (or the electronic equivalent). Its value lies in comparing it on a monthly basis to a control balance. The control balance starts with the previous month's balance, then adds receipts from the Trust Receipts Journal and subtracts disbursements from the Trust Disbursements Journal. Once the total matches the trial balance, the reconciliation readily follows by adding amounts of any outstanding checks and subtracting any deposits not credited by the bank at month's end. This balance should agree with the bank statement. Monthly reconciliation is required by this rule.

[6] In some situations, documentation in addition to that listed in paragraphs (a) through (i) of Rule 1 is necessary for a complete understanding of a trust account transaction. The type of document that a lawyer must retain under paragraph (j) because it is "reasonably related" to a client trust transaction will vary depending on the nature of the transaction and the significance of the document in shedding light on the transaction. Examples of documents that typically must be retained under this paragraph include correspondence between the client and lawyer relating to a disagreement over fees or costs or the distribution of proceeds, settlement agreements contemplating payment of funds, settlement statements issued to the client, documentation relating to sharing litigation costs and attorney fees for subrogated claims, agreements for division of fees between lawyers, guarantees of payment to third parties out of proceeds recovered on behalf of a client, and copies of bills, receipts or correspondence related to any payments to third parties on behalf of a client (whether made from the client's funds or from the lawyer's funds advanced for the benefit of the client).

RULE 2. CLIENT TRUST ACCOUNT SAFEGUARDS

With respect to client trust accounts required by Rule 1.15 of the South Carolina Rules of Professional Conduct:

(a) only a lawyer admitted to practice law in this jurisdiction or a person under the direct supervision of the lawyer shall be an authorized signatory or authorize transfers from a client trust account;

(b) receipts shall be deposited intact and records of deposit should be sufficiently detailed to identify each item; and

(c) withdrawals shall be made only (i) by check payable to a named payee and not to cash, or (ii) by authorized electronic transfer.

[Adopted effective September 9, 2011.]

Comment

[1] Rule 2 enumerates minimal accounting controls for client trust accounts. It also enunciates the requirement that only a lawyer admitted to the practice of law in this jurisdiction or a person who is under the direct supervision of the lawyer shall be the authorized signatory or be permitted to authorize electronic transfers from a client trust account. While it is permissible to grant nonlawyer access to a client trust account, such access should be limited and closely monitored by the lawyer. If a lawyer chooses to grant nonlawyer access to a client trust account, the nonlawyer must be an individual under the direct supervision and control of the lawyer. A lawyer should never grant access to closing companies or other, similar entities. The lawyer has a nondelegable duty to protect and preserve the funds in a client trust account and can be disciplined for failure to supervise subordinates who misappropriate client funds. See Rules 5.1 and 5. 3 of the South Carolina Rules of Professional Conduct.

[2] The requirement in paragraph (b) that receipts shall be deposited intact means that a lawyer cannot deposit one check or negotiable instrument into two or more accounts at the same time, a practice commonly known as a split deposit.

RULE 3. AVAILABILITY OF RECORDS

Records required by Rule 1 may be maintained by electronic, photographic, or other media provided that they otherwise comply with these Rules and that printed copies can be produced. These records shall be readily accessible to the lawyer.

[Adopted effective September 9, 2011.]

Comment

Rule 3 allows the use of alternative media for the maintenance of client trust account records if printed copies of necessary reports can be produced. If trust records are computerized, a system of regular and frequent (preferably daily) backup procedures is essential. If a lawyer uses third-party electronic or internet based file storage, the lawyer must make reasonable efforts to ensure that the company has in place, or will establish reasonable procedures to protect the confidentiality of client information. See ABA Formal Ethics Opinion 398 (1995). Records required by Rule 1 shall be readily accessible and shall be readily available to be produced upon request of a client or third person who has an interest as provided in Rule 1.15 of the South Carolina Rules of Professional Conduct, or upon official request of a disciplinary authority, including but not limited to, a subpoena *duces tecum*. Personally identifying information in records produced upon request of a client, third person, or disciplinary authority shall remain confidential and shall be disclosed only in a manner to ensure client confidentiality as otherwise required by law or court rule.

RULE 4. DISSOLUTION OF LAW FIRM OR SALE OF LAW PRACTICE

Upon dissolution of a law firm or of any legal professional corporation or the sale of a law practice, the partners shall make reasonable arrangements for the maintenance of the client trust account records specified in Rule 1.

[Adopted effective September 9, 2011.]

Comment

This rule provides for the preservation of a lawyer's trust account records in the event of dissolution or sale of a law practice. Regardless of the arrangements the partners or shareholders make among themselves for maintenance of the records, each partner may be held responsible for ensuring the availability of these records. For the purposes of these Rules, the terms "law firm," "partner," and "reasonable" are defined in accordance with Rules 1.0(e), (i), and (j) of the South Carolina Rules of Professional Conduct.

RULE 5. AUTHORIZED ELECTRONIC TRANSFERS

Authorized electronic transfers involving client trust accounts shall be limited to:

(a) money required for payment to a client or third person on behalf of a client;

(b) expenses properly incurred on behalf of a client, such as filing fees or payment to third persons for services rendered in connection with the representation;

(c) money transferred to the lawyer for fees that are earned in connection with the representation and are not in dispute; and

(d) money transferred from one client trust account to another client trust account.

[Adopted effective September 9, 2011.]

RULE 6. NO BEARER ITEMS

No item shall be drawn on a trust account or fiduciary account made payable to cash or bearer, and no cash shall be withdrawn from a trust account or fiduciary account by means of a debit card or ATM card.

[Adopted effective September 9, 2011.]

RULE 418. ADVERTISING AND SOLICITATION BY UNLICENSED LAWYERS

(a) Unlicensed Lawyer Defined. "Unlicensed lawyer" means any person who is admitted to practice law in another jurisdiction but who is not admitted to practice law in South Carolina under Rules 402, 405, 414 or 415, SCACR.

(b) Rules of Professional Conduct Applicable. Any advertising or solicitation by an unlicensed lawyer shall comply with Rules 7.1 through 7.5 of the Rules of Professional Conduct contained in Rule 407, SCACR, when the advertising or solicitation is:

(1) An in-person contact with a potential client which occurs in South Carolina;

(2) A telephone communication (to include a facsimile of other electronic transmission) to a potential client at a telephone number in South Carolina;

(3) A letter or other document sent to a potential client through the U.S. mail or a private carrier to an address in South Carolina;

(4) An advertisement on a radio or television station located in South Carolina;

(5) An advertisement in a South Carolina a newspaper or any other publication which is primarily distributed in South Carolina; or

(6) Any other form of advertising or solicitation which is specifically targeted at potential clients in South Carolina.

(c) Misconduct; Procedure. For any advertising or solicitation covered by (b) above, it shall be misconduct for an unlicensed lawyer to violate or attempt to violate Rules 7.1 through 7.5 of the Rules of Professional Conduct, knowingly assist or induce another to do so, or do so through the acts of another. The Commission on Lawyer Conduct shall have jurisdiction over allegations that an unlicensed lawyer has committed misconduct. The procedure for investigating and hearing these allegations shall be the same as that provided by the Rules for Lawyer Disciplinary Enforcement contained in Rule 413, SCACR, for allegations that a lawyer admitted to practice law in this State has committed misconduct, to include the immunity and confidentiality provisions contained in those rules.

(d) Sanctions for Misconduct. An unlicensed lawyer who commits misconduct under this rule may receive a letter of caution or any form of discipline contained in Rule 7(b)(4)-(10) of the Rules for Lawyer Disciplinary Enforcement. In addition, an unlicensed lawyer who has committed misconduct under this rule may be ordered to refund all fees paid to the unlicensed lawyer pursuant to any contract of employment arising out of the advertising or solicitation. Misconduct under this rule may also be punished as a contempt of the Supreme Court, and the Supreme Court may issue injunctions against future violations.

(e) Unauthorized Practice of Law Unaffected. Nothing in this rule shall be construed to allow an unlicensed attorney to engage in the practice of law in South Carolina.

[Adopted effective July 1, 1999.]

RULE 419. ADMINISTRATIVE SUSPENSIONS

(a) Applicability. This rule governs suspensions by the South Carolina Bar, pursuant to the Bylaws of the South Carolina Bar, for failure to pay annual license fees, including the Lawyers' Fund for Client Protection assessment, and/or by the Commission for Continuing Legal Education and Specialization, pursuant to the Regulations for Mandatory Continuing Legal Education for Judges and Active Members of the South Carolina Bar, for failure to file a report establishing compliance with mandatory continuing legal education requirements and failure to pay the annual filing fee.

(b) Due Date of Fees and Reports.

(1) Annual license fees and assessments required by the Bylaws of the South Carolina Bar and Rule 411(d)(1), SCACR, shall be due not later than January 1. A lawyer who has failed to pay the annual license fees and assessments, including payment of any penalty established by the Bar, by January 31 will be automatically suspended by the Bar. With the exception of retired members, the Bar shall not accept a license fee or assessment unless the lawyer provides the Bar with a current e-mail address.

(2) Reports of compliance with continuing legal education requirements required by the Regulations for Mandatory Continuing Legal Education for Judges and Active Members of the South Carolina Bar shall be due not later than March 1. A lawyer who has failed to file a report of compliance and pay the annual filing fee, including payment of any penalty by the Commission, by March 31 will be automatically suspended by the Commission. The reporting period for lawyers and judges shall run from March 1 through the last day in February, annually.

(c) Failure to Comply.

(1) Promptly after January 31, the Bar shall notify the lawyers who have failed to pay the annual license fees and assessments, including payment of any penalty established by the Bar, that they have been suspended and that, if they have not complied and been reinstated by the Bar by March 1, their names will be published in the Advance Sheets.

(2) Promptly after March 31, the Commission shall notify the lawyers who have failed to file a report of compliance and pay the annual filing fee, including payment of any penalty by the Commission, that they have been suspended and that, if they have not complied and been reinstated by the Commission by May 1, their names will be published in the Advance Sheets.

(d) Reinstatement by Bar and Commission.

(1) The Bar shall forward a list of the lawyers who remain suspended after March 1 for failure to pay the annual license fees and assessments, including payment of any penalty established by the Bar, to the

Clerk of the Supreme Court. The names of those lawyers shall be published in the Advance Sheets. The suspended lawyers shall have until April 1 to comply and seek reinstatement through the Bar.

(2) The Commission shall forward a list of lawyers who remain suspended after May 1 for failure to file a report of compliance and pay the annual filing fee, including payment of any penalty by the Commission, to the Clerk of the Supreme Court. The names of those lawyers shall be published in the Advance Sheets. The suspended lawyers shall have until June 1 to seek reinstatement through the Commission.

(e) Suspension by Supreme Court.

(1) Promptly after April 1, the Bar shall forward a list of the lawyers who remain suspended for failure to pay annual license fees to the Clerk of the South Carolina Supreme Court. Those lawyers shall be suspended by order of the South Carolina Supreme Court and shall thereafter forward their certificate of admission to practice law in this state to the Clerk of the South Carolina Supreme Court.

(2) Promptly after June 1, the Commission shall forward a list of the lawyers who remain suspended for failure to file reports of compliance with continuing legal education requirements to the Clerk of the South Carolina Supreme Court. Those lawyers shall be suspended by order of the South Carolina Supreme Court and shall thereafter forward their certificate of admission to practice law in this state to the Clerk of the South Carolina Supreme Court.

(f) Reinstatement by Supreme Court. Any lawyer seeking reinstatement after April 1, in the case of a lawyer suspended for failing to pay license fees, and June 1, in the case of a lawyer suspended for failing to file reports of Continuing Legal Education compliance must petition the South Carolina Supreme Court. The petition for reinstatement shall comply with the requirements of Rule 32, RLDE, Rule 413, SCACR, to include a filing fee of $200. The Court may take such action as it deems appropriate in acting on the petition for reinstatement, including, but not limited to, requiring the lawyer to appear before the Court for a hearing, referring the petition to the Committee on Character and Fitness or referring the petition to the Commission on Lawyer Conduct for investigation and a recommendation as to the propriety of reinstatement.

(g) Termination. If a lawyer fails to seek reinstatement within three (3) years of being suspended by the Court, the lawyer's membership in the South Carolina Bar shall be terminated and the lawyer's name shall be removed from the roll of attorneys. The lawyer must thereafter comply with Rule 402, SCACR, to be readmitted to the practice of law in this state.

[Adopted effective September 6, 2000. Amended effective April 7, 2004; May 3, 2006.]

RULE 420. CHIEF JUSTICE'S COMMISSION ON THE PROFESSION

(a) Purpose. The Chief Justice's Commission on the Profession is created in recognition of the need for the emphasis upon and encouragement of professionalism in the practice of law.

(b) Membership. The Commission's chairperson will be the Chief Justice or the Chief Justice's designee. The Chief Justice will appoint the Commission's other members as follows.

(1) *State Judges:* Two Circuit Court Judges, two Family Court Judges; and additional judges from either the state appellate or trial bench as the Chief Justice may deem necessary.

(2) *Practicing Lawyers:* Seven practicing lawyers, giving due regard for diversity of representation, nominated by the Board of Governors of the South Carolina Bar.

(3) *Law School Faculty:* Two members of the faculty of a South Carolina Law School.

(4) *Instructor/Administrator:* One person who is involved in the instruction of legal assistants, is involved in instruction at the undergraduate or technical college level, or serves as a law office administrator.

In addition, the Chief Justice may extend an invitation to serve on the Commission to a U.S. District Court Judge from the District of South Carolina.

(c) Responsibilities. The Commission shall ensure that the practice of law remains a high calling which serves clients and the public good. Its major responsibilities are:

(1) To monitor and coordinate South Carolina's professionalism efforts in the bar, the courts and the law school;

(2) To monitor professionalism efforts in other jurisdictions;

(3) To plan and conduct symposiums, seminars, and other meetings on professionalism;

(4) To ensure the presence of a professionalism component in Bridge the Gap;

(5) To make recommendations to the Court, the South Carolina Bar, voluntary bar associations and the law school concerning additional means by which professionalism can be enhanced;

(6) To receive and administer grants and to make expenditures therefrom as the Commission shall deem prudent; and

(7) To receive and respond to inquiries concerning professionalism from the judiciary and the bar. The Commission shall have no authority to respond to complaints within the province of the Commission on Lawyer Conduct or the Commission on Judicial Conduct.

(d) Commission Regulations. Regulations may be promulgated by the Court or the Commission. Regulations will be effective only upon approval of the Court.

[Adopted effective November 22, 2000. Amended effective June 12, 2003; October 6, 2004.]

RULE 421. CERTIFICATION OF ATTORNEYS IN DEATH PENALTY CASES

(a) Classes of Certified Attorneys. There shall be two classes of attorneys certified to handle death penalty cases: lead counsel and second counsel.

(b) Lead Counsel. Lead counsel shall have at least five years experience as a licensed attorney and at least three years experience in the actual trial of felony cases. The application for certification to act as lead counsel shall be on a form designated by the Supreme Court.

(c) Second Counsel. Second counsel shall have at least three years experience as a licensed attorney. Second counsel is not required to be further certified to be eligible for appointment.

[Adopted effective September 1, 2001.]

RULE 422. COMMISSION ON ALTERNATIVE DISPUTE RESOLUTION

(a) Purpose. The Commission on Alternative Dispute Resolution is created to assist the courts, practitioners and the public with issues related to arbitration and mediation in the judicial system.

(b) Membership of Commission. The Commission's Chair will be the Chief Justice or the Chief Justice's designee. The Supreme Court will appoint the Commission's other members as follows:

(1) *State Judges:* One Circuit Court judge, one Family Court judge; one judge from the state appellate bench; one summary court judge; two judges from any state court.

(2) *Practicing Lawyers:* Six practicing lawyers, at least four of whom are certified arbitrators and/or mediators, with due regard for diversity of practices among the members.

(3) Two public members who may be certified arbitrators or mediators.

(4) A clerk of court from a county subject to mandated alternative dispute resolution rules.

(5) The Director of Court Administration or the Director's designee.

(6) The Chair of the House of Representatives Judiciary Committee or the Chair's designee.

(7) The Chair of the Senate Judiciary Committee or the Chair's designee.

(8) The Chair of the South Carolina Bar's Alternative Dispute Resolution Section.

(c) Duties. The Commission shall be responsible for the efficient administration of court-connected arbitration and mediation in South Carolina. Its responsibilities include:

(1) To serve as the principal resource for and coordinate efforts in the use of alternative dispute resolution in the resolution of civil and family litigation in the judicial system of South Carolina;

(2) To collect and analyze data on the effectiveness of those alternative dispute resolution programs;

(3) To approve training programs for the certification of arbitrators and mediators (hereinafter referred to as neutrals);

(4) To nominate five persons from its membership to serve as the Board of Arbitrator and Mediator Certification as established by the Circuit Court Alternative Dispute Resolution (ADR) Rules and the Family Court Mediation Rules (hereinafter referred to as the ADR Rules);

(5) To set certification and recertification fees subject to approval by the Supreme Court;

(6) To recommend funds needed at the state level to support the court-connected programs and administrative costs, and to allocate and expend funds received for any of the purposes within the scope of the Commission;

(7) To promote educational opportunities for all users;

(8) To monitor alternative dispute resolution efforts in other jurisdictions;

(9) To make recommendations to the Supreme Court, the South Carolina Bar, voluntary bar associations and the law school concerning additional means by which the use and practice of alternative dispute resolution can be improved and expanded; and

(10) To recommend to the Supreme Court amendments or additions to the ADR rules.

(d) Promulgation of Regulations. Regulations may be promulgated by the Commission. Regulations will be effective only upon approval of the Supreme Court.

[Adopted effective September 1, 2002.]

RULE 423. CERTIFICATES OF GOOD STANDING

A certificate of good standing may be issued by the Clerk of the Supreme Court to a person admitted to practice law in this state or to a person who holds a limited certificate to practice law in this state if the person is a member in good standing with the South Carolina Bar and is not under suspension for any reason. A person admitted or holding a limited certificate may request a certificate of good standing by submitting a written request to the Clerk of the Supreme Court accompanied by a filing fee in the amount of $25. If multiple copies are requested, an additional fee of $5 shall be charged for the second or subsequent copy of the certificate.

[Adopted effective April 7, 2004.]

RULE 424. LICENSING OF FOREIGN LEGAL CONSULTANTS

(a) Qualifications for Admission. In its discretion, the Supreme Court of the State of South Carolina may license to practice in this State as a foreign legal consultant, without examination, an applicant who:

(1) is a member in good standing of a recognized legal profession in a foreign country, the members of which are admitted to practice as attorneys or counselors at law or the equivalent and are subject to effective regulation and discipline by a duly constituted professional body or a public authority;

(2) for at least five of the seven years immediately preceding his or her application has been a member in good standing of such legal profession and has actually been engaged in the practice of law in the said foreign country or elsewhere substantially involving or relating to the rendering of advice or the provision of legal services concerning the law of the said foreign country;

(3) possesses the good moral character and general fitness requisite for a member of the Bar of this State;

(4) is at least twenty-six years of age; and

(5) intends to practice as a foreign legal consultant in this State and to maintain an office in this State for that purpose.

(b) Proof Required. An applicant under this Rule shall file an application in triplicate with the Clerk of the Supreme Court. The application shall be accompanied by a non-refundable application fee of $1,000. The application shall include the following:

(1) a certificate from the professional body or public authority in such foreign country having final jurisdiction over professional discipline, certifying as to the applicant's admission to practice and the date thereof, and as to his or her good standing as such attorney or counselor at law or the equivalent;

(2) a letter of recommendation from one of the members of the executive body of such professional body or public authority or from one of the judges of the highest law court or court of original jurisdiction of such foreign country;

(3) a duly authenticated English translation of such certificate and such letter if, in either case, it is not in English; and

(4) such other evidence as to the applicant's educational and professional qualifications, good moral character and general fitness, and compliance with the requirements of Section (a) of this Rule as the Supreme Court of the State of South Carolina may require.

(c) Scope of Practice. A person licensed to practice as a foreign legal consultant under this Rule may render legal services in this State subject, however, to the limitations that he or she shall not:

(1) appear for a person other than himself or herself as attorney in any court, or before any magistrate, administrative body, or other judicial officer, in this State;

(2) prepare any deed, mortgage, assignment, lease, or any other instrument effecting the transfer or registration of title to real estate located in the United States of America;

(3) prepare:

(A) any will or trust instrument effecting the disposition on death of any property located in the United States of America and owned by a resident thereof, or

(B) any instrument relating to the administration of a decedent's estate in the United States of America;

(4) prepare any instrument in respect to the marital or parental relations, rights, or duties of a resident of the United States of America, or the custody or care of the children of such a resident;

(5) render professional legal advice on the laws of this State, the laws of any other state, the laws of the District of Columbia, the laws of the United States of America or of any territory or possession thereof, or the laws of any foreign country other than the country in which the foreign legal consultant is admitted to practice as an attorney or the equivalent thereof;

(6) be, or in any way hold himself or herself out as, a member of the Bar of this State; or

(7) carry on his or her practice under, or utilize in connection with such practice, any name, title, or designation other than one or more of the following:

(A) his or her own name;

(B) the name of the law firm with which he or she is affiliated;

(C) his or her authorized title in the foreign country of his or her admission to practice, which may be used in conjunction with the name of such country; and

(D) the title "foreign legal consultant," which shall be used in conjunction with the words "admitted to the practice of law in [name of the foreign country of his or her admission to practice]" and also stating "Not a member of the South Carolina Bar."

(d) Rights and Obligations. Subject to the limitations set forth in Section (c) of this Rule, a person licensed as a foreign legal consultant under this Rule shall be considered a lawyer affiliated with the Bar of this State and shall be entitled and subject to:

(1) the rights and obligations set forth in the Rules of Professional Conduct of Rule 407, South Carolina

Appellate Court Rules. With respect to continuing legal education requirements of Rule 408(a), a person licensed as a foreign legal consultant shall annually attend at least two (2) hours of approved Continuing Legal Education (CLE) courses devoted to legal ethics/professional conduct; and

(2) the rights and obligations of a member of the Bar of this State with respect to:

(A) affiliation in the same law firm with one or more members of the Bar of this State, including by:

(i) employing one or more members of the Bar of this State;

(ii) being employed by one or more members of the Bar of this State or by any partnership (or professional corporation) which includes members of the Bar of this State or which maintains an office in this State; and

(iii) being a partner in any partnership (or shareholder in any professional corporation) which includes members of the Bar of this State or which maintains an office in this State; and

(B) attorney–client privilege, work-product privilege, and similar professional privileges.

(e) Disciplinary Provisions: A person licensed to practice as a foreign legal consultant under this Rule shall be subject to professional discipline in the same manner and to the same extent as members of the Bar of this State and to this end:

(1) every person licensed to practice as a foreign legal consultant under these Rules:

(A) shall be subject to control by the Supreme Court and to admonition, reprimand, or suspension of his or her license to practice by the Supreme Court of the State of South Carolina and shall otherwise be governed by Rule 407, South Carolina Appellate Court Rules; and

(B) shall execute and file with the Clerk of the Supreme Court, in such form and manner as such court may prescribe:

(i) his or her commitment to observe the Rules of Professional Conduct Rule 407, South Carolina Appellate Court Rules, to the extent applicable to the legal services authorized under Section (c) of this Rule;

(ii) a written undertaking to notify the Supreme Court of any change in such person's good standing as a member of the foreign legal profession referred to in Section (a)(1) of this Rule and of any final action of the professional body or public authority referred to in (b)(1) of this Rule imposing any disciplinary censure, suspension, or any other sanction upon such person; and

(iii) a duly acknowledged instrument, in writing, setting forth his or her address in this State and designating the Clerk of the Supreme Court as his or her agent upon whom process may be served, with like effect as if served personally upon him or her, in any action or proceeding thereafter brought against him or her and arising out of or based upon any legal services rendered or offered to be rendered by him or her within or to residents of this State whenever, after due diligence, service cannot be made upon him or her at such address or at such new address in this State as he or she shall have filed in the office of such Clerk by means of a duly acknowledged supplemental instrument in writing.

(2) Service of process on the Clerk of the Supreme Court, pursuant to the designation filed as aforesaid, shall be made by personally delivering to and leaving with such Clerk, or with a deputy or assistant authorized by him or her to receive such service, at his or her office, duplicate copies of such process together with a fee of $10. Service of process shall be complete when such Clerk has been so served. Such Clerk shall promptly send one of such copies to the foreign legal consultant to whom the process is directed, by certified mail, return receipt requested, addressed to such foreign legal consultant at the address specified by him or her as aforesaid.

(f) License Fees. A person licensed as a foreign legal consultant shall pay license fees in the same amount as paid by active members who have been admitted to practice law in this State or any other jurisdiction for three years or more, as set forth in Rule 410(c), South Carolina Appellate Court Rules.

(g) Revocation of License. In the event the Supreme Court of the State of South Carolina determines that a person licensed as a foreign legal consultant under this Rule no longer meets the requirements for licensure set forth in Section (a)(1) or Section (a)(3) of this Rule, it shall revoke the license granted to such person hereunder.

(h) Admission to Bar. In the event a person licensed as a foreign legal consultant under this Rule is subsequently admitted as a member of the Bar of this State under the provisions of the Rules governing such admission, the license granted to such person hereunder shall be deemed terminated by the license granted to such person to practice law as a member of the Bar of this State.

(i) Application for Waiver of Provisions. The Supreme Court of the State of South Carolina, upon application, may in its discretion vary the application or waive any provision of this Rule where strict compliance will cause undue hardship to the applicant. Such application shall be in the form of a verified petition setting forth the applicant's name, age, and residence address, together with the facts relied upon and a prayer for relief. Such application shall be accompanied by a filing fee of $75.00.

(j) Confidentiality. The files and records maintained by the Clerk relating to the licensing of foreign legal consultants shall be confidential and shall not be disclosed except as necessary by the Clerk to carry out his or her own responsibilities. The Clerk may disclose information to the National Conference of Bar Examiners and to the bar admission authorities in other jurisdictions, and may disclose the names of those persons who are licensed as foreign legal consultants and date of their licensing. The Supreme Court may authorize the release of confidential information to other persons or agencies.

[Adopted effective November 2, 2006. Amended effective December 3, 2010; April 22, 2011.]

APPENDICES TO PART IV

APPENDIX A. RULES OF THE BOARD OF LAW EXAMINERS

(Promulgated Pursuant to Rule 402(a)(4), SCACR)

A. General Rules.

1. Bar examinations shall be held twice each year on the last Monday, Tuesday and Wednesday in February and July.

2. At the conclusion of every morning and afternoon session, each applicant will certify that the applicant has not given or received any assistance of any nature whatsoever in connection with the examination.

3. Questions requiring essay type answers will be given on Monday and Tuesday of each examination. The essay portion of the examination may cover any of the following subjects: Corporations, Agency and Partnership, State and Federal Civil Practice and Procedure, Uniform Commercial Code—Articles 2, 3, 4 and 9, Equity, Legal Writing and Research, Wills, Trusts and Estates, Trial Advocacy, Domestic Relations, and Insurance. An applicant should be familiar with principles of law which prevail in this State with respect to the foregoing subjects and any aspects of the law which are peculiar to this State. The grade an applicant receives will be based both upon the candidate's knowledge of the applicable law as well as the candidate's ability to analyze and apply the law to the facts set forth in the questions.

4. All answers to the essay questions will be legibly written in examination booklets. Booklets and pens will be provided by the Clerk of the Supreme Court.

5. The Multistate Bar Examination as provided by the National Conference of Bar Examiners will be given on Wednesday of each examination. The Multistate Bar Examination, which is a multiple choice type examination, will cover the following subjects: Constitutional Law, Contracts, Torts, Real Property, Evidence, and Criminal Law. The Clerk of the Supreme Court will provide pencils for this portion of the examination.

B. Special Accommodations for Disabled Applicants.

1. *Policy.* It is the policy of the Board of Law Examiners of the State of South Carolina to provide reasonable accommodations for disabled applicants including persons with learning disabilities and persons with health impairments. The bar examination will be administered to all eligible applicants in a manner that does not discriminate against those applicants with disabilities.

2. *Application Procedure.*

(a) Persons needing special accommodations on examinations should make a written request to the Board to obtain the necessary information, procedures and written forms. Appropriate current documentation is required by the Board.

(b) Upon written request to the Board, the manner in which the examination is administered to an applicant may be modified while maintaining the security and integrity of the examination.

(c) An applicant must submit a written request for special testing accommodations on forms prescribed by the Board no later than November 1st for the February examination and April 1st for the July examination. This filing deadline may be extended upon good cause as determined by the Chairman of the Board.

(d) Applicants must submit a current medical verification prepared by a licensed professional qualified to diagnose such disability who can describe the nature and extent of the disability.

(e) The Board may require the applicant to provide additional information in support of the applicant's request. This information may include, but is not limited to, information concerning special accommodations provided during the applicant's law school education including certification from official representatives of the school where such accommodations were provided. The Board may also require the applicant to undergo a physical/psychological examination to be conducted by a licensed professional designated by the Board verifying the nature and extent of the impairment. The Board may also appoint an expert to analyze the documentation submitted by the applicant and to make a recommendation to the Board concerning appropriate accommodations.

(f) In addition, an applicant seeking special testing accommodations due to a learning disability or attention deficit/hyperactivity disorder must provide appropriate documentation provided by a licensed professional qualified to diagnose such disability including, but not limited to, a licensed physician, learning disability specialist or psychologist. Learning disability and attention deficit/hyperactivity disorder evaluations must meet all requirements stated on the Board's written forms and should be completed or updated within the past three (3) years. An updated evaluation does not necessarily need to be a full, comprehensive diagnostic evaluation, but must provide information concerning relevant treatment, course of condition, current impairment, and rationale for current accommodation requests. The previous comprehensive diagnostic evaluation must be submitted with the updated evaluation. It is the applicant's responsibility to insure the Board is provided with a complete record fully demonstrating the existence and extent of impairment.

3. *General Standards and Procedures.*

(a) Depending on the nature and extent of an applicant's disability, the exam may be administered to the applicant in a separate room. Applicants assigned to a separate testing room will be monitored by a proctor approved by the Secretary of the Board.

(b) At the request of a blind or sight impaired applicant, the Board may provide the examination in braille or in large print; provided, the request is made no later than November 1st for the February exam and April 1st for the July exam.

(c) The Board may allow the applicant to use the services of a special assistant. This person may not provide substantive assistance to the applicant, but may read the essay and/or the Multistate Bar Examination questions to the applicant. The special assistant may type or write the applicant's answers to the essay questions and fill in the Multistate Bar Examination answer sheet at the applicant's direction. If the applicant chooses to use a special assistant, the applicant must provide background information regarding the special assistant to the Board. The special assistant shall not have any legal related employment or education. The Secretary of the Board must approve the special assistant.

(d) The Board may allow a disabled applicant additional time to complete the Multistate Bar Examination and the essay portions of the examination. The additional time on each section of the examination shall not exceed one and one half (1 1/2) times the normal time allotted for the section. In addition, longer rest and/or lunch breaks may be permitted; however, in no event shall the entire examination extend beyond two (2) additional days.

(e) The Board shall determine the measures necessary to ensure that any special accommodations approved under this policy do not compromise the security or integrity of the examination or the integrity of the applicant's answers.

(f) The Board will notify the applicant of its decision on the request for special accommodations in writing at least thirty (30) days prior to the scheduled examination. Provided, the Chairman of the Board may approve later notification when the filing deadline is extended pursuant to Paragraph B(2)(c) of these Rules.

(g) An applicant dissatisfied with the decision of the Board may appeal to the Supreme Court within ten (10) days after service of the written decision of the Board. This appeal is to be made by filing a motion with the Clerk of the Supreme Court in compliance with Rule 240, South Carolina Appellate Court Rules.

(h) The Secretary of the Board shall serve as the Americans with Disabilities Act coordinator for the Board and shall ensure that the provisions of this Rule are fully implemented.

[Adopted effective February 1, 1980. Amended effective September 22, 1988; August 26, 1993; September 30, 1996; December 2, 1999; September 8, 2000; May 21, 2004; June 6, 2008; April 29, 2009; July 22, 2010.]

APPENDIX B. RULES AND REGULATIONS OF THE COMMITTEE ON CHARACTER AND FITNESS

1. PURPOSE

The primary purpose of the Committee on Character and Fitness is to screen Applicants before admission to the bar for the protection of the public and the system of justice. The public is inadequately protected unless our system evaluates character and fitness as those elements relate to the practice of law. The public interest requires that the public be secure in its expectation that those who are admitted to the bar are worthy of the trust and confidence clients may reasonably place in their lawyers.

2. ORGANIZATION AND FUNDING

The Committee on Character and Fitness is appointed by and responsible to the Supreme Court of South Carolina. The Committee is charged with the duty and responsibility to administer character and fitness screening. It performs its duties in a manner that assures the protection of the public by recommending for admission only those who qualify. The Supreme Court provides funding and staffing to permit appropriate investigation of all information pertaining to applicants' character and fitness.

3. THE INVESTIGATIVE PROCESS

The Committee on Character and Fitness places upon the applicant the burden of producing information. Each investigation is initiated by requiring the applicant to execute under oath a thorough application and to sign an authorization and release form that extends to the Committee and to any persons or institutions supplying information to the Committee. The applicant is informed of the consequences of failing to produce information requested by the application and of making material omissions or misrepresentations. The Committee frames each question on the application in a manner that renders the scope of inquiry clear and unambiguous. The Committee has the power to cause the witnesses and documents or other records to be subpoenaed and to administer oaths or affirmations.

4. CONFIDENTIALITY AND DUE PROCESS

The Committee on Character and Fitness respects the confidentiality of records and sources and the need to protect the applicant, the sources and the public. This rule provides for confidentiality of records and sources except for cooperation with another bar examining authority. The Committee respects due process and has specified procedures which include notice to applicants and an opportunity to appear, with right to counsel, before the Committee prior to a final adverse determination.

5. STANDARD OF CHARACTER AND FITNESS

A lawyer should be one whose record of conduct justifies the trust of clients, adversaries, courts and others with respect to the professional duties owed to them. A record manifesting a deficiency in the honesty, trustworthiness, diligence or reliability of an applicant may constitute a basis for denial of admission.

6. RELEVANT CONDUCT

The revelation or discovery of any of the following will be treated as cause for further inquiry before the Committee decides whether the applicant possesses the character and fitness to practice law: unlawful conduct; academic misconduct; making of false statements, including omissions; misconduct in employment; acts involving dishonesty, fraud, deceit or misrepresentations; abuse of legal process; neglect of financial responsibilities; neglect of professional obligations; violation of an order of a court; evidence of mental or emotional instability; evidence of drug or alcohol dependency; denial of admission to the bar in another jurisdiction on character and fitness grounds; disciplinary action by a lawyer disciplinary agency or other professional disciplinary agency of any jurisdiction.

This list is not exclusive but is representative. Circumstances in individual cases may cause inquiry into other areas.

7. USE OF INFORMATION

The Committee on Character and Fitness determines whether the present character and fitness of an applicant qualifies the applicant for admission. In making this determination through the processes described above, the following factors, among others, will be considered in assigning weight and significance to prior conduct: applicant's age at the time of the conduct; recency of the conduct; reliability of the information concerning the conduct; seriousness of the conduct; factors underlying the conduct; cumulative effect of conduct or information; evidence of rehabilitation; applicant's positive social contributions since the conduct; applicant's candor in the admissions process; materiality of any omissions or misrepresentations.

APPENDIX C. REGULATIONS FOR MANDATORY CONTINUING LEGAL EDUCATION FOR JUDGES AND ACTIVE MEMBERS OF THE SOUTH CAROLINA BAR

I. PURPOSE

These Regulations implement Rules 408, 419, and 504, SCACR.

II. REQUIREMENTS

A. Active Members of the South Carolina Bar.

1. Except as otherwise provided in Regulation III, each active member of the South Carolina Bar, as defined in the By–Laws of the South Carolina Bar, shall complete a minimum of 14 hours of accredited continuing legal education (CLE) each annual reporting period.

2. At least 2 of the 14 hours shall be devoted to legal ethics/professional responsibility (LEPR). LEPR shall include, but not be limited to, instruction focusing on the Rules of Professional Conduct as they relate to law firm management, malpractice avoidance, lawyer fees, legal ethics, and the duties of lawyers to the judicial system, the public, clients and other lawyers.

3. As part of the legal ethics/professional responsibility (LEPR) requirement set forth in paragraph 2, at least once every three annual reporting periods, each lawyer must complete one hour of LEPR devoted exclusively to instruction in substance abuse or mental health issues and the legal profession.

4. An active member who accumulates in excess of 14 hours credit in an annual reporting period may carry a maximum of 14 hours forward to the next annual reporting period, of which a maximum of 2 hours may be LEPR credit (earned LEPR credit in excess of the required 2 hours may be applied to CLE requirements and/or carried forward not to exceed the maximum of 14 hours).

B. Judicial Members.

1. *Minimum Requirements.*

Judicial members specified in Rule 504(a), SCACR, shall complete a minimum of 15 hours of accredited judicial continuing legal education (JCLE) each annual reporting period. JCLE credit accumulated in any annual reporting period in excess of 15 hours may be carried forward to the next annual reporting period; provided, however, that not more than 30 hours credit may be carried forward to the next annual reporting period. At least once every three annual reporting periods, each judicial member must complete one hour of JCLE devoted exclusively to instruction in substance abuse or mental health issues and the legal profession.

2. *Mandatory Attendance at Designated Educational Activities.*

Without regard to any JCLE credit accumulated pursuant to the requirements of Regulation II(B)(1), judicial members shall attend any educational activity designated as mandatory by the Supreme Court of South Carolina or the Commission on Continuing Legal Education and Specialization (Commission). "Educational activity" means any seminar, program, conference, roundtable, or other activity which has been accredited for JCLE purposes and which has been designated mandatory for judicial members. Attendance at an educational activity may be designated as mandatory for all judicial members or only for certain specified categories of judicial members (for example: mandatory for probate judges only).

III. Exemptions

The following shall be exempt from the requirements of Regulation II:

A. Active members of the South Carolina Bar who are at least 60 years old, who have been admitted to practice law for 30 or more years and who submit to the Commission affidavits establishing that fact and requesting exemption (exempt status pursuant to this provision shall apply to both the CLE and LEPR requirements);

B. Certified specialists who comply with the CLE requirements of their specialty; provided, however, that at least 2 hours of the CLE credits completed by certified specialists shall be devoted to LEPR and that any certified specialist who completes more than 2 hours of LEPR credit may carry forward to the next annual reporting period up to 2 hours of such credit.

C. Newly admitted lawyers in the year in which they are licensed.

D. For JCLE requirements imposed by Regulation II(B), judicial members in the year in which they are sworn into office, provided they have satisfied the CLE requirements for active members of the South Carolina Bar.

IV. Hours and Accreditation

A. General.

One (1) hour of accredited CLE means 60 minutes of instruction as teacher or student at any CLE program which has been accredited by the Commission or which is sponsored or co-sponsored by an accredited organization. A list of currently accredited sponsors can be obtained from the Commission.

B. Application for Accredited Sponsor Status.

A sponsor wishing to apply for sponsor accreditation shall submit to the Commission:

1. An application for status as an accredited sponsor of CLE activities (forms available from the Commission);

2. Copies of written materials described in that application form; and

3. Any further information the Commission requires.

Except for accredited sponsors designated by the Commission, sponsor accreditation must be renewed every 5 years; provided, however, that sponsor accreditation may be withdrawn for cause at any time after 60 days notice to the sponsor and the South Carolina Bar.

C. Accreditation of Courses Sponsored by Non-accredited Sponsors.

CLE courses presented by sponsors which have not been granted sponsor accreditation will be considered for accreditation on an individual basis. An application for accreditation of a program may be obtained from the Commission and must be submitted to the Commission by the sponsor or by a lawyer who desires credit for attending the program. Except as provided in IV(D), the Commission will consider applications for the retroactive as well as prospective accreditation of programs.

D. In–House CLE.

In-house CLE, which is defined as CLE courses, training, programs, etc., sponsored or offered by law firms (individually or collectively), corporate legal departments, and similar organizations (but excluding public/governmental organizations and their subdivisions, agencies, etc.) primarily for the education of their members and employees, may be approved for credit under the rules and regulations applicable to other sponsors, subject to the following additional conditions:

1. The courses shall be submitted for approval on a course-by-course rather than an approved-sponsor basis;

2. The courses, including all written material related thereto, must be filed with an application for accreditation on or before the date on which the course is to be held;

3. The courses must be attended by at least 5 lawyers, not including the instructors; and

4. Not more than one-half of the approved credits for any reporting period may be earned through in-house programs.

E. Client Seminars.

Client seminars, which are defined as educational activities sponsored by a law firm in which the target audience is clients or potential clients of the sponsoring law firm, shall not be accredited even though the educational activities otherwise satisfy the accreditation standards specified in Regulation V. For this purpose, a law firm may be a professional corporation, professional association, partnership, sole practitioner or any other association of lawyers engaged in the private practice of law.

F. Fees.

Fees for the processing of applications for accreditation of individual programs or applications for accredited sponsor status and fees for other applications and purposes shall be as specified by the Commission.

G. Enhanced Credit for Teaching.

Upon application to the Commission, enhanced CLE credit may be earned through teaching at an accredited CLE activity. Information regarding the enhanced credit, including qualifications for the credit, the formula for calculating the credit, and exceptions to the credit, may be obtained from the Commission.

H. CLE Credit for Legal Writing.

Upon application to the Commission, CLE credit may be earned through authorship of articles or books concerning substantive or procedural law which are published or accepted for publication in approved third party publications. Information about this credit may be obtained from the Commission.

V. Accreditation Standards

The following standards will be considered by the Commission in the granting, denying, or withdrawal of accreditation of sponsors, programs, or parts of programs:

A. Courses must have significant intellectual or practical content;

B. Subject matter must deal primarily with the theory, practice, or ethics of law and the legal profession;

C. Courses must be directed to and intended for an audience of lawyers or judges;

D. Faculty members must be qualified by practical or academic experience to teach the subject;

E. High quality written materials must be distributed to participants;

F. Suitable classroom or laboratory setting must be provided for participants;

G. Ethical considerations pertaining to the subject matter should be included in the program;

H. Audio–Visual and Media Presentations.

1. Audio–visual or media presentations, including telephone and on-line seminars, are acceptable provided:

(a) A faculty member is in attendance or available by telephone hook-up to comment and answer questions; or

(b) Other appropriate mechanisms, as determined by the Commission, are present to enable the attendee to participate or react with the presenters and other attendees. Appropriate mechanisms include quizzes or examinations, response tracking, user prompts, and instant messaging.

2. In addition to meeting the standards of A through G, above, audio–visual or media presentations must:

(a) Utilize some mechanism to monitor course participation and completion in such a manner that certification of attendance is controlled by the provider. Courses must not be susceptible to a "fast forward" finish by attendees;

(b) High quality written materials must be available to be downloaded or otherwise furnished so that the attendees will have the ability to refer to such materials during and subsequent to the presentation;

(c) Telephone and on-line educational activities must be pre-approved by the Commission;

(d) Telephone activities will be accredited for the actual time spent to a maximum of 90 minutes per activity, and on-line educational activities, to include live webcasts, will be accredited for the actual time spent to a maximum of 6 hours per activity; and

(e) Providers shall furnish to the Commission password and/or log-in capabilities for accredited programs. Access will allow for review of course mechanisms, such as interactive functionality. Any such activity may be audited by 1 or more representatives of the Commission without charge.

3. CLE credit earned through audio-visual or media presentations and applied to the annual 14 hour minimum requirement shall not exceed 6 hours of credit per annual reporting period.

I. A written report of attendees shall be submitted to the Commission within 30 days of the course/program.

VI. Reports and Fees

A. Active Members.

On forms prepared by the Commission and available through its offices (or a reasonable facsimile), each active member of the South Carolina Bar not exempt from Regulation II(A) shall, not later than March 1 of each year, file with the Commission a sworn annual report of compliance for the preceding annual reporting period and pay an annual filing fee of $ 20.00. Any active member submitting a report of compliance after March 1 shall pay, in addition to the annual filing fee, a late filing fee of $ 50.00. The late filing fee shall be doubled for any member who files after the filing deadline and who has filed late and paid a late filing fee on any prior occasion.

B. Judicial Continuing Legal Education (JCLE).

On forms prepared by the Commission and available through its offices (or a reasonable facsimile), each judicial member specified in Rule 504(a), SCACR, shall, not later than April 15 of each year, file with the Commission an annual report of compliance for the preceding educational period and pay an annual filing fee of $ 20.00. Any judicial member submitting a report of compliance after April 15 shall pay, in addition to the annual filing fee, a late fee of $ 50.00.

C. Amended Reports of Compliance.

For the purposes of these Regulations, an amended report of compliance is one that seeks to change a report of compliance previously submitted to the Commission. A report of compliance may be amended within 1 year from the date that the original report was received by the Commission or 1 year from the filing deadline for the original report, whichever date is later. An amended report shall be executed in the same manner as the report it is amending and shall be accompanied by the filing fees specified for such original report, to include late filing fees if appropriate.

D. Revenue From Filing and Other Fees.

The fees specified in these Regulations and fees paid by certified specialists shall be used only to defray operating expenses of the Commission and its staff and may be adjusted by the Commission from time to time in order to produce the actual income required for the expenditures, plus a reasonable reserve fund.

VII. Non–compliance

A. Active Members.

1. *Automatic Suspension.* An active member of the South Carolina Bar who is neither exempt nor excused from the requirements of Regulation II(A) and/or VI(A) and who has failed to comply with these requirements by March 31 shall be automatically suspended from the practice of law.

2. *Notice of Suspension.* Notice of suspension will be provided to suspended members, the Clerk of the South Carolina Supreme Court, and to the judge or judges of the judicial circuit in which any suspended lawyer principally practices and/or maintains a principal residence. Suspended members will also be advised that unless they comply and are reinstated by the Commission by May 1, their names will be published in the Advance Sheets.

3. *Publication of Names of Suspended Lawyers.* The names of suspended lawyers who have not been reinstated by May 1 shall be provided to the Clerk of the South Carolina Supreme Court for publication in the Advance Sheets.

B. Judicial Members.

Any judicial member specified in Rule 504(a), SCACR, who is not exempt from the requirements of Regulation II(B)(1), II(B)(2), and/or VI (B) and who is in violation thereof shall be notified of the violation by certified mail at the judicial member's last known address. The judicial member shall then have 60 days after the date the notice was mailed to file an affidavit responding to the notice. Any response may include documents establishing that the judicial member concerned has cured the deficiency. If any judicial member fails to respond to the notice of violation or if after considering a judicial member's response the Commission believes the judicial member is still in violation of Rule 504, SCACR, and these Regulations, the Commission shall report the matter to the South Carolina Supreme Court for action as deemed appropriate by the Court.

VIII. Petition for Reinstatement

A. Reinstatement by the Commission.

An active member of the South Carolina Bar who has been suspended for failure to comply with these Regulations may petition the Commission for reinstatement. Petitions for reinstatement by the Commission must be received by the Commission not later than June 1. Each petition for reinstatement shall be accompanied by proof that the petitioner is then in compliance and that a reinstatement fee of $ 200.00 plus filing fees and late fees have been paid. If the petitioner is found to be in compliance by the Commission, to include payment of all fees, the petition shall be granted and the Commission will notify the petitioner, the Clerk of the South Carolina Supreme Court, and the judge or judges of the judicial circuit in which the petitioner principally practices and/or maintains a principal residence. The Commission shall inform the petitioner of the curative actions necessary for reinstatement if the petition is found not to be in compliance.

B. Reinstatement After June 1.

Petitions received after June 1 will be returned to the petitioner who will be informed that the petition for reinstatement must be filed with the Clerk of the South Carolina Supreme Court.

C. Notice to the Clerk of South Carolina Supreme Court.

Promptly after June 1, the Commission shall provide to the Clerk of the South Carolina Supreme Court the names of all lawyers who remain suspended.

IX. Waivers and Extensions

A. Waivers.

In individual cases involving extraordinary hardship or extenuating circumstances, the Commission may waive or modify the requirements of Regulation II(A) or extend the requirements of Regulation VI(A). When appropriate, and as a condition for any such waiver or modification, the Commission may proportionally increase the member's requirements for the succeeding annual reporting period. For example, if a member receives a waiver of 6 hours credit for one annual reporting period, the requirement for the following annual reporting period may be increased by 6 hours.

B. Extensions.

The Commission has no authority to extend the deadlines for compliance reporting or automatic suspension and all requests for such extensions made to the Commission will be denied.

X. Reconsideration

Any judicial member or active member of the South Carolina Bar or any sponsor aggrieved by a decision or action of the Commission may request reconsideration. A request for reconsideration must be submitted to the Commission (a) in writing, (b) within 30 days from the mailing of notice of the decision to the requesting judge or active member of the South Carolina Bar or sponsor or the publication of notice of the action in the South Carolina Bar News (or successor publication), and (c) may be accompanied by supporting evidence or documentation including affidavits. The request for reconsideration may, but need not, include a demand for a hearing. If a hearing is demanded, the judicial member, active member, or sponsor requesting the hearing will be heard by the Commission or by a committee appointed by the Commission for that purpose and may present evidence and argument in support of the request for reconsideration.

XI. Appeals

Any person aggrieved by the operation of these Regulations and who has exhausted all other remedies available hereunder, may petition the South Carolina Supreme Court for redress; provided, however, that any appeal must be submitted to the Court, in writing, not later than 30 calendar days after notice of final action by the Commission is mailed (via United States Postal Service) to the individual concerned.

[Approved by the Supreme Court on October 12, 2001. Amended effective September 1, 2003; July 6, 2006; September 7, 2006; January 4, 2007; amended August 5, 2010, effective March 1, 2011.]

APPENDIX D. REGULATIONS FOR LEGAL SPECIALIZATION IN SOUTH CAROLINA

I. PURPOSE

These Regulations implement the specialization plan promulgated by the Supreme Court of South Carolina in Rule 408, SCACR.

II. DEFINITIONS

As used in these Regulations:

A. "Court" means the Supreme Court of South Carolina.

B. "Commission" means the Supreme Court Commission on Continuing Legal Education and Specialization.

C. "Advisory Board" means a board appointed by the Commission to administer a field of law designated a specialty area.

D. "ABA" means the American Bar Association.

E. "CLE" means continuing legal education.

F. "Independent certifying organization" means an organization, bar association, group or entity other than the Supreme Court of South Carolina which certifies or intends to certify lawyers as specialists.

G. "Specialty field" and "specialty area" mean a field of the law in which lawyers are certified as specialists by the Court or an independent certifying organization.

III. JURISDICTION

Pursuant to Rule 408, SCACR, the Commission has jurisdiction over all matters pertaining to specialization in the practice of law in South Carolina. The Commission's responsibilities include, but are not limited to:

A. Administration of a program to recognize and regulate specialization in the law.

B. Designation and definition of fields of law in which certificates of certification may be issued by the Court.

C. Publication of reasonable and nondiscriminatory standards concerning education, experience, proficiency, and other relevant matters for granting certification to lawyers in designated and defined fields of law.

D. Approval and accreditation of independent organizations to certify lawyers as specialists in specialty fields in which certification is not offered by the Court.

E. Establishment of Advisory Boards in each field of law designated by the Commission in which certification shall be offered and appointment of members of such Boards.

F. Designation of filing and other fees to defray the expense of administering the specialization program.

IV. EXECUTIVE DIRECTOR

The Commission's Executive Director is responsible for the execution of the policies and directives of the Commission with respect to all specialization activities. The Executive Director, or a staff member designated by the Executive Director for that purpose, shall be ex officio a member of each Advisory Board and in that capacity, shall serve as Secretary to the Advisory Board, performing all duties that may be required of Secretary by these Regulations to include keeping and transcribing Minutes of all Advisory Board meetings.

V. ADVISORY BOARDS

A. General. Advisory Boards to the Commission shall be established for each field of law in which certification is to be offered by the Court.

B. Composition and Terms. Each Advisory Board shall consist of not less that five (5) members who are certified in the specialty field and who are appointed by the Commission to serve for three (3) years and until their successors are appointed. With respect to members initially appointed to an Advisory Board, such members must be lawyers who practice substantially in the specialty field and their terms shall be staggered so that not more than two (2) members' terms shall expire at the same time. No person shall be appointed for more than two (2) consecutive terms. One (1) member of each Advisory Board shall be designated as chairperson by the Commission.

C. Responsibilities. See Rule 408(d), SCACR. Advisory Boards shall advise and assist the Commission in carrying out its objectives and in the conduct and development of the program of specialization in the law. Standards and procedures for certification and recertification shall be prepared by each Advisory Board for approval by the Commission and the Court. The Advisory Board for each field of law shall be charged with actively administering the program in its particular field in cooperation with and under the general guidance of the Commission.

VI. INDEPENDENT CERTIFYING ORGANIZATIONS

A. Application for Approval. An independent certifying organization seeking approval from this Commission to issue certificates of specialization to South Carolina lawyers shall file an application requesting such approval. Application may be by letter and shall be accompanied by evidence of accreditation by the ABA and a complete copy of its application for accreditation which it submitted to the ABA (including any amendments or supplements thereto). An applicant shall specify each field of law for which it is seeking approval to issue certificates of specialization in South Carolina.

B. Designation of Specialty Fields—Limitations. Each field of law in which certification is to be offered by an independent certifying organization in South Carolina must be susceptible of meaningful definition and be an area in which a significant number of South Carolina Lawyers regularly practice.

C. Standards for Approval. An independent certifying organization, whose standards and procedures equal or exceed the minimum standards for certification specified in Rule 408, SCACR, and these Regulations, which has been accredited by the ABA, may be approved to issue certificates of specialization to South Carolina lawyers. However, such certificates of specialization may be offered only in those fields of the law in which specialization is not available from the Court. For this purpose, if specialization is available from the Court in any sub-area of a field of law in which an independent certifying organization offers or proposes to offer certification, that field of law shall be considered one in which specialization is available from the Court. Applications from independent certifying organizations that have not been accredited by the ABA will be rejected.

D. Fees. See Regulation IX, infra.

E. Term of Authorization to Issue Certificates. Approval of an independent certifying organization to issue certificates of specialization in South Carolina shall be for a term of three (3) years. To retain approval to issue certificates of specialization, a certifying organization shall be required to reapply at or near the end of the third (3rd) year of its initial approval period and every three (3) years thereafter.

F. Revocation/Termination of Authority to Issue Certificates.

1. *Revocation.* In any case in which an approved independent certifying organization ceases to exist, has its ABA accreditation withdrawn or suspended, fails to pay the annual administrative fee specified in Regulation IX E, infra, or fails to comply with the provisions of these Regulations, its approved status shall be revoked automatically.

2. *Termination.* In the event the Commission ceases to exist, its jurisdiction over South Carolina's specialization program is revoked, or its authority to approve the issuing of certificates of specialization by independent certifying organizations is withdrawn, the authority for independent certifying organizations to issue certificates of specialization to South Carolina lawyers shall terminate automatically.

G. Publication of Certified Status. After an independent certifying organization is authorized to issue certificates of specialization in South Carolina, any South Carolina lawyer certified as a specialist by that organization may publicize his or her certification, provided the communication states the name of the certifying organization and is not false or misleading. (For example, a lawyer certified by the ABC Board of Trial Advocacy as a civil trial specialist could publicize that fact in this manner: "Certified Civil Trial Specialist—ABC Board of Trial Advocacy.") In the event the authority of an independent certifying organization to issue certificates of specialization is revoked or terminated for any reason, South Carolina lawyers may not publicize a certification from that organization.

H. Required Reports. An independent certifying organization approved to issue certificates of specialization to South Carolina lawyers shall report to the Commission:

1. The name, South Carolina Bar number, mailing address, field of law in which certified, and period of certification (beginning and ending dates) of any South Carolina lawyer certified by it.

2. The name, South Carolina Bar number, and mailing address of any South Carolina lawyer certified by it whose certificate of specialization is revoked, suspended, modified, or whose certificate expires and is not renewed.

3. The name, South Carolina Bar number, and mailing address of any South Carolina lawyer certified by it who fails to comply with its CLE requirements.

4. Notice of renewal, revocation, modification, or suspension of its ABA accreditation.

5. Notice of any change in its constitution, bylaws, articles of incorporation, or other governing document or of any change to its standards and procedures for certification and recertification of specialists.

6. Any other information that may be required.

VII. APPLICATIONS FOR CERTIFICATION AND RECERTIFICATION

A. General. Applications shall be typewritten on forms provided by the Commission. Each question shall be answered responsively or shown as "not applicable." Applications and the information included therein shall be sworn to by the applicant as being true and complete.

B. Completion of Requirements for Certification. An applicant shall complete all requirements prior to application; provided, however, that:

1. Oral interview/examination and written examination will be completed after an application is filed.

2. The period of law practice and substantial involvement in the specialty field required by the standards and procedures of that specialty field may be completed after an application is filed, but must be completed not more than three (3) months after the application is received in the Commission's offices.

3. CLE requirements may be completed after an application is submitted provided the applicant furnishes proof of satisfaction of the requirements within three (3) months of the date his or her application is received in the Commission's offices.

C. Requirement for Additional Information. To assist in determining an applicant's entitlement to certification, the Commission, its Executive Director, or the Advisory Board may require an applicant to submit information in addition to that called for on the application form.

D. Payment of Application Fees. An application shall not be deemed complete until the application fee in the amount specified by the Commission has been paid.

E. References. Advisory Boards shall require applicants to provide names and addresses of at least five (5) lawyers or judges, or both, who can attest to the applicant's competence in the specialty field. Such references should be certified or should practice substantially in the specialty field and may not be related to or in practice with the applicant. Members of the Advisory Board and the Commission are not eligible to serve as references. In addition to references provided by an applicant, the Commission, its Executive Director, or the Advisory Board may solicit at random additional lawyers and/or judges to submit statements concerning the applicant's competence. Statements of references concerning an applicant shall be submitted on forms approved and furnished by the Commission.

F. Minimum CLE Requirements. CLE requirements to enter a specialty field, annual CLE requirements to maintain certification, and CLE requirements to qualify for recertification shall be specified by each specialty field's Advisory Board. However, the minimum CLE requirements to enter a specialty field shall not be less than thirty-six (36) hours of participation in CLE in the specialty area during the three (3) year period preceding a lawyer's application for certification, the annual CLE requirement for certified lawyers shall not be less than twelve (12) hours, and the CLE requirement to qualify for recertification shall not be less than seventy-five (75) hours of CLE in the specialty area.

G. Substantial Involvement in the Specialty Field. Substantial involvement is measured by the type and number of cases or matters handled and the amount of time spent practicing the specialty area. To qualify for certification in a specialty area, time spent practicing the specialty shall be no less than twenty-five percent (25%) of the total practice of a lawyer engaged in a normal full-time practice.

H. Processing of Applications.

1. The Executive Director and/or a member of the Executive Director's staff shall check each application upon receipt to assure that all portions of the application have been completed and that the applicant has complied with all requirements of the specialty field.

2. An application incomplete on its face or one in which it appears that the applicant does not meet the minimum practice (including substantial involvement in the specialty area) or CLE requirements for certification shall be returned to the applicant with a letter specifying the deficiencies in his or her application.

I. Burden of Proof. An applicant has the burden of establishing that he or she has met the requirements for certification in the specialty field. That burden is satisfied only if the Advisory Board is convinced, by clear and convincing evidence, that the applicant's involvement, experience, competency, practice, and education in the specialty field concerned meets or exceeds the minimum standards specified for certification in the specialty field and that he or she is a person of good character and reputation.

J. Failure of Written Examination. An applicant who fails a specialty field's written examination may not be certified unless he or she reapplies for certification and thereafter makes a passing score on the specialty's written examination. The application for certification of any applicant who has failed a specialty field's written examination three (3) times shall be rejected.

K. Requirements for Recertification. Recertification shall require similar evidence of competence as that required for initial certification in substantial involvement, peer review, and evidence of good standing. Minimum CLE requirements for recertification are indicated in Regulation VII F, supra.

L. Certification When Malpractice Claims or Ethical Complaints are Pending. An Advisory Board should not decline to recommend certification or recertification of an applicant it finds otherwise qualified simply because of a malpractice claim or ethical complaint filed or threatened. In cases involving such claims or complaints, the Advisory Board should undertake a due diligence review of the facts and circumstances of the claim or complaint and then determine its action with respect to the application for certification or recertification.

VIII. WRITTEN EXAMINATION

A. Requirement. Advisory Boards will require applicants to pass a written examination as a prerequisite to initial certification. An applicant who has not taken a specialty field's written examination within two (2) years of the date his or her application was received in the Commission's offices shall be required to reapply for certification.

B. Time and Place. Written examination for applicants shall be conducted in such place and on such date as fixed by the applicable Advisory Board in coordination with the Executive Director.

C. Grading. The grade given an applicant's written examination by the grader or graders shall be final in all cases except where the written examination is subject to review as indicated hereafter (see Regulation VIII F, infra).

D. Destruction of Examination Booklets and Answer Sheets. Examination booklets and answer sheets of applicants who pass a specialty field's written examination will be destroyed after grading. Examination booklets and answer sheets of an applicant who fails a specialty field's written examination will be destroyed fifteen (15) days after the applicant was mailed notice (by certified mail) by the Executive Director that he or she failed the written examination unless, within that fifteen (15) day period, the applicant has filed with the Executive Director a written request to review his or her examination.

E. Review of Written Examination. Within fifteen (15) days of the mailing of notice by the Executive Director that an applicant has failed the written examination, the applicant may request in writing to review his or her examination. If a written request to review the examination is timely submitted, the applicant will be permitted to review the examination in the Commission's offices at a time designated by the Executive Director. To prevent compromise of the written examination, the applicant shall not be permitted to remove the examination from the Commission's offices or to copy the examination.

F. Petition for Grade Review. After reviewing his or her examination, any applicant who feels errors were made in grading may file with the Commission a Petition for Grade Review. That petition must be filed within fifteen (15) days of the date he or she reviewed his or her written examination in the Commission's offices. The petition should set out in detail the errors the applicant believes were made in the grading of his or her examination. An applicant may file supporting information to substantiate his or her petition. A petition not timely filed shall not be considered.

G. Review Procedure. The Executive Director will submit an applicant's Petition for Grade Review, examination, and answer sheet to the specialty's Advisory Board. All information will be submitted to the Advisory Board in blind form with no identifying information on any document furnished the Advisory Board. The Advisory Board shall review the entire examination of any applicant requesting a review of his or her grade and shall recommend to the Commission that the applicant's grade remain the same or be changed. The Advisory Board's recommendation to the Commission shall be in writing, shall specify the reasons why the Advisory Board reached its recommendation, and shall be submitted within sixty (60) days from the receipt of the Petition for Grade Review unless that period is extended by the Executive Director for good cause.

H. Decision of the Commission. The Commission shall consider a Petition for Grade Review and the recommendation of the Advisory Board pertaining thereto at its first meeting following receipt of the Advisory Board's recommendation. The Commission's decision on whether the applicant passed or failed the examination shall be final.

IX. SPECIALIZATION FEES

The following fees, which may be adjusted as necessary, have been established for the specialization program:

A. Application Fee. A fee as specified by the Commission shall be assessed for each application for certification that is submitted. The applicant is not entitled to a refund of the application fee or any portion thereof if his or her application is returned, rejected or withdrawn.

B. Examination Fee. An examination fee may be instituted if deemed necessary by the Commission to help defray the expense of administering the specialization program.

C. Certification Fee. A fee as specified by the Commission is due and payable by an applicant who has been notified that he or she has been approved for certification by the Court. Payment of the certification fee is a prerequisite to issuance of a certificate of specialization.

D. Application Fee for Approval as an Independent Certifying Organization. Independent certifying organizations filing applications for approval to issue certificates of specialization to South Carolina lawyers shall pay a nonrefundable application fee as specified by the Commission for each field of the law in which an applicant proposes to offer specialization.

E. Annual Administrative Fee. Each independent certifying organization approved to issue certificates of specialization to South Carolina lawyers shall pay an annual administrative fee as specified by the Commission for each field of the law in which it is approved to issue certificates of specialization.

F. Filing Fees. When reporting compliance with a specialty field's annual CLE requirements, each certified specialist shall pay an annual filing fee in an amount specified by the Commission for each such report he or she files with the Commission. Reports filed after the reporting deadline of March 1 (as determined by USPS postmark) shall be assessed a late filing fee in an amount equal to the late filing fee charged active South Carolina Bar members who do not file reports of compliance by March 1.

X. REPORTING COMPLIANCE WITH CLE REQUIREMENTS

A. Specialists Certified by the Court.

1. *Reports of Compliance.* On forms prepared by the Commission and available through its offices, each specialist certified by the Court shall, not later than March 1 of each year, file a report of compliance with the CLE requirements of each of the relevant specialty field. In addition to CLE requirements imposed by the specialty field, the specialist shall annually report at least two (2) hours of LEPR. Any specialist who reports more than two (2) hours of LEPR credit in any annual reporting period may carry forward up to two (2) hours of LEPR credit to the next annual reporting period.

2. *Annual Certified Specialist Statement.* On forms prepared by the Commission, and available

though its offices, each certified specialist shall, not later than March 31 of each year, file a statement pertaining to the nature of the specialist's practice and disclosing whether, during the preceding year, the specialist has been the subject of disciplinary actions, malpractice claims (including claims settled by payments), and/or any criminal convictions, excluding minor traffic offenses. Failure or refusal to file this report may result in revocation of certification.

B. Specialists Certified by Independent Certifying Organizations. Lawyers who are certified by approved independent certifying organizations shall comply with the annual CLE requirements of such organizations and shall, not later than March 1 of each year, file an annual CLE report with the Commission on forms prepared by and available through the Commission's offices. Requirements of an independent certifying organization notwithstanding, each such specialist shall complete and report annually to the Commission a minimum of fourteen (14) hours of approved CLE of which at least two (2) hours must be directed to LEPR. Specialists reporting more than two (2) hours of LEPR credit in any annual reporting period may carry forward to the next annual reporting period up to two (2) hours of his or her excess LEPR credit.

XI. HEARING AND APPEAL

A. Denial of Certification or Recertification. An applicant denied certification or recertification by an Advisory Board may request a hearing by petitioning the pertinent Advisory Board (through the Commission's Executive Director) within thirty (30) days after notice is mailed by the Commission that his or her certification or recertification has been denied. However, an applicant who is denied certification because of his or her failure to receive a passing score on a specialty field's written examination may not petition for a hearing pursuant to this paragraph, but may review his or her examination and petition for a review of his or her grade as provided in Regulation VIII, supra. No particular form is prescribed for a petition requesting a hearing pursuant to this paragraph, but such a petition shall be in writing and shall set forth in detail the basis upon which the appeal is predicated. Any petition for a hearing not timely filed shall be rejected.

B. Hearing Procedures.

1. *Notice: Time and Place of Hearing.* The pertinent Advisory Board shall fix a time and place for the hearing as soon as practical after a petition requesting a hearing is received and shall notify the applicant thereof. Such notice shall be given to the applicant at least fifteen (15) days prior to the time fixed for the hearing. Hearings shall normally be held in the South Carolina Bar Building located at 950 Taylor Street in Columbia, South Carolina; however consideration shall be given to any special circumstances affecting the applicant's ability to travel to Columbia.

2. *Quorum.* A majority of the Advisory Board shall constitute a quorum. All decisions by the Advisory Board shall be by majority vote of those members present and voting.

3. *Conduct of Hearings: Rights of Parties.*

(a) Hearings shall be reported by a certified court reporter. The applicant shall pay the reporter's fees and shall not be provided a transcript until those fees are paid. In its sole discretion, the Commission may pay or refund to the applicant the reporting and transcript costs. The applicant shall be entitled to counsel at all stages of the investigation and at all hearings and shall have the right to attend all hearings with his or her counsel. The Advisory Board may seek the services of the Office of the Attorney General. Oral evidence shall be taken on oath or affirmation. The applicant shall have the right to testify in his or her behalf unless that right is waived or the applicant fails to appear at the hearing. An applicant who does not testify on his or her behalf may be called and examined, as if under cross-examination, by the Board, the Executive Director, or any attorney appointed by the Advisory Board to represent it. Failure to appear at a hearing ordered by an Advisory Board, after receiving written notice, shall constitute a waiver by the applicant of his or her right to appeal to the Commission and the Court. The applicant is responsible for all costs associated with his or her appearance including, in addition to the reporter's fees indicated above, travel and lodging costs, counsel fees, witness fees, and fees for document reproduction.

(b) At any hearing, the applicant, the Advisory Board, Executive Director, and any attorney appointed by the Advisory Board to represent it, shall have the right to call and examine witnesses; to introduce exhibits; to cross examine witnesses pertaining to any matter relevant to the issues; to impeach witnesses; and to rebut evidence.

(c) The Chairperson of the Advisory Board or a member appointed by the Chairperson shall preside at the hearing. Strict rules of evidence shall not apply, but the presiding officer is authorized to make evidentiary rulings.

(d) Any hearing may be recessed or adjourned from time to time at the discretion of the Advisory Board to allow for the development of additional evidence if such is deemed necessary to a full, fair, and just determination of the issues before the Advisory Board.

(e) The hearing shall be completed within ninety (90) days after receiving applicant's request for hearing.

(f) Within thirty (30) days after completing the hearing, the Advisory Board shall notify the applicant and the Commission of its action on applicant's appeal.

4. *Oaths.* The presiding member of an Advisory Board shall have the authority to administer oaths to witnesses appearing before the Advisory Board.

5. *Notices.* Notices required by this Regulation and by Regulations VIII and XII may be served by delivering a copy of the notice or the document to be served to the party to be served, or his or her attorney of record, either in person or by registered or certified mail at his or her last known address.

C. Appeals.

1. *Appeal to the Commission.* An appeal may be taken to the Commission from a decision of an Advisory Board which denies certification or recertification to an applicant or which revokes a specialist's certification. Any such appeal must be received by the Commission not later than thirty (30) days after notice of the Advisory Board's decision was delivered or mailed to the applicant. No particular form is prescribed for such appeals, but the basis for the appeal should be set forth in detail.

2. *Supreme Court.*

(a) Except as provided otherwise in Regulation VIII, supra, with respect to issues pertaining to a failure to achieve a passing grade on a specialty field's written examination, an applicant may appeal to the Court an adverse decision of the Commission concerning his or her certification, recertification, or revocation of certified status. An appeal is accomplished by filing written notice of intention to appeal within ten (10) days after receipt of the Commission's adverse decision. Notice of appeal shall be filed with the Clerk of the Court and with the Commission's Executive Director.

(b) Procedures for the appeal shall be prescribed by the Court after an applicant files notice of intention to appeal.

XII. REVOCATION OF CERTIFICATION

A. General. See Rule 408(g), SCACR. An Advisory Board may revoke certification of any attorney if the certification program for that specialty field is terminated or if it is determined, after hearing on appropriate notice, that:

1. Certification was granted contrary to the Advisory Board's Standards and Procedures, the Commission's Regulations, or the Court's Rules; or

2. Certification was granted to an attorney who was not eligible for certification in the specialty or who made any false representations or misstatements of material facts; or

3. A certified lawyer has failed to abide by all Advisory Board Standards and Procedures, Commission Regulations, and Court Rules, as amended from time to time; or

4. A certified lawyer has failed to meet the continuing legal education requirements of the specialty field or to file the annual CLE report or to pay the fees prescribed by the Commission; or

5. A certified lawyer no longer meets the minimum standards for certification established by the Advisory Board's Standards and Procedures, including practice of law and substantial involvement requirements.

B. Hearing Procedures. The rules specified in Regulation XI B, supra, shall govern hearings held by Advisory Boards for the purpose of revoking an attorney's certification. However, provisions of Regulation XI B to the contrary notwithstanding, a certified attorney shall be entitled to thirty (30) days notice of the time and place of the hearing to determine if his or her certification should be revoked and he or she shall not be required to pay the court reporter's fees.

C. Report to Certified Attorney and the Commission. Within thirty (30) days after completing its hearing, unless that period is extended by the Executive Director for good cause, the Advisory Board shall notify the certified lawyer and the Commission of its decision with respect to revocation of the attorney's certification.

D. Appeals. See Regulation XI C, supra.

E. Disbarment. Disbarment or suspension of a certified attorney shall automatically revoke his or her certification.

XIII. EFFECTIVE DATE

These Regulations shall be effective May 1, 1994 or whenever approved by the Supreme Court of South Carolina, whichever date is later.

[Approved by the Supreme Court on May 5, 1994. Amended effective November 15, 2001; March 1, 2003; September 1, 2003; September 7, 2006; January 4, 2007.]

APPENDIX E. REGULATIONS FOR SPECIALTY FIELDS

BANKRUPTCY AND DEBTOR–CREDITOR LAW SPECIALIZATION ADVISORY BOARD

EMPLOYMENT AND LABOR LAW SPECIALIZATION ADVISORY BOARD

ESTATE PLANNING AND PROBATE LAW SPECIALIZATION ADVISORY BOARD

TAXATION LAW SPECIALIZATION ADVISORY BOARD

BANKRUPTCY AND DEBTOR–CREDITOR LAW SPECIALIZATION ADVISORY BOARD

STANDARDS AND PROCEDURES FOR CERTIFICATION, RECERTIFICATION AND DECERTIFICATION

By virtue of the authority vested in the Bankruptcy and Debtor–Creditor Law Specialization Advisory Board (Board) and the Commission on Continuing Lawyer Competence (Commission) by the South Carolina Supreme Court (Court), the Board prescribes the following standards and procedures for certification, recertification, and decertification as a specialist in bankruptcy law (see Rule 408, SCACR, and Commission Regulations).

I. GENERAL REQUIREMENTS AND DEFINITIONS

A. Nothing herein shall in any manner limit the right of an attorney certified in bankruptcy law to practice in all fields of law. Any lawyer, alone or in association with any other lawyer, shall have the right to practice in all fields of law, even though certified in bankruptcy law.

B. No lawyer shall be required to obtain a certificate in bankruptcy law before practicing in that field. Any lawyer, alone or in association with any other lawyer, shall have the right to practice in the field of bankruptcy law, even though not certified therein.

C. All applicants for certification or recertification in bankruptcy law must be active members in good standing with the South Carolina Bar, entitled to practice before the United States District Court for the District of South Carolina, and shall meet the requirements for certification or recertification prescribed by the Board.

D. Certification in bankruptcy law is individual and voluntary. Requirements for and benefits derived from certification may not be fulfilled by or attributed to a law firm, corporation, company, or other entity of which the certified lawyer is a member or employee.

E. Forms, documents, applications, questionnaires, and examinations involved in the certification, recertification, or decertification process, as well as fees required of applicants and certified lawyers shall be as prescribed by the Board and/or Commission.

F. Certification shall be for a period of five (5) years at the end of which time recertification shall be permitted as indicated in § IV, below.

G. Bankruptcy and Debtor–Creditor Law is defined as the practice of law dealing with all aspects of federal bankruptcy law, including, but not limited to: personal and business bankruptcies; reorganizations and liquidations; the rights, obligations and remedies of debtors, creditors, trustees, and other parties in interest; state insolvency laws, including, but not limited to foreclosure, claim and delivery, collection, receivership, and attachment proceedings; and practice before the United States Bankruptcy Court and other federal and state courts.

H. Applicants for certification or recertification shall furnish satisfactory evidence of their good character and reputation. Unless otherwise prohibited by the Rules for Lawyer Disciplinary Enforcement, they shall also provide information in whatever form required by the Board as to whether they are now subject to an investigation, complaint, inquiry, or other disciplinary proceedings by any segment of the Bar, including but not limited to any local, state, or other grievance board, committee, or commission (hereinafter committee); and if so, the details of such investigation, complaint, inquiry, or proceedings including whether they have ever been reprimanded, suspended, disbarred, or otherwise disciplined by any court or grievance committee.

The Board may deny certification or recertification on a finding of a grievance committee, a court, or administrative agency or other governmental agency that an applicant has been guilty of professional misconduct, or defer certification or recertification based upon the pendency of such proceedings. However, the Board will consider the seriousness of the underlying facts of the grievance, the passage of time since such discipline, the applicant's experience since that time, and any history of other disciplinary actions or pending actions. Failure to disclose such information is a material misrepresentation and may be cause for rejection.

I. Applicants for certification or recertification will provide information in whatever form required by the Board as to whether they have ever been convicted, given probation, fined, or otherwise punished for any crime except a minor traffic offense, regardless of whether the conviction and/or punishment resulted from a plea of guilty, nolo contendere, or from a verdict after trial or otherwise and regardless of the pendency of an appeal. The Board may deny certification or recertification if an applicant has been convicted, given probation, fined, or otherwise punished for any crime except a minor traffic offense.

J. An applicant shall apply for certification or recertification as a specialist by completing and filing with the Board an application form furnished by the Board calling for information indicative of and relevant to the applicant's involvement, experience, competency, and practice in the field of bankruptcy law. By completing and filing such application, the applicant shall be deemed to have authorized the Board to take all appropriate action to resolve any questions with respect to the applicant's involvement, experience, competency, and practice in the field of bankruptcy law and to verify the information furnished by the applicant in making the application.

In the appraisal of each applicant, the Board will take such steps as it deems advisable or necessary under the circumstances to assure that the applicant presented to the Court for certification as a specialist is a lawyer who is technically competent in the field and of whom the Board has no notice of any personal or ethical deficiencies that might impair his/her professional performance as a specialist. Accordingly, the Board shall require applicants to disclose any information needed to determine whether to present his/her application to the Court for certification. The Board may not only verify information submitted by the applicant, but may, in its discretion, conduct its own investigation into the applicant's competency, experience, involvement, and reputation. Should the Board determine that an applicant's competency, character, experience, involvement, or reputation does not support his/her application for certification, the Board shall reject the application subject to such rights of hearing and appeal as may be promulgated by the Commission and the Court.

K. Each applicant shall submit the names and addresses of five (5) lawyers engaged in the "practice of law" (as that term is defined in § II A) who are familiar with the applicant's practice; who do not practice in the same firm, company, association or office as the applicant; and who are not members of this Board or the Commission, to be contacted as references to attest to the applicant's experience, involvement, and competency in the practice of bankruptcy law. At least one (1) of the five (5) lawyers must be currently engaged in the practice of bankruptcy law as defined in § I G. Provided, however, that at least one (1) of the five (5) lawyers whose names are provided as references must be currently certified bankruptcy law specialists. The Board may, in its discretion and without notice to an applicant, secure information concerning any particular applicant's practice, involvement, experience, and competency in the specialty area from lawyers and judges other than those whose names are submitted by an applicant.

L. In addition to any requirement heretofore or hereinafter listed, the Board may, in its sole discretion, require additional information from a particular applicant when in its judgment such additional information is necessary to a decision with respect to certification, recertification, or decertification.

II. MINIMUM STANDARDS FOR CERTIFICATION

A. Required Period Of Law Practice

Applicants shall have been engaged in the practice of law for a period of five (5) years on a full-time basis. "Practice of law" means full-time legal work done primarily for the purpose of legal advice or representation. Service, after admission to the Bar of any state or the District of Columbia, as a judge of any court of record shall be considered practice of law. Corporate or government service, including military service, as an attorney, after admission to the Bar of any state or the District of Columbia, shall be considered practice of law if the work done was legal in nature and primarily for the purpose of giving legal advice to, or representation of, the corporation or government agency or individuals primarily connected with the corporation or government agency. Practice of law which otherwise satisfies these requirements but which is on a part-time basis will satisfy the requirement if the balance of the applicant's activity is work such as law teaching or legal writing which, although legal in nature, may not qualify as practice of law.

B. Substantial Involvement

Applicants must show substantial involvement and special competency in bankruptcy law practice during the five (5) years immediately preceding application by providing such information as may be required by the Board. During each of the five (5) years immediately preceding application, applicants must show:

1. that they have devoted a minimum of 35% of their time practicing bankruptcy law as defined herein (see § I G) and

2. that their time devoted to the practice of bankruptcy law equals at least 35% of a full-time practice of law.

The test for substantial involvement has two parts. The first part is subjective, relating to the individual applicant's practice, and requires that at least 35% of that practice be devoted to bankruptcy law. The second part is objective and (considering an eight (8) hour work day, five (5) days per week as average or normal) requires an applicant to spend (on average) at least two and eight-tenths (2.8) hours a day and 14 hours per week involved in bankruptcy law practice.

C. Continuing Legal Education—Minimum Requirements

During the five (5) years preceding application for initial certification, applicants must have earned, in approved educational activities directed to the subject of bankruptcy law, not less than 60 hours of continuing legal education credit. Not more than 15 hours of the required 60 hours of continuing legal education credit may be in trial advocacy type courses.

For this purpose "approved educational activities" shall mean courses/programs accredited by the Board for the bankruptcy law specialty or courses/programs that would qualify for such accreditation.

D. Examination

Applicants for initial certification must pass an oral interview/examination and upon successful completion thereof, must take and pass a written examination to demonstrate sufficient knowledge, proficiency, competency, and experience in bankruptcy law to justify the representation of special competency to the legal profession and to the public. The written examination shall be administered only once during each calendar year, provided applications are pending, at a time and place to be determined by the Board, giving due consideration to the convenience of such applicants.

E. Fees

Applicants shall timely pay the fees established from time to time by the Board and/or Commission, including but not limited to application fees, filing fees, examination fees, and certification fees.

F. Failure To Furnish Information; Misrepresentation

Certification or recertification may be denied because of an applicant's failure to furnish requested information or because of misrepresentation of any material fact requested by the Board.

III. REQUIREMENTS FOLLOWING CERTIFICATION

A. During each annual reporting period all certified specialists in bankruptcy law shall complete not less than 12 hours of approved specialty continuing legal education. "Approved specialty continuing legal education" means educational activities accredited by the Board for the specialty (see § IV C concerning CLE credit required for recertification).

B. A certified specialist must report annually to the Commission his/her compliance with § III A and pay such filing fees, including late fees, as the Commission may from time to time prescribe. Failure to file and/or pay required fees may result in suspension from the practice of law in accordance with Commission Regulations in addition to revocation of certification.

C. During the period of certification, all certified specialists must continue to practice law and to be substantially involved in the practice of bankruptcy law (see § II A & B regarding the meaning of "practice of law" and "substantially involved in the practice of bankruptcy law"). Should any certified specialist cease to practice law or to be substantially involved in the practice of bankruptcy law, he/she shall promptly notify the Board for such action with respect to decertification as the Board shall deem to be appropriate. The failure of a certified specialist to notify the Board that he/she is no longer engaged in the practice of law or substantially involved in the practice of bankruptcy law may constitute grounds for decertification of the individual concerned.

D. During any period of initial or subsequent certification, all certified specialists shall report to the Commission any administrative action or malpractice claim in which settlement is made or suit filed and, unless otherwise prohibited by the Rules for Lawyer Disciplinary Enforcement, shall likewise report to the Commission any case in which any certified specialist learns that he/she is the subject of an investigation, inquiry, or other disciplinary proceedings by any segment of the Bar, including but not limited to any local, state, or other grievance board, committee, or commission.

IV. RECERTIFICATION

A. Renewal of certification under the program shall be required every five (5) years.

B. Applicants must demonstrate their continuing substantial involvement and special competency in the practice of bankruptcy law as may be required by the Board. Provided, however, that requirements for recertification shall not exceed the requirements for original certification except as noted in § IV C, below.

C. To qualify for recertification, applicants must demonstrate the completion of a minimum of seventy-five (75) hours of approved specialty continuing legal education in the five (5) years since their original or latest certification. Not more than 15 hours of the required 75 hours of approved specialty continuing legal education credit may be in trial advocacy type courses.

V. REVOCATION OF CERTIFICATION

The Board may revoke the certification of any lawyer if the certification program for this field is terminated, if a lawyer wishes to withdraw from the specialty and submits a letter resigning his/her certification, or if it is determined after hearing, on appropriate notice, that:

A. Certification was granted contrary to the Board's Standards and Procedures, Commission Regulations, or the South Carolina Appellate Court Rules; or

B. Certification was granted to a lawyer who was not eligible for certification or who made any false representation; or

C. A certified lawyer has failed to abide by all Board Standards and Procedures, Commission Regulations, and the South Carolina Appellate Court Rules, as amended from time to time; or

D. A certified lawyer has failed to meet the continuing legal education requirements of § III A or to file the annual report and/or pay the fees prescribed by § II E and § III B; or

E. A certified lawyer no longer meets the minimum standards for certification established by the Board's

Standards and Procedures, including practice of law and substantial involvement requirements (see § II A & B).

VI. WAIVERS

In cases of rare and unusual circumstances, the Board may waive compliance with any of the standards herein for the purpose of certifying or recertifying an individual as a specialist in bankruptcy law except that a waiver may not be granted to certify an applicant who has not practiced law for at least five (5) years, an applicant who has not been substantially involved in the practice of bankruptcy law for at least the preceding three (3) years, or to excuse an applicant from the requirement to take and pass a written examination. In any case in which a waiver is granted pursuant to this section, notification to the Court recommending certification or recertification shall indicate that a waiver has been granted and will specify the reason(s) therefor.

VII. EFFECTIVE DATE

These Standards and Procedures shall be effective November 1, 1992, or whenever approved by the South Carolina Supreme Court, whichever date is later.

[Approved November 6, 1992 by Order of the Supreme Court of South Carolina.]

EMPLOYMENT AND LABOR LAW SPECIALIZATION ADVISORY BOARD

STANDARDS AND PROCEDURES FOR CERTIFICATION, RECERTIFICATION, AND DECERTIFICATION

By virtue of the authority vested in the Employment and Labor Law Specialization Advisory Board (Board) and the Commission on Continuing Legal Education and Specialization (Commission) by the South Carolina Supreme Court (Court), the Board prescribes the following standards and procedures for certification, recertification, and decertification as a specialist in employment and labor law (see Rule 408, SCACR, and Commission Regulations).

I. GENERAL REQUIREMENTS AND DEFINITIONS

A. Nothing herein shall in any manner limit the right of an attorney certified in employment and labor law to practice in all fields of law. Any lawyer, alone or in association with any other lawyer, shall have the right to practice in all fields of law, even though certified in employment and labor law.

B. No lawyer shall be required to obtain a certificate in employment and labor law before practicing in that field. Any lawyer, alone or in association with any other lawyer, shall have the right to practice in the field of employment and labor law, even though not certified therein.

C. All applicants for certification or recertification in employment and labor law must be active members in good standing with the South Carolina Bar and shall meet the requirements for certification or recertification prescribed by the Board.

D. Certification in employment and labor law is individual and voluntary. Requirements for and benefits derived from certification may not be fulfilled by or attributed to a law firm, corporation, company, or other entity of which the certified lawyer is a member or employee.

E. Forms, documents, applications, questionnaires, and examinations involved in the certification, recertification, or decertification process, as well as fees required of applicants and certified lawyers shall be as prescribed by the Board and/or Commission.

F. Certification shall be for a period of five years at the end of which time recertification shall be permitted as indicated in § IV below.

G. Employment and Labor Law is the practice of law dealing with all aspects of employment relations (public and private) including, but not limited to, unfair labor practices, collective bargaining, contract administration, the rights of individual employees and union members, employment discrimination; all matters arising under the National Labor Relations Act (Wagner Act), Labor Management Relations Act (Taft–Hartley Act), Labor Management Reporting and Disclosure Act (Landrum–Griffin Act), Fair Labor Standards Act, Title VII of the Civil Rights Act of 1964, other federal statutes and analogous state statutes; practice before the National Labor Relations Boards, analogous state boards, federal and state courts, and arbitrators.

H. Applicants for certification or recertification shall furnish satisfactory evidence of their good character and reputation. Unless otherwise prohibited by the the Rules for Lawyer Disciplinary Enforcement, they shall also provide information in whatever form required by the Board as to whether they are now subject to an investigation, complaint, inquiry or other disciplinary proceedings by any segment of the Bar, including but not limited to any local, state, or other grievance board, committee, or commission; and if so, the details of such investigation, complaint, inquiry, or proceedings including whether they have ever been reprimanded, suspended, disbarred, or otherwise disciplined by any court or grievance committee.

The Board may deny certification or recertification on a finding of a grievance committee, a court, or administrative agency or other governmental agency that an applicant has been guilty of professional misconduct, or defer certification or recertification based upon the pendency of such proceedings. However, the Board will consider the seriousness of the underlying facts of the grievance, the passage of time since such discipline, the applicant's experience since that time, and any history of other disciplinary actions or pending actions. Failure to disclose such information is a material misrepresentation and may be cause for rejection.

I. Applicants for certification or recertification will provide information in whatever form required by the Board as to whether they have ever been convicted, given probation, fined, or otherwise punished for any crime punishable by confinement for one (1) year or more, regardless of whether the conviction and/or punishment resulted from a plea of guilty, nolo contendere, or from a verdict after trial or otherwise and regardless of the pendency of an appeal. The Board may deny certification or recertification if an applicant has been convicted, given probation, fined, or otherwise punished for any crime punishable by confinement for one (1) year or more.

J. An applicant shall apply for certification or recertification as a specialist by completing and filing with the Board an application form furnished by the Board calling for information indicative of and relevant to the applicant's involvement, experience, competency, and practice in the field of employment and labor law. By completing and filing such application, the applicant shall be deemed to have authorized the Board to take all appropriate action to resolve any questions with respect to the applicant's involvement, experience, competency, and practice in the field of employment and labor law and to verify the information furnished by the applicant in making the application. In the appraisal of each applicant, the Board will take such steps as it deems advisable or necessary under the circumstances to assure that the applicant presented to the Court for certification as a specialist is a lawyer who is technically competent in the field and of whom the Board has no notice of any personal or ethical deficiencies that might impair his/her professional performance as a specialist. Accordingly, the Board shall require each applicant to disclose any information needed to determine whether to present his/her application to the Court for certification. The Board not only may verify information submitted by the applicant, but may, in its discretion, conduct its own investigation into the applicant's competency, experience, involvement, and reputation. Should the Board determine that an applicant's competency, character, experience, involvement, or reputation does not support his/her application for certification, the Board shall reject the application subject to such rights of hearing and appeal as may be promulgated by the Commission and the Court.

K. Applicants shall submit the names and addresses of two (2) or more federal judges or federal administrative law judges, hearing officers, arbitrators, or mediators before whom they have appeared or practiced. At least one (1) reference from a federal judge or U.S. District Court magistrate judge is preferred; however, the other references listed will be acceptable. Additionally, applicants must submit the names and addresses of five (5) lawyers engaged in the "practice of law," as defined in § II A, who are familiar with the applicant's practice and who are not partners, associates, or members of this Board or the Commission, to be contacted as references to attest to the applicant's experience, involvement, and competency in the practice of employment and labor law. At least one (1) of the five (5) lawyers must be an employment and labor law specialist currently certified by the Supreme Court of South Carolina. The Board may, in its discretion and without notice to an applicant, secure information concerning an applicant's practice, involvement, experience, and competency in the specialty area from lawyers and judges other than those whose names are submitted by an applicant.

L. In addition to other requirements herein, the Board may, in its sole discretion, require additional information from a particular applicant when in its judgment such additional information is necessary to a decision with respect to certification, recertification, or decertification.

II. MINIMUM STANDARDS FOR CERTIFICATION

A. Required Period Of Law Practice

Applicants shall have been engaged in the practice of law for a period of five (5) years on a full-time basis. "Practice of law" means full-time legal work done primarily for the purpose of providing legal advice or representation. Service, after admission to the Board of any state or District of Columbia, as a judge of any court of record, as an administrative law judge, arbitrator, law teacher or judicial clerk (at state and federal courts and administrative agencies) shall be considered the practice of law. Corporate or government service, including military service, as an attorney, after admission to the Board of any state or the District of Columbia, shall be considered practice of law if the work done was legal in nature and primarily for the purpose of giving legal advice to, or representation of, the corporation or government agency or individuals primarily connected with the corporation or government agency.

B. Substantial Involvement

Applicants must show substantial involvement and special competency in employment and labor law practice during the five (5) years immediately preceding application by providing such information as may be required by the Board. During each of the five (5) years immediately preceding application, applicants must show:

1. that their time devoted to the practice of employment and labor law as defined herein (see § I G) was not less than 40% of a normal full-time practice of law, and

2. that their practice of employment and labor law has included substantial experience in at least two (2)

of the five (5) employment and labor law areas indicated below:

a. Labor–Management Relations Act (union elections; unfair labor practices)

b. Collective Bargaining Agreements (negotiation, arbitration, and § 301 actions)

c. Employment Discrimination (Title VII, Age Discrimination in Employment Act, Equal Pay Act, Americans with Disability Act, South Carolina Human Affairs Law, and Compliance with E.O. 11,246)

d. Individual Employment Rights (wrongful discharge—handbook cases, public policy cases, breach of duty of "good faith," and intentional infliction of emotional distress; workers' compensation retaliation claims, whistle blower claims; covenants not to compete; drug/alcohol testing; and miscellaneous privacy issues)

e. Miscellaneous (Landrum–Griffin Act, public employee issues—both statutory and constitutional, Occupational Safety and Health Act, Employee Retirement Income Security Act, Fair Labor Standards Act, Davis–Bacon Act, state-law wage payment claims, Railway Labor Act, Immigration Reform & Control Act, WARN — plant closings, veterans' employment rights, and negligent hiring/supervision).

C. Continuing Legal Education—Minimum Requirements

During the five (5) years preceding application for initial certification (or appropriate lesser period if any of the practice or substantial involvement requirements of § II A & B are waived), applicants must have earned credit for not less than sixty (60) hours of continuing legal education (CLE) in approved courses or programs dealing with employment and labor law. Not more than twenty (20) hours of the required sixty (60) hours of CLE may be in trial advocacy type courses. For the purpose of this requirement, "approved courses or programs" shall mean courses/programs accredited by the Board for the employment and labor law specialty or courses/programs that would qualify for such accreditation.

D. Oral Interview/Examination

Applicants for initial certification must appear personally before the Board for an oral interview/examination. Applicants must demonstrate sufficient knowledge, proficiency, competency, and experience in employment and labor law to justify the representation of special competency to the legal profession and to the public.

E. Fees

Applicants shall timely pay the fees established from time to time by the Board and/or Commission, including but not limited to application fees, filing fees, examination fees, and certification fees.

F. Failure To Furnish Information; Misrepresentation

Certification or recertification may be denied because of an applicant's failure to furnish requested information or because of misrepresentation of any material fact requested by the Board.

III. REQUIREMENTS FOLLOWING CERTIFICATION

A. During each annual reporting period, all certified specialists in employment and labor law shall complete not less than twelve (12) hours of approved specialty continuing legal education. "Approved specialty continuing legal education" means educational activities accredited by the Board for the specialty (see § IV C which requires seventy-five (75) hours of approved CLE for recertification). Provided, however, that for reporting period 2008–2009, a minimum of fifteen (15) hours of approved specialty credit shall be required and at least nine (9) hours of specialty credit must be completed without regard to carry forward credit from the prior reporting period.

B. Each certified specialist must report annually to the Commission his/her compliance with § III A and pay such filing fees, including late fees, as the Commission may from time to time prescribe. Failure to file and/or pay required fees may result in suspension from the practice of law in accordance with Commission Regulations in addition to revocation of certification.

C. During the period of certification, all certified specialists must continue to practice law and to be substantially involved in the practice of employment and labor law (see § II A & B, regarding the meaning of "practice of law" and "substantially involved in the practice of employment and labor law"). Should any certified specialist cease to practice law or to be substantially involved in the practice of employment and labor law, he/she shall promptly notify the Board for such action with respect to decertification as the Board shall deem to be appropriate. The failure of a certified specialist to notify the Board that he/she is no longer engaged in the practice of law or substantially involved in the practice of employment and labor law may constitute grounds for decertification of the individual concerned.

D. During any period of initial or subsequent certification, each certified specialist shall report to the Commission any administrative action or malpractice claim in which settlement is made or suit is filed and unless otherwise prohibited by the Rules for Lawyer Disciplinary Enforcement, shall likewise report to the Commission any case in which he/she learns that he/she is the subject of an investigation, inquiry or other disciplinary proceedings by any segment of the Bar, including, but not limited to, any local, state or other grievance board, committee or commission.

IV. RECERTIFICATION

A. Renewal of certification under the program shall be required every five (5) years.

B. Applicants must demonstrate their continuing substantial involvement and special competency in the practice of employment and labor law as may be required by the Board. However, except as provided in § IV C below, requirements for recertification shall not exceed the requirements for original certification.

C. To qualify for recertification, applicants must demonstrate the completion of a minimum of seventy-five (75) hours of approved specialty continuing legal education (CLE) in the five (5) years since their original or latest certification. Of the seventy-five (75) hours CLE required for recertification, not more than thirty (30) hours may be in trial advocacy type courses.

V. REVOCATION OF CERTIFICATION

The Board may revoke the certification of any lawyer if the certification program for this field is terminated, if a lawyer wishes to withdraw from the specialty and submits a letter resigning his/her certification or if it is determined after hearing, on appropriate notice, that:

A. Certification was granted contrary to the Board's Standards and Procedures, Commission Regulations, or South Carolina Appellate Court Rules; or

B. Certification was granted to a lawyer who was not eligible for certification or who made any false representation; or

C. A certified lawyer has failed to abide by all Board Standards and Procedures, Commission Regulations, and South Carolina Appellate Court Rules, as amended from time to time; or

D. A certified lawyer has failed to meet the continuing legal education requirements of § III A or to file the annual report and/or pay the fees prescribed by § II E and § III B; or

E. A certified lawyer no longer meets the minimum standards for certification established by the Board's Standards and Procedures, including practice of law and substantial involvement requirements (see § II A & B).

VI. WAIVERS

In cases of rare and unusual circumstances, the Board may waive compliance with any of the standards herein for the purpose of certifying or recertifying an individual as a specialist in employment and labor law except that a waiver may not be granted to certify an individual who has not practiced law for at least three (3) years and who has not been substantially involved in the practice of employment and labor law for at least three (3) years. In any case in which a waiver is granted pursuant to this section, notification to the Court recommending certification or recertification shall indicate that a waiver has been granted and will specify the reason(s) therefor.

VII. EFFECTIVE DATE

These Standards and Procedures shall be effective November 1, 1992, or whenever approved by the South Carolina Supreme Court, whichever date is later, and supersede all prior Employment and Labor Law Specialization Advisory Board Standards and Procedures for Certification, Recertification, and Decertification.

[Approved by the South Carolina Supreme Court December 8, 1992.]

ESTATE PLANNING AND PROBATE LAW SPECIALIZATION ADVISORY BOARD

STANDARDS AND PROCEDURES FOR CERTIFICATION, RECERTIFICATION, AND DECERTIFICATION

By virtue of the authority vested in the Estate Planning and Probate Law Specialization Advisory Board (Board) and the Commission on Continuing Lawyer Competence (Commission) by the South Carolina Supreme Court (Court), the Board prescribes the following standards and procedures for certification, recertification, and decertification as a specialist in estate planning and probate law (see Rule 408, SCACR, and Commission Regulations).

I. GENERAL REQUIREMENTS AND DEFINITIONS

A. Nothing herein shall in any manner limit the right of an attorney certified in estate planning and probate law to practice in all fields of law. Any lawyer, alone or in association with any other lawyer, shall have the right to practice in all fields of law, even though certified in estate planning and probate law.

B. No lawyer shall be required to obtain a certificate in estate planning and probate law before practicing in that field. Any lawyer, alone or in association with any other lawyer, shall have the right to practice in the field of estate planning and probate law, even though not certified therein.

C. All applicants for certification or recertification in estate planning and probate law must be active members in good standing with the South Carolina Bar, and shall meet the requirements for certification or recertification prescribed by the Board.

D. Certification in estate planning and probate law is individual and voluntary. Requirements for and benefits derived from certification may not be fulfilled by or attributed to a law firm, corporation, company, or other entity of which the certified lawyer is a member or employee.

E. Forms, documents, applications, questionnaires, and examinations involved in the certification, recertification, or decertification process, as well as fees required of applicants and certified lawyers shall be as prescribed by the Board and/or Commission.

F. Certification shall be for a period of five years at the end of which time recertification shall be permitted as indicated in § IV, below.

G. Estate Planning and Probate Law is the practice of law dealing with all aspects of the analysis and planning for the conservation and disposition of estates, giving due consideration to: applicable tax consequences; the preparation of legal instruments in order to effectuate estate plans; and the administration of estates, including all tax-related matters.

H. Applicants shall furnish satisfactory evidence of their good character and reputation. They shall also provide information in whatever form required by the Board as to whether they are now subject to an investigation, complaint, inquiry, or other disciplinary proceedings by any segment of the Bar, including but not limited to any local, state, or other grievance board, committee, or commission (hereinafter committee); and if so, the details of such investigation, complaint, inquiry, or proceedings including whether they have ever been reprimanded, suspended, disbarred, or otherwise disciplined by any court or grievance committee.

The Board may deny certification or recertification on a finding of a grievance committee or a court that an applicant has been guilty of professional misconduct, or defer certification or recertification based upon the pendency of such proceedings. However, the Board will consider the seriousness of the underlying fact of the grievance, the passage of time since such discipline, the applicant's experience since that time, and any history of other disciplinary actions or pending actions. Failure to disclose such information is a material misrepresentation and may be cause for rejection.

I. Applicants will provide information in the form required by the Board as to whether they have ever been convicted, given probation, fined, or otherwise punished for any crime except a minor traffic offense, regardless of whether the conviction and/or punishment resulted from a plea of guilty, nolo contendere, or from a verdict after trial or otherwise and regardless of the pendency of an appeal.

The Board may deny certification or recertification if an applicant has been convicted, given probation, fined, or otherwise punished for any crime except a minor traffic offense.

J. An applicant shall apply for certification as a specialist by completing and filing with the Board an application form furnished by the Board calling for information indicative of and relevant to the applicant's involvement, experience, competency, and practice in the field of estate planning and probate law. By completing and filing such application, the applicant shall be deemed to have authorized the Board to take all appropriate action to resolve any questions with respect to the applicant's involvement, experience, competency, and practice in the field of estate planning and probate law and to verify the information furnished by the applicant in making the application. In the appraisal of each applicant, the Board will take such steps as it deems advisable or necessary under the circumstances to assure that the applicant presented to the Court for certification as a specialist is a lawyer who is technically competent in the field and of whom the Board has no notice of any personal or ethical deficiencies that might impair his/her professional performance as a specialist. Accordingly, the Board shall require applicants to disclose any information needed to determine whether to present his/her application to the Court for certification. The Board not only may verify information submitted by the applicant, but may, in its discretion, conduct its own investigation into the applicant's competency, experience, involvement, and reputation. Should the Board determine that an applicant's competency, character, experience, involvement, or reputation does not support his/her application for certification, the Board shall reject the application subject to such rights of hearing and appeal as may be promulgated by the Commission and the Supreme Court.

K. Each applicant shall submit the names and addresses of five (5) lawyers engaged in the "practice of law," as defined in § II A, who are familiar with the applicant's practice and who are not partners or associates or members of this Board or the Commission, to be contacted as references to attest to the applicant's experience, involvement and competency in the practice of estate planning and probate law. The Board may, in its discretion and without notice to an applicant, secure information concerning any particular applicant's practice, involvement, experience, and competency in the specialty area from lawyers and judges other than those whose names are submitted by an applicant.

L. In addition to any requirement heretofore or hereinafter listed, the Board may, in its sole discretion, require additional information from a particular applicant when in its judgment such additional information is necessary to a decision with respect to certification, recertification, or decertification.

II. MINIMUM STANDARDS FOR CERTIFICATION

A. Required Period of Law Practice

Applicants shall have been engaged in the practice of law for a period of five (5) years on a full-time basis. "Practice of law" means full-time legal work done primarily for the purpose of legal advice or representation. Service, after admission to the Bar of any state or the District or Columbia, as a judge of any court of record shall be considered practice of law. Corporate or government service, including military service, as an attorney, after admission to the Bar of any state or the District of Columbia, shall be considered practice of law if the work done was legal in nature and primarily for the purpose of giving legal advice to, or representation of, the corporation or government agency or individuals primarily connected with the corporation or government agency. Practice of law which otherwise satisfies these requirements but which is on a part-time basis will satisfy the requirement if the balance of applicant's activity is work such as law teaching or legal writing which, although legal in nature, may not qualify as practice of law.

B. Substantial Involvement

Applicants must show substantial involvement and special competency in estate planning and probate law practice during the five (5) years immediately preceding application by providing such information as may be required by the Board.

During each of the five (5) years immediately preceding application, applicants must have devoted a minimum of 35% of their time practicing estate planning and probate law as defined herein (see § I G). Applicants must show such substantial involvement and special competency in estate planning and probate law during each of such five (5) years by providing information as may be required by the Board regarding both the following categories:

1. *Estate Planning*

Requires, to the satisfaction of the Board, an adequate involvement in a substantial portion of the activities described in each of the following paragraphs:

(a) Counseled persons in estate planning, including giving advice with respect to wills, powers of attorney, trusts, transfers, business arrangements and agreements, and other matters primarily involving estate planning, including but not limited to the tax aspects of the activities listed herein.

(b) Prepared or supervised the preparation of estate planning instruments, e.g., simple and complex wills, including provisions for testamentary trusts, marital deduction, and elections; revocable and irrevocable inter vivos trusts, including short-term and minor trusts; business planning agreements including stock agreements; and estate and gift tax liability and returns including representations before the Internal Revenue Service in connection with such liability or returns.

2. *Estate Administration (Probate).* Requires, to the satisfaction of the Board, an adequate involvement in a substantial portion of the activities described in each of the following paragraphs:

(a) Handled, advised, or supervised with respect to the probate and/or administration of decedent's estates, trusts, guardianships, conservatorships, determinations of heirship, will contests, construction suits, and court proceedings held thereon.

(b) Prepared, reviewed, supervised, or gave advice concerning the preparation of Federal Estate Tax Returns, state inheritance/estate tax returns, and U.S. Fiduciary Income Tax returns, including representation before the Internal Revenue Service, South Carolina or other state taxing authorities, or the courts in connection with such tax returns and related tax controversies.

C. Continuing Legal Education—Minimum Requirements

During each of the five (5) years preceding application, applicants must have earned credit for not less than twelve (12) hours of continuing legal education in approved courses or programs dealing with estate planning and probate law. For this purpose "approved courses or programs" shall mean courses/programs accredited by the Board for the estate planning and probate law specialty or courses/programs that would qualify for such accreditation.

D. Examination

Applicants for certification must pass an oral interview/examination and upon successful completion thereof, must take and pass a written examination to demonstrate sufficient knowledge, proficiency, and experience in estate planning and probate law to justify the representation of special competency to the legal profession and to the public. The written examination shall be administered only once during each calendar year, provided applications are pending, at a time and place to be determined by the Board, giving due consideration to the convenience of such applicants.

E. Fees

Applicants shall timely pay the fees established from time to time by the Board, including but not limited to application fees, filing fees, examination fees, and certification fees.

F. Failure to Furnish Information; Misrepresentation

Certification or recertification may be denied because of an applicant's failure to furnish requested information or because of misrepresentation of any material fact requested by the Board.

III. REQUIREMENTS FOLLOWING CERTIFICATION

A. During each annual reporting period all certified specialists in estate planning and probate law shall complete not less than fifteen (15) hours of approved specialty continuing legal education. "Approved specialty continuing legal education" means educational activities accredited by the Board for the specialty (see § IV C which requires one hundred (100) hours of CLE credit for recertification). Provided, however, that for reporting period 2008–2009, a minimum of twelve (12) hours of approved specialty continuing legal education shall be required.

B. A certified specialist must report annually to the Commission his/her compliance with § III A and pay such filing fees, including late fees, as the Commission may from time to time prescribe. Failure to file and/or pay required fees may result in suspension from the practice of law in accordance with Commission Regulations.

C. During the period of certification, all certified specialists must continue to practice law and to be substantially involved in the practice of estate planning and probate law (see § II A & B, regarding the meaning of "practice of law" and "substantially involved in the practice of estate planning and probate law"). Should any certified specialist cease to practice law or to be substantially involved in the practice of estate planning and probate law, he/she shall promptly notify the Board for such action with respect to decertification as the Board shall deem to be appropriate. The failure of a certified specialist to notify the Board that he/she is no longer engaged in the practice of law or substantially involved in the practice of estate planning and probate law may constitute grounds for decertification of the individual concerned.

IV. RECERTIFICATION

A. Renewal of certification under the program shall be required every five (5) years.

B. Applicants must demonstrate their continuing substantial involvement and special competency in the practice of estate planning and probate law as may be required by the Board. Provided, however, that requirements for recertification shall not exceed the requirements for original certification except as noted in § IV C, below.

C. To qualify for recertification, applicants must demonstrate the completion of a minimum of one hundred (100) hours of approved specialty continuing legal education in the five (5) years since their original or latest certification. Provided, however, that for applications for recertification received prior to January 1, 2011, only ninety (90) hours of approved specialty continuing legal education shall be required.

V. REVOCATION OF CERTIFICATION

The Board may revoke the certification of any lawyer if the certification program for this field is terminated or if it is determined after hearing, on appropriate notice, that:

A. Certification was granted contrary to the Board's Standards and Procedures, Commission Regulations, or South Carolina Appellate Court Rules; or

B. Certification was granted to a lawyer who was not eligible for certification or who made any false representation; or

C. A certified lawyer has failed to abide by all Board standards and procedures, Commission regulations, and South Carolina Appellate Court Rules, as amended from time to time; or

D. A certified lawyer has failed to meet the continuing legal education requirements of § III A or to file the annual report and/or pay the fees prescribed by § II E and § III B; or

E. A certified lawyer no longer meets the minimum standards for certification established by the Board's standards and procedures, including practice of law and substantial involvement requirements (see § II A & B).

VI. WAIVERS

In cases of rare and unusual circumstances, the Board may waive compliance with any of the standards herein for the purpose of certifying or recertifying an individual as a specialist in estate planning and probate law except that a waiver may not be granted to certify an individual who has not practiced law for at least three (3) years or to excuse any applicant from the requirement to take and pass a written examination. In any case in which a waiver is granted pursuant to this section, notification to the Court recommending certification or recertification shall indicate that a waiver has been granted and will specify the reason(s) therefor.

VII. EFFECTIVE DATE

These Standards and Procedures shall be effective October 31, 1990, or whenever approved by the South Carolina Supreme Court, whichever date is later, and supersede all prior Estate Planning and Probate Law Specialization Advisory Board Standards and Procedures for Certification, Recertification, and Decertification.

TAXATION LAW SPECIALIZATION ADVISORY BOARD

STANDARDS AND PROCEDURES FOR CERTIFICATION, RECERTIFICATION, AND DECERTIFICATION

By virtue of the authority vested in the Taxation Law Specialization Advisory Board (Board) and the Commission on Continuing Lawyer Competence (Commission) by the South Carolina Supreme Court (Court), the Board prescribes the following standards and procedures for certification, recertification, and decertification as a specialist in taxation law (see Rule 408, SCACR, and Commission Regulations).

I. GENERAL REQUIREMENTS AND DEFINITIONS

A. Nothing herein shall in any manner limit the right of an attorney certified in taxation law to practice in all fields of law. Any lawyer, alone or in association with any other lawyer, shall have the right to practice in all fields of law, even though certified in taxation law.

B. No lawyer shall be required to obtain a certificate in taxation law before practicing in that field. Any lawyer, alone or in association with any other lawyer, shall have the right to practice in the field of taxation law, even though not certified therein.

C. All applicants for certification or recertification in taxation law must be active members in good standing with the South Carolina Bar, entitled to practice before the Internal Revenue Service, and shall meet the requirements for certification or recertification prescribed by the Board.

D. Certification in taxation law is individual and voluntary. Requirements for and benefits derived from certification may not be fulfilled by or attributed to a law firm, corporation, company, or other entity of which the certified lawyer is a member or employee.

E. Forms, documents, applications, questionnaires, and examinations involved in the certification, recertification, or decertification process, as well as fees required of applicants and certified lawyers shall be as prescribed by the Board and/or Commission.

F. Certification shall be for a period of five (5) years at the end of which time recertification shall be permitted as indicated in § IV, below.

G. Taxation Law is defined as the practice of law dealing with all matters arising under the Internal Revenue Code and the taxation provisions of the Employee Retirement Income Security Act (ERISA), and state and local tax laws, including counseling and practice before federal and state courts and governmental agencies with respect thereto.

H. Applicants for certification or recertification shall furnish satisfactory evidence of their good character and reputation. Unless otherwise prohibited by the Rules for Lawyer Disciplinary Enforcement, they shall also provide information in whatever form required by the Board as to whether they are now subject to an investigation, complaint, inquiry, or other disciplinary proceedings by any segment of the Bar, including but not limited to any local, state, or other grievance board, committee, or commission (hereinafter committee); and if so, the details of such investigation, complaint, inquiry, or proceedings including whether they have ever been reprimanded, suspended, disbarred, or otherwise disciplined by any court or grievance committee.

The Board may deny certification or recertification on a finding of a grievance committee, a court, or administrative agency or other governmental agency that an applicant has been guilty of professional misconduct, or defer certification or recertification based upon the pendency of such proceedings. However, the Board will consider the seriousness of the underlying fact of the grievance, the passage of time since such discipline, applicant's experience since that time, and any history of other disciplinary actions or pending actions. Failure to disclose such information is a material misrepresentation and may be cause for rejection.

I. Applicants for certification or recertification will provide information in whatever form required by the Board as to whether they have ever been convicted, given probation, fined, or otherwise punished for any crime except a minor traffic offense, regardless of whether the conviction and/or punishment resulted from a plea of guilty, nolo contendere, or from a verdict after trial or otherwise and regardless of the pendency of an appeal. The Board may deny certification or recertification if an applicant has been convicted, given probation, fined, or otherwise punished for any crime except a minor traffic offense.

J. An applicant shall apply for certification or recertification as a specialist by completing and filing with the Board an application form furnished by the Board calling for information indicative of and relevant to the applicant's involvement, experience, competency, and practice in the field of taxation law. By completing and filing such application, the applicant shall be deemed to have authorized the Board to take all appropriate action to resolve any questions with respect to the applicant's involvement, experience, competency, and practice in the field of taxation law and to verify the information furnished by the applicant in making the application. In the appraisal of each applicant, the Board will take such steps as it deems advisable or necessary under the circumstances to assure that the applicant presented to the Court for certification as a specialist is a lawyer who is technically competent in the field and of whom the Board has no notice of any personal or ethical deficiencies that might impair his/her professional performance as a specialist. Accordingly, the Board shall require an applicant to disclose any information needed to determine whether to present his/her application to the Court for certification. The Board not only may verify information submitted by the applicant, but may, in its discretion, conduct its own investigation into the applicant's competency, experience, involvement, and reputation. Should the Board determine that an applicant's competency, character, experience, involvement, or reputation does not support his/her application for certification, the Board shall reject the application subject to such rights of hearing and appeal as may be promulgated by the Commission and the Supreme Court.

K. Each applicant shall submit the names and addresses of five (5) lawyers engaged in the "practice of law," as defined in § II A, who are familiar with the applicant's practice and who are not partners or associates or members of this Board or the Commission, to be contacted as references to attest to the applicant's experience, involvement, and competency in the practice of taxation law. At least two (2) of the five (5) lawyers must be currently certified taxation law specialists. The Board may, in its discretion and without notice to an applicant, secure information concerning any particular applicant's practice, involvement, experience, and competency in the specialty area from lawyers and judges other than those whose names are submitted by an applicant.

L. In addition to any requirement heretofore or hereinafter listed, the Board may, in its sole discretion, require additional information from a particular applicant when in its judgment such additional information is necessary to a decision with respect to certification, recertification, or decertification.

II. MINIMUM STANDARDS FOR CERTIFICATION

A. Required Period of Law Practice

Applicants shall have been engaged in the practice of law for a period of five (5) years on a full-time basis. "Practice of law" means full-time legal work done primarily for the purpose of legal advice or representation. Service, after admission to the Bar of any state or the District or Columbia, as a judge of any court of record shall be considered practice of law. Corporate or government service, including military service, as an attorney, after admission to the Bar of any state or the District of Columbia, shall be considered practice of law if the work done was legal in nature and primarily for the purpose of giving legal advice to, or representation of, the corporation or government agency or individuals primarily connected with the corporation or government agency. Practice of law which otherwise satisfies these requirements but which is on a part-time basis will satisfy the requirement if the balance of applicant's activity is work such as law teaching or legal writing which, although legal in nature, may not qualify as practice of law.

B. Substantial Involvement

Applicants must show substantial involvement and special competency in taxation law practice during the five (5) years immediately preceding application by providing such information as may be required by the Board.

1. During each of the five (5) years immediately preceding application, applicants must show:

(a) that they have devoted a minimum of 50% of their time practicing taxation law as defined herein (see § I G) and

(b) that their time devoted to the practice of taxation law equals at least 50% of a full-time practice of law.

Thus, the test for substantial involvement has two parts. The first part is subjective, relating to the individual applicant's practice, and it requires that at least 50% of that practice be devoted to taxation law. The second part is objective and (considering an eight (8) hour work day, five (5) days per week as average or normal) requires an applicant to spend (on average) at least four (4) hours a day and twenty (20) hours per week involved in taxation law practice.

2. In satisfying the 50% requirement in § II B 1 (a), an applicant may count, as time devoted to the practice of taxation law, the entire time devoted to a matter involving both taxation and other fields or areas of law, provided that at least one-half of the applicant's time devoted to such mixed matters is spent on taxation law. However, an applicant may not satisfy more than one-half of the 50% requirement in § II B 1 (a) by the time devoted to practice in a mixed taxation and non-taxation field of law for which a certified specialty is available under Rule 408, SCACR. For example, if an applicant devotes 20% of his/her practice to income taxation, 60% to estate planning, and 20% to other areas or fields, he/she could satisfy no more than one-half of that 50% requirement by his/her estate planning practice since a certified specialty is available in estate planning and probate law. The applicant in this illustration would, therefore, fail the 50% requirement of § II B 1 (a) since he/she could count only 25% from estate planning (1/2 of 50%) and 20% from income taxation, giving a total of 45% of his/her time devoted to taxation practice (5% short of the 50% requirement).

C. Continuing Legal Education—Minimum Requirements

During each of the five (5) annual reporting periods preceding application for initial certification (or appropriate lesser period if any of the practice or substantial involvement requirements of § II A & B are waived), applicants must have completed not less than fifteen (15) hours of continuing legal education in approved courses or programs dealing with taxation law. For this purpose "approved courses or programs" shall mean courses/programs accredited by the Board for the taxation law specialty or courses/programs that would qualify for such accreditation. Provided, however, that for applications for initial certification received prior to January 1, 2010, in the five (5) years preceding application, applicants must have completed at least seventy-five (75) hours of continuing legal education in approved courses or programs dealing with taxation law.

D. Examination

Applicants for initial certification must pass an oral interview/examination and upon successful completion thereof, must take and pass a written examination to demonstrate sufficient knowledge, proficiency, competency, and experience in taxation law to justify the representation of special competency to the legal profession and to the public. The requirement for a written examination may be waived for any applicant who has been awarded a Masters degree (LLM) in taxation by an ABA accredited law school not more than five (5) years prior to receipt of his/her application by the Commission. The written examination shall be administered only once during each calendar year, provided applications are pending, at a time and place to be determined by the Board, giving due consideration to the convenience of such applicants. The requirement for a written examination shall apply to all applications received after March 1, 1992.

E. Fees

Applicants shall timely pay the fees established from time to time by the Board and/or Commission, including but not limited to application fees, filing fees, examination fees, and certification fees.

F. Failure to Furnish Information; Misrepresentation

Certification or recertification may be denied because of an applicant's failure to furnish requested information or because of misrepresentation of any material fact requested by the Board.

III. REQUIREMENTS FOLLOWING CERTIFICATION

A. During each annual reporting period all certified specialists in taxation law shall complete not less than fifteen (15) hours of approved specialty continuing legal education. "Approved specialty continuing legal education" means educational activities accredited by the Board for the specialty (see § IV C concerning CLE credit required for recertification.)

B. Certified specialists must report annually to the Commission his/her compliance with § III A and pay such filing fees, including late fees, as the Commission may from time to time prescribe. Failure to file and/or pay required fees may result in suspension from the practice of law in accordance with Commission Regulations in addition to revocation of certification.

C. During the period of certification, all certified specialists must continue to practice law and to be substantially involved in the practice of taxation law (see § II, A & B, regarding the meaning of "practice of law" and "substantially involved in the practice of taxation law"). Should any certified specialist cease to practice law or to be substantially involved in the practice of taxation law, he/she shall promptly notify the Board for such action with respect to decertification as the Board shall deem to be appropriate. The failure of a certified specialist to notify the Board that he/she is no longer engaged in the practice of law or substantially involved in the practice of taxation law may constitute grounds for decertification of the individual concerned.

D. During any period of initial or subsequent certification, all certified specialists shall report to the Commission any administrative action or malpractice claim in which settlement is made or suit is filed and unless otherwise prohibited by the Rules for Lawyer Disciplinary Enforcement, shall likewise report to the Commission any case in which he/she learns that he/she is the subject of an investigation, inquiry or other disciplinary proceedings by any segment of the Bar, including but not limited to any local, state or other grievance board, committee or commission.

IV. RECERTIFICATION

A. Renewal of certification under the program shall be required every five (5) years.

B. Applicants must demonstrate their continuing substantial involvement and special competency in the practice of taxation law as may be required by the Board. Provided, however, that requirements for recertification shall not exceed the requirements for original certification except as noted in § IV C, below.

C. To qualify for recertification, applicants must demonstrate the completion of a minimum of 120 hours of approved specialty continuing legal education in the five (5) years since their original or latest certification.

V. REVOCATION OF CERTIFICATION

The Board may revoke the certification of any lawyer if the certification program for this field is terminated or if it is determined after hearing, on appropriate notice, that:

A. Certification was granted contrary to the Board's Standards and Procedures, Commission Regulations, or South Carolina Appellate Court Rules; or

B. Certification was granted to a lawyer who was not eligible for certification or who made any false representation; or

C. A certified lawyer has failed to abide by all Board standards and procedures, Commission regulations, and South Carolina Appellate Court Rules, as amended from time to time; or

D. A certified lawyer has failed to meet the continuing legal education requirements of § III A or to file the annual report and/or pay the fees prescribed by § II E and § III B; or

E. A certified lawyer no longer meets the minimum standards for certification established by the Board's standards and procedures, including practice of law and substantial involvement requirements (see § II A & B).

VI. WAIVERS

In cases of rare and unusual circumstances, the Board may waive compliance with any of the standards herein for the purpose of certifying or recertifying an individual as a specialist in taxation law except that a waiver may not be granted to certify an individual who has not practiced law for at least three (3) years and who has not been substantially involved in the specialty for at least three (3) years. In any case in which a waiver is granted pursuant to this section, notification to the Court recommending certification or recertification shall indicate that a waiver has been granted and will specify the reason(s) therefor.

VII. EFFECTIVE DATE

These Standards and Procedures shall be effective October 31, 1991, or whenever approved by the South Carolina Supreme Court, whichever date is later, and supersede all prior Taxation Law Specialization Advisory Board Standards and Procedures for Certification, Recertification, and Decertification.

[Adopted effective December 4, 1991. Amended effective September 7, 2006; August 22, 2008; July 22, 2010.]

APPENDIX F. REGULATIONS FOR THE CHIEF JUSTICE'S COMMISSION ON THE PROFESSION

(Promulgated Pursuant to Rule 420, SCACR)

I. SCOPE

These regulations implement Rule 420, SCACR. The purposes of the Chief Justice's Commission on the Profession shall be as set forth in Rule 420(c).

II. MEMBERSHIP

A. The membership is defined in Rule 420(b). Members will serve for a term of three years provided, however, that initial appointments and subsequent appointments may be for terms less than three years to accomplish staggered terms.

B. Termination of membership of a member other than upon completion of a term will be upon resignation of that member or upon vote of two-third's of the other members and approval of the chairperson.

III. OFFICERS AND COMMITTEE CHAIRPERSONS; STAFF

A. The chairperson may designate officers and committee chairpersons as needed.

B. The Commission is empowered to hire or contract for staff as it deems necessary.

IV. MEETINGS; QUORUM; VOTING

A. The Commission will meet at least twice annually at the call of the chairperson. Notice of the time and place will be given at least two weeks in advance of the meeting. The meeting may be convened by telephone conference call, videoconference or Internet conference.

B. At all meetings eight members will constitute a quorum. The latest edition of Robert's Rules of Order will govern proceedings.

C. Voting may be in person, by proxy, by letter, by telephone, by fax or by email. Any matter or proposition will not be action of the Commission without affirmative vote of at least seven members.

VI. EFFECTIVE DATE; DISSOLUTION

A. These regulations will be effective upon adoption by the Court.

B. Upon dissolution of the Commission all assets will revert to the Supreme Court of South Carolina.

[Adopted effective November 22, 2000.]

APPENDIX G. REGULATIONS FOR THE COMMISSION ON ALTERNATIVE DISPUTE RESOLUTION

I. SCOPE AND PURPOSE

These regulations implement Rule 422, SCACR.

II. MEMBERSHIP

A. The membership is defined in Rule 422. Members appointed under sections b(1)—(4) will serve for a term of three years provided, however, that initial appointments and subsequent appointments may be for terms less than three years to accomplish staggered terms.

B. Termination of membership of a member other than upon completion of a term will be upon resignation of that member or upon vote of two-thirds of the other members and approval of the Chair.

III. COMMITTEES; STAFF

A. The Commission may empower committees to act in the intervals between Commission meetings. The Chair will name committee chairs and members.

B. The South Carolina Bar will provide administrative assistance to the Commission from funds provided through the certification process and by the Judicial Department. The Bar may use the funds to hire administrative staff and for other purposes including but not limited to the following:

1. To purchase equipment, supplies and services necessary to operate;

2. To deposit at interest in federally insured banks or savings and loan associations located in the State of South Carolina, with interest or other investment income to become a part of the fund; and

3. To invest any portion of the funds as may not be needed currently with interest or other investment income to become a part of the fund.

C. The Commission may delegate to staff administrative responsibilities for certification and other matters.

IV. MEETINGS; QUORUM; VOTING

A. The Commission will meet at least four times annually at the call of the Chair. Notice of the time and place will be given at least two weeks in advance of the meeting. The meeting may be held in person, convened by telephone conference call or video conference, or a combination thereof.

B. At all meetings ten members will constitute a quorum. The latest edition of Robert's Rules of Order will govern proceedings.

C. Voting may be in person, by letter, by telephone, by fax or by email. Members may vote by proxy if the proxy is in writing, signed and received by the Chair prior to the convening of the meeting. Any matter or proposition will not be action of the Commission without affirmative vote of at least eight members.

V. SOUTH CAROLINA BOARD OF ARBITRATOR AND MEDIATOR CERTIFICATION

A. Purpose.

The Board of Arbitrator and Mediator Certification (hereinafter referred to as Board) is established as set forth in the Circuit Court Alternative Dispute Resolution (ADR) Rules and the Family Court Mediation Rules (hereinafter referred to as the ADR Rules). These regulations are implemented to govern the Board in the certification, recertification, decertification and discipline of mediators/arbitrators (hereinafter referred to as neutrals) and the approval of training courses for neutrals.

B. Applications for Certification of Neutrals.

1. Applications shall be typewritten on forms provided by the Board. Each question shall be answered responsively or shown as "not applicable." The signature of the applicant shall constitute a certification that the information furnished in the application is true and correct.

2. To assist in determining an applicant's entitlement to certification, the Board may require an applicant to submit information in addition to that called for on the application form.

3. An application shall be deemed incomplete until the application fee, as set by the Supreme Court, has been paid.[1]

4. *Processing of Applications.*

a. The Board shall check each application to assure that all portions of the application have been properly completed and that the applicant has complied with all requirements of the Board and the applicable ADR Rules.

b. An application not approved by the Board shall be returned to the applicant with a letter specifying the deficiencies in the application. The applicant may submit additional documentation/information.

5. An applicant has the burden of establishing that the requirements for certification have been met. That burden is satisfied only if the Board is convinced by clear and convincing evidence that the application meets or exceeds the standards specified for certification by the applicable ADR Rules and this Board.

6. A decision of the Board not to approve an application may be appealed to the Commission by filing written notice to the Commission's Chair, c/o South Carolina Bar, P.O. Box 608, Columbia, SC 29202. The appeal must be made no later than thirty (30) days after mailing of a copy of the notice denying approval. The Board shall supply a copy of all material filed in support of the application. The decision of the Board will be reviewed by all members of the Commission except those who serve on the Board using the same standard set forth in paragraph five above.

7. Recertification of neutrals shall require that the applicant submit a recertification application on or before December 31st of each year together with a recertification fee as set by the Supreme Court.[2] Failure to submit a recertification application by the referenced deadline will result in an additional late fee for recertification.

C. Roster of Certified Neutrals. The Board shall maintain at the South Carolina Bar rosters of approved neutrals. The Board shall furnish the clerks of the pilot counties updated rosters of certified neutrals on a periodic basis. A neutral who has failed to submit a recertification application and fee by January 15 of each year shall be removed from the rosters.

D. Decertification, Discipline and Processing of Complaints of Misconduct.

1. Decertification, discipline and processing of complaints of misconduct by neutrals certified by the Board shall be in accordance with the ADR Rules.

2. No particular form is prescribed with respect to processing complaints of misconduct of neutrals. Any such complaint shall be in writing and shall set forth in detail the basis upon which decertification or discipline is warranted.

3. The complaint shall be filed with the person employed by the Bar and assigned to serve the Commission (hereinafter "Staff").

4. Staff shall provide the neutral written notice of the complaint sent to the neutral's address maintained with the South Carolina Bar and may require the neutral to file a response.

5. The Executive Director of the Bar, or his or her designee (hereinafter "Counsel"), after review of the complaint and response, if any, may investigate the matter and advise the Board when probable cause exists. Such investigation may include meeting with the neutral, the complainant or both.

6. Upon review of the complaint and the neutral's response, if any, together with any results of investigation, the Board may dismiss any complaint that it finds to be without merit. A decision to dismiss is final and not subject to review.

7. Notwithstanding any other provision herein, the Board may request that the neutral and complainant meet with one or more members of the Board to resolve the matter. This resolution may include sanctions if agreed by the neutral. If sanctions are accepted, all relevant documentation shall be forwarded to the Supreme Court.

8. If probable cause exists and the matter cannot otherwise be resolved, the Board shall notify the Commission Chair who shall appoint three (3) members of the Commission, who have not been involved previously in the matter, as a Hearing Panel. Neither the Chair of the Commission nor the members of the Board shall participate as members of the Hearing Panel. The Commission Chair shall designate one member as Chair of the Hearing Panel. The Hearing Panel shall schedule a hearing in accordance with the ADR Rules and these Regulations. The Hearing Panel may petition the Supreme Court to temporarily suspend a neutral's certification pending outcome of the hearing. Counsel shall prosecute the matter.

9. In matters of decertification, discipline and processing of complaints, three (3) members of the Board or the Hearing Panel shall constitute a quorum. In the event that members of the Board or Hearing Panel disqualify themselves in a pending matter leaving less than a quorum, the Commission Chair shall appoint *ad hoc* members to restore the Board or Hearing Panel to full membership in that matter. Decisions and recommendations shall be by majority vote.

10. *Access to Disciplinary Information.*

a. Except as otherwise provided in the ADR Rules and these Regulations or ordered by the Supreme Court, all complaints, proceedings, records, information or orders relating to an allegation of misconduct shall be confidential and shall not be disclosed to the public. While the matter remains confidential, the members of the Board, the ADR Commission, the staff of the Commission, the members of the Supreme Court and the staff of the Supreme Court shall not in any way reveal the existence of the complaint except to persons directly involved in the matter and then only to the extent necessary for the proper disposition of the matter. A violation of this provision may be punished as a contempt of the Supreme Court.

b. When charges are filed regarding allegations of misconduct, the charges and any answer shall become public 30 days after a hearing panel is appointed. Thereafter, except as otherwise provided in the ADR Rules and these Regulations or by the Supreme Court, all subsequent records and proceedings relating to the misconduct allegations shall be open to the public inclusive of any sanction imposed after the filing of charges. If allegations of incapacity are raised during the misconduct proceedings, all records, information and proceedings relating to these allegations shall be held confidential.

c. The Board and/or Commission may, however, disclose information at any stage of the proceedings:

i. When the chair, vice chair or a panel of the Commission has determined that there is a need to notify another person to protect that person or to notify a government agency in order to protect the public or the administration of justice;

ii. To appropriate law enforcement officials when the chair, vice chair or a panel of the Commission determines that it is in possession of reliable information indicating that a person has violated the criminal laws of this state, any other state, the District of Columbia or the United States;

iii. Upon waiver in writing by the neutral; or

iv. To the appropriate disciplinary authority in any jurisdiction in which a neutral is admitted to practice law or any other profession or has applied for admission to practice law or any other profession concerning a matter where there is evidence the neutral committed misconduct under the alternative dispute rules or regulations of that jurisdiction or where a neutral receives any sanction under these regulations.

d. In order to protect the interests of a complainant, witness, third party or neutral, the hearing panel may, upon application of any person and for good cause shown, issue a protective order prohibiting the disclosure of specific information otherwise privileged or confidential and direct that the proceedings be conducted in a manner to preserve the confidentiality of the information that is the subject of the application.

e. Either party may disclose in proceedings before a hearing panel statements and other evidence gathered prior to the matter becoming public after a filing of charges, that were subject to discovery under the ADR Rules and these Regulations to the extent admissible under the South Carolina Rules of Civil Procedure or South Carolina Rules of Evidence.

11. Communications to the Board, Commission or their staffs relating to misconduct or incapacity in testimony given in the proceedings shall be absolutely privileged, and no civil lawsuit predicated thereon may be initiated against any Complainant or witness. Members of the Board, Commission and staff shall be absolutely immune from civil suit for all conduct in the course of their official duties.

E. Hearing Procedures.

1. The Hearing Panel shall provide the complainant and the neutral written notice of the hearing at least ten (10) days prior to the scheduled hearing. Any such notice shall be in writing and given by registered or certified mail; UPS or other reputable carrier; or by telecopy (FAX) addressed to the complainant's and neutral's last known address.

2. Subpoenas for the attendance of witnesses and the production of documentary evidence may be issued by the Chair of the Hearing Panel or, if the Chair of the Hearing Panel is absent or unavailable, by any other member of the Hearing Panel. Such subpoena may be served in any manner provided by law for the service of witness subpoenas in a civil action. Any person who, without adequate excuse, fails to obey a duly served subpoena may be held in contempt of the Supreme Court.

3. The hearing may be conducted informally but with decorum.

4. The rules of evidence shall generally be observed in the conduct of the hearing, and all testimony shall be under oath or affirmation. Upon a showing of good cause to the Hearing Panel, testimony of any party or witness may be presented over the telephone.

5. The proceedings shall be transcribed. Costs associated with the transcription shall be borne by the Commission but may be assessed by order of the Supreme Court against the neutral.

6. Absent a showing of good cause, if the complainant fails to appear at the hearing, the Hearing Panel may dismiss the action for want of prosecution. Such a dismissal is final. If the neutral fails to appear, absent a showing of good cause, the hearing shall proceed.

7. If, after conducting the hearing, the Hearing Panel determines that decertification or other disciplinary action is not warranted, it shall dismiss the matter. A decision to dismiss is final and not subject to review.

8. If, after conducting the hearing, the Hearing Panel determines that decertification or other disciplinary action is appropriate, it shall make a written recommendation to the Supreme Court and provide a copy to the complainant and neutral. A copy of the transcript of hearing and all exhibits shall be filed with the Supreme Court.

9. Within fifteen (15) days after the Hearing Panel submits its recommendation to the Supreme Court, the neutral or Counsel may file a response to the Hearing Panel's action. The Supreme Court shall then take such action as it deems appropriate.

F. Reinstatement.

1. A neutral who has been decertified may be reinstated as a certified neutral provided, however, no application for reinstatement may be tendered within two (2) years after the date of decertification.

2. A petition for reinstatement, together with five (5) copies, shall be made in writing under oath and filed with the Board, with a fee which is twice the application fee.

3. A petition for reinstatement shall contain:

a. The name, age, residence and address of the petitioner;

b. The offense or misconduct upon which the decertification was based, together with the date of such decertification; and

c. A concise statement of facts claimed to justify reinstatement as a certified neutral.

4. The Board shall refer the petition for reinstatement along with its recommendation to the Supreme Court. The Supreme Court shall take such action as it deems appropriate.

VI. TRAINING PROGRAMS

A. Mediator and arbitrator training programs sponsored by the South Carolina Bar's CLE Division or any other provider of ADR programs may be approved by the Board. Applications for approval of training programs by such other providers must be accompanied by a $25 application fee. Approval of the program is valid for one year after which the applicant must reapply and submit the application fee.

B. The Commission shall maintain at the South Carolina Bar a roster of approved training programs.

C. An applicant or provider requesting approval of a mediator or arbitrator training has the burden of establishing that the training has met the requirements of the Rules for approval. That burden is satisfied only if the Board is convinced by clear and convincing evidence that the training program meets or exceeds the standards specified by the applicable Rules and the Commission.

D. The Board's decision not to approve a mediator or arbitrator training program may be reviewed by the Court upon petition by the unsuccessful applicant.

VII. EFFECTIVE DATE

These regulations will be effective upon adoption by the Supreme Court.

[Adopted effective June 27, 2002. Amended effective October 15, 2003; September 4, 2008.]

1 By Order dated June 27, 2002, the application fee was set at $250.

2 By Order dated June 27, 2002, the recertification fee was set at $50 and the late fee was set at $50.

V. RULES GOVERNING THE JUDICIARY, EMPLOYEES OF THE JUDICIAL DEPARTMENT, AND OTHERS ASSISTING THE JUDICIARY

RULE 501. CODE OF JUDICIAL CONDUCT

PREAMBLE

Our legal system is based on the principle that an independent, fair and competent judiciary will interpret and apply the laws that govern us. The role of the judiciary is central to American concepts of justice and the rule of law. Intrinsic to all sections of this Code are the precepts that judges, individually and collectively, must respect and honor the judicial office as a public trust and strive to enhance and maintain confidence in our legal system. The judge is an arbiter of facts and law for the resolution of disputes and a highly visible symbol of government under the rule of law.

The Code of Judicial Conduct is intended to establish standards for ethical conduct of judges. It consists of broad statements called Canons, specific rules set forth in Sections under each Canon, a Terminology Section, an Application Section and Commentary. The text of the Canons and the Sections, including the Terminology and Application Sections, is authoritative. The Commentary, by explanation and example, provides guidance with respect to the purpose and meaning of the Canons and Sections. The Commentary is not intended as a statement of additional rules. When the text uses "shall" or "shall not," it is intended to impose binding obligations the violation of which can result in disciplinary action. When "should" or "should not" is used, the text is intended as hortatory and as a statement of what is or is not appropriate conduct but not as a binding rule under which a judge may be disciplined. When "may" is used, it denotes permissible discretion or, depending on the context, it refers to action that is not covered by specific proscriptions.

The Canons and Sections are rules of reason. They should be applied consistent with constitutional requirements, statutes, other court rules and decisional law and in the context of all relevant circumstances. The Code is to be construed so as not to impinge on the essential independence of judges in making judicial decisions.

The Code is designed to provide guidance to judges and candidates for judicial office and to provide a structure for regulating conduct through disciplinary agencies. It is not designed or intended as a basis for civil liability or criminal prosecution. Furthermore, the purpose of the Code would be subverted if the Code were invoked by lawyers for mere tactical advantage in a proceeding.

The text of the Canons and Sections is intended to govern conduct of judges and to be binding upon them. It is not intended, however, that every transgression will result in disciplinary action. Whether disciplinary action is appropriate, and the degree of discipline to be imposed, should be determined through a reasonable and reasoned application of the text and should depend on such factors as the seriousness of the transgression, whether there is a pattern of improper activity and the effect of the improper activity on others or on the judicial system.

The Code of Judicial Conduct is not intended as an exhaustive guide for the conduct of judges. They should also be governed in their judicial and personal conduct by general ethical standards. The Code is intended, however, to state basic standards which should govern the conduct of all judges and to provide guidance to assist judges in establishing and maintaining high standards of judicial and personal conduct.

TERMINOLOGY

Terms explained below are noted with an asterisk (*) in the Sections where they appear. In addition, the Sections where terms appear are referred to after the explanation of each term below.

"Appropriate authority" denotes the authority with responsibility for initiation of disciplinary process with respect to the violation to be reported. *See* Sections 3D(1) and 3D(2).

"Candidate." A candidate is a person seeking selection for or retention in judicial office by election or appointment. A person becomes a candidate for judicial office as soon as he or she makes a public announcement of candidacy, declares or files as a candidate with the election or appointment authority, or authorizes solicitation or acceptance of contributions or support. The term "candidate" has the same meaning when applied to a judge seeking election or appointment to non-judicial office. *See* Preamble and Sections 5A, 5B, 5C and 5E.

"Continuing part-time judge." A continuing part-time judge is a judge who serves repeatedly on a part-time basis by election or under a continuing appointment, including a retired judge subject to recall who is permitted to practice law. *See* Application Section C.

"Court personnel" does not include the lawyers in a proceeding before a judge. *See* Sections 3B(7)(c) and 3B(9).

"De minimis" denotes an insignificant interest that could not raise reasonable question as to a judge's impartiality. *See* Sections 3E(1)(c) and 3E(1)(d).

"Economic interest" denotes ownership of a more than de minimis legal or equitable interest, or a relationship as officer, director, advisor or other active participant in the affairs of a party, except that:

(i) ownership of an interest in a mutual or common investment fund that holds securities is not an economic interest in such securities unless the judge participates in the management of the fund or a proceeding pending or impending before the judge could substantially affect the value of the interest;

(ii) service by a judge as an officer, director, advisor or other active participant in an educational, religious, charitable, fraternal or civic organization, or service by a judge's spouse, parent or child as an officer, director, advisor or other active participant in any organization does not create an economic interest in securities held by that organization;

(iii) a deposit in a financial institution, the proprietary interest of a policy holder in a mutual insurance company, of a depositor in a mutual savings association or of a member in a credit union, or a similar proprietary interest, is not an economic interest in the organization unless a proceeding pending or impending before the judge could substantially affect the value of the interest;

(iv) ownership of government securities is not an economic interest in the issuer unless a proceeding pending or impending before the judge could substantially affect the value of the securities. See Sections 3E(1)(c) and 3E(2).

"Fiduciary" includes such relationships as executor, administrator, trustee, conservator, and guardian. *See* Sections 3E(2) and 4E.

"Knowingly," "knowledge," "known" or "knows" denotes actual knowledge of the fact in question. A person's knowledge may be inferred from circumstances. *See* Sections 3D, 3E(1), and 5A(3).

"Law" denotes court rules as well as statutes, constitutional provisions and decisional law. *See* Sections 2A, 3A, 3B(2), 3B(6), 4B, 4C, 4D(5), 4F, 4I, 5A(2), 5A(3), 5B(2), 5C(1), 5C(3) and 5D.

"Member of the candidate's family" denotes a spouse, child, grandchild, parent, grandparent or other relative or person with whom the candidate maintains a close familial relationship. *See* Section 5A(3)(a).

"Member of the judge's family" denotes a spouse, child, grandchild, parent, grandparent, or other relative or person with whom the judge maintains a close familial relationship. *See* Sections 4D(2), 4D(3), 4E and 4G.

"Member of the judge's family residing in the judge's household" denotes any relative of a judge by blood or marriage, or a person treated by a judge as a member of the judge's family, who resides in the judge's household. *See* Sections 3E(1) and 4D(5).

"Nonpublic information" denotes information that, by law, is not available to the public. Nonpublic information may include but is not limited to: information that is sealed by statute or court order, impounded or communicated in camera; and information offered in grand jury proceedings, presentencing reports, dependency cases or psychiatric reports. *See* Section 3B(11).

"Periodic part-time judge." A periodic part-time judge is a judge who serves or expects to serve repeatedly on a part-time basis but under a separate appointment for each limited period of service or for each matter. *See* Application Section D.

"Political organization" denotes a political party or other group, the principal purpose of which is to further the election or appointment of candidates to political office. *See* Sections 5A(1), 5B(2) and 5C(1).

"Pro tempore part-time judge." A pro tempore part-time judge is a judge who serves or expects to serve once or only sporadically on a part-time basis under a separate appointment for each period of service or for each case heard. *See* Application Section E.

"Public election." This term includes primary and general elections; it includes partisan elections, nonpartisan elections and retention elections. *See* Section 5C.

"Require." The rules prescribing that a judge "require" certain conduct of others are, like all of the rules in this Code, rules of reason. The use of the term "require" in that context means a judge is to exercise reasonable direction and control over the conduct of those persons subject to the judge's direction and control. *See* Sections 3B(3), 3B(4), 3B(6), 3B(9) and 3C(2).

"Serious Crime." Any felony; any lesser crime that reflects adversely on the lawyer's honestly, trustworthiness or fitness as a lawyer in other respects; or, any crime a necessary element of which, as determined by the statutory or common law definition of the crime, involves interference with the administration of justice, false swearing, misrepresentation, fraud, deceit, bribery, extortion, misappropriation, theft, willful failure to file income tax returns, or an attempt, conspiracy or solicitation of another to commit a serious crime.

"Third degree of relationship." The following persons are relatives within the third degree of relationship: great-grandparent, grandparent, parent, uncle, aunt, brother, sister, child, grandchild, great-grandchild, nephew or niece. *See* Section 3E(1)(d).

CANON 1. A JUDGE SHALL UPHOLD THE INTEGRITY AND INDEPENDENCE OF THE JUDICIARY

A. An independent and honorable judiciary is indispensable to justice in our society. A judge should participate in establishing, maintaining and enforcing high standards of conduct, and shall personally observe those standards so that the integrity and independence of the judiciary will be preserved. The provisions of this

Code are to be construed and applied to further that objective.

Commentary

Deference to the judgments and rulings of courts depends upon public confidence in the integrity and independence of judges. The integrity and independence of judges depends in turn upon their acting without fear or favor. Although judges should be independent, they must comply with the law, including the provisions of this Code. Public confidence in the impartiality of the judiciary is maintained by the adherence of each judge to this responsibility. Conversely, violation of this Code diminishes public confidence in the judiciary and thereby does injury to the system of government under law.

CANON 2. A JUDGE SHALL AVOID IMPROPRIETY AND THE APPEARANCE OF IMPROPRIETY IN ALL OF THE JUDGE'S ACTIVITIES

A. A judge shall respect and comply with the law* and shall act at all times in a manner that promotes public confidence in the integrity and impartiality of the judiciary.

Commentary

Public confidence in the judiciary is eroded by irresponsible or improper conduct by judges. A judge must avoid all impropriety and appearance of impropriety. A judge must therefore accept restrictions on the judge's conduct that might be viewed as burdensome by the ordinary citizen and should do so freely and willingly.

The prohibition against behaving with impropriety or the appearance of impropriety applies to both the professional and personal conduct of a judge. Because it is not practicable to list all prohibited acts, the proscription is necessarily cast in general terms that extend to conduct by judges that is harmful although not specifically mentioned in the Code. Actual improprieties under this standard include violations of law, court rules or other specific provisions of this Code. The test for appearance of impropriety is whether the conduct would create in reasonable minds a perception that the judge's ability to carry out judicial responsibilities with integrity, impartiality and competence is impaired. See also Commentary under Section 2C.

B. A judge shall not allow family, social, political or other relationships to influence the judge's judicial conduct or judgment. A judge shall not lend the prestige of judicial office to advance the private interests of the judge or others; nor shall a judge convey or permit others to convey the impression that they are in a special position to influence the judge. A judge shall not testify voluntarily as a character witness.

Commentary

Maintaining the prestige of judicial office is essential to a system of government in which the judiciary functions independently of the executive and legislative branches. Respect for the judicial office facilitates the orderly conduct of legitimate judicial functions. Judges should distinguish between proper and improper use of the prestige of office in all of their activities. For example, it would be improper for a judge to allude to his or her judgeship to gain a personal advantage such as deferential treatment when stopped by a police officer for a traffic offense. Similarly, judicial letterhead must not be used for conducting a judge's personal business.

A judge must avoid lending the prestige of judicial office for the advancement of the private interests of others. For example, a judge must not use the judge's judicial position to gain advantage in a civil suit involving a member of the judge's family. In contracts for publication of a judge's writings, a judge should retain control over the advertising to avoid exploitation of the judge's office. As to the acceptance of awards, see Section 4D(5)(a) and Commentary.

Although a judge should be sensitive to possible abuse of the prestige of office, a judge may, based on the judge's personal knowledge, serve as a reference or provide a letter of recommendation. However, a judge must not initiate the communication of information to a sentencing judge or a probation or corrections officer but may provide to such persons information for the record in response to a formal request.

Judges may participate in the process of judicial selection by cooperating with appointing authorities and screening committees seeking names for consideration, and by responding to official inquiries concerning a person being considered for a judgeship. See also Canon 5 regarding use of a judge's name in political activities.

A judge must not testify voluntarily as a character witness because to do so may lend the prestige of the judicial office in support of the party for whom the judge testifies. Moreover, when a judge testifies as a witness, a lawyer who regularly appears before the judge may be placed in the awkward position of cross-examining the judge. A judge may, however, testify when properly summoned. Except in unusual circumstances where the demands of justice require, a judge should discourage a party from requiring the judge to testify as a character witness.

C. A judge shall not hold membership in any organization that practices invidious discrimination on the basis of race, sex, religion or national origin.

Commentary

Membership of a judge in an organization that practices invidious discrimination gives rise to perceptions that the judge's impartiality is impaired. Section 2C refers to the current practices of the organization. Whether an organization practices invidious discrimination is often a complex question to which judges should be sensitive. The answer cannot be determined from a mere examination of an organization's current membership rolls but rather depends on how the organization selects members and other relevant factors, such as that the organization is dedicated to the preservation of religious, ethnic or cultural values of legitimate common interest to its members, or that it is in fact and effect an intimate, purely private organization whose membership limitations could not be constitutionally prohibited. Absent such factors, an organization is generally said to discriminate invidiously if it arbitrarily excludes from membership on the basis of race, religion, sex or national origin persons who would otherwise be admitted to membership. See *New York State Club Ass'n. Inc. v. City of New York, 487 U.S. 1, 108 S. Ct. 2225, 101 L. Ed. 2d 1 (1988); Board of Directors of Rotary International v. Rotary Club of Duarte, 481 U.S. 537, 107 S. Ct. 1940, 95 L. Ed. 2d 474 (1987); Roberts v. United States Jaycees, 468 U.S. 609, 104 S. Ct. 3244, 82 L. Ed. 2d 462 (1984).*

An organization dedicated to the preservation of religious, spiritual, charitable, civic or cultural values, or a sororal, fraternal, alumni, or other college, university or school related organization, is not considered to discriminate invidiously if it does not stigmatize any excluded persons as inferior and therefore unworthy of membership.

Although Section 2C relates only to membership in organizations that invidiously discriminate on the basis of race, sex, religion or national origin, a judge's membership in an organization that engages in any discriminatory membership practices prohibited by the law of the jurisdiction also violates Canon 2 and Section 2A and gives the appearance of impropriety. In addition, it would be a violation of Canon 2 and Section 2A for a judge to arrange a meeting at a club that the judge knows practices invidious discrimination on the basis of race, sex, religion or national origin in its membership or other policies, or for the judge to regularly use such a club. Moreover, public manifestation by a judge of the judge's knowing approval of invidious discrimination on any basis gives the appearance of impropriety under Canon 2 and diminishes public confidence in the integrity and impartiality of the judiciary, in violation of Section 2A.

When a person who is a judge on the date this Code becomes effective learns that an organization to which the judge belongs engages in invidious discrimination that would preclude membership under Section 2C or under Canon 2 and Section 2A, the judge is permitted, in lieu of resigning, to make immediate efforts to have the organization discontinue its invidiously discriminatory practices, but is required to suspend participation in any other activities of the organization. If the organization fails to discontinue its invidiously discriminatory practices as promptly as possible (and in all events within a year of the judge's first learning of the practices), the judge is required to resign immediately from the organization.

CANON 3. A JUDGE SHALL PERFORM THE DUTIES OF JUDICIAL OFFICE IMPARTIALLY AND DILIGENTLY

A. Judicial Duties in General. The judicial duties of a judge take precedence over all the judge's other activities. The judge's judicial duties include all the duties of the judge's office prescribed by law.* In the performance of these duties, the following standards apply.

B. Adjudicative Responsibilities.

(1) A judge shall hear and decide matters assigned to the judge except those in which disqualification is required.

(2) A judge shall be faithful to the law* and maintain professional competence in it. A judge shall not be swayed by partisan interests, public clamor or fear of criticism.

(3) A judge shall require* order and decorum in proceedings before the judge.

(4) A judge shall be patient, dignified and courteous to litigants, jurors, witnesses, lawyers and others with whom the judge deals in an official capacity, and shall require* similar conduct of lawyers, and of staff, court officials and others subject to the judge's direction and control.

Commentary

The duty to hear all proceedings fairly and with patience is not inconsistent with the duty to dispose promptly of the business of the court. Judges can be efficient and businesslike while being patient and deliberate.

(5) A judge shall perform judicial duties without bias or prejudice. A judge shall not, in the performance of judicial duties, by words or conduct manifest bias or prejudice, including but not limited to bias or prejudice based upon race, sex, religion, national origin, disability or age, and shall not permit staff, court officials and others subject to the judge's direction and control to do so.

Commentary

A judge must refrain from speech, gestures or other conduct that could reasonably be perceived as sexual harassment and must require the same standard of conduct of others subject to the judge's direction and control.

A judge must perform judicial duties impartially and fairly. A judge who manifests bias on any basis in a proceeding impairs the fairness of the proceeding and brings the judiciary into disrepute. Facial expression and body language, in addition to oral communication, can give to parties or lawyers in the proceeding, jurors, the media and others an appearance of judicial bias. A judge must be alert to avoid behavior that may be perceived as prejudicial.

(6) A judge shall require* lawyers in proceedings before the judge to refrain from manifesting, by words or conduct, bias or prejudice based upon race, sex, religion, national origin, disability or age, against parties, witnesses, counsel or others. This Section 3B(6) does not preclude legitimate advocacy when race, sex, religion, national origin, disability, age, or other similar factors, are issues in the proceeding.

(7) A judge shall accord to every person who has a legal interest in a proceeding, or that person's lawyer, the right to be heard according to law.* A judge shall not initiate, permit, or consider ex parte communications, or consider other communications made to the judge outside the presence of the parties concerning a pending or impending proceeding except that:

(a) Where circumstances require, ex parte communications for scheduling, administrative purposes or emergencies that do not deal with substantive matters or issues on the merits are authorized; provided:

(i) the judge reasonably believes that no party will gain a procedural or tactical advantage as a result of the ex parte communication, and

(ii) the judge makes provision promptly to notify all other parties of the substance of the ex parte communication and allows an opportunity to respond.

(b) A judge may obtain the advice of a disinterested expert on the law* applicable to a proceeding before the judge if the judge gives notice to the parties of the person consulted and the substance of the advice, and affords the parties reasonable opportunity to respond.

(c) A judge may consult with court personnel* whose function is to aid the judge in carrying out the judge's adjudicative responsibilities or with other judges.

(d) A judge may, with the consent of the parties, confer separately with the parties and their lawyers in an effort to mediate or settle matters pending before the judge.

(e) A judge may initiate or consider any ex parte communications when expressly authorized by law* to do so.

Commentary

The proscription against communications concerning a proceeding includes communications from lawyers, law teachers, and other persons who are not participants in the proceeding, except to the limited extent permitted.

To the extent reasonably possible, all parties or their lawyers shall be included in communications with a judge.

Whenever presence of a party or notice to a party is required by Section 3B(7), it is the party's lawyer, or if the party is unrepresented the party, who is to be present or to whom notice is to be given.

An appropriate and often desirable procedure for a court to obtain the advice of a disinterested expert on legal issues is to invite the expert to file a brief amicus curiae.

Certain ex parte communication is approved by Section 3B(7) to facilitate scheduling and other administrative purposes and to accommodate emergencies. In general, however, a judge must discourage ex parte communication and allow it only if all the criteria stated in Section 3B(7) are clearly met. A judge must disclose to all parties all ex parte communications described in Sections 3B(7)(a) and 3B(7)(b) regarding a proceeding pending or impending before the judge.

Examples when an *ex parte* communication may be expressly authorized by law include the issuance of a temporary restraining order under certain limited circumstances [Rule 65(b), SCRCP], the issuance of a writ of supersedeas under exigent circumstances [Rule 225(d)(6), SCACR], the determination of fees and expenses for indigent capital defendants [S.C. Code Ann. § 16–3–26 (Supp. 1995)], the issuance of temporary orders related to child custody and support where conditions warrant [S.C. Code Ann. § 63–17–390 (Supp. 2008)], and the issuance of a seizure order regarding delinquent insurers [S.C. Code Ann. § 38–27–220 (Supp. 1995)].

A judge must not independently investigate facts in a case and must consider only the evidence presented.

A judge may request a party to submit proposed findings of fact and conclusions of law, so long as the other parties are apprised of the request and are given an opportunity to respond to the proposed findings and conclusions.

A judge must make reasonable efforts, including the provision of appropriate supervision, to ensure that Section 3B(7) is not violated through law clerks or other personnel on the judge's staff.

If communication between the trial judge and the appellate court with respect to a proceeding is permitted, a copy of any written communication or the substance of any oral communication should be provided to all parties.

(8) A judge shall dispose of all judicial matters promptly, efficiently and fairly.

Commentary

In disposing of matters promptly, efficiently and fairly, a judge must demonstrate due regard for the rights of the parties to be heard and to have issues resolved without unnecessary cost or delay. Containing costs while preserving fundamental rights of parties also protects the interests of witnesses and the general public. A judge should monitor and supervise cases so as to reduce or eliminate dilatory practices, avoidable delays and unnecessary costs. A judge should encourage and seek to facilitate settlement, but parties should not feel coerced into surrendering the right to have their controversy resolved by the courts.

Prompt disposition of the court's business requires a judge to devote adequate time to judicial duties, to be punctual in attending court and expeditious in determining matters under submission, and to insist that court officials, litigants and their lawyers cooperate with the judge to that end.

(9) A judge shall not, while a proceeding is pending or impending in any court, make any public comment that might reasonably be expected to affect its outcome or impair its fairness or make any nonpublic comment that might substantially interfere with a fair trial or hearing. The judge shall require* similar abstention on the part of court personnel* subject to the judge's direction and control. This Section does not prohibit judges from making public statements in the course of their official duties or from explaining for public information the procedures of the court. This Section does not apply to proceedings in which the judge is a litigant in a personal capacity.

Commentary

The requirement that judges abstain from public comment regarding a pending or impending proceeding continues during any appellate process and until final disposition. This Section does not prohibit a judge from commenting on proceedings in which the judge is a litigant in a personal capacity, but in cases such as a writ of mandamus where the judge is a litigant in an official capacity, the judge must not comment publicly. The conduct of lawyers relating to trial publicity is governed by Rule 3.6 of the Rules of Professional Conduct contained in Rule 407, SCACR.

(10) A judge shall not commend or criticize jurors for their verdict other than in a court order or opinion in a proceeding, but may express appreciation to jurors for their service to the judicial system and the community.

Commentary

Commending or criticizing jurors for their verdict may imply a judicial expectation in future cases and may impair a juror's ability to be fair and impartial in a subsequent case.

(11) A judge shall not disclose or use, for any purpose unrelated to judicial duties, nonpublic information* acquired in a judicial capacity.

C. Administrative Responsibilities.

(1) A judge shall diligently discharge the judge's administrative responsibilities without bias or prejudice and maintain professional competence in judicial

administration, and should cooperate with other judges and court officials in the administration of court business.

(2) A judge shall require* staff, court officials and others subject to the judge's direction and control to observe the standards of fidelity and diligence that apply to the judge and to refrain from manifesting bias or prejudice in the performance of their official duties.

(3) A judge with supervisory authority for the judicial performance of other judges shall take reasonable measures to assure the prompt disposition of matters before them and the proper performance of their other judicial responsibilities.

(4) A judge shall not make unnecessary appointments. A judge shall exercise the power of appointment impartially and on the basis of merit. A judge shall avoid nepotism and favoritism. A judge shall not approve compensation of appointees beyond the fair value of services rendered.

Commentary

Appointees of a judge include assigned counsel, officials such as referees, commissioners, special masters, receivers and guardians and personnel such as clerks, secretaries and bailiffs. Consent by the parties to an appointment or an award of compensation does not relieve the judge of the obligation prescribed by Section 3C(4).

D. Disciplinary Responsibilities.

(1) A judge who receives information indicating a substantial likelihood that another judge has committed a violation of this Code should take appropriate action. A judge having knowledge* that another judge has committed a violation of this Code that raises a substantial question as to the other judge's fitness for office shall inform the appropriate authority.*

(2) A judge who receives information indicating a substantial likelihood that a lawyer has committed a violation of the Rules of Professional Conduct contained in Rule 407, SCACR, should take appropriate action. A judge having knowledge* that a lawyer has committed a violation of the Rules of Professional Conduct that raises a substantial question as to the lawyer's honesty, trustworthiness or fitness as a lawyer in other respects shall inform the appropriate authority.*

(3) Acts of a judge, in the discharge of disciplinary responsibilities, required or permitted by Sections 3D(1) and 3D(2) are part of a judge's judicial duties and shall be absolutely privileged, and no civil action predicated thereon may be instituted against the judge.

(4) A judge who is arrested for or has been charged by way of indictment, information or complaint with a serious crime shall inform the Commission on Judicial Conduct in writing within fifteen days of being arrested or being charged by way of indictment, information or complaint.

Commentary

Appropriate action may include direct communication with the judge or lawyer who has committed the violation, other direct action if available, and reporting the violation to the appropriate authority or other agency or body.

E. Disqualification.

(1) A judge shall disqualify himself or herself in a proceeding in which the judge's impartiality might reasonably be questioned, including but not limited to instances where:

Commentary

Under this rule, a judge is disqualified whenever the judge's impartiality might reasonably be questioned, regardless whether any of the specific rules in Section 3E(1) apply. For example, if a judge were in the process of negotiating for employment with a law firm, the judge would be disqualified from any matters in which that law firm appeared, unless the disqualification was waived by the parties after disclosure by the judge.

A judge should disclose on the record information that the judge believes the parties or their lawyers might consider relevant to the question of disqualification, even if the judge believes there is no real basis for disqualification.

By decisional law, the rule of necessity may override the rule of disqualification. For example, a judge might be required to participate in judicial review of a judicial salary statute, or might be the only judge available in a matter requiring immediate judicial action, such as a hearing on probable cause or a temporary restraining order. In the latter case, the judge must disclose on the record the basis for possible disqualification and use reasonable efforts to transfer the matter to another judge as soon as practicable.

(a) the judge has a personal bias or prejudice concerning a party or a party's lawyer, or personal knowledge* of disputed evidentiary facts concerning the proceeding;

(b) the judge served as a lawyer in the matter in controversy, or a lawyer with whom the judge previously practiced law served during such association as a lawyer concerning the matter, or the judge has been a material witness concerning it;

Commentary

A lawyer in a government agency does not ordinarily have an association with other lawyers employed by that agency within the meaning of Section 3E(1)(b); a judge formerly employed by a government agency, however, should disqualify himself or herself in a proceeding if the judge's impartiality might reasonably be questioned because of such association.

(c) the judge knows* that he or she, individually or as a fiduciary, or the judge's spouse, parent or child wherever residing, or any other member of the judge's family residing in the judge's household,* has an economic interest* in the subject matter in controversy or in a party to the proceeding or has any other more than de minimis* interest that could be substantially affected by the proceeding;

(d) the judge or the judge's spouse, or a person within the third degree of relationship* to either of them, or the spouse of such a person:

(i) is a party to the proceeding, or an officer, director or trustee of a party;

(ii) is acting as a lawyer in the proceeding;

(iii) is known* by the judge to have a more than de minimis* interest that could be substantially affected by the proceeding;

(iv) is to the judge's knowledge* likely to be a material witness in the proceeding.

Commentary

The fact that a lawyer in a proceeding is affiliated with a law firm with which a relative of the judge is affiliated does not of itself disqualify the judge. Under appropriate circumstances, the fact that "the judge's impartiality might reasonably be questioned" under Section 3E(1), or that the relative is known by the judge to have an interest in the law firm that could be "substantially affected by the outcome of the proceeding" under Section 3E(1)(d)(iii) may require the judge's disqualification.

(2) A judge shall keep informed about the judge's personal and fiduciary* economic interests,* and make a reasonable effort to keep informed about the personal economic interests of the judge's spouse and minor children residing in the judge's household.

F. Remittal of Disqualification. A judge disqualified by the terms of Section 3E may disclose on the record the basis of the judge's disqualification and may ask the parties and their lawyers to consider, out of the presence of the judge, whether to waive disqualification. If following disclosure of any basis for disqualification other than personal bias or prejudice concerning a party, the parties and lawyers, without participation by the judge, all agree that the judge should not be disqualified, and the judge is then willing to participate, the judge may participate in the proceeding. The agreement shall be incorporated in the record of the proceeding.

Commentary

A remittal procedure provides the parties an opportunity to proceed without delay if they wish to waive the disqualification. To assure that consideration of the question of remittal is made independently of the judge, a judge must not solicit, seek or hear comment on possible remittal or waiver of the disqualification unless the lawyers jointly propose remittal after consultation as provided in the rule. A party may act through counsel if counsel represents on the record that the party has been consulted and consents. As a practical matter, a judge may wish to have all parties and their lawyers sign the remittal agreement.

CANON 4. A JUDGE SHALL SO CONDUCT THE JUDGE'S EXTRA-JUDICIAL ACTIVITIES AS TO MINIMIZE THE RISK OF CONFLICT WITH JUDICIAL OBLIGATIONS

A. Extra-Judicial Activities in General. A judge shall conduct all of the judge's extra-judicial activities so that they do not:

(1) cast reasonable doubt on the judge's capacity to act impartially as a judge;

(2) demean the judicial office; or

(3) interfere with the proper performance of judicial duties.

Commentary

Complete separation of a judge from extra-judicial activities is neither possible nor wise; a judge should not become isolated from the community in which the judge lives.

Expressions of bias or prejudice by a judge, even outside the judge's judicial activities, may cast reasonable doubt on the judge's capacity to act impartially as a judge. Expressions which may do so include jokes or other remarks demeaning individuals on the basis of their race, sex, religion, national origin, disability or age. See Section 2C and accompanying Commentary.

B. Avocational Activities. A judge may speak, write, lecture, teach and participate in other extra-judicial activities concerning the law,* the legal system, the administration of justice and non-legal subjects, subject to the requirements of this Code.

Commentary

As a judicial officer and person specially learned in the law, a judge is in a unique position to contribute to the improvement of the law, the legal system, and the administration of justice, including revision of substantive and procedural law and improvement of criminal and juvenile justice. To the extent that time permits, a judge is encouraged to do so, either independently or through a bar association, judicial conference or other organization dedicated to the improvement of the law. Judges may participate in efforts to promote the fair administration of justice, the independence of the judiciary and the integrity of the legal profession and may express opposition to the persecution of lawyers and judges in other countries because of their professional activities.

In this and other Sections of Canon 4, the phrase "subject to the requirements of this Code" is used, notably in connection with a judge's governmental, civic or charitable activities. This phrase is included to remind judges that the use of permissive language in various Sections of the Code does not relieve a judge from the other requirements of the Code that apply to the specific conduct.

C. Governmental, Civic or Charitable Activities.

(1) A judge shall not appear at a public hearing before, or otherwise consult with, an executive or legislative body or official except on matters concerning the law,* the legal system or the administration of justice or except when acting pro se in a matter involving the judge or the judge's interests.

Commentary

See Section 2B regarding the obligation to avoid improper influence.

(2) A judge shall not accept appointment to a governmental committee or commission or other governmental position that is concerned with issues of fact or policy on matters other than the improvement of the law,* the legal system or the administration of justice. A judge may, however, represent a country, state or

locality on ceremonial occasions or in connection with historical, educational or cultural activities.

Commentary

Section 4C(2) prohibits a judge from accepting any governmental position except one relating to the law, legal system or administration of justice as authorized by Section 4C(3). The appropriateness of accepting extra-judicial assignments must be assessed in light of the demands on judicial resources created by crowded dockets and the need to protect the courts from involvement in extra-judicial matters that may prove to be controversial. Judges should not accept governmental appointments that are likely to interfere with the effectiveness and independence of the judiciary.

Section 4C(2) does not govern a judge's service in a nongovernmental position. See Section 4C(3) permitting service by a judge with organizations devoted to the improvement of the law, the legal system or the administration of justice and with educational, religious, charitable, fraternal or civic organizations not conducted for profit. For example, service on the board of a public educational institution, unless it were a law school, would be prohibited under Section 4C(2), but service on the board of a public law school or any private educational institution would generally be permitted under Section 4C(3).

(3) A judge may serve as an officer, director, trustee or non-legal advisor of an organization or governmental agency devoted to the improvement of the law,* the legal system or the administration of justice or of an educational, religious, charitable, fraternal or civic organization not conducted for profit, subject to the following limitations and the other requirements of this Code.

Commentary

Section 4C(3) does not apply to a judge's service in a governmental position unconnected with the improvement of the law, the legal system or the administration of justice; see Section 4C(2).

See Commentary to Section 4B regarding use of the phrase "subject to the following limitations and the other requirements of this Code." As an example of the meaning of the phrase, a judge permitted by Section 4C(3) to serve on the board of a fraternal institution may be prohibited from such service by Sections 2C or 4A if the institution practices invidious discrimination or if service on the board otherwise casts reasonable doubt on the judge's capacity to act impartially as a judge.

Service by a judge on behalf of a civic or charitable organization may be governed by other provisions of Canon 4 in addition to Section 4C. For example, a judge is prohibited by Section 4G from serving as a legal advisor to a civic or charitable organization.

(a) A judge shall not serve as an officer, director, trustee or non-legal advisor if it is likely that the organization

(i) will be engaged in proceedings that would ordinarily come before the judge, or

(ii) will be engaged frequently in adversary proceedings in the court of which the judge is a member or in any court subject to the appellate jurisdiction of the court of which the judge is a member.

Commentary

The changing nature of some organizations and of their relationship to the law makes it necessary for a judge regularly to reexamine the activities of each organization with which the judge is affiliated to determine if it is proper for the judge to continue the affiliation. For example, in many jurisdictions charitable hospitals are now more frequently in court than in the past. Similarly, the boards of some legal aid organizations now make policy decisions that may have political significance or imply commitment to causes that may come before the courts for adjudication.

(b) A judge as an officer, director, trustee or non-legal advisor, or as a member or otherwise:

(i) may assist such an organization in planning fund-raising and may participate in the management and investment of the organization's funds, but shall not personally participate in the solicitation of funds or other fund-raising activities, except that a judge may solicit funds from other judges over whom the judge does not exercise supervisory or appellate authority;

(ii) may make recommendations to public and private fund-granting organizations on projects and programs concerning the law,* the legal system or the administration of justice;

(iii) shall not personally participate in membership solicitation if the solicitation might reasonably be perceived as coercive or, except as permitted in Section 4C(3)(b)(i), if the membership solicitation is essentially a fund-raising mechanism;

(iv) shall not use or permit the use of the prestige of judicial office for fund-raising or membership solicitation.

Commentary

A judge may solicit membership or endorse or encourage membership efforts for an organization devoted to the improvement of the law, the legal system or the administration of justice or a nonprofit educational, religious, charitable, fraternal or civic organization as long as the solicitation cannot reasonably be perceived as coercive and is not essentially a fund-raising mechanism. Solicitation of funds for an organization and solicitation of memberships similarly involve the danger that the person solicited will feel obligated to respond favorably to the solicitor if the solicitor is in a position of influence or control. A judge must not engage in direct, individual solicitation of funds or memberships in person, in writing or by telephone except in the following cases: 1) a judge may solicit for funds or memberships other judges over whom the judge does not exercise supervisory or appellate authority, 2) a judge may solicit other persons for membership in the organizations described above if neither those persons nor persons with whom they are affiliated are likely ever to appear before the court on which the judge serves and 3) a judge who is an officer of such an organization may send a general membership solicitation mailing over the judge's signature.

Use of an organization letterhead for fund-raising or membership solicitation does not violate Section 4C(3)(b) provided the letterhead lists only the judge's name and office or other position in the organization, and, if comparable designations are listed for other persons, the judge's judicial designation. In addition, a judge must also make reasonable efforts to ensure that the judge's staff, court officials and others subject to the judge's direction and control do not solicit funds on the judge's behalf for any purpose, charitable or otherwise.

A judge must not be a speaker or guest of honor at an organization's fund-raising event, but mere attendance at such an event is permissible if otherwise consistent with this Code.

D. Financial Activities.

(1) A judge shall not engage in financial and business dealings that:

(a) may reasonably be perceived to exploit the judge's judicial position, or

(b) involve the judge in frequent transactions or continuing business relationships with those lawyers or other persons likely to come before the court on which the judge serves.

Commentary

The Time for Compliance provision of this Code (Application, Section F) postpones the time for compliance with certain provisions of this Section in some cases.

When a judge acquires in a judicial capacity information, such as material contained in filings with the court, that is not yet generally known, the judge must not use the information for private gain. See Section 2B; see also Section 3B(11).

A judge must avoid financial and business dealings that involve the judge in frequent transactions or continuing business relationships with persons likely to come either before the judge personally or before other judges on the judge's court. In addition, a judge should discourage members of the judge's family from engaging in dealings that would reasonably appear to exploit the judge's judicial position. This rule is necessary to avoid creating an appearance of exploitation of office or favoritism and to minimize the potential for disqualification. With respect to affiliation of relatives of judges with law firms appearing before the judge, see Commentary to Section 3E(1) relating to disqualification.

Participation by a judge in financial and business dealings is subject to the general prohibitions in Section 4A against activities that tend to reflect adversely on impartiality, demean the judicial office, or interfere with the proper performance of judicial duties. Such participation is also subject to the general prohibition in Canon 2 against activities involving impropriety or the appearance of impropriety and the prohibition in Section 2B against the misuse of the prestige of judicial office. In addition, a judge must maintain high standards of conduct in all of the judge's activities, as set forth in Canon 1. See Commentary for Section 4B regarding use of the phrase "subject to the requirements of this Code."

(2) A judge may, subject to the requirements of this Code, hold and manage investments of the judge and members of the judge's family,* including real estate, and engage in other remunerative activity.

Commentary

This Section provides that, subject to the requirements of this Code, a judge may hold and manage investments owned solely by the judge, investments owned solely by a member or members of the judge's family, and investments owned jointly by the judge and members of the judge's family.

(3) A judge may serve as an officer, director, manager, general partner, advisor or employee of a business entity if that service does not conflict with the judge's judicial duties, create the appearance of impropriety or otherwise violate any provision of this Code.

Commentary

A judge may participate in a business if that participation does not conflict with the judge's judicial duties, create the appearance of impropriety or violate any other provision of this Code. For example, a judge may be prohibited from participation if the business entity frequently appears before the judge's court or the participation requires significant time away from judicial duties. Similarly, a judge must avoid participation if the judge's participation would involve misuse of the prestige of office.

(4) A judge shall manage the judge's investments and other financial interests to minimize the number of cases in which the judge is disqualified. As soon as the judge can do so without serious financial detriment, the judge shall divest himself or herself of investments and other financial interests that might require frequent disqualification.

(5) A judge shall not accept, and shall urge members of the judge's family residing in the judge's household,* not to accept, a gift, bequest, favor or loan from anyone except for:

Commentary

Section 4D(5) does not apply to contributions to a judge's campaign for judicial office, a matter governed by Canon 5.

Because a gift, bequest, favor or loan to a member of the judge's family residing in the judge's household might be viewed as intended to influence the judge, a judge must inform those family members of the relevant ethical constraints upon the judge in this regard and discourage those family members from violating them. A judge cannot, however, reasonably be expected to know or control all of the financial or business activities of all family members residing in the judge's household.

(a) a gift incident to a public testimonial, books, tapes and other resource materials supplied by publishers on a complimentary basis for official use, or an invitation to the judge and the judge's spouse or guest to attend a bar-related function or an activity devoted to the improvement of the law,* the legal system or the administration of justice;

Commentary

Acceptance of an invitation to a law-related function is governed by Section 4D(5)(a); acceptance of an invitation paid for by an individual lawyer or group of lawyers is governed by Section 4D(5)(h).

A judge may accept a public testimonial or a gift incident thereto only if the donor organization is not an organization whose members comprise or frequently represent the same side in litigation, and the testimonial and gift are otherwise in compliance with other provisions of this Code. See Sections 4A(1) and 2B.

(b) a gift, award or benefit incident to the business, profession or other separate activity of a spouse or other family member of a judge residing in the judge's household, including gifts, awards and benefits for the use of both the spouse or other family member and the judge (as spouse or family member), provided the gift, award or benefit could not reasonably be perceived as intended to influence the judge in the performance of judicial duties;

(c) ordinary social hospitality;

(d) a gift from a relative or friend, for a special occasion, such as a wedding, anniversary or birthday, if the gift is fairly commensurate with the occasion and the relationship;

Commentary

A gift to a judge, or to a member of the judge's family living in the judge's household, that is excessive in value raises questions about the judge's impartiality and the integrity of the judicial office and might require disqualification of the judge where disqualification would not otherwise be required. See, however, Section 4D(5)(e).

(e) a gift, bequest, favor or loan from a relative or close personal friend whose appearance or interest in a case would in any event require disqualification under Section 3E;

(f) a loan from a lending institution in its regular course of business on the same terms generally available to persons who are not judges;

(g) a scholarship or fellowship awarded on the same terms and based on the same criteria applied to other applicants;

(h) any other gift, bequest, favor or loan, only if: the donor is not a party or other person who has come or is likely to come or whose interests have come or are likely to come before the judge; and, if its value exceeds $150.00, the judge reports it in the same manner as the judge reports compensation in Section 4H; or

(i) a judicial portrait or memorial which complies with the requirements of Rule 3.5(d) of the Rules of Professional Conduct contained in Rule 407, SCACR.

Commentary

Section 4D(5)(h) prohibits judges from accepting gifts, favors, bequests or loans from lawyers or their firms if they have come or are likely to come before the judge; it also prohibits gifts, favors, bequests or loans from clients of lawyers or their firms when the clients' interests have come or are likely to come before the judge.

E. Fiduciary Activities.

(1) A judge shall not serve as executor, administrator or other personal representative, trustee, guardian, conservator, attorney in fact or other fiduciary.* Further, a judge should not be a signatory on a joint account with a guardian, conservator, attorney in fact, or personal representative, or otherwise exercise influence or control over the investment or use of such funds and property as are within the jurisdiction of the court. A judge may, however, serve in one of these capacities for the estate, trust or person of a member of the judge's family,* but only if such service will not interfere with the proper performance of judicial duties.

(2) A judge shall not serve as a fiduciary * if it is likely that the judge as a fiduciary will be engaged in proceedings that would ordinarily come before the judge, or if the estate, trust or ward becomes involved in adversary proceedings in the court on which the judge serves or one under its appellate jurisdiction.

(3) The same restrictions on financial activities that apply to a judge personally also apply to the judge while acting in a fiduciary * capacity.

Commentary

The Time for Compliance provision of this Code (Application, Section F) postpones the time for compliance with certain provisions of this Section in some cases.

The restrictions imposed by this Canon may conflict with the judge's obligation as a fiduciary. For example, a judge should resign as trustee if detriment to the trust would result from divestiture of holdings the retention of which would place the judge in violation of Section 4D(4).

F. Service as Arbitrator or Mediator. A judge shall not act as an arbitrator or mediator or otherwise perform judicial functions in a private capacity unless expressly authorized by law.* However, a retired judge may act as an arbitrator or mediator and remain available for assignment as a judge by the Chief Justice of the Supreme Court, provided the judge is disqualified: (1) from mediation and arbitration in matters in which the judge served as judge; and (2) as a judge from matters in which the judge participated as mediator or arbitrator.

G. Practice of Law. A judge shall not practice law. Notwithstanding this prohibition, a judge may act pro se and may, without compensation, give legal advice to and draft or review documents for a member of the judge's family.* This prohibition on the practice of law becomes effective immediately upon taking the oath of office and applies to any case in the judge's former practice that was not completed when judicial duties were assumed.

Commentary

This prohibition refers to the practice of law in a representative capacity and not in a pro se capacity. A judge may act for himself or herself in all legal matters, including matters involving litigation and matters involving appearances before or other dealings with legislative and other governmental bodies. However, in so doing, a judge must not abuse the prestige of office to advance the interests of the judge or the judge's family. See Section 2B.

The Code allows a judge to give legal advice to and draft legal documents for members of the judge's family, so long as the judge receives no compensation. A judge must not, however, act as an advocate or negotiator for a member of the judge's family in a legal matter.

H. Compensation, Reimbursement and Reporting.

(1) *Compensation and Reimbursement.* A judge may receive compensation and reimbursement of ex-

penses for the extra-judicial activities permitted by this Code, if the source of such payments does not give the appearance of influencing the judge's performance of judicial duties or otherwise give the appearance of impropriety.

(a) Compensation shall not exceed a reasonable amount nor shall it exceed what a person who is not a judge would receive for the same activity.

(b) Expense reimbursement shall be limited to the actual cost of travel, food and lodging reasonably incurred by the judge and, where appropriate to the occasion, by the judge's spouse or guest. Any payment in excess of such an amount is compensation.

(2) *Public Reports.* A judge shall report the date, place and nature of any activity for which the judge received compensation, and the name of the payor and the amount of compensation so received. Compensation or income of a spouse attributed to the judge by operation of a community property law is not extra-judicial compensation to the judge. The judge's report shall be made at least annually and shall be filed as a public document in the Office of Court Administration.

Commentary

See Section 4D(5) regarding reporting of gifts, bequests and loans.

The Code does not prohibit a judge from accepting honoraria or speaking fees provided that the compensation is reasonable and commensurate with the task performed. A judge should ensure, however, that no conflicts are created by the arrangement. A judge must not appear to trade on the judicial position for personal advantage. Nor should a judge spend significant time away from court duties to meet speaking or writing commitments for compensation. In addition, the source of the payment must not raise any question of undue influence or the judge's ability or willingness to be impartial.

I. Disclosure of a judge's income, debts, investments or other assets is required only to the extent provided in this Canon and in Sections 3E and 3F, or as otherwise required by law.*

Commentary

Section 3E requires a judge to disqualify himself or herself in any proceeding in which the judge has an economic interest. See "economic interest" as explained in the Terminology Section. Section 4D requires a judge to refrain from engaging in business and from financial activities that might interfere with the impartial performance of judicial duties; Section 4H requires a judge to report all compensation the judge received for activities outside judicial office. A judge has the rights of any other citizen, including the right to privacy of the judge's financial affairs, except to the extent that limitations established by law are required to safeguard the proper performance of the judge's duties.

CANON 5. A JUDGE OR JUDICIAL CANDIDATE SHALL REFRAIN FROM INAPPROPRIATE POLITICAL ACTIVITY

A. All Judges and Candidates.

(1) Except as authorized in Sections 5B(2), 5C(1) and 5C(3), a judge or a candidate * for election or appointment to judicial office shall not:

(a) act as a leader or hold an office in a political organization *;

(b) publicly endorse or publicly oppose another candidate for public office;

(c) make speeches on behalf of a political organization;

(d) attend political gatherings; or

(e) solicit funds for, pay an assessment to or make a contribution to a political organization or candidate, or purchase tickets for political party dinners or other functions.

Commentary

A judge or candidate for judicial office retains the right to participate in the political process as a voter.

Where false information concerning a judicial candidate is made public, a judge or another judicial candidate having knowledge of the facts is not prohibited by Section 5A(1) from making the facts public.

Section 5A(1)(a) does not prohibit a candidate for elective judicial office from retaining during candidacy a public office such as county prosecutor, which is not "an office in a political organization."

Section 5A(1)(b) does not prohibit a judge or judicial candidate from privately expressing his or her views on judicial candidates or other candidates for public office.

A candidate does not publicly endorse another candidate for public office by having that candidate's name on the same ticket.

(2) A judge shall resign from judicial office upon becoming a candidate * for a non-judicial office either in a primary or in a general election, except that the judge may continue to hold judicial office while being a candidate for election to or serving as a delegate in a state constitutional convention if the judge is otherwise permitted by law * to do so.

(3) A candidate * for a judicial office:

(a) shall maintain the dignity appropriate to judicial office and act in a manner consistent with the integrity and independence of the judiciary, and shall encourage members of the candidate's family * to adhere to the same standards of political conduct in support of the candidate as apply to the candidate;

Commentary

Although a judicial candidate must encourage members of his or her family to adhere to the same standards of political conduct in support of the candidate that apply to the candidate, family members are free to participate in other political activity.

(b) shall prohibit employees and officials who serve at the pleasure of the candidate,* and shall discourage other employees and officials subject to the candidate's direction and control from doing on the candidate's behalf what the candidate is prohibited from doing under the Sections of this Canon;

(c) except to the extent permitted by Section 5C(2), shall not authorize or knowingly * permit any other person to do for the candidate * what the candidate is prohibited from doing under the Sections of this Canon;

(d) shall not:

(i) make pledges or promises of conduct in office other than the faithful and impartial performance of the duties of the office;

(ii) make statements that commit or appear to commit the candidate with respect to cases, controversies or issues that are likely to come before the court; or

(iii) knowingly * misrepresent the identity, qualifications, present position or other fact concerning the candidate or an opponent;

Commentary

Section 5A(3)(d) prohibits a candidate for judicial office from making statements that appear to commit the candidate regarding cases, controversies or issues likely to come before the court. As a corollary, a candidate should emphasize in any public statement the candidate's duty to uphold the law regardless of his or her personal views. See also Section 3B(9), the general rule on public comment by judges. Section 5A(3)(d) does not prohibit a candidate from making pledges or promises respecting improvements in court administration. Nor does this Section prohibit an incumbent judge from making private statements to other judges or court personnel in the performance of judicial duties. This Section applies to any statement made in the process of securing judicial office, such as statements to commissions charged with judicial selection and tenure and legislative bodies confirming appointment. See also Rule 8.2 of the Rules of Professional Conduct contained in Rule 407, SCACR.

(e) may respond to personal attacks or attacks on the candidate's record as long as the response does not violate Section 5A(3)(d).

B. Candidates Seeking Appointment to Judicial or Other Governmental Office.

(1) A candidate * for appointment to judicial office or a judge seeking other governmental office shall not solicit or accept funds, personally or through a committee or otherwise, to support his or her candidacy.

(2) A candidate * for appointment to judicial office or a judge seeking other governmental office shall not engage in any political activity to secure the appointment except that:

(a) such persons may:

(i) communicate with the appointing authority, including any selection or nominating commission or other agency designated to screen candidates;

(ii) seek support or endorsement for the appointment from organizations that regularly make recommendations for reappointment or appointment to the office, and from individuals to the extent requested or required by those specified in Section 5B(2)(a); and

(iii) provide to those specified in Sections 5B(2)(a)(i) and 5B(2)(a)(ii) information as to his or her qualifications for the office;

(b) a non-judge candidate * for appointment to judicial office may, in addition, unless otherwise prohibited by law *:

(i) retain an office in a political organization,*

(ii) attend political gatherings, and

(iii) continue to pay ordinary assessments and ordinary contributions to a political organization or candidate and purchase tickets for political party dinners or other functions.

Commentary

Section 5B(2) provides a limited exception to the restrictions imposed by Sections 5A(1) and 5D. Under Section 5B(2), candidates seeking reappointment to the same judicial office or appointment to another judicial office or other governmental office may apply for the appointment and seek appropriate support.

Although under Section 5B(2) non-judge candidates seeking appointment to judicial office are permitted during candidacy to retain office in a political organization, attend political gatherings and pay ordinary dues and assessments, they remain subject to other provisions of this Code during candidacy. See Sections 5B(1), 5B(2)(a), 5E and Application Section.

C. Judges and Candidates Subject to Public Election.

(1) A judge or a candidate * subject to public election * may, except as prohibited by law *:

(a) at any time

(i) purchase tickets for and attend political gatherings;

(ii) identify himself or herself as a member of a political party; and

(iii) contribute to a political organization *;

(b) when a candidate for election

(i) speak to gatherings on his or her own behalf;

(ii) appear in newspaper, television and other media advertisements supporting his or her candidacy;

(iii) distribute pamphlets and other promotional campaign literature supporting his or her candidacy; and

(iv) publicly endorse or publicly oppose other candidates for the same judicial office in a public election in which the judge or judicial candidate is running.

Commentary

Section 5C(1) permits judges subject to election at any time to be involved in limited political activity. Section 5D, applicable solely to incumbent judges, would otherwise bar this activity.

(2) A candidate * shall not personally solicit or accept campaign contributions or personally solicit publicly stated support. A candidate may, however, establish committees of responsible persons to conduct campaigns for the candidate through media advertisements, brochures, mailings, candidate forums and other means not prohibited by law. Such committees may solicit and accept reasonable campaign contributions, manage the expenditure of funds for the candidate's campaign and obtain public statements of support for his or her candidacy. Such committees are not prohibited from soliciting and accepting reasonable campaign contributions and public support from lawyers. A candidate's committees may solicit contributions and public support for the candidate's campaign no earlier than one year before an election and no later than 90 days after the last election in which the candidate participates during the election year. A candidate shall not use or permit the use of campaign contributions for the private benefit of the candidate or others.

Commentary

Section 5C(2) permits a candidate, other than a candidate for appointment, to establish campaign committees to solicit and accept public support and reasonable financial contributions. At the start of the campaign, the candidate must instruct his or her campaign committees to solicit or accept only contributions that are reasonable under the circumstances. Though not prohibited, campaign contributions of which a judge has knowledge, made by lawyers or others who appear before the judge, may be relevant to disqualification under Section 3E.

Campaign committees established under Section 5C(2) should manage campaign finances responsibly, avoiding deficits that might necessitate post-election fund-raising, to the extent possible.

Section 5C(2) does not prohibit a candidate from initiating an evaluation by a judicial selection commission or bar association, or, subject to the requirements of this Code, from responding to a request for information from any organization.

(3) Except as prohibited by law,* a candidate * for judicial office in a public election * may permit the candidate's name: (a) to be listed on election materials along with the names of other candidates for elective public office, and (b) to appear in promotions of the ticket.

Commentary

Section 5C(3) provides a limited exception to the restrictions imposed by Section 5A(1).

D. Incumbent Judges. A judge shall not engage in any political activity except (i) as authorized under any other Section of this Code, (ii) on behalf of measures to improve the law,* the legal system or the administration of justice, or (iii) as expressly authorized by law.

Commentary

Neither Section 5D nor any other section of the Code prohibits a judge in the exercise of administrative functions from engaging in planning and other official activities with members of the executive and legislative branches of government. With respect to a judge's activity on behalf of measures to improve the law, the legal system and the administration of justice, see Commentary to Section 4B and Section 4C(1) and its Commentary.

E. Applicability. Canon 5 generally applies to all incumbent judges and judicial candidates *. A successful candidate, whether or not an incumbent, is subject to judicial discipline for his or her campaign conduct; an unsuccessful candidate who is a lawyer is subject to lawyer discipline for his or her campaign conduct. A lawyer who is a candidate for judicial office is subject to Rule 8.2(b) of the Rules of Professional Conduct contained in Rule 407, SCACR.

APPLICATION OF THE CODE OF JUDICIAL CONDUCT

A. Anyone, whether or not a lawyer, who is an officer of the unified judicial system and who performs judicial functions, including an officer such as a magistrate, master-in-equity or special referee, is a judge within the meaning of this Code. All judges shall comply with this Code except as provided below.

Commentary

The four categories of judicial service in other than a full-time capacity are necessarily defined in general terms because of the widely varying forms of judicial service. For the purposes of this Section, as long as a retired judge is subject to recall the judge is considered to "perform judicial functions." The determination of which category and, accordingly, which specific Code provisions apply to an individual judicial officer, depend upon the facts of the particular judicial service.

Administrative law judges are not officers of the unified judicial system. By statute, they are, however, subject to the requirements of this Code. S.C.Code Ann. § 1-23-560 (Supp. 1995).

B. Retired Judge Subject to Recall. A retired judge subject to recall who by law is not permitted to practice law is not required to comply:

(1) except while serving as a judge, with Section 4F;

(2) at any time with Section 4E; and

(3) with the requirement to file a report under Section 4H(2) in any reporting year in which the judge is not assigned to hold court; provided, however, that a retired judge subject to recall who does not file a report for any year shall not thereafter be assigned to hold court unless a report under Section 4H(2) has been filed covering the calendar year immediately preceding the calendar year in which the assignment is to be made.

C. Continuing Part-Time Judge. A continuing part-time judge *:

(1) is not required to comply:

(a) except while serving as a judge, with Section 3B(9); and

(b) at any time with Sections 4C(2), 4D(3), 4E(1), 4F, 4G, 4H, 5A(1), 5B(2) and 5D.

(2) shall not practice law in the court on which the judge serves or in any court subject to the appellate jurisdiction of the court on which the judge serves, and shall not act as a lawyer in a proceeding in which the judge has served as a judge or in any other proceeding related thereto.

Commentary

When a person who has been a continuing part-time judge is no longer a continuing part-time judge, including a retired judge no longer subject to recall, that person may act as a lawyer in a proceeding in which he or she has served as a judge or in any other proceeding related thereto only with the express consent of all parties pursuant to Rule 1.12(a) of the Rules of Professional Conduct contained in Rule 407, SCACR.

D. Periodic Part-Time Judge. A periodic part-time judge *:

(1) is not required to comply:

(a) except while serving as a judge, with Section 3B(9);

(b) at any time, with Sections 4C(2), 4C(3)(a), 4D(1)(b), 4D(3), 4D(4), 4D(5), 4E, 4F, 4G, 4H, 5A(1), 5B(2) and 5D.

(2) shall not practice law in the court on which the judge serves or in any court subject to the appellate jurisdiction of the court on which the judge serves, and shall not act as a lawyer in a proceeding in which the judge has served as a judge or in any other proceeding related thereto.

Commentary

When a person who has been a periodic part-time judge is no longer a periodic part-time judge (no longer accepts appointments), that person may act as a lawyer in a proceeding in which he or she has served as a judge or in any other proceeding related thereto only with the express consent of all parties pursuant to Rule 1.12(a) of the Rules of Professional Conduct contained in Rule 407, SCACR.

E. Pro Tempore Part-Time Judge. A pro tempore part-time judge *:

(1) is not required to comply:

(a) except while serving as a judge, with Sections 2A, 2B, 3B(9) and 4C(1);

(b) at any time with Sections 2C, 4C(2), 4C(3)(a), 4C(3)(b), 4D(1)(b), 4D(3), 4D(4), 4D(5), 4E, 4F, 4G, 4H, 5A(1), 5A(2), 5B(2) and 5D.

(2) A person who has been a pro tempore part-time judge * shall not act as a lawyer in a proceeding in which the judge has served as a judge or in any other proceeding related thereto except as otherwise permitted by Rule 1.12(a) of the Rules of Professional Conduct contained in Rule 407, SCACR.

F. Time for Compliance. A person to whom this Code becomes applicable shall comply immediately with all provisions of this Code except Sections 4D(2), 4D(3) and 4E and shall comply with these Sections as soon as reasonably possible and shall do so in any event within the period of one year.

Commentary

If serving as a fiduciary when selected as judge, a new judge may, notwithstanding the prohibitions in Section 4E, continue to serve as fiduciary but only for that period of time necessary to avoid serious adverse consequences to the beneficiary of the fiduciary relationship and in no event longer than one year. Similarly, if engaged at the time of judicial selection in a business activity, a new judge may, notwithstanding the prohibitions in Section 4D(3), continue in that activity for a reasonable period but in no event longer than one year.

RULE 502. RULES FOR JUDICIAL DISCIPLINARY ENFORCEMENT

RULE 1. PURPOSE

The regulation of judicial conduct is critical to preserving the integrity of the judiciary and enhancing public confidence in the judicial system. These rules provide the procedure for resolving allegations that a judge has committed ethical misconduct or that a judge suffers from a physical or mental condition which adversely affects the judge's ability to perform judicial functions.

[Adopted effective January 1, 1997.]

RULE 2. TERMINOLOGY

The following terminology is used throughout these rules:

(a) Admonition: a sanction imposed on a judge by an investigative panel of the Commission or by the Supreme Court. See Rule 7(b)(5) and Rule 19(d)(2). A confidential admonition cannot be imposed by an investigative panel after the filing and service of formal charges. If imposed by the Supreme Court after the disciplinary proceeding has become public under Rule 12(b), the order imposing the admonition shall not be published, but shall be a matter of public record. Only in cases of minor misconduct, when there is little or no injury to the public, the legal system, or the profession, should an admonition be imposed.

(b) Closed, But Not Dismissed: a manner of disposing of a matter where a panel of the Commission makes a finding that the matter should not be dismissed, but it is either impossible or impractical to proceed with the matter because it appears that the judge is deceased, disappeared, incarcerated, physically or mentally incapacitated, or removed from judicial duties, or for other good cause.

(c) Commission: the Commission on Judicial Conduct.

(d) Commission Counsel: the lawyer drafting reports, providing legal advice to the Commission and performing other duties assigned by the Commission. See Rule 6.

(e) Complaint: information in any form from any source received by the Commission that alleges or from which a reasonable inference can be drawn that a judge committed misconduct or is incapacitated. If there is no written complaint from another person, disciplinary counsel's written statement of the allegations constitutes the complaint.

(f) Conviction: any conviction resulting from a trial or any type of plea, including a plea of nolo contendere or a plea pursuant to *North Carolina v. Alford*, 400 U.S. 25 (1970).

(g) Deferred Discipline Agreement: a confidential agreement between the judge and an investigative panel of the Commission for the judge to undergo treatment, participate in education programs or take other corrective action. It is only available as a response to misconduct that is minor and can be addressed through treatment or a rehabilitation program. A deferred discipline agreement can only be entered into prior to the filing and service of formal charges.

(h) Disciplinary Counsel: the lawyer in charge of screening and investigating complaints, prosecuting formal charges and performing other duties assigned by the Supreme Court. See Rule 5.

(i) Formal Charges: the document that charges the judge with specific acts of misconduct or with a specific incapacity.

(j) Hearing Panel: the panel of the Commission that conducts hearings on formal charges. See Rule 4.

(k) Hearing: the public proceeding at which the issues of law and fact raised by the formal charges and answer are tried. See Rule 26.

(*l*) Incapacity: a mental or physical condition that adversely affects a judge's ability to perform judicial functions. Incapacity is distinguished from a disability that does not adversely affect a judge's performance of judicial functions.

(m) Incapacity Inactive Status: non-disciplinary suspension of a judge from office based on incapacity.

(n) Interim Suspension: temporary suspension from office pending a final determination in any proceeding under these rules. See Rule 17.

(*o*) Investigation: an inquiry into allegations of misconduct, including a search for and examination of evidence concerning the allegations. See Rule 19.

(p) Investigative Panel: the panel of the Commission that considers the recommendations of disciplinary counsel with regard to the disposition of cases and acceptance of agreements for resolution of disciplinary matters. The investigative panel also determines whether formal charges will be filed. See Rule 4.

(q) Letter of Caution: a written caution or warning about past or future conduct issued when it is determined that no misconduct has been committed or that only minor misconduct not warranting the imposition of a sanction has been committed. A letter of caution may be issued by disciplinary counsel, an investigative panel or the Supreme Court. The issuance of a letter of caution is not a sanction under these rules and does not constitute a finding of misconduct. The fact that a letter of caution has been issued shall not be considered in a subsequent disciplinary proceeding against the judge unless the caution or warning contained in the letter of caution is relevant to the misconduct alleged in the proceedings.

(r) Judge: anyone, whether or not a lawyer, who is an officer of the unified judicial system, and who is eligible to perform judicial functions, including an officer such as a magistrate, master-in-equity or special referee, is a judge within the meaning of these rules. This term includes a retired judge who has elected to be eligible for appointment under S.C. Code Ann. § 9–8–120 (Supp. 2009). This term does not include arbitrators, mediators, or administrative law judges.

(s) Misconduct: any conduct by a judge constituting grounds for discipline. See Rule 7(a).

(t) Proceedings: all steps in the discipline and incapacity system set forth in these rules.

(u) Public Members: members of the Commission who have never been a judge or been admitted to practice law in any jurisdiction.

(v) Public Reprimand: a reprimand by the Supreme Court in the form of a written decision which shall be imposed in person or served upon the respondent by certified mail.

(w) Reasonable Cause: a reasonable ground for belief in the existence of facts warranting the filing of formal charges for discipline or a petition for transfer to incapacity inactive status.

(x) Record: all documents filed in the case beginning with the formal charges. The record includes a transcript of the hearing on the formal charges.

(y) Respondent: a judge or former judge against whom formal charges have been filed.

(z) Screening: examination of a complaint or other information coming to the attention of disciplinary counsel to determine whether the Commission has jurisdiction. See Rule 19(a).

(aa) Serious Crime: any felony; any lesser crime that reflects adversely on the judge's honesty, trustworthiness or fitness as a judge in other respects; or, any crime a necessary element of which, as determined by the statutory or common law definition of the crime, involves interference with the administration of justice, false swearing, misrepresentation, fraud, deceit, bribery, extortion, misappropriation, theft, willful failure to file income tax returns, or an attempt, conspiracy or solicitation of another to commit a serious crime.

(bb) Supreme Court: the Supreme Court of South Carolina.

[Adopted effective January 1, 1997. Amended effective May 22, 1997; August 7, 1997; June 8, 2000; September 1, 2003; April 4, 2007; January 1, 2010; January 19, 2011.]

RULE 3. THE COMMISSION ON JUDICIAL CONDUCT

(a) Commission Created. There is hereby created a Commission on Judicial Conduct.

(b) Jurisdiction.

(1) *Judges.* The Commission has jurisdiction over judges regarding allegations that misconduct occurred before or during service as a judge and regarding allegations of incapacity during service as a judge.

(2) *Former Judges.* The Commission has continuing jurisdiction over former judges regarding allegations that misconduct occurred during service as a judge. The Commission shall also have jurisdiction over allegations that a former judge has made false statements or presented false evidence, or has committed conduct which would be a ground for discipline under Rule 7(a)(2), during a disciplinary proceeding against the former judge even if the conduct did not occur during the time of service as a judge, and the Commission may recommend the imposition of a sanction under Rule 7(b) or may recommend that a finding of criminal contempt be made by the Supreme Court for this conduct.

(c) Appointment. The Commission shall be composed of 26 members appointed by the Supreme Court. 10 members shall be judges from the circuit court or family court or masters-in-equity. 4 members shall be judges from the magistrate, municipal or probate courts. 4 members shall be active members of the South Carolina Bar who have never held a judicial office. 8 members shall be public members.

(d) Terms. Commission members shall serve for a term of 4 years and shall be eligible for reappointment. A member assigned to a hearing panel may continue to participate in the hearing and decision of a matter despite the expiration of the member's term if the hearing began before the expiration of the term.

(e) Removal. The Supreme Court may remove any member of the Commission.

(f) Vacancies. A vacancy shall occur when a Commission member ceases to be eligible to represent the category from which the member was appointed, is removed, or becomes unable to serve for any reason. An appointment to fill the vacancy shall be made by the Supreme Court. A member selected to fill a vacancy shall hold office for the duration of the unexpired term.

[Adopted effective January 1, 1997. Amended effective July 6, 2000; January 1, 2010.]

RULE 4. ORGANIZATION AND AUTHORITY OF THE COMMISSION

(a) Officers. The Supreme Court shall appoint one member to serve as the chair and another to serve as the vice-chair of the Commission. The vice-chair shall perform the duties of the chair whenever the chair is absent or unable to act.

(b) Panels and Meetings. The members of the Commission, other than the chair, vice-chair and public members, shall be divided by the chair into 4 panels of 6 members. Each panel shall be composed of 2 members who are judges from the circuit court, judges from the family court or masters-in-equity; 1 member who is a judge from the magistrate, municipal or probate courts; 1 attorney member; and 2 public members. The panels shall be assigned to serve as an investigative panel or a hearing panel as designated by the chair. If the panel is assigned to serve as an investigative panel, the chair shall add either the chair or the vice-chair to the panel to increase its membership to 7. The chair may rotate the assignments of the panels as investigative or hearing panels, and may rotate membership on the panels; provided, however, that no member shall sit on both the investigative and hearing panel for the same proceeding. Panels shall meet when scheduled by the Commission. The full Commission shall meet periodically as determined by the Commission to consider administrative matters. Meetings of the Commission other than periodic meetings may be called by the chair upon the chair's own motion and shall be called by the chair upon the written request of 3 members of the Commission.

(c) Quorum. 10 members of the full Commission, 5 members of an investigative panel and 3 members of a hearing panel shall constitute a quorum for the transaction of business. Where necessary to obtain a quorum for a panel, the chair of the Commission may appoint substitute members from another panel; provided, however, that no member who has served on an investigative panel in a matter may be appointed to serve on the hearing panel for that matter.

(d) Expenses. Subject to such policies as the Office of Finance and Personnel of the Judicial Department may establish, members shall be reimbursed for reasonable and necessary expenses incurred pursuant to their duties.

(e) Powers and Duties of the Commission.

(1) The Commission shall have the duty and authority to:

(A) adopt its own rules of procedure for discipline and incapacity proceedings subject to the approval of the Supreme Court; and

(B) propose amendments to the Code of Judicial Conduct and these Rules for Judicial Disciplinary Enforcement to the Supreme Court.

(2) In addition to the duties assigned to Commission counsel in Rule 6, the Commission may delegate to Commission counsel the duty and authority to:

(A) maintain the Commission's records;

(B) maintain statistics concerning the operation of the Commission and make them available to the Commission and the Supreme Court;

(C) prepare an annual report of the Commission's activities for presentation to the Supreme Court and the public;

(D) inform the public of the existence and operation of the judicial discipline system, including the Commission's address and telephone number and the disposition of each matter in which public discipline is imposed;

(E) monitor judges for compliance with conditions of discipline and deferred discipline and refer judges who fail to comply to disciplinary counsel for contempt proceedings; and,

(F) supervise attorneys, court reporters, and other staff as the Supreme Court may provide to the Commission.

(f) Powers and Duties of Investigative Panel. An investigative panel shall have the duty and authority to:

(1) review the recommendations of disciplinary counsel after investigation and either issue a letter of caution, issue notice of intent to impose a confidential admonition, enter into a deferred discipline agreement, consider an agreement for discipline by consent, authorize formal charges, refer the matter to another agency, or dismiss the complaint;

(2) designate a member of the panel to preside over the investigative panel in the absence of the chair or vice-chair of the Commission; and

(3) declare a matter closed but not dismissed prior to the filing of formal charges; and,

(4) after proper notice, re-open a matter that has been previously dismissed or closed but not dismissed.

(g) Powers and Duties of Hearing Panel. A hearing panel shall have the duty and authority to:

(1) rule on pre-hearing motions, conduct hearings on formal charges and make findings, conclusions, and recommendations to the Supreme Court for the disposition of the case, pursuant to Rule 26;

(2) designate a member of the panel to serve as the chair of the panel; and

(3) declare, after proper notice, a matter closed, but not dismissed, after the filing of formal charges.

(h) Recusal. A member of the Commission shall recuse himself or herself in any matter in which recusal would be required of a judicial officer under the Code of Judicial Conduct.

(i) Complaints Against Members of the Commission. If a complaint is filed against a member of the Commission who is a judge, the Commission member against whom the complaint has been filed shall not participate in the investigation or adjudication of the matter.

[Adopted effective January 1, 1997. Amended effective July 6, 2000; September 1, 2003; March 1, 2004; May 26, 2006; April 4, 2007; January 1, 2010; January 19, 2011.]

RULE 5. DISCIPLINARY COUNSEL

(a) Appointment. The Supreme Court shall appoint an active member of the South Carolina Bar as disciplinary counsel. Disciplinary counsel may be removed by a majority vote of the Supreme Court. Disciplinary counsel shall not otherwise engage in the practice of law, except to the extent a staff attorney would be authorized to do so under Rule 506, SCACR, or serve in a judicial capacity.

(b) Powers and Duties. Disciplinary counsel shall have the authority and duty to:

(1) receive and screen complaints, dismiss complaints, issue letters of caution, refer complaints to other agencies when appropriate, conduct investigations, notify complainants about the status and disposition of their complaints, make recommendations to an investigative panel on the disposition of complaints after investigation, file formal charges when directed to do so by an investigative panel, prosecute formal charges, and file briefs and other appropriate petitions with the Supreme Court;

(2) maintain permanent records of the operations of disciplinary counsel's office, including receipt of complaints, screening, investigation, and filing of formal charges in judicial discipline and incapacity matters, subject to the requirements of Rule 20;

(3) compile statistics to aid in the administration of the system, including but not limited to a log of all complaints received, investigative files, and statistical summaries of docket processing and case dispositions;

(4) supervise such other attorneys, investigators and staff as the Supreme Court or the Attorney General may provide;

(5) employ private investigators or experts as necessary to investigate and process matters before the Commission and the Supreme Court;

(6) initiate and prosecute proceedings before the Commission and the Supreme Court to enforce orders related to disciplinary proceedings or related to the conduct of judicial duties by judges and to seek restraining orders and sanctions in connection with violations thereof;

(7) dismiss a matter where a judge subject to a pending complaint dies prior to an agreement for discipline by consent or report of the hearing panel being submitted to the Supreme Court; and,

(8) perform other duties at the direction of the Commission or the Supreme Court.

(c) Appointment of Attorneys to Assist Disciplinary Counsel. The Supreme Court may appoint such additional active members of the South Carolina Bar as it deems appropriate to assist disciplinary counsel in performing disciplinary counsel's duties under this rule. Subject to such policies as the Office of Finance and Personnel of the Judicial Department may establish, these attorneys shall be reimbursed for reasonable and necessary expenses incurred pursuant to their duties.

[Adopted effective January 1, 1997. Amended effective September 1, 2003; May 26, 2006; November 15, 2007; January 1, 2010; January 19, 2011.]

RULE 6. COMMISSION COUNSEL

(a) Appointment. The Supreme Court may appoint a Commission counsel to assist the Commission.

(b) Powers and Duties. The Commission may delegate functions to the Commission counsel, including but not limited to the duty and authority to:

(1) advise the hearing panel during its deliberations and draft decisions, orders, reports and other documents on behalf of the hearing panel;

(2) supervise other staff necessary to the performance of the Commission's duties; and

(3) perform other duties at the direction of the Commission.

[Adopted effective January 1, 1997.]

RULE 7. GROUNDS FOR DISCIPLINE; SANCTIONS IMPOSED; DEFERRED DISCIPLINE AGREEMENT

(a) Grounds for Discipline. It shall be a ground for discipline for a judge to:

(1) violate or attempt to violate the Code of Judicial Conduct or the Rules of Professional Conduct or any other applicable ethics codes;

(2) willfully violate a valid order of the Supreme Court, Commission or panels of the Commission in a proceeding under these rules, willfully fail to appear personally as directed, willfully fail to comply with a subpoena issued under these rules, or knowingly fail to respond to a lawful demand from a disciplinary authority to include a request for a response or appearance under Rule 19(b)(1), (c)(3) or (c)(4);

(3) be convicted of a crime of moral turpitude or a serious crime;

(4) persistently fail to perform judicial duties or persistently perform judicial duties in an incompetent or neglectful manner;

(5) be habitually intemperate;

(6) consistently fail to timely issue orders, decrees, opinions or otherwise perform official duties without just cause or excuse;

(7) willfully violate a valid court order issued by a court of this state or another jurisdiction;

(8) willfully fail to comply with the terms of a finally accepted deferred disciplinary agreement or any terms of a finally accepted agreement for discipline by consent;

(9) violate the Judge's Oath of Office contained in Rule 502.1, SCACR.

(b) Sanctions. Misconduct shall be grounds for one or more of the following sanctions:

(1) *removal From Office by the Supreme Court.* The removal shall operate as a permanent injunction prohibiting the judge from holding any judicial office within the unified judicial system in South Carolina. On petition, the Supreme Court may dissolve this permanent injunction;

(2) *suspension by the Supreme Court.* The Supreme Court may also make a recommendation to the appropriate authority that the judge not be reappointed to the office at the end of the judge's term;

(3) public reprimand;

(4) admonition by an investigative panel of the Commission or by the Supreme Court with the consent of the judge, provided that an admonition may be used in subsequent proceedings as evidence of prior misconduct solely upon the issue of sanction to be imposed;

(5) admonition, provided that an admonition may be used in subsequent proceedings as evidence of prior misconduct solely upon the issue of sanction to be imposed;

(6) assessment of the costs of the proceeding, including the cost of hearings, investigations, service of process and court reporter services;

(7) limitations on the nature and extent of the judge's performance of judicial duties; or

(8) any other sanction or requirement as the Supreme Court may determine is appropriate.

[Adopted effective January 1, 1997. Amended effective January 1, 1997; August 7, 1997; June 8, 2000; September 1, 2003; September 22, 2004; April 4, 2007.]

RULE 8. PROOF

Charges of misconduct or incapacity shall be established by clear and convincing evidence, and the burden of proof of the charges shall be on the disciplinary counsel. The burden of proof in proceedings seeking reinstatement following suspension or transfer to judicial incapacity inactive status is on the judge by clear and convincing evidence.

[Adopted effective January 1, 1997.]

RULE 9. CIVIL RULES APPLICABLE

Except as otherwise provided in these rules, the South Carolina Rules of Evidence applicable to nonjury civil proceedings and the South Carolina Rules of

Civil Procedure apply in judicial discipline and incapacity cases when formal charges have been filed. The right to discovery, however, shall be limited to that provided by Rule 25.

[Adopted effective January 1, 1997. Amended effective September 1, 2003.]

RULE 10. RIGHT TO COUNSEL

The judge shall be entitled to retain counsel and to have the assistance of counsel at every stage of these proceedings. The Commission may appoint counsel to represent the judge in incapacity proceedings. See Rule 28(b)(3). After appearing as counsel for a judge in a matter under these rules, counsel for the judge may only withdraw upon leave of the chair, vice chair, or a panel of the Commission after 10 days notice to disciplinary counsel and the judge or, prior to formal charges having been filed, upon stipulation of the judge, the withdrawing counsel and disciplinary counsel. Provided, after a matter has been forwarded to the Supreme Court for action, counsel can only withdraw from representation upon leave of the Supreme Court after due notice to the client and disciplinary counsel.

[Adopted effective January 1, 1997. Amended effective September 1, 2003.]

RULE 11. EX PARTE CONTACTS

Members of the Commission and Commission counsel shall not engage in *ex parte* communications regarding a case, except that before making a determination to file formal charges in a case pursuant to Rule 19(d)(4), members of the investigative panel assigned to that case may communicate with disciplinary counsel as required to perform their duties in accordance with these rules and the chair and vice-chair may entertain requests for permissive disclosure pursuant to Rule 12(c) made by disciplinary counsel without notice to the judge. Where disciplinary counsel makes a request to the chair or vice-chair pursuant to either Rule 12(c) or 19(b) without notice to the judge, the request shall so state and set forth the reason that notice is not being given. *Ex parte* communications shall include any communication which would be prohibited by Section 3B(7) of the Code of Judicial Conduct, Rule 501, SCACR, if engaged in by a judge.

[Adopted effective January 1, 1997. Amended effective September 1, 2003; January 1, 2010.]

RULE 12. ACCESS TO DISCIPLINARY INFORMATION

(a) General Rule. Except as otherwise provided in these rules or ordered by the Supreme Court, the members of the Commission, the staff of the Commission, disciplinary counsel, the staff of disciplinary counsel, the members of the Supreme Court and the staff of the Supreme Court shall not in any way reveal the existence of the complaint, while the matter remains confidential, except to persons directly involved in the matter and then only to the extent necessary for a proper disposition of the matter. A violation of this provision may be punished as a contempt of the Supreme Court.

(b) When Misconduct Proceedings Become Public. When formal charges are filed regarding allegations of misconduct, the formal charges and any answer shall become public 30 days after the filing of the answer or, if no answer is filed, 30 days after the expiration of the time to answer under Rule 23. Thereafter, except as otherwise provided by these rules or the Supreme Court, all subsequent records and proceedings relating to the misconduct allegations shall be open to the public inclusive of a letter of caution or admonition issued after the filing of formal charges. If allegations of incapacity are raised during the misconduct proceedings, all records, information and proceedings relating to these allegations shall be held confidential.

(c) Permissive Disclosure by Commission. The Commission may, however, disclose information at any stage of the proceedings:

(1) when the chair, vice-chair or a panel of the Commission has determined that there is a need to notify another person to protect that person or to notify a government agency in order to protect the public or the administration of justice;

(2) to appropriate law enforcement officials when the chair, vice-chair or a panel of the Commission determines that it is in possession of reliable information indicating that a person has violated the criminal laws of this State, any other state, the District of Columbia, or the United States;

(3) upon waiver in writing by the judge;

(4) to persons from whom and entities from which it appears that a judge has misappropriated monies or other property when the chair or vice-chair or a panel of the Commission has determined that the disclosure of the information will tend to prevent further misappropriation or likely facilitate restitution, recovery, or compensation; or,

(5) to the appropriate disciplinary authority in any jurisdiction in which a judge is admitted to practice law or has applied for admission to practice law concerning a matter where there is evidence the judge committed misconduct under any lawyer or judicial disciplinary rules of that jurisdiction or where a judge receives any sanction under Rule 7(b).

(d) Protective Orders. In order to protect the interests of a complainant, witness, third party or respondent, the hearing panel may, upon application of any person and for good cause shown, issue a protective order prohibiting the disclosure of specific information otherwise privileged or confidential and direct that the proceedings be conducted in a manner to preserve the confidentiality of the information that is the subject of the application.

(e) Work Product and Deliberations. Disciplinary counsel's work product, Commission deliberations, and records of the Commission's deliberations shall not be disclosed.

(f) Permissive disclosure by the parties. Either party may disclose in proceedings before a hearing panel statements and other evidence, gathered prior to the matter becoming public after the filing of formal charges, that were subject to discovery under Rule 25 to the extent admissible under the South Carolina Rules of Civil Procedure or South Carolina Rules of Evidence.

[Adopted effective January 1, 1997. Amended effective March 6, 1997; September 1, 2003; January 1, 2010.]

RULE 13. IMMUNITY FROM CIVIL SUITS

Communications to the Commission, Commission counsel, disciplinary counsel, or their staffs relating to misconduct or incapacity and testimony given in the proceedings shall be absolutely privileged, and no civil lawsuit predicated thereon may be instituted against any complainant or witness. Members of the Commission, Commission counsel and staff, and disciplinary counsel and staff shall be absolutely immune from civil suit for all conduct in the course of their official duties.

[Adopted effective January 1, 1997.]

RULE 14. TIME, SERVICE AND FILING

(a) Computation of Time. Computation of time under these rules shall be in the manner provided by Rule 263, SCACR.

(b) Extending and Diminishing Time Prescribed by These Rules.

(1) *By the Commission.* The chair of the Commission, the vice-chair of the Commission, or the chair of the hearing panel before which the matter is pending, may extend or shorten the period of time to perform any act required by Rules 19–26. Any request for an extension by an investigative panel or hearing panel shall be considered by the chair or vice-chair of the Commission. No extension over 30 days shall be granted except upon good cause shown. The grant or denial of an extension shall not be subject to an interlocutory appeal.

(2) *By Disciplinary Counsel.* Disciplinary counsel may extend the time for responses due from a judge under Rule 19 for one or more periods not to exceed 30 days in the aggregate for each.

(3) *By the Parties.* Disciplinary counsel and the judge may, by written agreement, extend the time to respond under Rule 19 or 23(a) after the execution and delivery by both parties of an agreement for discipline by consent or deferred disciplinary agreement for the duration of the period the agreement is awaiting a final disposition and for a period of 30 days thereafter if the Agreement is not accepted.

(4) *By the Supreme Court.* Except for those periods of time that may be extended by the Commission under (1) above, the Supreme Court or any justice thereof may grant an extension of time to perform any act required by these rules. The Supreme Court or any justice thereof may shorten any time period prescribed by these rules.

(c) Service. Service upon the judge of formal charges in any disciplinary or incapacity proceedings shall be made by personal service upon the judge or the judge's counsel by any person authorized by the chair of the Commission, or by registered or certified mail, return receipt requested, to the judge's last known address. If service cannot be so made, service shall be deemed complete when deposited in the U.S. Mail, provided the formal charges were sent by registered or certified mail, return receipt requested, to the address the judge provided to the South Carolina Bar pursuant to Rule 410(e), SCACR, and to the judge's last known address, if those addresses differ. Service of all other documents shall be made in the manner provided by Rule 262(b), SCACR.

(d) Filing. When these rules require filing of a document with the Commission or the Supreme Court, the filing may be accomplished by:

(1) Delivering the document to the Commission or the clerk of the Supreme Court; or

(2) Depositing the document in the U.S. mail, properly addressed to the Commission or the clerk of the Supreme Court, with sufficient first class postage attached.

The date of filing shall be the date of delivery or the date of mailing. Any document filed with the Supreme Court or the Commission shall be accompanied by proof of service of such document on all other parties. An electronically transmitted facsimile copy of a document may be accepted for filing; however, an original of the document must be immediately sent by U.S. mail to the clerk of the Supreme Court or the Commission.

[Adopted effective January 1, 1997. Amended effective September 1, 2003; November 15, 2007; January 1, 2010; March 22, 2010.]

RULE 15. OATHS; SUBPOENA POWER

(a) Oaths. Oaths and affirmations may be administered by any member of the Commission, disciplinary counsel, or any other person authorized by law to administer oaths and affirmations.

(b) Subpoenas for Investigation.

(1) Disciplinary counsel may compel by subpoena the attendance of the judge or witnesses and the production of pertinent books, papers, documents (whether in typed, written, digital, electronic or other format), and other tangible evidence, for the purposes of investigation.

(2) The Commission chair, vice-chair, or Commission counsel may issue subpoenas for specific witnesses or documents at the request of the judge under investigation or direct disciplinary counsel to subpoena witnesses or documents and provide the subpoenaed information to the Commission chair, vice-chair or Commission counsel.

(c) Subpoenas for Deposition or Hearing. After formal charges are filed, disciplinary counsel and respondent may compel by subpoena the attendance of witnesses and the production of pertinent books, papers, and documents at a deposition or hearing held under these rules.

(d) Enforcement of Subpoenas. The willful failure to comply with a subpoena issued under this rule may be punished as a contempt of the Supreme Court. Upon proper application, the Supreme Court may enforce the attendance and testimony of any witnesses and the production of any documents subpoenaed.

(e) Quashing Subpoenas. Any attack on the validity of a subpoena shall be heard and determined by the investigative or hearing panel before which the matter is pending. Any resulting order shall not be subject to an interlocutory appeal; instead, these decisions must be challenged by filing objections or a brief pursuant to Rule 27(a).

(f) Subpoena Pursuant to Law of Another Jurisdiction. Whenever a subpoena is sought in this State pursuant to the law or disciplinary rules of another jurisdiction for use in lawyer or judicial disciplinary or disability proceedings, and where the issuance of the subpoena has been duly approved under the applicable laws or rules of the other jurisdiction, the chair or vice-chair or a panel of the Commission upon a showing of good cause, may issue a subpoena to compel the attendance of witnesses and the production of documents in the county where the witness resides or is employed or elsewhere in this state as agreed by the witness. Service, enforcement, or challenges to such subpoenas shall be as provided in these rules.

[Adopted effective January 1, 1997. Amended effective April 18, 1997; September 1, 2003; November 15, 2007; January 1, 2010.]

RULE 16. JUDGES CHARGED WITH OR CONVICTED OF A CRIME

(a) Transmittal of Charging Documents. The clerk of any court in this state shall transmit a certified copy of any indictment, information or complaint charging a judge with a crime to the disciplinary counsel within 10 days of the filing of such charging document.

(b) Transmittal of Certificate of Conviction. The clerk of any court in this state in which a judge is convicted of a crime shall, within 10 days after the conviction, transmit a certified copy of the judgment of conviction to disciplinary counsel.

(c) Action by Disciplinary Counsel. Upon receiving competent evidence that a judge has been charged or convicted of a crime, disciplinary counsel shall determine whether the crime involved is a serious crime as defined by Rule 2(aa). If the crime is a serious crime, disciplinary counsel may seek an interim suspension under Rule 17(a) if the judge has been charged with a serious crime, and shall seek an interim suspension under Rule 17(a) if the judge has been convicted of a serious crime. If the crime is not a serious crime, disciplinary counsel shall process the matter in the same manner as any other information coming to the attention of the Commission.

(d) Conviction as Conclusive Evidence. A certified copy of a judgment of conviction constitutes conclusive evidence that the judge committed the crime, and the sole issue in any disciplinary proceedings based on the conviction shall be the nature and extent of the discipline imposed.

(e) Stay of Hearing; Effect of Acquittal, Dismissal of Charges, or Reversal or Vacation of Conviction. The hearing under Rule 26 shall not be held until all direct appeals from the conviction are exhausted. An acquittal, dismissal of the criminal charges, or reversal or vacation of a conviction shall not automatically terminate any proceeding then pending against the judge, and the Commission may proceed on the basis of the available evidence other than the charge or the conviction.

[Adopted effective January 1, 1997.]

RULE 17. INTERIM SUSPENSION

(a) Criminal Prosecution or Conviction for a Serious Crime. Without the necessity of Commission action, the Supreme Court may place a judge on interim suspension upon notice of the filing of an indictment, information or complaint charging the judge with a serious crime, and shall immediately place a judge on interim suspension on receipt of a certified copy of a judgment of conviction or other competent evidence showing that the judge has been convicted of a serious crime. The fact that sentencing may be delayed or an appeal may be taken shall not prevent the Supreme Court from imposing an interim suspension.

(b) Other Misconduct or Incapacity. Upon receipt of sufficient evidence demonstrating that a judge poses a substantial threat of serious harm to the public or to the administration of justice, the Supreme Court may suspend the judge or transfer the judge to incapacity inactive status pending a final determination in any proceeding under these rules.

(c) Failure to Respond to Notice of Investigation, Subpoena, or Notice of Appearance. Upon receipt of sufficient evidence demonstrating that a judge has failed to fully respond to a notice of investigation, has failed to fully comply with a proper subpoena issued in connection with an investigation or formal charges, has failed to appear at and fully respond to inquiries at an appearance required pursuant to Rule 19(c)(3), or has failed to respond to inquiries or directives of the Commission or the Supreme Court, the Supreme Court may place that judge on interim suspension.

(d) Motion for Reconsideration. A judge placed on interim suspension or transferred to incapacity inactive status may apply to the Supreme Court for reconsideration of the order. A copy of the motion shall be filed with the Commission and served on disciplinary counsel.

(e) Order to Be Public. The order of interim suspension or transfer to incapacity inactive status shall be public. Unless the Supreme Court determines that it is appropriate to do so, an order transferring a judge to incapacity inactive status shall not disclose the nature of the incapacity.

[Adopted effective January 1, 1997. Amended effective September 1, 2003; January 1, 2010; June 1, 2010.]

RULE 18. NOTIFICATION TO COMPLAINANT; LIMITED RIGHT TO REVIEW

(a) Notification to Complainant. Disciplinary counsel shall provide written acknowledgment of every complaint, if the complainant is known, and notify the complainant in writing of the final disposition of a proceeding under these rules. Notification in writing shall be mailed within 20 days of the decision disposing of the proceeding.

(b) Limited Right to Review. Although entitled to notice, a complainant is not a party to the proceeding. However, upon notice of a dismissal by disciplinary counsel pursuant to Rule 19(d)(1), a complainant may seek review by the investigative panel. Disciplinary counsel shall inform the complainant of the following review process in the notice of dismissal. The complainant may seek review by submitting a request to disciplinary counsel in writing within 30 days of the date of the notice of dismissal. Upon receipt of the request for review, disciplinary counsel shall provide the judge with a copy of the request. The judge may submit a written response within 15 days. Disciplinary counsel shall submit the complainant's request and the judge's response, if any, for consideration at the next meeting of the investigative panel. Notification in writing shall be mailed to the complainant and the judge within 20 days of the investigative panel's decision. The complainant is not entitled to appeal or otherwise seek review of a dismissal or referral by disciplinary counsel pursuant to Rule 19(a) or of any decision, action, or disposition by the investigative panel, the hearing panel, the Commission chair or vice-chair, or the Supreme Court.

[Amended effective January 1, 2010.]

RULE 19. SCREENING AND INVESTIGATION

(a) Screening. Disciplinary counsel shall evaluate all information coming to disciplinary counsel's attention by complaint or from other sources that alleges judicial misconduct or incapacity. If the information would not constitute misconduct or incapacity if it were true, disciplinary counsel shall dismiss the complaint or, if appropriate, refer the matter to another agency. If the information raises allegations that would constitute judicial misconduct or incapacity if true, disciplinary counsel shall conduct an investigation.

(b) Investigation. Disciplinary counsel shall conduct all investigations. Disciplinary counsel may issue subpoenas pursuant to Rule 15(b), conduct interviews and examine evidence to determine whether grounds exist to believe the allegations of complaints. Disciplinary counsel shall issue a notice of investigation to the judge with a copy of the complaint or information received, requesting that the judge file a response to the allegations in the notice; provided, however, that disciplinary counsel may seek permission of the chair or vice-chair to dispense with the requirement to make this request or to dispense with the requirement to provide the judge with a copy of the complaint or information received. The judge shall file a written response within 15 days of notice to do so from disciplinary counsel. The written response must include the judge's verification that it is complete and accurate to the best of the judge's knowledge and belief.

(c) Requirements of Notice of Investigation.

(1) When issuing notice of investigation pursuant to Rule 19(b), disciplinary counsel shall give the following notice to the judge:

(A) a specific statement of the allegations being investigated and the canons or other ethical standards allegedly violated, with the provision that the investigation can be expanded if deemed appropriate by disciplinary counsel;

(B) the judge's duty to respond pursuant to Rule 19(b);

(C) the judge's opportunity to meet with disciplinary counsel pursuant to Rule 19(c)(3); and,

(D) the name of the complainant unless the investigative panel determines that there is good cause to withhold that information.

(2) The investigative panel may defer the giving of notice but, when notice is deferred, disciplinary counsel must give notice to the judge before making a recommendation as to a disposition.

(3) Before disciplinary counsel or the investigative panel determines its disposition of the complaint under Rule 19(d), either disciplinary counsel or the judge may request that the judge appear before disciplinary counsel to respond to questions. The appearance shall be on the record and the testimony shall be under oath

or affirmation. If disciplinary counsel requests the judge's appearance, disciplinary counsel must give the judge 20 days' notice.

(4) Any person giving testimony pursuant to either Rule 19 shall be entitled to obtain a transcript of his or her testimony from the transcribing court reporter upon paying the subscribed charges unless otherwise directed by an investigative panel for good cause shown.

(d) Disposition After Investigation.

(1) Upon completion of investigation, if disciplinary counsel believes that no misconduct has been committed, and a written caution or warning is not appropriate to conclude the matter, disciplinary counsel may dismiss the complaint.

(2) If disciplinary counsel believes that no misconduct has been committed, but a written caution or warning is appropriate to conclude the matter, disciplinary counsel may issue a letter of caution.

(3) If disciplinary counsel believes there is evidence supporting the allegations against a judge, disciplinary counsel may:

(A) propose an agreement for discipline by consent to the judge pursuant to Rule 21;

(B) recommend to an investigative panel that the matter be concluded with a letter of caution or a confidential admonition; or,

(C) recommend to an investigative panel that formal charges be filed.

(4) The investigative panel may adopt, reject or modify the recommendations of disciplinary counsel.

(A) If the investigative panel finds no violation or a violation pursuant to Rule 7 for which the imposition of a sanction is not warranted, it may dismiss or issue a letter of caution.

(B) If the investigative panel finds that there is reasonable cause to believe the judge committed misconduct for which the imposition of a sanction is warranted, it may accept an agreement for discipline by consent pursuant to Rule 21; it may execute a deferred discipline agreement; it may admonish the judge pursuant to the provisions of Rule 19(d)(5); or, it may direct disciplinary counsel to file formal charges.

(C) If the investigative panel finds that the matter should not be dismissed, but it is either impossible or impractical to proceed with the matter because it appears that the judge is deceased, disappeared, incarcerated, or physically or mentally incapacitated, or for other good cause, the panel may designate the matter closed but not dismissed. If the judge files a written objection with the Commission and serves a copy of that objection on disciplinary counsel within 10 days of service of notice that the matter was closed, but not dismissed, the matter shall be deemed re-opened and in the investigation phase. Any objection need not contain any grounds for objecting. Before a matter can be re-opened after being closed, but not dismissed, an investigative panel of the Commission must make a finding that there has been a change in the circumstances that were the basis for the matter to be closed, but not dismissed, or that there is other good cause for it to be re-opened. Before a motion can be considered by an investigative panel of the Commission to re-open a matter that has been previously closed, but not dismissed, disciplinary counsel shall serve a copy of the motion to do so containing the grounds to re-open on the judge and then the judge shall have 10 days to respond thereto. Disciplinary counsel shall notify both the judge and the complainant when a matter is closed, but not dismissed and when the matter is re-opened. If the panel declines to re-open the matter, disciplinary counsel shall so advise the judge.

(5) When the investigative panel finds reasonable cause to conclude that the judge has committed misconduct, but finds that public discipline is not warranted, it may issue notice to the judge that it intends to impose a confidential admonition as a final disposition of the matter(s). Notice to the judge shall include a copy of the confidential admonition and shall be served on the judge in accordance with Rule 14(c). The notice of intent shall state the judge's right to object and that any such objection need not include any grounds therefor. The confidential admonition shall thereafter be imposed unless the judge both files with the Commission and serves on disciplinary counsel a written objection within 30 days of mailing of the notice. If the judge objects to the imposition of the confidential admonition in conformity with the requirements of this rule, disciplinary counsel shall file formal charges.

[Adopted effective January 1, 1997. Amended effective April 18, 1997; August 7, 1997; June 8, 2000; September 1, 2003; May 26, 2006; April 4, 2007; January 1, 2010; January 19, 2011.]

RULE 20. MOTION BY DISCIPLINARY COUNSEL TO RE-OPEN DISMISSED COMPLAINTS

If a complaint has been dismissed, the allegations made in that complaint shall not be used for any purpose unless the complaint is re-opened by the Commission. A complaint dismissed prior to the filing of formal charges may be re-opened by an investigative panel upon motion of disciplinary counsel upon a finding by the investigative panel that there is new information concerning the matter dismissed, an additional complaint has been filed against the same judge involving related or similar allegations, or other good cause. Prior to a motion to re-open being decided, a copy of the motion to reopen containing the grounds therefor shall be served on the judge by disciplinary counsel, and the judge shall then have 10 days thereafter to file a written response with the Commission.

The judge and the complainant shall be notified by disciplinary counsel as to the panel's decision on the motion to re-open.

[Adopted effective January 1, 1997. Amended effective September 1, 2003; January 1, 2010.]

RULE 21. DISCIPLINE BY CONSENT

(a) Agreement. At any stage in the proceedings, the judge and disciplinary counsel may agree to the imposition of a stated sanction(s) or the issuance of a letter of caution in exchange for the judge's admission of any or all of the allegations of misconduct involved in the proceedings. If the agreement is entered into after the filing of the formal charges, the agreement shall admit or deny the allegations contained in the formal charges. If the agreement is entered into before the filing of the formal charges, the agreement shall contain the specific factual allegations which the judge admits he or she has committed and the applicable provisions of the Code of Judicial Conduct or other ethical or disciplinary provisions that the judge has violated. The agreement shall be signed by disciplinary counsel, by the judge and, if the judge is represented by counsel, by the judge's counsel. The signature of the judge's counsel on the agreement shall indicate that counsel has advised the judge regarding the agreement and that counsel believes the judge is voluntarily entering into the agreement with a full understanding of the effect of the agreement.

(b) Affidavit. The judge shall also sign an affidavit stating that:

(1) the judge consents to the sanction(s) or letter of caution;

(2) the consent is voluntarily given;

(3) the matters admitted in the agreement and the facts stated in the affidavit are true.

(c) Submission to Panel. The agreement and affidavit shall be submitted to an investigative panel if formal charges have not been filed, or to a hearing panel if formal charges have been filed on any of the allegations. Provided, if formal charges have been filed but not heard, an investigative panel can consider the proposed agreement and affidavit if the parties both agree in writing. The panel shall either reject the agreement, or submit the agreement and affidavit to the Supreme Court if it determines the agreement should be accepted. An investigative panel shall, however, finally approve or disapprove an agreement for an admonition, a deferred discipline agreement or a letter of caution and, if approved, shall impose the sanction or issue the letter of caution without submitting the matter to the Supreme Court.

(d) Action by Supreme Court. If the panel submits the matter to the Supreme Court, the Supreme Court shall either reject the agreement or issue a decision disciplining the judge which shall be based on the agreement. The decision shall comply with the requirements of Rule 27(e).

(e) Effect of Rejection of Agreement. If an agreement is rejected by the panel or the Supreme Court, the proceedings shall continue. The rejected agreement and affidavit shall be withdrawn and shall not be used against the judge in any further proceedings.

(f) Confidentiality. The agreement, affidavit and any statement or other documents submitted in mitigation shall remain confidential until the Supreme Court enters a decision disciplining the judge at which time the agreement, affidavit and any statement or other documents submitted in mitigation shall be available to the public. An agreement and affidavit which are rejected or which result in the imposition of an admonition, a deferred discipline agreement or a letter of caution by an investigative panel, shall not be available to the public at any time, nor shall any statement or other documents in mitigation filed therewith.

(g) Briefs and Oral Arguments. The Supreme Court may require the parties to submit briefs or participate in oral arguments in connection with the agreement. Either the judge or disciplinary counsel may move before the Supreme Court for permission for the parties to file briefs, to have oral arguments, or both in connection with the agreement, but the Supreme Court, in its discretion, may proceed to take action on the agreement without briefs, without oral arguments, or without either, not withstanding a request from one or both of the parties.

[Adopted effective January 1, 1997. Amended effective May 22, 1997; August 7, 1997; July 21, 1999; June 8, 2000; September 1, 2003.]

RULE 22. FORMAL CHARGES

The formal charges shall give fair and adequate notice of the nature of the alleged misconduct or incapacity. Disciplinary counsel shall file the formal charges with the Commission. Disciplinary counsel shall cause a copy of the formal charges to be served upon the respondent or respondent's counsel and shall file proof of service with the Commission.

[Adopted effective January 1, 1997.]

RULE 23. ANSWER

(a) Time. The respondent shall file a written answer with the Commission and serve a copy on disciplinary counsel within 30 days after service of the formal charges, unless the time is extended by the hearing panel.

(b) Waiver of Privilege. The raising of a mental or physical condition as a defense constitutes a waiver of any medical privilege pursuant to Rule 28(d)(4).

[Adopted effective January 1, 1997.]

RULE 24. FAILURE TO ANSWER; FAILURE TO APPEAR

(a) Failure to Answer. Failure to answer the formal charges shall constitute an admission of the factual allegations.

(b) Failure to Appear. If the respondent should fail to appear when specifically so ordered by the hearing panel or the Supreme Court, the respondent shall be deemed to have admitted the factual allegations which were to be the subject of such appearance and to have conceded the merits of any motion or recommendations to be considered at such appearance. Absent good cause, the hearing panel or Supreme Court shall not continue or delay proceedings because of the respondent's failure to appear. A willful failure to appear before a hearing panel or the Supreme Court may be punished as a contempt of the Supreme Court.

[Adopted effective January 1, 1997.]

RULE 25. DISCOVERY

(a) Initial Disclosure. Within 20 days of the filing of an answer, disciplinary counsel and respondent shall exchange:

(1) the names and addresses of all persons known to have knowledge of the relevant facts;

(2) non-privileged evidence relevant to the formal charges;

(3) the names of expert witnesses expected to testify at trial and affidavits setting forth their opinions and the bases therefor; and,

(4) other material only upon good cause shown to the chair of the hearing panel.

Disciplinary counsel or the respondent may withhold such information only with permission of the chair of the hearing panel or the chair's designee, who shall authorize withholding of the information only for good cause shown, taking into consideration the materiality of the information possessed by the witness and the position the witness occupies in relation to the judge. The chair's review of the withholding request is to be in camera, but the party making the request must advise the opposing party of the request without disclosing the subject of the request.

(b) Pre–Hearing Disclosure. Within 20 days of the date of the filing of an answer, the administrative chair of the hearing panel shall set a date for the exchange of witness lists and exhibits no later than 30 days prior to the scheduled hearing. Disciplinary counsel and respondent shall exchange exhibits to be presented at the hearing, names and addresses of witnesses to be called at the hearing, witness statements, and summaries of interviews with witnesses who will be called at the hearing (for purposes of this paragraph, a witness statement is a written statement signed or otherwise adopted or approved by the person making it, or a stenographic, mechanical, electrical, or other recording, or a transcription thereof, which is a substantially verbatim recital of an oral statement by the person making it and contemporaneously recorded). Copies of transcripts of testimony taken by a court reporter pursuant to Rule 15(b) or Rule 19(c) may be obtained by the parties from the court reporter at the expense of the requesting party and need not be made available to the requesting party by the opposing party unless not otherwise available or otherwise directed by the Commission under Rule 25(h).

(c) Depositions. Depositions shall only be allowed if agreed upon by disciplinary counsel and the respondent, or if the chair of the hearing panel or the chair's designee grants permission to do so based on a showing of good cause. The chair or the chair's designee may place restrictions or conditions on the manner, time and place of any authorized deposition.

(d) Exculpatory Evidence. Notwithstanding any other provision of this rule, disciplinary counsel shall provide respondent with exculpatory evidence relevant to the formal charges.

(e) Duty of Supplementation. Both parties have a continuing duty to supplement information required to be exchanged under this rule.

(f) Completion of Discovery. All discovery shall be completed within 60 days of the filing of the answer.

(g) Failure to Disclose. If a party fails to timely disclose a witness's name and address, any statements by the witness, summaries of witness interviews, or other evidence required to be disclosed or exchanged under this rule, the hearing panel may grant a continuance of the hearing, preclude the party from calling the witness or introducing the document, or take such other action as may be appropriate. In the event disciplinary counsel has not timely disclosed exculpatory material, the hearing panel may require the matter to be disclosed and grant a continuance, or take such other action as may be appropriate.

(h) Resolution of Disputes. Disputes concerning discovery shall be determined by the hearing panel. Review of these decisions shall not be subject to an interlocutory appeal; instead these decisions must be challenged by filing objections or a brief pursuant to Rule 27(a).

(i) Pre–Hearing Conferences. The hearing panel may require the respondent and disciplinary counsel to participate in a pre-hearing conference in person or by telephone. Either party may request a pre-hearing conference. Scheduling of a pre-hearing conference is at the sole discretion of the chair of the hearing panel.

[Adopted effective January 1, 1997. Amended effective September 1, 2003; November 15, 2007; January 1, 2010.]

RULE 26. HEARING

(a) Scheduling. Upon receipt of the respondent's answer or upon expiration of the time to answer, the hearing panel of the Commission shall schedule a public hearing and notify disciplinary counsel and respondent of the date, time, and place of the hearing.

(b) Hearing Panel. The hearing shall be conducted by three or more members of the hearing panel of the Commission. See Rule 4(g).

(c) Conduct of Hearing.

(1) All testimony shall be given under oath or affirmation.

(2) Disciplinary counsel shall present evidence on the formal charges.

(3) Disciplinary counsel may call the respondent as a witness.

(4) Both parties shall be permitted to present evidence and produce and cross-examine witnesses.

(5) The hearing shall be recorded verbatim and a transcript shall be promptly prepared and filed with the Commission. A copy of the transcript shall be made available to the respondent at respondent's expense.

(6) Disciplinary counsel and the respondent may submit proposed findings, conclusions, and recommendations for dismissal, letter of caution, sanction(s), or transfer to judicial incapacity inactive status to the members of the hearing panel who conducted the hearing.

(d) Submission of the Report. Within 60 days after the filing of the transcript, the hearing panel shall file with the Supreme Court the record of the proceeding and a report setting forth a written summary, proposed findings of fact, conclusions of law, any minority opinions, and recommendations for dismissal, letter of caution, sanction(s), transfer to judicial incapacity inactive status, or removal or retirement based on incapacity. The hearing panel shall at the same time serve the report upon the respondent and disciplinary counsel.

(e) Combining Cases for Hearing. Upon motion of either party after 10 days notice to the opposing party, a hearing panel may combine for hearing two or more formal charges pending against a judge which have not been heard or may reconvene to hear additional formal charges against a judge filed prior to the hearing panel issuing a panel report concerning formal charges against the judge already heard by that panel.

[Adopted effective January 1, 1997. Amended effective August 7, 1997; September 1, 2003; April 4, 2007; March 22, 2010.]

RULE 27. REVIEW BY SUPREME COURT

(a) Briefs of Disciplinary Counsel and Respondent. Within 30 days of the service of the hearing panel report, disciplinary counsel and/or respondent may serve and file a brief setting forth and arguing any exceptions taken to the findings, conclusions or recommendations made by the hearing panel. Within 30 days after service of the brief, any opposing party may serve and file a brief in response. Within 15 days of the service of the response, the party who filed the brief containing exceptions may serve and file a reply brief. The failure of a party to file a brief taking exceptions to the report constitutes acceptance of the findings of fact, conclusions of law, and recommendations.

(b) Form, Content and Number of Briefs. The form and content of the briefs shall to the extent possible comply with the requirements of Rules 208 and 267, SCACR. The number of briefs to be served and filed shall be the same as that required for final briefs under Rule 211(a), SCACR.

(c) Supplementary Filings and Oral Argument.

(1) If the Supreme Court desires an expansion of the record or additional findings, it shall remand the case to the hearing panel with appropriate directions, retain jurisdiction, and withhold action pending receipt of the additional filing.

(2) The Supreme Court may order additional briefs or oral arguments as to the entire case or specified issues.

(d) Stay for Further Proceedings. If during review by the Supreme Court the Commission receives another complaint against the respondent, disciplinary counsel shall advise the Supreme Court. The Supreme Court may stay its review pending the Commission's determination of the second complaint. The Supreme Court may impose a single sanction covering all recommendations for discipline from the Commission against a respondent.

(e) Decision.

(1) The Supreme Court shall file a written decision dismissing the case, containing a letter of caution, imposing a sanction(s), or transferring the judge to incapacity inactive status. Any order relating to incapacity shall comply with Rule 28(g). Unless otherwise ordered by the Supreme Court, the decision shall be effective upon filing.

(2) The Supreme Court may accept, reject, or modify in whole or in part the findings, conclusions and recommendations of the Commission.

(3) The Supreme Court may assess costs against the respondent if it finds the respondent has committed misconduct. Unless otherwise ordered by the court, costs shall be paid within 30 days of the filing of the opinion or order assessing costs.

(f) Rehearing. A petition for rehearing must be served and filed within 15 days after the filing of the decision or order.

(g) Recusal. A justice of the Supreme Court shall not participate in any proceeding involving allegations of misconduct or incapacity against the justice, or in any proceeding where recusal is required under the Code of Judicial Conduct. Upon notice of recusal, the

Chair of the Commission on Judicial Conduct may appoint a lawyer who is not an employee of the Judicial Department to act as disciplinary counsel in the matter. Following recusal of the affected justice, the Chief Justice (or Acting Chief Justice) shall appoint an acting justice to replace the recused justice for the duration of the case.

[Adopted effective January 1, 1997. Amended effective August 7, 1997; September 9, 1999; January 1, 2010.]

RULE 28. CASES INVOLVING ALLEGATIONS OF MENTAL OR PHYSICAL INCAPACITY

(a) Initiation of Incapacity Proceeding. An incapacity proceeding may be initiated by complaint, by a claim of inability to defend in a disciplinary proceeding, or by an order of involuntary commitment or adjudication of incompetency.

(b) Proceedings to Determine Incapacity Generally. All incapacity proceedings shall be conducted in accordance with the procedures for disciplinary proceedings, except:

(1) the purpose of the incapacity proceedings shall be to determine whether the judge suffers from a physical or mental condition that adversely affects the judge's ability to perform judicial functions;

(2) all of the proceedings, information and documents shall be confidential except as provided in Rule 28(g);

(3) the Commission, if it deems it appropriate, may appoint counsel to represent the judge if the judge is without representation;

(4) the Commission may appoint a guardian ad litem for the judge;

(5) the hearing panel shall designate one or more qualified medical, psychiatric, or psychological experts to examine the judge prior to the hearing on the matter. The hearing panel may designate an expert agreed upon by disciplinary counsel and the judge. The expert or experts shall report to the hearing panel and the parties;

(6) if the Supreme Court concludes that the judge suffers from a physical or mental condition that adversely affects the judge's ability to hold judicial office, it may enter any order appropriate to the circumstances, the nature of the incapacity and probable length of the period of incapacity, including:

(A) retiring or removing the judge from office if the incapacity seriously interferes with the judge's performance of judicial duties and the incapacity is, or is likely to become, of a permanent character;

(B) transferring the judge to judicial incapacity inactive status;

(C) placing restrictions or conditions on the judge, to include limiting the judge's performance of judicial functions or requiring the judge to undergo appropriate treatment;

(D) transferring the judge to the lawyer incapacity status if the judge is a lawyer and the Supreme Court determines the judge is incapacitated to practice law;

(E) deferring any disciplinary proceeding based on misconduct pending against the judge if the Supreme Court determines that the judge is unable to assist in his or her own defense pursuant to Rule 28(d)(2).

(c) Involuntary Commitment or Adjudication of Incompetency. If a judge has been judicially declared incompetent or is involuntarily committed on the grounds of incompetency or incapacity by a final judicial order after a judicial hearing, the Supreme Court, upon receipt of a certified copy of the order, shall enter an order immediately transferring the judge to judicial incapacity inactive status. If the judge is a lawyer, the order shall also transfer the judge to the lawyer incapacity inactive status. A copy of the order shall be served, in the manner the Supreme Court shall direct, upon the judge, the judge's guardian, or the director of the institution to which the judge has been committed.

(d) Inability to Properly Defend in a Disciplinary Proceeding.

(1) If in the course of a disciplinary proceeding based on misconduct, a judge alleges an inability to assist in the defense due to mental or physical incapacity, disciplinary counsel shall notify the Supreme Court. The Supreme Court shall immediately transfer the judge to judicial incapacity inactive status and, if the judge is a lawyer, to the lawyer incapacity inactive status, pending a determination by the Supreme Court of the incapacity pursuant to Rule 28(b). A determination by the Commission that the judge is able to assist in his or her own defense is interlocutory and may not be appealed before entry of a final order in the proceeding.

(2) If, pursuant to Rule 28(b), the Supreme Court determines the claim of inability to defend is valid, the disciplinary proceeding based on misconduct shall be deferred. Any investigation of the disciplinary complaint may continue. The judge shall remain on judicial and lawyer incapacity inactive status until the Supreme Court grants a petition for reinstatement to active status as a judge or lawyer. If the Supreme Court determines that a petition for reinstatement to active status should be granted, the Supreme Court shall also determine the disposition of the interrupted disciplinary proceedings.

(3) If, pursuant to Rule 28(b), the Supreme Court determines that the claim of inability to defend is invalid, the disciplinary proceeding based on misconduct shall resume. The judge shall, however, be retained on judicial and lawyer incapacity inactive

status pending completion of the disciplinary proceedings.

(4) The raising of mental or physical condition as a defense to, or in mitigation of, formal charges constitutes a waiver of any medical privilege.

(e) Stipulated Disposition.

(1) After receipt of the examination report of the expert or experts designated by the hearing panel, disciplinary counsel and the judge may agree upon proposed findings of fact, conclusions, and recommended disposition. The stipulated disposition shall be submitted to the hearing panel for a recommendation to the Supreme Court of approval or rejection. The final decision on the recommendation shall be made by the Supreme Court.

(2) If the Supreme Court accepts the stipulated disposition, it shall enter an order in accordance with its terms. If the stipulated disposition is rejected by the Supreme Court, it shall be withdrawn and cannot be used against the judge in any proceedings. If the Supreme Court rejects the stipulated disposition, the Supreme Court shall order that the hearing proceed.

(f) Reinstatement From Incapacity Inactive Status.

(1) *Generally.* No judge transferred to incapacity inactive status may resume active status except by order of the Supreme Court.

(2) *Petition.* Any judge transferred to incapacity inactive status shall be entitled to petition for transfer to active status once a year or at whatever shorter intervals the Supreme Court may direct in the order transferring the judge to incapacity inactive status or any modifications thereof. The judge shall serve a copy of the petition on disciplinary counsel, and shall file 10 copies filed with the Clerk shall be accompanied by proof of service showing service on disciplinary counsel.

(3) *Examination.* Upon the filing of a petition for transfer to active status, the Supreme Court may take or direct whatever action it deems necessary or proper to determine whether the incapacity has been removed, including a direction for an examination of the judge by qualified medical or psychological experts designated by the Supreme Court. In its discretion, the Supreme Court may direct that the expense of the examination be paid by the judge.

(4) *Required Disclosure.* With the filing of a petition for reinstatement to active status, the judge shall be required to disclose the name of each psychiatrist, psychologist, physician and hospital or other institution by whom or in which the judge has been examined or treated since the transfer to incapacity inactive status. The judge shall furnish to the Supreme Court written consent to the release of information and records relating to the incapacity if requested by the Supreme Court or court-appointed medical or psychological experts.

(5) *Granting of Petition for Transfer to Active Status.* The Supreme Court shall grant the petition for transfer to active status upon a showing by clear and convincing evidence that the incapacity has been removed.

(6) *Judicial Declaration of Competency.* If a judge transferred to incapacity inactive status on the basis of a judicial determination of incompetence has been declared to be competent, the Supreme Court may dispense with further evidence that the incapacity has been removed and may immediately direct reinstatement to active status as a judge and as a lawyer.

(g) Orders to Be Public. An order transferring a judge to incapacity inactive status or reinstating a judge to active status following transfer to incapacity inactive status shall be public; the order shall not, however, disclose the nature of the incapacity. All other orders issued in an incapacity proceeding shall be confidential.

[Adopted effective January 1, 1997. Amended effective July 21, 1999.]

RULE 502.1. JUDGE'S OATH

All members of the Unified Judicial System in this state shall take the following oath of office:

I do solemnly swear (or affirm) that:

I am duly qualified, according to the Constitution of this State, to exercise the duties of the office to which I have been appointed, and that I will, to the best of my ability, discharge those duties and will preserve, protect and defend the Constitution of this State and of the United States;

I pledge to uphold the integrity and independence of the judiciary;

I pledge, in the discharge of my duties, to treat all persons who enter the courtroom with civility, fairness, and respect;

I pledge to listen courteously, sit impartially, act promptly, and rule after careful and considerate deliberation;

I pledge to seek justice, and justice alone;

[So help me God.]

[Adopted effective September 22, 2004.]

RULE 503. ADVISORY COMMITTEE ON STANDARDS OF JUDICIAL CONDUCT

Section A

There is hereby created an Advisory Committee on Standards of Judicial Conduct. The purpose of the Committee shall be to render written advisory opinions to inquiring judges concerning the propriety of contemplated judicial and nonjudicial conduct.

Section B

The Committee shall consist of one Circuit Court judge, one Family Court judge, and one active member of the South Carolina Bar who does not hold and has never held a judicial office.

Committee members shall be appointed by the Supreme Court and shall hold office for a period of three (3) years. The terms of the members shall be staggered so that one term expires each year. The Supreme Court shall appoint one of the members of the Committee as the Chairman.

Section C

Two members of the Committee shall constitute a quorum for the transaction of any Committee business, including the issuance of any advisory opinion, whether in a meeting or by circulated writing.

Section D

All opinions shall be advisory in nature only. No opinion shall bind the Commission on Judicial Conduct in any proceeding properly before that body. However, in the discretion of the Commission on Judicial Conduct, an opinion of the Committee may be considered as evidence of a good faith effort to comply with the Code of Judicial Conduct.

Section E

All requests for opinions shall be in writing, addressed to the Committee and signed by the requesting judge. All opinions rendered by the Committee shall be in writing and shall, within the body of the opinion, state the facts on which it is based. The name of the requesting judge and any other party or parties shall not be contained in the opinion and shall remain confidential. A copy of each opinion shall be filed with the Clerk of the Supreme Court and with the Commission on Judicial Conduct. Upon filing with the Clerk of the Supreme Court, opinions shall become a matter of public record. All other files and records of the Committee shall be confidential and shall not be disclosed except upon order of the Supreme Court.

Section F

No member of the Committee shall participate in any matter before the Committee in which he has a direct or indirect interest.

Section G

Any determination of the propriety or impropriety of particular conduct by the Commission on Judicial Conduct shall supersede any conflicting opinion of the Committee.

Section H

No individual shall serve simultaneously on the Advisory Committee on Standards of Judicial Conduct and the Commission on Judicial Conduct.

[Former Supreme Court Rule 42 adopted as Rule 503, SCACR, effective September 1, 1990. Amended effective July 13, 1993; August 26, 1993; January 1, 1997.]

RULE 504. CONTINUING LEGAL EDUCATION OF THE JUDICIARY

(a) Purpose. Only by continuing their legal education can the Judiciary fulfill its obligation to competently serve the State. This Rule establishes minimum requirements for such continuing legal education and the means by which the requirements shall be enforced. For the purposes of this Rule, the term "judge" means all justices of the South Carolina Supreme Court, all judges of the Court of Appeals, all judges of the circuit court, all full-time and part-time masters-in-equity, all family court judges, and all probate judges (including associate and deputy probate judges and other persons, regardless of job description or title, who perform the duties of a probate judge either full-time or part-time). Nothing in this Rule shall be construed as preventing the Supreme Court from requiring mandatory attendance of judges at designated continuing legal education programs.

(b) Continuing Legal Education Requirement. A judge shall complete a minimum of 15 hours of continuing legal education approved by the Commission on Continuing Legal Education and Specialization (Commission) each year. The annual reporting period for purposes of this Rule shall run from March 1 through the last day in February. A judge may be given credit in one or more succeeding reporting periods, not exceeding 3 such periods, for completing more than 15 hours of approved education during any one reporting period.

(c) Annual Report. On or before April 15 of each year, each judge shall make a written report to the Commission, on a form approved by the Commission, concerning his or her completion of approved continuing legal education during the preceding year. The form shall be accompanied by filing fees prescribed by the Commission.

(d) Non-compliance.

(1) If it appears to the Commission that a judge has failed to comply with the requirements of this Rule, the Commission shall notify the judge in writing of this apparent non-compliance by certified mail, addressed to him or her at his or her last known address. The judge shall then have sixty (60) days after the mailing of the notice to file an affidavit responding to it. The response may include documents demonstrating that the judge has cured any deficiency. If after receiving the judge's response the Commission believes the judge is still in violation of this Rule, the Commission shall report the matter to the Supreme Court. Upon receiving a report of non-compliance, the Supreme Court may take such action as it deems appropriate.

(2) In addition, any judge who willfully fails to comply with this rule may be subject to disciplinary action under Rule 502, SCACR.

(3) For good cause shown, the Commission may, in individual cases involving hardship or extenuating circumstances, grant waivers of the minimum education requirements or extensions of time within which to fulfill the same or make the required reports.

[Former Supreme Court Rule 35 adopted as Rule 504, SCACR, effective September 1, 1990. Amended effective October 23, 1990; July 1, 1992; January 7, 1993; June 14, 1995; May 3, 2006.]

Publisher's Notes

The CLE Regulations are published as "Appendix C" in the "Appendices to Part IV".

RULE 505. JUDGES' DISABILITY AND RETIREMENT

Disability shall be considered to be the inability of a judicial officer to perform the functions of his office for medical or psychiatric reasons. Any justice of the Supreme Court, or any judge of the Court of Appeals, Circuit Court, or Family Court, who becomes disabled due to physiological or psychiatric impairment for a period of ninety (90) days shall submit to the Supreme Court, or shall have someone designated by him submit on his behalf, the following materials:

A. (1) A statement acknowledging permanent or prolonged medical disability and a request for early retirement due to disability,

or

(2) A statement advising the Court of the extent and expected duration of the disability and the judge's intentions towards returning to active service,

and

B. Two statements from qualified medical doctors of the judge's choosing. These statements will specify the nature of the disability, the degree of impairment, the prognosis for recovery to the extent that the judge may resume his official functions, and the probability of relapse or recurrence.

If the judge does not submit the required materials, the Court shall initiate the necessary actions to secure compliance with A(1) or (2) and B. The Court may make the determination of when the alleged impairment has existed for a period of ninety (90) days.

In the Court's decision whether disability retirement may be initiated, it may consider other medical evidence, the work product of the judge and the nature of the duties required. If the Court wishes to consider other medical evidence, the Court shall require an examination of the judge by at least two qualified physicians appointed by the Court. The expenses of the examination shall be borne by the judge. After a hearing, the Court shall determine whether the disability is likely to be permanent or prolonged to the extent that the best interests of the judicial system and the judge would not be well served by his continuance in office. Should the disability appear permanent or prohibitively protracted, the Court shall immediately order the judge's retirement on the basis of his medical disability. The judge shall be given ten (10) days in which to petition the Court for reconsideration of its order.

Should the Court determine the disability to be of a temporary nature, the judge shall be so informed and shall be directed to submit, on a quarterly basis, reports stating the status of his health and the date of his expected return to service. Such statements shall be accompanied by reports from two qualified medical doctors of the judge's choosing who will evaluate his current condition and rate of recovery.

Upon receipt of each quarterly report, the Court shall evaluate the nature and extent of the disability in conjunction with reports submitted earlier. The Court shall determine on the basis of each report whether the disability appears permanent or protracted to the extent that the best interests of the judicial system and the judge would not be well served by his continuance in office, or, whether there is a substantial possibility of recovery to the extent that the judge will fully resume his functions. The Court shall notify the submitting judge of its decision and either order retirement due to medical disability or direct that quarterly reports continue to be submitted. Any judge for whom the Court orders retirement after receipt of a quarterly report shall be granted a hearing by the Court if he petitions the Court for a rehearing within ten (10) days after the order is entered.

The confidentiality provisions of Rule 12 contained in Rule 502, SCACR, shall be applicable to proceedings and files under this Rule. An order directing retirement shall, however, be public.

[Former Supreme Court Rule 54 adopted as Rule 505, SCACR, effective September 1, 1990. Amended effective August 26, 1993; January 1, 1997.]

RULE 506. CODE OF CONDUCT FOR STAFF ATTORNEYS AND LAW CLERKS

CANON 1. A STAFF ATTORNEY OR LAW CLERK SHOULD UPHOLD THE INTEGRITY AND INDEPENDENCE OF THE JUDICIARY AND OF HIS[1] OFFICE

An independent and honorable judiciary is indispensable to justice in our society. A staff attorney or law clerk should himself observe, and should impart to anyone under his supervision, high standards of conduct so that the integrity and independence of the judiciary may be preserved and his office may reflect a devotion to serving the public. The provisions of this Code should be construed and applied to further those objectives. Enforcement of the standards of this Code is generally in the discretion of the employing court, but such enforcement shall not preclude enforcement pursuant to law, court order, or the Rules of Professional Conduct. The standards established by this Code shall not preclude other more stringent standards required by law, court order or by the Rules of Professional Conduct. For the purpose of this Code, the term 'staff attorney' includes any attorney who is employed by the Judicial Department other than a law clerk or a member of the judiciary.

[Canon 1 of former Supreme Court Rule 44 adopted as Canon 1 of Rule 506, SCACR, effective September 1, 1990. Amended effective May 3, 1995.]

[1] In the interest of verbal economy, masculine pronouns shall be read to incorporate the feminine gender throughout the Code.

CANON 2. A STAFF ATTORNEY OR LAW CLERK SHOULD AVOID IMPROPRIETY AND THE APPEARANCE OF IMPROPRIETY IN ALL HIS ACTIVITIES

A staff attorney or law clerk should not engage in any activities that would put into question the propriety of his conduct in carrying out the duties of his office. He should not allow his family, social, or other relationships to influence his official conduct or judgment. He should not lend the prestige of his office to advance the private interests of others; nor should he convey or permit others to convey the impression that they are in a special position to influence him.

[Canon 2 of former Supreme Court Rule 44 adopted as Canon 2 of Rule 506, SCACR, effective September 1, 1990.]

CANON 3. A STAFF ATTORNEY OR LAW CLERK SHOULD PERFORM THE DUTIES OF HIS OFFICE IMPARTIALLY AND DILIGENTLY

The official duties of a staff attorney or law clerk take precedence over all his other activities. His official duties include all the duties of his office assigned by the employing court. In the performance of these duties the following standards apply:

A. A staff attorney or law clerk shall respect and comply with the law and should conduct himself at all times in a manner that promotes public confidence in the integrity and impartiality of the judiciary and of his office.

B. A staff attorney or law clerk shall be faithful to the highest standards of his profession and maintain professional competence in it. He should be patient, dignified, courteous, and fair to all persons with whom he deals in his official capacity and should expect similar conduct of others subject to his direction and control. He should diligently discharge the responsibilities of his office in an efficient, fairminded, and professional manner.

C. A staff attorney or law clerk should avoid any favoritism, unfairness, or nepotism in connection with the hiring, discharge, or treatment of subordinates.

D. A staff attorney or law clerk should never perform any discretionary or ministerial function, including the assignment of cases, in a manner which improperly favors any litigant or attorney, nor should he imply that he is in a position to do so.

E. A staff attorney or law clerk shall disqualify himself in a matter in which his impartiality might reasonably be questioned, including but not limited to instances where:

(1) he has a personal bias or prejudice concerning the matter;

(2) he served as a lawyer in the matter in controversy; or a lawyer with whom he previously was associated in private practice, either as lawyer or law clerk, served during such association as a lawyer concerning the matter;

(3) he, or a relative by blood or marriage, is known to have an interest that could be substantially affected by the outcome of the proceeding;

(4) he is related by blood or marriage to a party to the proceeding, or to an officer, director, or trustee of a party, or to a lawyer in the proceeding.

[Canon 3 of former Supreme Court Rule 44 adopted as Canon 3 of Rule 506, SCACR, effective September 1, 1990.]

CANON 4. A STAFF ATTORNEY OR LAW CLERK MAY ENGAGE IN ACTIVITIES TO IMPROVE THE LAW, THE LEGAL SYSTEM, AND THE ADMINISTRATION OF JUSTICE

A staff attorney or law clerk, subject to the proper performance of his official duties, may engage in the following quasi-official activities:

A. He may speak, write, lecture, teach, and participate in other activities concerning the law, the legal system, court administration, and the administration of justice.

B. He may serve as a member, officer, or director of an organization or governmental agency devoted to the improvement of the law, the legal system, or the administration of justice, but should not participate in fund-raising activities for such an organization or agency.

C. He may promote the development of professional organizations and foster the interchange of technical information and experience with others in his profession. He may make himself available to the public at large for speaking engagements and public appearances designed to enhance the public's knowledge of the operation of the court system.

[Canon 4 of former Supreme Court Rule 44 adopted as Canon 4 of Rule 506, SCACR, effective September 1, 1990.]

CANON 5. A STAFF ATTORNEY OR LAW CLERK SHOULD REGULATE HIS EXTRA–OFFICIAL ACTIVITIES TO MINIMIZE THE RISK OF CONFLICT WITH HIS OFFICIAL DUTIES

A. Avocational Activities. A staff attorney or law clerk may write, lecture, teach, and speak on non-legal subjects, and engage in the arts, sports, and other social and recreational activities, if such avocational activities do not detract from the dignity of his office or interfere with the performance of his official duties.

B. Civic and Charitable Activities. A staff attorney or law clerk may participate in civic and charitable activities that do not detract from the dignity of his office or interfere with the performance of his official duties. He may serve as an officer, director, trustee, or non-legal advisor of an educational, religious, charitable, fraternal, or civic organization and solicit funds for any such organization, subject to the following limitations:

(1) He should not use or permit the use of the prestige of his office in the solicitation of funds.

(2) He should not solicit his subordinates to contribute to or participate in any civic or charitable activity, but he may call his subordinates' attention to a general fund-raising campaign such as the United Way.

(3) He should not solicit funds from lawyers or persons likely to come before the court he serves.

C. Financial Activities.

(1) A staff attorney or law clerk should refrain from financial and business dealings that tend to detract from the dignity of his office, interfere with the proper performance of his official duties, exploit his official position, or involve him in frequent transactions with lawyers or persons likely to come before the court he serves. Before or during a clerkship or tenure as a staff attorney, a law clerk or staff attorney may seek and obtain employment to commence after the completion of that job; if any law firm, lawyer, or entity with whom a law clerk or staff attorney has been employed or is seeking or has obtained future employment appears in any matter pending before the appointing judge, the law clerk or staff attorney should promptly bring this fact to the attention of the appointing judge or justice, the Court, or his or her attorney supervisor, and they shall determine the extent of the law clerk's or staff attorney's performance of duties in connection with such matter. In relation to such future employment, the law clerk or staff attorney may accept payment of bar examination related expenses, including reasonable living expenses while preparing for a bar examination, and relocation expenses from the future employer.

(2) Neither a staff attorney or law clerk nor a member of his family residing in his household should accept a gift, bequest, favor, or loan from any person under circumstances that might reasonably be regarded as influencing the performance of his official duties. He shall report the value of any gift or bequest, other than from a relative by blood or marriage, as required by law.

D. Practice of Law. A staff attorney or law clerk shall not practice law in any federal, state, or local court, except in his official capacity as a staff attorney or law clerk, or undertake to perform legal services for any private client in return for remuneration. This prohibition, however, shall not be construed to preclude the performance of legal work necessary to the management of the personal affairs of the staff attorney or law clerk, his spouse or minor child, so long as:

(1) such work is done without compensation;

(2) it does not require any act, including the entry of an appearance in a court of this State or of the United States, that would suggest that his position is being misused, that preferential treatment is being sought by virtue of the holding of that position, or that would otherwise be inconsistent with his primary responsibility to the employing court;

(3) such activity does not conflict or reasonably appear to conflict with court duties or will not reflect adversely on the court or create the appearance of impropriety.

This provision shall not be construed to prohibit a staff attorney or law clerk from qualifying to practice law in South Carolina under Rule 403, SCACR.

This provision shall not be construed to preclude staff attorneys or law clerks who are members of the reserve components of the armed forces or National Guard from fulfilling the duties in those organizations.

[Canon 5 of former Supreme Court Rule 44 adopted as Canon 5 of Rule 506, SCACR, effective September 1, 1990. Amended effective May 3, 1995.]

CANON 6. A STAFF ATTORNEY OR LAW CLERK SHOULD REGULARLY FILE REPORTS OF COMPENSATION RECEIVED FOR QUASI–OFFICIAL AND EXTRA–OFFICIAL ACTIVITIES

A staff attorney or law clerk may receive compensation and reimbursement of expenses for quasi-official and extra-official activities permitted by these guidelines, if the source of such payments does not influence or give the appearance of influencing him in the performance of his official duties or otherwise give the appearance of impropriety, subject to the following restrictions:

A. Compensation. Compensation should not exceed a reasonable amount nor should it exceed that normally received by others for the same activity.

B. Expense Reimbursement. Expense reimbursement should be limited to the actual cost of travel, food, and lodging reasonably incurred by a staff attorney or law clerk and, where appropriate to the occasion, by his spouse. Any payment in excess of such an amount is compensation.

C. Public Reports. A staff attorney or law clerk shall make and file such reports as may be prescribed by law.

[Canon 6 of former Supreme Court Rule 44 adopted as Canon 6 of Rule 506, SCACR, effective September 1, 1990.]

CANON 7. A STAFF ATTORNEY OR LAW CLERK SHOULD REFRAIN FROM CERTAIN POLITICAL ACTIVITY

A staff attorney or law clerk may engage in political activity that does not tend to reflect adversely on the dignity of the court or his office, or interfere with the proper performance of his official duties, subject to the following limitations:

A. he should not use the prestige of his office to advance political interests of others;

B. he should not act as a leader or hold any office in a political organization;

C. he should not solicit funds for a political organization, candidate, or event;

D. he should not become a candidate for political office; and

E. he should not make speeches for or publicly endorse a political organization or candidate.

[Canon 7 of former Supreme Court Rule 44 adopted as Canon 7 of Rule 506, SCACR, effective September 1, 1990.]

CANON 8. A STAFF ATTORNEY OR LAW CLERK SHOULD NOT REVEAL THE CONFIDENCES GAINED IN THE COURSE OF HIS EMPLOYMENT

The relationship between the staff attorney or law clerk and his employing court is sensitive and privileged. The highest standard of care is required because of the degree to which the lives of others may be affected by even the inadvertent disclosure of confidential information gained in the course of employment. Disclosure of such confidential information is highly prejudicial to the administration of justice. Therefore:

A. He shall never reveal confidences gained in the course of his employment except where disclosure is specifically permitted by his employing court.

B. He shall insure that all confidential documents are protected from disclosure except where specifically permitted by the employing court.

C. He shall never employ such information for his own or another's personal gain.

D. He shall exercise due care to insure that those employees under his supervision do not reveal confidential information gained in the course of their employment.

[Canon 8 of former Supreme Court Rule 44 adopted as Canon 8 of Rule 506, SCACR, effective September 1, 1990.]

RULE 507. POLITICAL ACTIVITY OF JUDICIAL DEPARTMENT EMPLOYEES AND OFFICERS

Section 1. An employee or officer of the Judicial Department may not:

A. Use his or her official authority or influence for the purpose of interfering with or affecting the result of an election or a nomination for office;

B. Directly or indirectly coerce, attempt to coerce, command or advise a State officer or employee to pay, lend, or contribute anything of value to a party, committee, organization, agency, or person for political purposes;

C. Be a candidate for elective office in a partisan election; or

D. Actively participate in the campaign of any political party or candidate.

Section 2. The Commission on Judicial Conduct is authorized to enforce this rule in accordance with the procedures established in Rule 502, SCACR. The Advisory Committee on Standards of Judicial Conduct may issue advisory opinions concerning this rule in accordance with the procedures established in Rule 503, SCACR.

[Former Supreme Court Rule 45 adopted as Rule 507, SCACR, effective September 1, 1990. Amended effective January 1, 1997.]

RULE 508. COURT REPORTERS

Court reporters shall report to the Office of Court Administration the gross income from fees they collected under Rule 607(h), SCACR, during the preceding quarter on January 1, April 1, July 1 and October 1 each year.

Upon failure of the court reporter to file such reports within ten days from the due date, the court reporter shall forfeit right to salary until such time as the reports are made.

The court reporter of the Judicial Department is a fulltime employee and is not allowed to accept outside employment as a reporter. Provided, however, that the Office of Court Administration may grant permission to any stenotype court reporter to accept outside employment as a reporter if the reporter has acquired computer-aided transcription equipment which is acceptable to the Office of Court Administration. The Office of Court Administration may also grant permission to stenotype reporters to associate with other persons in business ventures if, in the judgment of the Office of Court Administration, such arrangements will promote the use of computer-aided transcription equipment. The Office of Court Administration, as a condition of granting permission to a stenotype reporter to accept outside employment, may require financial reports and workload reports from reporters engaged in the operation of computer-aided transcription equipment. The Office of Court Administration, as a further condition of granting permission to a stenotype reporter to accept outside employment, may regulate the extent of outside employment accepted by a reporter. The fees charged by reporters for work performed outside of the Judicial Department shall not be regulated by the Judicial Department. The official work of a reporter within the Judicial Department shall receive priority over outside employment engaged in by reporters.

[Former Supreme Court Rule 37 adopted as Rule 508, SCACR, effective September 1, 1990. Amended effective August 1, 1998.]

RULE 509. CERTIFICATION OF MAGISTRATES AND MUNICIPAL JUDGES

(a) Board of Magistrate and Municipal Judge Certification.

(1) *Membership and Terms of Office.* The Board of Magistrate and Municipal Judge Certification ("Board") shall consist of nine (9) members. The Board members shall be appointed by the Supreme Court for three (3) year terms and shall be eligible for reappointment. In case of a vacancy on the Board, the Supreme Court shall appoint a member to serve the remainder of the unexpired term. The Supreme Court shall appoint a chairperson of the Board from among the Board's membership. The Director of South Carolina Court Administration ("Director") shall serve as secretary of the Board *ex officio.*

(2) *Duties.* It shall be the duty of the Board to determine whether magistrates and municipal judges in South Carolina possess the necessary legal knowledge for appointment and reappointment, pursuant to the provisions of S.C. Code Ann. §§ 22–1–10 and 14–25–15. Subject to the approval of the Supreme Court, the Board is empowered to make rules and regulations for conducting the required training program curriculum and examinations, including a list of the subjects upon which applicants may be tested. Thirty (30) days notice must be given of any changes to the rules and regulations.

(b) Application for Certification or Recertification Examination. Members in good standing of the South Carolina Bar are exempt from certification and recertification examinations requirements. For purposes of this Rule, ministerial magistrates and municipal ministerial recorders are considered magistrates and municipal judges, and are subject to certification and recertification requirements. Examinations for certification or recertification of non-lawyer magistrates and municipal judges shall be conducted at least three times each year at such times as the Board shall specify. Any person desiring to take the Examination shall file an application with the Director on a form prescribed by the Board. Applications shall be accepted up to the first day of the month in which the examination is given. Only active magistrates and municipal judges may apply for examination.

An application will not be considered filed until it is fully completed and received by the Director.

(c) Review of Examination Results. The Certification and Recertification Examinations shall consist of such sections as may be specified by the Board. The Board shall certify whether an applicant passed or failed for each section of the examination to the Director who shall promptly then notify the applicants. An applicant must pass each section of the examination but need not pass every section of the examination during the same trimester. Once the applicant passes a particular section, he or she shall not be retested on that section again for purposes of the immediate certification or recertification being sought.

An applicant who fails to pass any section of the Certification Examination may, within fifteen (15) days after notification of the failure, request in writing the Director's permission to inspect that section of the examination, the model answers, and the applicant's answers. Within ten (10) days of receipt of the request, the Director shall notify the applicant of the date and time when the inspection will be permitted and where it will occur. The inspection must take place within thirty (30) days of the Director's receipt of the request.

After reviewing the examination papers, an applicant who feels an error has been made in grading an answer may petition the Supreme Court to have the answer regraded. The original and seven (7) copies of the petition, accompanied by a filing fee of twenty-five ($25.00) dollars, must be filed with the Supreme Court within ten (10) days of the applicant's review of the examination and must enumerate the alleged errors in grading. No briefing or argument is permitted. The only identifying mark to be placed on the petition is an identification number assigned to the applicant by the Board. Neither the applicant nor any agent of the applicant shall contact any member of the Board or any justice of the Supreme Court regarding the questions on any section of the Certification Examination, grading, procedures, or an applicant's answers.

(d) Re-examination. Any applicant who has failed to pass any section of the examination may apply to be re-examined on those sections as often as the examinations are offered. The application shall be made on a form furnished by the Director. The time limits applicable to filing initial applications shall be applicable to applications for re-examination.

(e) Confidentiality. The files and records maintained by the Board relating to applications, examinations, and re-examinations shall be confidential and shall not be disclosed except as necessary for the Board to carry out its responsibilities. The Board may disclose the names of those persons who have successfully completed the certification process. The Supreme Court may authorize the release of confidential information to other persons or agencies.

(f) Failure to Obtain Certification or Recertification. If a magistrate fails to obtain certification or recertification within the time period prescribed by § 22–1–10, the Board shall send a written notice to the Governor that the magistrate has failed to timely obtain certification or recertification, that the magistrate's office is vacant and that the Governor should appoint a successor. A copy of the notification shall be sent to the magistrate.

If a municipal judge fails to obtain certification or recertification within the time prescribed by § 14–25–15, the Board shall send a written notice to the City Council that the municipal judge has failed to timely obtain certification or recertification, that the municipal judge's office is vacant, and that the Council should appoint a successor. A copy of the notification shall be sent to the municipal judge.

[Adopted as Rule 415 and redesignated as Rule 509, SCACR, effective October 6, 1993. Amended effective December 7, 1993; February 8, 1996; October 20, 2000.]

RULE 510. CONTINUING LEGAL EDUCATION FOR MAGISTRATES AND MUNICIPAL JUDGES

(a) Purpose. Being mindful of the improvements in the administration of justice that have resulted from our mandatory continuing legal education requirements for judges and active members of the South Carolina Bar (see Rules 408 and 504, SCACR), this Rule establishes minimum requirements for continuing legal education (CLE) for magistrates and municipal judges and the means by which those requirements shall be enforced. Nothing in this Rule shall be construed as preventing the Supreme Court from requiring mandatory attendance of magistrates and municipal judges at designated continuing legal education programs.

(b) Continuing Legal Education Requirements.

(1) *Magistrates.* During each reporting year, which begins on July 1 and ends on June 30, all magistrates are required to attend at least 18 hours of accredited CLE. At least 6 of the 18 hours shall be devoted to civil law issues and at least 6 of the 18 hours shall be devoted to criminal law issues and at least 2 of the 18 hours shall be devoted to ethical issues. To obtain credit for an accredited educational activity which has a testing component, the testing component must be completed satisfactorily.

(2) *Municipal Judges.* During each reporting year, which begins on July 1 and ends on June 30, all municipal judges shall be required to attend at least 12 hours of accredited continuing legal education pertaining to criminal law issues, and practice and procedure in municipal courts, and at least two of the hours shall be devoted to ethical issues. To obtain credit for an accredited educational activity which has a testing component, the testing component must be completed satisfactorily.

(3) *Newly Appointed Magistrates and Municipal Judges.* For the year in which a magistrate or municipal judge is appointed to office, the required initial training shall satisfy the requirements of this Rule. If a magistrate or municipal judge is appointed in one reporting year and completes the required training at the next scheduled training session, which is in the succeeding reporting year, the requirements of this Rule shall be satisfied for both reporting years.

(4) *Carry Forward Credit.* A magistrate who completes more than 18 hours of CLE credit in any reporting year may carry a maximum of 12 hours of the excess credit forward to the next reporting year. A municipal judge who completes more than 12 hours of CLE credit in any reporting year may carry a maximum of 6 hours of the excess credit forward to the next reporting year.

(c) Accreditation of Courses for Magistrates and Municipal Judges. The Board of Magistrate and Municipal Court Certification (Board) or its designee, shall determine whether a course is appropriate for credit pursuant to this Rule and if so, the credit it should be assigned. Course outlines and materials shall be submitted to the Board no later than fifteen days prior to the date the course is scheduled to be held. The Board is authorized to designate certain sponsors as accredited sponsors, who shall not be required to comply with the requirements of this section of this Rule. Accredited sponsor status may be withdrawn by the Board for cause after 60 days notice to the sponsor.

When accrediting a course, the Board shall determine what portion of a course is devoted to civil law, criminal law, or ethics, and designate the course appropriately. When making this designation, if the Board determines that the content of a course is inseparably composed of both civil and criminal elements, the Board shall designate those hours as civil/criminal. Magistrates and municipal judges may utilize such courses to fulfill their civil or criminal requirements, as described in subsections (b)(1) and (b)(2) above.

For the purpose of determining credit to be assigned to a course, an instructional hour means 60 minutes of instruction as a teacher or student. Only courses accredited by the Board may be applied to satisfy the CLE requirements established by this Rule. In determining whether a course should be accredited, the Board will be guided by the following standards:

(1) Courses should have significant intellectual or practical content;

(2) The subject matter should deal with legal theory or practical aspects of proceedings in magistrate or municipal courts;

(3) Faculty members must be qualified by practical or academic experience to teach the subject;

(4) High quality written materials should be distributed to participants;

(5) Suitable classroom or other setting should be provided for participants;

(6) Ethical and professional considerations pertaining to the subject matter should be included in the program; and

(7) Programs should encourage magistrates and municipal judges to develop contacts and resources of information in conjunction with their instructors and fellow magistrates or municipal judges.

The Board shall promptly provide the Commission on Continuing Legal Education and Specialization (Commission) with information concerning the courses it accredits pursuant to this Rule. Information provided should include program title and sponsor, date(s) and place(s) program will be presented, credit assigned to the program, and whether any portion of the program is devoted to civil or criminal issues.

(d) Duties of Sponsors of Accredited Courses. To assist in verifying course attendance, sponsors of courses accredited by the Board shall prepare a list of course attendees and retain that list for a minimum of 2 years. Within 30 days after a program is completed, sponsors will provide the Commission with a list of attendees, with SC Bar numbers, if available, which indicates the credit each attendee has earned.

(e) Reports and Fees.

(1) On forms prepared by the Commission and available through its offices, each magistrate and municipal judge shall, not later than July 15, file with the Commission a sworn annual report of compliance for the previous reporting year. The compliance reporting form will be accompanied by filing fees as prescribed by Regulation VI(B) of the Commission's *Regulations for Mandatory Continuing Legal Education for Judges and Active Members of the South Carolina Bar*.

(2) Magistrates and municipal judges who are active members of the South Carolina Bar and required to satisfy the requirements of the Commission's *Regulations for Mandatory Continuing Legal Education for Judges and Active Members of the South Carolina Bar*, may satisfy the requirements specified in those Regulations by showing compliance with the CLE and fee requirements in this Rule. However, active members of the Bar are still required to complete the 2 hours of Ethics CLE required by Rule 408(a), SCACR.

(f) Non–Compliance. If it appears to the Commission that a magistrate or municipal judge has failed to comply with the requirements of this Rule, the Commission shall notify the judge in writing by certified mail, addressed to the judge's last known address. The judge shall then have 30 days after the mailing of the notice to file an affidavit in response. The response may include documents demonstrating that the judge has cured the perceived deficiency. If after receiving the response, the Commission believes the judge has failed to comply with this Rule, the Commission will report the matter to the Supreme Court. Upon finding the judge has failed to comply with this Rule, the Supreme Court may suspend the judge, find the judge in contempt of court, or take any other action it deems appropriate.

(g) Waivers. For good cause shown, the Commission may, in individual cases involving extraordinary hardship or extenuating circumstances, waive or modify the requirements of subparagraphs (b)(1)&(2) and (e)(1). When appropriate, and as a condition for any waiver or modification, the Commission may proportionally increase CLE requirements for the succeeding reporting year.

[Adopted effective March 1, 2003. Amended effective October 10, 2003.]

RULE 511. RULES OF PROFESSIONAL CONDUCT FOR COURT INTERPRETERS

PREAMBLE

Many persons who come before the courts are partially or completely excluded from full participation in the proceedings due to limited English proficiency (LEP) or a speech or hearing impairment. It is essential that this communication barrier be removed, as much as possible, so that these persons are placed in the same position as a similarly situated person for whom there is no such barrier. A non–English speaker should be able to understand just as much as an English speaker with the same level of education and intelligence.

As officers of the court, interpreters help assure that such persons may enjoy equal access to justice and that court proceedings and court support services function efficiently and effectively. Interpreters are highly skilled professionals who fulfill an essential role in the administration of justice. Anyone serving as a court interpreter should be required to understand and abide by the precepts set out in these Rules. Judges and attorneys should also become familiar with the Rules and expect conduct from interpreters that is consistent with them.

[Adopted effective June 21, 2006.]

APPLICABILITY

These Rules shall guide and be binding upon all persons, agencies and organizations who administer, supervise use of, or deliver interpreting services to the judiciary.

[Adopted effective June 21, 2006.]

RULE 1. ACCURACY AND COMPLETENESS OF INTERPRETATION

Interpreters shall render a complete and accurate interpretation, or sight translation, without altering, omitting or adding anything to what is stated or written, and without explanation or summarization.

The interpreter shall preserve the nuances and level of formality, or informality, of the speech.

[Adopted effective June 21, 2006.]

Commentary

The interpreter has a two-fold duty: (1) to ensure that the proceedings in English reflect precisely what was said by a non–English speaking person, and (2) to place the non–English speaking person on an equal footing with those who understand English. This creates an obligation to conserve every element of information contained in a source language communication when it is rendered in the target language.

Therefore, interpreters are obligated to apply their best skills and judgment to preserve faithfully the meaning of what is said in court, including the style or register of speech. Verbatim, "word for word," or literal oral interpretations are not appropriate when they distort the meaning of the source language. Every spoken statement, even if it appears non-responsive, obscene, rambling, or incoherent should be interpreted. This includes apparent misstatements.

Interpreters should never interject their own words, phrases, or expressions. If the need arises to explain an interpreting problem (e.g., a term or phrase with no direct equivalent in the target language or a misunderstanding that only the interpreter can clarify), the interpreter should ask the court's permission to provide an explanation. Interpreters should convey the emotional emphasis of the speaker without reenacting or mimicking the speaker's emotions, or dramatic gestures.

Sign language interpreters, however, must employ all of the visual cues that the language they are interpreting for requires, including facial expressions, body language, and hand gestures. Sign language interpreters, therefore, should ensure that court participants do not confuse these essential elements of the interpreted language with inappropriate interpreter conduct.

The obligation to preserve accuracy includes the interpreter's duty to correct any error of interpretation discovered by the interpreter during the proceeding. Interpreters should demonstrate their professionalism by objectively analyzing any challenge to their performance.

RULE 2. REPRESENTATION OF QUALIFICATIONS

Interpreters shall accurately and completely represent their certifications, training, and pertinent experience.

[Adopted effective June 21, 2006.]

Commentary

Acceptance of a case by an interpreter conveys linguistic competency in legal settings. Withdrawing or being asked to withdraw from a case after it begins causes a disruption of court proceedings and is wasteful of scarce public resources. It is, therefore, essential that interpreters present a complete and truthful account of their training, certification and experience prior to appointment so the officers of the court can fairly evaluate their qualifications for delivering interpreting services.

RULE 3. IMPARTIALITY AND AVOIDANCE OF CONFLICT OF INTEREST

Interpreters shall be impartial and unbiased and shall refrain from conduct that may give an appearance of bias. Interpreters shall disclose any real or perceived conflict of interest.

[Adopted effective June 21, 2006.]

Commentary

The interpreter serves as an officer of the court and the interpreter's duty in a court proceeding is to serve the court and the public to which the court is a servant. This is true regardless of whether the interpreter is publicly retained at government expense or retained privately at the expense of one of the parties.

The interpreter should avoid any conduct or behavior that presents the appearance of favoritism toward any of the parties. Interpreters should maintain professional relationships with their clients, and should not take an active part in any of the proceedings. The interpreter should discourage a non–English speaking party's personal dependence.

During the course of the proceedings, interpreters should not converse with parties, witnesses, jurors, attorneys, or with friends or relatives of any party, except in the discharge of their judicial functions. It is especially important that interpreters, who are often familiar with attorneys or other members of the courtroom work group, including law enforcement officers, refrain from casual and personal conversations with anyone in court that may convey an appearance of a special relationship or partiality to any of the court participants.

The interpreter should strive for professional detachment. Verbal and non-verbal displays of personal attitudes, prejudices, emotions, or opinions should be avoided at all times.

Should an interpreter become aware that a proceeding participant views the interpreter as having a bias or being biased, the interpreter should disclose that knowledge to the presiding judge. Any condition that interferes with the objectivity of an interpreter constitutes a conflict of interest and must be disclosed to the judge. An interpreter should not serve in any matter in which payment for their services is contingent upon the outcome of the case.

Before providing services in a matter, court interpreters must disclose to all parties and the presiding judge any prior involvement, whether personal or professional, that could be reasonably construed as a conflict of interest. This disclosure should not include privileged or confidential information.

The following are circumstances that create potential conflicts of interest that must be disclosed:

(1) The interpreter is a friend, associate, or relative of a party or counsel for a party involved in the proceedings;

(2) The interpreter has served in an investigative capacity for any party involved in the case;

(3) The interpreter has previously been retained by a law enforcement agency to assist in the preparation of the criminal case at issue;

(4) The interpreter or the interpreter's spouse or child has a financial interest in the subject matter in controversy or in a party to the proceeding, or any other interest that would be affected by the outcome of the case;

(5) The interpreter has been involved in the choice of counsel or law firm for that case;

(6) The interpreter is an attorney in the case;

(7) The interpreter has previously been retained for private employment by one of the parties to interpret in the case;

(8) For any other reason, the interpreter's independence of judgment would be compromised in the course of providing services.

The existence of any of the above-mentioned circumstances does not alone disqualify an interpreter from providing services as long as the interpreter is able to render services objectively. An interpreter may serve if the judge and all parties consent. If an actual or apparent conflict of interest exists, the interpreter may, without explanation to any of the parties or the judge, decline to provide services.

Should an interpreter become aware that a non-English speaking participant views the interpreter as having a bias, or being biased, the interpreter should disclose that knowledge to the judge.

RULE 4. PROFESSIONAL DEMEANOR

Interpreters shall conduct themselves in a manner consistent with the dignity of the court and shall be as unobtrusive as possible.

[Adopted effective June 21, 2006.]

Commentary

Interpreters should know and observe the established protocol, rules, and procedures for delivering interpreting services. When speaking in English, interpreters should speak at a rate and volume that enables them to be heard and understood throughout the courtroom, but the interpreter's presence should otherwise be as unobtrusive as possible. Interpreters should work without drawing undue or inappropriate attention to themselves. Interpreters should dress in a manner that is consistent with the dignity of the proceedings of the court. Interpreters should avoid obstructing the view of any of the individuals involved in the proceedings. However, interpreters who use sign language or other visual modes of communication must be positioned so that hand gestures, facial expressions, and whole body movement are visible to the person for whom they are interpreting.

Interpreters are encouraged to avoid personal or professional conduct that could discredit the court.

RULE 5. CONFIDENTIALITY

Interpreters shall protect the confidentiality of all privileged and other confidential information.

[Adopted effective June 21, 2006.]

Commentary

The interpreter shall protect and uphold the confidentiality of all privileged information obtained during the course of her or his duties. It is especially important that the interpreter understand and uphold the attorney-client privilege, which requires confidentiality with respect to any communication between attorney and client. This rule also applies to other types of privileged communication.

Interpreters must also refrain from repeating or disclosing information obtained by them in the course of their employment that may be relevant to the legal proceeding.

In the event that an interpreter becomes aware of information that suggests imminent harm to someone or relates to a crime being committed during the course of the proceedings, the interpreter should immediately disclose the information to the presiding judge. If the judge is not available, the interpreter should disclose the information to an appropriate authority in the judiciary.

RULE 6. RESTRICTION OF PUBLIC COMMENT

Interpreters shall not publicly discuss, report, or offer an opinion concerning a matter in which they are, or have been, engaged even when that information is not privileged or required by law to be confidential.

[Adopted effective June 21, 2006.]

Commentary

Generally, interpreters should not discuss outside of the interpreter's official duties, interpreter assignments, persons involved or the facts of the case. However, interpreters may share information for training and educational purposes. Interpreters should only share as much information as is required to accomplish their purpose. An interpreter must not reveal privileged or confidential information.

RULE 7. SCOPE OF PRACTICE

Interpreters shall limit themselves to interpreting or translating, and shall not give legal advice, express personal opinions to individuals for whom they are interpreting, or engage in any other activities which may be construed to constitute a service other than interpreting or translating while serving as an interpreter.

[Adopted effective June 21, 2006.]

Commentary

Since interpreters are responsible only for enabling others to communicate, they should limit themselves to the activity of interpreting or translating only. Interpreters should refrain from initiating communications while interpreting unless it is necessary for assuring an accurate and faithful interpretation. Interpreters may be required to initiate communications during a proceeding when they find it necessary to seek assistance in performing their duties. Examples of such circumstances include seeking direction when unable to understand or express a word or thought, requesting speakers to moderate their rate of communication or repeat or rephrase something, correcting their own interpreting errors, or notifying the court of reservations about their ability to satisfy an assignment competently. In such instances they should make it clear that they are speaking for themselves.

An interpreter may convey legal advice from an attorney to a person only while that attorney is giving it. An interpreter should not explain the purpose of forms, services, or otherwise act as counselors or advisors unless they are interpreting for someone who is acting in that official capacity. The interpreter may translate language on a form for a person who is filling out the form, but may not explain the form or its purpose for such a person.

The interpreter should not personally serve to perform official acts that are the official responsibility of other court officials including, but not limited to, court clerks, pre-trial release investigators or interviewers, or probation counselors.

RULE 8. ASSESSING AND REPORTING IMPEDIMENTS TO PERFORMANCE

Interpreters shall assess at all times their ability to deliver their services. When interpreters have any reservation about their ability to satisfy an assignment competently, they shall immediately convey that reservation to the presiding judge.

[Adopted effective June 21, 2006.]

Commentary

If the communication mode or language of the non-English-speaking person cannot be readily interpreted, the interpreter should notify the presiding judge.

Interpreters should notify the presiding judge of any environmental or physical limitation that impedes or hinders their ability to deliver interpreting services adequately (e.g., the court room is not quiet enough for the interpreter to hear or be heard by the non-English speaker, more than one person at a time is speaking, or principals or witnesses of the court are speaking at a rate of speed that is too rapid for the interpreter to adequately interpret). Sign language interpreters must ensure that they can both see and convey the full range of visual language elements that are necessary for communication, including facial expressions and body movement, as well as hand gestures. Interpreters should notify the presiding judge of the need to take periodic breaks to maintain mental and physical alertness and prevent interpreter fatigue. Interpreters should recommend and encourage the use of team interpreting whenever necessary.

Interpreters are encouraged to make inquiries as to the nature of a case whenever possible before accepting an assignment. This enables interpreters to match more closely their professional qualifications, skills, and experience to potential assignments and more accurately assess their ability to satisfy those assignments competently.

Even competent and experienced interpreters may encounter cases where routine proceedings suddenly involve technical or specialized terminology unfamiliar to the interpreter (e.g., the unscheduled testimony of an expert witness). When such instances occur, interpreters should request a brief recess to familiarize themselves with the subject matter. If familiarity with the terminology requires extensive time or more intensive research, interpreters should inform the presiding judge.

Interpreters should refrain from accepting a case if they feel the language and subject matter of that case is likely to exceed their skills or capacities. Interpreters should notify the presiding judge if they feel unable to perform competently, due to lack of familiarity with terminology, preparation, or difficulty in understanding a witness or defendant.

Interpreters should notify the presiding judge of any personal bias they may have involving any aspect of the proceedings. For example, an interpreter who has been the victim of a sexual assault may wish to be excused from interpreting in cases involving similar offenses.

RULE 9. DUTY TO REPORT ETHICAL VIOLATIONS

Interpreters shall report to the proper judicial authority any effort to impede their compliance with any law, any provision of these Rules, or any other judicial policy governing court interpreting and legal translating.

[Adopted effective June 21, 2006.]

Commentary

Because the users of interpreting services frequently misunderstand the proper role of the interpreter, they may ask or expect the interpreter to perform duties or engage in activities that conflict with the provisions of these Rules or other laws, regulations, or policies governing court interpreters. It is incumbent upon the interpreter to inform such persons of his or her professional obligations. If, having been apprised of these obligations, the person persists in demanding that the interpreter violate them, the interpreter should report it to the presiding judge.

RULE 10. PROFESSIONAL DEVELOPMENT

Interpreters shall continually improve their skills and knowledge and advance the profession through activities such as professional training and education, and interaction with colleagues and specialists in related fields.

[Adopted effective June 21, 2006.]

Commentary

Interpreters must continually strive to increase their knowledge of the languages they work in professionally, including past and current trends in technical, vernacular, and regional terminology as well as their application within court proceedings. Interpreters should keep informed of all statutes, rules of courts and policies of the judiciary that relate to the performance of their professional duties.

An interpreter should seek to elevate the standards of the profession through participation in workshops, professional meetings, interaction with colleagues, and reading current literature in the field.

VI. RULES GOVERNING THE ADMINISTRATION OF THE COURTS

RULE 601. CONFLICTS IN HEARING DATES

(a) Order of Priority as Between Tribunals. In the event an attorney of record is called to appear simultaneously in actions pending in two or more tribunals of this State, the following list shall establish the priority of his obligations to those tribunals:

(1) The Supreme Court.

(2) The Court of Appeals.

(3) The Commission on Judicial Conduct, the Commission on Lawyer Conduct, and the Committee on Character and Fitness.

(4) The Circuit Court—General Sessions.

(5) The Family Court—merits hearings involving child abuse, child neglect and termination of parental rights upon approval of the Chief Judge for Administrative Purposes for the Family Court and notice to the Chief Judge for Administrative Purposes for the Circuit Court five days prior to the term of the Circuit Court.

(6) The Circuit Court—Common Pleas, Jury Term.

(7) The Family Court—all cases not referenced in (5) above.

(8) The Circuit Court—Common Pleas, Non–Jury Term.

(9) The Administrative Law Court.

(10) Alternative Dispute Resolution Conferences conducted pursuant to the SC Court–Annexed ADR Rules.

(11) The Probate Court.

(12) Magistrates and Municipal Courts.

(13) Other Administrative Bodies or Officials.

When a party or his counsel is in the process of a hearing or trial before a tribunal, he may not be required to appear in another tribunal having greater priority unless the tribunal with less priority grants a recess or continuance for that purpose.

(b) Conflict With Federal Courts. When times set for appearances before state and federal courts are in conflict, appearance shall have such priority as is appropriate. Courts and counsel shall have the obligation to adjust schedules to accord with the spirit of comity between the state and federal courts.

(c) Attorney to Give Notice. An attorney who cannot make a scheduled appearance because of the priority established by paragraph (a) of this rule shall notify the affected tribunals as soon as the conflict becomes apparent.

[Adopted effective September 1, 1990. Amended effective July 1, 1993; January 1, 1997; January 7, 2000; September 1, 2003; May 3, 2006; May 14, 2010.]

RULE 602. DEFENSE OF INDIGENTS

Rules promulgated under the Defense of Indigents Act (Act No. 309) passed by the General Assembly and approved by the Governor on June 17, 1969, were adopted by this Court on January 1, 1970. By Order of this Court dated September 20, 1972, the Rules were amended and now read as follows:

(a) Every person arrested for the commission of a crime within the jurisdiction of the Court of General Sessions, every juvenile to be brought before any court on any charge for which he may be imprisoned, and every person charged with the violation of a probationary sentence shall be taken as soon as practicable before the Clerk of the Court of General Sessions in the county where the charges are preferred, or such other officer or officers as may be designated by the resident judge of the circuit, for the purpose of securing to the accused the right to counsel.

In cases involving criminal charges within the jurisdiction of magistrates' courts, municipal courts, or other courts with like jurisdiction, if a prison sentence is likely to be imposed following any conviction, the presiding judge of the court in which the matter is to be determined shall inform the accused as provided in Rule 2 when the case is called for disposition. The procedures concerning juveniles, as provided in Rule 1 and Rule 2 hereof, shall continue to be followed.

(b) The officer before whom the arrested person is taken shall:

(1) Inform the accused of the charges against him and of the nature of the charges.

(2) Advise the accused of his right to counsel and of his right to the appointment of counsel by the court, if the accused is financially unable to employ counsel.

(3) If the accused represents that he is financially unable to employ counsel, take his application for the appointment of counsel or for the services of the Public Defender where the latter is available in the county.

Upon examination of a completed Affidavit of Indigency (Form II), the officer designated to make a determination of indigency shall determine if the accused is indigent. If that officer is unable to make this determination, the final determination whether the accused is indigent shall be made by a judge of the court in which the matter is to be heard.

For purposes of this rule, a person is indigent if that person is financially unable to employ counsel. In making a determination whether a person is indigent, all factors concerning the person's financial condition should be considered including income, debts, assets and family situation. A presumption that the person is indigent shall be created if the person's net family income is less than or equal to the Poverty Guidelines established and revised annually by the United States Department of Health and Human Services and published in the Federal Register. Net income shall mean gross income minus deductions required by law.

(c) If application for counsel is approved for the accused, the Clerk of Court or other officer shall immediately notify the Office of Public Defender, if one exists in the county, and the Public Defender shall immediately thereafter enter upon the representation of the accused. If there is no Public Defender for the county, then the Clerk of Court or other officer shall immediately notify the court, or such person as the resident judge may designate, of the request for counsel and appointment of counsel shall be made immediately with prompt notification thereof to the accused and counsel so appointed.

The initial designation of the Public Defender of appointment of counsel to represent an accused shall be subject to review by the court if it subsequently appears that the accused is in fact financially able to employ counsel, has obtained counsel of his own, or for other good cause shown.

If counsel shall have been retained and partially paid for his services in either the trial or appeal stages, no reimbursement may be had from indigent funds. However, upon the completion of the trial stage, the defendant may be brought before the designated officer of the county for the purpose of a redetermination of indigency. Upon a finding of indigency, and upon the appointment of counsel, the fees and costs of representation may be had from indigent funds as prescribed in these rules.

(d) The appointment of private counsel pursuant to Section V of the Act shall be made or confirmed in a written order, showing the date and time of the appointment; which shall be filed with the Clerk of Court, with copies thereof provided to the accused and to the appointed counsel. Where representation is by a Public Defender, he shall file with the Clerk of Court a written certificate setting forth the date and time at which he undertook such representation, and shall keep and report the hours in court and hours out of court and extraordinary expenses incurred applicable to each case for which representation is made.

(e)(1) Trial counsel, whether retained, appointed, or Public Defender, shall continue representation of an accused until final judgment, including any proceeding on direct appeal, except as hereinafter provided.

(2) During the trial stage, trial counsel may be relieved only for good cause upon written petition to and by written order of the trial judge. In all cases where relief from representation is sought by trial counsel, a copy of the petition shall be served on the accused and the prosecuting attorney. The Public Defender also shall be served when relief is sought by retained or appointed counsel. If trial counsel is relieved for good cause, the trial court shall immediately appoint substitute counsel.

(3) After conviction of an accused who has been represented by appointed counsel or Public Defender, the Office of Appellate Defense shall represent the accused until final judgment. After serving and filing a Notice of Appeal for an accused who desires to appeal, appointed counsel and Public Defenders shall be automatically relieved as appellate counsel for the accused, without obtaining leave to withdraw as provided in Rule 264, SCACR. However, the Public Defender or appointed counsel shall assist in representing the accused in any manner necessary to properly perfect the appeal or as otherwise requested by the Office of Appellate Defense.

(4) When an accused who desires to appeal claims to be indigent at the conclusion of the trial, his retained counsel must first serve and file a Notice of Appeal as required by Rule 203, SCACR. The accused shall then request a determination of his indigency status from the Office of Appellate Defense. If the Office of Appellate Defense determines that the accused is not indigent, retained counsel shall continue representation of the accused during the appeal, unless granted leave to withdraw under Rule 264, SCACR.

If the Office of Appellate Defense determines that the accused is indigent, it will represent the accused until final judgment, including any proceeding on direct appeal, without retained trial counsel's obtaining leave to withdraw under Rule 264, SCACR. However, retained counsel shall assist in representing the accused in any manner necessary to properly establish the indigency of the accused and properly perfect the appeal, including but not limited to obtaining an affidavit of indigency from the accused, obtaining a Court Order declaring the accused's indigency from either the trial judge or the Chief Administrative Judge of the Circuit, and in any other manner requested by the Office of Appellate Defense.

(f) Where a Defender Corporation is established in a county and representation of a defendant is by an attorney other than the Public Defender, no claim for reimbursement of such appointed counsel shall be submitted to the State Treasurer, but he shall be paid out of other available funds.

(g)(1) The application for counsel fees and/or expenses under the terms of this Act shall be made on such forms as prescribed and furnished by the South Carolina Court Administration. Vouchers for fees or expenses should be submitted upon the completion of each stage of representation, trial and appeal stages, respectively. No voucher for fees or expenses except where specifically permitted by written order of the court shall be submitted prior to the completion of a state of representation.

After the completion of services in a state of representation, appointed counsel or public defenders must submit their voucher for fees and/or expenses within thirty (30) days after such completion to the

Clerk of Court of the county in which the services were performed.

(2) Vouchers submitted for fees must show with specificity the hours of in-court and out-of-court time, with an explanation as to the nature of each entry.

Necessary expenses which must be approved by the trial judge by written order, prior to their being incurred, are fees of expert witnesses, costs of scientific tests or exhibits for trial demonstration, costs of psychiatric examinations, and extraordinary travel expenses. The cost of long distance telephone calls should be submitted on the voucher. No other expenses may be submitted for reimbursement from the fund. All claims for expense against the defense fund must be shown on the voucher and must be accompanied by an original or copy of the bills documenting such claim.

Appointed counsel or public defenders involved in representation of defendants against whom the death penalty is sought are subject to the provisions of these Rules of the Defense of Indigents Act except as contravened by the special provisions of Act 555 of 1978.

(3) The court reporter's fee for providing the transcript of the trial proceeding may be reimbursed only after direct submission, by the court reporter, of a letter of transmittal showing the case name and number, the nature of the proceeding, the reporter's name, address, and social security number, a copy of the written request for transcript, a copy of the order of appointment of the requesting party as counsel and a completed court reporter's bill (Form SCCA DI–4). The providing of transcripts and billing rates are to conform to the guidelines set out in Rule 508, SCACR, and are applicable to state court reporters as well as independent court reporters.

Only the cost of one original or one copy of any transcript per defendant, regardless of the number of counsel, may be reimbursed out of the defense fund.

(4) After April 15, 1978, no local reproduction or printing of a transcript or brief for the purpose of an appeal may be reimbursed out of the defense fund. For the purpose of appeal, the transcript and brief should be prepared for reproduction, and forwarded to the Clerk of the Supreme Court. Such papers should be accompanied by a letter of transmittal showing the attorney's name, a return address, a copy of the order of appointment of that attorney as counsel and a copy of the Notice of Appeal.

Upon approval of the papers as submitted, printing, filing and service as required by South Carolina Appellate Court Rules will be administratively accomplished, with a copy returned to the attorney submitting the papers. Any appeal papers not in compliance with South Carolina Appellate Court Rules may be returned for revision.

(5) In cases in which the death penalty is sought, one original of the trial proceeding should be prepared immediately by the court reporter and submitted to the Clerk of the Supreme Court for the purpose of the automatic review by the Supreme Court. Upon such provision to the Clerk, copies of the transcript will be provided to defendant's counsel and no original or copy of a transcript in a case in which the death penalty is sought, otherwise provided to appointed counsel or a public defender by a court reporter, may be paid for out of the defense fund.

(6) In any trial or appeal in which an indigent defendant intends to represent himself, no expenses related to his representation may be paid from the defense fund without his having first appeared before the court, or such designated officer, for the purpose of a determination of indigency and his having obtained a written order of the court finding that defendant competent to represent himself.

Where an indigent defendant represents himself, after first obtaining leave of court, expenses of representation at trial or appeal must be submitted to Court Administration in conformity with these Rules and the Defense of Indigents Act except that any vouchers or court reporter's bills submitted must be accompanied by written evidence of defendant's compliance with this Rule. In any trial or appeal wherein representation is by the defendant himself, no fees of counsel may be allowed.

In post-conviction relief matters, expenses related to representation and fees of appointed counsel may be paid where permitted and as prescribed in these Rules and the Defense of Indigents Act. No defendant representing himself in a post-conviction relief matter may receive fees for representation but may be reimbursed for expenses allowed by these rules and statutes.

(h) In any case in which more than one attorney is appointed to represent a defendant, the combined fees paid to such attorneys shall not exceed the maximum amounts as provided by statute relating to indigent representation.

In all cases of multiple appointed counsel for single defendants, no single defendant is entitled to have the cost of more than one original or one copy of any transcript paid for from the defense fund regardless of the number of counsel.

In cases involving several defendants represented by appointed counsel who are tried together and who intend to appeal jointly, arrangements should be made, where possible, to share the transcripts between defendants and attorneys.

In any case in which a defendant represented by appointed counsel and a defendant represented by retained counsel intend to appeal jointly, the procedures for the provision of transcripts and printing, and the payment of the costs thereof, shall be pursuant to these Rules and the Defense of Indigents Act. The

Office of Court Administration shall thereafter apportion an estimated amount of that cost and shall be reimbursed by the defendant who had retained counsel.

(i) The forms in Appendix A of Part VI shall be furnished by the Clerk of the Supreme Court to the office of the Clerk of Court in each county for use in administering the provisions of the Act as implemented by these Rules.

[Former Supreme Court Rule 51 adopted as Rule 602, SCACR, effective September 1, 1990. Amended effective September 1, 2001; April 29, 2009.]

RULE 603. PAPER SIZE

All papers filed in all courts of this State, other than papers filed as exhibits in their original form or as copies of their original form, shall be prepared on letter-size (8½ by 11) paper. This Rule shall become mandatory July 1, 1983. Until that time, the Clerks of the various courts of this State shall accept papers of either letter-size or legal-size (8½ by 11 or 8½ by 14).

[Former Supreme Court Rule 47 adopted as Rule 603, SCACR, effective September 1, 1990.]

RULE 604. ATTORNEYS OR COURT OFFICERS AS SURETY

(a) An attorney or other officer of any court of this State shall not:

(1) Be, directly or indirectly, a surety upon any recognizance or undertaking in any court of this State;

(2) Be, directly or indirectly, involved in the surety business or in business with any person or persons becoming surety upon any recognizance or undertaking in any court in this State;

(3) Refer a person, directly or indirectly, to any surety or bondsman who is an immediate family member of the attorney or court officer. An immediate family member includes the spouse, father, mother, father-in-law, mother-in-law, son, daughter, brother, sister, brother-in-law, and sister-in-law.

(b) A clerk of court shall not accept any recognizance or undertaking on which an attorney or other officer of any court of this State has acted, directly or indirectly, as a surety.

(c) An attorney or court officer violating a provision of this Rule shall be guilty of contempt. The prohibitions contained in this Rule shall not apply to any recognizance or undertaking in which the attorney, the court officer, an immediate family member of the attorney or court officer, or an agent or employee of the attorney or court officer is the principal.

[Former Supreme Court Rule 14 adopted as Rule 604, SCACR, effective September 1, 1990. Amended effective May 17, 1993.]

RULE 605. BROADCASTING, TELEVISING, RECORDING OR PHOTOGRAPHING COURT PROCEEDINGS

(a) Definitions.

(1) "Media" means any recognized news-gathering or news-reporting agency and the individual persons involved, and includes newspapers, radio, television, radio and television networks, news services, magazines, trade papers, in-house publications, professional journals, or other news-reporting or news-gathering agency whose function is to inform the public or some segment thereof.

(2) "Presiding judge" means the judge, justice, master or other judicial officer who is scheduled to preside or is presiding over the proceeding. Presiding judge in the appellate court shall refer to the Chief Justice or Chief Judge of the court, or the senior justice or judge if the Chief Justice or Chief Judge is not participating in the proceeding.

(3) "Proceeding" means any trial, hearing, motion, argument or other matter held in open court which the public is entitled to attend.

(b) General Rule. Except as provided by (c) through (f) below, the broadcasting, televising, recording, or taking photographs in the courtroom and areas immediately adjacent thereto during sessions of court or recesses between sessions is prohibited.

(c) Use for Judicial Administration. A presiding judge may authorize the use of electronic or photographic means for the presentation of evidence, for the perpetuation of a record, or for other purposes of judicial administration.

(d) Ceremonial Proceedings. A presiding judge may authorize the broadcasting, televising, recording, or photographing of investitive or ceremonial proceedings.

(e) Educational Use. A presiding judge may authorize the photographic or electronic recording and reproduction of appropriate court proceedings under the following conditions:

(1) the means of recording will not distract participants or impair the dignity of the proceedings;

(2) the parties have consented, and the consent to being depicted or recorded has been obtained from each witness appearing in the recording and reproduction;

(3) the reproduction will not be exhibited until after the proceeding has been concluded and all direct appeals have been exhausted; and

(4) the reproduction will be exhibited only for instructional purposes in educational institutions.

(f) Media Coverage.

(1) *General Provisions.*

(i) Subject to the requirements of this Rule, representatives of the media may use video, still cameras or recorders to cover proceedings in the courts of this State.

(ii) Media representatives must give reasonable notice to the presiding judge of a request to cover a proceeding. If written notice is required by the presiding judge, Form 1 should be used. In the absence of reasonable notice, the presiding judge may refuse to permit media coverage, after giving due regard for the public educational benefits flowing from the photographing and recording of court proceedings.

(iii) The presiding judge may refuse, limit, or terminate media coverage of an entire case, portions thereof, or testimony of particular witnesses as may be required in the interests of justice.

(iv) No direct public expense is to be incurred for equipment, wiring, or personnel needed to provide media coverage.

(v) Nothing in this Rule shall prevent a judge from placing additional reasonable restrictions, or prohibiting altogether, photographing, recording, or broadcasting in court facilities other than the courtroom.

(2) *Limitations.*

(i) Coverage of proceedings which are otherwise closed to the public is prohibited.

(ii) There shall be no audio pickup or broadcast of conferences which occur in a court facility between attorneys and their clients, between co-counsel of a client, between adverse counsel or between counsel and the presiding judge.

(iii) The members of the jury may not be photographed except when they happen to be in the background of other subjects being photographed. Camera and audio coverage of prospective jurors during selection is prohibited.

(3) *Equipment and Personnel.*

(i) No more than two television cameras, operated by no more than one camera person each, shall be permitted in any proceeding.

(ii) No more than one radio recorder, operated by no more than one person, shall be permitted in any proceeding.

(iii) No more than two still photographers, utilizing no more than two cameras and related equipment each, shall be permitted in any proceeding.

(iv) If two or more media representatives have given notice under section (f)(1)(ii) above, the presiding judge shall notify the applicants that no coverage may begin until all the representatives have agreed upon a pooling arrangement for their respective news media. Such pooling arrangements shall include the designation of pool operators, procedures for cost sharing, access to and dissemination of material, and selection of a pool representative if appropriate. The presiding judge may not be called upon to mediate or resolve any dispute as to these pooling arrangements.

(v) Equipment or clothing shall not bear the insignia or marking of any media agency. Media personnel operating cameras shall wear appropriate business attire.

(vi) Reporters, in the interest of accuracy, may use hand-held micro-cassette tape recorders that are no more sensitive than the human ear, provided they are not used in violation of section (f)(2)(ii).

(4) *Sound and Light Criteria.*

(i) Equipment shall not produce distracting sound or light. Signal lights or devices to show when equipment is operating shall not be visible. Moving lights, flash attachments, or sudden light changes shall not be used.

(ii) Except as otherwise approved by the presiding judge, existing courtroom sound and light systems shall be used without modification. Audio pickup for all purposes shall be accomplished from existing audio systems present in the court facility or from a television camera's built-in microphone. If no technically suitable audio system exists in the court facility, microphones and related wiring essential for media purposes shall be unobtrusive and shall be located in places designated in advance of any proceeding by the presiding judge.

(iii) Court proceedings shall not be interrupted by reporter or technician because of a technical or equipment problem. If any problem occurs, that piece of equipment shall be turned off while the proceeding is in session. No attempt shall be made to correct the technical or equipment problem until the proceeding is in recess or has concluded.

(5) *Location of Equipment and Personnel.*

(i) The presiding judge shall designate the location in the courtroom for media equipment and operators.

(ii) During proceedings, operating personnel shall not move about nor shall there be placement or removal of equipment.

(6) *Compliance.* Any media representative who fails to comply with this Rule shall be subject to an appropriate sanction as determined by the presiding judge.

(7) *Review.* It is not intended that a grant or denial of media coverage be subject to appellate review insofar as it pertains to and arises under this Rule, except as otherwise provided by law.

(8) *Impermissible Use of Media Material.* None of the video, photographs or recordings of proceedings under subsection (f) of this Rule shall be admissible as evidence in the proceeding out of which it arose, any proceedings subsequent and collateral thereto, or upon any retrial or appeal of such proceeding.

[Adopted effective September 21, 1993. Amended effective October 1, 1996.]

Notes

See also, "APPENDIX B. MEDIA COVERAGE OF COURT PROCEEDINGS FORM" in the APPENDICES TO PART VI.

RULE 606. RETENTION AND DISPOSITION OF EXHIBITS IN THE CIRCUIT AND FAMILY COURTS

(a) Duty of Clerk. Unless otherwise directed by the court or this rule, the clerk of court for the county shall retain possession of all exhibits admitted into evidence or marked for identification during a hearing or trial before the circuit or family court.

(b) Release of Exhibits. The clerk may temporarily release exhibits to the court reporter during the hearing or trial or when necessary to prepare the transcript, to a person designated by order of an appellate court when exhibits are needed for an appellate proceeding, or to any other person as may be ordered by the court.

(c) Retention Period by Clerk.

(1) *Criminal Cases (Including Juvenile Delinquency Cases).*

(A) Capital Cases. In any criminal case in which a sentence of death has been imposed, the exhibits shall be retained by the clerk and shall not be disposed of except upon order of the Supreme Court or upon the death of the defendant. In the event of the death of the defendant, the circuit court shall direct a disposition of the exhibits.

(B) Non–Capital Cases. The clerk of court shall retain the exhibits in non-capital cases (including juvenile delinquency cases) for at least eighteen (18) months after sentence is imposed or, if an appeal is taken, for eighteen (18) months after the remittitur is sent by the appellate court. For the purpose of this rule, the term "sentence" shall include commitment or other care and treatment imposed at the dispositional hearing in a juvenile delinquency case. After the expiration of this retention period, the clerk shall dispose of the exhibits as provided by (d)(1)(B) and (d)(1)(C) below. In the event the defendant should die during this retention period, the exhibits may be immediately disposed of as provided by (d)(1)(C) below even for offenses covered by the Preservation of Evidence Act (S.C. Code Ann. §§ 17–28–300 to –360).

(2) *Civil Cases.*

(A) Collateral Challenges Regarding Capital Cases. In any post-conviction relief case or other civil collateral proceeding challenging a criminal case involving a sentence of death, the exhibits shall be retained by the clerk and shall not be disposed of except upon order of the Supreme Court or upon the death of the criminal defendant. In the event of the death of the defendant, the circuit court shall direct a disposition of the exhibits.

(B) All Other Civil Cases. The clerk shall retain the exhibits in all other civil cases for sixty (60) days after the entry of the final judgment in the matter or, if an appeal is taken, sixty (60) days after the remittitur is sent by the appellate court. After the expiration of this retention period, the clerk shall dispose of the exhibits as provided by (d)(2)(B) below.

(d) Disposition of Exhibits by Clerk.

(1) *Criminal Cases (Including Juvenile Delinquency Cases).*

(A) Capital Cases. As indicated by (c)(1)(A) above, the clerk shall not dispose of exhibits in a capital case except upon order of the Supreme Court or upon the death of the defendant. In the event of the death of the defendant, the circuit court shall direct a disposition of the exhibits.

(B) Disposition of Exhibits in Cases Involving Crimes Listed in the Preservation of Evidence Act. In any non-capital case involving one of the offenses listed in the Preservation of Evidence Act or accessory before the fact to one of those offenses, a custodian designated by the governing body of the county or, if such designation has not been made, the sheriff of the county, shall be responsible for obtaining the exhibits from the clerk after the expiration of the time period specified in (c)(1)(B) above. Unless otherwise ordered by the court under S.C. Code Ann. § 17–28–340, the designated custodian, or the sheriff if no other custodian has been designated, shall be responsible for retaining the exhibits for the periods specified by the Preservation of Evidence Act. After notice from the clerk, the designated custodian, or the sheriff if no other custodian has been designated, shall have thirty (30) days to take custody of the exhibits and provide the clerk with a receipt for the exhibits. Failure to do so may be treated as contempt of the circuit or family court.

(C) All Other Criminal Cases. Unless the court has ordered some other disposition of the exhibit, the party introducing an exhibit shall immediately reclaim the exhibit from the clerk after the expiration of the retention period specified in (c)(1)(B) above. The party shall sign a receipt for the exhibit. For exhibits that are not reclaimed, the clerk may dispose of an exhibit:

(i) Forty-five (45) days after the mailing of a notice to the party introducing the exhibit advising the party that the exhibit will be destroyed or disposed of if not reclaimed within thirty (30) days. This notice shall not be sent prior to the expiration of the retention period specified in (c)(1)(B) above. The notice shall be sent to the party's last counsel of record as shown by the case file or, if the party has no counsel of record, to the party at the party's last known address as shown by the case file; or

(ii) Regardless whether notice is given under (i) above, twenty-four (24) months after the sentence was imposed or, if an appeal was taken, twenty-four (24) months after the remittitur was issued.

(2) *Civil Cases.*

(A) Collateral Challenges Regarding Capital Cases. As indicated by (c)(2)(A) above, the clerk shall not dispose of exhibits in a post-conviction relief case or other civil collateral proceeding challenging a criminal case involving a sentence of death except upon order of the Supreme Court or upon the death of the criminal defendant. In the event of the death of the defendant, the circuit court shall direct a disposition of the exhibits.

(B) All Other Civil Cases. Unless the court has ordered some other disposition of the exhibit, the party introducing an exhibit shall immediately reclaim the exhibit from the clerk of court after the expiration of the retention period specified in (c)(2)(B). The party shall sign a receipt for the exhibit. For exhibits which are not reclaimed, the clerk may dispose of the exhibit:

(i) Forty-five (45) days after the mailing of a notice to the party introducing the exhibit advising the party that the exhibit will be destroyed or disposed of if not reclaimed within thirty (30) days. This notice shall not be sent prior to the expiration of the retention period specified in (c)(2)(B) above. The notice shall be sent to the party's last counsel of record as shown by the case file or, if the party has no counsel of record, to the party at the party's last known address as shown by the case file; or

(ii) Regardless whether notice is given under (i) above, six (6) months after the entry of final judgment in the matter or, if an appeal was taken, six months after the remittitur was issued.

(e) Effect of the Failure to Reclaim Exhibits; Liability of Clerk. The failure of a party to reclaim an exhibit within thirty (30) days after the time the party is authorized to do so under (d)(1)(C) or (d)(2)(B) shall be construed as the party's consent to destroy or otherwise dispose of the exhibit, and no cause of action shall lie against the clerk for the destruction or other disposition of the exhibit. Except as otherwise provided by law, this rule or order of the court, an exhibit which is not reclaimed under (d)(1)(C) or (d)(2)(B) shall become the property of the county and the clerk shall deliver the exhibit to the county; provided, however, if the exhibit has no value or de minimis value, the clerk may destroy the exhibit.

(f) Record of Disposition. A record of exhibits which have been disposed of by the clerk under (d) above shall be maintained. At a minimum, the case file should contain a description, copy or photograph of the exhibit; the date any notice under (d)(1)(C)(i) or (d)(2)(B)(i) was mailed; the date of the disposition of the exhibit; the nature of the disposition including the name of the party, person or agency to whom it was returned if applicable; and a copy of the receipt for the exhibit if the exhibit was returned.

(g) Illegal Items. This rule shall not authorize the return of an exhibit to any person when the exhibit is a weapon, controlled substance, poison, explosive or any other kind of property which the person may not lawfully possess. In such cases, the exhibit shall be disposed of in the manner provided by law or in a manner ordered by the court.

(h) Authority of Court. The court may, on motion by a party or its own motion, direct the release of an exhibit at any time, and may allow the substitution of a copy, photograph or description in place of the exhibit. If such substitution is allowed, the copy, photograph or description shall be admissible in any subsequent proceedings to the same extent that the exhibit would have been admissible. The court may, on motion by a party or its own motion, direct the retention of an exhibit beyond the period specified by this rule upon a showing of good cause. The court may, on motion by a party or someone having an interest in the exhibit, direct that an exhibit be returned to someone other than the party who introduced the exhibit. In cases involving one of the offenses listed in the Preservation of Evidence Act or accessory before the fact to one of those offenses, no substitution, return or other disposition of the exhibit shall be made unless the requirements of S.C. Code Ann. § 17–28–340 have been satisfied.

[Adopted effective September 1, 1997. Amended effective April 29, 2009.]

RULE 607. COURT REPORTER TRANSCRIPTS AND TAPES

(a) Applicability. This rule is applicable to court reporter transcripts and tapes relating to proceedings before the family and circuit court, to include proceedings before masters-in-equity. A court reporter for such a proceeding, regardless whether the court reporter is a Judicial Department employee or a private court reporter, shall comply with the requirements of this rule.

(b) Ordering Transcripts. Transcripts of proceedings which are needed for an appeal or appellate review of a post-conviction relief action before the Supreme Court or Court of Appeals shall be ordered as provided by Rules 207(a) or 243(b), SCACR. In all other cases, the request for the transcript shall be made, in writing, to the court reporter, and a copy of the request shall be served as provided by Rule 262(b), SCACR, on all parties to the proceeding which is to be transcribed and, if the transcript is requested for use in another case, on all parties in that case. A copy of the request shall also be provided to the Office of Court Administration. The names and addresses of all persons who are to be served with a copy shall be included on the request for the transcript.

(c) Preparation of Transcript. The transcript shall be prepared in the manner prescribed by the Court Reporters Manual published by the Office of Court Administration.

(d) Delivery of Transcripts. A court reporter shall transcribe and deliver the transcript no later than sixty (60) days after the date of the request. Records shall be transcribed by the court reporter in the order in which the requests for transcripts are made; provided, however, that requests to transcribe post-conviction relief proceedings challenging a sentence of death shall be given priority as provided by S.C.Code Ann. § 17–27–160(E).

(e) Extension of Time to Deliver. If a court reporter anticipates continuous engagement in the performance of other official duties which make it impossible to prepare a transcript within the time specified in (d) above, the reporter shall promptly notify the Office of Court Administration in writing of the fact, setting forth the caption of the case involved, the length of time required to complete the transcript, and the nature and probable duration of the conflicting official duties. The Office of Court Administration may grant an extension of up to ninety (90) days. An extension in excess of ninety days (90) days shall not be allowed except by order of the Chief Justice.

(f) Notice of Extension. Upon the granting of any extension of time for delivery of the transcript, the Office of Court Administration shall notify the parties and, if the transcript has been requested for an appeal or other proceeding before the Supreme Court or the Court of Appeals, the Clerk of that Court.

(g) Failure to Receive Transcript. If the requesting party has not received the transcript within the allotted time nor received notification of an extension within ten (10) days after the allotted time, the requesting party shall notify, in writing, the Office of Court Administration, the court reporter and, if the transcript has been requested for an appeal or other proceeding before the Supreme Court or the Court of Appeals, the Clerk of that Court.

(h) Fees for Transcription and Other Services.

(1) *By Judicial Department Court Reporter.* A court reporter shall receive the following fees:

(A) A fee of Three Dollars and Twenty–Five Cents ($3.25) per page for producing an original transcript.

(B) A fee of Seventy–Five Cents ($.75) per page for furnishing a copy of a previously prepared transcript.

(C) A fee of One Dollar and Fifty Cents ($1.50) per page for each person receiving Real-time output when a Real-time Request is signed by the requestor.

(D) A fee of One Dollar and Fifty Cents ($1.50) per page for unedited (rough copy) ASCII Disks when no request for an original transcript has been made.

(E) A fee of Thirty–Five Dollars ($35) for edited ASCII disks. This service is only available to a requestor who has requested an original or a copy of the transcript.

(F) A fee of One Dollar ($1) per page for condensed transcripts, which contain no more than four pages of text. This service is only available to a requestor who has requested an original or a copy of the transcript.

(G) A fee of Fifty Cents ($.50) per page for Keyword Indexing. This service is only available to a requestor who has requested an original or a copy of the transcript.

(H) A fee of Thirty–Five Dollars ($35) for e-mailed transcripts. This service is only available to a requestor who has requested an original or a copy of the transcript.

(I) A fee of One Dollar and Fifty Cents ($1.50) per page for unedited (rough draft) e-mailed transcripts.

(J) The following per page costs apply to requests to produce a transcript on an expedited basis:

(i) A fee of Four Dollars and Twenty–Five Cents ($4.25) for original transcripts delivered within seven days of the request and Seventy–Five Cents ($.75) for a copy.

(ii) A fee of Five Dollars and Twenty–Five Cents ($5.25) for original transcripts delivered overnight and One Dollar ($1.00) for a copy.

(iii) A fee of Six Dollars and Twenty–Five Cents ($6.25) for original transcripts delivered on a daily basis and One Dollar ($1.00) for a copy.

(2) *By Private Court Reporter.* In the event the court reporter is not an employee of the Judicial Department, the fees to be charged shall be that agreed upon by the court reporter and the parties. The transcript produced by the Judicial Department court reporter is the official transcript.

(i) Retention of Tapes. Except as provided below, a court reporter shall retain the primary and backup tapes of a proceeding for a period of at least five (5) years after the date of the proceeding, and the court reporter may reuse or destroy the tapes after the expiration of that period. If the proceeding was a hearing or trial which lasted for more than one day, the time shall be computed from the last day of the hearing or trial. In any proceeding which has been transcribed, the court reporter shall retain the primary and backup tapes which have been transcribed for a period of at least thirty (30) days after the original transcript is sent to the requesting party, to allow any party to challenge the accuracy of the transcription. If no challenge is received by the court reporter within the thirty (30) day period, the tapes may be reused or destroyed.

(j) Failure to Comply. The wilful failure of a court reporter to comply with the provisions of this Rule shall constitute contempt of court enforceable by order of the Supreme Court.

[Adopted effective August 1, 1998. Amended effective June 8, 2000; August 6, 2003; September 1, 2006; August 27, 2008; April 29, 2009.]

RULE 608. APPOINTMENT OF LAWYERS FOR INDIGENTS

(a) Purpose. This rule provides a uniform method of managing the appointment of lawyers to serve as counsel for indigent persons in the circuit and family courts pursuant to statutory and constitutional mandates.

(b) Terminology. The following terminology is used in this rule:

(1) *Active Member:* Any active member of the South Carolina Bar as defined by the Bylaws of the Bar. For the purpose of this rule, a person holding a limited certificate to practice law in South Carolina shall not be considered an active member.

(2) *Appointment Year:* The period from July 1 to June 30.

(3) *Supreme Court:* The Supreme Court of South Carolina.

(4) *Indigent:* Any person who is financially unable to employ counsel. In making a determination of indigency, all factors concerning the person's financial condition should be considered including income, debts, assets, and family situation. A presumption that the person is indigent shall be created if the person's net family income is less than or equal to the Poverty Guidelines established and revised annually by the United States Department of Health and Human Services and published in the Federal Register. Net income shall mean gross income minus deductions required by law.

(5) *Death Penalty Case:* Any criminal case in which the solicitor has given notice of the intent to seek the death penalty and any post-conviction relief action challenging a proceeding in which a death sentence was imposed.

(6) *Family Member:* A spouse, child, grandchild, parent, grandparent, or other person with which the member maintains a close familial relationship.

(c) Lists.

(1) For each appointment year, the South Carolina Bar shall prepare two lists for each county:

(A) Criminal List. A list of all active members who have been certified by the Supreme Court to serve as lead counsel in death penalty cases (see Rule 421, SCACR) who are eligible for appointment in the county, and all other active members who normally represent at least three (3) clients before the court of general sessions during a calendar year and are eligible for appointment in the county. The list shall indicate which members are death penalty certified as lead counsel, the date on which each member was admitted to practice law in South Carolina, and whether the member has completed or is exempt from the trial experiences required by Rule 403, SCACR. This list shall be used to appoint counsel for indigents in death penalty cases [see (b)(5) above] and criminal cases, including juvenile delinquency matters.

(B) Civil List. A list of all other active members eligible for appointment in the county. This list shall indicate the date on which each member was admitted to practice law in South Carolina, and whether the member has completed or is exempt from the trial experiences required by Rule 403, SCACR. This list shall be used for the appointment of counsel for indigents in all cases other than those specified in (A) above, including post-conviction relief matters that are not death penalty cases.

These lists shall be arranged alphabetically and shall be provided to the county clerks of court at least thirty (30) days prior to the beginning of the appointment year. In compiling the lists, the South Carolina Bar shall place each lawyer's name on a list in the county designated in (c)(2)(A). The lawyer's name shall also be placed on a list in one of the counties designated in (c)(2)(B), in the discretion of the South Carolina Bar, to meet the needs of counties which require additional lawyers for appointment.

(2) Active members shall, at the time of payment of annual license fees to the South Carolina Bar, provide the following information to the Bar:

(A) the county in which they primarily practice in South Carolina or, if they do not practice law in South Carolina, the county in which they reside in South Carolina;

(B) all counties in which they maintain an office, provide a significant amount of legal services, or disseminate advertisements via television, radio, billboards, newspapers, magazines, or telephone directories;

(C) whether they are certified by the Supreme Court to serve as lead counsel in a death penalty case;

(D) if they are not death penalty certified as lead counsel, whether their names should be placed on the criminal or civil list based on the criteria given in (c)(1) above;

(E) if admitted after March 1, 1979, whether they have completed the trial experiences required by Rule 403, SCACR; and

(F) the number of appointments they received in the reporting year, the number of appointments still pending at the close of the reporting year, and the total number of hours expended on appointments in the reporting year.

(3) Active members shall notify the South Carolina Bar within thirty (30) days of any changes in the county in which they reside, primarily practice, maintain an office, provide a significant amount of legal services, or advertise as defined in (2)(B). Active members who wish to provide service to indigents in additional counties shall notify the Bar with the name of the additional county at the time of payment of annual license fees. The Bar shall transfer the names of those members to the appropriate list(s) and notify the appropriate clerk(s) of court.

(4) If a member ceases to be an active member, the Bar shall delete that member's name from the list(s) and notify the appropriate clerk(s) of court.

(5) If a member becomes certified to serve as lead counsel in a death penalty case, the member shall, within thirty (30) days of the date of the certification, notify the South Carolina Bar. If not already on the criminal list(s), the Bar shall transfer the member's name to the criminal list(s). The Bar shall notify the appropriate clerk(s) of court of the certification and any transfer.

(6) If a member would, due to conflicts of interest, be prevented from accepting cases in a county in which the member would be subjected to appointment under (c)(2), the member will designate a county in which the conflicts will not arise.

(d) Active Members Who Are Exempt from Appointment.

(1) The following active members shall be exempt from appointment:

(A) Members who are prohibited by federal or state law from taking such appointments. While not intended to be an exclusive list, this includes:

(i) Law Clerks and Staff Attorneys for the Judicial Department under Canon 5(D), Rule 506, SCACR.

(ii) Public Defenders who are prohibited from engaging in any private practice of law under S.C. Code Ann. § 17–3–580(A).

(iii) Appellate Defenders who are prohibited from engaging in the private practice of law by S.C. Code Ann. §§ 17–4–40 and –50.

(B) Members who are solicitors or assistant solicitors for a judicial circuit if those members do not engage in the private practice of law.

(C) Members who are employed by the Office of the South Carolina Attorney General or by the United States Attorney if those members do not engage in the private practice of law.

(D) Members who are employed by any court of this state or by any Federal Court if those members do not engage in the private practice of law.

(E) Members who are employed by the South Carolina Administrative Law Court or by any Federal Administrative Law Judge if those members do not engage in the private practice of law.

(F) Members who are engaged in providing legal assistance supported in whole or in part by the Legal Services Corporation established under 42 U.S.C. § 2996a if those members do not engage in the private practice of law outside that program.

(G) Members who have been admitted to practice law in this State or another jurisdiction for thirty-five (35) years or have attained sixty-five (65) years of age.

(H) Members who have neither an office nor a principal residence in this State, and who do not engage in the private practice of law in this State.

(I) Members who are full time employees of the United States to include members employed by the armed forces of the United States. To be exempt, these members may not engage in the private practice of law in this State.

(J) Members who are full time employees of the State of South Carolina, or a political subdivision of the State, to include counties, school districts, municipalities, and public service districts. To be exempt, these members may not engage in the private practice of law in this State.

(K) Members who are full time care givers for a family member and do not derive any income from the practice of law in this State.

(L) Members who have been designated pursuant to S.C. Code Ann. § 63–11–500 to represent guardians ad litem in Department of Social Services cases. Each qualifying program may designate up to two members in each county and these members are expected to provide representation in all such cases unless there is a conflict or other good cause for not providing the representation.

(M) Members who are serving as members or associate members of the Board of Law Examiners.

(N) Members who are serving as members of the Committee on Character and Fitness.

(O) Members who are serving as members of the Commission on Lawyer Conduct.

(P) Members who are serving as members of the Commission on Judicial Conduct.

(Q) Members who are serving as members of the General Assembly.

(2) For the purpose of determining if a member is exempt, members shall not be considered to have engaged in the private practice of law by volunteering for an appointment under section (h)(1), by representing an indigent as part of the pro bono program of the South Carolina Bar, or by providing legal services for themselves or a family member as long as the services are provided without compensation.

(3) Active members shall claim an exemption at the time they file with the Bar under section (c)(2) above. The claim for exemption must be accompanied by sufficient information to confirm that the lawyer is in fact eligible for exemption. The Bar shall determine if the member is exempt or non-exempt.

(4) A member who is denied an exemption by the Bar may seek review of that determination by filing a petition with the Supreme Court within ten (10) days of receiving notice of the Bar's determination. The petition shall comply with the requirements of Rule 240, SCACR, including the filing fee required by that rule.

(5) If an active member is non-exempt and becomes exempt, or is exempt and becomes non-exempt, the member shall notify the Bar of this change in status within thirty (30) days of the change. Any member claiming to have become exempt shall provide the Bar with sufficient information to confirm that the member is in fact eligible for exemption. The Bar shall add to, or delete from, the appropriate list the name of the member and notify the appropriate clerks of court of any additions or deletions.

(e) Active Members Who Have Not Completed the Trial Experiences Required by Rule 403, SCACR. An active member who has not completed the trial experiences required by Rule 403, SCACR, but has been admitted to practice law in South Carolina for six months or more, shall be fully eligible for appointment under this rule, and, at his or her expense, will be expected to associate another lawyer if necessary to carry out the appointment.

(f) Appointments, Process of Appointments, and Relief from Appointments.

(1) *Appointments.*

(A) Lead Counsel in Death Penalty Cases. The appointment of a lead counsel to represent an indigent defendant in a death penalty case shall be made from the list of members specified in (c)(1)(A) above who have been death penalty certified as lead counsel by the Supreme Court; provided, however, that lawyers who are not certified may be appointed as lead counsel in a post-conviction relief action for a death-sentenced inmate if they have previously represented a death-sentenced inmate in a state or federal post-conviction relief proceeding as provided by S.C. Code Ann. § 17-27-160.

(B) Other Criminal Cases. The appointment of counsel in all other criminal cases, including juvenile delinquency matters, shall be made from the criminal list specified in (c)(1)(A) above. A member who is death penalty certified may be appointed to a non-death penalty case.

(C) All Other Cases. The appointment of members as counsel in all other cases, including post-conviction relief matters that are not death penalty cases, shall be made from the civil list specified in (c)(1)(B).

(2) *Appointment Process.*

(A) Sequence of Appointments. Appointments shall be made beginning with the name of the member whose name would follow that of the last person appointed alphabetically on the list for the preceding year and shall thereafter proceed alphabetically down the list unless there is good reason, as determined by the clerk of court or the judge, to alter the sequence. A good reason for altering the sequence may include, but is not limited to, the necessity to obtain a lawyer with sufficient experience to serve as second counsel in a capital case, when a reason for disqualification is known at the time the appointment is being made, or when a deviation is necessary to insure that counsel is competent to handle the matter. Once the end of the list is reached, appointments will be made from the beginning of the list.

(B) Notification of Appointment. Once appointments have been made, the clerk of court shall mail a copy of the order of appointment to the attorney within two business days and notify the attorney electronically where feasible.

(C) Documenting Appointments. Upon making an appointment, the clerk of court shall:

(i) promptly mark the names of those members who have received appointments; and

(ii) promptly record the total number of appointments the member has received in the county during the appointment year.

(3) *Relief from Appointments.* If a member is unable to serve for any reason, the member shall, within five (5) days of the date of receipt of the order of appointment, file a motion to be relieved with the clerk of court. A member who becomes aware of a reason for being relieved after the expiration of the five (5) day period shall promptly file a motion to be relieved with the clerk of court.

The Chief Judge for Administrative Purposes of the court before which the matter is pending shall then consider the request to be relieved and may relieve the member if the judge finds good cause to do so.

If relieved, the member shall not receive credit for the appointment unless the order relieving the member affirmatively finds that the member has substantially performed the responsibilities of the appointment prior to being relieved.

(4) *Limitations on Numbers of Appointments.*

(A) Number of Appointments in a County per Month. A member will not receive more than one (1) appointment in any county during a calendar month. Once all of the members on a list have received one (1) appointment in a calendar month, the county clerk of court will contact the clerk in the Lead Regional County identified in the table below. The clerk from the Lead Regional County will provide the next names available for appointment from the list in that county and note that those members have received appointments from other Counties in the Region. The clerk will provide sufficient names to cover the pending appointments.

(B) Death Penalty Cases. A member who receives an appointment as lead or second counsel in a death penalty case shall be exempt from being appointed to another death penalty case until six (6) months after the date of sentencing or, if the matter does not result in a sentence, the date when the case ends. When a member is appointed as lead or second counsel in a death penalty case, the clerk shall mark the list to reflect the period of exemption. Although a member may be temporarily exempt from further death penalty appointments, nothing shall prevent the member from volunteering for an appointment under (h)(1) below.

(C) A member who receives an appointment as an attorney to protect under Rule 31, Rules for Lawyer Disciplinary Enforcement, contained in Rule 413, SCACR, or receives an assignment to investigate a matter as an attorney to assist disciplinary counsel under Rule 5(c), Rules for Lawyer Disciplinary Enforcement, shall receive credit for the appointment under this rule. The Office of Disciplinary Counsel shall notify the appropriate clerk of court of the appointment, and the clerk shall mark the list to reflect the appointment. If the member is relieved of this appointment before it is substantially completed, the Supreme Court or the Office of Disciplinary Counsel shall notify the clerk so that the credit may be withdrawn.

(D) A member who serves as a member of the Resolution of Fee Disputes Board and completes an assignment under Rule 416, SCACR, shall receive credit for the appointment under this rule. The Circuit Chair of the Resolution of Fee Disputes Board shall notify the appropriate clerk of court of the completed assignment, and the clerk shall mark the list to reflect the appointment. A member serving as Circuit Chair or Executive Chair shall receive credit for two appointments during the appointment year. The Executive Chair or the South Carolina Bar shall notify the appropriate clerk of court, and the clerk shall mark the list to reflect the appointments.

(5) *Number of Appointments per Year.* A member will be subject to no more than seven (7) appointments during an appointment year. After each member on the list has received seven (7) appointments, the county clerk of court will contact the clerk in the Lead Regional County identified at the end of this section. The clerk from the Lead Regional County will provide the next names available for appointment from the list in that county and note that those members have received appointments from other counties in the Region. The clerk will provide sufficient names to cover the pending appointments. After members in the Lead Regional County have received seven (7) appointments, members in the other counties in that Region shall receive appointments until all members in the Region have received seven (7) appointments. If further appointments in a Region are needed, other Lead Regional Counties should be contacted to provide names for appointments, beginning with the next closest Lead Regional County.

County Designations

Region	Lead Regional County	Other Counties in the Region
1	Beaufort	Allendale, Bamberg, Barnwell, Hampton, Jasper
2	Charleston	Berkeley, Clarendon, Colleton, Dorchester, Orangeburg, Williamsburg
3	Greenville	Abbeville, Anderson, Cherokee, Greenwood, Laurens, Oconee, Pickens, Spartanburg, Union
4	Lexington	Aiken, Edgefield, McCormick, Saluda
5	Richland	Calhoun, Chester, Chesterfield, Darlington, Fairfield, Kershaw, Lancaster, Lee, Marlboro, Newberry, Sumter, York
6	Horry* (Florence and Horry Counties will split appointments in Dillon	Dillon, Florence* , Georgetown, Marion

County. From January 1 through June 30, Florence County will supply overflow attorneys to Dillon County. From July 1 through December 31, Horry County will supply overflow attorneys to Dillon County.

(6) A member who has received an appointment in a county other than the county in which the attorney primarily practices or resides may receive authorization to be present by telephone or, where available, by videoconference for hearings. This provision does not apply to evidentiary hearings.

(g) Minimizing Appointments.

(1) The unnecessary appointment of lawyers to serve as counsel places an undue burden on the lawyers of this State. Before making an appointment, a circuit or family court judge must insure that the person on whose behalf the appointment is being made is in fact indigent. Further, a lawyer should not be appointed as counsel for an indigent unless the indigent has a right to appointed counsel under the state or federal constitution, a statute, a court rule, or the case law of this State.

(2) A lawyer should only be appointed as counsel under this rule when counsel is not available from some other source. For example, an appointment under the rule for a criminal defendant should not be made when there is a public defender available to take the appointment.

(h) Volunteers and Substitute Counsel.

(1) Nothing in this rule shall prohibit a circuit or family court judge from appointing an active member or any other category of member of the South Carolina Bar who may lawfully provide the representation if the member volunteers to represent an indigent. A lawyer may volunteer for an appointment at any time regardless of whether the lawyer has completed the maximum number of appointments provided by (f)(4) or (f)(5) above.

(2) Nothing in this rule shall prevent an appointed lawyer from obtaining a substitute counsel to take the appointment as long as the substitute counsel is eligible to take the appointment and the substitution is approved by the circuit or family court. If the substitution is approved, only the member who originally received the appointment shall receive credit for the appointment.

(i) Records. Any records maintained by the South Carolina Bar, the circuit court, the family court, or a clerk of court relating to appointments under this rule shall be made available for review by any active member upon written request of that member. The clerk of court in each county shall, quarterly, furnish the South Carolina Bar with a list setting forth the total number of appointments and the type of each appointment made by the clerk of court in that quarter. Specifically, the clerk of court of each county shall report, on a form prepared by the South Carolina Bar:

(1) the total number of lawyers appointed, transferred to, or received from other counties pursuant to (f)(5).

(2) the type of appointments made, including the total number of appointments in:

(A) death penalty matters in the court of general sessions;

(B) general criminal matters in the court of general sessions;

(C) post-conviction relief matters in the court of common pleas;

(D) sexually violent predator matters in the court of common pleas;

(E) juvenile delinquency matters in the family court;

(F) family court matters, to include whether the member was appointed as counsel for a parent, child, or guardian ad litem;

(G) any other type of appointment.

[Adopted effective March 4, 1999. Amended effective November 4, 1999; September 1, 2001; January 24, 2002; July 1, 2003; September 1, 2003; December 14, 2005; February 5, 2009; April 29, 2009; July 22, 2009; July 1, 2010.]

RULE 609. RULES ADVISORY COMMITTEE

(a) Members. The Rules Advisory Committee (Committee) shall consist of the following members who shall be appointed by the Supreme Court for four (4) year terms:

(1) a circuit court judge who shall serve as the chair of the Committee;

(2) a circuit court judge or a master-in-equity;

(3) a family court judge;

(4) a probate judge;

(5) a magistrate or municipal court judge;

(6) four active members of the South Carolina Bar; and,

(7) a non-voting reporter.

For the initial appointments, half of the members shall be appointed for two (2) year terms and half of the members shall be appointed for four (4) year terms. In case of a vacancy on the Committee, the Supreme Court shall appoint a member to serve the remainder of the unexpired term. A quorum shall consist of five members not counting the reporter.

(b) Duties. The Committee shall make recommendations regarding the adoption or amendment of rules governing the administration of or the practice and procedure before the trial courts of this State. This shall include, but is not limited to, the South Carolina Rules of Civil Procedure, the South Carolina Rules of Criminal Procedure, the South Carolina Rules of Family Court, the South Carolina Rules of Probate Court, the South Carolina Rules of Magistrates Court and the South Carolina Rules of Evidence. Further, the Supreme Court may refer proposed rules or issues to the Committee for its consideration. The recommendations of the Committee shall be in writing and shall contain the language of any proposed rule or amendment along with an explanation and analysis of the recommendations made by the Committee. For any proposed rule or amendment which must be submitted to the South Carolina General Assembly under Article V, § 4A, of the South Carolina Constitution, the recommendations of the Committee must be submitted to the Supreme Court by October 1st.

(c) Subcommittees. The Committee may divide itself into subcommittees to consider and make recommendations to the Committee. Additionally, the Supreme Court may appoint a Special Subcommittee when it determines that additional personnel are necessary to study and make recommendations regarding a particular rule or set of rules. If appointed, a Special Subcommittee shall make their recommendations to the Committee.

(d) Power of Supreme Court. Nothing in this Rule shall prevent the Supreme Court from promulgating a rule or rule amendment without submitting the matter to the Committee. Further, the Supreme Court may refer a proposed rule or amendment to other groups for their recommendations.

[Adopted effective July 1, 2008.]

APPENDICES TO PART VI

APPENDIX A. DEFENSE OF INDIGENTS FORMS

FORM 1. A STATEMENT OF THE RIGHTS OF AN ACCUSED

A STATEMENT OF THE RIGHTS OF AN ACCUSED

You have been arrested and charged with the crime of ______________________________
____

You are advised:

(a) You have a right to employ counsel to represent you.

(b) In the event you are financially unable to employ counsel, the State will provide you with counsel by appointment or with the services of the Public Defender of this County. If you desire the State to provide you with counsel, you may make application for counsel on a form which I will give to you.

This form has been read to the accused, ______________, in my presence, at ___ o'clock p.m. – a.m., this ____ day of ________, __.

____
Clerk of Court or Other Officer

(If the accused cannot employ counsel and does not wish the State to provide him with counsel at this time, he shall be asked to execute the following statement.)

WAIVER OF RIGHT TO HAVE APPOINTED
COUNSEL OR SERVICES OF PUBLIC DEFENDER

The undersigned certifies that he has been informed of the charges against him and the nature thereof, and that he is unable to employ counsel. However, the undersigned now states that he does not at this time desire to apply for the appointment of counsel or for the services of the Public Defender, and expressly waives his desire to services of counsel provided by the State at this time, which he understands he has a right to do.

____
Defendant

Executed before me this ____ day of ________, __.

____
Signature of Clerk
of Court or Officer

FORM 2. AFFIDAVIT OF INDIGENCY AND APPLICATION FOR COUNSEL

STATE OF SOUTH CAROLINA COUNTY OF ________________	IN THE FAMILY COURT ____JUDICIAL CIRCUIT
______________________________ Plaintiff,	**AFFIDAVIT OF INDIGENCY AND APPLICATION FOR COUNSEL** (Defense of Indigency Act, Form No.2)
vs.	
______________________________ Defendant.	Docket No. ________________________

NAME OF APPLICANT	
ADDRESS	
TELEPHONE NUMBER(S)	
DATE OF BIRTH	
SOCIAL SECURITY NO.	
NAMES OF CO-DEFENDANTS	

1. **Are you presently employed?** Yes ☐ No ☐

   a. If "yes", state the amount of your salary or wages per month, and give the name and address of your employer.

SALARY OR WAGES PER MONTH	NAME AND ADDRESS OF EMPLOYER

If "no", state the name and address of last employment, date of termination of employment, and amount of your salary or wages per month.

SALARY OR WAGES PER MONTH	NAME AND ADDRESS OF EMPLOYER	TERMINATION DATE

2. **Include employment information for the spouse, if applicable.**

SALARY OR WAGES PER MONTH	NAME AND ADDRESS OF EMPLOYER

If the spouse is not currently employed, state the name and address of last employment, date of termination of employment, and amount of salary or wages per month.

SALARY OR WAGES PER MONTH	NAME AND ADDRESS OF EMPLOYER	TERMINATION DATE

SCACRVIFORM02DR (12/2009)

3. List by name, age and relationship to you, any persons who are dependent upon you for support. Indicate beside each how much you contribute toward their support.

NAME	AGE	RELATIONSHIP	AMOUNT OF SUPPORT

4. **Have you received within the past twelve months any money from any of the following sources?**

a. Business, profession or form of self-employment? Yes ☐ No ☐

b. Rent payments, interest or dividends? Yes ☐ No ☐

c. Pensions, annuities or life insurance payments? Yes ☐ No ☐

d. Gifts or inheritances? Yes ☐ No ☐

e. Any other sources? Yes ☐ No ☐

If the answer to any of the above is "yes", describe each source of money and state the amount received from each during the past twelve months.

SOURCE OF MONEY	AMOUNT

5. **Do you own cash, or do you have any money in a checking or savings account?**

Yes ☐ No ☐

If the answer is "yes", state the total amount of the cash owned. ____________

6. **Do you own any real estate, stocks, bonds, notes, or other valuable property (excluding ordinary household furnishings and clothing)?**

Yes ☐ No ☐

If the answer is "yes", describe the property and state the appropriate value of the items owned.

____

____

____

7. **What kind of motor vehicle do you own?** ____________

Is it paid for? Yes ☐ No ☐

If not, what are the payments? ____________

8. **How much do you owe (on liens, mortgages, other encumbrances or debts)?** ____________

____

SCACRVIFORM02DR (12/2009)

I do solemnly swear that the account by me delivered into this court with my application for counsel does contain a true and full account of all my real and personal estate, debts, credits and effects whatsoever without exception, which I or any person in trust for me have or at the time of my possession had, or am, or was, in any respect, entitled to, in possession, remainder or reversion and that I have not at any time since charges were made against me or before, directly or indirectly sold, leased, assigned or otherwise disposed of or made over, in trust for myself or otherwise, other than is mentioned herein.

I understand the appointment of counsel creates a claim against the assets and estate of the person who is provided counsel or the parents or legal guardians of a juvenile in an amount equal to the cost of representation less the amount paid to appointed counsel, the public defender office and/or the Commission on Indigent Defense. I understand that such claim shall be filed in the office of the Clerk of Court in the county where I, my child, or ward are assigned counsel, but that the filing of a claim shall not constitute a lien against my real or personal property unless, in the discretion of the court, part of all of such claim is reduced to judgment by appropriate order of the court after serving me with at least thirty (30) days notice that judgment will be entered.

I understand that, pursuant to §17-3-30(b), I am required to pay a non-refundable $40.00 application fee to the Clerk of Court for public defender services or other appointed counsel.

I am financially unable to employ counsel and request that counsel be assigned to represent me. I understand that I am entitled to at least thirty days' notice before a claim against me may be reduced to judgment, and I do hereby waive the right to such notice.

This _____ day of ______________________, ______ ________________________________
Applicant

Subscribed and sworn to before me this
__________ day of ________________, ________

____(L.S.)
Notary Public for South Carolina
My Commission Expires: ____________

The applicant's request for court-appointed counsel is hereby ☐ **granted** / ☐ **denied.**

Dated: ____________________ ________________________________
Judge/Clerk or Deputy Clerk

_____________, South Carolina

SCACRVIFORM02DR (12/2009)

STATE OF SOUTH CAROLINA) IN THE COURT OF GENERAL SESSIONS
) _____ JUDICIAL CIRCUIT
COUNTY OF ________________)
)
) **AFFIDAVIT OF INDIGENCY**
THE STATE OF SOUTH CAROLINA) **AND**
) **APPLICATION FOR COUNSEL**
vs.) (Defense of Indigency Act, Form No.2)
)
________________________)

CRIMINAL CHARGING DOCUMENT NO. ________________________

NAME OF APPLICANT	
ADDRESS	
TELEPHONE NUMBER(S)	
DATE OF BIRTH	
SOCIAL SECURITY NO.	
NAMES OF CO-DEFENDANTS	

1. **Are you presently employed?** Yes ☐ No ☐

a. If "yes", state the amount of your salary or wages per month, and give the name and address of your employer.

SALARY OR WAGES PER MONTH	NAME AND ADDRESS OF EMPLOYER

If "no", state the name and address of last employment, date of termination of employment, and amount of your salary or wages per month.

SALARY OR WAGES PER MONTH	NAME AND ADDRESS OF EMPLOYER	TERMINATION DATE

2. **Include employment information for the spouse, if applicable.**

SALARY OR WAGES PER MONTH	NAME AND ADDRESS OF EMPLOYER

If the spouse is not currently employed, state the name and address of last employment, date of termination of employment, and amount of salary or wages per month.

SALARY OR WAGES PER MONTH	NAME AND ADDRESS OF EMPLOYER	TERMINATION DATE

SCACRVIFORM02GS (02/2009)

3. List by name, age and relationship to you, any persons who are dependent upon you for support. Indicate beside each how much you contribute toward their support.

NAME	AGE	RELATIONSHIP	AMOUNT OF SUPPORT

4. **Have you received within the past twelve months any money from any of the following sources?**

a. Business, profession or form of self-employment? Yes ☐ No ☐

b. Rent payments, interest or dividends? Yes ☐ No ☐

c. Pensions, annuities or life insurance payments? Yes ☐ No ☐

d. Gifts or inheritances? Yes ☐ No ☐

e. Any other sources? Yes ☐ No ☐

If the answer to any of the above is "yes", describe each source of money and state the amount received from each during the past twelve months.

SOURCE OF MONEY	AMOUNT

5. **Do you own cash, or do you have any money in a checking or savings account?**

Yes ☐ No ☐

If the answer is "yes", state the total amount of the cash owned. ____________________

6. **Do you own any real estate, stocks, bonds, notes, or other valuable property (excluding ordinary household furnishings and clothing)?**

Yes ☐ No ☐

If the answer is "yes", describe the property and state the appropriate value of the items owned.

____

____

____

7. **What kind of motor vehicle do you own?** ____________________

Is it paid for? Yes ☐ No ☐

If not, what are the payments? ____________________

8. **How much do you owe (on liens, mortgages, other encumbrances or debts)?** ____________________

____

SCACRVIFORM02GS (02/2009)

I do solemnly swear that the account by me delivered into this court with my application for counsel does contain a true and full account of all my real and personal estate, debts, credits and effects whatsoever without exception, which I or any person in trust for me have or at the time of my possession had, or am, or was, in any respect, entitled to, in possession, remainder or reversion and that I have not at any time since charges were made against me or before, directly or indirectly sold, leased, assigned or otherwise disposed of or made over, in trust for myself or otherwise, other than is mentioned herein.

I understand the appointment of counsel creates a claim against the assets and estate of the person who is provided counsel or the parents or legal guardians of a juvenile in an amount equal to the cost of representation less the amount paid to appointed counsel, the public defender office and/or the Commission on Indigent Defense. I understand that such claim shall be filed in the office of the Clerk of Court in the county where I, my child, or ward are assigned counsel, but that the filing of a claim shall not constitute a lien against my real or personal property unless, in the discretion of the court, part of all of such claim is reduced to judgment by appropriate order of the court after serving me with at least thirty (30) days notice that judgment will be entered.

I understand that, pursuant to §17-3-30(b), I am required to pay a non-refundable $40.00 application fee to the Clerk of Court for public defender services or other appointed counsel.

I am financially unable to employ counsel and request that counsel be assigned to represent me. I understand that I am entitled to at least thirty days' notice before a claim against me may be reduced to judgment, and I do hereby waive the right to such notice.

This ____day of ________________, _____ ______________________________
Defendant or Parent/Guardian if applicable

Subscribed and sworn to before me this
________ day of ______________, ______

______________________________(L.S.)
Notary Public for South Carolina
My Commission Expires: ________

The applicant's request for court-appointed counsel is hereby ☐ **granted** / ☐ **denied.**

Dated: ________________ ______________________________
Judge/Clerk or Deputy Clerk

__________, South Carolina

SCACRVIFORM02GS (02/2009)

STATE OF SOUTH CAROLINA	)	IN THE FAMILY COURT
	)	_____JUDICIAL CIRCUIT
COUNTY OF ___________________	)	
	)	
	)	**AFFIDAVIT OF INDIGENCY**
A JUVENILE	)	**AND**
	)	**APPLICATION FOR COUNSEL**
________________________________	)	(Defense of Indigency Act, Form No.2)
	)	
	)	
A Child under Seventeen (17) Years of Age	)	Docket No. ________________________

NAME OF APPLICANT	
ADDRESS	
TELEPHONE NUMBER(S)	
DATE OF BIRTH	
SOCIAL SECURITY NO.	
NAMES OF CO-DEFENDANTS	

1. **Are you presently employed?** Yes ☐ No ☐

   a. If "yes", state the amount of your salary or wages per month, and give the name and address of your employer.

SALARY OR WAGES PER MONTH	NAME AND ADDRESS OF EMPLOYER

If "no", state the name and address of last employment, date of termination of employment, and amount of your salary or wages per month.

SALARY OR WAGES PER MONTH	NAME AND ADDRESS OF EMPLOYER	TERMINATION DATE

2. **Include employment information for the spouse, if applicable.**

SALARY OR WAGES PER MONTH	NAME AND ADDRESS OF EMPLOYER

If the spouse is not currently employed, state the name and address of last employment, date of termination of employment, and amount of salary or wages per month.

SALARY OR WAGES PER MONTH	NAME AND ADDRESS OF EMPLOYER	TERMINATION DATE

SCACRVIFORM02JU (12/2009)

3. List by name, age and relationship to you, any persons who are dependent upon you for support. Indicate beside each how much you contribute toward their support.

NAME	AGE	RELATIONSHIP	AMOUNT OF SUPPORT

4. **Have you received within the past twelve months any money from any of the following sources?**

a. Business, profession or form of self-employment? Yes ☐ No ☐

b. Rent payments, interest or dividends? Yes ☐ No ☐

c. Pensions, annuities or life insurance payments? Yes ☐ No ☐

d. Gifts or inheritances? Yes ☐ No ☐

e. Any other sources? Yes ☐ No ☐

If the answer to any of the above is "yes", describe each source of money and state the amount received from each during the past twelve months.

SOURCE OF MONEY	AMOUNT

5. **Do you own cash, or do you have any money in a checking or savings account?**

Yes ☐ No ☐

If the answer is "yes", state the total amount of the cash owned. ______________

6. **Do you own any real estate, stocks, bonds, notes, or other valuable property (excluding ordinary household furnishings and clothing)?**

Yes ☐ No ☐

If the answer is "yes", describe the property and state the appropriate value of the items owned.

____

____

____

7. **What kind of motor vehicle do you own?** ______________________

Is it paid for? Yes ☐ No ☐

If not, what are the payments? ______________________

8. **How much do you owe (on liens, mortgages, other encumbrances or debts)?** ____________

SCACRVIFORM02JU (12/2009)

I do solemnly swear that the account by me delivered into this court with my application for counsel does contain a true and full account of all my real and personal estate, debts, credits and effects whatsoever without exception, which I or any person in trust for me have or at the time of my possession had, or am, or was, in any respect, entitled to, in possession, remainder or reversion and that I have not at any time since charges were made against me or before, directly or indirectly sold, leased, assigned or otherwise disposed of or made over, in trust for myself or otherwise, other than is mentioned herein.

I understand the appointment of counsel creates a claim against the assets and estate of the person who is provided counsel or the parents or legal guardians of a juvenile in an amount equal to the cost of representation less the amount paid to appointed counsel, the public defender office and/or the Commission on Indigent Defense. I understand that such claim shall be filed in the office of the Clerk of Court in the county where I, my child, or ward are assigned counsel, but that the filing of a claim shall not constitute a lien against my real or personal property unless, in the discretion of the court, part of all of such claim is reduced to judgment by appropriate order of the court after serving me with at least thirty (30) days notice that judgment will be entered.

I understand that, pursuant to §17-3-30(b), I am required to pay a non-refundable $40.00 application fee to the Clerk of Court for public defender services or other appointed counsel.

I am financially unable to employ counsel and request that counsel be assigned to represent me.

I understand that I am entitled to at least thirty days' notice before a claim against me may be reduced to judgment, and I do hereby waive the right to such notice.

This _____day of ___________________, _____ ________________________________
Juvenile

This _____day of ___________________, _____ ________________________________
Parent/Guardian (if applicable)

Subscribed and sworn to before me this
_________ day of _______________, ________

______________________________________(L.S.)
Notary Public for South Carolina
My Commission Expires: ___________

....

The applicant's request for court-appointed counsel is hereby ☐ **granted** / ☐ **denied.**

Dated: ___________________ ________________________________
Judge/Clerk or Deputy Clerk

_____________, South Carolina

SCACRVIFORM02JU (12/2009)

FORM 3. CERTIFICATE OF JUDGE

CERTIFICATE OF JUDGE

I hereby certify that the above-named defendant has been fully informed in open Court of the charges against him and of his right to have counsel appointed by the Court to represent him in this case; that he has elected in open Court to be tried in this case without the appointment of counsel; and that he has executed the above waiver in my presence after its meaning and effect have been fully explained to him.

This ____ day of ________, __

____

Judge

CERTIFICATE OF JUDGE

I hereby certify that the above-named defendant has been fully informed in open Court of the charges against him and of his right to have counsel appointed by the Court to represent him in this case; that he has elected in open Court to be tried in this case without the appointment of counsel; and that he has refused to sign a waiver.

This ____ day of ________, __

____

Judge

FORM 4. NOTICE OF APPOINTMENT FOR LEGAL COUNSEL IN THE COURT OF COMMON PLEAS

STATE OF SOUTH CAROLINA	)	IN THE COURT OF COMMON PLEAS
County of ______________	)	______ Judicial Circuit
______________ Petitioner	)	
vs.	)	NOTICE OF APPOINTMENT FOR LEGAL COUNSEL
STATE OF SOUTH CAROLINA	)	Case Number ______ -CP- _____ - _____
Defendant	)	

To: ______________________________ , Attorney at Law

By order of the Chief Administrative Judge and pursuant to Rule 608, SCACR, you are hereby appointed to act as attorney for ______________________ , the Petitioner, in this action.

This ______ day of ____________ , 20 _____ .

____
Judge/Clerk of Court

SCCA 265 (2/04)

FORM 5. NOTICE OF APPOINTMENT FOR LEGAL COUNSEL IN THE COURT OF GENERAL SESSIONS

STATE OF SOUTH CAROLINA	)	IN THE COURT OF GENERAL SESSIONS
County of ______________________	)	_______ Judicial Circuit
STATE OF SOUTH CAROLINA Petitioner	)	
	)	NOTICE OF APPOINTMENT FOR LEGAL COUNSEL
vs.	)	
______________________ Defendant	)	

To: ______________________________, Attorney at Law

By order of the Chief Administrative Judge and pursuant to Rule 608, SCACR, you are hereby appointed to act as attorney for ____________________________, the Defendant, in this action.

This ______ day of _____________, ________.

____
Clerk of Court

SCCA 266 (2/04)

FORM 6. APPOINTMENT OF COUNSEL OR GAL

STATE OF SOUTH CAROLINA	**IN THE COURT OF** (*Select one.*)
COUNTY OF ________________	☐ **COMMON PLEAS** ☐ **FAMILY COURT**
	____________ **JUDICIAL CIRCUIT**
________________________,	**CASE NO.:** ________________
Plaintiff(s),	**APPOINTMENT OF COUNSEL OR GAL**
-vs-	(*Select one.*)
________________________,	☐ **ORDER**
Defendant(s).	☐ **AMENDED ORDER**

TYPE OF CASE/PROCEEDING: (*Select one.*)

☐ Post-Conviction Relief (PCR)/habeas case	☐ Adoption	☐ Juvenile
☐ SVP case	☐ Custody and/or Visitation	☐ Abuse and Neglect
☐ Minor Name Change	☐ Other:	

It appears that____, who is a litigant in this case, is entitled to court-appointed counsel or a guardian ad litem.

It further appears that: (*Select one.*)

☐ counsel/guardian ad litem has not yet been appointed by the court; therefore, an appointment for counsel/guardian ad litem is necessary.

☐ counsel/guardian ad litem was previously appointed by the court but has indicated either a possible conflict of interest, an entitlement to exemption, or other good cause warranting the appointment of new counsel or GAL based on: ________________________

☐ counsel was previously appointed by the court but has not indicated that the litigant has retained private counsel and is no longer entitled to appointed counsel.

☐ court appointed counsel has obtained ________________________, Esquire as substitute counsel pursuant to Rule 608(h)(2); provided, however, only the member who originally received the appointment and who sought substitute counsel shall receive credit.

☐ Other:____

Therefore, it is ordered that____, hereby is appointed as (*Select only one.*)

☐ counsel ☐ lead counsel (*if capital PCR case*) ☐ guardian ad litem

for the above-named person. Any counsel or GAL previously appointed is/are hereby relieved.

☐ (*If Death Penalty PCR Case*) It is further ordered that________________________, Esquire, is hereby appointed as second counsel in this capital PCR case.

The clerk of court is directed to forward a copy of this order to all persons entitled to notice.

IT IS SO ORDERED THIS _____ DAY OF ________________________, 20__.

____

☐Circuit Judge ☐Clerk of Court

NOTICE: SC Supreme Court Order of September 29, 2006, requires appointed counsel entitled to payment from the Office of Indigent Defense (OID) to register the case online with OID within fifteen (15) days of this appointment at www.sccid.sc.gov, and further directs that reimbursement vouchers be submitted directly to SCCID and not to the trial judge or clerk of court. See SCCID website for further details.

SCCA/267 (03/07)

FORM 7. APPOINTMENT OF COUNSEL

STATE OF SOUTH CAROLINA	)	**IN THE COURT OF** (*Select one.*)
COUNTY OF____________________	)	☐ **GENERAL SESSIONS** ☐ **FAMILY COURT**
	)	______ **JUDICIAL CIRCUIT**
State of South Carolina,	)	**CASE NO.:** ____________________
Plaintiff,	)	**APPOINTMENT OF COUNSEL**
-vs-	)	(*Select one.*)
____________________________,	)	☐ **ORDER**
☐ **Defendant** ☐ **Juvenile.**	)	☐ **AMENDED ORDER**

Offense(s): ____

____

It appears that the above named person is entitled to court-appointed counsel or a guardian ad litem.

It further appears that: (*Select only one.*)

☐ the public defender now represents another person involved herein and that a conflict would arise if that office represents the above-named individual.

☐ the public defender has indicated a possible conflict of interest or other good cause warranting the appointment of counsel based on:

____

☐ the public defender or court-appointed counsel has indicated that the named individual has now retained private counsel and is no longer entitled to appointed counsel.

☐ court-appointed counsel has claimed an exemption or has demonstrated good cause pursuant to Rule 608 warranting the appointment of new counsel based on:

☐ court-appointed counsel has obtained substitute counsel named below pursuant to Rule 608(h)(2); only the member who originally received the appointment and who sought substitute counsel shall receive credit for the appointment.

Therefore, it is ordered that________________________, Esquire hereby is appointed as

(*Select only one.*) ☐ counsel ☐ lead counsel (*if capital PCR case*)

for the above-named person. Counsel previously appointed is/are hereby relieved as counsel.

☐ (*If Death Penalty PCR Case*) It is further ordered that________________________, Esquire, is hereby appointed as second counsel in this capital case.

The clerk of court is directed to forward a copy of this order to all persons entitled to notice.

IT IS SO ORDERED THIS ______ DAY OF __________________, 20____.

____

☐ Circuit Judge ☐ Clerk of Court

NOTICE: SC Supreme Court Order of September 29, 2006, requires appointed counsel entitled to payment from the Office of Indigent Defense (OID) to register the case online with OID within fifteen (15) days of this appointment at www.sccid.sc.gov, and further directs that reimbursement vouchers be submitted directly to SCCID and not to the trial judge or clerk of court. See SCCID website for further details.

SCCA/268 (03/07)

APPENDIX B. MEDIA COVERAGE OF COURT PROCEEDINGS FORM

FORM 1. MEDIA COVERAGE OF COURT PROCEEDINGS

STATE OF SOUTH CAROLINA)
COUNTY OF______________________)
) IN THE COURT _______________
____________________________)
____________________________)
-vs-)
____________________________)
____________________________)

Request for Electronic and Photographic Coverage
Of Judicial Proceedings

Pursuant to Rule 605, South Carolina Appellate Court Rules, the undersigned hereby requests permission to use equipment in order to record, photograph or televise all or portions of the proceedings in the above captioned case.

Consistent with Rule 605, the undersigned desires to use the following equipment:

____

____

The proceedings that the undersigned desires to record, photograph or televise commence on:

____

The personnel who will be responsible for the operation of this equipment are:

____

____

The undersigned hereby certifies that the operation of the equipment and the conduct of the personnel will be in conformity with Rule 605.

This _____ day of _______, __.

____
(Individual Signature)

____
(Representing/Firm)

RECEIVED:

____
(Position)

Date: ____________________

____
(Address)

________________________ ______________________________
Presiding Judge (Telephone Number)

INDEX TO SOUTH CAROLINA APPELLATE COURT RULES

SOUTH CAROLINA RULES OF CIVIL PROCEDURE

Westlaw Electronic Research

These rules may be searched electronically on Westlaw in the SC-RULES *database; updates to these rules may be found on Westlaw in* SC-RULESUP-DATES. *For search tips and a summary of database content, consult the Westlaw Scope Screen for each database.*

I. SCOPE OF RULES—ONE FORM OF ACTION

RULE 1. SCOPE OF RULES

These rules govern the procedure in all South Carolina courts in all suits of a civil nature whether cognizable as cases at law or in equity, with the exceptions stated in Rule 81. They shall be construed to secure the just, speedy, and inexpensive determination of every action.

RULE 2. ONE FORM OF ACTION

There shall be one form of action to be known as "civil action."

Notes

These Rules are the same as Federal Rules 1 and 2 except the name of the State. Rule 81 provides that the Rules will apply also to Magistrate's, Probate and Family Courts where not inconsistent with the rules of those courts. Rule 2 is substantially identical to Code Sections 15-1-80 and 90. This Rule also abolishes the mostly cosmetic differences between "actions" and "special proceedings". A special proceeding is really only a civil action in which some special remedy is sought; i.e., writ of mandamus, writ of habeas corpus, etc.

II. COMMENCEMENT OF ACTION—SERVICE OF PROCESS, PLEADINGS, MOTIONS AND ORDERS

RULE 3. COMMENCEMENT OF ACTION

(a) Commencement of civil action. A civil action is commenced when the summons and complaint are filed with the clerk of court if:

(1) the summons and complaint are served within the statute of limitations in any manner prescribed by law; or

(2) if not served within the statute of limitations, actual service must be accomplished not later than one hundred twenty days after filing.

(b) Filing *In Forma Pauperis*.

(1) Except as provided in (2) below, a plaintiff who desires to file an action *in forma pauperis* shall file in the court a motion for leave to proceed *in forma pauperis*, together with the complaint proposed to be filed and an affidavit showing the plaintiff's inability to pay the fee required to file the action. If the motion is granted, the plaintiff may proceed without further application and file the complaint in the court without payment of filing fees.

(2) Where a party is represented in a civil action by an attorney working on behalf of or under the auspices of a legal aid society or a legal services or other nonprofit organization funded in whole or substantial part by funds appropriated by the United States Government or the General Assembly of the State of South Carolina, which has as its primary purpose the furnishing of legal services to indigent persons, or the South Carolina Bar Pro Bono Program, fees related to the filing of the action shall be waived without the necessity of a motion and court approval. Before the filing fees will be waived, the attorney representing the party must file with the clerk a written certification that representation is being provided on behalf of or under the auspices of the society, organization or program, and that the party is unable to pay the filing fees.

[Amended effective July 1, 1994; May 5, 2003; April 27, 2004; April 28, 2011.]

Notes

Note to 2004 Amendment

This amendment rewrote subsection (a), deleted subsection (b), and renumbered subsection (c) as subsection (b). These changes are intended to reflect the legislative intent expressed in § 15–3–20 as amended by 2002 S.C. Act No. 281, § 1.

Note to 2011 Amendment

This amendment added the language of (b) (2) which allows for the waiver of the filing fees for an action when a party is represented by an attorney working on behalf of or under the auspices of a legal aid society, a legal services or other nonprofit organization, or the South Carolina Pro Bono Program.

RULE 4. PROCESS

(a) Summons: Issuance. The summons shall be issued by plaintiff or plaintiff's attorney. Copies of the original summons shall be served upon each defendant.

(b) Same: Form. The summons shall be signed by the plaintiff or his attorney, contain the name of the State and county, the name of the court, the file number of the action, and the names of the parties, be directed to the defendant, state the name and address of the plaintiff's attorney, if any, otherwise the plaintiff's address, and the time within which these rules require the defendant to appear and defend, and shall notify him that in case of his failure to do so judgment by default will be rendered against him for the relief demanded in the complaint.

(c) By Whom Served. Service of summons may be made by the sheriff, his deputy, or by any other person not less than eighteen (18) years of age, not an attorney in or a party to the action. Service of all other process shall be made by the sheriff or his deputy or any other duly constituted law enforcement officer or by any person designated by the court who is not less than eighteen (18) years of age and not an attorney in or a party to the action, except that a subpoena may be served as provided in Rule 45.

(d) Summons: Personal Service. The summons and complaint must be served together. The plaintiff shall furnish the person making service with such copies as are necessary. Voluntary appearance by defendant is equivalent to personal service; and written notice of appearance by a party or his attorney shall be effective upon mailing, or may be served as provided in this rule. Service shall be made as follows:

(d)(1) *Individuals.* Upon an individual other than a minor under the age of 14 years or an incompetent person, by delivering a copy of the summons and complaint to him personally or by leaving copies thereof at his dwelling house or usual place of abode with some person of suitable age and discretion then residing therein, or by delivering a copy to an agent authorized by appointment or by law to receive service of process.

(d)(2) *Minors, Incompetents and Persons Confined.* Upon a minor under the age of 14 years, a person judicially declared incapable of conducting his own affairs, or an incompetent person by delivering a copy of the summons and complaint to such minor, or incompetent personally and also a copy to (a) the guardian or committee of such person, or if there be none such within the State upon (b) a parent or other person having the care and control of such person, or (c) any competent person with whom he resides or (d) in whose service he is employed. If the individual upon whom service is made is a minor between the ages of 14 and 18, who lives with a parent or guardian, a copy of the summons and complaint shall likewise be served upon said parent or guardian, if said parent or guardian resides within the State. Service on imprisoned persons or persons confined in a state hospital or similar institution, in or out of this State, shall be made by delivering a copy of the summons and complaint to the confined person personally; and service shall be made by the sheriff of the county in which the person is imprisoned or confined. In cases of persons imprisoned, and patients in a state hospital or similar institution, personal service of process may be made by the superintendent of the institution or by the director of the prison system or by assistants duly designated by the superintendent or the director in writing for the purpose of making service of process, instead of the sheriff. The superintendent or the director or their designated assistants shall not be entitled to any costs therefore. Service on confined or imprisoned persons shall also conform to the provisions of § 15–9–510, S.C.Code, 1976.

(d)(3) *Corporations and Partnerships.* Upon a corporation or upon a partnership or other unincorporated association which is subject to suit under a common name, by delivering a copy of the summons and complaint to an officer, a managing or general agent, or to any other agent authorized by appointment or by law to receive service of process and if the agent is one authorized by statute to receive service and the statute so requires, by also mailing a copy to the defendant.

(d)(4) *State of South Carolina.*

(A) When State a Party. Upon the State of South Carolina by delivering a copy of the summons and complaint to the Attorney General, or when another official is designated to be served by the statute permitting such action by delivering a copy of the summons and complaint to that official and sending a copy of the summons and complaint by registered or certified mail to the Attorney General at Columbia.

(B) When Unconstitutionality of Statute Is Asserted. In any action attacking the Constitutionality of a State statute when the State, officer or agency is not made a party, a copy of the summons and complaint shall be sent by registered or certified mail to the Attorney General.

(d)(5) *State Officer or Agency.* Upon an officer or agency of the State by delivering a copy of the summons and complaint to such officer or agency and by sending a copy of the summons and complaint by registered or certified mail to the Attorney General at Columbia. If the agency is a corporation the copy shall be delivered as provided in paragraph (3) of this subdivision of this rule.

(d)(6) *Governmental Subdivision.* Upon a municipal corporation, county or other governmental or political subdivision subject to suit, by delivering a copy of the summons and complaint to the chief executive officer or clerk thereof, or by serving the summons and complaint in the manner prescribed by statute for the service of summons and complaint or any like process upon any such defendant.

(d)(7) *Statutory Service.* Service upon a defendant of any class referred to in paragraph (1) or (3) of this subdivision of this rule is also sufficient if the summons and complaint are served in the manner prescribed by statute.

(d)(8) *Service by Certified Mail.* Service of a summons and complaint upon a defendant of any class referred to in paragraph (1) or (3) of this subdivision of this rule may be made by the plaintiff or by any person authorized to serve process pursuant to Rule 4(c), including a sheriff or his deputy, by registered or certified mail, return receipt requested and delivery restricted to the addressee. Service is effective upon the date of delivery as shown on the return receipt. Service pursuant to this paragraph shall not be the basis for the entry of a default or a judgment by default unless the record contains a return receipt showing the acceptance by the defendant. Any such default or judgment by default shall be set aside pursuant to Rule 55(c) or Rule 60(b) if the defendant demonstrates to the court that the return receipt was signed by an unauthorized person. If delivery of the process is refused or is returned undelivered, service shall be made as otherwise provided by these rules.

(e) Same: Other Service. Whenever a statute or an order of court provides for service of a summons and complaint or of a notice, or an order upon a party not an inhabitant of or found within the State, service shall be made under the circumstances and in the manner prescribed by the statute, rule, or order.

(f) Territorial Limits of Effective Service. All process other than a subpoena may be served anywhere within the territorial limits of the State, and, when a statute so provides, beyond the territorial limits of the State. A subpoena may be served within the territorial limits provided in Rule 45.

(g) Proof and Return. The person serving the process shall make proof of service thereof promptly and deliver it to the officer or person who issued same. If served by the sheriff or his deputy, he shall make proof of service by his certificate. If served by any other person, he shall make affidavit thereof. If served by publication, the printer or publisher shall make an affidavit thereof, and an affidavit of mailing shall be made by the party or his attorney if mailing of process is permitted or required by law. Failure to make proof of service does not affect the validity of the service. The proof of service shall state the date, time and place of such service and, if known, the name and address of the person actually served at the address of such person, and if not known, then the date, time and place of service and a description of the person actually served. If service was by mail, the person serving process shall show in his proof of service the date and place of mailing, and attach a copy of the return receipt or returned envelope when received by him showing whether the mailing was accepted, refused, or otherwise returned. If the mailing was refused, the return shall also make proof of any further service on the defendant pursuant to paragraph (8) of subdivision (d) of this rule. The return along with the receipt or envelope and any other proof shall be promptly filed by the clerk with the pleadings and become a part of the record.

(h) Proof of Service Without the State. When the service is made out of the State the proof of such service may be made, if within the United States, by affidavit before:

(1) Any person in this State authorized to make an affidavit;

(2) A commissioner of deeds for this State;

(3) A notary public who shall affix thereto his official seal; or

(4) A clerk of a court of record who shall certify the same by his official seal; and,

(5) If made without the limits of the United States, before a consul, vice-consul or consular agent of the United States who shall use in his certificate his official seal.

(i) Amendment. At any time in its discretion and upon terms as it deems just, the court may, by written order, allow any process or proof of service thereof to be amended, unless it clearly appears that material prejudice would result to the substantial rights of the party against whom the process issued.

(j) Acceptance of Service. No other proof of service shall be required when acceptance of service is acknowledged in writing and signed by the person served or his attorney, and delivered to the person making service. The acknowledgement shall state the place and date service is accepted.

[Amended effective May 1, 1986; July 1, 1994; July 1, 1995.]

Notes

This Rule 4(a) differs from the Federal Rule by continuing the present State practice of the plaintiff or his attorney issuing the summons, rather than having it issued by the Clerk of Court. The second sentence requires only copies of the original summons to be served with the complaint on each defendant. Rule 4(b) is substantially identical to the Federal Rule, being modified only to conform to State practice as set out in Rule 4(a). The first sentence of Rule 4(c) continues present State practice. The second sentence makes more definite the requirement of Code § 15–9–1030 that an official person must serve all other process such as rules and orders, except subpoenas. Rule 4(d) conforms to present State and Federal Practice, and states specifically, as does Code § 15–9–70, that voluntary appearance is equivalent to personal service. It also preserves Circuit Rule 17 as to notice of appearance.

Rules 4(d)(1) through 4(d)(8) conform to the present State practice and the Federal practice, which refers matters of service of process generally to local State practice. Rule 4(d)(1) preserves the requirements of Code § 15–9–520.

Rule 4(d)(2) preserves and conforms to present practice under Code §§ 15–9–480 and 15–9–490. Service on persons confined in State penal or mental facilities will continue to conform also to Code §§ 15–9–500 and 15–9–510.

This Rule 4(d)(3) conforms to both the Federal Rule and preserves and supplements Code §§ 15–9–210 through 15–9–330. Rules 4(d)(7) and 4(d)(8) preserve other forms of statutory service on particular classes of defendants, such as non-resident motorists.

These Rules 4(d)(4) through 4(d)(6) conform to the Federal Rules and clarify State practice concerning service on the State, its officers or agencies, and on political subdivisions.

Rule 4(d)(7) conforms to the Federal Rule, and preserves State statutory requirements as to service on particular individuals or corporations, partnerships and unincorporated associations. Rule 4(d)(8) is the new Federal Rule permitting service of summons and complaint by registered or certified mail.

This catch-all provision is the same as the Federal Rule, and is necessary to cover unusual cases, principally when a court orders service on a person or party.

This Rule 4(f) modifies the Federal Rule to cover service outside the State.

This Rule 4(g) is a restated version of Code § 15–9–80 and present Circuit Rule 5. The final sentence conforms to the new Federal Rule on service by mail, as well as Rule 4(d)(8).

Rule 4(h) replaces Code § 15–9–90, in the same language, and follows the Federal Rule. Rule 4(i) is same as Federal Rule and Code § 15–9–100.

This Rule 4(j) is the same as the Federal Rule and follows State practice.

Notes to 1986 Amendments

Rule 4(c), as originally adopted, could be construed to broaden the definition of "process" and unduly restrict those who could serve process and other orders. These amendments conform to prior practice which permitted other law enforcement officials, and those appointed by the court to serve process. Orders which are not necessary to establish jurisdiction of person or property, including temporary restraining orders, are not required to be served by the sheriff unless ordered by the court. The age requirement is changed to conform to similar language in Rule 45(c).

In Rule 4(d)(2), the reference to Sec. 15–9–500 is deleted because that provision has been repealed.

The phrase "in lieu of summons" is deleted from Rule 4(e) as originally adopted to avoid the implication that an action can be commenced other than by service of summons and complaint.

Notes to 1994 Amendments

This amendment to Rule 4(g) deletes "of and" following the word "envelope" to make the sentence read correctly.

Note to 1995 Amendment

Rule 4(d)(2) is amended to add a provision for the service of the summons and complaint on persons confined in a prison or state hospital. The language is drawn from S.C.Code Ann. § 15–9–500 (1976) (repealed) which governed this situation prior to the adoption of the Rules of Civil Procedure in 1985.

RULE 5. SERVICE AND FILING OF PLEADINGS AND OTHER PAPERS

(a) Service: When Required. Unless otherwise ordered by the court because of numerous defendants or other reasons, all (1) written orders; (2) pleadings subsequent to the original summons and complaint, which includes answers, counterclaims, cross claims, replies and amended complaints; (3) written motions, other than ones which may be heard ex parte; (4) written notices; (5) discovery requests and responses; (6) appearances; (7) demands; (8) offers of judgment; (9) designations of record or case; (10) grounds or exceptions on appeal; and (11) other similar papers shall be served upon each of the parties of record. No service need be made on parties in default for failure to appear, except that pleadings asserting new or additional claims for relief against them shall be served upon them in the manner provided for serving of summons in Rule 4, and notice of any trial or hearing on unliquidated damages shall also be given to parties in default.

(b)(1) *Same: How Made.* Whenever under these rules service is required or permitted to be made upon a party represented by an attorney the service shall be made upon the attorney unless service upon the party himself is ordered by the court. Service upon the attorney or upon a party shall be made by delivering a copy to him or by mailing it to him at his last known address or, if no address is known, by leaving it with the clerk of court. Delivery of a copy within this rule means: handing it to the attorney or to the party; or leaving it at his office with his clerk or other person in charge thereof; or, if there be no one in charge, leaving it in a conspicuous place therein; or, if the office is closed or the person to be served has no office, leaving a copy at his dwelling place or usual place of abode with some person of suitable age and discretion then residing therein. Service by mail is complete upon mailing of all pleadings and papers subsequent to service of the original summons and complaint.

(b)(2) *Service on Sunday.* Civil process may be served on Sundays, provided that no person may be served going to or from or attending a regularly or specially scheduled church or religious service on Sunday.

(b)(3) *Service of Proposed Orders and Other Papers.* Any party providing a proposed order, proposed findings of fact or conclusions of law, or proposed judgment or other paper to the court for its consideration in any pending matter shall serve the same on all counsel of record at the same time and by the same means.

(c) Same: Numerous Defendants. In any action in which there are unusually large numbers of defendants, the court, upon motion or of its own initiative, may order that service of the pleadings of the defendants and replies thereto need not be made as between the defendants and that any cross-claim, counterclaim, or matter constituting an avoidance or affirmative defense contained therein shall be deemed to be denied or avoided by all other parties and that the filing of any such pleadings and service thereof upon the plaintiff constitutes due notice of it to the parties. A copy of every such order shall be served upon the parties in such manner and form as the court directs.

(d) Filing. All papers required to be served upon a party except as provided in Rule 26(g)(1), shall be filed with the court within five (5) days after service thereof. The summons and complaint shall be filed before service. Proof of service shall be filed within ten (10) days after service of the summons and complaint. Upon failure to serve the summons and complaint, the action may be dismissed by the court on the court's own initiative or upon application of any party. Upon failure of a party to file other pleadings, motions, or papers, the court may permit filing or proceed as though the same had not been served.

(e) Filing With the Court Defined. The filing of pleadings and other papers with the court as required by these rules shall be made by filing them with the clerk of the court, except that the judge may permit the papers to be filed with him, in which event he shall note thereon the filing date and forthwith transmit them to the office of the clerk. Upon any trial or hearing, the clerk shall furnish the original record in the action to the judge, who shall return same to the clerk immediately upon completion of such trial or hearing. Copies of the record may be furnished instead of the original by permission of the judge. Upon change of venue the original record shall be transferred to the clerk of court to which the action is transferred.

[Amended effective July 1, 1993; July 1, 1994; September 1, 2001; Last amended by order dated April 27, 2005.]

Notes

This Rule 5(a) is substantially the same as Federal Rule, and restates Code §§ 15–9–910 and 15–9–970 with no change in practice.

This Rule 5(b)(1) is the same as Federal Rule 5(b) and substantially restates Code §§ 15–9–920, 15–9–930, 15–9–980 and 15–9–990; with no resulting change in State practice. Rule 5(b)(2) is the same as Code § 15–9–1010, except permitting subpoenas to be served on Sunday.

This Rule 5(c) is the same as the Federal Rule. It has no parallel in State practice, but is a needed addition.

This Rule 5(d) encompasses present Circuit Rule 68 and former Rule 75, as well as Code § 15–9–1000. It is a more concise statement, and provides more specific sanctions in the court's discretion.

This Rule 5(e) is the same as the Federal Rule. It restates and clarifies present Circuit Rules 32 and 67.

Notes to 1993 Amendments

Rule 5(d) was amended to add language permitting the court to dismiss an action on its own initiative if it has been filed but not served upon the defendant. The prior rule required a motion by a party.

Notes to 1994 Amendments

Rule 5(b)(3) clarifies the intent of Rule 5(a) and requires that proposed orders, findings of fact and conclusions of law and other materials provided to the court are to be served on all counsel of record. The material is to be provided to all other counsel at the same time and by the same means as they are provided to the court. Thus opposing counsel will have the opportunity to review and comment on the proposed order before it is signed. The rule does not require the court to delay entering any proposed order.

Note to 2001 Amendment

Rule 5(b)(2) is rewritten to reflect the enactment of S.C. Code Ann. § 15–9–17, 2000 S.C. Acts No. 360, which allows for the service of process on Sundays with the stated exceptions.

Note to 2005 Amendment

This amendment to subsection (a) makes explicit that all major documents and papers, including, but not limited to, pleadings and amended pleadings, discovery requests and responses, motions and similar papers are to be served on every party of record. The amendment also adds the word "grounds" in subsection (a)(10).

RULE 6. TIME

(a) Computation. In computing any period of time prescribed or allowed by these rules, by order of court, or by any applicable statute, the day of the act, event, or default after which the designated period of time begins to run is not to be included. The last day of the period so computed is to be included, unless it is a Saturday, Sunday or a State or Federal holiday, in which event the period runs until the end of the next day which is neither a Saturday, Sunday nor such holiday. When the period of time prescribed or allowed is less than seven days, intermediate Saturdays, Sundays and holidays shall be excluded in the computation. A half holiday shall be considered as other days and not as a holiday.

(b) Enlargement. When by these rules or by notice given thereunder or by order of court an act is required or allowed to be done at or within a specified time, the time may be extended by written agreement of counsel for an additional period not exceeding the original time provided in these rules, or the court for cause shown may at any time in its discretion (1) with or without written motion or notice order the period enlarged if request therefor is made before the expiration of the period as originally prescribed or extended or (2) upon motion made after the expiration of the specified period, for good cause shown, permit the act to be done. The time for taking any action under rules 50(b), 52(b), 59, and 60(b) may not be extended except to the extent and under the conditions stated in them. The time for filing notice of intent to appeal is jurisdictional and may not be extended by consent or order.

(c) Unaffected by Expiration of Term. The period of time provided for the doing of any act or the taking of any proceeding is not affected or limited by the continued existence or expiration of a term of court. The continued existence or expiration of a term of court in no way affects the power of a court to do any act or take any proceeding in any civil action which has been pending before it.

(d) For Motions—Affidavits. A written motion other than one which may be heard ex parte, and notice of the hearing thereof, shall be served not later than ten days before the time specified for the hearing, unless a different period is fixed by these rules or by an order of the court. Such an order may for cause shown be made on ex parte application. When a motion is to be supported by affidavit, the affidavit shall be served with the motion; and, except as otherwise provided in Rule 59(c), additional or opposing affidavits may be served not later than two days before the hearing, unless the court permits them to be served at some other time. The moving party may serve reply affidavits at any time before the hearing commences. In all cases where a motion shall be granted on payment of costs or on the performance of any condition, or where an order shall require such payment or performance, the party whose duty it shall be to comply therewith shall have 20 days for that purpose, unless otherwise directed in the order.

(e) Additional Time After Service by Mail or Upon Statutory Agent. Whenever a party has the right or is required to do some act or take some proceedings within a prescribed period after the service of a notice or other paper upon him and the notice or paper is served upon him by mail or upon a person designated by statute to accept service, five days shall be added to the prescribed period.

[Amended effective May 1, 1986.]

Notes

This Rule 6(a) replaces and considerably clarifies Code § 15–1–20; particularly as to computing time when there are consecutive holidays.

This Rule 6(b) is the same as the Federal Rule, which is in turn a more concise statement of Code §§ 15–13–90 and 15–27–120 and Circuit Rule 62, except that the Rule continues the present State practice of allowing one limited extension of time by agreement of counsel.

This Rule 6(c) was deleted from the Federal Rule in 1966, but was retained here as a much-needed clarification of State practice. The confusion as to the powers of the court with the modern advent of many "special terms" is eliminated. Time limits on such matters are now stated in the applicable rule; i.e., Rule 59 as to time for motions for new trial.

This Rule 6(d) is the same as the Federal Rule, except that the Rule has enlarged notice time from 5 to 10 days. The last sentence is added to preserve Circuit Rule 62.

This Rule 6(e) is the same as the Federal Rule except that the additional time to take an act after service is by mail is increased from 3 to 5 days. This replaces the very unclear meaning of Code § 15–9–950.

Notes to 1986 Amendments

This amendment [to Rule 6(b)] authorizes the court to permit an act to be done after the expiration of time upon a showing of good cause. This is the standard applied by courts in practice and is found in Rule 55(c) for relief from entry of default. The change distinguishes the test under Rule 6(b) which is applicable when filings are untimely, from that used when a party has obtained a judgment. Post-judgment relief under Rule 60(b) remains governed by the stricter standard of excusable neglect which has a precise meaning under state precedents. See also Rule 55(c).

III. PLEADINGS AND MOTIONS

RULE 7. PLEADINGS ALLOWED; FORM OF MOTIONS

(a) Pleadings. There shall be a complaint and an answer; and a reply to a counterclaim denominated as such; an answer to a cross-claim, if the answer contains a cross-claim; a third-party complaint, if a person who was not an original party is summoned under Rule 14, and there shall be a third-party answer, if a third-party complaint is served. No other pleadings shall be allowed, except that the court may order a reply to an answer or a third-party answer; and there may be a reply to affirmative defenses as provided in Rule 8(c).

(b) Motions and Other Papers.

(1) An application to the court for an order shall be by motion which, unless made during a hearing or trial in open court with a court reporter present, shall be made in writing, shall state with particularity the grounds therefor, and shall set forth the relief or order sought. The requirement of writing is fulfilled if the motion is stated in a written notice of the hearing of the motion.

(2) The rules applicable to captions, signing, and other matters of form of pleadings apply to all motions and other papers provided for by these rules.

(c) Demurrers, Pleas, etc. Abolished. Demurrers, pleas, and exceptions for insufficiency of a pleading shall not be used.

Notes

This Rule 7(a) is identical to the Federal Rule, and the provisions of Code §§ 15–13–10, 15–13–210, 15–13–310 and 15–

13–610. There is no change to State practice, except the references to third-party pleadings.

This Rule 7(b) is identical to the Federal Rule and preserves the pertinent parts of Circuit Rules 56 and 65. The Rule also requires that motions must also be reduced to writing if made in open court with no court reporter or recorder present. "Petitions" for special relief are simply stated as motions. For example, under Rule 65, a motion for a temporary restraining order accompanies the summons and complaint rather than characterizing it as a separate petition.

This Rule 7(c) is the same as the Federal Rule. Since common law pleas, and exceptions for insufficiency of a pleading have been abolished since 1870, this last step abolishes the outmoded demurrer. The defenses now raised by demurrer are raised by motion under Rule 12.

RULE 8. GENERAL RULES OF PLEADING

(a) Claims for Relief. A pleading which sets forth a cause of action, whether an original claim, counterclaim, cross-claim, or third-party claim, shall contain (1) a short and plain statement of the grounds including facts and statutes upon which the court's jurisdiction depends, unless the court already has jurisdiction to support it, (2) a short and plain statement of the facts showing that the pleader is entitled to relief, and (3) a prayer or demand for judgment for the relief to which he deems himself entitled. Relief in the alternative or of several different types may be demanded. Relief for a sum certain in money may be demanded for actual damages, but claims for punitive or exemplary damages shall be in general terms only and not for a stated sum, provided however, a party may plead that the total amount in controversy shall not exceed a stated sum which shall limit the claim for all purposes.

(b) Defenses; Form of Denials. A party shall state in short and plain terms the facts constituting his defenses to each cause of action asserted and shall admit or deny the averments upon which the adverse party relies. If he is without knowledge or information sufficient to form a belief as to the truth of an averment, he shall so state and this has the effect of a denial. Denials shall fairly meet the substance of the averments denied. When a pleader intends in good faith to deny only a part or a qualification of an averment, he shall specify so much of it as is true and material and shall deny only the remainder. Unless the pleader intends in good faith to controvert all the averments of the preceding pleading, he may make his denials as specific denials of designated averments or paragraphs, or he may generally deny all the averments except such designated averments or paragraphs as he expressly admits; but, when he does so intend to controvert all its averments, including averments of the grounds upon which the court's jurisdiction depends, he may do so by general denial subject to the obligations set forth in Rule 11.

(c) Affirmative Defenses; Reply. In pleading to a preceding pleading, a party shall set forth affirmatively the defenses: accord and satisfaction, arbitration and award, assumption of risk, condonation, contributory negligence, discharge in bankruptcy, duress, fraud, illegality, injury by fellow servant, laches, license, misrepresentation, mistake, payment, plene administravit or the administration of the estate is closed, recrimination, release, res judicata, statute of frauds, statute of limitations, waiver, and any other matter constituting an avoidance or affirmative defense. When a party has mistakenly designated a defense as a counterclaim or a counterclaim as a defense, the court shall treat the pleading as if there had been a proper designation. A party may file a reply to any of the foregoing affirmative defenses.

(d) Effect of Failure to Deny. Averments in a pleading to which a responsive pleading is required, other than those as to the amount of damage, are admitted when not denied in the responsive pleading. Averments in a pleading to which no responsive pleading is required or permitted shall be taken as denied or avoided.

(e) Pleading to Be Concise and Direct; Consistency.

(1) Each averment of a pleading shall be simple, concise, and direct. No technical forms of pleading or motions are required.

(2) A party may set forth two or more statements of a cause of action or defense alternatively or hypothetically, either in one count or defense or in separate counts or defenses. When two or more statements are made in the alternative and one of them if made independently would be sufficient, the pleading is not made insufficient by the insufficiency of one or more of the alternative statements. A party may also state as many separate causes of action or defenses as he has regardless of consistency and whether based on legal or on equitable grounds or on both. All statements shall be made subject to the obligations set forth in Rule 11.

(f) Construction of Pleadings. All pleadings shall be so construed as to do substantial justice to all parties.

[Amended effective May 1, 1986; July 1, 1995.]

Notes

This Rule 8(a) is in the same general language as the Federal Rule with the important distinction that the State practice requiring pleading of the facts (rather than a "statement of the claim") is retained. The prayer or demand for relief is also designated as a part of the pleading to finally eliminate confusion on that point. Liberal rules as to amendment throughout (i.e., Rule 15) enable the parties to conform the pleadings to the facts and relief demanded, as they develop. See Rule 54(c). The final sentence is added to eliminate prayers for exaggerated and sensational claims for damages.

This Rule 8(b) is the same as the Federal Rule. It abolishes the "general denial" unless the pleader can controvert every allegation of the complaint, including the jurisdictional allegations. Every allegation must be specifically admitted or denied. Failure to deny constitutes admission. An answer neither admitting nor denying but "demanding proof thereof" is insufficient. The pleader must deny in good faith all parts of an averment not admitted.

This Rule 8(c) is the same as the Federal Rule except for some affirmative defenses added to the list as a guide. The aim is to avoid the "surprise" defenses permissible under the old general denial answer, and require the defendant also to stick to "fact" pleading. The last sentence permits a fact pleading reply to all affirmative defenses. This reinforces the intent to fix the facts by the pleadings, an important departure from the Federal Rules approach to pleadings.

This Rule 8(d) is simply a restatement of Code § 15–13–80.

These Rules 8(e) and 8(f) substantially restate Code §§ 15–15–40 and 15–13–20, and are no change to State practice. This Rule does not allow "jumbling" of two or more causes of action in one count.

Notes to 1986 Amendments

Rule 8(a) is amended because the amount in controversy may determine the jurisdiction of the State and Federal courts, as well as the methods of discovery available in State courts. As originally adopted a general plea seeking punitive damages placed no limit on the amount sought and could expand the scope of the case unduly. This amendment avoids an exaggerated interpretation of a claim for punitive damages and permits the pleader to keep the case proportionate to the actual injury suffered.

Rule 8(b) is amended to make clear that fact pleading is required for both the complaint and answer.

The affirmative defenses of condonation and recrimination are added to Rule 8(c) because they are often asserted in pleadings in Family Courts.

Note to 1995 Amendment

Rule 8(c) is amended to add the affirmative defense of duress to conform the rule to the comparable federal rule. The amendment does not change substantive or procedural law because duress is recognized as an affirmative defense, and the concluding clause of the first sentence requires it to be asserted as a matter of avoidance.

RULE 9. PLEADING SPECIAL MATTERS

(a) Capacity. It is not necessary to aver the capacity of a party to sue or be sued or the authority of a party to sue or be sued in a representative capacity or the legal existence of an organized association of persons that is made a party, except to the extent required to show the jurisdiction of the court. When a party desires to raise an issue as to the legal existence of any party or the capacity of any party to sue or be sued or the authority of a party to sue or be sued in a representative capacity, he shall do so by specific negative averment, which shall include such supporting particulars as are within the pleaders' knowledge.

(b) Fraud, Mistake, Condition of Mind. In all averments of fraud or mistake, the circumstances constituting fraud or mistake shall be stated with particularity. Malice, intent, knowledge, and other condition of mind of a person may be averred generally.

(c) Conditions Precedent. In pleading the performance or occurrence of conditions precedent, it is sufficient to aver generally that all conditions precedent have been performed or have occurred. A denial of performance or occurrence shall be made specifically and with particularity.

(d) Official Document or Act. In pleading an official document or official act it is sufficient to aver that the document was issued or the act was done in compliance with law.

(e) Judgment. In pleading a judgment or decision of a domestic or foreign court, judicial or quasi-judicial tribunal, or of a board or officer, it is sufficient to aver the judgment or decision without setting forth matter showing jurisdiction to render it.

(f) Time and Place. For the purpose of testing the sufficiency of a pleading, averments of time and place are material and shall be considered like all other averments of material matter.

(g) Special Damage. When items of special damage are claimed, they shall be specifically stated.

(h) Libel or Slander. In pleading libel or slander it is not necessary to state in the pleading any extrinsic facts for the purpose of showing the application to the pleader of the defamatory matter out of which the action arose; but it is sufficient to state generally that the same was published or spoken concerning the pleader. In such case, the opposing party may in his answer, allege both the truth of the matter charged as defamatory, and any mitigating circumstances reducing the amount of damages and, whether he prove the justification or not, he may give in evidence the mitigating circumstances.

(i) Verification of Account. In an action on an account the pleader shall attach a verified copy of the account to the pleading, or if the items of the account are set forth in the pleading, it must be verified.

Notes

All parts of Rules 9(a) through 9(g) conform to the Federal Rules and to present State practice. Rule 9(h) was added to preserve Code §§ 15–13–760 and 15–13–770 as to pleading libel and slander. Rule 9(i) preserves Code § 15–13–710.

RULE 10. FORM OF PLEADINGS

(a) Caption, Name of Parties. Every pleading shall contain a caption setting forth the name of the State and County, the name of the Court, the title of the action, the file number and a designation as in Rule 7(a). In the summons and complaint the title of the action shall include the names of all parties, but in other pleadings it is sufficient to state the name of the first party on each side with an appropriate indication of other parties.

(1) *Unknown Parties.* When a party does not know the name of an adverse party he may state that fact in

the pleadings and designate such adverse party by any name and the words "whose true name is unknown," and when his true name is discovered the pleadings must be amended accordingly.

(b) Paragraphs; Separate Statements. All averments of the facts of a cause of action or defense and demands for relief shall be made in consecutive numbered paragraphs, the contents of each of which shall be limited as far as practicable to a statement of a single set of circumstances; and a paragraph may be referred to by number in all succeeding pleadings. Each cause of action and each defense shall be stated in a separate cause of action or defense.

(c) Adoption by Reference; Exhibits. Statements in a pleading may be adopted by reference in a different part of the same pleading or in another pleading or in any motion. A copy of any plat, photograph, diagram, document, or other paper which is an exhibit to a pleading is a part thereof for all purposes if a copy is attached to such pleading.

(d) Manner of Preparing Papers. Pleadings and other papers shall be on legal cap paper, eight and one-half by eleven inches in size. They shall be plainly written with adequate spacing between lines or typewritten with not less than one and one-half spacing between lines. Each page shall be numbered consecutively and pages shall be fastened at the top so as to read continuously. Papers in handwriting or typewriting must have a blank margin of an inch and one-half on the left. Plats, photographs, diagrams, documents, and other paper exhibits or copies thereof may be submitted in their actual size; but should be reduced if practicable to eight and one-half by eleven inches if such reduction does not impair legibility and clarity.

(e) Filing Refused. The clerk of the court shall not file any pleadings or other papers not prepared in accordance with this rule; except plats, photographs, diagrams, documents, and other paper exhibits as provided in paragraph 10(c).

[Amended effective September 1, 1990.]

Notes

This Rule 10(a) is substantially the same as the Federal Rule and conforms to present State practice.

This Rule 10(a)(1) preserves Code § 15–13–70 as to unknown parties.

This Rule 10(b) is substantially the same as the Federal Rule and restates Circuit Rule 18, paragraph one. The Rule adheres to fact pleading by reference to "cause of action" instead of the word "claim" in the Federal Rule.

This Rule 10(c) is the same as the Federal Rule, except that it requires copies of exhibits to be attached to the pleading, if they are to be considered a part thereof.

Rule 10(d) is added to the Federal Rules to conform to the new State Rules as to form and style of papers as prescribed by Supreme Court Rule 5, and Circuit Court Rule 13.

This Rule 10(e) is added to preserve Code § 15–9–1000, and Circuit Court Rule 12.

Notes to 1990 Amendments

This amendment [to Rule 10(d)] deletes a reference to the Supreme Court Rules which have been repealed.

RULE 11. SIGNING OF PLEADINGS; ATTORNEYS

(a) Signature. Every pleading, motion or other paper of a party represented by an attorney shall be signed in his individual name by at least one attorney of record who is an active member of the South Carolina Bar, and whose address and telephone number shall be stated. A party who is not represented by an attorney shall sign his pleading, motion or other paper and state his address. Except when otherwise specifically provided by rule or statute, pleadings need not be verified or accompanied by affidavit. The signature of an attorney or party constitutes a certificate by him that he has read the pleading, motion or other paper; that to the best of his knowledge, information and belief there is good ground to support it; and that it is not interposed for delay.

All motions filed shall contain an affirmation that the movant's counsel prior to filing the motion has communicated, orally or in writing, with opposing counsel and has attempted in good faith to resolve the matter contained in the motion, unless the movant's counsel certifies that consultation would serve no useful purpose, or could not be timely held. There is no duty of consultation on motions to dismiss, for summary judgment, for new trial, or judgment NOV, or on motions in Family Court for temporary relief pursuant to Family Court Rule 21, or in real estate foreclosure cases, or with pro se litigants.

If a pleading, motion or other paper is not signed or does not comply with this Rule, it shall be stricken unless it is signed promptly after the omission is called to the attention of the pleader or movant. If a pleading, motion, or other paper is signed in violation of this Rule, the court, upon motion or upon its own initiative, may impose upon the person who signed it, a represented party, or both, an appropriate sanction, which may include an order to pay to the other party or parties the amount of the reasonable expenses incurred because of the filing of the pleading, motion or other paper, including a reasonable attorney's fee.

(b) Change of Attorney. An attorney may be changed by consent, or upon cause shown, and upon such terms as shall be just, upon application, by order of the Court, and not otherwise. Written notice of change of attorney must be served as provided by Rule 5.

(c) Affidavits and Verifications. Affidavits or verifications authorized or permitted under these Rules shall be written statements or declarations by a party or his attorney of record or of a witness, sworn to or affirmed before an officer authorized to administer oaths, that the affiant knows the facts stated to be true of his own knowledge, except as to those matters stated on information and belief and as to those matters that he believes them to be true. When a corporation is a party the verifications may be made by any officer or agent thereof. When a partnership or other unincorporated association is the party under a common name the verification may be made by a member or officer thereof. When the State or any officer thereof in its behalf is a party, verifications may be made by any person acquainted with the facts.

(d) Attorney as Surety. No attorney or other officer of the court shall become surety upon any undertaking or bond filed in any action.

[Amended effective May 1, 1986; July 1, 1989; July 1, 1993.]

Notes

This Rule 11(a) is substantially the Federal Rule, with one addition, that the pleadings must be signed by the party or, if he has an attorney, by an attorney who practices in the State. Important as this change is, it is not as significant as the Rule itself, which eliminates the verification of pleadings and places on the lawyer who signs a pleading the duty of good faith in preparing the pleading. The lawyer may be disciplined if he violates this duty. This version of Rule 11(a) is not nearly so stringent as the latest version of the Federal Rule which became effective August 1, 1983; but it represents a substantial forward step in lawyer responsibility.

This Rule 11(b) retains the requirements of Circuit Court Rule 7, and represents no change in State or Federal practice.

Rules 11(c) and 11(d) are added to the Federal Rule to preserve the requirements of Code § 15–1–240, and Circuit Court Rule 9.

Notes to 1986 Amendments

The amendment to Rule 11(a) makes explicit that the certification requirement applies to all motions or papers filed by the attorney or party. The requirement that an attorney of record must be a resident or maintain an office in the State is deleted. The conditions under which a person may appear of record are more properly within the exclusive power of the Supreme Court to govern the admission to practice, rather than a matter of trial court procedure.

Rule 11(c) is amended to permit an employee of an attorney to probate affidavits or verifications on pleadings or other papers, although a deposition cannot be taken before such employee under Rule 28(c).

Notes to 1989 Amendments

The amendment to Rule 11(a) requires that a movant make a "good faith" effort to resolve any dispute before filing a motion and to so certify in the motion unless the consultation would serve no useful purpose or could not be timely held. This is similar to the Local Federal Rule. As in the Local Federal Rule, there is no duty to consult with pro se litigants, or about certain motions. Consultation may be oral or written.

The change makes clear that the court may impose sanctions for violations of this Rule and replaces the ambiguous language that "an attorney may be subject to appropriate disciplinary action." The change is more consistent with the language on sanctions for discovery abuse. The amendment does not change the standard for imposing sanctions which remains that of the pre-1983 Federal Rule.

Notes to 1993 Amendments

Rule 11(a) was amended to add a requirement that the signer of pleadings include his telephone number.

RULE 12. DEFENSES AND OBJECTIONS—WHEN AND HOW PRESENTED—BY PLEADING OR MOTION—MOTION FOR JUDGMENT ON PLEADINGS

(a) When Presented. A defendant shall serve his answer within 30 days after the service of the complaint upon him, unless the Court directs otherwise when service of process is made pursuant to Rule 4(e), and provided further that the State of South Carolina shall answer or otherwise respond to an application for post-conviction relief within 60 days after service of the application, if it arises out of a guilty plea, and 90 days if it arises out of a trial. A party served with a pleading stating a cross-claim against him shall serve an answer thereto within 30 days after the service upon him. The plaintiff shall serve his reply to a counterclaim in the answer within 30 days after service of the answer or, if a reply is ordered by the court, within 30 days after service of the order, unless the order otherwise directs. The service of a motion permitted under this rule alters these periods of time as follows, unless a different time is fixed by order of the Court: (1) if the Court denies the motion or postpones its disposition until the trial on the merits, the responsive pleading shall be served within 15 days after notice of the Court's action; (2) if the Court grants a motion for a more definite statement the responsive pleading shall be served within 15 days after the service of the more definite statement, and a responsive pleading, if necessary, shall be served within 15 days after notice of the court's action on a motion to strike.

(b) How Presented. Every defense, in law or fact, to a cause of action in any pleading, whether a claim, counterclaim, cross-claim, or third-party claim, shall be asserted in the responsive pleading thereto if one is required, except that the following defenses may at the option of the pleader be made by motion: (1) lack of jurisdiction over the subject matter, (2) lack of jurisdiction over the person, (3) improper venue, (4) insufficiency of process, (5) insufficiency of service of process, (6) failure to state facts sufficient to constitute a cause of action, (7) failure to join a party under Rule 19, (8) another action is pending between the same parties for the same claim. A motion making any of these defenses shall be made before pleading if a further pleading is permitted. No defense or objection is waived by being joined with one or more other defenses or objections in a responsive pleading or motion. If a pleading sets forth a cause of action or defense to which an adverse party is not required to serve a responsive pleading, he may assert at the trial any defense in law or fact to that cause of action or defense. If, on a motion asserting the defense numbered (6) to dismiss for failure of the pleading to state facts sufficient to constitute a cause of action, matters outside the pleading are presented to and not excluded by the Court, the motion shall be treated as one for summary judgment and disposed of as provided in Rule 56, and all parties shall be given reasonable opportunity to present all material made pertinent to such a motion by Rule 56.

(c) Motion for Judgment on the Pleadings. After the pleadings are closed but within such time as not to delay the trial, any party may move for judgment on the pleadings. If, on a motion for judgment on the pleadings, matters outside the pleadings are presented to and not excluded by the Court, the motion shall be treated as one for summary judgment and disposed of as provided in Rule 56, and all parties shall be given reasonable opportunity to present all material made pertinent to such a motion by Rule 56.

(d) Preliminary Hearings. The defenses specifically enumerated (1)–(8) in subdivision (b) of this rule, whether made in a pleading or by motion, motions for judgment on the pleadings under subdivision (c) of this rule, and motions for summary judgment under Rule 56, shall be heard and determined before trial on application of any party, unless the Court orders that the hearing and determination thereof be deferred until the trial.

(e) Motion for More Definite Statement. If a pleading to which a responsive pleading is permitted is so vague or ambiguous that a party cannot reasonably be required to frame a responsive pleading, he may move for a more definite statement before interposing his responsive pleading. The motion shall point out the defects complained of and the details desired. If the motion is granted and the order of the Court is not obeyed within 15 days after notice of the order or within such other time as the Court may fix, the Court may strike the pleading to which the motion was directed or make such order as it deems just.

(f) Motion to Strike. Upon motion pointing out the defects complained of, and made by a party before responding to a pleading or, if no responsive pleading is required within 30 days after the service of the pleading upon him or upon the court's own initiative, at any time the court may order stricken from any pleading any insufficient defense or any redundant, immaterial, impertinent or scandalous matter.

(g) Consolidation of Defenses in Motion. A party who makes a motion under this rule may join with it any other motions herein provided for and then available to him. If a party makes a motion under this rule but omits therefrom any defense or objection then available to him which this rule permits to be raised by motion, he shall not thereafter make a motion based on the defense or objection so omitted, except a motion as provided in subdivision (h)(2) hereof on any of the grounds there stated.

(h) Waiver or Preservation of Certain Defenses.

(1) A defense of lack of jurisdiction over the person, improper venue, insufficiency of process, insufficiency of service of process, or that another action is pending between the same parties for the same claim is waived (A) if omitted from a motion in the circumstances described in subdivision (g) or (B) if it is neither made by motion under this rule nor included in a responsive pleading or an amendment thereof permitted by Rule 15(a) to be made as a matter of course.

(2) A defense of failure to state a cause of action upon which relief can be granted, a defense of failure to join a party indispensable under Rule 19, and an objection of failure to state a legal defense to a claim may be made in any pleading permitted or ordered under Rule 7(a), or by motion for judgment on the pleadings, or at the trial on the merits.

(3) Whenever it appears by suggestion of the parties or otherwise that the court lacks jurisdiction of the subject matter, the court shall dismiss the action.

[Amended effective May 1, 1986; July 1, 1995.]

Notes

This Rule 12(a) is identical to the Federal Rule except that it changes the time to answer from 20 to 30 days, and the time to plead after motion denied from 10 to 15 days. No other changes in State practice are affected by the Rule.

This important Rule 12(b) enables a party to: (1) raise by motion or answer all of the defenses now raised by demurrer, and (2) eliminates the necessity of the awkward "special appearance to object to jurisdiction" under present State practice. The motion should be made before answer for early disposition of cases; but the defenses enumerated may be made in the responsive pleading and are not waived by being stated in a pleading rather than by motion. The last sentence eliminates the so-called "speaking demurrer" at trial, by treating such late motion as a motion for Summary Judgment under Rule 56.

This Rule 12(c) preserves the present common law practice in this State; and it is more important than the Federal Rule, because of the requirement for fact pleading. It may also be treated as a motion for summary judgment in proper circumstances.

This Rule 12(d) is the same as the Federal Rule, and assures timely disposal of 12(b) and 12(c) motions to dismiss or for judgment prior to trial.

This Rule 12(e) is the same as the Federal Rule and effects no change in present practice, except time for compliance is changed from 10 days to 15 days.

This Rule 12(f) preserves present State practice under Code § 15–13–60 and § 15–13–440 verbatim.

This Rule 12(g) is the same as the Federal Rule. It is new material to help prevent piecemeal presentation of defenses by separate motions.

This Rule 12(h) should be read together with Rule 12(g) in defining those defenses which are waived if not presented by pleading or motion.

Notes to 1986 Amendments

The amendment to Rule 12(a)(2) sets the time for response after a motion to strike at 15 days, which is the same time set for pleading after a successful motion for a more definite statement.

The amendment to the fourth sentence of Rule 12(b) clarifies the litigant's right to assert at trial any defenses as well as any claims he could have raised in a permissive pleading but chose not to do so. Consequently, the election not to reply to an affirmative defense does not waive the right to contest that affirmative defense.

The amendment to Rule 12(f) makes clear that a motion to strike must point out the defects complained of, and is consistent with the language of Rule 12(e).

Note to 1995 Amendment

Rule 12(a) is amended to provide special time periods for the State to respond to applications for post-conviction relief because the thirty day time period for civil litigation is often extended so that the State may obtain a transcript of the proceeding before responding.

RULE 13. COUNTERCLAIM AND CROSS–CLAIM

(a) Compulsory Counterclaims. A pleading shall state as a counterclaim any claim which at the time of serving the pleading the pleader has against any opposing party, if it arises out of the transaction or occurrence that is the subject matter of the opposing party's claim and does not require for its adjudication the presence of third parties of whom the court cannot acquire jurisdiction. But the pleader need not state the claim if (1) at the time the action was commenced the claim was the subject of another pending action, or (2) the opposing party brought the suit upon his claim by attachment or other process by which the court did not acquire jurisdiction to render a personal judgment on that claim, and the pleader is not stating any counterclaim under this Rule 13.

(b) Permissive Counterclaims. A pleading may state as a counterclaim any claim against an opposing party not arising out of the transaction or occurrence that is the subject matter of the opposing party's claim.

(c) Counterclaim Exceeding Opposing Claim. A counterclaim may or may not diminish or defeat the recovery sought by the opposing party. It may claim relief exceeding in amount or different in kind from that sought in the pleading of the opposing party.

(d) Counterclaim Against the State. These rules shall not be construed to enlarge beyond the limits fixed by law the right to assert counterclaims or to claim credits against the State of South Carolina or an officer, agency, or governmental or political subdivision thereof.

(e) Counterclaim Maturing or Acquired After Pleading. A claim which either matured or was acquired by the pleader after serving his pleading may, with the permission of the court, be presented as a counterclaim by supplemental pleadings.

(f) Omitted Counterclaim. When a pleader fails to set up a counterclaim through oversight, inadvertence, or excusable neglect, or when justice requires, he may by leave of court set up the counterclaim by amendment.

(g) Cross-Claim Against Co-party. A pleading may state as a cross-claim any claim by one party against a co-party arising out of the transaction or occurrence that is the subject matter either of the original action or of a counterclaim therein or relating to any property that is the subject matter of the original action. Such cross-claim may include a claim that the party against whom it is asserted is or may be liable to the cross-claimant for all or part of a claim asserted in the action against the cross-claimant.

(h) Joinder of Additional Parties. Parties other than those to the original action may be made parties to a counterclaim or cross-claim in accordance with Rules 19 and 20.

(i) Separate Trials. Separate Judgments. If the court orders separate trials as provided in Rule 42(b), judgment on a counterclaim or cross-claim may be rendered in accordance with the terms of Rule 54(b) even if the claims of the opposing party have been dismissed or otherwise disposed of.

(j) Transfer. In an action brought in a court of limited jurisdiction, in the event the counterclaim or cross-claim tendered for filing is in excess of the jurisdictional amount or otherwise beyond the jurisdiction of said court, upon the payment of any fees required by statute, the action shall be transferred to the circuit court of the county to be there considered and tried as if the action had been there originally filed. If such counterclaim be a permissive counterclaim allowed under Rule 13(b), the transfer shall be in the discretion of the court in which the action is brought. If such permissive counterclaim is not transferred in the discretion of the court, the judgment in such action shall not be a bar to the claim if and when brought thereafter in another action.

Notes

Rules 13(a) through (i) are the same as the Federal Rules on counterclaims and cross-claims. These include and expand Code §§ 15–13–420, 15–15–30, 15–15–40, 15–15–50 and 15–15–70. Counterclaims arising out of the same transaction or occurrence that is the subject of the action are "compulsory" under Rule 13(a) and are barred by res judicata or estoppel by judgment if not asserted. All other counterclaims whether legal or equitable in nature are permissive, and may be pleaded against the opposing party. Separate trials on claims not directly related to the original action may be ordered by the court under Rule 13(i). Rule 13(j) is added to conform to State practice, in which there are courts of differing jurisdiction. This Rule 13 considerably broadens present State practice as to counterclaims, but will avoid much litigation and dispute whether the counterclaim or cross-claim is allowable under the old 1870 Code practice.

RULE 14. THIRD PARTY PRACTICE

(a) When Defendant May Bring in Third Party. At any time after commencement of the action a defending party, as a third-party plaintiff, may cause a summons and complaint to be served upon a person not a party to the action who is or may be liable to him for all or part of the plaintiff's claim against him. The third-party plaintiff need not obtain leave to make the service if he files the third-party complaint not later than 10 days after he serves his original answer. Otherwise he must obtain leave on motion upon notice to all parties to the action. The person served with the summons and third-party complaint, hereinafter called the third-party defendant, shall make his defenses to the third-party plaintiff's claim as provided in Rule 12 and his counterclaims against the third-party plaintiff and cross-claims against other third-party defendants as provided in Rule 13. The third-party defendant may assert against the plaintiff any defenses which the third-party plaintiff has to the plaintiff's claim. The third-party defendant may also assert any claim against the plaintiff arising out of the transaction or occurrence that is the subject matter of the plaintiff's claim against the third-party plaintiff. The plaintiff may assert any claim against the third-party defendant arising out of the transaction or occurrence that is the subject matter of the plaintiff's claim against the third-party plaintiff, and the third-party defendant thereupon shall assert his defenses as provided in Rule 12 and his counterclaims and cross-claims as provided in Rule 13. Any party may move to strike the third-party claim, or for its severance or separate trial. A third-party defendant may proceed under this rule against any person not a party to the action who is or may be liable to him for all or part of the claim made in the action against the third-party defendant.

(b) When Plaintiff May Bring in Third Party. When a counterclaim is asserted against a plaintiff, he may cause a third party to be brought in under circumstances which under this rule would entitle a defendant to do so.

(c) Joinder as Plaintiff or Defendant. Upon motion of any party, or on its own motion, the Court may order that a party designated as a third-party defendant be joined as a plaintiff or defendant under Rules 19 or 20, when the ends of justice and efficiency in proceedings would be served thereby. In event such joinder is ordered, designation of such party or his pleading as "third party" shall thereafter be dropped.

Notes

These Rules 14(a) through (c) are substantially the same as the Federal Rule, except for the omission of references to admiralty and maritime practice, and the addition of Rule 14(c) as to joinder. There is no counterpart to "third-party practice" in present State procedure, but the liberal State practice as to joinder and interpleader render the procedure less novel than appears on its face. The development of third-party practice in the Federal courts over the years has led to more use of joinder under Rules 19 and 20, rather than increased use of third-party practice. Therefore, Rule 14(c) is added to encourage that result where appropriate.

RULE 15. AMENDED AND SUPPLEMENTAL PLEADINGS

(a) Amendments. A party may amend his pleading once as a matter of course at any time before or within 30 days after a responsive pleading is served or, if the pleading is one to which no responsive pleading is required and the action has not been placed upon the trial roster, he may so amend it at any time within 30 days after it is served. Otherwise a party may amend his pleading only by leave of court or by written consent of the adverse party; and leave shall be freely given when justice so requires and does not prejudice any other party. A party shall plead in response to an amended pleading within the time remaining for response to the original pleading or within fifteen days after service of the named amended pleading, whichever period may be the longer, unless the court otherwise orders.

(b) Amendments to Conform to the Evidence. When issues not raised by the pleadings are tried by express or implied consent of the parties, they shall be treated in all respects as if they had been raised in the pleadings. Such amendment of the pleadings as may be necessary to cause them to conform to the evidence and to raise these issues may be made upon motion of any party at any time, even after judgment; but failure so to amend does not affect the result of the trial of these issues. If evidence is objected to at the trial on the ground that it is not within the issues made by the pleadings, the court may allow the pleadings to be amended and shall do so freely when the presentation of the merits of the action will be subserved thereby and the objecting party fails to satisfy the court that the admission of such evidence would prejudice him in maintaining his action or defense upon the merits. The court shall upon motion grant a continuance reasonably necessary to enable the objecting party to meet such evidence. Upon allowing any such amendment or evidence the Court shall state in the record the reason or reasons for allowing the amendment or evidence. In the event the Court should try issues not raised by the pleadings, it shall state in the record all such issues tried and the reason therefor.

(c) Relation Back of Amendments. Whenever the claim or defense asserted in the amended pleading arose out of the conduct, transaction or occurrence set forth or attempted to be set forth in the original pleadings, the amendment relates back to the date of the original pleading.

An amendment changing the party against whom a claim is asserted relates back if the foregoing provision is satisfied and, within the period provided by law for commencing the action against him the party to be brought in by amendment (1) has received such notice of the institution of the action that he will not be prejudiced in maintaining his defense on the merits, and (2) knew or should have known that, but for a mistake concerning the identity of the proper party, the action would have been brought against him.

(d) Supplemental Pleadings. Upon motion of a party the court may, upon reasonable notice and upon such terms as are just, permit him to serve a supplemental pleading setting forth transactions or occurrences or events which have happened since the date of the pleading sought to be supplemented, whether or not the original pleading is defective in its statement of a cause of action or defense. If the court deems it advisable that the adverse party plead thereto, it shall so order, specifying the time therefor.

Notes

This Rule 15(a) is substantially the same as the Federal Rule, and preserves present State practice under Code §§ 15–13–910 and 15–13–920. The Rule increases the time to amend a pleading without court order from 20 to 30 days, and the time to plead in response to an amended pleading from 10 to 15 days. It also adds the requirement that the court not allow amendment prejudicial to another party, which is a statement of existing case law.

This Rule 15(b) broadens the court's power to allow amendments to conform the pleadings to the evidence under Code § 15–13–920; but this is necessary if the philosophy of the Rules, that the pleadings must state the issues, is to be consistent. The Rule also circumscribes the use of amendment at late stages in a trial by requiring the court to grant continuance of the trial as necessary, and stating in the record the reasons for allowing the amendment.

This Rule 15(c) is the same as the Federal Rule.

This Rule 15(d) is the same as the Federal Rule. State practice since 1870 has followed this procedure. McClaslan v. Latimer, 17 S.C. 123 (1882); Francis Marion Hotel v. Chicco, 131 S.C. 344, 127 S.E. 436 (1924).

RULE 16. PRE–TRIAL PROCEDURE: FORMULATING ISSUES

(a) Pre-trial Hearings. In any action after the issues are joined by the actual filing and service of all pleadings, the court may in its discretion or upon motion of any party direct the attorneys for the parties to appear before it for a hearing to consider:

(1) The simplification of the issues;

(2) The necessity or desirability of amendments to the pleadings;

(3) The possibility of obtaining admissions of fact and of documents which will avoid unnecessary proof;

(4) The limitation of the number of expert witnesses;

(5) The limitation of the time allowed for discovery;

(6) The advisability of reference of issues to a master: (a) for findings to be used as evidence when the trial is to be by jury, or (b) disposition of non-jury issues;

(7) The disposition of pending motions;

(8) Such other matters as may aid in the disposition of the action.

The attorneys at such pre-trial hearing shall be prepared, as to each party, to:

(1) State the facts which can be proven whether or not alleged in the pleadings;

(2) State the questions of law involved, with citations of legal authority substantiating the party's position thereon;

(3) State with particularity all items of damages claimed and the measure of the damages;

(4) Provide copies of all relevant medical statements or records;

(5) Make good faith offers of settlement;

(6) Exchange lists of witnesses, including expert witnesses;

(7) Agree upon all facts not in controversy;

(8) Exchange lists of all exhibits proposed to be offered at trial.

(b) Pre-trial Orders. The court shall make a written order which recites the action, if any, taken at the hearing, the amendments allowed to the pleadings, and the agreements made by the parties as to any of the matters considered, and which limits the issues for trial to those not disposed of by admissions or agreements of counsel; and such order when entered controls the subsequent course of the action, unless modified on motion, or at the trial to prevent manifest injustice. The order may, in the court's discretion, also: (1) provide that exhibits or witnesses not listed at the hearing may not be called or admitted in evidence at the trial, unless such witness or exhibit is discovered after pre-trial hearing and promptly disclosed to opposing parties; (2) provide that all motions pending at the time of the hearing which are not presented for disposition are deemed abandoned; (3) provide that all or part of the pre-trial hearing be continued to a future time, or that additional pre-trial hearings be scheduled to promote the orderly and efficient disposition of the action; (4) establish provisions for disclosure or discovery of electronically stored information; and (5) include any agreements the parties reach for asserting claims of privilege or of protection as trial preparation material after production.

(c) Pre-trial Briefs. At or prior to a pre-trial hearing, counsel for each party shall provide to the judge a uniform brief containing the matters listed below. The pre-trial brief shall be provided to the judge and served on all parties or counsel of record at the same time and by the same means.

(1) A concise, non-argumentative statement of the facts of the case.

(2) An objective statement of the facts in controversy.

(3) The legal issues involved. This includes the law applicable to the cause of action and the defense.

(4) A listing of exhibits, indicating those to which there is disagreement and a listing of witnesses who

may be called and, if available, their address and phone number.

(5) Any unusual problems relating to evidence to be introduced, such as "Business Records as Evidence Act," hearsay, use of depositions, etc.

(6) Any unusual question or matter which should be brought to the attention of the court.

(7) A statement that settlement negotiations were attempted before the date of the pre-trial hearing and the status of settlement negotiations.

The pre-trial brief is solely for the use of the court at the pre-trial hearing, and shall not be filed with or made part of the record in the action.

(d) Pre-trial Calendar. The Chief Judge for Administrative Purposes in any circuit may establish a pre-trial hearing calendar on which actions may be placed for consideration as above provided and set thereon all actions in which a pre-trial hearing has been ordered or which, in his discretion, such hearing should be ordered. If a motion for such hearing is pending, the administrative judge shall hear or assign for hearing such motion. If the motion is granted the action shall be placed on the pre-trial calendar.

(e) Status Conferences. Whether or not a formal pre-trial hearing has been held in an action, the trial judge may hold an informal conference before trial to dispose of any remaining matters, including disposition of any pending motions and consideration of settlement. No pre-trial brief or other formal procedures set forth in paragraphs (a) through (d) of this Rule 16 shall be required for such conferences; however, any briefs and memoranda submitted in support of pending motions shall be served on all parties at the same time and by the same means used to serve the court. [Amended effective July 1, 1993; April 28, 2011.]

Notes

This Rule 16 is similar to the Federal Rule, with the exceptions noted below. The proposal preserves present Circuit Rule 43, as revised in 1981, except to denote the pre-trial as a hearing, and by requiring a pre-trial order, reciting the action taken at the pre-trial hearing. The session is a "hearing" rather than a "conference." Present State pre-trial conferences often do not produce concrete results since no court order follows. Rule 16(e) is added to allow an informal status conference shortly before trial to dispose of any remaining matters. An order may be entered in writing or stated upon the record on any ruling the court deems necessary when this informal conference may be held in the action. The aim of the Rule is to produce a meaningful pre-trial hearing in complex and difficult cases, and to avoid such hearings in routine actions. The allowance for informal conferences immediately before trial enables the court to dispose of remaining pre-trial matters, including settlements, in any and all cases.

Notes to 1993 Amendments

The amendment provides that all pre-trial briefs and memoranda, required by 16(c) or permitted under 16(e), be served upon all parties at the same time and by the same means as is used to serve the court. The pre-trial brief is solely for the use of the court and does not restrict a party in the presentation of its case.

Note to 2011 Amendments

The amendments to Rules 16, 26, 33, 34, 37 and 45 of the South Carolina Rules of Civil Procedure concerning electronic discovery are substantially similar to the corresponding provisions in the Federal Rules of Civil Procedure. The rules concerning electronic discovery are intended to provide a practical, efficient and cost-effective method to assure reasonable discovery. Pursuit of electronic discovery must relate to the claims and defenses asserted in the pleadings and should serve as a means for facilitating a just and cost-effective resolution of disputes.

IV. PARTIES

RULE 17. PARTIES PLAINTIFF AND DEFENDANT: CAPACITY

(a) Real Party in Interest. Every action shall be prosecuted in the name of the real party in interest. An executor, administrator, guardian, bailee, trustee of an express trust, a party with whom or in whose name a contract has been made for the benefit of another, or a party authorized by statute may sue in his own name without joining with him the party for whose benefit the action is brought; and when a statute so provides, an action for the use or benefit of another shall be brought in the name of the State. No action shall be dismissed on the ground that it is not prosecuted in the name of the real party in interest until a reasonable time has been allowed, after objection, for ratification of commencement of the action by, or joinder or substitution of, the real party in interest; and such ratification, joinder, or substitution shall have the same effect as if the action had been commenced in the name of the real party in interest.

(b) Capacity to Sue or Be Sued. The capacity of a party to sue or be sued shall be determined by the law of this State.

(c) Minor or Incompetent Persons. Whenever a minor or incompetent person has a representative, such as a general guardian, committee, conservator, or other like fiduciary, the representative may sue or defend on behalf of the minor or incompetent person. If a minor or incompetent person does not have a duly appointed representative he may sue by his next friend or by guardian ad litem. The court shall appoint a guardian ad litem for a minor or incompetent person not otherwise represented in an action or shall make such order as it deems proper for the protection of the minor or incompetent person. A person imprisoned outside this State shall appear by guardian ad litem in an action by or against him; but if imprisoned in this

State, and not a minor or incompetent, the court may, in its discretion appoint a guardian ad litem or order him to be brought personally to the trial to testify in accordance with Rule 43(a).

(d) Guardians Ad Litem. Guardians ad litem appearing in the courts of this State, or before any agency, board or commission from which an appeal to the courts of this State shall lie, shall be qualified and appointed in accordance with the provisions of this rule.

(1) *Who May Appoint.* Guardians ad litem may be appointed by the court in which the action is pending, the judge of probate, the clerk of court, or the master-in-equity of the county wherein the minor, or incompetent or imprisoned person resides, or in the county in which the action is pending or is to be filed.

(2) *Who May Be Appointed.* The general guardian of a minor or incompetent person may be appointed guardian ad litem, if he has no interest adverse to that of the person whom he represents in the action. No other person may be appointed guardian ad litem of a minor or incompetent or imprisoned person unless he be fully competent to understand and protect the rights of the person whom he represents, has no interest adverse to that of the person whose interest he represents, is not connected or associated with the attorney or counsel of the adverse party, and is not the attorney for the adverse party. If the guardian ad litem is an attorney, it shall not be necessary that he be represented by an additional attorney; but the attorney of the adverse party shall not represent the guardian ad litem.

(3) *Minors.* The guardian ad litem for a minor party shall be appointed upon the application of the minor, if he be of the age of 14 years or over; if under that age upon the application of his parent, general or testamentary guardian; or of a relative or friend. If application be made by a relative or friend, other than a parent, notice thereof must first be given to the minor's general or testamentary guardian, if he has one; if he has none, then to the person with whom such minor resides.

(4) *Imprisoned Persons.* The guardian ad litem for an imprisoned person shall be appointed upon application of such person or of a relative or friend. If application be made by a relative or friend, notice thereof must first be given to such imprisoned person.

(5) *Incompetent Persons.* The guardian ad litem for an incompetent person shall be appointed upon the application of his guardian or committee or of a relative or friend. If application be made by a relative or friend, notice thereof must be first given to the incompetent person's guardian if he has one; if he has none, then to the person with whom such incompetent person resides.

(6) *Failure to Apply.* If no application for appointment of a guardian ad litem be made by or in behalf of a minor, imprisoned, or incompetent party within thirty (30) days after service of the summons upon such party, then the guardian ad litem may be appointed upon application of any other party to the action, after first giving notice of such application to the person or persons to whom notice of application must be given under subsections (3), (4), and (5) of this rule.

(7) *Out-of-State Party.* When a minor, imprisoned or incompetent party resides out of the State or is absent therefrom, the court shall make such orders allowing additional time, or other orders as may be necessary to protect the interest of such parties.

(e) Unknown Owners or Heirs as Parties. In all actions or proceedings to obtain title or possession, or to remove adverse claim of title, or to quiet title, or for partition, or for sale, or for foreclosure of any encumbrance, or enforcement of any trust, or specific performance of any contract, or for any other disposition of any property, real, personal, or mixed, situated within the State including choses in action either situated within or due or claimed to be due from persons, firms or corporations resident within the State, persons may be made parties defendant either on the filing of the complaint, counterclaim or cross-claim, as the case may be, or at any time thereafter by amendment thereof, by the name and description of unknown owners, or unknown heirs or unknown devisees of any deceased persons, or by any such designations.

(f) Actions for Partition of Real Estate of Deceased Person. In an action for partition of real estate of a deceased person, the legal representative shall be a party to the action unless the estate of the deceased person has been closed and the legal representative discharged or it appears to the court that there are no debts chargeable against the estate of the deceased. In all actions for partition all tenants in common shall be parties, but if the consent of anyone who should be joined cannot be obtained, he may be made a defendant.

[Amended effective May 1, 1986.]

Notes

This Rule 17(a) is current Federal Rule 17(a). The first sentence and the first clause of the second sentence are substantially the same as Code §§ 15–5–70 and 80. The Federal Rule adds to those who may sue in the name of others, "guardian" and "bailee." Those listed in the rule are considered illustrative and do not mean that others may not also fall into the category of those who can sue in the name of another. The last clause of the second sentence permits an action for the use or benefit of another to be brought in the name of the State. This is obviously needed but not provided for in §§ 15–5–70 and 80. The last sentence of the rule is intended to prevent forfeiture in those cases in which the determination of the proper party to sue is difficult or when there has been an honest mistake. This provision may change existing State law, because precedents hold that lack of the proper party is jurisdictional. Hodges v. Lake Summit Co., 155 S.C. 436, 152 S.E. 658 (1928); Wilson v. Gibbes Machine Co., 189 S.C. 426, 1 S.E.2d 490 (1938). Therefore, the filing of the suit might not bar the applicable statute of limitations, absent this provision.

This Rule 17(b) is the first sentence of the Federal Rule and includes the conflicts law of the State. The remainder of Federal Rule 17(b) provides for problems peculiar to Federal courts and is deleted. The rule does not attempt to define the capacities of parties to sue or be sued, but refers to the law that defines these matters.

This Rule [17(c)] retains the principal provisions of Code § 15–5–310. The last sentence, which does not appear in Federal Rule 17(c), retains the provisions in Code § 15–5–320 as to guardians ad litem for imprisoned persons. The Rule narrows existing practice by providing for a guardian ad litem only when the person is imprisoned outside the State. Thus in the most common civil cases involving prisoners, post-conviction relief proceedings, a guardian would not be required for an in-state prisoner who is normally represented by appointed or retained counsel; but the court has the discretion to appoint a guardian for an in-state prisoner.

This provision [Rule 17(d)] does not appear in the Federal Rule. It is a restatement of Code §§ 15–5–310 to 380. These provisions were added to Rule 17 as the Federal Rule refers to the State law on this subject.

This Rule 17(d)(1) is drawn principally from Code § 15–5–310 and Code § 15–5–360 dealing with the appointment of guardians for minors and incompetent persons.

This Rule 17(d)(2) is drawn from Circuit Court Rule 6 with minor textual changes.

This Rule 17(d)(3) is drawn from Code § 15–5–330 with minor textual changes.

This Rule 17(d)(4) is drawn from Code § 15–5–370 with minor textual changes.

This Rule 17(d)(5) is drawn from Code § 15–5–360.

This Rule 17(d)(6) provides for the appointment of a guardian upon motion of any other party, if an application for the appointment has not been received within 30 days after the service of summons, and is similar language to Code §§ 15–5–340, 360 and 370. The provision incorporates the thirty day period for answering a complaint contained in Circuit Court Rule 102.

This Rule 17(d)(7) is similar to Code § 15–5–350, and states the obvious proposition that the court has the authority to protect the interest of the individuals for whom guardians have not been appointed.

This Rule 17(e) is added to supplement Rule 10(a) as to unknown parties, providing for the use of fictitious names similar to Code § 15–13–70. Actions against unknown parties are peculiar to State Court jurisdiction and this section is added to the Federal Rule to complete the procedure.

This Rule 17(f) does not appear in the Federal Rules. It is drawn from the first paragraph of present Circuit Court Rule 54. The intent of the provision is to insure that the debtors of the estate may reach the proceeds from the partition of the real estate which technically becomes the property of the heirs or beneficiaries upon the death of the deceased. Requiring the legal representative to be joined in all cases, except discharge or where there are no debts, serves this purpose. This Rule is not jurisdictional and partition will occur even if the legal representatives are not named or none has been appointed. See Smith v. Hawkins, 254 S.C. 423, 175 S.E.2d 824 (1970). The provisions of the second paragraph of Circuit Court Rule 54 and all of Circuit Court Rule 55, as to actions for partition of separate tracts, are contained in Rule 53 of these Rules. See also Rule 71 of these Rules for procedure on foreclosure and partition actions.

Notes to 1986 Amendments

This amendment [to Rule 17(d)(1)] permits a guardian ad litem to be appointed before the action is filed.

RULE 18. JOINDER OF CLAIMS AND REMEDIES

(a) Joinder of Claims. A party asserting a cause of action as an original claim, counterclaim, cross-claim, or third-party claim, may join, either as independent or as alternate claims, as many claims, legal, or equitable, as he has against the opposing party.

(b) Joinder of Remedies; Fraudulent Conveyances. Whenever a claim is one heretofore cognizable only after another claim has been prosecuted to a conclusion, the two claims may be joined in a single action; but the court shall grant relief in that action only in accordance with the relative substantive rights of the parties. In particular, a plaintiff may state a claim for money and a claim to have set aside a conveyance fraudulent as to him, without first having obtained a judgment establishing the claim for money.

(c) Separate Trials. The court may make such orders as will prevent a party from being embarrassed, delayed or put to unnecessary expense by the joinder of independent or disassociated claims, and may order separate trials or make other orders to prevent delay or prejudice.

Notes

This Rule 18(a) is the same as the Federal Rule. This Rule substantially modifies current State practice under Code § 15–15–10 which limits for purposes of pleading, the joinder of claims. Under this Rule 18(a) there are no limitations on the joinder of claims for pleading purposes. Under Rule 18(c), the court does have power to grant separate trials on the different claims when it would be more convenient or fair. This Rule refers only to joinder of claims for pleading purposes. Rules 19–22 govern joinder of parties.

This [Rule 18(b)] is the language of current Federal Rule 18(b) and provides that in a single action a party should be accorded all the relief, legal, equitable or both to which that party is entitled. The last sentence of the Rule is in accordance with the Uniform Fraudulent Conveyance Act, but joinder of the two claims is permissive, not mandatory.

This provision [Rule 18(c)] is not in Federal Rule 18. Similar provisions are in Rules 13(i), 20(b), 21, and 43. The only problem from liberal joinder of claims is possibly the inconvenience of trying various claims in one lawsuit. This Rule provides the court authority to resolve such problems by appropriate orders.

RULE 19. JOINDER OF PERSONS NEEDED FOR JUST ADJUDICATION

(a) Persons to Be Joined if Feasible. A person who is subject to service of process and whose joinder will not deprive the court of jurisdiction over the subject matter of the action shall be joined as a party in the action if (1) in his absence complete relief cannot be accorded among those already parties, or (2) he claims an interest relating to the subject of the action and is so situated that the disposition of the action in his absence may (i) as a practical matter impair or impede his ability to protect that interest or (ii) leave any of the persons already parties subject to a substantial risk of incurring double, multiple, or otherwise inconsistent obligations by reason of his claimed interest. If he has not been so joined, the court shall order that he be made a party. If he should join as a plaintiff but refuses to do so, he may be made a defendant, or, in a proper case, an involuntary plaintiff.

(b) Determination by Court Whenever Joinder Not Feasible. If a person as described in subdivision (a)(1)–(2) hereof cannot be made a party, the court shall determine whether in equity and good conscience the action should proceed among the parties before it, or should be dismissed, the absent person being thus regarded as indispensable. The factors to be considered by the court include: first, to what extent a judgment rendered in the person's absence might be prejudicial to him or those already parties; second, the extent to which, by protective provisions in the judgment, by the shaping of relief, or other measures, the prejudice can be lessened or avoided; third, whether a judgment rendered in the person's absence will be adequate; fourth, whether the plaintiff will have an adequate remedy if the action is dismissed for nonjoinder.

(c) Pleading Reasons for Nonjoinder. Any pleading asserting a cause of action for relief shall state the names, if known to the pleader, of any persons described in subdivision (a)(1)–(2) hereof who are not joined, and the reasons why they are not joined.

(d) Exception of Class Actions. This rule is subject to the provisions of Rule 23 in class actions.

Notes

This Rule 19(a) is the same as the Federal Rule. The principle behind this Rule is that whenever possible persons materially interested in the action should be joined so that they may be heard and a complete determination had. When this joinder is not possible, the case should be examined pragmatically and a choice made between proceeding without the particular interested party or dismissing the action. Dean Lightsey, in Code Pleading, notes that the number of cases in which there is truly an "indispensable party" in whose absence the court should not proceed are very rare. Id. at 109–110. The Rule provides for joining such a party as a defendant or involuntary plaintiff similar to Code § 15–5–40. Case law interpreting the Federal Rule makes it clear that the absence of a party does not automatically deprive the court of jurisdiction to resolve the interests of the parties before it. This changes some older state precedents which have held that such defects were jurisdictional. See, Green v. Niver, 43 S.C. 359, 21 S.E. 263 (1894); Gooch v. Elliott, 120 S.C. 245, 113 S.E. 72 (1922).

When a party described in Rule 19(a) cannot be joined, the court must decide whether to proceed with the case in that party's absence. This Rule 19(b) provides the practical factors for the court to consider in reaching its determination, and are not meant to be exclusive. Only if pragmatic considerations strongly indicate that it would be preferable to dismiss the action rather than proceed with the parties before it, should the court conclude that the absent party is truly "indispensable." Under Rule 12(h)(1) the lack of an "indispensable" party in this sense can be raised as late as the trial on the merits. However, if the purpose of the motion is to protect the movant from an apparently unfavorable situation, rather than to protect the absent party, the court may properly consider delay in making the motion as a reason against dismissing the action.

This Rule 19(c) is substantially the same as the Federal Rule. Rule 19(d) simply refers to Rule 23 for joinders in class actions.

RULE 20. PERMISSIVE JOINDER OF PARTIES

(a) Permissive Joinder. All persons may join in one action as plaintiffs if they assert any right to relief jointly, severally, or in the alternative in respect of or arising out of the same transaction, occurrence, or series of transactions or occurrences and if any question of law or fact common to all these persons will arise in the action. All persons may be joined in one action as defendants if there is asserted against them jointly, severally, or in the alternative, any right to relief in respect of or arising out of the same transaction, occurrence, or series of transactions or occurrences and if any question of law or fact common to all defendants will arise in the action. A plaintiff or defendant need not be interested in obtaining or defending against all the relief demanded. Judgment may be given for one or more of the plaintiffs according to their respective rights to relief, and against one or more defendants according to their respective liabilities.

(b) Separate Trials. The court may make such orders as will prevent a party from being embarrassed, delayed, or put to expense by the inclusion of a party against whom he asserts no claim and who asserts no claim against him, and may order separate trials or make other orders to prevent delay or prejudice.

Notes

This Rule 20(a) is substantially the same as the Federal Rule. This rule liberalizes joinder in State practice. It overrules cases like Hellams v. Switzer, 24 S.C. 39 (1885) which denied joinder to upstream farmers damaged by defendant's dam, because their interests were not identical as to damages required.

This Rule 20(b) provides additional authority for separate trials when liberal joinder may produce prejudice or inconvenience for some of the parties.

RULE 21. MISJOINDER AND NON-JOINDER OF PARTIES

Misjoinder of parties is not ground for dismissal of an action. Parties may be dropped or added by order of the court on motion of any party or of its own initiative at any stage of the action and on such terms as are just. Any claim against a party may be severed and proceeded with separately.

Notes

This Rule 21 is the same as the Federal Rule. Presently, Code § 15–13–320(4) permits a demurrer for "defect" of parties, and dismissal of the action is possible. The demurrer is abolished by Rule 7(c), but Rule 12(b)(7) permits a motion to dismiss for failure to join a truly "indispensable" party. With this situation provided for, there is no practical reason why misjoinder should result in dismissal, and this Rule 21 empowers the court to add or drop parties as may be appropriate.

RULE 22. INTERPLEADER

(a) Interpleader May Be Required. Persons having claims against the plaintiff may be joined as defendants and required to interplead when their claims are such that the plaintiff is or may be exposed to double or multiple liability. It is not ground for objection to the joinder that the claims of the several claimants or the titles on which their claims depend do not have a common origin or are not identical but are adverse to and independent of one another, or that the plaintiff avers that he is not liable in whole or in part to any or all of the claimants. A defendant exposed to similar liability may obtain such interpleader by way of cross-claim or counter-claim. The provisions of this rule supplement and do not in any way limit the joinder of parties permitted in Rule 20.

(b) Release From Liability, Deposit, Delivery, or Bond. Any party seeking interpleader, as provided in subdivision (a) of this rule, may deposit with the court the amount claimed, or deliver to the court or as otherwise directed by the court the property claimed, or give bond payable to the clerk of the court in such amount and with such surety as the court may deem proper, conditioned upon the compliance by the plaintiff with the further order of judgment of the court with respect to the subject matter of the controversy. The court may thereupon order such party discharged from liability as to such claims, and the action continued as between claimants of such money or property.

Notes

This Rule 22(a) is the same as the Federal Rule. Federal Rule 22(b) is deleted because it refers to the Federal Interpleader Act which is inapplicable in State procedure. Rule 22(a) broadens the remedy of interpleader permitted under Code § 15–5–200. First, the remedy is of right and not in the discretion of the court. Second, interpleader may be brought by the applicant whether or not he is a party to the pending action. The remedy is not limited to defensive interpleader. Third, the traditional requirement that "the same debt or property" be claimed by the competing claimants gave rise to many technical and unjust decisions and has been abolished. Fourth, the plaintiff may aver that he is not liable in whole or in part to any or all of the claimants, and may remain in the litigation as a party. Fifth, there is no requirement that the applicant file an affidavit denying collusion. Thus the historical common law requirements of bills of interpleader or bills in the nature of interpleader are abolished.

This Rule 22(b) is new, and not in the Federal Rule. It is added to provide expressly for payment into court and discharge from liability as is now provided by Code § 15–5–200.

RULE 23. CLASS ACTIONS

(a) Prerequisites to a Class Action. One or more members of a class may sue or be sued as representative parties on behalf of all only if the court finds (1) the class is so numerous that joinder of all members is impracticable, (2) there are questions of law or fact common to the class, (3) the claims or defenses of the representative parties are typical of the claims or defenses of the class, (4) the representative parties will fairly and adequately protect the interests of the class, and (5) in cases in which the relief primarily sought is not injunctive or declaratory with respect to the class as a whole, the amount in controversy exceeds one hundred dollars for each member of the class.

(b)(1) *Derivative Actions by Shareholders.* In a derivative action brought by one or more shareholders or members to enforce a right of a corporation or of an unincorporated association, the corporation or association having failed to enforce a right which may properly be asserted by it, the complaint shall be verified and shall allege that the plaintiff was a shareholder or member at the time of the transaction of which he complains or that his share or membership thereafter devolved on him by operation of law. The complaint shall also allege with particularity the efforts, if any, made by the plaintiff to obtain the action he desires from the directors or comparable authority and, if necessary, from the shareholders or members, and the reasons for his failure to obtain the action or for not making the effort. The derivative action may not be maintained if it appears that the plaintiff does not fairly and adequately represent the interests of the shareholders or members similarly situated in enforcing the right of the corporation or association. The action shall not be dismissed or compromised without the approval of the court and notice of the proposed dismissal or compromise shall be given to shareholders or members in such manner as the court directs.

(2) *Actions Relating to Unincorporated Associations.* An action brought by or against the members of an unincorporated association as a class by naming certain members as representative parties may be maintained only if it appears that the representative parties will fairly and adequately protect the interests of the association and its members. In the conduct of

the action, the court may make appropriate orders corresponding with those described in Rule 23(d), and the procedure for dismissal or compromise of the action shall correspond with that provided in Rule 23(c).

(c) Dismissal or Compromise. A class action shall not be dismissed or compromised without the approval of the court, and notice of the proposed dismissal or compromise shall be given to all members of the class in such manner as the court directs.

(d) Orders in the Conduct of Actions. In the conduct of actions to which this rule applies, the court may make appropriate orders: (1) As soon as practicable, after the commencement of an action brought as a class action, the court shall determine by order whether it is to be so maintained. An order under this subdivision may be conditional, and may be altered or amended before the decision on the merits. (2) The court may at any time impose such terms as shall fairly and adequately protect the interest of the persons on whose behalf the action is brought or defended. It may order that notice be given in such a manner as it may direct of the pendency of the action by the party seeking to maintain the action on behalf of the class. It may order that notice be given in such manner as it may direct of a proposed settlement, of entry of judgment, or any other proceedings in the action including notice to the absent persons that they may come in and present claims and defenses if they so desire. (3) Whenever the representation appears to the court inadequate fairly to protect the interests of absent persons who may be bound by the judgment, the court may at any time impose additional conditions on the representative parties, or order an amendment of the pleadings, eliminating therefrom all reference to the representation of the absent persons, and in that event the court shall order entry of the judgment in such form as to affect only the parties to the action and those adequately represented.

Notes

This language [Rule 23(a)] is drawn principally from Federal Rule 23(a) and contains essentially the same requirements as Code § 15–5–50, except that subsection (3), the requirement that the claims of the representative be typical is not mentioned, although it could be inferred from the language of the statute. Subsection (5), which requires that when money damages are the primary relief sought, each class member have a claim exceeding one hundred dollars is new. It is intended to limit class actions when the amount sought may be small in comparison with the costs incurred in the litigation. Although not stated in the federal rules, a similar requirement exists when jurisdiction is based upon diversity of citizenship, for then each member of the class must meet the jurisdictional amount, Zahn v. International Paper Co., 414 U.S. 291 [94 S.Ct. 505, 38 L.Ed.2d 511] (1973). Present State practice permits a class action where the relief sought is primarily equitable, even though small monetary damages are sought, Miller v. Borg-Warner Acceptance Corp., [279 S.C. 90] 302 S.E.2d 340 (1983).

This Rule 23(b)(1) is the language of present Federal Rule 23.1. Existing State practice permits a class action in these circumstances. See e.g., Hernlen v. Vandiver, 145 S.C. 412, 143 S.C. 222 (1928) (action on behalf of depositors, stockholders, and creditors of bank against directors of bank for mismanagement) and Black v. Simpson, 94 S.C. 312, 77 S.E. 1023 (1913) (suit by stockholders against director and general manager for fraudulent acquisition of control). The Rule simply provides more specific guidance for the procedure.

This Rule 23(b)(2) is current Federal Rule 23.2. It is included here because it is similar to the requirements for derivative actions. In addition, present State practice recognizes a class action in similar circumstances.

This is the language of current Federal Rule 23(e). It is necessary to protect the rights of all members of the class.

This Rule 23(d) is found in Federal Rules 23(c) and (d) in slightly different language, and describes the present State procedure in specific language. This Rule requires those seeking to maintain an action on behalf of a class to notify the members of the class of the pendency of the action.

RULE 24. INTERVENTION

(a) Intervention of Right. Upon timely application anyone shall be permitted to intervene in an action: (1) when a statute confers an unconditional right to intervene; or (2) when the applicant claims an interest relating to the property or transaction which is the subject of the action and he is so situated that the disposition of the action may as a practical matter impair or impede his ability to protect that interest, unless the applicant's interest is adequately represented by existing parties.

(b) Permissive Intervention. Upon timely application anyone may be permitted to intervene in an action: (1) when a statute confers a conditional right to intervene; or (2) when an applicant's claim or defense and the main action have a question of law or fact in common. When a party to an action relies for ground of claim or defense upon any statute or executive order administered by a federal or state governmental officer or agency or upon any regulation, order, requirement or agreement issued or made pursuant to the statute or executive order, the officer or agency upon timely application may be permitted to intervene in the action. In exercising its discretion the court shall consider whether the intervention will unduly delay or prejudice the adjudication of the rights of the original parties.

(c) Procedure; Notice to State When Validity of Statute Questioned. A person desiring to intervene shall serve a motion to intervene upon the parties as provided in Rule 5. The motion shall state the ground therefor and shall be accompanied by a pleading setting forth the claim or defense for which intervention is sought. The same procedure shall be followed when a statute of this State gives a right to intervene. When the constitutionality of a statute is drawn in question in any action in which the State or an officer, agency or employee thereof is not a party, the party shall also serve the motion on the Attorney General.

Notes

This [Rule 24(a)] is the same as Federal Rule 24(a). Intervention of right under this Rule is a counterpart to Rule 19(a) on joinder of persons needed for a just adjudication; where, upon motion of a party in an action, an absentee should be joined so that he may protect his interest which as a practical matter may be substantially impaired by the disposition of the action, he ought to have a right to intervene in the action on his own motion. The Rule expands intervention of right as provided by Code § 15–5–200, and Circuit Court Rule 22.

This [Rule 24(b)] is the language of current Federal Rule 24(b) with one minor change to delete an unnecessary reference to federal law. It provides a needed procedure to permit intervention by parties who ought to be allowed to intervene, but have no direct right to intervene under Rule 24(a).

This language [Rule 24(c)] is a modification of Federal Rule 24(c). The last two sentences, providing that the same procedure will be followed when a statute permits intervention, and for notice to the Attorney General when a statute is alleged to be unconstitutional, are modified slightly to make them applicable to State practice. Code § 15–33–80 gives the Attorney General a statutory right to intervene in declaratory judgment actions. The language of the Federal Rule on these matters is preferred because Rule 24(c) is procedural, and designed for notice to the Attorney General so that he may decide whether or not to intervene in any case challenging the constitutionality of a statute, while the present statute apparently applies only to declaratory judgment actions.

RULE 25. SUBSTITUTION OF PARTIES

(a) Death.

(1) If a party dies and the claim is not thereby extinguished, the court may order substitution of the proper parties. The motion for substitution may be made by any party or by the successors or representatives of the deceased party and, together with the notice of hearing shall be served on the parties as provided in Rule 5 and upon persons not parties in the manner provided by Rule 4 for the service of summons. If substitution is not made within a reasonable time, the action may be dismissed as to the deceased party. Counsel of record for such deceased party shall give notice to all other parties of the death of such party as soon as practicable after obtaining such knowledge and of the name and address of the proper parties who should be substituted.

(2) In the event of the death of one or more of the plaintiffs or of one or more of the defendants in an action in which the right sought to be enforced survives only to the surviving plaintiffs or only against the surviving defendants, the action does not abate. The death shall be suggested upon the record and the action shall proceed in favor of or against the surviving parties.

(3) After a judgment has been rendered in any action for any wrong, such action shall not abate by the death of any party, but shall proceed thereafter in the same manner as in cases where the action survives by law.

(b) Incompetency. If a party becomes incompetent, the court upon motion served as provided in subdivision (a) of this rule may allow the action to be continued by or against his representative.

(c) Transfer of Interest. In case of any transfer of interest, the action may be continued by or against the original party, unless the court upon motion directs the person to whom the interest is transferred to be substituted in the action or joined with the original party. Service of the motion shall be made as provided in Rule 25(a)(1).

(d) Public Officers; Death or Separation From Office.

(1) When a public officer is a party to an action in his official capacity and during its pendency dies, resigns, or otherwise ceases to hold office, the action does not abate and his successor is automatically substituted as a party. Proceedings following the substitution shall be in the name of the substituted party, but any misnomer not affecting the substantial rights of the parties shall be disregarded. An order of substitution may be entered at any time, but the omission to enter such an order shall not affect the substitution.

(2) When a public officer sues or is sued in his official capacity, he may be described as a party by his official title rather than by name; but the court may require his name to be added.

(e) Substitution at Any Stage. Substitution of parties under the provision of this rule may be made by the trial court either before or after judgment, or pending appeal, by the appellate court.

[Amended effective November 20, 2008.]

Notes

This Rule 25(a)(1) is substantially the same as Federal Rule 25(a). In the Federal Rule the motion for substitution is to be made within 90 days after notice of death is suggested upon the record. This Rule substitutes "a reasonable time" after such knowledge is obtained.

This Rule 25(a)(2) is the same as the Federal Rule. It provides in specific language a procedure to avoid dismissing and restarting an action as to surviving parties.

This Rule 25(a)(3) is new but does not change State practice. It repeats substantially the language of the second paragraph of Code § 15–5–180.

This [Rule 25(c)] is the language of current Federal Rules 25(b) and (c) but represents present State practice.

This Rule 25(d) is the language of Federal Rule 25(d). It applies only when the officer is sued in his official capacity. In the event he is sued as an individual then the provisions of Rule 25(a) apply. Rule 25(d)(2) provides that the officer sued in his official capacity may be described as a party by his official title rather than by his personal name. If it is desirable to have the official's name the court has the power to add it.

This provision [Rule 25(e)] does not appear in the Federal Rules. It is added to preserve State practice.

V. DEPOSITIONS AND DISCOVERY

RULE 26. GENERAL PROVISIONS GOVERNING DISCOVERY

(a) Discovery Methods. Parties may obtain discovery by one or more of the following methods: depositions upon oral examination or written questions; written interrogatories; production of documents or things or permission to enter upon land or other property, for inspection and other purposes; physical and mental examinations; and requests for admissions. The frequency or intent of use of discovery methods set forth in subdivision (a) shall be limited by the court if it determines that: (i) the discovery sought is unreasonably cumulative or duplicative, or is obtainable from some other source that is more convenient, less burdensome, or less expensive; (ii) the party seeking discovery has had ample opportunity by discovery in the action to obtain the information sought; or (iii) the discovery is unreasonably burdensome or expensive taking into account the needs of the case, the amount in controversy, limitations on the parties' resources, and the importance of the issues at stake in the litigation. The court may act upon its own initiative after reasonable notice or pursuant to a motion under subdivision (c) of this Rule.

(b) Scope of Discovery. Unless otherwise limited by order of the court in accordance with these rules, the scope of discovery is as follows:

(1) *In General.* Parties may obtain discovery regarding any matter, not privileged, which is relevant to the subject matter involved in the pending action, whether it relates to the claim or defense of the party seeking discovery or to the claim or defense of any other party, including the existence, description, nature, custody, condition and location of any books, documents, or other tangible things and the identity and location of persons having knowledge of any discoverable matter. It is not ground for objection that the information sought will be inadmissible at the trial if the information sought appears reasonably calculated to lead to the discovery of admissible evidence.

(2) *Insurance Agreements.* A party may obtain discovery of the existence and contents of any insurance agreement under which any person carrying on an insurance business may be liable to satisfy part or all of a judgment which may be entered in the action or to indemnify or reimburse for payments made to satisfy the judgment. Information concerning the insurance agreement is not by reason of disclosure admissible in evidence at trial. For purposes of this paragraph, an application for insurance shall not be treated as part of an insurance agreement.

(3) *Trial Preparation: Materials.* Subject to the provisions of subdivision (b)(4) of this rule, a party may obtain discovery of documents and tangible things otherwise discoverable under subdivision (b)(1) of this rule and prepared in anticipation of litigation or for the trial by or for another party or by or for that other party's representative (including his attorney, consultant, surety, indemnitor, insurer, or agent) only upon a showing that the party seeking discovery has substantial need of the materials in the preparation of his case and that he is unable without undue hardship to obtain the substantial equivalent of the materials by other means. In ordering discovery of such materials when the required showing has been made, the court shall protect against disclosure of the mental impressions, conclusions, opinions, or legal theories of an attorney or other representative of a party concerning the litigation.

A party may obtain without the required showing a statement concerning the action or its subject matter previously made by that party. Upon request, a person not a party may obtain without the required showing a statement concerning the action or its subject matter previously made by that person. If the request is refused, the person may move for a court order. The provisions of Rule 37(a)(4) apply to the award of expenses incurred in relation to the motion. For purposes of this paragraph, a statement previously made is (A) a written statement signed or otherwise adopted or approved by the person making it, or (B) a stenographic, mechanical, electrical, or other recording, or a transcription thereof, which is a substantially verbatim recital of an oral statement by the person making it and contemporaneously recorded.

(4)(A) Trial Preparation: Experts. Discovery of facts known and opinions held by experts, otherwise discoverable under the provisions of subdivision (b)(1) of this rule and acquired or developed in anticipation of litigation or for trial, may be obtained by any discovery method subject to subdivisions (b)(4)(B) and (C) of this rule, concerning fees and expenses.

(B) A party may discover facts known or opinions held by an expert who has been retained or specially employed by another party in anticipation of litigation or preparation for trial and who is not expected to be called as a witness at trial, only as provided in Rule 35(b) or upon a showing of exceptional circumstances under which it is impracticable for the party seeking discovery to obtain facts or opinions on the same subject by other means. A party is not required to disclose nor produce an expert who was only consulted informally, or consulted and not retained or specially employed.

(C) Upon the request of the party seeking discovery, unless the court determines otherwise for good cause shown, or the parties agree otherwise, a party retaining an expert who is subject to deposition shall produce such expert in this state for the purpose of taking his deposition, and the party seeking discovery shall pay the expert a reasonable fee for time and expenses spent in travel and in responding to discovery and upon motion the court may require the party seeking discovery to pay the other party a fair portion of the fees and expenses reasonably incurred by the latter party in obtaining facts and opinions from the expert.

(5) *Claims of Privilege or Protection of Trial Preparation Materials.*

(A) Information Withheld. When a party withholds information otherwise discoverable under these rules by claiming that it is privileged or subject to protection as trial preparation material, the party shall make the claim expressly and shall describe the nature of the documents, communications, or things not produced or disclosed in a manner that, without revealing the information itself privileged or protected, will enable other parties to assess the applicability of the privilege or protection.

(B) Information Produced. If information produced in discovery is subject to a claim of privilege or of protection as trial preparation material, the party making the claim may notify any party that received the information of the claim and the basis for it. After being notified, a party must promptly return, sequester, or destroy the specified information and any copies it has and may not use or disclose the information until the claim is resolved. A receiving party may promptly present the information to the court under seal for a determination of the claim. If the receiving party disclosed the information before being notified, the receiving party must take reasonable steps to retrieve the information. The producing party must preserve the information until the claim is resolved.

(6) *Electronically Stored Information.*

(A) A party need not provide discovery of electronically stored information from sources that the party identifies to the requesting party as not reasonably accessible because of undue burden or cost. On motion to compel discovery or for a protective order, the party from whom discovery is sought must show that the information is not reasonably accessible because of undue burden or cost. If that showing is made, the court may nonetheless order discovery from such sources if the requesting party shows good cause, considering the limitations of Rule 26(b)(6)(B). The court may specify conditions for the discovery, including allocation of expenses associated with discovery of the electronically stored information.

(B) On motion or on its own motion, the court shall limit the frequency or extent of discovery otherwise allowed by these rules if the court determines that:

(i) the discovery sought is unreasonably cumulative or duplicative, or is obtainable from some other source that is more convenient, less burdensome, or less expensive;

(ii) the party seeking discovery has had ample opportunity by discovery in the action to obtain the information sought; or

(iii) the burden or expense of the proposed discovery outweighs its likely benefit, taking into account the needs of the case, the amount in controversy, the parties' resources, the importance of the issues at stake in the litigation, and the importance of the proposed discovery in resolving the issues. The court may act upon its own initiative after reasonable notice or pursuant to a motion under Rule 26(c).

(c) Protective Orders. Upon motion by a party or by the person from whom discovery is sought, and for good cause shown, the court in which the action is pending or alternatively, on matters relating to a deposition, the court in the circuit where the deposition is to be taken may make any order which justice requires to protect a party or person from annoyance, embarrassment, oppression, or undue burden by expense, including one or more of the following: (1) that the discovery not be had; (2) that the discovery may be had only on specified terms and conditions, including a designation of the time or place; (3) that the discovery may be had only by a method of discovery other than selected by the party seeking discovery; (4) that certain matters not be inquired into or that the scope of the discovery be limited to certain matters; (5) that discovery be conducted with no one present except persons designated by the court; (6) that a deposition after being sealed be opened only by order of the court; (7) that a trade secret or other confidential research, development, or commercial information not be disclosed or be disclosed only in a designated way; (8) that the parties simultaneously file specified documents or information enclosed in sealed envelopes to be opened as directed by the court.

If the motion for a protective order is denied in whole or in part, the court may, on such terms and conditions as are just, order that any party or person provide or permit discovery. The provisions of Rule 37(a)(4) apply to the award of expenses incurred in relation to the motion.

(d) Sequence and Timing of Discovery. Unless the court upon motion, for the convenience of parties and witnesses and in the interests of justice, orders otherwise, methods of discovery may be used in any sequence and the fact that a party is conducting discovery, whether by deposition or otherwise, shall not operate to delay any other party's discovery.

(e) Supplementation of Responses. A party who has responded to a request for discovery with a response that was complete when made is under no duty to supplement his response to include information thereafter acquired, except that requests for discovery under Rules 31, 33, 34, and 36 shall be deemed to continue from the time of service until the time of trial of the action so that information sought, which comes to the knowledge of a party, or his representative or attorney, after original answers have been submitted, shall be promptly transmitted to the other party.

In addition, a party is under a duty seasonably to supplement his response with respect to any question directly addressed to (1) the identity and location of persons having knowledge of discoverable matters, and (2) the identity of each person expected to be called as an expert witness at trial, the subject matter on which he is expected to testify, and the substance of his testimony.

(f) Discovery Conference. At any time after commencement of an action the court may direct the attorneys for the parties to appear before it for a conference on the subject of discovery. The court shall do so upon motion by the attorneys for any party if the motion includes:

(1) A statement of the issues as they then appear;

(2) A proposed plan and schedule of discovery;

(3) Any limitations proposed to be placed on discovery;

(4) Any other proposed orders with respect to discovery;

(5) A statement of any issues relating to discovery of electronically stored information, including the form or forms in which it should be produced;

(6) A statement of any issues relating to claims of privilege or of protection as trial preparation material, including—if the parties agree on a procedure to assert such claims after production—whether the parties wish to have the court include their agreement in an order; and

(7) A statement showing that the attorney making the motion has made a reasonable effort to reach agreement with opposing attorneys on the matters set forth in the motion. Each party and his attorney are under a duty to participate in good faith in the framing of a discovery plan if a plan is proposed by the attorney for any party. Notice of the motion shall be served on all parties. Objections or additions to matters set forth in the motion shall be served not later than 10 days after service of the motion.

Following the discovery conference, the court shall enter an order tentatively identifying the issues for discovery purposes, establishing a plan and schedule for discovery, setting limitations on discovery, if any; and determining such other matters, including the allocation of expenses, as are necessary for the proper management of discovery in the action. An order may be altered or amended whenever justice so requires. Subject to the right of a party who properly moves for a discovery conference to prompt convening of the conference, the court may combine the discovery conference with a pretrial hearing authorized by Rule 16.

(g) Signing of Discovery Requests, Responses, and Objections. Every request for discovery or response or objection thereto made by a party represented by an attorney shall be signed by at least one attorney of record in his individual name, whose address shall be stated. A party who is not represented by an attorney shall sign the request, response, or objection and state his address. The signature of the attorney or party constitutes a certification in accordance with Rule 11.

(1) *Filing, Service and Custody.* Except as provided in Rule 30(h), the party requesting discovery shall serve the request on other counsel or parties, but not file the notice or materials or matters discovered. The requesting party shall retain the originals and shall file the originals with the clerk of court when the same are to be used at a hearing or at trial.

(2) *Destruction.* One year after the final termination of an action in which discovery other than depositions has been taken, the party taking the other discovery or the clerk of court, as the case may be, may destroy or otherwise dispose of the original discovery requests and responses.

[Amended effective May 1, 1986; June 30, 1996; April 28, 2011.]

Notes

This [Rule 26(a)] is the language of Federal Rule 26(a) as amended August 1, 1983. The second part was added to address the problem of duplicative, redundant, and excessive discovery by encouraging judges to identify instances of needless discovery and to limit the uses of the various discovery devices accordingly. This rule changes State procedure by permitting discovery by deposition upon written questions and also mental and physical examinations.

This [Rule 26(b)(1)] is the language of Federal Rule 26(b). It is substantially equivalent to the language of Circuit Court Rule 87B with minor editorial changes. In particular it has the same scope of discovery—"relevant to the subject matter."

This [Rule 26(b)(2)] is the language of the Federal Rule 26(b)(2) and authorizes discovery of insurance agreements by any discovery method. Circuit Court Rule 90(e) presently authorizes an interrogatory to discover the names and addresses of all insurance companies which have liability insurance relating to the claim and the numbers and amounts of the policies. Thus, this language does not produce any significant change in existing State practice.

This [Rule 26(b)(3), first paragraph] is the language of Federal Rule 26(b)(3). There is no equivalent Circuit Court Rule on this subject although there is existing common law providing similar protection. This provision is added to clarify and standardize the law on the issue.

This [Rule 26(b)(3), second paragraph] is a continuation of paragraph (b)(3), of the Federal Rule and provides for the discovery of statements by parties and witnesses. This is comparable to Circuit Court Rule 90(e)(1) which provides for the discovery of the existence of statements taken from witnesses.

Rule 26(b)(4) is based upon the comparable Federal Rule. The language is changed to permit discovery of an expert expected to testify at trial by any means and without any special showing of need. There is also a requirement that the party is not required to disclose an expert casually or informally consulted or one consulted but not specially employed. This is similar to the result reached under the federal rules and its Advisory Notes to 26(b)(4)(B). 26(b)(4)(C) is changed to require a party producing an expert for deposition to do so in this state. The discovering party is specifically made responsible for reasonable fees and expenses incurred in traveling to this state, as well as the time spent in responding to the discovery.

This [Rule 26(c)] is the language of Federal Rule 26(c). Exactly the same language was recently adopted as Circuit Court Rule 96.

This [Rule 26(d)] is the language of Federal Rule 26(d). There is no equivalent in the Circuit Court Rules. The purpose of the paragraph is to prevent the idea of "priority" in the taking of discovery, resulting in delay. The court however retains power to set the order of discovery if necessary.

This Rule 26(e) is the language of Federal Rule 26(e). A like duty to supplement the special interrogatories permitted under present Circuit Court Rule 90 is imposed by that rule and is substantially the same as the Federal Rule. In these discovery Rules the Federal language is adopted for all discovery except Rule 33(b) standard interrogatories. The Circuit Court Rule 90 provision is retained as to answers to those special interrogatories because the interrogatories are limited in number, the continuing duty to update them is not burdensome, and it preserves the existing State practice.

This [Rule 26(f)] is the language of Federal Rule 26(f). Its purpose is to prevent discovery abuse by encouraging the court to intervene when abuse occurs, or when an attorney has failed to obtain the cooperation of opposing counsel and should have the assistance of the court. Routine matters should be resolved by Rule 26(c) Motions for protective orders or Rule 37 Motions to compel. The discovery conference is discretionary with the court, and may be combined with a pretrial hearing.

This language [Rule 26(g)] is drawn from the first three sentences of Federal Rule 26(g) and has been slightly modified to incorporate reference to Rule 11. The more strict standard of the Federal Rules contained in Rules 11, 16 and 26 has not been adopted.

This paragraph [Rule 26(g)(1) and (2)] conforms to Circuit Court Rule 97 and provides that, except for videotaped depositions under Rule 30(h), the requesting party retains the original discovery request and response until it is needed for a motion or trial, then it is filed with the court.

Notes to 1986 Amendments

This amendment to Rule 26(b)(4)(C) replaces the "manifest injustice" standard with that of "good cause shown" to conform to similar references to the standard for controlling discovery practice in other Rules.

Notes to 1996 Amendments

Rule 26 is amended to add paragraph (b)(5) requiring a party to notify the other parties that it is withholding information otherwise discoverable on grounds of privilege or work product. The party must also provide sufficient information to enable other parties to evaluate the applicability of the claimed privilege or protection. The rule does not specify the detail required which will depend upon the facts of each case. The rule applies to material otherwise discoverable, and does not require disclosure of information that is privileged. A motion challenging the claim of privilege or work product normally is decided by the court after an in camera inspection of the materials. Non-parties have a similar obligation when responding to a subpoena under Rule 45(d)(2), SCRCP, and there is similar language in the comparable federal rules.

Rule 26(e) is amended to make applicable the language of Rule 33(b) on the duty to supplement the standard interrogatories to discovery requests under Rule 31 Depositions Upon Written Questions, Rule 33 Interrogatories to Parties, Rule 34 Production of Documents and Tangible Things, and Rule 36 Request for Admission. Discovery requests under these rules are deemed to be continuing and the responding party must update the answers promptly when new information comes to the attention of the party, a representative of the party or counsel. This duty to supplement does not apply to discovery under Rule 30 Depositions Upon Oral Examination. However, there is an additional duty to provide supplemental information on expert witnesses and witnesses with knowledge of the facts of the case regardless of the form of the discovery request. The obligation to supplement prior discovery responses includes the duty to amend or supplement answers which are found to be incorrect or misleading so former subparagraph (e)(2) has been deleted, as has former subparagraph (e)(3) which is now redundant.

Note to 2011 Amendments

The amendments to Rules 16, 26, 33, 34, 37 and 45 of the South Carolina Rules of Civil Procedure concerning electronic discovery are substantially similar to the corresponding provisions in the Federal Rules of Civil Procedure. The rules concerning electronic discovery are intended to provide a practical, efficient and cost-effective method to assure reasonable discovery. Pursuit of electronic discovery must relate to the claims and defenses asserted in the pleadings and should serve as a means for facilitating a just and cost-effective resolution of disputes.

RULE 27. DEPOSITIONS BEFORE ACTION OR PENDING APPEAL

(a) Before Action.

(1) *Petition.* A person who desires to perpetuate his own testimony or that of another person regarding any matter that may be cognizable in any court of the State may file a verified petition in the court in the Circuit of the residence of any expected adverse party. The petition shall be entitled in the name of the petitioner and shall show: 1. that the petitioner expects to be a party to an action cognizable in a court of the State but is presently unable to bring it or cause it to be brought; 2. the subject matter of the expected action and his interest therein; 3. the facts which he

desires to establish by the proposed testimony and his reasons for desiring to perpetuate it; 4. the names or a description of the persons he expects will be adverse parties and their addresses so far as known; and 5. the names or a description of the persons to be examined and the substance of the testimony which he expects to elicit from each, and shall ask for an order authorizing the petitioner to take the depositions of the persons to be examined named in the petition, for the purpose of perpetuating their testimony.

(2) *Notice and Service.* The petitioner shall thereafter serve a notice upon each person named in the petition as an expected adverse party, together with a copy of the petition, stating that the petitioner will apply to the court, at a time and place named therein, for the order described in the petition. At least 20 days before the date of hearing the notice shall be served either within or without the circuit or state in the manner provided in Rule 4(d) for service of summons; but if such service cannot with due diligence be made upon any expected adverse party named in the petition, the court may make such order as is just for service by publication or otherwise, and shall appoint, for persons not served in the manner provided in Rule 4(d), an attorney who shall represent them, and, in case they are not otherwise represented, shall cross-examine the deponent. If any expected adverse party is a minor or incompetent the provisions of Rule 17(c) apply.

(3) *Order and Examination.* If the court is satisfied that the perpetuation of the testimony may prevent a failure or delay of justice, it shall make an order designating or describing the persons whose depositions may be taken and specifying the subject matter of the examination and whether the depositions shall be taken upon oral examination or written interrogatories. The depositions may then be taken in accordance with these rules; and the court may make orders of the character provided for by Rules 34 and 35. For the purpose of applying these rules to depositions for perpetuating testimony, each reference therein to the court in which the action is pending shall be deemed to refer to the court in which the petition for such deposition was filed.

(4) *Use of Deposition.* If a deposition to perpetuate testimony is taken under these rules or if, although not so taken, it would be admissible in evidence in the courts of the state in which it is taken, it may be used in any action involving the same subject matter subsequently brought in a court of this State in accordance with the provisions of Rule 32(a).

(b) Pending Appeal. If an appeal has been taken from a judgment of a court or before the taking of an appeal if the time therefor has not expired, the court in which the judgment was rendered may allow the taking of the depositions of witnesses to perpetuate their testimony for use in the event of further proceedings in the court. In such case the party who desires to perpetuate the testimony may make a motion in the court for leave to take the depositions, upon the same notice and service thereof as if the action was pending in the circuit court. The motion shall show (1) the names and addresses of persons to be examined and the substance of the testimony which he expects to elicit from each; (2) the reasons for perpetuating their testimony. If the court finds that the perpetuation of the testimony is proper to avoid a failure or delay of justice, it may make an order allowing the depositions to be taken and may make orders of the character provided for by Rules 34 and 35, and thereupon the depositions may be taken and used in the same manner and under the same conditions as are prescribed in these rules for depositions taken in actions pending in the circuit court.

(c) Perpetuation by Action. This rule does not limit the power of a court to entertain an action to perpetuate testimony.

Notes

At present Code §§ 19–17–40 et seq. provide for depositions de bene esse. This proposal, drawn from Federal Rule 27 with minor modifications, provides an easy method for perpetuating testimony prior to the filing of suit. It has been consistently held that it is not a method of discovery before suit is brought. As provided in paragraph (a)(1) the verified petition must establish that the petitioner expects to be a party but is unable to do so at the present time, and also must specify the proposed testimony and the names of the deponents, which indicates that the petitioner must know in advance the information sought to be perpetuated. In appropriate cases the rule also permits the use of Rules 34 and 35 if necessary. There are similar provisions for retaining the testimony if the case is on appeal.

RULE 28. PERSONS BEFORE WHOM DEPOSITIONS MAY BE TAKEN; DEPOSITIONS IN OUT-OF-STATE ACTIONS

(a) Within the United States. Within any state or within a territory or insular possession subject to the jurisdiction of the United States, depositions shall be taken before an officer authorized to administer oaths by the laws of the United States or of the place where the examination is held, or before a person appointed by the court in which the action is pending. A person so appointed has power to administer oaths and take testimony. The term officer as used in Rules 30, 31 and 32 includes a person appointed by the court or designated by the parties under Rule 29.

(b) In Foreign Countries. In a foreign country, depositions may be taken (1) on notice before a person authorized to administer oaths in the place in which the examination is held, either by the law thereof or by the law of the United States, or (2) before a person commissioned by the court, and a person so commissioned shall have the power by virtue of his commission to administer any necessary oath and take testimony, or (3) pursuant to a letter rogatory. A commission or a letter rogatory shall be issued on application and notice and on terms that are just and appropriate. It is not requisite to the issuance of a commission or a letter rogatory that the taking of the deposition in any other manner is impracticable or inconvenient; and both a commission and a letter rogatory may be issued in proper cases. A notice or commission may designate the person before whom the deposition is to be taken either by name or descriptive title. A letter rogatory may be addressed "To the Appropriate Authority in (here name the country)." Evidence obtained in response to a letter rogatory need not be excluded merely for the reason that it is not a verbatim transcript or that the testimony was not taken under oath or for any similar departure from the requirements for depositions taken within the United States under these rules.

(c) Disqualification for Interest. No deposition shall be taken before a person who is a relative or employee or attorney or counsel of any of the parties, or is a relative or employee of such attorney or counsel, or is financially interested in the action.

(d) Depositions or Production in Out-of-State Actions.

(1) When the deposition of a witness or production of documents or other things, is to be done in this State for use in an out-of-state action or proceeding, an attorney, licensed to practice law in this State, or the clerk of court, may issue a subpoena, including a subpoena duces tecum, compelling the attendance of such witness at that deposition, or the production of documents or other things pursuant to this rule and subject to all of the requirements of Rule 45 and Rule 11, only after payment of the filing fee set[1] by Administrative Rule, and after filing with the Clerk of Court:

(A) A certified copy of any mandate, writ, or commission issued by a court of record in any other state, territory, district, or foreign jurisdiction directing that such deposition be taken or documents or other things produced; or

(B) a certified copy of a notice or written agreement filed in a court of record in any other state, territory, district, or foreign jurisdiction directing that such deposition be taken or documents or other things produced.

(2) Such witness may be compelled to attend a deposition only in the county where he resides, where he is employed, or where he transacts his business in person.

(3) Such witness or a party may obtain a protective order pursuant to Rule 26(c) upon application to the court in the county from which the subpoena is issued.

(4) If such witness fails to obey the subpoena or refuses to answer any question propounded upon oral examination, the provisions of Rule 37(a) and (b) shall apply, and the party requesting the deposition shall make application for such order to the court of the county from which the subpoena was issued.

(5) Such witness is entitled to the same compensation as provided to a witness pursuant to Rule or statute.

(6) The clerk of court, shall, upon receipt of the above described filing fee, file all papers received by him pursuant to this Rule.

[Amended effective May 1, 1986; July 1, 1995.]

[1] By order dated February 21, 2003, effective March 1, 2003, the filing fee was set at $50.

Notes

Rule 28(a)–(c) is substantially the same as Federal Rule 28. The language of 28(d) is the same as in Circuit Court Rule 100, with minor changes to conform to the new organization and rearrangement of these rules.

Rule 28(d) is consistent with the South Carolina Uniform Interstate Depositions and Discovery Act, which is codified at S.C. Code Ann. § 15–47–100 et seq.

Notes to 1986 Amendments

This change [to Rule 28(d)(1)] permits the filing fee to be set by administrative rule of the Supreme Court rather than by amendment of procedural rules.

Note to 1995 Amendment

Rule 28(d) governing depositions and document production in South Carolina for use in an out-of-state action is amended to conform to recently revised Rule 45. The amended rule permits an attorney licensed to practice law in South Carolina or the clerk of court to issue the subpoena. In addition, as provided in Rule 45(a)(1)(D) the subpoena may be for the production of documents without the necessity of a deposition. The filing fee and file the required documents must be filed with the clerk of the court in the appropriate county before the attorney or the clerk may issue the subpoena. The attorney is subject to all of the provisions in Rule 11 and Rule 45, particularly 45(c)(1) regarding the duty to avoid imposing undue burden or expense on a person subject to the subpoena.

RULE 29. STIPULATIONS REGARDING DISCOVERY PROCEDURE

Unless the court orders otherwise, the parties may by written stipulation (1) provide that depositions may be taken before any person, at any time or place, upon any notice, and in any manner and when so taken may be used like other depositions, and (2) to the extent allowed by Rule 6(b), modify the procedures provided by these rules for other methods of discovery.

[Amended effective September 1, 2001.]

Notes

The language above is the current Federal Rule which permits stipulations for means of discovery, and insures that a court may vary the stipulations. The parties, however, cannot by stipulation extend the time for response to interrogatories, document requests, and requests to admit.

Note to 2001 Amendment

The 2001 amendment eliminates the requirement of court approval for requests for extensions regarding discovery procedure where the parties agree to the extension in writing. Extensions are limited by Rule 6(b) which allows the parties to stipulate to only one extension and for the original time provided.

RULE 30. DEPOSITIONS UPON ORAL EXAMINATION

(a)(1) *When Depositions May Be Taken.* After commencement of an action any party may take the testimony of any person, including a party, by deposition upon oral examination. Leave of court, granted with or without notice, must be obtained only if the plaintiff seeks to take a deposition prior to the expiration of 30 days after service of summons and complaint upon any defendant, except that leave is not required if a defendant has served a notice of taking depositions or otherwise sought discovery as provided in these Rules. The deposition of a person confined in prison may be taken only by leave of court on such terms as the court prescribes.

(2) *Limitations.* A witness may be compelled to attend in the county in which he resides or is employed or transacts his business in person, or at such other convenient place as is fixed by an order of the court. A party may be compelled to attend in the county in which the subject civil action is pending, or in the county in which he resides or is employed or transacts business, or at such other convenient place as is fixed by an order of the court.

The deposition of any party or witness may only be taken one time in any case except by agreement of the parties through their counsel or by order of the court for good cause shown.

A witness attending any deposition held pursuant to these rules shall receive for each day's attendance and for the time necessarily occupied in going to and returning from the same, $25.00 per day, and mileage for going from and returning to his place of residence, in the same amounts as provided by law for official travel of state officers and employees.

This rule shall not apply to those cases where the amount in controversy is less than the sum of $10,000.00, unless the parties or their counsel agree otherwise, or unless the court should so order upon good cause shown.

(b) Notice of Examination: General Requirements; Special Notice; Non-stenographic Recording; Production of Documents and Things; Deposition of Organization; Deposition by Telephone.

(1) A party desiring to take the deposition of any person upon oral examination shall give ten (10) days notice in writing to every other party to the action. The notice shall state the time and place for taking the deposition and the name and address of each person to be examined, if known, and if the name is not known, a general description sufficient to identify him or the particular class or group to which he belongs. If a subpoena duces tecum is to be served on the person to be examined, the designation of the materials to be produced as set forth in the subpoena shall be attached to or included in the notice.

(2) Leave of court is not required for the taking of a deposition by plaintiff if the notice (A) states that the person to be examined is about to go more than 100 miles from the place of trial, or is about to go out of the State, or is bound on a voyage to sea, and will be unavailable for examination unless his deposition is taken before expiration of the 30-day period provided in Rule 30(a)(1), and (B) sets forth facts to support the statement. The plaintiff's attorney shall sign the notice, and his signature constitutes a certification by him that to the best of his knowledge, information, and belief the statement and supporting facts are true. The sanctions provided by Rule 11 are applicable to the certification. If a party shows that when he was served with notice under this subdivision (b)(2) he was unable through the exercise of diligence to obtain counsel to represent him at the taking of the deposition, the deposition may not be used against him.

(3) The court may for cause shown enlarge or shorten the time for taking the deposition.

(4) The parties may stipulate in writing or the court may upon motion order that the testimony at a deposition be recorded by other than stenographic means. The stipulation or order shall designate the person before whom the deposition shall be taken, the manner of recording, preserving and filing the deposition, and may include other provisions to assure that the recorded testimony will be accurate and trustworthy. A party may arrange to have a stenographic transcription made at his own expense. Any objection under Rule 30(c), any changes made by the witness, his signature identifying the deposition as his own or the statement of the officer that is required if the witness does not sign, as provided in Rule 30(e), and the certification of the officer required by Rule 30(f) shall be set forth in writing to accompany a deposition recorded by non-stenographic means.

(5) The notice to a party deponent may be accompanied by a request made in compliance with Rule 34 for the production of documents and tangible things at the taking of the deposition. The procedure of Rule 34 shall apply to the request.

(6) A party may in his notice and in a subpoena name as the deponent a public or private corporation or a partnership or association or governmental agency and describe with reasonable particularity the matters on which examination is requested. In that event, the organization so named shall designate one or more officers, directors or managing agents, or other persons who consent to testify on its behalf, and may set forth, for each person designated, the matters on which he will testify. A subpoena shall advise a non-party organization of its duty to make such a designation. The persons so designated shall testify as to matters

known or reasonably available to the organization. This subdivision (b)(6) does not preclude taking a deposition by any other procedure authorized in these rules.

(7) The parties may stipulate in writing or the court may upon motion order that a deposition be taken by telephone. For the purposes of this rule and Rules 28(a), 37(a)(1), 37(b)(1) and 45(d), a deposition taken by telephone is taken at the same place where the deponent is to answer questions propounded to him. The notary before whom the deposition is taken shall be at the same place as the deponent during the taking of the deposition.

(c) Examination and Cross-Examinations; Record of Examination; Oath; Objections. Examination and cross-examination of witnesses may proceed as permitted at the trial under the provisions of the South Carolina Rules of Evidence except Rules 103 and 615. The officer before whom the deposition is to be taken shall put the witness on oath and shall personally, or by someone acting under his direction and in his presence, record the testimony of the witness. The testimony shall be taken stenographically or recorded by any other means ordered in accordance with subdivision (b)(4) of this rule. If requested by one of the parties, the testimony shall be transcribed. All objections made at time of the examination to the qualifications of the officer taking the deposition, or to the manner of taking it, or to the evidence presented, or to the conduct of any party, and any other objection to the proceedings, shall be noted by the officer upon the deposition. Evidence objected to shall be taken subject to the objections. In lieu of participating in the oral examination, parties may serve written questions in a sealed envelope on the party taking the deposition and he shall transmit them to the officer, who shall propound them to the witness and record the answers verbatim.

(d) Motion to Terminate or Limit Examination. At any time during the taking of the deposition, on motion of a party or the deponent and upon a showing that the examination is being conducted in bad faith or in such manner as unreasonably to annoy, embarrass, or oppress the deponent or party, the court in which the action is pending or the court in the place where the deposition is being taken may order the officer conducting the examination to cease forthwith from taking the deposition, or may limit the scope and manner of the taking of the deposition as provided in Rule 26(c). If the order made terminates the examination, it shall be resumed thereafter only upon the order of the court in which the action is pending. Upon demand of the objecting party or deponent, the taking of the deposition shall be suspended for the time necessary to make a motion for an order. The provisions of Rule 37(a)(4) apply to the award of expenses incurred in relation to the motion.

(e) Submission to Witness; Changes; Signing. When the testimony is fully transcribed the deposition shall be submitted to the witness for examination and shall be read to or by him unless such examination and reading are waived by the witness and by the parties. Any changes in form or substance which the witness desires to make shall be entered upon the deposition by the officer with a statement of the reasons given by the witness for making them. The deposition shall then be signed by the witness, unless the parties by stipulation waive the signing or the witness is ill or cannot be found or refuses to sign. If the deposition is not signed by the witness within 30 days of its submission to him, the officer shall sign it and state on the record the fact of the waiver or of the illness or absence of the witness or the fact of the refusal to sign together with the reason, if any, given therefor; and the deposition may then be used as fully as though signed unless on a motion to suppress under Rule 32(d)(4) the court holds that the reasons given for the refusal to sign require rejection of the deposition in whole or in part.

(f) Certification and Delivery by Officer; Exhibits; Copies; Notice of Filing.

(1) The officer transcribing a deposition shall certify on the deposition that the witness was duly sworn by him and that the deposition is a true record of the testimony given by the witness. He shall then securely seal the deposition in an envelope endorsed with the title of the action and marked "Deposition of (herein insert name of witness)" and shall promptly deliver it or send it by registered or certified mail to the party taking the deposition who shall retain the original and become the custodian. The custodian shall promptly file the original deposition with the clerk of court when the same is to be used at a hearing or at trial.

Documents and things produced for inspection during the examination of the witness, shall, upon the request of a party, be marked for identification and annexed to the deposition and may be inspected and copied by any party, except that if the person producing the materials desires to retain them he may (A) offer copies to be marked for identification and annexed to the deposition and to serve thereafter as originals if he affords to all parties fair opportunity to verify the copies by comparison with the originals, or (B) offer the originals to be marked for identification, after giving to each party an opportunity to inspect and copy them, in which event the materials may then be used in the same manner as if annexed to the deposition. Any party may move for an order that the originals be annexed to and returned with the deposition to the court, pending final disposition of the case.

(2) Upon payment of reasonable charges therefor, the officer shall furnish a copy of the deposition to any party or to the deponent.

(3) The party taking the deposition shall give prompt notice of its filing to all other parties.

(4) One year after final termination of an action in which a deposition has been taken, the party taking the

deposition or the clerk of court, as the case may be, may destroy or otherwise dispose of the original deposition.

(g) Failure to Attend or to Serve Subpoena; Expenses.

(1) If the party giving the notice of the taking of a deposition fails to attend and proceed therewith and another party attends in person or by attorney pursuant to the notice, the court may order the party giving the notice to pay to such other party the reasonable expenses incurred by him and his attorney in attending, including reasonable attorney's fees.

(2) If the party giving the notice of the taking of a deposition of a witness fails to serve a subpoena upon him and the witness because of such failure does not attend, and if another party attends in person or by attorney because he expects the deposition of that witness to be taken, the court may order the party giving the notice to pay such other party the reasonable expenses incurred by him and his attorney in attending, including reasonable attorney's fees.

(h) Videotaped Depositions.

(1) The provisions of this rule apply only to civil actions in which the prayer for relief involves an amount of one hundred thousand dollars or more or in which the court has granted permission for the use of videotape by court order.

(A) When a party taking a deposition, in addition to having the testimony taken stenographically and transcribed, also desires to have the testimony videotaped, the party shall include notice of the videotaping of the deposition in the written notice required. Neither the provisions of this Rule [1] shall preclude the parties from agreeing that a written transcript will not be presented with respect to a particular deposition.

(B) The officer before whom a videotape deposition is taken shall be one of the officers enumerated herein.

(2)(A) At the beginning of the deposition, and prior to the deponent being sworn, the videotape operator shall record an identification sign. As the sign is being recorded, the operator shall, in addition, vocally record the information on the sign. The identification sign shall indicate the caption of the action, the docket number of the action, the name of the deponent, the date, the time, and the name of the officer before whom the videotaped deposition is being taken.

After the identification sign has been recorded, each participant shall identify himself or herself on camera, stating clearly the name, the address, and the role of the participant.

(B) After the identification required by subsection (a) above has been completed, the witness shall be put on oath as required; the swearing shall be on camera.

(C) After the witness has been sworn, testimony shall be taken in accord with the provisions herein. The taking of such testimony shall be videotaped in its entirety.

(D) During the taking of a videotape deposition under this rule, the officer before whom the deposition is taken shall assure that the videotape records the witness in a standard fashion at all times during the deposition, unless all counsel agree otherwise, or unless on motion before the court, the court directs otherwise. In no event shall the officer use, or permit the use of, videotape camera techniques such as close-up views of the witness or other similar techniques to vary the view which is being recorded for presentation in the courtroom unless agreed upon or ordered by the court as recited above. As an exemption to the foregoing, the officer shall, at the request of the attorney questioning the witness, cause a close-up view of a deposition exhibit to be taken while the witness is being questioned concerning the exhibit.

(3) When a videotape deposition has been taken the videotape shall be shown immediately to the witness for examination, unless such showing and examination are waived by the witness and the parties.

(4) The officer before whom a videotape deposition is taken shall cause to be attached to the original videotape recording a certification that the witness was sworn by him and that the videotape recording is a true record of the testimony given by the witness. If the witness has not waived his right to a showing and examination of the videotape deposition, the witness shall also sign the certification. If the witness has exercised his right pursuant to section (3) above to examine the videotape and, having done so, refuses to certify that the videotape recording is a true record of his testimony, the officer before whom the videotape deposition was taken shall so note on the certification form and shall further state the reasons given by the witness for refusing to certify that the videotape recording is a true record of his testimony.

(5) The videotape deposition, together with the officer's certification and the certification of the cameraman, shall be filed by the officer before whom the deposition was taken at the same time and in the same manner the written transcript of a deposition is filed pursuant to the provisions of these rules.

(6) Upon payment of reasonable charges therefor, the officer before whom the deposition was taken shall furnish a copy of the videotape deposition in the form of a videotape or an audio recording to any party or to the deponent.

(7) Except upon order of the trial judge and upon such terms as he may provide, the videotape recordings on file with the clerk of court shall not be available for inspection or viewing after their filing and prior to their use at the trial of the case or their disposition in accordance with this rule. The clerk may release the

videotape to the officer before whom the deposition was taken, without the order of the trial judge, for the purpose of preparing a copy for a party or a deponent as provided in section (6) above.

(8) If objections have been made by any of the parties during the course of the deposition, upon the written request of any of the parties submitted to the clerk of court, the videotape depositions, with the written transcript and the certifications required hereinabove, shall be submitted by the clerk of court to the trial judge for the purpose of obtaining rulings on the objections. An audio copy of the sound track may be submitted in lieu of the videotape for this purpose. For the purpose of ruling on the objections, the trial judge may review the written transcript, view the entire videotape recording, view only those parts of the videotape recording pertinent to the objections made, or he may listen to an audiotape recording submitted in lieu of the videotape recording. The trial judge shall rule on the objections prior to the date set for the trial of the action and shall return the recording to the officer with notice to the parties of his rulings and of his instruction as to editing. The editing shall reflect the rulings of the trial judge and shall remove all reference to the objections. The officer shall then cause the videotape to be edited in accordance with the court's instructions and shall cause both the original videotape recording and the edited version of that recording, each clearly identified, to be filed with the clerk of court.

(9) If an objection is made at the time of trial when objection has not previously been raised and ruled upon, such objection shall be made before the videotape deposition is presented and shall be ruled upon by the trial judge in advance of the presentation. If such objection is sustained, that portion of the videotape deposition containing the objectionable testimony shall not be presented to the jury.

(10) The party taking the deposition shall be responsible for assuring that the necessary equipment for videotaping the deposition is present at the time the deposition is taken. The party desiring to use the videotape deposition for any purpose subsequent to the taking of the deposition shall be responsible for assuring that the necessary equipment for playing the videotape deposition back is available when the videotape deposition is to be used. When a videotape deposition is used during a hearing, a trial, or any other court proceeding, the party first using the videotape deposition in whole or in part shall assure the availability of the same or comparable videotape playback equipment to any other party for such other party's use in further showing the videotape deposition during the hearing, the trial, or other court proceeding in question.

(11) The cost of videotape, as a material, shall be borne by the party taking the videotape deposition. Where an edited version is required, the cost of videotape, as a material, shall be borne by the party who caused to be recorded testimony or other evidence subsequently determined to be objectionable and ordered stricken from the tape by the court. The cost of recording the deposition testimony on videotape shall be borne by the party taking videotape deposition. The cost of producing an edited version of the videotape recording for use at trial shall be borne by the party who caused to be recorded testimony or other evidence subsequently determined to be objectionable and ordered stricken from the tape by the court.

(12) The ownership of the videotape used in recording testimony shall remain with the party taking the videotape deposition. The ownership of the videotape used in producing an edited videotape recording shall remain with the party who caused to be recorded testimony or other evidence subsequently determined to be objectionable and ordered stricken from the tape by the court. Videotape may be reused for the recording of other testimony, but the proponent shall be responsible for the submission of a recording of acceptable quality. The trial court may authorize the clerk of court to release the original videotape recording and the edited videotape recording to the owner of the videotape:

(A) upon the final disposition of the case when no trial is had,

(B) upon the expiration of the appeal period following the trial of the case, provided no appeal is taken, or

(C) upon the final determination of the case, if an appeal is taken.

(13) The cameraman who videotaped a deposition pursuant to the provisions of this rule shall execute the following written certificate prior to the beginning of the videotape deposition:

"I ______ hereby affirm that I am familiar with the provisions of Rule 30(h) pertaining to videotape depositions and will assure that the videotaping of this deposition is done in compliance with the provisions of Rule 30(h) and in an impartial manner."

Such written certification will be filed in accordance with section (7) above.

(i) Use of Depositions of Treating Physicians and Other Specified Treating Health Care Providers. The deposition of any licensed physician, psychologist, chiropractor, osteopathic physician or dentist who provided actual medical treatment to a party may be taken by any party to an action in which the physician, psychologist, chiropractor, osteopathic physician or dentist may be called as a witness, on notice to each party or attorney as provided in the rules. Notwithstanding the provisions of Rule 32(a)(3) regarding the location of a witness, an evidence deposition, otherwise admissible, may be received in evidence at a trial or hearing. The deposition may be taken by stenographic means, or videotape as provided in these rules or in such other manner as may be provided by these rules.

The notice shall specify that the purpose of the deposition is for evidence at a trial or hearing pursuant to this rule, and shall further specify the manner in which the deposition is to be taken. The cost of the deposition, including materials and fees, shall be borne by the party noticing the deposition. Before the evidence deposition, any party may obtain discovery from the witness as permitted by Rule 26. This rule shall not be the exclusive method of obtaining the testimony of the specified health care providers, nor shall the existence of an evidence deposition prevent any party from using any deposition otherwise admissible under Rule 32, or subpoenaing the deposed witness to testify at the trial or hearing. Provided, however, a party who noticed the evidence deposition must provide 2 days notice of the intent to call the treating health care provider as a witness and once that notice is given, must call that witness unless leave of court is granted.

(j) Conduct During Depositions.

(1) At the beginning of each deposition, deposing counsel shall instruct the witness to ask deposing counsel, rather than the witness' own counsel, for clarifications, definitions, or explanations of any words, questions or documents presented during the course of the deposition. The witness shall abide by these instructions.

(2) All objections, except those which would be waived if not made at the deposition under Rule 32(d)(3), SCRCP, and those necessary to assert a privilege, to enforce a limitation on evidence directed by the Court, or to present a motion pursuant to Rule 30(d), SCRCP, shall be preserved.

(3) Counsel shall not direct or request that a witness not answer a question, unless that counsel has objected to the question on the ground that the answer is protected by a privilege [2] or a limitation on evidence directed by the court or unless that counsel intends to present a motion under Rule 30(d), SCRCP. In addition, counsel shall have an affirmative duty to inform a witness that, unless such an objection is made, the question must be answered. Counsel directing that a witness not answer a question on those grounds or allowing a witness to refuse to answer a question on those grounds shall move the court for a protective order under Rule 26(c), SCRCP, or 30(d), SCRCP, within five business days of the suspension or termination of the deposition. Failure to timely file such a motion will constitute waiver of the objection, and the deposition may be reconvened.

(4) Counsel shall not make objections or statements which might suggest an answer to a witness. Counsel's objections shall be stated concisely and in a non-argumentative and non-suggestive manner, stating the basis of the objection and nothing more.

(5) Counsel and a witness shall not engage in private, off-the-record conferences during depositions or during breaks or recesses regarding the substance of the testimony at the deposition, except for the purpose of deciding whether to assert a privilege or to make an objection or to move for a protective order.

(6) Any conferences which occur pursuant to, or in violation of, section (5) of this rule are proper subjects for inquiry by deposing counsel to ascertain whether there has been any witness coaching and, if so, to what extent and nature.

(7) Any conferences which occur pursuant to, or in violation of, section (5) of this rule shall be noted on the record by the counsel who participated in the conference. The purpose and outcome of the conference shall be noted on the record.

(8) Deposing counsel shall provide to opposing counsel a copy of all documents shown to the witness during the deposition, either before the deposition begins or contemporaneously with the showing of each document to the witness. If the documents are provided (or otherwise identified) at least two business days before the deposition, then the witness and the witness' counsel do not have the right to discuss the documents privately before the witness answers questions about them. If the documents have not been so provided or identified, then counsel and the witness may have a reasonable amount of time to privately discuss the documents before the witness answers questions concerning the document.

(9) Violation of this rule may subject the violator to sanctions under Rule 37, SCRCP.

[Amended effective July 1, 1994; September 3, 1995; July 1, 2000; September 1, 2001; April 27, 2005.]

1 So in original.

2 For purposes of this rule, the term "privilege" includes but is not limited to: attorney-client privilege; work product protection; trade secret protection and privileges based on the United States Constitution and the South Carolina Constitution.

Notes

This language [Rule 30(a)(1)] is similar to that currently found in Circuit Court Rule 87A. It is drawn from the current Rule 30(a) of the Federal Rules.

The above language [Rule 30(a)(2)] is not contained in the current Federal Rule. However, the first two paragraphs are contained in Circuit Court Rule 87A and reflect limitations on the use of discovery in present State practice. The third paragraph is the language of Circuit Court Rule 87I and provides for statutory fees. The fourth paragraph is the language of Circuit Court Rule 87J and states that depositions should not be routinely available in cases involving less than $10,000 in controversy.

The change [Rule 30(b)(1)] alters the Federal Rule which requires reasonable notice of deposition to conform to present State practice requiring ten days notice of deposition. Rule 30(b)(3) permits the court to shorten or lengthen this period.

This [Rule 30(b)(2)] is the language of the Federal Rule, slightly modified to delete a reference to the deponents departing from the county where the trial will be held. Sufficient protection is provided by the remaining factors including travel more than 100 miles from the place where the action is pending.

This [Rule 30(b)(3)] is the language of Federal Rule 30, and makes no change in existing State practice.

This [Rule 30(b)(4)] permits stipulation of the parties or the court to order the recording of a deposition by other than stenographic means. It is meant to encourage the use of other mechanisms including videotape. The rule requires a fairly extensive order or stipulation. Videotape depositions are presently authorized by Circuit Rule 99 which is reproduced in paragraph (h) of this rule.

This [Rule 30(b)(5)] is the existing Federal Rule and makes clear what often occurs in practice, that a deposition and document request may be made returnable at the same time.

This [Rule 30(b)(6)] permits a party seeking discovery to require of the other party that it designate the appropriate individual or individuals to respond to the deposition and thereby provides flexibility for a knowledgeable individual to be presented for a deposition. It is an expansion of language which now is in Circuit Court Rule 87C.

This section [Rule 30(b)(7)] permits a deposition by telephone. Although such a deposition is permissible under present rules, this section makes the procedure explicit.

This [Rule 30(c)] is the language of the Federal Rule with the deletion of a reference to the Federal Rules of Evidence. It is consistent with Circuit Court Rule 87C. It specifically requires that evidence to which objection is made be taken subject to that objection. The last sentence changes existing State practice by permitting the use of written questions in lieu of personal attendance. This is intended for those multiparty depositions in which a party may only be interested in a small portion of the expected testimony.

This language [Rule 30(d)] is substantially similar to Circuit Court Rule 87H(2), which was drawn from a previous version of Federal Rule 30(d). The language above permits an objection to be filed in the court where the action is pending, and also in the court in the place where the deposition is taking place. This is a change from the existing Circuit Court Rule which deleted the reference to the district where the deposition is taking place.

This [Rule 30(e)] is similar to the language currently found in Circuit Court Rule 87H(4), and the language of the current Federal Rule.

This Rule 30(f) is the Federal Rule modified to conform to State practice with regard to custody and destruction of deposition materials. See Rule 26(g)(2) as to destruction of other discovery materials.

This [Rule 30(g)] is the language of the current Federal Rule. It contains substantially the same material that is presently in Circuit Court Rule 87H(7).

This [Rule 30(h)] is the language of Circuit Court Rule 99, Videotaped Depositions. This is the same language as in Code §§ 15–28–10 and 20. There is no comparable detailed language in the Federal Rule, which authorizes videotaped depositions by court order or stipulation and contemplates that many of the matters contained in Circuit Court Rule 99 will be resolved by the stipulation or order.

Notes to 1994 Amendment

Rule 30 is amended to add paragraph (i) which provides that the depositions of specified health care providers may be introduced in evidence at trial or hearing notwithstanding that the witness is otherwise subject to subpoena. The restriction in Rule 32(a)(3)(B) that a deposition can only be used if the witness is more than 100 miles from the place of trial does not apply to a deposition taken pursuant to this paragraph. Moreover, this paragraph does not affect a deposition otherwise admissible under the rules. The rule authorizes the evidence deposition of the designated witnesses by stenographic or videotape as otherwise provided in the rules. The notice of the deposition must specify that the purpose is to obtain an evidence deposition and that it may be taken by videotape. The other parties may obtain discovery of the witness before the evidence deposition by any means, including deposition, authorized by Rule 26. The costs of the evidence deposition is borne by the party noticing the deposition. Once an evidence deposition has been obtained, the party noticing the evidence deposition must give 2 days notice of the intent to call the treating health care provider as a witness, and must call the witness unless the leave of court is granted.

Note to 1995 Amendment

This amendment, which changed the first sentence of Rule 30(c), was made as a result of the adoption of the South Carolina Rules of Evidence. With this amendment, the first sentence is identical to the Federal Rule except for the substitution of the phrase "South Carolina Rules of Evidence" in place of the phrase "Federal Rules of Evidence."

Note to 2000 Amendment

Rule 30 is amended by adding Paragraph (j) which provides deposition guidelines similar to those used in federal district court in South Carolina. The final subsection differs from the federal rule by making the imposition of sanctions for violations of the rule discretionary. The intent of the amendment is to help eliminate conduct tending to interfere with or impede depositions.

Note to 2001 Amendment

Rule 30(j) is amended to clarify that any consultation between lawyer and client permitted by Rule 30 will be private.

Note to 2005 Amendment

Rule 30(a)(2) previously established the counties in which a witness, but not a party, could be deposed. The rule is amended to add that a party may be deposed in the county where the action is pending, as well as where the deponent resides, or is employed or transacts business in person, or where set by order of the court.

RULE 31. DEPOSITIONS UPON WRITTEN QUESTIONS

(a) Serving Questions; Notice. After commencement of the action, any party may take the testimony of any person, including a party, by deposition upon written questions. The attendance of witnesses may be compelled by the use of subpoena as provided in Rule 45. The deposition of a person confined in prison may be taken only by leave of court on such terms as the court prescribes.

A party desiring to take a deposition upon written questions shall serve them upon every other party with a notice stating (1) the name and address of the person who is to answer them, if known, and if the name is not known, a general description sufficient to identify him or the particular class or group to which he belongs, and (2) the name or descriptive title and address of the officer before whom the deposition is to be taken. A deposition upon written questions may be taken of a public or private corporation or a partnership or association or governmental agency in accordance with the provisions of Rule 30(b)(6).

Within 30 days after the notice and written questions are served, a party may serve cross questions upon all other parties. Within 10 days after being served with cross questions, a party may serve redirect questions upon all other parties. Within 10 days after being served with redirect questions, a party may serve recross questions upon all other parties. The court may for cause shown enlarge or shorten the time.

(b) Officer to Take Responses and Prepare Record. A copy of the notice and copies of all questions served shall be delivered by the party taking the deposition to the officer designated in the notice, who shall proceed promptly, in the manner provided by Rule 30(c), (e), and (f), to take the testimony of the witness in response to the questions and to prepare, certify, and deliver or mail the deposition, attaching thereto the copy of the notice and the questions received by him, to the party taking the deposition.

(c) Notice of Filing. When the deposition is received the party taking it shall promptly give notice thereof to all other parties.

Notes

This is the language of the Federal Rule. There is no counterpart to this discovery device in State practice. It is a useful device to determine if a distant witness had relevant knowledge without the expense of an oral deposition. It may also be useful to establish the evidentiary foundation of documents held by third parties.

RULE 32. USE OF DEPOSITIONS IN COURT PROCEEDINGS

(a) Use of Depositions. At the trial or upon the hearing of a motion or an interlocutory proceeding, any part or all of a deposition, so far as admissible under the rules of evidence applied as though the witness were then present and testifying, may be used against any party who was present or represented at the taking of the deposition or who had reasonable notice thereof, in accordance with any of the following provisions:

(1) Any deposition may be used by any party for the purpose of contradicting or impeaching the testimony of deponent as a witness, or for any other purpose permitted by the rules of evidence.

(2) The deposition of a party or of anyone who at the time of taking the deposition was an officer, director, or managing agent, or a person designated under Rule 30(b)(6) or 31(a) to testify on behalf of a public or private corporation, partnership or association or governmental agency which is a party may be used by an adverse party for any purpose.

(3) The deposition of a witness, whether or not a party, may be used by any party for any purpose if the court finds:

(A) that the witness is dead; or

(B) that the witness is at a greater distance than 100 miles from the place of trial or hearing, or is out of the State, unless it appears that the absence of the witness was procured by the party offering the deposition; or

(C) that the witness is unable to attend or testify because of age, illness, infirmity, or imprisonment; or

(D) that the party offering the deposition has been unable to procure the attendance of the witness by subpoena; or

(E) upon application and notice, that such exceptional circumstances exist as to make it desirable, in the interest of justice and with due regard to the importance of presenting the testimony of witnesses orally in open court, to allow the deposition to be used.

(4) If only part of a deposition is offered in evidence by a party, an adverse party may require him to introduce any other part which ought in fairness to be considered with the part introduced, and any party may introduce any other parts.

(5) *Excerpts From Depositions to Be Offered at Trial.* At least 1 day prior to offering excerpts from a deposition in the case in chief counsel, unless otherwise ordered by the trial judge, shall furnish to the trial judge and, at the same time and by the same means, furnish to all opposing counsel the excerpts from depositions (by page and line number) and a list of deposition exhibits which counsel expects to introduce in the case in chief at trial. When the deposition excerpt is offered at trial counsel for the adverse party shall furnish to the trial judge and, at the same time and by the same means, furnish to all opposing counsel any objections (by page and line number) to opposing counsel's deposition excerpts and any additional excerpts from the depositions (by page and line number) which counsel expects to be read pursuant to SCRCP (a)(4), as well as a list of deposition exhibits to be used. With reasonable notice to the trial judge and all counsel, other excerpts may be read.

Substitution of parties pursuant to Rule 25 does not affect the right to use depositions previously taken; and when an action has been brought in any court of the United States or of any State and another action involving the same subject matter is afterward brought between the same parties or their representatives or successors in interest, all depositions lawfully taken and duly filed in the former action may be used in the latter as if originally taken therefor. A deposition previously taken may also be used as permitted by the rules of evidence.

(b) Objections to Admissibility. Subject to the provisions of Rule 28(b) and subdivision (d)(3) of this rule, objection may be made at the trial or hearing to receiving in evidence any deposition or part thereof for any reason which would require the exclusion of the evidence if the witness were then present and testifying.

(c) Effect of Taking or Using Depositions. A party does not make a person his own witness for any purpose by taking his deposition. The introduction in evidence of the deposition or any part thereof for any purpose other than that of contradicting or impeaching the deponent makes the deponent the witness of the party introducing the deposition, but this shall not apply to the use by an adverse party of a deposition under subdivision (a)(2) of this rule. At the trial or hearing any party may rebut any relevant evidence contained in a deposition whether introduced by him or by any other party.

(d) Effect of Errors and Irregularities in Depositions.

(1) *As to Notice.* All errors and irregularities in the notice for taking a deposition are waived unless written objection is promptly served upon the party giving the notice.

(2) *As to Disqualification of Officer.* Objection to taking a deposition because of disqualification of the officer before whom it is to be taken is waived unless made before the taking of the deposition begins or as soon thereafter as the disqualification becomes known or could be discovered with reasonable diligence.

(3) *As to Taking of Deposition.*

(A) Objections to the competency of a witness or to the competency, relevancy, or materiality of testimony are not waived by failure to make them before or during the taking of the deposition, unless the ground of the objection is one which might have been obviated or removed if presented at that time.

(B) Errors and irregularities occurring at the oral examination in the manner of taking the deposition, in the form of the questions or answers, in the oath or affirmation, or in the conduct of parties, and errors of any kind which might be obviated, removed, or cured if promptly presented, are waived unless seasonable objection thereto is made at the taking of the deposition.

(C) Objections to the form of written questions submitted under Rule 31 are waived unless served in writing upon the party propounding them within the time allowed for serving the succeeding cross or other questions and within 5 days after service of the last questions authorized.

(4) *As to Completion and Return of Deposition.* Errors and irregularities in the manner in which the testimony is transcribed or the deposition is prepared, signed, certified, sealed, indorsed, transmitted, filed, or otherwise dealt with by the officer under Rules 30 and 31 are waived unless a motion to suppress the deposition or some part thereof is made with reasonable promptness after such defect is, or with due diligence might have been, ascertained.

Objections to the competency of a witness, or to the competency, relevancy, or materiality of testimony are not so waived but reserved for consideration by the court either at a pre-trial conference or prior to the deposition being admitted.

[Amended effective July 1, 1994.]

Notes

This [Rule 32(a)] is current Federal Rule 32(a), which is an amended version of the Federal Rule which served as the guide for Circuit Court Rule 87D. There are minor changes in the wording of the rule, but no significant alterations.

This [Rule 32(b)] is the current Federal Rule which is an amended version of the Federal Rule which served as the guide for Circuit Court Rule 87E. There are minor clarifying amendments.

This [Rule 32(c)] is the language of the Federal Rule which is an amended version of the Federal Rule which served as the guide for Circuit Court Rule 87(f). There are minor modifications in the language of the rule. This provision was deleted from the Federal rules in 1972 because of the adoption of the Federal Rules of Evidence. It was added here because the State has not adopted Rules of Evidence.

This [Rule 32(d)] is the language of current Federal Rule 32(d). There is no counterpart of this provision in the Circuit Court Rules. In essence these provisions provide that errors or irregularities in the procedure of taking the deposition, or in depositions under written interrogatories, or in the transcription, certification, and filing are waived if not made at the time the error could have been corrected.

Notes to 1994 Amendment

Rule 32(a)(5) requires that excerpts of depositions and deposition exhibits that are to be used in the party's case in chief are to be provided to the judge and counsel 1 day before use. Adverse counsel shall identify the portions of the deposition and its exhibits that will be used at the time the excerpts are offered. This rule does not apply to excerpts that are to be used for impeachment purposes.

RULE 33. INTERROGATORIES TO PARTIES

(a) Availability; Procedures for Use. Except as limited by paragraph (b)(9), any party may serve upon any other party written interrogatories to be answered by the party served or, if the party served is a public or private corporation or a partnership or association or governmental agency, by any officer or agent, who shall furnish such information as is available to the party. Interrogatories may, without leave of court, be served upon the plaintiff after commencement of the action and upon any other party with or after service of the summons and complaint upon that party.

Each interrogatory shall be answered separately and fully in writing under oath, unless it is objected to, in which event the reasons for objection shall be stated in lieu of an answer. The answers are to be signed by the person making them, and the objections signed by the attorney making them. The party upon whom the interrogatories have been served shall serve a copy of the answers, and objections if any, within 30 days after the service of the interrogatories, except that a defendant may serve answers or objections within 45 days after service of the summons and complaint upon that defendant. The court may allow a shorter or longer time. The party submitting the interrogatories may move for an order under Rule 37(a) with respect to any objection to or other failure to answer an interrogatory.

(b) Standard Interrogatories. In all cases the following standard interrogatories may be served by one party upon another unless otherwise ordered by the court for good cause shown. The interrogatories shall be deemed to continue from the time of service, until the time of trial of the action so that information sought, which comes to the knowledge of a party, or his representative or attorney, after original answers to interrogatories have been submitted, shall be promptly transmitted to the other party.

(1) Give the names and addresses of persons known to the parties or counsel to be witnesses concerning the facts of the case and indicate whether or not written or recorded statements have been taken from the witnesses and indicate who has possession of such statements.

(2) Set forth a list of photographs, plats, sketches or other prepared documents in possession of the party that relate to the claim or defense in the case.

(3) In cases involving personal injury set forth the names and addresses of all physicians who have treated the party and all hospitals to which the party has been committed in connection with said injuries and also set forth a statement of all medical costs involved.

(4) Set forth the names and addresses of all insurance companies which have liability insurance coverage relating to the claim and set forth the number or numbers of the policies involved and the amount or amounts of liability coverage provided in each policy.

(5) Set forth an itemized statement of all damages, exclusive of pain and suffering, claimed to have been sustained by the party.

(6) List the names and addresses of any expert witnesses whom the party proposes to use as a witness at the trial of the case.

(7) For each person known to the parties or counsel to be a witness concerning the facts of the case, set forth either a summary sufficient to inform the other party of the important facts known to or observed by such witness, or provide a copy of any written or recorded statements taken from such witnesses.

(8) *[Defendants only.]* If the defendant is improperly identified, give the proper identification and state whether counsel will accept service of an amended summons and pleading reflecting the correct information.

(9) *Limitations.* In addition to the standard interrogatories authorized by this paragraph, the court may order additional interrogatories for good cause shown in any case. In all actions in which the amount in controversy is not less than $25,000, and in all actions for declaratory or injunctive relief, a party may serve additional interrogatories including more than one set of interrogatories upon any other party; but the total number of general interrogatories to any one party shall not exceed fifty questions including subparts, except by leave of court upon good cause shown.

(c) Option to Produce Business Records. Where the answer to an interrogatory may be derived or ascertained from the business records, including electronically stored information, of the party upon whom the interrogatory has been served or from an examination, audit or inspection of such business records, including a compilation, abstract or summary thereof, and the burden of deriving or ascertaining the answer is substantially the same for the party serving the interrogatory as for the party served, it is a sufficient answer to such interrogatory to specify the records from which the answer may be derived or ascertained and to afford to the party serving the interrogatory reasonable opportunity to examine, audit or inspect such records and to make copies, compilations, abstracts or summaries. A specification shall be in sufficient detail to permit the interrogating party to locate and to identify, as readily as can the party served, the records from which the answer may be ascertained.

(d) Scope; Use at Trial. Interrogatories may relate to any matters which can be inquired into under Rule 26(b), and the answers may be used to the extent permitted by the rules of evidence. An interrogatory otherwise proper is not necessarily objectionable merely because an answer to the interrogatory involves an opinion or contention that relates to fact or the application of law to fact, but the court may order that such an interrogatory need not be answered until after designated discovery has been completed or until a pre-trial hearing or other later time.

[Amended effective May 1, 1986; May 1, 1988; May 1, 2008; February 5, 2009; April 28, 2011.]

Notes

This Rule 33(a) is the language of current Federal Rule except the first line. This language permits interrogatories to any party, not just an adverse party, and increases the time within which a party may object or respond to 30 days.

Rule 33(b)(5) amends present Circuit Court Rule 90 to require an "itemized" statement of all special damages exclusive of pain and suffering. 33(b)(8) is amended to make clear that in certain cases additional interrogatories are permitted beyond the standard interrogatories. Paragraphs 33(b)(1) through (4) and (6) are verbatim the standard interrogatories permitted by present Circuit Court Rule

90(e)(A) through (D) and (F). Paragraph (b)(7) is new and provides for a summary of the facts known to the witnesses in the case. The rule requires a detailed summary so as to avoid the problem encountered with the interrogatories directed to experts in Federal Rule 26(b)(4)(A)(i) which often results in a short, vague summary of expected testimony. On the other hand, it is limited to important facts known or observed by the witness so that the summary is restricted to the actual knowledge of the witness. Paragraph (b)(8) is added to provide for additional special interrogatories to parties in complex cases. The $10,000 limitation follows the approach set by present Circuit Court Rule 87J. The limit of fifty such interrogatories follows present local rules of the Federal courts.

This Rule 33(c) is the Federal Rule and permits the party responding to discovery interrogatories to supply the documents from which the information can be obtained when the burden of extracting the information is the same for either party. It places on the requesting party the burden of obtaining the information if he specially needs it.

Notes to 1985 Amendments

The changes to Rule 33(b)(8) raise the amount in controversy necessary to authorize general interrogatories as a matter of course from $10,000 to $25,000. The rule is clarified to permit up to fifty general interrogatories in addition to the seven standard interrogatories.

Notes to 1988 Amendments

Rule 33(b)(8) is amended to make clear that the court has the discretion to permit additional interrogatories in any case for good cause shown.

Notes to 2008 Amendment

This amendment added section (b)(8) relating to defendants.

Note to 2011 Amendments

The amendments to Rules 16, 26, 33, 34, 37 and 45 of the South Carolina Rules of Civil Procedure concerning electronic discovery are substantially similar to the corresponding provisions in the Federal Rules of Civil Procedure. The rules concerning electronic discovery are intended to provide a practical, efficient and cost-effective method to assure reasonable discovery. Pursuit of electronic discovery must relate to the claims and defenses asserted in the pleadings and should serve as a means for facilitating a just and cost-effective resolution of disputes.

RULE 34. PRODUCTION OF DOCUMENTS AND THINGS AND ENTRY UPON LAND FOR INSPECTION AND OTHER PURPOSES

(a) Scope. Any party may serve on any other party a request (1) to produce and permit the party making the request, or someone acting on his behalf, to inspect and copy, any designated documents, or electronically stored information (including writings, drawings, graphs, charts, photographs, phonorecords, and other data compilations from which information can be obtained, translated, if necessary, by the respondent through detection devices into reasonably usable form), or to inspect and copy, test, or sample any tangible things which constitute or contain matters within the scope of Rule 26(b) and which are in the possession, custody or control of the party upon whom the request is served; or (2) to permit entry upon designated land or other property in the possession or control of the party upon whom the request is served for the purpose of inspection and measuring, surveying, photographing, testing, or sampling the property or any designated object or operation thereon, within the scope of Rule 26(b).

(b) Procedure. The request may, without leave of court, be served upon the plaintiff after commencement of the action and upon any other party with or after service of the summons and complaint upon that party. The request shall set forth the items to be inspected either by individual item or by category, and describe each item and category with reasonable particularity. The request shall specify a reasonable time, place, and manner of making the inspection and performing the related acts. The request may specify the form or forms in which electronically stored information is to be produced.

The party upon whom the request is served shall serve a written response within 30 days after the service of the request, except that a defendant may serve a response within 45 days after service of the summons and complaint upon that defendant. The court may allow a shorter or longer time. The response shall state, with respect to each item or category, that inspection and related activities will be permitted as requested, unless the request is objected to, including an objection to the requested form or forms for producing electronically stored information, in which event the reasons for objection shall be stated. If objection is made to part of an item or category, the part shall be specified. If objection is made to the requested form or forms for producing electronically stored information (or if no form was specified in the request) the responding party must state the form or forms it intends to use. The party submitting the request may move for an order under Rule 37(a) with respect to any objection to or other failure to respond to the request or any part thereof, or any failure to permit inspection as requested. A party who produces documents for inspection shall produce them as they are kept in the usual course of business or shall organize and label them to correspond with the categories in the request.

Unless the parties otherwise agree, or the court otherwise orders:

(1) If a request does not specify the form or forms for producing electronically stored information, a responding party must produce the information in a form or forms in which it is ordinarily maintained or in a form or forms that are reasonably usable; and

(2) a party need not produce the same electronically stored information in more than one form.

(c) Persons Not Parties. A person not a party may be compelled to produce documents or things or submit to an inspection only as provided in Rule 45. This rule does not preclude an independent action against a person not a party for production of documents and things and permission to enter upon land.

[Amended effective July 1, 1993; April 28, 2011.]

Notes

This [Rule 35(b)] is the language of the current Federal Rule, and is an amended version of the rule which served as a guide for present Circuit Court Rule 88. The major change is that the requirement of good cause is eliminated because it was an erratic and uncertain guide for decisions by the court. It also saves the court having to handle the matter unless there is an objection to the document requests. Thirty days are permitted for a response, and there is provision for an independent action for discovery against persons not parties to the action.

Notes to 1993 Amendments

Rule 34 applies only to production from parties, and was amended specifically to provide that production from non-parties is governed only by Rule 45.

Note to 2011 Amendments

The amendments to Rules 16, 26, 33, 34, 37 and 45 of the South Carolina Rules of Civil Procedure concerning electronic discovery are substantially similar to the corresponding provisions in the Federal Rules of Civil Procedure. The rules concerning electronic discovery are intended to provide a practical, efficient and cost-effective method to assure reasonable discovery. Pursuit of electronic discovery must relate to the claims and defenses asserted in the pleadings and should serve as a means for facilitating a just and cost-effective resolution of disputes.

RULE 35. PHYSICAL AND MENTAL EXAMINATIONS

(a) Order for Examination. In any case in which the amount in controversy exceeds $100,000 actual damages, and the mental or physical condition (including the blood group) of a party, or of a person in the custody or under the legal control of a party, is in controversy, the court in which the action is pending may order the party to submit to a physical or mental examination by a physician or to produce for examination the person in his custody or legal control. The order may be made only on motion for good cause shown and upon notice to the person to be examined and to all parties and shall specify the time, place, manner, conditions and scope of the examination and the person or persons by whom it is to be made, and shall be delivered to the person or persons making the examination.

The physician of the party to be examined may be present at the examination. Unless the parties agree, or the court for good cause shown determines otherwise, the examination shall be in the county where the person to be examined, or his physician, resides. Special consideration shall be given to the convenience of the person to be examined and that of his physician in setting the time and place of the examination, and reasonable consideration shall be given to the convenience of the examining physician. Upon reasonable objection to the physician designated to make the examination, and if the parties shall fail to agree as to who shall make the examination, the court may designate a physician; but the fact that a physician was so designated shall not be admissible upon the trial.

(b) Report of Examining Physicians.

(1) If requested by the party against whom an order is made under Rule 35(a) or the person examined, the party causing the examination to be made shall deliver to him a copy of a detailed written report of the examining physician setting out his findings, including results of all tests made, diagnoses and conclusions, together with like reports of all earlier examinations of the same condition. After delivery the party causing the examination shall be entitled to request and receive from the party against whom the order is made a like report of any examination, previously or thereafter made, of the same condition, unless, in the case of a report of examination of a person not a party, the party shows that he is unable to obtain it. The court on motion may make an order against a party requiring delivery of a report on such terms as are just, and if a physician fails or refuses to make a report the court may exclude his testimony if offered at the trial.

(2) By requesting and obtaining a report of the examination so ordered or by taking the deposition of the examiner, the party examined waives any privilege he may have in that action or any other involving the same controversy, regarding the testimony of every other person who has examined or may thereafter examine him in respect of the same mental or physical condition.

(3) This subdivision applies to examinations made by agreement of the parties, unless the agreement expressly provides otherwise. This subdivision does not preclude discovery of a report of an examining physician or the taking of a deposition of the physician in accordance with the provisions of any other rule.

[Amended effective May 1, 1987.]

Notes

The language [of Rule 35(a)] in the first paragraph reflects the existing Federal Rule on the subject, except the $100,000 limitation. The language changes are minor and only to clarify the operation of the rule. The second paragraph is new and is not in the Federal Rule. It establishes limitations on the use of the device, particularly that the party examined may have his physician present during the examination and that the examination may take place only in the county of residence of the patient or his physician. The new material also permits objection to be made to the examining physician.

This [Rule 35(b)] is the language of the current Federal Rule 35(b) and authorizes the party examined to request a copy of the report of the examination ordered by the court. Upon delivery the party who obtained the order for the physical examination may obtain from the examined party, copies of all of its reports on the same subject. Conceivably that party could obtain the same information by deposing the physicians who made other examinations, but it certainly is easier and more efficient to provide for the automatic exchange of medical reports on the same condition. The purpose of the rule is to encourage settlement when it is apparent that there is no significant difference in the medical opinion of the respective experts.

Notes to 1986 Amendments

The Rule as originally written imposed some absolute restrictions on the location and timing of a medical examination. The amendments [to Rule 35(a)] give the court discretion to make exceptions to those requirements if justified by the facts.

RULE 36. REQUEST FOR ADMISSION

(a) Request for Admission. A party may serve upon any other party a written request for the admission, for purposes of the pending action only, of the truth of any matters within the scope of Rule 26(b) set forth in the request that relate to statements or opinions of fact or of the application of law to fact, including the genuineness of any documents described in the request. Copies of documents shall be served with the request unless they have been or are otherwise furnished or made available for inspection and copying. The request may, without leave of court, be served upon the plaintiff after commencement of the action and upon any other party with or after service of the summons and complaint upon that party.

Each matter of which an admission is requested shall be separately set forth. The matter is admitted unless, within 30 days after service of the request, or within such shorter or longer time as the court may allow or as stipulated in writing by the parties pursuant to Rules 29 and 6(b), the party to whom the request is directed serves upon the party requesting the admission a written answer or objection addressed to the matter, signed by the party or by his attorney, but, unless the court shortens the time, a defendant shall not be required to serve answers or objections before the expiration of 45 days after service of the summons and complaint upon him. If objection is made, the reasons therefor shall be stated. The answer shall specifically deny the matter or set forth in detail the reasons why the answering party cannot truthfully admit or deny the matter. A denial shall fairly meet the substance of the requested admission, and when good faith requires that a party qualify his answer or deny only a part of the matter of which an admission is requested, he shall specify so much of it as is true and qualify or deny the remainder. An answering party may not give lack of information or knowledge as a reason for failure to admit or deny unless he states that he has made reasonable inquiry and that the information known or readily obtainable by him is insufficient to enable him to admit or deny. A party who considers that a matter of which an admission has been requested presents a genuine issue for trial may not, on that ground alone, object to the request; he may, subject to the provisions of Rule 37(c), deny the matter or set forth reasons why he cannot admit or deny it.

The party who has requested the admissions may move to determine the sufficiency of the answers or objections. Unless the court determines that an objection is justified, it shall order that an answer be served. If the court determines that an answer does not comply with the requirements of this rule, it may order either that the matter is admitted or that an amended answer be served. The court may, in lieu of these orders, determine that final disposition of the request be made at a pre-trial conference or at a designated time prior to trial. The provisions of Rule 37(a)(4) apply to the award of expenses incurred in relation to the motion.

(b) Effect of Admission. Any matter admitted under this rule is conclusively established unless the court on motion permits withdrawal or amendment of the admission. Subject to the provisions of Rule 16 governing amendment of a pre-trial order, the court may permit withdrawal or amendment when the presentation of the merits of the action will be subserved thereby and the party who obtained the admissions fails to satisfy the court that withdrawal or amendment will prejudice him in maintaining his action or defense on the merits. Any admission made by a party under this rule is for the purpose of the pending action only and is not an admission by him for any other purpose.

(c) Limitation. A party may serve on any other party more than one set of requests to admit, but the total number of all requests to one party shall not exceed twenty requests, including subparts, except by leave of court upon good cause shown. Requests to admit the genuineness of documents or tangible things are not limited to any number of documents or things.

[Amended effective September 1, 2001.]

Notes

This is the language of current Federal Rule 36, as well as substantially the language of Circuit Court Rule 89, with the addition of the limitation in 36(c) which is new matter.

Note to 2001 Amendment

The second sentence of the second paragraph of Rule 36(a) is amended to reflect the change in Rule 29 allowing the parties, under certain circumstances, to stipulate to extensions.

RULE 37. FAILURE TO MAKE OR COOPERATE IN DISCOVERY: SANCTIONS

(a) Motion for Order Compelling Discovery. A party, upon reasonable notice to other parties and all persons affected thereby, may apply for an order compelling discovery as follows:

(1) *Appropriate Court.* An application for an order to a party may be made to the court in which the action

is pending, or, on matters relating to a deposition in progress, to the court where the deposition is being taken. An application for an order to a deponent who is not a party shall be made to the court in the place where the deposition is being taken.

(2) *Motion.* If a deponent fails to answer a question propounded or submitted under Rule 30 or 31, or a corporation or other entity fails to make a designation under Rule 30(b)(6) or 31(a), or a party fails to answer an interrogatory submitted under Rule 33, or if a party, in response to a request for inspection submitted under Rule 34, fails to respond that inspection will be permitted as requested or fails to permit inspection as requested, the discovering party may move for an order compelling an answer, or a designation, or an order compelling inspection in accordance with the request. When taking a deposition on oral examination, the proponent of the question may complete or adjourn the examination before he applies for an order.

If the court denies the motion in whole or in part, it may make such protective order as it would have been empowered to make on a motion made pursuant to Rule 26(c).

(3) *Evasive or Incomplete Answer.* For purposes of this subdivision an evasive or incomplete answer is to be treated as a failure to answer.

(4) *Award of Expenses of Motion.* If the motion is granted, the court shall, after opportunity for hearing, require the party or deponent whose conduct necessitated the motion or the party or attorney advising such conduct or both of them to pay to the moving party the reasonable expenses incurred in obtaining the order, including attorney's fees, unless the court finds that the opposition to the motion was substantially justified or that other circumstances make an award of expenses unjust. If the motion is denied, the court shall, after opportunity for hearing, require the moving party or the attorney advising the motion or both of them to pay to the party or deponent who opposed the motion the reasonable expenses incurred in opposing the motion, including attorney's fees, unless the court finds that the making of the motion was substantially justified or that other circumstances make an award of expenses unjust.

If the motion is granted in part and denied in part, the court may apportion the reasonable expenses incurred in relation to the motion among the parties and persons in a just manner.

(b) Failure to Comply With Order.

(1) *Sanctions by Court in Circuit Where Deposition Is Taken.* If a deponent fails to be sworn or to answer a question after being directed to do so by the court the failure may be considered a contempt of that court.

(2) *Sanctions by Court in Which Action Is Pending.* If a party or an officer, director, or managing agent of a party or a person designated under Rule 30(b)(6) or 31(a) to testify on behalf of a party fails to obey an order to provide or permit discovery, including an order made under subdivision (a) of this rule or Rule 35, or if a party fails to obey an order entered under Rule 26(f), the court in which the action is pending may make such orders in regard to the failure as are just, and among others the following:

(A) An order that the matters regarding which the order was made or any other designated facts shall be taken to be established for the purposes of the action in accordance with the claim of the party obtaining the order;

(B) An order refusing to allow the disobedient party to support or oppose designated claims or defenses, or prohibiting him from introducing designated matters in evidence;

(C) An order striking out pleadings or parts thereof, or staying further proceedings until the order is obeyed, or dismissing the action or proceeding or any part thereof, or rendering a judgment by default against the disobedient party;

(D) In lieu of any of the foregoing orders or in addition thereto, an order treating as a contempt of court the failure to obey any orders except an order to submit to a physical or mental examination;

(E) Where a party has failed to comply with an order under Rule 35(a) requiring him to produce another for examination, such orders as are listed in paragraphs (A), (B), and (C) of this subdivision, unless the party failing to comply show that he is unable to produce such person for examination.

In lieu of any of the foregoing orders or in addition thereto, the court shall require the party failing to obey the order or the attorney advising him or both to pay the reasonable expenses, including attorney's fees, caused by the failure, unless the court finds that the failure was substantially justified or that other circumstances make an award of expenses unjust.

(c) Expenses on Failure to Admit. If a party fails to admit the genuineness of any document or the truth of any matter as requested under Rule 36, and if the party requesting the admissions thereafter proves the genuineness of the document or the truth of the matter, he may apply to the court for an order requiring the other party to pay him the reasonable expenses incurred in making that proof, including reasonable attorney's fees. The court shall make the order unless it finds that (1) the request was held objectionable pursuant to Rule 36(a), or (2) the admission sought was of no substantial importance, or (3) the party failing to admit had reasonable ground to believe that he might prevail on the matter, or (4) there was other good reason for the failure to admit.

(d) Failure of Party to Attend at Own Deposition or Serve Answers to Interrogatories or Respond to Request for Inspection. If a party or an officer, director or managing agent of a party or a person designated under Rule 30(b)(6) or 31(a) to testify on behalf of a party fails (1) to appear before the officer who is to take his deposition, after being served with a proper notice, or (2) to serve answers or objections to interrogatories submitted under Rule 33, after proper service of the interrogatories, or (3) to serve a written response to a request for inspection submitted under Rule 34, after proper service of the request, the court in which the action is pending on motion may make such orders in regard to the failure as are just, and among others it may take any action authorized under paragraphs (A), (B), and (C) of subdivision (b)(2) of this rule. In lieu of any order or in addition thereto, the court shall require the party failing to act or the attorney advising him or both to pay the reasonable expenses, including attorney's fees, caused by the failure, unless the court finds that the failure was substantially justified or that other circumstances make an award of expenses unjust.

The failure to act described in this subdivision may not be excused on the ground that the discovery sought is objectionable unless the party failing to act has applied for a protective order as provided by Rule 26(c).

(e) Failure to Participate in the Framing of a Discovery Plan. If a party or his attorney fails to participate in good faith in the framing of a discovery plan by agreement as is required by Rule 26(f), the court may, after opportunity for hearing, require such party or his attorney to pay to any other party the reasonable expenses, including attorney's fees caused by the failure.

(f) Electronically Stored Information. Absent exceptional circumstances, a court may not impose sanctions under these rules on a party for failing to provide electronically stored information lost as result of the routine, good-faith operation of an electronic information system.

[Amended effective April 28, 2011.]

Notes

This Rule 37 is the language of the Federal Rule with minor changes. The Federal Rule provides that a motion to compel discovery or for sanctions may be brought either in the court where the action is pending or in the place where the discovery or deposition is taken. Thus, if a deposition were being taken in another state or Federal district, the parties do not have to adjourn the deposition and return to the court where the action is pending for assistance. However, this Rule 37 deletes that provision with reference to the deposition of a party. Such motion may be brought only in the court where the action is pending. A motion to compel a witness deponent (not a party) to proceed, however, may be brought in the circuit court in the place where the deposition is being taken, usually the county of residence of the deponent.

Note to 2011 Amendments

The amendments to Rules 16, 26, 33, 34, 37 and 45 of the South Carolina Rules of Civil Procedure concerning electronic discovery are substantially similar to the corresponding provisions in the Federal Rules of Civil Procedure. The rules concerning electronic discovery are intended to provide a practical, efficient and cost-effective method to assure reasonable discovery. Pursuit of electronic discovery must relate to the claims and defenses asserted in the pleadings and should serve as a means for facilitating a just and cost-effective resolution of disputes.

VI. TRIALS

RULE 38. JURY TRIAL OF RIGHT

(a) Right Preserved. The right of trial by jury as declared by the Constitution or as given by a statute of South Carolina shall be preserved to the parties inviolate. Issues of fact in an action for the recovery of money only or of specific real or personal property must be tried by a jury, unless a jury trial be waived.

(b) Demand. Any party may demand a trial by jury of any issue triable of right by a jury by serving upon the other parties a demand therefor in writing at any time after the commencement of the action and not later than 10 days after the service of the last pleading directed to such issue. Such demand may be endorsed upon a pleading of the party.

(c) Same: Specification of Issues. In his demand a party may specify the issues which he wishes so tried; otherwise he shall be deemed to have demanded trial by jury for all the issues so triable. If he has demanded trial by jury for only some of the issues, any other party within 10 days after service of the demand or such lesser time as the court may order, may serve a demand for trial by jury of any other or all of the issues of fact in the action.

(d) Waiver. The failure of a party to serve a demand as required by this rule and to file it as required by Rule 5(d) constitutes a waiver by him of trial by jury. A demand for trial by jury made as herein provided may not be withdrawn without the consent of the parties, except where an opposing party is in default under Rule 55(a).

Notes

This Rule 38 is substantially the Federal Rule. The last sentence is added to Paragraph 38(a) to preserve the language of Code § 15–23–60. Paragraph 38(e) of the Federal Rule, referring to admiralty and maritime claims, is inapplicable to State practice.

RULE 39. TRIAL BY JURY OR BY THE COURT

(a) By Jury. When trial by jury has been demanded as provided in Rule 38, the action shall be designated upon the calendar and the clerk's filebook as a jury action. The trial of all issues so demanded shall be by jury, unless (1) the parties or their attorneys of record, by written stipulation filed with the court or by an oral stipulation made in open court and entered in the record, consent to trial by the court sitting without a jury or (2) the court upon motion or its own initiative finds that a right of trial by jury of some or all of those issues does not exist.

(b) By the Court. Issues of law and issues not demanded for trial by jury as provided in Rule 38 shall be tried by the court or may be referred to a master as provided in Rule 53; but, notwithstanding the failure of a party to demand a jury in an action in which such a demand might have been made of right, the court in its discretion upon motion may order a trial by jury of any or all issues.

(c) Advisory Jury and Trial by Consent. In all actions not triable of right by a jury the court upon motion or of its own initiative may try any issue with an advisory jury or the court, with the consent of both parties may order a trial by jury whose verdict has the same effect as if trial had been a matter of right.

Notes

This Rule 39 is substantially the Federal Rule. Paragraph 39(b) preserves the State practice of reference to masters of appropriate non-jury cases. The Rule preserves State practice with no real change. Present Circuit Rule 28, and the substance of Code §§ 15–23–70, 15–27–90, 15–23–60 and 15–33–20 are retained.

RULE 40. GENERAL DOCKET, TRIAL ROSTERS, AND CALL OF CASES FOR TRIAL

(a) Dockets and Trial Rosters; Designation by Party.

(1) *Clerk to Maintain Docket and Trial Rosters.* The Clerk of Court shall maintain: (1) a General Docket of all cases filed in the Circuit Court; (2) a Jury Trial Roster of all cases transferred from the General Docket wherein the case is, by agreement of counsel, scheduling order, or expiration of time, deemed ready for jury trial; (3) a Nonjury Docket of all nonjury matters including all motions filed in the Circuit Court.

(2) *Pleading or Motion to Designate Type of Matter.* At the time of filing of a complaint or responsive pleading thereto, the party shall inform the clerk, or the pleadings shall state in the caption, subject to Rule 38(b), whether the matter is to be heard by a jury or to be heard by the court as a nonjury matter. In the absence of such statement the clerk shall file it as a nonjury matter, subject to a motion to transfer to the appropriate docket. All motions relating to discovery matters, scheduling orders or emergency matters shall state in the caption: Priority Matter.

(b) General Docket, Transfer of Cases to Jury Trial Roster; Call of Cases Only From Jury Trial Roster; Order of Call. The clerk initially shall place all cases in which a jury has been requested on the General Docket. A case may not be called for trial until it has been transferred to the Jury Trial Roster. Trial shall be had no earlier than 30 days from the date the case first appears on the Jury Trial Roster. Cases shall be called for trial in the order in which they are placed on the Jury Trial Roster, unless the court in a Scheduling Order has set a date certain for the trial, or, after the case has been set on the Jury Trial Roster, the court, upon motion, grants a continuance as provided in (i) below. The first 20 cases on the Jury Trial Roster at the opening of court on the first day of a term, excluding those previously dismissed, continued or otherwise resolved before the opening of that term of court, may be called for trial. For each additional judge sitting during that term of court an additional 20 cases are subject to call. All other cases may be called for trial in that term only upon no less than 24 hours notice. Notwithstanding the foregoing, no action may be called for trial until 180 days after service of the last pleading which adds a new party to the action, unless all parties consent in writing.

(c) Transfer to Jury Trial Roster by Agreement. A case may be moved from the General Docket to the Jury Trial Roster at any time by agreement of all counsel of record. If agreement is reached, counsel shall notify the clerk in writing who shall immediately transfer the case to the Jury Trial Roster.

(d) Transfer to Jury Roster Within Six to Nine Months of Filing.

(1) *Agreement or Objection.* No earlier than 180 days after the date the case was filed, any party may file and serve upon all other parties a Request to Transfer that case from the General Docket to the Jury Trial Roster. Within 10 days of the service of the Request to Transfer all other parties shall file and serve either an Agreement to Transfer, or, an Objection to the Request to Transfer. Absent a timely filing indicating a position, the same shall be waived. If all parties have agreed to the transfer, the requesting party shall notify the clerk in writing of the agreement and the clerk shall place the case on the Jury Trial Roster, and it may be called for trial as provided in paragraph (b). If any party files an Objection to Transfer, the case may not be transferred to the Jury Trial Roster within 9 months of filing of the complaint except by agreement or as provided in (d)(2) below.

(2) *Objection Shall State Proposed Date of Transfer.* Any party who objects to the transfer to the Jury Trial Roster shall also state in its Objection to Transfer whether it will consent to the transfer of the case to the Jury Trial Roster within 9 months of the date of the filing of the complaint, and the date on which it will consent to the transfer. Absent a timely filing indicating a position, the same shall be waived. If all nonmoving parties specify a date within 9 months of the filing of the action on which the case may be transferred, the requesting party shall notify the clerk in writing of the agreement to transfer the case to the Jury Trial Roster on the latest date specified by any party that is less than 9 months after filing.

(e) Transfer to Jury Roster Nine Months to Twelve Months After Filing.

(1) *Request and Response.* No earlier than 9 months after the case was filed, any party in any case on the General Docket may file or re-file and serve upon all other parties a Request to Transfer to the Jury Trial Roster. Within 10 days of the service of the Request to Transfer all non-moving parties shall file and serve either an Agreement to Transfer on the date requested, or a Request for a Scheduling Order as provided in (e)(2) below. No other response is permitted. Absent a timely filing indicating a position, the same shall be waived. If all counsel of record have agreed to the transfer, the moving party shall notify the clerk in writing of the agreement, and the clerk shall place the case on the Jury Trial Roster and it may be called for trial as provided in (b).

(2) *Mandatory Scheduling Order.* If any party requests a Scheduling Order, that party, and all other parties, within 10 days thereafter, shall file and serve a Response to the Request for a Scheduling Order which shall include: (1) all matters deemed relevant by counsel that may be raised in a Pre–Trial Hearing under Rule 16 including all motions outstanding, and all dispositive motions to be filed; (2) all discovery remaining to be completed or other discovery matters governed by Rule 26(f) Discovery Conference; (3) any other matter affecting the trial date, including the disposition of all previous requests to transfer the case to the Jury Trial Docket; and (4) the date on which all pre-trial matters shall be completed and the case ready for trial. The clerk shall promptly set the request for a Scheduling Order for a hearing before the Chief Judge for Administrative Purposes which shall take priority as provided in (h) below, at which time the Chief Judge for Administrative Purposes shall review the matter and, in its discretion, set a date on which the case is to be transferred to the Jury Trial Roster, and may set a date before which the case may not be called for trial or a date certain for trial. The Scheduling Order may be amended by a subsequent Chief Judge for Administrative Purposes.

(f) Automatic Transfer. The clerk shall review the General Docket and shall transfer to the Jury Trial Roster all cases which have remained on the General Docket for 12 months and in which the court has not entered a Scheduling Order setting the date when the case is to be transferred to the Jury Trial Roster or in which there is no pending motion for a Scheduling Order in the file. The clerk shall notify counsel of record of the transfer, but publication of the Jury Trial Roster also shall be deemed notice of the automatic transfer.

(g) Motion to Strike From Jury Trial Roster. A party may move to strike a case from the Jury Trial Roster if upon timely motion that party establishes that it did not consent to the transfer as represented to the clerk, or that at the time the case was automatically transferred under (f) above, there was in effect a scheduling order setting another date for the transfer, or a pending motion for such order.

(h) Nonjury Docket; Priority of Matters. The clerk shall immediately transfer all matters designated as nonjury matters from the General Docket to the Nonjury Docket. All motions on the Motions Calendar and motions filed in any case shall be immediately placed on the Nonjury Docket. The Chief Judge for Administrative Purposes, in cooperation with the clerk, is responsible for setting all matters on the Nonjury Docket for disposition. Motions may be scheduled for hearing at any time after the period for notice of the motion required by these rules. Priority in scheduling hearings on nonjury matters and scheduling motions at any other time shall be given to all motions designated Priority Matter which includes emergency matters, discovery motions, and all requests for Scheduling Orders as specified in (a)(2) above. Provided, however, that no contested nonjury action may be called for trial on the merits until 120 days after the filing of the summons and complaint, or the last pleading that adds a new party to the action, unless agreed to in writing by all parties.

(i) Continuance.

(1) *For Cause.* As actions are called, counsel may request that the action be continued. If good and sufficient cause for continuance is shown, the continuance may be granted by the court. Ordinarily such continuances shall be only until the next term of court. Each scheduled calendar week of circuit court shall constitute a separate term of court.

(2) *For Absence of Witness.* No motion for continuance of trial shall be granted on account of the absence of a witness without the oath of the party, his counsel or agent, to the following effect, to wit: That the testimony of the witness is material to the support of the action or defense of the party moving; that the motion is not intended for delay; but is made solely because the party cannot go safely to trial without such testimony; that there has been due diligence to procure the testimony of the witness or of such other circumstances as will satisfy the court that the motion is not intended for delay. In all such cases where a subpoena has been issued, the original shall be produced, with proof of service, or the reason why not served, endorsed thereon, or attached thereto; or, if lost, the same proof shall be offered with additional proof of the loss of the original subpoena. A party applying for such postponement on account of the absence of a witness shall set forth under oath in addition to the foregoing matters what fact or facts he believes the witness if present would testify to, and the grounds for such belief.

(j) Case Stricken From Docket by Agreement. A party may strike its complaint, counterclaim, cross-claim or third party claim from any docket one time as a matter of right, provided that all parties adverse to that claim, counterclaim, cross-claim or third party claim agree in writing that it may be stricken, and all further agree that if the claim is restored upon motion made within 1 year of the date stricken, the statute of limitations shall be tolled as to all consenting parties during the time the case is stricken, and any unexpired portion of the statute of limitations on the date the case was stricken shall remain and begin to run on the date that the claim is restored. A party moving to restore a case stricken from the docket shall provide all parties notice of the motion to restore at least 10 days before it is heard. Upon being restored, the case shall be placed on the General Docket and proceed from that date as provided in this rule.

(k) Alternate Method of Transfer to Jury Roster. Notwithstanding any other provision of this rule, any party may file and serve on all other parties a Request to Transfer that case from the General Docket to the Jury Trial Roster no earlier than 120 days after the case was filed. The Request must certify that the party is ready to go to trial and must indicate any outstanding pre-trial matters. Within 10 days after service of the Request to Transfer, any party may file a Response to the Request. If the Response opposes the transfer, it shall indicate in what respect the case is not ready for trial. Once the time to file Responses has expired, the clerk shall promptly set the Request for Transfer for a hearing before the Chief Judge for Administrative Purposes. The hearing shall be given priority as provided by subdivision (h) of this rule. After a hearing, the Chief Judge may, as a matter of discretion, transfer the case to the Jury Trial Roster.

[Amended effective January 1, 1995; August 30, 1998; September 1, 2001; May 3, 2007.]

Notes

This Rule 40 is substantially a compendium of present Circuit Court Rules governing preparation of trial rosters, setting the order of cases for trial, and granting postponement or continuance. The Federal rule simply directs that the District Courts shall provide local rules on these matters. See also Rule 79 as to clerks of court maintaining calendars (File Book).

Note to 1986 Amendment

The amendment to Rule 40(b)(2) permits the clerk to place actions on the appropriate trial roster 120 days after filing, and assures that counsel will have at least 120 days from the date of filing of the original summons and complaint, or the last pleading which brings in a new party, before the case can be tried so that there will be adequate time to prepare the case. Assertion of new claims between existing parties does not extend the time automatically.

Notes to 1994 Amendments

Rule 40 addresses problems in the scheduling of cases and substantially revises the way jury cases are called for trial. Previously, under Rule 40(b)(2) a case could not be called for trial for 120 days after it was filed or the last party was joined. This short period and the lack of specific procedures meant that attorneys could not predict accurately when a case would be called, and some were called without adequate notice or opportunity to complete discovery. Former Rule 40(c)(3) often was used to dismiss and refile many of these cases causing confusion in the docket and the status of those cases.

This rule addresses these problems and provides counsel an adequate time to prepare for trial, yet prevents unnecessary delay by fixing a time when the case must be placed on the Jury Roster. The rule has four parts. First, the rule sets the procedure for placing a case on the Jury Roster and provides a minimum period within which it cannot be called without the consent of the parties, and also a time when it must be scheduled for trial. Second, the rule establishes procedures for the call of cases on the Jury Roster during a term of court. Third, the rule provides that Priority Motions, those involving emergency matters, motions for scheduling orders and discovery motions, must be given precedence when hearings are scheduled. Prompt resolution of these motions speeds trial preparation. Fourth, the procedure in former Rule 40(c)(3) used to dismiss a case has been revised and limited.

Rule 40(a) establishes the dockets and rosters and describes how cases are filed initially. All cases are placed on the General Docket. Rule 40(b). Counsel must inform the clerk or the pleadings must state whether it is a jury or nonjury matter. Rule 40(a)(2). However, the time for demanding a jury remains governed by Rule 38. Jury cases remain on the General Docket until transferred by consent, Scheduling Order or expiration of time. Rule 40(b). Nonjury cases are transferred immediately to the Nonjury Docket. Rule 40(h). In the absence of a designation as jury or nonjury, the matter is placed on the Nonjury Docket, subject to a motion to transfer. Rule 40(a)(2). At any time the case can be transferred to the Jury Trial Roster with the consent of all parties.

The first major section is paragraphs (c)–(h) which governs the transfer of a case from the General Docket to the Jury Trial Roster. The rule divides the pre-trial period into three parts. Rule 40(d) governs the first year after the case is filed. During that period the case can be transferred only with the consent of all parties. Rule 40(c) and (d)(1). The rule, however, establishes a way to determine if the case may be transferred to the Jury Roster within a year of its being filed. Six months after the filing of the case any party may file and serve a Request for Transfer. A Response is mandatory within 10 days and a failure to do so is deemed consent to the transfer. Rule 40(d)(1). The Response to a Request to Transfer is either consent or an objection to the transfer. If objecting, a party must also state whether it consents to a transfer within a year of the case's filing date. Therefore within 10 days of the Request to Transfer, the parties will have determined if the case can be immediately transferred, or transferred within a year of filing. If the parties consent but suggest different dates for transfer within the first year, the latest date controls. Rule 40(d)(2). The moving party notifies the clerk of court of the date of transfer. Rule 40(d)(1). A transfer made without consent or in violation of the rule may be challenged under Rule 40(g). If any party objects to a transfer on any date within the first year it remains on the General Docket. Rule 40(d)(1).

Rule 40(e) governs transfers between one year and eighteen months after the case is filed. A Request to Transfer filed during this period results either in a transfer to the Jury Trial Roster or a Scheduling Order issued by the Chief Judge for Administrative Purposes. In either event scheduling now comes under the control of the court. Any party may file a Request to Transfer after one year. Rule 40(e)(1). Only two responses are permitted. A consent to the transfer or a

Request for a Scheduling Order. A failure to respond is deemed consent. If there is consent the moving party notifies the clerk and the case is transferred. Rule 40(e)(1). A transfer made without consent or in violation of the rule may be challenged by a motion to strike from the Jury Roster. Rule 40(g). If no party requests a transfer the case remains on the general docket and may not be transferred without the consent of all parties.

A Request for a Scheduling Order requires that each party file and serve within 10 days a Response to a Request for a Scheduling Order which is a detailed statement describing the status of the case so the court has enough information to set an appropriate time to place the case on the Jury Trial Roster. The Response to a Request for a Scheduling Order shall contain all matters that may be raised at a pre-trial hearing, all outstanding motions, the remaining discovery, all matters that affect the trial date, and the date on which the case will be ready for trial. The Request for a Scheduling Order is a Priority Matter and must be so designated on the motion. Rule 40(a)(2). Priority Matters are given precedence whenever motions and non-jury matters are scheduled. Rule 40(h). At the hearing on the Scheduling Order the Chief Judge for Administrative Purposes can set a date for the case to be transferred to the Jury Roster, set a date certain for trial, or set a date before which it cannot be called for trial. The Scheduling Order can be amended by any judge acting as Chief Administrative Judge to take into account subsequent developments.

After eighteen months every case is subject to the control of the court regardless of the actions of counsel. Rule 40(f) requires automatic transfer of any case which is not subject to a Scheduling Order, or has a pending motion for a Scheduling Order. The clerk should notify counsel of the transfer but publishing the Jury Trial Roster is deemed notice of the transfer.

Rule 40(b) is the second major section of the rule and governs the call of cases on the Jury Roster. The principal features of this paragraph are provisions providing adequate notice of when the case may be called for trial. Cases are called in the order in which they appear on the Jury Roster. But a case must be on the Jury Roster for 30 days before it may be called for trial. More importantly, the rule restricts the number of cases that are subject to trial on the first day of a term of court. The Jury Roster at the opening of the first day of the term of court fixes the number that may be immediately called. The first twenty cases on the Jury Trial Roster that, before the opening of that term of court, have not been dismissed, continued or otherwise resolved, may be called immediately. All cases after the first twenty require at least 24 hours before they may be called for trial. For each additional judge sitting in a term, another twenty cases are subject to immediate call. Once called the court may in its discretion grant a continuance as provided in Rule 40(i) which is the same as former Rule 40(b)(1) and (2). Or, a party may strike the case from the docket by agreement under Rule 40(j) which is more restrictive than the former Rule 40(c)(3).

The third major section of the Rule addresses motion practice to ensure that certain ones are promptly scheduled and resolved to prevent unnecessary delay in trial preparation. Rule 40(h) designates certain motions as priority matters including emergency matters, discovery motions and Requests for a Scheduling Order. Counsel must so designate those motions when filing them. Rule 40(a)(2). All motions are placed on the Nonjury Docket, and the Chief Judge and clerk of court must give the Priority Motions preference when scheduling the nonjury matters or setting motions for hearing at any other time. Counsel generally must give 10 days notice to opposing counsel of any motion, as in Rule 6(d) and 56(c), and once that period has expired, motions may be called at any time. Nonjury trials, however, may not be called for trial until 120 days after filing or the joinder of the last party to the action as is the current practice.

Rule 40(j) is the final section of the rule and substantially revises the procedure for dismissing a case previously found in Rule 40(c)(3). Rule 40(j) now requires all adverse parties to consent to the dismissal in writing, but, the consent also operates to toll the statute of limitations for one year after the case is stricken from the docket as to each consenting party. Any remaining portion of the statute of limitations begins to run one year after the case was stricken unless the case has previously been restored to the General Docket. A party moving to restore a case must give 10 days notice of the motion, and upon being restored the case is placed on the General Docket where it proceeds as a newly filed action on the General Docket. A case can also be dismissed voluntarily under Rule 41(a).

Note to 1998 Amendment

This amendment added subsection (k) to the rule. It provides an alternative procedure for transferring a case to the jury roster and is based on a March 14, 1995 order of the South Carolina Supreme Court.

Note to 2001 Amendments

Rule 40(d), (e)(1), (f), and (k) are amended to shorten the time period before cases move to the Jury Trial Roster.

Note to 2007 Amendment

The last sentence of Rule 40(b) establishes a minimum period of time following the joinder of a new party during which the action may not be called for trial without the consent of all parties. The 2007 amendment extends this period from 120 days to 180 days, and measures this period from the date the newly joined party is served with process, rather than the filing date of the pleading adding the new party. As before, the 180 day exclusion may be waived with the consent of all parties.

RULE 41. DISMISSAL OF ACTIONS; NON-SUIT

(a) Voluntary Dismissal: Effect Thereof.

(1) *By Plaintiff; By Stipulation.* Subject to the provisions of Rule 23(c), of Rule 66(a), and of any statute, an action may be dismissed by the plaintiff without order of court (A) by filing and serving a notice of dismissal at any time before service by the adverse party of an answer or motion for summary judgment, whichever first occurs, or (B) by filing a stipulation of dismissal signed by all parties who have appeared in the action. Unless otherwise stated in the notice of dismissal or stipulation, the dismissal is without prejudice, except that a notice of dismissal operates as an adjudication upon the merits when filed by a plaintiff who has once dismissed in any court of the United States or of any state an action based on or including the same claim.

(2) *By Order of Court.* Except as provided in paragraph (1) of this subdivision of this rule, an action shall not be dismissed at the plaintiff's instance save upon order of the court and upon such terms and conditions as the court deems proper. If a counterclaim has been pleaded by a defendant prior to the service upon him of the plaintiff's motion to dismiss, the action shall not be dismissed against the defendant's objection unless the counterclaim can remain pending for independent adjudication by the court. Unless otherwise specified in the order, a dismissal under this paragraph is without prejudice.

(b) Involuntary Dismissal: Non-suit; Effect Thereof. For failure of the plaintiff to prosecute or to comply with these rules or any order of court, a defendant may move for dismissal of an action or of any claim against him. After the plaintiff in an action tried by the court without a jury has completed the presentation of his evidence, the defendant, without waiving his right to offer evidence in the event the motion is not granted, may move for a dismissal on the ground that upon the facts and the law the plaintiff has shown no right to relief.

The court as trier of the facts may then determine them and render judgment against the plaintiff or may decline to render any judgment until the close of all the evidence. If the court renders judgment on the merits against the plaintiff, the court shall make findings as provided in Rule 52(a). Unless the court in its order for dismissal otherwise specifies, a dismissal under this subdivision and any dismissal not provided for in this rule, other than a dismissal for lack of jurisdiction or for improper venue or for failure to join a party under Rule 19, operates as an adjudication upon the merits.

(c) Dismissal of Counterclaim, Cross-Claim or Third Party Claim. The provisions of this rule apply to the dismissal of any counterclaim, cross-claim, or third-party claim. A voluntary dismissal by the claimant alone pursuant to paragraph (1) of subdivision (a) of this rule shall be made before a responsive pleading is served or, if there is none, before the introduction of evidence at the trial or hearing.

(d) Costs of Previously-Dismissed Action. If a plaintiff who has once dismissed an action in any court commences an action based upon or including the same claim against the same defendant, the court may make such order for the payment of costs of the action previously dismissed as it may deem proper and may stay the proceedings in the action until the plaintiff has complied with the order.

Notes

This Rule 41 is the same as the Federal Rule, except that it requires service as well as filing the notice of voluntary dismissal by plaintiff if taken before answer or motion to dismiss is served. This Rule amends present State practice as to dismissal (non-suit); but clarifies Circuit Rules 29, 30, 59 and 76, which this Rule 41 and Rule 50 (directed verdict) replace. It is particularly helpful when the court tries a law action without a jury, and specifies the court's duty on such procedure. Rule 41(b) also makes clear when involuntary dismissal operates as an adjudication on the merits.

RULE 41.1. SEALING DOCUMENTS AND SETTLEMENT AGREEMENTS

(a) Purpose. Because South Carolina has a long history of maintaining open court proceedings and records, this Rule is intended to establish guidelines for governing the filing under seal of settlements and other documents. Article I, § 9, of the South Carolina Constitution provides that all courts of this state shall be public and this Rule is intended to ensure that that Constitutional provision is fulfilled. However, the Court recognizes that as technology advances, court records will be more readily available and this Rule seeks to balance the right of public access to court records with the need for parties to protect truly private or proprietary information from public view and to insure that rules of court are fairly applied. This Rule does not apply to private settlement agreements and shall not be interpreted as approving confidentiality provisions in private settlement agreements where the parties agree to have the matter voluntarily dismissed under Rule 41(a)(1), SCRCP, without court involvement. The enforceability of those provisions is governed by general legal principles, not by this Rule.

(b) Filing Documents Under Seal. Should Rule 26(b)(5), SCRCP, be inapplicable, and absent another governing rule, statute, or order, any party seeking to file documents under seal shall file and serve a "Motion to Seal." The motion shall identify, with specificity, the documents or portions of documents for which sealing is considered necessary, shall contain a non-confidential description of the documents, and shall be accompanied by a separately sealed attachment labeled "Confidential Information to be submitted to Court in Connection with the Motion to Seal." The attachment shall contain the documents for the court to review *in camera*. The motion shall state the reasons why sealing is necessary, explain why less drastic alternatives to sealing will not afford adequate protection, and address the following factors:

(1) the need to ensure a fair trial;

(2) the need for witness cooperation;

(3) the reliance of the parties upon expectations of confidentiality;

(4) the public or professional significance of the lawsuit;

(5) the perceived harm to the parties from disclosure;

(6) why alternatives other than sealing the documents are not available to protect legitimate private interests as identified by this Rule; and

(7) why the public interest, including, but not limited to, the public health and safety, is best served by sealing the documents.

The burden is on the party seeking to seal documents to satisfy the court that the balance of public and private interests favors sealing the documents. In family court matters, the judge shall also consider whether documents: 1) contain material which may expose private financial matters which could adversely affect the parties; and/or 2) relate to sensitive custody issues, and shall specifically balance the special interests of the child or children involved in the family court matter.

Unless otherwise ordered by the court, the clerk of court shall treat the motion to seal in a manner similar to all other motions filed with the court. The motion shall be entered in the Clerk's File Book and on the Motion Calendar and a hearing on the motion shall be held.

(c) Sealing Settlements. A proposed settlement agreement submitted for the court's approval shall not be conditioned upon its being filed under seal. Under no circumstances shall a court approve sealing a settlement agreement which involves a public body or institution.

Simultaneously with the filing of a motion seeking court approval of a settlement, or after a settlement has been approved, any party to the litigation may file a motion seeking to have all or part of the settlement filed under seal.

If the agreement is approved, and a motion to seal has been filed, the procedure set forth in **(b)** above shall be followed with the exception that the factors for sealing a settlement set forth below shall be addressed.

In determining whether to approve the filing of the settlement documents, in whole or in part, under seal, the court shall consider:

(1) the public or professional significance of the lawsuit;

(2) the perceived harm to the parties from disclosure:

(3) why alternatives other than sealing the documents are not available to protect legitimate private interests as identified by this Rule; and,

(4) why the public interest, including, but not limited to, the public health and safety, is best served by sealing the documents.

In family court matters, the judge shall also consider whether the settlement: 1) contains material which may expose private financial matters which could adversely affect the parties; and/or 2) relates to sensitive custody issues, and shall specifically balance the special interests of the child or children involved in the family court matter.

(d) Orders Sealing Documents. All orders sealing documents or all or parts of settlements shall set forth with specificity the reasons that require they be sealed.

[Adopted effective May 5, 2003.]

Notes

Rule 41.1 was enacted to set forth with clarity the fact that the courts of this State are presumed to be open and to set forth with particularity when documents and settlement agreements, submitted to a court for approval, may be sealed.

RULE 42. CONSOLIDATION; SEPARATE TRIALS

(a) Consolidation. When actions involving a common question of law or fact are pending before the court, it may order a joint hearing or trial of any or all matters in issue in the action; it may order all the actions consolidated; and it may make such orders concerning proceedings therein as may tend to avoid unnecessary costs or delay.

(b) Separate Trials. The court, in furtherance of convenience or to avoid prejudice, or when separate trials will be conducive to expedition and economy, may order a separate trial of any claim, cross-claim, counterclaim, or third-party claim, or of any separate issue or of any number of claims, cross-claims, counterclaims, third-party claims, or issues, always preserving inviolate the right of trial by jury as declared by the Constitution or as given by a statute of the State.

Notes

This Rule 42 is substantially identical with the Federal Rule. Rule 42(b) as to ordering separate trials is similar to State procedure, under Code § 15–27–20. Rule 42(a) as to consolidation of cases for trial is new to State procedure, but a valuable and needed addition. The parties and pleadings are not merged, and each action retains its own identity; but consolidation for trial can save much time and cost, as when all claims arise out of one auto accident, or several claims are based upon identical contracts.

RULE 43. CONDUCT OF TRIAL

(a) Form and Admissibility. In all trials the testimony of witnesses shall be taken orally in open court, unless otherwise provided by these rules. All evidence shall be admitted which is admissible under the statutes or rules of evidence heretofore applied in the courts of this State. In any case, the statute or rule which favors the reception of the evidence governs and the evidence shall be presented according to the most convenient method prescribed in any of the statutes or rules to which reference is herein made. The competency of a witness to testify shall be determined in like manner.

(b) Scope of Examination and Cross–Examination. Deleted

(1) *Examination, Leading Questions.* Deleted

(2) *Hostile and Adverse Witnesses.* Deleted

(c) Record of Excluded Evidence. Deleted

(1) *Reservation of Rights Unnecessary.* If an objection has once been made at any stage to the admission of evidence, it shall not be necessary thereafter to reserve rights concerning the objectionable evidence.

(d) Affirmation in Lieu of Oath. Whenever under these rules an oath is required to be taken, a solemn affirmation may be accepted in lieu thereof.

(e) Evidence on Motions. When a motion is based on facts not appearing of record the court may hear the matter on affidavits presented by the respective parties, but may direct that the matter be heard wholly or partly on oral testimony or depositions.

(f) Interpreters. When a witness does not speak the English language sufficiently to testify, the court may appoint an interpreter of its own selection and may fix his reasonable compensation. The compensation shall be paid out of funds provided by law or by one or more of the parties as the court may direct, and may be taxed ultimately as costs, in the discretion of the court.

(g) Statement of Pleadings to Jury. Counsel for any party may read his pleadings to the jury or make a statement to the jury of the facts alleged in the pleadings and the theory of his case; but counsel shall not argue his case during his opening statement. The pleadings shall not be submitted to the jury for its deliberations.

(h) Examination of Witness. One counsel only for each party shall examine or cross-examine a witness. During examination in open court, the examining counsel shall stand. For the purpose of this subdivision of this rule, two or more parties who have pleaded jointly shall be considered one party.

(i) Argument. Counsel shall not attempt to further argue any matter after he has been heard and the ruling of the court has been pronounced. No argument shall be made on objections to admissibility of evidence or conduct of trial unless specifically requested by the court. No more than two hours shall be taken by each side in final argument or sum up, without permission of the court. Counsel shall not address or refer to by name any member of the jury he is addressing, or otherwise personally appeal to any member thereof.

(j) Right to Open and Close. The moving party upon a motion shall have the right to open and close argument, and the plaintiff shall have the right to open and close upon the trial; except that a party admitting the adverse party's claim in his pleading, and taking upon himself the burden of proof, shall have the like privilege. The party having the right to open shall be required to open in full, and in reply may respond in full but may not introduce any new matter.

(k) Agreements of Counsel. No agreement between counsel affecting the proceedings in an action shall be binding unless reduced to the form of a consent order or written stipulation signed by counsel and entered in the record, or unless made in open court and noted upon the record, or reduced to writing and signed by the parties and their counsel. Settlement agreements shall be handled in accordance with Rule 41.1, SCRCP.

(*l*) Subsequent Applications for Order After Refusal. If any motion be made to any judge and be denied, in whole or in part, or be granted conditionally, no subsequent motion upon the same state of facts shall be made to any other judge in that action.

(m) Expert Testimony. Deleted

(1) *Testimony by Experts.* Deleted

(2) *Bases of Opinion Testimony by Experts.* Deleted

(3) *Opinion on Ultimate Issue.* Deleted

(4) *Disclosure of Facts or Data Underlying Expert Opinion.* Deleted

[Amended effective May 1, 1986; April 23, 1987; July 1, 1990; September 3, 1995; May 5, 2003; April 29, 2009.]

Notes

This Rule 43 substantially preserves present State practice as to evidence and conduct of trial. The present Federal Rule differs because of the adoption of the Federal Rules of Evidence in 1975; however, the practitioner will notice little change in present practice. Rules 43(a) through 43(d) restate present State practice under statutes, rules and case law. Rule 43(d) preserves Code § 19–1–40. Rule 43(c)(1) preserves new Circuit Rule 101. Rule 43(f) is new matter but is implied by the court's powers under Title 14, Chapter 15 of the Code. Rule 43(g) preserves Circuit Rule 85, except it prohibits submitting the pleadings to the jury for its deliberations, a needed change to avoid the jury treating pleadings as evidence or having information therefrom contrary to the judge's charge and instructions.

Note to 1986 Amendments

The amendment to Rule 43(b)(2) clarifies the right of a litigant to call an adverse party, or a witness who may bind an adverse party, and use leading questions and impeach him if justified by the facts. The amendments to paragraphs (f) and (h) correct inadvertent omissions in those paragraphs.

Note to 1987 Amendments

Rule 43(f) is amended to delete the reference to the hearing impaired whose interpreters are to be provided by statute.

Note to 1990 Amendments

Rule 43(m) Expert Testimony is taken from Rules 702 to 705 of the Federal Rules of Evidence. The language in subdivision (3) is that of Federal Rule of Evidence 704 prior to its amendment in 1984. The Advisory Committee Notes to the Federal Rules of Evidence provide commentary and useful guidance on the use of expert testimony under this Rule.

Note to 1995 Amendments

This amendment deleted subsections (b), (c) [but not (c)(1)], and (m). These matters are now governed by the South Carolina Rules of Evidence.

Note to 2003 Amendments

This amendment changed the title of the Rule to be more reflective of its content and added the final sentence to Rule 43(k), **Agreements of Counsel** to provide that agreements regarding sealing settlements will be handled according to Rule 41.1, SCRCP.

Note to 2009 Amendments

The amendment to Rule 43(k) provides a settlement agreement is also binding if the agreement is reduced to writing and signed by the parties and their counsel.

RULE 44. PROOF OF OFFICIAL RECORD; FOREIGN LAW

(a) Authentication.

(1) *Domestic.* An official record or an entry therein, when admissible for any purpose, may be evidenced by an official publication thereof or by a copy attested by the officer having legal custody of the record, or by his deputy, and accompanied with a certificate that such officer has the custody. If the office in which the record is kept is within the United States or within a territory or insular possession subject to the dominion of the United States, the certificate may be made by a judge of a court of record of the district or political subdivision in which the record is kept, authenticated by the seal of the court, or may be made by any public officer having a seal of office and having official duties in the district or political subdivision in which the record is kept, authenticated by the seal of his office. If the office in which the record is kept is in a foreign state or country, the certificate may be made by a secretary of embassy or legation, consul general, consul, vice consul, or consular agent or by any officer in the foreign service of the United States stationed in the foreign state or country in which the record is kept and authenticated by the seal of his office.

(2) *Foreign.* A foreign official record, or an entry therein, when admissible for any purpose, may be evidenced by an official publication thereof; or a copy thereof, attested by a person authorized to make the attestation, and accompanied by a final certification as to the genuineness of the signature and official position (A) of the attesting person, or (B) of any foreign official whose certificate of genuineness of signature and official position relating to the attestation. A final certification may be made by a secretary of embassy or legation, consul general, consul, vice consul, or consular agent of the United States, or a diplomatic or consular official of the foreign country assigned or accredited to the United States. If reasonable opportunity has been given to all parties to investigate the authenticity and accuracy of the documents, the court may, for good cause shown, (A) admit an attested copy without final certification or (B) permit the foreign official record to be evidenced by an attested summary with or without a final certification.

(b) Lack of Record. A written statement that after diligent search no record or entry of a specified tenor is found to exist in the records designated by the statement, authenticated as provided in subdivision (a)(1) of this rule in the case of a domestic record, or complying with the requirements of subdivision (a)(2) of this rule for a summary in the case of a foreign record, is admissible as evidence that the records contain no such record or entry.

(c) Other Proof. This rule does not prevent the proof of official records or of entry or lack of entry therein by any other method authorized by law.

(d) Foreign Law. A party who intends to raise an issue concerning the law of a foreign jurisdiction shall give notice in his pleadings or by other reasonable written notice or applicable motion. The court, in determining foreign law, may consider any relevant material or source, including testimony, whether or not submitted by a party or admissible under the law of evidence. The court's determination shall be treated as a ruling on a question of law.

[Amended effective May 1, 1986.]

Notes

This Rule 44 is substantially the Federal Rule. It conforms to present practice and Code §§ 19–5–10, 19–5–20, 19–5–40 and 19–5–220. Rule 44(d) is new. It conforms to present practice but is a more precise statement.

Notes to 1986 Amendments

This amendment [to Rule 44(d)] permits the issue of foreign law to be raised by any written notice rather than only in the pleadings or a motion. It is similar to Federal Rule 44.1 and supplements the Uniform Judicial Notice of Foreign Law Act, S.C. Code § 19–3–110 et seq.

RULE 45. SUBPOENA

(a) Form; Issuance.

(1) Every subpoena shall:

(A) state the name of the court from which it is issued; and

(B) state the title of the action, the name of the court in which it is pending, and its civil action number; and

(C) command each person to whom it is directed to attend and give testimony or produce and permit inspection and copying of designated books, documents or tangible things in the possession, custody or control of that person, or to permit inspection of premises, at a time and place therein specified; and

(D) set forth the text of subdivisions (c) and (d) of this rule.

A command to produce evidence or to permit inspection may be joined with a command to appear at trial or hearing or at deposition, or may be issued separately. A subpoena may specify the form or forms in which electronically stored information is to be produced.

(2) A subpoena commanding attendance at a trial or hearing shall issue from the court for the county in

which the hearing or trial is to be held. A subpoena for attendance at a deposition shall issue from the court for the county designated by the notice of deposition as the county in which the deposition is to be taken. If separate from a subpoena commanding the attendance of a person, a subpoena for production or inspection shall issue from the court for the county in which production or inspection is to be made. Provided, however, that a subpoena to a person who is not a party or an officer, director or managing agent of a party, commanding attendance at a deposition or production or inspection shall issue from the court for the county in which the non-party resides or is employed or regularly transacts business in person.

(3) The clerk shall issue a subpoena, signed but otherwise in blank, to a party requesting it, who shall complete it before service. An attorney as officer of the court may also issue and sign a subpoena on behalf of a court in which the attorney is authorized to practice.

(b) Service.

(1) A subpoena may be served by any person who is not a party and is not less than 18 years of age. Service of a subpoena upon a person named therein shall be made in the same manner prescribed for service of a summons and complaint in Rule 4(d) or (j), and, if the person's attendance is commanded, by tendering to that person the fees for one day's attendance of $25.00 and the mileage allowed by law for official travel of State officers and employees. When the subpoena is issued on behalf of the State of South Carolina or an officer or agency thereof, fees and mileage need not be tendered. Unless otherwise ordered by the court, prior notice in writing of any commanded production of documents and things or inspection of premises before trial shall be served on each party in the manner prescribed by Rule 5(b) at least 10 days before the time specified for compliance.

(2) Subject to the provisions of clause (ii) of subparagraph (c)(3)(A) of this rule, a subpoena may be served at any place within the State. Provided, however, that a subpoena to a person who is not a party or an officer, director or managing agent of a party, commanding attendance at a deposition or production or inspection shall issue from the court for the county in which the non-party resides or is employed or regularly transacts business in person and be served in that county.

(3) Proof of service when necessary shall be made by filing with the clerk of the court by which the subpoena is issued a statement of the date and manner of service and of the names of the persons served, certified by the person who made the service.

(c) Protection of Persons Subject to Subpoenas.

(1) A party or an attorney responsible for the issuance and service of a subpoena shall take reasonable steps to avoid imposing undue burden or expense on a person subject to that subpoena. The court on behalf of which the subpoena was issued shall enforce this duty and impose upon the party or attorney in breach of this duty an appropriate sanction, which may include, but is not limited to, lost earnings and a reasonable attorney's fee.

(2)(A) A person commanded to produce and permit inspection and copying of designated electronically stored information, books, papers, documents or tangible things, or inspection of premises need not appear in person at the place of production or inspection unless commanded to appear for deposition, hearing or trial. A party or an attorney responsible for the issuance and service of a subpoena for production of books, papers and documents without a deposition shall provide to another party copies of documents so produced upon written request. The party requesting copies shall pay the reasonable costs of reproduction.

(B) Subject to paragraph (d)(2) of this rule, a person commanded to produce and permit inspection and copying may, within 14 days after service of the subpoena or before the time specified for compliance if such time is less than 14 days after service, serve upon the party or attorney designated in the subpoena written objection to inspection or copying of any or all of the designated materials or of the premises—or to producing electronically stored information in the form or forms requested. If objection is made, the party serving the subpoena shall not be entitled to inspect and copy the materials or inspect the premises except pursuant to an order of the court by which the subpoena was issued. If objection has been made, the party serving the subpoena may, upon notice to the person commanded to produce, move at any time in the court that issued the subpoena for an order to compel the production. Such an order to compel production shall protect any person who is not a party or an officer of a party from significant expense resulting from the inspection and copying commanded.

(3)(A) On timely motion, the court by which a subpoena was issued, or regarding a subpoena commanding appearance at a deposition, or production or inspection directed to a non-party, the court in the county where the non-party resides, is employed or regularly transacts business in person, shall quash or modify the subpoena if it:

(i) fails to allow reasonable time for compliance; or

(ii) requires a person who is not a party nor an officer, director or managing agent of a party, nor a general partner of a partnership that is a party, to travel more than 50 miles from the county where that person resides, is employed or regularly transacts business in person, except that, subject to the provisions of clause (c)(3)(B)(iii) of this rule, such a person may in order to attend trial be commanded to travel from any such place within the state in which the trial is held; or

(iii) requires disclosure of privileged or otherwise protected matter and no exception or waiver applies; or

(iv) subjects a person to undue burden.

(B) If a subpoena:

(i) requires disclosure of a trade secret or other confidential research, development, or commercial information, or

(ii) requires disclosure of an unretained expert's opinion or information not describing specific events or occurrences in dispute and resulting from the expert's study made not at the request of any party, or

(iii) requires a person who is not a party nor an officer, director or managing agent of a party, nor a general partner of a partnership that is a party, to incur substantial expense to travel from the county where that person resides, is employed or regularly transacts business in person, the court may, to protect a person subject to or affected by the subpoena, quash or modify the subpoena or, if the party in whose behalf the subpoena is issued shows a substantial need for the testimony or material that cannot be otherwise met without undue hardship and assures that the person to whom the subpoena is addressed will be reasonably compensated, the court may order appearance or production only upon specified conditions.

(d) Duties in Responding to Subpoena.

(1)(A) A person responding to a subpoena to produce documents shall produce them as they are kept in the usual course of business or shall organize and label them to correspond with the categories in the demand.

(B) If a subpoena does not specify the form or forms for producing electronically stored information, a person responding to a subpoena must produce the information in a form or forms in which it is ordinarily maintained or in a reasonably usable form or forms.

(C) A person responding to a subpoena need not produce the same electronically stored information in more than one form.

(D) A person responding to a subpoena need not provide discovery of electronically stored information from sources that the person identifies as not reasonably accessible because of undue burden or cost. On motion to compel discovery or to quash, the person from whom discovery is sought must show that the information sought is not reasonably accessible because of undue burden or cost. If that showing is made, the court may nonetheless order discovery from such sources if the requesting party shows good cause, considering the limitations of Rule 26(b)(6)(B). The court may specify conditions for the discovery.

(2)(A) When information subject to a subpoena is withheld on a claim that it is privileged or subject to protection as trial preparation materials, the claim shall be made expressly and shall be supported by a description of the nature of the documents, communications, or things not produced that is sufficient to enable the demanding party to contest the claim.

(B) If information produced in response to a subpoena is subject to a claim of privilege or of protection as trial preparation material, the person making the claim may notify any party that received the information of the claim and the basis for it. After being notified, a party must promptly return, sequester, or destroy the specified information and any copies it has and may not use or disclose the information until the claim is resolved. A receiving party may promptly present the information to the court under seal for a determination of the claim. If the receiving party disclosed the information before being notified, the receiving party must take reasonable steps to retrieve the information. The person who produced the information must preserve the information until the claim is resolved.

(e) Contempt. Failure by any person without adequate excuse to obey a subpoena served upon that person may be deemed a contempt of the court from which the subpoena issued. An adequate cause for failure to obey exists when a subpoena purports to require a non-party to attend a deposition, permit an inspection, or produce at a place not within the limits provided by clause (ii) of subparagraph (c)(3)(A); or if served without an adequate time to respond as provided in Rule 45(b)(1); or if service is made upon an individual under Rule 4(d)(1) and the individual did not receive or acknowledge the subpoena.

[Amended effective July 1, 1989; July 1, 1993; July 1, 1995; September 1, 2002; April 28, 2011.]

Notes

This Rule 45 is substantially the same as the Federal Rule, modified to the limits of State court jurisdiction. Rule 45(b) is modified to conform to new Circuit Court Rule 106. The Federal Rule has been little changed for 40 years and is familiar to South Carolina practitioners. It offers several simplifications of present State practice: (1) The Clerk of Court issues the subpoena "duces tecum" under Rule 45(b), as well as the subpoena to compel attendance of witnesses. (A "standard form" is provided for all clerks, which may be issued to counsel in advance for use as needed.). (2) Service runs statewide and is not confined to one county. (3) One form replaces the old "subpoena writ" with "tickets" attached for each witness. Rule 45(g) is added to provide reasonable per diem and mileage for witnesses. The "Uniform Act to Secure Attendance of Witness from Without the State in Criminal Proceedings," Code § 19-7-50, et seq., is not affected.

Notes to 1993 Amendments

Rule 45 is amended to conform to federal Rule 45, as amended in December 1991. The major purposes of that amendment, which are adopted here, are to simplify the procedure for issuing a subpoena and to clarify and enlarge the protection of non-parties who are compelled to assist the court in the proceedings, as well as to facilitate access to materials without the necessity of a deposition. The federal rule made other changes in the methods of issuing subpoenas in districts other than the one in which the action is pending which are not relevant to state practice.

Much of the practice remains the same including who may serve the subpoena, the right to object to production in writing, and to require the issuing party to obtain a court order before inspecting the documents. The major changes are: (1) the attorney signs and issues the subpoena on behalf of the court; (2) documents, materials or an inspection can be obtained from a non-party without obtaining a deposition; and (3) the non-party's rights are expanded and clarified. In this context, paragraph (a)(2) provides that a subpoena for trial is issued by the court where the action is pending and under paragraph (b)(2) may be served throughout the state. The subpoenaed person may move under (c)(3)(A) to quash or modify the subpoena in the issuing court, which is the court where the action is pending, and may obtain relief if the subpoena requires travel of more than 50 miles from where the non-party resides, is employed or regularly transacts business.

The rights of a non-party subpoenaed for a deposition are enlarged and clarified. Under paragraph (a)(2) the subpoena for a non-party deposition, production or inspection is issued by the court in the county where the person resides, is employed or regularly transacts business, and served there. Under paragraph (c)(3)(A) the non-party can object to the subpoena in his home county, if different from the place where the action is pending. Finally, paragraph (e) makes clear that a subpoena to a non-party for a deposition, inspection or production, requiring travel beyond 50 miles of the county where the individual resides, is employed or regularly transacts business, provides an adequate excuse for failure to respond, and avoids a sanction for contempt.

The following material discusses each provision of the new rule. Paragraph (a)(1) defines the form of the subpoena. It no longer requires that the subpoena bear the seal of the court. Subparagraph (D) now requires that the subpoena contain language of paragraphs (c) Protection of Persons Subject to Subpoenas, and (d) Duties in Responding to Subpoena, to alert the person subpoenaed about the rights and obligations under Rule 45.

Paragraphs (a)(1) and (c)(2)(A) permit a subpoena for the production of documents or inspection without requiring a deposition. This adopts a common practice which was not authorized by the prior rule which required the deposition of a non-party to obtain production or inspection from a non-party. The last sentence of paragraph (b)(1) requires ten (10) days written notice to other parties if production is requested without a deposition.

Paragraph (a)(2) states that the subpoena for trial or hearing is issued by the court for the county where the action is pending. A subpoena for a deposition is issued by the county where the deposition is to take place. A subpoena for the deposition of a non-party is issued where the non-party resides, is employed or regularly transacts business in person. Specifying the court that issues the subpoena is important because motions to quash or enforce a non-party subpoena are brought in the issuing court which might be different from the court where the action is pending.

Paragraph (a)(3) provides that the clerk is to issue the subpoena in blank if the subpoena is requested by an unrepresented party, but the attorney is also authorized to sign the subpoena on behalf of any court in which he is licensed to practice. There is no requirement that the subpoena bear the seal of the court. The attorney signs and issues it as an officer of the court.

Paragraph (b)(1) defines who can serve a subpoena, and specifies that it is by delivery to the person subpoenaed along with tendering the witness fee and mileage. This clarifies the procedure for service.

Paragraph (b)(2) provides that subpoenas may be served throughout the state subject to two exceptions. First, (c)(2)(A)(ii) requires the appropriate court to quash or modify a subpoena on several grounds. Second, a non-party subpoena can only be issued and served in the county where the non-party resides, is employed or regularly transacts business in person. Paragraph (b)(3) describes how proof of service of the subpoena is to be made.

Paragraph (c)(1) states the duty of the attorney to avoid undue burden on the subpoenaed person and authorizes the issuing court to enforce this duty by imposing sanctions including, but not limited to, lost earnings and reasonable attorney's fees.

Paragraph (c)(2)(A) permits a subpoena for the production of documents without the necessity of also scheduling a deposition. Ten (10) days written notice to other parties is required under the last sentence of (b)(1) if there is no deposition. Rule 30 requires similar notice of all depositions.

Paragraph (c)(2)(B) is taken from former Rule 45(d) which authorized a person subpoenaed to object in writing to the production, and required the person seeking the information to obtain a court order before inspecting the documents. This order is obtained from the court that issued the subpoena, and, in the case of a non-party, would be the court in the county where the non-party resides, is employed or regularly transacts business in person, if different from the court where the action is pending.

Paragraph (c)(3)(A) states that the court shall quash or modify the subpoena if there is no reasonable time to comply, requires excessive travel, calls for privileged material or creates an undue burden. Paragraph (c)(3)(B)(i) authorizes the court to quash or modify the subpoena if it requires disclosure of trade secrets. Sub-paragraph (ii) protects the intellectual property of unretained experts, while providing a means for obtaining it if necessary, and the expert is properly compensated. Paragraph (c)(3)(B)(iii) adds additional protection for witnesses subpoenaed for trial. The court may modify or quash the subpoena if it requires travel over 50 miles to attend the trial, unless the other party can demonstrate a substantial need for the information that could not be obtained otherwise without substantial hardship, and that the person subpoenaed will be reasonably compensated.

Paragraph (d)(1) requires those served with the subpoena to produce the documents in the order in which they are kept in the ordinary course of business or label them to correspond to the categories in the demand. This is the same requirement imposed on parties responding to a document request under Rule 34. Paragraph (d)(2) imposes a new obligation to support an objection to production on grounds of privilege by providing a description of the documents or things not produced sufficiently to allow the claim to be contested.

Paragraph (e) provides authority for the court to impose sanctions through the contempt power for failure to comply with a subpoena. The paragraph does have a new sentence that states that it is an adequate excuse for failure to comply with the subpoena that it required a non-party to appear at a deposition, permit inspection or produce materials outside of the geographical limits set by the rule.

Notes to 1995 Amendments

Rule 45(c)(3)(A)(ii) and 45(c)(3)(B)(iii) are amended to make clear that a non-party general partner of a partnership that is a party, is treated the same as an officer, director or managing agent of a party for purposes of trial subpoenas. Rule 45(c)(3) provides a non-party, subpoenaed to appear at trial more than fifty miles from the place of service, the opportunity to move to quash the subpoena unless a special showing of need is made and reasonable compensation is provided to the witness. These special provisions are not available to parties or officers, directors and managing agents of parties. The amendment extends the exclusion to a general partner of a partnership that is a party. The amendment does not affect limited partners.

Notes to 2002 Amendments

The first 2002 amendment amends Rule 45(b)(1) to permit service of subpoenas by the same method as used to serve a summons and complaint. First, in addition to in hand service of the subpoena, service on an individual could be made by leaving the subpoena at the person's home or usual place of abode with a person of suitable age and discretion then residing there as provided in Rule 4(d)(1). Second, a subpoena could be served on an individual, a corporation, or a partnership by registered or certified mail, return receipt requested and delivery restricted to the addressee under Rule 4(d)(8). In addition, the person or the person's attorney may accept service under Rule 4(j).

The second 2002 amendment amends Rule 45(e), to make clear the circumstances when service is effective and may be enforced through the contempt power.

Note to 2011 Amendments

The amendments to Rules 16, 26, 33, 34, 37 and 45 of the South Carolina Rules of Civil Procedure concerning electronic discovery are substantially similar to the corresponding provisions in the Federal Rules of Civil Procedure. The rules concerning electronic discovery are intended to provide a practical, efficient and cost-effective method to assure reasonable discovery. Pursuit of electronic discovery must relate to the claims and defenses asserted in the pleadings and should serve as a means for facilitating a just and cost-effective resolution of disputes.

RULE 46. EXCEPTIONS UNNECESSARY

Formal exceptions to rulings or orders of the court are unnecessary; but for all purposes for which an exception has heretofore been necessary it is sufficient that a party, at the time the ruling or order of the court is made or sought, makes known to the court the action which he desires the court to take or his objection to the action of the court and his grounds therefor; and, if a party has no opportunity to object to a ruling or order at the time it is made, the absence of an objection does not thereafter prejudice him.

Notes

This Rule 46 is the same as the Federal Rule and presents no change in State practice. It does not apply, of course, to formal "exceptions" from the reports of masters as provided by Rule 53 or "exceptions on appeal" under Supreme Court Rules. (Editor's Note: Effective September 1, 1990, the Supreme Court Rules were repealed by the South Carolina Appellate Court Rules.)

RULE 47. JURORS

(a) Examination of Jurors. The court may permit the parties or their attorneys to conduct the examination of prospective jurors or may itself conduct the examination. In the latter event, the court shall permit the parties or their attorneys to supplement the examination by such further inquiry as it deems proper or shall itself submit to the prospective jurors such additional questions submitted by the parties or their attorneys as it deems proper.

(b) Alternate Jurors. The court may direct that not more than six jurors in addition to the regular petit jury panel be called and impanelled to sit as alternate jurors. Alternate jurors in the order in which they are called shall replace jurors who, prior to the time the jury retires to consider its verdict, become or are found unable or disqualified to perform their duties. Alternate jurors shall be drawn in the same manner, shall have the same qualifications, shall be subject to the same examination and challenges, shall take the same oath, and shall have the same functions, powers, facilities, and privileges as the regular jurors. An alternate juror who does not replace a regular juror shall be discharged after the jury retires to consider its verdict. Each side is entitled to 1 peremptory challenge in addition to those otherwise allowed by law if 1 or 2 alternate jurors are to be impanelled, 2 peremptory challenges if 3 or 4 alternate jurors are to be impanelled, and 3 peremptory challenges if 5 or 6 alternate jurors are to be impanelled. The additional peremptory challenges may be used only against an alternate juror and the other peremptory challenges allowed by law shall not be used against an alternate juror.

(c) Separation of Jury. If it appears that the jury deliberations may extend into the night, the court may order that the jury be taken to suitable sleeping quarters for the night; and on the following morning they shall resume their deliberations. The jury shall be kept together and separate from the public, and as far as practicable during all times shall be under the surveillance of the bailiffs. Any juror or jurors may be separated for the night from any other juror or jurors. There shall be no communication with any member of the jury by any third person, and the jury shall be fully protected from any outside influence.

Notes

These Rules 47(a) and (b) are substantially the present Federal Rule. They represent no material change from present State practice, and are consistent with Code §§ 14-7-390, 14-7-1020, 14-7-1120 and 14-7-1340. Rule 47(c) is added to preserve Circuit Court Rule 80.

RULE 48. JURIES OF LESS THAN TWELVE; MAJORITY VERDICT

The jury shall be composed of twelve persons and their verdict shall be unanimous, except that the parties may stipulate that the jury shall consist of any number less than twelve, or less than six in civil action in magistrate's courts, or that a verdict or a finding of a stated majority of the jurors be taken as the verdict or finding of the jury.

Notes

This Rule 48 is substantially identical to the Federal Rule. Except in capital felony cases (State v. Hall, 137 S.C. 261, 101 S.E. 662 (1919)), there is no constitutional barrier to waiver of the 12 person or unanimous verdict requirements. The Rule should be particularly useful in cases where a juror becomes disabled and there is no alternate juror available. The clause concerning magistrate's courts is to conform to Code § 22–3–240.

RULE 49. SPECIAL VERDICTS AND INTERROGATORIES

(a) Special Verdicts. The court may require a jury to return only a special verdict in the form of a special written finding upon each issue of fact. In that event the court may submit to the jury written questions susceptible of categorical or other brief answer or may submit written forms of the several special findings which might properly be made under the pleadings and evidence; or it may use such other method of submitting the issues and requiring the written findings thereon as it deems most appropriate. The court shall give to the jury such explanation and instruction concerning the matter thus submitted as may be necessary to enable the jury to make its findings upon each issue. If in so doing the court omits any issue of fact raised by the pleadings or by the evidence, each party waives his right to a trial by jury of the issue so omitted unless before the jury retires he demands its submission to the jury. As to an issue omitted without such demand the court may make a finding; or if it fails to do so, it shall be deemed to have made a finding in accord with the judgment on the special verdict.

(b) General Verdict Accompanied by Answer to Interrogatories. The court may submit to the jury, together with appropriate forms for a general verdict, written interrogatories upon one or more issues of fact the decision of which is necessary to a verdict. The court shall give such explanation or instruction as may be necessary to enable the jury both to make answers to the interrogatories and to render a general verdict, and the court shall direct the jury both to make written answers and to render a general verdict. When the general verdict and the answers are harmonious, the appropriate judgment upon the verdict and answers shall be entered pursuant to Rule 58. When the answers are consistent with each other but one or more is inconsistent with the general verdict, judgment may be entered pursuant to Rule 58 in accordance with the answers, notwithstanding the general verdict, or the court may return the jury for further consideration of its answers and verdict or may order a new trial. When the answers are inconsistent with each other and one or more is likewise inconsistent with the general verdict, judgment shall not be entered, but the court shall return the jury for further consideration of its answers and verdict or shall order a new trial.

(c) Verdict in Action for Personal Property. In an action for the recovery of specific personal property, if the property has not been delivered to the plaintiff, or if it has and the defendant demands its return, the jury shall assess the value of the property if the verdict be in favor of the plaintiff or if they find that the defendant is entitled to a return of the property. The jury may at this time assess the damages, both actual and punitive, which the prevailing party has sustained by reason of the detention or taking and withholding of such property.

Notes

These Rules 49(a) and (b) are the same as the Federal Rules. They essentially preserve present State practice as to general and special verdicts under Code §§ 15–33–20, 15–33–30 and 15–33–40, with the important innovation that under Rule 49(a) the court may require only a special verdict in any case, rather than both a general and a special verdict under the old Code procedure. This innovation has proven increasingly valuable in complex litigation after 40 years of experience with the Federal Rule. Rule 49(c) is added to preserve Code §§ 15–33–30 and 15–69–210, as to special findings required in actions for claim and delivery.

RULE 50. MOTION FOR A DIRECTED VERDICT AND FOR JUDGMENT NOTWITHSTANDING THE VERDICT

(a) Motion for Directed Verdict: When Made: Effect. When upon a trial the case presents only questions of law the judge may direct a verdict. A party who moves for a directed verdict at the close of the evidence offered by an opponent may offer evidence in the event that the motion is not granted, without having reserved the right so to do and to the same extent as if the motion had not been made. A motion for a directed verdict which is not granted is not a waiver of trial by jury even though all parties to the action have moved for directed verdicts. A motion for a directed verdict shall state the specific grounds therefor. The order of the court granting a motion for a directed verdict is effective without any assent of the jury.

(b) Motion for Judgment Notwithstanding the Verdict. Whenever a motion for a directed verdict made at the close of all the evidence is denied or for any reason is not granted, the court is deemed to have submitted the action to the jury subject to a later determination of the legal questions raised by the motion. A party who has moved for a directed verdict may move to have the verdict and any judgment entered thereon set aside and to have judgment entered in accordance with his motion for a directed verdict; or if a verdict was not returned, such party may move for judgment in accordance with his motion for a directed verdict. A motion for a new trial may be joined with this motion, or a new trial may be prayed for in the alternative. If a verdict was returned the court may allow the judgment to stand or may reopen the judgment and either order a new trial or direct the entry of judgment as if the requested verdict had been directed. If no verdict was returned the court may direct the entry of judgment as if the requested verdict had been directed or may order a new trial.

(c) Same: Conditional Rulings on Grant of Motion.

(1) If the motion for judgment notwithstanding the verdict, provided for in subdivision (b) of this rule, is granted, the court shall also rule on motion for a new trial, if any, by determining whether it should be granted if the judgment is thereafter vacated or reversed, and shall specify the grounds for granting or denying the motion for the new trial. If the motion for a new trial is thus conditionally granted, the order thereon does not affect the finality of the judgment. In case the motion for a new trial has been conditionally granted and the judgment is reversed on appeal, the new trial shall proceed unless the appellate court has otherwise ordered. In case the motion for a new trial has been conditionally denied, the respondent on appeal may assert error in that denial; and if the judgment is reversed on appeal, subsequent proceedings shall be in accordance with the order of the appellate court.

(2) The party whose verdict has been set aside on motion for judgment notwithstanding the verdict may promptly after notice of the judgment serve a motion for a new trial pursuant to Rule 59.

(d) Same: Denial of Motion. If the motion for judgment notwithstanding the verdict is denied, the party who prevailed on that motion may, on appeal, assert grounds entitling him to a new trial in the event the appellate court concludes that the trial court erred in denying the motion for judgment notwithstanding the verdict. If the appellate court reverses the judgment, nothing in this rule precludes it from determining that a party is entitled to a new trial, or from directing the trial court to determine whether a new trial shall be granted.

(e) Time for Motion; Appeal; End of Term. The motion for judgment n.o.v. shall be made promptly after the jury is discharged, or in the discretion of the court not later than 10 days thereafter. The time for appeal for all parties shall be stayed by a timely motion for judgment n.o.v. and shall run from the receipt of written notice of entry of the order granting or denying such motion. The time within which to make the motion shall not be affected by the ending of a term of court or departure of the judge from the circuit, and the trial judge shall retain jurisdiction of the action for the purpose of hearing and disposing of such motion if not heard and disposed during the term. Except by consent of the parties, argument on the motion shall be heard in the circuit where the trial was held. The motion may in the discretion of the court be determined on briefs filed by the parties without oral argument.

(f) Judge to be Provided with Copy. A party filing a written motion under this rule shall provide a copy of the motion to the judge within ten (10) days after the filing of the motion.

[Amended effective May 1, 1986; August 30, 1998.]

Notes

This Rule 50 conforms to the Federal Rule, and to present State practice, with four stated changes.

1. The language of Code § 15–33–10 is added as the first sentence to Rule 50(a).

2. The motion for directed verdict may be made at the close of plaintiff's evidence, as well as at the close of all the evidence. This is an alternative to the present motion for involuntary dismissal (non-suit) which is also available.

3. The motion for judgment n.o.v. and for a new trial may be made in the alternative, which is also familiar to State practice.

4. The only substantive change in State procedure is that the parties may be allowed up to ten (10) days to file the motions, and the end of a term of court does not deprive the trial judge of jurisdiction to hear and determine them. Rule 50(e) is added for this purpose. This does not preclude the motions being made in open court, which will continue to be the practice in most cases, but the grounds for the motion and the ruling must be stated in writing or entered on the record to assist the appellate court in its decision in event of appeal.

Notes to 1986 Amendments

Post-trial motions are made promptly at the end of the trial, or at that time the court, upon motion, may grant an additional ten days to make them. The amendment to Rule 50(e) provides that the time for appeal commences upon the receipt of written notice of entry of the order disposing of post-trial motions, rather than the date when the order is signed by the court. Similar changes are made in Rules 52 and 59.

Note to 1998 Amendment

This amendment adds Rule 50(f). It is intended to help insure that the judge is promptly notified that the motion has been filed.

RULE 51. INSTRUCTIONS TO JURY: OBJECTION

At the close of the evidence or at such earlier time during the trial as the court reasonably directs, any party may file written requests that the court instruct the jury on the law as set forth in the requests. The court shall inform counsel of its proposed action upon the requests prior to their arguments to the jury, but the court shall instruct the jury after the arguments are completed. No party may assign as error the giving or the failure to give an instruction unless he objects thereto before the jury retires to consider its verdict, stating distinctly the matter to which he objects and the grounds for his objection. Opportunity shall be given to make the objection out of the hearing of the jury.

Notes

This is the language of Federal Rule 51. This Rule, as does the Federal Rule, requires the court to inform the lawyers of its proposed action on their requested instructions prior to argument. The language preserves Code § 15–27–100, opportunity to object to charge or request additional charge out of presence of the jury, and present Circuit Court Rule 11.

RULE 52. FINDINGS BY THE COURT

(a) Effect. In all actions tried upon the facts without a jury or with an advisory jury, the court shall find the facts specially and state separately its conclusions of law thereon, and judgment shall be entered pursuant to Rule 58; and in granting or refusing interlocutory injunctions the court shall similarly set forth the findings of fact and conclusions of law which constitute the grounds of its action. Requests for findings are not necessary for purposes of review. The findings of a master, to the extent that the court adopts them, shall be considered as the findings of the court. If an opinion or memorandum of decision is filed, it will be sufficient if the findings of fact and conclusions of law appear therein. Findings of fact and conclusions of law are unnecessary on decisions of motions under Rules 12 or 56 or any other motion except as provided in Rule 41(b).

(b) Amendment. Upon motion of a party made not later than 10 days after receipt of written notice of entry of judgment the court may amend its findings or make additional findings and may amend the judgment accordingly, and the motion may be made with a timely motion for a new trial. When findings of fact are made in actions tried by the court without a jury, the question of the sufficiency of the evidence to support the findings may thereafter be raised whether or not the party raising the question has made in the trial court an objection to such findings or has made a motion to amend them or a motion for judgment.

(c) Time for Appeal; End of Term. The time for appeal for all parties shall be stayed by a timely motion to amend the judgment and shall run from the receipt of written notice of entry of the order granting or denying such motion. The time within which to make the motion under this Rule shall not be affected by the ending of a term of court or departure of the judge from the circuit, and the trial judge shall retain jurisdiction of the action for the purpose of hearing and disposing of such motion if not heard and disposed during the term. Except by consent of the parties, argument on the motion shall be heard in the circuit where the trial was held. The motion may in the discretion of the court be determined on briefs filed by the parties without oral argument.

(d) Judge to be Provided with Copy. A party filing a written motion under this rule shall provide a copy of the motion to the judge within ten (10) days after the filing of the motion.

[Amended effective May 1, 1986; August 30, 1998.]

Notes

Rules 52(a) and (b) are the language of the Federal Rule. They incorporate the provisions of Code §§ 15–36–110, 15–35–130, and 15–35–140 on judgments and decrees in nonjury trials. Rule 52(c) is added to meet the needs of State practice. Rule 52(b), Motion to amend, as indicated by the words "In such actions," does not apply to cases tried by jury, but expands the right presently available in equity cases to all actions tried by the court without a jury. It is not to be confused with the right to correct clerical errors and omissions under Rule 60(a), or to open up judgments under Rule 60(b). The last sentence of Rule 52(b) makes clear that a motion to amend is optional, not a prerequisite to the right to appeal.

Notes to 1986 Amendments

The third sentence in the original Rule 52(a) could be construed to alter the scope of review of appellate courts when the "two judge" rule is inapplicable and, therefore, is deleted. The amendments to Rule 52(b) and (c) provide that the time for appeal commences upon the receipt of written notice of entry of the order disposing of such motions, rather than the date when the court signed the order. Similar amendments are made in Rules 50(e) and 59.

Note to 1998 Amendment

This amendment adds Rule 52(d). It is intended to help insure that the judge is promptly notified that the motion has been filed.

RULE 53. MASTERS AND SPECIAL REFEREES

(a) Master and Special Referee Defined. The term "master" means the master-in-equity for the county. The term "special referee" means a member of the South Carolina Bar to whom a matter has been referred under S.C. Code Ann. § 14–11–60.

(b) References. In an action where the parties consent, in a default case, or an action for foreclosure, some or all of the causes of action in a case may be referred to a master or special referee by order of a circuit judge or the clerk of court. In all other actions, the circuit court may, upon application of any party or upon its own motion, direct a reference of some or all of the causes of action in a case. Any party may request a jury pursuant to Rule 38 on any or all issues triable of right by a jury and, upon the filing of a jury demand, the matter shall be returned to the circuit court. A case shall not be referred to a master or special referee for the purpose of making a report to the circuit court. The clerk shall promptly provide the master or special referee with a copy of the order of reference.

(c) Powers. Once referred, the master or special referee shall exercise all power and authority which a circuit judge sitting without a jury would have in a similar matter.

(d) Compensation of Special Referees. The compensation of the special referee shall be paid by the parties in such amount as shall be set by the special referee, subject to review by the circuit court upon objection by any party within ten (10) days of receipt of the order.

(e) Appeals. When a matter has been referred, any appeal from any order or judgment issued by the master or special referee shall be to the Supreme Court or the Court of Appeals as provided by the South Carolina Appellate Court Rules.

[Amended effective May 1, 1986; July 1, 1994; June 1, 1999; September 1, 2001; September 1, 2002.]

Notes

This Rule 53 follows the Federal Rule as to form but is considerably modified to conform to State practice and needs. References in Federal Courts are rare, but absolutely necessary in State Courts, particularly to handle a large volume of State litigation such as foreclosures, partitions, and other equity matters. The State practice allowing judgment to be entered on the master's report in appropriate cases is preserved, as is the allowance of 10 days to file exceptions to the report. Other post-trial motions, such as a motion to amend judgment under Rule 52(b), would apply when the order of reference directs that judgment be entered on the master's report, just as they apply in actions tried by the court.

Notes to 1986 Amendments

Rule 53(c) is amended to make clear that the master has the same powers as a court sitting without a jury unless the order of reference limits his authority. Changes in that paragraph as well as Rule 53(d) leave the scheduling of the time and place of the hearings to the master. Rule 53(e)(1) is amended to remove the need for filing the transcript of proceedings if one has not been prepared, but Rule 53(e)(2) allows any party to obtain the transcript of proceedings before any hearing on exceptions to the master's report. Rule 53(e)(5) now authorizes the master to request briefs or proposed orders from counsel.

Note to 1994 Amendment

This Rule 53(b) amendment clarifies the authority of the clerk of court to issue orders of reference in default cases and where all the parties consent.

Note to 1999 Amendment

This amendment substantially revises this rule. It eliminates the practice of referring a matter for the purpose of making a report to the circuit court. Under the revised rule, the master or special referee will enter final judgment on any matter which is referred and any appeal from a decision of the master or special referee is to the Court of Appeals or the Supreme Court as provided by the South Carolina Appellate Court Rules. The detailed discussion of the powers of masters and special referees, and the procedure to be followed in matters pending before them, has been eliminated as unnecessary since the master or special referee has all the powers that a circuit court judge sitting without a jury would have in the matter and the procedure is that provided by the South Carolina Rules of Civil Procedure.

Note to 2001 Amendment

Rule 53(d) is amended to provide that fees for special referees are set by the special referee subject to review by the circuit court if a party timely objects.

Note to 2002 Amendment

The 2002 amendment permits referral of foreclosure cases to the master-in-equity by order of the clerk of court. If there are counterclaims requiring a jury trial, any party may file a demand for a jury under Rule 38 and the case will be returned to the circuit court.

VII. JUDGMENT

RULE 54. JUDGMENTS: COSTS

(a) Definition; Form. "Judgment" as used in these rules includes any decree or order which dismisses the action as to any party or finally determines the rights of any party. A judgment need not contain a recital of pleadings, the report of a master, or the record of prior proceedings.

(b) Judgment Upon Multiple Claims or Involving Multiple Parties. When more than one claim for relief is presented in an action, whether as a claim, counterclaim, cross-claim, or third-party claim, or when multiple parties are involved, the court may direct the entry of a final judgment as to one or more but fewer than all of the claims or parties only upon an express determination that there is no just reason for delay and upon an express direction for the entry of judgment. In the absence of such determination and direction, any order or other form of decision, however designated, which adjudicates fewer than all the claims or the rights and liabilities of fewer than all the parties shall not terminate the action as to any of the claims or parties, and the order or other form of decision is subject to revision at any time before the entry of judgment adjudicating all the claims and the rights and liabilities of all the parties.

(c) Demand for Judgment. A judgment by default shall not be different in kind from or exceed in amount that prayed for in the demand for judgment. Except as to a party against whom a judgment is entered by default, every final judgment shall grant the relief to which the party in whose favor it is rendered is entitled, even if the party has not demanded such relief in his pleadings.

(d) Costs. Except when express provision therefor is made either in a statute or in these rules, costs shall be allowed as of course to the prevailing party unless the court otherwise directs; but costs against the

State, its officers, and agencies shall be imposed only to the extent permitted by law. A motion for costs, supported by an affidavit that the costs are correct and were necessarily incurred in the action, may be filed by the prevailing party within 10 days of the receipt of written notice of the entry of final judgment. Upon notice that the matter has been appealed, the clerk may delay the taxation of costs until the appeal is completed. A party who prevails for the first time on appeal may file a motion for costs, as provided herein, within 10 days of written notice of the entry of the final judgment after appeal. After an appeal, the clerk shall include the costs incurred in the appeal as taxable costs as provided in Rule 58(b). Costs may be taxed by the clerk on one day's notice. On motion served within 10 days after receipt of notice, the action of the clerk may be reviewed by the court. Upon allowance, the costs shall be included in the judgment or decree.

(e) **Taxable Costs.** Taxable costs shall include:

(1) *Costs Authorized by Statute and Sanctions Imposed in Favor of Prevailing Party.* All sanctions including reasonable attorneys fees, if ordered, imposed upon another party and in favor of the prevailing party under any statute or Rule of Civil Procedure are taxable;

(2) *Fees of the Clerk.* All filing and recording fees charged by the clerk of the court in which the action was pending, or fees or costs taxed under Rule 222, SCACR, are taxable;

(3) *Fees of the Sheriff.* All fees and costs chargeable by the sheriff for service of summons and complaint, or subpoenas for trial witnesses who testified at trial or for the production of documents and materials actually used at trial, and all costs actually incurred by the sheriff in serving other process necessarily required in the case, including costs incurred attaching property, in caring for property attached, or in conducting the sale of attached property, including any bond, guarantee, sales commissions or insurance premiums, if required, are taxable;

(4) *Fees Incurred in Service of Process.* All fees and costs incurred in the service of summons and complaint, or subpoenas for the witnesses who testified at trial, or for the production of documents and materials actually used at trial, in an amount not to exceed that which may be charged by the sheriff for comparable services, are taxable;

(5) *Witnesses' Fees.* All witness fees and mileage actually traveled as specified in Rule 45(b)(1), paid to persons who were subpoenaed and testified at trial, are taxable;

(6) *Fees for Exemplification and Copies of Papers Necessarily Obtained for Trial.* The costs of one copy of a document introduced in evidence in lieu of the original; the fees of officials for certification of proof of the non-existence of documents; the cost of securing translation if the document translated is taxable or the translation is necessary for exemplification of matters before the court; the cost of maps and one copy of a photograph introduced into evidence, are taxable.

[Amended effective July, 1, 1993.]

Notes

Rule 54(a) adopts generally the definition of judgment found in Code § 15–35–10, rather than the language of the Federal Rule. The simple form of judgment as set out in the Appendix of Forms is sufficient, but may be expanded to include other matters as the court deems necessary. The judgment under Rule 58 is a separate document, distinct from underlying opinions, decisions and other orders. Its use will simplify entry, execution, enforcement and proof of judgment, and should state simply and directly the recovery or relief granted. It should be prepared by the court or by the clerk, but may be prepared by the prevailing party and submitted for signature by the judge, or by the clerk in appropriate cases. Rules 54(b)–(d) are substantially the Federal Rule; they represent the flexibility of the Rules procedure but with very little change from the provisions of Code §§ 15–35–40, 50, 70, 90, and 100.

Notes to 1993 Amendments

Rule 54(d) is amended to provide the procedure for filing for costs. The motion, supported by affidavit, shall be filed by the prevailing party within 10 days of notice of the entry of the final judgment. A later motion is untimely unless it is filed by a party who prevailed for the first time on appeal. The clerk may delay taxation of the costs until the completion of an appeal, and as required by Rule 58(b), add the taxable costs incurred on appeal at that time. The clerk taxes the costs on one day's notice to the opposing party, who has 10 days after the clerk's action to request a review by the trial court. Upon allowance, the taxable costs become part of the judgment.

Rule 54(e) provides a list of taxable costs. It is based upon the comparable local federal rule, and follows generally the state statutes that previously authorized taxable costs.

RULE 55. DEFAULT

(a) **Entry.** When a party against whom a judgment for affirmative relief is sought has failed to plead or otherwise defend as provided by these rules and that fact is made to appear by affidavit or otherwise, the clerk shall enter his default upon the calendar (file book).

(b) **Judgment.** Judgment by default may be entered as follows:

(1) *Cases Involving Liquidated Damages or Sum Certain Amounts.* When the claim of a party seeking judgment by default is for a liquidated amount, a sum certain or a sum which can by computation be made certain, the judge, upon motion or application of the party seeking default, and upon affidavit of the amount due, shall enter judgment for that amount and costs against the party against whom judgment by default is sought, if that party has been defaulted for failure to appear and if such party is not a minor or incompetent person. A verified pleading may be used in lieu of an

affidavit when the pleading contains information sufficient to determine or compute the sum certain.

(2) *All Other Cases.* In all other cases, the party entitled to a judgment by default shall apply to the court therefor; but no judgment by default shall be entered against a minor or incompetent person unless represented in the action by a guardian ad litem who has appeared therein. If the party against whom judgment by default is sought has appeared in the action, the party (or, if appearing by representative, the party's representative) shall be served with written notice of the motion or application for judgment at least 3 days prior to the hearing on such application. If, in order to enable the court to enter judgment or to carry it into effect, it is necessary to take an account or to determine the amount of damages or to establish the truth of any averment by evidence or to make an investigation of any other matter, the court may conduct such hearing or order such references as it deems necessary and proper and shall accord a right of trial by jury to the parties if a proper demand therefor has been made pursuant to Rule 38 and not withdrawn, or when and as required by any statute. Pursuant to Rule 5(a), notice of any trial or hearing on unliquidated damages shall also be given to parties in default by first class mail to the last known address of such party whether or not such party has appeared in the action.

(3) *Attorneys Fees.* If a party seeks to recover attorneys fees in connection with a default judgment, a hearing pursuant to subdivision (b)(2) of this rule shall be required unless: (i) the party seeking attorneys fees specifies in the motion for default judgment that such motion includes a request that the court award attorneys fees and also files an affidavit of attorneys fees; (ii) notice of such motion and affidavit is provided to the defaulted party by first class mail to the last known address of such party; and (iii) no objection is filed by the opposing party within 10 days of service of such motion and affidavit.

(4) *Judgments After Service by Publication; Affidavit; Undertaking.* In actions for the recovery of money only, when the summons has been served by publication and the defendant is a non-resident of the State, no default judgment shall be rendered unless the plaintiff or his agent at or before the time of making the application for judgment shall have been examined on oath respecting any payments that have been made to the plaintiff or any one for his use on account of the demand mentioned in the complaint, and shall show by affidavit that an attachment has been issued in the action and levied upon property belonging to the defendant, which affidavit shall contain a specific description of such property, and a statement of its value and shall be filed with proof of publication. Before judgment is rendered the plaintiff shall, unless the court in its discretion dispenses with the same, cause to be filed an undertaking in such amount as shall be ordered by the court with security to be approved by the court or the clerk thereof, that the plaintiff will abide the order of the court touching the restitution of any estate or effects which may be directed by such judgment to be transferred or delivered, or the restitution of any money that may be collected under, or by virtue of, such judgment, in event the defendant or his representative shall apply and be admitted to defend the action and shall succeed in such defense.

(c) Setting Aside Default. For good cause shown the court may set aside an entry of default and, if a judgment by default has been entered, may likewise set it aside in accordance with Rule 60(b).

(d) Plaintiffs, Counterclaimants, Cross-Claimants. The provisions of this rule apply whether the party entitled to the judgment by default is a plaintiff, a third-party plaintiff, or a party who has pleaded a cross-claim or counterclaim. In all cases a judgment by default is subject to the limitations of Rule 54(c).

(e) Judgment Against the State and Certain Other Parties. No judgment by default shall be entered against the State of South Carolina or an officer or agency thereof, against minors, incompetents, or parties to a suit for divorce or annulment of marriage or against a party upon whom service of summons was made by publication, and who did not subsequently make appearance in the action, or in any in rem action, unless the claimant establishes his claim to relief by evidence satisfactory to the Court.

[Amended effective May 1, 1986; August 30, 1998; June 1, 1999.]

Notes

These Rules 55(a) and 55(b)(1) are drawn from Federal Rule 55 with two changes. This Rule 55(a) requires that the Court enter all judgments by default and preserves Circuit Rule 15. Federal Rule 55(b) permits the Clerk to enter judgments by default for sums certain, if there has been no appearance, and if the defendant is not a minor or incompetent person; and that provision was deleted. The language directing the Clerk to enter the default upon the calendar and a reference to Rule 38, Jury Trial of Right, is added. These changes clarify, but do not change, the operation of the Rule.

This Rule 55(b)(2) does not appear in the Federal Rule. It is added to preserve Circuit Court Rule 38, requiring attachment of property against which the money judgment may be collected, when defendant has not been personally served and does not appear in the action.

Rules 55(c) and 55(d) are identical to the Federal Rules. Rule 55(e) has been modified to make reference to State government, and add all minors, incompetents, and divorce and annulment actions, to the category of cases in which the claimant must establish the claim by evidence in the event of default.

Notes to 1986 Amendments

This amendment [to Rule 55(e)] includes in rem actions in those which the court takes proof on the value of the claim, to insure that a default judgment in any in rem action is limited to the value of the claim rather than the value of the property seized.

Note to the 1998 Amendments

The language of Rule 55(b)(1) is new and is based on the federal rule. The phrase "liquidated damages" contained in the first sentence was added since this is the terminology which has traditionally been used in South Carolina. The last sentence relating to verified pleadings is not contained in the federal rule.

The language of Rule 55(b)(2) is substantially the language of Rule 55(b)(1) prior to these amendments with the addition of the last sentence. The last sentence simply incorporates the notice requirements of Rule 5(a) into the text of this rule.

Rule 55(b)(3) is new and has no counterpart in the federal rules. It provides a procedure for requesting attorneys fees as part of a default judgment. Rule 55(b)(4) is the language of Rule 55(b)(2) prior to these amendments.

Note to 1999 Amendments

The 1998 Amendments to Rule 55 gave a clerk of court authority to enter default judgments in cases where judgment is sought for a liquidated amount or for a sum certain. These amendments remove that authority and provide that default judgments, regardless of the nature of the damages being sought, may only be entered by a judge.

RULE 56. SUMMARY JUDGMENT

(a) For Claimant. A party seeking to recover upon a claim, counterclaim, or cross-claim or to obtain a declaratory judgment may, at any time after the expiration of 30 days from the commencement of the action or after service of a motion for summary judgment by the adverse party, move with or without supporting affidavits for a summary judgment in his favor upon all or any part thereof.

(b) For Defending Party. A party against whom a claim, counterclaim, or cross-claim is asserted or a declaratory judgment is sought may, at any time, move with or without supporting affidavits for a summary judgment in his favor as to all or any part thereof.

(c) Motions and Proceedings Thereon. The motion shall be served at least 10 days before the time fixed for the hearing. The adverse party may serve opposing affidavits not later than two days before the hearing. The judgment sought shall be rendered forthwith if the pleadings, depositions, answers to interrogatories, and admissions on file, together with the affidavits, if any, show that there is no genuine issue as to any material fact and that the moving party is entitled to a judgment as a matter of law. A summary judgment, interlocutory in character, may be rendered on the issue of liability alone although there is a genuine issue as to the amount of damages.

(d) Case Not Fully Adjudicated on Motion. If on motion under this rule judgment is not rendered upon the whole case or for all the relief asked and a trial is necessary, the court at the hearing of the motion, by examining the pleadings and the evidence before it and by interrogating counsel, shall if practicable ascertain what material facts exist without substantial controversy and what material facts are actually and in good faith controverted. It may thereupon make an order specifying the facts that appear without substantial controversy, including the extent to which the amount of damages or other relief is not in controversy, and directing such further proceedings in the action as are just. Upon the trial of the action the facts so specified shall be deemed established, and the trial shall be conducted accordingly.

(e) Form of Affidavits; Further Testimony; Defense Required. Supporting and opposing affidavits shall be made on personal knowledge, shall set forth such facts as would be admissible in evidence, and shall show affirmatively that the affiant is competent to testify to the matters stated therein. Sworn or certified copies of all papers or parts thereof referred to in an affidavit shall be attached thereto or served therewith. The court may permit affidavits to be supplemented or opposed by depositions, answers to interrogatories, or further affidavits. When a motion for summary judgment is made and supported as provided in this rule, an adverse party may not rest upon the mere allegations or denials of his pleading, but his response, by affidavits or as otherwise provided in this rule, must set forth specific facts showing that there is a genuine issue for trial. If he does not so respond, summary judgment, if appropriate, shall be entered against him.

(f) When Affidavits Are Unavailable. Should it appear from the affidavits of a party opposing the motion that he cannot for reasons stated present by affidavit facts essential to justify his opposition, the court may refuse the application for judgment or may order a continuance to permit affidavits to be obtained or depositions to be taken or discovery to be had or may make such order as is just.

(g) Affidavits Made in Bad Faith. Should it appear to the satisfaction of the court at any time that any of the affidavits presented pursuant to this rule are presented in bad faith or solely for the purpose of delay, the court shall forthwith order the party employing them to pay to the other party the amount of the reasonable expenses which the filing of the affidavits caused him to incur, including reasonable attorney's fees, and any offending party or attorney may be adjudged guilty of contempt.

[Amended effective May 1, 1986.]

Notes

This is the language of Federal Rule 56. Present Circuit Court Rule 44, Summary Judgment, is substantially the same as the Federal Rule except for the following:

Rule 56(d) Case Not Fully Adjudicated on Motion, does not appear in the present Circuit Court Rule. This Rule makes the findings of uncontested facts discretionary with the court rather than mandatory; but is valuable in disposing of uncontested issues at trial.

Present Circuit Court Rule 44 has minor textual matters that do not appear in the Federal Rule. Paragraphs (a) and (b) of the Circuit Court Rule have the concluding phrase, "notice of motion shall state the grounds for the motion", which is rendered unnecessary by Rule 7(b). The second sentence of Rule 56(e) permits other relevant materials to be considered by the court, and is a needed addition.

Notes to 1986 Amendments

This change [to Rule 56(c)] conforms the time for serving affidavits in opposition to a motion for summary judgment with the general standard in Rule 6(d).

RULE 57. DECLARATORY JUDGMENTS

The procedure for obtaining a declaratory judgment pursuant to Code §§ 15–53–10 through 15–53–140, shall be in accordance with these rules, and the right to trial by jury may be demanded under the circumstances and in the manner provided in Rules 38 and 39. The existence of another adequate remedy does not preclude a judgment for declaratory relief in cases where it is appropriate. The court may order a speedy hearing of an action for a declaratory judgment and may advance it on the calendar.

Notes

This is the same as the language of Federal Rule 57 except that the appropriate State Code references are substituted for the Federal statute.

RULE 58. ENTRY OF JUDGMENT

(a) Entry Upon Verdict or Decision. Subject to the provisions of Rule 54(b):

(1) upon a general verdict of a jury, or upon a decision by the court that a party shall recover only a sum certain or costs or that all relief shall be denied, the clerk, unless the court otherwise orders, shall forthwith prepare, sign, and enter the judgment without awaiting any direction by the court;

(2) upon a decision by the court granting other relief, or upon a special verdict or a general verdict accompanied by answers to interrogatories, the court shall promptly prepare the form of the judgment, or direct counsel to promptly prepare the form of judgment, to which may be attached the decision, order or opinion of the court, and after review and approval by the court, the clerk shall promptly enter it.

Every judgment shall be set forth on a separate document. A judgment is effective only when so set forth and entered in the record. Entry of the judgment should not be delayed for the taxing of costs.

(b) Judgments of Appellate Court. When a judgment rendered by an appellate court is remitted to the trial court the clerk shall adjust the costs and disbursements in the appellate court to which any party may be entitled upon due notice, as provided in the case of adjustment of costs in the trial court; and he shall record such judgment and enter an abstract thereof in like manner as provided in the case of judgments rendered by the trial court. Cross references shall be made to both the judgment of the trial court appealed from and the judgment of the appellate court at the place of their entries upon the calendar and upon the abstracts of judgment.

[Amended effective May 1, 1986.]

Notes

Rule 58(a) is the same as the Federal Rule. The requirement of old Circuit Court Rule 3, that judgments on jury verdicts or orders of judgment rendered during the term should be entered at the expiration of five days after the court has adjourned for the term, is abolished. The current rule that each week of court is a separate term has eliminated the necessity for this provision. Rule 58(b) is added to preserve Circuit Court Rule 40.

Notes to 1986 Amendments

This amendment [to Rule 58(a)] clarifies and simplifies the procedure for entry of judgment in cases where there is not a general verdict, a recovery of a sum certain or the denial of all relief. When more complex relief is ordered, the court is responsible for preparing the form of judgment which may be accomplished by attaching the decision or order of the court to the judgment form, or in appropriate cases, the court may direct counsel to prepare the judgment form which the court then reviews and, if approved, the judgment is entered by the clerk.

RULE 59. NEW TRIALS; AMENDMENT OF JUDGMENTS

(a) Grounds. A new trial may be granted to all or any of the parties and on all or part of the issues (1) in an action in which there has been a trial by jury, for any of the reasons for which new trials have heretofore been granted in actions at law in the courts of the State; and (2) in an action tried without a jury, for any of the reasons for which rehearings have heretofore been granted in the courts of the State. On a motion for a new trial in an action tried without a jury, the court may open the judgment if one has been entered, take additional testimony, amend findings of fact and conclusions of law or make new findings and conclusions, and direct the entry of a new judgment.

(b) Time for Motion. The motion for a new trial shall be made promptly after the jury is discharged, or in the discretion of the court not later than 10 days thereafter. In non-jury actions the motion shall be made not later than 10 days after the receipt of written notice of the entry of judgment or of the filing of an order disposing of the action, if no judgment has been entered.

(c) Time for Serving Affidavits. When a motion for new trial is based upon affidavits they shall be served with the motion. The opposing party has 10 days after such service within which to serve opposing affidavits, which period may be extended for an additional period not exceeding 20 days either by the court for good cause shown or by the parties by written stipulation. The court may permit reply affidavits.

(d) On Initiative of Court. Not later than 10 days after entry of judgment, the court of its own initiative may order a new trial for any reason for which it might have granted a new trial on motion of a party. After giving the parties notice and an opportunity to be heard on the matter, the court may grant a motion for a new trial, timely served, for a reason not stated in the motion. In either case, the court shall specify in the order the grounds therefor.

(e) Motion to Alter or Amend a Judgment. A motion to alter or amend the judgment shall be served not later than 10 days after receipt of written notice of the entry of the order.

(f) Time for Appeal; End of Term. The time for appeal for all parties shall be stayed by a timely motion under this Rule and shall run from the receipt of written notice of entry of the order granting or denying such motions. The time within which to make the motions under this Rule shall not be affected by the ending of a term of court or departure of the judge from the circuit, and the trial judge shall retain jurisdiction of the action for the purpose of hearing and disposing of such motion if not heard and disposed during the term. Except by consent of the parties, argument on the motion shall be heard in the circuit where the trial was held. The motion may in the discretion of the court be determined on briefs filed by the parties without oral argument.

(g) Judge to be Provided with Copy. A party filing a written motion under this rule shall provide a copy of the motion to the judge within ten (10) days after the filing of the motion.

[Amended effective May 1, 1986; August 30, 1998.]

Notes

This Rule 59 is substantially the Federal Rule. It is consistent with Code § 15-27-150. Rule 59(b) provides that if the motions are not made and heard during the term, the more precise and definite Federal practice of allowing 10 days after the entry of judgment to make the motion is more equitable. Rule 59(f) is added to provide that departure from the circuit does not deprive the trial judge of jurisdiction to rule on motions under this Rule and Rules 50, 52 and 60. It also provides flexibility for the trial judge to determine the motions on briefs without oral argument.

Notes to 1986 Amendments

In jury trials, post-trial motions are made promptly at the end of the trial, or at that time the court, upon motion, may grant an additional ten days to make them. These amendments to Rules 59(b) and (e) and (f) conform the language to that of Rules 50 and 52, and provide that the time for appeal commences upon the receipt of written notice of entry of the order disposing of such motions which was prior state practice, rather than the date when the court signed the order which is the practice in the federal courts.

Note to 1998 Amendment

This amendment adds Rule 59(g). It is intended to help insure that the judge is promptly notified that the motion has been filed.

RULE 60. RELIEF FROM JUDGMENT OR ORDER

(a) Clerical Mistakes. Clerical mistakes in judgments, orders or other parts of the record and errors therein arising from oversight or omission may be corrected by the court at any time of its own initiative or on the motion of any party and after such notice, if any, as the court orders. During the pendency of an appeal, leave to correct the mistake must be obtained from the appellate court. The ending of a term of court or departure from the circuit shall not operate to deprive the trial judge of jurisdiction to correct such mistakes. A party filing a written motion under this rule shall provide a copy of the motion to the judge within ten (10) days after the filing of the motion.

(b) Mistakes; Inadvertence; Excusable Neglect; Newly Discovered Evidence; Fraud, etc. On motion and upon such terms as are just, the court may relieve a party or his legal representative from a final judgment, order, or proceeding for the following reasons:

(1) mistake, inadvertence, surprise, or excusable neglect;

(2) newly discovered evidence which by due diligence could not have been discovered in time to move for a new trial under Rule 59(b);

(3) fraud, misrepresentation, or other misconduct of an adverse party;

(4) the judgment is void;

(5) the judgment has been satisfied, released, or discharged, or a prior judgment upon which it is based has been reversed or otherwise vacated, or it is no longer equitable that the judgment should have prospective application.

The motion shall be made within a reasonable time, and for reasons (1), (2), and (3) not more than one year after the judgment, order or proceeding was entered or taken. A motion under this subdivision (b) does not affect the finality of a judgment or suspend its operation. This rule does not limit the power of a court to entertain an independent action to relieve a party from a judgment, order, or proceeding, or to set aside a judgment for fraud upon the court. During the pendency of an appeal, leave to make the motion must be obtained from the appellate court. Writs of coram nobis, coram vobis, audita querela, and bills of review and bills in the nature of a bill of review, are abolished, and the procedure for obtaining any relief from a judgment shall be by motion as prescribed in these rules or by an independent action.

[Amended effective July 1, 1994; August 30, 1998.]

Note

This Rule 60 is drawn from the Federal Rule. There are minor changes in the language of the Federal Rule. The last sentence of 60(a) was added permitting the trial judge to correct clerical errors even after departure from the circuit. Rule 60(b) deletes subsection (6) of the Federal Rule which permits relief for "any other reason justifying relief from the operation of the judgment." In the Federal Rule subsection (6) has created ambiguity about what is included.

Finally, Rule 60(b) provides, leave to make the motion need not be obtained from any appellate court except during such time as an appeal from the judgment is actually before the appellate court. This permits the motion to be made before the trial court. The United States Supreme Court approved a similar result in Standard Oil Co. v. U.S., 429 U.S. 17, 97 S.Ct. 31, 50 L.Ed.2d 21 (1976). This change will not, except in civil actions, affect S.C. Supreme Court Rule 24, Motions for New Trial upon After-discovered Evidence, which now requires leave by the Supreme Court before the motion can be made in the trial court.

Rule 60(b) is substantially the same as Code § 15-27-130. There are two differences. First, existing State law provides for relief from a "judgment taken against him through his mistake." Rule 60(b) deletes "his" and thus there may be a motion for relief from other mistakes. Second, the statute provides that the relief must be sought within one year. This Rule retains the one year limitation for Rule 60(b)(1)-(3) for mistake, inadvertence, excusable neglect, newly-discovered evidence, and fraud; but permits relief under Rule 60(b)(4) and (5) after one year, but within a "reasonable time" when the judgment is void or the judgment has been satisfied, avoiding the necessity of bringing a new action to set aside the judgment in such cases after one year. (Editor's Note: Effective September 1, 1990, the Supreme Court Rules were repealed by the South Carolina Appellate Court Rules.)

Notes to 1994 Amendments

The amendment to Rule 60(a) and (b) clarifies that leave of the appellate court is necessary to correct a clerical mistake or to make a motion to set aside an order of judgment while the appeal is pending. An appeal is pending from the time the notice of appeal is served until the issuance of the remittitur. See Rules 203, 204 and 221(b), SCACR.

Note to 1998 Amendment

This amendment adds a requirement to Rule 60(a) that a copy of any written motion be provided to the judge. It is intended to help insure that the judge is promptly notified that the motion has been filed.

RULE 61. HARMLESS ERROR

No error in either the admission or the exclusion of evidence and no error or defect in any ruling or order or in anything done or omitted by the court or by any of the parties is ground for granting a new trial or for setting aside a verdict or for vacating, modifying or otherwise disturbing a judgment or order, unless refusal to take such action appears to the court inconsistent with substantial justice. The court at every stage of the proceeding must disregard any error or defect in the proceeding which does not affect the substantial rights of the parties.

Notes

This is the language of Federal Rule 61, and retains the effect of Code § 15-27-140.

RULE 62. STAY OF PROCEEDINGS TO ENFORCE A JUDGMENT

(a) Automatic Stay; Exceptions—Injunctions, Receivership, and Accountings. Except as stated herein, no execution shall issue upon a judgment nor shall proceedings be taken for its enforcement until the expiration of 10 days after its entry. Unless otherwise ordered by the court, an interlocutory or final judgment in an action for an injunction or in a receivership action, or a judgment or order directing an accounting, shall not be stayed during the period after its entry and until an appeal is taken or during the pendency of an appeal. The provisions of subdivision (c) of this rule govern the suspending, modifying, restoring, or granting of an injunction during the pendency of an appeal.

(b) Stay on Motion for New Trial or for Judgment. In its discretion and on such conditions for the security of the adverse party as are proper, the court may stay the execution of or any proceedings to enforce a judgment pending the disposition of a motion for a new trial or to alter or amend a judgment made pursuant to Rule 59, or of a motion for relief from a judgment or order made pursuant to Rule 60, or of a motion for judgment in accordance with a motion for a directed verdict made pursuant to Rule 50, or of a motion for amendment to the findings or for additional findings made pursuant to Rule 52(b).

(c) Injunction Pending Appeal. When an appeal is taken from an interlocutory or final judgment granting, dissolving, or denying an injunction, the court in its discretion may suspend, modify, restore, or grant an injunction during the pendency of the appeal upon such terms as to bond or otherwise as it considers proper for the security of the rights of the adverse party.

(d) Stay Upon Appeal. When an appeal is taken, a party, by giving a supersedeas bond, may obtain a stay subject to the exceptions contained in subdivision (a) of this rule and the South Carolina Appellate Court Rules. The bond may be given at or after the time of filing the notice of appeal or of procuring the order allowing the supersedeas as the case may be. The stay is effective when the supersedeas bond is approved by the court.

(e) Stay in Favor of the State or Agency Thereof. When an appeal is taken by the State or an officer or agency thereof or by direction of any department of the Government of the State and the operation or enforcement of the judgment is stayed, no bond, obligation, or other security shall be required from the appellant.

(f) Stay According to Statute. The provisions of this Rule 62 shall be considered as cumulative to and not superseding the right of any party to a stay of execution accorded by statute; except that the time limits and provision for supersedeas bond provided by this Rule 62 shall apply in all proceedings for stay of execution or order of supersedeas.

(g) Power of Appellate Court Not Limited. The provisions in this rule do not limit any power of an appellate court or of a judge or justice thereof to stay proceedings during the pendency of an appeal or to suspend, modify, restore, or grant an injunction during the pendency of an appeal or to make any order appropriate to preserve the status quo or the effectiveness of the judgment subsequently to be entered. An application for such relief should first be made to the trial court under Rule 62(c) or (d), but when such application is not practicable it may first be made to an appellate court or a judge or justice thereof.

(h) Stay of Judgment as to Multiple Claims or Multiple Parties. When a court has ordered a final judgment under the conditions stated in Rule 54(b), the court may stay enforcement of that judgment until the entering of a subsequent judgment or judgments and may prescribe such conditions as are necessary to secure the benefit thereof to the party in whose favor the judgment is entered.

[Amended effective September 1, 1990.]

Notes

This Rule 62 is drawn from the Federal Rule. Rule 62(a) provides for an automatic stay of execution for 10 days in all but injunctive actions or those involving receiverships or accounting. Stays in those proceedings, as well as motions for new trial under Rule 59, for relief from judgment under Rule 60, or for judgment in accordance with a motion for directed verdict under Rule 50, or for amendment of findings under Rule 52(b) are discretionary with the court. Stays of injunctive actions or those on appeal are covered by Rule 62(c) and (d). Rule 62(h) permits stays when some, but not all, claims have been reduced to judgment under Rule 54(b). This Rule replaces Circuit Court Rules 64, 65 and 66, without substantial change. Likewise, Supreme Court Rule 18, which permits the Supreme Court in actions pending in that court to stay proceedings in the court below, is not affected because of the specific language of Rule 62(g).

Notes to 1990 Amendments

This amendment modifies Rule 62(d) to make reference to the South Carolina Appellate Court Rules which have replaced the Supreme Court Rules.

RULE 63. DISABILITY OF A JUDGE

If at any time after a trial or hearing has been commenced, but before the final order or judgment has been issued, the judge is unable to proceed, a successor judge shall be assigned. The successor judge may proceed upon certifying familiarity with the record and determining that the proceedings may be completed without prejudice to the parties. In a hearing or a trial without a jury, the successor judge shall, at the request of a party, recall any witness whose testimony is material and disputed and who is available to testify without undue burden. A successor judge may also provide for the recall of any witnesses.

[Amended effective April 27, 2004.]

Notes

Note to 2004 Amendment

The 2004 Amendment rewrote this Rule to provide a clear procedure when a judge who has heard some or all of a case is unable to proceed. The language is similar to Rule 63 of the Federal Rules of Civil Procedure.

VIII. PROVISIONAL AND FINAL REMEDIES AND SPECIAL PROCEEDINGS

RULE 64. REMEDIES FOR SEIZURE, REMEDIES NOT PROVIDED

(a) Seizure of Person or Property. At the commencement of and during the course of an action all remedies providing for seizure of person or property for the purpose of securing satisfaction of the judgment ultimately to be entered in the action are available under the circumstances and in the manner provided by law.

(b) Remedies Not Provided. In any case where no provision is made by statute or by these rules, the procedures and remedies shall be according to the practice as it has heretofore existed in the courts of this State.

Notes

This Rule 64(a) is the language of the first sentence of the Federal Rule, the remainder being applicable only to actions in Federal Courts. Rule 64(b) is added to preserve all remedies not addressed by statute or these Rules, but the procedure must conform to the Rules when the remedy is specifically included; i.e., Rule 65, Injunctions and Mandamus; Rule 71, Foreclosure, etc.

RULE 65. INJUNCTIONS; MANDAMUS, HABEAS CORPUS, AND OTHER REMEDIAL WRITS

(a) Temporary Injunction; Notice. No temporary injunction shall be issued without notice to the adverse party.

(b) Temporary Restraining Order; Notice; Hearing; Duration. No temporary restraining order shall be granted without notice of motion for the order to the adverse party unless it clearly appears from specific facts shown by affidavit or by a verified complaint that immediate and irreparable injury, loss or damage will result to the applicant before notice can be served and a hearing had thereon. Every temporary restraining order granted without notice shall be endorsed with the date and hour of issuance; shall be filed forthwith in the clerk's office and entered of record; shall be served, together with a summons and complaint in the event no summons and complaint have previously been served in the action, upon the adverse party in accordance with the provisions of Rule 4; shall define the injury and state why it is irreparable and why the order was granted without notice; and shall expire by its terms within such time after entry, not to exceed 10 days, as the court fixes, unless within the time so fixed the order, for good cause shown, is extended for a like period or unless the party against whom the order is directed consents that it may be extended for a longer period. The reasons for the extension shall be entered of record. In case a temporary restraining order is granted without notice, the motion for a temporary injunction shall be set down for hearing at the earliest possible time and takes precedence of all matters except older matters of the same character; and when the motion comes on for hearing the party who obtained the temporary restraining order shall proceed with the application for a temporary injunction and, if he does not do so, the court shall dissolve the temporary restraining order. On two days' notice to the party who obtained the temporary restraining order without notice or on such shorter notice to that party as the court may prescribe, the adverse party may appear and move its dissolution or modification and in that event the court shall proceed to hear and determine such motion as expeditiously as the ends of justice require.

(c) Security. Except in divorce, child custody and non-support actions where the giving of security is discretionary, no restraining order or temporary injunction shall issue except upon the giving of security by the applicant, in such sum as the court deems proper, for the payment of such costs and damages as may be incurred or suffered by any party who is found to have been wrongfully enjoined or restrained. No such security shall be required of the State or of an officer or agency thereof. A surety upon a bond or undertaking under this rule submits himself to the jurisdiction of the court and irrevocably appoints the clerk of court as his agent upon whom any papers affecting his liability on the bond or undertaking may be served. His liability may be enforced on motion without necessity of an independent action. The motion and such notice of the motion as the court prescribes may be served on the clerk of court who shall forthwith mail copies to the persons giving the security if their addresses are known.

(d) Form and Scope of Injunction or Restraining Order. Every order granting an injunction and every restraining order shall set forth the reasons for its issuance; shall be specific in terms; shall describe in reasonable detail, and not by reference to the complaint or other document, the act or acts sought to be restrained; and is binding only upon the parties to the action, their officers, agents, servants, employees, and attorneys, and upon those persons in active concert or participation with them who receive actual notice of the order by personal service or otherwise.

(e) Injunction to Suspend Business. No temporary restraining order shall be granted to suspend the general and ordinary business of an individual, partnership, association or corporation. Same may be suspended only by injunction after notice.

(f)(1) *Remedial Writs.* No writ of mandamus, habeas corpus, or other remedial writ shall be granted without notice of motion for the writ to the adverse party, which notice shall be served, together with the summons and complaint, in event no summons and complaint have previously been filed and served in the action, upon the adverse party in accordance with the provisions of Rules 4 and 5. Such notice and motion shall be supported by affidavit or verified complaint setting forth clearly the facts entitling the moving party to such writ. The motion shall be heard upon such notice as the court may prescribe, and the court shall proceed to hear and determine such motion as expeditiously as the ends of justice require. Unless a different time be prescribed by the court, the adverse party shall plead to the complaint and respond to such motion in the time prescribed by these rules for other civil actions.

(2) *Damages; Costs; Fees.* A claim for any other relief to which a party may be entitled in the action may be joined with a claim for writ of mandamus, habeas corpus, or other remedial writ, in accordance with these rules, including a claim for damages. The prevailing party upon the motion for such writ shall be entitled to recover costs in accordance with the practice as it heretofore existed in the courts of this State, including attorneys fees where proper.

[Amended effective May 1, 1986.]

Notes

This Rule 65, except for the additions concerning mandamus, habeas corpus and other remedial writs, is substantially the Federal Rule which, in turn, is very much the same as present State practice. To conform to the "one form of action" requirement of Rule 2, a summons and verified complaint must be filed and served with the notice and motion for temporary injunction, unless the action has already been commenced by filing and service of the summons and complaint. An action may no longer be commenced by the service of an order or "rule to show cause" only. This Rule 65 makes it clear that the various remedial writs are not causes of action but remedies or relief, the right to which must be supported by the law and the facts. Therefore, the injunction or other writ granted does not become permanent or final until final judgment in the action. Rule 65(f) is added to the Federal Rule to both preserve and modernize the procedure for obtaining other remedial writs in addition to injunction.

Notes to 1986 Amendments

This amendment [to Rule 65(c)] makes clear that the court may, but need not, order the applicant seeking an injunction or restraining order in a Family Court case to give security.

RULE 66. RECEIVERS

(a) Action Where Receiver Appointed. An action in which a receiver has been appointed shall not be dismissed except by order of the court. The practice in the administration of estates by receivers or by other similar officers appointed by the court shall be in accordance with the laws of this State. In all other respects the action in which the appointment of a receiver is sought or which is brought by or against a receiver is governed by these rules.

(b) Powers of Receiver. In addition to the powers conferred by law, every receiver of the property and effects of a debtor shall, unless restricted by order of the court, have general power and authority to sue for and collect the debts, demands and rents belonging to the debtor, and to compromise and settle such as are of a doubtful value. He may also sue and defend in the name of the debtor where it is necessary or proper for him to do so.

Notes

This Rule 66(a) is substantially identical to the Federal Rule and the present State practice. Rule 66(b) is added to preserve present Circuit Court Rule 69.

RULE 67. DEPOSIT IN COURT

In an action in which any part of the relief sought is a judgment for a sum of money or the disposition of a sum of money or the disposition of any other thing capable of delivery, a party, upon notice to every other party, and by leave of court, may deposit with the court all or any part of such sum or thing, whether or not that party claims all or any part of the sum or thing. Money paid into the court under this rule shall be deposited as directed by the court in any bank or institution authorized to receive public funds, and shall be withdrawn only upon the check of the clerk of court in favor of the party to whom the order of the court directs.

Notes

This Rule 67 is substantially the Federal Rule, modified in the second sentence to conform to State statutes governing deposit of public funds. It expands present practice to permit any party, not simply trustees, to make such deposit with leave of the court.

Notes to 1986 Amendments

The phrase at the end of the first sentence was inadvertently deleted in the printing of the original rule.

RULE 68. OFFER OF JUDGMENT

(a) Offer of Judgment. Any party in a civil action, except a domestic relations action, may file, no later than twenty days before the trial date, a written offer of judgment signed by the offeror or his attorney, directed to the opposing party, offering to take judgment in the offeror's favor, or to allow judgment to be taken against the offeror for a sum stated therein, or to the effect specified in the offer. Service of the offer of judgment shall be made as provided in these rules. Within twenty days after service of the offer of judgment or at least ten days prior to the trial date, whichever date is earlier, the offeree or his attorney may file a written acceptance of the offer of judgment. Upon the filing, the court shall immediately issue the judgment and the clerk shall enter the judgment as provided in the offer of judgment. If the offer of judgment is not accepted within twenty days after notification, or prior to or on the tenth day before the actual trial date, whichever date occurs first, the offer shall be considered rejected and evidence thereof is not admissible except in a proceeding after trial to fix costs, interest, attorney's fees, and other recoverable monies. Any offeror may withdraw an offer of judgment prior to its acceptance or prior to the date on which it would be considered rejected by giving notice to the offeree or his attorney as provided in these rules. Any offeror may file a subsequent offer of judgment in any amount which supersedes any earlier offer that was rejected by the offeree or withdrawn by the offeror, and, on filing and service, terminates any rights to interest or costs under the superseded offer. An offer is not considered rejected by a counter offer and shall remain effective until accepted, rejected, or withdrawn as provided in this subsection. All offers of judgment and any acceptance of offers of judgment must be included by the clerk in the record of the case.

(b) Consequences of Non–Acceptance. If an offer of judgment is not accepted and the offeror obtains a verdict or determination at least as favorable as the rejected offer, the offeror shall recover from the offeree: (1) any administrative, filing, or other court costs from the date of the offer until the entry of the judgment; (2) if the offeror is a plaintiff, eight percent interest computed on the amount of the verdict or award from the date of the offer to the entry of judgment; or (3) if the offeror is a defendant, reduction from the judgment or award of eight percent interest computed on the amount of the verdict or award from the date of the offer to the entry of the judgment.

(c) This rule shall not abrogate the contractual rights of any party concerning the recovery of attorney's fees or other monies in accordance with the provision of any written contract between the parties to the action.

[Amended effective May 1, 1986; July 1, 1994; May 3, 2006.]

Notes

This Rule 68 is essentially Code §§ 15–21–40, 15–21–50, and 15–65–130 and is not identical to the Federal Rule.

Notes to 1986 Amendments

This material [last sentence of Rule 68(a); Rule 68(b)] was formerly found in S.C. Code §§ 15–21–10, 30 and 40, and is added to make the procedure under the rule consistent with prior practice.

Notes to 1994 Amendments

Rule 68(a) and (b) are amended to permit a defending party to recover costs when the plaintiff fails to recover any judgment in his favor as well as when the plaintiff's recovery is less than the offer of judgment.

Note to 2006 Amendment

This amendment makes this provision consistent with S.C. Code Ann. Section 15–35–400, which became effective July 1, 2005.

RULE 69. EXECUTION

Process to enforce a judgment for the payment of money shall be a writ of execution, unless the court directs otherwise. The procedure on execution, in proceedings supplementary to and in aid of a judgment, and in proceedings on and in aid of execution shall be as provided by law. In the aid of the judgment or execution, the judgment creditor or his successor in interest when that interest appears of record, may examine any person, including the judgment debtor, in the manner provided in these rules for obtaining discovery.

Notes

This Rule 69 is substantially the Federal Rule, omitting references to Federal statutes. It preserves by reference present State practice under S.C.Code Sections 15–39–10 through 15–39–150, and also brings to the assistance of the judgment creditor the right to obtain discovery under Rules 26 through 37.

RULE 70. JUDGMENT FOR SPECIFIC ACTS: VESTING TITLE

If a judgment directs a party to execute a conveyance of land or to deliver deeds or other documents or to perform any other specific act and the party fails to comply within the time specified, the court may direct the act to be done at the cost of the disobedient party by some other person appointed by the court and the act when so done has like effect as if done by the party. On application of the party entitled to performance, the court may issue a writ of attachment or sequestration against the property of the disobedient party to compel obedience to the judgment. The court may also in proper cases adjudge the party in contempt. If real or personal property is within the state, the court in lieu of directing a conveyance thereof may enter a judgment divesting the title of any party and vesting it in others and such judgment has the effect of a conveyance executed in due form of law. When any order or judgment is for the delivery of possession, the party in whose favor it is entered is entitled to a writ of execution or assistance upon application to the clerk.

Notes

This Rule 70 is the same as the Federal Rule except changing references to the State rather than the United States. It preserves the practice of allowing the clerk to issue writs of attachment or sequestration to obtain delivery of possession of property. The Rule represents no change to present State practice, but defines the court's powers more precisely.

RULE 71. FORECLOSURE AND PARTITION

(a) Proceedings, Reference. Actions to foreclose liens or obtain partition of real property shall be tried by the court, and shall ordinarily be referred to a master pursuant to Rule 53. In foreclosure actions the judge or master shall compute the amounts due the plaintiff and any other claimants, which amounts when determined shall be the total debt due to each. The total debt shall as a minimum set forth clearly the principal due upon default, the rate of interest and interest from date of default to hearing date, any other relevant interest charged, any amounts due or to be credited on escrow items, the taxable costs of collection prior to hearing, and the amount of allowable attorneys fees due and anticipated through conclusion of the action. Also included shall be the rate of interest to accrue until the date of the judgment and the post judgment interest rate. The judge or master may also establish the priority and compute the amounts due of any other liens when a determination of lien priorities appears necessary or desirable prior to a foreclosure sale. Any party who has appeared in the action may present proof that the debt may be satisfied by selling the property in parcels, rather than selling the whole to satisfy the claims. Only parties who have appeared and filed pleadings in the action shall be entitled to the usual notice of hearings and other proceedings unless the pleadings state an unliquidated claim. In all cases proof shall be made of the facts and circumstances alleged in the pleadings and evidence given as to any payments which have been made or credits due. Prior to the filing of the master's report or final order of judgment, the judge or master shall assure that the plaintiff and all other claimants have complied with the statutes pertaining to the filing of notices of lis pendens. In all actions a record of hearings shall be made and preserved in the case file in the office of the clerk of court.

(b) Judgment and Sale on Foreclosure. The judgment shall direct that the mortgaged premises (or part thereof as required to satisfy the claims established) be sold by or under direction of the master or, in counties where there is no master, other appropriate court officer. The judgment shall also contain a good and sufficient legal description of the property being sold, a provision for the necessary legal advertisement, the time and location of the sale, and notice of any senior liens, taxes, or other rights to which the property to be sold is subject. The judgment shall also specify the amount of good faith deposit necessary at the time of the sale, and the date that compliance must be made with the bid. The plaintiff or any other party may be a purchaser on such sale. Unless the pleadings state that no personal or deficiency judgment is demanded or any right to such judgment is expressly waived in writing, the bidding shall not be closed upon the day of sale but shall remain open until the thirtieth day after such sale exclusive of the day of the sale. The manner and conduct of the bidding when a deficiency has been demanded shall be as required by law.

The master or other court officer making the sale shall execute a deed to the purchaser. Out of the proceeds of the sale he shall pay the costs of the sale, any amounts ordered to be paid by the judgment, then to the parties or their attorneys of record the amounts of their total claims and interest or so much of the purchase money as will pay the same. Notwithstanding the fact that the foreclosure action may have been referred to the master for final judgment, the master or other officer conducting the sale shall file a report with the court as to the sale and the receipts and disbursements made. Any surplus moneys arising from the sale shall be held by the officer making the sale and shall be paid pursuant to Rule 71(c).

(c) Disposition of Surplus. In the event of a surplus fund resulting from the sale, the master or other officer conducting the sale shall at the time he makes his report to the court on the sale and disbursements, cause to be furnished to all parties appearing in the action a notice advising of the surplus fund. Unless otherwise provided therein, the original order of reference in a foreclosure action shall be considered to extend to the disposition of the surplus fund.

Any party to the action, or any person who had a lien on the mortgaged premises at the time of the sale, upon filing with the master or other officer conducting the sale a claim of entitlement to the surplus fund, may have a hearing to determine such entitlement. All such claims must be verified or supported by affidavit and must be filed with the master or other officer conducting the sale within forty-five (45) days from the date of the filing of the statement of receipts and disbursements provided in Rule 71(b). If a claim is not filed within the said forty-five (45) day period, the same shall be considered abandoned and waived as to such surplus. The claim must contain the name of the claimant, the nature of the claim, the date the claim arose, and a calculation of the amount claimed. At the expiration of the claim filing period, the master or other officer conducting the sale shall set a hearing to accept proof of the claims filed. Only those who have filed a timely claim are entitled to notice of the hearing. In the event no claims are filed against the surplus funds, the fund shall be paid over to the mortgagor or lienor entitled to the fund. If such mortgagor or lienor cannot be readily determined or located, the fund shall be disposed of as an abandoned fund in the manner provided by law. When the proceedings have been completed, a report of the same shall be made to the court and filed in the action.

(d)(1) *Parties to Partition Actions.* In addition to the requirements of these rules for the joinder in an action of all parties in interest, pursuant to Rule 17(f) no partition of real property of a deceased person shall be had unless the legal representative or representatives of such deceased person be made parties to the action and it be made to appear to the court that the debts of such deceased person are fully paid or that the personal estate in the hands of the personal representative or representatives is sufficient for the payment of the debts of such deceased person. If the partition action involves real property of a deceased person whose estate has not been administered or is not being administered at the time of the bringing of the action, then all known encumbrancers of the estate of the deceased person shall be made parties to the action and no decree in partition shall be entered unless due provision is made for the payment of the debts found due such encumbrancers. In all actions for partition, all heirs at law or devisees of the deceased person shall likewise be made parties.

(2) *Partitioning Several Tracts.* Where several tracts or parcels of land lying in this State are owned by the same persons as tenants in common, no separate action shall be brought for partition of a part thereof without the consent of all the cotenants. If such action be brought without such consent, the share or shares of the plaintiff(s) may be charged with all of the costs of the action.

(3) *Attorneys Fees and Costs.* Attorneys fees and costs may be awarded the attorney for any party(s) from any common fund generated by the partition to the extent that attorney's efforts benefited all parties; otherwise, his fee shall be paid by the party(s) he represents or from the party(s) share(s) only. The court may order the payment of costs from the proceeds of sale of the common property or may equitably assess the costs against shares of the parties.

(4) *Lien Against Undivided Interest of Cotenants.* A lien against the undivided interest of a tenant in common is subordinate to the right of cotenants to compel partition; and when partition is made, the lien is transferred to the portion assigned to the debtor in severalty, or to his share of proceeds from the sale of the property.

(e) Actions When Title Is at Issue. In foreclosure or partition actions when title to real property is at issue the court or master to whom the action is referred shall take testimony and receive evidence as to the title and interest in the premises of the several parties. In all such actions the judge or master shall ascertain the rights and interests of the several parties and set forth in the report or order of judgment the conveyances or probate estates, if any, through which the rights or interests were acquired. In all such actions a transcript of record shall be made and preserved in the case file in the office of the clerk of court.

(f)(1) *Writs of Partition.* Writs of partition shall be issued and directed to five persons. Two of such persons shall be nominated by the plaintiff, two by the defendant and the fifth by the officer issuing the writ, and in cases when the defendant fails to appear or answer the plaintiff shall nominate three persons and the officer two. The writ shall command them, or a majority of them, within one month thereafter, fairly and impartially, according to the best of their judgment, to make partition of the premises described in the complaint among the parties entitled thereto, according to their several rights.

(2) *Oath of Commissioners.* Before acting under such writ of partition the commissioners therein named shall be duly sworn for the purpose of complying with the command of the writ.

(3) *Return by Commissioners When Property Cannot Be Divided in Kind.* When the estate or property cannot, in the opinion of the commissioners, be fairly and equally divided between the parties interested therein without manifest injury to them, or some one of them, they shall make a special return of the whole property and the value thereof, truly appraised, and certify their opinion to the court whether it will be most for the benefit of all parties to deliver over to one or more of the parties interested therein the property which cannot be fairly divided, upon the payment of a sum of money to be assessed by the commissioners, or to sell the property at public auction, and the court shall proceed to consider and determine the same.

(4) *Allotment or Sale.* If it shall appear to the court that it will be for the benefit of all parties interested in the estate or property that it should be vested in one or more of the persons entitled to a portion of it, on the payment of a sum of money assessed as provided in Rule 71(f)(3), the court shall determine accordingly, and the person or persons, on the payment of the consideration money, shall be vested with the estate so adjudged to such person or persons. But if it shall appear to the court that it would be more for the interest of the parties interested in the estate or property that it should be sold and the proceeds of sale be divided among them, then the court shall direct a sale to be made upon such terms as the court shall deem right.

(5) *Partition or Sale Without Writ.* Nothing in this Rule shall be construed to affect the power of the court to dispense with the issuing of a writ of partition when, in the judgment of the court, it would involve unnecessary expense to issue such writ. And the court may in all proceedings in partition, without recourse to such writ, determine by means of testimony taken before the proper officer and reported to the court whether a partition in kind among the parties be practicable or expedient and, when such partition cannot be fairly and equally made, may order a sale of the property and a division of the proceeds according to the rights of the parties.

[Amended effective May 1, 1986; July 1, 1990.]

Notes

These Rules 71 and 71(f) replace old Circuit Rules 51 through 55, and contain the changes in procedure on foreclosure and partition that have developed through case law and practice in the nearly 100 years since those rules were adopted. They should eliminate the considerable differences in application and interpretation of the old rules that have developed in the various counties and circuits, and make the procedure uniform statewide.

Notes to 1986 Amendments

Rule 71(a) is amended so that a record of the hearings, but not necessarily a typed transcript, is preserved in the file. Rule 71(b) now requires waiver of the demand for a deficiency judgment in the pleadings or in writing, before the bidding will be closed on the day of sale. The report concerning the sale shall include receipts and disbursements. Rule 71(c) now requires filing of claims against the surplus within 45 days of the filing of the statement of the sale rather than the date the court confirms the sale.

Notes to 1990 Amendments

Rule 71 is amended to add paragraph 71(f) incorporating procedures for the appointment of commissioners to recommend a partition in kind. The procedures were formerly found in S.C.Code Ann. §§ 15–61–60 to 90 (1976) (repealed 1985), and readopted by the Supreme Court in Anderson v. Anderson, 299 S.C. 110, 382 S.E.2d 897 (1989). The language of the Rule follows the language of the repealed statutes and S.C.Code Ann. § 15–61–100 (1976).

RULE 71.1. POST–CONVICTION RELIEF ACTIONS

(a) Procedure. The procedure for post-conviction relief is provided by the Uniform Post–Conviction Procedure Act (Act), S.C.Code Ann. §§ 17–27–10 to –120 (1985). The South Carolina Rules of Civil Procedure shall apply to the extent that they are not inconsistent with the Act.

(b) Time and Form of Application. An application for post-conviction relief cannot be made while an appeal from the conviction or sentence is pending or during the time in which an appeal may be perfected. All applications shall be made on the form set out in the Appendix of Forms. The Office of Court Administration shall insure that an adequate quantity of these forms are available to the circuit court clerks for distribution to persons seeking post-conviction relief.

(c) Independent Action. An application filed under the Act is an independent civil action which should be separately filed and indexed by the clerk of court. The caption in all post-conviction relief actions shall read: *Full Name and Prison number (if any) of Applicant v. State of South Carolina.*

(d) Appointment of Counsel for Hearing. If, after the State has filed its return, the application presents questions of law or fact which will require a hearing, the court shall promptly appoint counsel to assist the applicant if he is indigent. Counsel shall be given a reasonable time to confer with the applicant. Counsel shall insure that all available grounds for relief are included in the application and shall amend the application if necessary.

(e) Burden of Proof. The applicant has the burden of establishing his entitlement to relief by a preponderance of the evidence.

(f) Filing and Service of Order. The post-conviction relief judge shall submit the signed final order or judgment to the clerk for filing and the clerk of court shall provide notice of entry of judgment and serve a copy of the order or judgment to the parties as provided in Rule 77(d), SCRCP.

(g) Appellate Review; Continuing Representation. A final decision entered under the Act shall be reviewed according to the procedure specified by Rule 243, SCACR. If an applicant represented by counsel desires to appeal, counsel shall serve and file a Notice of Appeal as required by Rule 243, SCACR, and shall continue to represent the applicant on appeal unless automatically relieved under Rule 602, SCACR, or allowed to withdraw under Rule 264, SCACR. If the applicant is indigent, counsel shall assist the applicant in obtaining representation by the Division of Appellate Defense of the Office of Indigent Defense.

[Adopted effective September 1, 1990. Amended effective September 1, 2001; April 27, 2004; May 3, 2007; April 29, 2009.]

Notes

Note to 1990 Amendment

This rule is based in part on former Supreme Court Rule 50(1)–(8), and has no counterpart in the Federal Rules.

Note to 2001 Amendments

These amendments consolidate former Rule 71.1(f) and (g) and change the method of appointment of counsel for indigents on appeal to conform to Rule 602, SCACR.

Note to 2004 Amendment

The 2004 Amendment clarifies the process for filing and notification of parties of filed orders in post-conviction relief actions.

Note to 2007 Amendment

In 2005, the Office of Appellate Defense became a division of the Office of Indigent Defense. This amendment reflects this organizational change.

Note to 2009 Amendment

References to the South Carolina Appellate Court Rules in Rule 71.1 were amended to reflect changes in the numbering of those rules by Orders of the South Carolina Supreme Court dated January 29, 2009 and April 29, 2009.

IX. APPEALS AND ARBITRATION

RULE 72. JUDGMENTS AND ORDERS SUBJECT TO APPEAL

Appeal may be taken, as provided by law, from any final judgment or appealable order.

[Amended effective July 1, 1989.]

Notes

This Rule 72 parallels, in part, S.C. Code § 14–3–330, but is designed to reduce appeals from interlocutory or intermediate orders in an action. It accords with the modern decisions of the Supreme Court narrowing "dilatory appeals" from such interlocutory orders as grant or deny motions addressed to the pleadings, motions at trial, and the like. All such questions are left to the appeal from final judgment or order of dismissal. There is no conflict with the Supreme Court jurisdictional statutes and all statutory rights to appeal are preserved specifically by subdivision (6).

Notes to 1989 Amendments

The jurisdiction of all courts is determined by the Constitution, the jurisdictional statutes, and the case law interpreting those provisions. Rule 72 as originally written created confusion and unintended arguments that the civil rules changed the scope of appeal. Rule 72 was not intended to alter, amend or supercede previously existing law concerning appeals. The amendment rephrases Rule 72 as a general statement that appeals are as provided by law, and is consistent with Rule 73 which states that the procedure on appeal is governed by the Rules of the Supreme Court.

Article V, § 5, of the Constitution sets forth the jurisdiction of the Supreme Court. Some of the relevant statutes are § 14–3–320 (equitable matters); § 14–3–330 (matters of law); § 17–17–140 (habeas corpus). Some of the important cases are: North Carolina Federal Savings and Loan Ass'n v. Twin States Dev. Corp., 289 S.C. 480, 347 S.E.2d 97 (1986) (§ 14–3–330 controls appeals not Rule 72); Coleman v. Keels, 30 S.C. 614, 9 S.E. 270 (1889) (certiorari); Ex parte Mackey, 15 S.C. 322 (1880) (mandamus); Southern Railway Co. v. Coltex, 285 S.C. 213, 329 S.E.2d 736 (1985) (new trial because of error of law); Simms v. Phillips, 46 S.C. 149, 24 S.E. 87 (1896) (subject matter jurisdiction); Nat. Exchange Bank v. Stelling, 32 S.C. 102, 10 S.E. 766 (1890) (personal jurisdiction); Godley v. Uniroyal, Inc., 278 S.C. 571, 300 S.E.2d 78 (1983) (venue not immediately appealable).

RULE 73. PROCEDURE ON APPEAL TO SUPREME COURT OR COURT OF APPEALS

Procedure on appeal to the South Carolina Supreme Court or the South Carolina Court of Appeals shall be in accordance with the South Carolina Appellate Court Rules.

[Amended effective September 1, 1990.]

Notes

This Rule 73 is to conform to the Supreme Court's action in 1978 deleting Circuit Court Rules 47 through 50, concerning procedure on appeals, and transferring them to the Supreme Court Rules.

Notes to 1990 Amendments

This amendment modifies the rule to make reference to the South Carolina Appellate Court Rules which have replaced the Supreme Court Rules.

RULE 74. PROCEDURE ON APPEAL TO THE CIRCUIT COURT

Except for the time for filing the notice of appeal, the procedure on appeal to the circuit court from the judgment of an inferior court or decision of an administrative agency or tribunal shall be in accordance with the statutes providing such appeals. Notice of appeal to the circuit court must be served on all parties within thirty (30) days after receipt of written notice of the judgment, order or decision appealed from. In all such appeals the notice of intention to appeal shall be filed with the clerk of the court to which the appeal is taken and with the inferior court or administrative agency or tribunal within the time provided by the statute, or by this rule when no time is fixed by statute, for service of the notice of intention to appeal. The proceedings in the circuit court shall be in accordance with these rules, and priority shall be given to the hearing and disposition of such appeals in accordance with law.

[Amended effective May 1, 1986.]

Notes

[See Notes following Rule 75.]

Notes to 1986 Amendments

This amendment makes the time for filing a notice of appeal to the circuit court thirty days in all cases and conforms to the Administrative Procedures Act.

RULE 75. RECORD ON APPEAL TO THE CIRCUIT COURT: TRANSMITTAL

Appeals to the circuit court shall be made upon the original record in the lower court or administrative agency or tribunal. Upon filing of notice of appeal in an action the original record shall be certified by the clerk of the inferior court or administrative agency or tribunal and transmitted within thirty (30) days to the clerk of the court to which the appeal is taken. If the lower court, agency or tribunal has no clerk, then the original record shall be certified and transmitted by the judge or chief official of the lower court, agency or tribunal. Upon motion for good cause shown, the court may extend the time for the lower court, agency or tribunal to prepare and certify the record. Upon receipt of the certified record, the clerk of the circuit court shall give notice in writing to the parties that the record has been filed.

[Amended effective May 1, 1986.]

Notes

These Rules 74 and 75 are added to make uniform the procedure on appeals to the Circuit Court where there is no provision by statute. They do not replace any provisions as to such appeals in Title 18 of the Code, or other statutes providing for appeals from administrative decisions; but are added to supply omissions in these statutes where no provision is made for the time to file notice of intention to appeal, the form of the record on appeal, or how it shall be transmitted.

Notes to 1986 Amendments

This amendment requires the record to be certified to the circuit court within thirty days, and provides that the court may grant additional time for good cause shown.

RULE 76. ARBITRATION: AUTOMOBILE REPARATION

(a) Arbitration Panels. Resident circuit judges, by order of reference, shall designate attorneys to constitute a panel of arbitrators for automobile reparation actions under the South Carolina Automobile Reparation Reform Act of 1974. To insure a sufficient number of arbitrators in each county, more particularly those counties with fewer attorneys, a panel of arbitrators for each county shall consist of all attorneys in good standing, duly admitted to practice law and actively engaged in the practice of law in the State whose principal offices now or hereafter are located within the judicial circuit of which such county is a part.

(b) Depositions in Arbitration. The procedure for the taking of depositions in arbitration actions shall be the same as set forth in Rules 26 through 32. The monetary limitation for the taking of depositions under the provisions of Rule 30(a)(2) shall not be applicable in the taking of depositions in arbitration proceedings.

(c) Arbitration Docket. The arbitration docket required by the Act to be maintained by the clerks of court shall be on a form specified by the Director, South Carolina Court Administration, and the claims submitted to arbitration shall be assigned a case file number using a numbering system similar to that set forth in "Instructions for Filing, Indexing, Numbering and Preserving Records within the Judicial System of South Carolina," issued by the Office of South Carolina Court Administration.

Notes

This Rule 76 is added to preserve Circuit Court Rule 91, changed only to reflect reference to new Rule numbers in these Rules.

X. COURTS AND CLERKS

RULE 77. COURTS AND CLERKS

(a) Courts Always Open. The courts of this State shall be deemed always open for the purpose of filing any pleading or other proper paper, or issuing and returning mesne and final process, and of making and directing all interlocutory motions, orders and rules.

(b) Trials and Hearings; Orders in Chambers. All trials upon the merits shall be conducted in open court and so far as convenient in a regular courtroom.

All other acts or proceedings may be done or conducted by a judge in chambers, without the attendance of the clerk or other court officials and at any place either within or without the circuit, but no hearing, other than one ex parte or one upon motions subsequent to trial, shall be conducted outside the circuit without the consent of all parties affected thereby.

(c) Clerk's Office and Orders by Clerk. The clerk's office with the clerk or a deputy in attendance shall be open during business hours on all days except Saturdays, Sundays and legal holidays. All motions and applications in the clerk's office for issuing mesne process, for issuing final process to enforce and execute judgments, for entering defaults, and for other proceedings which do not require allowance or order of the court are grantable of course by the clerk; but his action may be suspended or altered or rescinded by the court upon motion for cause shown.

(d) Notice of Orders or Judgments. Immediately upon the entry of an order or judgment the clerk shall serve a notice of the entry by first class mail upon every party affected thereby who is not in default for failure to appear, and shall make a note in the case file or docket sheet of the mailing. Such mailing shall not be necessary to parties who have already received notice. Such mailing is sufficient notice for all purposes for which notice of the entry of an order or judgment is required by these rules; but any party may in addition serve a notice of entry on any other party in the manner provided in Rule 5 for the service of such papers. In addition to the above, in post-conviction relief actions, the post-conviction relief judge shall submit the signed order or judgment to the clerk of court for filing and the clerk shall promptly provide notice of the entry of judgment and serve a copy of the signed order to the parties. Pursuant to Rule 5(b) service shall be made solely on the attorney when the applicant is represented by counsel and, where an applicant is proceeding *pro se*, service shall be made upon the applicant at the last known address provided to the clerk by the applicant.

(e) Cancelling or Ordering Terms of Court. No term of court shall be cancelled nor additional term scheduled without the prior approval of the Chief Justice. When the local bar requests that a week of common pleas court be not held, or the solicitor requests that a week of general sessions court be not held, the clerk shall immediately notify the Court Administrator of this State.

[Amended effective April 28, 2004.]

Notes

This Rule 77 is substantially identical to the Federal Rule and present State practice. The only additions are the requirement in Rule 77(d) that the Clerk mail notice of entry of orders or judgment, unless (as is customary) they have been notified, usually by the judge; and Rule 77(e) preserves present Circuit Court Rule 83.

Note to 2004 Amendment

The 2004 amendment clarified the process for clerks of court providing notice of entry of judgment and copies of the final signed order to the parties. It made clear that service is to be made on the attorney of a represented applicant and only on applicants when they are proceeding *pro se*.

RULE 78. CLERKS OF COURT; RECORDS, ABSTRACTS, BOOKS

(a) Records to Be Kept; Penalties. Subject to the approval of the Supreme Court, the Office of Court Administration shall establish procedures for creating, maintaining, removing, and destroying all records and other court documents by the clerks of court, probate courts, municipal courts, magistrate's courts, court administrators, and other officers and employees of the courts, and for the furnishing of information and statistical data relative to the work of the courts and to the expenditure of public moneys for their maintenance and operation. Failure to comply with the requirements of this rule, or any procedures established pursuant hereto, shall subject the party so failing to penalties as for contempt of court.

(b) Abstracts of Civil Judgments and Orders. The clerk shall enter an abstract of every final judgment or order affecting title to or lien upon real or personal property, and any other order which the court may direct to be entered in the "Abstracts of Judgments" book. Suitable indices of every such civil judgment or order shall be kept by the clerk.

(c) Other Books and Records of the Clerk. The clerk shall also keep such other books and records as may be required, and shall produce the Code of Laws, the rules, the calendars and the file book upon request of the court.

Notes

This Rule 78(a) is present new (1983) Circuit Court Rule 84. Rules 78(b) and (c) conform to present State statutes and practice.

RULE 79. CALENDAR OF CIVIL ACTIONS; FILE BOOK

(a) File Book. The clerk of court shall consolidate the calendars of civil actions in the circuit court and provide for the filing and keeping of papers with respect to civil actions in the manner provided in this rule. The clerk of court for each county shall keep a Calendar, hereinafter referred to as "File Book," relating to civil actions in the circuit court in which there shall be entered and cross-indexed all proceedings of a civil nature which are instituted in the circuit civil court for the county or are appealed to that court from a magistrate's court, municipal court, other inferior court, or any administrative agency for which provision is made for an appeal to the circuit court.

The clerk of court shall maintain only one file book for the circuit civil court as required by this rule.

(b)(1) *Civil Action Number.* When a summons and complaint or notice of intention to appeal to the circuit court are filed, the action or appeal shall receive a number in keeping with the numbering system approved by the Supreme Court by order dated March 11, 1974, as now or hereafter amended, and thereafter all papers filed in the proceeding shall be similarly numbered and kept together in a file bearing the same number.

(2) *Notice of Jury Matters.* The plaintiff at the time of filing the complaint in any proceeding shall inform the clerk of court of the nature of the issue and shall designate whether the case shall be tried non-jury or by a jury.

(c) Entry Required. No jury or nonjury action and no appeal to the circuit civil court from a magistrate's court, municipal court, other inferior court, or any administrative agency, whether for interlocutory action or final disposition, shall be heard by the court until the action has been first entered in the file book and all pleadings in the action filed with the clerk of court.

(d) Entries on File Book. Entries may be made on the file book only by a judge of the court or by the clerk of court or his deputy.

(e) Motion Calendar. In addition to the file book, each clerk of court shall maintain a motion calendar in such form as prescribed by the Office of South Carolina Court Administration. The clerk of court shall place on the motion calendar all pending motions and other matters requiring a summary hearing before the judge. The motion calendar shall contain the case number, date of request, name of the action, attorneys involved and the nature of the motion to be presented.

(f) Notice or Order of Dismissal. No action listed in the file book which thereafter is settled or disposed of in any manner, shall be dismissed, marked ended, or stricken from the file book unless and until:

(1) plaintiff shall file and serve a notice of dismissal or stipulation of dismissal pursuant to the provisions of Rule 41; or

(2) counsel in the action shall have prepared and filed an order signed by the appropriate judge, or the clerk of court pursuant to the provisions of Section 15–35–30 [1], Code of Laws of South Carolina, 1976, and bearing the written consent of all interested parties to the action showing that it has been ended; or

(3) dismissal is ordered by the court.

The clerk of court shall bring the file book forward from time to time as may be necessary.

(g) Failure to Comply. Failure to comply with the requirements of this rule shall subject the party so failing to penalties as for contempt of court; which contempt shall be enforced by the court on motion of any aggrieved party or by the court on its own motion.

[Amended effective May 1, 1986.]

Notes

This Rule 79 together with Rule 40 preserves generally present Circuit Court Rule 26, as amended through 1981 by the Supreme Court except that references to roster meetings to be called by the clerk of court are eliminated. Rule numbers and paragraph numbers are changed to conform to the numbering system of these Rules, and the word "action" is substituted for the word "case" to conform to Rule 2.

Notes to 1986 Amendments

These amendments [to Rules 79(b)(2) and (e)] on responsibilities for notifying the clerk of the type of trial requested, and the placing of all summary matters on the motion calendar are designed to improve the administration of the dockets.

RULE 80. STENOGRAPHIC REPORT OF TRANSCRIPT AS EVIDENCE

Whenever the testimony of a witness at a trial or hearing which was stenographically reported is admissible in evidence at a later trial, it may be offered in evidence by a copy of the transcript thereof duly certified by the person who reported the testimony or the clerk of court having custody of the original transcript.

Notes

This Rule 80 is substantially the same as the Federal Rule. It avoids the need to produce the original notes, or the stenographer, to prove the transcript of a trial or hearing.

XI. GENERAL PROVISIONS

RULE 81. APPLICABILITY

These rules, or any of them, shall apply to every trial court of civil jurisdiction within this state, within the limits of the jurisdiction and powers of the court provided by law, and the procedure therein shall conform to these rules insofar as practicable. They shall apply insofar as practicable in magistrate's courts, probate courts, and family courts to the extent they are not inconsistent with the statutes and rules governing those courts. In any case where no provision is made by statute or these Rules, the procedure shall be according to the practice as it has heretofore existed in the courts of this State.

Notes

This Rule 81 covers the same subject as the Federal Rule but is drafted to conform to the State court system, and to make the procedure in all civil courts as uniform as possible.

RULE 82. JURISDICTION AND VENUE

(a) Jurisdiction Unaffected. These rules shall not be construed to extend or limit the jurisdiction of any

[1] Pub. Note: Section 15–35–30 was repealed effective July 1, 1985.

See Rule 41(a) for provisions governing voluntary dismissal.

court of this State or, except as provided in Rule 82(b), the venue of any action.

(b) Venue of Action. When an action is brought in the wrong county or in the wrong court, the court shall not dismiss the action but shall transfer it to any proper county or court in which it could have been brought.

(c) Removal to Federal Courts. When a petition for the removal of any action pending in any court of this State to any court of the United States is filed, no order accepting the petition or directing the action to be removed shall be required.

Notes

This Rule 82(a), similar to the Federal Rule, is a rule of construction, to insure that these Rules are not held to have made any change in jurisdictional or venue requirements and limitations. Rule 82(b) is similar to that adopted by many states to avoid having an action dismissed only to be commenced again in the proper jurisdiction. Rule 82(c) conforms to present practice.

RULE 83. [RESERVED]

RULE 84. FORMS

The Supreme Court shall prescribe the content and format of forms required by these rules. The use of the forms as prescribed is mandatory.

[Amended effective May 1, 1986.]

Notes

This Rule 84 preserves the forms required under present Circuit Court Rule 10 (Security for Costs), 93 (Juror Summons), and 94 (Juror Information); and provides forms for Judgments as required by Rules 54 and 58 of these Rules. As indicated by these rules, additional material may be inserted in the standard forms of Judgment, but as a minimum must follow the forms.

Notes to 1986 Amendments

This amendment permits the Supreme Court to prescribe the forms by administrative order rather than the more cumbersome process of amending procedural rules.

RULE 85. TITLE; CRIMINAL PROCEDURE; RULES REPEALED

(a) These rules shall be entitled South Carolina Rules of Civil Procedure and may be cited by Rule number and the letters SCRCP, i.e., Rule ______, SCRCP.

(b) Those certain of the Rules of Practice for the Circuit Courts of South Carolina pertaining to practice and procedure in criminal cases and heretofore numbered Rules 4, 25, 35, 61, 72, 95, 98, 103, 104 and 105, contained in the Appendix of Criminal Practice Rules, shall be renumbered as Criminal Practice Rules 1 through 10, and continue in full force and effect.

(c) All other of the Rules of Practice for the Circuit Courts of this State heretofore adopted are repealed as of the effective date of these South Carolina Rules of Civil Procedure.

Notes

This Rule 85 is similar to the Federal Rule, and of other States adopting the Rules of Civil Procedure.

Editor' Note: The appendix of Criminal Practice Rules was repealed by Rule 39, SCRCrimP.

RULE 86. EFFECTIVE DATE

(a) These rules shall take effect on July 1, 1985. They govern all proceedings in civil actions brought after they take effect and also all further proceedings in actions then pending, except to the extent that in the opinion of the court their application in a particular action pending when the rules take effect would not be feasible or would work injustice, in which event the former procedure applies.

(b) The 1986 amendments to these rules shall take effect on May 1, 1986.

[Amended effective May 1, 1986.]

Notes

This Rule 86 is similar to the Federal Rule, making these rules immediately applicable to pending actions, as of the effective date, except where the Court finds this not feasible.

APPENDIX OF FORMS

(Pursuant to Rule 84, S.C. Rules of Civil Procedure)

FORM 1. SECURITY FOR COSTS—FORM OF UNDERTAKING

FORM 1
SECURITY FOR COSTS – FORM OF UNDERTAKING

If the plaintiff resides beyond the State, security for costs may be required. Whenever security for costs shall be required the following form and no other shall be regarded as a compliance with the order:

STATE OF SOUTH CAROLINA
________________ County

A. B.
vs
C. D.

Complaint For

I (or we as the case may be) acknowledge myself (or ourselves) liable for the costs of this case in the sum ____________ dollars, and consent that if the plaintiff fail to recover, the defendant may have execution for his cost against me (or us as the case may be) for not exceeding said sum.

Given under __________ hand this ____ day of ____________ A.D. 2______.

E.F.
Witness:
Approved:
G.H.
C.C.C.P. & G.S

The amount to be inserted in this Form shall be fixed by the clerk of court after careful examination of the pleadings filed in the action. If the amount set is, in the opinion of any party to the action, insufficient, a motion may be made to the court for an order fixing the amount for which such security shall be given.

Deposit in Lieu of Undertaking. When security for costs is required, the plaintiff or other for him may deposit the required sum of money with the clerk of court, in lieu of this form.

JUROR SUMMONS FOR CIRCUIT COURT

STATE OF SOUTH CAROLINA **JUROR SUMMONS FOR CIRCUIT COURT**

COUNTY OF	FOR TERM BEGINNING WEEK OF:	JUROR NUMBER:

You are hereby summoned to appear at ______________ on _________________________, at _____ to answer this summons to serve as a (check applicable box) ☐ petit juror ☐ grand juror for the Court of Common Pleas and General Sessions. Failure to appear at the address above at the specified time may subject you to penalties as prescribed by

CLERK OF COURT, Phone

NAME AND ADDRESS OF JUROR	IMPORTANT INFORMATION AND INSTRUCTIONS
	Fill in the requested information in the "Juror Information Section" and the appropriate contact information below. After reading all of the conditions listed in the "Juror Response Section," mark any condition that applies to you. Separate the top and bottom portions of this page at the line indicated below and WITHIN THREE DAYS OF RECEIPT return the bottom portion of the form using the self-addressed envelope provided.

NOTE: PERSONS FAILING TO RETURN THESE FORMS AS REQUESTED MAY BE SUBJECT TO CHARGES OF CONTEMPT OF COURT.

Separate this top portion from bottom portion at the dotted line. Retain this top portion for your reference.

Return this bottom portion as instructed using the self-addressed envelope provided.

JUROR INFORMATION SECTION

(PLEASE PRINT OR TYPE CLEARLY.)

FOR TERM BEGINNING WEEK OF: ______ JUROR NUMBER: ______

CITY, COUNTY, STATE OF BIRTH	AGE	DATE OF BIRTH	# OF CHILDREN	MARRIED ☐	SINGLE ☐	WIDOWED ☐	DIVORCED ☐

YOUR OCCUPATION	PRESENT OR FORMER EMPLOYER	YEARS
LEVEL OF FORMAL EDUCATION COMPLETED	**NAME OF SPOUSE**	
SPOUSE'S OCCUPATION	**SPOUSE'S PRESENT OR FORMER EMPLOYER**	**YEARS**

HAVE YOU EVER SERVED ON A ☐ CIVIL JURY, OR ☐ CRIMINAL JURY? IF SO, WHEN?

HAVE YOU EVER BEEN A PARTY TO A CIVIL LAWSUIT? ☐ YES ☐ NO

HAVE YOU EVER BEEN CONVICTED OF A CRIME (OTHER THAN A MINOR TRAFFIC OFFENSE)? ☐ YES ☐ NO

NAME AND/OR ADDRESS CORRECTION: If the information below is incorrect, please write in the correct information in the space provided to the left.

INFORMATION BELOW WILL BE MADE AVAILABLE ONLY TO OFFICERS OF THE COURT.

HOME PHONE #	BUSINESS PHONE #	SPOUSE'S BUSINESS PHONE #	EMERGENCY PHONE #	E-MAIL ADDRESS

JUROR RESPONSE SECTION INSTRUCTIONS

Retain the top portion of this form for your reference and return the bottom portion of the form along with any required affidavits or written statements in the self-addressed envelope provided.
NOTE: Unless the clerk of court otherwise notifies you, you must report for jury duty as requested.

DISQUALIFICATIONS

☐ I am not a U.S. citizen.
☐ I am not a resident of this county. (Note correct address above.)
☐ I cannot read, write, speak, or understand the English language.
Translator's name and telephone #: ____________________

☐ I have less than a sixth grade education or its equivalent.
☐ I have a mental or physical condition that prevents me from serving as a juror. (Doctor's statement required)
☐ I have been convicted in a state or federal court of a crime that carries a sentence of more than one year of imprisonment and I have not been pardoned or given amnesty for that conviction. List offenses, when and where convicted: ____________________

☐ I am a clerk of court, deputy clerk of court, constable, sheriff, commissioned law enforcement officer, probate judge, county commissioner, magistrate, or county officer, or I am employed within the walls of a courthouse. Occupation: ____________
☐ I have served on a circuit court jury within this calendar year.
Date of Service: ________________ County: ____________

EXEMPTIONS

☐ I am 65 years of age or older and wish to be excused. (If you do not wish to serve on a jury, you may **telephone** the clerk of court to be excused. Unless you are excused by the clerk of court prior to the term for which you are summoned, you must report for jury duty.)
☐ I am the primary caretaker of a disabled person or a person age 65 or older who cannot care for himself.***
☐ I have legal custody and duty of care of a child under the age of seven and I cannot provide adequate childcare while serving as a juror.***
☐ I am a guard, keeper, employee, or other officer at a state penitentiary.
☐ I have served on a circuit court jury during the previous two calendar years, or I have served on a grand jury during the previous four calendar years. Date of Service: ____________ County: ____________
Jury Type: ☐ Circuit Court ☐ Grand Jury
☐ I am a student or a school employee and wish to be transferred to a later date that will not conflict with my school term.
Date Available for Service: ____________
[When you return this form, you must also send evidence of school enrollment or employment.]
***An affidavit (notarized statement) must be returned with this form attesting to the above statements.

☐ I HAVE READ THE CONDITIONS FOR DISQUALIFICATION AND EXEMPTION ABOVE AND NONE OF THE CONDITIONS LISTED APPLY TO ME.

NOTE: THE FURNISHING OF FALSE OR MISLEADING INFORMATION OR THE FAILURE TO FURNISH INFORMATION TO THE COURT MAY SUBJECT YOU TO PENALTIES AS PRESCRIBED BY LAW.

YOUR SIGNATURE ______________________________

SCCA 235E (12/2010) NOTE: Participation of all eligible citizens as jurors is encouraged. If you need specific accommodations, courthouse staff will be available for assistance.

FORM 5. APPLICATION FOR POST–CONVICTION RELIEF

FORM 5

STATE OF SOUTH CAROLINA	)	IN THE COURT OF COMMON PLEAS
County of ______________________	)	
______________________	)	
Full name and prison number (if any) of Applicant	)	
v.	)	**APPLICATION FOR**
State of South Carolina	)	**POST-CONVICTION RELIEF**

INSTRUCTIONS - READ CAREFULLY

In order for this application to receive consideration by the Court, it shall be in writing (legibly handwritten or typewritten), signed by the applicant and verified (notarized), and it shall set forth in concise form the answers to each applicable question. If necessary, applicant may furnish his answer to a particular question on the reverse side of the page or on an additional page. Applicant shall make clear to which question any such continued answer refers.

Since every application must be sworn under oath, any false statement of a material fact therein may serve as the basis of prosecution and conviction for perjury. Applicants should, therefore, exercise care to assure that all answers are true and correct.

If the application is taken in forma pauperis, it shall include an affidavit (attached at the back of the form) setting forth information which establishes that applicant will be unable to pay the fees and costs of the proceedings. When the application is completed, the original shall be mailed to the Clerk of Court for the County in which the applicant was convicted.

1. Place of detention ______________________

____

2. Name and location of Court which imposed sentence ______________________

____

3. Name(s) of co-defendant(s) (if any) ______________________

____

4. The indictment number or numbers (if known) upon which and the offenses for which sentence was imposed:

(a) ______________________

(b) ______________________

(c) ______________________________

5. The date upon which sentence was imposed and the terms of the sentence:

(a) ______________________________

(b) ______________________________

(c) ______________________________

6. Check whether a finding of guilty was made:

(a) after a plea of guilty ______________________________

(b) after a plea of not guilty ______________________________

(c) after a plea of nolo contendere ______________________________

7. Did you appeal from the judgment of conviction or the imposition of sentence?

____

8. If you answered "yes" to (7), list:

(a) the name of each Court to which you appealed:

i. ______________________________

ii. ______________________________

iii. ______________________________

(b) the result in each such Court to which you appealed:

i. ______________________________

ii. ______________________________

iii. ______________________________

(c) the date of each such result:

i. ______________________________

ii. ______________________________

iii. ______________________________

(d) if known, citations of any written opinion or orders entered pursuant to such results:

i. ______________________________

ii. ______________________________

iii. ______________________________

9. If you answered "no" to (7), state your reasons for not so appealing:

(a) ______________________________

(b) ______________________________

(c) ______________________

10. State concisely the grounds on which you base your allegation that you are being held in custody unlawfully:

(a) ______________________

(b) ______________________

(c) ______________________

11. State concisely and in the same order the facts which support each of the grounds set out in (10):

(a) ______________________

(b) ______________________

(c) ______________________

12. Prior to this application have you filed with respect to this conviction:

(a) any petition in a State Court under South Carolina Law? ______________________

(b) any petition in State or Federal Courts for habeas corpus or post-convictions relief? ______________________

(c) any petition in the United States Supreme Court for certiorari other than petitions, if any, already specified in (8)? ______________________

(d) any other petitions, motions or applications in this or any other Court? ________

13. If you answered "yes" to any part of (12), list with respect to each petition, motion or application:

(a) the specific nature thereof:

i. ______________________

ii. ______________________

iii. ______________________

iv. ______________________

(b) the name and location of the Court in which each was filed:

i. ______________________

ii. ______________________

iii. ______________________

iv. ______________________

(c) the disposition thereof:

i. ______________________________

ii. ______________________________

iii. ______________________________

iv. ______________________________

(d) the date of each such disposition:

i. ______________________________

ii. ______________________________

iii. ______________________________

iv. ______________________________

(e) if known, citations of any written opinions or orders entered pursuant to each such disposition:

i. ______________________________

ii. ______________________________

iii. ______________________________

iv. ______________________________

14. Has any ground set forth in (10) been previously presented to this or any other Court, State or Federal, in any petition, motion or application which you have filed?

____

____

15. If you answered "yes" to (14) identify:

(a) which grounds have been presented:

i. ______________________________

ii. ______________________________

iii. ______________________________

(b) the proceedings in which each ground was raised:

i. ______________________________

ii. ______________________________

iii. ______________________________

Revised 3/2003

16. If any ground set forth in (10) has not previously been presented to any Court, State or Federal, set forth the ground and state concisely the reasons why such ground has not previously been presented:

(a) ______________________________

(b) ______________________________

(c) ______________________________

17. Were you represented by an attorney at any time during the course of:

(a) your arraignment and plea? ______________________________

(b) your trial, if any? ______________________________

(c) your sentencing? ______________________________

(d) your appeal, if any, from the judgment of conviction or the imposition of sentence? ______________________________

(e) preparation, presentation or consideration of any petitions, motions or applications with respect to this conviction, which you filed?

____

18. If you answered "yes" to one or more parts of (17), list:

(a) the name and address of each attorney who represented you:

i. ______________________________

____

ii. ______________________________

____

iii. ______________________________

____

(b) the proceedings at which each such attorney represented you:

i. ______________________________

____

ii. ______________________________

____

iii. ______________________________

____

Revised 3/2003

19. State clearly the relief you seek in filing this application:

____

____

____

20. Are you now under sentence from any other court that you have not challenged?

____

____

STATE OF SOUTH CAROLINA)
) VERIFICATION
County of ______________________)

I, ____, being duly sworn upon my oath, depose and say that I have subscribed to the foregoing application; that I know the contents thereof; that it includes every ground known to me for vacating, setting aside or correcting the conviction and sentence attacked in this application; and that the matters and allegations therein set forth are true.

____

SWORN to and subscribed before me this _________
day of ________________________, _______.

__________________________________ (L.S.)
Notary Public

My Commission Expires: ____________________

Revised 3/2003

APPLICATION TO PROCEED WITHOUT PAYMENT OF COSTS AND AFFIDAVIT IN SUPPORT THEREOF

I, ____, hereby apply for leave to proceed in this action without prepayment of fees or costs or security therefor. In support of my application I declare under penalty of perjury that the following facts are true:

(1) I am the applicant in this action and I believe I am entitled to redress.

(2) Because of my poverty I am unable to pay the costs of said proceeding or give security thereof.

____
Applicant

SWORN or affirmed to and subscribed before me this ______ day of ________________, _______.

____
Notary Public

My Commission Expires: ________________

Revised 3/2003

SUBPOENA IN A CIVIL CASE

STATE OF SOUTH CAROLINA

ISSUED BY THE ________________________ COURT IN THE COUNTY OF ______________________

________________________________, Plaintiff

v. SUBPOENA IN A CIVIL CASE

________________________________, Defendant Case Number: __________________________

Pending in ________________________ County

TO: ____

☐ YOU ARE COMMANDED to appear in the above named court at the place, and time specified below to testify in the above case.

PLACE OF TESTIMONY ________________	COURTROOM ______________________
	DATE AND TIME ____________, __________

☐ YOU ARE COMMANDED to appear at the place, date, and time specified below to testify at the taking of a deposition in the above case.

PLACE OF DEPOSITION	DATE AND TIME ____________, __________

☐ YOU ARE COMMANDED to produce and permit inspection and copying of the following documents or objects in your possession, custody or control at the place, date and time specified below (list documents of objects:

____

PLACE	DATE AND TIME ____________, __________

☐ YOU ARE COMMANDED to permit inspection of the following premises at the date and time specified below.

PREMISES	DATE AND TIME ____________, __________

ANY SUBPOENAED ORGANIZATION NOT A PARTY TO THIS IS HEREBY DIRECTED TO RULE 30(b)(6), SOUTH CAROLINA RULES OF CIVIL PROCEDURE, TO FILE A DESIGNATION WITH THE COURT SPECIFYING ONE OR MORE OFFICERS, DIRECTORS, OR MANAGING AGENTS, OR OTHER PERSONS WHO CONSENT TO TESTIFY ON ITS BEHALF, SHALL SET FORTH, FOR EACH PERSON DESIGNATED, THE MATTERS ON WHICH HE WILL TESTIFY OR PRODUCE DOCUMENTS OR THINGS. THE PERSON SO DESIGNATED TESTIFY AS TO MATTERS KNOWN OR REASONABLY AVAILABLE TO THE ORGANIZATION

I CERTIFY THAT THE SUBPOENA IS ISSUED IN COMPLIANCE WITH RULE 45(c)(1), AND THAT NOTICE AS REQUIRED BY RULE 45(b)(1) HAS BEEN GIVEN TO ALL PARTIES.

____

Attorney/Issuing Officer's Signature Date Print Name
Indicate if Attorney for Plaintiff or Defendant
Attorney's Address and Telephone Number :

____

____

____

Clerk of Court/Issuing Officer's Signature Date Print Name
Pro Se Litigant's Name, Address and Telephone Number :

____

____

SCCA 254 (05/2011) (See Rule 45, South Carolina Rules of Civil Procedure, Parts (c) & (d) on next page)

PROOF OF SERVICE

SERVED	DATE	FEES AND MILEAGE TENDERED TO WITNESS
	PLACE	☐YES ☐NO AMOUNT $
SERVED ON		MANNER OF SERVICE
SERVED BY		TITLE

DECLARATION OF SERVER

I certify that the foregoing information contained in the Proof of Service is true and correct.

Executed on______________________

____
SIGNATURE OF SERVER

____
ADDRESS OF SERVER

Rule 45, South Carolina Rules of Civil Procedures, Parts (c) and (d):

(c) Protection of Persons Subject to Subpoenas.

(1) A party or an attorney responsible for the issuance and service of a subpoena shall take reasonable steps to avoid imposing undue burden or expense on a person subject to that subpoena. The court on behalf of which the subpoena was issued shall enforce this duty and impose upon the party or attorney in breach of this duty an appropriate sanction, which may include, but is not limited to, lost earnings and a reasonable attorney's fee.

(2) (A) A person commanded to produce and permit inspection and copying of designated books, papers, documents or tangible things, or inspection of premises need not appear in person at the place of production or inspection unless commanded to appear for deposition, hearing or trial. A party or an attorney responsible for the issuance and service of a subpoena for production of books, papers and documents without a deposition shall provide to another party copies of documents so produced upon written request. The party requesting copies shall pay the reasonable costs of reproduction.

(B) Subject to paragraph (d)(2) of this rule, a person commanded to produce and permit inspection and copying may, within 14 days after service of the subpoena or before the time specified for compliance if such time is less than 14 days after service, serve upon the party or attorney designated in the subpoena written objection to inspection or copying of any or all of the designated materials or of the premises. If objection is made, the party serving the subpoena shall not be entitled to inspect and copy the materials or inspect the premises except pursuant to an order of the court by which the subpoena was issued. If objection has been made, the party serving the subpoena may, upon notice to the person commanded to produce, move at any time in the court that issued the subpoena for an order to compel the production. Such an order to compel production shall protect any person who is not a party or an officer of a party from significant expense resulting from the inspection and copying commanded.

(3) (A) On timely motion, the court by which a subpoena was issued, or regarding a subpoena commanding appearance at a deposition, or production or inspection directed to a non-party, the court in the county where the non-party resides, is employed or regularly transacts business in person, shall quash or modify the subpoena if it:

i. fails to allow reasonable time for compliance; or

ii. requires a person who is not a party nor an officer, director or managing agent of a party, nor a general partner of a partnership that is a party, to travel more than 50 miles from the county where that person resides, is employed or regularly transacts business in person, except that, subject to the provisions of clause (c)(3)(B)(iii) of this rule, such a person may in order to attend trial be commanded to travel from any such place within the state in which the trial is held; or

iii. requires disclosure of privileged or otherwise protected matter and no exception or waiver applies; or

iv. subjects a person to undue burden.

(B) If a subpoena:

i. requires disclosure of a trade secret or other confidential research, development, or commercial information, or

ii. requires disclosure of an unretained expert's opinion or information not describing specific events or occurrences in dispute and resulting from the expert's study made not at the request of any party, or

iii. requires a person who is not a party nor an officer, director or managing agent of a party, nor a general partner of a partnership that is a party, to incur substantial expense to travel from the county where that person resides, is employed or regularly transacts business in person,

the court may, to protect a person subject to or affected by the subpoena, quash or modify the subpoena or, if the party in whose behalf the subpoena is issued shows a substantial need for the testimony or material that cannot be otherwise met without undue hardship and assures that the person to whom the subpoena is addressed will be reasonably compensated, the court may order appearance or production only upon specified conditions.

(d) Duties in Responding to Subpoena.

(1) A person responding to a subpoena to produce documents shall produce them as they are kept in the usual course of business or shall organize and label them to correspond with the categories in the demand.

(2) When information subject to a subpoena is withheld on a claim that it is privileged or subject to protection as trial preparation materials, the claim shall be made expressly and shall be supported by a description of the nature of the documents, communications, or things not produced that is sufficient to enable the demanding party to contest the claim.

INDEX TO SOUTH CAROLINA RULES OF CIVIL PROCEDURE

*

SOUTH CAROLINA RULES OF CRIMINAL PROCEDURE

Westlaw Electronic Research

These rules may be searched electronically on Westlaw in the SC-RULES *database; updates to these rules may be found on Westlaw in* SC-RULESUPDATES. *For search tips and a summary of database content, consult the Westlaw Scope Screen for each database.*

I. PRETRIAL MATTERS

RULE 1. SHERIFF TO FILE AFFIDAVITS ON ARREST

The Sheriff and/or law enforcement officer shall file with the appropriate magistrate the affidavit and/or proof of service on which the arrest is made within five days after the arrest.

[Adopted effective September 1, 1988.]

Notes

Rule 1 is based upon the language of Criminal Practice Rule 1.

RULE 2. PRELIMINARY HEARINGS

(a) Notice of Right. Any defendant charged with a crime not triable by a magistrate shall be brought before a magistrate and shall be given notice of his right to a preliminary hearing solely to determine whether sufficient evidence exists to warrant the defendant's detention and trial. In the case of bailable offenses, the notice shall be given at the bond hearing. In the case of non-bailable offenses, the notice shall be given no later than would be required if the offense were bailable. Notice shall be given orally and also by means of a simple form providing the defendant an opportunity to request a preliminary hearing by signing the form and returning it to the advising magistrate. In all cases, the request for a preliminary hearing shall be made within ten days after the notice.

(b) Time for Hearing. If the defendant requests a preliminary hearing, the hearing shall be held within ten days following the request. The hearing shall not be held, however, if the defendant is indicted by a grand jury or waives indictment before the preliminary hearing is held. The defendant may appear by counsel or in person or both.

(c) Probable Cause. If probable cause be found by the magistrate, the defendant shall be bound over to the Court of General Sessions. If there be a lack of probable cause, the defendant shall be discharged; but his discharge shall not prevent the State from instituting another prosecution for the same offense.

(d) Conclusion of Hearing. After concluding the hearing the magistrate shall transmit forthwith to the Clerk of the Court his findings together with all papers in the hearing.

(e) Delays. Any delay in the holding of a preliminary hearing shall not be grounds for a delay in the prosecution of the case in the Court of General Sessions.

[Adopted effective September 1, 1988.]

Notes

Rule 2 is the language of Criminal Practice Rule 9.

RULE 3. DISPOSITION OF ARREST WARRANTS

(a) Transmittal to Clerk. Magistrates, municipal judges, and other officials authorized to issue warrants shall, in all cases within the jurisdiction of the Court of General Sessions, forward to the Clerk of the Court of General Sessions all documents pertaining to the case including, but not limited to, the arrest warrant and bond, within fifteen (15) days from the date of arrest in the case of an arrest warrant and date of issuance in the case of other documents. Transmittal shall be pursuant to procedures now or hereafter promulgated by the Office of South Carolina Court Administration.

(b) Transmittal to Solicitor. The Clerk of the Court of General Sessions shall forward a copy of any arrest warrant received pursuant to paragraph (a) above to the solicitor within two (2) business days from date of receipt from the issuing official.

(c) Action on Warrant. Within ninety (90) days after receipt of an arrest warrant from the Clerk of Court, the solicitor shall take action on the warrant by (1) preparing an indictment for presentment to the grand jury, which indictment shall be filed with the Clerk of Court, assigned a criminal case number, and presented to the Grand Jury; (2) formally dismissing the warrant, noting on the face of the warrant the action taken; or (3) making other affirmative disposition in writing and filing such action with the Clerk of Court.

(d) Extensions of Time. The solicitor may petition the circuit court for an order delaying action on the warrant, as set forth above, for successive ninety (90) day periods if the circuit court specifically finds good cause for such delay for each successive ninety day period.

(e) Record of Proceedings. Any action taken pursuant to paragraphs (a), (b), and (c) above shall be entered in the records of the Clerk of Court pursuant to procedures now or hereafter promulgated by the Office of South Carolina Court Administration.

[Adopted effective September 1, 1988.]

Notes

Rule 3 is the language of Criminal Practice Rule 6.

RULE 4. MOTIONS IN GENERAL

(a) Form of Motions. An application to the court for an order shall be by motion which, unless made during a hearing or trial in open court with a court reporter present, shall be made in writing, shall state with particularity the grounds therefor, and shall set forth the relief or order sought. The requirement of writing is fulfilled if the motion is stated in a written notice of the hearing of the motion.

(b) Subsequent Applications for Order After Refusal. If any motion be made to any judge and be denied, in whole or in part, or be granted conditionally, no subsequent motion upon the same set of facts shall be made to any other judge in that action. If upon such subsequent motion any order be made, it shall be void.

[Adopted effective September 1, 1988.]

Notes

Section (a) is the language of Rule 7(b)(1), SCRCP, and Section (b) is the language of Rule 43(1), SCRCP. The last sentence of Section (b) is taken from Circuit Court Rule 60.

RULE 5. DISCLOSURE IN CRIMINAL CASES

(a) Disclosure of Evidence by the Prosecution.

(1) *Information Subject to Disclosure.*

(A) Statement of Defendant. Upon request by a defendant, the prosecution shall permit the defendant to inspect and copy or photograph: any relevant written or recorded statements made by the defendant, or copies thereof, within the possession, custody or control of the prosecution, the existence of which is known, or by the exercise of due diligence may become known, to the attorney for the prosecution; the substance of any oral statement which the prosecution intends to offer in evidence at the trial made by the defendant whether before or after arrest in response to interrogation by any person then known to the defendant to be a prosecution agent.

(B) Defendant's Prior Record. Upon request of the defendant, the prosecution shall furnish to the defendant such copy of his prior criminal record, if any, as is within the possession, custody, or control of the prosecution, the existence of which is known, or by the exercise of due diligence may become known, to the attorney for the prosecution.

(C) Documents and Tangible Objects. Upon request of the defendant the prosecution shall permit the defendant to inspect and copy books, papers, documents, photographs, tangible objects, buildings or places, or copies or portions thereof, which are within the possession, custody or control of the prosecution, and which are material to the preparation of his defense or are intended for use by the prosecution as evidence in chief at the trial, or were obtained from or belong to the defendant.

(D) Reports of Examinations and Tests. Upon request of a defendant the prosecution shall permit the defendant to inspect and copy any results or reports of physical or mental examinations, and of scientific tests or experiments, or copies thereof, which are within the possession, custody, or control of the prosecution, the existence of which is known, or by the exercise of due diligence may become known, to the attorney for the prosecution, and which are material to the preparation of the defense or are intended for use by the prosecution as evidence in chief at the trial.

(2) *Information Not Subject to Disclosure.* Except as provided in paragraphs (A), (B), and (D) of subdivision (a)(1), this rule does not authorize the discovery or inspection of reports, memoranda, or other internal prosecution documents made by the attorney for the prosecution or other prosecution agents in connection with the investigation or prosecution of the case, or of statements made by prosecution witnesses or prospective prosecution witnesses provided that after a prosecution witness has testified on direct examination, the court shall, on motion of the defendant, order the prosecution to produce any statement of the witness in the possession of the prosecution which relates to the subject matter as to which the witness has testified; and provided further that the court may upon a sufficient showing require the production of any statement of any prospective witness prior to the time such witness testifies.

(3) *Time for Disclosure.* The prosecution shall respond to the defendant's request for disclosure no later than thirty (30) days after the request is made, or within such other time as may be ordered by the court.

(b) Disclosure of Evidence by the Defendant.

(1) *Information Subject to Disclosure.*

(A) Documents and Tangible Objects. If the defendant requests disclosure under subdivision (a)(1)(C) or (D) of this rule, upon compliance with such request by the prosecution, the defendant, on request of the prosecution, shall permit the prosecution to inspect and copy books, papers, documents, photographs, tangible objects, or copies or portions thereof, which are within the possession, custody, or control of the defendant and which the defendant intends to introduce as evidence in chief at the trial.

(B) Reports of Examinations and Tests. If the defendant requests disclosure under subdivision (a)(1)(C) or (D) of this rule, upon compliance with such request by the prosecution, the defendant, on request of the prosecution, shall permit the prosecution to inspect and copy any results or reports of physical or mental examinations and of scientific tests or experiments made in connection with the particular case, or copies thereof, within the possession or control of the defendant, which the defendant intends to introduce as evidence in chief at the trial or which were prepared by a witness whom the defendant intends to call at trial when the results or reports relate to his testimony.

(2) *Information Not Subject to Disclosure.* Except as to scientific or medical reports, this subdivision does not authorize the discovery or inspection of reports, memoranda, or other internal defense documents made by the defendant, or his attorneys or agents in connection with the investigation or defense of the case, or of statements made by the defendant, or by prosecution or defense witnesses, or by prospective prosecution or defense witnesses, to the defendant, his agents or attorneys.

(c) Continuing Duty to Disclose. If, prior to or during trial, a party discovers additional evidence or material previously requested or ordered, which is subject to discovery or inspection under this rule, he shall promptly notify the other party or his attorney or the court of the existence of the additional evidence or material.

(d) Regulation of Discovery.

(1) *Protective and Modifying Orders.* Upon a sufficient showing the court may at any time order that the discovery or inspection be denied, restricted, or deferred, or make such other order as is appropriate. Upon motion by a party, the court may permit the party to make such showing, in whole or in part, in the form of a written statement to be inspected by the judge alone. If the court enters an order granting relief following such an *ex parte* showing, the entire text of the party's statement shall be sealed and preserved in the records of the court to be made available to the appellate court in the event of an appeal.

(2) *Failure to Comply With a Request.* If at any time during the course of the proceedings it is brought to the attention of the court that a party has failed to comply with this rule, the court may order such party to permit the discovery or inspection, grant a continuance, or prohibit the party from introducing evidence not disclosed, or it may enter such other order as it deems just under the circumstances. The court may specify the time, place and manner of making the discovery and inspection and may prescribe such terms and conditions as are just.

(e) Notice of Alibi.

(1) *Notice of Alibi by Defendant.* Upon written request of the prosecution stating the time, date and place at which the alleged offense occurred, the defendant shall serve within ten days, or at such time as the court may direct, upon the prosecution a written notice of his intention to offer an alibi defense. The notice shall state the specific place or places at which the defendant claims to have been at the time of the alleged offense and the names and addresses of the witnesses upon whom he intends to rely to establish such alibi.

(2) *Disclosure by Prosecution.* Within ten days after defendant serves his notice, but in no event less than ten days before trial, or as the court may otherwise direct, the prosecution shall serve upon the defendant or his attorney the names and addresses of witnesses upon whom the State intends to rely to establish defendant's presence at the scene of the alleged crime.

(3) *Continuing Duty to Disclose.* Both parties shall be under a continuing duty to promptly disclose the names and addresses of additional witnesses whose identity, if known, should have been included in the information furnished under subdivisions (1) or (2).

(4) *Failure to Disclose.* If either party fails to comply with the requirements of this rule, the court may exclude the testimony of any undisclosed witness offered by either party. Nothing in this rule shall limit the right of the defendant to testify on his own behalf.

(f) Notice of Insanity Defense or Plea of Guilty but Mentally Ill. Upon written request of the prosecution, the defendant shall within ten days or at such time as the court may direct, notify the prosecution in writing of the defendant's intention to rely upon the defense of insanity at the time of the crime or to enter a plea of guilty but mentally ill. If the defendant fails to comply with the requirements of the subdivision, the court may exclude the testimony of any expert witness offered by the defendant on the issue of his mental state. The court may, for good cause shown, allow late filing of the notice or grant additional time to the parties to prepare for trial or make such other order as is appropriate.

(g) Waiver. The court may, for good cause shown, waive the requirements of this rule.

[Adopted effective September 1, 1988.]

Notes

Rule 5 is the language of Criminal Practice Rule 8. Section (a)(3) has been added to establish time limits for disclosure by the State, and Section (f) has been amended to provide for notification when a defendant intends to enter a plea of guilty but mentally ill.

RULE 6. RULE FOR CHEMICAL ANALYSIS AND CHAIN OF CUSTODY

(a) Report of Chemical Analysis. For the purpose of establishing the physical evidence of a controlled substance or other substance regulated by Title 44, Chapter 53 of the Code of Laws or Rule 61–4 of the Department of Health and Environmental Control, a report signed by the chemist or analyst who performed the test or tests required concerning its nature shall be evidence that the material delivered to him or her was properly tested under procedures approved by the State Law Enforcement Division (SLED), that those procedures are legally reliable and that the material is or contains the substance or substances stated. The report shall be admitted without the necessity of the chemist or analyst personally being present or appearing in court provided:

(1) the report, at a minimum, identifies each item tested, the kind of test or tests conducted on each item, and the chemist's or analyst's conclusion whether the item is or contains a controlled or other regulated substance (to include weight or quantity, if appropriate) in language which can be understood by a juror without the necessity for expert testimony; and,

(2) the report is accompanied by an affidavit of the chemist or analyst who performed the test or tests that:

(A) he or she is certified by SLED as qualified under standards approved by SLED to analyze those substances;

(B) sets forth his or her training and experience as a chemist or analyst, to include the number of times he or she has been qualified as an expert witness and testified in court; and,

(C) he or she conducted the test or tests shown on the report using procedures approved by SLED and that the report accurately reflects his or her opinion regarding the results of those tests.

The defendant or opposing party may object to the introduction of a chemist's or analyst's report at a preliminary hearing, or if no preliminary hearing is held, not later than ten (10) days prior to the trial of the case. If such objection is properly made, the trial judge shall require the chemist or analyst to be present at trial for the purpose of personally testifying.

(b) Certified or Sworn Statement. For the purpose of establishing a chain of physical custody or control of evidence entered under Part A of this Rule, a certified or sworn statement signed by each successive person having custody of the evidence that he or she delivered it to the person stated is evidence that the person had custody and made delivery as stated without the necessity of the person who signed the statement being present in court provided: (1) the statement contains a sufficient description of the substance or its container to distinguish it; and (2) the statement says the substance was delivered in substantially the same condition as when received.

The defendant or his attorney may demand appearance in court of the persons within the chain of custody in the same manner as provided in Section (a).

(c) Disclosure. In a criminal prosecution any reports or papers mentioned in Sections (a) or (b) shall be made available to the defendant or his attorney at the preliminary hearing or if no hearing is held, not later than eleven (11) days prior to the trial of the case.

(d) Waiver of Rights. Nothing in this Rule shall preclude the right of any defendant to obtain an expert chemist or analyst to test a substance in his behalf, provided it is tested under the supervision of the authority having custody of the substance or of SLED. Nothing in this Rule shall preclude the right of any party to introduce any evidence supporting or contradicting reports or papers entered into evidence under this Rule.

[Adopted effective September 1, 1988. Amended effective July 1, 1994.]

Notes

Rule 6 is the language of Criminal Practice Rule 7.

Notes to 1994 Amendment

This amendment changes Rule 6(a). Under the former rule, all the requirements of this rule were intended to be shown by a single report. This amendment allows the report of the chemist or analyst containing the results of the testing to be a separate document from the affidavit of the chemist or analyst establishing the remaining requirements of this rule. Additionally, the amendment makes minor changes to clarify the meaning of the rule.

RULE 7. CONTINUANCES

(a) Authority to Grant. The chief administrative judge for General Sessions in each circuit shall have exclusive authority to grant continuances of cases scheduled for trial or expected to be called for trial. Continuances may be granted by a presiding judge during a term of court at which he presides only upon written request by counsel, and any order granting a continuance shall be in writing, shall be made only upon a showing of good and sufficient legal cause and shall be filed forthwith with the clerk of court. A continuance granted by a presiding judge cannot extend beyond the next term of court without the approval of the chief administrative judge.

(b) Continuance Because of Absence of Witness. No motion for continuance of trial shall be granted on account of the absence of a witness without the oath of the party, his counsel, or agent to the following effect: the testimony of the witness is material to the support of the action or defense of the party moving; the motion is not intended for delay, but is made solely because he cannot go safely to trial without such testimony; and has made use of due diligence to procure the testimony of the witness or of such other circumstances as will satisfy the court that his motion is not intended for delay.

(1) When a subpoena has been issued, the original shall be produced with proof of service or the reason why not served endorsed thereon or attached thereto; or if lost the same proof shall be offered with additional proof of the loss of the original subpoena.

(2) A party applying for such postponement on account of the absence of a witness shall set forth under oath in addition to the foregoing matter what fact or facts he believes the witness if present would testify to and the grounds for such belief.

(c) Continuance for Good Cause. If other good sufficient cause for continuance is shown, a continuance may be granted by the chief administrative judge for General Sessions Court.

[Adopted effective September 1, 1988.]

Notes

This replaces Circuit Court Rule 27. The language is substantially the language of Rule 40(c), SCRCP, with additional language regulating the granting of continuances by the chief administrative judge and presiding judges.

RULES 8 to 12. [RESERVED]

II. TRIAL

RULE 13. SUBPOENAS

(a) Issuance of Subpoenas. Upon the request of any party, the clerk of court shall issue subpoenas or subpoenas duces tecum for any person or persons to attend as witnesses in any cause or matter in the General Sessions Court. The subpoena shall state the name of the court, the title of the action, and shall command each person to whom it is directed to attend and give testimony, or otherwise produce documentary evidence at time and place therein specified. The subpoena shall also set forth the name of the party requesting the appearance of such witness and the name of counsel for the party, if any.

(b) Service. A subpoena may be served by the sheriff of any county in which the witness may be found, by his deputy or by any other person who is not a party and is not less than eighteen years of age. Service of a subpoena upon an individual may be made by delivering a copy to him personally, or by leaving copies thereof at his dwelling house or usual place of abode with some person of suitable age and discretion then residing therein, or by delivering a copy to an agent authorized by appointment or by law to receive service. Service may be made on any day of the week.

[Adopted effective September 1, 1988.]

Notes

This rule replaces S.C. Code Ann. Section 19–7–10 (1976) repealed by Act No. 100 of 1985. The language is taken from Section 19–7–10 (1976) and Rule 4(d), 45(c), SCRCP.

RULE 14. TRIAL BY JURY

(a) Number of Jurors. A jury shall be composed of twelve members, but at any time before verdict, the parties may agree in writing with the approval of the court that the jury shall consist of any number less than twelve or that a valid verdict may be returned by a jury of less than twelve should the court find it necessary to excuse one or more jurors for any just cause after trial commences.

(b) Waiver. A defendant may waive his right to a jury trial only with the approval of the solicitor and the trial judge.

(c) Protection of Right. In all cases, the trial judge shall ensure that the defendant's rights under the state and federal constitutions to a trial by jury are preserved.

[Adopted effective September 1, 1988.]

Notes

This replaces Circuit Court Rule 46. The language is based on Rule 23, Fed. R. Crim. P.

RULE 15. [RESERVED]

RULE 16. PRESENCE OF ACCUSED AT TRIAL

Except in cases wherein capital punishment is a permissible sentence, a person indicted for misdemeanors and/or felonies may voluntarily waive his right to be present and may be tried in his absence upon a finding by the court that such person has received notice of his right to be present and that a warning was given that the trial would proceed in his absence upon a failure to attend the court.

[Adopted effective September 1, 1988.]

Notes

Rule 16 is the language of Criminal Practice Rule 3.

RULE 17. RESERVATION OF OBJECTIONS

If an objection has once been made at any stage to the admission of evidence, it shall not be necessary thereafter to reserve rights concerning the objectionable evidence.

[Adopted effective September 1, 1988.]

Notes

This replaces Circuit Court Rule 101. The language is taken from Rule 43(c)(1), SCRCP.

RULE 18. ARGUMENT ON OBJECTIONS

(a) Argument After Ruling. Counsel shall not attempt to further argue any matter after he has been heard and the ruling of the court has been pronounced.

(b) Argument on Objection. No argument shall be made on objections to admissibility of evidence or conduct of trial unless specifically requested by the court.

(c) Interruption of Argument. No attorney shall interrupt another in the course of his argument.

[Adopted effective September 1, 1988.]

Notes

This replaces the first paragraph of Circuit Court Rule 11. The language is taken from Rule 43(i), SCRCP. Section (c) is taken from Circuit Court Rule 11 regarding interrupting an attorney during argument.

RULE 19. DIRECTED VERDICT

(a) Grounds for Motion. On motion of the defendant or on its own motion, the court shall direct a verdict in the defendant's favor on any offense charged in the indictment after the evidence on either side is closed, if there is a failure of competent evidence tending to prove the charge in the indictment. In ruling on the motion, the trial judge shall consider only the existence or non-existence of the evidence and not its weight.

(b) Defendant's Right to Present Evidence. If a defendant's motion for directed verdict at the close of the evidence offered by the State is not granted, the defendant may offer evidence without having reserved the right.

(c) Submission of Case to Jury. Submission of any charge to the jury shall constitute a denial of any motion for directed verdict previously made by the defendant and not ruled upon.

[Adopted effective September 1, 1988.]

Notes

This is substantially the substance of Circuit Court Rule 76. The language is taken from Rule 29(a), Fed. R. Crim. P. and the common law.

RULE 20. INSTRUCTIONS

(a) Time for Request. All requests for legal instructions to the jury shall be submitted at the close of the evidence, or at such earlier time as the trial judge shall reasonably direct. All requests must include accurate citation to authorities relied upon.

(b) Objections to Charge. Notwithstanding any request for legal instructions, the parties shall be given the opportunity to object to the giving or failure to give an instruction before the jury retires, but out of the hearing of the jury. Any objection shall state distinctly the matter objected to and the grounds for objection. Failure to object in accordance with this rule shall constitute a waiver of objection.

[Adopted effective September 1, 1988.]

Notes

This rule replaces Circuit Court Rule 11, and is taken from Rule 51, SCRCP, and Rule 30, Fed. R. Crim. P. (version effective prior to August 1, 1987).

RULE 21. [RESERVED]

RULE 22. ADDRESSING THE JURY

In arguing before a jury, no attorney shall address or refer to by name or otherwise any member of the jury he is addressing, or otherwise make any personal appeal to any or all members of the jury.

[Adopted effective September 1, 1988.]

Notes

This is substantially the language of Circuit Court Rule 77.

RULE 23. SEPARATION OF JURY

If it appears that jury deliberations may extend into the night, the court, in its discretion, may order that the jury be taken to suitable sleeping quarters; and on the following morning they shall resume their deliberations. The jury shall be kept together, separately from the public, and as far as practicable, shall at all times, be under the surveillance of bailiffs. Any juror or jurors may be separated for the night from any other juror or jurors. There shall be no unauthorized communication with any member of the jury by any third person and the jury shall be fully protected from any outside influence.

[Adopted effective September 1, 1988.]

Notes

This replaces Circuit Court Rule 80. The language is taken from Rule 47(c), SCRCP, with minor modifications for clarity.

RULE 24. EXPERT TESTIMONY [DELETED]

[Deleted effective September 3, 1995.]

Notes

Note to 1990 Amendment

Rule 24 Expert Testimony is taken from Rules 702 to 705 of the Federal Rules of Evidence. The language in paragraph (c) is that of Federal Rule of Evidence 704 prior to its amendment in 1984. The Advisory committee Notes to the Federal Rules of Evidence provide commentary and useful guidance on the use of expert testimony under this Rule.

Note to 1995 Amendment

This amendment deleted Rule 24, SCRCrimP. Expert testimony is now governed by Rules 702–705 of the South Carolina Rules of Evidence.

RULES 25 to 27. [RESERVED]

III. POST-TRIAL MATTERS

RULE 28. AFFIDAVIT IN MITIGATION—HOW SUBMITTED

After verdict against him, the defendant shall not be permitted to submit any affidavit to the court which goes to deny matters of fact, but he may submit affidavits as to matters in extenuation or mitigation; provided, they are filed so as to allow the Attorney General or Solicitor a reasonable time to answer them.

[Adopted effective September 1, 1988.]

Notes

Rule 28 is substantially the language of Criminal Practice Rule 4.

RULE 29. POST-TRIAL MOTIONS

(a) Generally. Except for motions for new trials based on after-discovered evidence, post-trial motions shall be made within ten (10) days after the imposition of the sentence. In cases involving appeals from convictions in magistrate's or municipal court, post-trial motions shall be made within ten (10) days after receipt of written notice of entry of the order or judgment disposing of the appeal. The time for appeal for all parties shall be stayed by a timely post-trial motion and shall run from the receipt of written notice of entry of the order granting or denying such motion. The time within which to make the motion shall not be affected by the ending of a term of court or departure of the judge from the circuit, and the circuit judge shall retain jurisdiction of the action for the purpose of hearing and disposing of the motion if not heard and disposed of during the term. Except by consent of the parties, argument on the motion shall be heard in the circuit where the trial or hearing was held. The motion may, in the discretion of the court, be determined on briefs filed by the parties without oral argument.

(b) New Trials Based on After-Discovered Evidence. A motion for a new trial based on after-discovered evidence must be made within one (1) year after the date of actual discovery of the evidence by the defendant or after the date when the evidence could have been ascertained by the exercise of reasonable diligence. A motion for a new trial based on after-discovered evidence may not be made while the case is on appeal unless the appellate court, upon motion, has suspended the appeal and granted leave to make the motion. Leave of the appellate court is not required if no appeal has been taken or if the appeal has been finally decided in the appellate court.

[Adopted effective September 1, 1988. Amended effective September 1, 1990; June 30, 1991; April 28, 2011.]

Notes

The first sentence of this rule is taken from the common law rule that post trial motions be made and heard before the end of the term of court. This rule replaces Criminal Practice Rule 5.

Note to 1990 Amendment

This amendment deletes reference to Supreme Court Rule 24 which has been repealed. It adds language indicating when a motion for a new trial based on after-discovered evidence may be made in the trial court and when leave from an appellate court must be obtained to make the motion. It modifies the prior practice under Supreme Court Rule 24 by not requiring leave from the appellate court after the conviction has been affirmed.

Note to 1991 Amendment

This amendment reorganizes Rule 29. It changes prior practice by allowing the parties up to ten (10) days to file post trial motions and by providing the circuit judge jurisdiction to hear and determine these motions despite the end of the term. The amendment also provides flexibility for the circuit judge to determine motions on briefs without oral arguments.

Note to 2011 Amendment

This amendment places a one year limit on the time to make a motion for a new trial based on after-discovered evidence.

RULE 30. PROCESSING AND MAINTAINING BENCH WARRANTS

(a) Procedure. Subject to the approval of the Chief Justice, the Office of Court Administration shall establish procedures for processing and maintaining bench warrants.

(b) Form. Bench warrants shall be in the form prescribed in these rules and shall require either the signature of the trial judge or the signature of the respective clerk of court at the direction of the trial judge.

(c) Service. It is the continuing duty of the sheriff, and of other appropriate law enforcement agencies in the county, to make every reasonable effort to serve bench warrants and to make periodic reports to the court concerning the status of unserved warrants.

[Adopted effective September 1, 1988.]

Notes

Rule 30 is the language of Criminal Practice Rule 10.

RULES 31 to 35. [RESERVED]

IV. GENERAL PROVISIONS

RULE 36. FORMS

The Supreme Court shall prescribe the content and format of forms required by these rules. The use of the forms as prescribed is mandatory.

[Adopted effective September 1, 1988.]

Notes

The language of this rule is taken from Rule 84, SCRCP.

RULE 37. APPLICABILITY

These rules shall apply to every trial court of criminal jurisdiction within this State, within the limits of the jurisdiction and the powers of the court provided by law, and the procedure therein shall conform to these rules insofar as practicable. They shall apply insofar as practicable in magistrate's courts, municipal courts, and family courts to the extent they are not inconsistent with the statutes and rules governing those courts. In any case where no provision is made by statute or these rules, the procedure shall be according to the practice as it has heretofore existed in the courts of the State.

[Adopted effective September 1, 1988.]

Notes

The language of this rule is substantially taken from Rule 81, SCRCP.

RULE 38. TITLE AND CITATION

These rules shall be entitled the South Carolina Rules of Criminal Procedure and shall be cited by rule number and the abbreviation SCRCrimP, i.e., Rule __, SCRCrimP.

[Adopted effective September 1, 1988.]

Notes

The language of this rule is taken from Rule 85(c), SCRCP.

RULE 39. RULES REPEALED

All other existing Criminal Practice Rules heretofore adopted are repealed as of the effective date of these South Carolina Rules of Criminal Procedure.

[Adopted effective September 1, 1988.]

Notes

The language of this rule is taken from Rule 85(c), SCRCP.

RULE 40. EFFECTIVE DATE

These rules shall take effect on September 1, 1988. They govern all proceedings in criminal actions brought after they take effect and also all further proceedings then pending, except to the extent that in the opinion of the court their application in a particular action pending when the rules take effect would not be feasible or would work injustice, in which event the former procedure applies.

[Adopted effective September 1, 1988.]

Notes

The language of this rule is taken from Rule 86(a), SCRCP.

APPENDIX OF FORMS

FORM A. (Rule 6) AFFIDAVIT OF CHEMIST OR CHEMICAL ANALYST

Control No. ________________
Print All Information Except Where Signature Is Required

FORM A (Rule 6)

AFFIDAVIT OF CHEMIST OR CHEMICAL ANALYST

RE: Report Number ________________

I, ________________________________, am a Chemist / Chemical Analyst employed by ________________________________, and certified by SLED as qualified to perform testing and analysis for controlled substances or other substances regulated by Title 44, Chapter 53 of the Code of Laws or Rule6-4 of the Department of Health and Environmental Control.

I have had ________ years and ________ months experience as a Chemist / Chemical Analyst. During that period, I have been qualified as an expert witness and testified in court no fewer that ________ times. I have received the following training as a Chemist / Chemical Analyst:

(List schools of courses attended; other training received; organizations and honors received.)

____
____
____
____
____
____
____
____
____

I certify that I tested the items listed in the above referenced report using laboratory procedures approved by SLED and that the report accurately reflects my opinion regarding the results of the test of tests performed.

Sworn before me this	)	________________________________
______ day of ______________ , 2______	)	(Signature of Chemist of Analyst)
	)	
________________________________	)	________________________________
Notary Public for South Carolina	)	(Place)
	)	________________________________
My Commission expires ______________	)	(Date)

SCRCrimP APP-1

FORM B. (Rule 6) CERTIFICATE OF PROOF OF CHAIN OF PHYSICAL CUSTODY OR CONTROL (INITIAL CUSTODY)

CONTROL NO. ________

PRINT ALL INFORMATION EXCEPT WHERE SIGNATURE IS REQUIRED

FORM B (RULE 6)

CERTIFICATE OF PROOF OF CHAIN OF PHYSICAL CUSTODY OR CONTROL
(Initial Custody)

This is to certify that I ______________________ am employed by
(Name)

______________________________ and that on,
(Name of Agency or Department)

__________, ,2____, I seized from ______________________
(Name)

pursuant to ______________________________
(State Whether Subject to a Warrant, Lawful Arrest or Otherwise)

at or near ______________________________
(Place Where Seized)

the following substance(s) or container(s):
(Describe substance or container with sufficient particularity to distinguish it.)

____

____

____

____

On ________________, ,2____, I made delivery of the above described substance(s) or container(s) to ______________________ of
(Name)

______________________ in substantially the same condition
(Law Enforcement Agency)

as when I received it.

____
(Signature)

(Place): ______________
(Date): ______________

Sworn before me this ____ day of ______, 2____

____
Notary Public for South Carolina

My Commission expires __________

FORM C. (Rule 6) CERTIFICATE OF PROOF OF CHAIN OF PHYSICAL CUSTODY OR CONTROL (SUBSEQUENT CHANGE OF CUSTODY)

CONTROL NO. ________

PRINT ALL INFORMATION EXCEPT WHERE SIGNATURE IS REQUIRED

FORM C (RULE 6)

CERTIFICATE OF PROOF OF CHAIN OF PHYSICAL CUSTODY OR CONTROL
(Subsequent Change of Custody)

This is to certify that I ______________________ (Name) am employed by ______________________ (Name of Agency or Department) as ______________________ (Capacity of Employment) and that on ____________ (Date), 2___ I received ______________________ (Specify Whether by Mail or in Person) from ______________________ (Name of Person) of ______________________ (Law Enforcement Agency) the following substance(s) or container(s) which were originally seized by ______________________ (Name of Person Making Original Seizure)

(Describe substance or container with sufficient particularity to distinguish it.)

____

____

____

____

On ______________________ 2___, I made delivery of the above described substance(s) or container(s) to ______________________ (Name) of ______________________ (Law Enforcement Agency) in substantially the same condition as when I received it.

____
(Signature)

(Place): ______________

(Date): ______________

Sworn before me this ____ day of ______, 2___

____

Notary Public for South Carolina

My Commission expires ________

FORM D. BENCH WARRANT

STATE OF SOUTH CAROLINA
County of __________

____

vs.

____
____
____

BENCH WARRANT

____

Bench Warrant No. ____________________
Issued ____________________, 20________
Court ____________________________
Home Address _______________________
____
Business Address ______________________
____
Sex ________ Race ________ DOB __________
Height ______________ Weight ____________
Eyes ______________ Hair ____________
Social Security No. ____________________

. . . .

Return of Service

Note:

This return of service shall be printed or TYPED to the left of the above Bench Warrant information, both on the back of the warrant.

RETURN OF SERVICE

Date Served __________________________
Served by ___________________________
-or-
Date Returned ________________________
Reason for Return _____________________
____

FORM E. SUBPOENA IN A CRIMINAL CASE

SUBPOENA IN A CRIMINAL CASE

SOUTH CAROLINA COURT	COUNTY
V.	CASE NO.
	SUBPOENA FOR ☐ PERSON ☐ DOCUMENT(S) OR OBJECT(S)

TO:

☐ YOU ARE HEREBY COMMANDED to appear in the above–named court at the place, date, and time specified below to testify in the above-entitled case.

PLACE	COURTROOM
	DATE AND TIME

☐ YOU ARE ALSO COMMANDED to bring with you the following document(s) or object(s).

LIST DOCUMENT(S) OR OBJECT(S)

This subpoena shall remain in effect until you are granted leave to depart by the court or by an officer acting on behalf of the court.

CLERK OF COURT	DATE
(BY) DEPUTY CLERK	
THIS SUBPOENA IS ISSUED UPON APPLICATION OF THE: ☐ SOLICITOR ☐ DEFENDANT	NAME AND ADDRESS OF ATTORNEY or DEFENDANT (IF PRO SE/SELF REPRESENTED)

SCCA 253 (JULY 1, 1993)

PROOF OF SERVICE

SERVED	DATE	PLACE
SERVED ON (PRINT NAME)		MANNER OF SERVICE
SERVED BY (PRINT NAME)		TITLE

DECLARATION OF SERVER

I certify that the foregoing information contained in the Proof of Service is true and correct.

Executed on ____________________ ____________________

SIGNATURE OF SERVER

ADDRESS OF SERVER

FORM F. GENERAL SESSIONS SENTENCING SHEET

STATE OF SOUTH CAROLINA) IN THE COURT OF GENERAL SESSIONS
)
)
COUNTY OF)

STATE) INDICTMENT/CASE#: _____-GS-______-____________
VS.)
) A/W#: ____________________
AKA: ____________________) Date of Offense: ____________________
Race: ______ Sex: ______ Age: ______) S.C. Code §: ____________________
DOB: ______ SS#: ____________) CDR Code #: ____________________
Address: ____________________)
City, State, Zip: ____________________) **SENTENCE SHEET**
DL# ____________ * SID# ____________)
*CDL Yes ☐ No ☐ CMV Yes ☐ No ☐ Hazmat Yes ☐ No ☐

In disposition of the said indictment comes now the Defendant who was ☐ CONVICTED OF or ☐ PLEADS TO: ____________________
In violation of § ____________ of the S.C. Code of Laws, bearing CDR Code # ________
☐ NON-VIOLENT ☐ VIOLENT ☐ SERIOUS ☐ MOST SERIOUS ☐ Mandatory GPS (CSC w/minor 1st or Lewd Act) ☐ §17-25-45
The charge is: ☐ As indicted, ☐ Lesser Included Offense, ☐ Defendant Waives Presentment to Grand Jury. (def.'s initials)
The plea is: ☐ Without Negotiations or Recommendation, ☐ Negotiated Sentence, ☐ Recommendation by the State.
ATTEST:

Solicitor SC Bar # Defendant Attorney for Defendant SC Bar #

WHEREFORE, the Defendant is committed to the ☐ **State Department of Corrections** ☐ **County Detention Center,** for a determinate term of ________ days/months/years or ☐ under the **Youthful Offender Act** not to exceed ______ years and/or to pay a fine of $ ________ ; provided that upon the service of ____________ days/months/years and or payment of $ ________ ; plus costs and assessments as applicable*; the balance is suspended with **probation** for ____________ months/years and subject to South Carolina Department of Probation, Parole and Pardon Services standard conditions of probation, which are incorporated by reference.
☐ CONCURRENT or ☐ CONSECUTIVE to sentence on: ____________________
☐ The Defendant is to be given credit for time served pursuant to S.C. Code §24-13-40 to be calculated and applied by the State Department of Corrections.
☐ The Defendant is to be placed on Central Registry of Child Abuse and Neglect pursuant to S.C. Code §17-25-135.
Pursuant to 18 U.S.C. Section 922, it is unlawful for a person convicted of a violation of Section 16-25-20 or 16-25-65 (Criminal Domestic Violence) to ship, transport, possess, or receive a firearm or ammunition.

SPECIAL CONDITIONS:

☐ **RESTITUTION:** ☐ **Deferred** ☐ **Def. Waives Hearing** ☐ **Ordered**

Total: $ ________ plus 20% fee: ______ $ ________

Payment Terms: ____________________

☐ Set by SCDPPPS

Recipient: ____________________

*Fine: ____________		$ ______
§14-1-206 (Assessments 107.5%)		$ ______
§14-1-211 (A)(1)(Conv. Surcharge)	$100	$ ______
§14-1-211 (A)(2)(DUI Surcharge)	$100	$ ______
§56-5-2995 (DUI Assessment)	$12	$ ______
§56-1-286 (DUI Breath Test)	$25	$ ______
Proviso 47.9 (Public Def/Prob)	$500	$ ______
§14-1-212 (Law Enforce. Funding)	$25	$ ______
§14-1-213 (Drug Court Surcharge)	$150	$ ______
§50-21-114 (BUI Breath Test Fee)	$50	$ ______
§56-5-2942(J) (Vehicle Assessment)	$40/ea	$ ______
Proviso 90.5 (SCCJA Surcharge)	$5	$ ______
3% to County (if paid in installments)		$ ______
TOTAL		$ ______
		$ ______

Clerk of Court/Deputy Clerk ____________________
Court Reporter: ____________________

PTUP ____________________
________ days/hours Public Service Employment
Obtain GED ☐
Attend Voc. Rehab. Or Job Corp. ________
May serve W/E beginning ________
Substance Abuse Counseling ☐
Random Drug/Alcohol Testing ☐
Fine may be pd. in equal consecutive weekly/monthly pmts. of $ ______ Beginning ______
$ ________ Paid to Public Defender Fund
Other: ____________________

☐ Appointed PD or appointed other counsel, §47.12 requires $500 be paid to Clerk during probation.

Presiding Judge ____________________
Judge Code: ____________________
Sentence Date ____________________

SCCA/217 (03/2011)

INDEX TO SOUTH CAROLINA RULES OF CRIMINAL PROCEDURE

*

[illegible]

SOUTH CAROLINA RULES OF EVIDENCE

Westlaw Electronic Research

These rules may be searched electronically on Westlaw in the SC-RULES *database; updates to these rules may be found on Westlaw in* SC-RULESUP-DATES. *For search tips and a summary of database content, consult the Westlaw Scope Screen for each database.*

ARTICLE I

GENERAL PROVISIONS

RULE 101. SCOPE

Except as otherwise provided by rule or by statute, these rules govern proceedings in the courts of South Carolina to the extent and with the exceptions stated in Rule 1101.

[Adopted effective September 3, 1995.]

Notes

This rule differs from the federal rule in two regards. First, the phrase "except as otherwise provided by rule or by statute" is added to make it clear that statutes or other rules promulgated by the Supreme Court may limit the applicability of these rules. An example of such a rule is Rule 11 of the South Carolina Administrative and Procedural Rules for Magistrate's Court which provides that the rules of evidence apply in civil actions before the magistrate's court, but allows those rules to be relaxed in the interest of justice. Second, the phrase "courts of South Carolina" has been substituted for the phrase "courts of the United States, and before the United States bankruptcy judges and United States magistrate judges." Rule 1101 provides greater detail regarding the applicability of these rules in various proceedings.

RULE 102. PURPOSE AND CONSTRUCTION

These rules shall be construed to secure fairness in administration, elimination of unjustifiable expense and delay, and promotion of growth and development of the law of evidence to the end that the truth may be ascertained and proceedings justly determined.

[Adopted effective September 3, 1995.]

Notes

This rule is identical to the federal rule.

RULE 103. RULINGS ON EVIDENCE

(a) Effect of Erroneous Ruling. Error may not be predicated upon a ruling which admits or excludes evidence unless a substantial right of the party is affected, and

(1) *Objection.* In case the ruling is one admitting evidence, a timely objection or motion to strike appears of record, stating the specific ground of objection, if the specific ground was not apparent from the context; or

(2) *Offer of Proof.* In case the ruling is one excluding evidence, the substance of the evidence and the specific evidentiary basis supporting admission were made known to the court by offer or were apparent from the context.

(b) Record of Offer and Ruling. The court may add any other or further statement which shows the character of the evidence, the form in which it was offered, the objection made, and the ruling thereon. It may direct the making of an offer in question and answer form.

(c) Hearing of Jury. In jury cases, proceedings shall be conducted, to the extent practicable, so as to prevent inadmissible evidence from being suggested to the jury by any means, such as making statements or offers of proof or asking questions in the hearing of the jury.

[Adopted effective September 3, 1995.]

Notes

This rule is identical to the federal rule with the exception of the omission of subsection (d) relating to plain error. The rule of plain error contained in the federal rule is inconsistent with the law in South Carolina. Cf. *State v. Torrence,* 305 S.C. 45, 406 S.E.2d 315 (1991) (abolishing in favorem vitae review in capital cases and holding that error must be preserved by contemporaneous objection in the trial court). It should be noted that the Supreme Court has recognized a very few limited circumstances in which it will review issues raised for the first time on appeal. Cf. *Toyota of Florence, Inc. v. Lynch,* 314 S.C. 257, 442 S.E.2d 611 (1994) (challenge to abhorrent and outrageous argument raised for first time on appeal); *State v. Pace,* 316 S.C. 71, 447 S.E.2d 186 (1994) (failure to make contemporaneous objection to judge's comments excused where judge's tone and tenor made it clear that any objection would have been futile). Further, the failure to adopt a rule of plain error in no way limits the authority of trial judges to raise evidentiary issues on their own motion.

Subsection (a) means that reversal on appeal is only required where a substantial right of a party has been affected; error which is harmless does not affect a substantial right. Graham, *Handbook of Federal Evidence,* § 103.1 (3rd ed. 1981). This is equivalent to South Carolina law holding that reversal is not required unless an error is prejudicial and not harmless. *State v. Sosebee,* 284 S.C. 411, 326 S.E.2d 654 (1985) (probable prejudice must be shown); *State v. Gaskins,* 284 S.C. 105, 326 S.E.2d 132 (1985) (a new trial is not required for harmless error), cert. denied, 471 U.S. 1120, 105 S.Ct. 2368, 86 L.Ed.2d 266 (1985), overruled on other grounds, *State v. Torrence,* 305 S.C. 45, 406 S.E.2d 315 (1991); *Watts v. Bell Oil Co.,* 266 S.C. 61, 221 S.E.2d 529 (1976) (prejudice must be shown).

Subsection (a)(1) is generally in accord with prior South Carolina law which required a contemporaneous objection with specific grounds to preserve an error for review. *State v. Hoffman,* 312 S.C. 386, 440 S.E.2d 869 (1994) (contemporaneous objection); *White v. Wilbanks,* 298 S.C. 225, 379 S.E.2d 298 (Ct.App.1989) (contemporaneous objection), rev'd on other grounds, 301 S.C. 560, 393 S.E.2d 182 (1990); *State v. Bailey,* 253 S.C. 304, 170 S.E.2d 376 (1969) (specific grounds required; general objection preserves nothing). It does somewhat relax the requirement of stating specific grounds where the grounds are apparent from the context. The better practice, however, is for counsel to always give, and the court always to require, specific grounds for an objection; this will avoid later disputes regarding what was apparent from the context. It should be noted that Rule 43(i), SCRCP, Rule 18, SCRCrimP, and Rule 9(b), SCRFC, do not prevent counsel from stating the grounds for an objection, but merely control argument on the grounds for the objection. This rule does not alter the prior practice regarding motions in limine, which allowed the motion to exclude evidence to be made at the pretrial stage, *State v. Glenn*, 285 S.C. 384, 330 S.E.2d 285 (1985), but required a contemporaneous objection when the evidence is actually offered into evidence at the trial to preserve the issue for review. *State v. Schumpert*, ___ S.C. ___, 435 S.E.2d 859 (1993); *Parr v. Gaines*, 309 S.C. 477, 424 S.E.2d 515 (Ct.App.1992).

Subsection (a)(2) is the federal rule modified to require the grounds for admission to be stated. As modified, this rule is consistent with South Carolina law which requires a proffer of the excluded evidence and the grounds for admission to be stated to preserve the trial court's ruling for review. *State v. Cabbagestalk*, 281 S.C. 35, 314 S.E.2d 10 (1984); *State v. Cox*, 258 S.C. 114, 187 S.E.2d 525 (1972); *Legrande v. Legrande*, 178 S.C. 230, 182 S.E. 432 (1935); *Gold Kist, Inc. v. Citizens & Southern Nat'l Bank*, 286 S.C. 272, 333 S.E.2d 67 (Ct.App. 1985). The rule does change South Carolina law by dispensing with the requirement of a proffer and a statement of the grounds for admissibility where the substance of the evidence and the grounds are apparent from the context. The prior law only dispensed with the requirement of a proffer where the judge refused to allow a proffer. *State v. Schmidt*, 288 S.C. 301, 342 S.E.2d 401 (1986). To avoid later disputes over what was apparent from the context, however, the better practice is for a proffer and a statement of the grounds to always be made.

The first sentence of subsection (b) is similar to language contained in former Rule 43(c), SCRCP. Although no specific South Carolina case can be found to support the second sentence, requiring an offer to be made in question and answer form is within the discretion of the judge.

Subsection (c) is in accord with prior South Carolina law. *Chandler v. People's Nat'l Bank*, 140 S.C. 433, 138 S.E. 888 (1927); Rule 43(c), SCRCP.

RULE 104. PRELIMINARY QUESTIONS

(a) Questions of Admissibility Generally. Preliminary questions concerning the qualification of a person to be a witness, the existence of a privilege, or the admissibility of evidence shall be determined by the court, subject to the provisions of subdivision (b). In making its determination it is not bound by the rules of evidence except those with respect to privileges.

(b) Relevancy Conditioned on Fact. When the relevancy of evidence depends upon the fulfillment of a condition of fact, the court shall admit it upon, or subject to, the introduction of evidence sufficient to support a finding of the fulfillment of the condition.

(c) Hearing of Jury. Hearings on the admissibility of confessions or statements by an accused, and pretrial identifications of an accused shall in all cases be conducted out of the hearing of the jury. Hearings on other preliminary matters shall be so conducted when the interests of justice require, or when an accused is a witness and so requests.

(d) Testimony by Accused. The accused does not, by testifying upon a preliminary matter, become subject to cross-examination as to other issues in the case.

(e) Weight and Credibility. This rule does not limit the right of a party to introduce before the jury evidence relevant to weight or credibility.

[Adopted effective September 3, 1995.]

Notes

Except for subsection (c), this rule is identical to the federal rule.

The first sentence of subsection (a) is in accord with prior South Carolina law. *Wright v. Pub. Sav. Life Ins. Co.*, 262 S.C. 285, 204 S.E.2d 57 (1974). No South Carolina authority has been found which specifically determines whether a judge must apply the rules of evidence in conducting a hearing on the admissibility of evidence. Cf. *Congdon v. Morgan*, 14 S.C. 587 (1880) (passing comment that judge did not violate rules of evidence during hearing on admissibility of evidence).

Subsection (b) addresses situations where the relevancy of an item of evidence depends upon the existence of a particular preliminary fact. Prior South Carolina case law has recognized that a judge commits no error in admitting evidence where its relevancy is established later in the trial. *Perry v. Jefferies*, 61 S.C. 292, 39 S.E. 515 (1901) (evidence of acts of defendant's agents admitted before any evidence of agency introduced).

Subsection (c) modifies the federal rule by adding the phrase "or statements made by an accused, and pretrial identifications of an accused." This addition is made to emphasize the fact that hearings on the admissibility of all statements made by a criminal defendant, whether inculpatory or exculpatory, must be made outside the presence of the jury. *State v. Primus*, 312 S.C. 256, 440 S.E.2d 128 (1994); *State v. Lee*, 255 S.C. 309, 178 S.E.2d 652 (1971). The addition also requires all hearings regarding the admissibility of pretrial identifications (to include any assertion that an in-court identification should be excluded as a result of a pretrial identification) to be heard outside the presence of the jury. *State v. Simmons*, 308 S.C. 80, 417 S.E.2d 92 (1992).

No South Carolina cases have been found which address the matters stated in subsections (d) and (e).

RULE 105. LIMITED ADMISSIBILITY

When evidence which is admissible as to one party or for one purpose but not admissible as to another party or for another purpose is admitted, the court, upon request, shall restrict the evidence to its proper scope and instruct the jury accordingly.

[Adopted effective September 3, 1995.]

Notes

This rule is identical to the federal rule and is in accord with prior South Carolina law. *State v. Bottoms*, 260 S.C. 187, 195 S.E.2d 116 (1973); *State v. Bagwell*, 201 S.C. 387, 23 S.E.2d 244 (1942).

RULE 106. REMAINDER OF OR RELATED WRITINGS OR STATEMENTS

When a writing, or recorded statement, or part thereof is introduced by a party, an adverse party may require the introduction at that time of any other part or any other writing or recorded statement which ought in fairness to be considered contemporaneously with it.

[Adopted effective September 3, 1995.]

Notes

The law in this State has been that, when a part of a document or writing is introduced into evidence, the remainder may be introduced by the other party. *Dukes v. Smoak,* 181 S.C. 182, 186 S.E. 780 (1936). The same rule was applicable to conversations. *State v. Jackson,* 265 S.C. 278, 217 S.E.2d 794 (1975). However, the party seeking to bring out the remainder had to wait until cross-examination or the presentation of that party's case to do so. This rule, which is identical to the federal rule, changes the prior law as to written or recorded statements. The party seeking to introduce the remainder of a written or recorded statement can now require the remainder to be introduced at the same time the other part of the written or recorded statement is introduced. This rule does not change the order of proof as to the remainder of an unrecorded conversation; the party seeking to bring out the remainder must do so during cross-examination or during that party's case.

ARTICLE II

JUDICIAL NOTICE

RULE 201. JUDICIAL NOTICE OF ADJUDICATIVE FACTS

(a) Scope of Rule. This rule governs only judicial notice of adjudicative facts.

(b) Kinds of Facts. A judicially noticed fact must be one not subject to reasonable dispute in that it is either (1) generally known within the territorial jurisdiction of the trial court or (2) capable of accurate and ready determination by resort to sources whose accuracy cannot reasonably be questioned.

(c) When Discretionary. A court may take judicial notice, whether requested or not.

(d) When Mandatory. A court shall take judicial notice if requested by a party and supplied with the necessary information.

(e) Opportunity to Be Heard. A party is entitled upon timely request to an opportunity to be heard as to the propriety of taking judicial notice and the tenor of the matter noticed. In the absence of prior notification, the request may be made after judicial notice has been taken.

(f) Time of Taking Notice. Judicial notice may be taken at any stage of the proceeding.

(g) Instructing Jury. The court shall instruct the jury to accept as conclusive any fact judicially noticed.

[Adopted effective September 3, 1995.]

Notes

Except for subsection (g), this rule is identical to the federal rule. As stated by subsection (a), this rule governs only judicial notice of adjudicative facts. Adjudicative facts are "facts about the particular event which gave rise to the lawsuit and . . . [help] explain who did what, when, where, how and with what motive and intent." Legislative facts, on the other hand, are the factual grounds on which judges base their opinions "when deciding upon the constitutional validity of a statute, interpreting a statute, or extending or restricting a common law rule." C. McCormick, *McCormick on Evidence* §§ 328 and 331 (4th ed. 1992). The courts of this State continue to have authority to take judicial notice of legislative facts. *Cf. Davenport v. City of Rock Hill,* 315 S.C. 114, 432 S.E.2d 451 (1993) (history of tax anticipation notes considered).

Subsection (b) is consistent with prior case law in this State. *See In Re Harry C.,* 280 S.C. 308, 313 S.E.2d 287 (1984); *State v. Broad River Power Co.,* 177 S.C. 240, 181 S.E. 41 (1935). This rule does not allow a judge to take judicial notice of a fact merely because it is within his personal knowledge, and the case of *Gamble v. Price,* 289 S.C. 538, 347 S.E.2d 131 (Ct.App.1986) is inconsistent with this rule.

Regarding subsection (c), no South Carolina case has been found discussing this matter.

Subsection (d) is consistent with prior case law in this State. *See Toole v. Salter,* 249 S.C. 354, 154 S.E.2d 434 (1967); *State v. Broad River Power Co.,* 177 S.C. 240, 181 S.E. 41 (1935).

Regarding subsection (e), the law of this State has not previously entitled a party to be heard on the issue of taking judicial notice. This opportunity appears to be a useful safeguard to protect a party's rights. J. Weinstein and M. Berger, *Weinstein's Evidence,* ¶ 201[05] (1994).

Subsection (f) is consistent with prior case law in this State. *Cf. State v. Squires,* 311 S.C. 11, 426 S.E.2d 738 (1992) (Supreme Court took judicial notice that infrared spectroscopy process had gained general acceptance in the scientific community); *McCoy v. Town of York,* 193 S.C. 390, 8 S.E.2d 905 (1940) (Supreme Court took judicial notice of dangerous qualities of gasoline and kerosene).

Subsection (g) requires a court to instruct the jury to accept as conclusive any fact judicially noticed. The rule differs from the federal rule in that it makes no distinction between civil and criminal cases. The language of the rule is taken from the 1974 Uniform Rules of Evidence, Rule 201.

ARTICLE III

PRESUMPTIONS IN CIVIL ACTIONS AND PROCEEDINGS

RULE 301. PRESUMPTIONS IN GENERAL IN CIVIL ACTIONS AND PROCEEDINGS

In all civil actions and proceedings not otherwise provided for by statute or by these rules, a presumption imposes on the party against whom it is directed the burden of going forward with evidence to rebut or meet the presumption, but does not shift to such party the burden of proof in the sense of the risk of nonpersuasion, which remains throughout the trial upon the party on whom it was originally cast.

[Adopted effective September 3, 1995.]

Notes

This rule is the same as the federal rule. It is consistent with the case law in this State. *See Long v. Metropolitan Life Insurance Co.,* 228 S.C. 498, 90 S.E.2d 915 (1956); *Ford v. Atlantic Coast Line R. Co.,* 169 S.C. 41, 168 S.E. 143 (1932).

ARTICLE IV

RELEVANCY AND ITS LIMITS

RULE 401. DEFINITION OF "RELEVANT EVIDENCE"

"Relevant evidence" means evidence having any tendency to make the existence of any fact that is of consequence to the determination of the action more probable or less probable than it would be without the evidence.

[Adopted effective September 3, 1995.]

Notes

This rule is identical to the federal rule and is consistent with South Carolina law. *State v. Alexander,* 303 S.C. 377, 401 S.E.2d 146 (1991); *State v. Schmidt,* 288 S.C. 301, 342 S.E.2d 401 (1986).

RULE 402. RELEVANT EVIDENCE GENERALLY ADMISSIBLE; IRRELEVANT EVIDENCE INADMISSIBLE

All relevant evidence is admissible, except as otherwise provided by the Constitution of the United States, the Constitution of the State of South Carolina, statutes, these rules, or by other rules promulgated by the Supreme Court of South Carolina. Evidence which is not relevant is not admissible.

[Adopted effective September 3, 1995.]

Notes

This rule is the federal rule amended to reference South Carolina law. The rule reflects the law in South Carolina. *Levy v. Outdoor Resorts of South Carolina,* 304 S.C. 427, 405 S.E.2d 387 (1991); *State v. Petit,* 144 S.C. 452, 142 S.E. 725 (1928).

RULE 403. EXCLUSION OF RELEVANT EVIDENCE ON GROUNDS OF PREJUDICE, CONFUSION, OR WASTE OF TIME

Although relevant, evidence may be excluded if its probative value is substantially outweighed by the danger of unfair prejudice, confusion of the issues, or misleading the jury, or by considerations of undue delay, waste of time, or needless presentation of cumulative evidence.

[Adopted effective September 3, 1995.]

Notes

This rule is identical to the federal rule and is consistent with the law in South Carolina. *State v. Alexander,* 303 S.C. 377, 401 S.E.2d 146 (1991) (relevant evidence may be excluded where its probative value is substantially outweighed by the danger of unfair prejudice); *State v. Hess,* 279 S.C. 14, 301 S.E.2d 547 (limitation of defense testimony upheld where it was merely cumulative to other testimony), cert. denied, 464 U.S. 827, 104 S.Ct. 100, 78 L.Ed.2d 105 (1983); *State v. Gregory,* 198 S.C. 98, 16 S.E.2d 532 (1941) (trial judge properly limited the defendant's presentation of certain evidence to guard against confusion of the jury by the injection of collateral issues).

RULE 404. CHARACTER EVIDENCE NOT ADMISSIBLE TO PROVE CONDUCT; EXCEPTION; OTHER CRIMES

(a) Character Evidence Generally. Evidence of a person's character or a trait of character is not admissible for the purpose of proving action in conformity therewith on a particular occasion, except:

(1) *Character of Accused.* Evidence of a pertinent trait of character offered by an accused, or by the prosecution to rebut the same;

(2) *Character of Victim.* Evidence of a pertinent trait of character of the victim of the crime offered by an accused, or by the prosecution to rebut the same, or evidence of a character trait of peacefulness of the victim offered by the prosecution in a homicide case to rebut evidence that the victim was the first aggressor;

(3) *Character of Witness.* Evidence of the character of a witness, as provided in Rules 607, 608, and 609.

(b) Other Crimes, Wrongs, or Acts. Evidence of other crimes, wrongs, or acts is not admissible to prove the character of a person in order to show action in conformity therewith. It may, however, be admissible to show motive, identity, the existence of a common scheme or plan, the absence of mistake or accident, or intent.

[Adopted effective September 3, 1995.]

Notes

Rule 404(a) is identical to the federal rule and is consistent with the law in South Carolina. *State v. Peake,* 302 S.C. 378, 396 S.E.2d 362 (1990).

Rule 404(a)(1) is identical to the federal rule and is consistent with the law in South Carolina. *State v. Lyles,* 210 S.C. 87, 41 S.E.2d 625 (1947) (a defendant may put in evidence of his good character); *State v. Major,* 301 S.C. 181, 391 S.E.2d 235 (1990) (when the accused offers evidence of his good character regarding specific character traits relevant to the crime charged, the state may cross-examine as to acts relating to the traits focused on by the accused).

Rule 404(a)(2) identical to the federal rule and is consistent with the law in South Carolina. *State v. Boyd,* 126 S.C. 300, 119 S.E. 839 (1923).

Rule 404(b) differs in two respects from the federal rule. First, unlike the federal rule which does not limit the purposes for which evidence of other crimes may be admitted, the South Carolina rule limits the use of evidence of other crimes, wrongs, or acts to those enumerated in *State v. Lyle,* 125 S.C. 406, 118 S.E. 803 (1923). *See also Citizens Bank of Darlington v. McDonald,* 202 S.C. 244, 24 S.E.2d 369 (1943) (Lyle applicable in civil cases). Second, the South Carolina rule does not contain the requirement which is in the federal rule that, upon request by an accused, the prosecution must provide reasonable notice of the general nature of any evidence it intends to introduce under the rule. With the exception of notice of evidence to be used in aggravation in the sentencing phase of capital cases, S.C.Code Ann. § 16–3–20(B) (Supp.1993), there is no similar requirement under South Carolina law. The rule does not set forth the burden of proof required for the admission of evidence of bad acts not the subject of a conviction and, therefore, case law would control. *State v. Smith,* 300 S.C. 216, 387 S.E.2d 245 (1989) (in a criminal case, evidence of other crimes or bad acts must be clear and convincing if the acts are not the subject of a conviction). Further, when the prejudicial effect of evidence substantially outweighs its probative value, the evidence may be excluded under Rule 403 which is consistent with prior case law. *State v. Garner,* 304 S.C. 220, 403 S.E.2d 631 (1991).

RULE 405. METHODS OF PROVING CHARACTER

(a) Reputation or Opinion. In all cases in which evidence of character or a trait of character of a person is admissible, proof may be made by testimony as to reputation or by testimony in the form of an opinion. On cross-examination, inquiry is allowable into relevant specific instances of conduct.

(b) Specific Instances of Conduct. In cases in which character or a trait of character of a person is an essential element of a charge, claim, or defense, proof may also be made of specific instances of that person's conduct.

[Adopted effective September 3, 1995.]

Notes

Rule 405(a) is identical to the federal rule and changes the law in South Carolina in one respect. Formerly, only testimony as to a person's general reputation was allowed. *State v. Groome,* 274 S.C. 189, 262 S.E.2d 31 (1980); *In re Greenfield's Estate,* 245 S.C. 595, 141 S.E.2d 916 (1965). Rule 405(a) allows evidence of character to be in the form of opinion or reputation evidence. The portion of Rule 405(a) regarding cross-examination as to specific acts is consistent with the law in South Carolina. *State v. Major,* 301 S.C. 181, 391 S.E.2d 235 (1990) (when the accused offers evidence of his good character regarding specific character traits relevant to the crime charged, the state may cross-examine as to particular bad acts or conduct relating to the traits focused on by the accused).

Rule 405(b) is identical to the federal rule and is consistent with South Carolina law. *State v. Amburgey,* 206 S.C. 426, 34 S.E.2d 779 (1945).

RULE 406. HABIT; ROUTINE PRACTICE

Evidence of the habit of a person or of the routine practice of an organization, whether corroborated or not and regardless of the presence of eyewitnesses, is relevant to prove that the conduct of the person or organization on a particular occasion was in conformity with the habit or routine practice.

[Adopted effective September 3, 1995.]

Notes

This rule is identical to the federal rule and makes it clear that the presence or absence of eyewitnesses does not affect the relevancy of evidence of habit or routine practice. To the extent that South Carolina law regarding evidence of habit or routine was previously read to require the absence of eyewitnesses, this rule constitutes a change in the law. *Compare Laney v. Atlantic Coast Line Railway Co.,* 211 S.C. 328, 45 S.E.2d 184 (1947); *State v. Hester,* 137 S.C. 145, 134 S.E. 885 (1926); *Dowling v. Fenner,* 131 S.C. 62, 126 S.E. 432 (1922) *with Holcombe v. Watson Supply Co.,* 171 S.C. 110, 171 S.E. 604 (1933).

RULE 407. SUBSEQUENT REMEDIAL MEASURES

When, after an event, measures are taken which, if taken previously, would have made the event less likely to occur, evidence of the subsequent measures is not admissible to prove negligence or culpable conduct in connection with the event. This rule does not require the exclusion of evidence of subsequent measures when offered for another purpose, such as proving ownership, control, or feasibility of precautionary measures, if controverted, or impeachment.

[Adopted effective September 3, 1995.]

Notes

This rule is identical to the federal rule. The general rule that evidence of subsequent measures is inadmissible to establish negligence is consistent with South Carolina law. *Green v. Atlantic Coast Line R. Co.*, 136 S.C. 337, 134 S.E. 385 (1926). Under South Carolina law another stated purpose for admitting evidence of subsequent measures is to show the conditions existing at the time of the event or accident. *Taylor v. Nix*, 307 S.C. 551, 416 S.E.2d 619 (1992); *Plunkett v. Clearwater Bleachery Mfg. Co.*, 80 S.C. 310, 61 S.E. 431 (1906); *see also Eargle v. Sumter Lighting Co.*, 110 S.C. 560, 96 S.E. 909 (1918).

RULE 408. COMPROMISE AND OFFERS TO COMPROMISE

Evidence of (1) furnishing or offering or promising to furnish, or (2) accepting or offering or promising to accept, a valuable consideration in compromising or attempting to compromise a claim which was disputed as to either validity or amount, is not admissible to prove liability for or invalidity of the claim or its amount. Evidence of conduct or statements made in compromise negotiations is likewise not admissible. This rule does not require the exclusion of any evidence otherwise discoverable merely because it is presented in the course of compromise negotiations. This rule also does not require exclusion when the evidence is offered for another purpose, such as proving bias or prejudice of a witness, negativing a contention of undue delay, or proving an effort to obstruct a criminal investigation or prosecution.

[Adopted effective September 3, 1995.]

Notes

This rule is identical to the federal rule. It is generally the rule in South Carolina that evidence relating to settlements is not admissible to prove liability. *Hunter v. Hyder*, 236 S.C. 378, 114 S.E.2d 493 (1960); *see also Woodward v. Southern Railway*, 88 S.C. 453, 70 S.E. 1060 (1911) (evidence of disclosures made by either party to the other, directly or indirectly, in negotiations for a compromise is not admissible). Evidence of an offer to compromise may be admissible for some other purpose. *Meehan v. Commercial Casualty Ins. Co.*, 166 S.C. 496, 165 S.E. 194 (1932) (evidence of offers of compromise made by alleged agent of a party admissible for purpose of proving agency).

RULE 409. PAYMENT OF MEDICAL AND SIMILAR EXPENSES

Evidence of furnishing or offering or promising to pay medical, hospital, or similar expenses occasioned by an injury is not admissible to prove liability for the injury.

[Adopted effective September 3, 1995.]

Notes

This rule is identical to the federal rule. Formerly, South Carolina law, while generally prohibiting the admission of evidence of offers to pay, or payment of, medical or other expenses, *McIntire v. Winn Dixie Greenville, Inc.*, 275 S.C. 323, 270 S.E.2d 440 (1980), did allow its admission if the circumstances surrounding the payment indicated an admission of liability rather than an act of benevolence. *Crosby v. Southeast Zayre, Inc.*, 274 S.C. 519, 265 S.E.2d 517 (1980). The rule strictly prohibits the admission of evidence of offers to pay, or payment of, medical or other similar expenses.

RULE 410. INADMISSIBILITY OF PLEAS, PLEA DISCUSSIONS, AND RELATED STATEMENTS

Except as otherwise provided in this rule, evidence of the following is not, in any civil or criminal proceeding, admissible against the defendant who made the plea or was a participant in the plea discussions:

(1) a plea of guilty which was later withdrawn;

(2) a plea of nolo contendere;

(3) any statement made in the course of any court proceedings regarding either of the foregoing pleas; or

(4) any statement made in the course of plea discussions with an attorney for the prosecuting authority which do not result in a plea of guilty or which result in a plea of guilty later withdrawn.

However, such a statement is admissible (i) in any proceeding wherein another statement made in the course of the same plea or plea discussions has been introduced and the statement ought in fairness be considered contemporaneously with it, or (ii) in a criminal proceeding for perjury or false statement if the statement was made by the defendant under oath, on the record and in the presence of counsel.

[Adopted effective September 3, 1995.]

Notes

Except for subsection (3), this rule is identical to the federal rule. Subsection (3) was amended because South Carolina has no equivalent to Rule 11 of the Federal Rules of Criminal Procedure. It should be noted that convictions based on pleas of nolo contendere are admissible under Rule 609 for impeachment. The rule is consistent with prior South Carolina law. *State v. Mathis*, 287 S.C. 589, 340 S.E.2d 538 (1986); *State v. Lynn*, 277 S.C. 222, 284 S.E.2d 786 (1981).

RULE 411. LIABILITY INSURANCE

Evidence that a person was or was not insured against liability is not admissible upon the issue whether the person acted negligently or otherwise wrongfully. This rule does not require the exclusion of evidence of insurance against liability when offered for another purpose, such as proof of agency, ownership, or control, or bias or prejudice of a witness.

[Adopted effective September 3, 1995.]

Notes

This rule is identical to the federal rule and is consistent with the law in South Carolina. *Dunn v. Charleston Coca-Cola Bottling Co.*, 311 S.C. 43, 426 S.E.2d 756 (1993) (the fact that a defendant is protected from liability by insurance shall not be made known to the jury); *Sarvis v. Register*, 288 S.C. 236, 341

S.E.2d 791 (1986) (generally, the existence of insurance should not be brought to the attention of the jury).

RULE 412. ADMISSIBILITY OF EVIDENCE CONCERNING VICTIM'S SEXUAL CONDUCT IN CRIMINAL SEXUAL CONDUCT CASES

In prosecutions for criminal sexual conduct or assault with intent to commit criminal sexual conduct, the admissibility of evidence concerning the victim's sexual conduct is subject to the limitations contained in S.C. Code Ann. § 16-3-659.1 (1985).

[Adopted effective September 3, 1995.]

Notes

In a prosecution for criminal sexual conduct or assault with intent to commit criminal sexual conduct, the admissibility of evidence of the victim's sexual conduct is controlled by S.C. Code Ann. § 16–3–659.1 (1985). Unlike the federal rule which contains the standards and procedures governing the admissibility of such evidence, this rule merely references the statute.

ARTICLE V

PRIVILEGES

RULE 501. GENERAL RULE

Except as required by the Constitution of South Carolina, by the Constitution of the United States or by South Carolina statute, the privilege of a witness, person or government shall be governed by the principles of the common law as they may be interpreted by the courts in the light of reason and experience.
[Adopted effective September 3, 1995.]

Notes

This rule modifies the federal rule to refer to the South Carolina Constitution and statutes. Like the federal rule, this rule does not set forth a list of privileges. Among those privileges which would be covered by this rule are: husband and wife (S.C. Code Ann. § 19-11-30); priest and penitent (S.C. Code Ann. § 19-11-90); certain mental health professionals and clients (S.C. Code Ann. § 19-11-95); news media and sources (S.C. Code Ann. § 19-11-100); attorney and client [*Drayton v. Industrial Life & Health Ins. Co.,* 205 S.C. 98, 31 S.E.2d 148 (1944)]; privilege against self-incrimination (U.S. Const. amend. V; S.C. Const. art. I, § 12; S.C. Code Ann. § 19-11-80); and the identity of a confidential informant [*State v. Hayward,* 302 S.C. 75, 393 S.E.2d 918 (1990)].

ARTICLE VI

WITNESSES

RULE 601. COMPETENCY

(a) General Rule. Every person is competent to be a witness except as otherwise provided by statute or these rules.

(b) Disqualification of a Witness. A person is disqualified to be a witness if the court determines that (1) the proposed witness is incapable of expressing himself concerning the matter as to be understood by the judge and jury either directly or through interpretation by one who can understand him, or (2) the proposed witness is incapable of understanding the duty of a witness to tell the truth.

[Adopted effective September 3, 1995.]

Notes

Subsection (a) differs from the federal rule which provides that the only exceptions to the competency rule are those set forth in the Rules of Evidence. Because legislation such as the Dead Man's Statute, S.C. Code Ann. § 19–11–20 (1985), still exists limiting witness competency, the rule also refers to exceptions provided by statute.

At common law, there were numerous grounds which would render a witness incompetent. Legislation has eliminated many of these common law disqualifications resulting in a liberalization of the rules regarding competency. *See, e.g.,* S.C. Code Ann. §§ 19–11–10 (1985) (party competent to be witness); 19–11–30 (Supp. 1993) (spouse of party competent); 19–11–40 (1985) (witness having interest in action is not disqualified); 19–11–50 (1985) (criminal defendant may testify); 19–11–60 (1985) (convicted person may testify). Subsection (a) continues this trend of liberalization by creating a general rule of competency.

This rule will result in a change in the law regarding competency of children. Under prior South Carolina law, proof of competency for children under the age of fourteen was required unless the child was a victim of abuse or neglect, as defined in the Children's Code, who was testifying concerning the abuse or neglect. *South Carolina Department of Social Services v. Doe,* 292 S.C. 211, 355 S.E.2d 543 (Ct. App.1987); S.C. Code Ann. § 19–11–25 (Supp.1993). Under this rule, children are presumed to be competent unless it is shown otherwise.

The federal rule does not contain a subsection (b). This provision was added to establish a minimum standard for competency of a witness and to make it clear that the determination of a witness' competency is within the sound discretion of the trial judge. *In re Robert M.,* 294 S.C. 69, 362 S.E.2d 639 (1987); *State v. Camele,* 293 S.C. 302, 360 S.E.2d 307 (1987); *State v. Pitts,* 256 S.C. 420, 182 S.E.2d 738 (1971).

RULE 602. LACK OF PERSONAL KNOWLEDGE

A witness may not testify to a matter unless evidence is introduced sufficient to support a finding that the witness has personal knowledge of the matter. Evidence to prove personal knowledge may, but need not, consist of the witness' own testimony. This rule is subject to the provisions of Rule 703, relating to opinion testimony by expert witnesses.

[Adopted effective September 3, 1995.]

Notes

This rule is identical to the federal rule and is consistent with South Carolina law. *See Gentry v. Watkins-Carolina Trucking Co.,* 249 S.C. 316, 154 S.E.2d 112 (1967); *Wilson v. Clary,* 212 S.C. 250, 47 S.E.2d 618 (1948).

RULE 603. OATH OR AFFIRMATION

Before testifying, every witness shall be required to declare that the witness will testify truthfully, by oath or affirmation administered in a form calculated to awaken the witness' conscience and impress the witness' mind with the duty to do so.

[Adopted effective September 3, 1995.]

Notes

This rule is identical to the federal rule which sets forth the common law tenet that a witness is required to take an oath or affirmation to tell the truth before being allowed to testify. *See* 98 C.J.S. *Witnesses* § 320(a) (1957). The use of an affirmation instead of an oath is consistent with prior law. *See* S.C. Code Ann. § 19-1-40 (1985); Rule 43(d), SCRCP.

RULE 604. INTERPRETERS

An interpreter is subject to the provisions of these rules relating to qualification as an expert and the administration of an oath or affirmation to make a true translation.

[Adopted effective September 3, 1995.]

Notes

This rule is identical to the federal rule. The qualification of an interpreter is within the discretion of the trial judge and depends on the circumstances of each case. *Peoples National Bank v. Manos Brothers,* 226 S.C. 257, 84 S.E.2d 857 (1954).

RULE 605. COMPETENCY OF JUDGE AS WITNESS

The judge presiding at the trial may not testify in that trial as a witness.

[Adopted effective September 3, 1995.]

Notes

This rule is identical to the first sentence of the federal rule and is consistent with South Carolina law providing that a judge may not testify as a witness in a case being tried before that judge. *State v. Bagwell,* 201 S.C. 387, 23 S.E.2d 244 (1942). The second sentence of the federal rule dispenses with the requirement of an objection to a judge being a witness. This sentence was deleted as being inconsistent with the law of this state. *See State v. Torrence,* 305 S.C. 45, 406 S.E.2d 315 (1991).

RULE 606. COMPETENCY OF JUROR AS WITNESS

(a) At the Trial. A member of the jury may not testify as a witness before that jury in the trial of the case in which the juror is sitting. If the juror is called so to testify, the opposing party shall be afforded an opportunity to object outside the presence of the jury.

(b) Inquiry Into Validity of Verdict or Indictment. Upon an inquiry into the validity of a verdict or indictment, a juror may not testify as to any matter or statement occurring during the course of the jury's deliberations or to the effect of anything upon that or any other juror's mind or emotions as influencing the juror to assent to or dissent from the verdict or indictment or concerning the juror's mental processes in connection therewith, except that a juror may testify on the question whether extraneous prejudicial information was improperly brought to the jury's attention or whether any outside influence was improperly brought to bear upon any juror. Nor may a juror's affidavit or evidence of any statement by the juror concerning a matter about which the juror would be precluded from testifying be received for these purposes.

[Adopted effective September 3, 1995.]

Notes

The language of this rule is identical to the federal rule. Subsection (a) of this rule changes the law in South Carolina in two regards. First, while prior law allowed a juror to testify as to venue, *State v. Vari,* 35 S.C. 175, 14 S.E. 392 (1892) (juror allowed to testify as to isolated, particular matter such as value or venue but not as to general facts and circumstances of the offense), this subsection would prohibit such testimony. Second, the prior law did not require that the party opposing the calling of a juror as a witness be given an opportunity to object outside the presence of the jury.

Subsection (b) is consistent with the general rule that a juror may not present testimony as to the deliberations in the jury room; as to any mistake, irregularity, or misconduct on the part of the jurors; or which would impeach the verdict or contradict the record. *Barsh v. Chrysler Corp.,* 262 S.C. 129, 203 S.E.2d 107 (1974); *State v. Wells,* 249 S.C. 249, 153 S.E.2d 904 (1967); *Caines v. Marion Coca-Cola Bottling Co.,* 196 S.C. 502, 14 S.E.2d 10 (1941). An affidavit of a juror has been admitted on a post-trial motion "with great hesitation" when there was an allegation that a party had attempted to influence the juror. *Cohen v. Robert,* 33 S.C.L. (2 Strob.) 410 (1848). The rule is also consistent with South Carolina cases holding that no one may invade the secrecy of a grand jury's deliberations. *State v. Sanders,* 251 S.C. 431, 163 S.E.2d 220 (1968); *Margolis v. Telech,* 239 S.C. 232, 122 S.E.2d 417 (1961).

RULE 607. WHO MAY IMPEACH

The credibility of a witness may be attacked by any party, including the party calling the witness.

[Adopted effective September 3, 1995.]

Notes

This rule is identical to the federal rule. However, it is contrary to the former law in this State that a party must vouch for its own witness and may not impeach its witness unless the witness is declared hostile upon a showing of actual surprise and harm, or unless the party is required to call someone, such as a subscribing witness to a deed or will, as a witness. *State v. Anderson,* 304 S.C. 551, 406 S.E.2d 152 (1991); *Hicks v. Coleman,* 240 S.C. 227, 125 S.E.2d 473 (1962); *White v. Southern Oil Stores, Inc.,* 198 S.C. 173, 17 S.E.2d 150 (1941).

RULE 608. EVIDENCE OF CHARACTER, CONDUCT AND BIAS OF WITNESS

(a) Opinion and Reputation Evidence of Character. The credibility of a witness may be attacked or supported by evidence in the form of opinion or reputation, but subject to these limitations: (1) the evidence may refer only to character for truthfulness or untruthfulness, and (2) evidence of truthful character is admissible only after the character of the witness for truthfulness has been attacked by opinion or reputation evidence or otherwise.

(b) Specific Instances of Conduct. Specific instances of the conduct of a witness, for the purpose of attacking or supporting the witness' credibility, other than conviction of crime as provided in Rule 609, may not be proved by extrinsic evidence. They may, however, in the discretion of the court, if probative of truthfulness or untruthfulness, be inquired into on cross-examination of the witness (1) concerning the witness' character for truthfulness or untruthfulness, or (2) concerning the character for truthfulness or untruthfulness of another witness as to which character the witness being cross-examined has testified.

The giving of testimony, whether by an accused or by any other witness, does not operate as a waiver of the accused's or the witness' privilege against self-incrimination when examined with respect to matters which relate only to credibility.

(c) Evidence of Bias. Bias, prejudice or any motive to misrepresent may be shown to impeach the witness either by examination of the witness or by evidence otherwise adduced.

[Adopted effective September 3, 1995.]

Notes

Except for the addition of subsection (c), this rule is identical to the federal rule.

Subsection (a) of this rule permits a witness' truthfulness to be impeached by opinion or reputation evidence. The general rule in South Carolina is that a witness' general reputation for truth and veracity is placed in issue when taking the witness stand. *See State v. Major,* 301 S.C. 181, 391 S.E.2d 235 (1990); *State v. Robertson,* 26 S.C. 117, 1 S.E. 443 (1887); *State v. Hale,* 284 S.C. 348, 326 S.E.2d 418 (Ct. App.1985), cert. denied, 286 S.C. 127, 332 S.E.2d 533 (1985). Formerly, although evidence of a person's general reputation in the community was admissible, opinion testimony was not admissible. *State v. Groome,* 274 S.C. 189, 262 S.E.2d 31 (1980); *In re: Greenfield's Estate,* 245 S.C. 595, 141 S.E.2d 916 (1965). The provision prohibiting bolstering of a witness until after the witness' credibility is attacked is consistent with prior South Carolina law. *State v. Lynn,* 277 S.C. 222, 284 S.E.2d 786 (1981); *Woods v. Thrower,* 116 S.C. 165, 107 S.E. 250 (1921). However, there was an exception allowing bolstering prior to attack when the witness was a stranger to the community. *State v. Lynn,* supra; *Woods v. Thrower,* supra. This exception is not included in the rule.

As to subsection (b), no South Carolina cases have been found which permit cross-examination regarding specific acts to show truthfulness. The use of specific acts to attack credibility is similar to prior South Carolina case law which allowed a witness to be cross-examined about prior bad acts if they constituted crimes of moral turpitude. *State v. Outlaw,* 307 S.C. 177, 414 S.E.2d 147 (1992); *State v. Major,* 301 S.C. 181, 391 S.E.2d 235 (1990); *State v. McGuire,* 272 S.C. 547, 253 S.E.2d 103 (1979). The cross-examiner was required to take the answer given by the witness and could not use extrinsic evidence or other testimony to prove the bad act. *State v. Outlaw,* supra; *State v. Major,* supra. Additionally, the inquiry could only go so far as to bring out the general nature of the misconduct and could not go into specific details. *State v. Outlaw,* supra; *State v. Major,* supra.

Subsection (b), like its federal counterpart, does not set forth what conduct may adversely affect a witness' credibility. The former case law standard, which allowed impeachment if the conduct was a crime of moral turpitude, is not the appropriate standard in light of the Court's decision to abandon the moral turpitude standard under Rule 609. Instead, the trial courts should be guided by the decisions of the federal courts which limit inquiry into those specific instances of misconduct which are "clearly probative of truthfulness or untruthfulness" such as forgery, bribery, false pretenses, and embezzlement. *See Weinstein's Evidence,* ¶ 608[05] (1994). This will reduce the kinds of misconduct which can be inquired into from that permitted under prior law. Further, this rule, like the prior case law, does not allow a cross-examiner to go on a "fishing expedition" in the hopes of finding some misconduct. *State v. McGuire,* supra. The decision whether to allow such impeachment remains in the discretion of the trial judge. Id.

Subsection (c) was added to address impeachment by showing bias or impartiality. *State v. Brewington,* 267 S.C. 97, 226 S.E.2d 249 (1976); *North Greenville College v. Sherman Const. Co., Inc.,* 270 S.C. 553, 243 S.E.2d 441 (1978).

RULE 609. IMPEACHMENT BY EVIDENCE OF CONVICTION OF CRIME

(a) General Rule. For the purpose of attacking the credibility of a witness,

(1) evidence that a witness other than an accused has been convicted of a crime shall be admitted, subject to Rule 403, if the crime was punishable by death or imprisonment in excess of one year under the law

under which the witness was convicted, and evidence that an accused has been convicted of such a crime shall be admitted if the court determines that the probative value of admitting this evidence outweighs its prejudicial effect to the accused; and

(2) evidence that any witness has been convicted of a crime shall be admitted if it involved dishonesty or false statement, regardless of the punishment.

For the purposes of this rule, a conviction includes a conviction resulting from a trial or any type of plea, including a plea of *nolo contendere* or a plea pursuant to *North Carolina v. Alford,* 400 U.S. 25 (1970).

(b) Time Limit. Evidence of a conviction under this rule is not admissible if a period of more than ten years has elapsed since the date of the conviction or of the release of the witness from the confinement imposed for that conviction, whichever is the later date, unless the court determines, in the interests of justice, that the probative value of the conviction supported by specific facts and circumstances substantially outweighs its prejudicial effect. However, evidence of a conviction more than 10 years old as calculated herein, is not admissible unless the proponent gives to the adverse party sufficient advance written notice of intent to use such evidence to provide the adverse party with a fair opportunity to contest the use of such evidence.

(c) Effect of Pardon, Annulment, or Certificate of Rehabilitation or Other Equivalent Procedure. Evidence of a conviction is not admissible under this rule if (1) the conviction has been the subject of a pardon, annulment, certificate of rehabilitation, or other equivalent procedure based on a finding of the rehabilitation of the person convicted, and that person has not been convicted of a subsequent crime which was punishable by death or imprisonment in excess of one year, or (2) the conviction has been the subject of a pardon, annulment, or other equivalent procedure based on a finding of innocence.

(d) Juvenile Adjudications. Evidence of a juvenile adjudication is admissible under this rule if conviction of the crime would be admissible to attack the credibility of an adult.

(e) Pendency of Appeal. The pendency of an appeal therefrom does not render evidence of a conviction inadmissible. Evidence of the pendency of an appeal is admissible.

[Adopted effective September 3, 1995.]

Notes

Except for subsections (a) and (d), this rule is identical to the federal rule.

Subsection (a) is identical to the federal rule except for the addition of the last sentence. This addition was made to make it clear that the term "conviction" includes a conviction resulting from a trial or any type of plea, to include a plea of nolo contendere or a plea pursuant to *North Carolina v. Alford,* 400 U.S. 25, 91 S.Ct. 160, 27 L.Ed.2d 162 (1970). Allowing a plea of nolo contendere to be used for impeachment is consistent with the prior law. *State v. Lynn,* 277 S.C. 222, 284 S.E.2d 786 (1981). Subsection (a) does change the law in South Carolina. The prior law was that a witness could be impeached by evidence that the witness had been convicted of a crime of moral turpitude. *State v. Hale,* 284 S.C. 348, 326 S.E.2d 418 (Ct.App.1985), cert. denied, 286 S.C. 127, 332 S.E.2d 533 (1985); *State v. Harvey,* 275 S.C. 225, 268 S.E.2d 587 (1980). Further, the standard for balancing probative value against prejudicial effect was the same for all witnesses, to include the accused in a criminal case. *Green v. Hewett,* 305 S.C. 238, 407 S.E.2d 651 (1991). This subsection does not use the moral turpitude standard, but instead allows impeachment with a conviction for any crime which carries a maximum sentence of death or imprisonment for more than one year. Further, the rule provides for a different standard for balancing probative value and prejudicial effect for an accused who is a witness.

Regarding subsection (b), the adoption of a general ten year limit on the use of convictions for impeachment constitutes a change in South Carolina law. The former case law did not set forth a time limit on the use of convictions for impeachment. *Green v. Hewett,* supra. Instead, the determination whether a conviction was too remote rested in the discretion of the trial judge. *Horton v. State,* 306 S.C. 252, 411 S.E.2d 223 (1991); *State v. Livingston,* 282 S.C. 1, 317 S.E.2d 129 (1984); *State v. Johnson,* 271 S.C. 485, 248 S.E.2d 313 (1978). The ten year limit was adopted to help guide trial courts in making uniform determinations in this area.

Subsection (c) regulates the effect of a pardon, annulment, certificate of rehabilitation or other equivalent procedures on the admissibility of a conviction for impeachment purposes. As to the effect of pardons issued by South Carolina, this subsection is arguably more restrictive than S.C. Code Ann. § 24–21–990(5) (Supp. 1993) which provides that a witness cannot be impeached by a conviction for which the witness received a pardon unless the crime indicates a lack of veracity.

The language of subsection (d) of the federal rule, which allows evidence of juvenile adjudications only in criminal cases and does not allow such evidence against the accused, was not used so that the South Carolina rule would conform with state law. Juvenile adjudications are admissible in this state to impeach any witness, including the accused, if the conduct would be criminal if it were committed by an adult. *State v. Mallory,* 270 S.C. 519, 242 S.E.2d 693 (1978). It should be noted that S.C. Code Ann. § 20–7–780 (Supp.1993), which makes juvenile records confidential unless otherwise ordered by the family court, may limit access to records of juvenile adjudications.

No South Carolina authority existed as to the effect of the pendency of an appeal on the admissibility of evidence of the conviction. Subsection (e) of the federal rule was adopted verbatim.

RULE 610. RELIGIOUS BELIEFS OR OPINIONS

Evidence of the beliefs or opinions of a witness on matters of religion is not admissible for the purpose of showing that by reason of their nature the witness' credibility is impaired or enhanced.

[Adopted effective September 3, 1995.]

Notes

No changes were made to the language of the federal rule. The South Carolina Supreme Court has held that a belief in God is not a prerequisite to allowing the witness to testify. *State v. Green,* 267 S.C. 599, 230 S.E.2d 618 (1976); *State v. Hicks,* 257 S.C. 279, 185 S.E.2d 746 (1971). However, in *State v. Turner,* 36 S.C. 534, 15 S.E. 602 (1892), the State was allowed to question the accused concerning comments ridiculing religion which he had allegedly made in order to impeach his credibility. This case is inconsistent with the rule.

RULE 611. MODE AND ORDER OF INTERROGATION AND PRESENTATION

(a) Control by Court. The court shall exercise reasonable control over the mode and order of interrogating witnesses and presenting evidence so as to (1) make the interrogation and presentation effective for the ascertainment of the truth, (2) avoid needless consumption of time, and (3) protect witnesses from harassment or undue embarrassment.

(b) Scope of Cross–Examination. A witness may be cross-examined on any matter relevant to any issue in the case, including credibility.

(c) Leading Questions. Leading questions should not be used on the direct examination of a witness except as may be necessary to develop the witness' testimony. Ordinarily leading questions should be permitted on cross-examination. When a party calls a hostile witness, an adverse party, or a witness identified with an adverse party, interrogation may be by leading questions.

(d) Re-examination and Recall. A witness may be re-examined as to the same matters to which he testified only in the discretion of the court, but without exception he may be re-examined as to any new matter brought out during cross-examination. After the examination of the witness has been concluded by all the parties to the action, that witness may be recalled only in the discretion of the court. This rule shall not limit the right of any party to recall a witness in rebuttal.

[Adopted effective September 3, 1995.]

Notes

The language of subsection (a) of this rule is identical to that used in the federal rule. It is consistent with the general rule in this State that the conduct of the trial, including the examination of witnesses, is within the sound discretion of the trial judge. *See McMillan v. Ridges,* 229 S.C. 76, 91 S.E.2d 883 (1956); *State v. Nathari,* 303 S.C. 188, 399 S.E.2d 597 (Ct. App. 1990). It should be noted that Rule 614 controls the calling and interrogation of witnesses by the court.

Under South Carolina law, cross-examination is limited only by the requirement that the inquiry relate to matters pertinent to the issues involved or to impeachment of the witness. *See State v. Ham,* 259 S.C. 118, 191 S.E.2d 13 (1972); *Hansson v. General Insulation and Acoustics,* 234 S.C. 177, 107 S.E.2d 41 (1959). The scope of cross-examination is within the discretion of the trial judge. *State v. Sherard,* 303 S.C. 172, 399 S.E.2d 595 (1991). Subsection (b) rejects the more restrictive language of the federal rule which limits cross-examination to the subject matter of direct examination and matters affecting the credibility of the witness.

Subsection (c) is consistent with former law. *See* Rule 43(b)(1), SCRCP; Rule 43(b)(2), SCRCP. The use of leading questions when examining a child, *State v. Hale,* 284 S.C. 348, 326 S.E.2d 418 (Ct. App. 1985), cert. denied, 286 S.C. 127, 332 S.E.2d 533 (1985), is still permissible under the first sentence of subsection (c) which allows leading questions when "necessary to develop the witness' testimony."

There was no provision in the federal rule as to re-examination and recall of witnesses. The provision concerning re-examination and recall of witnesses was added to the rule to make it consistent with South Carolina law. *See Levy v. Outdoor Resorts of South Carolina, Inc.,* 304 S.C. 427, 405 S.E.2d 387 (1991); *State v. Stroman,* 281 S.C. 508, 316 S.E.2d 395 (1984); *Huff v. Latimer,* 33 S.C. 255, 11 S.E. 758 (1890).

RULE 612. WRITING USED TO REFRESH MEMORY

If a witness uses a writing to refresh memory for the purpose of testifying, either—

(1) while testifying, or

(2) before testifying, if the court in its discretion determines it is necessary in the interests of justice, an adverse party is entitled to have the writing produced at the hearing, to inspect it, to cross-examine the witness thereon, and to introduce in evidence those portions which relate to the testimony of the witness. If it is claimed that the writing contains matters not related to the subject matter of the testimony the court shall examine the writing in camera, excise any portions not so related, and order delivery of the remainder to the party entitled thereto. Any portion withheld over objections shall be preserved and made available to the appellate court in the event of an appeal. If a writing is not produced or delivered pursuant to order under this rule, the court shall make any order justice requires, except that in criminal cases when the prosecution elects not to comply, the order shall be one striking the testimony or, if the court in its discretion determines that the interests of justice so require, declaring a mistrial.

[Adopted effective September 3, 1995.]

Notes

Except for the deletion of a reference to federal law, no changes were made to the federal rule. Requiring a party to provide a copy of a memorandum used by a witness to refresh recollection so that it may be used on cross-examination of the witness is consistent with prior law. *State v. Hamilton,* 276 S.C. 173, 276 S.E.2d 784 (1981); *State v. Tyner,* 273 S.C. 646, 258 S.E.2d 559 (1979). Rule 37(b)(2), SCRCP, and Rule 5(d)(2), SCRCrimP, are similar to the provision in this rule concerning the trial judge's authority to decide the remedy for failure to produce a document for the adverse party.

RULE 613. PRIOR STATEMENTS OF WITNESSES

Subject to the provisions of S.C. Code Ann. §§ 19–1–80, 19–1–90 and 19–1–100:

(a) Examining Witness Concerning Prior Statement. In examining a witness concerning a prior statement made by the witness, whether written or not, the statement need not be shown nor its contents disclosed to the witness at that time, but on request the same shall be shown or disclosed to opposing counsel.

(b) Extrinsic Evidence of Prior Inconsistent Statement of Witness. Extrinsic evidence of a prior inconsistent statement by a witness is not admissible unless the witness is advised of the substance of the statement, the time and place it was allegedly made, and the person to whom it was made, and is given the opportunity to explain or deny the statement. If a witness does not admit that he has made the prior inconsistent statement, extrinsic evidence of such statement is admissible. However, if a witness admits making the prior statement, extrinsic evidence that the prior statement was made is inadmissible. This provision does not apply to admissions of a party-opponent as defined in Rule 801(d)(2).

[Adopted effective September 3, 1995.]

Notes

The language at the beginning of this rule was added to provide that the rule is subject to the provisions of S.C. Code Ann. §§ 19–1–80 to –100 (1985) regarding written statements made to public employees.

Subsection (a) is identical to the federal rule. This provision was included in the federal rule to abolish the holding in *The Queen's Case,* 2 Br. & B. 284, 129 Eng. Rep. 976 (1820), that a witness must be shown a prior statement before being examined about the statement. Although no South Carolina case has been found adopting the holding in *The Queen's Case,* the language of the federal rule eliminating the requirement of showing the witness the prior statement has been included in the South Carolina rule.

Subsection (b) of the federal rule was amended to provide that a proper foundation must be laid before admitting a prior inconsistent statement. A witness must be permitted to admit, deny, or explain a prior inconsistent statement. *McMillan v. Ridges,* 229 S.C. 76, 91 S.E.2d 883 (1956). Extrinsic evidence of the statement is not admissible unless the witness is advised of the substance of the statement, the time and place it was allegedly made, and the person to whom it was made. *State v. Galloway,* 263 S.C. 585, 211 S.E.2d 885 (1975). In addition, language was added to subsection (b) to set forth the rule that if the witness admits making the prior statement, the witness has been impeached and no further extrinsic evidence of the statement, including the statement itself, is admissible. *State v. Lynn,* 277 S.C. 222, 284 S.E.2d 786 (1981); *McMillan v. Ridges,* supra.

RULE 614. CALLING AND INTERROGATION OF WITNESSES BY COURT

(a) Calling by Court. In extraordinary circumstances, the court may, on its own motion or at the suggestion of a party, call witnesses, and all parties are entitled to cross-examine witnesses thus called. Before calling a court's witness, the court shall afford the parties a hearing on the matter outside the presence of the jury.

(b) Interrogation by Court. When required by the interests of justice only, the court may interrogate witnesses.

[Adopted effective September 3, 1995.]

Notes

Subsection (a) is the federal rule modified in two respects. First, the phrase "[i]n extraordinary circumstances" was added to emphasize that under our adversarial system the decision whether to call a witness should generally be made by the parties, and the power of the court to call a witness ought to be sparingly used. The formulation of this rule differs from the rule established in *State v. Anderson,* 304 S.C. 551, 406 S.E.2d 152 (1991), although the circumstances in that case would be extraordinary circumstances justifying a court in calling a witness under this rule. Second, the federal rule was modified to require the court to afford the parties a hearing outside the presence of the jury before a witness is called by the court. This modification is consistent with prior case law. Id.; *Riddle v. State,* 314 S.C. 1, 443 S.E.2d 557 (1994). Allowing all parties to cross-examine a court's witness is also consistent with the prior case law. *Riddle v. State,* supra; *State v. Anderson,* supra.

Subsection (b) is the federal rule modified by adding the phrase "[w]hen required by the interests of justice only." This language was added to emphasize that this power, like the power to call a court's witness, should be used sparingly. If the court does interrogate a witness, the court must be careful not to intimate any opinion as to the force and effect of the testimony by its questions. *Fowler v. Laney Tank Lines, Inc.,* 263 S.C. 422, 211 S.E.2d 231 (1975).

The federal rule contains a subsection (c) which may obviate the need for a timely objection to the calling of a court's witness or the interrogation of a witness by the court in certain circumstances. This provision is inconsistent with the law of South Carolina and was deleted. *See State v. Torrence,* 305 S.C. 45, 406 S.E.2d 315 (1991).

RULE 615. EXCLUSION OF WITNESSES

At the request of a party the court may order witnesses excluded so that they cannot hear the testimony of other witnesses, and it may make the order of its own motion. This rule does not authorize exclusion of (1) a party who is a natural person, or (2) an officer or employee of a party which is not a natural person designated as its representative by its attorney, or (3) a person whose presence is shown by a party to be essential to the presentation of the party's cause.

[Adopted effective September 3, 1995.]

Notes

The federal rule requires sequestration of witnesses upon the request of a party. The South Carolina rule adheres to prior state practice which leaves the sequestration decision in the sound discretion of the trial judge. *See State v. Jackson,* 265 S.C. 278, 217 S.E.2d 794 (1975); *State v. Miokovich,* 257

S.C. 225, 185 S.E.2d 360 (1971). Otherwise, the South Carolina rule is consistent with the federal rule.

ARTICLE VII

OPINIONS AND EXPERT TESTIMONY

RULE 701. OPINION TESTIMONY BY LAY WITNESSES

If the witness is not testifying as an expert, the witness' testimony in the form of opinions or inferences is limited to those opinions or inferences which (a) are rationally based on the perception of the witness, (b) are helpful to a clear understanding of the witness' testimony or the determination of a fact in issue, and (c) do not require special knowledge, skill, experience or training.

[Adopted effective September 3, 1995.]

Notes

Except for the addition of subsection (c) and minor grammatical changes, this rule is identical to the federal rule. The language of subsection (c) is based on language contained in the rules of evidence of Florida and Tennessee, and is intended to emphasize the fact that lay persons may not give expert opinions.

Subsection (a) appears to be consistent with prior law. *Cf. State v. Bottoms,* 260 S.C. 187, 195 S.E.2d 116 (1973) (opinion must be based upon the personal observations of the witness and not merely upon the statements of another witness).

As to subsection (b), the prior case law has held that opinion evidence is admissible as long as it is not superfluous. *State v. McClinton,* 265 S.C. 171, 217 S.E.2d 584 (1974). This is roughly equivalent to saying that opinion evidence must be helpful.

As to subsection (c), the Court of Appeals has stated that expert testimony is essential where the topic is not a matter within the common knowledge and experience of most lay persons. *Spartanburg Regional Med. Center v. Bulsa,* 308 S.C. 322, 417 S.E.2d 648 (Ct. App. 1992); *Armstrong v. Union Carbide,* 308 S.C. 235, 417 S.E.2d 597 (Ct. App. 1992). Subsection (c) merely states this proposition in the reverse.

RULE 702. TESTIMONY BY EXPERTS

If scientific, technical, or other specialized knowledge will assist the trier of fact to understand the evidence or to determine a fact in issue, a witness qualified as an expert by knowledge, skill, experience, training, or education, may testify thereto in the form of an opinion or otherwise.

[Adopted effective September 3, 1995.]

Notes

The rule is identical to the federal rule, and to former Rule 43(m)(1), SCRCP, and former Rule 24(a), SCRCrimP.

RULE 703. BASES OF OPINION TESTIMONY BY EXPERTS

The facts or data in the particular case upon which an expert bases an opinion or inference may be those perceived by or made known to the expert at or before the hearing. If of a type reasonably relied upon by experts in the particular field in forming opinions or inferences upon the subject, the facts or data need not be admissible in evidence.

[Adopted effective September 3, 1995.]

Notes

The rule is identical to the federal rule and former Rule 43(m)(2), SCRCP, and former Rule 24(b), SCRCrimP. This rule makes it clear that an expert may rely on facts or data in giving an opinion which are not admitted into evidence.

RULE 704. OPINION ON ULTIMATE ISSUE

Testimony in the form of an opinion or inference otherwise admissible is not objectionable because it embraces an ultimate issue to be decided by the trier of fact.

[Adopted effective September 3, 1995.]

Notes

This rule is identical to former Rule 43(m)(3), SCRCP, and former Rule 24(c), SCRCrimP. It is identical to the federal rule as it existed prior the 1984 amendment which added subsection (b) to the rule to prohibit expert testimony on the ultimate issue of whether a criminal defendant is insane.

RULE 705. DISCLOSURE OF FACTS OR DATA UNDERLYING EXPERT OPINION

The expert may testify in terms of opinion or inference and give reasons therefor without first testifying to the underlying facts or data, unless the court requires otherwise. The expert may in any event be required to disclose the underlying facts or data on cross-examination.

[Adopted effective September 3, 1995.]

Notes

The rule is identical to the federal rule. It differs from former Rule 43(m)(4), SCRCP, and former Rule 24(d), SCRCrimP, which contained the phrase "without prior disclosure of" in place of the phrase "without first testifying to."

ARTICLE VIII

HEARSAY

RULE 801. DEFINITIONS

The following definitions apply under this article:

(a) Statement. A "statement" is (1) an oral or written assertion or (2) nonverbal conduct of a person, if it is intended by the person as an assertion.

(b) Declarant. A "declarant" is a person who makes a statement.

(c) Hearsay. "Hearsay" is a statement, other than one made by the declarant while testifying at the trial or hearing, offered in evidence to prove the truth of the matter asserted.

(d) Statements Which Are Not Hearsay. A statement is not hearsay if—

(1) *Prior Statement by Witness.* The declarant testifies at the trial or hearing and is subject to cross-examination concerning the statement, and the statement is (A) inconsistent with the declarant's testimony, or (B) consistent with the declarant's testimony and is offered to rebut an express or implied charge against the declarant of recent fabrication or improper influence or motive; provided, however, the statement must have been made before the alleged fabrication, or before the alleged improper influence or motive arose, or (C) one of identification of a person made after perceiving the person, or (D) consistent with the declarant's testimony in a criminal sexual conduct case or attempted criminal sexual conduct case where the declarant is the alleged victim and the statement is limited to the time and place of the incident; or

(2) *Admission by Party–Opponent.* The statement is offered against a party and is (A) the party's own statement in either an individual or a representative capacity, or (B) a statement of which the party has manifested an adoption or belief in its truth, or (C) a statement by a person authorized by the party to make a statement concerning the subject, or (D) a statement by the party's agent or servant concerning a matter within the scope of the agency or employment, made during the existence of the relationship, or (E) a statement by a coconspirator of a party during the course and in furtherance of the conspiracy.

[Adopted effective September 3, 1995.]

Notes

With the exception of subsection (d)(1), this rule is identical to the federal rule.

While case law has not defined the words "statement" and "declarant," the definitions in subsections (a) and (b) are consistent with how those words are used in numerous cases discussing the hearsay rule. Prior law recognized that wordless conduct intended as a communication may be hearsay. *State v. Williams,* 285 S.C. 544, 331 S.E.2d 354 (Ct. App. 1985).

Subsection (c) is consistent with South Carolina law. *Player v. Thompson,* 259 S.C. 600, 193 S.E.2d 531 (1972).

Subsection (d)(1) changes the law in South Carolina. Previously, where the declarant testified at trial and was subject to cross-examination, the general rule was that prior statements made by the declarant/witness were admissible regardless of the hearsay nature of the statements. *See State v. Garner,* 304 S.C. 220, 403 S.E.2d 631 (1991); *State v. Caldwell,* 283 S.C. 350, 322 S.E.2d 662 (1984); *State v. Plyler,* 275 S.C. 291, 270 S.E.2d 126 (1980); *but see State v. Munn,* 292 S.C. 497, 357 S.E.2d 461 (1987) (all out-of-court statements made by alleged victim not necessarily admissible simply because victim testifies at trial). Subsection (d)(1), however, treats prior statements of a witness as not being hearsay in only four instances. Subsection (A) omits the requirement of the federal rule that the declarant's prior inconsistent statement be given under oath. This modification renders the rule consistent with South Carolina law. *See State v. Copeland,* 278 S.C. 572, 300 S.E.2d 63 (1982), cert. denied, 460 U.S. 1103, 103 S.Ct. 1802, 76 L.Ed.2d 367 (1983). It should be noted that the foundation requirements of Rule 613(b) must be met before extrinsic evidence of a prior inconsistent statement is admissible. Subsection (B) is the federal rule modified by adding the phrase "provided, however, the statement must have been made before the alleged fabrication, or before the alleged improper influence or motive arose." This modification, which is taken from the United States Supreme Court's interpretation of Rule 801(d)(1)(B) of the Federal Rules of Evidence in *Tome v. United States,* 513 U.S. 150, 130 L.Ed.2d 574, 115 S.Ct. 696 (1995), is somewhat similar to the limitation previously contained in the case law that a prior consistent statement is admissible only where it was made prior to the declarant's relation to the cause. *Jolly v. State,* 314 S.C. 17, 443 S.E.2d 566 (1994); *Burns v. Clayton,* 237 S.C. 316, 117 S.E.2d 300 (1960). Subsection (C) is identical to the federal rule and consistent with South Carolina law that evidence regarding pre-trial identifications, which are not the product of unconstitutional procedures, are admissible. *State v. Stewart,* 275 S.C. 447, 272 S.E.2d 628 (1980); *State v. Gambrell,* 274 S.C. 587, 266 S.E.2d 78 (1980). Subsection (D), which is not contained in the federal rule, was added to make admissible in criminal sexual conduct cases evidence that the victim complained of the sexual assault, limited to the time and place of the assault. Subsection (D) is consistent with South Carolina law. *Jolly v. State,* 314 S.C. 17, 443 S.E.2d 566 (1994).

Subsection (d)(2)(A) is consistent with South Carolina law. *Bunch v. Cobb,* 273 S.C. 445, 257 S.E.2d 225 (1979) (admission against interest of a party opponent is admissible); *State v. Good,* 308 S.C. 313, 417 S.E.2d 643 (Ct. App. 1992) (an out of court admission of a criminal defendant is admissible). Subsection (B) is consistent with South Carolina law. *State v. Sharpe,* 239 S.C. 258, 122 S.E.2d 622 (1962) (testimony that defendant was silent in response to an accusation by a third party admissible), *rev'd on other grounds, State v. Torrence,* 305 S.C. 45, 406 S.E.2d 315 (1991); *Coleman & Lipscomb v. Frazier,* 38 S.C.L. (4 Rich.) 146 (1850) (where party received a statement and acted on it as true, statement admissible). Subsection (C) is consistent with South Carolina law. *Harper v. American Ry. Express Co.,* 139 S.C. 545, 138 S.E. 354 (1927) (statements by a person authorized to speak are admissible). Subsection (D) is consistent with South Carolina law that statements made by an agent in the scope of his authority were admissible. *Hunter v. Hyder,* 236 S.C. 378, 114 S.E.2d 493 (1960). Subsection (E) is consistent with South Carolina law. *State v. Sullivan,* 277 S.C. 35, 282 S.E.2d 838 (1981); *Yeager v. Murphy,* 291 S.C. 485, 354 S.E.2d 393 (Ct. App. 1987) (statements made by co-conspirators in furtherance of the conspiracy are admissible).

RULE 802. HEARSAY RULE

Hearsay is not admissible except as provided by these rules or by other rules prescribed by the Supreme Court of this State or by statute.

[Adopted effective September 3, 1995.]

Notes

The rule replaces the words "by the Supreme Court pursuant to statutory authority or by Act of Congress" found in the federal rule with "by the Supreme Court of this State or by statute." It is consistent with the general rule that hearsay is not admissible unless it fits within an exception to the hearsay rule. *Jolly v. State,* 314 S.C. 17, 443 S.E.2d 566 (1994); *Lee v. Gulf Ins. Co.,* 248 S.C. 296, 149 S.E.2d 639 (1966).

RULE 803. HEARSAY EXCEPTIONS; AVAILABILITY OF DECLARANT IMMATERIAL

The following are not excluded by the hearsay rule, even though the declarant is available as a witness:

(1) Present Sense Impression. A statement describing or explaining an event or condition made while the declarant was perceiving the event or condition, or immediately thereafter.

(2) Excited Utterance. A statement relating to a startling event or condition made while the declarant was under the stress of excitement caused by the event or condition.

(3) Then Existing Mental, Emotional, or Physical Condition. A statement of the declarant's then existing state of mind, emotion, sensation, or physical condition (such as intent, plan, motive, design, mental feeling, pain, and bodily health), but not including a statement of memory or belief to prove the fact remembered or believed unless it relates to the execution, revocation, identification, or terms of declarant's will.

(4) Statements for Purposes of Medical Diagnosis or Treatment. Statements made for purposes of medical diagnosis or treatment and describing medical history, or past or present symptoms, pain, or sensations, or the inception or general character of the cause or external source thereof insofar as reasonably pertinent to diagnosis or treatment; provided, however, that the admissibility of statements made after commencement of the litigation is left to the court's discretion.

(5) Recorded Recollection. A memorandum or record concerning a matter about which a witness once had knowledge but now has insufficient recollection to enable the witness to testify fully and accurately, shown to have been made or adopted by the witness when the matter was fresh in the witness' memory and to reflect that knowledge correctly. If admitted, the memorandum or record may be read into evidence but may not itself be received as an exhibit unless offered by an adverse party.

(6) Records of Regularly Conducted Activity. A memorandum, report, record, or data compilation, in any form, of acts, events, conditions, or diagnoses, made at or near the time by, or from information transmitted by, a person with knowledge, if kept in the course of a regularly conducted business activity, and if it was the regular practice of that business activity to make the memorandum, report, record, or data compilation, all as shown by the testimony of the custodian or other qualified witness, unless the source of information or the method or circumstances of preparation indicate lack of trustworthiness; *provided, however,* that subjective opinions and judgments found in business records are not admissible. The term "business" as used in this subsection includes business, institution, association, profession, occupation, and calling of every kind, whether or not conducted for profit.

(7) Absence of Entry in Records Kept in Accordance With the Provisions of Subsection (6). Evidence that a matter is not included in the memoranda, reports, records, or data compilations, in any form, kept in accordance with the provisions of subsection (6), to prove the nonoccurrence or nonexistence of the matter, if the matter was of a kind of which a memorandum, report, record, or data compilation was regularly made and preserved, unless the sources of information or other circumstances indicate lack of trustworthiness.

(8) Public Records and Reports. Records, reports, statements, or data compilations, in any form, of public offices or agencies, setting forth (A) the activities of the office or agency, or (B) matters observed pursuant to duty imposed by law as to which matters there was a duty to report, excluding, however, in criminal cases matters observed by police officers and other law enforcement personnel; *provided, however,* that investigative notes involving opinions, judgments, or conclusions are not admissible. Accident reports required by S.C. Code Ann. §§ 56–5–1260 to –1280 (1991) are not admissible as evidence of negligence or due care in an action at law for damages.

(9) Records of Vital Statistics. Records or data compilations, in any form, of births, fetal deaths, deaths, or marriages, if the report thereof was made to a public office pursuant to requirements of law.

(10) Absence of Public Record or Entry. To prove the absence of a record, report, statement, or data compilation, in any form, or the nonoccurrence or nonexistence of a matter of which a record, report, statement or data compilation, in any form, was regularly made and preserved by a public office or agency, evidence in the form of a certification in accordance with Rule 902, or testimony, that diligent search failed to disclose the record, report, statement, or data compilation, or entry.

(11) Records of Religious Organizations. Statements of births, marriages, divorces, deaths, legitimacy, ancestry, relationship by blood or marriage, or other similar facts of personal or family history, contained in a regularly kept record of a religious organization.

(12) Marriage, Baptismal, and Similar Certificates. Statements of fact contained in a certificate that the maker performed a marriage or other ceremony or administered a sacrament, made by a clergyman, public official, or other person authorized by the rules or practices of a religious organization or by law to perform the act certified, and purporting to have been issued at the time of the act or within a reasonable time thereafter.

(13) Family Records. Statements of fact concerning personal or family history contained in family Bibles, genealogies, charts, engravings on rings, inscriptions on family portraits, engravings on urns, crypts, or tombstones, or the like.

(14) Records of Documents Affecting an Interest in Property. The record of a document purporting to establish or affect an interest in property, as proof of the content of the original recorded document and its execution and delivery by each person by whom it purports to have been executed, if the record is a record of a public office and an applicable statute authorizes the recording of documents of that kind in that office.

(15) Statements in Documents Affecting an Interest in Property. A statement contained in a document purporting to establish or affect an interest in property if the matter stated was relevant to the purpose of the document, unless dealings with the property since the document was made have been inconsistent with the truth of the statement or the purport of the document.

(16) Statements in Ancient Documents. Statements in a document in existence twenty years or more the authenticity of which is established.

(17) Market Reports, Commercial Publications. Market quotations, tabulations, lists, directories, or other published compilations, generally used and relied upon by the public or by persons in particular occupations.

(18) Learned Treatises. To the extent called to the attention of an expert witness upon cross-examination or relied upon by the expert witness in direct examination, statements contained in published treatises, periodicals, or pamphlets on a subject of history, medicine, or other science or art, established as a reliable authority by the testimony or admission of the witness or by other expert testimony or by judicial notice. If admitted, the statements may be read into evidence but may not be received as exhibits. This rule is in addition to any statutory provisions on this subject.

(19) Reputation Concerning Personal or Family History. Reputation among members of a person's family by blood, adoption, or marriage, or among a person's associates, or in the community, concerning a person's birth, adoption, marriage, divorce, death, legitimacy, relationship by blood, adoption, or marriage, ancestry, or other similar fact of personal or family history.

(20) Reputation Concerning Boundaries or General History. Reputation in a community, arising before the controversy, as to boundaries of or customs affecting lands in the community, and reputation as to events of general history important to the community or State or nation in which located.

(21) Reputation as to Character. Reputation of a person's character among associates or in the community.

(22) Judgment of Previous Conviction. Evidence of a final judgment (to include final judgments in juvenile delinquency matters), entered after a trial or upon a plea of guilty (but not upon a plea of nolo contendere), adjudging a person guilty of a crime punishable by death or imprisonment in excess of one year, to prove any fact essential to sustain the judgment, but not including, when offered by the Government in a criminal prosecution for purposes other than impeachment, judgments against persons other than the accused. The pendency of an appeal may be shown but does not affect admissibility.

(23) Judgment as to Personal, Family or General History, or Boundaries. Judgments as proof of matters of personal, family or general history, or boundaries, essential to the judgment, if the same would be provable by evidence of reputation.

[Adopted effective September 3, 1995.]

Notes

Except for modifications to subsections (4), (6), (8), (18), and (22), and the deletion of subsection (24) which contained a "catchall" or residual hearsay exception, this rule is identical to the federal rule.

Subsections (1) and (2): These subsections constitute a change in South Carolina law. Previously, a statement had to meet the conditions of both subsections (1) and (2) before it would be admissible under the res gestae exception to the hearsay rule. *State v. Harrison*, 298 S.C. 333, 380 S.E.2d 818 (1989).

Subsection (3): This subsection is consistent with prior state practice. *Winburn v. Minnesota Mut. Life Ins. Co.*, 261 S.C. 568, 201 S.E.2d 372 (1973); *Sligh v. Newberry Elec. Coop., Inc.*, 216 S.C. 401, 58 S.E.2d 675 (1950); *Ervin v. Myrtle Grove Plantation*, 206 S.C. 41, 32 S.E.2d 877 (1945); *Lazar v. Great Atl. & Pac. Tea Co.*, 197 S.C. 74, 14 S.E.2d 560 (1941); *Spires v. Spires*, 111 S.C. 373, 97 S.E. 847 (1919).

Subsection (4): The first part of this subsection is identical to the federal rule and is consistent with state practice. *State v. Camele,* 293 S.C. 302, 360 S.E.2d 307 (1987) (physician's testimony should include only those statements related to him by the patient upon which the physician relied in reaching medical conclusions); *Gentry v. Watkins–Carolina Trucking Co.,* 249 S.C. 316, 154 S.E.2d 112 (1967) (statements of present condition and past symptoms made to a physician consulted as a potential witness are admissible, not as substantive evidence, but, in the absence of fraud or bad faith, as information upon which the physician relied in reaching a professional opinion). The final phrase was added to the subsection to provide that the admissibility of statements made after commencement of the litigation is within the trial judge's discretion. *Gentry v. Watkins–Carolina Trucking Co.*, supra.

Subsection (5): This subsection is similar to previous state law which allowed a witness to testify from a writing when it was the original document prepared by the witness contemporaneously with the event for the purpose of preserving the memory of it. *Gwathmey v. Foor Hotel Co.,* 121 S.C. 237, 113 S.E. 688 (1922); *The Bank of Charleston Nat'l Banking Ass'n v. Zorn,* 14 S.C. 444 (1881). The provision of this rule limiting the introduction of the writing to when it is offered by an adverse party is a change in South Carolina law.

Subsection (6): This subsection differs from the federal rule in that the word "opinions" in the first sentence is deleted and the phrase, "*provided, however,* that subjective opinions and judgments found in business records are not admissible" is added to the federal rule to make it consistent with state law. *Kershaw County Dep't of Social Serv. v. McCaskill,* 276 S.C. 360, 278 S.E.2d 771 (1981); *see also State v. Rich,* 293 S.C. 172, 359 S.E.2d 281 (1987) (admission of properly authenticated fingerprints); Uniform Business Records as Evidence Act, S.C. Code Ann. § 19–5–510 (1985).

Subsection (7): While the case law has recognized the admissibility of negative evidence to prove the non-existence of records of regularly conducted activity, the courts have not recognized this as a separate hearsay exception. *E.g., Peoples Nat'l Bank v. Manos Bros., Inc.,* 226 S.C. 257, 84 S.E.2d 857 (1955); *see also Flowers v. South Carolina Dep't of Highways and Pub. Transp.,* 309 S.C. 76, 419 S.E.2d 832 (Ct. App. 1992) (citing federal rule).

Subsection (8): This subsection differs from the federal rule in that it does not include item (C). The subsection also contains two limitations not included in the federal rule. First, investigative notes involving opinions, judgments, or conclusions are not admissible. Further, accident reports required by statute are not admissible as evidence of negligence or due care in actions for damages. As modified, this subsection is consistent with prior state practice. *State v. Pearson,* 223 S.C. 377, 76 S.E.2d 151 (1953); S.C. Code Ann. § 56–5–1290 (1991); *see also State v. Rich,* 293 S.C. 172, 359 S.E.2d 281 (1987) (admission of properly authenticated fingerprints).

Subsection (9): This subsection constitutes a change in South Carolina law. Prior case law limited admissions of such reports to matters within the knowledge of the person making the report. *Williams v. Metropolitan Life Ins. Co.,* 116 S.C. 277, 108 S.E. 110 (1921).

Subsection (10): While the case law has recognized the admissibility of negative evidence to prove the non-existence of public records, the courts have not recognized this as a separate hearsay exception. *See Peoples Nat'l Bank v. Manos Bros., Inc.,* 226 S.C. 257, 84 S.E.2d 857 (1955) (introduction of evidence of the non-existence of public record entries); *Flowers v. South Carolina Dep't of Highways and Pub. Transp.,* 309 S.C. 76, 419 S.E.2d 832 (Ct.App.1992) (citing federal rule). See also Rule 44(b), SCRCP.

Subsection (11): There does not appear to be any South Carolina law concerning this exception to the hearsay rule.

Subsection (12): No prior South Carolina authority has been found which states the hearsay exception expressed in this subsection.

Subsection (13): This exception is apparently consistent with prior case law in this State. *See Dobson v. Cothran,* 34 S.C. 518, 13 S.E. 679 (1891) (entry in family Bible of the birth date of a person is admissible as evidence of the person's age only where better evidence cannot be obtained).

Subsection (14): This subsection is consistent with statutory and case law in this State. *Wilson v. Moseley,* 113 S.C. 278, 102 S.E. 330 (1920) (a record book from a clerk's office, wherein a deed was authorized to be recorded and was recorded, is admissible to prove the existence and contents of the deed if sufficient evidence is presented to prove that the original deed is not available); S.C. Code Ann. § 19–5–10 (1985) (admissibility of certified copies or certified photostatic copies of documents).

Subsection (15): This provision is apparently consistent with prior case law in this State. *See Smith v. Williams,* 141 S.C. 265, 139 S.E. 625 (1927) (husband's statements in a deed and accompanying memorandum purporting to convey an interest in property admissible to show whether family agreement had been made following husband's death entitling widow to retain use and possession of the property).

Subsection (16): The ancient document exception to the hearsay rule in subsection (16) is consistent with prior case law in this State. However, prior case law qualified a document as "ancient" if the document was thirty years old or older. *Atlantic Coast Line R.R. Co. v. Searson,* 137 S.C. 468, 135 S.E. 567 (1926) (map more than thirty years old could be introduced as ancient document); *Johnson v. Pritchard,* 302 S.C. 437, 395 S.E.2d 191 (Ct. App. 1990) (duly authenticated ancient documents of thirty years or more constitute an exception to the hearsay rule). Subsection (16) qualifies a document as "ancient" if it is twenty years old or older.

Subsection (17): This provision is consistent with prior case law in this State. *Peoples Nat'l Bank v. Manos Bros., Inc.,* 226 S.C. 257, 84 S.E.2d 857 (1954) (on the issue of domicile, a city directory is admissible); *Kirkpatrick v. Hardeman,* 123 S.C. 21, 115 S.E. 905 (1923) (accredited current price lists and market reports, including those published in trade journals or newspapers, which are accepted as trustworthy, are admissible on the question of market value of stock).

Subsection (18): This exception is identical to the federal rule except for the addition of the last sentence. This rule changes and expands previous South Carolina law which held that medical books are not admissible into evidence to be read to the court and jury except in the situations set forth in S.C. Code Ann. § 19–5–410 (1985). *See LaCount v. General Asbestos & Rubber Co.,* 184 S.C. 232, 192 S.E. 262 (1937); *Baker v. Southern Cotton Oil Co.,* 161 S.C. 479, 159 S.E. 822 (1931); *Edwards v. Union Buffalo Mills Co.,* 162 S.C. 17, 159 S.E. 818 (1931). This rule is consistent with the case of *Baker v. Port City Steel Erectors, Inc.,* 261 S.C. 469, 200 S.E.2d 681 (1973), which states that a scientific textbook can be used for the purpose of impeaching an expert witness.

Subsection (19): This exception is consistent with prior state law. *Hazelwood v. Mayes,* 111 S.C. 23, 96 S.E. 672 (1918); *Horry v. Glover,* 11 S.C.Eq. (2 Hill Eq.) 515 (1837).

Subsection (20): This exception is consistent with prior state law. *Culbertson v. Culbertson,* 273 S.C. 103, 254 S.E.2d 558 (1979) (boundary); *County of Darlington v. Perkins,* 269 S.C. 572, 239 S.E.2d 69 (1977) (general history).

Subsection (21): There is no South Carolina law dealing with this exception. This section is included in the rules to insure that reputation evidence is not excluded on the basis of hearsay. *See Weinstein's Evidence* ¶ 803(21)[01] (1994). Rules 404, 405, and 608 deal with when reputation evidence may be admissible.

Subsection (22): This subsection is identical to the federal rule except for the addition of the phrase "to include final judgments in juvenile delinquency matters." This addition makes it clear that a final judgment in a juvenile delinquency matter is to be treated in the same manner as an adult conviction under this subsection; to determine if the crime is punishable by death or imprisonment in excess of one year, the maximum punishment an adult would receive for the offense is controlling. Traditionally, evidence of a judgment in a criminal case was not admissible in a civil case as evidence of the facts upon which the conviction was based. *Fontville v. Atlanta & Charlotte Air Line Ry. Co.,* 93 S.C. 287, 75 S.E. 172 (1910). This traditional rule has, however, been eroded in several cases. *South Carolina State Board of Dental Examiners v. Breeland,* 208 S.C. 469, 38 S.E.2d 644 (1946) (at least where the police power of the state is involved in a civil case, a criminal conviction based on a jury verdict is admissible); *Globe & Rutgers Fire Ins. Co. v. Foil,* 189 S.C. 91, 200 S.E. 97 (1938) (evidence of a conviction based on a guilty plea is admissible in a civil case as an admission against the criminal defendant). The adoption of this rule now allows criminal judgments based on a plea of guilty or a trial for an offense which carries a maximum punishment of death or imprisonment for more than one year to be admissible in almost all civil actions to prove the facts essential to the criminal judgment. Not allowing a criminal judgment based on a plea of nolo contendere to be used to prove the facts on which the judgment is based is consistent with the prior case law. *Kibler v. State,* 267 S.C. 250, 227 S.E.2d 199 (1976) (plea of nolo cannot be used as an admission in a civil case); *see also In re Anderson,* 255 S.C. 56, 177 S.E.2d 130 (1970) (attorney disciplinary proceeding). It should be noted that S.C. Code Ann. § 56–5–6160 (1991) limits the admissibility of evidence of a conviction for a traffic offense. Further, S.C. Code Ann. § 20–7–780 (Supp. 1993), which makes juvenile records confidential unless otherwise ordered by the family court, may limit access to final judgments in juvenile delinquency matters.

Subsection (23): This exception is consistent with prior state law. *Bradley v. Calhoun,* 116 S.C. 7, 106 S.E. 843 (1921).

RULE 804. HEARSAY EXCEPTIONS; DECLARANT UNAVAILABLE

(a) Definition of Unavailability. "Unavailability as a witness" includes situations in which the declarant—

(1) is exempted by ruling of the court on the ground of privilege from testifying concerning the subject matter of the declarant's statement; or

(2) persists in refusing to testify concerning the subject matter of the declarant's statement despite an order of the court to do so; or

(3) testifies to a lack of memory of the subject matter of the declarant's statement; or

(4) is unable to be present or to testify at the hearing because of death or then existing physical or mental illness or infirmity; or

(5) is absent from the hearing and the proponent of a statement has been unable to procure the declarant's attendance (or in the case of a hearsay exception under subdivision (b)(2), (3), or (4), the declarant's attendance or testimony) by process or other reasonable means.

A declarant is not unavailable as a witness if exemption, refusal, claim of lack of memory, inability, or absence is due to the procurement or wrongdoing of the proponent of a statement for the purpose of preventing the witness from attending or testifying.

(b) Hearsay Exceptions. The following are not excluded by the hearsay rule if the declarant is unavailable as a witness:

(1) *Former Testimony.* Testimony given as a witness at another hearing of the same or a different proceeding, or in a deposition taken in compliance with law in the course of the same or another proceeding, if the party against whom the testimony is now offered, or, in a civil action or proceeding, a predecessor in interest, had an opportunity and similar motive to develop the testimony by direct, cross, or redirect examination.

(2) *Statement Under Belief of Impending Death.* In a prosecution for homicide or in a civil action or proceeding, a statement made by a declarant while believing that the declarant's death was imminent, concerning the cause or circumstances of what the declarant believed to be impending death.

(3) *Statement Against Interest.* A statement which was at the time of its making so far contrary to the declarant's pecuniary or proprietary interest, or so far tended to subject the declarant to civil or criminal liability, or to render invalid a claim by the declarant against another, that a reasonable person in the declarant's position would not have made the statement unless believing it to be true. A statement tending to expose the declarant to criminal liability and offered to exculpate the accused is not admissible unless corroborating circumstances clearly indicate the trustworthiness of the statement.

(4) *Statement of Personal or Family History.* (A) A statement concerning the declarant's own birth, adoption, marriage, divorce, legitimacy, relationship by blood, adoption, or marriage, ancestry, or other similar fact of personal or family history, even though declarant had no means of acquiring personal knowledge of the matter stated; or (B) a statement concerning the foregoing matters, and death also, of another person, if the declarant was related to the other by blood,

adoption, or marriage or was so intimately associated with the other's family as to be likely to have accurate information concerning the matter declared.

[Adopted effective September 3, 1995.]

Notes

Subsection (a) is identical to the federal rule and consistent with South Carolina law. *Riddle v. State*, 314 S.C. 1, 443 S.E.2d 557 (1994) (witness unavailable who refuses to testify even after being threatened with contempt); *State v. Doctor*, 306 S.C. 527, 413 S.E.2d 36 (1992) (witness who asserts a privilege is unavailable); *State v. Steadman*, 216 S.C. 579, 59 S.E.2d 168, cert. denied, 340 U.S. 850, 71 S.Ct. 78, 95 L.Ed. 623 (1950) (witness who is absent from the jurisdiction and cannot be found is unavailable); *State v. Rogers*, 101 S.C. 280, 85 S.E. 636 (1914) (witness who is dead, insane, beyond the seas, or kept away by the contrivance of the opposing party is unavailable).

Subsection (b) omits subsection (5), the "catch all" or residual hearsay exception found in the federal rule, but is otherwise identical to the federal rule. Subsection (1) is consistent with South Carolina law. *State v. Steadman*, 216 S.C. 579, 59 S.E.2d 168, cert. denied, 340 U.S. 850, 71 S.Ct. 78, 95 L.Ed. 623 (1950). It should be noted that S.C. Code Ann. § 19–11–50 (1985), which provides that the testimony of a criminal defendant may not be used in any subsequent criminal case against him except prosecution for perjury founded on that testimony, may place some limit on the admissibility of evidence under this subsection. Subsection (2) broadens the admissibility of dying declarations by making them admissible in civil cases. *See Sligh v. Newberry Electric Co-op.*, 216 S.C. 401, 58 S.E.2d 675 (1950). The rigid requirement that the declarant must actually have died, *State v. Dawson*, 203 S.C. 167, 26 S.E.2d 506 (1943), is relaxed under the Rule which only requires the death of the declarant in a homicide prosecution. Subsection (3) is consistent with South Carolina law. *State v. Doctor*, 306 S.C. 527, 413 S.E.2d 36 (1992). Subsection (4) is consistent with South Carolina law. *McLain v. Woodside*, 95 S.C. 152, 79 S.E. 1 (1913).

RULE 805. HEARSAY WITHIN HEARSAY

Hearsay included within hearsay is not excluded under the hearsay rule if each part of the combined statements conforms with an exception to the hearsay rule provided in these rules.

[Adopted effective September 3, 1995.]

Notes

The rule is identical to the federal rule and is consistent with prior South Carolina case law. *Bain v. Self Memorial Hosp.*, 281 S.C. 138, 314 S.E.2d 603 (Ct. App. 1984).

RULE 806. ATTACKING AND SUPPORTING CREDIBILITY OF DECLARANT

When a hearsay statement, or a statement defined in Rule 801(d)(2)(C), (D), or (E) has been admitted in evidence, the credibility of the declarant may be attacked, and if attacked may be supported, by any evidence which would be admissible for those purposes if declarant had testified as a witness. Evidence of a statement or conduct by the declarant at any time, inconsistent with the declarant's hearsay statement, is not subject to any requirement that the declarant may have been afforded an opportunity to deny or explain. If the party against whom a hearsay statement has been admitted calls the declarant as a witness, the party is entitled to examine the declarant on the statement as if under cross-examination.

[Adopted effective September 3, 1995.]

Notes

The rule is identical to the federal rule. However, it is a departure from prior South Carolina case law. There are cases which have addressed a similar matter by holding that a declarant who made a dying declaration could not be impeached with an inconsistent statement that did not independently fall within a hearsay exception. *State v. Brown*, 108 S.C. 490, 95 S.E. 61 (1918); *State v. Taylor*, 56 S.C. 360, 34 S.E. 939 (1900).

ARTICLE IX

AUTHENTICATION AND IDENTIFICATION

RULE 901. REQUIREMENT OF AUTHENTICATION OR IDENTIFICATION

(a) General Provision. The requirement of authentication or identification as a condition precedent to admissibility is satisfied by evidence sufficient to support a finding that the matter in question is what its proponent claims.

(b) Illustrations. By way of illustration only, and not by way of limitation, the following are examples of authentication or identification conforming with the requirements of this rule:

(1) *Testimony of Witness With Knowledge.* Testimony that a matter is what it is claimed to be.

(2) *Nonexpert Opinion on Handwriting.* Non-expert opinion as to the genuineness of handwriting, based upon familiarity not acquired for purposes of the litigation.

(3) *Comparison by Trier or Expert Witness.* Comparison by the trier of fact or by expert witnesses with specimens which have been authenticated.

(4) *Distinctive Characteristics and the Like.* Appearance, contents, substance, internal patterns, or other distinctive characteristics, taken in conjunction with circumstances.

(5) *Voice Identification.* Identification of a voice, whether heard firsthand or through mechanical or electronic transmission or recording, by opinion based

upon hearing the voice at any time under circumstances connecting it with the alleged speaker.

(6) *Telephone Conversations.* Telephone conversations, by evidence that a call was made to the number assigned at the time by the telephone company to a particular person or business, if (A) in the case of a person, circumstances, including self-identification, show the person answering to be the one called, or (B) in the case of a business, the call was made to a place of business and the conversation related to business reasonably transacted over the telephone.

(7) *Public Records or Reports.* Evidence that a writing authorized by law to be recorded or filed and in fact recorded or filed in a public office, or a purported public record, report, statement, or data compilation, in any form, is from the public office where items of this nature are kept.

(8) *Ancient Documents or Data Compilation.* Evidence that a document or data compilation, in any form, (A) is in such condition as to create no suspicion concerning its authenticity, (B) was in a place where it, if authentic, would likely be, and (C) has been in existence 20 years or more at the time it is offered.

(9) *Process or System.* Evidence describing a process or system used to produce a result and showing that the process or system produces an accurate result.

(10) *Methods Provided by Statute or Rule.* Any method of authentication or identification provided by statute or by other rules promulgated by the Supreme Court.

[Adopted effective September 3, 1995.]

Notes

In considering the rules in Article IX, it is important to remember that these rules relate to how a party authenticates evidence to show it is what the party claims. Even when evidence is properly authenticated, it must still be admissible under the other rules of evidence. *See State v. Jeffcoat,* 279 S.C. 167, 303 S.E.2d 855 (1983).

With the exception of subsection (b)(10) which is discussed below, this rule is identical to the federal rule.

Subsection (a) is consistent with South Carolina law which requires authentication as a condition precedent to admissibility. *See State v. Rich,* 293 S.C. 172, 359 S.E.2d 281 (1987). As noted in the Advisory Committee's Notes to the Federal Rules, the requirement of showing authentication or identity falls in the category of relevancy dependent upon fulfillment of a condition of fact and is governed by the procedure set forth in Rule 104(b).

Subsection (b) contains illustrations of how evidence may be authenticated. These illustrations are consistent with the prior case law indicating that evidence in support of authentication can be direct or circumstantial. *Winburn v. Minnesota Mutual Life Ins. Co.,* 261 S.C. 568, 201 S.E.2d 372 (1973); *State v. Wilson,* 246 S.C. 580, 145 S.E.2d 20 (1965).

Subsection (b)(1) is in accord with the prior law in this state. *Williams v. Milling–Nelson Motors, Inc.,* 209 S.C. 407, 40 S.E.2d 633 (1946); *Brazeale v. Piedmont Mfg. Co.,* 184 S.C. 471, 193 S.E. 99 (1937).

Subsection (b)(2) is generally consistent with state law *State v. Jeffcoat,* 279 S.C. 167, 303 S.E.2d 855 (1983) (signature on check identified by signator's bookkeeper); *Weaver v. Whilden,* 33 S.C. 190, 11 S.E. 686 (1890) (no error in refusing to allow nonexpert witness who was unfamiliar with handwriting to testify as to genuineness of signature). There does not appear to be any South Carolina law that states that the familiarity cannot have been acquired for the purposes of litigation.

Subsection (b)(3) is in accord with the prior case law in South Carolina. *Pee Dee Production Credit Ass'n v. Joye,* 284 S.C. 371, 326 S.E.2d 650 (1984); *Benedict, Hall & Co. v. Flanigan,* 18 S.C. 506 (1883); *Boman v. Plunkett,* 13 S.C.L. (2 McCord) 518 (1823) (comparison by jury was permitted in aid of doubtful proof). South Carolina has also recognized that nonexperts can make such comparisons. *State v. Ezekial,* 33 S.C. 115, 11 S.E. 635 (1890); *Benedict, Hall & Co. v. Flanigan,* 18 S.C. 506 (1883).

Subsection (b)(4) is consistent with prior law. *Kershaw, Cty. Bd. of Educ. v. U.S. Gypsum,* 302 S.C. 390, 396 S.E.2d 369 (1990); *IKT Company Inc. v. Hardwick,* 274 S.C. 413, 265 S.E.2d 510 (1980); *State v. Hightower,* 221 S.C. 91, 69 S.E.2d 363 (1952). A common form of authentication permissible under this subsection is the reply doctrine which provides that once a letter, telegram, or telephone call is shown to have been mailed, sent, or made, a letter, telegram or telephone call shown by its contents to be in reply is authenticated without more. Graham, *Handbook of Federal Evidence,* § 901.4 (2nd ed. 1986). This appears to be the law in South Carolina. *Leesville Mfg. Co. v. Morgan Wood & Iron Works,* 75 S.C. 342, 55 S.E. 768 (1906) (reply letter is presumed genuine).

Subsection (b)(5) is consistent with the law in South Carolina. *State v. Stewart,* 275 S.C. 447, 272 S.E.2d 628 (1980) (identification of defendant's voice as that of armed robber was admissible in criminal prosecution where circumstances demonstrate reliability of evidence); *State v. Plyler,* 275 S.C. 291, 270 S.E.2d 126 (1980) (sufficient testimony as to recognition of the voice warrants its admission); *State v. Vice,* 259 S.C. 30, 190 S.E.2d 510 (1972) (voice identification permissible; further, jury can compare recorded telephone call and defendant's voice, recorded prior to trial, for purposes of comparison); *State v. Porter,* 251 S.C. 393, 162 S.E.2d 843 (1968) (identification of party with whom witness talked need not be known at time of conversation, but is sufficient if knowledge enabling witness to identify other party is later obtained), cert. denied, 393 U.S. 1079, 89 S.Ct. 859, 21 L.Ed.2d 773 (1969); *State v. Steadman,* 216 S.C. 579, 59 S.E.2d 168 (1950); *State v. Smith,* 307 S.C. 376, 415 S.E.2d 409 (Ct.App. 1992) (dispatcher allowed to identify voice of anonymous caller as that of defendant, even though no prior voice identification training).

Subsection (b)(6) is in accord with the prior law in this State. *Fielding Home for Funerals v. Pub. Sav. Life Ins. Co.,* 271 S.C. 117, 245 S.E.2d 238 (1978) (business); *State v. Steadman,* 216 S.C. 579, 59 S.E.2d 168 (1950); *Gilliland & Gaffney v. Southern Ry.,* 85 S.C. 26, 67 S.E. 20 (1910) (business).

Section (b)(7) is consistent with South Carolina law. *State v. Pearson,* 223 S.C. 377, 76 S.E.2d 151 (1953); *Ex parte Steen,* 59 S.C. 220, 37 S.E. 829 (1901). As to the authentication of police fingerprint records, see *State v. Rich,* 293 S.C. 172, 359 S.E.2d 281 (1987).

Subsection (b)(8) is in accord with prior case law with the exception that the prior cases required 30 years before a document was classified as ancient rather than 20 years as required by this subsection. *See Atlantic Coast Line Ry. v. Searson*, 137 S.C. 468, 135 S.E. 567 (1926); *Polson v. Ingram*, 22 S.C. 541 (1885); *Thompson v. Brannon*, 14 S.C. 542 (1881); *Johnson v. Pritchard*, 302 S.C. 437, 395 S.E.2d 191 (Ct. App. 1990). *See also*, Rule 803(16), which also reduces the minimum period for receipt of "ancient" records under the hearsay rule.

Subsection (b)(9) appears to be in accord with South Carolina law. *See State v. Hester*, 137 S.C. 145, 134 S.E.2d 885 (1926).

Subsection (b)(10) is the federal rule modified to make the language applicable to South Carolina statutes and rules. An example of such a rule is Rule 44, SCRCP, which deals with the authentication of official records.

RULE 902. SELF-AUTHENTICATION

Extrinsic evidence of authenticity as a condition precedent to admissibility is not required with respect to the following:

(1) Domestic Public Documents Under Seal. A document bearing a seal purporting to be that of the United States, or of any State, district, Commonwealth, territory, or insular possession thereof, or the Panama Canal Zone, or the Trust Territory of the Pacific Islands, or of a political subdivision, department, officer, or agency thereof, and a signature purporting to be an attestation or execution.

(2) Domestic Public Documents Not Under Seal. A document purporting to bear the signature in the official capacity of an officer or employee of any entity included in subsection (1) hereof, having no seal, if a public officer having a seal and having official duties in the district or political subdivision of the officer or employee certifies under seal that the signer has the official capacity and that the signature is genuine.

(3) Foreign Public Documents. A document purporting to be executed or attested in an official capacity by a person authorized by the laws of a foreign country to make the execution or attestation, and accompanied by a final certification as to the genuineness of the signature and official position (A) of the executing or attesting person, or (B) of any foreign official whose certificate of genuineness of signature and official position relates to the execution or attestation or is in a chain of certificates of genuineness of signature and official position relating to the execution or attestation. A final certification may be made by a secretary of embassy or legation, consul general, consul, vice consul, or consular agent of the United States, or a diplomatic or consular official of the foreign country assigned or accredited to the United States. If reasonable opportunity has been given to all parties to investigate the authenticity and accuracy of official documents, the court may, for good cause shown, order that they be treated as presumptively authentic without final certification or permit them to be evidenced by an attested summary with or without final certification.

(4) Certified Copies of Public Records. A copy of an official record or report or entry therein, or of a document authorized by law to be recorded or filed and actually recorded or filed in a public office, including data compilations in any form, certified as correct by the custodian or other person authorized to make the certification, by certificate complying with subsection (1), (2), or (3) of this rule or complying with any statute or rule promulgated by the Supreme Court.

(5) Official Publications. Books, pamphlets, or other publications purporting to be issued by public authority.

(6) Newspapers and Periodicals. Printed materials purporting to be newspapers or periodicals.

(7) Trade Inscriptions and the Like. Inscriptions, signs, tags, or labels purporting to have been affixed in the course of business and indicating ownership, control, or origin.

(8) Acknowledged Documents. Documents accompanied by a certificate of acknowledgment executed in the manner provided by law by a notary public or other officer authorized by law to take acknowledgments.

(9) Commercial Paper and Related Documents. Commercial paper, signatures thereon, and documents relating thereto to the extent provided by general commercial law.

(10) Presumptions Under Statutes. Any signature, document or other matter declared by statute to be presumptively or prima facie genuine or authentic.

[Adopted effective September 3, 1995.]

Notes

With the exception of subsections (4) and (10) which are discussed below, this rule is identical to the federal rule.

Subsection (1): South Carolina law has previously permitted self-authentication of certain classes of domestic public documents under seal. *See* e.g., S.C. Code Ann. § 19-5-220 (1985) (proof of various documents under seal of any city or state).

Subsection (2): There does not appear to be any South Carolina law permitting self-authentication in these circumstances.

Subsection (3) is similar to Rule 44(a)(2), SCRCP.

Subsection (4) is identical to the federal rule except that it is amended so as to also allow compliance with "any statute or rule prescribed by the Supreme Court." Examples of such statutes and rules include: S.C. Code Ann. § 19-5-10 (1985) (admissibility of certified copies or certified photostatic copies of documents); S.C. Code Ann. § 19-5-30 (Supp. 1993) (admissibility of photostatic or certified copies of certain motor vehicle records); Rule 44(a)(1), SCRCP (authentication of domestic records); Rule 6, SCRCrimP (self-authentication of chemist's or analyst's report of nature of "controlled dangerous substances").

Subsection (5): There does not appear to be any South Carolina authority for this proposition.

Subsection (6) appears to be consistent with South Carolina law. *See Kirkpatrick v. Hardeman*, 123 S.C. 21, 115 S.E. 905 (1923) (although unclear if Court treated as hearsay or authentication problem, newspaper reports of stock quotations were admitted for purpose of proving market value of stock).

Subsection (7): There does not appear to be any South Carolina authority for this proposition.

Subsection (8): This is similar to South Carolina Code Ann. §§ 19–5–220 and 19–5–230 (1985) which allow the self-authentication of certain documents of city, state or foreign governments under seal of a notary public.

Subsection (9): Under the Uniform Commercial Code, certain items are self-authenticating. See S.C. Code Ann. § 36–1–202 (1976) (includes bills of lading, insurance policies or any document authorized by the contract to be issued by third party); § 36–3–307 (1976) (signatures, unless specifically denied in the pleadings); § 36–3–510 (1976) (formal certificate of protest, a stamp by drawee that payment was refused, or bank records showing dishonor are all admissible in evidence and create a presumption of dishonor); § 36–8–105(3) (Supp. 1993) (signatures on a certificated security, in a necessary indorsement, on an initial transaction statement or on an instruction is admitted unless put into issue).

Subsection (10): This subsection differs from the federal rule only in that "declared by statute" is substituted for "declared by Act of Congress." An example of a statute under this subsection is S.C. Code Ann. § 39–15–140 (1985) (certificate of trademark registration issued by the Secretary of State).

RULE 903. SUBSCRIBING WITNESS' TESTIMONY UNNECESSARY

The testimony of a subscribing witness is not necessary to authenticate a writing unless required by statute or by the laws of the jurisdiction whose laws govern the validity of the writing.

[Adopted effective September 3, 1995.]

Notes

This rule adds "by statute" to the federal rule. The law in South Carolina is that the testimony of a subscribing witness is generally not necessary for authentication. *Edgar v. Brown*, 15 S.C.L. (4 McCord) 91 (1827); S.C. Code Ann. § 19-1-120 (1985) (the absence of a witness to any bond or note shall not be deemed a good cause by any court for postponing a trial, but the signature may be proved by other testimony); S.C. Code Ann. § 62-2-503 (Supp. 1993) (Uniform Probate Code's provision for self-proved wills); §§ 62-3-405 and -406 (Supp. 1993) (requirements of proof of execution when will not self-proved and submitted for formal probate).

ARTICLE X

CONTENTS OF WRITINGS, RECORDINGS, AND PHOTOGRAPHS

RULE 1001. DEFINITIONS

For purposes of this article the following definitions are applicable:

(1) Writings and Recordings. "Writings" and "recordings" consist of letters, words, sounds, or numbers, or their equivalent, set down by handwriting, typewriting, printing, photostating, photographing, magnetic impulse, mechanical or electronic recording, or other form of data compilation.

(2) Photographs. "Photographs" include still photographs, X-ray films, video tapes, motion pictures or other similar methods of recording information.

(3) Original. An "original" of a writing or recording is the writing or recording itself or any counterpart intended to have the same effect by a person executing or issuing it. An "original" of a photograph includes the negative or any print therefrom. If data are stored in a computer or similar device, any printout or other output readable by sight, shown to reflect the data accurately, is an "original".

(4) Duplicate. A "duplicate" is a counterpart produced by the same impression as the original, or from the same matrix, or by means of photography, including enlargements and miniatures, or by mechanical or electronic re-recording, or by chemical reproduction, or by other equivalent techniques which accurately reproduces the original.

[Adopted effective September 3, 1995.]

Notes

This rule is identical to the federal rule except that the word "sounds" is added to subdivision (1) and "other similar methods of recording information" was added to subdivision (2). This additional language does not significantly alter the rule, and provides for advances in technology.

RULE 1002. REQUIREMENT OF ORIGINAL

To prove the content of a writing, recording, or photograph, the original writing, recording, or photograph is required, except as otherwise provided in these rules or by statute.

[Adopted effective September 3, 1995.]

Notes

This rule is better known as the best evidence rule. This rule is identical to the federal rule except the words "by statute" were substituted at the end of the rule in place of the words "by Act of Congress."

The proposed rule is consistent with current case law as it applies to writings. *See, e.g., Riddle v. City of Greenville*, 251 S.C. 473, 163 S.E.2d 462 (1968); *Sample v. Gulf Refining Co.*, 183 S.C. 399, 191 S.E. 209 (1937); *Cain v. Whitlock*, 178 S.C. 289, 182 S.E. 752 (1935); *Mull v. Easley Lumber Co.*, 121 S.C. 155, 113 S.E. 356 (1922); *Guinarin v. So. Life & Trust Co.*, 106 S.C. 37, 90 S.E. 319 (1916); *Mayfield v. So. Ry.*, 85 S.C. 165, 67 S.E. 132 (1910); *McCoy v. Atl. Coast Line Ry.*, 84 S.C. 62, 65 S.E. 939 (1909).

There are no cases which deal with the applicability of the best evidence rule to photographs and only one case in which the best evidence rule has been applied to recordings. *State v. Worthy*, 239 S.C. 449, 123 S.E.2d 835 (1962), *overruled on other grounds*, *State v. Torrence*, 305 S.C. 45, 406 S.E.2d 315 (1991).

Examples of statutes that have an effect on the requirement to produce the original are: S.C. Code Ann. § 19-1-110 (1985) (instruments of common carriers); S.C. Code Ann. § 19-5-10 (1985) (public documents); S.C. Code Ann. § 19-5-210 (1985) (grants issued by North Carolina); S.C. Code Ann. §§ 19-5-310 and -320 (1985) (missing person reports); S.C. Code Ann. § 19-5-510 (1985) (business records).

RULE 1003. ADMISSIBILITY OF DUPLICATES

A duplicate is admissible to the same extent as an original unless (1) a genuine question is raised as to the authenticity of the original or (2) in the circumstances it would be unfair to admit the duplicate in lieu of the original.

[Adopted effective September 3, 1995.]

Notes

This rule is identical to the federal rule. There is no case law in this State on the admissibility of a duplicate in this context, only on the admissibility of a duplicate as secondary evidence. See Note following Rule 1004.

RULE 1004. ADMISSIBILITY OF OTHER EVIDENCE OF CONTENTS

The original is not required, and other evidence of the contents of a writing, recording, or photograph is admissible if—

(1) Originals Lost or Destroyed. All originals are lost or have been destroyed, unless the proponent lost or destroyed them in bad faith; or

(2) Original Not Obtainable. No original can be obtained by any available judicial process or procedure; or

(3) Original in Possession of Opponent. At a time when an original was under the control of the party against whom offered, that party was put on notice, by the pleadings or otherwise, that the contents would be a subject of proof at the hearing, and that party does not produce the original at the hearing; or

(4) Collateral Matters. The writing, recording, or photograph is not closely related to a controlling issue.

[Adopted effective September 3, 1995.]

Notes

This rule is identical to the federal rule and is consistent with our case law. It has long been the law in South Carolina that secondary evidence is admissible under the circumstances outlined in this rule. *See*, e.g., *Pee Dee Prod. Credit Ass'n v. Love*, 284 S.C. 371, 326 S.E.2d 650 (1984) (original lost); *Windham v. Lloyd*, 253 S.C. 568, 172 S.E.2d 117 (1970) (original lost); *Wynn v. Coney*, 232 S.C. 346, 102 S.E.2d 209 (1958) (original in possession of opponent); *Greer v. Equitable Life Assur. Soc'y*, 180 S.C. 162, 185 S.E. 68 (1936) (collateral matter); *Rose v. Winnsboro Nat'l Bank*, 41 S.C. 191, 19 S.E. 487 (1894) (original in possession of opponent).

RULE 1005. PUBLIC RECORDS

The contents of an official record, or of a document authorized to be recorded or filed and actually recorded or filed, including data compilations in any form, if otherwise admissible, may be proved by copy, certified as correct in accordance with Rule 902 or testified to be correct by a witness who has compared it with the original. If a copy which complies with the foregoing cannot be obtained by the exercise of reasonable diligence, then other evidence of the contents may be given.

[Adopted effective September 3, 1995.]

Notes

This rule is identical to the federal rule and is substantially similar to S.C. Code Ann. § 19-5-10 (1985) and Rule 44, SCRCP.

RULE 1006. SUMMARIES

The contents of voluminous writings, recordings, or photographs which cannot conveniently be examined in court may be presented in the form of a chart, summary, or calculation, provided the underlying data are admissible into evidence. The originals, or duplicates, shall be made available for examination or copying, or both, by other parties at reasonable time and place. The court may order that they be produced in court.

[Adopted effective September 3, 1995.]

Notes

This rule is identical to the federal rule except for the language "provided the underlying data are admissible into evidence" and is consistent with South Carolina case law. *Adamson v. Marianne Fabrics, Inc.*, 301 S.C. 204, 391 S.E.2d 249 (1990); *Zemp Constr. Co. v. Harmon Bros. Constr. Co.*, 225 S.C. 361, 82 S.E.2d 531 (1954); *Crowley v. Spivey*, 285 S.C. 397, 329 S.E.2d 774 (Ct. App. 1985); *Butler v. Sea Pines Plantation Co.*, 282 S.C. 113, 317 S.E.2d 464 (Ct. App. 1984). It should be noted that the case of *Peagler v. Atlantic Coast Line R.R.*, 234 S.C. 140, 107 S.E.2d 15 (1959), is inconsistent with these prior cases and has been effectively overruled.

RULE 1007. TESTIMONY OR WRITTEN ADMISSION OF PARTY

Contents of writings, recordings, or photographs may be proved by the testimony or deposition of the party against whom offered or by that party's written admission, without accounting for the nonproduction of the original.

[Adopted effective September 3, 1995.]

Notes

This rule is identical to the federal rule. The case law has not previously recognized any limitation on the form of the statement or admission which can be used. *Gardner v. City of Columbia Police Dep't*, 216 S.C. 219, 57 S.E.2d 308 (1950). Therefore, this rule may be somewhat narrower since it limits the statements or admissions which can be used to those contained in testimony, deposition or written admission.

RULE 1008. FUNCTIONS OF COURT AND JURY

When the admissibility of other evidence of contents of writings, recordings, or photographs under these rules depends upon the fulfillment of a condition of fact, the question whether the condition has been fulfilled is ordinarily for the court to determine in accordance with the provisions of Rule 104. However, when an issue is raised (a) whether the asserted writing even existed, or (b) whether another writing, recording, or photograph produced at the trial is the original, or (c) whether other evidence of contents correctly reflects the contents, the issue is for the trier of fact to determine as in the case of other issues of fact.

[Adopted effective September 3, 1995.]

Notes

This rule is identical to the federal rule. It has long been held in this State that a question as to whether to admit a document under the best evidence rule is addressed to the discretion of the trial judge. *Shirer v. O.W.S. & Associates*, 253 S.C. 232, 169 S.E.2d 621 (1969); *Vaught v. Nationwide Mut. Ins. Co.*, 250 S.C. 65, 156 S.E.2d 627 (1967); *Drayton v. Industrial Life & Health Ins. Co.*, 205 S.C. 98, 31 S.E.2d 148 (1944); *Sample v. Gulf Refining Co.*, 183 S.C. 399, 191 S.E. 209 (1937); *Atlantic Coast Line R.R. v. Dawes*, 103 S.C. 507, 88 S.E. 286 (1916); *Leesville Mfg. Co. v. Morgan Wood & Iron Works*, 75 S.C. 342, 55 S.E. 768 (1906); *Wayne Smith Constr. Co., Inc. v. Wolman, Duberstein, and Thompson*, 294 S.C. 140, 363 S.E.2d 115 (Ct. App. 1987). There are no cases discussing the role of the trier of fact in this area.

ARTICLE XI

MISCELLANEOUS RULES

RULE 1101. APPLICABILITY OF RULES

(a) Courts and Judges. Except as otherwise provided by rule or statute, these rules apply to the courts of South Carolina. The term "judge" in these rules includes justices of the Supreme Court; judges of the Court of Appeals; judges of the circuit, family, probate and municipal courts; magistrates; masters-in-equity; and special referees.

(b) Proceedings Generally. These rules apply generally to civil actions and proceedings, to criminal cases and proceedings, and to contempt proceedings except those in which the court may act summarily.

(c) Rule of Privilege. The rule with respect to privileges applies at all stages of all actions, cases, and proceedings.

(d) Rules Inapplicable. The rules (other than with respect to privileges) do not apply in the following situations:

(1) *Preliminary Questions of Fact.* The determination of questions of fact preliminary to admissibility of evidence when the issue is to be determined by the court under Rule 104.

(2) *Grand Jury.* Proceedings before grand juries.

(3) *Miscellaneous Proceedings.* Proceedings for extradition; preliminary hearings in criminal cases; sentencing (except in the penalty phase of capital trials as required by statute), dispositional hearings in juvenile delinquency matters, or granting or revoking probation; issuance of warrants for arrest, criminal summonses, and search warrants; and proceedings with respect to release on bail or otherwise.

[Adopted effective September 3, 1995.]

Notes

Except for subsections (a), (b), and (d)(3), this rule is identical to the federal rule.

In subsection (a), the federal rule has been amended by adding the phrase "except as otherwise provided by rule or statute." See Note to Rule 101. Further, the phrase "courts of South Carolina" replaces the list of courts in the federal rule, and the term "judge" is modified to include all levels of the unified judiciary. These changes emphasize the fact that these rules are applicable to all levels of the unified judiciary.

Subsection (b) indicates that these rules apply generally to all civil and criminal proceedings except for summary criminal contempt. This exception is consistent with the relaxed procedural requirements for the imposition of summary contempt. *Cf. State v. Weinberg*, 229 S.C. 286, 92 S.E.2d 842 (1956).

Regarding subsection (c), no South Carolina authority has been found to support the proposition that the rules of privilege remain applicable even if the other rules of evidence are inapplicable.

Regarding subsection (d)(1), no South Carolina authority has been found regarding this proposition.

Subsection (d)(2) is consistent with the case law in South Carolina. *See State v. Williams*, 301 S.C. 369, 392 S.E.2d 181 (1990) (the validity of an indictment is not affected by the character of the evidence considered by the grand jury and, if valid on its face, the indictment may not be challenged on the ground that the grand jury acted on the basis of incompetent evidence); *State v. Williams*, 263 S.C. 290, 210 S.E.2d 298

(1974) (a grand jury indictment is not subject to dismissal on the basis that it was founded upon hearsay evidence).

To be consistent with the terminology used in this State, the phrase "preliminary hearings" in subsection (d)(3) replaces the phrase "preliminary examinations" in the federal rule. In addition, the phrase "dispositional hearings in juvenile delinquency matters" has been added to subsection (d)(3). Although no cases have been found regarding the application of the rules of evidence to extradition proceedings, subsection (d)(3) is generally consistent with prior law in this State. *See State v. Dingle,* 279 S.C. 278, 306 S.E.2d 223 (1983) (rules concerning hearsay inapplicable in preliminary hearings); *State v. Franklin,* 267 S.C. 240, 226 S.E.2d 896 (1976) (before imposing a sentence, judge may appropriately conduct an inquiry largely unlimited either as to the kind of information he may consider or the source from which it may come); *State v. Sullivan,* 267 S.C. 610, 230 S.E.2d 621 (1967) (a search warrant may be issued on an affidavit even when the affidavit is based on hearsay statements); *State v. Hill,* 5 S.C.L. (3 Brev.) 89, 6 S.C.L. (1 Tread.) 242 (1812) (the court may hear and consider affidavits when determining whether to admit a defendant to bail). However, as to probation revocation, the rule may constitute a change in the law. *See State v. White,* 218 S.C. 130, 61 S.E.2d 754 (1950) (hearsay rules applied in review of probation revocation).

RULE 1102. AMENDMENTS

Amendments to the South Carolina Rules of Evidence may be made by the South Carolina Supreme Court.

[Adopted effective September 3, 1995.]

Notes

This is the federal rule modified to apply to South Carolina.

RULE 1103. TITLE AND EFFECTIVE DATE

(a) Title. These rules shall be entitled South Carolina Rules of Evidence, and may be cited by rule number and the letters SCRE, i.e., Rule ___, SCRE.

(b) Effective Date. These rules shall become effective September 3, 1995.

[Adopted effective September 3, 1995.]

Notes

The language of subsection (a) is based on Rule 85(a), SCRCP. The federal rules do not contain a counterpart to subsection (b).

INDEX TO SOUTH CAROLINA RULES OF EVIDENCE

SOUTH CAROLINA RULES OF FAMILY COURT

Westlaw Electronic Research

These rules may be searched electronically on Westlaw in the SC-RULES *database; updates to these rules may be found on Westlaw in* SC-RULESUPDATES. *For search tips and a summary of database content, consult the Westlaw Scope Screen for each database.*

I. GENERAL PROVISIONS

RULE 1. TITLE

These rules shall be entitled the South Carolina Rules of Family Court and may be cited by Rule number and the letters SCRFC, i.e., Rule ___, SCRFC.

RULE 2. APPLICABILITY AND REPEALER

(a) Domestic Relations Actions. In addition to the rules set forth in Sections I, II and III of these Rules of Family Court, the South Carolina Rules of Civil Procedure (SCRCP) shall be applicable in domestic relations actions to the extent permitted by Rule 81, SCRCP. The following SCRCP, however, shall be inapplicable: 5(a) to the extent it does not require notice to a defendant of every hearing, 8(d) to the extent it provides that the failure to file a responsive pleading constitutes an admission, 12(b) to the extent it permits a 12(b)(6) motion to be converted to a summary judgment motion, 12(c), 13(j), 18, 23, 38, 39, 40(a & b), 42 to the extent it refers to trial by jury, 43(b)(1) to the extent it limits the use of leading questions to cross-examination, 43(i & j), 47, 48, 49, 50, 51, 54(c) to the extent it permits the court to grant relief not requested in the pleadings, 55, 56, 68, 69, 71, 72, 78, 79, and 84.

(b) Juvenile Actions. In addition to the rules set forth in Sections I, II, and IV of these Rules of Family Court, Rules 5, 6, 24, and 29, South Carolina Rules of Criminal Procedure, shall be applicable in juvenile actions.

(c) Other Actions. Procedure in other actions shall be as provided by statute.

(d) Repealer. All Rules of Practice for the Family Courts of this State heretofore adopted are repealed as of the effective date of the South Carolina Rules of Family Court.

(e) Administrative Orders. No administrative orders shall be issued which conflict with these rules.

[Amended effective July 1, 1989; July 1, 1990.]

RULE 3. FORMS

The Office of Court Administration, subject to approval by the Chief Justice, may develop forms for use in the Family Courts in domestic relations and juvenile matters. Use of a particular form may be mandatory, exclusive or discretionary, as directed by the Chief Justice.

RULES 4 and 5. [RESERVED]

II. PROVISIONS APPLICABLE TO ALL ACTIONS IN FAMILY COURTS

RULE 6. FAMILY COURT RECORDS

(a) File Book.

(1) *Domestic Relations Actions in Family Court.* The clerk of court shall provide for the filing and keeping of papers with respect to domestic relations actions in the manner provided in this rule. The clerk of court for each county shall keep a File Book, relating to domestic relations actions in the family court, in which there shall be entered and cross-indexed all proceedings of a domestic relations nature which are instituted in the family court for the county. The clerk of court shall maintain only one file book for domestic relations actions in the family court as required by this rule.

(2) *Juvenile Actions in Family Court.* The clerk of court shall provide for the filing and keeping of papers with respect to juvenile actions in the manner provided in this rule. The clerk of court for each county shall keep a File Book, relating to juvenile actions in the family court, in which there shall be entered and cross-indexed all proceedings of a juvenile action nature which are instituted in the family court for the county. The clerk of court shall maintain only one file book for juvenile actions in the family court as required by this rule.

(b) File Number. When a summons and complaint or juvenile petition are filed, the action shall receive a number in keeping with such case numbering system as the Office of South Carolina Court Administration shall develop, and thereafter all papers filed in the proceeding shall be similarly numbered and kept together in a file bearing the same number.

(c) Entry Required. No domestic relations or juvenile actions, whether for interlocutory action or final disposition, shall be heard by the court until the action has been first entered in the appropriate file book and all pleadings in the action filed with the clerk of court.

(d) Entries on File Books. Entries may be made on the file books only by a judge of the court or by the clerk of court or his deputy.

(e) Motion Calendar. In addition to the file books, each clerk of court shall maintain a family court motion calendar in such form as prescribed by the Office of South Carolina Court Administration. Attorneys shall advise the clerk of court to note on the motion calendar all requests for appearance on preliminary motions and other matters requiring a summary hearing before a family court judge. The family court motion calendar shall contain the case number, date of request, name of the action, attorneys involved and the nature of the motion to be presented.

(f) Order of Dismissal. No action listed in a file book which thereafter is settled or disposed of in any manner shall be dismissed, marked ended, or stricken from a file book unless and until:

(1) plaintiff shall file and serve a notice of dismissal or stipulation of dismissal pursuant to the provisions of Rule 41(a), SCRCP; or

(2) counsel in the action shall have prepared and filed an order signed by the appropriate judge and bearing the written consent of all interested parties to the action showing that it has been ended; or,

(3) dismissal is ordered by the court.

The clerk of court shall keep the file books current from time to time as may be necessary.

(g) Failure to Comply. Failure to comply with the requirements of this rule shall subject the person so failing to penalties as for contempt of court; which contempt shall be enforced by the court on motion of any aggrieved party or by the court on its own motion.

RULE 7. ADMISSIBILITY OF CERTAIN DOCUMENTS

The following documents and written statements shall be admissible in evidence without requiring that the persons or institution issuing the documents or statements be present in court:

(a) A written statement of a child's attendance at school, signed by a school principal or duly authorized school official.

(b) The school report card showing a child's records of attendance, grades on subjects taught and other pertinent information, provided that this be a report sent out at periodic intervals by the school.

(c) The written statement by a physician showing that a patient was treated at certain times and the type of ailment.

(d) Except in cases where the particular agency is a party, a written report of the Department of Social Services or other agency, reporting the home investigation or any other report required by the court.

(e) A written statement of an employer showing wages either weekly or monthly for a given period of time and W–2 statement, income tax returns and other reports of like nature.

RULE 8. APPEARANCE OF COUNSEL

Upon retention of counsel in a proceeding in family court, counsel shall immediately notify the court and opposing counsel, if any, of his appearance. The notification shall include the attorney's current address and telephone number.

RULE 9. CONDUCT OF HEARINGS

(a) Procedure. All hearings in the family courts shall be conducted by the court without a jury. Hearings shall be conducted in a judicial atmosphere, with the judge wearing a black judicial robe.

(b) Argument. Counsel shall not attempt to further argue any matter after he has been heard and the ruling of the court has been pronounced. No argument shall be made on objections to admissibility of evidence or conduct of trial unless specifically requested by the court.

RULE 10. JUDGES' ABSENCE FROM STATE

No family court judge shall absent himself from this State without leavc first granted by the Chief Justice.

RULE 11. JURISDICTION OF JUDGE OF ADJOINING CIRCUIT

In case any judicial circuit is without a resident family court judge, by reason of death, absence, disqualification or otherwise, and no other family court judge, special or regular, is presiding therein, then jurisdiction in all matters arising in such circuit is conferred upon and shall be exercised by a resident family court judge of any adjoining circuit or by any family court judge presiding therein. Any judge exercising such jurisdiction shall first satisfy himself of the necessity of doing so by affidavit of the moving party.

RULE 12. ATTORNEYS FOR GUARDIANS AD LITEM

If a guardian ad litem is represented by an attorney, the court in its discretion may assess reasonable attorneys' fees and costs.

RULE 13. BENCH WARRANTS

(a) Procedure. Subject to the approval of the Chief Justice, the Office of South Carolina Court Administration shall establish procedures for processing and maintaining bench warrants.

(b) Form. Bench warrants shall be in the form prescribed by the Supreme Court and shall require either the signature of the trial judge, or the signature of the respective clerk of court at the direction of the trial judge.

(c) Service. It is the continuing duty of the sheriff, and of other appropriate law enforcement agencies in the county, to promptly serve bench warrants and to make periodic reports to the court concerning the status of unserved warrants.

RULES 14 and 15. [RESERVED]

III. PROVISIONS APPLICABLE TO DOMESTIC RELATIONS ACTIONS

RULE 16. CONTINUING JURISDICTION

The family court has jurisdiction of the parties and control of all subsequent proceedings from the time of service of the summons and complaint.

RULE 17. FAILURE TO FILE ANSWER

(a) Appearance by Defendant. In domestic relations matters, even though the defendant does not file an answer, notice of the time and date of the merits hearing shall be given to the defendant. If the defendant is not represented by counsel, notice as required by this rule shall be sufficient if mailed to the defendant at his last known address, by certified mail, return receipt requested. The defendant may be heard at the merits hearing on issues of custody of children, visitation, alimony, support, equitable distribution, and counsel fees.

(b) Default. In domestic relations matters, the provisions of Rule 55, SCRCP, regarding orders of default shall be made in the final order issued by the family court.

RULE 18. FAILURE OF DEFENDANT TO COUNTERCLAIM FOR DIVORCE

Failure of the defendant in a domestic relations action to counterclaim for divorce shall not bar a subsequent action therefor.

RULE 19. LIS PENDENS

In domestic relations actions any party may record a notice of pendency of the proceeding under the circumstances and in the manner provided in other civil actions.

RULE 20. FINANCIAL DECLARATION

(a) When Required. In any domestic relations action in which the financial condition of a party is relevant or is an issue to be considered by the court, a current financial declaration in the form prescribed by the Supreme Court shall be served and filed by all parties.

(b) Filing and Service. Financial declarations shall be filed and served prior to or at the first hearing, or no later than 45 days after the complaint is served, whichever occurs first.

(c) Effect of Default. If the defendant fails to timely answer or otherwise plead, the plaintiff shall not be required to serve a financial declaration on the defendant prior to the final hearing.

(d) Sanctions. Reasonable sanctions may be imposed upon an attorney or a party for willful noncompliance with this rule.

RULE 21. TEMPORARY RELIEF

(a) Motion for Temporary Relief. A written motion for temporary relief, and notice of the hearing thereof, shall be served not later than five days before the time specified for the hearing, unless a different period is fixed by order of the court. In an emergency situation, such order may be made on ex parte application.

(b) Evidence at Hearing. Evidence received by the court at temporary hearings shall be confined to pleadings, affidavits, and financial declarations unless good cause is shown to the court why additional evidence or testimony may be necessary.

(c) Service of Affidavits. Notwithstanding the provisions of Rule 6(d), SCRCP, affidavits filed at a temporary hearing need not be served on the opposing party prior to the temporary hearing.

RULE 22. INTERVIEW WITH CHILD

In all matters relating to children, the family court judge shall have the right, within his discretion, to talk with the children, individually or together, in private conference. Upon timely request, the court, in its discretion, may permit a guardian ad litem for a child who is being examined, and/or the attorneys representing the parents, if any, to be present during the interview.

RULE 23. PRESENCE OR TESTIMONY OF CHILD

(a) Presence in Courtroom. Generally, in actions of parents against each other, or where the conduct of either parent is an issue, the children should not be allowed in the courtroom during the taking of testimony.

(b) Testimony. Children should not be offered as witnesses as to the misconduct of either parent, except, when, in the discretion of the court, it is essential to establish the facts alleged.

RULE 24. AUTOMATIC ENFORCEMENT OF CHILD SUPPORT AND PERIODIC ALIMONY

(a) Determination of Arrearage. Clerks of court shall review all child support and periodic alimony accounts paid through the clerk of court. This review shall be conducted at least once a month. An account shall be considered in arrears if a scheduled payment has not been received when review is made and at least five working days have passed.

(b) Rule to Show Cause and Affidavit. Whenever an account is in arrears, the clerk of court shall issue a rule to show cause and an affidavit identifying the order of the court which requires such payments to be made and the amount of the arrearage, directing the party in arrears to appear in court at a specific time and date. This rule shall have the same force and effect as a rule to show cause issued by a judge.
[Amended effective July 1, 1990.]

RULE 25. DISCOVERY

Recognizing the unique nature of the court's jurisdiction and the need for a speedy determination thereof, the prompt voluntary exchange of information and documents by parties prior to trial is encouraged. However, formal depositions or discovery shall be conducted only by stipulation of the parties or by court order upon application therefor in writing. Such an order may prescribe the manner, time, conditions and restrictions pertaining to the deposition or discovery.

RULE 26. ORDERS

(a) Findings of Fact. An order or judgment pursuant to an adjudication in a domestic relations case shall set forth the specific findings of fact and conclusions of law to support the court's decision.

(b) Certification. By signing his name to an order in a domestic relations case, the judge certifies compliance with this rule.

(c) Time for Issuing. Except under exceptional circumstances, an order in a domestic relations case shall be issued as soon as possible after the hearing, but not later than 30 days thereafter.

RULE 27. ENFORCEMENT OF VISITATION

(a) When a family court order provides for specific periods of visitation for a non-custodial person, and the custodial person fails to comply with the provisions regarding visitation, the non-custodial person may ask the family court, by pro se affidavit, for a hearing to determine whether the custodial person shall be held in contempt or the visitation provisions should be modified.

(b) When a family court order provides for specific periods of visitation for the non-custodial person and the non-custodial person refuses to return the child to the custodial person at the end of the period of visitation, the custodial person may ask the family court, by pro se affidavit, for a hearing to determine whether the non-custodial person should be held in contempt and for an order requiring return of the child.

(c) Whenever a person requests relief pursuant to this rule, the clerk of court shall issue a rule to show cause, and shall attach the pro se affidavit and a copy of the visitation order allegedly violated, directing the other person to appear in court at a specific time and date. The hearing shall be scheduled within thirty days of the date the pro se affidavit is filed. A rule issued pursuant to this section shall have the same force and effect as a rule to show cause issued by a judge. The petitioning person shall be responsible for arrangements and costs of serving the rule, affidavit, and order.

(d) If requested in the pro se affidavit or at the hearing, the court may include in its final order a provision modifying the terms of visitation if the best interests of the child would be served thereby.

RULES 28 to 30. [RESERVED]

IV. PROVISIONS APPLICABLE TO JUVENILE ACTIONS

RULE 31. PRE-ADJUDICATORY DETENTION

Upon a finding by the judge that detention is necessary for protection of the community or to serve the best interest of a child, and that such detention is likely to be for a period in excess of 48 hours, the judge upon adequate evidence and testimony may by appropriate order, extend such detention for a period not to exceed 7 days. Additional extensions not to exceed 7 days each may be made by subsequent orders of the court. Such order shall be in writing or reduced to writing and shall recite appropriate findings of fact.

RULE 32. DETENTION HEARING

At the detention hearing the family court may admit any evidence relevant to the necessity for detaining the child. The detention hearing may be held without the presence of the child's parents if they cannot be located after reasonable effort. If the parents are not located, the court shall appoint a guardian ad litem for the child.

RULE 33. TRANSFER OF VENUE

(a) Pre-adjudicatory Transfer. Upon the filing of a petition involving a child who is a resident of another county in the State, the judge may direct immediate transfer of the case to the county in which the child resides if the child has returned to his home and if it appears that the petitioner and local witnesses will not be inconvenienced. If the judge orders a transfer, a copy of such order along with all other documents and papers in the file shall be forwarded to the court in the county in which the child resides, and shall be received and processed in the same manner as if filed initially in the latter county.

(b) Post-adjudicatory Transfer. If the judge decides that an immediate transfer should not be made, and an adjudicatory hearing is held and the case is not dismissed, the judge may order its transfer to the county of the child's residence for disposition.

RULE 34. WAIVER HEARING

If jurisdiction of a delinquency matter is retained in the family court after a waiver hearing, the judge who presided over the waiver hearing shall not preside over the adjudicatory hearing.

RULE 35. ADJUDICATORY HEARING

(a) Date for Hearing. The date for the adjudicatory hearing shall be set at the earliest practicable date but no later than 40 days from the filing of the petition unless otherwise delayed by order of the court, which order shall set forth the reasons for the delay. Failure to schedule the adjudicatory hearing within the prescribed 40 day period shall not operate as a ground for dismissal except upon an affirmative showing of material prejudice.

(b) Notice of Hearing. Notice of the adjudicatory hearing shall be served on both parents and both shall be ordered to be present, and if the child is not living with the parents, the guardians or persons with whom the child resides. The parent or guardian shall be required to be present and not excused from attendance except by the judge upon a showing of sickness or other justifiable cause.

RULE 36. RIGHT TO COUNSEL

In every delinquency proceeding, there shall be served upon the child, his parents, guardians, or persons with whom the child resides, a notice that he has a right to be represented by an attorney and if the parents are not able to employ an attorney, that an attorney will be appointed by the court to represent the child. In appropriate cases the court may appoint counsel for the child and assess costs against the parents.

RULE 37. DISPOSITIONAL HEARING

The judge who presided at the adjudicatory hearing shall preside at the dispositional hearing except as provided for in Rule 33(b), SCRFC, or unless otherwise unavailable.

RULES 38 to 40. [RESERVED]

V. OTHER PROVISIONS

RULE 41. COUNSEL AND GUARDIAN AD LITEM FEES IN ABUSE AND/OR NEGLECT PROCEEDINGS

(a) Limitation on Fees. In all child abuse and neglect proceedings, the court shall grant to legal counsel appointed for the child subject to child abuse and/or neglect proceedings, a fee not to exceed One Hundred ($100.00) Dollars. The court shall grant to a guardian ad litem appointed for a child subject to such proceedings a fee not to exceed Fifty ($50.00) Dollars.

(b) Exceptions. If the court determines that extraordinary circumstances require the award of a fee larger than that which is specified in this rule, the court shall set forth in its order the salient facts upon which the extraordinary circumstances are based and shall award a fee to appointed legal counsel or guardian ad litem in an amount which the court determines to be just and proper.

APPENDIX OF FORMS

Note: For Family Court forms, see http://www.judicial.state.sc.us/forms

INDEX TO SOUTH CAROLINA RULES OF FAMILY COURT

SOUTH CAROLINA RULES OF MAGISTRATES COURT

Westlaw Electronic Research

These rules may be searched electronically on Westlaw in the SC-RULES *database; updates to these rules may be found on Westlaw in* SC-RULESUP-DATES. *For search tips and a summary of database content, consult the Westlaw Scope Screen for each database.*

SCOPE & PURPOSE

These rules govern civil procedure in the magistrates courts. They are to be known and cited as the "South Carolina Rules of Magistrates Court." They shall be construed to secure the just, speedy, and inexpensive determination of every civil case within the jurisdiction of the magistrates court. All civil actions in the magistrates court shall be conducted in such a manner as to do substantial justice between the parties according to the rules of substantive law. Provided, however, the time limits for taking any actions under these rules shall not apply where different time limits are specified by statute.

[Adopted effective May 1, 2008.]

RULE 1. DEFINITIONS

"Amendment" means making a change in a complaint, answer, or counterclaim.

"Answer" means the paper filed by the party responding to the complaint.

"Complaint" means the paper containing the claim filed by the plaintiff.

"Counterclaim" means the paper containing a claim by a defendant against a plaintiff.

"Court" means the judge of the magistrates court.

"Default" means failure to respond to the complaint or failure to appear at trial.

"Defendant" means the party against whom the plaintiff has filed a complaint.

"Execution" means enforcement of the judgment.

"Judgment" means the decision of the court on the case.

"Party" means either a plaintiff or a defendant.

"Plaintiff" means the party filing the complaint.

"Subpoena" means an order of the court requiring a witness to attend and testify at a specified place and time.

"Summons" means the paper issued by the court which orders the defendant to respond to the complaint.

"Working day" means a day which is not a Saturday, Sunday, or legal holiday under state or federal law.

[Adopted effective May 1, 2008.]

RULE 2. APPLICATION OF STATUTORY LAW AND CIRCUIT COURT PRACTICE IN ABSENCE OF RULE

These rules shall govern all civil suits in the magistrates court. If no procedure is provided by these rules, the court shall proceed in a manner consistent with the statutory law applicable to magistrates and with circuit court practice in similar situations but not inconsistent with these rules.

[Adopted effective May 1, 2008.]

RULE 3. COMPUTATION OF TIME PERIODS

In computing any period of time prescribed or allowed by these rules, by order of the court, or by any applicable statute, the day of the act, event, or default after which the designated period begins to run is not to be included. The last day of the period so computed is to be included in the period unless it is not a working day, in which event the period runs until the end of the next day which is a working day. When the period of time prescribed or allowed is less than seven days, Saturdays, Sundays, and holidays shall be excluded in the computation. A half holiday shall be construed as a working day.

[Adopted effective May 1, 2008.]

RULE 4. FILING CIVIL ACTION; ACTION AGAINST CORPORATION; LONG ARM STATUTE

(a) A civil action may be filed in any magistrates court in the county in which at least one defendant resides or where the most substantial part of the cause of action arose, except that civil actions against domestic corporations may be filed in the county where such corporation shall have its principal place of business.

(b) A civil action may be filed in any magistrates court in the county in which the plaintiff resides or where the cause of action arose when the defendant does not reside in this State and jurisdiction is based upon S.C. Code Ann. § 36–2–803.

[Adopted effective May 1, 2008.]

RULE 5. COMPLAINT

(a) A suit is commenced by filing with the magistrates court a short and plain written statement of the facts showing what the plaintiff claims and why the claim is made. Provided, however, upon a personal appearance, the plaintiff may make an oral statement which shall be reduced to writing. The court or court personnel shall assist the plaintiff in reducing the statement to writing if the court determines assistance is required. This statement shall be called a complaint. A plaintiff may combine as many claims as the plaintiff has against a defendant in one case and may sue more than one defendant in one case if the claim involves all of the defendants.

(b) The plaintiff shall state on the complaint the address to which the court may mail notices and correspondence concerning the case. If the plaintiff's mailing address changes, the plaintiff must advise the court in writing. The court may notify the plaintiff of all proceedings incident to the case by mailing the notice by regular mail to the plaintiff at the address provided.

(c) A plaintiff who desires to file an action without costs shall file a motion for leave to proceed *in forma pauperis*, together with the complaint proposed to be filed and an affidavit showing the plaintiff's inability to pay the fee required to file the action. If the motion is granted, the plaintiff may proceed without further application and file the complaint in the court without payment of filing fees.

[Adopted effective May 1, 2008.]

RULE 6. SUMMONS; SERVICE

(a) Upon the filing of the complaint and a copy with any attachments for each defendant, the court shall issue a summons. A copy of the original summons, along with a copy of the complaint and any attachments, shall be served on each defendant.

(b) The summons shall contain the name of the State and county, the name of the court, the file number of the action, and the names of the parties, be directed to the defendant, and shall state the time within which these rules require the defendant to file an answer and any counterclaim, and shall notify the defendant that in case of failure to do so, judgment by default will be rendered against the defendant for the relief demanded in the complaint.

(c) Service of the summons may be made by the sheriff, the sheriff's deputy, a magistrate's constable, or by any other person not less than eighteen (18) years of age, who is not an attorney in or a party to the action. Service of all other process shall be made by the sheriff or the sheriff's deputy, a magistrate's constable, or any other duly constituted law enforcement officer, or by any person designated by the court who is not less than eighteen (18) years of age and who is not an attorney in or a party to the action.

(d) The summons and complaint must be served together. The plaintiff shall furnish the person making service with as many copies as are necessary. Voluntary appearance made by the defendant is equivalent to personal service. Service shall be made as follows:

(1) *Individuals.* Upon an individual other than a minor under the age of fourteen (14) years or an incompetent person, by delivering a copy of the summons and complaint to the individual personally or by leaving copies of the summons and complaint at the individual's dwelling house or usual place of abode with a resident of suitable age and discretion, or by delivering a copy to an agent authorized by appointment or by law to receive service of process.

(2) *Minors and Incompetents.* Upon a minor under the age of fourteen (14) years, a person judicially declared incapable of conducting the person's own affairs, or an incompetent person, by delivering a copy of the summons and complaint to the minor or incompetent person personally and also a copy to (a) the person's guardian or committee or, if there is no guardian or committee within the State, upon (b) a parent or other person having care and control of the

person, or (c) any competent person with whom the person resides or (d) by whom the person is employed. If the individual upon whom service is made is a minor between the ages of fourteen (14) and eighteen (18) who lives with a parent or guardian, a copy of the summons and complaint shall also be served upon the parent or guardian if the parent or guardian resides within the State. Service on persons confined shall also conform to the provisions of S.C. Code Ann. § 15–9–510.

(3) *Corporations and Partnerships.* Upon a corporation, a partnership, or other unincorporated association which is subject to suit under a common name, by delivering a copy of the summons and complaint to an officer, a managing or general agent, or to any other agent authorized by appointment or by law to receive service of process, and if the agent is one authorized by statute to receive service and the statute requires it, by also mailing a copy to the defendant.

(4) *Governmental Subdivision.* Upon a municipal corporation, county, or other governmental or political subdivision subject to suit in the magistrates court, by delivering a copy of the summons and complaint to the governmental subdivision's chief executive officer or clerk, or by serving the summons and complaint in the manner prescribed by statute for the service of summons and complaint or any similar process upon this type of defendant.

(5) *Statutory Service.* Service upon a defendant of any class referred to in paragraph (d)(1) or (d)(3) of this rule is also sufficient if the summons and complaint are served in the manner prescribed by statute.

(6) *Service by Certified Mail.* Service of a summons, complaint, and any appropriate attachments upon a defendant of any class referred to in paragraph (d)(1) or (d)(3) of this rule may be made by certified mail, return receipt requested and delivery restricted to the addressee. Service is effective upon the date of delivery as shown on the return receipt. Service pursuant to this paragraph shall not be the basis for the entry of a default judgment unless the record contains a return receipt showing the acceptance by the defendant. Any default judgment shall be set aside pursuant to Rule 12 if the defendant demonstrates to the court that the return receipt was signed by an unauthorized person. If delivery is refused or is returned undelivered, service shall be made as otherwise provided by these rules.

(e) Same: Other Service. Whenever a statute or an order of the court provides for service of a summons and complaint, or an order upon a party not an inhabitant or found within the county of the court's jurisdiction, service shall be made under the circumstance and in the manner prescribed by the statute, rule, or order.

(f) Territorial Limits of Effective Service. All process other than a subpoena may be served anywhere within the territorial limits of the State and, when a statute so provides, beyond the territorial limits of the State. A subpoena may be served within the county of the court's jurisdiction. Nothing in this subdivision is meant to extend the jurisdiction of the magistrates court beyond the limits otherwise established by law.

(g) Proof and Return. The person serving the process shall promptly make proof of service and deliver it to the court. If served by the sheriff, the sheriff's deputy, or a magistrate's constable, proof of service shall be made by certificate. If served by any other person, the person shall make an affidavit of service. If served by publication, the printer or publisher shall make an affidavit of publication, and an affidavit of mailing shall be made to the party or the party's attorney if mailing of process is permitted or required by law. Failure to make proof of service does not affect the validity of service. The proof of service shall state the date, time, and place of service and a description of the person actually served. If service was by mail, the person serving process shall show in the proof of service the date and place of mailing, and attach a copy of the return receipt or the returned envelope showing whether the mailing was accepted, refused, or otherwise returned. If the mailing was refused, the return shall also show proof of any further service on the defendant pursuant to paragraph (d)(6) of this rule. The return along with the receipt or envelope and any other proof shall be promptly filed with the court with the pleadings and become a part of the record.

(h) Proof of Service Outside the State. When the service is made outside of the State, the proof of service may be made by affidavit before:

(1) Any person in this State authorized to make an affidavit;

(2) A commissioner of deeds for this State;

(3) A notary public who shall affix to the proof of service an official seal;

(4) A clerk of court of record who shall certify the same by an official seal; or,

(5) If made outside the limits of the United States, a consul, vice-consul, or consular agent of the United States who shall use in the certificate an official seal.

(i) Amendment. At any time in its discretion and upon terms it deems just, the court may, by written order, allow any process or proof of service to be amended, unless it clearly appears that material prejudice would result to the substantial rights of the party against whom the process issued.

(j) Acceptance of Service. No other proof of service shall be required when acceptance of service is acknowledged in writing and signed by the person served or the person's attorney and delivered to the court. The acknowledgement shall state the place and date service is accepted.

(k) Dismissal of Summons and Complaint. Subject to the provisions of any statute, rule, or order, a magistrate may dismiss a summons and complaint against any or all defendants without prejudice to the plaintiff if service of process cannot be obtained within one hundred twenty (120) days of the filing of the complaint.

[Adopted effective May 1, 2008.]

RULE 7. ANSWER AND COUNTERCLAIM; TIME FOR FILING

(a) The defendant may reply to the plaintiff's complaint by filing a written statement in a form approved by the magistrate or by personally appearing and making an oral statement. This reply shall be called an "answer." If the defendant personally appears within the specified time period and makes an oral answer, it shall be reduced to writing. The court or court personnel shall assist the defendant in reducing the answer to writing if the court determines assistance is required. The defendant's answer may deny in total or in part any or all of the material allegations made in the plaintiff's complaint, and/or allege any new matter constituting a defense. The court shall deliver a copy of the answer to the plaintiff in a manner provided for in Rule 8.

(b) A defendant shall file an answer and any appropriate counterclaims with the court within thirty (30) days from the first day after the date of service. When service is by some other means, as provided for in Rule 6, the defendant shall file the answer and any appropriate counterclaims with the court within the time period designated by the statute, rule, or order, and the time period shall be stated in the summons.

[Adopted effective May 1, 2008.]

RULE 8. DELIVERY AND FILING OF PLEADINGS AND OTHER PAPERS

(a) Delivery: When Required. Every order, pleading after the original summons and complaint, written motion, written notice, appearance, demand, offer of judgment, or similar documents shall be delivered to each of the parties unless otherwise ordered by the court.

(b) Same: How Made. Whenever under these rules delivery of documents is required to be made upon a party represented by an attorney, delivery of the documents shall be made to the attorney unless otherwise ordered by the court. Delivery of a document to a party shall be made by delivering it to that party or by mailing it to the party's last known address or, if no address is known, by filing it with the court. Delivery of a copy within this rule means: handing it to the attorney or to the party; or leaving it at the office of the attorney or the party with a clerk or other person in charge of the office; or, if there is no one in charge, leaving it at the party's usual place of abode with a resident of suitable age and discretion; or mailing it to the last known address of that party. Delivery by mail of all pleadings and papers after service of the original summons and complaint is complete upon mailing.

(c) Service or Delivery on Sunday. Civil process may be served on Sundays, provided that no person may be served going to or from or attending a regularly or specially scheduled church or religious service on Sunday.

[Adopted effective May 1, 2008.]

RULE 9. COUNTERCLAIM

(a) At any time within the time period specified in these rules for answering the complaint, the defendant may assert a counterclaim which grows out of the same transaction or occurrence as the plaintiff's claim by filing a written statement in a form approved by the magistrate or by personally appearing and making an oral statement. If the defendant personally appears within the specified time period and makes an oral counterclaim, it shall be reduced to writing. The court or court personnel shall assist the defendant in reducing the counterclaim to writing if the court determines assistance is required. The counterclaim shall be delivered to the plaintiff by the court in a manner provided for in Rule 8. The claims contained in the counterclaim shall be deemed denied by the plaintiff and no answer or reply is required to be filed by the plaintiff in response to a counterclaim filed by the defendant.

(b) The defendant in a counterclaim may waive the excess of the claim over the jurisdictional maximum to bring it within the jurisdiction of the magistrates court. If the defendant elects to waive a portion of the counterclaim, a separate action for the remainder of the claim may not be maintained. If the defendant does not waive the excess, the entire action shall be transferred to the circuit court of the county to be considered and tried as if the action had been originally filed in the circuit court as provided for in Rule 13(j), SCRCP.

[Adopted effective May 1, 2008.]

RULE 10. TRIAL DATE; NOTICE; FAILURE TO ANSWER

(a) Upon the filing of an answer by the defendant, the magistrate shall set the date of trial and deliver notice of the trial date to both parties in a manner provided for in Rule 8.

(b) If the defendant has failed to answer within the time period specified by these rules, the magistrate shall set a hearing date and shall deliver notice of the hearing date to both parties in a manner provided for in Rule 8 when the hearing is necessary for the entering of a default judgment in a manner consistent with Rule 11. At the default hearing, the defendant may participate only by cross-examining witnesses and objecting to evidence.

[Adopted effective May 1, 2008.]

RULE 11. DEFAULT JUDGMENT; DISMISSAL OF ACTION; DAMAGES

(a) If the defendant does not answer the complaint within the time period specified by these rules or answers within the specified time period but fails to appear at the time set for trial, judgment may be given for the plaintiff by default if the amount of the claim is liquidated. If the claim is unliquidated, and the defendant fails to answer within the time period specified by these rules or answers within the specified time period but then fails to appear at the time set for trial, judgment may be given to the plaintiff by default as in the case of liquidated claims if (1) the plaintiff itemizes the account and attaches an affidavit that it is true and correct and that no part of the sum sued for has been paid by discount or otherwise and (2) a copy of the account and affidavit was served with the summons on the defendant. In all other cases when the defendant fails to appear or answer, the plaintiff cannot recover without proving damages.

(b) If the plaintiff does not appear at trial, or if neither the plaintiff nor the defendant appears at the time and place specified for trial, the court may enter an order dismissing the action.

(c) If the defendant has filed a counterclaim against the plaintiff and the plaintiff fails to appear at the time set for trial, judgment may be given for the defendant by default if the claim is liquidated. If the claim is unliquidated, and the plaintiff fails to appear at the time set for trial, judgment may be given to the defendant by default as in the case of liquidated demands if (1) the defendant itemizes the account and attaches an affidavit that it is true and correct and that no part of the sum sued for has been paid by discount or otherwise and (2) a copy of the account and affidavit is filed with the answer and is delivered to the plaintiff as provided for in Rule 8. In all other cases when the plaintiff fails to appear, the defendant cannot recover on a counterclaim without proving damages.

(d) If a default hearing is conducted at the time set for trial because either the plaintiff or the defendant failed to appear, no further notice need be given of the default hearing, provided both parties were properly delivered notice of the time set for trial in a manner provided for in Rule 8.

(e) For good cause shown, the court may set aside a default or a default judgment in accordance with Rule 12.

[Adopted effective May 1, 2008.]

RULE 12. RELIEF FROM JUDGMENT OR ORDER

(a) Clerical mistakes and errors arising from oversight or omission in judgments, orders, or other parts of the record may be corrected by the court at any time of its own initiative or on the motion of any party and after any notice that the court orders. During the pendency of an appeal, leave to correct the mistake must be obtained from the appellate court.

(b) On motion and upon terms that are just, the court may relieve a party or the party's legal representative from a final judgment, order, or proceeding for the following reasons: (1) mistake, inadvertence, surprise, or excusable neglect; (2) newly discovered evidence which by due diligence could not have been discovered in time to move for a new trial under Rule 19; (3) fraud, misrepresentation, or other misconduct of an adverse party; (4) the judgment is void; (5) the judgment has been satisfied, released, or discharged, or a prior judgment upon which it is based has been reversed or otherwise vacated, or it is no longer equitable that the judgment should have prospective application. The motion shall be made within a reasonable time, and for reasons (1), (2), and (3), not more than one year after the judgment, order, or proceeding was entered or taken. A motion under this subdivision does not affect the finality of a judgment or suspend its operation. This rule does not limit the power of the court to entertain an independent action to relieve a party from a judgment, order, or proceeding, or to set aside a judgment for fraud upon the court. During the pendency of an appeal, leave to make the motion must be obtained from the appellate court. The procedure for obtaining any relief from judgment shall be by motion as prescribed in these rules, by appeal, or by an independent action.

[Adopted effective May 1, 2008.]

RULE 13. CONDUCT OF TRIAL; JURY TRIALS; WITNESSES; SUBPOENAS

(a) Trials should be conducted in an informal manner and the South Carolina Rules of Evidence shall apply but shall be relaxed in the interest of justice. In the trial of a civil action, in which one or both parties are unrepresented by legal counsel, the court shall question the parties and witnesses in order to assure that all claims and defenses are fully presented.

(b) Notice of the fact that court personnel will explain to all parties the procedure of the magistrates court and will assist them, if such assistance is required, to fill out all forms that may be necessary or appropriate shall be conspicuously posted in the magistrates office in the following form:

NOTICE TO ALL PARTIES IN CIVIL ACTIONS

THIS OFFICE WILL EXPLAIN THE PROCEDURE OF THE COURT, AND WILL HELP YOU PREPARE PAPERS RELATED TO YOUR ACTION, IF THE COURT DETERMINES SUCH HELP IS REQUIRED.

(c) If either party wants a jury trial, it must be requested in writing at least five (5) working days prior to the original date set for trial.

(d) All testimony shall be given under oath or affirmation.

(e) The court shall have the power to issue subpoenas to compel the attendance of witnesses. The court may issue a subpoena, signed but otherwise in blank, to a party requesting it, who shall complete it before service. An attorney as officer of the court may also issue and sign a subpoena on behalf of a court in which the attorney is authorized to practice.

[Adopted effective May 1, 2008.]

RULE 14. AMENDMENT OF COMPLAINTS, ANSWERS, AND COUNTERCLAIMS; CONTINUANCES

The court shall be lenient in the allowance of changes or amendments to complaints, answers, and counterclaims, and in granting continuances of trials for good cause shown when necessary to serve the ends of justice. However, except in unusual circumstances, no party shall be allowed more than one continuance in any case and all continuances must have the specific approval of the court. Continuances shall be for as short a period as possible, and, where feasible, the wishes of the party not requesting the continuance shall be considered in scheduling a new hearing date. Raising a claim, defense, or counterclaim for the first time at trial shall constitute grounds for a continuance when necessary to serve the ends of justice.

[Adopted effective May 1, 2008.]

RULE 15. EXCHANGE OF INFORMATION BETWEEN PARTIES; SETTLEMENT

(a) Recognizing the unique nature of the court's jurisdiction and the need for a speedy determination of actions filed in the court, the prompt voluntary exchange of information and documents by parties prior to trial is encouraged, but in no event shall the court require such exchange.

(b) The court, with both parties present, shall confer with the parties before any trial whenever it appears that a conference might simplify the issues, shorten the trial, or lead to a voluntary exchange of information which might promote settlement. The court in its discretion may order that a list of exhibits a party intends to offer into evidence at the trial be furnished to the opposing party and/or that the opposing party be given a reasonable opportunity to copy or examine the exhibits.

[Adopted effective May 1, 2008.]

RULE 16. DIRECTED VERDICT; JUDGMENT NOTWITHSTANDING THE VERDICT

(a) At the close of evidence offered by a party, if the case presents only questions of law, the court may direct a verdict on its own motion or on motion of either party. The order of the court granting a directed verdict is effective without any assent of a jury.

(b) If, at the close of all the evidence, a directed verdict is not granted, the court is deemed to have submitted the action to the jury subject to a later determination of the legal questions raised during the trial of the case if the case is being tried before a jury. If a jury verdict is returned, the court may allow the judgment to stand or may reopen the judgment and either order a new trial or direct the entry of judgment as if a directed verdict had been granted. A jury verdict is final if no motion for a new trial or judgment notwithstanding the verdict is filed with the court within five (5) days of the rendering of the jury verdict and the court has not on its own motion ordered a new trial or directed a verdict notwithstanding the jury verdict.

[Adopted effective May 1, 2008.]

RULE 17. COSTS; NOTICE OF JUDGMENT; ENFORCEMENT

(a) The party recovering judgment shall also recover those costs provided for by law, which shall not be included when determining the jurisdictional amount of the court.

(b) The court shall deliver written notice of judgment to all parties or their attorneys using the procedure described in Rule 8, except that no written notice need be delivered to a party if the judgment is announced at the trial in the presence of that party or the party's attorney.

(c) The process to enforce a judgment for the payment of money shall be by writ of execution and shall be conducted as provided by law.

(d) Upon payment in full, the judgment creditor shall file a statement of collection with the magistrates court and with the Clerk of the Circuit Court, if the judgment had been previously filed with the Clerk of the Circuit Court.

[Adopted effective May 1, 2008.]

RULE 18. APPEALS

(a) All appeals of judgments rendered by the magistrates court shall be to the circuit court of the county where the judgment was rendered. Within thirty (30) days after delivery of written notice of judgment to the parties or their attorneys, a party wishing to appeal shall serve on the respondent and file a notice of appeal containing a statement of the grounds for appeal with the magistrate rendering the judgment and with the Circuit Court of the County where the judgment was rendered. If the judgment is announced at the trial in the presence of the parties or their attorneys, the notice of appeal shall be served and filed within thirty (30) days of the date the judgment is announced. At the time of the filing of the notice of appeal, the appropriate filing fee shall be paid by the appellant to the clerk of the circuit court to which the appeal is taken, unless a motion for leave to proceed *in forma pauperis* and an affidavit showing the appellant's inability to pay the fee required to appeal the action accompanies the filing of the notice of appeal. The right of appeal from a judgment exists for thirty (30) days after the denial of a motion for a new trial.

(b) Within thirty (30) days of the date of filing of the notice of appeal with the Circuit Court, the magistrate shall file the return to the notice of appeal with the Clerk of the Circuit Court for the county wherein the judgment was rendered, together with the record, a statement of all proceedings in the case, and, if necessary, the testimony taken at trial. Upon motion for good cause shown, the Circuit Court may allow a definite extension of time in which to file the return.

(c) Pursuant to Rule 75, SCRCP, upon receipt of the magistrate's return, the clerk of the Circuit Court to which the appeal is taken shall give notice in writing to the parties that the return has been filed.

[Adopted effective May 1, 2008.]

RULE 19. NEW TRIAL; AMENDMENT OF JUDGMENTS

(a) A new trial may be granted to all or any of the parties and on all or part of the issues for any of the reasons for which new trials previously have been granted in the courts of this state. On motion for a new trial in an action tried without a jury, the court may open the judgment, if one has been entered, may take additional testimony, may amend findings of fact and conclusions of law, may make new findings and conclusions, and may direct the entry of a new judgment.

(b) The motion for a new trial shall be made in writing and filed with the court no later than five (5) days after notice of the judgment. The court shall notify all opposing parties that the motion has been filed and shall provide those parties a copy of the motion in a manner provided for in Rule 8.

(c) Not later than five (5) days after entry of judgment, the court, on its own initiative, may order a new trial for any reason for which it might have granted a new trial on motion of a party. After giving the parties notice and an opportunity to be heard on the matter, the court may grant a motion for a new trial, timely served, for a reason not stated in the motion. In either case, the court shall specify in the order the grounds for granting a new trial.

(d) A motion to alter or amend the judgment shall be filed no later than five (5) days after notice of the judgment. The court shall notify all opposing parties that the motion has been filed and shall provide those parties a copy of the motion in a manner provided for in Rule 8.

(e) Except by consent of the parties, argument on a motion for a new trial or to alter or amend the judgment shall be heard by the magistrate before whom the trial was held. However, the motion may, in the discretion of the court, be decided on briefs filed by the parties without oral argument.

[Adopted effective May 1, 2008.]

RULE 20. OFFER OF JUDGMENT; CONSEQUENCES OF NON–ACCEPTANCE

(a) Offer of Judgment. No later than ten (10) days prior to trial, either party may serve upon the adverse party an offer to allow judgment to be taken against the party for the money or property or to the effect specified in the offer with costs accrued to the date of the offer. If, within ten (10) days after service of the offer, or at least five (5) days prior to the trial date, whichever date is earlier, the adverse party serves written notice that the offer is accepted, either party may then file the offer and notice of acceptance together with proof of service, and the court shall enter judgment. An offer that is not accepted shall be deemed rejected and evidence of the offer is not admissible except in a proceeding to determine costs.

(b) Consequences of Non–Acceptance. If an offer of judgment is not accepted and the offeror obtains a verdict or determination at least as favorable as the rejected offer, the offeror shall recover from the offeree: (1) any administrative, filing, or other court costs from the date of the offer until the entry of the judgment; (2) if the offeror is a plaintiff, eight percent interest computed on the amount of the verdict or award from the date of the offer to the entry of judgment; or (3) if the offeror is a defendant, reduction from the judgment or award of eight percent interest computed on the amount of the verdict or award from the date of the offer to the entry of the judgment.

(c) This rule shall not abrogate the contractual rights of any party concerning the recovery of attorney's fees or other monies in accordance with the provision of any written contract between the parties to the action.

[Adopted effective May 1, 2008.]

RULE 21. BUSINESS REPRESENTATION

A business, as defined by S.C. Code Ann. § 33–1–103, may be represented in a civil magistrates court proceeding by a non-lawyer officer, agent, or employee, including attorneys licensed in other jurisdictions and those possessing Limited Certificates of Admission pursuant to Rule 405, SCACR. The representation may be compensated and shall be undertaken at the business's option and with the understanding that the business assumes the risk of any problems incurred as the result of the representation. The court shall require a written authorization from the entity's president, chairperson, general partner, owner, or chief executive officer, or in the case of a person possessing a Limited Certificate, a copy of that certificate, before permitting the representation.

[Adopted effective May 1, 2008.]

RULE 22. ARGUMENTS ON MOTIONS AND AT TRIAL

The moving party upon a motion shall have the right, at that party's option, to both open and close argument, and the plaintiff shall have the option to have the right to open and close argument upon the trial; except that a party admitting the adverse party's claim in his pleading, and taking upon him the burden of proof, shall have the same privilege. The party having the right to open shall be required to open in full, and in reply may respond in full but may not introduce any new matter.

[Adopted effective May 1, 2008.]

RULE 23. SUBPOENAS

(a) Any magistrate, on the application of any party to a cause pending in the magistrates court, shall issue a subpoena citing any person whose testimony may be required in the cause to appear and give evidence. The Court may issue a subpoena, signed but otherwise in blank, to a party requesting it, who shall complete it before service. An attorney as officer of the court may also issue and sign a subpoena on behalf of a court in which the attorney is authorized to practice. Every subpoena shall state the name of the court, and the title of the action, and shall command each person to whom it is directed to attend and give testimony at a time and place specified.

(b) A subpoena may be served by the sheriff of any county in which the witness may be found, by the sheriff's deputy, by a constable of the court, or by any other person who is not a party and is not less than eighteen (18) years of age. Service of a subpoena upon a person named in the subpoena shall be made as provided by Rule 6 and Rule 8 (c).

(c) No subpoena shall require a witness to appear in any proceeding not held within the county where that witness resides.

(d) Failure by any person without adequate excuse to obey a subpoena served upon the person may be deemed in contempt of court from which the subpoena issued.

(e) A witness subpoenaed to attend a proceeding under these rules shall receive for each day's attendance and for the time necessarily occupied in going to and returning from the proceeding $25.00 per day and mileage in the same amount as provided by law for official travel of State officers and employees.

(f) In case it shall appear to the satisfaction of any magistrate that the attendance of any witness whose testimony may be required in any case pending before the magistrate cannot be had because of just cause for the witness' absence, extreme age, sickness or infirmity, or when the witness does not reside in the county of the court's jurisdiction, the magistrate may take the examination of such witness or cause it to be done by another magistrate or other officer authorized by law to administer oaths, to be used in evidence on the trial of the case. All parties to the cause shall have notice of the examination so that they may examine or cross-examine the witness. When the examination is made by another, it shall be recorded and sealed, with the title of the case endorsed, and conveyed by a disinterested person to the magistrate authorizing it or mailed postage prepaid to that magistrate.

[Adopted effective May 1, 2008.]

RULE 24. FORMS

Note: For Magistrates Court forms, see http://www.judicial.state.sc.us/forms

The use of the following forms in the magistrates court is recommended. The magistrates court shall make these forms available without charge to any person who is a litigant in an action before the court. Subject to the approval of the Supreme Court, the Office of Court Administration shall make amendments to these forms and add forms as is deemed appropriate.

[1] SUMMONS

[2] COMPLAINT

[3] INSTRUCTIONS TO DEFENDANT

[4] ANSWER

[5] JUDGMENT

[6] COUNTERCLAIM

[7] INSTRUCTIONS TO PLAINTIFF

[8] AMENDMENT TO COMPLAINT

[9] SUBPOENA OF WITNESS

[10] DISMISSAL

[11] SATISFACTION OF JUDGMENT

[12] PARTIAL SATISFACTION OF JUDGMENT

[13] PETITION AND ORDER FOR APPOINTMENT OF GUARDIAN AD LITEM

[14] NOTICE OF INTENTION TO SEEK CHANGE OF VENUE

[15] AFFIDAVIT FOR CHANGE OF VENUE

[16] ORDER FOR CHANGE OF VENUE

[17] AFFIDAVIT AND ITEMIZATION OF ACCOUNTS

[18] AFFIDAVIT OF DEFAULT

[19] NOTICE OF EXCEPTION TO SURETIES

[20] NOTICE

[21] NOTICE OF CIVIL APPEAL

[22] NOTICE OF DEFAULT JUDGMENT

[23] JURY SUMMONS

[24] JURY DUTY CERTIFICATION

[25] BOND UNDERTAKING AND ORDER

[26] MEMORANDUM OF COSTS

[27] AFFIDAVIT (Claim and Delivery)

[28] AFFIDAVIT AND CLAIM FOR IMMEDIATE DELIVERY OF PROPERTY (Claim and Delivery)

[29] ORDER OF IMMEDIATE POSSESSION

[30] UNDERTAKING BY SURETY AND APPROVAL (Claim and Delivery)

[31] NOTICE OF RIGHT TO A PRESEIZURE HEARING (Claim and Delivery)

[32] ORDER RESTRAINING DAMAGE OR CONCEALMENT OF PROPERTY (Claim and Delivery)

[33] APPLICATION FOR EJECTMENT (Eviction)

[34] RULE TO VACATE OR SHOW CAUSE (Eviction)

[35] WRIT OF EJECTMENT (Eviction)

[36] AFFIDAVIT OF PLAINTIFF (Distraint)

[37] NOTICE OF PREDISTRESS HEARING (Distraint)

[38] AFFIDAVIT OF ABANDONMENT (Distraint)

[39] AFFIDAVIT (Attachment)

[40] BOND UNDERTAKING AND APPROVAL (Attachment)

[41] WARRANT OF ATTACHMENT

[42] MOTION AND AFFIDAVIT TO PROCEED *IN FORMA PAUPERIS*

[43] MOTION AND AFFIDAVIT FOR EMERGENCY HEARING (Protection from Domestic Abuse Act)

[44] SUMMONS (Protection from Domestic Abuse Act)

[45] PETITION FOR ORDER OF PROTECTION (Protection from Domestic Abuse Act)

[46] ORDER OF PROTECTION (Protection from Domestic Abuse Act)

[47] ORDER DENYING RELIEF (Protection from Domestic Abuse Act)

[48] TRANSMITTAL FORM FOR DOCUMENTS (Protection from Domestic Abuse Act)

[49] AFFIDAVIT OF SERVICE

[50] COMPLAINT AND MOTION FOR RESTRAINING ORDER (Harassment and Stalking)

[51] SUMMONS (RESTRAINING ORDER) (Harassment and Stalking)

[52] RESTRAINING ORDER (Harassment and Stalking)

[53] MOTION AND AFFIDAVIT FOR EMERGENCY HEARING (TEMPORARY RESTRAINING ORDER) (Harassment and Stalking)

[54] TEMPORARY (EX PARTE) RESTRAINING ORDER (Harassment and Stalking)

[55] NOTICE AND MOTION TO EXTEND RESTRAINING ORDER (Harassment and Stalking)

[56] RULE TO SHOW CAUSE (Harassment and Stalking)

[57] COMPLAINT FOR INTERPLEADER

[58] SUMMONS (INTERPLEADER)

[59] ANSWER TO COMPLAINT IN INTERPLEADER

[60] ORDER FOR INTERPLEADER AND SUMMONS FOR HEARING

[61] JUDGMENT IN INTERPLEADER ACTION

[62] AUTHORIZATION FOR NON–LAWYER REPRESENTATIVE

[63] AUTHORIZATION FOR NON–LAWYER REPRESENTATIVE

[Adopted effective May 1, 2008.]

INDEX TO SOUTH CAROLINA RULES OF MAGISTRATES COURT

SOUTH CAROLINA RULES OF PROBATE COURT

Westlaw Electronic Research

These rules may be searched electronically on Westlaw in the SC-RULES *database; updates to these rules may be found on Westlaw in* SC-RULESUPDATES. *For search tips and a summary of database content, consult the Westlaw Scope Screen for each database.*

RULE

RULE 1. [REUSE OF TAPES USED TO RECORD PROCEEDINGS]

Tapes used to record proceedings in the probate courts of South Carolina may be reused when:

(1) the complete record of the proceeding has been transcribed; or

(2) a period of six (6) months has elapsed since the date of the final order in the proceeding.

[Rule 1 of the former Rules of Practice for the Probate Courts of South Carolina adopted effective September 2, 1980. Adopted as Rule 1 of the renamed South Carolina Rules of Probate Court effective September 1, 1990.]

RULE 2. DUTY OF PROBATE JUDGE

Each probate judge has the continuing duty to monitor every matter pending in the probate court and to enforce prompt compliance with all requirements imposed by law upon administrators, executors, guardians and attorneys in the performance of their duties before the probate court.

[Rule 2 of the former Rules of Practice for the Probate Courts of South Carolina adopted effective July 1, 1982. Adopted as Rule 2 of the renamed South Carolina Rules of Probate Court effective September 1, 1990.]

RULE 3. PROCEDURES TO BE HANDLED IN PROCESSING PROBATE MATTERS, MAINTAINING RECORDS, AND SUBMITTING REPORTS OF THE COURTS

Subject to the approval of the Chief Justice, the Office of Court Administration shall establish procedures for processing probate matters, for maintaining records by all probate courts, and for furnishing information and statistical data relative to the work of the courts and to the expenditure of public moneys for their maintenance and operation.

The Probate Courts shall keep in their respective offices a standardized file, as prescribed by the Office of Court Administration, in which there shall be entered all matters which are instituted in the probate court.

As soon as a matter is initiated in the probate court it shall receive a number in keeping with such case numbering system as Court Administration shall develop for the probate courts. All papers pertaining to a matter must be kept together in a folder bearing the uniform case number and filed sequentially as directed by Court Administration.

Failure to comply with the requirements of the Rule, or any procedures established thereto, shall subject the party so failing to penalties as for contempt of Court.

[Rule 3 of the former Rules of Practice for the Probate Courts of South Carolina adopted effective March 8, 1983. Adopted as Rule 3 of the renamed South Carolina Rules of Probate Court effective September 1, 1990.]

RULE 4. PROCEDURES FOR ENDING DEFUNCT CASES

When an estate matter has been assigned a file number and entered in the pending file, and appears to be defunct in fact and not susceptible to ending by letters dismissory, the court shall strike the case from the active file with leave to restore upon good cause being shown why the case should be continued as a pending case.

When a guardianship or committeeship is defunct in fact and not susceptible to ending by normal final accounting, notification, and final discharge procedures, the court shall issue a final discharge upon its own initiative, provided that prior notice of such discharge shall be given in a newspaper published in the county, or if there be no newspaper published in the county, in the newspaper having the greatest circulation therein, once a week for four consecutive weeks, that on a certain day final discharge will be made. When a final accounting has not been made, no final discharge granted pursuant to this rule shall affect the rights of any ward or mentally incompetent person.

[Rule 4 of the former Rules of Practice for the Probate Courts of South Carolina adopted effective March 8, 1983. Adopted as Rule 4 of the renamed South Carolina Rules of Probate Court effective September 1, 1990.]

COURT-ANNEXED ALTERNATIVE DISPUTE RESOLUTION (ADR) RULES

Westlaw Electronic Research

These rules may be searched electronically on Westlaw in the SC-RULES *database; updates to these rules may be found on Westlaw in* SC-RULESUP-DATES. *For search tips and a summary of database content, consult the Westlaw Scope Screen for each database.*

RULE 1. SCOPE OF RULES

These rules shall be construed to secure the just, speedy, inexpensive and collaborative resolution in every action to which they apply. These rules govern Alternative Dispute Resolution (ADR) processes in the courts of this State as follows:

(a) With the exceptions stated in Rule 3, these rules govern court-annexed ADR processes in South Carolina Circuit Courts in civil suits, and in South Carolina Family Courts in domestic relations actions:

(1) in counties designated by the Supreme Court of South Carolina for mandatory ADR;[1]

(2) as required by statute; or

(3) as ordered by a court of competent jurisdiction.

(b) With the exception of Rules 3, 4, 5, 6, 7(e) and (f), 9(b) and (d), and Rule 10(a), these rules shall govern ADR processes that are neither court mandated nor required by statute in all cases pending in the courts of this State.

(c) These rules shall govern all mediations in Medical Malpractice actions as required by S.C. Code Ann. § 15–79–120 and S.C. Code Ann. § 15–79–125(C).

[Adopted effective May 3, 2006. Amended effective April 29, 2009.]

1 See Supreme Court Order dated September 16, 2009. See Editor's Note below.

RULE 2. DEFINITIONS

(a) Mediation. An informal process in which a third-party mediator facilitates settlement discussions between parties. Any settlement is voluntary. In the absence of settlement, the parties lose none of their rights to trial.

(b) Mediator. A neutral person who acts to encourage and facilitate the resolution of a dispute. The mediator does not decide the issues in controversy or impose settlement.

(c) Arbitration. An informal process in which a third-party arbitrator issues an award deciding the issues in controversy. The award may be binding or non-binding as specified in these rules.

(d) Arbitrator. A neutral person who acts to decide the issues in controversy of a dispute.

(e) Neutral. A mediator or arbitrator.

(f) Certified. A mediator or arbitrator who is approved by the Board of Arbitrator and Mediator Certification to be eligible for court appointment pursuant to these rules.

(g) Alternative Dispute Resolution (ADR) Conference. A mediation or arbitration. Arbitration conferences may also be referred to as hearings.

(h) Roster. The official list of certified neutrals maintained and published by the South Carolina Supreme Court Board of Arbitrator and Mediator Certification.

(i) Board. The South Carolina Supreme Court Board of Arbitrator and Mediator Certification.

[Adopted effective May 3, 2006.]

RULE 3. ACTIONS SUBJECT TO ADR

(a) Mediation. All civil actions filed in the circuit court, all cases in which a Notice of Intent to File Suit is filed pursuant to the provisions of S.C. Code § 15–79–125(A), and all contested issues in domestic relations actions filed in family court, except for cases set forth in Rule 3(b) or (c), are subject to court-ordered mediation under these rules unless the parties agree to conduct an arbitration. The parties may select their own neutral and may mediate or arbitrate at any time.

(b) Exceptions. ADR is not required for:

(1) special proceedings, or actions seeking extraordinary relief such as mandamus, habeas corpus, or prohibition;

(2) requests for temporary relief;

(3) appeals;

(4) post–conviction relief (PCR) matters;

(5) contempt of court proceedings;

(6) forfeiture proceedings brought by governmental entities;

(7) mortgage foreclosures;

(8) family court cases initiated by the South Carolina Department of Social Services; and

(9) cases that have been previously subjected to an ADR conference, unless otherwise required by this rule or by statute.

(c) Motion to Refer Case to Mediation. In cases not subject to ADR, the Chief Judge for Administrative Purposes, upon the motion of the court or of any party, may order a case to mediation.

[Adopted effective May 3, 2006. Amended effective May 3, 2007.]

RULE 4. SELECTION OR APPOINTMENT OF NEUTRAL

(a) Eligibility. A neutral may be a person who:

(1) is a certified neutral under Rule 15; or

(2) is not a certified neutral but in the opinion of all of the parties is otherwise qualified by training or experience to mediate or arbitrate all or some of the issues in the action.

(b) Roster of Certified Neutrals. The Board shall maintain a current roster ("Roster") of neutrals certified under Rule 15 who are willing to serve in each county. The Board shall make the Roster available to the clerks of court for each county. A certified neutral shall notify the Supreme Court's Board of Arbitrator and Mediator Certification if the neutral desires to be added to or deleted from the Roster. The Board and clerk of court for each county shall make this roster available to the public.

(c) Appointment of Mediator by Circuit Court. In circuit court cases subject to ADR in which no Proof of ADR has been filed on the 210th day after the filing of the action, the Clerk of Court shall appoint a primary mediator and a secondary mediator from the current Roster on a rotating basis from among those mediators agreeing to accept cases in the county in which the action has been filed. A Notice of ADR appointing the mediators shall be issued upon a form approved by the Supreme Court or its designee. In the event of a conflict of interest with the primary mediator, the secondary mediator shall serve. In the event of a conflict of interest with the secondary mediator, and if the parties have not agreed to the selection of an alternative mediator, the plaintiff or the plaintiff's attorney shall immediately file with the Clerk of Court a written notice advising the court of this fact and requesting the appointment of two more mediators. In lieu of mediation, the parties may select non-binding arbitration pursuant to these rules.

In medical malpractice cases subject to pre-suit mediation as required by S.C. Code § 15–79–125(C), the Notice of Intent to File Suit shall be filed in accordance with procedures for filing a lis pendens and requires the same filing fee as provided by S.C. Code § 8–21–310(11)(b). The Notice of Intent to File Suit shall contain language directed to the defendant(s) that the dispute is subject to pre-suit mediation within 120 days and must contain a place for the names of the primary and secondary mediators. At the time the Notice of Intent to File Suit is filed, the Clerk of Court shall appoint a primary mediator and a secondary mediator in the manner set forth in the paragraph above. The plaintiff shall serve the defendants with the Notice of Intent to File Suit containing the mediator appointment. Notwithstanding the clerk's appointments, the parties by agreement may choose a different mediator at any time.

(d) Appointment of Mediator by Family Court. In family court cases subject to ADR, early mediation is encouraged.

(1) If there are unresolved issues of custody or visitation, an early mediation of those issues is required. In such event, the court shall appoint a mediator at a temporary hearing. If there is no temporary hearing, then the parties shall agree upon a mediator or notify the court for the appointment of a mediator within fifteen (15) days of the joinder of the issues of custody or visitation. In the event a mediation has not already been held to attempt resolution of the issues of custody and visitation, the temporary order shall designate a mediator in language substantially complying with the form approved by the Su-

preme Court or its designee. The designation shall include the name, address and phone number of the primary mediator, whether the mediator was selected or appointed, and if appointed, the name, address and phone number of a secondary mediator. E–mail addresses shall be included, if available.

(2) If issues other than custody or visitation are in dispute and no Proof of ADR has been filed certifying that the issues have been mediated, the parties must mediate those issues prior to the scheduling of a hearing on the merits; provided, however, the parties may submit the issues of property and alimony to binding arbitration in accordance with subparagraph (5). A mediator shall be designated in the following manner:

(A) When the parties file a request for a merits hearing, the request shall include the name of the stipulated mediator or a request for appointment of a mediator. The court shall not schedule a hearing on the merits until a Proof of ADR has been filed.

(B) If a mediator has not been stipulated in the request for merits hearing, the clerk of court shall appoint a primary mediator and a secondary mediator from the current Roster on a rotating basis from among those mediators agreeing to accept cases in the county in which the action has been filed. A Notice of ADR appointing the mediators shall be issued upon a form approved by the Supreme Court or its designee.

(3) In the event of a conflict of interest with the primary mediator, the secondary mediator shall serve. In the event of a conflict of interest with the secondary mediator, and if the parties have not agreed to the selection of an alternative mediator, the plaintiff or the plaintiff's attorney shall immediately file with the Clerk of Court a written notice advising the court of this fact and requesting the appointment of two more mediators.

(4) An initial mediation conference must occur within thirty (30) days of appointment or selection. The parties must complete mediation and file a Proof of ADR with the clerk's office before a merits hearing can be scheduled.

(5) In lieu of mediation, the parties may elect to submit issues of property and alimony to binding arbitration in accordance with the Uniform Arbitration Act, S.C. Code § 15–48–10 et seq.

(e) By agreement. By agreement, the parties may choose a neutral at any time. In any event, the ADR conference shall be held on or before the deadlines provided for in these rules.

(f) Notice to Neutral. The parties shall notify the selected or appointed neutral to initiate scheduling of the ADR Conference.

[Adopted effective May 3, 2006. Amended effective May 3, 2007.]

RULE 5. THE ADR CONFERENCE

(a) Location of the Conference. The ADR Conference is to be held within the county where the case is filed at a site designated by the neutral or any other site agreed upon by the parties and the neutral.

(b) Discovery and Motions. The ADR conference shall not be cause for delay of other proceedings in the case, including the completion of discovery, the filing and hearing of motions, or any other matter that would delay preparation of the case for trial, except by order of the court.

(c) Recesses. The neutral may recess the ADR conference at any time and may set times for reconvening. No further notification is required for persons present at the recessed conference.

(d) Privacy. ADR conferences are private. Other persons may attend only with the permission of the parties, their attorneys and the mediator.

(e) Motion to Defer or Exempt from ADR. A party may file a motion to defer an ADR conference or exempt a case from ADR for case specific reasons. For good cause, the Chief Judge for Administrative Purposes of the circuit may grant the motion. For example, it may be appropriate to defer an ADR conference or completely exempt a case from the requirement of ADR where a party is unable to participate due to incarceration or mental or physical condition.

(f) Deadline for the ADR Conference in Circuit Court. The ADR conference shall be held on or before three hundred (300) days from the date of the filing of the action. The case shall not be on the circuit court trial roster until a Proof of ADR is filed.

Pre-suit medical malpractice mediations required by S.C. Code § 15–79–125 shall be held not later than 120 days after all defendants are served with the Notice of Intent to File Suit or as the Court directs.

(g) Scheduling in Family Court. The parties shall contact and cooperate with the mediator to set the schedule for conferences and the mediator may recess a conference at any time and may set times for reconvening. No further notification is required for persons present at the recessed conference. The case shall not be docketed in family court for trial until a Proof of ADR is filed.

[Adopted effective May 3, 2006. Amended effective May 3, 2007.]

RULE 6. DUTIES OF THE PARTIES, REPRESENTATIVES AND ATTORNEYS—MEDIATION

(a) Duty to Inform. In cases subject to ADR under these rules, all attorneys should fairly and objectively inform their clients about mediation and arbitration.

(b) Attendance. The following persons shall physically attend a mediation settlement conference unless otherwise agreed to by the mediator and all parties or as ordered or approved by the Chief Judge for Administrative Purposes of the circuit:

(1) The mediator;

(2) All individual parties; or an officer, director or employee having full authority to settle the claim for a corporate party; or in the case of a governmental agency, a representative of that agency with full authority to negotiate on behalf of the agency and recommend a settlement to the appropriate decision-making body of the agency;

(3) The party's counsel of record, if any; and

(4) For any insured party against whom a claim is made, a representative of the insurance carrier who is not the carrier's outside counsel and who has full authority to settle the claim.

(c) Identification of Matters in Dispute. The mediator may require, prior to the scheduled mediation conference, that each party provide a brief memorandum setting forth their position with regard to the issues that need to be resolved. The memorandum should be no more than five (5) pages in length unless permitted by the mediator. With the consent of all parties, such memoranda may be mutually exchanged by the parties.

(d) Cooperation. The parties and their representatives shall cooperate with the mediator.

(e) Confidentiality. Communications during the mediation settlement conference shall be confidential in accordance with Rule 8.

(f) Agreement in Circuit Court. Upon reaching an agreement, the parties shall, before the adjournment of the mediation, reduce the agreement to writing and sign along with their attorneys. If the parties envision a more formal agreement, the mediator shall assign one of the parties' attorneys to prepare the agreement. A consent judgment or voluntary dismissal shall be filed with the court by such persons as may be designated by the mediator.

(g) Agreement in Family Court. Parties must participate in at least three (3) hours of mediation unless an agreement is reached sooner. Upon the parties reaching an agreement, the mediator shall provide a Memorandum of Agreement to the parties, attorneys of record, and guardians ad litem of record. It is the obligation of the parties to seek approval of the agreement by the family court.

[Adopted effective May 3, 2006.]

RULE 7. AUTHORITY AND DUTIES OF MEDIATORS

(a) Authority of Mediators. The mediator shall at all times be authorized to control the conference and the procedures to be followed.

(b) Duties. The mediator shall set up the mediation conference. The mediator shall define and describe the following to the parties:

(1) The mediation process, including the difference between mediation and other forms of conflict resolution;

(2) The facts that the mediation conference is not a trial; the mediator is not a judge, jury or arbitrator; and the parties retain the right to trial if they do not reach a settlement;

(3) The inadmissibility of conduct and statements as evidence in any arbitral, judicial or other proceeding;

(4) The circumstances under which the mediator may meet alone with either of the parties or with any other person;

(5) Whether and under what conditions communications with the mediator will be held in confidence during the conference;

(6) The duties and responsibilities of the mediator and the parties;

(7) The fact that any agreement must be reached by mutual consent of the parties; and

(8) The costs of the mediation settlement conference.

(c) Confidentiality. The mediator must comply with Rule 8 regarding confidentiality.

(d) Duty of Impartiality/Disclosure. The mediator has a duty to be impartial and to disclose any circumstance likely to affect impartiality or independence, including any bias, prejudice or financial or personal interest in the result of the mediation or any past or present relationship with the parties or their representatives.

(e) Declaring Impasse. It is the duty of the mediator to timely determine when the mediation is not viable, that an impasse exists, or that the mediation should end. A mediation cannot be unilaterally ended without the permission of the mediator.

(f) Reporting Results of Conference. Within ten (10) days of conclusion of the conference, the mediator shall file with the Clerk of Court a Proof of ADR on a form approved by the Supreme Court or its designee. Any request for a final hearing in a contested case subject to ADR under these rules shall include a copy of a Proof of ADR. South Carolina Court Administration or the South Carolina Commission on Alternative Dispute Resolution may require the mediator to provide additional statistical data for evaluation of the program.

In pre-suit medical malpractice mediations required by S.C. Code § 15–79–125, the Clerk of Court shall serve notice of entry of the Proof of ADR by first class mail upon all attorneys and unrepresented parties. The 60–day period in which to file a summons and complaint in accordance with S.C. Code § 15–79–125

(E)(1) shall commence upon receipt of written notice of entry of the Proof of ADR from the Clerk of Court.

(g) Immunity. The mediator shall have immunity from liability to the same extent afforded judicial officers of this state.

[Adopted effective May 3, 2006. Amended effective May 3, 2007.]

RULE 8. CONFIDENTIALITY

(a) Confidentiality. Communications during a mediation settlement conference shall be confidential. Additionally, the parties, their attorneys and any other person present must execute an Agreement to Mediate that protects the confidentiality of the process. To that end, the parties and any other person present shall maintain the confidentiality of the mediation and shall not rely on, or introduce as evidence in any arbitral, judicial or other proceeding, any oral or written communications having occurred in a mediation proceeding, including, but not limited to:

(1) Views expressed or suggestions made by another party or any other person present with respect to a possible settlement of the dispute;

(2) Admissions made in the course of the mediation proceeding by another party or any other person present;

(3) Proposals made or views expressed by the mediator;

(4) The fact that another party had or had not indicated willingness to accept a proposal for settlement made by the mediator; or

(5) All records, reports or other documents created solely for use in the mediation.

(b) Limited Exceptions to Confidentiality. This rule does not prohibit:

(1) Disclosures as may be stipulated by all parties;

(2) A report to or an inquiry from the Chief Judge for Administrative Purposes regarding a possible violation of these rules;

(3) The mediator or participants from responding to an appropriate request for information duly made by persons authorized by the court to monitor or evaluate the ADR program;

(4) Threats of harm or attempts to inflict physical harm made during the mediation sessions; and

(5) Any disclosures required by law or a professional code of ethics.

(c) Private Consultation/Confidentiality. The mediator may meet and consult individually with any party or parties or their counsel during a mediation conference. The mediator without consent shall not divulge confidential information disclosed to a mediator in the course of a private consultation.

(d) No Waiver of Privilege. No communication by a party or attorney to the mediator in private session shall operate to waive any attorney-client privilege.

(e) Mediator Not to be Called as Witness. The mediator shall not be compelled by subpoena or otherwise to divulge any records or to testify in regard to the mediation in any adversary proceeding or judicial forum. All records, reports and other documents received by the mediator while serving in that capacity shall be confidential.

[Adopted effective May 3, 2006. Amended effective May 1, 2008.]

RULE 9. COMPENSATION OF NEUTRAL

(a) By Agreement. When the parties stipulate the neutral, the parties and the neutral shall agree upon compensation.

(b) By Court Order—Mediation. When the mediator is appointed by the court, the mediator shall be compensated by the parties at a rate of $175 per hour, provided that the court-appointed mediator shall charge no greater than one hour of time in preparing for the initial mediation conference. Travel time shall not be compensated. Expense reimbursement shall be limited to actual expenses not exceeding $50, unless otherwise ordered by the Chief Judge for Administrative Purposes of the circuit. An appointed mediator may charge no more than $175 for cancellation of an ADR Conference.

(c) Payment of Compensation by the Parties. Unless otherwise agreed to by the parties or ordered by the court, fees and expenses for the ADR conference shall be paid in equal shares per party. Payment shall be due upon conclusion of the conference unless other arrangements are made with the neutral, or unless a party advises the neutral of his or her intention to file a motion to be exempted from payment of neutral fees and expenses pursuant to Rule 9(d).

(d) Indigent Cases. Where a mediator has been appointed, a party may move before the Chief Judge for Administrative Purposes to be exempted from payment of neutral fees and expenses based upon indigency. Applications for indigency shall be filed no later than ten (10) days after the ADR conference has been concluded. Determination of indigency shall be in the sole discretion of the Chief Judge for Administrative Purposes.

[Adopted effective May 3, 2006.]

RULE 10. SANCTIONS

(a) Proof of ADR. If by the time required by these rules, no Proof of ADR has been filed with the Office of the Clerk of Court and the case has not been exempted or deferred from ADR by court order, the court may issue a Rule to Show Cause why sanctions should not be imposed, including the dismissal of an action without prejudice or the striking of a pleading. The court may also manage such cases through status conferences and/or scheduling orders.

(b) Sanctions. If any person or entity subject to the ADR Rules violates any provision of the ADR Rules without good cause, the court may, on its own motion or motion by any party, impose upon that party, person or entity, any lawful sanctions, including, but not limited to, the payment of attorney's fees, neutral's fees, and expenses incurred by persons attending the conference; contempt; and any other sanction authorized by Rule 37(b), SCRCP.

[Adopted effective May 3, 2006.]

RULE 11. DUTIES OF THE PARTIES, REPRESENTATIVES AND ATTORNEYS—ARBITRATION

(a) Attendance. The following persons shall physically attend an arbitration unless otherwise agreed to by the arbitrator and all parties or as ordered or approved by the Chief Judge for Administrative Purposes:

(1) The arbitrator;

(2) All individual parties; or an officer, director, or employee for a corporate party; or in the case of a governmental agency, a representative of that agency; and

(3) The party's counsel of record, if any.

(b) Identification of Matters of Dispute. The arbitrator may require, prior to the scheduled arbitration conference, that each party provide a brief memorandum setting forth their position with regard to the issues that need to be resolved. The memorandum should be no more than five (5) pages in length unless permitted by the arbitrator. Such memoranda shall be exchanged by the parties at the same time and in the same manner as the memoranda are furnished to the arbitrator.

(c) Cooperation. The parties and their representatives shall cooperate with the arbitrator.

[Adopted effective May 3, 2006.]

RULE 12. NON-BINDING ARBITRATION HEARING AND AWARD

(a) Scope. This rule applies only to non-binding arbitrations. Nothing in this rule shall be construed to apply to binding arbitration pursuant to the Uniform Arbitration Act as adopted in South Carolina. Arbitrations selected by the parties under these rules are deemed non-binding arbitrations unless otherwise expressly agreed by the parties.

(b) Arbitration Hearings. The following shall apply to arbitration hearings, unless otherwise expressly agreed by the parties:

(1) Witnesses may be compelled to testify under oath or affirmation and produce evidence by the same authority and to the same extent as if the hearing were at trial. The arbitrator is empowered and authorized to administer oaths and affirmations.

(2) Rule 45, SCRCP, shall apply to subpoenas for attendance of witnesses and production of documentary evidence at an arbitration hearing under these rules.

(3) The arbitrator shall have the authority of a trial judge to govern the conduct of hearings, except for the power to punish for contempt. The arbitrator shall refer all contempt matters to the Chief Judge for Administrative Purposes.

(4) The South Carolina Rules of Evidence do not apply, except as to privilege, in an arbitration hearing but shall be considered as a guide toward full and fair development of the facts. The arbitrator shall consider all evidence presented and give it the weight and effect the arbitrator determines appropriate.

(5) No *ex parte* communications between the parties or their counsel and the arbitrator are permitted.

(6) The arbitration hearing shall be limited to two hours unless the arbitrator determines that more time is necessary to insure fairness and justice to the parties. The arbitrator is not required to receive repetitive or cumulative evidence.

(7) No recording or transcript of an arbitration hearing shall be made.

(c) Award. Unless otherwise expressly agreed by the parties:

(1) The award shall be in writing, signed by the arbitrator. Within ten (10) business days after the hearing is concluded, the arbitrator shall serve the original award on the prevailing party, copies of the award on all other parties, and a Proof of ADR with the court, together with a certificate of service. The arbitration hearing is concluded when all the evidence is in and any arguments or post-hearing briefs the arbitrator permits have been completed or received.

(2) The award must resolve all issues raised by the pleadings.

(3) Findings of facts and conclusions of law or opinions supporting an award are not required.

(d) Trial De Novo as a Right. Any party not in default for a reason subjecting that party to judgment by default who is dissatisfied with an arbitrator's award may have a trial de novo of right upon filing a written demand for trial de novo with the court, and service of the demand on all parties on a form approved by the Supreme Court or its designee within thirty (30) days after receipt of the arbitrator's award. No evidence that there has been an arbitration proceeding or any fact concerning the arbitration may be admitted in a trial, or in any subsequent proceeding involving any of the issues in or parties to the arbitration, without the consent of all parties and the court's approval.

(e) Judgment Entered on Award. If the case is not terminated by agreement of the parties, and no party files a demand for trial de novo under Rule 12(d), the prevailing party shall submit to the Chief Judge for Administrative Purposes a proposed order directing the entry of judgment on the award, which when entered, shall have the same effect as a consent judgment in the action and may be enforced accordingly.

[Adopted effective May 3, 2006.]

RULE 13. AUTHORITY AND DUTIES OF ARBITRATORS

(a) Authority of Arbitrators. The arbitrator shall at all times be authorized to control the hearing and the procedures to be followed.

(b) Duties. The arbitrator shall set up the arbitration hearing. The arbitrator shall define and describe the following to the parties:

(1) The non-binding arbitration process, including the difference between arbitration and other forms of conflict resolution;

(2) The duties and responsibilities of the arbitrator and the parties; and

(3) The cost of the arbitration hearing.

(c) Arbitrator Not to be Called as Witness. The arbitrator shall not be compelled by subpoena or otherwise to divulge any records or to testify in regard to the arbitration in any adversary proceeding or judicial forum. All records, reports and other documents received by the arbitrator while serving in that capacity shall be confidential.

(d) Duty of Impartiality/Disclosure. The arbitrator has a duty to be impartial and to disclose any circumstance likely to affect impartiality or independence, including any bias, prejudice or financial or personal interest in the result of the arbitration or any past or present relationship with the parties or their representatives.

(e) Reporting Results of Hearing. Within ten (10) days of conclusion of the hearing as set forth in Rule 12(c), the arbitrator shall file with the Clerk of Court Proof of ADR on a form approved by the Supreme Court or its designee. South Carolina Court Administration or the South Carolina Commission on Alternative Dispute Resolution may require the arbitrator to provide additional statistical data for evaluation of the program.

(f) Immunity. The arbitrator shall have immunity from liability to the same extent afforded judicial officers of this state.

[Adopted effective May 3, 2006.]

RULE 14. BOARD OF ARBITRATOR AND MEDIATOR CERTIFICATION

There is hereby established a Board of Arbitrator and Mediator Certification. The Board will be composed of five (5) persons appointed by the Supreme Court for a term of three (3) years or until a replacement member is appointed. In the event of a vacancy on the Board, the Supreme Court shall appoint someone to fill the unexpired term. Three members of the Board shall constitute a quorum. In the event that members of the Board disqualify themselves in a pending matter leaving less than a quorum, the Supreme Court may appoint *ad hoc* members to restore the Board to full membership in that matter.

[Adopted effective May 3, 2006.]

RULE 15. CERTIFICATION OF COURT-APPOINTED NEUTRALS

The Board of Arbitrator and Mediator Certification ("Board") shall receive and approve applications for certifications of persons to be appointed as mediators or arbitrators. The application shall be on a form approved by the Supreme Court or the Board. Recertification of a neutral who, by virtue of current job restrictions is prohibited from serving under these rules, is allowed if the neutral submits the appropriate recertification paperwork, pays the applicable fee and agrees upon termination of the prohibiting employment to promptly supplement the application to list at least one county for court appointments.

(a) Circuit Court Certification. For circuit court certification, a person must:

(1) Either:

(A) Be admitted to practice law in this State for at least three (3) years and be a member in good standing of the South Carolina Bar; or

(B) Be admitted to practice law in the highest court of another state or the District of Columbia for at least three (3) years and:

(i) Be at least 21 years old;

(ii) Have received a juris doctorate degree or its equivalent from a law school approved by the American Bar Association;

(iii) Be a member in good standing in each jurisdiction where he or she is admitted to practice law;

(iv) Be an associate member of the South Carolina Bar in good standing; and

(v) Agree to be subject to the Rules of Professional Conduct, Rule 407, SCACR, and the Rule on Disciplinary Procedure, Rule 413, SCACR, to the same extent as an active member of the South Carolina Bar.

(2) Be of good moral character;

(3) Have not, within the last five (5) years, been:

(A) Disbarred or suspended from the practice of law;

(B) Denied admission to a bar for character or ethical reasons; or

(C) Publicly reprimanded or publicly disciplined for professional conduct;

(4) Pay all administrative fees and comply with all procedures established by the Supreme Court, the Board and the Commission on Alternative Dispute Resolution; and

(5) Agree to provide mediation/arbitration to indigents without pay.

(6) To be certified as a Mediator, a person must also:

(A) Have completed a minimum of forty (40) hours in a civil mediation training program approved by the Board, or any other training program attended prior to the promulgation of these rules or attended in other states and approved by the Board; and

(B) Demonstrate familiarity with the statutes, rules and practice governing mediation settlement conferences in South Carolina.

(7) To be certified as an Arbitrator, a person must also:

(A) Have served as a Master–in–Equity, Circuit or Appellate Court Judge; or

(B) Have completed a minimum of six (6) hours in a civil arbitration training program approved by the Board, or any other training program attended prior to the promulgation of these rules or attended in other states and approved by the Board; and

(C) Demonstrate familiarity with the statutes, rules and practice governing arbitration hearings in South Carolina;

(b) Family Court Mediator Certification. For family court mediator certification, a person must:

(1) Either:

(A) Be admitted to practice law in this State for at least three (3) years and be a member in good standing of the South Carolina Bar;

(B) Be admitted to practice law in the highest court of another state or the District of Columbia for at least three (3) years and:

(i) Be at least 21 years old;

(ii) Have received a juris doctorate degree or its equivalent from a law school approved by the American Bar Association;

(iii) Be a member in good standing in each jurisdiction where he or she is admitted to practice law;

(iv) Be an associate member of the South Carolina Bar in good standing; and,

(v) Agree to be subject to the Rules of Professional Conduct, Rule 407, SCACR, and the Rule on Disciplinary Procedure, Rule 413, SCACR, to the same extent as an active member of the South Carolina Bar; or,

(C) Be a psychologist, master social worker, independent social worker, professional counselor, associate counselor, marital and family therapist, or physician specializing in psychiatry, licensed for at least three (3) years under Title 40 of the 1976 Code of Laws, as amended.

(2) Have completed a minimum of forty (40) hours in a family court mediation training program approved by the Board, or any other training program attended prior to the promulgation of these rules or attended in other states and approved by the Board;

(3) Demonstrate familiarity with the statutes, rules and practice governing mediation settlement conferences in South Carolina;

(4) Be of good moral character;

(5) Have not, within the last five (5) years, been:

(A) Disbarred or suspended from the practice of law or a profession set forth in Rule 15(b)(1)(C);

(B) Denied admission to a bar or denied a professional license for character or ethical reasons; or

(C) Publicly reprimanded or publicly disciplined for professional conduct;

(6) Pay all administrative fees and comply with all procedures established by the Supreme Court, the Board and the Commission on Alternative Dispute Resolution; and

(7) Agree to provide mediation to indigents without pay.

[Adopted effective May 3, 2006. Amended effective April 29, 2009.]

RULE 16. APPROVAL OF TRAINING PROGRAMS

A training program must be approved by the Supreme Court or its designee, the Board of Arbitrator and Mediator Certification, before the program can be used for compliance with Rule 15(a)(6)(A) (certification of circuit court mediators), Rule 15(b)(2) (certification of family court mediators), or Rule 15(a)(7)(B) (certification of circuit court arbitrators). Approval need not be given in advance of training attendance. The Supreme Court may set administrative fees, which must be paid in advance of approval.

(a) Approval of Circuit Court Mediator Training Programs.

(1) An approved training program for mediators of the Court of Common Pleas civil actions shall consist of a minimum of forty (40) hours of instruction, unless otherwise provided by these rules. The curriculum of such programs shall at a minimum include:

(A) Conflict resolution and mediation theory;

(B) Mediation processes and techniques, including the process and techniques of trial court mediation;

(C) Standards of conduct and ethics for mediators;

(D) Statutes, rules and practice governing mediation settlement conferences in South Carolina;

(E) Demonstrations of mediation settlement conferences;

(F) Simulations of mediation settlement conferences, involving student participation as mediator, attorneys and disputants, which simulations shall be supervised, observed and evaluated by program faculty; and

(G) Such other requirements as the Supreme Court from time to time may decide are appropriate.

(2) Training programs completed in South Carolina or other states may be approved by the Board if:

(A) The program consisted of a minimum of 37 hours of instruction;

(B) The program covered all the topics enumerated in paragraph (a)(1) of this Rule except subparagraph (D) related to South Carolina law; and

(C) The applicant takes at least three (3) hours of supplemental training pre-approved by the Supreme Court or the Board, covering the South Carolina law topics enumerated in paragraph (a)(1), subparagraph (D) of this Rule.

(b) Approval of Family Court Mediator Training Programs.

(1) An approved training program for mediators in the Family Court shall consist of a minimum of forty (40) hours of instruction, unless otherwise provided by these rules. The curriculum of such programs shall at a minimum include:

(A) Statutes, rules and practice concerning family and related law in South Carolina, including the law regarding custody, visitation, support, division of property and alimony;

(B) Conflict resolution, family dynamics, and mediation theory in general, as well as specific training regarding domestic violence;

(C) Mediation processes and techniques, including the process and techniques of trial court mediation;

(D) Standards of conduct and ethics for mediators;

(E) Statutes, rules and practice governing mediation settlement conferences in South Carolina;

(F) Demonstrations of mediation conferences;

(G) Simulations of mediation settlement conferences, involving student participation as mediator, attorneys and disputants, which simulations shall be supervised, observed and evaluated by program faculty; and

(H) Such other requirements as the Supreme Court from time to time may decide are appropriate for good instruction.

(2) Training programs completed in South Carolina or other states may be approved by the Board if:

(A) The program consisted of a minimum of 37 hours of instruction;

(B) The program covered all the topics enumerated in paragraph (b)(1) of this Rule except subparagraphs (A) and/or (E) related to South Carolina law; and

(C) The applicant takes at least three (3) hours of supplemental training pre-approved by the Supreme Court or the Board, covering the South Carolina law topics enumerated in paragraph (b)(1), subparagraphs (A) and (E) of this Rule.

(c) Approval of Circuit Court Arbitrator Training Programs.

(1) An approved training program for arbitrators of the Court of Common Pleas civil actions shall consist of a minimum of six (6) hours of instruction, unless otherwise provided by these rules. The curriculum of such programs shall at a minimum include:

(A) Conflict resolution and arbitration theory;

(B) Arbitration processes and techniques, including the process and techniques of both binding and non-binding arbitration;

(C) Standards of conduct and ethics for arbitrators;

(D) Statutes, rules and practice governing arbitration hearings in South Carolina;

(E) Demonstrations of arbitration hearings; and

(F) Such other requirements as the Supreme Court from time to time may decide are appropriate.

(2) Training programs completed in South Carolina or other states may be approved by the Board if:

(A) The program consisted of a minimum of 6 hours of instruction;

(B) The program covered all the topics enumerated in paragraph (c)(1) of this Rule except subparagraph (D) related to South Carolina law; and

(C) The applicant takes at least three (3) hours of supplemental training pre-approved by the Supreme Court or the Board, covering the South Carolina law topics enumerated in paragraph (c)(1), subparagraph (D) of this Rule.

[Adopted effective May 3, 2006.]

RULE 17. STANDARDS OF CONDUCT, DECERTIFICATION AND DISCIPLINE OF NEUTRALS

(a) Standards of Conduct for Mediators. Any person serving as a mediator, whether certified or not, shall comply with the Standards of Conduct for Mediators, which is attached as Appendix B to these rules.

(b) Standards of Conduct for Arbitrators. Any person serving as an arbitrator, whether certified or not, shall comply with the Code of Ethics for Arbitrators, which is attached as Appendix A to these rules.

(c) Decertification of Neutrals. Certification under Rule 15 may be revoked at any time if it is shown that the neutral no longer meets the requirements to be certified under Rule 15 or that the neutral has failed to faithfully observe these rules, the ethical standards of Rules 17(a) or (b), or has engaged in any conduct showing an unfitness to serve as a neutral.

(d) Discipline of Neutrals. A neutral who violates these rules, the ethical standards of Rules 17(a) or (b), or who has engaged in any conduct showing an unfitness to serve as a neutral may, in addition to decertification under Rule 17(c), be subject to discipline by the Supreme Court. This discipline may include any sanction the Supreme Court determines is appropriate, to include an order publicly reprimanding the neutral for the conduct, an order barring the neutral from serving as a neutral in any court of this State for a definite or indefinite period of time, an order requiring the neutral to complete additional training, and/or the assessment of a fine. The fact that discipline is taken against an attorney under this Rule shall not preclude action against the attorney under Rule 413, SCACR, if the conduct is misconduct under that rule. The fact that discipline is taken under this Rule against a licensed professional listed in Rule 15(b)(1)(C) shall not preclude action against the professional under the rules or statutes governing that profession, if the conduct is misconduct under that rule or statute.

(e) Processing Complaints of Misconduct by Neutrals. Persons alleging that a neutral has engaged in misconduct may file a complaint with the Board of Arbitrator and Mediator Certification. Misconduct includes any conduct or other circumstances that would warrant decertification or discipline under Rule 17(c) or (d). Complaints of misconduct shall be investigated by the Board and, upon a finding of probable cause, forwarded to the Commission on Alternate Dispute Resolution for a hearing before a Hearing Panel consisting of three (3) members of the Commission. Subject to the requirements of Rule 422(d), SCACR, the Commission shall promulgate regulations governing the processing of these complaints.

[Adopted effective May 3, 2006. Amended effective May 3, 2007.]

RULE 18. CLERKS OF COURT

All circuit and family court Clerks of Court in each county shall perform whatever duties are required pursuant to these rules relating to record keeping, notification to the court, parties, or attorneys, docket control, maintenance of rosters, and service of orders.

[Adopted effective May 3, 2006.]

RULE 19. LOCAL RULE–MAKING

These rules shall be uniform for all counties in which they are applicable. Local rules may be allowed only upon approval of the Supreme Court. Unless otherwise specified by these rules, all motions related to ADR or to these rules should be directed to the Chief Judge for Administrative Purposes.

[Adopted effective May 3, 2006.]

RULE 20. APPLICATION OF RULES

These rules shall apply to cases filed in circuit or family court on or after the effective date of any statute mandating ADR or Supreme Court order designating that county or court as subject to these rules.

[Adopted effective May 3, 2006.]

APPENDICES

APPENDIX A. CODE OF ETHICS FOR ARBITRATORS [1]

CANON I. AN ARBITRATOR SHOULD UPHOLD THE INTEGRITY AND FAIRNESS OF THE ARBITRATION PROCESS

A. Fair and just processes for resolving disputes are indispensable in our society. Commercial arbitration is an important method for deciding many types of disputes. In order for commercial arbitration to be effective, there must be broad public confidence in the integrity and fairness of the process. Therefore, an arbitrator has a responsibility not only to the parties but also to the process of arbitration itself, and must observe high standards of conduct so that the integrity and fairness of the process will be preserved. Accordingly, an arbitrator should recognize a responsibility to the public, to the parties whose rights will be decided, and to all other participants in the proceeding. The provisions of this code should be construed and applied to further these objectives.

B. It is inconsistent with the integrity of the arbitration process for persons to solicit appointment for themselves. However, a person may indicate a general willingness to serve as an arbitrator.

C. Persons should accept appointment as arbitrators only if they believe that they can be available to conduct the arbitration promptly.

D. After accepting appointment and while serving as an arbitrator, a person should avoid entering into any financial, business, professional, family or social relationship, or acquiring any financial or personal interest, which is likely to affect impartiality or which might reasonably create the appearance of partiality or bias. For a reasonable period of time after the decision of a case, persons who have served as arbitrators should avoid entering into any such relationship, or acquiring any such interest, in circumstances which might reasonably create the appearance that they had been influenced in the arbitration by the anticipation or expectation of the relationship or interest.

E. Arbitrators should conduct themselves in a way that is fair to all parties and should not be swayed by outside pressure, by public clamor, by fear of criticism or by self-interest.

F. When an arbitrator's authority is derived from an agreement of the parties, the arbitrator should neither exceed that authority nor do less than is required to exercise that authority completely. Where the agreement of the parties sets forth procedures to be followed in conducting the arbitration or refers to rules to be followed, it is the obligation of the arbitrator to comply with such procedures or rules.

G. An arbitrator should make all reasonable efforts to prevent delaying tactics, harassment of parties or other participants, or other abuse or disruption of the arbitration process.

H. The ethical obligations of an arbitrator begin upon acceptance of the appointment and continue throughout all stages of the proceeding. In addition, wherever specifically set forth in this code, certain ethical obligations begin as soon as a person is requested to serve as an arbitrator and certain ethical obligations continue even after the decision in the case has been given to the parties.

CANON II. AN ARBITRATOR SHOULD DISCLOSE ANY INTEREST OR RELATIONSHIP LIKELY TO AFFECT IMPARTIALITY OR WHICH MIGHT CREATE AN APPEARANCE OF PARTIALITY OR BIAS

Introductory Note. This code reflects the prevailing principle that arbitrators should disclose the existence of interests or relationships that are likely to affect their impartiality or that might reasonably create an appearance that they are biased against one party or favorable to another. These provisions of the code are intended to be applied realistically so that the burden of detailed disclosure does not become so great that it is impractical for persons in the business world to be arbitrators, thereby depriving parties of the services of those who might be best informed and qualified to decide particular types of cases.[2]

1 This code is based on the Code of Ethics for Arbitrators promulgated by the American Bar Association and the American Arbitration Association.

2 In applying the provisions of this code relating to disclosure, it might be helpful to recall the words of the concurring opinion, in a case decided by the US Supreme Court, that arbitrators "should err on the side of disclosure" because "it is better that the relationship be disclosed at the outset when the parties are free to reject the arbitrator or accept him with knowledge of the relationship." At the same time, it must be recognized that "an arbitrator's business relationships may be diverse indeed, involving more or less remote commercial connections with great numbers of people." Accordingly, an arbitrator "cannot be expected to provide the parties with his complete and unexpurgated business biography," nor is an arbitrator called on to disclose interest or relationships that are merely "trivial" (a concurring opinion in *Commonwealth Coatings Corp. v. Continental Casualty Co.*, 393 US 145, 131–152, 1968).

This code does not limit the freedom of parties to agree on whomever they choose as an arbitrator. When parties, with knowledge of a person's interests and relationships, nevertheless desire that individual to serve as an arbitrator, that person may properly serve.

Disclosure.

A. Persons who are requested to serve as arbitrators should, before accepting, disclose

(1) any direct or indirect financial or personal interest in the outcome of the arbitration;

(2) any existing or past financial, business, professional, family or social relationships which are likely to affect impartiality or which might reasonably create an appearance of partiality or bias. Persons requested to serve as arbitrators should disclose any such relationships which they personally have with any party or its lawyer, or with any individual whom they have been told will be a witness. They should also disclose any such relationships involving members of their families or their current employers, partners or business associates.

B. Persons who are requested to accept appointment as arbitrators should make a reasonable effort to inform themselves of any interests or relationships described in the preceding paragraph A.

C. The obligation to disclose interests or relationships described in the preceding paragraph A is a continuing duty which requires a person who accepts appointment as an arbitrator to disclose, at any stage of the arbitration, any such interests or relationships which may arise, or which are recalled or discovered.

D. Disclosure should be made to all parties unless other procedures for disclosure are provided in the rules or practices of an institution which is administering the arbitration. Where more than one arbitrator has been appointed, each should inform the others of the interests and relationships which have been disclosed.

E. In the event that an arbitrator is requested by all parties to withdraw, the arbitrator should do so. In the event that an arbitrator is requested to withdraw by less than all of the parties because of alleged partiality or bias, the arbitrator should withdraw unless either of the following circumstances exists.

(1) If an agreement of parties, or arbitration rules agreed to by the parties, establishes procedures for determining challenges to arbitrators, then those procedures should be followed; or,

(2) if the arbitrator, after carefully considering the matter, determines that the reason for the challenge is not substantial, and that he or she can nevertheless act and decide the case impartially and fairly, and that withdrawal would cause unfair delay or expense to another party or would be contrary to the ends of justice.

CANON III. AN ARBITRATOR IN COMMUNICATING WITH THE PARTIES SHOULD AVOID IMPROPRIETY OR THE APPEARANCE OF IMPROPRIETY

A. If an agreement of the parties or applicable arbitration rules referred to in that agreement establishes the manner or content of communications between the arbitrator and the parties, the arbitrator should follow those procedures notwithstanding any contrary provision of the following paragraphs B and C.

B. Unless otherwise provided in applicable arbitration rules or in an agreement of the parties, arbitrators should not discuss a case with any party in the absence of each other party, except in any of the following circumstances.

(1) Discussions may be had with a party concerning such matters as setting the time and place of hearings or making other arrangements for the conduct of the proceedings. However, the arbitrator should promptly inform each other party of the discussion and should not make any final determination concerning the matter discussed before giving each absent party an opportunity to express its views.

(2) If a party fails to be present at a hearing after having been given due notice, the arbitrator may discuss the case with any party who is present.

(3) If all parties request or consent to it, such discussion may take place.

C. Unless otherwise provided in applicable arbitration rules or in an agreement of the parties, whenever an arbitrator communicates in writing with one party, the arbitrator should at the same time send a copy of the communication to each other party. Whenever the arbitrator receives any written communication concerning the case from one party which has not already been sent to each other party, the arbitrator should do so.

CANON IV. AN ARBITRATOR SHOULD CONDUCT THE PROCEEDINGS FAIRLY AND DILIGENTLY

A. An arbitrator should conduct the proceedings in an evenhanded manner and treat all parties with equality and fairness at all stages of the proceedings.

B. An arbitrator should perform duties diligently and conclude the case as promptly as the circumstances reasonably permit.

C. An arbitrator should be patient and courteous to the parties, to their lawyers and to the witnesses and should encourage similar conduct by all participants in the proceedings.

D. Unless otherwise agreed by the parties or provided in arbitration rules agreed to by the parties, an arbitrator should accord to all parties the right to appear in person and to be heard after due notice of the time and place of hearing.

E. An arbitrator should not deny any party the opportunity to be represented by counsel.

F. If a party fails to appear after due notice, an arbitrator should proceed with the arbitration when authorized to do so by the agreement of the parties, the rules agreed to by the parties or by law. However, an arbitrator should do so only after receiving assurance that notice has been given to the absent party.

G. When an arbitrator determines that more information than has been presented by the parties is required to decide the case, it is not improper for the arbitrator to ask questions, call witnesses, and request documents or other evidence.

H. It is not improper for an arbitrator to suggest to the parties that they discuss the possibility of settlement of the case. However, an arbitrator should not be present or otherwise participate in the settlement discussions unless requested to do so by all parties. An arbitrator should not exert pressure on any party to settle.

I. Nothing in this code is intended to prevent a person from acting as a mediator or conciliator of a dispute in which he or she has been appointed as arbitrator, if requested to do so by all parties or where authorized or required to do so by applicable laws or rules.

J. When there is more than one arbitrator, the arbitrators should afford each other the full opportunity to participate in all aspects of the proceedings.

CANON V. AN ARBITRATOR SHOULD MAKE DECISIONS IN A JUST, INDEPENDENT AND DELIBERATE MANNER

A. An arbitrator should, after careful deliberation, decide all issues submitted for determination. An arbitrator should decide no other issues.

B. An arbitrator should decide all matters justly, exercising independent judgment, and should not permit outside pressure to affect the decision.

C. An arbitrator should not delegate the duty to decide to any other person.

D. In the event that all parties agree upon a settlement of issues in dispute and request an arbitrator to embody that agreement in an award, an arbitrator may do so, but is not required to do so unless satisfied with the propriety of the terms of settlement. Whenever an arbitrator embodies a settlement by the parties in an award, the arbitrator should state in the award that it is based on an agreement of the parties.

CANON VI. AN ARBITRATOR SHOULD BE FAITHFUL TO THE RELATIONSHIP OF TRUST AND CONFIDENTIALITY INHERENT IN THAT OFFICE

A. An arbitrator is in a relationship of trust to the parties and should not, at any time, use confidential information acquired during the arbitration proceeding to gain personal advantage or advantage for others, or to affect adversely the interest of another.

B. Unless otherwise agreed by the parties, or required by applicable rules or law, an arbitrator should keep confidential all matters relating to the arbitration proceedings and decision.

C. It is not proper at any time for an arbitrator to inform anyone of the decision in advance of the time it is given to all parties. In a case in which there is more than one arbitrator, it is not proper at any time for an arbitrator to inform anyone concerning the deliberations of the arbitrators. After an arbitration award has been made, it is not proper for an arbitrator to assist in postarbitral proceedings, except as is required by law.

D. In many types of arbitration it is customary practice for the arbitrators to serve without pay. However, in some types of cases it is customary for arbitrators to receive compensation for their services and reimbursement for their expenses. In cases in which any such payments are to made, all persons who are requested to serve, or who are serving as arbitrators, should be governed by the same high standards of integrity and fairness as apply to their other activities in the case. Accordingly, such persons should scrupulously avoid bargaining with parties over the amount of payments or engaging in any communications concerning payments which would create an appearance of coercion or other impropriety. In the absence of governing provisions in the agreement of the parties or in rules agreed to by the parties or in applicable law, certain practices, relating to payments are generally recognized as being preferable in order to preserve the integrity and fairness of the arbitration process. These practices include the following.

(1) It is preferable that before the arbitrator finally accepts appointment the basis of payment be established and that all parties be informed thereof in writing.

(2) In cases conducted under the rules or administration of an institution that is available to assist in making arrangements for payments, the payments should be arranged by the institution to avoid the necessity for communication by the arbitrators directly with the parties concerning the subject.

(3) In cases where no institution is available to assist in making arrangement for payments, it is preferable that any discussions with arbitrators concerning payments should take place in the presence of all parties.

APPENDIX B. STANDARDS OF CONDUCT FOR MEDIATORS [1]

I. SELF–DETERMINATION: A MEDIATOR SHALL RECOGNIZE THAT MEDIATION IS BASED ON THE PRINCIPLE OF SELF–DETERMINATION BY THE PARTIES

Self-determination is the fundamental principle of mediation. It requires that the mediation process rely upon the ability of the parties to reach a voluntary, uncoerced agreement.

COMMENTS

The mediator may provide information about the process, raise issues, and help parties explore options. The primary role of the mediator is to facilitate a voluntary resolution of a dispute. Parties shall be given an opportunity to consider all proposed options.

A mediator cannot personally ensure that each party has made a fully informed choice to reach a particular agreement, but it is a good practice for the mediator to make the parties aware of the importance of consulting other professionals, where appropriate, to help them make informed decisions.

II. IMPARTIALITY: A MEDIATOR SHALL CONDUCT THE MEDIATION IN AN IMPARTIAL MANNER

The concept of mediator impartiality is central to the mediation process. A mediator shall mediate only those matters in which she or he can remain impartial and evenhanded. If at any time the mediator is unable to conduct the process in an impartial manner, the mediator is obligated to withdraw.

COMMENTS

A mediator shall avoid conduct that gives the appearance of partiality toward one of the parties. The quality of the mediation process is enhanced when the parties have confidence in the impartiality of the mediator.

When mediators are appointed by a court or institution, the appointing agency shall make reasonable efforts to ensure that mediators serve impartially.

A mediator should guard against partiality or prejudice based on the parties' personal characteristics, background or performance at the mediation.

III. CONFLICTS OF INTEREST: A MEDIATOR SHALL DISCLOSE ALL ACTUAL AND POTENTIAL CONFLICTS OF INTEREST REASONABLY KNOWN TO THE MEDIATOR. AFTER DISCLOSURE, THE MEDIATOR SHALL DECLINE TO MEDIATE UNLESS ALL PARTIES CHOOSE TO RETAIN THE MEDIATOR. THE NEED TO PROTECT AGAINST CONFLICTS OF INTEREST ALSO GOVERNS CONDUCT THAT OCCURS DURING AND AFTER THE MEDIATION

A conflict of interest is a dealing or relationship that might create an impression of possible bias. The basic approach to questions of conflict of interest is consistent with the concept of self-determination. The mediator has a responsibility to disclose all actual and potential conflicts that are reasonably known to the mediator and could reasonably be seen as raising a question about impartiality. If all parties agree to mediate after being informed of conflicts, the mediator may proceed with the mediation. If, however, the conflict of interest casts serious doubt on the integrity of the process, the mediator shall decline to proceed.

A mediator must avoid the appearance of conflict of interest both during and after the mediation. Without consent of all parties, a mediator shall not subsequently establish a professional relationship with one of the parties in a related matter, or in an unrelated matter under circumstances which would raise legitimate questions about the integrity of the mediation process.

COMMENTS

A mediator shall avoid conflicts of interest in recommending the services of other professionals. A mediator may make reference to professional referral services or associations which maintain rosters of qualified professionals.

Potential conflicts of interest may arise between administrators of mediation programs and mediators and there may be strong pressures on the mediator to settle a particular case or cases. The mediator's commitment must be to the parties and the process. Pressures from outside of the mediation process should never influence the mediator to coerce the parties to settle.

IV. COMPETENCE: A MEDIATOR SHALL MEDIATE ONLY WHEN THE MEDIATOR HAS THE NECESSARY QUALIFICATIONS TO SATISFY THE REASONABLE EXPECTATIONS OF THE PARTIES

Any person may be selected as a mediator, provided that the parties are satisfied with the mediator's qualifications. Training and experience in mediation, however, are often necessary for effective mediation. A person who offers herself or himself as available to serve as a mediator gives parties and the public the expectation that she or he has the competency to mediate effectively. In court-connected or other forms of mandated mediation, it is essential that mediators assigned to the parties have the requisite training and experience.

COMMENTS

Mediators should have available for the parties information regarding their relevant training, education and experience.

The requirements for appearing on a list of mediators must be made public and available to interested persons.

[1] These standards are taken from the Standards of Conduct for Mediators promulgated by the American Bar Association, the American Arbitration Association and the Society of Professionals in Dispute Resolution.

When mediators are appointed by a court or institution, the appointing agency shall make reasonable efforts to ensure that each mediator is qualified for the particular mediation.

V. CONFIDENTIALITY: A MEDIATOR SHALL MAINTAIN THE REASONABLE EXPECTATIONS OF THE PARTIES WITH REGARD TO CONFIDENTIALITY

The reasonable expectations of the parties with regard to confidentiality shall be met by the mediator. The parties' expectations of confidentiality depend on the circumstances of the mediation and any agreements they may make. A mediator shall not disclose any matter that a party expects to be confidential unless given permission by all parties or unless required by law or other public policy.

COMMENTS

The parties may make their own rules with respect to confidentiality, or the accepted practice of an individual mediator or institution may dictate a particular set of expectations. Since the parties' expectations regarding confidentiality are important, the mediator should discuss these expectations with the parties.

If the mediator holds private sessions with a party, the nature of these sessions with regard to confidentiality should be discussed prior to undertaking such sessions.

In order to protect the integrity of the mediation, a mediator should avoid communicating information about how the parties acted in the mediation process, the merits of the case, or settlement offers. The mediator may report, if required, whether parties appeared at a scheduled mediation.

Where the parties have agreed that all or a portion of the information disclosed during a mediation is confidential, the parties' agreement should be respected by the mediator.

Confidentiality should not be construed to limit or prohibit the effective monitoring, research, or evaluation of mediation programs by responsible persons. Under appropriate circumstances, researchers may be permitted to obtain access to statistical data and, with the permission of the parties, to individual case files, observations of live mediations, and interviews with participants.

VI. QUALITY OF THE PROCESS: A MEDIATOR SHALL CONDUCT THE MEDIATION FAIRLY, DILIGENTLY, AND IN A MANNER CONSISTENT WITH THE PRINCIPLE OF SELF-DETERMINATION BY THE PARTIES

A mediator shall work to ensure a quality process and to encourage mutual respect among the parties. A quality process requires a commitment by the mediator to diligence and procedural fairness. There should be adequate opportunity for each party in the mediation to participate in the discussions. The parties decide when and under what conditions they will reach an agreement or terminate a mediation.

COMMENTS

A mediator may agree to mediate only when he or she is prepared to commit the attention essential to an effective mediation.

Mediators should only accept cases when they can satisfy the reasonable expectations of the parties concerning the timing of the process. A mediator should not allow a mediation to be unduly delayed by the parties or their representatives.

The primary purpose of a mediator is to facilitate the parties' voluntary agreement. This role differs significantly from other professional client relationships. Mixing the role of a mediator and the role of a professional advising a client is problematic, and mediators must strive to distinguish between the roles. A mediator should therefore refrain from providing professional advice.

Where appropriate, a mediator should recommend that parties seek outside professional advice, or consider resolving their dispute through arbitration, counseling, neutral evaluation, or other processes. A mediator who undertakes, at the request of the parties, an additional dispute resolution role in the same matter assumes increased responsibilities and obligations that may be governed by the standards of other professions.

A mediator shall withdraw from a mediation when incapable of serving or when unable to remain impartial.

A mediator shall withdraw from a mediation or postpone a session if the mediation is being used to further illegal conduct, or if a party is unable to participate due to drug, alcohol, or other physical or mental incapacity.

Mediators should not permit their behavior in the mediation process to be guided by a desire for a high settlement rate.

VII. ADVERTISING AND SOLICITATION: A MEDIATOR SHALL BE TRUTHFUL IN ADVERTISING AND SOLICITATION FOR MEDIATION

Advertising or any other communication with the public concerning services offered or regarding the education, training, and expertise of the mediator shall be truthful. Mediators shall refrain from promises and guarantees of results.

COMMENTS

It is imperative that communication with the public educate and instill confidence in the process.

In an advertisement or other communication to the public, a mediator may make reference to meeting state, national, or private organization qualifications only if the entity referred to has a procedure for qualifying mediators and the mediator has been duly granted the requisite status.

VIII. FEES: A MEDIATOR SHALL FULLY DISCLOSE AND EXPLAIN THE BASIS OF COMPENSATION, FEES, AND CHARGES TO THE PARTIES

The parties should be provided sufficient information about fees at the outset of a mediation to determine if they wish to retain the services of a mediator. If a mediator charges fees, the fees shall be reasonable considering, among other things, the mediation service, the type and complexity of the matter, the expertise of the mediator, the time required, and the rates customary in the community. The better practice in reaching an understanding about fees is to set down the arrangements in a written agreement.

COMMENTS

A mediator who withdraws from a mediation should return any unearned fees to the parties.

A mediator should not enter into a fee agreement which is contingent upon the result of the mediation or amount of the settlement.

Co-Mediators who share a fee should hold to standards of reasonableness in determining the allocation of fees.

A mediator should not accept a fee for referral of a matter to another mediator or to any other person.

IX. OBLIGATIONS TO THE MEDIATION PROCESS

Mediators have a duty to improve the practice of mediation.

COMMENTS

Mediators are regarded as knowledgeable in the process of mediation. They have an obligation to use their knowledge to help educate the public about mediation; to make mediation accessible to those who would like to use it; to correct abuses; and to improve their professional skills and abilities.

APPENDIX C. ALTERNATIVE DISPUTE RESOLUTION (ADR) FORMS

CIRCUIT COURT

SUGGESTED LANGUAGE TO BE INCLUDED ON NOTICE OF INTENT TO FILE SUIT IN A PROFESSIONAL NEGLIGENCE CASE AS REQUIRED BY ADR RULE 4 (c)

NOTICE: THIS DISPUTE IS SUBJECT TO A MANDATORY PRE-SUIT MEDIATION REQUIREMENT WITHIN 120 DAYS AS SET FORTH IN S.C. CODE § 15-79-125 (C) AND ADR RULE 5 (f).

In the event the parties are unable to agree upon a mediator, the Court hereby appoints ______________________________ to serve as mediator. In the event the aforementioned mediator has a conflict of interest or is unable to serve, the alternative mediator is ______________________________ .

SCADR 101 (5/2007)

STATE OF SOUTH CAROLINA	)	IN THE COURT OF COMMON PLEAS
COUNTY OF	)	
Plaintiff,	)	NOTICE OF ADR
vs.	)	
Defendant.	)	Case File Date:

Pursuant to the Standing Order for Alternative Dispute Resolution, dated ________, you are required to participate in the following methods of Alternative Dispute Resolution (ADR): mediation or arbitration (binding or non-binding); on or before 300 days from the date of filing of this action. The parties have a right to mutually agree upon the form of ADR and a neutral person(s) to conduct that ADR process. In the event the parties are unable to agree upon the form of ADR, the court hereby designates mediation as the default process of ADR. In the event the parties are unable to agree upon a mediator, the court hereby appoints ____________________

____________________ to serve as mediator. In the event the aforementioned mediator has a conflict of interest or is unable to serve, the alternate mediator is ____________________

____

The parties and/or their lawyers shall contact the court-appointed mediator directly regarding scheduling and payment of the court-mandated fee.

A Rule to Show Cause why sanctions should not be imposed may be issued in all cases that fail to file a Proof of ADR or Exemption form indicating evidence of participation in or exemption from an ADR process within 300 days from the date of filing of the action or 90 days from the date of this notice.

Date: ____________ ____________________
Clerk of Court

Notice of this Order was given by facsimile transmission, or if no fax number is shown, by first class mail or email to the attorneys of record on ____________________

Plaintiff's Lawyer: ____________________
Defendant's Lawyer: ____________________

Clerk's Initials: ____________

SCADR 102 (5/2007)

CIRCUIT COURT

RULE TO SHOW CAUSE

Lawyer's name and address

RE:

Dear:

According to court records, you have not submitted the Proof of ADR or Exemption form required by the Standing Order for Alternative Dispute Resolution. We are now required to issue a Rule to Show Cause why sanctions should not be imposed in this case.

Please contact me immediately at __________ or fax me at __________ , if my records are incorrect.

Sincerely,

ADR Coordinator

Letter to: Opposing Counsel

SCADR 103 (5/2007)

STATE OF SOUTH CAROLINA	)	IN THE COURT OF COMMON PLEAS
COUNTY OF	)	
	)	PROOF OF ADR OR EXEMPTION
Plaintiff,	)	
vs.	)	FILE NO.:
Defendant.	)	

(An original and copy of this form is to be completed and filed with the Office of the Clerk of Court and a copy forwarded to the attorneys for the parties within 10 days of the conclusion of ADR, or within 300 days of the filing date of the action, whichever is earlier.)

PURSUANT to the Court's Standing Order for Alternative Dispute Resolution dated ____________

A. ______ I certify that this case is exempt from ADR for the following reason and the parties wish to exercise that exemption:

Plaintiff/Attorney for Plaintiff	Defendant/Attorney for Defendant
Print Name	Print Name
Phone/Fax	Phone/Fax
Date: ____________	

B. ______ 1. Alternative Dispute Resolution (ADR) was conducted in the form of:

____

(Note: If binding arbitration has been chosen by the parties but not yet completed, an appropriate order of dismissal must be attached hereto.)

2. The neutral(s) was/were: (Name of arbitrator/mediator):

____

3. The ADR was conducted on ____________ , 200 ________

SCADR 104A (5/2007)

4. As a result of ADR, this case should be considered (please check one);

( ) Fully Settled.

( ) by Consent Judgment, to be filed by ____________

or ( ) Voluntary Dismissal to be filed by ____________

( ) Partially Settled.

( ) At an Impasse.

( ) In need of further ADR I ☐ am ☐ am not willing to continue as a neutral. I recommend that ADR resume as of ______________________________ .

5. Plaintiff ☐ was present ☐ was not present
Defendant ☐ was present ☐ was not present

6. Other partcipants were:

_______ Lawyer for Defendant ____________________
_______ Lawyer for Plaintiff ____________________
_______ Representative for Insurance Carrier ____________________
_______ Guardian *ad Litem* ____________________
_______ Experts ____________________
_______ Others ____________________

7. Choice of the neutral was by:

_______ Stipulation
_______ Court Order

8. The total number of hours spent in ADR was: ________ hours.

9. Further comments of the neutral: ____________________

____

____

____
Neutral's Signature

Date: ____

SCADR 104B (5/2007)

STATE OF SOUTH CAROLINA	)	IN THE FAMILY COURT
	)	____JUDICIAL CIRCUIT
COUNTY OF ____________________	)	
	)	
	)	**ADR RULE 4**
______________________________	)	**ORDER APPOINTING MEDIATOR**
Plaintiff,	)	
vs.	)	
	)	
______________________________	)	
Defendant.	)	Docket No. ____________________

Plaintiff Attorney: ____________________ Hearing Date: ____________________

Defendant Attorney: ____________________ Judge: ____________________

Guardian ad Litem: ____________________ Court Reporter: ____________________

It appears to the satisfaction of this Court that

☐ custody/visitation issues are contested; or,

☐ other issues are contested and the parties are ready to request a final hearing.

Therefore, pursuant to ADR Rule 4, counsel for the parties or the parties themselves

☐ agree to the following mediator:

Name:	
Address:	
Phone:	
Email:	
Fax:	

☐ have been unable to agree upon a mediator. As a result, the Court appoints the following mediators. In the event the primary mediator has a conflict of interest or is unable to serve, the alternate mediator is appointed.

	Primary Mediator	Alternate Mediator
Name:		
Address:		
Phone:		
Email:		
Fax:		

The parties and/or their attorneys shall contact the Court-appointed mediator directly regarding scheduling. Mediator's fees shall be due when billed.

Date: ____________________, 20___

____________________, S.C. ______________________________

Family Court Judge / Clerk of Court

SCCA 105 (12/2009)

STATE OF SOUTH CAROLINA	)	
	)	IN THE FAMILY COURT
COUNTY OF	)	
	)	
	)	
Plaintiff,	)	REQUEST FOR HEARING
	)	
vs.	)	CASE #
	)	
	)	
Defendant.	)	
______________________	)	

Attorney for Plaintiff: ______________________
Office Address: ______________________
Telephone: __________ Fax: __________
E-Mail Address: ______________________

Attorney for Defendant: ______________________
Office Address: ______________________
Telephone: __________ Fax: __________
E-Mail Address: ______________________

GAL: ______________________
Office Address: ______________________
Telephone: __________ Fax: __________
E-mail Address: ______________________

TYPE CASE: ______________ TIME NEEDED: __________

Is custody contested: ( ) YES ( ) NO If yes, add GAL information above
Are other issues contested? ( ) YES ( ) NO

If yes to either of the above, submit The Report of Mediator or Order Appointing Mediator.

Comments: ____

____

Hearing Requested By: ______________________ Date: __________

For: ( ) Plaintiff ( ) Defendant

Dates & Time Unavailable: ______________________________

SCADR 106A (5/2007)

COUNTY FAMILY COURT: FOR COURT USE ONLY
HEARING NOTICE BY FAX

PURSUANT TO YOUR REQUEST, THE ABOVE MATTER HAS BEEN SET FOR A HEARING ON

____________________ at ____________ JUDGE: ________________

TIME ALLOTTED: ____________________________________

SCADR 106B (5/2007)

STATE OF SOUTH CAROLINA COUNTY OF	IN THE FAMILY COURT
Plaintiff, vs. Defendant.	MEDIATION REPORT

Pursuant to the Court's Order Appointing Mediator:

1. Mediation was conducted by ______________________ on ________________

2. The following were issues mediated and are settled or contested as indicated.

		Settled	Contested
Paternity			
Custody			
Visitation			
Child Support			
Alimony			
Property & Debt Division			
Attorneys Fees			
Other:			
	a.		
	b.		
	c.		

SCADR 107A (5/2007)

3. A. Plaintiff ☐ was present ☐ was not present

   B. Defendant ☐ was present ☐ was not present

4. Other participants were:

   _______ Lawyer for Plaintiff
   _______ Lawyer for Defendant
   _______ Guardian *ad litem*
   _______ Experts
   _______ Others:

5. This case was co-mediated with: ______________________________

6. Choice of the mediator was by ☐ Stipulation of Mediator ☐ Selection ☐ Court Order.

7. The total number of hours spent in mediation was ________

8. Additional settlement conferences ☐ would ☐ would not be useful.

9. I ☐ am ☐ am not a lawyer.

10. Further comments of the mediator: ______________________________

11. After conferring with counsel and/or the parties, we estimate ________________ will be needed for a final hearing on settled and/or contested issues.

    A final hearing has not been set

    Or

    A final hearing has already been set for ________________________

____
Neutral's Signature

Date: ______________________

SCADR 107B (5/2007)

STATE OF SOUTH CAROLINA)
) IN THE COURT OF COMMON PLEAS
COUNTY OF ____________)
)
____________) CIVIL ACTION COVERSHEET
Plaintiff(s))
) ________-CP - _____- ________
vs.)
)
____________)
Defendant(s))

(Please Print)
Submitted By: ____________
Address: ____________
____

SC Bar #: ____________
Telephone #: ____________
Fax #: ____________
Other: ____________
E-mail: ____________

NOTE: The cover sheet and information contained herein neither replaces nor supplements the filing and service of pleadings or other papers as required by law. This form is required for the use of the Clerk of Court for the purpose of docketing. It must be filled out completely, signed, and dated. A copy of this cover sheet must be served on the defendant(s) along with the Summons and Complaint.

DOCKETING INFORMATION (*Check all that apply*)

If Action is Judgment/Settlement do not complete

☐ **JURY TRIAL** demanded in complaint. ☐ **NON-JURY TRIAL** demanded in complaint.
☐ This case is subject to **ARBITRATION** pursuant to the Court Annexed Alternative Dispute Resolution Rules.
☐ This case is subject to **MEDIATION** pursuant to the Court Annexed Alternative Dispute Resolution Rules.
☐ This case is exempt from ADR. (Proof of ADR/Exemption Attached)

NATURE OF ACTION (Check One Box Below)

Contracts	Torts - Professional Malpractice	Torts – Personal Injury	Real Property
☐ Constructions (100)	☐ Dental Malpractice (200)	☐ Assault/Slander/Libel (300)	☐ Claim & Delivery (400)
☐ Debt Collection (110)	☐ Legal Malpractice (210)	☐ Conversion (310)	☐ Condemnation (410)
☐ Employment (120)	☐ Medical Malpractice (220)	☐ Motor Vehicle Accident (320)	☐ Foreclosure (420)
☐ General (130)	Previous Notice of Intent Case #	☐ Premises Liability (330)	☐ Mechanic's Lien (430)
☐ Breach of Contract (140)	20____-CP-____-________	☐ Products Liability (340)	☐ Partition (440)
☐ Other (199)		☐ Personal Injury (350)	☐ Possession (450)
____________	☐ Notice/ File Med Mal (230)	☐ Wrongful Death (360)	☐ Building Code Violation (460)
	☐ Other (299)	☐ Other (399)	☐ Other (499)
	____________	____________	____________

Inmate Petitions	Judgments/Settlements	Administrative Law/Relief	Appeals
☐ PCR (500)	☐ Death Settlement (700)	☐ Reinstate Driver's License (800)	☐ Arbitration (900)
☐ Mandamus (520)	☐ Foreign Judgment (710)	☐ Judicial Review (810)	☐ Magistrate-Civil (910)
☐ Habeas Corpus (530)	☐ Magistrate's Judgment (720)	☐ Relief (820)	☐ Magistrate-Criminal (920)
☐ Other (599)	☐ Minor Settlement (730)	☐ Permanent Injunction (830)	☐ Municipal (930)
____________	☐ Transcript Judgment (740)	☐ Forfeiture-Petition (840)	☐ Probate Court (940)
	☐ Lis Pendens (750)	☐ Forfeiture—Consent Order (850)	☐ SCDOT (950)
	☐ Transfer of Structured Settlement Payment Rights Application (760)	☐ Other (899)	☐ Worker's Comp (960)
		____________	☐ Zoning Board (970)
	☐ Other (799) ________		☐ Public Service Commission (990)
			☐ Employment Security Comm (991)
			☐ Other (999)
			____________

Special/Complex /Other	
☐ Environmental (600)	☐ Pharmaceuticals (630)
☐ Automobile Arb. (610)	☐ Unfair Trade Practices (640)
☐ Medical (620)	☐ Out-of State Depositions (650)
☐ Other (699)	☐ Motion to Quash Subpoena in Out-of-County Action (660)
____________	☐ Sexual Predator (510)

Submitting Party Signature: ____________ **Date:** ________

Note: Frivolous civil proceedings may be subject to sanctions pursuant to SCRCP, Rule 11, and the South Carolina Frivolous Civil Proceedings Sanctions Act, S.C. Code Ann. §15-36-10 et. seq.

SCCA / 234 (01/2011) Page 1 of 2

FOR MANDATED ADR COUNTIES ONLY

Allendale, Anderson, Beaufort, Clarendon, Colleton, Florence, Greenville, Hampton, Horry, Jasper, Lee, Lexington, Pickens (Family Court Only), Richland, Sumter, Union, Williamsburg, and York

SUPREME COURT RULES REQUIRE THE SUBMISSION OF ALL CIVIL CASES TO AN ALTERNATIVE DISPUTE RESOLUTION PROCESS, UNLESS OTHERWISE EXEMPT.

You are required to take the following action(s):

1. The parties shall select a neutral and file a "Proof of ADR" form on or by the 210th day of the filing of this action. If the parties have not selected a neutral within 210 days, the Clerk of Court shall then appoint a primary and secondary mediator from the current roster on a rotating basis from among those mediators agreeing to accept cases in the county in which the action has been filed.

2. The initial ADR conference must be held within 300 days after the filing of the action.

3. Pre-suit medical malpractice mediations required by S.C. Code §15-79-125 shall be held not later than 120 days after all defendants are served with the "Notice of Intent to File Suit" or as the court directs. (Medical malpractice mediation is mandatory statewide.)

4. Cases are exempt from ADR only upon the following grounds:

   a. Special proceeding, or actions seeking extraordinary relief such as mandamus, habeas corpus, or prohibition;

   b. Requests for temporary relief;

   c. Appeals

   d. Post Conviction relief matters;

   e. Contempt of Court proceedings;

   f. Forfeiture proceedings brought by governmental entities;

   g. Mortgage foreclosures; and

   h. Cases that have been previously subjected to an ADR conference, unless otherwise required by Rule 3 or by statute.

5. In cases not subject to ADR, the Chief Judge for Administrative Purposes, upon the motion of the court or of any party, may order a case to mediation.

6. Motion of a party to be exempt from payment of neutral fees due to indigency should be filed with the Court within ten (10) days after the ADR conference has been concluded.

Please Note: **You must comply with the Supreme Court Rules regarding ADR. Failure to do so may affect your case or may result in sanctions.**

SCCA / 234 (01/2011) Page 2 of 2

STATE OF SOUTH CAROLINA)
) IN THE FAMILY COURT
COUNTY OF ______________) ____ JUDICIAL CIRCUIT
)
______________________________)
Plaintiff,) FAMILY COURT COVERSHEET
vs.)
)
______________________________)
Defendant.) Docket No. ______________

NOTE: The coversheet and information contained herein neither replaces nor supplements the filing and service of pleadings or other papers as required by law. This form is required for docketing purposes for the Clerk of Court and must be signed and dated, and filled out completely. A copy of this coversheet must be served on the defendant(s) along with the Summons and Complaint.

Submitted by: ______________ **SC Bar #** ______________
Address: ______________ **Telephone #** ______________
______________ **Fax #** ______________
Email: ______________ **Other:** ______________

DOCKETING INFORMATION (Check one box below if filing in a Mandatory Mediation County)
☐ This case is subject to MEDIATION pursuant to the Family Court Alternative Dispute Resolution Rules.
☐ This case is exempt from ADR (certificate attached).

Nature of Action Codes (Check One)	
Marital Dissolution	**Support**
☐ Divorce (110)	☐ Child Support – Private (501)
☐ Annulment (120)	☐ Child Support – Administrative Process (502)
☐ Separate Support and Maintenance (130)	☐ Child Support – Judicial Process (503)
☐ Registration of Foreign Divorce Decree – without support/custody (190)	☐ Registration of Foreign Order of Support (504)
☐ Registration of Foreign Divorce Decree – with support/custody (191)	☐ UIFSA – Outgoing (505)
☐ Marital Dissolution – Other (199) ______	☐ UIFSA – Incoming (506)
	☐ Modification of Child Support – Private (507)
	☐ Modification of Child Support – DSS (508)
Abuse and Neglect	☐ Modification of Alimony (525)
☐ Abuse and Neglect – Child (210)	☐ College Expenses (530)
☐ Abuse and Neglect – Adult (220)	☐ Support – Other (599) ______
☐ Abuse and Neglect – Other (299) ______	
	Custody/Visitation
	☐ Child Custody/Visitation (610)
Juvenile Delinquency	☐ Modification of Custody/Visitation (615)
☐ Truancy (311)	☐ Registration of Foreign Child Custody Order (690)
☐ Incorrigible (312)	☐ Custody/Visitation – Other (699) ______
☐ Runaway (313)	
☐ Criminal Offense (320)	**Miscellaneous Actions**
☐ Juvenile Delinquency – Other (399) ______	☐ Name Change (710)
	☐ Correction/Birth Record (720)
	☐ Judicial Bypass (730)
	☐ Adoption (740)
Protection from Domestic Abuse	☐ Foreign Adoption (741)
☐ Domestic Abuse – Intimate Partner (410)	☐ Post Dissolution Equitable Distribution (750)
☐ Domestic Abuse – Minor (420)	☐ Paternity – Private (761)
☐ Registration of Foreign Order of Protection (490)	☐ Paternity – DSS (762)
☐ Domestic Abuse – Other (499) ______	☐ Termination of Parental Rights – Private (771)
	☐ Termination of Parental Rights – DSS (772)
	☐ Miscellaneous Actions – Others (799) ______

Submitting Party Signature: ______________________ **Date:** ______________

Custodial Parent (if applicable): ______________________

Note: Frivolous civil proceedings are subject to sanctions pursuant to Rule 11, SCRCP and the South Carolina Frivolous Civil Proceedings Sanctions Act, S.C. Code Ann. § 15-36-10 et seq.

SCCA 467 (6/2011)

FOR MANDATED ADR COUNTIES ONLY

Allendale, Anderson, Beaufort, Clarendon, Colleton, Florence, Greenville, Hampton, Horry, Jasper, Lee, Lexington, Oconee (Family Court Only) Pickens (Family Court Only), Richland, Sumter, Union, Williamsburg, and York Counties.

SUPREME COURT RULES REQUIRE MEDIATION OF ALL CONTESTED DOMESTIC RELATIONS ACTIONS. IF THE DOCKETING INFORMATION ON PAGE 1 OF THIS COVERSHEET INDICATES THAT THIS CASE IS SUBJECT TO **MEDIATION** YOU ARE NOTIFIED THAT MEDIATED SETTLEMENT CONFERENCES ARE REQUIRED IN THIS CASE, AND THAT THE COURT-ANNEXED ADR RULES SHALL APPLY TO ALL CASES IN WHICH MEDIATION IS REQUIRED. FOR ADDITIONAL INFORMATION CONCERNING THE PROCESS AND TIME FRAMES, PLEASE CONSULT THE ADR RULES. KEY SECTIONS OF THE RULES ARE IDENTIFIED BELOW.

CONTESTED ACTIONS INVOLVING CUSTODY AND VISITATION

Rule 3	Actions Subject to ADR
Rule 4(d)(1)(3)(4) &(5)	Appointment of Mediator by Family Court
Rule 5(g)	Scheduling in Family Court
Rule 6(g)	Agreement in Family Court
Rule 7(f)	Reporting Results of Conference
Rule 9	Compensation of Neutral

ALL OTHER CONTESTED ACTIONS

Rule 3	Actions Subject to ADR
Rule 4(d)(2)(3)(4) &(5)	Appointment of Mediator by Family Court
Rule 5(g)	Scheduling in Family Court
Rule 6(g)	Agreement in Family Court
Rule 7(f)	Reporting Results of Conference
Rule 9	Compensation of Neutral

Indigent Cases: Where a mediator has been appointed, a party may move before the Chief Judge for Administrative Purposes to be exempted from payment of neutral fees and expenses based upon indigency. Applications for indigency shall be filed no later than ten (10) days after the ADR conference has been concluded. Determination of indigency shall be in the sole discretion of the Chief Judge for Administrative Purposes.

Please Note: Attendance at mediated settlement conferences is mandatory. You must comply with the Supreme Court rules regarding court-ordered mediation. Failure to do so may affect your case and may result in sanctions.

Note: Frivolous civil proceedings are subject to sanctions pursuant to Rule 11, SCRCP and the South Carolina Frivolous Civil Proceedings Sanctions Act, S.C. Code Ann. § 15-36-10 et seq.

SCCA 467 (6/2011)

INDEX TO ALTERNATIVE DISPUTE RESOLUTION RULES

*

RULES OF PROCEDURE FOR THE ADMINISTRATIVE LAW COURT

Westlaw Electronic Research

These rules may be searched electronically on Westlaw in the SC-RULES *database; updates to these rules may be found on Westlaw in* SC-RULESUPDATES. *For search tips and a summary of database content, consult the Westlaw Scope Screen for each database.*

I. GENERAL PROVISIONS

RULE 1. AUTHORITY AND APPLICABILITY

The promulgation of these Rules is authorized by S.C. Code Ann. § 1–23–650 (1976) (as amended). These Rules shall govern all proceedings before the Administrative Law Court, in which the right to a hearing (a) is provided by the Administrative Procedures Act; (b) is specifically required by other statutes or regulations; or (c) is required by due process under the South Carolina or United States Constitutions.
[Effective April 30, 2009.]

Notes

2009 Revised Notes

These Rules are applicable to all matters within the jurisdiction of the Court, whether they are contested cases under the Administrative Procedures Act or heard pursuant to a constitutional command for a hearing. ***Stono River EPA v. S.C. Dep't of Health and Envtl Control***, 305 S.C. 90, 406 S.E.2d 340 (1991); ***League of Women Voters v. Litchfield-by-the-Sea***, 305 S.C. 424, 406 S.E.2d 378 (1991).

RULE 2. DEFINITIONS

A. **Administrative Law Court** means an independent body of administrative law judges who preside over public hearings involving the promulgation of regulations, as authorized in S.C. Code Ann. § 1–23–111 and decide contested cases and appellate cases pursuant to the authority in S.C. Code Ann. § 1–23–310, et seq. and as otherwise provided by law.

B. **Administrative Law Judge** means a judge appointed pursuant to S.C. Code Ann. § 1–23–510 (1976) (as amended) who is assigned a particular matter by the Chief Administrative Law Judge, or if no administrative law judge has been assigned for a particular matter, the Chief Administrative Law Judge.

C. **Agency** means a state agency, department, board or commission whose action is the subject of a contested hearing, an appeal heard by an administrative law judge, or a public hearing on a proposed regulation presided over by an administrative law judge.

D. **Appeal** means the review conducted by an administrative law judge of an agency decision on the record established in the agency and any additional evidence presented to the administrative law judge pursuant to the Administrative Procedures Act.

E. **Contested Case** is defined in Section 1–23–310. It is a case for which a hearing is conducted pursuant to Article 3, Chapter 23 of Title 1, the South Carolina Administrative Procedures Act, and includes hearings conducted by the Administrative Law Court pursuant to Section 1–23–600(B), hearings required by due process under the South Carolina or United States Constitutions, or as otherwise provided by law.

F. **Court** means the Administrative Law Court.

G. **Docket** means the roster of matters pending before the Court, including contested cases, appeals, and hearings on proposed regulations.

H. **Party** means each person or agency named or admitted as a party or properly seeking and entitled to be admitted as a party, including a license or permit applicant. An applicant or licensee whose application or license is the subject of a request for a contested case hearing shall be deemed a party and shall be served with copies of all papers filed in the case.
[Effective April 30, 2009.]

Notes

2009 Revised Notes

The definition of a contested case includes matters which are heard pursuant to a constitutional command for a hearing and matters, such as county tax cases, which do not come directly from a state agency. The definition of a party makes it clear that the licensee or applicant is to be made a party to any matter which involves the license or permit, and that he shall be served with copies of all papers filed in the action.

RULE 3. TIME

A. **Computation.** In computing any period of time prescribed or allowed by these rules, by order of court, or by any applicable statute, the day of the act, event, or default after the designated period of time begins to run is not included. The last day of the period so computed is to be included, unless it is a Saturday, Sunday or a State or Federal holiday, in which event the period runs until the end of the next day which is neither a Saturday, Sunday nor such holiday. When the period prescribed is less than seven days, intermediate Saturdays, Sundays and holidays shall be excluded in the computation. A half holiday shall be considered as any other day and not as a holiday.

B. **Enlargement.** For good cause shown, the administrative law judge may extend or shorten the time to take any action, except as otherwise provided by rule or law.

C. **Service By Mail.** Whenever a party has the right or is required to do some act or take some proceedings within a prescribed period after the service of a notice or other paper upon him and the notice or paper is served upon him by mail, by e-mail, or upon a person designated by statute to accept service, five days shall be added to the prescribed period.
[Effective April 30, 2009. Amended effective May 1, 2011.]

Notes

2009 Revised Notes

The method of calculating time in Rule 6 (a) and 6 (e), SCRCP, is adopted. A simplified procedure for extending time is adopted rather than Rule 6 (b), SCRCP. The 10 day notice requirement for motions in Rule 6 (d) is not adopted, but the additional five days available if service is made by mail is included in this Rule.

Note to 2011 Amendments

The amendment to Rule 3(C) gives parties served with a notice or paper by the Court via e-mail in accordance with Rule 5 the same amount of time to respond as if the party had been served by mail.

RULE 4. FILING

A. Filing with Court. After the request for hearing and filing fee are delivered to the Court, all filings must be made with the administrative law judge assigned to the case and shall contain the docket number assigned. The Court will maintain its official file from the receipt of the request for hearing until a final order is issued by the administrative law judge.

B. Filing Defined. The date of the filing is the date of delivery or the date of mailing. Any document filed with the Court shall be accompanied by proof of service of such document on all parties, and, if filed by mail, shall be accompanied by a certificate of the date of mailing. A document, pleading or motion or other paper is deemed filed with the Court by:

(1) delivering the document to the Court;

(2) by depositing the document in the U.S. mail, properly addressed to the Court, with sufficient first class postage attached; or

(3) as otherwise approved by the Court through administrative order.

C. Paper Size. All papers filed with the Court shall be on letter-size (8½ by 11 inches) paper. Exhibits or copies of exhibits in their original form which exceed that size shall be reduced by photocopying or otherwise to letter-size so long as such documents remain legible after reduction.

[Effective April 30, 2009. Amended effective May 1, 2011.]

Notes

2009 Revised Notes

All filings are to be made with the assigned administrative law judge after the request for hearing and filing fee are delivered to the Court. All filed papers must be served upon all parties and, if filed by mail, must be accompanied by a certificate of service. All papers filed with the Court must be letter size. Exhibits or other documents that exceed that size are to be reduced before filing unless the process of reduction would make them illegible. The Court is responsible for the official record from the receipt of the request for a hearing until the administrative law judge issues the final order. Filing with the Court is defined as the date delivered to the Court or the date mailed by first class mail to the Court, along with a certificate of service.

Note to 2011 Amendments

Rule 4(B) is amended to provide that filing with the Court may be effectuated by methods which may be specifically approved by the Court through administrative order, as well as through the traditional methods of filing. Unless otherwise approved by administrative order of the Court, parties may not file documents with the Court by e-mail.

RULE 5. SERVICE

Any document, pleading, motion, brief or memorandum or other paper filed with the Court shall be served upon all parties to the proceeding. Service shall be made upon counsel if the party is represented, or if there is no counsel, upon the party. Service shall be made by delivery, by mail to the last known address, or as otherwise approved by the Court through administrative order. Service is deemed complete upon mailing. Service that complies with Rule 5(b)(1), SCRCP, also shall satisfy this Rule. A party who furnishes an e-mail address to the Court pursuant to Rule 6, Rule 11 or Rule 33 consents to the service of prehearing statements, notices of hearing, final orders, or other documents issued by the Court via e-mail.

[Effective April 30, 2009. Amended effective May 1, 2011.]

Notes

2009 Revised Notes

Service is required of all documents filed. It is complete upon mailing. The method of service is by delivery or mailing, but not fax. Any service that satisfies Rule 5, SCRCP also satisfies this Rule.

Note to 2011 Amendments

The amendment provides that service of documents may be effectuated by methods which may be specifically approved by the Court through administrative order, as well as through the traditional methods of service. The rule is further amended to provide that parties who furnish an e-mail address to the Court consent to the service of documents issued by the Court via e-mail. Unless otherwise approved by administrative order of the Court, e-mail service applies only to documents issued and served upon a party by the Court, such as prehearing statements, notices of hearing, or final orders, and parties may not serve documents by e-mail.

RULE 6. CONTENT OF PAPERS

The clerk of the Court shall assign a docket number to each case. All papers, pleadings, motions and orders thereafter shall be filed with the Court and a copy served on all other parties of record. All papers shall be signed and contain:

A. a caption setting forth the title of the case and a brief description of the document;

B. the case docket number assigned by the Court;

C. the name, address, telephone number and e-mail address of the person who prepared the document.

The party filing a document with the Court is responsible for redacting all identifying or personal information, such as social security numbers, from the document before it is filed with the Court. Once a document is filed with the Court, it is a public record subject to disclosure under the Freedom of Information Act.

[Effective April 30, 2009. Amended effective May 1, 2011.]

Notes

Note to 2011 Amendments

Rule 6 is amended to require that documents filed with the Court should contain the e-mail address of the person who prepared the document. The amendment further provides that the proponent of a document filed with the Court is responsible for redacting any personal or identifying information which is not subject to disclosure under FOIA from the document prior to filing it with the Court.

RULE 7. FORMS

The Court shall prescribe the content and format of forms required by these rules. The use of required forms as prescribed is mandatory. The Court may also prescribe the content and format of other forms which would facilitate administrative efficiency and judicial economy.

[Effective April 30, 2009.]

RULE 8. RIGHT OF PARTIES TO PARTICIPATE

A. Parties and Their Representatives. Parties in a contested case have the right to participate or to be represented in all hearings or pre-hearing conferences related to their case. Any party may be represented by an attorney admitted to practice, either permanently or pro hac vice. No one shall be permitted to represent a party where such representation would constitute the unauthorized practice of law. However, in tax cases, any party may be represented by a certified public accountant, and in cases arising under the Occupational Safety and Health Act, a partnership, corporation, or other business entity may be represented by an officer or employee. A party proceeding without legal representation shall remain fully responsible for compliance with these Rules and the Administrative Procedures Act. This Rule shall not be construed to permit law student practice except to the extent authorized by Rule 401 of the South Carolina Appellate Court Rules.

B. Notice of Appearance. After a case is assigned to an administrative law judge, an attorney or other person authorized to represent a party pursuant to this rule must file a notice of appearance with the presiding administrative law judge within ten days of being retained or authorized to represent the party.

C. Motion to Withdraw from Representation. An attorney or other person authorized to represent a party pursuant to these Rules must file a written motion to withdraw from representation.

[Effective April 30, 2009.]

Notes

2009 Revised Notes

A party may be represented only by an attorney, in tax related matters by a certified public accountant, or in OSHA cases only, a business entity may be represented by an officer or employee. Representation of a party before the Court is permitted only to the extent that such representation does not conflict with the rules governing the unauthorized practice of law. Parties representing themselves are not relieved of the responsibility to comply with these Rules and the Administrative Procedures Act. A representative who is retained after assignment of the case must file a notice of appearance with the presiding administrative law judge within ten days of being retained, and any person representing a party before the Court must file a written motion with the presiding judge to withdraw from representation of that party.

II. CONTESTED CASES

GENERAL PROCEDURES

RULE 9. POWERS AND DUTIES OF ADMINISTRATIVE LAW JUDGE

Upon assignment of a case, the administrative law judge shall rule on all motions, preside at the contested case hearing, rule on the admissibility of evidence, require the parties to submit briefs when appropriate, issue orders and rulings to insure the orderly conduct of the proceedings and issue the final order.

[Effective April 30, 2009.]

RULE 10. SIMPLIFICATION OF PROCEDURES

The administrative law judge, upon being assigned a contested case, shall review the request for a contested case hearing and determine the procedure appropriate to the complexity of the issues presented and the types of proof likely to be introduced so that the matter may be fully and fairly presented without unnecessary burden on either the agency or individuals involved in the hearing. The administrative law judge may limit the pre-hearing procedures and simplify the pre-hearing exchange of materials and otherwise take such reasonable measures so that the burdens of procedure do not unfairly prevent the presentation of the facts.

[Effective April 30, 2009.]

Notes

2009 Revised Notes

The statutory authority of the Court encompasses a wide range of administrative actions from the very simple review of hunting and fishing license revocations to complex environmental cases. This section provides specific direction to the administrative law judge to review the case and limit the pre-hearing procedures if they are unnecessary to a full development of the case. The administrative law judge, through the scheduling conference, which can be held by telephone, can consider the comments of the parties and then issue an appropriate order defining the pre-hearing procedures.

RULE 11. REQUEST FOR A CONTESTED CASE HEARING

A. Place of Filing. A request for a contested case hearing, accompanied by a filing fee as provided in Rule 71, must be filed with the clerk of the Court.

B. Service of Copies of the Request. A copy of the request must also be served on each party and on the affected agency or county official, in accordance with Rule 5. A certificate of service must be included with the request.

C. Time for Filing. Unless otherwise provided by statute, a request must be filed and served within thirty (30) days after actual or constructive notice of the agency's determination. In county tax matters and cases arising under the Setoff Debt Collection Act, the request must be filed and served within thirty (30) days after the date of the written decision. However, no request shall be filed more than ninety (90) days after the date of the issuance of the order or determination unless the administrative law judge assigned to the case finds that substantial cause exists for allowing the filing beyond the ninety (90) day period.

D. Content of the Request. The request may be submitted on a form prescribed by the Court and shall contain the following information:

1. The name, address, telephone number and e-mail address of the party requesting the hearing and the issue(s) for which the hearing is requested;

2. The caption or other information sufficient to identify the decision, order, letter, determination, action or inaction which is the subject of the hearing;

3. A copy of the written agency decision, order, letter or determination, if any, which gave rise to the request;

4. The relief requested.

E. Incomplete Requests. Any request which is incomplete or not in compliance with this rule or Rule 71 will not be assigned to an administrative law judge until all required information is received and the filing fee is processed.

[Effective April 30, 2009. Amended effective May 1, 2011.]

Notes

2009 Revised Notes

The request for a contested case hearing contains basic information so that the matter may be identified. The request must be filed directly with the clerk of the Court rather than with the affected agency. The request must be accompanied by a filing fee as provided in Rule 71, and a certificate of service upon all parties, including the affected agency or county official. The use of an official request form provided by the Court is optional. A copy of the written agency decision must also be included with the request for a hearing.

The thirty-day time period for filing a request for a contested case hearing begins to run when the party filing the request has actual or constructive notice of the agency order or determination. A request based upon failure to receive notice may not be filed more than 90 days after the date of the agency order or determination, unless for substantial cause shown the administrative law judge allows the filing to be made. For county tax matters and cases arising under the Setoff Debt Collection Act, the request must be filed and served within 30 days of the date of the written decision. A case will not be assigned to an administrative law judge until all information required by the rule, and the filing fee, is received.

Note to 2011 Amendments

The amendment requires parties requesting a contested case hearing to include their address, telephone number, and email address in the request.

RULE 12. AGENCY INFORMATION SHEET

The agency requesting a contested case hearing or receiving a notice of a request for a contested case hearing from a party shall, within ten (10) working days of the date of the notice of assignment of the case to an administrative law judge, file with the clerk of the Court and serve upon all parties an information sheet on the form prescribed by the Court, containing the following information:

A. the name of the affected agency, along with the name, telephone number, and e-mail address of the contact person in the agency responsible for the matter;

B. the name or title of the agency proceeding and the file number or any other identifying information of the agency action or inaction that is the subject of the hearing, and a copy of the written agency decision, if any, which gave rise to the request for a hearing;

C. the names, addresses, telephone numbers and e-mail addresses of all known parties, and their attorneys or authorized representatives;

D. the names, addresses and telephone numbers, if known, of any persons who have exercised their legal right to object to the issuance of a permit or license.

If the agency fails to file the requested materials with the Court within ten working days, the party requesting the hearing may move before the presiding administrative law judge for an order directing the agency to respond forthwith.

[Effective April 30, 2009. Amended effective May 1, 2011.]

Notes

2009 Revised Notes

Within ten working days from the date of the notice of assignment to an administrative law judge, the agency must file with the Court and serve upon all parties an agency information sheet on the form prescribed by the Court, containing the information formerly submitted in the agency transmittal form. A copy of the written agency decision must be included with the agency information sheet. If the agency fails to comply with this Rule, the party requesting the hearing may move for an order compelling the agency to respond.

Note to 2011 Amendments

Rule 12 is amended to provide that the agency information sheet must include the e-mail addresses of the agency's contact person, as well as the e-mail addresses of known parties and their representatives.

RULE 13. ASSIGNMENT OF CASE TO ADMINISTRATIVE LAW JUDGE

Upon receipt of the request for contested case hearing and filing fee the case shall be assigned to an administrative law judge as provided in S. C. Code Ann. § 1–23–570 (1976) (as amended).

[Effective April 30, 2009.]

Notes

2009 Revised Notes

The request for a contested case hearing and filing fee must be received before a contested case is assigned to an administrative law judge. Once a case is assigned to a judge, that judge will be responsible for all decisions in the case.

RULE 14. NOTIFICATION OF ASSIGNMENT AND REQUEST FOR INFORMATION

Upon receipt of the request for contested case hearing and filing fee, the Court shall notify all parties of the assignment of an administrative law judge, and the administrative law judge assigned to the case, by pre-hearing order, may request each party to prepare and return a Pre–Hearing Statement describing the contested case.

[Effective April 30, 2009.]

RULE 15. NOTICE OF CONTESTED CASE HEARING

The administrative law judge assigned to the case must issue a Notice of Contested Case Hearing at least thirty (30) days before the hearing date that sets forth the date, time, place, and purpose of the hearing, the administrative law judge who will conduct the hearing, and any other matters necessary for the prompt resolution of the matter. This Notice may be issued via e-mail pursuant to Rule 5.

[Effective April 30, 2009. Amended effective April 29, 2010; May 1, 2011.]

Notes

2009 Revised Notes

In accordance with the Administrative Procedures Act, the Court issues the notice of the contested case hearing at least 30 days before the hearing date.

Notes to 2010 Amendments

Rule 15 has been amended to clarify that the administrative law judge assigned to the case issues the Notice of Hearing.

Note to 2011 Amendments

The amendment provides that the Court may issue notices of hearing to the parties via e-mail. Parties are responsible for ensuring that the Court is provided with an accurate e-mail address.

RULE 16. PRELIMINARY RELIEF

The administrative law judge may issue remedial writs as are necessary to give effect to its jurisdiction and with respect to injunctions shall follow the procedure in Rule 65, SCRCP.

[Effective April 30, 2009.]

Notes

2009 Revised Notes

This section provides that the administrative law judge may issue remedial writs as provided in S. C. Code Ann. § 1–23–630 (2005) (as amended). The procedure for issuing the injunction is provided by Rule 65, SCRCP.

PRE–HEARING PROCEDURES

RULE 17. SCHEDULING CONFERENCES AND ORDERS

A. Scheduling Conference. At any time after the case has been assigned, the administrative law judge may hold a scheduling conference with the parties of record, by telephone if convenient, to determine:

(1) the necessity or desirability of pleadings or amendments;

(2) the simplification of the issues;

(3) the possibility of obtaining admissions of fact and of documents to avoid unnecessary proof;

(4) the limitation and exchange of expert testimony;

(5) the scheduling of discovery;

(6) the possibility of resolving the matter through settlement, reference to mediation or other alternative forms of dispute resolution.

B. Scheduling Order. The administrative law judge, after the conference, may issue an appropriate order containing the action, if any, taken at the scheduling conference.

[Effective April 30, 2009.]

Notes

2009 Revised Notes

This rule gives the judge the power to hold a pre-hearing conference in any case, preferably by telephone. The matters discussed include the opportunity for settlement conferences or alternative dispute resolution if appropriate. The administrative law judge issues an appropriate order to guide the prehearing proceedings.

RULE 18. PLEADING

The administrative law judge by order may require pleadings from the parties. If pleadings are required they shall be as follows:

A. A Petition shall be filed within 30 days after the order requiring pleadings, unless a different time is set by the judge. The petition shall state in separately numbered paragraphs the facts and the particular statutes and rules relied upon, and the relief requested. If the contested case arises out of an order or similar document containing specific findings of fact or conclusions of law, the petition shall admit or deny each specific finding. A party shall deny only that part of an averment that may be denied in good faith.

B. An Answer shall be filed within 30 days of service of the petition, unless otherwise ordered, and shall admit or deny or otherwise answer each allegation of the petition. Any allegation not denied shall be deemed admitted. The Answer shall assert any facts deemed to show an affirmative defense. Any defense not raised on the facts known to the parties may be deemed waived.

C. Any pleading, paper or document can be amended at any time upon motion and for good cause shown, unless the amendment would substantially prejudice any other party in the presentation of its case.

D. All pleadings shall contain the names, addresses, and telephone numbers of the parties or their attorneys or authorized representatives.

[Effective April 30, 2009.]

Notes

2009 Revised Notes

Pleadings are optional with the administrative law judge. If ordered, they must be in the form specified. If the case arises from the order, the petition must admit or deny the findings of the order. Amended pleadings are allowed upon motion and for good cause shown, in the discretion of the presiding administrative law judge.

RULE 19. MOTIONS

A. Content and Filing. All pre-hearing motions shall be written, contain the caption of the case and the title of the motion, the contested case docket number assigned by the Court and the name and address of the person preparing it. The motion shall also state the grounds for relief and the relief sought. All motions pertaining to the hearing shall be filed not later than ten (10) days before the hearing date, unless otherwise ordered by the administrative law judge. Any party may file a written response to the motion within ten (10) days unless the time is extended or shortened by the administrative law judge.

B. Motions for Continuance. A motion for continuance shall be in writing, state the reasons therefor, and be signed by the requesting party or representative. No application for a continuance may be made or granted ex parte (without notice) except in an emergency where notice is not feasible.

C. Motions Regarding Discovery. Any motion relating to discovery shall state that the moving party has made a good faith attempt to resolve all the issues raised by the motion with the opposing party. Opposing parties may respond within ten (10) days of the filing of the motion unless the time is otherwise altered by the administrative law judge, who may rule on the basis of the written motion and any response thereto, or may order argument on the motion.

D. Motions for Consolidation. When two or more hearings are to be held, and the same or substantially similar evidence is relevant and material to the matters at issue at each such hearing, the administrative law judge may upon motion by any party or on his own motion order that a consolidated hearing be conducted. Where consolidated hearings are held, a single record of the proceedings may be made and evidence introduced in one matter may be considered as introduced in others, and a separate or joint decision shall be made, at the discretion of the administrative law judge as appropriate.

[Effective April 30, 2009.]

Notes

2009 Revised Notes

Subsection (A) contains the requirement that motions be made at least ten days before the contested case hearing. A special rule for continuances was added because of their common usage. Notice to all parties is required. Subsection (C) contains a standard provision that the parties must consult with opposing counsel before filing of a discovery motion to discourage frivolous motions. Subsection (D) provides for consolidation of two or more cases in the event that the same or substantially similar evidence is relevant and material in the cases to be consolidated. The language of the subsection is adapted from 29 C.F.R., Part 18, Subpart A § 18.11, which is applicable to proceedings before Federal administrative law judges.

RULE 20. INTERVENTION

A. Motions for Intervention. A motion for leave to intervene shall be served on all parties and shall state the grounds for the proposed intervention, the position and interest of the proposed intervenor, and the possible impact of the intervention on the proceedings. A proposed answer or position in intervention shall be attached to the motion.

B. Grounds for Intervention. Any person may intervene in any pending contested case hearing upon a showing that:

(1) the movant will be aggrieved or adversely affected by the final order;

(2) the interests of the movant are not being adequately represented by existing parties, or that it is otherwise entitled to intervene;

(3) that intervention will not unduly prolong the proceedings or otherwise prejudice the rights of existing parties.

C. Time for Motion for Intervention. The motion for leave to intervene shall be filed as early in the proceedings as possible to avoid adverse impact on the existing parties or the disposition of the proceedings. Unless otherwise ordered by the administrative law judge, the motion to intervene shall be filed at least twenty (20) days before the hearing. Any later motion shall contain a statement of good cause for the failure to intervene earlier.

D. Conditions of Intervention. A person granted leave to intervene is a party to the proceeding. The intervenor shall be bound by any agreement, arrangement or other matter previously determined in the case. The order granting intervention may restrict the issues to be raised or otherwise condition the intervenor's participation in the proceeding. If appropriate, the administrative law judge may order consolidation of petitions and briefs and limit the number of representatives allowed to participate in the proceedings.

[Effective April 30, 2009.]

Notes

2009 Revised Notes

This rule contains the standard for intervention and specifically provides that the intervenor's participation can be limited in the discretion of the administrative law judge. The rule encourages early joinder of parties, and requires a good cause explanation if intervention is sought immediately before the hearing.

RULE 21. DISCOVERY

A. In General. Discovery shall be available as provided in S.C. Code Ann. § 1–23–320 (2005) (as amended), and as provided under these rules. Discovery shall be conducted according to the procedures in Rules 26–37, SCRCP, except that only the standard interrogatories provided by SCRCP 33(b), as applicable to the pending contested case, are permitted; there shall be no more than three (3) depositions per party under Rule 30, SCRCP; and no more than ten (10) requests to admit per party, including subparts under Rule 36, SCRCP. All discovery shall be completed within 90 days of the receipt of the Notice of Assignment and Request for Information. Upon motion for good cause shown or upon his own motion, discovery may be expanded or curtailed by the administrative law judge.

B. Discovery in Certificate of Need Cases. Discovery in Certificate of Need (CON) contested cases is limited to the issues raised during staff review in opposition to the issuance of the Certificate of Need. Only the standard interrogatories provided by Rule 33(b), SCRCP, as applicable to the pending contested case, and thirty (30) interrogatories (including subparts) to each party are permitted; there shall be no more than thirty (30) requests for production (including subparts); there shall be no more than ten (10) witnesses called by each party in their case in chief; and no more than ten (10) requests to admit (including subparts) to each party are permitted. Any permitted discovery shall be conducted according to the procedures in Rules 26–37, SCRCP. Discovery may be curtailed by the administrative law judge upon a showing of good cause or expanded by the administrative law judge upon a showing of substantial prejudice to the party seeking expanded discovery.

[Effective April 30, 2009. Amended effective May 1, 2011.]

Notes

2009 Revised Notes

The Administrative Procedures Act permits discovery by depositions, and this rule authorizes discovery by interrogatories, document production or requests to admit. The mechanism, timing and procedure of discovery is governed by the Rules of Civil Procedure, with specific limitations on interrogatories, depositions and requests to admit. The presiding administrative law judge may expand or curtail discovery either sua sponte or upon motion.

Note to 2011 Amendments

The amendment renumbers the former rule as subsection (A) and adds subsection (B) to provide parameters for discovery in Certificate of Need (CON) cases. The rule is designed to facilitate the resolution of CON cases in as prompt a manner as possible. The presiding administrative law judge in a CON case may establish a time frame for completion of discovery in a scheduling order.

RULE 22. SUBPOENAS

A. Issuance and Service. Subpoenas by or on behalf of any party shall be issued in blank by the clerk of the Court. The party requesting the subpoena shall complete the form and return the completed form to the clerk of the Court for signature before service, and shall file a copy of the subpoena and the return of service with the clerk of the Court upon service. An attorney authorized to practice before the courts of the State of South Carolina, as an officer of the court, may also issue and sign a subpoena on behalf of the Court. The attorney shall complete the form before service and file a copy of the subpoena and the return of service with the clerk of the Court upon service. The party requesting the subpoena shall be responsible for service of the subpoena and the payment of fees and mileage in accordance with Rule 45, SCRCP.

B. Enforcement. The administrative law judge shall enforce by proper proceedings the attendance and testimony of witnesses and the production and examination of records, books, and papers, and have the power to punish as for contempt of court, by fine or imprisonment or both, the unexcused failure or refusal to attend and give testimony or produce books, papers, and records that have been required by subpoena to be produced.

C. Motions to Quash or Modify Subpoenas. A person to whom a subpoena has been issued may move before the administrative law judge for an order quashing or modifying the subpoena.

[Effective April 30, 2009.]

Notes

2009 Revised Notes

Rule 22(A) provides the procedure for issuance and service of subpoenas. An unrepresented party requesting a subpoena must complete the blank form and return the completed form to the clerk for signature before service. However, attorneys may issue and sign subpoenas on behalf of the Court. Rule 22(C) provides the procedure for motions to quash or modify subpoenas. The administrative law judge has the power to enforce subpoenas and to sanction parties for failure to comply with subpoenas as for contempt.

RULE 23. ADVERSE DISPOSITION OF CONTESTED CASE

A. Default. The administrative law judge may dismiss a contested case or dispose of a contested case adverse to the defaulting party. A default occurs when a party fails to plead or otherwise prosecute or defend, fails to appear at a hearing without the proper consent of the judge or fails to comply with any interlocutory order of the administrative law judge. Any non-defaulting party may move for an order dismissing the case or terminating it adversely to the defaulting party.

B. Dismissal of Contested Case for Failure to Comply with the Rules. Upon motion of any party, or on its own motion, the Court may dismiss a contested case for failure to comply with any of the rules of procedure for contested cases, including the failure to comply with any of the time limits provided by this section.

[Effective April 30, 2009.]

Note

2009 Revised Notes

The administrative law judge may dispose of a contested case adverse to a defaulting party. Rule 23(B) allows the administrative law judge to dismiss a contested case for failure to comply with the rules of procedure for contested cases.

RULE 24. CONFIDENTIALITY

When, by statute or rule, a matter subject to the jurisdiction of the Court is required to be kept confidential, all pleadings, motions or other papers filed with the Court, and served on all parties, shall bear the designation "CONFIDENTIAL" and such documents shall be maintained so that only authorized individuals shall have access to those documents or pleadings. [Effective April 30, 2009.]

HEARING PROCEDURES

RULE 25. EVIDENCE

A. Governing Statute. S.C. Code Ann. § 1–23–330 (2005) (as amended) shall govern questions of evidence.

B. Objections. Objections to evidence shall be timely made and noted in the record. Whenever evidence is ruled inadmissible, the party offering that evidence may submit an offer of proof on the record. The party making the offer of proof for excluded oral testimony shall briefly summarize the testimony. If the evidence excluded consists of a document or exhibit, it shall be marked as part of an offer of proof and inserted in the record.

C. Preference for Stipulations, Documentary Evidence. Stipulations of law, fact and testimony are encouraged. Subject to these rules and when a hearing will be expedited and the interests of the parties will not be prejudiced substantially, any part of the evidence may be received in documentary form. [Effective April 30, 2009.]

Notes

2009 Revised Notes

This section establishes that the rules of evidence apply to administrative hearings as required by the Administrative Procedures Act. Stipulations are encouraged, and the judge may receive evidence in documentary form where appropriate. However, the use of prepared statements and exhibits in lieu of testimony, as formerly provided in Rule 25(D), is no longer permitted.

RULE 26. ADMISSIBILITY OF DOCUMENTS

The established rules of evidence as provided in S.C. Code Ann. § 1–23–330 shall be followed. The administrative law judge shall apply the tests under established rules of evidence otherwise relating to admissibility and credibility and determine the weight to be given such evidence. The administrative law judge may require the submitting party to identify the portions of voluminous records, or depositions that are relevant and material.

[Effective April 30, 2009.]

Notes

2009 Revised Notes

The established rules of evidence apply in all contested case proceedings, as provided in the Administrative Procedures Act. In lieu of the procedures formerly provided in this rule, parties may stipulate to the authenticity of documents in order to avoid delay or difficulty involved in establishing the foundation for those documents.

RULE 27. PRE–HEARING EXCHANGE OF EVIDENCE

Upon notice, the administrative law judge may, in appropriate cases, require the parties to exchange prior to the hearing:

A. a final list of witnesses the party reasonably expects to testify at the hearing;

B. a final list of all exhibits expected to be offered at the hearing;

C. a final list of all facts which the party intends to request be judicially noticed by the administrative law judge and the information supporting the judicial notice of the facts requested.

Any witness list or exhibit not exchanged prior to the hearing may be excluded from admission into evidence. Multiple documents submitted as one exhibit must be consecutively numbered. The pre-hearing exchange may be amended upon motion and for good cause shown, unless the amendment would substantially prejudice any other party in the presentation of its case.

[Effective April 30, 2009.]

Notes

2009 Revised Notes

This rule provides the administrative law judge another technique for limited pre-hearing exchange of information. It might be appropriate with other pre-hearing procedures in complex cases, or be the only disclosure in simple hearings. A procedure is provided for the amendment of the pre-hearing exchange. Multiple documents submitted as one exhibit, such as an agency file, must be consecutively numbered in order to facilitate reference to the individual documents during a hearing.

RULE 28. PRE–HEARING CONFERENCE

The administrative law judge may hold a pre-hearing conference prior to the hearing. The purpose is to obtain stipulations of law and fact, rule on the admissibility of evidence and to identify matters which any party intends to have judicially noticed. The administrative law judge may consider pending motions, and any other matter that will expedite the hearing.

[Effective April 30, 2009.]

Notes

2009 Revised Notes

This rule provides another tool to help the administrative law judge manage the case. This conference is discretionary and may be held shortly before the hearing to permit the pre-hearing resolution of any matter that would expedite the hearing itself.

RULE 29. CONTESTED CASE HEARINGS

A. Order of Proceedings. The administrative law judge shall conduct the hearing in the following manner:

(1) The administrative law judge shall give an opening statement briefly describing the nature of the proceeding.

(2) The parties shall be given an opportunity to briefly present opening statements.

(3) Parties shall present their evidence in the order determined by the administrative law judge. The party with the burden of proof will be the first to present evidence, all other parties being allowed to cross-examine in an orderly fashion. When that party rests, other parties will then be allowed to present their evidence, again allowing for orderly cross-examination. Rebuttal and surrebuttal evidence are allowed only in the discretion of the administrative law judge.

(4) Each witness shall be sworn or affirmed by the administrative law judge or the court reporter, and be subject to examination. In the discretion of the administrative law judge, witnesses may be sequestered during the hearing.

(5) Parties have the right to introduce evidence on the points at issue, to cross-examine witnesses present at the hearing as necessary for a full and true disclosure of the facts, to present evidence in rebuttal and to submit briefs.

(6) All objections to procedure, admission of evidence or any other matter shall be timely made and stated on the record.

(7) When all of the parties and witnesses have been heard, the parties shall be given the opportunity to present final arguments.

(8) Briefs and proposed findings of fact and conclusions of law may be requested by the administrative law judge, and if served upon the administrative law judge shall be served at the same time and by the same method on all parties. Briefs shall set forth the factual and legal position of the party and be served on the Court and on all parties of record.

B. Burden of Proof. In matters involving the assessment of civil penalties, the imposition of sanctions, or the enforcement of administrative orders, the agency shall have the burden of proof.

C. Decision. The administrative law judge shall issue the decision in a written order which shall include separate findings of fact and conclusions of law.

D. Motion for Reconsideration. Any party may move for reconsideration of a final decision of an administrative law judge in a contested case to alter or amend the final decision, subject to the grounds for relief set forth in Rule 59, SCRCP, as follows:

(1) Within ten (10) days after notice of the order concluding the matter before the administrative law judge, a party may move for reconsideration of the decision, provided that a notice of appeal from the decision has not been filed.

(2) The administrative law judge shall act on the motion for reconsideration within thirty (30) days after it is filed, and if no action is taken by the administrative law judge within that period, the inaction shall be deemed a denial of the relief sought in the motion.

(3) The filing of a motion for reconsideration shall not, of itself, stay the order of the administrative law judge or excuse or delay compliance with the order of the administrative law judge.

(4) The time for appeal for all parties shall be stayed by a timely motion for reconsideration, and shall run from receipt of an order granting or denying such motion, or if no order is filed regarding the motion, thirty (30) days from the date the motion is deemed denied pursuant to subsection (D)(2).

The filing of a motion for reconsideration is not a prerequisite to filing a notice of appeal from a final decision of an administrative law judge.

E. Stay of Final Order. An administrative law judge who issues a final order subject to judicial review may in the order stay its effect. At any time prior to the filing of a petition for judicial review, and upon the motion of any party, with notice to all parties, the administrative law judge may stay the final order upon appropriate terms. The filing of a motion for a stay does not alter the time for filing a petition for judicial review.

[Effective April 30, 2009. Amended effective May 1, 2011.]

Notes

2009 Revised Notes

This subsection permits the administrative law judge to stay the effect of any final order that is subject only to judicial review. The authority to stay the order is derived from S.C. Code Ann. § 1-23-380(A)(2) (2005) (as amended) which gives the agency or the reviewing court the power to stay an order. When the administrative law judge issues a final order subject only to judicial review, agency action is completed and the administrative law judge is the appropriate authority to consider the issue of a stay. Motions for stays do not alter the time for filing a petition for judicial review, which is jurisdictional.

2011 Revised Notes

Subsection (A) describes the procedure at the hearing which follows the standard civil trial format. In certain matters, such as enforcement actions, the agency has the burden of proof. The decision is to be written with separate statements of fact and law. Subsection (D) provides for a motion for reconsideration of the decision of an administrative law judge in a contested case. The motion for reconsideration is subject to the grounds for relief set forth in SCRCP 59. The administrative law judge must decide the motion within 30 days or it is deemed denied. The filing of a motion for reconsideration does not stay the effectiveness of the administrative law judge's order, but does toll the time for appeal until the motion is resolved. A motion for reconsideration made after a petition for judicial review has been filed is untimely because jurisdiction then resides in the Court of Appeals. The filing of a motion for reconsideration is not a prerequisite to filing a notice of appeal from the final decision of an administrative law judge.

Note to 2011 Amendments

The amendment eliminates the provision in Subsection (C) which "deemed denied" any issues raised in the contested case proceedings but not addressed in the written order. Rule 29(D) is further amended to provide that where the administrative law judge does not rule on the motion within thirty days, the time for appeal begins to run from the date the motion is deemed denied pursuant to subsection (D)(2).

RULE 30. RECORD AFTER FINAL DECISION

The record of the contested case shall consist of:

A. All pleadings, motions, intermediate rulings and depositions filed with the Court;

B. All evidence received or considered;

C. A statement of matters judicially noticed;

D. All proffers of proof of excluded evidence;

E. The final order or decision which is subject to judicial review;

F. The transcript of the testimony taken during the proceeding, if prepared.

[Effective April 30, 2009.]

RULE 31. APPEAL OF FINAL ORDER

The decision of the administrative law judge may be appealed as provided by law. An appellant shall file a copy of the notice of appeal with the clerk of the Court at the same time the notice of appeal is filed with the reviewing authority.

[Effective April 30, 2009.]

Notes

2009 Revised Notes

Pursuant to Act 387 of 2006, the South Carolina Appellate Court Rules govern the procedure for appealing a final order of an administrative law judge. A copy of the notice of appeal must be filed with the clerk of the Court at the same time the notice is filed with the Court of Appeals.

RULE 32. TRANSCRIPT

The hearings concerning a contested case shall be available for transcription as required by S.C. Code Ann. § 1–23–600 (a) (1976) (as amended). The cost of preparing a copy of a transcript shall be borne by the party requesting the transcript.

[Effective April 30, 2009.]

III. MATTERS HEARD ON APPEAL FROM FINAL DECISIONS OF CERTAIN AGENCIES

RULE 33. NOTICE OF APPEAL

The notice of appeal from the final decision of an agency shall be filed with the Court and a copy served on each party and the agency whose final decision is the subject of the appeal within thirty (30) days of receipt of the decision from which the appeal is taken. In appeals from decisions of the Department of Employment and Workforce, the notice of appeal must be filed and served within thirty (30) days of the date of the decision of the Department of Employment and Workforce Appellate Panel. The notice shall be accompanied by a filing fee as provided in Rule 71 and shall contain the following information:

A. the name, address, telephone number and e-mail address of the party requesting the appeal, and the name, address, telephone number and e-mail address of the attorney or other authorized representative, if any, representing that party;

B. a general statement of the grounds for appeal as provided in S.C. Code Ann. § 1–23–380(A)(6). The grounds for appeal may be amended, supplemented or modified in the statement of issues in the brief required by Rule 37(B)(1);

C. a copy of the final decision which is the subject of the appeal and the date received;

D. a copy of the request for a transcript;

E. a certificate of service of the notice of appeal on all parties.

Any notice of appeal which is incomplete or not in compliance with this rule or Rule 71 will not be assigned to an administrative law judge until all required information is received and the filing fee is processed.

[Effective April 30, 2009. Amended effective May 1, 2011.]

Notes

2009 Revised Notes

The notice of appeal is filed with the Court as the entity hearing the appeal. The time is set at 30 days because it is the same time for civil appeals. The notice of appeal should include a general statement of the issues on appeal, but the statement of issues in the brief shall be considered the final statement of the issues on appeal. The notice of appeal must be accompanied by a filing fee as provided in Rule 71. Any incomplete notice of appeal, or a notice not accompanied by the filing fee, will not be assigned to an administrative law judge until all required information and fees are received.

Note to 2011 Amendments

The amendment provides a time frame for filing the notice of appeal in Department of Employment and Workforce cases in accordance with the applicable statute. The Rule is further amended to require that the notice of appeal should include the e-mail addresses of the appellant and the appellant's attorney or authorized representative.

RULE 34. AUTOMATIC STAY OF PROCEEDINGS UPON APPEAL

The filing of an appeal from the final decision of an agency shall stay the final decision of that agency unless the effect of filing an appeal is otherwise established by statute, the Administrative Procedures Act notwithstanding; or the administrative law judge has entered an order regarding the effect of the proceedings in the agency. Notwithstanding the foregoing, upon the filing of an appeal from the final decision of an agency, any party may apply to the administrative law judge for an order regarding the effect of the appeal on the agency decision.

[Effective April 30, 2009.]

RULE 35. ORDERING AND FILING OF TRANSCRIPT

The party filing the notice of appeal shall be responsible for ordering a transcript and shall file a copy of the request for a transcript with the notice of appeal. Unless otherwise agreed by all parties in writing, the appellant must order the entire transcript. The administrative law judge may also order the agency to prepare a transcript. The transcript of the proceedings shall be filed with the clerk of the Court by the agency pursuant to Rule 36.

[Effective April 30, 2009.]

Notes

2009 Revised Notes

The party filing the notice of appeal must order the transcript at the same time as the service of the notice of appeal. A copy of the request for a transcript must be filed with the notice of appeal. The appellant must order the entire transcript unless the parties agree otherwise in writing.

RULE 36. RECORD ON APPEAL

A. Time for Service and Filing. Within forty-five (45) days of the date of the notice of assignment to an administrative law judge, the agency with possession of the Record shall file an original and one (1) copy of the Record with the Court and serve one (1) copy on each party to the appeal, unless the time for filing the Record is extended by the Administrative Law Judge assigned to the appeal. In appeals from decisions of the Department of Employment and Workforce, the Department must file and serve the Record within twenty (20) days of the date of the notice of assignment.

B. Content. The Record shall consist of the following:

(1) All pleadings, motions, and intermediate rulings;

(2) All evidence received or considered;

(3) A statement of matters judicially noticed;

(4) All proffers of proof of excluded evidence;

(5) The final order or decision which is subject to review;

(6) The transcript of the testimony taken during the proceeding.

The agency with possession of the Record is responsible for redacting all identifying or personal information, such as social security numbers, from the Record before it is filed with the Court. Once a document is filed with the Court, it is a public record subject to disclosure under the Freedom of Information Act.

C. Order of Record. The Record shall be arranged in the following order: the title page, index, orders, judgments, decrees, pleadings, transcript, exhibits, other materials or documents, and a certificate of service. Each page of the Record shall be numbered consecutively beginning with the index.

D. Title Page. The title page shall contain only the caption.

E. Index. Every Record shall contain an index to the principal matters therein, to include orders, judgments, pleadings, prehearing matters, opening statements, testimony, motions, closing arguments, posthearing motions, and exhibits. For witness testimony, the index shall show the pages on which direct, cross, redirect, and recross examination begins.

F. Exhibits. Photographs, plats and diagrams, and other paper exhibits shall be inserted in the Record where they can be reduced or drawn to a size which permits them to be printed and inserted in the Record, without folding more than one time. Where exhibits are larger, or do not reasonably lend themselves to accurate reproduction, they need not be included in the Record, but shall be filed separately. All exhibits other than paper exhibits must be delivered to the clerk of the Court.

G. Review Limited to Record. The Administrative Law Judge will not consider any fact which does not appear in the Record.

H. Cover of Record. The cover of the Record must be white in color and contain only the caption and the names, addresses, telephone numbers and e-mail addresses of counsel.

I. Margins and Bindings. Typewritten papers or reproductions must have a blank margin of an inch and a half on the left and must be securely fastened on the left margin.

[Effective April 30, 2009, amended effective April 29, 2010. Amended effective May 1, 2011.]

Notes

2010 Revised Notes

The agency with possession of the record in the contested case must file an original and one copy of the record with the Court within forty-five days of the date the case is assigned to an administrative law judge. This ensures that the agency must file the record only after the appellant has perfected the appeal by filing the notice of appeal and submitting the appropriate filing fee. The format of the Record on Appeal is similar to that used in the South Carolina Appellate Court Rules. The administrative law judge's review is limited to those facts appearing in the record.

Note to 2011 Amendments

Rule 36(A) is amended to provide a shorter time frame for the filing and service of the Record on Appeal in cases involving the Department of Employment and Workforce (DEW). The shortening of this time frame is designed to expedite the resolution of DEW appeals in accordance with S.C. Code Ann. § 41–35–750, as amended by Act 146 of 2010, which provides that these appeals must be heard in a summary manner. Rule 36(B) is amended to provide that the agency in possession of the record is responsible for redacting any identifying or personal information not subject to disclosure under FOIA prior to filing the Record on Appeal with the Court.

RULE 37. BRIEFS

A. Time for Filing. The party first noticing the appeal shall file an original and one copy of its brief with the Court within thirty (30) days after the filing of the Record on Appeal. Within thirty (30) days thereafter, the respondent and other parties shall file an original and one copy of their briefs in response. A reply brief and one copy may be filed ten (10) days thereafter. The principal briefs shall not exceed thirty (30) pages and the reply brief shall not exceed ten (10) pages. In appeals from the Department of Employment and Workforce, the appellant shall file its brief with the Court within twenty (20) days after the Record on Appeal is filed, and the respondent must file its brief within twenty (20) days after the date the appellant's brief is filed. The appellant may file a reply brief within ten (10) days after the respondent's brief is filed.

B. Content of Brief. Each brief shall contain:

(1) *Statements of the Issues on Appeal.* A statement of each of the issues presented for review. The statement shall be concise and direct as to each issue and may be stated in question form. Broad general statements may be disregarded by the Court. Ordi-

narily, no point will be considered that is not set forth in the statement of issues on appeal.

(2) *Statement of the Case.* The statement shall contain a concise history of the proceedings, insofar as necessary to an understanding of the appeal. The statement shall not contain contested matters and shall contain as a minimum, the following information: the date of the commencement of the action; the nature of the action; the nature of the defense or response; the date and nature of the agency action appealed from; the date of the service of the notice of appeal; the date of and description of any orders or proceedings in the agency as may have affected the appeal, or may throw light upon the questions involved in the appeal. Any matters stated or alleged in a party's statement shall be binding on that party.

(3) *Argument.* The brief shall be divided into as many parts as there are issues to be argued, and each such part shall bear an appropriate caption, followed by a discussion and citation of authority. A party may also include a separate statement of facts relevant to the issues presented for review, with reference to the record on appeal, which may include contested matters and summarize that party's contentions.

(4) *Conclusion.* A short conclusion stating the precise relief requested.

(5) *Certificate of Service.* A certificate showing the service of the brief on all parties of record.

C. Service of Brief. At the time of filing the brief with the Court, one copy of the brief and any appendix shall be served on each party to the appeal.

D. Cover of Brief. The cover of the appellant's brief shall be blue; that of the respondent red; that of an intervenor or amicus curiae green; and that of any reply brief gray. The cover of a brief shall contain only the caption and the names, addresses, telephone numbers and e-mail addresses of counsel. This subsection shall not apply to briefs filed by pro se litigants.

E. Margins and Bindings. Typewritten papers or reproductions must have a blank margin of an inch and a half on the left and must be securely fastened on the left margin.

[Effective April 30, 2009. Amended effective April 29, 2010; May 1, 2011.]

Notes

2010 Revised Notes

The appellant's brief must be filed within thirty days after the filing of the Record on Appeal, and the respondent's brief must be filed within thirty days after the appellant's brief is filed. These deadlines provide a readily ascertainable time for the submission of the briefs. Statements of fact set forth in the briefs are binding upon the proponent of the statement. The format of the briefs is similar to that used in the South Carolina Appellate Court Rules. The requirements of subsection (D), which specify the colors to be used for the cover of the briefs, do not apply to briefs filed by pro se litigants. The original and one copy of each brief must be filed with the Court.

Note to 2011 Amendments

The amendment provides a shorter time frame for the filing of briefs in appeals from the Department of Employment and Workforce (DEW). The shortening of this time frame is designed to expedite the resolution of DEW appeals in accordance with S.C. Code Ann. § 41–35–750, as amended by Act 146 of 2010, which provides that these appeals must be heard in a summary manner.

RULE 38. DISMISSAL OF APPEAL FOR FAILURE TO COMPLY WITH THE RULES

Upon motion of any party, or on its own motion, an administrative law judge may dismiss an appeal for failure to comply with any of the rules of procedure for appeals, including the failure to comply with any of the time limits provided by this section.

[Effective April 30, 2009.]

Notes

2009 Revised Notes

In all cases involving pro se litigants or those without substantial knowledge and experience in administrative matters, the administrative law judge may make reasonable efforts to assure fairness. Nevertheless, such litigants remain responsible for complying with these Rules and all applicable statutes.

RULE 39. ORAL ARGUMENT

The administrative law judge shall provide at least twenty (20) days notice of oral argument. The oral argument shall follow the procedure in Rule 218, SCACR. In the discretion of the administrative law judge, oral argument may not be required. Oral argument will ordinarily not be ordered by the Administrative Law Judge in appeals from the Office of Motor Vehicle Hearings or the Department of Employment and Workforce unless the proceeding involves a novel issue or a question of exceptional importance.

[Effective April 30, 2009. Amended effective May 1, 2011.]

Notes

2009 Revised Notes

The administrative law judge, rather than the clerk of the Court, provides the notice of oral argument. Oral argument is discretionary with the presiding judge, and is ordinarily not ordered in appeals from the Office of Motor Vehicle Hearings.

Note to 2011 Amendments

The amendment provides that oral argument is not ordinarily ordered in appeals from the Department of Employment and Workforce (DEW) unless the proceeding involves a novel issue or a question of exceptional importance. The elimination of oral argument in DEW appeals is designed to expedite the resolution of the appeals in accordance with S.C. Code Ann. § 41–35–750, as amended by Act 146 of 2010, which provides that these appeals must be heard in a summary manner.

RULE 40. OPINION

The administrative law judge shall render a decision in a written order which shall be served on all parties and filed with the clerk of the Court. The administrative law judge may affirm any ruling, order or judgment upon any ground(s) appearing in the Record and need not address a point which is manifestly without merit. Judicial review of any decision of the Court shall be as provided in S.C. Code Ann. § 1–23–610 (2005) (as amended). Motions for rehearing may be allowed in the discretion of the presiding administrative law judge. Any motion for rehearing must be filed within ten days of receipt of the order. The time for appeal is stayed by a timely motion for rehearing, and runs from receipt of an order granting or denying the motion. A motion for rehearing is not a prerequisite to filing a notice of appeal from the decision of the administrative law judge.

[Effective April 30, 2009. Amended effective May 1, 2011.]

Notes

2009 Revised Notes

The rules for hearing matters on appeal from the final decision of an agency are based on the South Carolina Appellate Court Rules as modified for the less complex matters heard by the Court. The South Carolina Appellate Court Rules should be examined to resolve novel issues of appellate procedure in the Court. The administrative law judge may affirm upon any ground appearing in the Record and may decline to address points which are without merit. Motions for rehearing must be filed within ten days of receipt of the order, and are only allowed in the discretion of the presiding judge. Motions for rehearing are not a prerequisite to filing a notice of appeal.

Note to 2011 Amendments

Rule 40 is amended to eliminate the provision which "deemed denied" any issues raised on appeal but not addressed in the order.

RULE 41. APPEAL OF FINAL ORDER

The appellant shall file a copy of the notice of appeal from the decision of the administrative law judge with the clerk of the Court.

[Effective April 30, 2009.]

Notes

2009 Revised Notes

Pursuant to Act 387 of 2006, the South Carolina Appellate Court Rules govern the procedure for appealing a final order of an administrative law judge.

IV. REGULATION HEARING PROCEDURES

RULE 42. REQUEST FOR HEARING ON PROPOSED REGULATION

An agency desiring a hearing on a proposed regulation pursuant to S.C. Code Ann. § 1–23–111 (1976) (as amended) shall file with the clerk of the Court a transmittal form including a description of the subject matter of the regulation and a request that a hearing be scheduled. Within five (5) days the chief administrative law judge shall assign an administrative law judge to preside over the proceedings.

[Effective April 30, 2009.]

RULE 43. DOCUMENTS FILED WITH REQUEST FOR HEARING

At the time the request for a hearing is made, the agency shall file with the clerk of the Court the following:

(a) a copy of the drafting notice for the proposed regulation as published in the State Register;

(b) the State Register Document Number of the proposed regulation;

(c) the proposed date of submission of the proposed regulation to the State Register for publication;

(d) the proposed date of publication in the State Register of the text or synopsis of the proposed regulation;

(e) a suggested date for the hearing.

[Effective April 30, 2009.]

Notes

2009 Revised Notes

The Request for a Hearing on Proposed Regulations should include documentation showing that the requirements for publication in the State Register have been met.

RULE 44. SCHEDULING OF HEARING ON PROPOSED REGULATION

Within ten (10) days of receipt of the request for a hearing and the required documents, the administrative law judge to whom the matter is assigned shall notify the agency of the location, date, and time of the hearing to allow participation by all affected interests and shall advise the agency to issue the proposed Notice of Hearing for the Proposed Regulation for publication in the State Register.

[Effective April 30, 2009.]

Notes

2009 Revised Notes

The administrative law judge notifies the agency of the hearing date, location, and time. The agency then publishes the Notice of Hearing for the Proposed Regulation in the State Register.

RULE 45. DOCUMENTS TO BE PRE–FILED WITH COURT

At least ten (10) days before the date scheduled for the hearing, the agency shall provide a statement confirming the need for a hearing as required by S.C. Code Ann. § 1–23–110 (1976) (as amended) on the basis that a request for a hearing was made by twenty-five (25) persons, a governmental subdivision or agency, or an association having not less than twenty-five (25) members.

A. Agency Statement of Need and Reasonableness. An agency desiring to adopt a regulation shall prepare and pre-file not later than ten (10) days before the date scheduled for the hearing, the full text of the proposed regulation, and a statement of need and reasonableness that contains a summary of anticipated evidence and argument to be presented by the agency at the hearing. The statement shall include citations to any statutes or case law, citations to any economic, scientific, or other manuals or treatises, and a list of any witnesses to be called by the agency to testify on its behalf with a summary of their anticipated testimony. The statement may contain evidence and argument in rebuttal of evidence and argument presented by the public.

B. Other Pre–Filed Documents. At the time the agency confirms the hearing, it also shall file a copy of the State Register containing the Notice; all materials received by the agency during the initial drafting period; a list of the agency personnel who will represent the agency at the hearing; a list of all persons who contacted the agency orally or in writing regarding the proposed regulation; and, a list of all persons expected to testify or present evidence at the hearing.

[Effective April 30, 2009.]

RULE 46. POWERS OF ADMINISTRATIVE LAW JUDGE

Consistent with law, the administrative law judge is authorized to do all things necessary and proper to the performance of the foregoing and to promote justice, fairness, and economy, including, but not limited to the power to preside at the hearing; administer oaths or affirmations; hear and rule on objections and motions; question witnesses when appropriate to make a complete record; rule on the admissibility of evidence; and strike from the record objectionable evidence, limit repetitive or immaterial oral statements and questions, and determine the order of making statements and questions.

[Effective April 30, 2009.]

RULE 47. ORDER OF PROCEEDINGS

All hearings held pursuant to S.C. Code Ann. § 1–23–111 (1976) (as amended) shall proceed substantially in the following manner:

A. Registration of Participants. All persons intending to present evidence or ask questions shall register with the administrative law judge before the hearing begins by legibly printing their names, addresses, telephone numbers, and names of any individuals or associations that the person represents on a register provided by the administrative law judge.

B. Notice of Procedure. The administrative law judge shall convene the hearing at the proper time, and shall explain to all persons present the purpose of the hearing and the procedure to be followed at the hearing so that all persons are treated fairly and impartially. The administrative law judge may impose time limitations on testimony by the agency or interested persons. The administrative law judge also shall announce when the record of the hearing is to be closed, and in its discretion may permit the filing of additional written statements and materials within five (5) days after the hearing. The time period may be extended in the discretion of the administrative law judge, but not later than twenty (20) days after the hearing ends.

C. Agency Presentation. The agency representatives will identify themselves and the witnesses expected to testify on the agency's behalf for the record, and make available copies of the proposed regulation at the hearing. The agency shall make its showing of the need for and the reasonableness of the regulation, and shall present any other evidence it considers necessary to fulfill all statutory or regulatory requirements. The agency may rely on its pre-filed Statement of Need and Reasonableness to satisfy its burden, and it may also present oral evidence.

D. Opportunity for Questions. Interested persons shall be given an opportunity to address questions to the agency representatives or witnesses or to interested persons making oral statements. Agency representatives may question interested persons making oral statements. Questioning may extend to the proposed regulations or a suggested modification, or may be conducted for other purposes, if material to the evaluation or formulation of the proposed regulations.

E. Opportunity for Presenting Statements and Evidence. Interested persons shall be given an opportunity to present oral and written statements and evidence regarding the proposed regulations.

F. Questioning by Administrative Law Judge. The administrative law judge may question all persons, including the agency representatives.

G. Further Agency Evidence. The agency may present any further evidence that it considers appropriate in response to statements made by interested persons. Upon presentation by the agency, interested persons may respond thereto.

H. Receipt of Written Materials. The administrative law judge may permit any interested person to submit written materials after the close of oral testimo-

ny on such terms and conditions as permit all parties an opportunity to comment on subsequent submissions.
[Effective April 30, 2009.]

RULE 48. REPORT OF ADMINISTRATIVE LAW JUDGE

After the time for the submission of all written materials, the administrative law judge shall issue a written report with findings as to the need and reasonableness of the proposed regulation, and if there is a finding of a lack of need or of reasonableness, may include suggested modifications to the proposed regulation.
[Effective April 30, 2009.]

RULE 49. RECORD OF PROCEEDING

The hearing record for the proposed regulations shall be closed on the date established by the administrative law judge, but not later than twenty (20) days after the hearing ends. The full record shall include:

A. all pre-filed documents submitted to the Court;

B. copies of all publications in the State Register pertaining to these rules;

C. all written petitions, requests, submissions or comments received by the agency or the administrative law judge pertaining to the substance and jurisdiction of the proceeding on the proposed regulation;

D. the proposed regulation as submitted to the administrative law judge;

E. the transcript of the proceedings, if one has been prepared; and

F. the report of the administrative law judge.
[Effective April 30, 2009.]

RULE 50. TRANSCRIPT

A transcript of the proceedings shall be prepared upon the order of the administrative law judge or the request of an agency or interested person. The party or person requesting the transcript shall pay for its production.
[Effective April 30, 2009.]

V. SPECIAL APPEALS

RULE 51. APPLICABILITY

The Rules in this section shall apply exclusively in matters heard on appeal from final decisions pursuant to Al–Shabazz v. State, 338 S.C. 354, 527 S.E.2d 742 (2000).
[Effective April 30, 2009.]

Notes

2009 Revised Notes

The Special Appeals Rules are the exclusive rules of procedure used in appeals from final decisions of the Department of Corrections and the Department of Probation, Parole and Pardon Services. The Court's jurisdiction to hear such matters is derived entirely from the decisions of the South Carolina Supreme Court in Al-Shabazz v. State, 338 S.C. 354, 527 S.E.2d 742 (2000), and Furtick v. S.C. Dep't of Probation, Parole and Pardon Services, 352 S.C. 594, 576 S.E.2d 146 (2003). These Rules are based upon the Court's existing general procedural and appellate rules, with adaptations for this specific type of appeal.

RULE 52. COMPUTATION OF TIME

In computing any period of time prescribed or allowed by these rules, by order of court, or by any applicable statute, the day of the act, event, or default after the designated period of time begins to run is not included. The last day of the period so computed is to be included, unless it is a Saturday, Sunday or a State or Federal holiday, in which event the period runs until the end of the next day which is neither a Saturday, Sunday nor such holiday. When the period prescribed is less than seven days, intermediate Saturdays, Sundays and holidays shall be excluded in the computation. A half holiday shall be considered as any other day and not as a holiday.
[Effective April 30, 2009.]

RULE 53. FILING

A. **Filing Defined.** The date of the filing is the date of delivery or the date of mailing as shown by the postmark or by the date stamp affixed by the mail room at the appellant's correctional institution. Any document filed with the Court shall be accompanied by proof of service of such document on all parties. A document, pleading or motion or other paper is deemed filed with the Court by:

(1) delivering the document to the Court; or

(2) depositing the document in the U.S. mail or in the mail room at the appellant's correctional institution, properly addressed to the Court, with sufficient first class postage attached.

B. **Paper Size.** All papers filed with the Court shall be on letter-size (8 ½ by 11 inches) paper. Exhibits or copies of exhibits in their original form which exceed that size shall be reduced by photocopying or otherwise to letter-size so long as such documents remain legible after reduction.
[Effective April 30, 2009.]

RULE 54. SERVICE

Any document, pleading, motion, brief or memorandum or other paper filed with the Court shall be served upon all parties to the proceeding. Service shall be made upon counsel if the party is represented, or if there is no counsel, upon the party. Service shall be made by delivery, or by mail to the last known address. Service is deemed complete upon mailing. Service that complies with Rule 5(b)(1), SCRCP, also shall satisfy this Rule.

[Effective April 30, 2009.]

RULE 55. DOCKET NUMBER AND SUBSEQUENT FILINGS

The clerk of the Court shall assign a docket number to each case. All papers, pleadings, motions and orders thereafter shall be filed with the presiding administrative law judge and a copy served on all other parties of record. All papers shall be signed and contain:

A. a caption setting forth the title of the case and a brief description of the document;

B. the case docket number assigned by the Court;

C. the name, address and telephone number of the person who prepared the document.

[Effective April 30, 2009.]

Notes

2009 Revised Notes

After the Clerk assigns a docket number to the case, all filings must be made with the presiding administrative law judge, must be served upon all parties, and must contain the information prescribed in the Rule.

RULE 56. LEGIBILITY OF DOCUMENTS

Any document, pleading, motion, brief or memorandum or other paper filed with the Court may be typewritten or handwritten, but in either event must be legible. In the discretion of the clerk of the Court, any illegible document may be returned unfiled to the party who submitted it.

[Effective April 30, 2009.]

RULE 57. FORMS

The Court shall prescribe the content and format of forms required by these rules. The use of required forms as prescribed is mandatory. The Court may also prescribe the content and format of other forms which would facilitate administrative efficiency and judicial economy.

[Effective April 30, 2009.]

RULE 58. RECORD AFTER FINAL DECISION

Where applicable, the record of the contested case shall consist of:

A. All pleadings, motions, intermediate rulings and depositions filed;

B. All evidence received or considered;

C. A statement of matters judicially noticed;

D. All proffers of proof of excluded evidence;

E. The final order or decision which is subject to administrative review;

F. Any transcript taken of the testimony during the proceeding.

[Effective April 30, 2009.]

RULE 59. NOTICE OF APPEAL

The notice of appeal from the final decision to be heard by the Administrative Law Court shall be filed with the Court and a copy served on each party, including the agency, within thirty (30) days of receipt of the decision from which the appeal is taken. The notice shall be on the form prescribed by the Court pursuant to Rule 57 and shall contain the following information:

A. the name, address, SCDC number, and telephone number of the party requesting the appeal, and the name, address, and telephone number of the attorney or other authorized representative, if any, representing that party;

B. a brief factual basis for each expressly and specifically asserted constitutional violation;

C. a copy of the final decision which is the subject of the appeal and the date received;

D. a certificate showing the service of the notice of appeal on all parties.

Any notice of appeal which is incomplete or not in compliance with this rule or Rule 71 will not be assigned to an administrative law judge until all required information is received and any applicable filing fee is processed. Within forty-five (45) days of the date the case is assigned to an Administrative Law Judge (date of assignment), the agency shall file the record with the Court, including a statement of the contents of the record, unless the time for filing the record is extended by the Administrative Law Judge assigned to the appeal.

[Effective April 30, 2009.]

Notes

2009 Revised Notes

The notice of appeal must be on the Court's prescribed form and must be filed and served within 30 days of receipt of the order appealed from. The notice must contain the prescribed information and must be accompanied by a certificate of service and any applicable filing fee. Notices which are not in compliance with this Rule or Rule 71 will not be assigned to an administrative law judge until all required information and applicable fees are received.

RULE 60. BRIEFS

A. Time for Filing Briefs. Unless otherwise ordered, the party first noticing the appeal shall file an original brief within sixty-five (65) days after the date of assignment. Within eighty-five (85) days after the date of assignment, the respondent shall file an original brief in response. A reply brief may be filed within ninety-five (95) days after the date of assignment. The principal briefs shall not exceed ten (10) pages and the reply brief shall not exceed five (5) pages.

B. Content of Brief. Each brief shall contain:

(1) *Statements of the Issues on Appeal.* A statement of each of the issues presented for review. The statement shall be concise and direct as to each issue and may be stated in question form. Broad general statements may be disregarded by the Court. Ordinarily, no point will be considered that is not set forth in the statement of issues on appeal.

(2) *Statement of the Case.* The statement shall contain a concise history of the proceedings, insofar as necessary to an understanding of the appeal. The statement shall not contain contested matters and shall contain as a minimum, the following information: the date of commencement of the action; the nature of the action; the nature of the defense or response; the date and nature of the agency action appealed from; the date of service of the notice of appeal; the date of and description of any orders or proceedings in the agency as may have affected the appeal, or may throw light upon the questions involved in the appeal. Any matters stated or alleged in a party's statement shall be binding on that party.

(3) *Argument.* The brief shall be divided into as many parts as there are issues to be argued, and each such part shall bear an appropriate caption, followed by a discussion and citation of authority. A party may also include a separate statement of facts relevant to the issues presented for review, with reference to the record on appeal, which may include contested matters and summarize that party's contentions. Any facts stated or alleged in a party's argument shall be binding on that party.

(4) *Conclusion.* A short conclusion stating the precise relief requested.

(5) *Certificate of Service.* A certificate showing the service of the brief on all parties of record.

C. Service of Brief. At the time of filing the brief with the Court, one copy of the brief and any appendix shall be served on each party to the appeal.

[Effective April 30, 2009.]

Notes

2009 Revised Notes

This rule provides the time frames for filing, format, and content of appellate briefs. Statements of fact set forth in the briefs are binding upon the proponent of the statement. The brief must be accompanied by a certificate of service.

RULE 61. RECORD ON APPEAL

The record on appeal shall consist of the transcript of the proceedings before the agency, if any, and the record of the contested case as described by Rule 58.

[Effective April 30, 2009.]

RULE 62. DISMISSAL OF APPEAL; SANCTIONS

Upon motion of any party, or on its own motion, an Administrative Law Judge may dismiss an appeal for failure to comply with any of the rules of procedure for appeals, including the failure to comply with any of the time limits provided by this section (V), or for the failure to provide a factual basis for each expressly and specifically asserted constitutional violation as prescribed by Rule 59(B). Notwithstanding the time frames established herein, the Administrative Law Judge has the discretion to determine that a document is timely filed upon a finding that the party who filed the document made a good faith effort to file the document within the applicable time limits. If the presiding judge determines that the appeal is frivolous or taken solely for purposes of delay, the judge may impose such sanctions as the circumstances of the case and discouragement of like conduct in the future may require.

[Effective April 30, 2009.]

Notes

2009 Revised Notes

Rule 62 allows an administrative law judge to dismiss an appeal for failure to comply with any applicable rule of procedure, and to impose appropriate sanctions for inmate appeals which are frivolous or taken solely for the purpose of delay.

RULE 63. MOTIONS

Any motions filed shall be in written form and shall state the grounds for relief and the relief sought. Any response to the motion must be filed within ten (10) days after receipt of the motion, unless the time is extended or shortened by the Administrative Law Judge. The filing of a motion does not toll any time limits imposed by these Rules.

[Effective April 30, 2009.]

Notes

2009 Revised Notes

This rule provides the procedure for filing motions. However, pursuant to Rule 65, motions for reconsideration or rehearing are not permitted and will not be considered by the administrative law judge.

RULE 64. ORAL ARGUMENT

In the discretion of the Administrative Law Judge, oral argument may not be required. Oral argument will ordinarily not be ordered by the Administrative Law Judge unless the proceeding involves a novel issue or a question of exceptional importance. If so ordered, at least twenty (20) days notice of oral argument shall be provided. The oral argument shall follow the procedure in Rule 218, SCACR.

[Effective April 30, 2009.]

RULE 65. OPINION

The Administrative Law Judge shall render a decision in a written order which shall be served on all parties and filed with the clerk of the Court. The Administrative Law Judge may affirm any ruling, order or judgment upon any ground(s) appearing in the Record and need not address a point which is manifestly without merit. The decision of the Administrative Law Judge is a final decision and motions for reconsideration will not be considered. Judicial review of any decision of the Court shall be as provided in S.C. Code Ann. § 1–23–610 (2005) (as amended).

[Effective April 30, 2009.]

Notes

2009 Revised Notes

Rule 65 incorporates the portion of Rule 220, SCACR, which allows the judge to affirm upon any ground appearing in the Record and to decline to address points which are without merit. Motions for reconsideration are not allowed.

RULE 66. APPEAL OF FINAL ORDER

The appellant shall file a copy of the notice of appeal from the decision of the Administrative Law Judge with the clerk of the Court.

[Effective April 30, 2009.]

Notes

2009 Revised Notes

Pursuant to Act 387 of 2006, the South Carolina Appellate Court Rules govern the procedure for appealing a final order of an administrative law judge.

VI. MISCELLANEOUS PROVISIONS

RULE 67. CLERICAL MISTAKES

Clerical mistakes in orders or other parts of the record and errors therein arising from oversight or omission may be corrected by the administrative law judge at any time of his own initiative or on the motion of any party and after such notice, if any, as the administrative law judge orders. During the pendency of an appeal from the decision of an administrative law judge, leave to correct the mistake must be obtained from the appellate court.

[Effective April 30, 2009.]

RULE 68. APPLICABILITY OF SOUTH CAROLINA RULES OF CIVIL PROCEDURE AND SOUTH CAROLINA APPELLATE COURT RULES

The South Carolina Rules of Civil Procedure and the South Carolina Appellate Court Rules may, in the discretion of the presiding administrative law judge, be applied in proceedings before the Court to resolve questions not addressed by these rules.

[Effective April 30, 2009.]

Notes

2009 Revised Notes

The South Carolina Appellate Court Rules may, in the discretion of the presiding administrative law judge, be applied in appellate proceedings before the Court to resolve questions which are not addressed by the Court's appellate rules.

RULE 69. APPLICABILITY OF RULES OF THE COURT

Once the Court acquires jurisdiction of a matter from an agency, the ALC Rules shall govern all procedural aspects of the matter, notwithstanding any other agency regulation or procedural rule.

[Effective April 30, 2009.]

Notes

2009 Revised Notes

Rule 69 provides for situations in which the procedural rules of the agency where the case arose differ from the ALC Rules. The Rule makes clear that the ALC Rules, rather than the rules of the agency, govern the proceedings once the Court acquires jurisdiction. Thus, questions of preliminary relief, content and form of pleadings, discovery and other procedural matters are resolved exclusively by the ALC Rules.

RULE 70. JUDGES SITTING EN BANC

A. Grounds for Consideration En Banc. A majority of the administrative law judges may order that a matter of law be considered by all the judges sitting en banc where (1) consideration by all the judges is necessary to serve or maintain uniformity of its decisions, or (2) when the proceeding involves a question of exceptional importance and public concern.

B. Quorum and Presiding Judge. When the administrative law judges sit en banc, a majority of the judges constitutes a quorum. A concurrence of a majority of the judges sitting is necessary for a decision. The Chief Administrative Law Judge shall preside at all en banc proceedings and in his absence, the administrative law judge next senior in service and who is present shall preside.

C. Petition for Consideration En Banc. No later than forty-five (45) days after the assignment of a case by the Chief Administrative Law Judge to an administrative law judge, a party may suggest the appropriateness of consideration of a matter en banc by filing a petition with the clerk of the Court. No response to the petition shall be required unless ordered by the assigned judge or by a majority of the judges. The presiding administrative law judge in a case may also request en banc consideration at any time during the proceedings. After receipt of the petition or request, the clerk will immediately circulate to the administrative law judges a vote sheet with the petition seeking an en banc hearing attached. No vote of the judges need be taken to determine whether the cause should be heard en banc unless a judge, within ten (10) days of receipt of the vote sheet, notifies the clerk in writing of his request for a vote of the judges on the suggestion. If no poll is requested, the Chief Administrative Law Judge will issue an order which bears the notation that no judge requested a poll. If a poll is requested and the hearing en banc is granted or denied, the Chief Administrative Law Judge will issue an order reflecting the decision.

D. Procedure. En banc consideration in an individual case is limited to only the particular issue(s) of law which meet the criteria set forth in paragraph A of this Rule 70. Upon a majority of the administrative law judges ordering a matter to be considered by the judges sitting en banc, notice will be given to the parties of the issue(s) under consideration. The parties may be required to file briefs and may be allowed to present oral argument on the issue(s). After the hearing, the Chief Administrative Law Judge will assign the authorship responsibility for the opinion.

E. En Banc Consideration Interlocutory. En banc consideration of a matter of law in a contested case or appellate case is an interlocutory measure. It is dispositive of the limited issue(s) addressed, but the decision is not final and conclusive until all factual issues and remaining legal issues in the contested case, or all issues in the appellate case, are resolved by the final order of the administrative law judge assigned to preside over the hearing in the case. Parties have no direct right of appeal from an en banc decision. Any appeal must follow the issuance of the final order on the merits of the case.

F. Effect of an En Banc Order. The issue(s) addressed in en banc decisions by the administrative law judges are binding upon all individual administrative law judges in all subsequent cases, unless a majority of the judges determine otherwise.

[Effective April 30, 2009.]

Notes

2009 Revised Notes

Rule 70 provides a procedure for en banc consideration of a matter of law in specified circumstances. If an issue in a case before the Court is considered en banc, that consideration must occur prior to the contested case or appeal hearing on the merits by the assigned administrative law judge. En banc consideration does not replace the contested case or appeals hearing before the administrative law judge. An en banc proceeding is not an evidentiary hearing and the administrative law judges sitting en banc cannot make findings of fact. After the judges sitting en banc render their decision, the assigned administrative law judge assigned to the case must conduct all further proceedings and render all further orders necessary in the matter.

RULE 71. FILING FEE

A. Cases for which Fee Required. Each request for a contested case hearing, notice of appeal, or request for injunctive relief before the Court must be accompanied by a filing fee in the amount set forth in Rule 71(C). A case will not be assigned to an administrative law judge and will not be processed until the filing fee has been paid or a waiver has been granted pursuant to Rule 71(B). This fee is not required for contested cases, appeals, or requests for injunctive relief brought by the State of South Carolina or its departments or agencies. For appeals brought pursuant to Al–Shabazz v. State, 338 S.C. 354, 527 S.E.2d 742 (2000), the fee will be assessed only for the third and subsequent appeals filed by an inmate during a given calendar year.

B. Request for Waiver. A party who is unable to pay the filing fee may request a waiver of the fee by filing a completed Request for Waiver form with the Clerk of the Court at the same time the request for a contested case, notice of appeal, or request for injunctive relief is filed with the Court. Request for Waiver forms shall be issued by the Clerk of the Court. If the filing fee is not waived, the party must pay the filing fee within ten days of the date of receipt of the order denying waiver of the filing fee. If the filing fee for a case is waived on behalf of a party, any motions filed by that party in that case are exempt from the motion fee as provided in Rule 71(D).

C. Schedule of Filing Fees. The filing fee will be assessed according to the following schedule:

Case Type	Fee
Dept. of Corrections (7th and subsequent filing per year)	$25
DHEC–Health Licensing/Individual Septic Tanks	$100
DHEC–(All other, including OCRM, CON and NAD)	$250
Dept. of Health and Human Services	$50
Dept. of Insurance–Rate Cases	$250

Case Type	Fee
Dept. of Insurance–Agent Application	$100
Dept. of Insurance–Agent Disciplinary	$100
Dept. of Insurance–All Other	$100
LLR—Wage Disputes (Department of Labor)	$50
LLR—Appeals (Professional and Occupational Licensing Boards)	$100
Dept. of Natural Resources—Hunting/Fishing	$50
Dept. of Natural Resources—Coastal Fisheries	$50
DOR–Alcoholic Beverage License Applications	$100
DOR–Alcoholic Beverage License Violations	$100
DOR–Bingo Violations	$100
DOR–State Tax Cases (<$500,000 in controversy)	$100
DOR–State Tax Cases (>$500,000 in controversy)	$250
County Tax Cases (Residential & Personal Property)	$50
County Tax Cases (Commercial)	$250
Dept. of Social Services (Day Care Appeals)	$100
Dept. of Social Services (All Other)	$50
Dept. of Transportation	$150
SLED	$100
Setoff Debt Collection Act	$50
Requests for Injunctive Relief	$150
Other Contested Cases and Appeals (including cases from agencies not listed herein)	$100

D. Motion Fees. A fee of $25 will be imposed for the following motions filed with the Court:

(1) Motion for Summary Judgment

(2) Motion to Intervene

(3) Motion to Dismiss

(4) Motion for Injunctive Relief (in a pending case).

(5) Motion to Compel

The fee must be submitted to the Clerk of the Court at the same time the motion is filed, unless a waiver of the filing fee in the case was previously granted to the party filing the motion. A motion will not be deemed filed until the fee is paid. The motion fee is not required for motions filed by the State of South Carolina or its departments or agencies.

[Effective April 30, 2009.]

Notes

2009 Revised Notes

Rule 71 provides for a schedule of filing fees as authorized by law. The filing fee varies according to the type and complexity of the case. The fee is required for all requests for a contested case hearing, notices of appeal, or requests for injunctive relief except for those brought by the State of South Carolina or its departments or agencies. For those appeals brought pursuant to Al-Shabazz v. State, 338 S.C. 354, 527 S.E.2d 742 (2000), the fee applies only to the third and subsequent filings by an inmate during a given calendar year. If a party is unable to pay the filing fee, he may request a waiver of the fee by filing the prescribed form with the Clerk of the Court. A case will not be assigned to an administrative law judge until the filing fee has been received or a waiver has been granted. Subsection (D) provides for a twenty-five dollar motion fee for certain motions filed with the Court. A motion will not be deemed filed with the Court until the fee has been paid. However, the motion fee is not required for motions filed by the State of South Carolina or its departments or agencies. In addition, if a party is granted a waiver of the filing fee, any fees for motions filed by that party are likewise waived.

RULE 72. SANCTIONS FOR FRIVOLOUS CASES

If the presiding administrative law judge determines that a contested case, appeal or motion is frivolous or taken solely for purposes of delay, the judge may impose such sanctions as the circumstances of the case and discouragement of like conduct in the future may require.

[Effective April 30, 2009.]

Notes

2009 Revised Notes

Rule 72 provides that an administrative law judge may impose sanctions for contested cases, appeals, or motions which are determined to be frivolous or taken for purposes of delay. In determining whether a case is frivolous, the administrative law judge may refer to S.C. Code Ann. § 15–36–10, the Frivolous Civil Proceedings Sanctions Act. The amount and type of sanction to be imposed is within the discretion of the presiding administrative law judge.

RULE 73. ADMISSION *PRO HAC VICE*

An attorney desiring to appear *pro hac vice* in a proceeding before the Court must file an Application for Admission *Pro Hac Vice* as provided in Rule 404, SCACR.

[Effective April 30, 2009.]

Notes

2009 Revised Notes

In accordance with the amendments to Rule 404, SCACR, effective March 1, 2005, Rule 73 provides that an attorney wishing to appear *pro hac vice* in a proceeding before the Court must file an application as provided in Rule 404.

INDEX TO RULES OF PROCEDURE FOR THE ADMINISTRATIVE LAW COURT

†